FROMMERS
DOLLARWISE
SOUTHEAST
ASIA

JOHN LEVY AND
KYLE McCARTHY

□

1989–1990

Published by Prentice Hall Trade Division
A Division of Simon & Schuster Inc.
Gulf + Western Building
One Gulf + Western Plaza
New York, NY 10023

ISBN 0-13-217753-6

ISSN 1040-9394

Text design by Levavi & Levavi, Inc.
Manufactured in the United States of America

*Although every effort was made to ensure the accuracy
of price information appearing in this book,
it should be kept in mind that prices
can and do fluctuate in the course of time.*

CONTENTS

I. AN INTRODUCTION TO SOUTHEAST ASIA 1
1. The Mysteries and Delights of Southeast Asia 4
2. A Common Culture 6
3. Planning Your Trip 9
4. Suggested Itineraries 16
5. How This Book Is Organized 17
6. Frommer's™ Dollarwise Travel Club—How to Save Money on All Your Travels 17

II. INTRODUCING BURMA 23
1. Introduction 24
2. Suggested Itineraries 30
3. Getting There and Getting Around 31
4. The ABCs of Burma (including Rangoon) 34

III. RANGOON 45
1. Orientation 46
2. Accommodations 48
3. Dining 49
4. What to See and Do in the City 51
5. Shopping 53
6. Day Trips from Rangoon 53

IV. EXPLORING BURMA 54
1. Pagan 54
2. Mandalay 62
3. Taunggyi and Inle Lake 70

V. HONG KONG 76
1. A Culture in Transition 76
2. Orientation and Transportation 80
3. The ABCs of Hong Kong 86
4. Accommodations 92

    5. Dining   101
    6. Sights, Shopping, and Nightlife   115
    7. The New Territories, Outlying Islands, and Day Trips to
       China   135
    8. Exploring Macau   139

VI. INTRODUCING INDONESIA   145

    1. Introduction   145
    2. Indonesian Culture   150
    3. Suggested Itineraries   155
    4. Getting There and Getting Around   155
    5. The ABCs of Indonesia   157
    6. Recommended Reading and Useful Phrases   163

VII. JAKARTA, THE NATION'S CAPITAL   165

    1. Orientation   167
    2. The ABCs of Jakarta   172
    3. Accommodations   175
    4. Dining   180
    5. Sights, Shopping, and Nightlife   187

VIII. EXPLORING JAVA   200

    1. Orientation   202
    2. Excursions from Jakarta: Pulau Seribu and Krakatoa   203
    3. Overland Across West Java: Bogor and Bandung   207
    4. Java's Cultural Capital: Yogyakarta   211
    5. Temples of Central Java: Borobudur, Prambanan, and
       Others   223
    6. Eastern Java: Solo, Mount Bromo, Transportation to Bali   227

IX. BALI, ISLAND OF THE GODS   233

    1. Orientation   233
    2. Balinese Culture   237
    3. The Beach Resorts: Sanur, Kuta Beach, and Nusa Dua   241
    4. Village Life: Ubud   256
    5. Exploring the Island   261
    6. Beyond Bali: Lombok and Komodo Island   270

X. INDONESIA OFF THE BEATEN PATH   274

    1. North Sumatra and Lake Toba   274
    2. West Sumatra, Land of the Minangkabau   288
    3. South Sulawesi: Tana Toraja   296
    4. Irian Jaya, Stone Age Tribes of the Baliem Valley   305

XI. INTRODUCING MALAYSIA   318
  1. Introduction   319
  2. Suggested Itineraries   324
  3. Getting There and Getting Around   325
  4. The ABCs of Malaysia   328
  5. Recommended Reading   337

XII. KUALA LUMPUR   339
  1. Orientation   340
  2. The ABCs of Kuala Lumpur   344
  3. Accommodations   349
  4. Dining   352
  5. What to See and Do in the City   356
  6. Shopping   359
  7. Nightlife   362

XIII. PENINSULAR MALAYSIA   364
  1. Cameron Highlands   364
  2. Penang   368
  3. The East Coast   379
  4. Malacca (Melaka)   384

XIV. EXPLORING BORNEO: SARAWAK AND SABAH 392
  1. Sarawak   393
  2. Sabah   404

XV. SINGAPORE   412
  1. An Introduction to Diverse Cultures   413
  2. The ABCs of Singapore   420
  3. Accommodations   425
  4. Dining   432
  5. Sights, Shopping, and Nightlife   440

XVI. INTRODUCING THAILAND   457
  1. Introduction   457
  2. Suggested Itineraries   466
  3. Getting There and Getting Around   466
  4. The ABCs of Thailand   469
  5. Recommended Reading   480

XVII. BANGKOK   482
  1. Orientation   483
  2. The ABCs of Bangkok   489

3. Accommodations 495
4. Dining 505
5. What to See and Do in the City 515
6. Shopping 525
7. Nightlife 529
8. Day Trips from Bangkok 531

**XVIII. CENTRAL THAILAND'S HISTORICAL
LEGACY**   541
1. Phitsanulok 541
2. Sukhothai and Si Satchanalai 545

XIX. CHIANG MAI AND THE NORTHERN HILLS 551
1. Orientation 552
2. Useful Information 554
3. Accommodations 557
4. Dining 562
5. What to See and Do in the City 565
6. Day Trips from the City 567
7. Shopping 571
8. Nightlife 575
9. Trekking in the Northern Hills 576

XX. SOUTHERN THAILAND: THE BEACHES   584
1. Pattaya 584
2. Koh Samui and Surat Thani 593
3. Phuket 601

INDEX   616

MAPS

Southeast Asia 2–3
Burma 25
Rangoon 47
Pagan/Mandalay 56
Hong Kong and Environs 82–83
Central District, Hong Kong 94
Kowloon (Tsimshatsui) 116
Indonesia 146–147
Jakarta 168
Java 204
Bali 242
Sumatra 275
South Sulawesi 290
Kuala Lumpur 341
Peninsular Malaysia 366
Borneo: Sarawak and Sabah 394
Singapore 416–417
Thailand 459
Bangkok 484–485
Northern Thailand 553
Chiang Mai 558
Southern Thailand 585

Acknowledgments

The fellow travelers and researchers who assisted us in this vast project have earned our deepest respect and gratitude: Ron Bozman, whose love of adventure and boundless energy informs this entire book, in particular the chapters on Indonesia, Hong Kong, and Singapore; Keith McCarthy, who trekked with us through Burma and Malaysia in search of the best values and the best turn of phrase; Emily Day, our spiritual guide through the wonders of Thailand; Joane Gil, the indefatigable shopper whose wise counsel guided us through Hong Kong; and Anne Fleming, whose research helped bring Malaysia and Burma to life for us and our readers.

And very special thanks to our friends: Rob Doughty, Maddy Cohen, Stephanie Welsh, and Dashiel Wham for their invaluable assistance.

A guidebook of this scope could not have been completed without the cooperation and generous hospitality of the tourism organizations in each country we visited. In particular we'd like to thank the following:

For Burma: the staff of the Consulate General of the Socialist Republic of the Union of Burma in New York City; and Robert Loftis of the U.S. Department of State and John Fredenburg of USIS in Rangoon, whose extraordinary assistance made it possible to include Burma in this guidebook.

For Hong Kong: Alex Cheung and Mary Bakht of the Hong Kong Tourist Association, New York; the efficient and knowledgeable Karisa Yuen-Ha Lui in HKTA's Hong Kong headquarters; and special thanks to Elena Ferretti for her generous spirit and assistance.

For Indonesia: Ms. Cri Murthi Adi at the Directorate General of Tourism and her assistant Peter Pangaribuan for their warm welcome; Stella Gunawan of the P.H.R.I. for her hospitality; Mr. Achjadi S. of the Direktorat Penerangan Luar Negeri for his unflagging support; and the Consul General of the Republic of Indonesia and his staff in New York, especially our friends Soehardjono S., Ann Saxon, and Ris Azehari.

Our research would have been impossible without the cooperation of the regional tourism offices led by Mohd. Saleh Tjakraamidjaja in D.K.I. Jakarta; R. Sjamsuddin, SH and S. Koesharjana in D.K.I. Yogyakarta; Tjok. Oka Pemayun and our guide Made Susanna in Bali; Soeroto Brodjo and our guide Amirrudin in Sulawesi Selatan; Mr. Boakorsyon and our guide Hans Menanti in Irian Jaya; H. Usman Ismail, our guide Sahat Sinaga, and Ch. L. Sitorus in Sumatra Utara; Sofjan Jusuf, our guide Hassan and H. Hawara Siddik in Sumatra Barat; Mr. Usman and Abdul Kadir in Lombok and all of their capable staff.

For Malaysia: Special thanks to Mokhtar Mohyat of the Malaysia Tourist Information Center for his interest and patience; and Jane Vong, of the Tourist Development Corporation of Malaysia in Kuala Lumpur, who made everything work with style.

For Singapore: Ms. Tan Seck Geok and our energetic guide Susan from the Singapore Tourist Promotion Board; Laura Boucher and Judith Ong for their tremendous cooperation; and Kevin Leong and the staff of the STPB in New York.

For Thailand: Sumonta Nakornthab, Chaiyasith Pongsakitch, and Nat Boonphanakit in the New York office of the Tourist Authority of Thailand, an extremely helpful, well-informed, and generous group; Paisan Wangsai in Central Thailand (and now New York) for his valuable assistance; and to the always diligent Mr. Beck and the tireless Ms. Piyavat Songkhao, who helped us all in the country we grew to love.

And real, heartfelt appreciation to the staff of Prentice Hall Travel: our leader Paul Pasmantier, our guru Marilyn Wood, and our dedicated editor Amit Shah, who stood by us from the inception of this book until its completion, at long last.

Thank you all

Travel in the younger sort, is a part of education; in the elder, a part of experience.
—*Francis Bacon*

INFLATION ALERT: In researching this book we have made every effort to obtain up-to-the-minute prices, but even the most conscientious researchers cannot keep up with the current pace of price changes. As we go to press, we believe we have obtained the most reliable data possible. Nonetheless, in the lifetime of this edition—particularly its second year (1990)—the wise traveler will add 15% to the prices quoted throughout these pages.

A DISCLAIMER: Although every effort was made to ensure the accuracy of the prices and travel information appearing in this book, it should be kept in mind that prices do fluctuate in the course of time, and that information does change under the impact of the varied and volatile factors that affect the travel industry.

A SPECIAL NOTE ABOUT TRAVELING TO BURMA: In the summer of 1988 Burmese citizens from around the country staged massive political demonstrations that ultimately brought about the resignation of Ne Win, the former military leader who had ruled the country since 1961. The military regained control in the fall by enforcing strict martial law with dusk-to-dawn curfews and shoot-to-kill orders for any demonstrators. At the same time, Burma closed its doors to all tourists.

This state of affairs changed just as we went to press, with limited seven-day travel permitted to tourists in groups only. Burma is still off-limits to all individual tourists. All of this is to say that before planning a trip to Burma, inquire about the availability of visas; inquiries should be made at the Burmese embassy or consulate in your country. We also recommend speaking with the United States Department of State Citizen's Emergency Center (tel. 202/647-5225) or the Burma desk (tel. 202/647-7108). Inquiries can also be made at the United States embassy in Bangkok.

CHAPTER I

AN INTRODUCTION TO SOUTHEAST ASIA

□ □ □

1. THE MYSTERIES AND DELIGHTS OF SOUTHEAST ASIA

2. A COMMON CULTURE

3. PLANNING YOUR TRIP

4. SUGGESTED ITINERARIES

5. HOW THIS BOOK IS ORGANIZED

6. FROMMER'S™ DOLLARWISE TRAVEL CLUB—HOW TO SAVE MONEY ON ALL YOUR TRAVELS

We met Bhek at dusk, entranced by our first ferry ride along Bangkok's magical Chao Phraya River. The young monk introduced himself, asked where we came from, and inquired about the reported decline of spirituality in the West. The sophistication of his questions startled us, breaking the river's spell. We assumed Bhek had studied abroad, but he denied having fulfilled this fantasy, saying he had learned about America in school. He continued with pride, envy, and resentment coloring his voice, "In our country, *we* must learn everything about *you.*"

Clearly, the "we" was not only his friends and colleagues, but his countrymen, and by extension, the people of Southeast Asia. By "you" he meant us, America and the West, the writers of this book, and you, the reader.

Bhek's comment has stayed with us, a reminder of the one-way view most of us have of the world. It's easy to see how the Hiltons, hamburgers, and hemlines of the West have influenced the great capitals of the East. Yet it's increasingly common to eat Thai or Chinese food, buy Malaysian-made cars or Singapore's newest computer clones, or wear Hong Kong–tailored suits and sneakers in any city—American, Canadian, European, or Australian—in the West. As our intermingling with Asia grows, so it becomes crucial for "us" to learn about "them."

SOUTHEAST ASIA

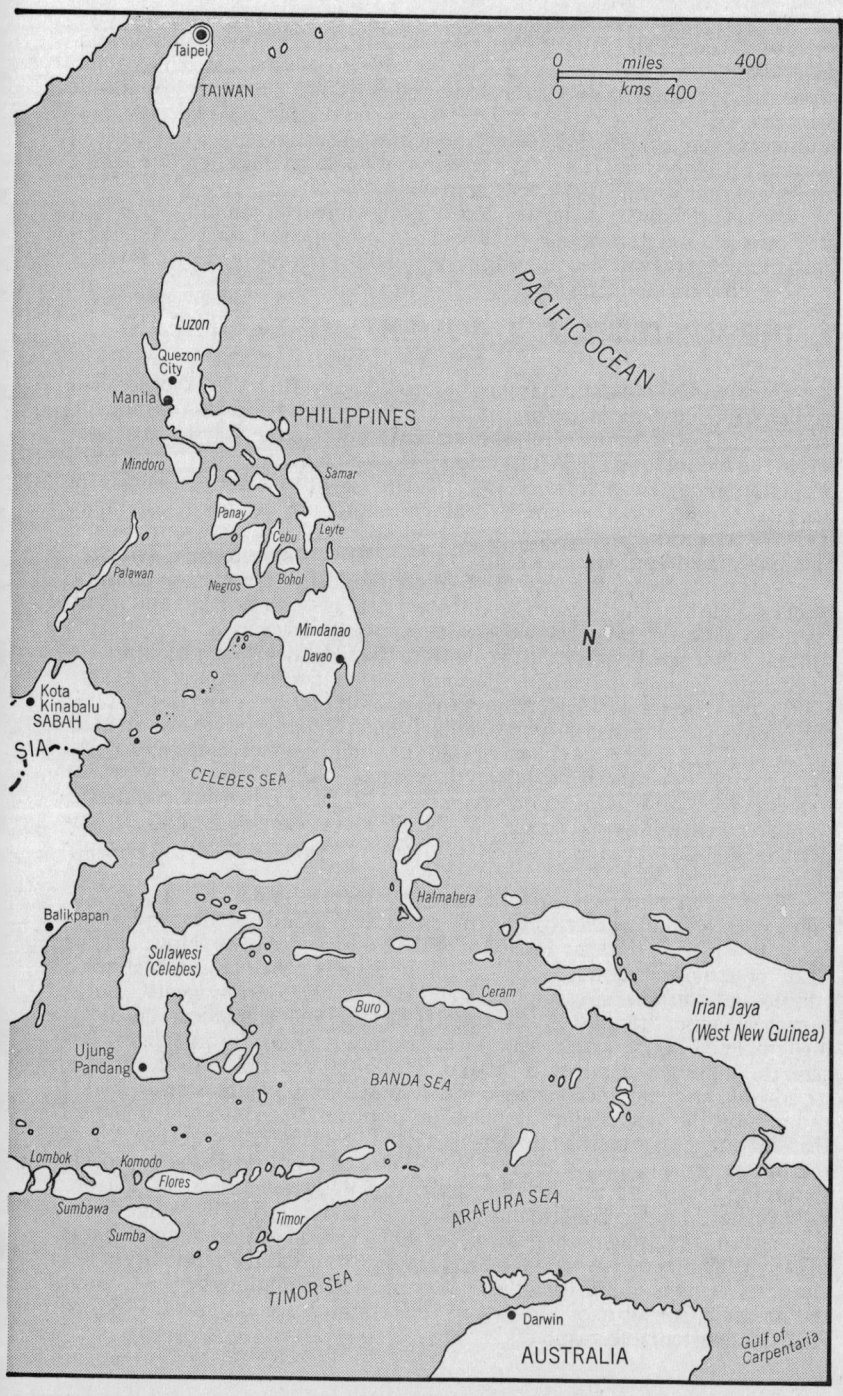

We have approached this travel guidebook with a desire to fathom the mysteries of the exotic and inscrutable Orient, and an equal emphasis on the mundane and knowable aspects of Asian life. We'll examine the temples and museums, monuments and archeology, religions and cultures of Southeast Asia. But we'll also explore the public transportation that makes personal encounters possible, the traditional-style lodgings and restaurants where you can live and eat as the locals do, and a traveling style respectful of cultures and a concept of time distinctly different from our own.

We have delighted in the wonders of Asia, while maintaining a regard for the needs and interests of our many readers, and hope that the recommendations found herein will lead you on an enlightening journey through one of the world's most intriguing regions.

1. THE MYSTERIES AND DELIGHTS OF SOUTHEAST ASIA

Since Marco Polo's return from China to Venice in A.D. 1292 the Occident has been trying to fathom the inscrutable Orient, source of odd customs and untold riches. One of history's ironies is that civilization in the "Mysterious East" was in full bloom for six millennia before Marco Polo discovered it. Soon, black pepper, spaghetti, gunpowder, the clock, and myriad other items we now take for granted began to flow along the sea routes meant for the lucrative silk and spice trade. Over time the East opened and then closed itself to Western scrutiny, and opinions ranged from admiration for its arts to derision of its pagan religions.

Today, hundreds of thousands of Western tourists seeking exotic cultures, beaches, and shopping bargains head toward Asia as Asian students and immigrants looking for advancement stream westward. There is no denying the cultural differences between the two worlds. The seductive West is often seen as diminishing the importance of religion and social welfare in the quest for material progress. The spiritual East ensures that tradition retains a role in economic development. Indonesian corporations install prayer rooms facing toward Mecca, Hong Kong race tracks enhance profits to build hospitals, Singapore executives consult geomancers to orient their desks. Nevertheless, the West *has* influenced this 10% of the world's population. As fast-food chains, pop music, computers, and miniskirts become widespread, it is increasingly important to understand the age-old values that these countries are trying to preserve in a rapidly changing world.

Burma, once the picnic spot of Asia under the British Raj, declined so radically under the military dictatorship of Gen. U Ne Win and his "Burmese Way to Socialism" that it's the least developed of the countries we cover. However, dirt roads, poor transportation, decrepit accommodations, a disappearing traditional cuisine, and usurious prices imposed by the omnipotent tourism agency, Tourist Burma, are more than offset by the country's exotic, fading grandeur, the decaying temples of Pagan, the elephants that share mountain roads through teak forests, the dignity and purity of devout Buddhists, and the intricate lacquer, woodwork, and embroidery that is widely sold. The ubiquitous black market prompts the Burmese people to be even more open and curious about foreigners than they might naturally be. In August 1988 U Ne Win retired as chairman of the Burma Socialist Program Party in response to months of violent protest, promising to schedule a referendum and eventually, general elections. Historically, his government restricted interaction with foreigners by only issuing seven-day visas and requiring the exchange of $100 U.S. on arrival in Rangoon, but as of early 1989 the country was off-limits to foreign tourists. The possibility of free elections seems no more likely than before the demonstrations began. Contact the Burmese Consulate or Embassy in your country (see Chapter II—Burma ABCs) for current information

In direct contrast is the tremendous vitality and hustle of **Hong Kong,** startling to all but the native New Yorker. Tourists see a small enclave of superb food and unbelievable shopping bargains, but Hong Kong is known to the ruling British government as the world's third-largest financial market and a dynamic shipping center. Because the predominantly Chinese population has been educated by the British, visitors will feel at home in the largely Christian, English-speaking environment. Yet there are colorful Confucian and Buddhist temples tucked into the old alleyways of the Central district, and waves of recent immigrants who've settled the New Territories to remind you that when Hong Kong reverts to the Chinese in 1997 it will soon seem as if it had always been part of the larger Chinese republic. Its colonial neighbor, the Portuguese territory of **Macau,** is an Indo/art deco refuge for architecture buffs and a casino gambler's mecca.

The Islamic **Republic of Indonesia** is the biggest of the countries covered, both geographically and in population. The diverse attractions of 13,677 islands and 360 ethnic groups delight ethnographers but make Indonesia a tour operator's nightmare. For, other than the truly paradisical island of Bali, it's difficult to encapsulate Indonesia's riches in sales pitches or ten-day tours. Every island group offers its own cultural treasures in a densely foliated, hot and steaming tropical package. The "Year of Indonesia" (sponsored by Indonesia's former foreign minister and the Nusantara Jaya Foundation, a private organization) is an ambitious arts and culture festival planned for 1990–1991 to educate the American and European public about the archipelago's delights. Visitors armed with knowledge can take up to 60 days riding a time machine between Irian Jaya's Stone Age and Jakarta's vision of the future.

The oldest rain forests on earth, predating the Ice Age and cherished by scientists as a learning resource, straddle the middle of peninsular **Malaysia.** One of the least-known tourist destinations, Malaysia startles the unsuspecting visitor with great natural beauty, an Asian blend of hospitable Malay, Chinese, and Indian citizens and a clean, modern environment. In contrast, Sabah and Sarawak, two Malaysian states on the island of Borneo, lure adventure travelers with jungle walks, river trips, and mountain treks through Dayak and Iban villages. Despite increasing industrialization, Malaysia remains Southeast Asia's best travel bargain, with the lowest average hotel and food costs in the entire region.

Singapore earns praise for its cleanliness, modernity, and efficiency. Touring the marvelous Singapore Zoo and Jurong Bird Park or shopping in Orchard Road's elegant, air-conditioned malls is easy, pleasurable, and inexpensive. Contemporary high-rises and two-story shop/houses are inhabited by a mix of Singapore's three ethnic groups; a prosperous Christian and Buddhist Chinese majority coexists peacefully with Muslim Malays and Hindu Indians. Despite criticism that the government handles litterbugs and intellectuals with the same heavy hand, Prime Minister Lee Kuan Yew deserves credit for the republic's stunning productivity and civility, modern-day wonders that never cease to amaze.

Since the 1987 celebration of King Bhumiphol's (Rama IX) 60th birthday, the **Kingdom of Thailand** has been overwhelmed by tourists who delight in its comfortable exoticism. Bangkok, the grande dame of Asian capitals, is a fascinating destination: dozens of gilded, multicolored wats throbbing with Buddhist monks, prayer bells, and devotees punctuating her increasingly modern, noisy, and sometimes maddeningly polluted skyline. The most welcoming of people, a subtle and piquant cuisine, rich archeological sites surrounding the ancient Siam capitals, and totally hedonistic beach resorts are only part of the appeal. Thailand has managed to remain distinctly Eastern while wholeheartedly embracing the West

Burma, Hong Kong, Macau, Indonesia, Malaysia, Singapore, and Thailand each have distinctive attributes that are more fully explored in subsequent chapters. Let's take a look at the aspects they have in common.

2. A COMMON CULTURE

The countries of present-day Southeast Asia share a common people and history, and languages and religions derived from the more advanced cultures of India and China.

A BRIEF HISTORY: Southeast Asia's history is primarily studied from Indian and Chinese texts, the accounts of European travelers, and an examination of its indigenous arts. However, G. Coedès in his fascinating book, *The Making of Southeast Asia* (Berkeley, Calif.: University of California Press, 1983), analyzed archeological finds and linguistic scholarship to create a theory of the region's prehistory.

Coedès has theorized that in Neolithic times the earliest Asian migration originated in China or Japan and spread south and west to Taiwan, the Philippines, Sulawesi, and the Moluccas, toward New Guinea and Melanesia and on to Australia, bypassing central Indochina. Possibly from continental Asia, another people, thought to be of Mongoloid stock and speaking Austro-Asiatic languages, migrated to the south coasts of these countries, parts of eastern India, and to much of Indochina.

Around 1500 B.C. primitive Austronesians, with similarities to a known Neolithic Chinese culture, migrated from China to Indochina, settling on the Malay peninsula among local tribes still living in the more primitive Paleolithic era. Evidence of contemporary primitive tribes indicates that the indigenous primitive Malay aborigines migrated by sea to parts of Indonesia, Borneo, the Philippines, Taiwan, and Japan.

Indochina was settled by descendants of mixed Austronesian and Austro-Asiatic stock. The art of pottery, bone tools and utensils, bead jewelry, houses built on stilts, and rice cultivation are characteristics of this period common to all Southeast Asia.

Linguistic studies show that the region soon divided into two language groups, those derived from the T'ai of southern China and related to Indonesian, and those derived from the Mon-Khmer. Both groups had acquired a basic knowledge and use of metals and navigational skills, pursued rice cultivation and the domestication of the ox and water buffalo, followed a matrilineal line of inheritance, and believed in ancestor worship, burial in jars, and the establishment of shrines on high ground.

After 200 B.C. the area was the focus of influence by the nearby highly civilized societies of India and China. China began its expansion southward at the end of the Warring States period, simultaneous with the arrival of the first Indian traders. Aspects of both civilizations were easily adopted because of the common heritage shared by the new immigrants and earlier Indochinese settlers.

The Hindu and Buddhist cultures of India were predominant throughout the region, maintained by a strong educated class and the common use of the Sanskrit and Pali languages. Absorption of Indian culture by indigenous peoples, its subsequent dilution, the waning of an educated aristocracy, and the introduction of Sinhalese Buddhism (the Theravada school from Sri Lanka) accelerated the decline of India's influence. The Mongol invasion of the 13th century, when the troops of Kublai Khan brought the customs and art of China to the region, was a turning point in Asian history.

This critical period witnessed the downfall of the Champa and Cham Kingdoms in Vietnam, the Khmer Empire of Cambodia, and the fall of the Kingdom of Pagan in Burma. Meanwhile Theravada Buddhism became widely adopted in Cambodia, ending an era of ornate, monumental temples like Angkor Wat, and signaling a return to indigenous visual arts in Java. It marked the birth of the Laotian Kingdom of Lan Ch'ang, the Siamese Kingdom of Sukhothai, the Lan Na Kingdom of Chiang Mai, and the T'ai principalities in Burma's Shan states.

From the 14th century until World War I the political and racial boundaries of the Southeast Asian states were roughly fixed. Instead these societies matured into the distinctive countries we know today under the cultural influences of China, the arrival of Islam, and the coming of the European traders.

THE WORLD'S GREAT RELIGIONS: The roughly 225 million residents of Burma, Hong Kong, Indonesia, Macau, Malaysia, Singapore, and Thailand coexist in varying states of harmony while following three major religions: Hinduism, Buddhism, and Islam. A brief introduction to the basic tenets of each should be helpful to travelers exploring the region. Large minorities practicing Christianity, Confucianism, and Taoism also exist, as well as several localized cults based on ancestor worship and traditional rituals.

Hinduism

Hinduism is the term scholars have used to describe the theology and social beliefs of the Indian subcontinent. Thought to have developed over several millennia among tribes believing in magic and ritual sacrifices, the tenets of Hinduism are based on the sacred text, *Veda*. The *Rig-Veda*, a collection of hymns, myths, liturgies, and philosophies preserved by Indian Brahmans (priests), was published between 1800 and 1300 B.C. It describes a pantheon of deities who personified the sky, earth, rain, thunder, streams, and other facets of nature.

Hinduism evolved over centuries in response to social needs. *The Upanishads,* the last section of the *Veda,* dating from the 6th century B.C., presented a new religious theory that moved beyond magic and sacrifices and toward the worship (*puja*) of specific icons in the home and in temples. It taught that life's goal was personal salvation from the needs of the material world. Life was an endless series of rebirths (*samsara*), daily suffering, and death according to the *karma* (the belief that every thought or deed has an inexorable consequence) of your previous life. Social actions were based on the quest for a better karma to ease the next life, and on *dharma,* the requisite conformity to social obligations. The principle of dharma solidified the abhorrent caste system, maintaining Indians in a status system derived from their color, rank at birth, and occupation, yet it also fortified government and societal rule over a huge and diverse mass of people. Hindus believed that the individual could obtain spiritual release (*moksha*) from the cycle of samsara through the mind-body discipline of yoga.

Hinduism continued to evolve, particularly after the growing popularity of the unorthodox theologies of Buddhism and Jainism. In the 1st century B.C. the influence of Greek invaders in the wake of Alexander the Great and of Buddhist ideas brought other deities into the Vedic pantheon. The lesser gods Siva (Shiva) and Vishnu became cult figures. (Siva the destroyer and regenerator of the material world, Vishnu the preserver, and Brahma the creator became the sacred Hindu triad.) The great Sanskrit epics, the *Mahabharata* and the *Ramayana,* are from around this time. The *Bhagavad-Gita* (a portion of the *Mahabharata*) outlined the new social and world views of Hinduism.

The introduction of Islam could not eradicate the strength of Hinduism in India, so for political expediency, Hinduism was granted the tolerated status of Christianity and Judaism. In Southeast Asia, where Hinduism was spread by Indian traders, local governments were established based on the notion of the god-king (*raja*), a ruler imbued with the power to mediate between the supernatural forces of the spiritual world and the daily problems of the material world. It became common to import Brahmans to the royal courts in order to reinforce the king's power.

Buddhism

The philosophy of Buddhism originated in the 6th century B.C., with the birth of Siddhartha Gautama. At the age of 29 this Indian prince renounced his worldly life, family, and possessions to devote himself to a spiritual quest. After six difficult years he abandoned asceticism and went west to Bodh Gaya in Bihar, India, to meditate under a bodhi tree. He achieved enlightenment (about 528 B.C.) and assumed the name of Buddha, or "Enlightened One." The Buddha began teaching his disciples that salvation could be achieved by the middle path, a life of moderation.

Scholars believe that Buddhism might have been an outgrowth of the Indian merchant class's opposition to the rigid roles imposed by Hinduism, the strict Vedic rules, and the excesses of Brahmans and rulers whose power was sanctified by the caste system. Buddhism was popularly accepted because it was based on rationality and the individual's quest for wisdom; ignorance caused misconceptions, which led to bad emotions and desire, which led to evil actions and suffering. The Buddha stressed that each individual was able to change his lot by education, thereby assuring the lower castes a greater opportunity for advancement.

Buddha's earliest teaching was the Four Noble Truths: that human existence is an endless cycle of rebirths, that ignorance of the spiritual world imprisons the soul in this painful cycle, that the elimination of ignorance and desire can lead to salvation (or Nirvana), and that life should be guided by the Eightfold Path (a combination of social rules, ethics, and principles of meditation).

Buddha stressed the importance of teaching and studying his philosophy rather than worshipping idols, but his disciples developed several sects of theology. The Mahayana (Universal or Greater Vehicle sect) Buddhists bestowed divinity on Buddha himself, and claimed that his most learned followers were *bodhisattvas,* or messiahs devoted to teaching the new faith. This sect spread to China, where it evolved into the Amitabha or Pure Land sect and eventually into Ch'an (Zen in Japanese) Buddhism. The Ch'an sects emphasized that enlightenment was within every person, not outside, and that physical hardship and intellectual pursuit, rather than religious practice, would eventually lead the individual to Nirvana.

The Theravada (or Lesser Vehicle) sect followed traditional Buddhism, stressing Buddha as an enlightened being and spiritual teacher rather than a god, and focusing on the study of his teachings. This sect began in Sri Lanka and moved east to Southeast Asia with Indian traders. The monastery was one of Buddha's concepts—a retreat for meditation and study. Buddhist monasteries developed throughout Southeast Asia into local schools, libraries, and hospitals that were vital to a village's daily life. Buddhism achieved its greatest following between the 7th and 9th centuries A.D., but declined as Confucianism, Taoism, and myriad local religions were combined with it. In modern times, the spread of Communism and its destruction of shrines, temples, and monasteries has most affected the Buddhist faith, greatly diminishing its numbers in China, Tibet, Vietnam, Cambodia, and Laos.

Islam

Muhammad, prophet and leader of the Muslim faith, was born in Mecca between A.D. 570 and 580. The beliefs of Islam were derived from Muhammad's knowledge of Judaism and Christianity, religions he admired for their discipline; he deplored the pagan Arab's idolatry. Allah (God) revealed himself to Muhammad in A.D. 611, and as His messenger, Muhammad tried to convince his friends (who later became caliphs) and others in Mecca to follow Allah. Few listened and in 622 he made the famous *hegira* or migration to Medina, a more receptive town in which he codified the laws of Islam and was pronounced its prophet and leader.

Muhammad led devoted followers against the idolators in Mecca and by 630 had captured it and the holy shrine, the Kaaba. At his death two years later, most of the Arabian peninsula had been converted to Islam. The tradition of *jihad* (holy war) had been instilled in Muslims, who felt guided by Allah to conquer infidels, spread his message, and protect Islamic lands from agression. Later the exigencies of running the vast Islamic empires would dictate the tolerance of Christianity, Judaism, Zoroastrianism, and even Hinduism, as long as nonbelievers paid their taxes.

Islam is basically a monotheistic religion, with Allah as the one supreme god. The *Koran* (Qu'ran or holy book) prescribes Islam's theology and rules by which to live. The Five Pillars of Islam are: that Muhammad is the messenger of Allah and the greatest of his prophets (but is not divine), that every Muslim must pray five times daily, that almsgiving to the community is a necessity, that Muslims must fast between sunrise and sunset during the month of Ramadan, and that all followers must attempt to make a pilgrimage (*hajj*) to the holy city of Mecca. The *Koran* also contains prohibitions against the consumption of alcohol and pork, and against gambling, usury, and the worship of images, although slavery and polygamy were condoned in moderation.

Islam spread from the Arabian peninsula to India and east through Asia by land and mercantile sea routes. Two major sects developed. The Sunni sect continued to follow the traditional teachings of the *Koran* as taught by caliphs and trained religious leaders. The Shi'ite sect believed that religious leaders should be descended from Muhammad (who had no surviving sons) and defined a line of teachers (*imams*) descended from Muhammad's cousin and son-in-law, Ali. The terrible war between Iraq and Iran (Sunni versus Shi'ite) indicates how complicated and serious the differences between these two sects became.

Scholars believe that Islam spread to Southeast Asia much earlier than written records indicate. Marco Polo reported it in A.D. 1292 while he was visiting a Muslim state in Sumatra. A journal dated 1300 notes the institution of Islam on the Malay peninsula, and shortly after the founding of Melaka (Malacca), the region's premier trading post in 1400, Arab merchants and their religion were firmly established. Today Indonesia has the largest Islamic population of any single country in the world.

3. PLANNING YOUR TRIP

Since a trip to Southeast Asia may be one of the most expensive and far-flung vacations you'll ever take, you probably want to make the most of it the first time around. How do you begin to plan such a trip? First, decide the ideal proportions of travel to staying put, sightseeing to relaxing, and museums to shopping; then review the "Suggested Itineraries" later in the chapter. The chapters specifically about each country provide much greater detail about the practical aspects of getting around and will give you a better feel for how much time you should allot to each destination.

Review the "Climate" section in each country's ABCs and try to plan your itinerary to avoid the monsoon or hot season. Consider how high heat and humidity will affect your traveling style and allow enough leeway in your plans to take it easy.

Many seasoned independent travelers find organized day trips, guided excursions, or special-interest tours a satisfying way to see those parts of Southeast Asia where communication or transportation is difficult, making sightseeing more a chore than a pleasure. We found our guided tours of Burma and the "off the beaten path" areas of Malaysia and Indonesia particularly efficient and enlightening, given the difficulty of getting around. (See the respective country chapters for recommended local tour operators.)

GETTING THERE: United Airlines offers the most complete service to Southeast Asia from North America, via San Francisco or Seattle (plus special add-on fares from Canadian cities) to Tokyo, Shanghai, Seoul, Manila, Taipei, Hong Kong, Bangkok, and Singapore.

United Airlines currently flies daily to Hong Kong and Singapore, three times a week to Bangkok, and plans to expand its flight schedule to meet increasing demand. Fares are computed according to mileage or routing (with lower fares for those who confine their flights exclusively to United), and modified by certain restrictions.

Recent roundtrip, economy class fares from New York to Hong Kong were $1,199, to Bangkok $1,369 and to Singapore $1,424. Economy class fares from San Francisco to Hong Kong or Bangkok were $1,120, and to Singapore $1,175. You can add additional stops to all of the above for $50 per stopover en route. In Business class, as luxurious as United's domestic First class, roundtrip fares from San Francisco to Hong Kong were $1,850, to Bangkok $2,020 and to Singapore $2,238. The super-deluxe, international First class, where guests are wined and dined by multi-lingual stewards and then bed down for the flight in even wider, fully reclining "sleeperettes," costs $3,880 to Hong Kong, and $4,238 to Bangkok or Singapore, roundtrip from San Francisco.

United Airlines has several special fare programs where you can save a lot of money by accepting certain restrictions on the day of departure, number of stopovers, advance ticket purchase, and duration of stay. For example, the 1989 restricted Economy class fares were as low as $850 roundtrip from San Francisco to Bangkok. The fares quoted above are low season rates, which are adjusted up by $50 to $100 depending on whether you fly in the busier spring and fall "shoulder" season or in the summertime "high" season. For children 2 to 11 years, United Airlines charges 67% of the excursion fare and 50% of the Business or First class fares. Children up to two years fly free, and bassinettes are provided for babies up to about 4 months of age.

Northwest Airlines (tel. 800/447-4747) also offers daily flights from New York or Los Angeles to the Orient. Their recent roundtrip excursion fares from New York to Hong Kong were $1,299 in Economy and $2,400 in Business class. Roundtrip excursion fares from Los Angeles were $850 in Economy and $1,850 in Business class, though several restrictions apply. Roundtrip Economy class excursion fares to Bangkok from New York were $1,299, and from Los Angeles, $1,000.

Canadian Airlines International (tel. 800/426-7000) flies to Hong Kong, Bangkok, and Singapore from Vancouver, B.C. Recent Economy class, low season excursion fares were $1,007, $1,175, and $1,217 from Vancouver to those cities respectively. Contact Canadian Airlines or your travel agent for information about special fares from Toronto or Montreal.

Japan Airlines (tel. 800/552-2746) services the Orient via Tokyo direct from New York, San Francisco or Los Angeles, Chicago, and Atlanta. Their Economy class excursion fare roundtrip from Los Angeles to Jakarta costs $1,759, a good value in that it includes two stopovers, though several restrictions apply.

Special Fares

Looking for the lowest fare ticket with the most flexibility can be a full time job in this age of airline deregulation. Shopping around is a must.

Travelers who want to combine the Orient and Southeast Asia with Australia and New Zealand or Europe should consult with a travel agent about various round-the-world fares. In 1989, United's Circle Pacific fare was $2,020 and its Round-the-World fare in the North Pacific was $2,099 for Economy class seating, using United and the services of its affiliate regional carriers. Tickets are valid for one year only and certain other restrictions apply. For fare information and reservations, travelers can call United Airlines directly at their toll-free number: 800/JET-AWAY. Northwest Airlines (tel. 800/447-4747) offers a round-the-world program in combination with one other airline (depending on your destination) for $2,099 in Economy class, with certain restrictions. Japan Airlines (tel. 800/552-2746) has a program with TWA; Economy class tickets cost $1,899 and certain restrictions apply.

For information about the rates and services provided by the national carriers of the countries covered in this guidebook, see the "Getting There" section in that country's introductory chapter.

Readers should consult the Sunday travel sections of their local newspapers, and the *New York Times* and *Los Angeles Times* for travel agencies advertising discount air fares. Many of these agencies can offer rock-bottom fares by using national carriers (such as China Airlines based in Taiwan, Korean Airlines based in Seoul, or Philppine Airlines based in Manila) who require a stopover in their home base. Be sure to obtain the necessary visas prior to departure if you are flying a multi-national route.

ALTERNATIVE TRAVEL: Many readers approach their trip to Southeast Asia with a special focus, desire, or curiosity. A region of such diverse cultures and countries offers many opportunities for study, adventure, and education. Each country's tourist information office (listed in the ABCs section) is the best source of information for alternative travel opportunities, particularly those requiring religious, professional, or academic affiliation. Choices include the following:

Study Tours

Several museums, societies, universities, and colleges plan escorted Southeast Asian tours for members, or alumni and their families. Two large institutions hosting frequent tours (with experts in the region's culture, history, arts, and politics) are the **Smithsonian Institution,** Associates Travel Program, 1100 Jefferson Dr. SW, Washington, DC 20560 (tel. 202/357-4700), and the **Asia Society,** Travel Department, 725 Park Ave., New York, NY 10021 (tel. 212/288-6400). Nonmembers can receive information about tours and pay the nominal membership fee with their reservations.

Adventure Travel

Travel could only be called adventurous in many parts of Southeast Asia. International enthusiasm for trekking, the sport of walking escorted by local guides and porters, has inspired several tour operators to provide services in the remote areas that are best visited on foot. One such area, infamous for its drug trade but known to hikers for its scrub-brush terrain, is the Golden Triangle, at Thailand's northern border. See Chapter XIX for more information about three-to five-day trekking tours (operating out of Chiang Mai) to visit northern Thailand's hill tribes.

Borneo's romantic appeal may have originated with stories of the Wild Man, one orangutan of hundreds that inhabit the huge island. Actually, Borneo is now divided into Kalimantan, the Indonesian majority; the independent sultanate of Brunei in the north; and Sabah and Sarawak, both part of Malaysia. The latter two

Malaysian states offer organized treks and boat tours along the jungle rivers that bisect Dayak and Iban villages. See Chapter XIV for more information about trips leaving from Kuching in Sabah or Kota Kinabalu in Sarawak.

A more arduous trek into remote and primitive regions is required to explore Irian Jaya, the Indonesian province on the island of New Guinea. Once permits are obtained from the local POLRI office, travelers can fly to Wamena or other villages that serve as missionary outposts, and begin their hiking there. The Indonesian province of North Sumatra can be explored on a river trek to view the flora and fauna of the densely forested jungle. Information about these and other adventure tours is contained in Chapter X.

Although Hong Kong seems too familiar and contemporary a city for adventure travel, there are several possibilities on the Outer Islands. Our favorite is a pleasingly rigorous overnight stay at the Po Lin Monastery on Lantau. Three vegetarian meals and admission to Buddhist chanting sessions is included in this spiritual package; see Chapter V for more information.

Bicycle touring is one of our favorite modes of travel, but most "off the beaten path" destinations have such poor roads that cycling is impractical. One exception is the divine Bali, a gently hilly, tropical island whose tranquil blacktop roads are well suited for cycling. **Backroads Bicycle Touring,** P.O. Box 1626-Q324, San Leandro, CA 94577 (tel. 415/895-1783), runs 12-day cycling tours, averaging 30 miles of riding per day, including sightseeing, beach time, and accommodations, which range from the best hotels to the most scenic camping. The tour departs from Los Angeles; an all-inclusive land package costs $1,300 without air fare.

Another company that offers a Bali bicycle tour and many other trips is **Sobek Expeditions,** P.O. Box 1089, Angels Camp, CA 95222 (tel. 209/736-4524), a longtime leader in the adventure travel field. Sobek offers an eight-day raft-floating trip on the Alas River in North Sumatra, through Southeast Asia's largest national park ($975 for the land package with a four-person minimum). Their guides also navigate the Mahakam River in Kalimantan, the Indonesian province on Borneo, to visit the longhouses of the Dayak villagers (seven-day land package for $895) and trek the highlands of the Baliem Valley to meet the Dani tribesmen (ten-day land package for $995). In Thailand, Sobek has arranged an exciting trek, elephant ride, and bamboo raft trip calling on many of the hill tribes and continuing south to Bangkok, to the River Kwai in Kanchanburi, and to the beaches at Phuket and Koh Phi Phi (24-day land package for $1,595).

Note: All prices quoted in this section were current as of December 1988.

Touring Vietnam

As of this writing, Americans are again on their way to Vietnam, though now as tourists! When organized group tours to Ho Chi Minh City and Saigon began in 1988 they received a tremendous amount of press and generated a great deal of misinformation. From the sources available to us, we've found that: U.S. Treasury Department regulations prohibit trade with Vietnam, therefore travel agents must use tour operators based outside the U.S. Airline schedules make it practical to begin Vietnam tours only from Manila or Bangkok. All travel agents offering a Vietnam tour from Bangkok must use the services of **Air People Tour and Travel Co.,** 30/7 Sala Daeng Rd., Bangkok 10500, Thailand (tel. 235-2668; FAX 662-2409003), the only licensed agents of Intourist and Vietnamtourism, the state-run agencies handling tourism in Communist-bloc countries.

This means that if you're interested in a seven-day Hanoi–Ho Chi Minh package ($1,150 including air fare from Bangkok, hotels, meals, etc.) or a seven-day Ho Chi Minh/Danang/Hue/Hanoi package ($1,220 all inclusive) you should contact Air People Tours directly. They will handle visa processing but require at least two weeks' advance notice. Travelers with limited time schedules can arrange to send photocopies of a passport and other vital information needed for the visa application, and will only have to spend a few days prior to departure in Bangkok.

Educational Travel

Travel is an education in and of itself, but students looking for organized classes have myriad opportunities. Contact the national tourist offices (listed in the ABCs section of each country's introductory chapter) for more information. Gourmets, cooking enthusiasts, and the many who find **cooking school** a wonderful way to tune into a culture's homelife should consider a week-long immersion in Thai cooking, given as part of an accommodations and tour package through the Oriental Hotel, Bangkok.

Those with a yen for Chinese can take long-term **Chinese-language courses** at the Towngas Centre, at the Leighton Centre, 77 Leighton Rd.; or the Home Management Centre, c/o the Hong Kong Electric Group, 1 Hysan Ave., second floor; or individual and short classes at the Chopsticks Cooking Centre, 116D Waterloo Rd., ground floor, Kowloon—all in Hong Kong.

Copeland Marks, noted scholar and author of cookbooks for Indian, Burmese, and Indonesian cooking, is planning **Indonesian cooking tours.** Two-week tours to several island groups will introduce participants to the specialties of each of Indonesia's ethnic groups. Contact the Indonesia Consulate General, 5 E. 68th St., New York, NY 10021 (tel. 212/879-0600), for more information.

Dancers can work out with professionals at the ASTI Academy in Denpasar, Bali, and musicians aspiring to play with a gamelan orchestra can study with private teachers there or in Yogyakarta. Health practitioners can explore the science of acupuncture in Hong Kong. Language students can perfect their Cantonese in Hong Kong or their Mandarin in Singapore, while staying with a local family. Contact the tourist offices of each country for more information about these and other educational programs.

TIPS FOR THE TRAVELER: Keep in mind that Southeast Asia is half a world away; if you plan for the most far-fetched problems, any that may occur will be much simpler to cope with.

Safety

Whenever you're traveling in an unfamiliar city or country, stay alert. Be aware of your immediate surroundings. Wear a moneybelt and don't sling your camera or purse over your shoulder; wear the strap diagonally across your body. This will minimize the possibility of your becoming a victim of crime. Every society has its criminals. It's your responsibility to be aware and alert even in the most heavily touristed areas. See specific chapters for more information.

Visas and Travel Documents

In the ABCs section for each country under the heading "Documents for Entry" there is specific information regarding entry formalities for U.S. and Commonwealth citizens, current as of late 1988. Be sure to consult with your travel agent or the embassies or consulates of the countries you plan to visit so that all your papers are in order.

If you're planning to visit a country that has recently been in the news for local disturbances (every one we cover was, at various stages in the preparation of this guide), contact the **Travel Advisory Service** of the U.S. Department of State (tel. 202/647-5225) to see if any recent travel advisories have been issued about the area.

Note that several countries require proof of onward passage in order for visas to be issued. For example, travelers arriving by air to Denpasar, Bali, and hoping to leave Indonesia by boat from Medan, Sumatra, must show their boat tickets upon arrival in Bali to be issued visas. If you're unsure about your travel plans it's always better to apply for a visa before reaching the country's port of entry (when harried Immigration officials may not want to take responsibility for "bending the rules").

Most countries require proof of vaccination against cholera, yellow fever, or other diseases found in neighboring Southeast Asian countries from travelers who have recently been to infected areas, which also include Africa and South America. Requirements for the World Health Organization's International Certificate of Vaccination change regularly; consult with your travel agent or the embassies or consulates of the countries you plan to visit before your departure.

If you're planning to rent a vehicle during your trip, we recommend obtaining an International Driver's License (available through most AAA or other automobile association offices), a requirement for car, motorcycle, or moped rental in some countries. You must obtain this before leaving your home country. However, vehicle insurance (rarely sold for motorcycles) is only valid if purchased in the country of rental.

Health Care for Travelers

John and Kyle, and researchers Keith and Ron, each had different opinions about how strongly worded this section should be. We know fellow travelers who can't be bothered to bring a toothbrush along, let alone a travel kit filled with aspirin, prescription medications, seasickness and diarrhea antidotes, snakebite kits, and Band-aids. On the other end of the scale, we have a friend who travels with a medical dictionary so he can be constantly on the alert for symptoms of internal parasites, viruses, and water-borne diseases. Of course, travel to the exotic and tropical countries of Southeast Asia does require more precaution than a weekend in London, and some health tips seem to be in order.

First, consult with your doctor regarding his/her recommendation on **immunizations and inoculations,** at least one month before departure because some immunizations require multiple inoculations administered over several weeks. Don't assume that you can obtain inoculations when you get to Southeast Asia. As of this writing, Burma, Indonesia, Malaysia, and Thailand have malaria-endemic areas and antimalarial pills are routinely prescribed for visitors. Bring enough of any prescription medications you normally take to last beyond your trip, in case of unforeseen delays.

For advice on inoculations, call the Centers for Disease Control (tel. 404/639-2572) or order the current edition of their book *Health Information for International Travel,* available for $4.75 by phone at 202/783-3238. VISA or MasterCard are also accepted.

Many common **nonprescription medications** are widely available in urban centers. However, we always carry a small first-aid kit with some antiseptic cream, sterile dressings and tape, blister pads, insect repellent, and sun block (lotions with an SPF higher than 8 are impossible to find in the region). We also carry a packet of tissues (public toilets rarely have toilet paper) and premoistened towelettes (good hygiene depends on keeping your hands clean).

Travelers with **eyeglasses** or contact lenses should always carry an extra pair, as well as a copy of the prescription.

The Balinese giggle about tourists stricken with "belly-belly," but unfortunately there can be more severe repercussions from what you eat and drink in this part of the world than a brief bout with **diarrhea.** Avoid the tapwater in every country except Hong Kong and Singapore, unless otherwise specified in the text. **Bottled water** is widely available and should be consumed in greater quantities than usual to prevent dehydration. Avoid all ice cubes and fresh fruit drinks diluted with water. Let the heat and humidity temper your usual intake of alcohol. Always remember to wash your hands carefully before each meal.

Except in the international hotels, only eat fruits that are peeled in front of you, and if you must, eat raw vegetables and salads only in the top hotels (where you may still be at risk). Exercise extreme caution when contemplating **"street food"** in any tropical country, and choose only things that are freshly cooked and served hot.

Never swim or wade in freshwater pools, streams, or lakes, which can be contaminated by runoff from fields fertilized by animal or human waste, a great source of infection. Never walk barefoot.

At the first sign of **health problems,** contact your own consulate or embassy (listed in the ABCs section of each country) to inquire about medical care. Medical care is inadequate in some of the countries covered in this guide, and serious illness would require evacuation to a proper medical facility, perhaps in another country. This can be staggeringly expensive.

Check your **insurance policy** before departure to make sure that overseas medical treatment, hospitalization, and medical evacuation are fully covered. Make arrangements with someone at home who will assume financial responsibility for your medical care or can wire transfer funds to you in case of emergency.

Several travel insurance and assistance companies offer short-term policies to cover trip cancellation costs, medical bills, and medical transportation. **International SOS Assistance,** P.O. Box 11568, Philadelphia, PA 19116 (tel. toll free 800/523-8930), provides emergency evacuation services to members for a small fee (an air ambulance evacuation with accompanying medical personnel can run as high as $25,000). **Access America,** 600 Third Ave., New York, NY 10163 (tel. toll free 800/851-2800), is a subsidiary of Blue Cross/Blue Shield that sells short-term travel insurance and evacuation coverage. Contact your insurance broker, travel agent, or these companies directly for more information about coverage.

A few minor precautions can make the difference between a pleasantly memorable trip and a disaster.

Traveling with Children

The natural innocence and curiosity of children make them delightful traveling companions, especially in Southeast Asia where children play a part in most daily activities. Although you'll probably find your movements somewhat restricted, a child's openness with strangers can win many friends and generate unexpected adventures.

Most of the countries covered in this guidebook are well organized for traveling families. There are many inexpensive, fun, and educational family activities, sights, and sports; most admission and tour fees are as much as 50% less for children up to 12 years old; most hotels have bargain triple-room rates or allow children up to 12 years to stay in the same room with their parents at no extra charge; babysitting service is widely available through the hotels and is usually inexpensive.

We do have some words of caution. Finding your favorite brand of baby products will be simple in Singapore but impossible in Indonesia. Car seats are a novelty unknown in most Asian countries and unheard of from rental-car companies. A portable stroller will facilitate sightseeing in most capital cities, but may be a burden in rural destinations where unpaved roads and no sidewalks are usually the norm. Above-average or adequate health care is available *only* in Hong Kong, Singapore, Bangkok, and Kuala Lumpur; consult with your family physician for advice on health precautions and procedures in case of emergency before your departure.

4. SUGGESTED ITINERARIES

In the introductory chapters for each country you'll find suggested itineraries for one-week, two-week, and one-month visits to the individual country. Here are suggestions for travelers who want to sample a bit of each country on their first visit to the region. All itineraries begin in Hong Kong and end in Singapore, the two gateways to Southeast Asia most frequently used by North American airlines.

TWO-MONTH ITINERARY: Days 1–5: Hong Kong, including a day trip to Macau. **Days 6–19:** Fly to Thailand and spend four days in Bangkok, fly north to Chiang Mai and spend three days, and take seven days to explore the archeological sites, beach resorts, or tribal villages. **Days 22–28:** Fly to Burma and take a packaged tour including Pagan and Inle Lake, then fly from Rangoon back to Bangkok. **Days 29–30:** Take the overnight train to Butterworth, Malaysia. **Days 30–42:** Relax for two days in the resort of Penang. Then drive from Penang to Kuala Lumpur with an overnight stop at the hill resort of Cameron Highlands, spend a day in Kuala Lumpur, and make an overnight excursion to the historical city of Malacca. Return to Kuala Lumpur. Fly to Kuching or Kota Kinabalu and spend five days exploring Sabah or Sarawak, Borneo, by climbing Mount Kinabalu, visiting the Niah or Mulu Caves, or joining a river tour through the jungle to longhouses and tribal villages. **Days 43–57:** Fly to Indonesia and spend a day in the capital, Jakarta. Take an overnight train and spend three days in Yogyakarta. Then fly to Bali and spend five days in a beach resort and two days in a hill village. **Days 58–61:** Fly to Singapore and spend three days before returning home.

ONE-MONTH ITINERARY: Days 1–4: Hong Kong. **Days 5–12:** Fly to Thailand and spend three days in Bangkok, fly north to Chiang Mai for two days, and take two days to explore the archeological sites; *or* spend four days at a beach resort. **Days 13–20:** Fly to Kuala Lumpur and spend two days, then fly to Kuching or Kota Kinabalu and spend five days exploring the natural beauty of Borneo; *or* fly round trip to Rangoon and take a seven-day package tour of the ancient Buddhist culture of Burma. **Days 21–27:** Fly to Indonesia and spend a day in Jakarta. Then fly on to Yogyakarta and spend three days. Fly to Bali and spend three days in a beach resort. **Days 28–30:** Fly to Singapore and spend two days before returning home.

THREE WEEKS OR LESS: We strongly suggest that readers with less than 21 days consider limiting their itinerary to two or three countries. There are several factors to bear in mind: the very long plane trip from North America or Europe usually means "jet lag" fatigue that may take a few days to overcome; the substantially hotter and more humid climate imposes a slower pace of sightseeing and shopping than most travelers are used to; every journey to a new country usually takes more time than anticipated because of transportation or weather delays, Customs and Immigration formalities, and exchanging currency. It's also important to remember that the pace of Southeast Asia itself is slower, and that the most delightful memories of travel are often those chance encounters, serendipitous wanderings, and unplanned forays that are only possible if you allow some flexibility in your schedule.

Therefore we recommend reading the introduction to each country and deciding which fits the vacation you have in mind. If it's a tropical beach, cruise to Thailand's south coast or Bali; for shopping, package Hong Kong and Bangkok with Singapore; for adventure travel, hike off the beaten path in Burma, Malaysia, and Indonesia; for Oriental arts, study the royal dances of Indonesia and Thailand; for a fabulous meal, dine in Hong Kong; for the past, admire Burma, and for the future, Singapore. Each country makes a first impression that longer visits can dispel—after 30 days in tiny Singapore you may learn more about Southeast Asia than if you'd stepped into every country in the table of contents of this guidebook.

5. HOW THIS BOOK IS ORGANIZED

This guidebook includes practical information on accommodations, dining, sightseeing, shopping, and getting around the following countries: Burma, Hong Kong and Macau, Indonesia, Malaysia, Singapore, and Thailand. It is the story of five colonies under the thumb of British, Dutch, and Portuguese imperialism that achieved independence as modern nations, and of two, Hong Kong and Macau, that will shortly revert to their original status as part of mainland China. (Only Thailand, through clever diplomacy, managed to escape foreign domination.)

Because the generic term "Southeast Asia" is often used broadly to define the huge area influenced by the powerful Indian and Chinese cultures, one may argue that several other modern countries should have been included in this guide. We agree, envisioning updates of this guidebook as an evolutionary process, and hope that some war-torn countries that could not be included in this edition (such as Cambodia, Laos, and Vietnam) will reopen their borders to foreigners who come in peace. We also hope that those countries that *are* included in this first edition will remain at peace and ready to welcome you.

As we go to press in 1989 one of the countries we did include, Burma, which had closed its borders to all foreign tourists, is now open to tourists in groups only. See Chapter II for more information.

CHOOSING THE BEST VALUE: In writing a Dollarwise® guide, we have sought out the best value in accommodations and dining in every price range. Any guide that runs the gamut from one of the world's best hotels at $245 per night (the Oriental in Bangkok) to a thatch-roofed *honay* at $4 per night (tribal huts in Indonesian New Guinea) has a tough job pleasing everyone. From the group of lodgings that have met our high standards of cleanliness and modest requirements for comfort, we recommend those whose character and commitment to service epitomize the values of Southeast Asia. Exploring a region known for its diverse and superb cuisines is no less difficult. Many first-time visitors are wary of sampling new foods in some of these exotic locales; therefore, we emphasize eateries where hygiene (including boiling drinking water) is as important as authentic regional cooking or a special ambience. Both gourmets searching for the best shark's fin in Hong Kong ($250 at Fook Lam Moon) and the homesick pining for a hamburger in Kuala Lumpur ($1 at McDonald's) will find a variety of recommendations.

TRADING INFORMATION: In addition to our discoveries, we count on yours. Your fellow travelers' "Reader's Selections," tales of inns and cafés encountered serendipitously, greatly enhance each new edition. Your feedback—praise for our favorite haunts, gripes about old standbys, news of others—helps us shape a better, more useful guide. Please direct your comments to us c/o Prentice Hall Trade Division, 1 Gulf + Western Plaza, New York, NY 10023.

6. FROMMER'S™ DOLLARWISE TRAVEL CLUB—HOW TO SAVE MONEY ON ALL YOUR TRAVELS

In this book, we'll be looking at how to get your money's worth in Southeast Asia, but there is a "device" for saving money and determining value on all your trips. It's the popular, international Frommer's Dollarwise Travel Club, now in its 28th successful year of operation. The club was formed at the urging of numerous readers of the $-A-Day and Dollarwise Guides, who felt that such an organization could provide continuing travel information and a sense of community to value-minded travelers in all parts of the world. And so it does!

In keeping with the budget concept, the annual membership fee is low and is immediately exceeded by the value of your benefits. Upon receipt of $18 (U.S. residents), or $20 U.S. by check drawn on a U.S. bank or via international postal money order in U.S. funds (Canadian, Mexican, and other foreign residents) to cover one year's membership, we will send all new members the following items:

(1) Any *two* of the following books

Please designate in your letter which two you wish to receive:

Frommer™ $-A-Day® Guides

Europe on $30 a Day
Australia on $30 a Day
Eastern Europe on $25 a Day
England on $40 a Day
Greece (including Istanbul and Turkey's Aegean Coast) on $30 a Day
Hawaii on $50 a Day
India on $25 a Day
Ireland on $35 a Day
Israel on $30 & $35 a Day
Mexico (plus Belize and Guatemala) on $25 a Day
New York on $50 a Day
New Zealand on $40 a Day
Scandinavia on $60 a Day
Scotland and Wales on $40 a Day
South America on $30 a Day
Spain and Morocco (plus the Canary Is.) on $40 a Day
Turkey on $30 a Day
Washington, D.C., and Historic Virginia on $40 a Day

($-A-Day Guides document hundreds of budget accommodations and facilities, helping you get the most for your travel dollars.)

Frommer Guides

Australia
Austria and Hungary
Belgium, Holland, & Luxembourg
Bermuda and The Bahamas
Brazil
Canada
Caribbean
Egypt
England and Scotland
France
Germany
Italy
Japan and Hong Kong
Portugal, Madeira, and the Azores
Southeast Asia
South Pacific
Switzerland and Liechtenstein
Alaska
California and Las Vegas
Florida
Mid-Atlantic States

New England
New York State
Northwest
Skiing USA—East
Skiing USA—West
Southeast and New Orleans
Southwest
Texas
USA

(Frommer Guides discuss accommodations and facilities in all price ranges, with emphasis on the medium-priced.)

Frommer™ Touring Guides

Australia
Egypt
Florence
London
Paris
Scotland
Thailand
Venice

(These new, color illustrated guides include walking tours, cultural and historic sites, and other vital travel information.)

Gault Millau

Chicago
France (avail. July 1989)
Italy (avail. July 1989)
Los Angeles
New England
New York
San Francisco
Washington, D.C.

(Irreverent, savvy, and comprehensive, each of these renowned guides candidly reviews over 1,000 restaurants, hotels, shops, nightspots, museums, and sights.

Serious Shopper's Guides

Italy
London
Los Angeles
Paris

(Practical and comprehensive, each of these handsomely illustrated guides lists hundreds of stores, selling everything from antiques to wine, conveniently organized alphabetically by category.)

A Shopper's Guide to the Caribbean

(Two experienced Caribbean hands guide you through this shopper's paradise, offering witty insights and helpful tips on the wares and emporia of more than 25 islands.)

Beat the High Cost of Travel

(This practical guide details how to save money on absolutely all travel items—accommodations, transportation, dining, sightseeing, shopping, taxes, and more. Includes special budget information for seniors, students, singles, and families.)

Bed & Breakfast—North America
(This guide contains a directory of over 150 organizations that offer bed & breakfast referrals and reservations throughout North America. The scenic attractions, and major schools and universities near the homes of each are also listed.)

Dollarwise Cruises
(This complete guide covers all the basics of cruising—ports of call, costs, fly-cruise package bargains, cabin selection booking, embarkation and debarkation and describes in detail over 60 or so ships cruising the waters of Alaska, the Caribbean, Mexico, Hawaii, Panama, Canada, and the United States.)

Dollarwise Skiing Europe
(Describes top ski resorts in Austria, France, Italy, and Switzerland. Illustrated with maps of each resort area. Includes supplement on Argentinian resorts.)

Frommer's Belgium
(Arthur Frommer unlocks the treasures of a country overlooked by most travelers to Europe. Discover the medieval charm, modern sophistication, and natural beauty of this quintessentially European country.)

Guide to Honeymoon Destinations
(A special guide for that most romantic trip of your life, with full details on planning and choosing the destination that will be just right in the U.S. [California, New England, Hawaii, Florida, New York, South Carolina, etc.], Canada, Mexico, and the Caribbean.)

Marilyn Wood's Wonderful Weekends
(This very selective guide covers the best mini-vacation destinations within a 200-mile radius of New York City. It describes special country inns and other accommodations, restaurants, picnic spots, sights, and activities—all the information needed for a two- or three-day stay.)

Manhattan's Outdoor Sculpture
(A total guide, fully illustrated with black and white photos, to more than 300 sculptures and monuments that grace Manhattan's plazas, parks, and other public spaces.)

Motorist's Phrase Book
(A practical phrase book in French, German, and Spanish designed specifically for the English-speaking motorist touring abroad.)

Paris Rendez-Vous
(An amusing and *au courant* guide to the best meeting places in Paris, organized for hour-to-hour use: from power breakfasts and fun brunches, through tea at four or cocktails at five, to romantic dinners and dancing 'til dawn.)

Swap and Go—Home Exchanging Made Easy
(Two veteran home exchangers explain in detail all the money-saving benefits of a home exchange, and then describe precisely how to do it. Also includes information on home rentals and many tips on low-cost travel.)

The Candy Apple: New York for Kids
(A spirited guide to the wonders of the Big Apple by a savvy New York grandmother with a kid's-eye view to fun. Indispensable for visitors and residents alike.)

The New World of Travel
(From America's #1 travel expert, Arthur Frommer, an annual sourcebook with the hottest news and latest trends that's guaranteed to change the way you travel —and save you hundreds of dollars. Jam-packed with alternative new modes of travel that will lead you to vacations that cater to the mind, the spirit, and a sense of thrift.)

Travel Diary and Record Book
(A 96-page diary for personal travel notes plus a section for such vital data as passport and traveler's check numbers, itinerary, postcard list, special people and places to visit, and a reference section with temperature and conversion charts, and world maps with distance zones.)

Where to Stay USA
(By the Council on International Educational Exchange, this extraordinary guide is the first to list accommodations in all 50 states that cost anywhere from $3 to $30 per night.)

(2) Any *one* of Frommer's™ City Guides
Amsterdam
Athens
Atlantic City and Cape May
Boston
Cancún, Cozumel, and the Yucatán
Chicago
Dublin and Ireland
Hawaii
Las Vegas
Lisbon, Madrid, and Costa del Sol
London
Los Angeles
Mexico City and Acapulco
Minneapolis and St. Paul
Montreal and Quebec City
New Orleans
New York
Orlando, Disney World, and EPCOT
Paris
Philadelphia
Rio
Rome
San Francisco
Santa Fe and Taos
Sydney
Washington, D.C.

(Pocket-size guides to hotels, restaurants, nightspots, and sightseeing attractions covering all price ranges.)

(3) A one-year subscription to *The Dollarwise® Traveler*
This quarterly eight-page tabloid newspaper keeps you up to date on fastbreaking developments in low-cost travel in all parts of the world, bringing you the latest money-saving information—the kind of information you'd have to pay $35 a year to obtain elsewhere. This consumer-conscious publication also features columns of special interest to readers: **Hospitality Exchange** (members all over the world who are willing to provide hospitality to other members as they pass through their home cities); **Share-a-Trip** (offers and requests from members

for travel companions who can share costs and help avoid the burdensome single supplement); and **Readers Ask . . . Readers Reply** (travel questions from members to which other members reply with authentic firsthand information).

(4) Your personal membership card

Membership entitles you to purchase through the club all Frommer publications for a third to a half off their regular retail prices during the term of your membership.

So why not join this hardy band of international budgeteers and participate in its exchange of travel information and hospitality? Simply send your name and address, together with your annual membership fee of $18 (U.S. residents) or $20 U.S. (Canadian, Mexican, and other foreign residents), by check drawn on a U.S. bank or via international postal money order in U.S. funds to: Frommer's Dollarwise Travel Club, Inc., Gulf + Western Building, One Gulf + Western Plaza, New York, NY 10023. And please remember to specify which *two* of the books in section (1) and which *one* in section (2) you wish to receive in your initial package of members' benefits. Or, if you prefer, use the order form at the end of the book and enclose $18 or $20 in U.S. currency.

Once you are a member, there is no obligation to buy additional books. No books will be mailed to you without your specific order.

CHAPTER II

INTRODUCING BURMA

□ □ □

1. INTRODUCTION
2. SUGGESTED ITINERARIES
3. GETTING THERE AND GETTING AROUND
4. THE ABC'S OF BURMA (INCLUDING RANGOON)

A SPECIAL NOTE ABOUT TRAVELING TO BURMA. In the summer of 1988 Burmese citizens from around the country staged massive political demonstrations that ultimately brought about the resignation of Ne Win, the former military leader who had ruled the country since 1961. The military regained control in the fall by enforcing strict martial law with dusk-to-dawn curfews and shoot-to-kill orders for any demonstrators. At the same time, Burma closed its doors to all tourists.

This state of affairs changed just as we went to press, with limited seven-day travel permitted to tourists in groups only. Burma is still off-limits to all individual tourists. All of this is to say that before planning a trip to Burma, inquire about the availability of visas; inquiries should be made at the Burmese embassy or consulate in your country. We also recommend speaking with the United States Department of State Citizen's Emergency Center (tel. 202/647-5225) or the Burma desk (tel. 202/647-7108). Inquiries can also be made at the United States embassy in Bangkok.

Dive below the surface of official Burma—rife with documents, papers, rules and regulations, and minor and major annoyances and inconveniences. Ignore the single-minded bureaucracy as much as you can. Instead of following Tourist Burma's suggestions (which often sound like admonitions), let Rudyard Kipling be your guide:

> . . . On the road to Mandalay
> Where the flying fishes play
> And the dawn comes up like thunder
> Over China 'crost the bay!

That's the Burma to look for and remember, the one that inspired the poets with its rugged beauty and fathomless mysteries of culture and temperament. Remember your precious few hours on Inle Lake, shrouded in early-morning mists, its waters dotted by the ghostly figures of fishermen setting off in their fragile, tiny, foot-rowed boats. Remember Pagan, the eloquent silence of its ruined, centuries-old temples murmuring volumes about a time when men spent lifetimes traveling the road to truth and enlightenment. And in the plains and plateaus, thousands of glittering pagodas burnish the horizon almost everywhere you cast your eye. The most inspiring examples offer a profound insight into the spirit of the people who built them: their faith is staggering.

At times the government seems determined to make your precious few days in Burma as complicated and uncomfortable as possible. Try not to let the government's paranoical mindset become the background music of your stay. A trip to Burma is by definition one filled with irony—you will find yourself wondering how a land characterized by such overwhelming beauty both in its people and vistas can be ruled by such a single-minded and, you suspect, inept government. How else to explain the fact that in natural resources and location Burma is one of the most fortunate nations in Southeast Asia, yet its people among the continent's most disadvantaged?

Although your seven-day visa (the current maximum) rules out a comprehensive experience of life in Burma, and the short list of places approved for travel somewhat restricts your movement, we think you will have time to develop an infatuation with the country. You will immerse yourself in Burma: in the sweetness and generosity of the people, in the remnants of ancient cultures. More than any other country in Southeast Asia, Burma may succeed in conducting you to confrontation with another way of life: the signposts of Western civilization are nonexistent in Burma, save for perhaps, and then only fleetingly, in Rangoon, your prescribed point of entry and departure.

The Burmese way to socialism and the Buddhist philosophy are profoundly disparate yet equally important ingredients in the country's philosophical bouillabaisse.

1. INTRODUCTION

The following is but a brief survey of Burmese culture and history.

THE LAND: Burma is filled with geographical drama: in the north lie the rugged, spectacular foothills of the Himalayas, giving way to the verdant plateaus of central Burma and finally the river valleys and marshlands of the southern coast. Burma occupies 261,000 square miles of Southeast Asia. Its longest border, on the east, is with Thailand, briefly with Laos, and for a long distance, China. The west coast is separated by the Bay of Bengal and the Andaman Sea from India; the northwest actually borders Bangladesh and India, while the northern border is with China. Because of its isolationist economic policies and ethnic skirmishes, the largely indefensible Thai, Laotian, and Chinese borders are veritable smuggling highways, allowing for the orderly exchange of Western goods for rubies, teak, and hard currency.

The main waterway is the Irrawaddy River, something akin to Burma's Mississippi, linking Mandalay with Pagan and Rangoon and spilling out to the Andaman Sea. Along this basin are the major agricultural areas and trading centers of the country, generally under control of the government. The more mountainous north and far east, inhabited by a multiplicity of tribal peoples (including Kachin, Shan, and Karen, to the south), is no more than a loose confederation of ethnically divided mini-states, which operate in perpetual conflict with official Burma. The west coast, in Rakhine state, is lined with fine beaches, mostly off-limits to foreign visitors.

THE PEOPLE: The Burmese are lovely, patient, friendly, and dignified. Far from tossing baleful glances at tourists, they seem genuinely delighted to welcome visitors, and are generous and helpful to foreigner and neighbor alike. It's nothing for a Burmese to offer a stranger food, advice, or even shelter.

Burmese culture is steeped in tradition and a passion for education and

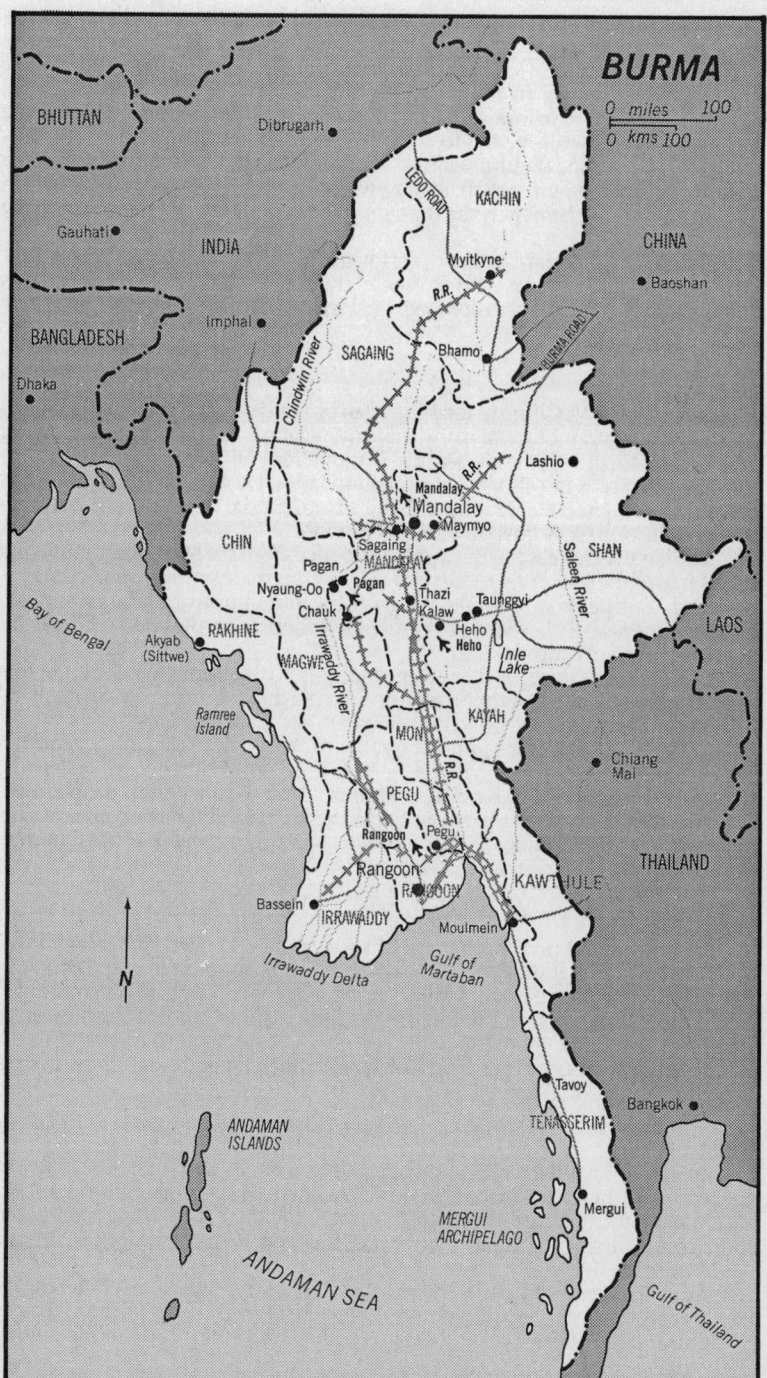

the fine arts. Over three-quarters of the population is literate, and a surprising number have gone on to university and graduate programs around the world. Craftsmen and artisans are accorded places of honor in society, and a great deal of respect is paid to the traditions and customs of the many races. Today the Burmese remain a deeply spiritual race, in part attributable to the Burmese way to socialism, an ideology that, in its abstract form, places the preservation of traditional culture above all else. Considering the hardships they endure as citizens of an ever-struggling nation governed by rulers hell-bent on forging an isolationist policy, the prevailing cheerfulness of the Burmese is truly amazing.

Take in a traditional evening of performance and music for a glimpse of Burmese humor and drama. The Burmese theater—spontaneous and fun—is known as *pwe*. Performances are staged anywhere, anytime, on nearly any occasion.

Ethnicity

Part of Burma's failure to establish itself as a unified nation lies in the continual disagreement among the many minority groups. The people of Burma are diverse and to this day still distinct. Nationalities are separated not only by cultural differences but also by political boundaries. Each of the significant tribes maintains its own state, often resembling a tiny fiefdom isolated from its neighbors and the one-party government in Rangoon.

The largest group is the Burmese, descended from the Mongols, numbering two-thirds of the country's population. The Burmese are settled in what the British called "Burma Proper," or the south-central lowlands surrounding Rangoon. Their ancestors are believed to have emigrated south from the eastern Himalayas in the 8th and 9th centuries.

The largest minority is the Shan group, comprising about 8% of the population. The Shans settled on the Shan plateau in northeast Burma. The Shan capital of Taunggyi is an ethereal city on the northern shores of Inle Lake.

Other, still smaller groups include the Mons, who arrived a few centuries before the Burmese, from the land known today as Cambodia; as well as the Chins, Rakhines, Kachins, Kayahs, and Karens. Many of these tribal people, especially the Karen, cross over between Burma and Thailand for an occasional skirmish with either Burmese or Thai forces who continually seek control in their own country of the northern territories.

Language

Burmese is the official language of the Republic, spoken by nearly 80% of the population. English is the second official language, and remains a course in the public school curriculum. In the countryside, older people will be more likely to be able to converse in English, albeit a little rustily. Children's command of English seems to be limited to a few key phrases calculated to reach out to the Western tourist ("School pens! School pens!" which translates as "Please bestow a plastic Bic ballpoint!").

Religion

Nearly 85% of Burma's population is Buddhist. By and large they adhere to the tenets of Theraveda Buddhism, which maintain that enlightenment and salvation are dependent on the actions of the individual. Theraveda is an older, more conservative philosophy than that of the more widely practiced Mahayana Buddhism.

With the establishment of the socialist Republic of Burma in 1974, religion has slipped from the central position it once held in the lives of the Burmese. Buddhism remains the most important (perhaps the only) aspect of life uniting the Burmese people, certainly more so than allegiance to the government, as demonstrated in the 1988 riots.

Other religious teachings have made nary an inroad into Burmese culture. A small group, mostly of Indian descent, practices Islam. British and American Christian missionaries established a precarious foothold among the tribes of the central region during the 19th century. Their followers today include a smattering of minorities, notably those of the Karen and Kachin tribes.

ECONOMY: By official government accounts Burma's economy today continues to expand and diversify, yet its people remain among the poorest on earth, lacking basic goods and services, and even clean water to drink. This in the face of a country that, not more than a few decades ago, could feed itself, export oil and rare hardwoods, and mine the most valuable gems in the world. Although exports have increased every year in the past decade, imports have increased at a faster pace, half of them paid for with foreign loans.

Since the decrease in oil production and exploration of the last few years, the cornerstone of the Burmese economy is rice—even though its production has slowed to such an extent that Burma is now a net rice importer. Ever since the British introduced its cultivation in the fertile Irrawaddy delta in the mid-1800s, Burma has depended on this one crop for the lion's share of its income. Today the rice growers themselves rarely profit from their labors. The government sets prices that barely cover the costs of production borne by the private farmer, who is not allowed to sell to anyone else.

Rice accounts for 40% of Burma's exports (though it is a net importer); timber products, most importantly teak, account for another 20%; mining of metals, minerals, and precious stones contributes 12%, while other products, mostly agricultural, make up the balance of Burma's outgoing trade.

The few imports allowed by the government are concentrated on capital and manufactured goods. Consumer products continue to arrive in a trickle and are largely supplemented by the activity of black market and smuggling operations.

Burma's infrastructure has deteriorated steadily since the departure of the British. Roads, utilities, and colonial-era buildings have not been touched in a generation. (It could be that Burma is attempting, though probably not intentionally, to erase all traces of outside rule.) Health and human services remain perennially low on the government's list of priorities. Instead, any gains made from trade are used mostly to fund military expansion and a scattering of new manufacturing ventures, the latter intended to reduce the country's dependence on agriculture.

HISTORY: Knowing the Burmese people, it comes as a shock when you reflect that their history for the last millennium or so has been written mainly in dispatches from the battlefield. Even today the country is in an uproar after the resignation of the despotic U Ne Win, for 26 years chairman of the Burmese Socialist Party and ruler of all Burma. A historical perspective will convince the observer that Burma is destined to be at odds with itself: the country's failure to establish itself as a major presence in Southeast Asia on the magnitude of Thailand or Singapore can be traced time and again to the disruptive effects of near-continual internal discord.

Neolithic Period

Earliest Burma is believed to have been inhabited by isolated tribes of people who left no deliberate record of their existence, although archeologists have uncovered evidence of some settlement.

The area's first documented discord is believed to have started soon after early settlers, the Mon, arrived in the region that is currently southern Burma in the first centuries after the birth of Christ. The Mon were soon at odds with the next arrivals, people from the eastern Himalayas whose descendants are considered Burma's indigenous race. A fitful struggle for control of the land ensued between these early groups, with the "Burmese" eventually ascendant.

Pagan

Pagan was the first Burmese kingdom whose records have survived to provide historians with clues to the life and times of ancient Burma. In 1057 Pagan's King Anawratha conquered the Mon people settled in the south and imported their Buddhist culture to his city, which to this day remains a showplace of exquisitely designed and constructed Buddhist temples. It was during this period that Burma achieved some degree of union, though it was to last for only a brief time.

In 1287 Pagan fell to Kublai Khan's Tartars in their march from the north country. The Mon took advantage of Pagan's defeat to return to the south, where they resumed development of their tiny kingdom. A new Mon capital was established in the early 15th century in Pegu, not far from present-day Rangoon. Over the next several hundred years control of the entire nation shifted continually from one kingdom to another, then back to the first. Burma's present-day major cities are built on the foundations of the earliest capitals.

Mandalay and Colonialism

Ironically, continued internal strife brought about Burma's dénouement as a resource-rich satellite of the British-India territories. Britain annexed Burma a chunk at a time, starting in 1826 (first Anglo-Burmese War) with the region near Assam bordering India. The defeated Burmese had been out trying to round up Assamese as a punitive measure for not paying tribute to the Burmese crown and had pressed farther into India than Britain cared for, although it took them nearly two years to mobilize and turn back the Burmese offensive.

Uneasy peace between the Burmese and British lasted less than 30 years. In the south the new Burmese king, Pagan Min, went on a genocidal rampage, executing nearly 6,000 people during the first two years of his reign. Britain responded more efficiently than it had during the Assam conflict and succeeded in gaining control of all of southern Burma, including Rangoon, in 1852.

To the north, in Burma's heartland, people lived in misery and terror under the corrupt and often inept rule of Burmese royalty. During the last half of the 19th century thousands of peasants fled to southern Burma to escape the oppression of their despotic rulers and the lawlessness of the land. In the marshy deltas of the Irrawaddy River they found plenty of work in British rice fields. The constant bickering and divisiveness of Mandalay's royal government weakened the city's resistance to the British, and in 1886, after dismantling a negligible defense, Britain took control of Mandalay and all of northern Burma, uniting the country for the first time in its tumultuous history, albeit as part and parcel of the British colonial empire.

It was not very long before the Burmese felt like displaced citizens in their own land. Thousands of Indians arrived with the British and were successful in developing Burma's burgeoning rice trade. The Burmese had never before had a national economy to speak of—perhaps in all the centuries of conflict they never had time to develop one—and now their land and resources were employed by the British and Indians to turn profits that never quite filtered down to the people. Growing resentment fueled a nationalist movement that remained relatively diffuse and unorganized until the 1920s and '30s. By then Britain could no longer ignore the rumblings of discontent and in 1937 Burma was separated from India. Internal conflicts among the various Burmese political groups prevented any further move toward independence until World War II, when Japan invaded and occupied the country.

By 1942 the Japanese had gained control of most of Burma and had driven out the British, Indian, and Chinese forces that had fought against their invasion. The Japanese military then helped Bogyoke Aung San, an activist who became known and loved by the Burmese as the father of the independence movement, to set up a national army. The Japanese, who wanted to run the show, soon antagonized Aung San and his followers, and by the end of the war these Burmese nationalists repledged their loyalties (and military strength) to the British.

Aung San was assassinated six months before the day of Independence, which came on January 4, 1948.

MODERN POLITICS: Burma's single-minded adherence to its own special brand of socialism since independence in 1948 is either a smashing success or a dismal failure, depending on who is telling the story. Theoretically the government's isolationist policies have succeeded in giving the country and its people a national identity and pride never possible in the centuries of outside rule. Statistically speaking, the average Burman lives a much harder life than his parents did before World War II.

Today the Burmese economy is a shambles, a Third World cliché. The country's phenomenal rice-growing capability is squandered, yet no other industry has been developed to fill the void in the country's earning power. National resources, among the world's most abundant, lie undisturbed. Public works built during British rule have not been maintained in a generation. Roads have deteriorated, the water supply is contaminated, and anything and everything that breaks is left broken, from toilets to telephones.

For nearly 30 years the reins of power in Burma have passed back and forth between the hands of two men. In 1958, after a decade of deteriorating and increasingly factional government, Prime Minister U Nu turned control over to General Ne Win, leader of the Burmese military. U Nu told the people of Burma that Ne Win's caretaker government was necessary to restore law and order and to guarantee free elections. This goal was in fact accomplished in 1960, and U Nu returned to power on the wave of popular vote. During the next two years he failed to unite the deeply divided country, and in fact antagonized the tribal states of the Shans and Kayahs into threatening secession. Once again Ne Win stepped in, this time uninvited, during a 1962 coup in which he disbanded the parliament and named himself ruler of Burma and head of a 15-member Revolutionary Council. The Council issued a manifesto called the Burmese Way to Socialism, a document stating the goals of its people in no uncertain terms.

U Nu spent his time in prison meditating on questions of Buddhist philosophy. After his release in 1966, Nu led various attempts to secure support for return to a parliamentary government. His appeals for money and support took him all over the globe.

In 1970 he actually succeeded in raising an army that launched a series of raids into Burma from Thailand. These gains were shortlived. Nu soon resigned from the rebel movement he had founded a few years earlier, the National United Liberation Front, and went into exile, first to the United States and finally to India. In 1981, under a special amnesty program announced by Ne Win, he returned to Rangoon.

Responding to global pressures to abolish the military government, Ne Win in 1974 announced the birth of the Socialist Republic of the Union of Burma. Until his resignation in mid-1988 Ne Win was the republic's only president. During the same time he also served as chairman of the Burma Socialist Party, an alleged civilian group in which former military leaders held 16 of 17 ministerial posts.

Today it's anyone's guess what Ne Win and his supporters have in store for the country, or the country for them. For the first time in Burma's history, millions of civilians are joining the various disgruntled student groups and rebel factions in demanding a return to democracy, free elections, and an end to one-party rule. Although he resigned in July 1988, Ne Win is still perceived by most observers to be calling the shots. Sadly, as we go to press in 1989, the announcement of military rule seems to render the possibility of genuine elections in the very near future remote.

Kyat	$U.S.	Kyat	$U.S.
0.25	0.04	150.00	25.00
0.50	0.08	200.00	33.33
0.75	0.13	250.00	41.67
1.00	0.17	300.00	50.00
2.00	0.33	350.00	58.33
3.00	0.50	400.00	66.67
4.00	0.67	450.00	75.00
5.00	0.83	500.00	83.33
6.00	1.00	550.00	91.67
7.00	1.17	600.00	100.00
8.00	1.33	650.00	108.33
9.00	1.50	700.00	116.67
10.00	1.67	750.00	125.00
15.00	2.50	800.00	133.33
20.00	3.33	850.00	141.67
25.00	4.17	900.00	150.00
30.00	5.00	950.00	158.33
35.00	5.83	1,000.00	166.67
40.00	6.67	1,050.00	175.00
45.00	7.50	1,100.00	183.33
50.00	8.33	1,150.00	191.67
75.00	12.50	1,200.00	200.00
100.00	16.67	1,250.00	208.33

2. SUGGESTED ITINERARIES

With such little time and so few destinations open to tourists, one might assume that planning an itinerary isn't important. This couldn't be farther from the truth, for a carefully mapped-out trip (with a few contingencies) will prove a real timesaver. Nearly all visitors to Burma travel along the "Golden Triangle," that is, the road from Rangoon to Mandalay and on to Pagan; however, if you intend to travel without a group, be aware that you may not be able to get to all of these destinations in seven days. Expect delays due to train, air, or bus failure or cancellations. Also know that as a free, independent tourist (F.I.T., in travel parlance), you are at the back of the queue for airline, train, and hotel reservations. In other words, don't be surprised when you show up in the country to discover that your favorite hotel is booked or that you can't get that perfect flight to Heho.

There are two basic questions for any itinerary to Burma: What are your interests? How do you want to travel (in a group or by yourself)?

Most people who visit Burma have some interest in Buddhist culture and history. If you are one of "most people," set your first sights on Pagan and allow yourself two full days to tour the area. The next most important stop is Mandalay, not only for the climb up Mandalay Hill, but also for visits to other nearby towns of interest such as Sagaing, Amarapura, Ava, and Mingun. Again, plan on spending two days in the Mandalay area. All visitors to Burma, no matter what their interest, should see the Shwe Dagon Pagoda in Rangoon; because of its central location, you'll need but a few hours to make this excursion. If you have the time, consider a day trip to Pegu, outside Rangoon, to see its excellent temples and shrines.

If you want to experience a bit of the old colonial style, make sure to find your way up to Maymyo, in the hills above Mandalay. There you can stay in a fantastic colonial-era club/manor house/hotel, while away the hours strolling through the country's finest botanical garden, or just breathe in the bracing air of Burma's most serene hill station. For those who want to explore the more ethnic side of Burma, in an area where the Shan people reside (the only contact authorized by Tourist Burma), a trip to Taunggyi and gorgeous Inle Lake will suffice.

Ordinarily we are inveterate independent travelers, the type who would rather not make the journey to a particular destination if done in a group than to suffer the indignity of being moved around as a herd. That said, we highly recommend taking an organized group tour of Burma. The advantages are several; the only disadvantage is cost. Groups get first priority on all transportation and accommodations—so much so that it's unlikely that you'll find a reservation at any of the exceedingly rare first-class rooms in any Burmese city. Group tours are, as much as possible in Byzantine Burma, efficiently run. If you're on your own, you'll end up spending much of your seven days making arrangements for travel that are unnecessary on an organized tour. In fact, you'll probably have less time in each destination traveling by yourself than if you travel by group. Most tours organized out of Bangkok include Rangoon, Pagan, and Mandalay only; more specialized tours can be arranged with Tourist Burma directly (see the ABCs for specific information). Group tours can be much more expensive, especially if you pay for everything in advance with hard currency.

Our most important tip for Burma travel is to try to design your itinerary in such a way as to depart Rangoon as soon as practical. All departures must be made from Rangoon, so you know that you'll get there by the end of the trip. A strategy used by many experienced Burma hands is to take the first flight out of the Rangoon airport after arriving in the country. In other words, instead of going into Rangoon proper, proceed directly to the Tourist Burma desk at the airport and try to get on the next flight out to Pagan, Mandalay, or Heho; if you intend to travel by train, try to buy a ticket for that evening's journey and head for the station (you'll also save the cost of a night's hotel room).

3. GETTING THERE AND GETTING AROUND

Getting to Burma is simple: you must arrive by air and Rangoon is the only allowable point of entry. Your choice of airline is further simplified by your intended date of arrival.

GETTING TO BURMA: The only carrier offering daily service to Rangoon, flying from Bangkok is the **Burma Airways Corporation (BAC);** as of late 1988 it also has Sunday and Wednesday flights from Singapore, Monday and Friday flights from Kathmandu, and is planning a route from Penang in Malaysia. Expect to pay about $200 for the round-trip ticket from Bangkok to Rangoon. Contact BAC in Rangoon at 104 Strand Rd. (tel. 84-566 or 84-567) near the Strand Hotel. **Thai Airways,** at 441 Tavoy House, Maha Bandoola Street, next to the Sule Pagoda (tel. 75-988 or 74-922), flies from Bangkok on Monday, Thursday, and Saturday.

Other international carriers with offices in Rangoon are **Biman Airways** (the national carrier of Bangladesh), at 106 Pansodan Rd. (tel. 74-199 or 70-736), with a flight on Tuesday from Dacca en route to Bangkok; **Royal Nepal Airways,** 22 York Rd. (tel. 71-347), with a flight on Thursday from Kathmandu;

Aeroflot (the national airline of the Soviet Union), at 18 Prome Rd., 7th Mile (tel. 61-066), with a Tuesday flight from Vientiane and Ho Chi Minh City en route to Moscow via Tbilisi; **Air France,** 69 Sule Pagoda Rd. (tel. 74-199); **KLM Royal Dutch Airlines,** 104 Strand Rd. (tel. 74-180); **SAS Scandinavian Airlines System,** 441-445 Tavoy House, Maha Bandoola St. (tel. 75-988); and **CAAC** (the Civil Aviation Administration of China), 67A Prome Rd. (tel. 75-714), offers Wednesday flights once every two weeks (once a week in winter) between Peking, Kunming, and Rangoon.

GROUP TRAVEL AND GETTING AROUND: Although many companies within the United States and Thailand (specifically Bangkok) offer tours to Burma, as of early 1989 all trips are arranged and supervised by Tourist Burma in Rangoon. In other words , it pays to shop around for the least expensive tour package, as you are likely to be placed in the serendipitous hands of Tourist Burma no matter which package you choose. (Generally, the cheapest deals will be available in Thailand rather than the United States). The most reliable and experienced outfit (but by no means the least expensive) is Diethelm Travel in the Kian Gwan Building on Wireless Road, Bangkok (tel. 255-9150). Several North American agencies also offer a one-week Burma tour; among them are Journeyworld International at 1061 First Avenue, Room 2A, New York, NY (tel. 212/752-8308), East Quest, 32 Pell St., New York, NY 10013 (212/406-2224), and Travcoa at 4000 MacArthur Blvd., Suite 650E, Newport Beach, CA 92660 (tel. 800/992-2003; within California 714/476-2800).

Most trips include visas, transfers, roundtrip airfare between Bangkok and Rangoon (insist on Thai Airways), hotels, and some meals, travel within the country (often via Burma Airways), and a guide. Expect to pay between $750 and $1,500 for a seven-day trip.

By Air

Before discussing the specifics of traveling around the country by air, a word needs to be mentioned about the relative merits of this mode of travel. Although flying can be speedy and relatively inexpensive, the key issue in Burma is safety. Unfortunately, the U.S. State Department felt compelled to issue a Traveler's Advisory in 1988 after two BAC planes crashed on routine domestic flights, both apparently due to maintenance failure. Since the upheavals of the past year, it is unlikely that the repair and safety level of the airline has improved markedly, so let your desire to race around the country be tempered by the risks of BAC's poor safety record. Also remember that airline flights are at least as likely as trains and buses to experience long delays.

BAC flights between Rangoon, Mandalay, Pagan, and Taunggyi (via Heho Airport) are quickly filled, with Burmese VIPs and tour groups given preference over the independent tourist; be prepared to be bumped from a flight.

The following fares and schedules from mid-1988 can be used to make rough approximations for your own planning:

There are six flights every morning connecting the major cities. In mid-1988 the one-way price for the 2½-hour flight from Rangoon to Pagan was 495 kyat ($82.50); for the half-hour flight from Pagan to Mandalay, 190 kyat ($31.75); for the 1½-hour flight from Heho Airport (serving Taunggyi) to Rangoon, 460 kyat ($76.75); for the half-hour flight from Mandalay to Heho, 205 kyat ($34.25); for the 2½-hour flight from Rangoon to Mandalay, 545 kyat ($90.75), with the same price charged for the flight originating in Mandalay and ending in Rangoon. The afternoon's flights reverse the morning's schedule.

If you do choose to fly, you'll have to make arrangements through **Tourist Burma**. They will reserve and sell Burma Airways tickets, but will only confirm your seat (unless you're in a pre-arranged group or an all-inclusive Tourist Burma package) the day before departure. The best advice is to reserve a seat after you arrive in a destination, don't pay, and return to the Tourist Burma office the day before the contemplated departure date to check on availability. They'll ask for a deposit, but if you choose not to fly, they won't refund your money! The only drawback is that you need to appear physically at the TB office with cash, normally before 11 a.m., in order to keep your seat; otherwise they'll sell it to local tourists.

In some cities, such as Pagan, TB may issue a voucher that you'll have to take to the BAC office to actually receive a ticket; in other cities a TB voucher taken at the airport will suffice. During the busy cool season, when reservations and, more important, confirmations may be hard to come by, some unscrupulous TB representatives will charge a special fee, *bakshish*, which can run as much as 100% of the ticket price. When an official at BAC explained this scam to us as an example of government corruption, he smiled and asked us, "Do you have a present for me?" Fortunately, this system isn't widespread, though one can imagine that it might become so.

In all destinations, TB will arrange for their bus to pick you up at your hotel or guesthouse for the transfer to the airport. They will also bus you into the main TB office in your destination, making that part of the process fairly efficient.

By Train

If you can reserve reclining seats in the top-class car, travel by train can be modestly comfortable—otherwise it ranges from spartan to truly hellish. We have usually managed to reserve the none-too-well-upholstered recliners by buying as early as possible; the key here is getting to Tourist Burma in the early morning. There are three daily trips made each way between Rangoon and Mandalay, along the main north-south line, leaving both cities at 6 a.m., 6:15 p.m., and 9 p.m., and arriving at the other end not sooner than 14 hours later. The first-class fare for an adult in mid-1988 was 110 kyat ($18.25). Sleepers are available for 138 kyats ($23). If you plan on traveling between Rangoon and Mandalay, try to get on the 6:15 p.m. run, as the approximately 14-hour journey will save the cost of a night's hotel room.

By Bus

Burma's bus service is not for the faint of heart. The trip from Mandalay to Taunggyi, for example, is a rugged, exhausting trip taking a minimum of 12 hours (longer, if mechanical problems arise) spent bouncing over bad roads and jostled among your many, many fellow passengers (we've counted as many as 30 people crammed in and on top of a Burma-style public bus, the latter most often a long-bed Toyota pickup truck outfitted with long wooden benches).

There are bus routes linking all the cities to which visitors are permitted to travel. Quite simply, TB will not sell you a ticket to more than half a dozen approved destinations, notably the historical cities of Mandalay, Taunggyi, and Pagan, and of course returning to gateway Rangoon.

By Taxi

Taxis are plentiful in the major cities (look for red license plates), vying for trade from the best hotels. They can also be rented for trips through the surrounding countryside. Be sure to agree on a fare before you leave on an excursion; although standardized rates are set for popular destinations, you may have to bargain your way to other places.

Horse-drawn carts often replace taxis for travel in and around Pagan and up in the hill country around Maymyo and Mandalay. Bicycle-driven trishaws are numerous in Mandalay and Rangoon. Travel in Burma will probably include all these conveyances and more—we've traveled in ox-drawn chicken carts and military trucks!

Whether you take a taxi, bicycle rickshaw, horse-drawn carriage, or ox cart, try to carry a card with basic names and destinations in Burmese, just in case you come to an impasse with your driver; most hotel concierges will help you by writing out the names of your desired destinations.

By Boat

Boat travel is an important means of transportation within the country for the Burmese people, but for the visitor on a seven-day visa it's one of the least practical—with one exception. The steamer journey from Mandalay to Pagan is the highlight of the trip for many foreign travelers to Burma. The expedition from Mandalay to Pagan takes 15 hours; the return trip upriver is longer. The boat leaves Mandalay every Sunday and Thursday at 5 a.m. The fare for cabin seating is 160 kyat ($26.75), as opposed to open deck for 31 kyat ($5.25).

4. THE ABC'S OF BURMA (INCLUDING RANGOON)

This section includes basic travelers' advice and provides an overview of the country, as well as information about Rangoon, Burma's capital. Quite simply, Rangoon is often the only place in Burma where the Western traveler will find goods and services bearing any resemblance to those readily available in a more developed nation. Consult the sections on each city in the next chapters for answers to more specific questions than those addressed here.

AIRLINES: The only carrier offering daily service to Rangoon, flying from Bangkok, as well as serving as the country's sole domestic carrier, is **Burmese Airways Corporation (BAC).** Contact BAC in Rangoon at 104 Strand Rd. (tel. 84-566 or 84-567), near the Strand Hotel. BAC tickets can also be purchased in Tourist Burma offices in Mandalay, Pagan, and Heho. For the addresses and telephone numbers of other international carriers, consult the section on "Getting to Burma."

AIRPORTS: Rangoon's **Mingaladon Airport** is the only point of entry—save for the rare cruise ship permitted to dock—to Burma for foreign travelers. The airport is 19 km (12 miles) northwest of the city. As part of the Customs-clearing process you are required to change at least $100 into Burmese currency and to show proof of onward passage. Changing currency offers an excellent introduction to the double-entendre ambience that pervades so much of Burmese life. Burma is the only Southeast Asian country we thought deserving of an entire ABC section devoted to the changing of money (see below).

After Customs, which is quite thorough, stop at the **Tourist Burma desk** in the terminal for maps and brochures. You'll also be able to make hotel reservations (although we advise having done so before arrival) and to purchase a taxi ticket, currently priced at 60 kyat ($10), for the ride to town. Hail your cab at the taxi stand outside and to the left of the terminal.

The restaurant located upstairs from the arrivals area serves typical, expensive, and fairly awful airport fare.

BANKS: Other than specialty finance agencies, the **Union Bank of Burma,** headquartered at 24/26 Sule Pagoda Rd. (tel. 85-300), is the only game in town.

A tourist's most pressing errands—money exchange and cashing traveler's checks—can also be completed in larger hotels and through licensed (and a vast network of unlicensed) moneychangers; at Tourist Burma offices (in Rangoon, at 77/79 Sule Pagoda Rd.); and the Foreign Trade Bank on Barr Street in Rangoon.

BATHROOMS: Burma is not high on any hygienist's list of must-sees in the world. Western-style toilets in various states of repair and cleanliness can be found in better hotels and larger cities. Most shops, small hotels, and guesthouses have an Asian toilet, that rustic little contraption flushed manually with water pail and ladle.

Carry your own toilet paper. (On your seven-day visa, one roll ought to do it.)

BUSINESS HOURS: Government offices in Burma are open Monday through Friday from 9:30 a.m. to 4 p.m. **Banking hours** are 10 a.m. to 2 p.m. Monday through Friday. Most restaurants close by 9 p.m. National television and radio go off the air shortly afterward. **Shops** in Rangoon and other cities are open seven days a week; hours may vary but not much past 10 p.m.

In mid-1988, owing to civilian unrest, rioting, and violence, the Burmese government imposed an 8 p.m. curfew in Rangoon and Mandalay. As of this writing the curfew was still in effect.

CLIMATE: Burma lies a few inconsequential degrees north of the equator. The tropical climate is divided into three distinct seasons: a hot and dry summer (March to mid-May), when temperatures can reach 113° in the central region; rainy (May through October); and cool (October through February), with temperatures in the 70° to 80° range. Temperatures and humidity average 80° and 80% year round, escaped only in the plateaus, where nighttime temperatures can drop to 40°.

Rainfall is plentiful, albeit concentrated to a few months a year and brief daily showers in every season.

CLOTHING: Let the climate be your first parameter when packing for Burma. Casual, loose-fitting clothing, neat and modest—in breathable fabrics such as cotton, rayon, silk, and linen—is essential. Men will not need a jacket and tie unless scheduled for a government or business meeting. Pack a sweater for nights in the country, and a bathing suit only if you promise not to dive into any body of water other than a hotel swimming pool.

You'll need lightweight raingear when traveling in the rainy season, and fast-drying or waterproof shoes.

CREDIT CARDS: Currently, **American Express** is the only charge card accepted in Burma. It can be used (at the official exchange rate) to pay for major hotels and transportation. Tourist Burma offices accept the card and are the only place to buy air, bus, rail, and tour tickets. Your American Express card will be listed on your currency card upon your arrival. Amex has no offices in the country; the closest office is in Bangkok (see "The ABCs of Bangkok" in Chapter XVI).

CUISINE: Burmese cooking, when you can find it, is spicy and pungent, emphasizing curry and fish; however, native cooking is currently in hiding and doesn't appear prominently on the Burmese restaurant scene. Instead, you'll find barely adequate Indian and Chinese fare the most common offering. Your only chance to sample real Burmese food may come with an invitation to someone's home, an opportunity not to be missed.

The larger hotels in Rangoon, Mandalay, Pagan, and Taunggyi all operate continental-style restaurants.

Seafood and rice are big exports for Burma, and are plentiful on every menu. Fish includes pomfret, mackerel, red snapper, cuttlefish, lobsters, and prawns. Raw fish should be avoided altogether; the waters are contaminated and only proper cooking renders seafood safe for consumption.

Coconuts, bananas, lemons, and limes are available year round. Seasonal fruits include guava, strawberries, jackfruit, watermelon, oranges, plums, and pomegranates, as well as less familiar bounty too numerous to enumerate. Wash and peel any fruit before eating it.

A colorful array of vegetables, heavy on legumes, rounds out the Burmese garden. Native dishes employ numerous varieties of beans, peas, chiles, onions, cabbages, carrots, kohlrabi, tomatoes, potatoes, and pumpkins.

Health considerations force us to recommend that you avoid the street food sold by hawkers and vendors.

CURRENCY: This section ought to be written in erasable ink. We report the state of affairs in mid-1988, when we did our research. The official unit of Burmese currency is the **kyat** (pronounced "chat"), currently exchanged at a rate of 6 kyat per U.S. dollar. All conversions to U.S. dollars in this section are according to this official rate.

Interestingly enough, the official version is not the only story. We point this out only because we would be remiss in not reporting that the black market for currency seems to be one of Burma's most thriving industries and biggest sports. From the moment you hail a cab at Mingaladon Airport until the moment, seven days later, when you prepare to board your departing flight, Burma's bustling parallel economy will manifest itself in subtle and not-so-subtle ways. On the black market kyat are discounted as much as 40 to the dollar. You will be offered a thousand opportunities to enter into this illegal transaction. We don't recommend one course of action over another. Perhaps one day, after three days' forbearance, you may throw caution to the wind and accept a less-than-kosher offer for those coveted Yankee dollars. The entire exchange will take less than 30 seconds and your buying power will suddenly be quadrupled. The risks involved are discussed in the next section on currency cards.

A further examination of Burmese currency offers insight into the country's domestic politics and policies. In 1987 the government "remonetarized" the currency and issued new money. Rendered worthless were the old kyat and pya denominations of 1, 5, 10, 25, and 50. New denominations of 45 and 90 were issued in 1988, as a way to force out all of those hoarding black-market kyat. The upshot was far more calamitous than that of mere fiscal housecleaning. Some Burmese lost their entire savings, earned largely on the black market. Their stashes of cash (unreportable, due to their clandestine origins) were not redeemable. Nor was so much as a month's grace period offered upon the announcement of the change.

CURRENCY CARD: This required document is incorporated into Burmese entry procedures. As part of Customs, foreigners are required to change at least $100 into kyat at the official exchange rate. At this time you are issued a currency card on which your initial exchange is recorded. Every subsequent major transaction is also recorded on the card, including payment for hotels, meals in larger restaurants, local travel, and the like. Upon departure, you are required to change any kyat you have left. Transactions on your card are calculated and the resulting balance must equal the kyat you surrender at departure. Try to spend all the kyat you have left before you reach Customs—the officials will redeem only one-fourth.

By now it may have occurred to you that, should you plan to exchange currency on the black market, you should take care to have the purchases and payments recorded on your currency card not exceed the money you have exchanged at the official rate. Otherwise you will have some explaining to do. In other words, try not to have your card filled in with too many transactions. Some people are known to say, "Oops, I must have forgotten to carry my card with me."

CUSTOMS: Visitors to Burma are allowed to carry 200 cigarettes and one liter of spirits into the country. Even if you abstain, we suggest purchasing these items before you leave Bangkok or Singapore. They are highly coveted and can be used as gifts. More important, they command, on average, about 600 kyat ($100) on the black market.

Clearing Customs on both arrival and departure is a thoroughly tedious, time-consuming process. Upon entry, travelers must declare all foreign currency, jewelry, and cameras. You are issued Customs and currency cards noting these items; the idea is to prevent you from selling your valuables on the black market. Video equipment will be impounded at the airport and returned when you leave; make sure to retain your receipt.

Burma enforces strict laws against the exportation of antiques. Gems and jewelry, both popular with tourists, are guaranteed export only when purchased at a Diplomatic Store: you will be required to show your official receipt for these items if they are found in your luggage.

When leaving, you must exchange any kyat you have left. Your currency form is inspected for discrepancies: again, don't make the mistake of paying for a hotel room or plane ticket (both purchases will be recorded on the currency form) with black-market kyat. Total currency exchanged on the card must equal purchases plus currency surrendered at departure. Save your whisky and cigarette windfall (if you go that route) to pay for meals, small gifts, and other transactions not typically recorded on the currency form.

DOCUMENTS FOR ENTRY: Tourists are granted non-negotiable seven-day visas for travel in Burma (children under 7 years of age are not required to procure a visa). You must be in possession of a valid passport and proof of onward or return passage. Visas are typically obtained at Burma's foreign consulates in Bangkok, Singapore, and Hong Kong. Be careful not to mention any controversial pastimes when applying: journalists are among the usual suspects denied entry. You'll need three passport-size photographs. Make sure to allow sufficient time (24 to 48 hours) for your visa to be approved and issued.

If you wish to apply for a visa in the United States, you may do so by contacting the Consulate-General of the Socialist Republic of Burma at 10 E. 77th St., New York, NY 10021 (tel. 212/535-1311). To apply by mail you'll need an arrival report form and two tourist application forms, three recent passport-size photographs, a visa fee of $5 U.S., and your original passport.

For those in other countries, you may apply for a visa from any Burmese embassy or consulate throughout the world. Visas are issued on passports only, not on other travel documents, Stateless Person Identity Cards, or Seaman's Permits. All visas are valid for three months from the date of issue.

Should you miss or be bumped from your departing flight, you must go to the Immigration and Manpower Office in Rangoon in the Government Office Complex on Strand Road (tel. 85-505), with a letter of explanation from your airline. You may be required to pay a small fine.

DRINKING WATER: *Don't drink tap water anywhere in Burma.* Consume only water you know has been boiled or bottled. Although Burma once set the highest standard for hygiene in Southeast Asia, those standards have been radically relaxed in recent years. Burma's water supply is contaminated by bacterial and viral organisms killed only by boiling for a minimum of 15 minutes.

DRUGSTORES: Western-style pharmacies are quite rare in Burma. Some very basic toiletries and pharmaceuticals are available at **Scott Markets** in Rangoon, on Bogyoke Aung San Road, near the intersection with Prome Road. A few imported medicines are also sold at **St. John's Market** in Rangoon and at the city's open-air market near 26th Street and Anawratha Road. If you need medical consultation or supplies, contact your embassy for advice or referrals.

ELECTRICITY: Standard wiring in Burma accommodates 220 volts, 50 cycles, A.C. You'll need to bring an adapter for American-made traveler's appliances, typewriters, etc.

EMBASSIES: More than 30 nations maintain diplomatic missions in Burma, all in Rangoon.

The **U.S. Embassy** is located at 581 Merchant St. (tel. 82-055), southeast of the Sule Pagoda. The British Embassy is at 80 Strand Rd. (tel. 81-700); the **Australian Embassy** is a few doors away at 88 Strand Rd. (tel. 80-711). The closest **Canadian Embassy** serving Burma is located in Dhaka (Bangladesh) at House 16A, Road 48, Gulshan, Dhaka, GPO Box 569 (tel. Dhaka 600-181).

EMERGENCIES: The following emergency telephone numbers are standard throughout Burma: **police,** 199; **ambulance,** 192; **fire,** 191. Consult your embassy for advice in handling medical emergencies.

ETIQUETTE: The Burmese are respectful people, showing great courtesy to each other and to visitors. Nearly 85% are Buddhist, whom you might offend by touching anywhere about the head and shoulders. Stick with a handshake rather than run the risk of delivering an insult by presuming too much familiarity. A Buddhist's spiritual center is the top of his head. The feet are considered unclean, and you should avoid pointing your toes at another person—very nearly a gesture of contempt! Remove your shoes and socks upon entering religious grounds or private homes.

FESTIVALS AND HOLIDAYS: The Burmese find something to celebrate nearly every month of the year. Holidays, complete with games, pranks, food, and sporting bouts, honor primitive deities, changes of season, the full moon, harvests, and events in the life of Buddha and local heroes. Check with your embassy or Tourist Burma when you arrive to learn what's going on during your week's stay. Many traditional events have no set date from year to year and are based on the lunar calendar. Following is a list of holidays celebrated throughout Burma:

January
Independence Day (January 4), the first day of a weeklong festival celebrated by hundreds of local fairs.

February
Union Day (February 12), celebrating a landmark day in 1947 during Burma's fight for independence when representatives from all the nation's ethnic factions sat down and agreed to pledge their cooperation.
The new moon is heralded this month in a **rice-harvest festival.**

March
Peasants' Day (March 2).
Resistance Day (March 27). Ah, the mighty resistance! Relived in parades and fireworks.

April
Thingyan (Water Festival). Absolutely our favorite Burmese holiday, it's the beginning of the new year, falling in the height (or depths) of the dry season, celebrated by throwing buckets of cold water at anyone and everyone. Other activities include dancing, singing, and performances. On a more reverential note, the soul and heart are cleansed in a ceremonial scrubdown for Buddha images and pagodas on New Year's Day.

May
Workers' Day (May 1), a state holiday honoring the laborer.
The full moon in May is celebrated as **Buddha's birthday.** Banyan trees are watered in a rite celebrating the tree under which Buddha attained enlightenment.

July
The **full moon** marks the beginning of a three-month period of heightened religious observance among Buddhists.
Martyrs' Day (July 19), in remembrance of Bogyoke Aung San, who was assassinated on this day in 1947.

September
Boat festivals are held throughout the country, complete with parades, pageantry, and pomp.

October
The Buddhist Lent, a period of prayer and contemplation, draws to a close. Weddings and other joyous occasions, frowned upon in the past three months, now proceed.
The **Festival of Lights,** celebrating Buddha's return from heaven, is a night of illumination of every description—from candles and oil lamps to fire balloons and light bulbs.

December
The season for many **festivals honoring spirits.**

FILM AND CAMERA: Film is expensive and hard to come by. Pack several rolls; Burma is well stocked in scenic vistas, mist-covered mountains, gleaming pagodas, and smiling faces. Purchasing a camera in Burma would be foolhardy. Try the Diplomatic Market in Rangoon for film, but again, if it's available it will be so only at premium prices.

HEALTH AND VACCINATIONS: Please take extra precautions to protect your health when traveling in Burma. Visitors need no special inoculations to gain entry save for those arriving within six days of travel in a cholera- or yellow-fever–infected area (typically in South America or Africa).
Launch an anti-malarial campaign two weeks prior to your arrival in Southeast Asia, and keep it up throughout your stay and until six weeks after leaving; many U.S. tropical disease experts recommend taking Aralen. Carry insect repellent and mosquito coils. If you're on a budget and plan to save on accommoda-

---

A SPECIAL NOTE ABOUT TRAVELING TO BURMA. In the summer of 1988 Burmese citizens from around the country staged massive political demonstrations that ultimately brought about the resignation of Ne Win, the former military leader who had ruled the country since 1961. The military regained control in the fall by enforcing strict martial law with dusk-to-dawn curfews and shoot-to-kill orders for any demonstrators. At the same time, Burma closed its doors to tourists.

This state of affairs changed just as we went to press, with limited seven-day travel permitted to tourists in groups only. Burma is still off-limits to all individual tourists. All of this is to say that before planning a trip to Burma, inquire about the availability of visas; inquiries should be made at the Burmese embassy or consulate in your country. We also recommend speaking with the United States Department of State Citizen's Emergency Center (tel. 202/647-5225) or the Burma desk (tel. 202/647-7108). Inquiries can also be made at the United States embassy in Bangkok.

---

tions, bring a sheet of mosquito netting—it's one of the first amenities to go in the downscale hotel scene.

Diarrhea is the most common traveler's ailment. Seek treatment if symptoms persist more than 48 hours or if they are accompanied by headaches, prolonged fever, and nausea.

As we instructed you before (and will again up ahead), *don't drink any water not boiled or bottled.* Also, the medical officer at the U.S. Embassy strongly suggests not drinking or eating any dairy products. Protect yourself from the sun by wearing a broad-brimmed straw hat, or by carrying a pretty handmade Burmese parasol.

HOSPITALS: Five out of five doctors who voiced an opinion agreed: Burmese medical care is woefully inadequate. Should you require medical services, contact your embassy (see above) at once for advice and assistance. The rural areas are especially wanting for basic care, but as a tourist on a seven-day visa, you probably won't have time (or be permitted) to roam very far from what help is available.

In Rangoon, there's the **Diplomatic Hospital** (also known as Kandawgyi Clinic), at Kat Natmouk on Royal Lake (tel. 50-149); **Rangoon General Hospital,** on Bogyoke Aung San Road (tel. 81-722); and **University Hospital,** on University Avenue (tel. 31-541).

LANGUAGE: Burmese is the official language in Burma, although English is considered a semi-official tongue. Most older Burmese speak English, learned in school in the years before Burma's independence in 1948. The elegant Burmese alphabet looks like two bubbles in an intricate ballet.

COMMONLY USED BURMESE WORDS AND EXPRESSIONS: One of the significant legacies of the British administration of Burma is the use of the English language throughout the country; however, we noticed that, although most of the older and educated people still speak English, the younger people tend to speak only a very few words in anything other than Burmese. The following list is intended to give you a mastery of a few Burmese words, enough to say hello, be polite, and hope that someone nearby speaks English.

Burmese	English
mingala ba	hello
thwahbaounmay	good-bye
hou kay	yes
mahou hapu	no
cheizu tin ba-de	thank you
kei sa mashibabu	you're welcome
mayela	how are you?
miyata	train
baska	bus
ahngaka	taxi
myou	city
lan	road or street
baska gai	bus station
miyata youn	train station
lei-zei	airport
zei	market
pyadai	museum
ho tey	hotel
sathau hasein	restaurant
sadai	post office

We recommend the *Burmese Phrasebook* (Victoria: Lonely Planet Publications, 1988) for a far more complete language guide.

LAUNDRY: Most hotels and guesthouses in Burma provide laundry services at very reasonable rates. Ask your concierge for details.

LIQUOR: Cocktail lounges are not exactly ubiquitous in Burma, but the larger hotels in Rangoon all have pleasantly air-conditioned watering holes where it's possible (when there isn't a "temporary" shortage, a state that seems perpetual) to sample Mandalay Beer—Burma's only suds—or a cocktail (perhaps poured from that bottle you brought into the country hours earlier). In smaller towns, government hotels dispense liquor to their own guests.

MEASURES: Burma uses a system of weights and measures little changed from British colonial days. Following are listed standard quantities and their American equivalents:

1 viss	=	3.6 pounds
1 tical	=	.58 ounces
1 cubit	=	18 inches
1 span	=	9 inches

THE METRIC SYSTEM—IN A NUTSHELL

Length
1 millimeter = 0.04 inches (*or* less than ¹⁄₁₆ in)
1 centimeter = 0.39 inches (*or* just under ½ in)
1 meter   = 1.09 yards (*or* about 39 inches)
1 kilometer = 0.62 mile (*or* about ⅔ mile)

To convert kilometers to miles, take the number of kilometers and multiply by .62 (for example, 25 km × .62 = 15.5 mi).

To convert miles to kilometers, take the number of miles and multiply by 1.61 (for example, 50 mi × 1.61 = 80.5 km).

Capacity
1 liter = 33.92 ounces
         = 1.06 quart
         = 0.26 gallons

To convert liters to gallons, take the number of liters and multiply by .26 (for example, 50 l × .26 = 13 gallons).

To convert gallons to liters, take the number of gallons and multiply by 3.79 (for example, 10 gal × 3.79 = 37.9 l).

Weight
1 gram   = 0.04 ounces (*or* about a paperclip's weight)
1 kilogram = 2.2 pounds

To convert kilograms to pounds, take the number of kilos and multiply by 2.2 (for example, 75 kg × 2.2 = 165 pounds).

To convert pounds to kilograms, take the number of pounds and multiply by .45 (for example, 90 lb × .45 = 40.5 kg).

Area
1 hectare (100m²) = 2.47 acres

To convert hectares to acres, take the number of hectares and multiply by 2.47 (for example, 20 ha × 2.47 = 49.4 acres).

To convert acres to hectares, take the number of acres and multiply by .41 (for example, 40 acres × .41 = 16.4 hectares).

Temperature

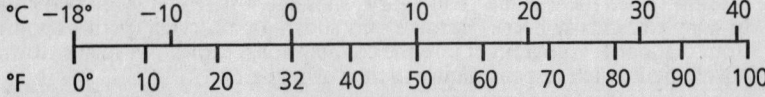

°C	−18°	−10		0	10	20	30	40
°F	0°	10	20	32	40	50	60	70	80	90	100

To convert degrees C to degrees F, multiply degrees C by 9, divide by 5, then add 32 (for example 9/5 × 20°C + 32 = 68°F).

To convert degrees F to degrees C, subtract 32 from degrees F, then multiply by 5, and divide by 9 (for example, 85°F − 32 × ⁵⁄₉ = 29°C).

NEWSPAPERS AND PERIODICALS: Nearly all publications are government owned and operated. Western printed media are almost impossible to obtain on a timely basis, although both the U.S. and British embassies have reading

rooms stocked with foreign publications. *The Working Man's Daily* and *The Guardian* are Burmese English-language newspapers offering extensive coverage of world news.

The **Information and Broadcasting Department of the State of Burma** operates libraries and reading rooms throughout the country, most of which subscribe to a few Western periodicals. In Rangoon the department's offices are on Pansodan Street near the Strand Hotel.

POSTAL SERVICE: The most reliable and efficient services are provided by the **General Post Office** in Rangoon, site also of Burma's only Poste Restante services. The post office is on Strand Road, next to the British Embassy; hours are 9:30 a.m. to 4 p.m. Monday through Friday. Check other cities' post office details in the "Useful Information" section in each chapter.

SAFETY AND SECURITY: Crimes against tourists are quite rare. We felt very safe traveling through Burma. The people are generous and trusting, and think nothing of offering a stranger food and lodging. As a precaution, it's probably a good idea to lock valuables in your hotel's safe.

TELEPHONE: Burma's international country code is 95. The city code for Rangoon is 01; for Mandalay, 02; Pagan, 35; Taunggyi, 81. Perhaps the preceding information is moot—*currently no direct service is provided either to or from the country.*

In Burma, **international telephone calls** can be placed from most major hotels, and also from the Central Telegraph Office in Rangoon, on the corner of Pandsodan Street and Maha Bandoola Road, several blocks east of Sule Pagoda, open from 7 a.m. to 8 p.m. seven days a week. A three-minute person-to-person call to New York City is incredibly pricey: 270 kyat, which works out to $45 at the official exchange rate. Connections, if made, can take up to several hours to complete.

Telex facilities are also available at the Central Telegraph Office and larger hotels.

TELEVISION AND RADIO: No doubt one of the reasons you spent time, money, and energy getting to Burma was to afford yourself the experience of television, Burmese style, a pleasant two-hour-a-day diversion featuring American and British kinescopes interspersed with heavily edited newscasts and inspiring reports from the government on national prosperity and harmony.

The Burmese Broadcasting System also operates a radio station broadcasting 16 hours a day. **English-language newscasts** are aired at 8:30 a.m., 1:30 p.m., and 9:15 p.m. every day.

TIME: Burma time is 6½ hours ahead of Greenwich Mean Time—a half hour ahead of Bangkok, 12½ hours ahead of New York, and 15½ hours ahead of Los Angeles.

TIPPING: Burma does not encourage tipping, although employees of hotels and restaurants in Rangoon seem not to take offense at the practice. Small gifts such as ballpoint pens, disposable lighters, and cosmetics are highly prized and graciously received.

TOURIST INFORMATION: The source for travelers in Burma is **Tourist Burma,** an arm of the government's Hotel and Tourist Corporation, with offices throughout the country. Knowing Tourist Burma's address in each city is as essential as knowing that of your hotel, for all major accommodations, tours, and transportation must be paid for with vouchers, and tickets must be purchased, at the Tourist Burma office. In Rangoon, Tourist Burma is located at 77-91 Sule Pagoda Rd. (tel. 78-376, 75-328, 74-281, and 80-321); hours are 8 a.m. to 8 p.m. Monday through Friday.

CHAPTER III

RANGOON

□ □ □

1. ORIENTATION
2. ACCOMMODATIONS
3. DINING
4. WHAT TO SEE AND DO IN THE CITY
5. SHOPPING
6. DAY TRIPS FROM RANGOON

It would be difficult to imagine a city of greater faded grandeur than Rangoon. Where once were wide, tree-lined boulevards with row upon row of stately neoclassical buildings there are now gray, crumbling, paint-peeling structures with vegetation growing out of fractured façades. The underground sewage system, once the state of the art in all of Asia, is now exposed, making a stroll down the street a relatively precarious affair. Perhaps the easiest way to imagine Rangoon past is to know that in its day, during the first third of this century, the city was hailed (and much studied) as a model urban area, much the way we regard Singapore today. Rangoon was designed for 300,000 inhabitants; today more than three million live in a 180-square-mile metropolitan area, exacerbating an already bad situation.

The flip side of this is that, like several cities in Eastern Europe, Rangoon has unintentionally avoided the banality of modern urban development. There are no glass-curtain high-rises, freeways, halogen street lights, or anything that can be construed as modern. Though not well preserved, Rangoon does retain much of its original character, making it a fascinating place to explore.

Since all travelers to Burma must pass through Rangoon, it's fortunate that it features one of the most important attractions in the country: the 2,500-year-old Shwe Dagon Pagoda, a lavish complex of Burmese temples, altars, and domes built around an enormous gold pagoda. This is one of the highlights on any itinerary through Southeast Asia.

As with the rest of the country, Rangoon is best visited during the cooler, winter season, from October to February, and avoided from March to May when the temperature averages 93°.

HISTORY: The city was founded in 1755 by King Alaungpaya near the original settlement of Dagon. In 1852 Rangoon was captured by the British during the Second Anglo-Burmese War and soon fired the British imagination with its potential to be developed as a major port and agricultural center in southern

Burma's rich river delta. Since then it has served as the nation's capital and commercial center.

1. ORIENTATION

The tourist infrastructure is fairly limited in Rangoon, though if you are willing to make an effort, most needs can be accommodated. Nearly all services and agencies likely to be needed by travelers are located in the core of the city, along the Rangoon River (the Strand) to the center of town at the Sule Pagoda. The Strand itself is a wide boulevard where you'll find embassies, hotels, and government organizations. Many tourist sites are away from the center of town and are best reached by taxi. Some hotels, such as the Strand and several low-price guesthouses, are in Rangoon center.

The core of the city is organized on a grid, and though distances between sights can be fairly long, it is still quite walkable. The Shwe Dagon Pagoda is only a short taxi or bus ride north from the center. The train station is located near the Scott Market on Bogyoke Aung San.

There are few useful maps of Rangoon, but one, known as *Rangoon: Where to Go, What to See,* by Erika Drucker (Bangkok: Craftsman Press Ltd., 1985), is a good and practical companion.

Listed below is a summary of Rangoon information. For more detailed information, consult "The ABCs of Burma (including Rangoon)" in the preceding chapter.

USEFUL INFORMATION: As with all other cities on the independent traveler's itinerary in this country, the most important place to visit is the **Tourist Burma** office, at 77-91 Sule Pagoda Rd. (tel. 78-376, 75-328, 74-281, or 80-321), across the street from the Sule Pagoda. Here you can reserve hotel rooms, tours, private cars, and rail and air tickets. All such reservations cover only travel from Rangoon; you'll have to make further connections in your ultimate destination. Other services at Tourist Burma include currency exchange, and on an informal basis, luggage storage. Hours at Tourist Burma are 8 a.m. to 8 p.m. daily.

The **police** can be reached by dialing 199. The **fire department** is at 191.

If you're feeling brave, **Burma Airways Corporation (BAC)** is located at 104 Strand Rd. (tel. 84-566).

The **telephone and telegraph office,** located on the corner of Maha Bandoola and Pansodan, is open Monday through Friday from 10 a.m. to 3 p.m. For phone-aholics, you'll find the five-minute limit on all domestic and international calls maddening, but at $45 for a three-minute call to the United States, you'll be happy for the restriction. The international telephone code for Burma is 95; Rangoon's **telephone area code** is 01.

The **General Post Office** is on Strand Road next to the British Embassy; Poste Restante is found on the first floor. Hours are 9:30 a.m. to 4 p.m. Monday through Friday.

There are public hospitals in Rangoon, but most visitors consult their embassies—see "The ABCs of Burma (including Rangoon)" in Chapter II—for medical attention. Apparently there are no drugstores to be found in Rangoon; only a paltry selection of medication and toiletries are available at **Scott's (Bogyoke) Market.**

Burmese Broadcasting Service (BBS) has news in English at 8:30 a.m., 1:30 p.m., and again at 9:15 p.m. There are open "stalls" selling Burmese and English-language books, many of which are miraculously rebound. **Pagan Book House,** at 100 37th St., offers an excellent selection of used English-language books, many on topics relating to Asia. Expect to spend a relative fortune for even the most modest paperback; prices range from 30 kyat ($5) to 100 kyat ($16.75). The most useful book about Rangoon is the United Nations Women's publication *Blue Book,* which is a compendium of references and tips for both the

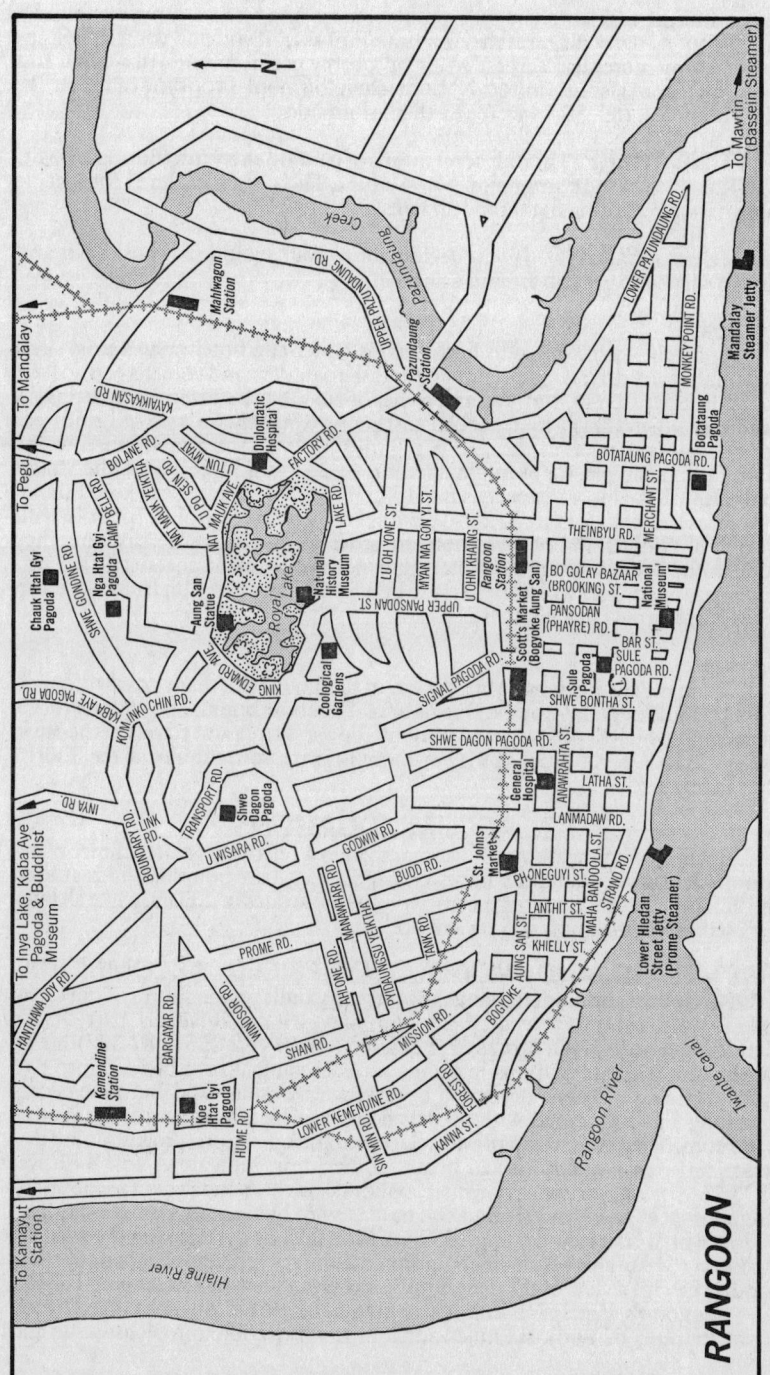

visitor and the resident. The only problem is finding a spare copy; we found a slightly out-of-date edition at the American Embassy. If you find yourself in Rangoon for any more than seven days, it's probably useful to unearth a copy. You could also contact the **United Nations Development Program** office, at 24 Manawhari Rd. (tel. 82-144), for further information.

GETTING THERE: The only legal means of gaining entry into Burma is by air, with Rangoon as the entry point. See "Getting There" in Chapter II for specific information regarding flights and air fares.

GETTING AROUND: If you decide not to walk, you'll find both taxis and buses available to get you around Rangoon.

By Taxi

By far the easiest place to find a taxi is either at a hotel or at tourist sites. Although many drivers speak enough English to understand you, it's best to have the address written in Burmese and to negotiate the price prior to departing. A large car, which can fit four people, costs approximately 75 kyat ($12.50) per hour; small cars are a bit cheaper. A typical run, from the Strand Hotel to the Shwe Dagon Pagoda, for example, should cost 25 kyat ($4.25); from the Strand to the Inya Lake Hotel, expect to pay 40 kyat ($6.75). Taxi drivers keep 30% of their fares and pay 75 kyat ($12.50) per imperial gallon of gasoline (petrol), with an official two-gallon-per-day ration. In order to procure more gasoline, they trade in the hard-currency black market, which is one reason that nearly any taxi driver you encounter will want to trade kyat for dollars at very high rates. See also "ABCs of Burma" in Chapter II.

By Bus

There is a fairly extensive bus system in Rangoon with many coaches leaving from the Sule Pagoda–Tourist Burma area. The most popular bus for visitors is the no. 37, which departs from in front of Tourist Burma and travels to the Shwe Dagon Pagoda for 1 kyat (15¢). For more information, inquire at the Tourist Burma office.

2. ACCOMMODATIONS

In comparison with rest of Burma, there is a relatively greater choice of accommodations in Rangoon; however, expect only bare-bones facilities at even the "luxury" hotels. Some of the pricier inns quote rates in dollars, while all budget establishments quote in kyat and dollars.

FIRST-CLASS AND MODERATELY PRICED ACCOMMODATIONS:
The eight modern bungalows recently built on the shores of the Royal Lakes, north-central of center city, on Kan Yeiktha Road, as part of the **Kandawgyi Hotel,** P.O. Box 1467, Rangoon (tel. 01/82-255 or 82-327), are by far the best accommodations in Rangoon. Each bungalow is divided into two spacious living quarters, decorated in carved teak, rattan, and Burmese fabrics and fully air-conditioned with a kitchenette, screened-in veranda, and marble bathroom. They even have a private telephone and television (programming daily at 7:30 p.m.). Such unusual luxury comes dear; bungalows cost 440 kyat ($73.25) for one or two. The main building of the Kandawgyi (pronounced "Kan-*doe*-gee") on Kan Yeiktha Road has 19 worn but spacious, air-conditioned rooms with a lake view costing 139 kyat ($23.25), or overlooking the road for 114 kyat ($19). There is an air-conditioned dining room, and a lakeside veranda for drinks with a view of the delightfully decorated Karaweik Restaurant barge.

Rangoon's largest lodging is the **Inya Lake Hotel,** on Kaba Aye Pagoda Road (tel. 01/62-866), six miles north of town overlooking picturesque and sprawling Inya Lake. The hotel is a faded and worn 1950s structure with a glitzy lobby, peeling paint, and aged plumbing. The 230 rooms are air-conditioned and each has a balcony, some with lake views. The seven-acre grounds are beautifully landscaped, with extensive paths and a swimming pool. Guest quarters are spacious but less than clean, with rates from $33.50 to $46 for a double and $26.50 to $36 for a single. We found that the restaurant serves above average fare.

Our favorite in-town Rangoon hotel is the venerable colonial-era **Strand Hotel,** located near the river at 92 Strand Rd. (tel. 01/81-532). In its day the Strand was on par with Raffles in Singapore and the Peninsula in Hong Kong, luxury palaces that played host to dignitaries, royalty, and the rich. Today the Strand is a mere shadow of its original incarnation, but there are hints of a grand past. The dimly lit, freshly painted lobby and dining rooms are ringed with palms, slowly revolving fans whirl from the vaulted ceiling, and a Burmese piano player croons in the bar during the evenings. Even though it's a very faded interior (what isn't in Burma?), the grace and charm of the British era live on, especially in the lost-and-found case with a 1940s Remington shaver awaiting the return of its owner! A huge standard guest room, with high ceilings and overhead fans (bath down the hall) is Rangoon's best value at $14 for two. Rooms with private bath run from $26.50 for a double to $34.50 for a junior suite. Finally, the Strand's location is ideal, next to the Burma Airways office and near the museum, river, and town center. Don't expect perfection (by a long shot) and you'll be in for a pleasant surprise.

BUDGET ACCOMMODATIONS: The **Garden Guest House** is just down the block from the Tourist Burma office, at 73 Sule Pagoda Rd. (tel. 01/71-516). It has 16 rooms, each with mosquito netting and overhead fan, and a large communal dormitory area that is used for sleeping when all the rooms are full, and as a "living room" otherwise. Each of the hotel's three floors has this communal area, from which the separate men's/women's toilets and showers extend. There is an adjacent restaurant on the first floor, making it easy to sleep and snack. A single here goes for $7; a double, for $9.50.

One of the better budget guesthouses is the 38-room **Pyin Oo Lwin,** at 183 Bar St. (tel. 01/70-001). The entryway isn't too promising: you ascend two rickety flights of stairs to reach the lobby, but once there, the facilities are reasonably clean. Guest rooms are extremely compact, fan-cooled, and utterly unadorned, with rates running 33 kyat ($5.50) per person in a single, double, or, triple configuration.

The **YWCA** is off Maha Bandoola on Bo Galay Bazaar Street near the YMCA (tel. 01/72-108), but accepts only women visitors. This faded colonial hostel dates from 1902 and its huge rooms are kept fairly clean. Single women travelers will feel comfortable with the friendly staff and flow of young Burmese women practicing on the lobby piano or taking karate or dressmaking lessons in the lounge. Dormitory rooms with twin beds rent for 25 kyat ($4.25) per bed with common cold-water shower and toilet down the hall.

The **YMCA** is located in the heart of Rangoon at 45th Street and Maha Bandoola (tel. 01/72-110), a ten-minute walk from the Tourist Burma Office, in a poorly maintained, weathered colonial structure. Bright high-ceilinged rooms are worn but clean, and have screened windows, overhead fans, and a writing desk. Doubles with private toilet and shower rent for 70 kyat ($11.75); with a common bathroom, for 55 kyat ($9.25). Dormitory beds are available to men only at 25 kyat ($4.25) per bed. The friendly management and good, inexpensive restaurant make the YMCA a good budget choice.

3. DINING
Rangoon can hardly be called a restaurant city—in fact, dining is the last reason to come to Burma. An impoverished economy, the scarcity of imported

foodstuffs, and the limited selection of locally grown produce are responsible for the disappearance of the authentic, delicately spiced Burmese cuisine, which can be sampled outside the country. Chinese, Indian, and vaguely continental dishes are the common fare in the few restaurants we recommend, although the generally poor hygiene and lack of refrigeration make dining in your hotel our first suggestion. Here's a look at the choices for those in guesthouses without restaurants.

Note: A 10% tax is added to all checks (tipping is not customary) and Mandalay beer, the only locally produced alcoholic beverage available, will add 25 kyat ($4.25) to 40 kyat ($6.75) to the tab.

The one supper worth recommending to all is at the **Karaweik Restaurant** located on the banks of the Royal Lake (tel. 52-533), the ornate stone barge modeled after the royal Karaweik bird, where Burmese cultural shows are presented nightly. Standard fare includes a beef or mutton curry, stir-fried vegetables, rice, cabbage salad, and fresh fruit. Reservations for the 7 p.m. supper and 8:15 p.m. cultural show should be made through Tourist Burma, although individual tourists can show up at the Karaweik and usually find a seat. The buffet dinner costs 35 kyat ($5.75) per person; the cultural show, 60 kyat ($10).

The **Nan Yu,** at 81 Pansodan St. (tel. 77-796), is near the telephone office downtown and serves good Chinese food in a clean and simple setting, considered rather luxurious by Rangoon standards. The ground floor has ceiling fans and tablecloths; the more intimate upstairs room is air-conditioned and equally comfortable. Favorites include the hot-and-sour duck, fried noodles with chicken, whole fish with curry powder, and the green-chile-spiced prawns. Nan Yu's food is well prepared, and two can sample three dishes for about 60 kyat ($10). Open daily from 10 a.m. to 8:30 p.m.

The **Strand Hotel,** at 92 Strand Rd. (tel. 81-532), is the most convenient for guesthouse residents. The Strand offers a set American breakfast for 25 kyat ($4.25) from 7 a.m. to 10:30 a.m. and a daily lunch and dinner with choice of soup, fish or meat entree, vegetables, and dessert for about 40 kyat ($6.75). It's overpriced by Rangoon standards, but the turn-of-the-century fan-cooled dining room is the gathering place for Burma travelers. A repast spent contemplating the tile floors, ceiling fans, and grand history of this colonial classic is well worthwhile.

A better-value, more flavorful meal can be had at the **Inya Lake Hotel** on Kaba Aye Pagoda Rd. (tel. 62-866), about six miles from downtown Rangoon. Meals are served in their coffeeshop/pâtisserie, in the comfortable Chinese restaurant (sometimes closed for private functions), or in their large, plush dining room. There are daily set menus with choices of European, Chinese, or Burmese entrees and a varied à la carte menu; dinners run 22 kyat ($3.75) to 40 kyat ($6.75). The hotel's scenic lakeside setting, lively bar, and bustling lobby scene make it a worthwhile excursion for those with time to spare.

The **White House,** near Inya Lake on Kaba Aye Pagoda Road (tel. 56-670), is popular with locals and expatriates for its huge menu and low prices.

Yan Kin at 1A Kan Be Rd. (tel. 50-545), near the Mogaung Pagoda, is another choice for Chinese-style Burmese food. The food is served in a garden setting, but be prepared to take a 15-minute taxi ride to get there. Expect to pay 50 kyat ($8.25) for the ride from central Rangoon and about 40 kyat ($6.75) for the food itself.

The **Burma Kitchen,** on Shwe Gon Dine Road (a cab ride away from the Shwe Dagon Pagoda and Reclining Buddha), is one of the few local eateries that tries to prepare typical Burmese cuisine. The result is a mixture of Indian, Chinese, and local entrees, served at medium prices.

We have yet to try it, but local friends tell us that they like the **Fursato Restaurant,** at 137 Shwe Gon Dine Rd. (tel. 52-265). The specialty here is Japanese food (only eat the cooked variety), with a meal for two running about 100 kyat ($16.75).

The **YMCA restaurant,** on the ground floor of the hostel at 45th Street and Maha Bandoola (tel. 72-110), is the best budget eatery. A full American breakfast costs 17 kyat ($2.75), but the tastier Burmese alternative, broad noodles with vegetables, chicken, and soup costs only 5 kyat (85¢). The YMCA also serves a large variety of snacks, including steamed buns with chicken or duck in pastry and vegetable fritters. It's open daily from 6 a.m. to 6 p.m.

In the "not bad" category is the **Ruby Restaurant,** at 50 Bo Aung Kyaw (Spark) St. (tel. 71-106), one block north of Strand Road. You'll have to suffer the rather grumpy Chinese owner and the high prices—entrees range from 30 kyat ($5) to 70 kyat ($11.75)—but the food is better than the usual Rangoon standard. Don't expect much from the not overly clean facilities.

Rangoon has several café-style snack and tea shops on its main avenues that serve Burmese milk tea or coffee and a variety of Oriental sweets, meat and vegetable pastries, and some Chinese dim sum. Use your discretion to judge cleanliness before sitting down, ask for fresh snacks instead of sampling from trays set out on the tables, and you can have a delicious and safe meal of typical foods for a pittance.

4. WHAT TO SEE AND DO IN THE CITY

The must-see activity in Rangoon, if not Burma, is a pilgrimage to the Shwe Dagon Pagoda, generally considered the most sacred and important religious site in the country. If you only wish to devote one day to seeing Rangoon, begin at the Shwe Dagon, northwest of city center, in the early morning (or end there in the evening), proceed to the Sule Pagoda, in the center of the city, and make a short trip to the National Museum. That should leave time for such other venues as the Reclining Buddha, Bogyoke Market, the Meditation Center, or the Synagogue.

SHWE DAGON PAGODA: From afar the golden Shwe Dagon Pagoda appears to sit serenely over much of hectic Rangoon. Yet after ascending the long staircase to reach the base of this holy site it is apparent that the central pagoda itself is only a part of a riot of Buddhist sounds, sights, and sensations. The central dome, one of the Buddhist world's largest, dates back over 2,500 years and is said to contain a relic of the Buddha. Supplicants from around the world have come to the pagoda to make an offering by placing gold leaf on the vast surface of this holy shrine. Though the central pagoda is of interest, we find the surrounding temples, monuments, pavilions, and lesser pagodas far more enchanting and visually arresting. As well, if one spends enough time at the Shwe Dagon there is bound to be a religious ceremony involving music, sprinkling of water, presentations of elaborate offerings, or other Buddhist rituals that brings this wonderful place to life. During late 1988 the Shwe Dagon was one of the important rallying points for citizens of Rangoon agitating for a more open form of government in Burma.

The Shwe Dagon Pagoda is open daily from about 4 a.m. until 9 p.m., when it is illuminated. You can reach it by taking the no. 37 bus, which stops in front of the Tourist Burma office; alternatively, you can take a taxi for about 25 kyat ($4.25). Ask your driver to wait while you make your visit.

There is a fine shopping arcade along the stairway leading to the top of the pagoda with all manner of highly negotiable objects.

SULE PAGODA: At this point in the development of Rangoon, it's difficult to determine whether the elaborately decorated Sule Pagoda is more of a geographic landmark or a religious center. For many it's the city center—and for most visitors it's a convenient marker across from the Tourist Burma office—but, like the Shwe Dagon, the Sule Pagoda is said to contain a relic of the Buddha. It was built some 2,000 years ago and its name translates into "the pagoda where a sacred hair relic is enshrined." The Sule Pagoda is open throughout the day and night; remember to remove your shoes before entering.

THE NATIONAL MUSEUM: Burma's National Museum, centrally located at 26 Phayre (Pansodan) St., around the corner from the Strand Hotel, is well worth a visit by those interested in the country's imperial past. A 25-foot-tall gilded lion throne used by the last Burmese monarch dominates the ground floor. Cases containing gold vessels, bejeweled costumes, weaponry, and ornaments—including a huge fan inlaid with rubies and emeralds—surround the throne. The gold and gem-studded regalia from the court of Mandalay, old photographs, and several models of the teakwood imperial pavilions will interest those who've seen the five miles of brick walls and moat that are the only remains of the huge complex.

Several galleries on the second floor are devoted to archeological finds from Beikthano and Srikhsetra, Buddhist settlements that flourished in the Pyu period from the 5th to 8th centuries. A gallery of arts and crafts includes ornately carved teak doors, Hindu statuary, embroidery, and a delightful display of marionettes. The top floor is devoted to showings of contemporary painting or temporary exhibits.

The museum is open daily from 10 a.m. to 3:30 p.m. Admission is 1 kyat (15¢) and compulsory bag check is 1 kyat (15¢).

KABA AYE PAGODA AND BUDDHIST MUSEUM: The Kaba Aye Pagoda, located north of Inya Lake, is a modern temple dedicated to world peace. The pagoda was built near a sacred cave, called Maha Pasana, where the Sixth World Buddhist Council was held. In the same complex is the Buddhist Museum featuring a small collection of religious objects and art including rare palm-leaf manuscripts. The best way to visit the Kaba Aye Pagoda is to take a taxi; expect to pay about 60 kyat ($10).

MEDITATION CENTER: For those interested in meditation there is the **Mahasi Meditation Center,** at 16 Thathana Yeiktha Rd. Full-time students come here from around the world to study with Buddhist masters. It is suggested that interested visitors write in advance of their visit for more information.

CHAUK HTAT GYI PAGODA: Though not on the scale or the artistic quality of Wat Po, Chauk Htat Gyi Pagoda is Rangoon's answer to Bangkok's Reclining Buddha. This prone giant with the smiling face measures out 230 feet and is set in a monastery north of the Royal Lakes on Shwe Gondine Road.

MUSMEAH YESHUA SYNAGOGUE: One of the more interesting sights in downtown Rangoon is the Musmeah Yeshua Synagogue, located at 85 26th St. We always enjoy finding churches and synagogues in unexpected places, and were delighted to discover this gem. The monumental building was constructed in 1897 and is still used, principally on major Jewish holidays. The pews and other furnishings are made of local wood and woven cane, and in comparison with most of the city, the structure and its decorations are in very good condition. To gain entry to the synagogue, call Mr. Samuels at 75-062 or ask one of the men at the knife-sharpening/locksmith's shop across the street.

BURMESE CULTURAL SHOW: The Burmese Cultural Show presented at the Karaweik Cultural Center (on Royal Lake near the Kandawgyi Hotel) is the only venue in this depressed economy to sample traditional Burmese music and dance. Other than the marionette performances that still thrive in Pagan, the performing arts are rarely performed in public. The *saing* (typical classic orchestra) is similar to a small Indonesian gamelan, a collection of drums, xylophone, gongs, oboe, and cymbals. In the performance, the saing is accompanied by the exotic *saung-gauk,* an ornately painted, gondola-shaped harp with a pleasing Oriental twang. Burmese music is based on the septonic scale and is difficult to appreciate from the limited melodies accompanying the dances.

The cultural show consists of nine segments, including folk dances, religious rituals, *chin-lone,* traditional court dances and a lively acrobatic display of a juggling game with a cane ball. Each dance is based on controlled small movements of the head, hands, hips, and feet. In one particular act, a marionette and dancer echo each other's steps flawlessly, illustrating the smooth moves of the best Burmese puppetry and the restrained, self-disciplined motions of classic dance. The Burmese Cultural Show is presented nightly at 8:15 p.m.; tickets can be obtained from Tourist Burma and the 60-kyat ($10) admission fee includes transport back to your hotel. There is a buffet supper available at the Karaweik Hall from 7 p.m. on for 35 kyat ($5.75).

5. SHOPPING

If Burma isn't much of a place for shopping, Rangoon ranks as its least interesting outlet, at least as far as the traveler is concerned.

The largest and best stocked of Rangoon's shopping venues is the **Bogyoke Market** (also known as Scott's Market), located near the train station. Here you will find everything from food to tourist souvenirs to black-market goods. Negotiating for anything is definitely in order.

We also like the surrounding streets with their shops carrying hand-painted postcards and other Burmese artifacts. One of the nicest and best shops we found was the **Thein U Post-Card Painting Shop** at 187 East Wing in the market (no telephone). Thein U Maung is the proprietor and resident artist here, and his watercolor cards and paintings are unique and wonderful (and make perfect gifts for friends). The prices ranged from 6 kyat ($1) to 60 kyat ($10) for a small painting.

The other interesting shopping center is found at the **Shwe Dagon Pagoda.** All sorts of Burmese goodies, as well as Buddhist offerings and other religious paraphernalia, are available at this, the closest thing to a Burmese shopping mall.

If you're in the market for gems, consider visiting one of the so-called **Diplomatic Stores.** We can't say very much good about the settings, but the gems are supposed to be genuine and are "guaranteed." (We have been told by experienced jewelers that the best rubies are sold at the gem auctions to professional buyers or are illegally smuggled into Thailand, with the remaining few lower-quality stones sold to the tourist market.) The other items for sale, such as silver, lacquerware, and other Burmese objets d'art, can be found in other parts of the country, particularly in Pagan and Mandalay, at lower prices and in generally more engaging and wide-ranging styles. Also, all purchases at the Diplomatic Stores must be made with hard currency. We suggest visiting these stores on an emergency basis only, such as when you must have that certain brand of Western shaving cream; otherwise, try to buy your souvenirs in other parts of the country.

6. DAY TRIPS FROM RANGOON

Most people traveling on the seven-day plan will choose to visit other parts of Burma, usually the northern cities in and around Taunggyi, Pagan, and Mandalay. If you're stuck in Rangoon, however, and are in search of a diversion, consider visiting Pegu, 50 miles northeast of Rangoon, the 15th-century Mon capital. There is train service as well as bus or taxi excursions; expect to spend about two hours getting to Pegu. Among the highlights are: Shwethalyaung, a huge reclining Buddha; the Shwemawdaw Pagoda; the Kyaikpun Pagoda, with its giant Buddhas; and Kalyani Sima. If you drive, you'll pass the War Memorial near Htaukkyant, dedicated to the 27,000 Allied soldiers who died during World War II.

CHAPTER IV

EXPLORING BURMA

□ □ □

1. PAGAN
2. MANDALAY
3. TAUNGGYI AND INLE LAKE

The race is on. You want to see everything. You've got just seven days—less, if you include travel time—to experience the wonder of travel in upcountry Burma. Reconcile yourself to the idea that you won't be able to accomplish your goal and if by chance you do, you'll be pleasantly surprised. Otherwise, just settle into the pace of life in Burma and you'll be amply rewarded by the serendipitous nature of just getting from here to there.

We list Pagan as our first stop, because for most travelers to Burma it represents the highlight of their trip. The thousands of pagodas, overwhelming at first, are there for exploration, astonishment, and contemplation. After that, it's on to Mandalay with its legendary hill, and especially the day trips and overnights to Sagaing and Maymyo (a lovely colonial hill station). Finally, our itinerary ends at Taunggyi and Inle Lake in the Shan state, one of the few opportunities to sample Burmese life in a setting that transcends all vestiges of foreign tourism.

1. PAGAN

Of all the cities in Burma, Pagan presents the richest evidence of an extraordinarily grand past, similar to Sukhothai in nearby Thailand. One senses that life in Pagan during its apogee, from the 11th to the 13th century, was equivalent to the Renaissance in Western Europe: a place full of spiritual light and cultural excellence.

This austere city, a 15-square-mile ruin spread out over a vast red-brick landscape, is located inland from the eastern bank of the Irrawaddy River, about 193 km (120 miles) south of Mandalay, within the so-called Mandalay Division. The physical manifestation of Pagan's former grandeur are the more than 5,000 pagodas dotting the rustic plain. The majority of these well- (and not-so-well-) preserved shrines offer evidence of a rich architectural heritage. They also convey, with great clarity, what Buddhist life nearly a millennium ago must have been like: a sublime symbiosis of Man, Nature, and Time. The most contemporary example of that superb chemistry is experienced at sunset over Pagan—it's like nothing you've ever seen before.

Life in modern-day Pagan, absent tourists, is dictated by the movement along the Irrawaddy River, roughly equivalent to the Mississippi of Burma. A steamboat plies the waters between Mandalay and Pagan, transporting locals from village to village and tourists from hearsay to wonder. Stilt villages sprout from the river, with families washing, defecating, and drinking from the mother river, as they've done for centuries. The banks are sandy or muddy, with recessed vegetation resembling the Florida Keys and deepest Africa. Whenever the steamer approaches a village it's cause for commotion, with village women preparing shrimp "brittle," grilled corn, and fresh oranges for weary ferry passengers, and rushing the bottom deck for the ten minutes or so that the boat is docked, only to leap off when there's no hope of further sales. And so it goes with every passing village.

Suffice it to say, Pagan is one of our favorite places in Burma: it's the Burma you long to see after reading Orwell and Kipling.

HISTORY: Although there is evidence of ancient Burmese feudal kingdoms in the Pagan area dating back as far as the 3rd century B.C., the first unified Burmese empire was organized during the reign of King Anawrahta between 1044 and 1077. Though this was the beginning of the first true Burmese dynasty, it marked the last period of great historical significance for Pagan. It was during this period and in subsequent reigns of the Pagan kings, spanning over 200 years, that most of the 5,000 pagodas were constructed. Subsequent to the 13th century Pagan was either overrun by competing capitals or laid waste by powerful earthquakes. In the case of Kublai Khan, who represented a foreign capital and struck like an earthquake, Pagan was just another way station on his blazing military itinerary: he laid waste to the city in 1287.

ORIENTATION: The village of Pagan is basically organized like a Wild West town, dominated by a dusty main street. The principal landmark is the Tharabha Gate, at the far northeastern end of town. Just a two-minute walk from the rubble-strewn gate is the all-important Tourist Burma office (see below); beyond you will find most of the hotels, restaurants, and shops. The vast majority of historic structures, such as the Ananda Temple, are to be found farther to the east in the broad plain.

USEFUL INFORMATION: The office of **Tourist Burma** is located near the Tharabha Gate and is open daily from 8 a.m. to 8 p.m. The office sells air, bus, ferry, and train tickets and can confirm reservations on all of these forms of transportation for Pagan-based travel only. They will also exchange money and make hotel reservations. The bus stop is in front of the Tourist Burma office. **Burma Airways Corporation (BAC)** has an office just about 100 yards down the main street on the other side of the road. After reserving and paying for your air ticket, you'll have to pick up the actual coupon at the BAC office.

Long-distance telephone calls can be made at the Thiripyitsaya Hotel (see below). The **telephone area code** for Pagan is 35.

The singularly best (and necessary) map for temple exploration is the "Tourist Burma Map of Pagan," available either at the Tourist Burma office or at a temple or pagoda near you—we bought ours at the Ananda Temple for 4 kyat (70¢).

GETTING THERE: We came to Pagan from Mandalay, the most common connecting destination. You can get to Pagan only from Rangoon, Mandalay, or Thazi by public transportation.

From Rangoon there is one two-hour flight daily, at a one-way fare of 445 kyat ($74.25), which leaves at 6:45 a.m. with a return flight at 4:30 p.m. (check with Tourist Burma for updated schedules). If you fly from Pagan to Rangoon, try to sit on the left side of the plane; you'll have a fine view of the pagoda fields as

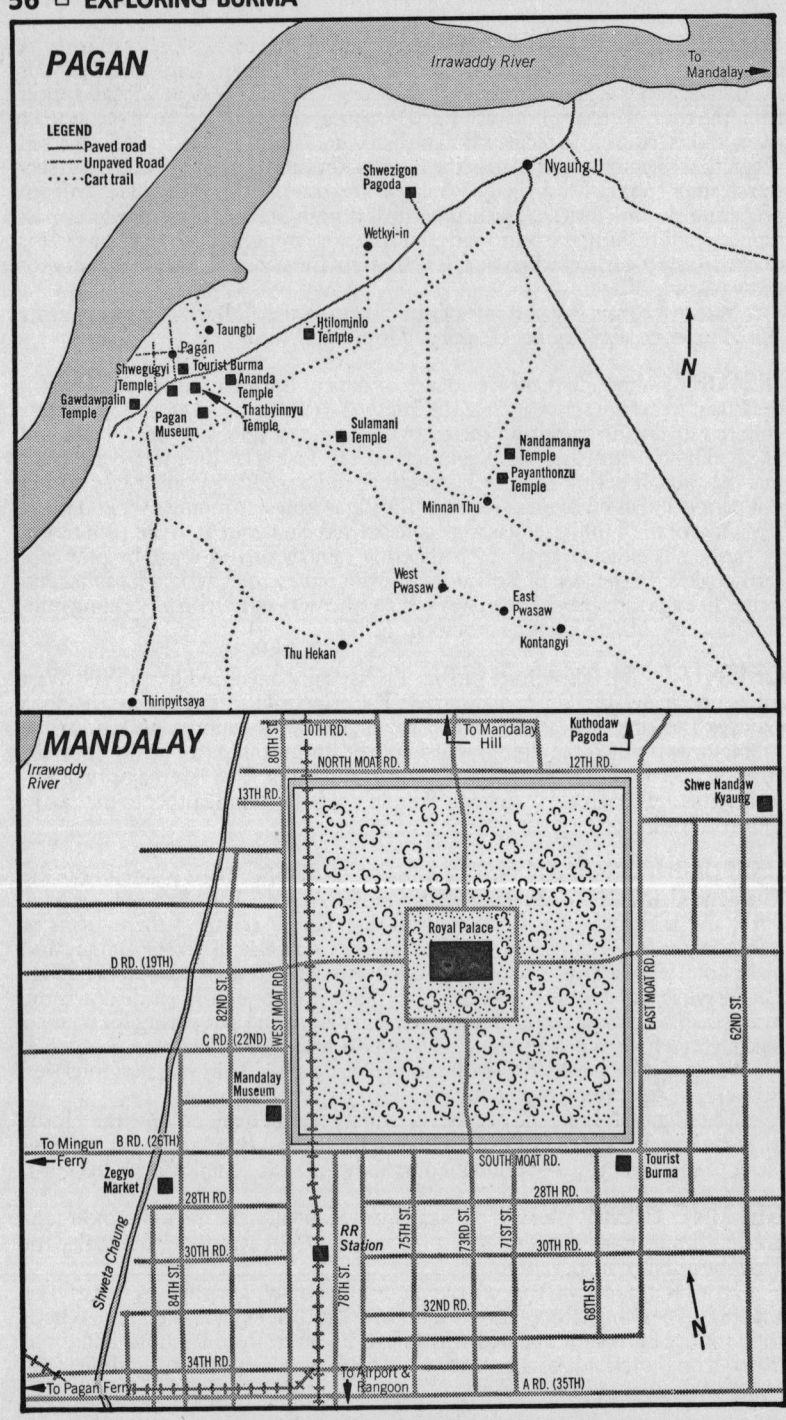

well as the Irrawaddy (if you're traveling from the capital up to Pagan, sit on the opposite side).

There is bus service **from Thazi** to Pagan for 55 kyat ($9.25); again, check with Tourist Burma as the hours and frequency seem to change as fast as the Burmese mind.

From Mandalay there is one half-hour flight each day at 3:40 p.m. for 190 kyat ($31.75), or you can take a 15-hour tramp steamer ride down the Irrawaddy River for just 31 kyat ($5.25) for open-deck seating or 160 kyat ($26.75) for cabin seating, a very romantic and interesting way to see a lot of Burma. We took the 15-hour steamer journey down the Irrawaddy from Mandalay, and it was an eye-opening experience: the villages that dot the landscape recall the "Darkest Africa" you grew up seeing on TV, with mud huts receding into a flat landscape surrounded by mountains. The Burmese travel on the lower deck, huddled around their cooking implements that are constantly burning on the wooden deck. Tourists are on the second level, splayed across deck chairs talking or sleeping; we met many travelers whom we happily kept running into later on in different cities. As the boat approaches various villages, the first sight you see are the fishermen in their *King and I* boats (canoe-like boats with decorative carvings at stern and bow), then the village women rushing the boats plying their snacks. The steamer leaves Mandalay at 5 a.m., arriving at 8 p.m. that evening, so there are many times when the idea of an impending dockside snack leaves a good taste in your mouth. The night in between can get very cool, so make sure you have a sweater or jacket with you. If you want to see a side of Burma you can't see any other way, and can afford the time, then this is the way to reach Pagan.

GETTING AROUND: There are several options in Pagan for getting about, but we suggest either walking (to the nearby sites), bicycling (to the not-so-far sites), or taking a horse cart (for more distant journeys).

Walking is best done in the early morning or late afternoon, as it gets extremely hot out there on the dusty pagoda plains.

Bicycles are for rent at nearly all guesthouses, but like all mechanical devices in Burma, are in various states of disrepair; check to make sure that the brakes work and, most important, that there is a modicum of rubber left on the tires. We enjoyed riding on the roads (there are very few cars and trucks), but it can get difficult when you have to bike on sandy paths. Before setting out on an extended trip, ask your host about the route and the condition of paths. Expect to pay 15 kyat ($2.50) for a half-day rental.

We rented a **horse-drawn carriage** to transport us to some of the more remote pagodas and villages. Each carriage can accommodate four passengers and has the added virtue of a driver who can usually double as a guide—most speak halting English—and who probably knows the local monks (good for gaining entry to those hard-to-find pagodas). Horse carriages are arranged as a private form of transportation (in other words, outside of Tourist Burma's long arm); the best place to get a carriage is at the unofficial stand, under the trees, midway on the main street on the eastern side of the road. It's best to make your arrangements in the evening for an early-morning start; most trips start at 7:30 a.m. and finish by 1 p.m., costing about 150 kyat ($25) for the carriage per half day.

If you need to arrange a **private car,** you can do so at the Tourist Burma office.

ACCOMMODATIONS: There are two hotels and 11 guesthouses in Pagan, most of which are primitively equipped but acceptable hostelries. If you're traveling independently, it's likely that you'll end up staying in a guesthouse instead of a hotel, given that most tour companies, including Tourist Burma, reserve the "luxury" rooms months in advance. In a remarkable example of effective price fixing, all the guesthouses charge the same rates: $17 single and $24 double.

Moderately Priced Accommodations

At the top end of accommodations in Pagan are the Thiripyitsaya Hotel and the Irra Inn. The **Thiripyitsaya Hotel,** located 1¼ miles west from the center of Pagan (tel. 01/89-000 in Rangoon), represents the apogee of luxury in Burma, and as such plays host to many foreign dignitaries and government officials. The grounds, well looked after, are laid out in a series of 17 chalets, each housing four air-conditioned double rooms with private bath. There is a swimming pool and a bar (which served only juice and bottled water when we were there) that overlooks the muddy Irrawaddy through a garden filled with oleanders and bougainvillea. One of our favorite features was the hotel's telephone, the only one in town from which you could make overseas calls. Our only complaint—other than that it's next to impossible to reserve a room here—is the relatively inattentive service. A single goes for $18.50 and a double costs $24.50, both with an additional 10% service charge.

The **Irra Inn,** located about half a mile northwest of the main road on Irra Inn Road (tel. 35/25), has 25 institutionally inspired rooms, mostly due to the fact that it was originally built in 1969 to house the Burmese Airways Corporation (which may also explain its relative opulence). Most rooms have balconies and range in price from 60 kyat ($10) for a single to 80 kyat ($13.25) for a double. All the rooms have Western-style bath/toilet facilities, mattresses, and closets. Don't think for a minute that this means comfort or luxury: there's no hot water, room service, or alcohol here.

Guesthouses

Nearly all of Pagan's guesthouses are on the main street, most within an easy walk from the Tourist Burma office and bus stop.

Two of our favorites are the **Mya Thi Da** and Sin Thu guesthouses. The Mya (no telephone) has 12 double rooms, all quite clean, with the requisite mosquito netting over each bed. The Mya has two showers, sinks, and toilets (Asian) in the back, and an assortment of popular magazines from many countries and eras in the front hall. The Mya is run by Aung Koont, a hardworking and happy guy who manages to keep his guests happy. We found that he served a very good breakfast, the sole exception among all the hotels in town. Mr. Koont also rents bicycles for less than other guesthouses, and they tend to be in better working order.

The **Sin Thu** (no telephone) has a "driveway" in which they work on their rental bicycles constantly. The rooms here are furnished with the straw-mat-on-wood-frame variety of bed, and Sin Thu can boast that two of the four toilets are Western style, a nice respite for the battered traveler. They also have (gasp!) a small color TV where we saw "Monty Python" one night—this is such a rarity in Burma that we were truly astonished. *Note:* The boiled water at Sin Thu is kept in a small Italian-style cooler as you come in the front door, with bowls available to the right (we were there two nights before we found it).

The **Pagan Guest House** (no telephone), with its nine double rooms and two singles, is also an alluring alternative because of its furnishings and its upstairs sitting room that looks out over flowering bougainvillea. The rooms actually have mattresses (thin), something we rarely saw anywhere in low-budget Burma, and ceiling fans to boot. They have three outdoor showers and toilets (one Western) in the back. The owner, Koo Koo Mon, is the Pagan's sweet and hospitable host.

Across the street from the Tourist Burma office, just to the right as you enter town, is Pagan's newest guesthouse, the **Paradise** (no telephone). Mr. Khin, who runs the place, is a fledgling Burmese rock 'n' roller who's happy to demonstrate some hot licks without request. We like the Paradise for its clean, newish rooms, but it seems to lack some of the homeyness of the other recommended inns.

DINING: You didn't come to Pagan for the food. Good, because the pickings are exceedingly slim. However, that didn't stop us from finding three reasonably good restaurants in town, all cheap: one Chinese, one Burmese(!), and one Indian vegetarian eatery. The latter, the **Marie-Min** (no telephone), is located on the right of the Tharabha Gate (across from Tourist Burma) as you enter Pagan. The food, all vegetarian, is tasty and their soup (similar to Chinese congee) is excellent. Eggplant, squash, and whatever greens are available in the market are combined into an astonishing array of dishes. One caveat: Though every place we ate had their "Dueling Mosquitos" quota, the Marie-Min had a greater concentration of flies than other places. The Marie-Min is open nearly all day and night, making it one of the very few places you can eat past 9:30 p.m.

Happily, we discovered that the food at **Soe Soe,** situated on the right-hand side of the main street (no telephone), exceeded the expectation based on their name—it's the best (maybe only) Chinese restaurant in town. The Soe Soe has an open façade and the interior walls are decorated with Burmese tapestries. The attraction here, though, is the food, specifically the chicken curry at 12 kyat ($2), fruit salad at 10 kyat ($1.75), and vegetable dishes at 7 kyat ($1.25), all scrumptious dishes that are among the best in town. Service is a mite slow, but well worth the wait; we often ate breakfast here and enjoyed their fried rice with eggs for 8 kyat ($1.25) and tomato-and-vegetable omelet for 7 kyat ($1.25) to launch another day of pagoda-climbing. Soe Soe is open daily from morning till night.

Ruby Restaurant, across the street and down from Soe Soe, is consistently the most crowded restaurant in Pagan. It also seems to be the favored place for locals to meet tourists. The host there, Po Pau, always smiles his beetlejuice smile as he recommends his hot-and-sour chicken, fried rice and noodles, or Siamese vegetable soup and yogurt, each prepared Burmese style. Prices run from 8 kyat ($1.25) for rice dishes to 15 kyat ($2.50) for the hot-and-sour chicken. The Ruby is open daily from 6 a.m. to 11 p.m.

WHAT TO SEE AND DO: Before the devastating earthquake on July 8, 1975, there were in excess of 5,000 pagodas in Pagan. There are now 2,217 left, most in partial ruin. Many sit serenely on the plain as a rubble of broken brick, but it takes little imagination to picture them in their original state, often whitewashed, some covered in gold. Even with this devastation, there are still so many incredible temples and trails to the past in Pagan that this list outlines just a fraction of what's there; these are simply some of our favorites. If you have the time, we encourage you to strike out on your own, to discover those indescribably beautiful temples and edifices that seem suffused with spiritual light from the past.

The best guide to the area, we repeat, is the "Tourist Burma Map of Pagan," available in the TB office or at the major temples.

Pagan Museum

A good place to start is the Pagan Museum, housing a small collection of locally excavated artifacts including a fine stone Buddha, and other smaller ceramic and bronze figurines (most in the "earth touching" attitude), and fragments of frescoes displayed inside the main building. The majority of the collection was gathered after the earthquake of 1975; there is a small exhibit about this devastating event. The museum is open Tuesday through Sunday from 9:30 a.m. to 4:30 p.m. and is located near the Gawdawpalin Temple, on the western side of Pagan. Admission is free.

Ananda Temple

One of the most visible of the pagodas on the Pagan horizon is the magnificent white Ananda Temple. Built in 1091 by King Kyansittha, this temple contains statues of the Buddha and exquisitely carved sculptures representing scenes in the Buddha's life. Ananda's architecture is unique (its ground plan is in the shape of a Greek cross) and is considered among the finest temples in Pagan. The best way to reach the Ananda Temple is by foot (15 minutes) or bicycle (5 minutes from the Tourist Burma office).

Thatbyinnyu Temple

The Thatbyinnyu Temple, located just south of the Ananda Temple and built by King Alaungsithu in the mid-12th century, commands one of the most extraordinary views of Pagan's wide plateau, and as such is the most popular tourist perch at magic hour. Like the Ananda, the temple is built on multiple levels, reaching a zenith of 220 feet and has a warren of caverns and staircases to explore. You can reach the Thatbyinnyu either by bike or on foot.

Shwegugyi Temple

The Shwegugyi, built during the reign of King Alaungsithu in 1131, is particularly worth visiting for its fine stonework and intricately carved molding and stucco decoration. The Shwegugyi is off the main street of Pagan, on the way to the museum.

Sulamani Temple

Upon arrival here, enter the temple from the front and proceed clockwise around the ground floor; this will ensure optimum enjoyment of what was probably our favorite landmark in Pagan. A great henna-red Buddha with powder-blue skirting and a gold canopy above him greets you with his silent smile, and as you continue to the left you see another, slightly smaller image of the great figure. Then another as you continue. And a fourth, on the same scale as the first. Just past this fourth Buddha you'll see a pale-red fresco of a reclining Buddha figure, which leads you to the fifth and final giant red Buddha. If you continue you'll reach the front entrance, where tucked away to the side you'll see a staircase leading to the top five levels of the temple. Climb up and find your level: the second level has a couple of Buddhas laid out like the ground floor, while all the other levels possess only a superb and unique view of Pagan, seen through the mist of the past.

It's best to take a bicycle to get to the Sulamani; continue on the path from the Ananda Temple.

Nandamannya Temple

This temple has two features that make it a must-see: the magnificence of its domed ceiling (as soon as you walk in, look up) with its intricate flowers and vinery connecting the Buddha images (with green halos), and the Pali (ancient Burmese/Buddhist language) tablet directly to your left as you enter. The frescoes on either side of the big Buddha are in fair shape; for some reason the ceiling is in perfect shape.

Nearby the temple you'll see a concrete silo: make sure you check it out. Recessed below the ground is a monastery, where for 40 years the most revered monk in Pagan stayed inside his room without ever leaving. He died in October 1987, and his room was turned into a shrine, with pictures of the soles of his feet adorning nearly every inch of wall space; these photos are proof of his holiness, and there are two shrines at the front of the room that are exquisite, made completely from gold and glass mosaics. The monk was interred in a small white house nearby, with its own pagoda.

The Nandamannya Temple is set away from the main group of pagodas and will require transportation, such as a horse cart (see "Getting Around").

Payanthonzu Temple

This small temple has exceptional frescoes of the young Buddha and Boddhisatvas (enlightened disciples of the Buddha who remain on earth to teach others), and three separate chambers that we much appreciated because they felt as though they were air-conditioned. (After bicycling around the temples during the day you learn to respect things like shade and fruit shakes.) The Payanthonzu is found in the same area as the Nandamannya, and requires horse-cart transport.

Shwezigon Pagoda

Because it was built in 1057 during the reign of King Anawrahta, the founder of Pagan's last and most significant dynasty, the golden-domed Shwezigon is considered the most historically significant temple in Pagan. From an architectural standpoint the Shwezigon is also important as it set the style for most of the other structures built in Pagan for the remaining period of the dynasty. Of specific interest are the glazed relief tablets of scenes from the Buddhist scriptures. This is a must-see sight.

Note: We were accosted at the Shwezigon by a throng of touts and moneychangers, all willing to buy the literal "shirt off your back."

The Shwezigon Pagoda is located just on the outskirts of Nyaung-Oo, a small village northeast of Pagan. To reach the Shwezigon, you'll either have to take a bike ride of about 20 minutes or take a Tourist Burma bus.

Htilominlo Temple

The Htilominlo is built in a style much the same as the Sulamni, that is, a two-storied structure with a central spire reaching a height of 165 feet. This 13th-century temple is worth exploring for its fine friezes and pilasters, several frescoes (in a regrettable state of repair), and a giant Buddha with three smaller matching images. As the Htilominlo is on the road toward Nyaung-Oo, most people visit the temple on the way to the Shwezigon.

Minnan Thu Village

Most horse-cart tours stop at Minnan Thu, one of the best examples of traditional Burmese village life open to tourists. The feeling here is a cross between a prairie farm in rural New Mexico and a *National Geographic* photo essay on primitive agrarian life. This was one of the highlights of our visit to Pagan.

The Temples in Thiripyitsaya

There is a series of fascinating pagodas on the road out of Pagan leading to the southern town of Chauk. Most people navigate this stretch by bicycle, but it's a long and sandy trip; we suggest that you walk your bike in the more difficult parts. Our favorite shrine in this area is the **Thingaraza,** a tiny temple housing two enormous Buddhas, one sitting, the other reclining. How do they do this, you ask? Briefly, this temple represents a political protest by an exiled Burmese prince who "imprisoned" the two oversize Buddhas in cell-like housing. The effect is to mirror his own status, and we found it incredibly affecting. We highly recommend a visit here.

Mount Popa

Allow at least a half day to see the temple- and pagoda-capped inactive volcano known as Mount Popa, located 60 km (37 miles) southeast of Pagan. The 5,000-foot-high rock formation is almost a perfect black stone column that can be climbed by a network of stairs, best accomplished in the early-morning hours —we did it in the midday sun and suffered accordingly. If you're fortunate enough to visit Pagan in late May or early June, you just might have the chance to attend the celebration of the Nats (Buddhist spirits).

SHOPPING: In comparison with other Southeast Asian countries, Burma isn't for shoppers. However, of all of the accessible tourist cities, we most appreciated the goods in Pagan. There are a few "shops" in town that are most interesting and worth a visit.

In the lobby of the **Thiripyitsaya Hotel** there is a small stand, where you can exploit the differential between the government and black-market currency rates to your advantage. They carry some lovely watercolors (each an original), some Burmese brown "socialist" uniforms (Nehru collars, etc.), and some very fine examples of Burmese bone jewelry.

In addition to its semiprecious jewels and tapestries, Burma is also well known and respected for its lacquerware, considered some of the finest in the world. The **Ma Moe Moe** family works, in the Ywar Thit quarter of town, is the premier place for lacquerware (and souvenirs, for that matter). Moe Moe, as she's called, is also a tough cookie at the bargaining table, so don't expect to get a huge discount for volume. Her trays, boxes, and plaques are among the best we found.

One of our favorite souvenirs were exquisite card-size watercolors that we found for sale at **Rama Arts and Crafts** on Irra Inn Road. The clarity of conception, depth of color, and the artist's trust in the world around him is amazing; these small cards are something special.

Our other favorite goody to buy in Pagan are **puppets,** still made and used (see "Nightlife") in the town's few remaining puppet theaters.

NIGHTLIFE: Our first choice of evening activity is attending a performance at the puppet theater, as described below. Other than that, there is one **café** in Pagan, just down from the Ruby Restaurant, where all during the day and until midnight you'll hear rock music blaring from badly duped tapes blasted through cheap plastic speakers—not anybody's idea of hi-fi.

Nightlife in Pagan is strolling down main street as young lovers walk arm in arm past pagodas that seemingly chaperone the night. We always found ourselves asleep by midnight, so as to get a very early start to avoid the heat that sizzles the city between noon and 4 p.m.

Last and certainly not least is the **Nay Che Puppet Theater,** one of two we found in town, and easily the finest. Two brothers put on the shows; one is the puppeteer, and the other makes the puppets and paints the backdrops. The performances are simply magical: you feel the same surge of excitement that you did when you were a child. The show consists of several vignettes, each a retelling of a Burmese fairy/folk tale or historical incident. The puppets execute backflips, dance (a dancing tiger nearly made us cry), duel, and love their way into your heart. Next door the theater has a shop where you can purchase incredible, three-foot-tall, handmade puppets for about $50, which make special gifts for special friends; they also sell less professional models for half the price. Don't miss this —there is one performance a night, though the brothers will give groups of four or more private shows for the same price, about 6 kyat ($1), after the regularly scheduled show at 8 p.m.

2. MANDALAY

Of the main cities on the approved itinerary, Mandalay is perhaps the most characteristically Burmese, reflecting much of contemporary culture. At one time it was the capital of the Burmese empire and home to the last dynasty of Burmese kings, but today it's among the country's more thriving market towns, with strong connections to the prosperous northern states. The city's small markets are perpetually filled with rare Burmese goods and even scarcer black-market items. Like Rangoon, Mandalay was one of the hotbeds of resistance during the political turmoil in 1988 and was placed under military control.

Though Mandalay is Burma's second-largest city, with a population approaching three-quarters of a million people, it is ordinarily a remarkably calm place whose pace is largely determined by the horse-drawn carriages, bicycle riders, and trishaw drivers who courteously share the road with rows of monks, schoolchildren, and workers strolling the city's wide streets. Even the city's motorized traffic, the typical Burmese blend of Willy's Jeeps, aged Mockvas and Humbers, and a sprinkling of shiny Japanese mini-trucks, seems to travel at half speed. When there is the slightest breeze the city seems to be enveloped in a dust cloud, lending an unearthly air to the early-evening cityscape. Mandalay's residents are affable and approachable, always willing to exchange a pleasantry—if not buy your name-brand Western clothing.

A trip to Mandalay should include some of the city's less famous, but equally fascinating, neighboring sites, particularly those at Sagaing, Amarapura, and Ava. We fondly remember making the 90-minute journey for an overnight to the largely undisturbed town of Maymyo, a hill station holdover from the British occupation of the 1920s.

HISTORY: Although rich in undisturbed images from the past, Mandalay is a young city, created as the capital in 1857 by King Mindon to be the gleaming jewel of his kingdom. Mindon, deeply religious, saw the city as the fulfillment of Buddha's prophecy made during his pilgrimage to nearby Mandalay Hill: that on the 2,400th anniversary of his death a city would be founded on the slopes of that sacred site. A thriving capital was established in Mandalay, but it lasted less than 30 years before being eclipsed by British-dominated Rangoon, 422 miles to the south. The centerpiece of the city, the elaborately constructed 19th-century Royal Palace, was completely destroyed in World War II during ferocious fighting between Japanese and Allied troops. Today the Royal Palace grounds are known as Fort Mandalay, a military base usually off-limits to tourists (entry requires an official government pass and escort).

ORIENTATION: Mandalay sprawls along the banks of the Irrawaddy River for miles and is not a city easily seen on foot. During the hot season the temperature often soars to over 100° Fahrenheit. You will probably want to rent a Jeep or other conveyance for the dusty trip to Mandalay Hill and other nearby sites.

Mandalay's wide, loosely paved streets are organized on an oddly designated grid, with most of the city's hotels, restaurants, and sights concentrated in the center to northeast quadrant. The main east-west thoroughfares have number (and some letter) designations, and run from 12th Road on the north to 41st Road on the south (D Road equals 19th Road, A Road equals 95th Road). The north-south lanes run from 86th Street on the west side to 62nd Street on the east end. Believe it or not, the system is easy to understand and navigate once you hit the streets.

The entire northern portion of Mandalay is dominated by the moat-enclosed ruins of the **Royal Palace,** as well as the 760-foot-high Mandalay Hill and surrounding temples.

The **train station** is in the center of town on 78th Street between A and B Roads. The **airport** is located on the southern perimeter of the town on the road leading to Rangoon. The **Tourist Burma** office is on the grounds of the Mandalay Hotel (tel. 22-540), about a mile from the train station; plan on taking a bicycle rickshaw for about 10 kyat ($1.75) for the pleasure.

USEFUL INFORMATION: In addition to the inconvenient main **Tourist Burma** office in the Mandalay Hotel (tel. 22-540), open daily from 8 a.m. to 8 p.m. (ticket sales until 2 p.m.), there are Tourist Information counters with erratic hours at the Mandalay airport (no telephone) and the railway station (tel. 22-541; open daily from 2 to 4 p.m.) as well as in Maymyo at the Maymyo Inn. If you do visit Tourist Burma, be sure to pick up a copy of their map of Mandalay—it's the best available.

The **post office** is located near the intersection of 81st and 22nd (C Road). On 26th Road (B Road) are the **PTT** and **Myanma Economic Bank.** The **telephone area code** is 02.

The **Mandalay People's Hospital** is located one block from the train station near 77th Street and 30th Road.

GETTING THERE: There is daily "express" **train** service between Rangoon and Mandalay; fares are 138 kyat ($23) for a reclining sleeper and 110 kyat ($18.25) for upper-class space. The thrice-daily journey is scheduled to take 12 hours, but plan on delays. If you want to save the cost of a hotel room, consider taking the popular night express that ordinarily (if on time) departs at 6:15 p.m. and should arrive in Mandalay at 8:30 a.m.

Mandalay is also connected to Rangoon and Pagan **by air** with fares of 545 kyat ($90.75) and 190 kyat ($31.75) respectively. The flight originates at Rangoon and takes about two hours while the Pagan commute is scheduled to take 30 minutes, but as always, plan for delays. If you do choose to fly, you'll be rewarded with an excellent view of the town, Mandalay Hill, and especially the moat and grounds of the Royal Palace and the gorgeous pagodas in nearby Sagaing.

One of the more intriguing ways to travel between Pagan and Mandalay is via the twice-weekly **steamer** on the Irrawaddy River (see "Getting There" in Section 1 on Pagan).

Finally, for real hard-seat adventure (and discomfort) there is the **bus** linking Taunggyi with Mandalay for 143 kyat ($23.75) and Pagan with Mandalay for 88 kyat ($14.75).

GETTING AROUND: One of the joys of Mandalay (especially after visiting Rangoon) is traversing the city's streets via **bicycle rickshaw.** Not only is the pace relaxing, but the patter of the driver is usually intriguing (at least a source of great stories, tips, unofficial currency swaps, and cultural insights). A typical ride about town should run about 7 kyat ($1.25). Prices are negotiable, so don't be shy about haggling. As with all parts of life in Burma, there is an improvisational aspect to local transportation. We agreed, once, to meet a driver for an efficient city tour in a Jeep. After greeting him outside the driveway of the Mandalay Hotel, we realized that we were to ride on the bars of his bicycle; there was no mention of the Jeep other than "The price of petrol too high today. Black market." Remember, you don't have much time, so choose your options carefully and don't be afraid to move on to another source. Expect to pay between 50 kyat ($8.25) and 100 kyat ($16.75) for an all-day trishaw.

There are official **cars** for rent courtesy of Tourist Burma for about ten times the rickshaw price (and they will insist on stamping your money form); the average quoted rate is 700 kyat ($116.75). If you do wish to reserve a cab, do so upon your arrival.

Less enchanting, but good for local sightseeing are the so-called "Mazdas," which are nothing more than noisy **motorized rickshaws** that will, almost certainly, break down on any lengthy excursion (we once went through four getting to Sagaing!).

It's possible to take the **public bus** (which might actually look like a bus, or more likely, some type of truck), but plan on getting to the bus stop (ask your hotel or rickshaw driver for the correct location) well in advance of the estimated departure time, lest you have to wait on line for tomorrow's run. Bus "stations" are not well marked on maps and depend on the route and ultimate destination.

Last, we have actually **hitchhiked** out of Mandalay up to Maymyo. This almost-unheard-of traveling technique in Burma will certainly provide you, as it did us, with a genuine life experience.

ACCOMMODATIONS: Mandalay has no first-class hotels, though there are a few spartanly furnished, clean, moderate to budget-priced inns.

The top alternative is the **Mandalay Hotel,** located one block south of the moat surrounding the palace ruins on the corner of 26th Road and 68th Street (tel. 02/22-540). The Mandalay isn't particularly convenient to the city center, but it is the Tourist Burma headquarters and easy for those on a prearranged tour. Guest rooms are clean but lacking any character. Check to see if the air conditioning actually works before agreeing to stay in a given room. There is a dining room that serves acceptable fare at high prices. Expect to pay $14 for a standard single and $23 for a double.

Along the same lines as the Mandalay Hotel is the nearby **Myamandala Hotel,** located around the corner on 25th Road (tel. 02/21-283). The 24 rooms are divided between the old and new wings; in both buildings we found clean rooms, private bathrooms, and in most quarters, air conditioning. Again, there isn't much style here, but at least it's reasonably tidy. Doubles are $17.50 in the old wing and $22 in the new building; singles are $7.75 and $10.50 respectively. The restaurant at the Myamandala is reputed to be better than average.

Moving west toward the center are a series of lower-priced (and lower standard) guesthouses. Out of the downtown throng is the **Myint Thidar Guesthouse** on 29th Road between 73rd and 74th Streets (tel. 02/26-021). This clean 20-room budget alternative has fan-cooled, mosquito-net accommodations; cold-water shower and Asian toilets are common. A double room rents for 36 kyat ($6); singles are 21 kyat ($3.50). The Myint Thidar maintains a 10 p.m. curfew.

The **Sabai Phyu Resthouse,** at 58 81st St., between 25th and 26th Streets (tel. 02/25-377), has 23 clean and modern rooms. The hotel is laid out in a box-like pattern, with all the rooms coming off a central sitting area, including the separate toilet and shower stalls. Mr. Soe Myind, the owner, is very friendly and seems to be a big wheel in town. A single here goes for 54 kyat ($9), a double for 108 kyat ($18), and a family room for 216 kyat ($36). All rooms have the requisite mosquito netting to ensure a tranquil evening of bedded bliss.

The **Taung Za Lat (Rhododendron) Resthouse,** on the corner of 26th Road and 81st Street (tel. 02/23-210), is a very basic, fairly clean establishment across the street from the Sabai Phyu. All facilities are shared and of primitive standard. Double rooms rent for 90 kyat ($15) while singles go for 45 kyat ($7.50).

DINING: As with most Burmese cities, Mandalay isn't renowned for its cuisine. Among the better dining rooms in the city is the **Shwe Nan Taw Restaurant,** also known as the Wooden Palace, 110 73rd St. between 28th and 29th Roads (tel. 24-588). The emphasis here is on Chinese specialties, including hot-and-sour prawns, chicken with vegetables, and a varied selection of duck and pork entrees. The ingredients and facilities seem clean by local standards and the food is quite acceptable. A meal for two runs about 100 kyat ($16.75).

One of the more attractive settings in Mandalay is the twin-story **Htaw Yin Restaurant,** 396 81st St., between 30th and 31st Roads (tel. 22-767), near the cross-country bus station. This Chinese eatery, with outdoor tables, serves such specialties as "fried chicken spicy," fish with soy sauce, deep-fried shrimp, shrimp and chicken with onion and dried chili, and stewed bean curd with shrimp. A full meal for two should cost approximately 80 kyat ($13.25).

The **TooToo Restaurant,** located at 79 27th St., between 74th and 75th Roads (no telephone), is a great local favorite; its 12 tables with tablecloths are usually occupied by locals scarfing down their vegetable casserole, spicy chicken, or meatball dishes with side orders of fried rice and corn. Prices range from 10 kyat ($1.50) to 15 kyat ($2.50); the TooToo is open from 11 a.m. to 8 p.m. daily.

The **Minn Sein Restaurant** is on 30th Street between 73rd and 74th Roads (no telephone), and is run by the same Mr. Soe Myind who is the owner of the Sabai Phyu Resthouse. Among the Sein's specialties are their fried bamboo root, sweet-and-sour chicken, and noodle and rice dishes. Prices range from 9 kyat ($1.50) to 15 kyat ($2.50) and the food is uniformly good.

Locals recommended the following restaurants in addition to the above: **Shwe Man Café,** between 79th and 80th Streets on 28th Road; **Shwe Nung Daw,** at 110 73rd St., between 27th and 28th Roads (tel. 24-588); **Shwe Hin La,** on 84th Street between 31st and 32nd Roads, for good Burmese food; and **Min Min,** on the corner of 26th Road and 83rd Street, for Muslim/Chinese cuisine (no pork but plenty of vegetables).

WHAT TO SEE AND DO: Most people who come to Mandalay expect only to see and climb its famous hill. Though the view is sensational, that isn't reason enough to make the visit. Among the more impressive sites are those located outside the town, such as the temples and knolls of Sagaing and the cool hill town of Maymyo.

One of the many tragedies experienced by Burma during World War II was the complete destruction of the wooden Royal Palace during a battle between Japanese and Allied forces. Although that was the physical and spiritual center of the city, there are many other impressive sites to explore within the city.

Mandalay Hill

Atop 760-foot-high Mandalay Hill one has an extraordinary view of the palace and surrounding temples, the Irrawaddy River, and the plains and hills in the distant countryside; however, you'll have to climb what locals claim to be 1,729 steps to reach the top. Along the way are small temples, pavilions, and rest stops where you might have the unique opportunity to chat with a monk. Although the stairs are covered, it's a good idea to do this climb in the early morning or evening to avoid Mandalay's intense midday heat.

Shwe Nandaw Kyaung

Our favorite building in all of Mandalay is the Shwe Nandaw Kyaung, a carved teak temple on the grounds of a still-functioning monastery northeast of center city. If you're on a one-day sightseeing blitz, take the time to thoroughly explore this elaborately decorated building as this will give you an idea about the intricate nature of Burmese craftsmanship. The Shwe Nandaw Kyaung is typical of the architecture and artistry that once characterized the Royal Palace. Across the street is another section of the monastery where a few very friendly English-speaking monks gather to drink tea; don't be surprised if they call you over to join them. At the entrance to the monastery is a stand selling Burmese bamboo horoscopes.

Kuthodaw Pagoda

This temple, located near the base of Mandalay Hill, is the Wat Po (in Bangkok) of Burma, mostly known for its 729 inscribed stone tablets, each one displaying a section of Buddhist philosophy from the scriptures. The slabs are artfully placed around the central pagoda in a maze-like layout. The shrine, actually more of a school or institute than a temple, was built by King Mindon in 1857 and is still in use by local monks.

Mandalay Royal Palace

The most dominant site in all of Mandalay is the Royal Palace, even though its presence is more phantom than actual. Nothing but the surrounding moat and pieces of wall survive, and the central section is inaccessible other than to military personnel, but the scale of the site (best appreciated from the top of Mandalay Hill) provides a clue to the lost grandeur of the palace. Built during the mid-19th century by King Mindon, the Royal Palace represented an almost Burmese baroque style of architecture, with buildings constructed in elaborate spirals (such as the famed tower) and with extraordinarily decorative carving. The Burmese themselves considered it decadent, though today it is appreciated as the last gasp of the ancient Burmese regime.

During World War II Burmese and Japanese troops (allies against the Western powers) were stationed inside the grounds of the palace, and fought a brutal battle with Allied (mostly British-Indian) troops. The largely wooden buildings caught fire, and within a short time all traces of the palace disappeared. A model and series of photographs of the palace are on display in the National Museum in Rangoon.

Maha Muni Pagoda

The most monumental Buddha in Mandalay is found on the southern perimeter of the city in the Maha Muni Pagoda. Set back from the road in the busy craftsman-lined stretch, thousands of devotees make pilgrimages to this, the holiest shrine in town. The Buddha was transported in 1784 by King Bodawpaya from the southern state of Rakhine after which he built the surrounding temple. Today a visit to the holy shrine is a popular activity for the city's many devout Buddhists, particularly in the morning when the monks wash the face of the Buddha. We found the trappings of the temple a bizarre combination of the reverent and the garish. The worship of the Buddha is done with the utmost seriousness, yet the sacred figure is framed by kitschy flashing lights. Be sure to visit the small side pavilion with its fine Khmer and Thai bronze figures.

As with the Shwe Dagon Pagoda in Rangoon, we enjoyed looking at the covered stalls leading up to the central Buddha. The usual panoply of Burmese goodies, from gold-leaf Buddhas to inflatable elephants, are on display for browsing and sale (don't forget to negotiate your price). It's best to arrange a taxi or Mazda for your visit to the Maha Muni Pagoda, as it's quite far from the center.

SHOPPING: Mandalay is still a center of traditional crafts, if only for the fact that it attracts a relatively large number of tourists. We found some excellent objects, including *kalaga* (Burmese tapestries), teak carvings, and puppets (like those found in Pagan).

One of the better craft shops in Mandalay is **Mann Shwe Gon,** on 29th Road, near the Myint Thidar Guesthouse. There you'll find a good assortment of Burmese kalaga, ranging in price from 30 kyat ($5) for a one-foot-square piece to 2,500 kyat ($416.75) for a 30-square-foot masterpiece. Puppets, made locally and in Rangoon, range from 50 kyat ($8.25) to 325 kyat ($54.25), depending on detail and age. Teak opium-scale boxes cost approximately 75 kyat ($12.50), while the weights to go with it run about 50 kyat ($8.25). As with all such establishments, we suggest very aggressive negotiations, and as part of the means of payment, consider bartering clothing, cosmetics, cigarettes, or alcohol for souvenirs.

One of Mandalay's oldest and best weaving concerns is **Acheik Lunyargyaw,** on 62nd Street off 19th Road. You'll recognize the façade by the sign incorporating an image of a flying white Pegasus. The main attraction here, other than to watch silk and cotton being woven by hundreds of experienced hands, is the sale of fine textiles. Though the cotton originates from India and the silk from China and Japan, the designers at Acheik Lunyargyaw weave some fine material, most of which is used to make saris and *longi* (sarong-like wrap-arounds worn by men and women). An average-price silk longi runs 1,100 kyat ($183.25) while its cotton cousin costs about 200 kyat ($33.25).

Zegyo Market
Although it's not great for the really fun touristy souvenirs, you should visit the Italian-inspired (built in the late '20s by Mr. Z, a peripatetic Italian) but thoroughly Byzantine Zegyo Market, in the city center across from the clock tower, for its amazing assortment of Burmese and black-market housewares and furnishings. We've yet to buy anything in the many covered stalls of the Zegyo, but it's one of the first places we stop, if only to get a feel for the mood of Mandalay. The market is open daily.

DAY TRIPS AND EXCURSIONS: You'll need to plan a full day of sightseeing to visit the three main ancient cities near Mandalay: Amarapura, Sagaing, and Ava. If you have the time, consider an overnight excursion to Maymyo, one of our favorite towns in the country.

Amarapura
With the growth of metropolitan Mandalay in full gear, it's understandable that its southern flank is about to overtake a historical town located a mere seven miles from the city center. Such is the case with Amarapura, one of many ancient Burmese capitals in the region. Although there is the not-so-fascinating Patodawgyi Pagoda, we particularly recommend visiting (and crossing) **U Pein's Bridge,** a longish teak affair that seems to be the busiest footpath in central Burma. The bridge crosses part of the Irrawaddy River and as such is an important link in the daily life of the local inhabitants. Apparently this famous bridge drowns during high water of the monsoon, but in the dry season it graces a lovely stretch of river, with paddies and farms near by.

Sagaing
Perhaps more impressive than Mandalay itself, Sagaing is our favorite historic day-trip destination. The area resembles the Mandalay region and, like its more famous neighbor, it, too, has a Buddha-built hill. The town is 21 km (13 miles) southwest of Mandalay, built along the western banks of the Irrawaddy River. The climb up Sagaing Hill is fairly taxing, especially on a hot day, but the view is outstanding and certainly justifies the effort. Along the way, monks will likely invite you to sit and talk or take you on a tour of their favorite pagoda. Gazing out over the surrounding hills and plains, across the Irrawaddy, are literally hundreds of gleaming pagodas, each seeming like something out of a fantastic tale of magic and mystery. At the top is a fine temple where, fortunately, they sell cool drinks.

There are two pagodas worth seeing in the town of Sagaing. The first is the **Kaunghmudaw Temple,** an enormous whitewashed breast-shaped pagoda that one can hardly look at in midday because of its sun-reflected brilliance. At the base of the pagoda are fine images of *nats,* Buddhist spirits who are known to live inside the temple. On the road back to Mandalay is the **Simyashin Pagoda** ("Elephant Pagoda"), a Sri Lankan–style building whose gates are well protected by two ten-foot-tall carved pachyderms. The periphery of the temple is also encircled with sculpted elephants.

Sagaing itself is a very typical Burmese village with a modest market, a restaurant or two, and a square where there's always something happening, often in what appears to be slow motion.

Ava

Yet again another former Burmese capital with lovely ruins, a few miles south of Amarapura, this time they are to be seen at the **Maha Aung Mye Bonzan Monastery,** which features excellent Burmese decorative masonry and carving.

Mingun

A trip to Mingun is in the opposite direction from Sagaing and Amarapura, and should be included on another day's excursion. Part of the pleasure of visiting Mingun is getting there: a boat travels seven miles upriver from Mandalay on the Irrawaddy River (this is especially recommended if you don't plan on taking the steamer from Mandalay to Pagan). Travelers call on Mingun principally to see the legendary **Mingun Bell,** reputed to be the largest ringing chime in the world (how does anyone know for sure, we ask?). While in Mingun, be sure to visit the **monastery,** still unfinished but a lovely example of Burmese architecture.

Maymyo

Ah, Maymyo! We read George Orwell's *Burmese Days* while in Maymyo, and what could have been more appropriate. The town was colonized by the British in the halcyon days of the Burma Oil Company and the Bombay Burma Timber Company, peaking in the 1920s. Then the town was the northern headquarters of these and other famous enterprises and the ranking officers of said companies were sent from sweaty Rangoon from March to May to the cool of the upcountry hills. Although real work was done in Maymyo, it also functioned as a retreat, replete with cricket, tennis, gin and tonics, and of course, a magnificent botanical garden. Today the town bears witness to its recent past, but it's a shadow of its former self. The central town is Burmese all the way, including a fine market (with some interesting crafts: also see the **Dream Merchant** tribal handcrafts shop on the main road). Transport is via *miem lay* (horse carts), which look like smaller versions of Wild West stagecoaches.

The colonial part of town is centered around the main lodging, the Candracraig Hotel, now known as the **Maymyo Hotel** (tel. 02/2047). This English country manor was built by a Canadian architect named Craig—thus the name—in 1904 to house the officers of the timber company; it was converted to a hotel in 1970, and since then it has tried to maintain certain traditions, all English. Other than at tea time, the Candracraig is most known for its roast beef dinner, complete with Yorkshire pudding and the trimmings. Although the meal doesn't match up to its billing in such a grand place, we still appreciate the theater of it all. The rooms in the Candracraig are enormous, most with fireplaces (essential in the winter; remember, Maymyo is over 3,300 feet high) and loaded with character. What's lacking in basic maintenance is more than compensated by atmosphere. Rooms run 60 kyat ($10) per night. Other amenities include tennis (they were repairing the court when we visited), bike rental, and that famous afternoon tea.

In town are two other guesthouses: the **Sa Kha Tha Guesthouse,** located on the main road (no telephone); and the **Namm Myaing Hotel,** also on the main road at the intersection of Mandalay and Lashio Roads, outside of the central village (tel. 02/2118), a 30-room inn with private baths, restaurant, and bar.

When in Maymyo, be sure to visit the **Botanical Gardens,** perhaps the single best-kept piece of earth in all Burma. We loved riding out to the 240-acre gardens and walking along its wonderfully landscaped paths. The Botanical Gardens are open daily with changing hours throughout the year. A bit farther on is the **Pwekauk Waterfall,** another lovely sight in this little piece of heaven. After all, how bad can any place be that considers strawberries and orchids its local specialties!

There is Jeep/bus/truck service between Maymyo and Mandalay on a daily basis, roughly whenever a vehicle is full, from 5:30 a.m. to 4 p.m.; expect to pay 20 kyat ($3.25) for the 69-km (42-mile) journey. Ask your concierge about the location of the nearest bus stop, as there are at least five scattered about the city.

3. TAUNGGYI AND INLE LAKE

One of the most interesting, picturesque, and prosperous parts of Burma lies in the northeast Shan state, home of Inle Lake, Taunggyi, and the infamous "Golden Triangle." If you include this area in your tour of Burma, you'll arrive from Rangoon at the beginning, or from Mandalay or Pagan at the end, of your seven days. In either case, this unique area of Burma will seem like the separate country it has attempted to be at various times in history.

The Shan plateau rises to the east from the central Irrawaddy River with rugged mountain ranges rising toward China to the northeast, Laos to the east, and Thailand to the southeast (the other sides of the opium-producing Golden Triangle). As you travel east, the air grows cooler and the landscape greener.

The Shan people constitute the largest minority in Burma and are historically related across current borders to both Thai and Chinese cousins. Within the Shan family tree are countless tribes, whose bright, distinctive wardrobe and varied facial features are evident at the weekly markets in the area. There are also Shan people living in former Shan principalities of northwestern Burma. Because of political conflicts, border skirmishes, and the flourishing drug trade in the far reaches of the province, tourists will only taste a small section of this diverse and dramatic area.

ORIENTATION: The centerpiece of northeastern Burma, **Inle Lake** is a high (2,800 feet above sea level), long (21 miles, by 3 miles wide), and shallow (10 feet average) natural lake that's home to over 70,000 Inthas, the local tribe that lives on the shores and islands of the lake. The Inthas, whose name means "son of the light," fish the waters of the lake and grow vegetables on sod embankments fashioned out of water hyacinths and lake-bottom mud, creating what could be the mightiest hydroponic garden in the world. Long, thin dugouts ply the tranquil lake, filled with vegetables, mud, fish, and village folk bound for market. You'll be astonished by the acrobatics of rowing: the boatman stands on the bow on one leg, holding the oar in one hand and hooking his other leg around the bottom of the oar, propelling the boat with the combined power of arm and leg. With his free hand the fisherman throws nets over the side while in motion, looking for the carp and small shrimp that are the staple of the local diet. The effect is spellbinding, a ballet mirrored in the glazed surface of the vast lake against the backdrop of the hills above.

Dotting the lake are small villages, the largest of which is **Ywama,** where the touring boats pause for lunch, a tour of the weaving shops, and every fifth day, the floating market, and a visit to the octagonally shaped Phaung-Daw-Oo Pagoda, whose Buddha statues are paraded on the lake in the annual October festival.

The boats that tour the lake embark from **Nyaungshwe,** a delightful little village on the north end of the lake whose simple guesthouses and restaurants offer the more adventuresome traveler a good base for exploring the area. If you arrive here on the right day of the week, you'll enjoy an unforgettably rich and teeming market, with tribespeople from the hills hawking their spices and vegetables, and lake people selling dried shrimp and fish. It provides a wonderful mix of local cultures. Nyaungshwe has a number of interesting pagodas, most of them in a state of decay, and provides a cool and pleasant venue to soak up Burmese village life.

From Nyaungshwe, you pass through **Shwenyaung,** located on the main highway, on your way up to **Taunggyi,** the largest city in the area, the highest major city in Burma (4,700 feet), and the capital of the Shan state. Taunggyi sits on the shoulder of the mountains that ring Inle Lake about 20 miles and an hour's bus ride east. Taunggyi is a bustling and prosperous town with the only

Western-standard hotel in the area, the Taunggyi Hotel, once called the Strand Hotel. The twice-weekly market here is even larger than the Nyaungshwe market, although many tribespeople frequent both. The Su-taung-pye Pagoda commands a dramatic spot on the edge of the mountain overlooking Inle Lake and provides one of the great sunset vistas in all of Asia. Beyond the market, the pagoda and the sometimes-open Taunggyi Museum, Taunggyi offers little of tourist interest.

USEFUL INFORMATION: Because this area has several important stopping points, the following information is organized around the two major destinations, Taunggyi and Nyaungshwe.

Taunggyi

Taunggyi is organized around the main road that runs from Shwenyaung through town into the mountains. The market is on the main road in the center of town. The **Taunggyi Hotel** is located on the southern edge of town, about a mile beyond the market and up the hill. The **Tourist Burma office** is located in its lobby, open daily from 8 a.m. to 7 p.m. The staff is very friendly, reasonably helpful, and provides the only official moneychanging service in the area. You can telephone them from the Tourist Burma office in Rangoon for hotel reservations, a good idea in high season (see "Accommodations").

Bus tickets to Pagan, Mandalay, and Inle Lake are sold only in the Tourist Burma office, along with air tickets from Heho to anywhere. *Note:* You cannot catch long-distance buses on the road without a ticket from this office. Tickets must be bought from Tourist Burma. Make your travel plans and buy the necessary tickets as soon as you get to Taunggyi.

The **telephone code** for Taunggyi is 081. You cannot make overseas calls from Nyaungshwe. Long-distance and overseas calls can be booked at the Taunggyi Hotel.

Street signs are written in Burmese, so all directions in this section will be approximate. Ask any local for help, most of whom speak English.

Nyaungshwe

Nyaungshwe lies on the northern shore of Inle Lake, at the end of a small road that forks from the Thazi–Taunggyi highway in the village of Shwenyaung. The **Tourist Burma** office is located on a canal of the lake. To get there from the bus stop, walk down the main road past the market, turn right at the pagoda, and continue straight past the open memorial fields until you hit the main canal. The office is open daily from 8 a.m. to 6 p.m. Boats with guides for touring the lake are rented here and it may be possible to change money, though overland and air travel arrangements must be made at Tourist Burma in Taunggyi. Don't assume that you can catch the Pagan or Mandalay buses on the main highway back in Shwenyaung. They will not pick you up without a proper ticket from the Tourist Burma office in Taunggyi. You should verify this situation with Tourist Burma in Rangoon or in Nyaungshwe. Buses and taxis from Shwenyaung to Nyaungshwe or Taunggyi are found on the edge of town as you enter.

GETTING THERE AND GETTING AROUND: All the usual caveats concerning internal travel in Burma apply to this region, especially so because there are proportionately fewer flights and buses to other major destinations. Plan on delays.

By Air

As with any trip in Burma, it's hard to get to Taunggyi from anywhere, but given the seven-day race against the clock, flying is the most efficient and certainly the most comfortable way. If you're on a tour, or have the money for the fare and the luck to get a seat, you'll probably fly from Rangoon, Mandalay, or Pagan to the airport at Heho, 22 km (14 miles) from Taunggyi, and be transported by Tourist Burma bus to the Taunggyi Hotel. Those travelers staying in Nyaungshwe can get off at the turnoff to Inle Lake in Shwenyaung and then catch a local bus for the seven-mile trip to Nyaungshwe. Individual tourists must be aggressive and find the Tourist Burma guide at the airport in order to get on the Tourist Burma bus (most of the attention from the guides goes to the tour groups). You may have to go show your passport at a military checkpoint at the airport.

Burma Airways (BAC) has one morning and one afternoon flight in and out of Heho Airport. The morning flight goes from Rangoon to Pagan to Mandalay to Heho to Rangoon. The afternoon flight goes from Rangoon to Heho to Mandalay to Pagan to Rangoon. Air fares range from 430 kyats ($71.75) for the Rangoon to Heho journey to 182 kyats ($30.50) for the Heho to Mandalay trip. Prices include transfer to and from the airport by a Tourist Burma bus. The bus will pick you up at your hotel in the town of departure.

Individual travelers not on a Tourist Burma tour who want to fly from Heho onward *must* go directly to the Tourist Burma office in Taunggyi (just stay on the bus) and book the next leg of your journey. You can book flights out of Heho, Mandalay, or Pagan only when you get to those cities. You cannot book a Heho–Mandalay ticket from Rangoon. Flights are heavily booked by tours, so it makes advance planning impossible unless you are part of a tour. To ignore this advice is to risk serious disruption of your travel plans.

Warning: We must report a U.S. Department of State travel advisory issued in the summer of 1988 that strongly warns travelers against flying Burma Airways during the rainy season (May to October) because of the high incidence of crashes (three in one year), all of which occurred in inclement weather.

By Train

To reach Inle Lake or Taunggyi by train, you must take either the day train or night train for the 11-hour journey north to Thazi, a rail-junction city in central Burma. You can then connect in some fashion to a pokey eastbound train for an 8-hour journey to Shwenyaung, the nearest railhead, where you can catch a local bus or taxi to Inle Lake or Taunggyi. The better alternative is to take the Tourist Burma bus from Thazi for a 5-hour drive to Taunggyi. The train-bus arrangement must be made at the Tourist Burma office in either Rangoon or Taunggyi, *not* at the train station. This becomes a 16-hour trip if the train is on schedule. It's not a trip for the faint-hearted. The cost of an ordinary seat on the day train from Rangoon to Thazi is 42 kyats ($7), 120 kyats ($20) for an upper-class seat, which is highly recommended. The ordinary seats are straight-backed and torturously uncomfortable. The night-sleeper seats run 160 kyats ($26.75). There is an additional charge for the bus connection to Taunggyi. The night train is recommended for saving you a day and for a cooler trip, but it's tiring, especially when capped by a 5-hour bus trip. Who said it would be easy?

By Bus

If you think the train is difficult, wait until you hear this one! You can travel by bus between Taunggyi and Pagan or Mandalay, but it's a new form of torture. Burmese private enterprise has reinvented the bus and given it the form of a Toyota long-wheel-base pickup with bench seats in the back. Into and on top of this vehicle are packed unbelievable numbers of people. At one point in our ten-hour journey we counted 36 people *inside* the back of the truck, plus 10 people and piles of baggage on top. We considered nominating the phenomenon for Guinness, but felt no one would believe the story. The Burmese people endure these trips with dignity, patience, and humor, and it's interesting for a Westerner to share the journey with them. However, we recommend it only to hardy travelers.

If you're still interested, the bus from Taunggyi to Mandalay (197 miles) leaves at 5:30 a.m. and takes ten hours. The bus to Pagan (190 miles) leaves at 5 a.m. and takes nine hours. Check with Tourist Burma for schedule updates. There is no bus service to Rangoon—fly or take a train. If you are staying at the Taunggyi Hotel, Tourist Burma will arrange for you to be picked up and taken to the bus station, which is at a location impossible to describe. If you are staying in Nyaungshwe, you must take a taxi to Shwenyaung and catch the bus there (local buses do not run that early).

Bus tickets can only be purchased at the Tourist Burma office in Taunggyi. The bus will stop every 50 yards to pick up local folk, but government regulations prohibit buses from carrying tourists without regulation tickets purchased from Tourist Burma. There are only a limited number of seats on these buses, so your first stop in Taunggyi should be at Tourist Burma to reserve your seat. When we were there, you couldn't buy these tickets at Tourist Burma in Nyaungshwe, only in Taunggyi, although you could board the bus in Shwenyaung with a ticket purchased in Taunggyi. All of these rules could have changed, so check with Tourist Burma in Rangoon to plan your trip. However, they are not always in touch with conditions in the far reaches of the Shan state, so it will be a wing and a prayer.

Buses from Mandalay or Pagan to Taunggyi also leave early in the morning and tickets must be purchased from the local Tourist Burma offices in those cities. If you are going straight to Inle Lake, you would get off the bus in Shwenyaung and take a local bus to Nyaungshwe. We would recommend going first to Tourist Burma in Taunggyi, however, and making arrangements for the next leg of your journey, then returning to Nyaungshwe by local bus.

The local buses from Taunggyi to Nyaungshwe and Inle Lake leave hourly from 7 a.m. for the 20-mile trip, which takes one hour. The buses leave from a street corner two blocks west of the north side of the town market. Walk from the Taunggyi Hotel turn left at the street just past the market. Walk two blocks and look for buses with a little lake symbol on top, and remember that the bus you're looking for will greatly resemble a Toyota pickup with a canvas top. Start asking locals as you pass the market. The fare is 12 kyat ($2).

In Nyaungshwe, you will get off the bus and meet it later at the edge of town. Ask for the departure time of the last bus, as we were told it would leave at 4:30 p.m. In fact, it left when it was *dolmush* (means "full" in Turkish), after 5 p.m. You don't want to miss the last bus, as you would then take a taxi to Shwenyaung and a second taxi or bus to Taunggyi. A taxi each way will cost you about 100 kyat ($16.75) for the whole trip, which may be worth it for the convenience.

By Private Car or Taxi

Tourist Burma will arrange for a private car to be at your disposal during the day, should you want to tour the area. The quoted rate was 550 kyat ($91.75). A Tourist Burma bus would cost 750 kyat ($125), and a guide, 100 kyats ($16.75). Check with Tourist Burma in Taunggyi for these arrangements. You can also make arrangements through Tourist Burma for a taxi to take you to Inle Lake.

Tourists have been known to make private arrangements with locals, by paying in dollars and avoiding the official restrictions. While this is illegal, we have heard of tourists who realized substantial savings and traveled very conveniently by private car.

ACCOMMODATIONS AND DINING: This is a short story. In Taunggyi, the only real choice is the **Taunggyi Hotel,** located off the road on the south side of town about a mile beyond the market (tel. 081/21-611 or 21-302), one of the nicer hotels in all of Burma. The building is a 1960s Russian nondescript structure beautifully situated in a forest at the foot of the mountain rising above

Taunggyi. Rooms are large, comfortable, and a fine value at 61 kyat ($10.25) to 79 kyat ($13.25) for singles and 108 kyat ($18) for two. A friendly and capable staff provides excellent service, the dining room serves above-average meals for this restaurant-scarce area, and the shower actually delivers hot water, making the Taunggyi Hotel the most luxurious base for travel in this area.

There are a few simple guesthouses in Taunggyi, the best of which is **San Pye Guest House,** located on the main road between the market and the Taunggyi Hotel (no telephone). It's a simple place, only moderately clean and recommended only in a pinch. The water specified for drinking may not have been boiled, however, so exercise great caution. Choose a room—and we use that term loosely—away from the road and expect to pay 25 kyat ($4.25) for the experience. The other guesthouses we looked at are not worthy of mention.

Dining in Taunggyi is similarly limited. The Taunggyi Hotel dining room serves acceptable but bland semi-Burmese food. We would advise à la carte selections rather than the official-issue set menus that always seem to begin with beef consommé. Our one and only outside favorite is the **Gone Yong Café,** an Indian restaurant and pâtisserie (believe it or not) on the main street (no telephone). It's located between the market and the Taunggyi Hotel on the same side of the road, and you must look closely for the name on the awning. A steaming cup of sturdy soup with roti (bread), hot from the oven in the back, is yours for a reasonable 5 kyat (85¢). Biryani (meat and rice with seasonings) and other Indian dishes complete the simple menu. Try tea and a delicious and sophisticated pastry for dessert. You'll have trouble spending over 35 kyat ($5.75) for two.

If you're really brave (and we make no guarantees of health safety), you'll sample some food at the town market, if you happen to be in town on market day. Miniature hotcakes cooked on a griddle caught our eye and seemed safe. Caveat eater.

More adventuresome travelers might want to stay closer to Inle Lake in the quieter village of Nyaungshwe, on the north bank of the lake. (Don't confuse this with Shwenyaung, where you turn off the main road to travel the seven miles to Nyaungshwe on the lake.) The **Inle Inn** (tel. 081/16) would be our recommendation, a simple place with thatch walls and small rooms with single beds opening off a central corridor. The common Asian toilet and cold-water shower are separate and moderately clean. It's not a bad choice by Burmese hotel standards, and certainly reasonable at 50 kyat ($8.25) per person. There is an adjacent restaurant serving good food at reasonable prices. To get there, walk from the bus stop past the market and turn left on the street bordering the market. Walk about a mile to find the Inle Inn on the left.

If there is no room in the Inle Inn, the nearby **Bamboo Inn** (no telephone) offers similar accommodation, though just a bit shabbier.

Dining in Nyaungshwe is a longer story than in Taunggyi. The **Friendship Restaurant,** near the market but one street closer to the lake (no telephone), has been a favorite eatery of visiting Westerners for years. There are two or three restaurants near the Tourist Burma office on the canal that cater to tourists waiting for a tour boat. All these restaurants have access to the lake fish and vegetables grown in the lake, so the food is fresher and better than in other parts of Burma.

On your tour of the lake, you'll probably stop at the **Intharlay Restaurant** (no telephone), located next to the Phaung-Daw-Oo Pagoda. The music is Western and the food is excellent, with fish and vegetables a real treat at about 40 kyat ($6.75) for two.

WHAT TO SEE AND DO: Inle Lake is the main attraction in this area, so you'll want to devote your attention to a **boat tour of Inle Lake,** one of the memorable experiences in any tour of Burma. These are easily arranged at the Tourist Burma office in Nyaungshwe (see "Useful Information" for directions), where the first boat leaves at 9 a.m. The tour boats are long, thin wooden vessels powered by outboard motors. They cost 600 kyat ($100) per boat, which seats up to ten, for the four- to six-hour trip. If you are not with a group, you must either pay the full amount or wait until a crowd gathers. It's best to go early, when the crowds are largest, so you can fill the boat and limit the individual cost. Don't forget a hat, sun block, and long-sleeved shirts, as the sun can be very fierce and the evenings cool.

The boat travels down the canal, passing village houses and Buddhist pagodas on the way into the lake. As you enter the long, narrow lake, you'll see boats of lake people on the way to market, carrying their crops and vegetables to sell in Nyaungshwe or Taunggyi. Long, thin fishing boats of dugout teak logs dot the lake, propelled by the leg-rowing techniques of the local fishermen, whose grace and strength are a wonder. They fish with loose nets and with conical nets which trap the fish on the shallow bottom.

Most of the 70,000 people living on the lake are of the Intha tribe, a word meaning "son of the light." The Inthas originally came from southeastern Burma and migrated here several hundred years ago to escape the fighting between the Burmese and Thai empires.

The first stop on the lake is a tour of the **"floating gardens,"** which don't necessarily float, but are an ingenious way of farming in the middle of the lake. Water hyacinths, the green floating plants you see everywhere, are gathered, then covered with piles of rich lake-bottom mud, until a mass is created that will sustain vegetables. You'll see vast areas of tomato gardens, pepper plants, bean vines, and fruit trees, a hydroponic garden of vast proportions. You pass through a small village, past pagodas and houses on stilts, making the village a collection of islands connected with wooden bridges.

The tour boat stops in **Ywama,** the largest village on the lake, where you visit a weaving factory and shop, and can purchase the skillfully woven bags, shawls, and fabrics. If you bargain a bit, you can save up to 40% over the asking price.

You walk down paths and across bridges to visit the **Phaung-Daw-Oo Pagoda,** a large octagonal pagoda whose six Buddha figures are paraded on the lake in the October festival each year. Lunch can be had at the nearby Intharlay Restaurant, after which the boat heads back toward Nyaungshwe. On the way back through Ywama, tour boats are met by the floating market of souvenir hawkers. The boat may stop at a **government resthouse** built on stilts in the middle of the lake, where you can go for a swim, though some medical advice would warn against that.

You then return to the Tourist Burma dock, passing lake villagers returning from the market. A stroll through the streets of **Nyaungshwe** can be very pleasant, as life is very quiet here. There are several pagodas throughout the town, though most are in advanced states of decay. Don't forget that the last bus to Taunggyi leaves quite early, around 4:30 or 5 p.m.

One or two days a week the **Nyaungshwe market** in the center of town comes to life, with lake villagers and hill-tribes people coming in to sell lush vegetables, colorful spices, fresh fish and dried shrimp, and all manner of household goods. It's a wildly colorful sight, which may also be enjoyed in Taunggyi on other days of the week.

Taunggyi is a bustling and prosperous commercial center, a large city compared to Nyaungshwe. You would enjoy the market here on the right day, the **Taunggyi Museum** (if it's open), and a visit to the pagodas that sit on the edge of the mountain overlooking Inle Lake, far below. The **Su-Taung-Pye Pagoda** has a particularly fine view at sunset.

After touring the lake, you will probably move on to Mandalay or Pagan. By road you'll pass through **Kalaw,** which was a British hill station and has an old resort hotel, the **Kalaw Hotel,** providing a base to visit the **Pindaya caves** in Pindaya, about 28 miles from Kalaw. These caves are famous for the thousands of Buddha images inside, some very old and richly gilded. Very few tourists will take the time for side visits like this, as time is short and traveling difficult.

CHAPTER V

HONG KONG

□ □ □

1. A CULTURE IN TRANSITION

2. ORIENTATION AND TRANSPORTATION

3. THE ABC'S OF HONG KONG

4. ACCOMMODATIONS

5. DINING

6. SIGHTS, SHOPPING, AND NIGHTLIFE

7. THE NEW TERRITORIES, OUTLYING ISLANDS, AND DAY TRIPS TO CHINA

8. EXPLORING MACAU

It's said that Hong Kong has the most beautiful harbor in the world and the most varied gourmet cuisine, that it is a land of unbridled consumption, excellent bargains, and endless shopping opportunities, that this 412-square-mile bundle of energy moves faster than many other great metropolises. Hong Kong is a land of superlatives, a tiny nation packed with an energetic and indefatigable people whose appreciation of life is contagious. If the 21st century belongs to the Pacific Rim, then Hong Kong is a microcosm of the future. And what more delightful introduction to tomorrow?

1. A CULTURE IN TRANSITION

Hong Kong, the island group synonomous with fast cash, mercantile chaos, and the headlong rush of East to meet West, is a culture in transition. On July 1, 1997, the People's Republic of China will take back the New Territories, land leased to the British 99 years ago. Its 5.6 million citizens will soon become the perpetrators of capitalism in a country of one billion socialists. Whether they will be hailed as advocates of an economic revolution or harbingers of libertarian doom can't be predicted. With seven years to go, the economic and social uncertainties of the Chinese takeover create tensions that can readily be felt by visitors, despite the fact that both countries share a common social and cultural heritage.

TRADITION IN DAILY LIFE: The people and government of Hong Kong relish their traditional ways as much as change. Frequent hand-puppet performances and martial arts demonstrations, standing-room-only cooking classes, family outings to the Sung Dynasty (ca. A.D. 960–1279) village re-creation, annual Dragon Boat Races, and celebrations like the Lantern Festival help keep alive the differences between East and West that make Hong Kong so special.

Even the most contemporary and sophisticated Hong Kong resident or business is guided by seemingly superstitious Chinese traditions that have evolved over 5,000 years of civilization. Government-subsidized estates, luxury condominiums, and the most expensive office towers in the world are built according to *fung shui,* or wind and water principles. For most projects geomancers are called in to align buildings, entrances, and even the workspace of occupants. (Notice how difficult it is to find a building's front door!) Individuals align their beds to sleep according to the eight elements of nature, in balance with the yin and yang (opposing female/male or cool/hot principles) of the universe, which is crucial for proper rest.

Food, the focal point of Chinese existence, is dominated by symbolism and ritual. To not serve long noodles at a birthday celebration would deprive the guest of honor of long life. In an old tradition rarely practiced today, the groom was supposed to bring a roast pig to his in-laws three days after his wedding to confirm the bride's virginity. At Chinese New Year, when houses cannot be swept for fear that good luck may be brushed out the door, dozens of auspicious dishes must be served. The customary Lai See, small red envelopes filled with new money for the new year, are handed out by all to the youngest and unmarried members of the household.

Chinese pictographs and numbers are used in combination to form fortuitous sounds or images. One of Hong Kong's biggest fundraisers is the annual government auction of "lucky" car license-plate numbers, for which people are willing to pay hundreds of thousands of dollars. Drawings of a dragon (symbol of the emperor and of masculinity) interlocked with a phoenix (symbol of the empress and femininity) are posted at wedding ceremonies, a typical use of symbols at all family events. The number three sounds like the word for life; the number eight, like that of prosperity; and nine, of eternity. As another example, the date August 8, 1988, a "double double eight" day (with four times the usual prosperity) in the Year of the Dragon (an astrological sign predicting times of wealth and success), was chosen by the Bank of China as the most propitious time to open its new Hong Kong headquarters.

It may seem that as rapidly as westernization takes place, old traditions become more firmly entrenched. *Dai pai dongs,* the street vendors whose noodles fed busy office workers for decades before the advent of McDonald's, are now licensed to operate outside the shopping malls overtaking the Central district. The classic Night Markets, outdoor flea markets that once provided a family's shopping needs, though fewer in number, have been immortalized on tourist maps or reincarnated in indoor malls. Mysterious and delightful contradictions abound. The glorious Hong Kong harbor, breathtakingly defined by a futuristic skyline, shelters sail-powered junks and sampans. Women can be seen in the high-necked *cheongsam* in five-star hotels or in the rice paddies on an outlying island, a fashion that predates the Great Wall.

A BRIEF HISTORY: Archeological evidence indicates that the sparsely populated island of Hong Kong first came under the control of mainland China about 2,200 years ago. Finds at the Li Cheung Uk tomb excavation in Kowloon confirm that the earliest settlers were Han Chinese; serious migration from the mainland began during the Sung dynasty in the 10th century. Until 1800, when some far-sighted Englishmen first noticed Hong Kong's strategic location at the mouth of the Pearl River, the Chinese colony was regarded by Europeans as "a barren island" of 5,000 fishermen and farmers.

In 1839 the Chinese forced out British traders established in Canton in efforts to quell the opium trade. The British needed to regain a trading post in the region. After their victory in the ensuing Opium Wars, they demanded the cession of Hong Kong as a British Crown Colony in 1842. Settlement proceeded apace and in the first five years of British rule the colony's population swelled almost fourfold with immigrant laborers.

The colorful story behind the landmark "Noon Day Gun" is one of the few reminders of this era. One of earliest developers was William Jardine, the original "Taipan" and founder of the Jardine Trading Company (known as the Noble House). He moved his offices from Canton and Macau to the first parcel of land auctioned by the British at East Point, and built a huge complex of offices, *godowns* (warehouses), and residences, since redeveloped as Causeway Bay. From the fortified Jardine outpost it was customary to fire off a gun salute whenever the Taipan's yacht was approaching port. A senior British naval officer, recently stationed in the colony, was outraged when he realized the gun salute was for a civilian. The tribute was forbidden and Jardine was ordered to deplete its gunpowder reserves (and become the colony's timekeeper) by firing a gun at noon each day, a practice that is still continued.

The Colony's Growth

The tiny colony prospered as a trading and warehousing entrepôt, expanding greatly in March 1860 when the Kowloon Peninsula and Stonecutter's Island were ceded in perpetuity to the British. Then unrest caused by the Taiping Rebellion (1851–1864) in mainland China forced thousands to immigrate to Hong Kong, ensuring that the colony remained a Chinese community. By 1861 the population had jumped to almost 120,000 (with fewer than 5,000 foreigners), although 20 years passed before the first Chinese representative was nominated to the Legislative Council. The long-established commodities trade between Britain, India, and China expanded from opium to include rice, sugar, and textiles, which were shipped throughout Southeast Asia and Japan.

On July 1, 1898, after the British prevented European interference in China during the Japanese conflict, the second Treaty of Peking sanctioned the lease of 588 km² of land (the New Territories) to Britain for 99 years. Although Shanghai remained the center of British investment, the now-sizable colony flourished. In 1904 tram lines were installed along the waterfront; their current inland location is tangible proof of the city's astonishing growth through land reclamation. Close contact was maintained with China; within a decade Kowloon and Canton were linked by railway. The colony's intellectuals were very influential in the 1911 overthrow of the last Manchu emperor, a rebellion that brought a new wave of migration from the north.

During the 1938 Japanese invasion of China half a million people fled. Within three years the Japanese had invaded Hong Kong from Canton, forcing the British to surrender on Christmas Day, 1941. Hardship, food shortages, and imprisonment made life very difficult for residents, many of whom were forced to leave. After 44 months of occupation, the population had decreased by 60%.

Since World War II

In 1946 the British appointed Sir Mark Young as governor and regained control of their colony. The fall of Shanghai to Communist troops in 1950 replenished Hong Kong's population with yet another wave of immigrants. This group included skilled craftsmen who established Hong Kong's textile industry, and it's still said that the best tailors are those who were trained in Shanghai.

Hong Kong recovered rapidly and became a prosperous, more industrialized, and urbanized city than before the war. After the population surge, the government became increasingly involved with Hong Kong's welfare; today more than two million inhabitants reside in government-subsidized housing. As textiles dominated the '50s economy, plastics dominated the '60s and electronics the '70s. In the Hong Kong of the '80s, where there are more Rolls-Royces per capita than anywhere else on earth, the business of finance dominates everything.

Despite its staggering growth and financial clout, Hong Kong always depended on mainland China for much of its foodstuffs and water supply. For centuries waves of migration were the only indirect effect of the mainland's turbulent political scene. Then, in 1967, leaders of China's Cultural Revolution began to incite student unrest in Hong Kong. Direct intervention, including the use of the Bank of China's loudspeaker system to broadcast protests of British imperialism, was employed to urge the overthrow of the government. Hong Kong survived, reaffirming its economic strength and loyalty to the Crown, and in the 1970s the designation "colony" was replaced by "British Administered Territory."

The 1970s were a period of continued growth for Hong Kong, a time when its proud status as a "NIC" (newly industrialized country) was evolving into that of a major financial center. Conflicts in Vietnam sent a wave of refugees—boat people—to Hong Kong, but strict immigration laws curbed an addition to the population. Amid growing nationalism, talks began in 1982 between Great Britain and the People's Republic of China over the future of Hong Kong after the 1997 expiration of Britain's lease on the New Territories. After discussing and considering several proposals, on December 19, 1984, an agreement was signed to return Hong Kong and the New Territories to China, but to maintain them as a special economic zone.

HONG KONG TODAY: At present Sir David Wilson, the 27th and perhaps the last of the governors appointed by Her Majesty, the Queen, is managing the territory under the gaze of senior Chinese official Xu Jiatun, head of the Hong Kong branch of the New China News Agency. The Sino-British agreement has fostered a great deal of mistrust among the middle class who feel that the British colluded with the Chinese to deny Hong Kong's residents a taste of democracy before the Chinese takeover. In the present political climate, the middle class (who prospered under capitalism) and the offspring of Shanghai émigrés (whose parents lived through the Communist takeover in 1950) are hoping to immigrate to Europe, Australia, or North America before 1997.

Hong Kong's political and economic scenes are rapidly changing. Secure investors are ploughing their money into Hong Kong's volatile stock market, which rebounded immediately after the Black Monday crash (October 19, 1987) in New York. The conservative are going into partnership with foreign companies, hoping that international status will ward off any Chinese nationalization schemes. Optimists are courting the Chinese government, trying to develop joint enterprises and open trade. The People's Republic has invested over $5 billion in businesses listed on the Hong Kong Stock Exchange; even the old-line British firms are promoting Chinese taipans. And the local Cantonese, who for years sought out the best (and the worst) of the West to imitate, are researching their Chinese roots. The privileged classes are learning to speak Mandarin, the principal dialect of the PRC, and many have returned to the provinces of their ancestors to reclaim the common links that eluded these neighbors for centuries.

What will the future bring? There's only one thing we can predict: that July 1, 1997, is as sure to bring change to the territory as the Chinese New Year is to bring red Lai See packets to the young.

HK$	$ U.S.	HK$	$ U.S.
0.25	0.03	150.00	19.23
0.50	0.06	200.00	25.64
0.75	0.10	250.00	32.05
1.00	0.13	300.00	38.46
2.00	0.26	350.00	44.87
3.00	0.38	400.00	51.28
4.00	0.51	450.00	57.69
5.00	0.64	500.00	64.10
6.00	0.77	550.00	70.51
7.00	0.90	600.00	76.92
8.00	1.03	650.00	83.33
9.00	1.15	700.00	89.74
10.00	1.28	750.00	96.15
15.00	1.92	800.00	102.56
20.00	2.56	850.00	108.97
25.00	3.21	900.00	115.38
30.00	3.85	950.00	121.79
35.00	4.49	1,000.00	128.21
40.00	5.13	1,050.00	134.62
45.00	5.77	1,100.00	141.03
50.00	6.41	1,150.00	147.44
75.00	9.62	1,200.00	153.85
100.00	12.82	1,250.00	160.26

2. ORIENTATION AND TRANSPORTATION

Hong Kong is one of the most modern cities in the world and easily accessible to the visitor: transportation is well organized and inexpensive, a wide range of printed information is readily available. English is widely spoken, and hotel concierges are well trained to answer the questions of a perplexed guest.

ORIENTATION: The glittering, skyscraper-blanketed isle known as Hong Kong is actually part of the British Trust Territory of Hong Kong that includes 235 other islands, the nearby Kowloon Peninsula, and the New Territories, mainland areas stretching north to the border of the People's Republic of China, which were deeded to the British during the 19th century. The aerial view that most newcomers get provides an excellent visual orientation. As you descend toward **Kai Tak International Airport,** precariously set on the Kowloon Peninsula, notice the narrow stretch of **Victoria Harbour** that separates **Kowloon** to the north from the densely developed island of **Hong Kong.** The famous Star Ferry shuttles commuters through one of the world's busiest ports and an incredibly dramatic setting, although since 1972 drivers have been able to use the less picturesque Cross Harbour Tunnel.

Business, government, and financial institutions based in Hong Kong are primarily in the district known as **Central,** where addresses are given by building names rather than street numbers. From the Star Ferry's point of view looking south, Central's biggest landmark is the Connaught Centre, a distinctive white office tower with round porthole windows. The Connaught Centre houses the Jardine Matheson Company (the real-life "Noble House" of James Clavell's novel whose scion is called "Taipan"), the main office of the Hong Kong Tourist Association (on the 35th floor), and the General Post Office and Star Ferry terminal at its base. Elevated walkways connect the Connaught Centre to Central's elegant Swire House, Prince's Building, Alexandra House, and the super-deluxe Landmark Tower shopping complex. The Mandarin Oriental Hotel is just beyond it on **Connaught Road, Central,** the main waterfront thoroughfare.

Heading east on **Gloucester Road** past the hi-tech, newly opened Hong Kong Bank Building (reputed to be the most expensive in the world) and the Far East Financial Centre, which resembles a bar of gold, you come to the neon, ticky-tacky commerce district of **Wanchai.** This district became famous in the '60s after the publication of Richard Mason's *The World of Suzie Wong,* but it, too, is becoming redeveloped. Beyond it is the more recently built-up **Causeway Bay.** This area is very popular with locals for its movie theaters, restaurants, shops, and cafés. It also has many hotels. The city is spreading along the water west of Central and into the **Western** district (marked by the red-trimmed, blue tower of the Hotel Victoria) whose new shopping facilities and hotels will soon lure more tourists.

The highest point (554 meters, 1,800 feet) on the island is **Victoria Peak;** Old Money and the territory's expatriate and Chinese elite reside on its hillsides. Below the peak on the island's south coast are the houseboat village at **Aberdeen,** the popular beach at **Repulse Bay,** and the celebrated outdoor market at **Stanley.**

Looking north from the ferry to Kowloon is almost as startling as looking at Hong Kong, the mainland areas having undergone tremendous development in the last decade. The Star Ferry Terminal is at the intersection of Canton and Salisbury Roads. **Canton Road,** the peninsula's west-coast waterfront roadway, houses one of Asia's largest shopping complexes behind the Star House offices, the Ocean Centre, Ocean Galleries, and Harbour City. **Salisbury Road** is the main waterfront thoroughfare facing south in this district known as **Tsimshatsui** (also written Tsim Shat Tsui or TST), which means "sharp, sandy point." Salisbury Road curves past the futuristic Space Museum (built on landfill) and the territory's grande dame, the Peninsula Hotel. The main north-south avenue in Tsimshatsui and the area most congested with shopping bargains is **Nathan Road,** also known as the Golden Mile.

·   Just east of this, and difficult to distinguish from its older neighbor, is **Tsimshatsui East.** Once a sandy coastline, **Chatham Road** now forms the western boundary of this triangular district of reclaimed land developed in the '80s. Both districts contain the greatest concentration of hotels, shops, and restaurants, and are a more convenient base for those whose primary goal is shopping. Vibrant Kowloon makes up only 12 km² of the 980.5 km² belonging to the increasingly developed New Territories and the Outlying Islands (see Section 7 for more details).

GETTING THERE: Hong Kong is the third-largest financial center in the world and it's no exaggeration to say that almost all roads lead there. In fact, it's included in this guidebook about Southeast Asia because it's one of the most common access points for travelers coming from North America. More than 30 carriers serve Kai Tak International Airport with regular flights. United Airlines has daily nonstop flights from San Francisco or Seattle to Hong Kong, with connections to dozens of other North American cities; the 1988 super-APEX fare was $850 to $1,000 round trip, depending on season. Hong Kong–based Cathay Pacific flies to 23 countries, with daily flights to San Francisco or Vancouver. Within Southeast Asia, Cathay Pacific flies three times daily to Bangkok, twice daily (only twice weekly nonstop) to Denpasar, Bali, or nonstop to Singapore, and daily to Jakarta or Kuala Lumpur.

Many luxury steamship companies operate South China Sea cruises, which originate at Hong Kong's Ocean Terminal; contact your travel agent for more information. Travelers to Hong Kong can visit the Portuguese protectorate of Macau by hydrofoil via the Pearl River estuary, or combine a hydrofoil or Hover-

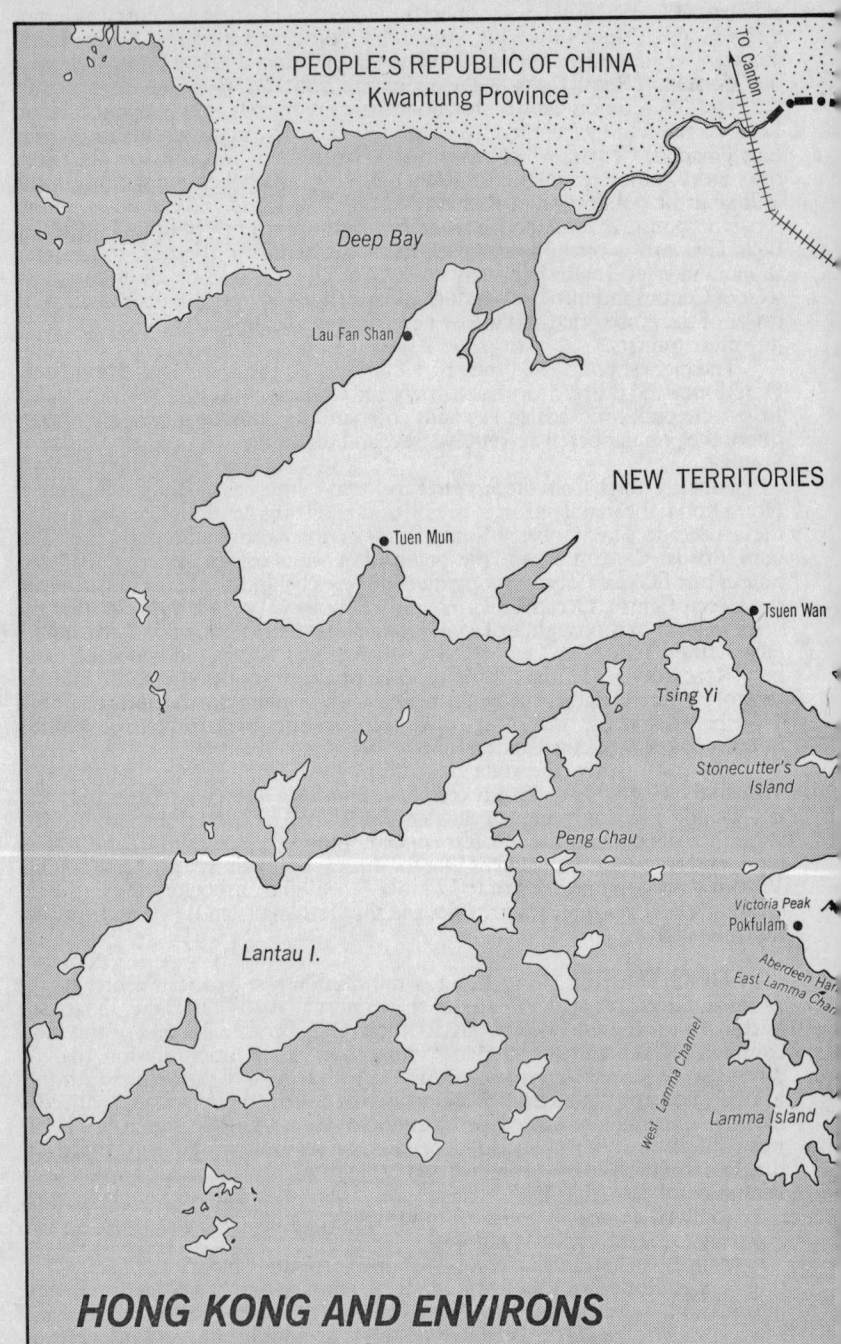

HONG KONG AND ENVIRONS

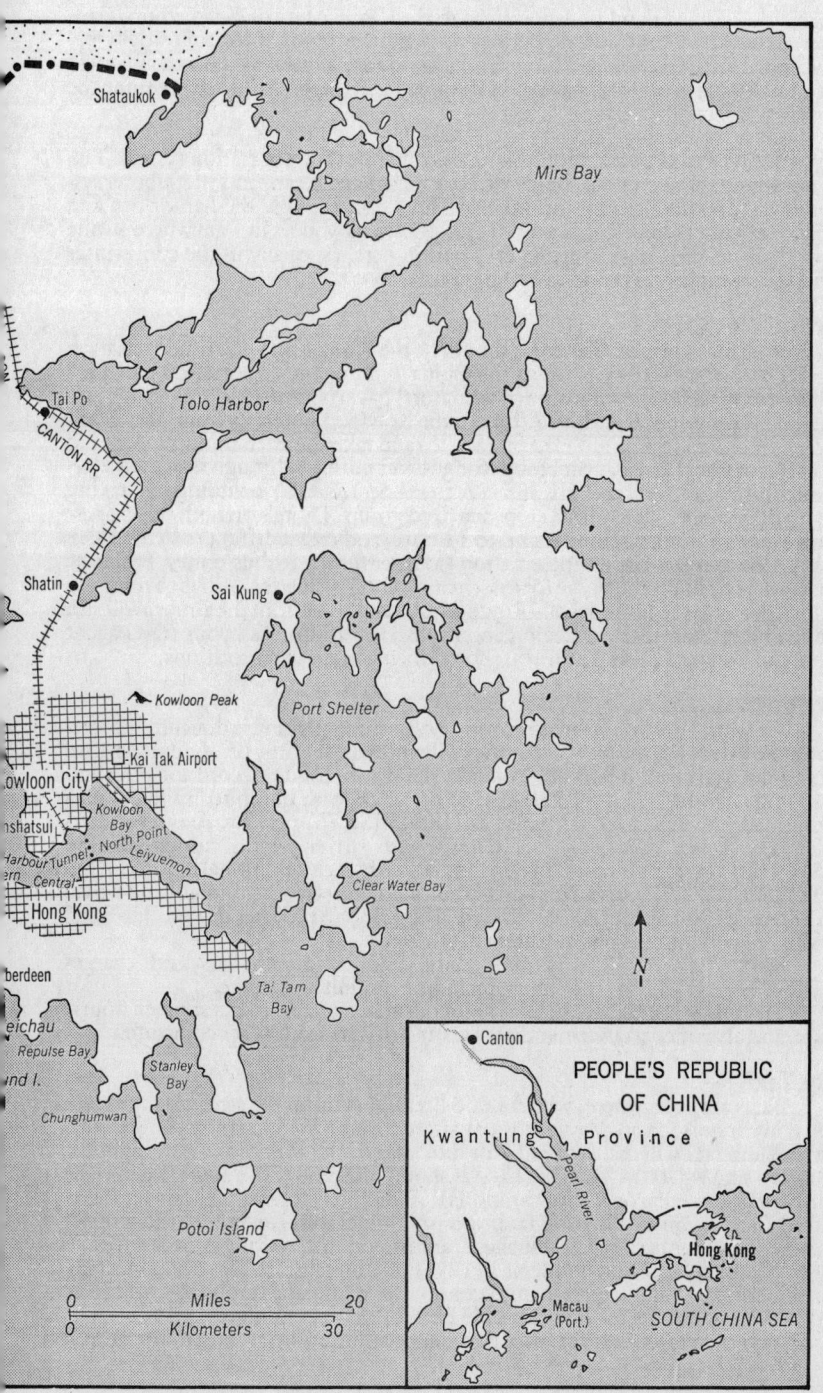

Shataukok

Mirs Bay

Tai Po

CANTON RR

Tolo Harbor

Shatin

Sai Kung

Kowloon Peak

Port Shelter

Kai Tak Airport

owloon City

Kowloon
Bay

nshatsui

North Point

Harbour Tunnel

Leiyuemon

ern

Central

Clear Water Bay

Hong Kong

berdeen

Tai Tam
Bay

eichau

Repulse Bay

nd I.

Stanley
Bay

Chunghumwan

Potoi Island

Miles   20

Kilometers   30

Canton

PEOPLE'S REPUBLIC
OF CHINA

Kwantung   Province

Pearl River

Hong Kong

Macau
(Port.)

SOUTH CHINA SEA

craft ride with overland transportation to the Chinese city of Guangzhou (Canton). The Kowloon-Canton Railway runs express trains three times daily between the main station in Hung Hom, Kowloon, and Lo Wu on the Chinese border. From here, visitors who have obtained visas beforehand can continue the journey to Guangzhou.

GETTING AROUND: Hong Kong has a first-rate transportation system. Taxis are abundant and cheap, buses well organized and clean, and the subway system a model of efficiency and luxury. The ferries that ply the harbor day and night provide as pleasant a way to get around as you'll find anywhere in the world. Then there's walking, an easy option here, especially in the cool winter and spring months. Let's look at the choices.

From the Airport

Your first stop after Customs should be the Hong Kong Tourist Association (HKTA) Information Centre in the Buffer Hall of the airport. You can then choose either a taxi, a limousine (if your hotel has arranged a pickup), or the efficient and economical Airbus. A **taxi** to the Kowloon hotels in Tsimshatsui will average HK$25 ($3.25) to HK$30 ($3.75) and take about 15 minutes. A taxi to Central or Causeway Bay on Hong Kong island must go through the Cross Harbour Tunnel, and will cost HK$55 ($7) to HK$60 ($7.75) including toll, taking up to 30 minutes. The **Airbus** stops at a fixed group of hotels on both sides, operates every 15 minutes from 7 a.m. to 11 p.m., and costs HK$6 (75¢) to HK$8 ($1). Check at the HKTA Information Counter for the Airbus routes. From the city, ask your hotel concierge for information about using the Airbus to return to the airport. Mercedes and Rolls-Royce **limousines** to or from the airport will run much more than taxis, averaging about HK$160 ($20). Ask your travel agent about arranging a pickup near your hotel when you make reservations.

By Car

We would not recommend renting a car here, as parking is difficult. However, those exploring the New Territories will find a car the only practical alternative to a tour. **Avis** (tel. 3-346-007) offers a self-drive Honda Accord for HK$300 ($38.50) per day or HK$1,750 ($224) per week, with unlimited mileage, plus collision damage waiver insurance at HK$45 ($5.75) per day. Avis also offers chauffeur-driven cars; a Toyota Crown with driver would run HK$1,050 ($134.50) for a minimum of ten hours, with each additional hour costing HK$135 ($17.25), plus a 20% surcharge for hours between midnight and 6 a.m. A Mercedes 300 limousine would cost HK$1,350 ($173) per day and HK$165 ($21.25) per hour beyond ten hours.

Hertz (tel. 5-221-013) rents only chauffeur-driven cars and charges HK$1,390 ($178.20) for 8 hours, including unlimited mileage.

The major hotels have their own limousines, available to guests at an hourly rate, and also offer arrangements for cars and drivers from other companies.

By Taxi

Taxis are everywhere, with 15,000 licensed taxis on the streets daily except on rainy or horse-racing days (Saturday afternoon and Wednesday evening). If it's available, a taxi will display a red "for hire" flag in the window, and at night the rooftop sign will be lit. Fares are fixed at about HK$5.50 (70¢) at the flag fall (the first two kilometers or 1.2 miles) and HK$2.80 (35¢) for every kilometer thereafter. In addition to the basic fare, you pay tunnel tolls (including the return), HK$2 (25¢) for each piece of luggage, animal, or bird, waiting time at HK$.70 (8¢) per ninety seconds, and HK$1 (12¢) for radio calls. Besides being inexpensive, clean, and comfortable, many taxis now have Chinatel carphones that can be used throughout the territory for only HK$2 (25¢) per minute.

Taxi drivers will expect a tip, that can be as little as rounding to the nearest dollar or as large as HK$3 (40¢) to HK$5 (65¢). Most speak some English, but it's advisable to have your concierge write down your destination in Chinese. If you have any complaints, note the taxi number and call the police hotline (tel. 5-277-177). There are legal restrictions on the areas taxis can pick up or drop passengers, so don't get angry if the driver doesn't deliver you to your exact location. Taxis usually wait at hotels or at taxi waiting stations, and are reluctant to just pull over if flagged. Some post signs indicating the direction they're willing to travel in as group taxis when they go off-duty, but tourists are unlikely to profit from this system. Restaurants will call a taxi if requested.

By Public Bus

Hong Kong's double-decker buses are a great way to sightsee and we'd recommend hopping on one from the Central terminal next to the Star Ferry for the scenic half-hour trip to Aberdeen, Stanley, or Repulse Bay (see Section 5 on sightseeing). The cream-and-blue **China Motor Bus Company** (tel. 5-658-556) services the island, and cream-and-red **Kowloon Motor Bus Company** (tel. 3-745-4466) buses are used in Kowloon. The bus service can get quite complicated if you're going to use it exclusively; check the HKTA brochures for bus routes and schedules or call the companies for information. Fares range from HK$1 (12¢) to HK$7 (90¢) and exact change must be deposited in the box as you enter. Bus service runs from 6 a.m. to midnight.

By Minibus and Maxicab

Yellow-and-red mini-vans (also called Light Buses) and some yellow-and-green maxi-cabs provide efficient transportation for shorter distances. Destinations are printed in both Chinese and English above the driver's seat. In both conveyances, call out when you want to stop. In the mini-vans, pay as you exit with fares ranging from HK$2 (25¢) to HK$6 (75¢). In the maxi-cab, pay as you enter, with fares ranging from HK$1 (12¢) to HK$4 (50¢). There's a mini-van terminal behind the Star Ferry terminal or you can spot these vehicles stopping at the main intersections, usually jammed with locals.

By Metro or Subway

Hong Kong's **Mass Transit Railway (MTR)** system, opened in 1979, is modern, comfortable, clean, and efficient. It's the fastest way to go between Kowloon and Hong Kong or to move about between districts. Pick up a route map from an MTR booth or any HKTA Information Centre. Fares range from HK$2.50 (30¢) to HK$6 (75¢), depending on distance, and tickets are purchased from machines in the station. Change is available from change machines or from the station information desk.

The HK$15 ($2) **Tourist Ticket** is a good buy, valid for that amount of MTR use anywhere in the system, with a bonus. (You must show your passport and purchase it within 14 days of arrival.)

Trams

For traveling east and west across the north side of Hong Kong (mostly between Wanchai, Causeway Bay, Central, and Western), you can enjoy the turn-of-the-century tram system, known in the U.S. as streetcars. You can go from Kennedy Town in the west to Shau Kei Wan in the east for the bargain fare of HK$.60 (7¢) for adults, HK$.20 (3¢) for children. You must deposit exact change in the box as you enter. For a real treat, ride the Antique Tram, a restored car complete with balconies and brass fittings (see the sightseeing section for more information).

Ferries

No one who comes to Hong Kong should miss the **Star Ferry**. It's not just one of the easiest ways to get from Kowloon to Hong Kong, it's a total treat offering views of that world-famous harbor, and yours for a mere pittance. From the Star Ferry Pier at the west end of Salisbury Road in Tsimshatsui, you can catch the ferry to the Central terminal as often as every three minutes from 6:30 a.m. to 11:30 p.m. (After hours, private *walla walla* or speedboats motor across for about HK$80 [$10] per trip.) The Star Ferry Pier in Central is located behind the distinctive Connaught Centre with its round porthole windows (see the sightseeing section). You can also take a Star Ferry from Central to Hung Hom to catch the train to China. That service runs from 7 a.m. to 7:20 p.m.

The **Hong Kong and Yaumatei Ferry Company** operates ferries to the Outlying Islands from a pier ten minutes west of the Star Ferry pier, near the Victoria Hotel. The journey to any of these islands averages about an hour, with almost hourly service to Cheung Chau and Lantau and ferries every other hour to Lamma (see "The Outlying Islands" for more information).

By Train

There is only one railway line, the **Kowloon-Canton Railway (KCR)**, which runs from Hung Hom in Kowloon to Sheung Shui on the Chinese border, where you can change for trains that run to China, Russia, and all the way to Europe. If your goal is much closer than Paris, you could stop at Mong Kok, Kowloon Tong, Tai Wai, Sha Tin Raceway, Tai Po Market, or Fanling, all in the New Territories. The ride is scenic and cheap. An ordinary-class ticket from Kowloon to Sheung Shui runs HK$5.20 (65¢), first-class tickets cost double that, and children's tickets, half. Express-train fares are about HK$16 ($2) for ordinary class and double that for first class. Call 0-609-9606 for information.

3. THE ABC'S OF HONG KONG

This section addresses the traveler's needs, but you can contact the **Hong Kong Tourist Association (HKTA)** at the addresses below for information prior to arrival. Don't forget to drop by one of their friendly information offices when you get to Hong Kong.

AIRLINES: Hong Kong is one of the primary transportation hubs for Southeast Asia, served by a wide range of airlines, including United Airlines, Cathay Pacific, Japan Air Lines, British Airways, Northwest, Qantas, Thai Airways, Singapore Airlines, and others. **United Airlines** is on the 29th floor of Gloucester Tower in the Landmark complex, Des Voeux Road, Central (tel. 5-810-4888). The Kowloon office is on the ground floor, Empire Building, on Salisbury Road, near the Holiday Inn Harbor View (tel. 3-829-8111). The Kowloon ticket offices of **Cathay Pacific Airlines** (tel. 3-723-6938) are in the second-floor shopping arcade of the Royal Garden Hotel, Mody Road, and on the ground floor of Ocean Centre, Canton Road. The Central office is on the ground floor of Swire House, Connaught Road (tel. 5-884-1488 for reservations).

AIRPORT: Hong Kong International Airport (also known as **Kai Tak**) is in the heart of Kowloon on the waterfront, with one of the most dramatic landing strips in the world. It's a 15-minute drive from the Kowloon hotels and 30 minutes from Central. After you clear Customs, pick up the information packet distributed by the HKTA and their giveaway A-O-A map. The Arrivals hall has a Hotel Reservations Service and a Macau Tourist Information desk. Departing passengers must pay a departure tax of HK$120 ($15.50) for adults, HK$60 ($7.75) for children, payable only in Hong Kong dollars. After paying, get in some last-minute shopping in a wide variety of duty-free shops.

AMERICAN EXPRESS: The American Express Travel Division office in Central is on the ground floor of New World Tower, 16-18 Queens Rd. (tel. 5-844-8668); it's open weekdays from 9:30 a.m. to 4 p.m., on Saturday till noon. The Kowloon office is in the Park Lane Shopper's Blvd. at 119 Nathan Rd. (tel. 3-

721-0179); it's open from 9 a.m. to 5 p.m. weekdays, on Saturday until noon. To report lost traveler's checks, call 5-843-1775 during business hours.

BANKS AND MONEY EXCHANGE: In the world's third-largest financial center (after New York and London), you'll find few problems with banking services. Although some banks charge a commission for foreign-exchange transactions (the airport moneychangers cannot charge more than 5%), one which does not is the Hong Kong and Shanghai Banking Corporation. Their Kowloon branch on Nathan Road near the Peninsula Hotel is especially convenient for shoppers.

In general, banks are open from 9 or 9:30 a.m. to 3 or 4 p.m. weekdays and until noon on Saturday. Most authorized moneychangers and hotels will change traveler's checks and foreign currency during extended hours.

BEAUTY PARLORS AND BARBERSHOPS: Every major hotel and most of the shopping malls have beauty parlors and barbershops. Consult with your hotel concierge or the HKTA for recommendations.

BOOKSTORES: One of the best English-language bookstores is the **Swindon Book Co.,** with outlets at 64 Nathan Rd. (tel. 3-662-046) and 249 Ocean Terminal (tel. 3-673-242), both in Kowloon. In Central, try **Bloomsbury Books Ltd.** at 20 On Lan St. (tel. 5-265-387), or **Kelly & Walsh Ltd.,** at 10C Ice House St. (tel. 5-225-743). For travel books, you won't do better than **Wanderlust Books,** 30 Hollywood Rd., Central (tel. 5-232-042).

BUSINESS HOURS: Most business offices operate six days a week and are open from 9 a.m. to 5 p.m. weekdays (with a lunch hour from 1 to 2 p.m.) and on Saturday from 9 a.m. to 1 p.m. Many Chinese businesses are open from 9 a.m. to 4:30 p.m. weekdays and 9 a.m. to 12:30 p.m. on Saturday. Shopping hours vary with the district (see "Shopping").

CLIMATE: Hong Kong has a subtropical climate, with warm summers and damp, chilly winters, much like San Francisco. Temperatures range from 86°F to 91°F (30°C to 33°C) in the summer and average 59°F (15°C) in the winter. Typhoon season is from July to September and the heaviest rainfall months are March to May.

CLOTHING: The traveler's dress code for Hong Kong is casual, but residents are serious followers of fashion. Light, cool clothing is recommended for summer. Although you can wear shorts and T-shirts, you'll feel out of place. Sweaters and outerwear (a lined raincoat is the most versatile) are a must in the winter and early spring. "Smart casual" is usually suitable for evenings, but for fancier restaurants, jackets and ties are recommended for men and dresses for women. We suggest traveling light to allow room for the bargain fashions you can purchase in this shopping paradise.

CREDIT CARDS: Major credit cards are accepted at most shops, restaurants, and all hotels. When charging purchases, remember to add the appropriate currency symbol (HK$) in front of the amount when you sign the sales slip. American Express (tel. toll free 800/227-4669), VISA (tel. toll free 800/227-6811), and MasterCard (tel. toll free 800/223-3320, 800/424-7787 in Canada) cardholders should contact their home offices regarding use of nearly 60 cash machines affiliated with Hong Kong banks.

CRIME: Hong Kong is famous for underworld crime and Tong wars, but the average tourist sees little of it. You can safely walk in almost any area, even at night, although the Night Markets and Wanchai District bars tend to attract pickpockets. We recommend that you leave valuables, airline tickets, and your passport in the hotel safe and carry a photocopy of your passport with you.

CURRENCY: The local currency is the **Hong Kong dollar (HK$)**, which comes in almost the same denominations as the U.S. dollar. Notes begin at denominations of HK$10, there are silver coins of HK$5, HK$2, HK$1, and there are bronze coins for Hong Kong cents. Since there is no central reserve bank, two private banks, the Standard Chartered and HongKongBank, print all the currency and you'll find that notes of the same denomination will look different. The exchange rate remains fairly constant at HK$7.8 = $1 U.S.

CUSTOMS: Visitors are allowed to bring in duty free one liter bottle of wine or spirits and up to 250 cigarettes, 50 cigars, or eight ounces of tobacco. Firearms must be declared and handed into custody until departure.

DENTISTS/DOCTORS: Hong Kong has a reputation for quality medical care. Most hotels have a doctor on call or can refer you to a qualified physician or dentist. You can also confer with your consulate for advice.

DOCUMENTS FOR ENTRY: Valid passports are required of any person entering Hong Kong. U.S. citizens plus citizens of 25 other countries, including certain Western European and South American countries, are permitted one-month visits without a visa. Citizens of some 25 other countries are allowed three-month stays without a visa. British citizens are allowed six-month stays without a visa. Check with the British consulate, high commission, or visa office in your home country for further information.

DRINKING WATER: Tap water is clean and safe to drink, although most locals boil their drinking water as they've done for centuries.

DRUGSTORES (CHEMISTS): Pharmaceutical supplies are readily available in the drug department of supermarkets, department stores, and shopping centers. Most are open only during normal business hours, but your hotel concierge can advise you of those with extended hours.

ELECTRICITY: Local voltage is 200 volts A.C., 50 cycles. Most hotel bathrooms have built-in transformers to reduce voltage to 110/120 volts.

EMBASSIES: The **United States Embassy and Consulate** is at 26 Garden Rd. (tel. 5-239-011), opposite the Peak Tram station in Central; it's open weekdays only from 8:30 a.m. to noon.

    British citizens with visa questions should see the General Enquiry Section of the Government Secretariat on Lower Albert Rd. (tel. 5-810-2717), up the hill from the Hilton Hotel, Central. The **Canadian High Commission** is on the 12th floor of Tower 1, Exchange Square, Connaught Road, Central (tel. 5-810-4321); it's open weekdays from 8 a.m. to 4:30 p.m. The **Australian High Commission** is on the 23rd and 24th floors of the Harbour Centre, 25 Harbour Rd., Wanchai (tel. 5-731-881); it's open weekdays from 9 to 11:30 a.m. and 1 to 4 p.m.

EMERGENCIES: For police, fire, or ambulance emergencies, dial 999. If you are in your hotel, contact the hotel operator or concierge.

FESTIVALS AND HOLIDAYS: The Chinese love a festival, and Hong Kong's calendar is rich with them. Check with the HKTA for specific dates.

January
New Year's Day (January 1), a public holiday.
Hong Kong Arts Festival, a month-long celebration of performing arts. Early booking is recommended.

February
Chinese New Year (may also fall in January), the most important festival in the Chinese calendar. The two or three days following New Year's Day are public holidays. Although it is primarily a family festival, the main shopping areas will be festively decorated and lion dances are presented in many neighborhoods and at the major hotels. Many businesses close for two or three days during this time and made-to-order goods will be delayed.
Lantern Festival, or Yuen Siu, marking the end of Chinese New Year. It's also known as Chinese Valentine's Day, marked by lanterns all over town and celebrations at Ko Shan Park in Kowloon or at the Sung Dynasty Village.

April
Ching Ming Festival, a family festival when visits are made to ancestral family graves.

May
Birthday of Tin Hau, Queen of Heaven and Goddess of the Sea. This very colorful festival is centered on the harbor, where fishermen decorate and converge on the waterfront and at temples dedicated to Tin Hau.
Cheung Chau Bun Festival, also known as the Festival of the Bun Hills, held on Cheung Chau Island. During a seven-day period, there are religious ceremonies, processions, Chinese opera, and the erection of 70-foot towers of pink-and-white buns in the courtyard of the Pak Tai Temple. It's a wildly exotic event, but difficult to plan for, as the precise dates are announced only three weeks ahead.
Birthday of Lord Buddha. In Buddhist temples the statues of the Buddha are bathed. Special pilgrimages are made to the Po Lin Monastery on Lantau as well as to the Miu Fat Monastery in the New Territories.

June
Dragon Boat Festival, commemorating the death of a national hero, Ch'n Yuen, who drowned himself in a protest against a corrupt government. There are many spirited races between dragon boats, long narrow vessels with the head and tail of a dragon on either end. The festival's highlight are the International Races, with teams from many nations competing in the harbor.
Birthday of Her Majesty, the Queen (June 11), a public holiday.

August
Festival of Hungry Ghosts. The Chinese believe that ghosts roam the world on a particular day. To appease them, people build small fires and burn paper cut-outs of money, fruit, and other items.

September
Mid-Autumn Festival, one of the major festivals of the Chinese year, similar to the western harvest festivals, also known as the Moon Cake Festival. Shops and streets are specially decorated and moon cakes, filled with a mixture of ground lotus and sesame seeds or dates are sold with festive lanterns. Families travel to the highest spot in town, light their lanterns, and watch the moon rise before eating their cakes.

October
Festival of Asian Arts, a wide selection of traditional dances, drama, and music from Asia. Write or call the HKTA for program information.

December
Christmas Day, a public holiday, along with the first and second weekday after Christmas.

FILM AND CAMERA: Good prices and a huge variety abound in cameras. Film is cheap (as much as 40% less than U.S. prices) and readily available. Inexpensive and adequate photo processing is available as quickly as 27 minutes.

HEALTH AND VACCINATIONS: No immunizations are required for entry (except cholera vaccinations, which are required of persons who have visited infected areas within 14 days of arrival). Call the British Embassy in your country if you have questions or check with your travel agent.

HOSPITALS: Hospitals with 24-hour emergency wards include **Hong Kong Adventist Hospital** at 40 Stubbs Rd. (tel. 5-764-211) and **Queen Mary Hospital** on Pokfulam Road (tel. 5-819-9211), both on Hong Kong.
In Kowloon, there is the **Queen Elizabeth Hospital,** on Wylie Road (tel. 3-710-2111).

LANGUAGE: English and Chinese are the official languages of Hong Kong. Cantonese is the most widely spoken Chinese dialect. Most shopkeepers, cab drivers, and all hotel personnel speak some English.

METRIC MEASURES: Hong Kong uses the metric system. For a table of metric conversions, see "The ABCs of Burma" in Chapter II.
In addition, there are two **local measures** used for fish, meats, and spices: 1 catty = 1⅓ pounds (604.8 grams) = 16 taels; thus 1 tael = approx. 1 ounce.

NEWSPAPERS: Local English-language newspapers include the *South China Morning Post,* the *Asian Wall Street Journal,* the *International Herald Tribune,* and the *Hong Kong Standard.*

POSTAL SERVICE: The **General Post Office** (tel. 5-231-071) is in Central just behind the Connaught Centre, next to the Star Ferry terminal. In Kowloon, the GPO is located at 405 Nathan Rd. (tel. 3-884-111), between the Jordan and Yau Ma Tei MTR Stations. Both are open from 8 a.m. to 6 p.m. daily except Sunday and holidays. Several other branches offer efficient, courteous service, Speedpost (an express mail), and FAX facilities, at premium prices.
The only **poste restante** service is at the Central General Post Office next to the Connaught Centre. Hours are 8 a.m. to 6 p.m. daily except Sunday. As always, you must present your passport for identification to pick up mail.
Shipping is simple but expensive; air parcels take two to three weeks to reach the U.S. and seamail takes six to eight weeks. Be advised of U.S. Customs regulations requiring an export license for shipping textiles and clothing to the U.S. (call the U.S. Consulate for advice). Most stores will ship their merchandise, but duties may be levied.

RAILWAY INFORMATION: The main **railroad station** (tel. 0-606-9606) for the Kowloon-Canton Railway is located in the Hung Hom district of Kowloon. Trains leave here regularly for the New Territories as far as Sheung Shui on the Chinese border.

RELIGIOUS SERVICES: For information about the many English-language religious services, consult the HKTA's *Hong Kong Guide,* or call them at 5-722-5555, or ask the concierge at your hotel.

TELEPHONE AND TELEGRAPH: Most hotels offer direct-dial international service, but with the usual usurious surcharges. To avoid hotel charges, you can place international calls or send telegrams or Telexes at the **Cable and Wireless Company** offices. Their Kowloon office at Hermes House on Middle Road, west of Nathan Road, is open 24 hours, as is the Central office in Room 102A, Tower 1 of Exchange Square. The Wanchai office, in New Mercury House, Gloucester Road, is open daily from 8 a.m. till midnight. The Cable and Wireless office at Hong Kong International Airport is open 24 hours. At these offices you can buy Cardphones, cards of varying value that can be used at certain public phones. For information on international service, call 3-732-4336.

Public telephones cost HK$1 (12¢) for local calls. Unless you're in the district, you must dial "5" in front of numbers for Hong Kong Island, "3" in front of Kowloon numbers, and "0" in front of numbers in the New Territories. (You may see business phones numbers written with an "H" or "K" in front of them, meaning the same thing.) Note that most Hong Kong island numbers are still six digits although recently installed Kowloon and New Territories phone numbers are commonly seven digits. For **directory assistance,** call 108.

The **country code** for Hong Kong is 852.

TIME: Hong Kong time is Greenwich Mean Time plus eight hours all year round making it 13 hours ahead of New York and 16 hours ahead of Los Angeles. American visitors should add one hour if Daylight Savings Time is in effect.

TIPPING: Tipping is customary in Hong Kong. Most restaurants add a 10% service charge, and if the service is good, an additional 5% should be added. In traditional Chinese restaurants the bill may not include the service charge, so a tip would be in order. In coffeeshops, local custom says to leave the loose change. Most hotels include a 10% service charge, but porters, bellmen, and hallmen expect tips (particularly appreciated in U.S. dollars) for service beyond the ordinary. Taxi drivers expect a tip in the range of HK$3 (35¢) to HK$5 (60¢) or, rounding off the meter to the nearest HK$5; airport porters, HK$3 (35¢) to HK$5 (60¢) per bag; hotel staff, HK$5 (60¢) to HK$10 ($1.20 or a U.S. $1 bill) per bag.

TOURIST INFORMATION: The **Hong Kong Tourist Association (HKTA)** has one of the best tourist information services in the world. They distribute wonderful and indispensable guides from their HKTA Information Centres, offices marked by the red junk symbol. Their **tourist hotline** (tel. 3-722-5555) provides a ready answer to any question from 8 a.m. to 6 p.m. weekdays and public holidays, 8 a.m. to 1 p.m. on Saturday and Sunday.

The **main office** of the HKTA is located on the 35th floor of Connaught Centre, Connaught Road (tel. 5-244-191), next to the Star Ferry Terminal in Central. It's open from 8 a.m. to 6 p.m. weekdays, until 1 p.m. on Saturday. The Information Centre at the Star Ferry Concourse **in Kowloon** is open the same hours, and also open from 8 a.m. to 1 p.m. on Sunday. The Information Centre at no. G8, Empire Center, 68 Mody Rd. **in Tsimshatsui East** (next to the Holiday Inn Harbour View), is open from 9 a.m. to 6 p.m. daily. The Information Centre **at Hong Kong International Airport,** open daily from 8 a.m. to 10:30 p.m., should be the first stop for any arriving tourist. Pick up a map, the "Official Hong Kong Guide" and the "Official Guide to Shopping and Eating Out" and you'll be in good shape for exploring.

Overseas Offices

Overseas, the HKTA has offices at 548 Fifth Ave., New York, NY 10036 (tel. 212/869-5008); at 421 Powell St., Suite 200, San Francisco, CA 94102 (tel. 415/781-4582); at 125 Pall Mall, London, SW1Y 5EA (tel. 01-930-4775); and on the 20th floor, National Australia Bank House, 255 George St., Sydney, NSW 2000, Australia (tel. 251-2885).

4. ACCOMMODATIONS

One aspect of Hong Kong's allure as a vacationland is superb hotels at more affordable rates than in the West. And as with many things in this city of contrasts, Hong Kong's hotels run the range from world-class luxury at $300 a night to windowless cubicles at $8. Most fall into an area in between that's good value although more costly than comparable accommodations in other Southeast Asian capitals. Even though the tourist high season is only October to late December, businesspeople keep hotel rooms full almost year round, so when it comes to rooms, bargaining can be tough!

We recommend making a reservation two to four weeks in advance of arrival, through a travel agent or by writing to the hotels directly and enclosing an International Money Order deposit equal to one night's stay. If you arrive without reservations, contact the Hong Kong Hotels Association desk at the airport (just after passing through Customs) for their assistance.

Of the 30,000 rooms in 70 hotels that will checker the region by 1990, the majority are "first class" to woo the business traveler and well-heeled tourist. Rooms are generally spacious, well appointed, and newly remodeled or recently constructed. Personalized service, a tradition of the Chinese imperial courts, is the pride of the best hotels, where every whim is catered to. Instead of booking the most expensive room in an undistinguished hotel, treat yourself to the lowest-price room in the best hotel you can afford and savor the imperial luxury that only Hong Kong offers.

Now a word about location. The majority of recommended hotels are on the more recently developed Kowloon side. The newest shopping malls, electronics and appliance stores cluster along Kowloon's waterfront and up the main artery, Nathan Road. Most hotels are an easy walk from shops and within walking distance of the Star Ferry to Hong Kong island's Central district for shopping or sightseeing. Hong Kong island is more diverse, with some older neighborhoods, some public parks, and the intense excitement of a world financial center. Business people will prefer the convenience of hotels in Central, Causeway Bay, or Wanchai (all districts on Hong Kong island), where taxis to nearby offices and government buildings are inexpensive and easily found.

LUXURY CHOICES: Hong Kong's top luxury hotels are constantly trading places in the "Ten Best Hotels in the World" polls conducted by magazines. Those who prefer grand style to an effective, 24-hour business center or French delicacies from room service will each cite the plusses of one of these three over the others; all are guaranteed to delight the traveler in search of Oriental splendor. Room rates range from HK$1,680 ($215) to HK$2,460 ($315), usually for one or two occupants to a room, plus 15% government tax and service charges.

For us, the most luxurious of the luxury hotels is the **Peninsula,** Salisbury Road, Kowloon (tel. 3-666-251), whose classic colonial façade graces the busy street within sight of the Star Ferry. The Peninsula opened in 1928 and quickly became the focus of the colony's British society. The grand lobby, its soaring Ionic columns crowned with ornate gilded plasterwork, was *the* place to meet. The British would take their place to the right of the grand staircase (toward the East Wing) and everyone else would be seated to the left (West Wing) at teatime, an unofficial tradition that lasted until the 1950s. Today the lobby has emerged from several renovations as majestic as ever, still the rendezvous for travelers the world over. And up the grand staircase are five floors of sumptuous accommodations, each attended by designated "room boys" (several old enough to be our grandfathers!) who will draw a bath, or lay out clothes, or deliver a pot of tea at a moment's notice.

The 190 recently renovated rooms are grand anew: all peach and jade chintz and English country finery. They're spacious enough to accommodate a work desk and a plush seating area with ease; the rich marble-tiled bathroom has twin sinks and a separate shower stall. Superior and deluxe suites occupy the harbor-facing wings of the hotel and are larger and even more opulently decorated. The Peninsula has kept one pace ahead of its peers by adding amenities considered de rigueur in this hotly competitive market—brass-trimmed digital alarm clocks, remote-control color TV, bathroom telephone, hair dryer tucked in a burlwood makeup table, computerized message delivery, light and air controls in the teak headboards, toiletries, personalized stationery—all are as charming as the hotel itself. The video laser disc players in the suites are housed in antiques, imported toiletries are enhanced by designer soaps, fragrant flower arrangements and fruit platters abound.

Of course the Peninsula excels beyond its rooms. There is Gaddi's, the famed continental dining room, and Cantonese, Japanese, and Swiss restaurants, a comfortable lounge and coffeeshop, an arcade filled with the most exclusive designer shops, business services provided by the concierge, and access to nearby sports facilities. The Peninsula Group is planning to enlarge its flagship by adding two 17-story towers (built in a similar style), which will include guest rooms, a swimming pool, health and business centers, and more shops. We've been assured by the management that they've planned this tremendous expansion with an eye to maintaining the attentive service and unique old-world charm that is the Peninsula's primary asset.

Until the renovation is complete, indulge yourself in a very grand hotel: rooms rent for HK$2,020 ($259) to HK$2,400 ($308), depending on floor and view; superior suites are HK$2,900 ($372) and deluxe suites range from HK$4,030 ($517) to HK$9,450 ($1,212) per day.

You certainly can't argue with critics who proclaim the **Regent,** at the corner of Salisbury and Nathan Roads, Kowloon (tel. 3-721-1211), one of the world's best hotels. With its unique waterfront location, the modern, black-glass Regent offers some of the world's best views of famous Hong Kong harbor. An elegant, polished marble lobby leads into a waterside coffeeshop with that unstoppable view, or left up a sweeping staircase of white Travertine marble that stunned residents when it was first installed.

Rooms are more subtle, luxurious, and tasteful, with golden earth tones used in silk-covered walls, contemporary furnishings, and marble bathrooms. Fine service begins with tea brought to arriving guests by an assistant manager and continues with the attentions of your floor waiter. A large pool and health club are on the premises as well as the super-luxe Lai Ching Heen Chinese restaurant, a continental restaurant, and steakhouse. Harbor-view rooms range from HK$2,120 ($272) to HK$2,460 ($315); plaza-view rooms start at HK$1,450 ($186). The Regent's corner suite with a terrace overlooking the Hong Kong harbor may just be the best room in town, but if you have to ask the price. . . .

The **Mandarin Oriental Hotel,** 5 Connaught Rd., Central (tel. 5-220-111), is Hong Kong's premier business district hotel. Newly renovated from its pink-and gray-marble lobby to its 547 jade and burnt-umber guest rooms, it is a luxurious blend of East and West regularly touted as one of the world's best hotels. Antique Peking lacquered chests used as night tables add a Chinese accent to the plush, modern rooms. Each has full marble baths, picture windows with city views and personalized valet service. The staff, trained in service customary to the Mandarin court, is prompt and efficient.

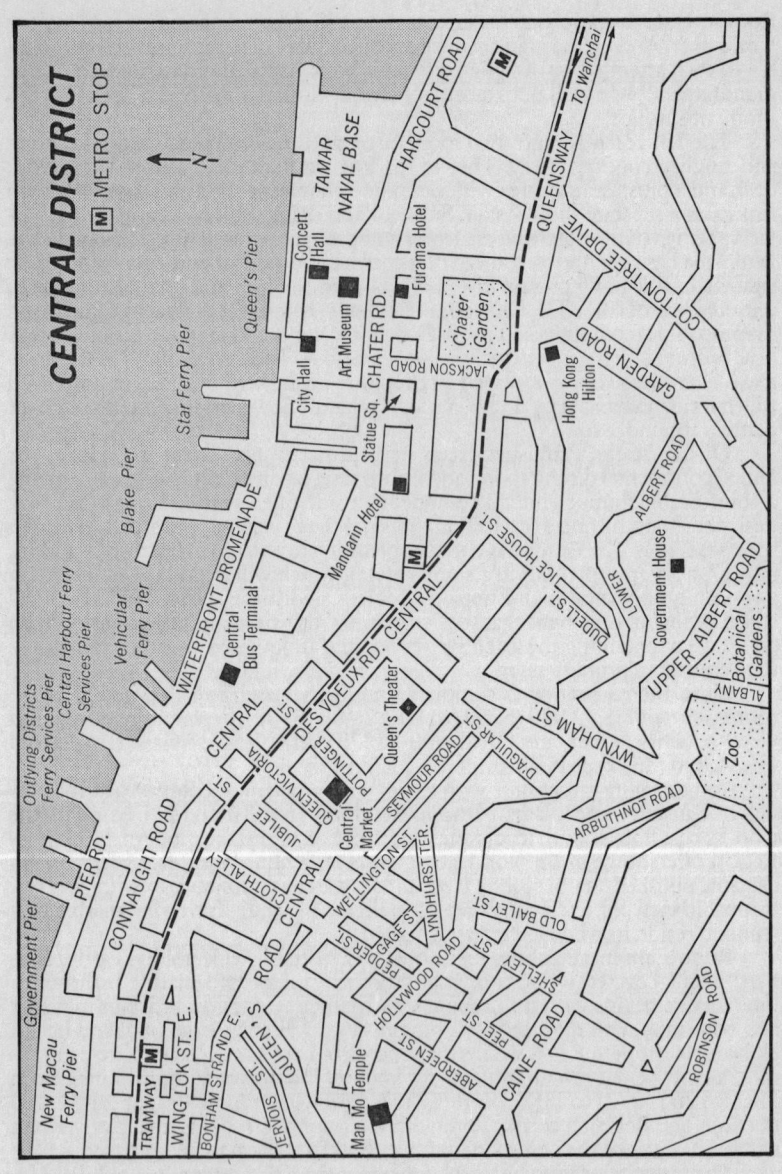

CENTRAL DISTRICT

M METRO STOP

The Mandarin Oriental's small health club is known for its fine facilities and neo-Greco, colonnaded swimming pool. The Man Wah Chinese restaurant is one of the island's best; guests also enjoy the gourmet Pierrot French restaurant, the Grill Room, and a popular bar featuring jazz. The tranquil mezzanine, overlooking the lobby's huge, astonishing 19th-century gold carving of a Han Dynasty birthday celebration, is a perfect spot at teatime. Room rates range from HK$1,640 ($210) to HK$2,205 ($283), depending on floor and view; fabulous suites range from HK$4,160 ($533) to HK$13,860 ($1,777).

Two other hotels offer facilities at comparable room rates and are excellent choices among top hotels. The **Hong Kong Hilton International,** 2 Queens Rd., Central (tel. 5-233-111), is at the foot of the Victoria Peak tram. The best of its newly renovated rooms overlook the harbor and pretty Chater Garden. As with the comfortably furnished public spaces, each room is tastefully decorated in muted tones and blond wood, a touch of subtlety in a sometimes garish world. All of the Hilton hotels in Asia have a reputation for excellent management and service; at the Hong Kong Hilton, 1,200 employees serve 789 rooms. Among the hotel's eight restaurants, the Eagle's Nest Chinese restaurant is considered one of the finest. The efficient business center, five executive floors with extra amenities and private lounges, and convenient central location make the Hilton particularly well suited to the business traveler. Rooms with a harbor view run HK$1,880 ($241) for a single occupant, HK$2,016 ($259) for two. Accommodations with less desirable city views cost about HK$330 ($42.25) less.

The **Shangri-La,** 64 Mody Rd., Tsimshatsui East (tel. 3-721-2111), is built along Kowloon's waterfront and commands one of the best views of the harbor and Hong Kong island. The lobby is so ornate that locals often come to have their portraits taken in front of its marble fountain. The staff at this large, busy hotel is attentive and friendly, and the restaurants, including the Shang Palace, the Chinese food outlet, are quite good. Perhaps the only disappointment with the Shangri-La are the guest rooms, which, since we first stayed there, have not been maintained to the high standards of the hotel's public spaces. (There is a plan to refurbish all 719 guest rooms before 1990.) Still, the vistas from the harbor-view rooms, at HK$2,460 ($315) for a double, rival those from the Regent; less desirable views rent out for about HK$550 ($70.50) less per night.

FIRST-CLASS HOTELS: First-class hotel rooms, those renting for HK$960 ($123) to HK$1,500 ($192.25) per night for two, plus 15% government tax and service charges, compete most actively for the business market and can often be a good buy for the traveler with a savvy travel agent. Price wars, incentive specials, and seasonal discounts (April, May, October, and November are the busiest months) can alter the prices listed below by about 20%; check with your travel agent or the nearest branch of the Hong Kong Tourist Association for the latest advertised specials. Typically, first-class hotels will offer 24-hour room service, a variety of in-house Oriental and Western restaurants, bars, business and health facilities, swimming pools, one-day laundry and dry-cleaning services, and amenities such as toiletries, color TV, and work desks in the guest rooms. We've divided recommended hotels into those on the Hong Kong and Kowloon sides and list them in order of preference. However, please note that when the competition gets tough for first-class hotels, the tough start renovating, and you may be pleasantly surprised by a "newer" hotel on arrival.

On Hong Kong Island

The new and stunning **Hotel Victoria,** 200 Connaught Rd. in Central (tel. 5-407-228), is atop the Shun Tak Centre, next to the Macau Ferry terminal and about a ten-minute walk west of the Star Ferry. The twin blue towers with a distinctive red stripe form one of the few hotels on the Hong Kong side situated directly on the waterfront. The rooms are totally contemporary and tasteful, with a seating area oriented toward the ever-changing harbor view, granite and marble bathrooms, and full amenities. The public spaces are equally elegant, with several restaurants, a fourth-floor pool, and a business center tucked in among the shops and facilities of the Shun Tak Centre. Room rates range from HK$1,080 ($138.50) for an impressive standard room with city views to HK$1,440 ($184.50) for a larger deluxe room with harbor view. A one-bedroom suite, ideal for those conducting meetings, runs HK$2,160 ($277). The executive-style Dynasty Club floors with private lounges, complimentary breakfast, tea, and cocktails are good value here at an additional HK$180 ($23) per night for two.

The **Excelsior Hotel** is well situated at the east end of Gloucester Road in Causeway Bay (tel. 5-767-365), and most rooms offer views over the bay and nearby Victoria Park. It's a large hotel (951 rooms), but the stylish grace of newly renovated halls and rooms makes it seem more personal, as befitting a member of the Mandarin Oriental Hotels chain. Modern rooms with built-in sofas and marble baths range from HK$960 ($123) for a lower-floor standard room to HK$1,500 ($192.25) for a harbor-view deluxe room. The Excelsior also boasts several fine restaurants, a disco, and the English-style Dickens pub. The surrounding Causeway Bay district, full of good restaurants and nightlife, is much livelier than other business areas.

The 570-room **Furama Intercontinental,** 1 Connaught Rd., Central (tel. 5-255-111), towers above the waterfront, distinguished by a saucer-like cap housing the famed La Ronda revolving restaurant. The lobby, one of Hong Kong's more lavish entryways, is sheathed top to bottom with pink and white Carrara marble. In contrast, guest quarters are on the plain and diminutive side, not quite living up to the promise of the downstairs entry. All rooms, ranging from HK$1,200 ($153.75) to HK$1,620 ($208), are fully equipped with a mini-bar and an electronic safe.

Fifteen years ago a commercial building on Hysan Avenue in Causeway Bay was converted to a fashionable, luxury lodging called the **Lee Gardens Hotel** (tel. 5-895-3311). Because of the retrofitting process, it was impossible to build a pool, but sandwiched in this giant structure are 800 compact rooms as well as restaurants, a business center, and a small shopping arcade, most of which cater to European groups. The Lee Gardens has lost a bit of its luster, there are signs of wear, and there are no grand views of the harbor, but for those who're working in the area, it is situated in a convenient location. Room rates for one or two range from HK$960 ($123) to HK$1,320 ($169.25).

On the Kowloon Side

New World Hotels International, operator of such class establishments as the Regent and Victoria, has built a top-notch facility on the Kowloon waterfront near the Star Ferry terminal. The **New World Hotel,** at 22 Salisbury Rd. in Tsimshatsui (tel. 3-694-111), is the jewel of the New World Centre, a suburban shopping mall that offers every service you could possibly need (including a hostess club). The ambience and décor parallel that at the Hotel Victoria, with its sleek, clean look, compact yet spacious rooms, and excellent service staff. In addition, the New World Hotel has a large outdoor pool. A standard double room rents for HK$1,225 ($157); for about HK$400 ($51.25) more you can have a suite with the extra amenities of a Dynasty Club floor.

Among the best values on the Kowloon side is the **Royal Garden Hotel** at 69 Mody Rd. (tel. 3-721-5215), set one block back from the harbor in Tsimshatsui East. This lavishly appointed but comfortable inn was built in 1982 by the Mandarin Oriental group, but is now independently managed. Guest rooms surround an atrium with cascading plants overflowing from each of the 15 floors. They are refined, somewhat smaller than those at more expensive hotels, but each room is outfitted with the latest amenities. The two main dining rooms, Lalique (decorated with Lalique art deco glass partitions) and the Falcon (which becomes a disco after 10 p.m.) serve good continental food. Superior rooms, single or double occupancy, run HK$1,320 ($169.25); partial harbor-view rooms cost HK$180 ($23) extra.

The lobby of the **Hyatt Regency,** centrally located at 67 Nathan Rd. in Tsimshatsui (tel. 3-311-1234), is beautifully detailed in Chinese deco inspired by the Shanghai hotels of the 1930s. Halls and restaurants carry the theme throughout in grand style. Rooms are well furnished in a contemporary international style though the "superior" rooms, at HK$1,236 ($158.50), are small; deluxe rooms, at HK$1,356 ($173.75), are more spacious. All rooms suffer from the convenience of the location, offering only views of neighboring buildings and the bustling Nathan Road shops.

Directly across the street from the Peninsula Hotel is the **Sheraton Hong Kong Hotel and Towers,** at 20 Nathan Rd. (tel. 3-691-111). It is encased within a giant shopping center, making shopping, quick meals, and banking easy. The Sheraton is quite luxurious; all double rooms are spacious and rates vary according to floor and view. A superior room for two costs HK$1,210 ($155). The top two floors have been christened the Sheraton Towers, a more service-oriented environment where guests enjoy a private elevator and check-in desk, complimentary continental breakfast, tea, drinks and snacks in an exclusive lounge, personalized stationery, and other perks of most business-class floors, at a premium of HK$400 ($51.25) per night.

Typical of hotels managed by this French chain, the **Hotel Regal Meridien Hong Kong,** centrally located at 71 Mody Rd. in Tsimshatsui East (tel. 3-772-1818), has five separate French restaurants on its premises, mostly to serve the European clientele who dominate the guest list. Rooms are cheerfully decorated in primary colors, with a pleasant desk and seating area, the latest in TVs, international direct-dial phones, stereo technology, and classy bathrooms. Though built as recently as 1983, the Meridien has not been as well maintained as some of its competitors. The best value here are the superior rooms facing a modest garden; singles run HK$1,368 ($175.50) and doubles are only HK$55 ($7) more.

The **Holiday Inn Harbor View Hong Kong,** 70 Mody Rd. (tel. 3-721-5161), shares with the big-ticket Regent and Shangri-La Hotels an unobstructed view of Hong Kong harbor, the absolute highlight of the hotel. Although it was entirely renovated in 1987, the Holiday Inn Harbor View's rooms and public spaces don't match the sophistication of other lodgings nearby. However, for a reasonable HK$1,740 ($223) two of you can enjoy an unsurpassed view.

The **Hong Kong Hotel,** 3 Canton Rd. (tel. 3-676-011), is one of the block towers rising above the harbor in Harbour City, near the Star Ferry terminal. The lobby is large and glitzy, and the rooms modern, comfortable, but undistinguished. The 758 rooms range from HK$780 ($100) for a tiny single to HK$1,080 ($138.50) for a standard room to HK$1,800 ($231) for a studio with harbor views. The Hong Kong Hotel also has a good pool and a variety of restaurants besides those in the surrounding shopping complex.

The **Holiday Inn Golden Mile,** at 46 Nathan Rd. (tel. 3-693-111), is nearby in a stretch known as the "Golden Mile." Kowloon's Nathan Road is a main artery where shops, hotels, and services crowd each other vying for attention. This Holiday Inn bears a passing resemblance to its American cousin, but it's a notch or two higher on the comfort/design/facilities level. There's a rooftop pool, several good eateries on or about the premises (including a deli), and a general feeling of all-American well-being. A double here can be had for HK$1,150 ($147.50); the superior rooms are the best value. The shopping arcade downstairs is old and of little interest save for its laundry, which will do shirts for half the price of hotels nearby.

THE MODERATE RANGE: There are a number of moderately priced hotels in the Tsimshatsui district of Kowloon. Built mainly for tourists and groups, they line the main shopping streets or nestle between malls and feature pleasant rooms, simple business facilities, and the occasional health center. The emphasis is on convenience rather than service and on cleanliness rather than luxury, but many are an excellent value with double rooms renting for HK$684 ($87.75) to HK$1,080 ($138.50), plus 15% government tax and service charges. These hotels are often block-booked in advance by tours (which extend the high season from May to December), so make your reservations at least four to eight weeks prior to arrival.

The new **Kowloon Hotel,** 19-21 Nathan Rd. (tel. 3-698-698), a member of the Peninsula group, is a mirrored-glass tower rising behind the Peninsula Hotel. It's a model of sleek efficiency, with 758 small rooms that vary only in the number of beds each contains. The rooms are comfortable, tasteful, and an exceptionally good value at HK$684 ($87.75); high-floor rooms with harbor views cost only HK$132 ($17) more. The Kowloon caters to many independent business travelers, and offers TV reception including broadcast channels, selected films, international stock quotations, a running account of your room bill, and other customized information. Restaurants on the second level include an extremely popular pizzeria.

The **Prince Hotel** is on Canton Road in Harbour City (tel. 3-723-7788), a complex of three shopping malls that makes this hotel very popular with visitors. Deluxe touches such as the beige marble lobby, welcome fruit basket, homey peach-and-cream upholstery, and complimentary toiletries bring Hong Kong's glitter to all 400 rooms. There are two bars, packed at day's end with travelers telling tales and displaying merchandise, a coffeeshop, and the fancier Rib Room grill. Another hotel under the same management with similar features is the **Marco Polo Hotel** (tel. 3-721-7049), about 100 yards away on Canton Road in the southern part of the Harbour City complex. Almost identical, modern rooms have sand and sky-blue tones, Breuer cane chairs, and all amenities. The Marco Polo's Brasserie is a popular cappuccino or snack stop and there is a restaurant, lobby bar, small business center, and hair salon. Rooms at both hotels cost HK$900 ($115.50) to HK$1,140 ($146.25), depending on floor and park/street views; double-bedded rooms are the best value because of the economy of space. Children under 12 can stay with their parents for no extra charge.

The **Grand Hotel,** 14 Carnarvon Rd. (tel. 3-669-331), is a 15-minute walk from the Star Ferry, but it's in central Tsimshatsui engulfed by restaurants, clubs, and shops. A contemporary bleached-wood and pastel color scheme creates a cool, soothing ambience. Rooms are small but compactly designed and spotless, with mini-bar and other amenities. The standard rooms, at HK$696 ($89.25), face the courtyard but the windows are imaginatively screened in rice paper; larger superior rooms, at HK$984 ($126.25), overlooking the street, are brighter but not as good value. The Grand's coffeeshop and Viking buffet restaurant are usually crowded with group tours.

The **Empress Hotel,** 17-19 Chatham Rd. (tel. 3-660-211), is a small hotel in a great location in the busiest part of Tsimshatsui. The already-renovated floor offers very tasteful, modern rooms while older rooms and unrenovated floors remain worn and shabby. However, once renovated, the entire hotel will represent good value. Standard rooms with no view rent for HK$720 ($92.25); larger superior and deluxe doubles have partial harbor views and rent for HK$960 ($123) to HK$1,080 ($138.50).

BUDGET HOTELS: In years past Hong Kong's budget lodgings used to crowd the Suzie Wong streets of the Wanchai district or cluster behind the office buildings of Causeway Bay. Newer choices have sprung up in Kowloon, north into the New Territories, and in the newly developing Western district, due west of the Central business district. The accommodations are usually smaller, with simple décor, air conditioning, TV, phone, and on-premises dining facilities, laundry service, and a mixed business/tourist clientele. Most of these hotels are less convenient: not within walking distance of where you want to be, but certainly easily accessible via the MTR or public bus. Double-room rates range from HK$384 ($49.25) to HK$744 ($95.50), plus 15% government tax and service charges.

The **Harbor View International House,** 4 Harbour Rd. (tel. 5-201-111), next to the prestigious Hong Kong Arts Centre, is the best value-for-money hotel in the Wanchai district. A YMCA-owned and -operated hotel, it is private, airy, and not at all like a youth hostel. Bright, spotless, modern rooms overlooking the harbor have European-style half-baths with shower in tidy attached bathrooms. We found the Harbor View's double rooms at HK$564 ($72.25) a better deal than the deluxe doubles at HK$672 ($86.25), the only difference being a little closet space. There are Cantonese and continental restaurants on hand, both good quality and moderately priced.

The **Ramada Inn,** 61 Lockhart Rd. (tel. 5-861-1000), is located in the heart of Wanchai. The Ramada caters primarily to a business clientele with elaborate and complete business facilities, including 24-hour stock market quotations on TV. The rooms are clean and comfortable, with that pre-fab, spill-proof feel familiar to cross-country American travelers. The staff is first-rate, efficient, and friendly. Two doors down is a spa, and nearby, the many restaurants, clubs, and neon of the district. A double at the Ramada costs HK$744 ($95.50).

The brand-new **Guangdong Hotel,** 18 Prat Ave. (tel. 3-739-3311), towers above the crowded lanes of central Tsimshatsui off Chatham Road South. It's a glitzy entrant in the sweepstakes to provide high-quality, inexpensive accommodation for the flood of business travelers now trading with China. The huge, deep-tan marble lobby, classic Chinese décor, and watercolors in each of the compact rooms give the Guangdong a luxe feel. There are Cantonese, Japanese, and Western restaurants and a business center specializing in Chinese periodicals and trade information. Small rooms with spacious bathrooms, full amenities, and a double bed start at HK$540 ($69.25); larger ones with personal toiletries and better city views range up to HK$816 ($104.50).

One of the better budget choices in the Yau Ma Tei district just north of Tsimshatsui is the **Bangkok Royal Hotel,** 2-12 Pilkem St. (tel. 3-679-181). This recently refurbished inn is one block off Nathan Road, making it more tranquil than some of its splashier-looking neighbors. The staff is friendly; they keep a clean lobby and tidy guest rooms (particularly the tiled '50s-style bathrooms). Doubles range from HK$384 ($49.25) to HK$552 ($70.75); single rooms cost HK$65 ($8.25) less.

The **Caravelle Hotel,** at 84 Morrisson Hill Rd. (tel. 5-754-455), is a worn, out-of-the-way, budget lodging that is a five-minute walk from the legendary Happy Valley Racetrack on Hong Kong island. It's too bad that an enormous highway ramp divides the hotel from its famous neighbor! Though the Caravelle's rooms are undistinguished, they are clean and have the usual amenities, including a mini-bar and television. Single occupants will pay HK$456 ($58.50); two will pay HK$504 ($64.50).

Our last selection is isolated on the fringe of the rice district in Western, removed from the action but on the main Connaught Road trolley line from Central. The **China Merchants Hotel,** 160 Connaught Rd. West (tel. 5-596-888), boasts new facilities including a health club with landscaped terrace and three California-style outdoor hot tubs! The rooms are small and comfortable, and many have a view of this working-class end of the busy harbor. All this in a clean, well-attended hotel rents for HK$560 ($71.75) for two in an average room, though prices climb higher with the story.

HOSTELS AND DORMITORIES: As might be expected in a country where

hotels are synonymous with luxury and service, the least expensive lodgings are the youth hostels, traveler's halts, and surplus dormitory space rented by religious and educational institutions on a transient basis. Our suggestions, culled from the inns licensed by the HKTA, are located in Kowloon near the Tsimshatsui and Yau Ma Tei stops on the MTR subway system. As in any international hostel, make sure to safeguard your valuables and travel documents, and to keep cameras, radios, etc., with you when not in your room.

Prices in private double rooms with attached baths average HK$380 ($48.75), but are as low as HK$110 ($14), and dorm beds with shared facilities are available from as little as HK$30 ($3.75)—all rates plus 5% to 15% tax and service charges. These hostels are fully booked almost year round, so reserving two months before arrival (by sending a money order deposit equal to one night's stay) is recommended. However, serendipitous travelers should always call first to check on last-minute cancellations.

Our first choice is the venerable **Salisbury YMCA,** 41 Salisbury Rd., Kowloon (tel. 3-692-211), long Hong Kong's best buy because of its location next door to the luxury Peninsula Hotel. A modern 13-story wing of large, comfortable, twin-bedded rooms, with air conditioning, phone, TV, and private bathroom, now competes with the nearby tourist hotels with rates of HK$432 ($55.50) for two. The colonial-era older wing has some worn but spotless doubles with high ceilings, a sink, and shared bath; some have partial harbor views and all have access to a sundeck. These rent for HK$234 ($30) for two occupants, HK$192 ($24.50) for singles; shared dorm rooms are HK$76 ($9.75) per bed. The Salisbury Y has a new air-conditioned restaurant as well as the classic streetside cafeteria where hostelers have met for decades. The pool and gym are available to hostel guests on a limited basis. What a bargain this place is!

The **YMCA International House,** 23 Waterloo Rd. (tel. 3-771-911), is another excellent value hostel one block from Nathan Road and the Yau Ma Tei MTR stop. It's not quite as convenient as the Salisbury Y and doesn't have a pool, but its gracious lobby and new wing meet international tourist hotel standards. Fully carpeted, large rooms with air conditioning, phone, TV, and private bathrooms are HK$396 ($50.75) for two, HK$384 ($49.25) for one. The newer rooms are a better deal than those at the same price in the older wing, which are worn, though with the same features.

Nearby is the **Salvation Army's Booth Lodge,** 11 Wing Sing Lane, Yau Ma Tei (tel. 3-319-266), just a block from Nathan and Waterloo Roads. The spotless, modern, functional reception and breakfast lounge is on the seventh floor of this white high-rise. Some of the 33 rooms, all air-conditioned with phone, minibar, TV, and private shower, have city views. They're worn but well kept and the friendly atmosphere warrants the HK$360 ($46.25) to HK$396 ($50.75) tariff.

The older **YWCA Guest House,** 5 Man Fuk Rd. (tel. 3-713-9211), is a short walk beyond the YMCA International House, on Waterloo Road Hill. This worn, aging hostel is another friendly, coed place where twin rooms with attached shower cost HK$383 ($49); double rooms with TV and attached bath are HK$409 ($52.50). The classic, long-favored YWCA institution on Hong Kong island closed recently for renovation and will return as an international-standard hostel by 1994.

After trying the Salisbury YMCA (the most convenient of hostels) and the Kowloon and International YMCAs (the best low-budget facilities), travelers should check out **Chungking Mansion,** 40 Nathan Rd., a 16-story housing block next to the Holiday Inn Golden Mile. Chungking Mansion has a street-level shopping arcade and five buildings (Blocks A to E) filled with small businesses and hotels. They have very spartan, tiny rooms in "hostels" of questionable security, which are often spread out with a few rooms on several floors. Often windowless cubicles with light wooden walls, hard, narrow beds, and adequately maintained common toilet and shower are basically places for overnight stays, and are only good value because of the excellent location. Women traveling alone should inspect their intended lodgings carefully before committing themselves.

Although Chungking Mansion is seedy-looking in the common guest areas, some of these hostels are well kept by proud Chinese owners trying to attract a more clean-cut clientele. The **Chung King** (tel. 3-665-362), on the fourth and fifth floor of A Block, is one of the few HKTA-licensed operators and has 82 small, neat rooms with attached cubicle showers ranging from HK$168 ($21.50) for one to HK$216 ($27.75) for two. At the **Double Seven Guest-house** (tel. 3-723-0148), on the seventh floor of A Block, there are several compact rooms with ceiling fans managed by Frank and Katherine Koo. These rent for HK$101 ($13) for one, HK$156 ($20) to HK$180 ($23) for two, depending on tiny-ness and access to a window. **Tom's Guesthouse** (tel. 3-722-4956), on the eighth floor of A Block, is another clean and friendly place with eight rooms, some tiny with private step-up toilet and shower, and some with common facilities across the hall. Rates start at HK$110 ($14) for two. The **Traveller's Hostel** (tel. 3-687-710), on the 16th floor of A Block, was one of the first traveler's halts and the meeting place for the $500-Around-the-World crowd. It still rents dorm beds at HK$30 ($3.75), but it's poorly maintained and the guest list seems to be dominated by sailors. However, its affiliate Time Travel, next door, is still a good place to shop for discount air fares and China visas, and its bulletin board has some good low-budget traveler's tips.

One last choice that's kept clean and tidy by a friendly staff is much less convenient. The **STB Hostel,** is on the first floor at Great Eastern Mansion, 255-261 Reclamation St., Yau Ma Tei (tel. 3-710-9199), a three-block walk from the Yau Ma Tei MTR stop. It's a commercial but colorful building in a neighborhood with auto-parts stores and commercial storefronts reminiscent of an older Hong Kong. Simple, small double rooms with attached toilet and shower rent for HK$264 ($33.75); six-bedded dorm rooms with shared facilities cost HK$51 ($6.50) per bed.

5. DINING

For the untold number of visitors who come only to eat, food is Hong Kong's greatest attraction. Residents thrive on the preparation, contemplation, and consumption of Cantonese and other regional Chinese cuisines. Here the adage "you don't live to eat, you eat to live" has been reversed. The fierce energy that goes into playing the stock market or peddling sportswear creates voracious appetites and lots of spending money. Hong Kong's population of five million supports more than 30,000 licensed restaurants! In ambience they range from imperial elegance to streetside *dai pai dongs* (street stalls); the only imperative is dining well.

It's difficult to escape the contagious enthusiasm for food; we dreamt of succulent dim sum (delightful dumplings served for breakfast or snacks) for weeks before our last visit. Fortunately for the health- or diet-conscious visitor, Chinese foods are prepared according to the Taoist belief in harmony and balance. The freshest vegetables, seafood, and soy-bean dishes, many vegetarian specialties, little beef, steaming and stir-frying techniques, and fresh fruit desserts combine to make a healthy, nutritious diet for even the most weight-conscious traveler.

Local gourmands, worldly business travelers, and droves of tourists have also assured the success of myriad foreign cuisines. Excellent European, continental, French, American, Japanese, Southeast Asian, and Indian restaurants abound. Often found in the best hotels or on the top floors of deluxe office towers, foreign eateries range from the Pizza Hut Formica to the crystal and chandeliers of Gaddi's at the Peninsula Hotel.

Though not cheap, Hong Kong's best Chinese or foreign cuisine can be had for much less than comparable meals in major European cities, and budget-watchers have dozens of fast-food outlets and street vendors to feast from. This section recommends some of Hong Kong's best (always disputable) restaurants, divided by regional cuisine, with emphasis on their specialties. In each category we've tried to include restaurants on both the Hong Kong and Kowloon sides, but all are worth the Star Ferry crossing and cab fare to get to.

Unless noted, restaurants are open seven days for lunch (about 11:30 a.m. to 3 p.m.) and dinner (about 6 p.m. to midnight), although schedules and menus change around the Chinese New Year (January/February). Attire and ambience are generally casual and reservations are strongly recommended at lunch or dinner. All the hotel restaurants and most larger, independent establishments accept major credit cards.

CULINARY HIGHLIGHTS: Some would say it takes chutzpah to even title a section "Culinary Highlights," but we've selected some Hong Kong dining events that promise a night to remember.

Resident and visiting gourmands agree that the best Chinese food in a deluxe atmosphere (usually a contradiction) is found at **Lai Ching Heen,** in the slick, modern Regent Hotel, Kowloon (tel. 3-721-1211). In keeping with the Regent style, Lai Ching Heen's décor combines subdued elegance and stunning harbor views, a favorite with the elite local and well-dressed foreign crowd. Small, rich details adorn the tables: ivory chopsticks resting on carved blocks of jade, polished gold cutlery with ornate jade handles, the finest imported crystal. From an intriguing menu of delicacies such as snake and mud carp, we sampled a crackling suckling pig, steamed scallops served on water chestnuts with lemon grass, crisp roast duckling, and a flavored rice steamed in lotus leaf. Each delicate portion was presented on beautiful porcelain, accompanied by velvety smooth Po Li tea. Lai Ching Heen is an ideal place to entertain or splurge for yourself. The set six- and seven-course banquets start at HK$385 ($49.50); à la carte, count on HK$550 ($70.50) per person.

One of Hong Kong's finest Western restaurants is **Gaddi's** located in the grand Peninsula Hotel, Tsimshatsui (tel. 3-666-251). Gaddi's elegant setting includes a rare 17th-century coromandel screen that contrasts with the colonial grandeur of cream paneled walls and high corniced ceilings. The lofty space is a backdrop for smartly attired businesspeople, bejeweled Oriental beauties, and young couples in romantic finery dancing to a popular trio. It's hard to imagine that Gaddi's, the territory's swan song to the colonial era, will remain the same after 1997!

French and continental cuisine is served by a small army of waiters. The tantalizing array of favorites, demanded by a century of repeat customers, includes wild duck with polenta and beetroot, medallions of garoupa with carrots and fennel, and Welsh lamb noisettes in red capsicum sauce. The prix-fixe lunch is a bargain at HK$165 ($21.25); à la carte dining will run upward of HK$675 ($86.50) per couple.

If there's a dining experience that should not be missed, it's feasting on seafood within sight of Hong Kong's spectacularly picturesque harbor. Visitors can choose between a small fishing village where fresh catch is custom-cooked and dining afloat on a chartered sampan, depending on the season.

Lei Yue Mun, on the slimmest part of the Kowloon peninsula, is a collection of fishing villages that boast several fine restaurants. **Hoi Tin** (tel. 3-481-482) is typical, and just a soothing, five-minute sampan glide for HK$6(75¢) from Sam Ka Tsuen pier. A narrow, unnamed path leads to Hoi Tin's indoor fishfest, dozens of tanks filled with hundreds of fish. It's an aquarium you can eat from, by picking out and purchasing your catch, then presenting it to your waiter with instructions on preparation and a choice of rice and vegetables. Hoi Tin has two large indoor dining rooms flanking the small, crowded outdoor patio. Though the outdoor area is noisy (directly in the airport flight path) and unadorned, it does afford a gorgeous view across the water to Hong Kong island. And the meal is great, the greens and rice are delicious, and the fish is . . . just as you like it. Dinner for five runs about HK$250 ($32) plus HK$180 ($23) for a huge amount of fish, crab, and prawn. Hoi Tin's charm is dining in a leisurely fashion (the service is excruciatingly slow when it's crowded) while watching the locals converse and party.

You can get to Lei Yue Mun by bus and MTR subway. Take the MTR from Central station to the Sai Wan Ho stop, exit on Tai On Street, and it's a 15-minute walk to the waterfront. At the Sam Ka Tsuen pier you can catch a sampan to Lei Yue Mun. From Kowloon you can catch the MTR at the Nathan Road Tsimshatsui stop to Kwung Tong, exit on the eastern side of Kwung Tong Road, and walk to the nearest bus stop for the no. 14C bus, or take a taxi for HK$12 ($1.50), to Sam Ka Tsuen pier. A taxi from the Star Ferry terminal in Kowloon will cost about HK$45 ($5.75).

You can't get any closer to the harbor than dining in it, afloat on a **sampan for hire** from the Causeway Bay Typhoon Shelter, next to the Excelsior Hotel. The typhoon shelters are just that, protected harbors to shelter small boats from the *tai fu* (literally "big wind"). In the mild months between May and September you can head down to the harbor about 7 p.m. and hire your own sampan seating up to eight for about HK$115 ($14.75) to HK$175 ($22.50) per hour. On a hot summer's night you'll find locals playing mah jong on sampans all night long. As you cruise among the dice games, pleasure craft and ferries, singsong boats bearing a full orchestra will float by and play your tune for about HK$8 ($1) per song. Beverages are provided by bar boats and surprisingly good Cantonese food by floating kitchens. Crab with ginger, steamed prawns, clams with black-bean sauce, and succulent seafood soups are typical selections; two will spend about HK$350 ($45) for a lavish supper passed over the gunwale. The starlight, the neon, and the ceaseless activity combine to make this an evening labeled "Made in Hong Kong."

CHINESE CUISINE: The Chinese culinary tradition is one of the most complex, sophisticated cuisines known to us. Even those who've graduated from a no. 3 "Sweet 'n' Sour Pork Combo Platter" to the spicy entrees of Szechuan (also spelled Sichuan) food will be amazed at the variety and creativity of the hundreds of dishes served. Sample any of the restaurants recommended below with an open mind and you'll be delighted at the different tastes that each region of China has produced.

A few suggestions should increase your dining pleasure. First, remember that the Chinese like to eat "family style," sharing each dish. An average portion will feed four (price is adjusted upward if your party is larger). For a typical meal count on ordering one dish per person plus an extra one for the table. Obviously, four to six people can sample more dishes and feast more economically than two, but don't let being two stop you.

A traditional Chinese restaurant will eschew set menus for a long listing of dishes, grouped by price and category. The Chinese believe in the curative and spiritual properties of food, and have assigned symbolic meaning to foods that are served on certain occasions or holidays. According to Taoist principles, a meal should balance the yin of dishes (coolness of light foods such as fish and vegetables) with the yang (heat of rich sauces and meats). Start with a light dish (perhaps stir-fried fish or steamed vegetables) to arouse the appetite, then choose a few varied entrees that appeal to you. Consult with the waiter for dishes (particularly seasonal specials noted on the daily menu) that will balance well with yours; it's common to continue ordering after you've begun the meal and safer than ordering too much at the outset. The HKTA produces an excellent pocket guide filled with pictures and the Chinese names of popular menu items from

Cantonese, Chiu Chow, Peking, Shanghai, Szechuan, and dim sum cooking; it's called the *Visitors Guide to Chinese Food in Hong Kong* and is available at all HKTA offices.

Chinese names for food are usually quite lyrical; it may be difficult to understand your waiter's interpretation of daily specials but the general menu will list each item's contents in English. Monosodium glutamate (the flavor enhancer known as MSG) is commonly used in its natural or chemical state, but at better restaurants the staff can eliminate it from your portion (at least, they say they can). Rice or noodles are traditionally served last as a filler, so specify if you'd like them served with the meal. A green or black tea (lift off the lid when the pot needs refilling), locally brewed San Miguel or imported Tsingdao beer, and cognac are residents' favorite beverages. Sweets and pastries are not the Chinese forte (nor are fortune cookies), but fresh fruit typically ends the meal. Don't be shy about asking for silverware, chopsticks lessons, prices on seasonal specials, fresh seafood, and the waiter's recommendations.

The Finest Cantonese Cuisine

Cantonese cuisine from the southern province of Guangdong is considered the most haute of all Chinese cuisines. It's a revelation to visitors raised on spareribs and fried rice (an overseas Chinese repertoire unheard of here). You can stumble into a brightly lit hall where some clients wolf down a $3 plate of beef noodles while others savor a $150 bowl of shark's fin soup. Freshness is the most distinctive characteristic of Cantonese cooking. Restaurants feature seasonal vegetables and tanks filled with live fish and crustaceans waiting to be ordered and cooked by quick stir-frying or steaming to retain the food's natural color, texture, and vitamins. Seafood, caught locally in the plentiful South China Sea, is the most popular, but pork, chicken, and vegetables are also essential to Cantonese cooking.

The Cantonese breakfast and snack food taken with tea is known as dim sum (literally, "to touch the heart"). Scrumptious dumplings filled with meat, poultry, or fish are steamed, fried, or baked and presented in small portions, perfect for gnoshers who want to sample a wide variety. Note that most Cantonese restaurants serve dim sum in the morning and at lunch, but we've listed separately below those that excel at this art.

The unpretentious nondécor of **Fook Lam Moon,** 459 Lockhart Rd. near Percival Road, Causeway Bay (tel. 5-891-2639), leaves many asking how this could be the finest Cantonese restaurant in Hong Kong. Yet when locals go, they have eyes only for the tanks filled with live crab, lobster, whelk, and abalone. Gourmands with an unlimited budget must sample some of their famous shark's fin (usually prepared in a rich broth) and then feast on braised superior abalone, steamed prawns, baked crab with rice noodles in hot pot, whelk, or bird's-nest delicacies ranging in price from HK$600 ($77) and up per person. Fook Lam Moon's extensive menu offers many meticulously prepared chicken, fish, and pork specialties at moderate prices, HK$90 ($11.50) and up per person. At lunch a variety of dim sum is served in a more casual setting; don't be surprised by the formal attire often seen at supper. A newer branch ("almost as good as the original," say locals) of Fook Lam Moon is at 31-35A Mody Rd., Kowloon (tel. 3-660-286).

Teak and lacquer tables and mocha marble walls make the **Eagle's Nest,** on the 25th floor of the Hilton International Hotel, 2 Queens Rd., Central (tel. 5-233-111, ext. 2501), one of the most elegant venues. Chinese couples in furs and silk, wealthy expatriates entertaining important guests, a live orchestra, and the superb harbor views compete for attention. The Eagle's Nest's expertise is its glorious preparation of Cantonese delicacies. Scallops with green vegetables are served in a woven basket of fried yam, baked lobster is spiced and then stuffed back into its shell, and the popular vagabond chicken, wrapped in lotus leaves then baked in ashes in a clay oven is an artistic presentation. Two people should count on spending HK$550 ($70.50) and up, especially if sampling the shark's-fin or bird's-nest specialties. Eagle's Nest draws a formal crowd and remains open until 1 a.m. weeknights and 2 a.m. on Friday and Saturday for dancing.

Connoisseurs also like **Man Wah,** on the 25th floor of the Mandarin Oriental Hotel, 5 Connaught Rd., Central (tel. 5-220-111, ext. 4025). The environment is stunning: rose and sapphire silk wall coverings and gold-lacquered woodcarvings vie with harbor and city views on all sides. Man Wah's daily specials are always seafood dishes prepared in classic ways. Gather up four people to sample their shark's-fin soup with crab coral (crab roe) and sautéed crystal prawns, and superior abalone and lobster entrees. For dessert, try the pudding-like double-boiled bird's nest in sweet almond cream, reputed to be good for your complexion. Four can expect to pay about HK$800 ($102.50) for an elegant repast.

If you've come to Hong Kong expecting to discover fantastically exotic Chinese delicacies, look no farther than to the pricey **Sun Tung Lok,** otherwise known as the Shark's Fin Restaurant, located at the intersection of Marsh Road and Lockhart Road, Causeway Bay (tel. 5-748-261). Yes, they offer a large variety of "superior" shark's-fin entrees, ranging from HK$75 ($9.50) for a mere taste to a full-blown HK$400 ($51.25) banquet, and several seasonally priced bird's-nest dishes. But if you really want to eat adventurously, consider the following: owl meat with vegetables, deer and turtle penis, cockerel testicles, and a wide assortment of snake dishes. All of these are priced according to local market rates, and we'd advise inquiring before ordering.

Yung Kee Restaurant, at 32-40 Wellington St. in the heart of Central (tel. 5-221-624), is another more modest favorite. The loud red-and-gilt décor, bright lighting, and perpetual motion of waiters wielding trays heaped with steaming dim sum and congee (a bland rice porridge enlivened with many condiments) hasn't changed in years. Yung Kee's real contribution to Cantonese cuisine is the crisp, whole roast goose. Start with thousand-year-old eggs (preserved duck eggs dipped in ginger and soy sauce) and then try the goose with seasonal vegetables and a noodle dish. Two can dine with a stylish "good food over ambience" crowd by night and with buzzing businessmen by day from HK$275 ($35.25). Reservations are recommended for weekends, particularly after 2 p.m. when dim sum is served.

The excellent Peninsula Hotel, at Salisbury Road, Kowloon, numbers among its several fine restaurants **Spring Moon (Kar Luen Lau)** (tel. 3-666-251), an elegant and contemporary Cantonese dining room. For those who would prefer to leave the ordering to the extremely capable staff, consider one of the two set-menu options. The more exotic of the two, served at lunch and dinner for HK$350 ($45), features moist, shredded barbecued duck served on a bed of jellyfish, shark's-fin soup, sautéed garoupa (a fleshy, tasty local fish), a decorative plate of piquant sweet-and-sour prawns, and three dessert courses including petit fours, sweet chestnut paste in a soupy concoction, and fresh fruit. A less elaborate but no less delicious lunch, featuring superb dim sum, is also highly recommended.

Dim Sum Teashops and Restaurants

Dim sum is, of course, that lunch/brunch/teatime fare of steamed, boiled, fried, and baked morsels of shrimp, beef, pork, or chicken gracefully wrapped in noodles, wonton, rice, or wheat-flour bundles. Favorites include cha siu bau (steamed or baked buns with minced-pork filling), har gau (whole shrimp steamed in a rice-flour wrapper), ngau yuk (slightly sweet, steamed beef balls), ngor mai gai (a bundle of lotus leaves tied together that contains steamed rice with Chinese sausage, spices, and beans), and chun guen (light, fried spring rolls). The dim sum tradition dates to the 10th century but is very much a part of the slick, new Hong Kong. Aficionados like to sip tea (the rich, dark Po Lei tea is preferred and drunk without milk or sugar) and read the morning paper, looking up only to peruse the passing carts stacked with bamboo baskets. Each is filled with bits of heaven, and waitresses are happy to show off their treats, leave some on your table, and mark off your price card.

The **Luk Yu Teahouse,** 24-26 Stanely St., Central (tel. 5-235-464), is the grandfather of dim sum parlors. Once a seedy, popular hangout for mainland smugglers in the Western district, all the carved-wood paneling and traders' acumen were transferred to the present location. Uniformed waiters, tablecloths, china teapots, and written dim sum menus (only in Chinese!) distinguish Luk Yu from most dim sum parlors. On any given day you'll find the same gentlemen sitting at tables they've occupied every workday for years. The dim sum is particularly fresh because it's made to order, and the selection is excellent, very varied, and changes daily. If you're not with friends who read Chinese, ask the waiter's advice or just point out passing dishes that look appealing. Luk Yu is also pleasant and low-key in the evening when fine Cantonese fare is served, but lunchtime is a classic scene. It is open from 7 a.m. to 9:30 p.m. daily; expect to pay about HK$50 ($6.50) per person for a dim sum extravaganza.

A more pedestrian but very typical, lively "coffeeshop" scene occurs between 7 and 10 a.m. daily at **King Bun,** a small, smoky den upstairs at 158 Queen's Rd., Central (tel. 5-434-256). King Bun is crowded with Central's mercantile and financial workers; it's casual and hectic. Tasty on-the-go dim sum costs about HK$8 ($1) per portion. In contrast, **Maxim's Palace** located on the first floor of the World Trade Center, next to the Excelsior Hotel, Causeway Bay (tel. 5-760-288), is a typical, but palatial dim sum venue. This den of ornate red and gold Oriental detailing is roughly the size of a football field and packed with voracious Chinese diners slurping up dumplings. Tourists can join the frenzy, surveying carts loaded with steaming dim sum, from 8 a.m. to 3 p.m. daily.

On the Kowloon side, the **Flower Lounge** (tel. 3-699-981) is a fun restaurant for dim sum or Cantonese standards. It's located on the first floor at 11 Canton Rd. next to the Harbour City shopping mall, with tables overlooking the constantly entertaining street bustle. If you choose a seat near the open kitchen, peer beyond the curtain of pressed ducks to the workings within. Although the Flower Lounge's menu doesn't offer a large dim sum selection, it's quite fresh and tasty, particularly if you come early (they open at 11 a.m.). The diced chicken with cashew nuts and sweet-and-sour prawn cutlets are Cantonese favorites; for dessert, try apple fritters. Two can eat heartily for HK$155 ($20) including a Chinese wine.

READER'S RESTAURANT SELECTION: "Every morning I walked around to the **Orchid Garden** for dim sum, it was so good. It's at 37 Hankow Rd. just off Nathan Road, TST" (Stan Mendoza, New York, N.Y.).

Casual Cantonese Dining

Hong Kong boasts hundreds of more casual, less specialized Cantonese restaurants where small menus, quick service, and low prices are ideal for those on-the-go.

There's no mistaking **Food Street,** Causeway Bay. It's a short pedestrian block off Gloucester Road (near the Excelsior Hotel) with at least ten restaurants from teriyaki to noodles joints, all casual places where reservations aren't expected and individuals can feel comfortable dining alone. **Boil and Boil Wonderful** (tel. 5-779-788) is a wildly popular eatery specializing in Chinese fare cooked in clay pots. Two can sample dumplings and soups galore for less than HK$200 ($25.50). The nearby **Riverside Restaurant** (tel. 5-779-733) serves more varied Cantonese fare in the same price range. **Phoenix Congee and Noodles** (tel. 5-777-973) lives up to its name, serving the thick rice porridge with flavorful toppings such as pork liver, duck sauce, or abalone. Congee or noodles dishes can satisfy two appetites for HK$60 ($7.75). You might try this for breakfast (they open at 7:30 a.m. daily) as the locals do. **Chiang Yip** (tel. 5-778-018) serves Taiwanese dishes like cuttlefish balls or fried eel with golden mushrooms, worth trying at only HK$135 ($17.25) for two.

West Villa offers very good food in a much more sophisticated, low-key setting. There are three convenient locations: at 1-5 On Lan St. (tel. 5-212-196) and 313-315 Des Voeux Rd. (tel. 5-437-388), both in Central, and on the ground floor of the Admiralty Center in Causeway Bay (tel. 5-298-333). West Villa is popular for its mixed seafood soup, baked crab with rice noodles served in a steaming hot pot, and the stewed beef roll with shitake mushrooms. The fashionable clientele pay HK$400 ($51.25) for a group of four.

Another low-key place with rose and cream upholstery and pristine tablecloths is **Full Moon,** 11 Barnton Court, Kowloon (tel. 3-679-131), a gracious respite from the shopping frenzy next door in Harbour City. The well-trained staff present platters of stuffed crab claws, braised pigeon with bean sauce, or sliced chicken with abalone and salted fish to tables of well-dressed shoppers. Expect to pay HK$175 ($22.50) to HK$225 ($28.75) for the refined ambience. At both West Villa and Full Moon, reservations are recommended in the evening.

Peking Cuisine

The Chinese food from the northern capital of Beijing (Peking) is usually equated with imperial cuisine, exquisitely prepared and displayed gourmet and exotic dishes favored by the royal court during the Ching Dynasty. Imperial banquets were defined to include 365 dishes, one for every day of the year, and often took several days to eat. Northern Chinese cuisine is generally hardier than the southern, with more poultry and meat dishes spiced with peppers, garlic, ginger, and leek. Instead of rice, whole-wheat noodles, steamed and baked breads and thick dumplings are eaten. Peking duck, crisp duck skin (baked according to the original 15,000-word recipe) wrapped in a thin pancake with scallion and a sweet plum sauce, is a justly famed example of this cuisine. Pairs of white Mandarin ducks bred for this specialty were said to be kidnapped and brought to the U.S. to sire today's well-known Long Island duckling. The barbecue and hot pot specialties of Mongolia are best sampled in Mongolian restaurants, which are listed separately.

One of the best restaurants for Peking food is **Spring Deer,** on the first floor at 42 Mody Rd. (tel. 3-664-012), next to the Empress Hotel in Kowloon. Its reputation for Peking duck is particularly well deserved. The waiter will slice the crispy skin (always served first) and tender bits of duck at your table, and will make the first "tacos" of pancakes, duck, scallions, cucumber, and hoisin sauce as an example. Other Peking specialties include crispy shredded beef, salted and deep-fried; onion cakes of dough filled with moist, sautéed onions; and fried prawns in chili sauce. Connoisseurs cite the chicken stuffed with shark's fin and baked in a clay pot, in the style of beggar's chicken (derived from the migrant workers who wrapped their meats and cooked them in bonfires out of sight of thieves). Spring Deer serves a crisp, greaseless fried rice and wonderful apple fritters with a honey sauce for dessert. It's a casual place that draws a lively crowd, though most come in groups and occupy the eight-person round tables, so reservations are always a must. A whole duck is too much for two and sometimes for four people to tackle, but there are other excellent duck dishes to try. Four should expect to pay about HK$420 ($53.75), including Tsingtao beer.

One of the best restaurants in Central's business district, thus more of a mob scene at lunch than at dinner, is **Peking Garden** in Alexandra House, just behind the Mandarin Hotel (tel. 5-266-456). (There is another location in Star House, in Tsimshatsui; tel. 3-698-211.) Peking Garden's clients are upscale enough to want tablecloths and a typical imperial style, with red-and-gold woodcarvings and silk-fringed lanterns. The Peking duck and a classic beggar's chicken, fragrantly spiced and enveloped in lotus leaves in a mud casing, are first-rate. Sliced mutton with leeks goes well with an order of steamed bread or long noodles with spring vegetables; four can feast for about HK$500 ($64).

The **American Restaurant** is the unlikely name of another Peking eatery at 20 Lockhart Rd., Wanchai (tel. 5-277-277). It has no visible décor, but it's favored by lawyers, civil servants, business people, and expatriates for delicious and inexpensive food. The cooks turn out pungent noodle dishes, tender duck, and spicy, fresh vegetables that come in a variety of sauces. Two can eat well for about HK$110 ($14).

Mongolian Hot Pot

The hot pot or "fire pot" tradition originated with the nomads who lived in the harsh steppes of Mongolia in northern China. Central cooking fires started in the vented animal-hide tents that some Mongolians still use, and preserved meats or vegetables were divided among the tribe. In Hong Kong this tradition has been adapted so that diners gather around a steaming cauldron to cook poultry, thinly sliced meat, fresh seafood, and vegetables fondue style at the table.

During the late 1970s Hong Kong gourmands made a culinary fad of Mongolian hot pot. One of the originals is the **Mongolian Barbecue Restaurant** at 54-58 Leighton Rd. (tel. 5-770-801), near the Leighton Center and the Lee Gardens Hotel. Don't expect anything from the ambience; it's a pretty run-down dining room, dimly lit with an industrial air. Cylindrical vents descend from the ceiling and hover over each table's hot pot burner. The system for ordering from the fire pot menu is to select an assortment of meat, fish, and vegetables, with a typical meal running about HK$165 ($21.25) for two.

Perhaps the best hot pot restaurants now are the **Seasons Barbecue** outlets in Kowloon. The most convenient of these is located at 22 Hillwood Rd. in Tsimshatsui (tel. 3-723-4609). These upscale eateries, popular with local business people, feature excellent seafood hot pot, with the favored ingredients including crab, prawns, octopus, grass fish, squid, fish balls, and clams. A meal for two averages HK$225 ($28.75). The two other venues are 21 Playing Field Rd. and 229 Sai Yee St.

Another choice in Wanchai is the **Genghis Khan Mongolian Grill and Hot Pot,** on Luard Street, just off Gloucester Road (tel. 5-861-2363). Though rarely visited by tourists, this is a terrific, if noisy place that features delicacies such as antelope, along with expected hot pot ingredients such as chicken, prawns, and beef. A mixed-grill platter (assorted barbecued meats and poultry) with soup and a beer will cost about HK$80 ($10.25). You may have to wait for a table, but the adventurous few will be well rewarded.

The Fiery Szechuan (or Sichuan) Cuisine

The cuisine of China's western Szechuan province has been heavily influenced by its nearby neighbors of Thailand, Malaysia, and India. Red chili peppers, salt, garlic, onions, and peppercorns are usually fried and used as a base for a variety of Szechuan sauces. Bean curd and bamboo shoots (Szechuan is the home of the vanishing panda, which thrives on bamboo) are commonly used to accentuate meats and poultry. Camphor-smoked duck, marinated in wine with orange peel and cinnamon, is a popular favorite. Consult with your waiter; you don't want your order so spicy that you can't tell what you're eating.

Szechuan restaurants have begun to multiply in Hong Kong the way they have in North America for the last few years, so consider our selections somewhat volatile. **Ziyang Szechuen Restaurant,** 45 Chatham Rd. South, Tsimshatsui (tel. 3-687-177), is a modern glass, brick, and chrome, currently hot spot that draws Hong Kong's yuppie elite. Well-presented food, an elegant crowd dressed to be admired, and gracious service make this fancier than your average Szechuan dive. Ziyang's beef, prawn, and fish (Szechuan seafood is a Hong Kong specialty) dishes are particularly good with any of their eggplant and bean-curd vegetable platters. Entrees are spiced per your request, but the menu includes mild choices like the rich broth with pork-filled dumplings. Diners will spend about HK$110 ($14) each, including beer.

The Causeway Bay shopping area is home to another venerable spicy food outlet, the **Red Pepper Szechuen Restaurant,** 7 Lan Fond Rd. (tel. 5-768-046), around the corner from the Lee Gardens Hotel. Although the Red Pepper is much frequented by tourists, it still delivers authentically prepared specialties such as kung pao chicken, prawns with chili sauce, and an excellent beef with orange flavor. Two can sup on the rich flavors for about HK$170 ($21.75).

Shanghai Cuisine

The cosmopolitan city of Shanghai has lent its name as the clearinghouse for the cuisines of China's eastern provinces. Cooking techniques such as stewing meats and poultry, braising and frying seasonal vegetables, and the "red cooking" technique of frying in very hot chili oil are common. As in the north, breads, noodles, and dumplings are used as often as rice. Salted fish, yellow fish (marinated in fermented wine), and hairy crabs (seasonal in October and November) are local favorites; newcomers usually order the famous beggar's chicken, originally from Hangzhou, or honey ham from Suzhou.

Lao Ching Hing, 6 Kai Chiu Rd. (tel. 5-771-554), behind the Lee Gardens Hotel, Causeway Bay, is our favorite for Shanghai cuisine. In a well-lit, comfortable wood-paneled first-floor dining room, dumplings, steamed bread, and thick, whole-wheat Shanghai noodles are served in generous portions. Shanghai delicacies such as braised yellow eels, bechdemer (sea cucumber), turtle soup, and the seasonal freshwater crab are available at Lao Ching Hing (not to be confused with the Regent Hotel's pricey Lai Ching Heen!), but their crisp rice with shrimp in tomato sauce, tasty fried onion cakes, or chicken in lotus leaf will delight even the most timid. A varied meal will run about HK$55 ($7) per person, higher if there are many seafood dishes.

One of the better eateries along Causeway Bay's frantic Hennessy Road is **Shanghai Garden,** located on the first floor of Hennessy Centre near Lee Garden Road (tel. 5-895-2200). In this slickly trimmed dining room, you can sample fine Shanghai entrees such as fried yellow fish with pine nuts, grilled beef with spring onions, or fried prawns in chili sauce. As with most restaurants in this busy shopping district, a lunchtime reservation is a wise idea. A complete meal for two averages HK$175 ($22.50).

Other Chinese Specialty Restaurants

The range of foods enjoyed by one billion Chinese is so diverse (snakes, bird's nests, jellyfish, bear paw, shark's fins, eel, garlic tops, and lotus root are some exotica) because their resourceful forefathers believed "that any living thing that turns its back to the sun" could be eaten. Imaginative chefs have taken this bounty of ingredients and created so many specialties that we don't even have space to mention them all—that's why they call Hong Kong an eating adventure.

SEAFOOD. In the "Culinary Highlights" section above, two seafood dining possibilities are mentioned—chartering a sampan and feasting off passing "kitchen boats," or negotiating with fishmongers selling fresh catches at Lei Yue Moon for a supper prepared at an open-air café. Here are three more conventional (if anything in Hong Kong could be called that) establishments.

Though the clientele ranges from staid corporate functionaries to boisterous sing-along groups, the **East Ocean Seafood Restaurant,** a classy eatery on the third floor of the modern Harbour Centre, 25 Harbour Rd., Wanchai (tel.

5-893-8887), gets a nod for its excellent shellfish. The rich seafood soup is stocked with fresh pink shellfish and delicate spices. Several prawn and crab dishes are excellent (we particularly liked the prawns with mandarin oranges); a wonderful accompaniment is the spicy, deep-fried bean curd with green pepper chunks and eggplant. Two can dive into this and relish a full-color, photo-souvenir menu for about HK$225 ($28.75), but if you double that you can splurge on superior shark's fin with crab roe—a real treat.

If you've got a car or are willing to make an excursion on the ultramodern MTR subway, we can recommend an excellent, country-style restaurant. The **Shatin Seafood Restaurant,** 14-15 Nam Hin Rd, in Kak Tin Village, Shatin, New Territories (tel. 0-691-1611), used to be in Hong Kong's countryside. (The New Territories is now comprised of futuristic housing "estates"—with their own shopping malls, schools, hospitals, and local government—that are being launched as satellite villages on the perimeters of Kowloon. The "villages" of Shatin, white mega-complexes jutting from the plains, house over 300,000.) In the restaurant, moved years ago from a cottage on the outskirts of the original Shatin village, traditional Chinese country fare such as barking deer, snake soup, and game imported from China are prepared as they were years ago. Large tanks outside the dining rooms are filled with live fish and crustaceans; once you've chosen, the fish is prepared to your liking. Steamed clams with ginger, chili crab with seasonal vegetables, whole steamed garoupa with black-bean sauce, even moist, paper-wrapped chicken and lamb with bamboo shoots are all delicious. Mr. K. Y. Tse, Shatin Seafood's owner, has assembled a surprisingly extensive wine collection over the years and is delighted to confer with guests (albeit in very limited English) on the best vintage to complement a meal. The food and wine is priced seasonally, but very reasonably, and truly unusual feasts can be had for HK$120 ($15.50) per person. The restaurant is about a half hour north of Tsimshatsui by car, or a HK$25 ($3.25) cab ride from the Kowloon Tong stop of the MTR. Ask your hotel concierge to make a reservation and call for directions before you set out.

One of Hong Kong's best-known eating adventures is a floating meal in Wong Chuk Hang, Aberdeen harbor, about 30 minutes and HK$35 ($3.75) by taxi from the Central hotels. The biggest and most ornate of the three floating restaurants is **Jumbo Floating Restaurant** (tel. 5-539-111), like its mates, built on a barge and to a scale that justifies its name. When seen from the sampan that ferries you from the mainland, Jumbo resembles the Rockefeller Center Christmas tree, a quilt of color reflected in the bay with hundreds of sampans and fishing boats bobbing around it. (Anyone who saw the mini-series "Taipan" may remember Peirce Brosnan leaping from its burning pagoda gables.) The interior is equally splashy, all red-and-gilt Chinese rococo with fringed lanterns illuminating the thousands of diners. It's no surprise that seafood is the specialty, but come for the spectacle rather than the mediocre, pricey fare that's presented with indifference by a harried staff. Jumbo is open daily from 10:30 a.m. to 11 p.m., but it's most lively at dinner, when Indian brides and Japanese businessmen create flashbulb chaos at the boat landing. Expect to pay from HK$140 ($18) each.

If Jumbo is full, try its smaller competitors, the **Sea Palace** (tel. 5-527-340) or **Tai Pak Seafood Restaurant** (tel. 5-525-953).

CHIU CHAU CUISINE. Chiu Chau cuisine, long known as the fare of dai pai dongs (street vendors), is the latest darling of local gourmands. Chiu Chau's heavy sauces, crispy chuenjew greens, vinegar-laced seafood, and full-bodied southern dishes satisfy locals the way home-style southern cooking does anywhere.

The **City Chiu Chau,** on the first floor of the East Ocean Centre, 98 Granville Rd., Tsimshatsui (tel. 3-723-6226), is one of the more attractive new venues. Each meal begins with a small cup of Iron Kwun Yom tea, which is intended as a palate cleanser but provides such a jolt of caffeine that you may want to limit your intake. When ready, sample the typical goose in soy sauce, crabmeat dishes, prawns with green onions, or lobster with tangy, mandarin orange dressing. Chiu Chau–style seafood dishes will elevate the approximately HK$100 ($12.75) per-person tariff to almost double.

VEGETARIAN CUISINE. The early followers of Buddhism created a sophisticated and varied vegetarian regimen that has contributed a number of imaginative vegetable dishes to Chinese cooking. Today Buddhist monasteries probably serve the greatest variety of vegetarian meals, and the Po Lin Monastery on Lantau (see Section 7 on the Outlying Islands) is well known for its visually stunning bean-curd creations. Although most Hong Kong restaurants serve some vegetarian entrees, the ones that are solely vegetarian tend to be small and casual eateries.

Vegi Food Kitchen, located near Victoria Park at 8 Cleveland St., Causeway Bay (tel. 5-890-6660), offers a wide range of delectable vegetarian Cantonese dishes with poetic names like Nest of Gems (diced vegetables in a deep-fried potato basket), Silver Frills (fried bean sprouts with shredded mushrooms), and Buddhist Delight (mixed sautéed vegetables). The food overall is superb but their vegetarian dim sum (offered daily from 11 a.m. to 3 p.m.) is a real treat. The **Bodhi Vegetarian Restaurant** is a sister establishment with the same menu at 386 Lockhart Rd., Wanchai (tel. 5-732-155).

OTHER ASIAN CUISINES: Hong Kong is at the crossroads of Asia both as a financial and culinary capital, with dozens of excellent showplaces for other exotic cuisines of the East.

Japanese
The recent surge in business activity has encouraged the opening of a number of new Japanese restaurants whose popularity, despite high prices, is gaining with locals.

For a very traditional meal, try **Hong Kong Kanetanaka,** on the top floor of East Point Center, 563 Hennessy Rd. next to the Sogo Department store, Causeway Bay (tel. 5-833-5617). At midday the tatami rooms fill with businessmen negotiating over teriyaki lunches at HK$160 ($20.50), while individuals prefer the sushi bar, at HK$225 ($28.75) to HK$400 ($51.25) for sushi specials. In the evening, the formality and price structure ascend rapidly.

For a fine Japanese steak, try the **Chitose Steak House,** on the 22nd floor of the East Point Centre (tel. 5-832-9068). Kobe steaks and American prime cuts are quick-fried on griddles embedded in each black lacquer table, while diners admire the city views as they eat. Prices start at about HK$320 ($41) for a complete dinner, but vary according to the weight of steaks chosen.

Benkay, in the basement of Gloucester Tower in the Landmark, Central (tel. 5-213-344), is a well-known spot for sushi and teppanyaki, popular with business people. At the teppanyaki grill tables, knife-wielding chefs skillfully stir-fry seafood, Kobe beef, and vegetable courses. Sushi specials are HK$165 ($21.25); count on HK$410 ($52.50) per person if ordering à la carte, including beer.

Vietnamese
Although Hong Kong has begun turning away "boat people," refugees from Vietnam, a small, flourishing Vietnamese community has established some excellent, authentic restaurants serving Vietnamese cuisine—a sophisticated blend of Chinese, Indian, and French traditions. The best when we dined there in '81, and still the top exponent of Vietnamese cooking is **The Golden Bull,** at no. 17, Level One of the New World Centre in Tsimshatsui (tel. 3-694-617). The Golden Bull's food is superb and varied, with 7 styles of beef, 11 seafood dishes, 6 piquant Vietnamese-style hot pots, and many noodle and side dishes. The ap-

petizer platter, designed to satisfy three, includes lightly fried beef, slim spring rolls with a tangy sauce, and delicious fish. Specials include jumbo prawns in garlic, freshwater lobsters, pigeon, oxtail with delicately scented lemongrass spice, and many seasonal vegetables with ginger and red chiles. Couples can enjoy the attentive service and a first-rate meal for about HK$350 ($45).

Indian

One of the strongest legacies of the British colonial era is the number of fine Indian restaurants.

Tandoor, at 75-77 Wyndham St., Central (tel. 5-218-363), is a newcomer to the Hong Kong scene but its soothing and elegant décor and skillful preparation of northern Indian cuisine has earned it many loyal fans. Tandoori dishes—usually meat, poultry, or fish bathed in lemon and spices and slowly baked in a tandoor clay oven—are favorites with diners who like a leaner meal or are scared off by some of the spicy curries. The spinach and rice side dishes, plus an assortment of baked and fried breads, are a wonderful accompaniment, and a mango lassi (yogurt-and-fruit drink) or kulfi (groundnut ice cream) round off the meal. Two will spend about HK$275 ($35.25) for supper.

Ashoka, down the block at 57-59 Wyndham (tel. 5-249-623), pioneered northern Indian cuisine 15 years ago and can still be counted on for excellent tandoori dishes. It has a cozier, more traditionally Indian feel with earth tones, rattan, gold screens, and lotus-blossom-shaped light fixtures. Ashoka's popular nine-dish lunch special at HK$45 ($5.75) is served southern Indian style on a silver *thali* (platter); the set dinner, at HK$50 ($6.50), includes ten different dishes.

The Cuisines of Southeast Asia

The cooking styles indigenous to the other countries explored in this guidebook are all represented in Hong Kong.

Spices, in a lovely rattan-and-batik space at 109 Repulse Bay Rd. on the ground floor of the rebuilt Repulse Bay Hotel (tel. 5-812-2711), is where the Association of South East Asian Nations (ASEAN) summits should convene; it offers an imaginative, diverse selection of favorites from every country. Diners can choose an Indian lamb vindaloo (spicy hot curry), Indonesian nasi goreng (fried rice with chicken and vegetables), Malaysian crab in chili, Thai duck curry, and many more taste treats. The daily luncheon buffet costs HK$60 ($7.75); dinner for two will average HK$190 ($24.50).

Our friends who do business in Bangkok claim that the **Chili Club,** on the first floor of 68 Lockhart Rd. in Wanchai (tel. 5-272-872), has the best, most authentic Thai food around. This small, casual, bright, and noisy eatery is in Wanchai, a district known as the Sixth Fleet haunt but certainly much tamer than Bangkok's own Patpong. The fresh fish steamed with chili and ginger, lemongrass-flavored tom yum gung soup, sautéed papaya with shrimp salad, and shredded beef with cucumber and chilis are refreshingly crisp and hot. A cold beer or tomato juice will quench the flames! Novices should ask the Chili Club's gracious staff to prepare their dishes "mild." Two can sweat out a fine meal for HK$250 ($32).

The **Satay Hut,** on the first floor of the Houston Centre opposite the Shangri-La Hotel, Tsimshatsui (tel. 3-723-3681), is a very small, inexpensive coffeeshop serving the foods of the Spice Islands. Opened by Singaporean Pearl Chu, the Satay Hut reflects her origins in a spotless environment, prompt service, and a slant toward Nonya cooking, the unique blend of Chinese and Malay cuisines found only in Singapore. Gourmands may recognize the Indonesian satays (skewered and barbecued beef, chicken, or pork with a peanut sauce) and Sumatran beef rendang (dried beef in a spicy curry). Start your meal with Singapore Rocket Fuel, a piquant sweet-and-sour seafood soup, explore the menu and finish with a gula melaka, Ms. Chu's special sago pudding in coconut cream. Two can dine heartily for a bargain HK$70 ($9).

For travelers who can't get to Burma, the **Rangoon Restaurant,** 265 Gloucester Rd., Causeway Bay (tel. 5-893-2281), offers a tasty sampling of that country's cuisine. In fact, travelers will find better food in this Rangoon than in the original one. You can feast on fiery Burmese curries or specially imported prawns and hilsa fish, or try the national dishes—mon hin gar (noodles in fish broth) or ohn no khauk (noodles with chicken curry and coconut milk). Two can dine amid Burmese art and antiques for HK$170 ($21.75).

WESTERN DINING: Last, and perhaps less interesting, though of excellent quality, are the hundreds of Western restaurants. They range from McDonald's and Pizza Hut or the Hong Kong equivalent, Maxim's, to the dear, formal, and stuffy salons in the great hotels. Our recommendations require advance reservations and suggest smarter, or more formal, attire.

Fine Continental Cuisine

One of Hong Kong's premier dining experiences awaits you at **Plume,** the renowned French restaurant at the Regent on Salisbury Road, Kowloon (tel. 3-721-1211). The décor is simple and elegantly modern. Once you've savored the delicious view of the harbor, turn your attention to the memorable cuisine. After the complimentary glass of champagne-myr (champagne with a touch of blueberry liqueur) and the Indian naan bread served with goose-liver pâté, you'll want to start with a salad of pan-fried quail breasts with herb vinaigrette, a cassolette of Irish oysters and caviar, or a cream of artichoke soup with beluga caviar. Then choose from delicate entrees like sautéed paupiettes of sea perch served with champagne butter, or venison ragoût and braised cabbage in a salmis sauce. You will undoubtedly want to accompany this feast with a fine vintage from the Plume's 8,000-bottle wine cellar. The combination of the view and the meal may make the substantial bill seem worthwhile; expect to pay HK$1,000 ($128.25) to HK$1,600 ($205) for two. Reservations are absolutely recommended and jacket and tie or dress is required.

Pierrot, on the top floor of the Mandarin Oriental Hotel, 5 Connaught Rd., Central (tel. 5-220-111), is another choice for French cuisine, where deep-red velvet walls, crystal chandeliers, and theatrical artwork lend formality. Clients come for Pierrot's souffléed scottish salmon with champagne sauce, tournedos of beef with goose liver, and an extensive (also expensive) wine list. Pierrot is open Monday through Friday for lunch, serving popular two- and three-course menus from HK$200 ($25.50). At supper nightly, couples will spend HK$1,250 ($160.25) and up.

Jimmy's Kitchen, at 1 Wyndham St., Central (tel. 5-265-293), has provided reliable, high-quality continental food since 1928. In a low-key, dark-wood-and-leather pub atmosphere, Jimmy Landau and his partners attend to the older business and expatriate crowd. The corned beef and cabbage, New York–cut sirloin, rack of lamb, and daily specials are familiar favorites, sure to satisfy the homesick palate. Jimmy also offers a snack and sandwich menu for off-hour dining; a complete meal with house wine will run about HK$250 ($32) for two. The Central location is older than the new digs on the first floor of the Kowloon Centre (tel. 3-684-027), though neither are the original. Jimmy also owns **Landau's,** at 257 Gloucester Rd., Causeway Bay (tel. 5-891-2901), a 1920s speakeasy replica with a wider-ranging continental menu and a more active, piano-bar scene.

If you're in the mood for romance, the **Verandah,** 109 Repulse Bay Rd. (tel. 5-812-2722), overlooking Repulse Bay, occupies one of Hong Kong's most enchanting settings. Although we mourn the loss of the venerable colonial classic Repulse Bay Hotel, the Peninsula Group has replaced the original structure with one that pays homage to the style of its predecessor. Dining at the Verandah is a strictly continental affair, with such specialties as wild forest mushrooms, lobster and artichoke gratiné, pepper steak, duck with mango confit, and an assortment of soufflés. Fixed-price meals run HK$115 ($14.75) and HK$400 ($51.25) for lunch and dinner respectively. The Bamboo Bar attached to the restaurant makes a fine midday or evening stop.

Steak aficionados can head to **The Steakhouse,** at the swank Regent Hotel, Tsimshatsui (tel. 3-721-1211), for a full plate from the salad bar, baked potatoes, onion rings, and imported U.S. beef. Dinner for two can run HK$675 ($86.50) and up, especially if you linger on the frozen margaritas.

Au Trou Normand, in a cellar at 6 Carnarvon Rd., just off bustling Nathan Road in Kowloon (tel. 3-668-754), is a cozy and casual bistro. Red-and-white checkered tablecloths are the background for a classic foie gras, escargots, filet of sole in oyster and white wine sauce, or the traditional coq au vin. Au Trou Normand's food is wonderful, it's less formal than the hotel restaurants, and it's moderately priced at HK$450 ($57.75) to HK$600 ($77) for two, including wine.

Casual Dining and Fast Food

A less tony steakhouse that's geared to nostalgia buffs is at 101 Barnton Court, Ocean Galleries in Harbour City. The **San Francisco Steak House** (tel. 3-722-7576) uses skyline photos, streetcar memorabilia, and a California wine list to add authenticity to hamburger platters, hero sandwiches, and 20-ounce San Francisco–cut steaks. A casual lunch runs about HK$60 ($7.75); a steak dinner, about HK$175 ($22.50). Reservations recommended on weekend evenings.

California, located on Lan Kwai Fong in Central (tel. 5-211-345), the liveliest nighttime street on the island, is a hot and happening place. It's easy to see why California is an expatriate favorite—Columbus Avenue–café/fern-bar décor and a daily California nouvelle cuisine menu complement each other and are both done well. The young professional clientele, pulsing music, and handsome help add to the attractive environment. Among the more interesting dishes are Caribbean pork, delicious tender crab quadrilles, lamb Marrakesh, and a surprisingly tart guacamole. Diners can count on Columbus Avenue prices with dinners running about HK$170 ($21.75) a head.

At **Casa Mexicana,** Victoria Centre on Watson Road, Causeway Bay (tel. 5-665-560), you can pig out on chips and salsa, guacamole, nachos, an enchilada/taco/tamale combo, and even an exotic baked chicken in lotus leaves, while enjoying the house mariachi band. The food is reasonably authentic and the décor would make El Fenix of Dallas proud. A fiesta for two with margaritas should run about HK$280 ($36). If Mexican isn't American enough, wander through Casa Mexicana and into the adjacent **Texas Rib House** (tel. 5-665-560). A salad bar and the Combo BBQ platter (barbecued chicken, ribs, sausage, and steak) with baked potato will make you feel at home for about HK$90 ($11.50).

The Queen's Café, an old-fashioned Shanghai-deco luncheonette, exists in a time warp at 39-41 Lee Garden Rd., Causeway Bay (tel. 5-762-658). It's a favorite of our local friends who treasure its delicious Eastern European cuisine. The Queen's Café has an old-world staff and old-world prices. You can enjoy rich beet borscht, chicken shashlik, ice cream, and sinful pastries for a bargain HK$68 ($8.75), and feel like you just dined at Schrafft's.

Our film industry friends favor the **Beverly Hills Deli,** at Level Two, no. 55, in the New World Centre, Tsimshatsui (tel. 3-698-695). It's just what the doctor ordered if you're in need of Empire kosher chicken noodle soup, served for two in one giant bowl at HK$45 ($5.75). Feeling homesick for a tuna melt? Maybe matzoh latkes with apple sauce? Texas chili with a vanilla egg cream? Filling meals start at HK$60 ($7.75). The Beverly Hills Deli delivers locally, and has a branch at 2 Lan Kwai Fong, basement level, Central.

A tranquil European-style tea parlor, all pink brocade and proper seating, is enough of a rarity in the territory's fast-food whirlwind to warrant attention, especially from shoppers. The **Gigi Coffee Lounge** is in Swire House (tel. 5-261-830), one of Central's premier office and shopping complexes. A full American breakfast at HK$30 ($3.75) or a variety of light, continental lunches or cappuccino and pastry at HK$84 ($10.75) can be had Monday through Saturday from 8 a.m. to 7 p.m.

Hong Kong has its own, locally spawned fast-food outlets that rival the better-known Western entrants such as **McDonald's, Kentucky Fried Chicken,** and **Burger King.** Of the home-grown chains, the most ubiquitous is **Maxim's,** a cross between a coffeeshop and industrial fast-food franchise, notable for its pink-striped sign and décor. The menu is familiar: hamburgers, french fries, and soda, with a few "exotic" extras such as chicken-and-pineapple salad and a decent tuna fish sandwich. A burger, fries, and Coke runs HK$11 ($1.50). Maxim's is in nearly every mall on both sides of the city; operating hours vary, but generally are daily from 8 a.m. to 9 p.m.

6. SIGHTS, SHOPPING, AND NIGHTLIFE

Most people think shopping (bargains! custom suits! new cameras!) when they envision Hong Kong, but the territory also has wonderful natural attractions, interesting cultural activities, and a wealth of nighttime adventures.

SIGHTSEEING AND SPORTS: Compact and well-organized Hong Kong is easy and fun to get around. Long walks turn up the least expected pleasures; the silent, high-speed MTR subway exemplifies 21st-century transport; double-decker public buses are an absolute bargain, and taxis are abundant and inexpensive. The HKTA's brochure "Places of Interest by Public Transport" details lesser-known attractions in Hong Kong, Kowloon, and the New Territories, and is a must for those who like to explore on their own. (If you're headed for more obscure places, remember to have your hotel write down your destination in Chinese!) Whatever your pleasure, an orientation to Hong Kong's Victoria Harbour, the dominant element in the territory's daily life, is essential to any itinerary.

The Star Ferry and Harbor Tours

A cross-harbor journey on the Star Ferry, the commercial and social link between Hong Kong island and the Kowloon mainland, is one of the world's most pleasant, least expensive excursions. The squat, broad-beamed, green-and-white ferries depart from the Star Ferry terminals next to the Connaught Centre on Connaught Road, Central, or next to Star House on Salisbury Road in Kowloon. Every three to ten minutes from 6:30 a.m. to 11:30 p.m. daily, the gates open and hundreds of commuters stream off the gangplank, as they've done since 1898. Tickets, purchased from booths at the gateway, cost HK$.60 (7¢) for the main level second class and HK$.80 (10¢) for the upper deck first class. The tranquil ten-minute journey offers breathtaking views of Victoria Peak on Hong Kong island and of the new high-rise estates sprouting north from Tsimshatsui.

If you're intrigued by the Chinese junks, sleek yachts, Arab tankers, and pleasure boats that ply the harbor, consider taking a **Star Ferry One Hour Harbour Cruise.** Six times daily a private ferryboat departs from the Star Ferry Hong Kong or Kowloon piers for a one-hour cruise that takes you past the Macau Ferry terminal in Western, the Yaumati Typhoon Shelter, along the coast of Tsimshatsui and Kai Tak International Airport, and by the Noon Day Gun mon-

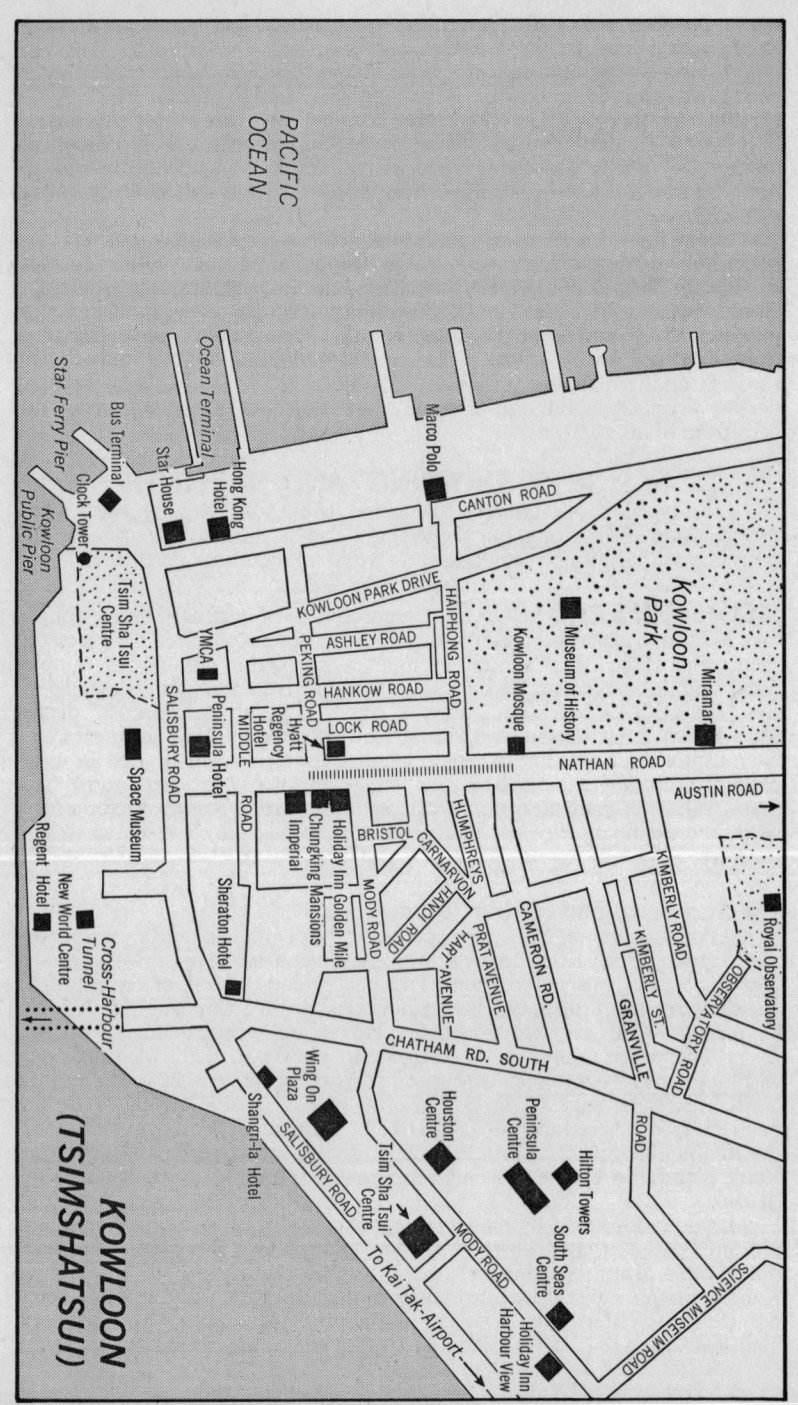

PACIFIC OCEAN

Ocean Terminal

Star Ferry Pier

Bus Terminal

Star House

Clock Tower

Kowloon Public Pier

Hong Kong Hotel

Marco Polo

CANTON ROAD

Kowloon Park

Tsim Sha Tsui Centre

SALISBURY ROAD

YMCA

KOWLOON PARK DRIVE

HAIPHONG ROAD

ASHLEY ROAD

PEKING ROAD

HANKOW ROAD

LOCK ROAD

Kowloon Mosque

Museum of History

Miramar

Peninsula Hotel

MIDDLE ROAD

Hyatt Regency Hotel

NATHAN ROAD

Space Museum

Sheraton Hotel

Holiday Inn Golden Mile

Chungking Mansions

Imperial

BRISTOL

MODY ROAD

HUMPHREY'S

CARNARVON

HANOI ROAD

HART AVENUE

PRAT AVENUE

CAMERON RD.

AUSTIN ROAD →

KIMBERLY ROAD

KIMBERLY ST.

GRANVILLE

OBSERVATORY ROAD

Royal Observatory

Regent Hotel

New World Centre

Cross-Harbour Tunnel

CHATHAM RD. SOUTH

Wing On Plaza

Shangri-la Hotel

SALISBURY ROAD

— To Kai Tak Airport —

Tsim Sha Tsui Centre

Houston Centre

Peninsula Centre

Hilton Towers

South Seas Centre

Holiday Inn Harbour View

MODY ROAD

GRANVILLE ROAD

SCIENCE MUSEUM ROAD

KOWLOON (TSIMSHATSUI)

ument in Causeway Bay. The fare is HK$60 ($7.75) for adults, HK$48 ($6.25) for children; this includes a guide, souvenirs, and beverages. Tickets can be purchased at Star Ferry ticket booths, through a travel agent or by calling 3-669-878.

Victoria Peak and the Peak Tramway

One of Hong Kong's highlights is a visit to its highest point, Victoria Peak, a vantage with the best views over Victoria Harbour and the skyscrapers of Central. The Peak Tramway was inaugurated May 30, 1888, to take heat-weary residents up to the heights of Hong Kong for cool breezes, picnics, and the most glorious view of the colony. The original trams were steam-powered until 1926, when electrical equipment was installed. The same equipment is still in use and they've never had an accident!

The tram ride itself is something else: eight minutes chugging up a 45° incline through lush greenery. On the way up there are four stops where schoolchildren and workmen clamber on as the tram slowly rolls backward. At the last stop, Victoria Peak, there's a shopping arcade and an observation platform with pay binoculars. Outside the modern station are other, older, observation platforms with dragons guarding the panoramic views now shared by residents of "The Peak." The Peak Tramway runs every 15 minutes from 7 a.m. to midnight daily; round-trip fares are HK$12 ($1.50) for adults, HK$5 (60¢) for children; one-way fares are HK$7 (90¢) for adults, HK$2.50 (30¢) for children. You can take a free shuttle from the Star Ferry pier, bus no. 15 from Exchange Square, or the green minibus no. 1 from City Hall to the terminal behind the Hong Kong Hilton International Hotel in Central, at the St. John's Building on Garden Road.

Exploring the Old and the New

Hong Kong's Central district, an amalgam of old and new, Chinese and international, is delightfully easy to explore on foot. Crowded back lanes contain tiny storefronts hung with paper lanterns, stocked with carved religious icons or herbal medicine jars, or shaded by freshly inked parchment calligraphy hung up to dry. On Jubilee Street bankers and brokers stop at dai pai dongs to examine the Chinese crullers (deep-fried dough sticks served in the morning with steaming bowls of milk). For a sit-down morning meal in the lyrical company of caged songbirds and their doting owners, try Han Wen (Hing Wan) at 119 Queen's Rd., Central. Strollers will find meters of silk and garishly printed polyester adorning Cloth Alley (Wing On Street), and Man Wah Lane humming with the carving of soapstone chops, the traditional seal used to identify letters and artworks. We recommend the HKTA's excellent "Central and Western District Walking Tour" booklet and map, available at all HKTA outlets, including the 35th floor of the Connaught Centre, for HK$10 ($1.30), which provides an informative and entertaining insider's view of these districts in a three-hour stroll.

An alternative tour of the old and new is the **Hong Kong Tramways Dim Sum Tour.** An open-roofed bus ushers tourists from the Star Ferry to the tram depot in Causeway Bay. There you'll ascend the iron stairs of a restored 1920s double-decker tram for a guided tour. In two hours you can munch on dim sum and peek down old lanes around the Happy Valley Race Course, the bargain stalls along Queensway, and the neon-lit R&R strip in Wanchai. Tours depart twice daily and cost HK$95 ($12.25) for adults, HK$70 ($9) for children; call 3-669-878 for more information.

Around the Island: Aberdeen, Repulse Bay, and Stanley

These three coastal communities are on the southern part of Hong Kong island and can be combined in a half-day excursion.

Several tour operators combine the Peak Tramway, Aberdeen, Repulse Bay, and Stanley into a six-hour guided coach-and-sampan tour. These tours cost HK$300 ($38.50) for adults, HK$175 ($22.50) for children 12 and under, and can be booked through your hotel or through the Gray Line of Hong Kong (tel. 3-687-111).

ABERDEEN. Aberdeen is called Hong Kong Tsai (Little Fragrant Harbor) in Chinese because its harbor retains many of the characteristics of old Hong Kong. Families live on houseboats as they have for centuries, operating shops, boatbuilding workshops, and kitchen boats on the water. The Aberdeen Typhoon Shelter, a protected harbor sheltered by Ap Lei Chau island, is still home to about 5,400 "boat people." Thousands more used to inhabit the colorful junks but most have been relocated to housing on the island (the junks marked with yellow numbers are scheduled to be relocated next). Motorized sampans steered by *tankas,* the old women who have traditionally transported Aberdeen's inhabitants, can be hired at the Aberdeen main pier for half-hour tours for about HK$60 ($7.75) per person. **Watertours of Hong Kong Ltd.** (tel. 3-673-031 or 5-254-808) also offers daily 20-minute tours with an English-speaking guide for HK$40 ($5) per adult, HK$30 ($3.75) per child, or in combination with other tours.
In the evening, three huge restaurants floating in the bay opposite the Shum Wan Ferry pier, **Jumbo** (see "Dining"), **Tai Pak,** and **Sea Palace,** are lit up like Christmas trees. Take their free shuttle from this pier, explore the wonderfully garish Oriental décor, and get a mini-tour of the harbor.
Aberdeen can be reached by taxi, or by public bus no. 7 or 70 for HK$3.50 (40¢) from the Central Bus Terminal. The HKTA publishes an excellent Aberdeen walking tour brochure that can be obtained at any of their offices. Nearby are **Ocean Park** and **Waterworld,** a marine amusement park with a roller coaster, marine mammal show, and waterside displays.

REPULSE BAY. About one hour from Central and east of Aberdeen is Repulse Bay, a district long favored by the wealthy and expatriate for its residential feeling, swimming beach, and less commercial development. The classic Repulse Bay Hotel, once a colonial landmark and linchpin for the wealthy community, was torn down in a 1970s development fever to make way for high-rises that were never built. The façade and lobby have recently been rebuilt as a shopping complex to house shops and restaurants.
The **Repulse Bay Beach** is like a spiritual theme park. Between the street and sand are an odd collection of multicolored statues dedicated to Kuan Yin, Goddess of Mercy, and Tin Hau, Goddess of Lifesaving and Seafarers. Lifeguards also watch over bathers daily between April and November, when the average sea temperature is 71°F/22°C.

STANLEY. The village of Stanley, beloved by tourists for its bargain clothes market, is on the shore of Hong Kong's southernmost peninsula. When the island was ceded to the British in 1842, Chuckchu was Hong Kong's largest fishing settlement and an important commercial center. (It was called Chuckchu, or "Robber's Lair," by the resident Hakka people because of the many pirates in the waters of Tai Tam Bay.) In 1845 it was renamed for Lord Stanley, secretary of state for the colonies, and has remained somewhat an enclave for expatriates.
The **Stanley Market** (see "Shopping"), an open-air tag sale of Calvin Klein, Banana Republic, Outback Red, and other labeled sportswear, foodstuffs, brass, and household items, is open daily from 10 a.m. to 6 p.m. There is a good, small Stanley Market Chinese Restaurant on the main street. The **Stanley Main Beach** is very crowded on weekends with local windsurfers and sun worshippers, and nearby **St. Stephen's Beach** has boating as well as swimming facilities. The HKTA publishes an informative Stanley walking-tour brochure available free from any of their offices.

You can reach Stanley by taxi direct from Central or from Kowloon via the tunnel for about HK$35 ($4.50), or by public bus no. 6 or 260 from the Exchange Square Bus Terminal for about HK$6 (80¢).

Cultural Activities

A re-creation of a 10th-century Chinese village, a cluster of small museums, an aquarium, and a planetarium are some organized cultural activities that are fun for the whole family.

In **Sung Dynasty Village** visitors can sample activities typical of village life during China's Sung Dynasty (A.D. 960–1279). This colorful complex of period temples, houses, and shops contains a candymaker, incense vendor, fan carver, fortune-tellers, food hawkers, roaming street musicians, dancers, and Kung-fu demonstrations. A carved-teak tavern run by women in traditional costumes serves plum wine to tourists and costumed actor customers. Trained monkeys, a wax museum of life-size historical figures, and an ornate restaurant offering Sung Dynasty specialties conspire to educate while entertaining the bemused spectator. Sung Dynasty Village receives guests via organized tours, operated four times daily (twice on weekends) to include lunch, snacks, or supper. The re-created village is in Kowloon at Kau Wa Ken, Lai Chi Kok, and the average tour takes about four hours. Tickets cost HK$210 ($27) for adults, HK$140 ($18) for children 3 to 11 years; call 3-741-5111 for reservations.

A quiet hour devoted to a slightly obscure interest can be spent at the **Flagstaff House Museum of Tea Ware,** located off Cotton Tree Drive east of the Hilton Hotel in Central (tel. 5-299-390). The museum is housed in a mid-19th-century Greek Revival building that from 1846 to 1978 was the residence and office of the British military commandant, and is the oldest surviving colonial building in Hong Kong. The verdant grounds are lush—a tropical escape in a forest of skyscrapers. The Flagstaff House offers exhibits from its amazingly varied collection of tea ware, and some excellent publications. The house, grounds, and collection of this quintessentially Oriental artform all warrant a visit. The museum is open six days from 10 a.m. to 5 p.m.; closed Wednesday and some holidays.

The **Hong Kong Museum of Art** is nearby, on the 10th and 11th floors of City Hall (tel. 5-224-127), a brief walk east of the Star Ferry pier. The museum specializes in fine art from all periods of Chinese history, but ceramics are the best represented. Early works of Chinese painting and calligraphy are also particularly beautiful. Visitors not drawn to Oriental art are sure to enjoy the prints, engravings, and old photographs of Hong Kong; scenes from the early colonial period are unrecognizable in today's metropolis. The museum is open daily except Thursday from 10 a.m. to 6 p.m. (on Sunday and holidays from 1 to 6 p.m.), and admission is free.

Hong Kong University houses the small **Fung Ping Shan Museum,** a collection of bronzes, ceramics, and other Oriental art given by university donors since 1953. It's located at 94 Bonham Rd. in the Western district, a brief walk from the no. 3 bus stop, which originates at the Connaught Centre, Central. The ceramic collection, with Han tomb pottery, three-color glazed pieces from the Tang Dynasty, the luminous celadons of the Song, and blue and white porcelains from the Ming and Ching, is wonderful to behold. Hong Kong University has regular lectures, tours, special exhibits, and courses on Oriental art; call (tel. 5-859-2114) for information. The museum is open daily except Sunday and holidays from 9:30 a.m. to 6 p.m., admission free.

Hong Kong's **Space Museum,** at 10 Salisbury Rd. (tel. 3-721-2361), on the harbor across from the Peninsula Hotel, was recently reopened after a program of renovation and expansion in 1988. Now it features sky shows and Omnimax presentations on a daily basis, as well as comprehensive displays about the exploration of space. The Space Museum is especially popular with families, both locals and tourists. Hours are Monday through Friday (except Tuesday) from 2 to 9:30 p.m., on Saturday from 1 to 9:30 p.m., and on Sunday from 10:30 a.m. to 9:30 p.m.; closed Tuesday. Admission is HK$18 ($2.25) for adults, HK$12 ($1.50) for children.

The **Museum of History,** in Kowloon Park in Tsimshatsui (tel. 3-671-124), is about a ten-minute walk from the Star Ferry pier and just two minutes from the MTR station. Opened in 1975, it chronicles the excavations and ethnography of Hong Kong and its peoples, displaying historical artifacts and photographs in comprehensive exhibits. Upstairs is a gallery devoted to temporary shows. A highlight of the museum is its bookshop, which has several excellent and inexpensive publications and catalogs that make great gifts. The museum is open Monday through Thursday and Saturday from 10 a.m. to 6 p.m., from 1 to 6 p.m. on Sunday and holidays; closed Friday. Admission is free.

The **Chinese University's Art Gallery,** at 12 miles Taipo Rd., Shatin, New Territories (tel. 0-695-2218), is a modern, well-lit exhibition space where Chinese ceramics, paintings, porcelain, bronze seals, and jade carvings are displayed for teaching purposes. The general collection and temporary exhibits are worth visiting for those interested in Oriental art, and an expedition to the campus in Shatin, New Territories, is an adventure in itself. The gallery is open daily from 9:30 a.m. to 4:30 p.m. (on Sunday and some holidays from 12:30 to 4:30 p.m.), and admission is free. The Kowloon Railway has regular service to University Station, where shuttle buses take you to the campus.

Two recently opened museums are also off the beaten path but promise to attract visitors by their unique exhibits. The **Sam Tung Uk Museum** at Kwu Uk Lane in Tsuen Wan, New Territories (tel. 0-411-2001), is a culture and history museum housed in an 18th-century Hakka family compound. Exhibits illuminating various aspects of Hong Kong's history will be mounted in one of the 12 renovated homes. After its completion the **Chai Wan Folk Museum** will be the area's first folk museum; crafts, tools, and folk art will be displayed along with old photographs and historical records. Contact the HKTA (tel. 3-722-5555 or 5-244-191) for information about hours and public transportation serving these new museums.

The **Aw Boon Haw Gardens** were built by Aw Boon Haw, the Tiger Balm salve magnate, in 1935 as a gift and a warning to the people of Hong Kong. Located on a hill above Tai Hang Road, Causeway Bay, it's about 5 km (3 miles) from Central. You can take bus no. 11 from the terminal next to the Star Ferry. Landscaped grounds, man-made grottoes, tiny pagodas, and brightly painted plaster statues of gods and goddesses remind visitors of traditional fables exhorting goodness, faithfulness, and the punishment of evil. The ornate Chinese mansion, eerie statues, and odd juxtaposition of religious icons will feel familiar to those who've been to Haw Par Villa (created by the Aw Boon brothers) in Singapore. It's an extremely photogenic outing—just make sure to pick up the HKTA's brochure describing the symbolism of each statue before you go. Aw Boon Haw Gardens is open daily from 9 a.m. to 4 p.m., admission free.

Ocean Park, on the south side of Hong Kong island, and easily reached from the Admiralty MTR station by the Ocean Park Citybus (tickets are available from MTR stations), is Asia's largest "oceanarium," marine displays on the coast of the South China Sea that feature seals, pelicans, and penguins. The 5,000 fish that idle nearby on Atoll Reef make this the world's largest aquarium. Visitors can wander through four levels and admire the fish, sea mammals, and huge goldfish collection. The marine displays are connected by cable car or by the world's longest outdoor escalator to an amusement park on the hillside. Middle Kingdom, a huge new cultural village on the model of Sung Dynasty Village but spanning 13 dynasties, will open in 1989. Roller coasters, restaurants, animal shows, a new aviary, Water World and its log flume rides, a children's zoo, a 360° movie screen in a round theater, Ferris wheels, and a host of other entertainment lures locals and their families in hordes on weekends and holidays. Midweek, Ocean

Park can really be a fun outing, especially for its picturesque setting. Several tour operators run coach tours to the amusement park for about HK$185 ($23.75) per person, including admission to most rides; call 5-532-2244 for more information.

Horse Racing

There is no more popular pastime in Hong Kong than gambling, which takes place in a variety of venues: legally on the stock market and in the lottery, illegally in the bird- and cock-fighting parlors around the city. The best place to sample betting Hong Kong style is at the horse races, held twice a week from September to May (plus some additional races on Chinese New Year). Alternating between historic **Happy Valley,** built on reclaimed swampland by the British in 1846 and home of the exclusive Royal Hong Kong Jockey Club, and the hi-tech $100-million grounds at **Shatin,** out in the New Territories, some HK$3 billion a year is wagered over the outcome of thoroughbred racing. The Jockey Club has supervised racing in Hong Kong for over 100 years, using profits to build projects such as Ocean Park, the Space Museum, the Jubilee Sports Center in Shatin, and the Hong Kong Academy for Performing Arts.

Racing is so popular that it's very difficult to get tickets to either track. Visitors (with a valid tourist stamp in their passports) can obtain an entry badge for HK$50 ($6.50) from the Jockey Club offices next to the Happy Valley racetrack up to 5 p.m. the day before a race. Entrance to the tracks can also be arranged through the Hong Kong Tourist Association (tel. 5-244-191) as part of a lunch or dinner inclusive tour. Each racing day, a limited number of guest badges is set aside for tourists who are over 18 years of age, carry a valid overseas passport (remember to bring it on the day of your tour), and have been visiting Hong Kong for less than three weeks. Depending on the day, typically Wednesday night, Saturday, or Sunday, the location shifts between Happy Valley and Shatin; consult the HKTA for the current schedule. The cost of the tour is HK$250 ($32) including transportation, Chinese lunch or dinner, and entrance to the Member's Enclosure at the track.

SPORTS AND RECREATION: Golf and tennis are popular with excercise-conscious visitors who are in Hong Kong for a longer stay, and the HKTA has made several sporting opportunities available. Their "Sports and Recreation Tour" is a one-day package to the ultra-elegant, private Clearwater Bay Golf and Country Club, on the Sai Kung peninsula. Visitors (a passport is required as the club is closed to nonmember residents) are welcome to use the club's professional 18-hole golf course, five all-weather and two indoor tennis courts, three squash courts, two badminton courts, swimming pool, and luxurious clubhouse. All sports equipment can be rented, and the new facilities share vistas over the South China Sea. The day tour costs HK$210 ($27) for adults, HK$165 ($21.25) for children under 12, including transportation, guides, lunch, and club admission fee, plus a HK$210 ($27) greens fee per 18 holes, or a HK$25 ($3.25) per-hour fee for tennis courts.

Visitors can also use the private facilities of the Royal Hong Kong Golf Club in Fanling, New Territories or the Discovery Bay Golf Club on Lantau Island as guests of members or by affiliation with several international clubs. The Urban Services Department manages 34 public tennis courts on Hong Kong island and 18 in Kowloon, most open from 6 a.m. to 11 p.m. daily, which can be reserved for use by visitors. Contact the HKTA (tel. 5-244-191) for more information about both private and public facilities.

For **jogging, hiking, and bicycling,** you'll have a choice of 21 park and 20 reservoir locations in which to work out. Kowloon Park adjoins Nathan Road, the famed "Golden Mile" shopping district, and offers quiet paths, benches to relax on, and a 700-yard Fitness Trail for joggers and exercise buffs. Victoria Park in Central and Lugard and Bowen Roads on Victoria Peak are also popular with local and visiting joggers; the peak roads offer dramatic vistas over the harbor and some aerobically challenging uphill runs as well. Several hotels will provide guests with jogging maps and warm-up suits for their workouts. Cycling is taken seriously in the territory. Bicycles can be rented at Shatin and Tai Mei Tuk, Taipo, two developments in the New Territories connected by a traffic-free cycling lane. Bicycles can also be rented at Silvermine Bay on Lantau Island and in Shek O on Hong Kong as well; contact the HKTA (tel. 5-244-191) for more information. Hikers will find a surprising number of parkland: the 50-km- (30-mile-) long Hong Kong trail, labeled trails and climbs on Lantau and in the New Territories, the 100-km (60-mile) MacLehose Trail stretching across eight country parks. Contact the HKTA or the Country Parks Authority, Agriculture and Fisheries Dept., 13th floor, 393 Canton Rd., Kowloon, for their leaflets, maps, and nature trail guides.

Victoria Park in Causeway Bay is one of the island's most pleasant enclaves, 19 acres of reclaimed land that hosts fitness buffs, songbird devotees, and strollers. Early birds can enjoy a fascinating ritual by joining the hundreds of locals who practice **Tai Chi Chuan** ("Supreme Ultimate Boxing") at 5 a.m. daily in the park. Tai Chi is a type of classic dance/movement for health and self-defense that's based on the philosophy of Lao Tzu. Students practice the slow, balanced moves and postures to physically develop their equilibrium, muscle control, and strength, as well as develop peace of mind and neutralize aggressive tendencies. It's the people's ballet at its best. In Kowloon Park there is an Aviary and Traditional Garden. Tai Chi practitioners can be found every morning between 7 and 8 a.m., practicing ancient, ritualized movements in large groups as the sun comes up.

Hong Kong is known for the Luk Chi Fu School, where the white crane system of **Kung fu,** based on the development of inner strength, is taught. Those seeking to perfect their self-defense skills with Kung fu can contact the Hong Kong Chinese Martial Arts Association (tel. 3-687-689) for additional information on local classes.

SHOPPING: Hong Kong offers a kaleidoscope of possibilities, with something for those who watch their pennies carefully as well as for those who have money to burn. The "Made in Hong Kong" label used to mean less than the best, but now Hong Kong's tailoring gives Savile Row plenty of competition, French and Italian haute couture is copied magnificently, and American ready-to-wear is manufactured here with quality control running as high as New York's Seventh Avenue. Jewelry and watches, porcelain, crystal, fabrics, and handcrafts are also made in myriad designs and price categories.

It's even easy to shop in the neighborhood where you're staying because many malls have branch shops in several districts. **Central,** the business district, is packed with malls, department stores, and retail boutiques that sell stylish, high-quality merchandise. The Landmark is a large, five-story atrium adjoining Gloucester and Edinburgh Tower, with the most exclusive imported designer shops. Swire House, the Prince's Building, Melbourne Plaza, Worldwide Plaza, and the Shun Tak Centre (below the new Hotel Victoria) all offer a varied selection of attractive merchandise. Reputable department stores include Lane Crawford, Dragon Seed, China Products, Sincere, and Wing On. For less pricey merchandise there are boutiques on Des Voeux Road, D'Aguilar Street, and Wyndham Street.

The district east of Central, **Causeway Bay,** is known for the Japanese department stores Mitzukoshi, Daimaru, Matsuzakaya, and Sogo. This area also has a Lane Crawford and China Products store. **Tsimshatsui,** on the Kowloon side of the harbor, is the shopping area that boggles the mind. Asia's largest shopping center is between the Star Ferry terminal and the Prince Hotel on Canton

Road. Within three huge blocks you'll find Ocean Terminal, Ocean Centre, and Harbour City; the large New World Centre is a few blocks east, on Salisbury Road.

The **Eastern** district has Taikoo Shing's Cityplaza, a huge shopping plaza that caters to locals. Two of the largest Japanese department stores are here—Uny, and across the street in Kornhill Plaza, Jusco (over 300,000 square feet).

There are more temptations at every turn, from your hotel lobby to the street vendors and Night Markets, shopping centers, back lanes filled with shop after boutique for cameras, shoes, luggage, eyeglasses, souvenirs, arts, crafts, toys, ginseng, and herbal medicines. The energy and fun send waves of desire over everyone, until traveler's checks, credit cards, and HK$ start to burn a hole in your pocket. But first. . . .

Some Shopping Tips

Any shop that displays the Hong Kong Tourist Association's logo (a little red Chinese junk) is a member of a reputable merchants' association that stands for quality and good business practices. The HKTA (in Hong Kong or abroad) will act on your behalf if you have any complaints regarding merchandise purchased from one of their member stores.

Each shopping district has its own timetable. In the Western district, shops are open from 10 a.m. to 6 p.m. In Central they're open from 10 a.m. to 9:30 p.m. On the Kowloon side, in Tsimshatsui East shops are open from 10:30 a.m. to 7:30 p.m. In Tsimashatsui and farther north of the harbor in Yau Ma Tei and Monkok shops are open from 10 a.m. to 9 p.m. Most shops are open daily; large department stores are usually closed Sunday. Street markets and some shops are open at night. If your visit is around the Chinese New Year (in January or February) you may find many shops closed and many custom items unavailable. During European and Christian holidays most of the shops remain open.

When shopping for clothing, remember that if you recognize a label, it can be a fake. Also, watch the kind of warranty or guarantee you get with any merchandise that is mechanical, electrical, or electronic. You want a Worldwide or International Guarantee, not a local guarantee or a local retailer's guarantee. Your guarantee should always carry a complete description, model number, and serial number for each item. Remember that Hong Kong dollars (HK$) are not U.S. dollars ($), and when charging something to a credit card make sure "HK" is written next to the price.

Most merchandise is not refundable or returnable and deposits are not refundable. Although a 50% deposit is generally requested, negotiate to leave no more than 20%. Always get a receipt for any major purchase. Although Hong Kong is a duty-free port (it doesn't charge import duties on certain goods), this doesn't mean that purchases are exempted from Customs duty when you return home. Double-check your home-country Customs regulations: how much you're allowed to import without paying duty, and how much duty will be owed on each type of merchandise. Your country's embassy in Hong Kong can give you this information.

Check the weight allotment on your international flight and consider carrying gifts back home. If shipping is most practical, you can do it yourself (see "The ABCs of Hong Kong" for postal information) or have the concierge at your hotel handle it.

And don't forget the maxims: "Let the buyer beware!"; "A fool and his money are soon parted"; "All that glitters is not gold"; "A penny saved is a penny earned"; "Cheap is expensive in the long run"; "You buy the best, you have the best." These adages have lasted for a very good reason since the earliest caravans traveled the ancient silk routes.

One last word of warning: Most of the new malls and plazas have marble floors, and after an hour or two of walking your feet may hurt. Buy foam rubber innersoles for your shoes to cushion the feet, and carry a few Band-Aids for sudden blisters.

What to Shop For

The popular saying goes that if you can't find it in Hong Kong, it doesn't exist. Hong Kong does have an incredible array of merchandise and services, often at hard-to-beat prices. However, in the land where commerce is king, there are people who will try to sell you anything, whether or not it's good value. Let's take a look at the most commonly bought items.

ART AND ANTIQUES. A warning—you'd better know antiques if you intend to spend a lot of money. There are recent copies of older works that fool even the experts; it's common to find a 19th-century copy of an 18th-century piece. We also believe that if you see something you like and are convinced you may never see it again, buy it for the price it's worth to you, regardless of whether it's "real" or not. Please note that some of the gallery and shop owners listed in this guidebook prefer to deal with other dealers, decorators, and importers, and sometimes discourage window-shoppers.

The outstanding area for antiques is **Hollywood Road in Central,** a street curving parallel to the harbor, a 15-minute walk inland (due south of the Macau or Central Harbour Ferry terminals) that's most easily reached by taxi. Hollywood Road is like an Oriental version of London's Portobello Road; the exotic and mysterious atmosphere of the shops will fascinate buffs. Go early or after lunch because the nearest restaurants are about a ten-minute walk downhill.

Tai Sing Company, at 122 Hollywood Rd. (tel. 5-491-289), carries a collection of antique celadon (very collectible pottery with a pale-green glaze) including exquisite pieces from the Ming Dynasty. Prices vary according to age and color, and range from HK$4,000 ($500) to HK$16,000 ($2,000). The management at Tai Sing's and at **Yue Po Chai Antiques,** no. 132-136 (tel. 5-404-374), are pleasant and helpful, graciously explaining the history of each piece. **Han Lau,** at no. 175, has a fine collection of antique Buddha statues ranging in price from HK$7,800 ($1,000) to HK$80,000 ($10,000) and some rare Tibetan rugs. The Buddhas are worth viewing; when you see them in great numbers they have a way of exuding their legendary calmness.

The **Shui Cheong Curio Store** at no. 179 (tel. 5-439-548), has much more affordable merchandise. Curios include art jewelry (1920s and '30s Chinese deco copies of classic styles), carved ivory, woodwork, porcelain, and cloisonné wares, the Chinese art of intricate multicolored enamels made popular by the French. The owner is straightforward about what's new and what's not, and prices are reasonable. Up the block at no. 225 is the **Morning Calm Gallery** (tel. 5-431-546), a small elegant shop that would fit in on Madison Avenue or Rodeo Drive. They have an assortment of tasteful reproductions—a pair of celadon teacups for HK$175 ($22.50)—and fine originals such as painted Korean chests for about HK$6,000 ($770).

You can't miss the **Man Mo Temple,** the oldest temple in Hong Kong, dedicated to Man, god of scholars, and Mo, god of warriors. Take a minute out of your shopping day to explore this popular shrine. Locals carrying chickens, baskets of oranges, bits of roast pork, candles, and incense thank the gods for their past and future good luck. Paper offerings are burnt in front of the altars so that the smoke will carry one's wishes to heaven. Man Mo Temple is by the steep stone staircase known as Ladder Street, one of the oldest streets on the island.

For aficionados of microcarving, that most demanding of arts, there's the **Kam Loon Court Company** in shop G4 of the Hollywood Centre at 233 Hollywood Rd. Fragments of ivory, jade, even human hair are precisely carved in such detail that they can only be appreciated under a magnifying glass. Several other stores along Hollywood Road have a selection of Foo dogs (the temple guardians), bronze Kuan Yin statues, Ho Tais, and other colorful curios. Bargaining (unless signposted otherwise) is encouraged in all the shops; start out with 65% of the asking price and see what you settle on.

Beyond the enclave of Hollywood Road there are dealers selling "new antiquities" and those whose museum-quality pieces justify an international reputation and international prices. The best of these are **Eileen Kershaw Ltd.,** in the lobby arcade of the Peninsula Hotel (tel. 3-664-083), whose extraordinary shop is filled with gold, jade, crystal, and ceramic wares; and **Charlotte Horstmann & Gerald Godfrey Ltd.,** whose elegant, two-story warehouse of art, sculpture, and furniture is at 104 Ocean Terminal (tel. 3-677-167), both in Kowloon. **Sammy Y. Lee and Wangs Co.** nearby at 29-31 Chatham Rd. South, have a collection of old rugs woven with rich, yet subtle, natural dyes. There are also several branches of the **China Arts and Crafts** department store (in Shell House, Central, and in Star House or the New World Centre in Kowloon) where you can find contemporary statuary, ceramics, and gift items.

If you still haven't found the perfect object, consider a museum replica manufactured by **Hoi Lung International** in Hong Kong (call 5-778-421 for their limited hours). Original techniques and materials are used to produce Oriental classics for such clients as the British Museum.

CAMERAS, COMPUTERS, AND ELECTRONICS. All are risky purchases because of problems with warranties, compatibility of make and model, and the plethora of unknown brand names, but intrepid shoppers can usually find a bargain.

Examine guarantees carefully. Many shops are able to sell these goods at discount prices because they are "gray market" products, intended for sale in their country of manufacture only and not inspected or guaranteed for sale or use outside the region.

Be a smart shopper! If you're planning to buy a camera or stereo, come armed with advertisements for discount stores back home (New York's 47th Street Photo and 47th Street Computer advertise in every Sunday *New York Times*). You'll find that discount stores that sell in volume can match the prices in most of Hong Kong's audio-visual outlets, and you can avoid the hassles of shipping and paying Customs duty on your purchase when it arrives. If you do find products at unbeatable prices, make sure that necessary accessories (the camera's strap, lens cap, lenses for the home VT minicam, A.C. power packs, hard disk drives) are included in the price you've bargained so hard for. Unless you've comparison-shopped, you won't know what the guy next door would charge for the same merchandise.

If your camera fell into the harbor while riding the Star ferry and you want an inexpensive "snapshot" camera, you'll find dozens of models made by known Japanese manufacturers and dozens of others by Asian manufacturers with similar names. You'll find the best buys in the latest gadgets and equipment; once they're on the market long enough to be discounted in America they are usually a better purchase there. If a store doesn't have the model you want but "can get it for you tomorrow," *do not leave a deposit*. Both **Esquire,** at 8 Cameron Rd. (tel. 3-721-3128), for camera and audio, and **Crown Photo Supplies,** at 27 Hankow Rd. (tel. 3-684-836), have several other branches in Central and Kowloon (see the HKTA "Official Guide to Shopping"). Stanley Street in Central and Canton and Nathan Roads in Kowloon also have dozens of camera/photo/stereo equipment shops to choose from.

Computer shopping is a problem area because many newcomers to the field confuse computer "clones" (reputable imitations of well-known brands, such as the Epson or Leading Edge) with "copies" of the IBM PC or Macintosh. Hong Kong sells several "copies": unknown, Asian-made brands of computer that are primarily for use in the region where they can be serviced and repaired. These usually don't carry International Warranties and often will not run common software programs. Computer buffs can find good buys in floppy disks, accessories, software, and some gadgets. Shop with care! The Golden Arcade shopping center in the Sham Shoi Po district has many small shops selling computers and supplies.

CARPETS AND RUGS. New Oriental carpets are generally a good buy and there are many carpet shops along Hollywood Road uphill from the antique shops. However, the most internationally famous carpet maker in Hong Kong, **Tai Ping Carpets,** in Hutchinson House, 10 Harcourt Rd., Central (tel. 5-227-138), has since 1956 been weaving its magic for the likes of the British royal family, Philip Morris headquarters in New York, the royal palaces at Riyadh and the Jamaican prime minister's office. Their rugs and carpets have graced the suites and ballrooms of nearly every leading hotel in the world. Every carpet is handmade to individual specifications, no matter how complex: full cut or loop pile, single or multi-ply yarn, embossed or carved designs, different weights of wool—they'll even copy a photograph or family pattern, and the workmanship is beautiful. Tai Ping Carpets has three showrooms, one in Hong Kong, one in Kowloon (tel. 3-694-061), and a factory in the New Territories. We took the factory tour, which proved instructive, but not as exciting as simply flipping through samples in the showroom. Prices start at about HK$1,200 ($153.75) to commission a carpet of your design from Tai Ping, which is about 20% less than it might cost back home.

CERAMICS, CRYSTAL, AND PORCELAIN. Glassware and tableware run 30% to 35% cheaper in Hong Kong for internationally known designers such as Spode, Wedgwood, Rosenthal, Lladro, and Waterford. The HKTA publishes a listing of member factories and department stores selling these goods, so shop around. If you decide not to hand-carry your purchase, you'll find that the crating and shipping may cost 10% to 15% of the purchase price, and if you have Customs duty to pay on arrival, your savings may not be worth the trouble.

What may be worthwhile is having table settings made up from your own pattern, to match fabric, wallpaper, a business logo, or to commemorate an event. The factories noted below are far from Kowloon and you'll probably need an interpreter, but try it. **Ah Chou Factory,** in the Hong Kong Industrial Centre, Castle Peak Road (tel. 3-745-1511), and **Hung Cheung Ceramic and China Manufacturer,** at 10 Fung Kat Heung, Yuen Long in the New Territories (tel. 0-712-153), are two choices, but call before you go. A nice alternative is the **Tao Fong Shan Monastery,** near Shatin in the New Territories (tel. 0-611-904), where the monks make ceramics. The prices are moderate and the patterns typical, plus these excellent souvenirs earn money for a worthy cause.

CLOTHING—CUSTOM-TAILORED. Everyone who has been to Hong Kong will suggest a favorite tailor; every hotel, arcade, and mall has one. Tailors require at least two or three fittings (often four or five) for custom-made men's or women's suits, which take three to five days to make; yes, for a price you can get a suit made in 24 hours, but not during the Chinese New Year holiday season. Suits range from HK$800 ($102) to HK$6,500 ($833), depending on the workmanship, fabric, and tailor's reputation. One rule of thumb is that the price of a custom-made Hong Kong suit should equal the cost of a similar ready-made suit at home, although the level of workmanship will be much higher. You'll be handed flyers as you window-shop in Kowloon for tailors who claim "We'll fit you for a silk or wool suit under HK$700 [$90] with a free shirt thrown in!" or "A formal tuxedo for only HK$1,000 [$128.25]!" You always get what you pay for.

Some fashionable New York visitors swear by **Elegante Tailor Ltd.,** in Han

Chun Mansions, Block A, second floor, 8-10 Hankow Rd., Kowloon (tel. 3-723-0921). Suit prices start at about HK$2,500 ($320.50), but Elegante specializes in copying suits from magazine photographs or from your own clothes. Other customers cite the attention to detail and excellent workmanship, but emphasize that when your tailor disagrees about styling details he's probably right. A suit can be turned out in five or six days and four fittings are required. Other well-known tailors (all HKTA members) are **A. Man Hing Cheong,** on the ground floor of the Mandarin Oriental Hotel, 5 Connaught Rd., Central (tel. 5-223-336), and **Jimmy Chen Custom Tailor,** with branches at B-62, Edinburgh Tower on Queen's Road, Central (tel. 5-259-605), and in shop MW4 at the arcade of the Peninsula Hotel, Salisbury Road, Kowloon (tel. 3-722-1888). You can bring your own fabrics or choose from each tailor's extensive collection.

The best-known name for custom-tailored shirts is **Ascot Chang** (tel. 3-662-398), with shops in the arcade of the Peninsula and Regent Hotels in Kowloon, and in the Prince's Building, Central. This tailor still draws longtime American clients even after opening a shop in New York City. In the old days a popinjay would have a shirt made in London at Turnbull and Asser and then ship it off to be copied by Ascot Chang. (For years a story circulated through Hollywood about a famous dandy who sent an expensive English shirt to Hong Kong and asked for a dozen exact copies. A dozen shirts arrived three weeks later with identical cigarette burns over the monogrammed pocket! The original had been copied *exactly*.) Shirts from Ascot Chang (either made-to-measure or copied from your own) cost between HK$300 ($38.50) and HK$850 ($112.75), depending on fabric and style.

Another reputable choice for custom shirts is **Jimmy's,** also in the arcade of the Peninsula Hotel. Jimmy's prices run about 30% less than those at Ascot Chang; shirts start at about HK$225 ($28.75).

Note: Although both suit and shirt tailors will package, insure, and ship your merchandise, clothing may be subject to a higher duty if you hand-carry it. At the time of writing, U.S. residents were allowed to bring in $400 worth of purchases without paying Customs duty on arrival. However, because of stringent trade quotas with Hong Kong, clothing shipped to the U.S. (regardless of the dollar value of what was hand-carried) is subject to a 21% duty, payable upon arrival. Contact your embassy in Hong Kong for the latest information on Customs regulations.

CLOTHING—READY-TO-WEAR. "Made in Hong Kong" indicates some of the best-quality workmanship available today. Good buys in clothing include the designs of Calvin Klein, Perry Ellis, The Limited, WilliWear, Esprit, and numerous other fashion houses whose clothes are manufactured in Hong Kong. While the majority of clothing is exported for sale in the West, many boutiques carry these goods (with or without labels) at prices up to 50% off what you're used to. (And for even better buys, see "The Markets" section.)

Top-of-the-line local designers include names such as **Diane Freis** (tel. 3-721-4342), whose clothes are sold in exclusive U.S. boutiques at double the cost of merchandise in her shops in the Prince's Building, Central, and in Ocean Terminal and Harbour City in Tsimshatsui. **Jenny Lewis** (tel. 3-673-750), **Ragence Lam** (tel. 3-954-243), and **Walter Ma** (tel. 5-250-197) have boutiques in the Swire House, Central, and in the Kowloon Hotel, Tsimshatsui. The fashions of **Eddie Lau** (tel. 3-765-6831) are found in the Mandarin Hotel, Central, and **Joseph Ho** (tel. 3-723-4985) has a shop in the Hong Kong Hotel on Canton Road, Tsimshatsui.

Several international couture designers have shops in the most elegant malls (the Landmark or Swire House, Central) and top hotel arcades (the Peninsula or the Mandarin). Best buys are garments manufactured in Hong Kong, China, or

Macau, but there are also small savings on European goods because they're imported duty free into Hong Kong and are sold without sales or VAT taxes. Designers include Basile, Bally, Bogner, Chanel, Daks, Étienne Aigner, Christian Dior, Karl Lagerfeld, Giorgio Armani, Hermès, Dunhill, Valentino, Matsuda, and many others.

We found great buys at some of the local boutiques, an adventuresome alternative when you've tired of the huge malls. The local **Crocodile** stores (with that familiar symbol copied from you-know-who) are ubiquitous. This chain (the main branch is in Crocodile House; tel. 5-415-499) caters to a modified preppy family with clothes that are sometimes more trendy than fashionable; however, their children's clothes are well made and adorable. Boys' and girls' clothing is well designed with detailing that would cost twice the price back home; the range of colors and sizes is large.

Another local shop with bargain clothing is **Bossini,** in Lows Industrial Plaza, sixth floor, 788 Cheung Sha Wan Rd., Kowloon. With a lower rent, they can afford to sell a variety of unisex, stylish clothing at extremely low prices. This is a good bet for movers and shakers with empty pockets. Pleated, 100% cotton trousers that are well cut cost only HK$110 ($14). **Julie House,** with shops at no. 262 in the Shun Tak Centre, Central, and on Wanchai Road (tel. 5-756-950), carries unknown French designer labels (Pierre Morrell, La Jean) and an assortment of stylish, well-made ladies' silk blouses for HK$175 ($22.50). They come in several colors, but hang side by side with polyester copies (forget what the label says and feel it).

EXOTICA. If you're one of those people who have to be first on your block with something, don't miss **Lee Sands Kobe Ltd.** in Star House, Tsimshatsui. This shop sells purses, wallets, attaché cases, and leather accessories in—hold on—chicken feet skin! You obviously can't comparison-shop on these items because you've never seen them before. How about snakeskin sneakers?

The **Comptesse Boutique,** in the arcade of the Peninsula Hotel, Tsimshatsui (tel. 3-724-4177), is a high-end version of exotica. There, babilla evening purses start at HK$8,000 ($1,026). For the noncognoscenti, babilla is baby crocodile. . . .

EYEWEAR AND OPTICAL STORES. Prescription eyeglasses, frames, designer sunglasses, and contact lenses are considered good buys in Hong Kong. There are several optical shops in each mall, but the **Professional Eye Care Center,** with shops at 10 D'Aguilar St. (tel. 5-233-711) and Shun Tak Centre no. 256 in Central (tel. 5-405-595), and at City Plaza II no. 204 (tel. 5-606-039) and the Hong Kong Hotel (tel. 3-688-408) in Kowloon, and the **Optical Shop Ltd.,** with shops in the Prince's Building no. 117 (tel. 5-238-385), and Shun Tak Centre no. 258 (tel. 5-481-633) in Central, and at Star House no. 12 (tel. 3-668-112) and Ocean Terminal no. 112 (tel. 3-668-733) in Kowloon, have some of the best prices around, and even discount another 10% for large orders. Before you custom-order something, make sure that you have enough time to get lenses corrected and/or refitted if necessary.

One of the best buys for friends who need reading glasses but refuse to wear them are the "half-magnifying glasses" that come in a gold-plated case with a pocket clip and sell for about HK$75 ($9.50); very convenient for Chinese menus too.

FACTORY OUTLETS. Hong Kong is the largest clothing exporter in the world. When items are manufactured with minor defects, in the wrong colors for foreign buyers, or in excess quantity, they are sent to the factory outlets for sale at a discount. However, many places list themselves as outlets but charge retail prices, so make sure you know what these items would cost in a retail store before you settle for inferior goods.

The best outlets for women are found in Kaiser Estate at 51 Man Yue Street in Hung Hom, a Kowloon area with few restaurants for the famished. **Four Seasons,** first floor, Block G1 (tel. 3-632-218), specializes in pure-silk goods and cashmere sweaters for men and women, with particularly good buys in sample size 8 separates. A complete line of men's cashmere sweaters with fashion detailing and a good thickness are as good as those from Scotland, but cost less than half the price at HK$585 ($75). They also have a large selection of men's and women's pure-silk kimonos, luxurious in jewel and pastel colors, and only HK$250 ($32).

Camberly Enterprises, on the ground floor (tel. 3-337-038), carries a full size and color range of classically styled, beautifully made Anne Klein II sportswear. Blouses and skirts start at HK$400 ($51.25); jackets, at HK$650 ($83.25); and tailored coats, at HK$825 ($105.75).

The **Oriental Pacific Retail** shop, in the Sands Building, Room 601-5, at 17 Hankow Rd., Tsimshatsui (tel. 3-724-2633), has an excellent selection of men's and women's sweaters, in brightly patterned synthetics and pure wools, from HK$80 ($10.25) and up.

Hong Kong's answer to Filene's Basement is **Shoppers World,** in Room 104 at 12 Pedder St., Central (tel. 5-231-950), or on the ground floor at 40 Waterloo Rd. in Yau Ma Tei (tel. 3-845-585). This place is like a roulette wheel—you never know what number will come up. The merchandise changes often, but big designer names with clothing for both sexes can be found at great prices.

Most of the factory outlets are open daily except Sunday from 9 a.m. to 6 p.m. and accept major credit cards. A complete list of outlets can be obtained from the HKTA. Flight attendants are another good source for shopping tips; they trade information with outgoing flight crews on the latest bargains and hot spots.

FURS. Furriers have come relatively recently to Hong Kong, because of the high-quality, inexpensive labor pool. Since costs of fur skins are governed by international fur auctions, prices are similar to those in New York's fur district. However, the most expensive furs are slightly less costly and no sales tax is charged; check with your embassy regarding Customs duty to see whether or not the savings is worthwhile.

The **Siberian Fur Store,** at 21 Chatham Rd. South, Kowloon (tel. 3-667-039), has been in business since 1935 and has a phenomenal selection of mink, sable, fox, and leopard (don't even think about purchasing endangered species). Owner Stephen Fong has a factory where fur skins are dressed and prides himself on doing it to perfection, yet a custom coat can be ready in three days! Prices range from about $1,000 to $20,000. Mr. Fong knows his business; his office walls are covered with photographs of himself with movie stars, celebrities, and political bigwigs. The Siberian Fur Store also exports to such U.S. retailers as Neiman Marcus and I. Magnin.

The **Celine Boutique Fourrure** is at 25A Chatham Rd. South, Kowloon (tel. 3-696-936). The furs of the celebrated French designer Celine are beautifully styled and excellently made. When we visited, a saga mink coat cost $13,000 but a stenciled lapin (rabbit) fun fur sold for $900. Occasionally the factory outlets or clothing stores mentioned above will carry fashionable, inexpensive fun furs at bargain prices.

Beware the furriers on Mody Road in Tsimshatsui East who stock ordinary styles and low-quality skins at prices considered high by knowledgeable fur buyers. Of course, knowledge is the key to good bargains and the Hong Kong Fur Federation or the HKTA (tel. 3-722-5555) can help you with your questions.

JEWELRY AND WATCHES. There are more than 1,300 retail jewelers in Hong Kong. The most prestigious international names such as Cartier and Van Cleef and Arpels have shops in prestigious hotels like the Peninsula. Baume Mercier, Piaget, Casio, Bulova, Omega, Rolex, and other known watchmakers all have their authorized sales agents; check the Hong Kong telephone directory or the HKTA for a list of authorized agents. Because this is a duty-free port and there is no sales tax, you'll find the authentic designer goods about 5% to 8% less expensive. Of course, the shops and street vendors who specialize in duplicating name designers charge much less.

Gold, diamonds, and jade are among the best buys. The standard gold used is 18 karat (though 22 karat is not uncommon), the European norm, which is softer and purer than the 14 karat usually sold in the U.S. The excellent workmanship, lower labor costs, and intense local competition mean that gold items can be an excellent value. The most popular jewelry purchases are small diamonds and precious stones set in gold. Diamond shopping requires a great deal of expertise and receipts should indicate the color, cut, clarity, and carat weight (all of which determine the cost of individual gems) so that the HKTA can follow up if there are problems with goods bought from their member shops. You can also get information from the **Diamond Importers Association,** Lane Crawford House, Room 1707, Central (tel. 5-235-497). Everyone has a trusted, favorite jeweler. Many expert shoppers swear by Kevin Mui at **Sammy's Jewellery Co.** in the Ambassador Hotel arcade (tel. 3-660-096).

Jade, in particular imperial jade, is quite expensive and, again, an experienced, knowledgeable shopper will do better on price and quality. Stick to shops that are members of the HKTA unless you're going for the inexpensive necklaces and charms readily found at the Jade Market (See "The Markets").

Pearls, particularly freshwater pearls, can be an excellent value. Most shopping centers carry them for as little as HK$32 ($4) a strand without a clasp. Cultured pearls, which need a clasp and knotting (very inexpensive if done locally), run about HK$375 ($48) a strand. Oriental pearls are rare and extremely expensive. For high-quality pearls, visit the **Trio Pearl Company Ltd.** in the Peninsula Hotel arcade, Tsimshatsui (tel. 3-679-171). After seeing the best, you'll be able to comparison-shop in other HKTA member shops. One of Hong Kong's most noted jewelers is **Kai-Yin Lo,** a designer who's been featured in *Vogue* and *Harper's Bazaar* for years. She incorporates gems, pearls, coral, jade, and other natural materials into imaginative gold pieces; her Hong Kong shops in the Peninsula (tel. 3-721-9693) and Mandarin Oriental Hotels (tel. 5-248-238) sell her unique, high-priced jewelry at a fraction of its cost in the finest U.S. department stores.

Chinese Art and Crafts (HK) Ltd. is a department store with an outstanding collection of real and costume Oriental jewelry. The range is so extensive that their well-crafted products range from HK$40 ($5) to HK$90,000 ($11,538). There are Chinese Arts and Crafts branches in Kowloon at the Star House (tel. 3-674-051), New World Centre (tel. 3-697-760), and the Silvercord Mall (tel. 3-722-6655) in Tsimshatsui, and at the Shell House (tel. 5-223-621), Central. The HKTA also has member jewelry manufacturers who welcome shoppers to their factory showrooms. It's interesting to see how every piece of jewelry is tracked through the production process by computer to facilitate cost control, inventory, and exports. A knowledgeable resident recommends the **Anju Jewellery Factory,** at 41 Man Yue St., Kowloon (tel. 3-659-081), run by the capable Ms. Suki Ng.

High-priced watches can be bought through authorized dealers at a small savings, or as copies from street vendors at HK$85 ($11) to HK$175 ($22.50). Always deal with an HKTA member store when buying a good watch. Dealers willing to bargain with Rolexes and Cartiers may be selling an authentic watch face, but have often replaced the straps, bands, or cases for copies. Even though the copied parts may be gold, silver, or whatever you've paid for, a watch repairman back home who's given a tampered-with product may refuse to honor the service warranty. Since it costs about $250 to clean an authentic Rolex at an authorized service shop in the U.S., this is a good gauge for what you might spend on a real gold or silver copy.

THE MARKETS. Once upon a time all shopping in Hong Kong was done at the street markets. By day or night vendors would ply their produce, chickens, discount clothing, cotton Chinese slippers, steaming bowls of wonton soup, tape cassettes, and any manner of goods and services from open-air stalls. Fortunetellers and noodle makers could avoid high overhead and catch passersby out looking for bargains. The few markets that remain have become something of an institution, maintained in parking lots or corners safeguarded from developers.

One of the most intriguing wet markets (those selling produce, meat, poultry, and goods that necessitate a regular washing down) is the **Central Market,** in a huge warehouse at Des Voeux Road and Victoria Street, Central. Nearby Wing On Street has been dubbed **Cloth Alley** because of the profusion of fabric and notions shops. Expert salespeople are ready to help you calculate the material you'll need to custom-tailor a suit. Another two shopping lanes, **Li Yuen Street East** and **Li Yuen Street West,** run uphill from Des Voeux Road, Central. You'll have to push your way through browsers, shopkeepers, outdoor stalls, and nomadic vendors with baskets of everything imaginable, from underwear to curios, from sneakers to costume jewelry.

In Wanchai, the **Wanchai Market,** at Queen's Road East and Wanchai Road, features traditional Chinese dry goods, such as wooden clogs, temple decorations, and kitchen utensils. Along Queens Road East there are still the old shops for calligrapher's tools, paper lanterns, traditional toys, rosewood furniture, and fabrics. **Jardine's Bazaar** is another popular street market in Causeway Bay.

One of the most famous markets is the **Stanley Market,** about 15 km (9 miles) from the Central district (40 minutes by no. 6 bus from Exchange Square next to the Connaught Centre) and well worth the trip for browsers of bazaars, souks, and flea markets. Stanley Market draws a large expatriate and tourist crowd to the tiny village of Stanley, where stalls crowd around a long main street. Blue jeans for under HK$120 ($15), T-shirts for under HK$40 ($5), imitation Cartier watches for HK$100 ($12.80), hundreds of silk ties for HK$8 ($1), cashmere sweaters for HK$250 ($32), linens, embroidered knickknacks, seconds of designer sportswear, fake ivory and jade, and dozens of sneakers are absolute bargains. Some of the merchandise is second quality, with uneven seams or irregular sizing; some of it is excess imports and available only in certain sizes or colors; and some of it is just plain fun. Lively sequined blouses (very popular for Chinese New Year) start at HK$250 ($32), brass icons begin at HK$25 ($3.25), and embroidered patches for kids' clothing are HK$15 ($2) each. The Stanley Market is open daily from 10 a.m. to 6 p.m. Come early and bargain madly here; the price plummets as you purchase in quantity.

The famed **Jade Market** is a tamer version of its former sprawling self at Kansu and Reclamation Street in Kowloon. Vendors who once squatted in the streets, their laps filled with priceless jade trinkets polished for inspection, now display goods on bridge tables set up side by side in two lots underneath the Gascoigne Road overpass (open from 10 a.m. to 4 p.m. daily). You have to trust your instincts when you buy here and shop around. Many dealers don't speak English, negotiating instead with flash cards and notepads, so you can bargain by jotting down numbers. Be firm! As you walk away, the pencil usually scratches out the last price and replaces it with a lesser figure. Dealers negotiate among themselves by using hand signals under the shield of a newspaper so that their competitors cannot see. If you take the time to study the jade pieces and learn the art of the traders, souvenir shopping becomes much more enjoyable.

Although jade (also jadeite or nephrite) comes in red, yellow, lavender, black, and white, green is the most typical and popular color with the Chinese. The best-quality jade has the strongest pure color, so translucent that it's like glass. The color should be evenly spread throughout the stone, with no visible splotches, fault lines, or cracks. The larger and thicker the stone, the more valuable. The Jade Market offers a variety of jewelry, trinkets, charms, medallions, and other small pieces that start at HK$8 ($1) and go up from there. Make sure that your purchase is not plastic by feeling it carefully (jade is cooler to the touch) and by watching the dealer package what you've chosen (so it's not replaced with a cheaper copy). Expensive purchases and investments in art jade should be confined to HKTA member jewelers and galleries, whose merchandise is guaranteed.

There are two **Night Markets** (also known as the "Poor Man's Nightclub") that operate in Hong Kong, albeit on a lesser scale than in the past. The larger and more exciting one is in Yau Ma Tei, off Shanghai Street between Public Square and Market Streets, called Yong Shue Tau. Nightly between 8 and 10 p.m. a myriad of foodstalls, sportswear and garment booths, tape cassette stalls, fix-it corners, shoe vendors, and fortune-tellers set up shop. Street singers, always in search of a modest tip, serenade passersby with Cantonese pop songs, thus earning the Night Market its nickname. The Yong Shue Tau Night Market is about a ten-minute walk south of the Yau Ma Tei/Waterloo Road MTR station.

The **Central Night Market** is off Connaught Road West, in front of the Macau Ferry pier. Imagine how it once spread over the acres now occupied by the high-rise Hotel Victoria and modern Shun Tak Centre. Vendors hawking designer (or fake designer) polo shirts and sequined Mickey Mouse jacket patches vie with seafood chefs and tape cassette vendors for attention with the aid of colored lights and streamers decorating their booths. Although this Poor Man's Nightclub is only a shadow of its former self, a seafood hotpot or pressed duck with rice feast can still be had harborside, under the stars, for less than HK$30 ($3.75) per person. The Central Night Market is a brief walk from the Sheung Wan/Macau Ferry MTR station. At both Night Markets, we advise extra precaution with your wallets, handbags, and valuables.

SMOKING SUPPLIES, PENS, AND LIGHTERS. Havana cigars are a real treat for those so inclined; they're available here and can be shipped abroad. A box of 25 cigars from **Davidoff's,** with shops in the Landmark in Central (tel. 5-255-428) and in the Peninsula Hotel in Kowloon (tel. 5-685-774), will cost about HK$850 ($109), plus HK$140 ($18) shipping (to the U.S.). Other gift ideas that are good buys include elegant writing tools such as Mont Blanc pens, designer-styled cigarette lighters, and personal accessories. The duty-free shop in the airport has a wide selection at good prices, but you can do about 10% to 15% better at the **Glory Pen Company** at 30-34M Queens Rd., Central (tel. 5-221-396), or the **Willing Pen Company** in Wing on House on Connaught Road Central (tel. 5-230-876).

SOUVENIRS. For good, old-fashioned souvenirs, the kind that say Hong Kong literally and figuratively, try the **Ben Lee Company,** at 39 Chatham Rd. in Tsimshatsui (tel. 3-724-0180). It's one of many, many such places, but Ben Lee's is spotless and pleasant with calm, charming salespeople. They sell embroidered linens, sweaters, and Chinese curios. Silk damask kimonos start at HK$150 ($19.25). A good last stop if there's anyone you've forgotten.

Your souvenirs of Hong Kong should be pleasant ones. If you're shopping at boutiques that are not members of the HKTA (identified by the little red junk sticker on their window), make sure to watch salespeople pack your merchandise.

It's not unusual to get home and find that what you picked out and paid for was switched for a cheaper item. This even applies to clothing; sometimes silk garments that are chosen off the rack are replaced by "fresh" rayon or polyester copies when packed.

And when you've bought all you cared to buy and more than you thought possible, remember that a serviceable, expandable nylon suitcase can be purchased on any street corner for about HK$80 ($10).

NIGHTLIFE: Elegant hotel bars, vast Chinese nightclubs with singers from Taiwan, legendary "Japanese-style" hostess clubs, romantic strolls around Victoria Peak, and a host of other pleasures await those who venture out after supper. For information on cultural events and new nightspots, contact the HKTA or pick up the daily *South China Morning Post* or the monthly *Hong Kong Visitor.* The weekend section of the *Hong Kong Standard,* called "The Buzz Weekender," has listings for everything, from clubs and hotels to discos and opera.

Night owls who expect to party may want to pick up the HKTA's handy **Yum Sing–Night on the Town Tour** package. This self-guided tour packet comes in two versions; the Grand Tour for HK$200 ($25.50) and the De Luxe Tour for HK$350 ($45). Both contain coupons that entitle the bearer (foreign passport holders only) to one or two free drinks in participating pubs, clubs, discos, and bars in addition to free admission. The De Luxe Tour also gives you access to hostess clubs, with one hour of free time with the hostess of your choice (more about that later). Either package is worth it if you want to check out various places without dropping a bundle, but bartenders did seem less than delighted when we presented coupons instead of cash. Both packages can be purchased at any HKTA Information and Gift Centre, HKTA member travel agency, and some hotel tour counters.

Bars, Clubs, and Discos

Hong Kong has bars and music lounges to suit every taste and budget and most don't even have a cover charge. Let's look at what the best hotels have to offer. The classy **Captain's Bar,** in the Mandarin Oriental on Connaught Road, Central (tel. 5-220-111), is a cozy place that caters to a young business crowd after working hours. Later on, tourists and well-dressed couples stop by when the regular bands start playing or drop in for a nightcap and the last set. In Tsimshatsui East, the Shangri-La Hotel's **Music Room** (tel. 3-721-2111) is splashier, with a more boisterous crowd who favor its jazz combos. The **Golden Carp Bar,** in the lounge of the Holiday Inn Harbour View (tel. 3-721-5161), has jazz playing all night. The regal **Peninsula Hotel** (tel. 3-666-251) has the celebrated chandelier-lit, gilded lobby where colonists and visiting foreign dignitaries spent decades sizing up women who sat on the "available" side of grand stairway, hoping to find company over a spot of sherry. The Royal Garden Hotel's popular **Lalique Room** (tel. 3-721-5215) serves up delightful cocktail music by a gifted pianist who can croon out show tunes and international ballads. **Dicken's Bar** at the Excelsior Hotel, Causeway Bay (tel. 5-767-365), draws hotel guests and expatriate regulars with draft English beer, fish 'n' chips, and live entertainment ranging from country-western bands to jazz quartets (particularly popular with locals).

There are many alternatives to the top hotels. Hong Kong's once-notorious Wanchai district, R&R headquarters for the Sixth Fleet and other troops since the Korean War, is calmer since its Suzie Wong heyday but still the place to find tattoo parlors and lots of neon. The **Fringe Club,** on Lower Albert Road, Central (tel. 5-217-251), is a private club where residents have a drink and appreciate new comedians, experimental music, or visiting bands. Visitors can obtain a temporary "nightly membership" for HK$12 ($1.50) and check out the territory's newest trends. **The Penthouse,** on the 18th floor of the New World Hotel,

Tsimshatsui (tel. 3-694-111), features colorful drinks, an elegant crowd, and dancing to live bands under a light canopy simulating the Milky Way and solar system. **Rick's Café,** at 4 Hart Ave., Tsimshatsui (tel. 3-672-939), alternately features jazz and reggae, and there's dancing from 9 p.m. to 3 a.m. The crowd here is mostly young. **Ned Kelly's Last Stand,** at 11A Ashley Rd., Tsimshatsui (tel. 3-660-562), is a good, local favorite. They feature Dixieland in the evening and on Sunday afternoons sponsor jam sessions.

For pop music in a lounge atmosphere, try the aptly named **The In Place,** at 42 Hankow Rd., Tsimshatsui (tel. 3-739-6331), it's heavy on the funk but light on the drink prices. We liked **Scottie's,** another fairly priced drinking man's club in Lan Kwai Fong (tel. 5-234-685), the Greenwich Village scene in Central. If you want to try an English-style pub, try the **Kangaroo Pub** at 11 Chatham Rd., Tsimshatsui (tel. 3-423-8293), or **Mad Dogs,** at 33 Wyndham St., Central.

Lan Kwai Fong, a busy square off D'Aguilar Street that throbs with nightlife, has several Western-style bars with great dance tapes, including **1997,** a basement club; **California,** a terrific eatery (see "Dining") that rocks at night; and several others, making it the ideal locale for an old-fashioned pub crawl.

If it's pure disco you're looking for, the hot ones as we go to press are **Canton,** at 161-16 World Finance Centre, Harbour City; **Hot Gossip,** in the Houston Centre (tel. 3-723-7908); and for the gay crowd, **Disco Disco,** at 40 D'Aguilar St. in Lan Kwai Fong (tel. 5-235-863), possibly the hottest of all. At Disco Disco the cover charge runs HK$120 ($15.50) including two drinks, pretty typical for these places. All get going about 10:30 p.m. and stay open until 2 a.m. **The Talk of the Town,** atop the Excelsior Hotel, Causeway Bay (tel. 5-767-365), draws a tamer crowd with its laser lighting, harbor views, and a glass-enclosed window area offering disco atmosphere at conversational sound levels.

Chinese Nightclubs and Hostess Clubs

Chinese nightclubs are usually huge banquet rooms where Cantonese fare is dished up to the tune of Taiwanese pop stars or the clatter of mainland Chinese jugglers spinning coffee tables. It can be a fun or confusing leap into the culture gap, since most of the performances are in Chinese and music and dance are geared to locals. Although it may not be your thing, the acrobatic numbers are terrific and it can be a memorable night. One of the grandest clubs is the **Ocean Palace Restaurant and Nightclub** in Kowloon's Ocean Centre complex (tel. 3-677-111). If you want to skip dinner, a HK$20 ($2.50) charge plus a two-drink minimum (drinks can be very expensive) will cover admission. In any case, call ahead for reservations.

Hostess clubs are currently the biggest thing in Hong Kong. These are large, opulently appointed establishments featuring courteous and gorgeous women of every race who sit, chat (they're multilingual), and pamper you while the meter runs at a very high rate. You are obliged to buy your "hostess" a drink for every one you have, and to provide some food as well. If you find her not to your liking, ask a floor manager for someone else. It may seem a bit bizarre and the pampering continues after hours, but it's very popular with visitors, particularly Japanese and Arab businessmen. It is also very expensive, with cognac costing up to HK$900 ($115.50) a bottle and a typical bill running HK$875 ($112.25) per person. Definitely not for the budget-minded.

In its own league as the most popular of all hostess clubs is the 70,000-square-foot **Club Volvo,** at Mandarin Plaza in Tsimshatsui East (tel. 3-692-883). This lavishly designed lounge recently went public on the Hong Kong stock exchange, causing several heads to turn. **Club Deluxe,** at L-301 New World Centre, Tsimshatsui (tel. 3-721-0277); **Club Dai-Ichi,** at 257 Gloucester Rd. (tel. 5-831-0935); **China City Night Club,** on the fourth floor of the Peninsula Centre, TST East; and **Club Celebrity,** at 178-190 Lockhao Rd., Wanchai, are all popular. Potential patrons are warned to check prices before accepting seating in private VIP rooms, to scrutinize credit-card charges, and to ask prices before ordering brandy or champagne.

Performing Arts and Evening Activities

There are performances nearly every night, be they touring musical companies, theater, or European ballets. There are five resident theater companies, the Hong Kong Philharmonic Orchestra, a 12,500-seat Coliseum, and several cinemas showing old and new films in French, German, English, and Chinese. The annual **Hong Kong Arts Festival** (tel. 5-823-0230) is held in January and February with international groups such as opera from China, Panama Francis and his Savoy Sultans or the classical Waverly Consort, and modern dance troupes from around the world. Contact the HKTA (tel. 5-244-191) for information about current events, the annual **Hong Kong International Film Festival,** the biannual **Asian Arts Festival,** and the weekly cultural shows held in the New World Centre, Tsimshatsui, and in City Plaza, Taikoo Shing. If you feel like staying in, there are two **TV channels** broadcasting in English, as well as a plethora of imported American shows. When we were there, "Dallas" and "Dynasty" were the big shows!

Nightbirds can go **shopping** or take a tram ride through Central and Causeway Bay (see "Sightseeing" for information). One of the most scenic expeditions is the **tram ride** to the top of Victoria Peak, then a 1½-hour stroll along Lugard Road, which circles the peak offering views of the skyscrapers and luxury mansions below. You can join an organized **harbor tour** or reserve seats on a floating Chinese nightclub, ferryboats set up for Cantonese banquets and dancing to local Canton pop crooners that are popular for family celebrations. The HKTA keeps updated information about these and other activities including street fairs, Night Markets, and religious celebrations.

7. THE NEW TERRITORIES, OUTLYING ISLANDS, AND DAY TRIPS TO CHINA

Hong Kong is only one of 236 islands in the South China Sea, many of which are worth exploring. Ferries run regularly from the Central piers to about half a dozen nearby islands. Others can be reached via inter-island ferries or by those with time to wait for their ship to come in. One of these islands is the tiny Portuguese protectorate of Macau, so near but another culture and country away. The New Territories is the huge peninsula south of China's Guangdong province that is part of the British Crown Colony of Hong Kong, but so recently developed that its very "newness" makes it worthy of inspection by those hoping to catch a glimpse of the future. And then, of course, there's the day trip to China itself, a titillating taste of the exotic just an invisible border away.

EXPLORING THE NEW TERRITORIES: Most visitors to Hong Kong, having completed a tour of Central, Kowloon, and Repulse Bay, consider that they've seen nearly all of the country. A few inquisitive travelers include Aberdeen, Stanley, and the Outlying Islands as part of their itinerary, but very few people explore the zone where Hong Kong is embracing the future, the vast expanse of land bordering mainland China called the New Territories.

The contrast of agrarian villages and densely populated industrial towns symbolizes the Chinese past and future. However, for the present one can still savor the pattern of ancient Chinese life in a tour of this fascinating zone.

Shatin

Perhaps the most staggering introduction to the New Territories is a visit to the burgeoning city of Shatin. This new city of over half a million was only begun in the 1970s. Prior to that the area was largely agricultural: rice paddies and small family farms dominated the landscape. Today it's a booming metropolis where the sounds of jackhammers, trucks, and other heavy equipment create a cacophony that's the New China in the making. The place has the feel of a sci-fi future, but in this booming sector such cities seem strangely organic. If anything, Shatin is emblematic of the shifting momentum of manufacturing to Asia.

Tao Fong Shan

Ironically, one of the most serene spots in the New Territories is a Chinese Christian retreat overlooking Shatin. Tao Fong Shan is a lovely, cool, pine-covered mountain that plays host to more birds and pilgrims than trucks and construction. The retreat was founded by a Norwegian priest who also built a Chinese-style church and organized a porcelain workshop. Guests are invited to stay overnight, with very spartan rooms renting for HK$90 ($11.50) for a single and HK$145 ($18.50) for a double. The workshop is open Monday through Saturday from 9 a.m. to 12:30 p.m. and 2 to 5 p.m., and on Sunday from 2 to 5 p.m.

Lok Ma Chau

Nearly all tours make a stop at the hilltop post overlooking mainland China. Back in the days when China was off-limits to foreigners, this was undoubtedly more of a thrill, but today it looks just like other parts of Hong Kong and in no way gives visitors a clue as to the essence of the real China. The only thing that's kind of fun are the kitschy souvenir stands at the bottom of the hill.

Ching Chung Koon Temple

One of the more interesting Taoist shrines in the New Territories is Ching Chung Koon, located next to a new highway and housing development on the outskirts of Tuen Mun. The grounds at this religious complex are interestingly landscaped with rock gardens (for meditation), ceremonial pavilions, and ancestral pavilions that contain photographs of departed souls. Ceremonies are frequently held to appease the spirits of dead ancestors. If you need to get a bite to eat after watching one of these ceremonies, you'll find a vegetarian outlet in the first pavilion (on the right) after you enter the main grounds.

Wong Tai Sin Temple

Located in Kowloon but visited on many New Territories tours is Hong Kong's most renowned fortune-telling temple, Wong Tai Sin. Tai Sin was a shepherd who was later venerated for his ability to cure the sick. Believers visit the shrine in hopes of having the spirit of Wong Tai Sin lend its special curative powers. Other supplicants visit the temple to consult the spiritual powers about their fate in business, love, and family affairs.

The air at the temple is redolent with the scent of sandlewood incense, which is considered the medium that carries hopeful messages to the spirits. Ascend the main stairs to the main pavilion; there, worshippers shake sticks from a bamboo case until one emerges. Each stick has a number and a corresponding fortune. Believers take that number and visit one of the numerous fortune-tellers in the booths outside the temple complex. There one can have a palm or face read, sticks interpreted, tarot cards examined, or (our absolute favorite) have birds peck out a fortune, all for HK$100 ($12.75) to HK$200 ($25.50). Locals actually pay about 10% of that amount, but they try to soak foreigners! Hunt around for a fortune-teller who speaks English or ask your guide, if you have one, to make the deal and translate.

The HKTA offers a popular, six-hour guided coach tour called "The Land Between" which explores the New Territories from Kowloon to the border of the People's Republic of China. The tour costs HK$200 ($25.50) for adults, HK$155 ($20) for children under 12 years, and includes a Chinese banquet lunch. Contact the HKTA (tel. 3-722-555 or 5-244-191) for reservations and information.

THE OUTLYING ISLANDS: Visitors who are weary of shopping and the urban landscape can easily flee Hong Kong for the Outlying Islands, three of which lie southwest and are easily accessible. Lantau, Cheung Chau, and Lamma are home to a mixture of fishermen, farmers, and a few new towns of urban workers who commute by boat to Hong Kong city.

CHEUNG CHAU. Just 40 minutes from Central and the smallest of these islands, Cheung Chau is made up of densely populated, bustling fishing and boatbuilding villages. The colorful northern harbor is thick with characteristic Chinese junks and sampans, built by local craftsmen from memory in the traditional style. The small village where the ferry lands is for pedestrians only, and a remarkable contrast to the world of Hong Kong one hour away.

There are several small Buddhist temples, the best of which is the oldest, the 200-year-old **Pak Tai Temple** (a ten-minute walk left of the ferry pier), built to honor Pak Tai, the god known as the Emperor of Dark Heaven and protector of all seafarers. Two powerful statues flank his effigy, the one to your right having a "Thousand Mile Eye" capable of seeing that distance, the one to the left having a "Favorable Wind Ear." Pak Tai is a favorite of the local fishermen, who look to him for blessings on the sea.

Each May there is a week-long **Festival of the Bun Hills,** a celebration including religious ceremonies, Chinese opera, costumed performances, and a marvelous parade of local women wearing hills of steamed buns as headdresses. Check the HKTA for the exact dates of the annual Cheung Chau Bun Festival.

LANTAU. Lantau is the largest of the Outlying Islands, with a population of only 16,000. It's primarily uninhabited, except for the small development at the main port of Silvermine, scattered weekend villas of the affluent, and a few fishing villages. **Tai O,** with its own ferry service on Sunday and holidays, is the most interesting fishing village. Tai O is a sleepy little hamlet where houses are built on stilts above a river that splits the village and that locals cross routinely in a small ferry.

The best reason to visit Lantau is the Buddhist **Po Lin Monastery,** situated on a plateau beneath the peak of Mount Phoenix. Built in 1921, the Po Lin compound is centered around a large main temple with three Grand Buddhas. You enter through the Protector Temple (photographs are forbidden here) and proceed to the original temple behind it. It houses a splendid white-jade Buddha. The smell of flowers and incense fill the air, sounds of clanging and chanting soothe the ear, and a sense of peace pervades this place, wooing you to stay. Visitors have an opportunity to do just that; the monastery offers spartan accommodations for HK$120 ($15.50) per night, including your own board to sleep on and three vegetarian meals. You can also come for a meal only, but either way, guests should check in at the monastery office.

The monastery will soon boast an amazing 34-meter- (110-foot-) tall bronze Buddha, which will sit on a hill above Po Lin on a huge lotus-shaped concrete base. Created at a cost of HK$60 million ($7.7 million) this Buddha will be the largest in Asia, and is designed to be seen from Macau. It is now being built in China and will be installed in late 1989.

LAMMA. The least celebrated of these islands, Lamma is a bucolic retreat for hikers or those seeking soothing walks away from it all. It is a pleasant 45-minute cruise from Central and has a school, several restaurants at each of its two ports, some homes and gazebos for viewing, and a one-person-wide cement path that belts the islands connecting both ports. The first thing you'll see are the seafood restaurants next to the **Sok Kwun Wan** ferry pier, each displaying the day's catch swimming in tanks. Our favorites are the **Lamma Regent** and the **Peach Garden,** both with pretty balconies overlooking the sea.

An interesting walk (it will take about 45 minutes and the ferries run about every 1½ hours) is to follow the cement path around the island to the main port of **Yung Shuw Wan.** Leaving Sok Kwun Wan you'll hear the clatter and chatter of the mah jong players, who gamble for high stakes in the tea shops. Past the groves of banana and papaya trees the path leads through dry brush resembling the Greek countryside. In 30 minutes of strolling you'll emerge to glimpse a stunning view of the rest of Lamma curved on the horizon before you. Shortly there's a gazebo from which to admire the blue tubing and industrial artscape of the majestic new hydroelectric plant that powers most of Hong Kong. The walk continues downhill through vegetable gardens filled with bok choy and Chinese herbs and past two-story homes with children playing out front. The traditional shops of Yung Shue Wan are stocked with medicine, dried herbs, religious icons, dried fish, and modern conveniences. Cars are prohibited and a jaunt from town to the ferry pier, again lined with a bevy of seafood restaurants, is a pleasant excursion.

Getting There

You can reach Lantau (the Silvermine Bay stop) and Cheung Chau by ferry from the Outlying Districts Services Pier, west of the waterfront promenade and the Jordan Road Vehicular Ferry Terminal. The ferries to Lamma leave from the Central Harbour Services Pier next to this; both are a short walk from the Connaught Road Central MTR station. **Ferry service** is frequent, particularly on weekends when many locals head to the beach, and most fares are less than HK$8 ($1). Contact the Hong Kong and Yaumati Ferry Company (tel. 5-423-081) or the HKTA (tel. 3-722-5555) for schedule and fare information.

Several tour operators offer day trips to Lantau for about HK$300 ($38.50) for a day cruise by junk including lunch and a swim, or 15% less with ferry transportation; and Cheung Chau for about HK$250 ($32) for a day trip including lunch at the Warwick Hotel and use of their beach facilities, or 20% more if combined with a trip to Lantau. Contact **Gray Line Tours of Hong Kong Ltd.** (tel. 3-687-111), **Winston Tours** (tel. 3-664-440), **President Tours and Travel** (tel. 3-694-808), or your hotel concierge for more information.

DAY TRIPS TO CHINA: Several tour operators offer day trips to destinations in southern China, an interesting if not altogether satisfying way to sample this country's riches. The most popular trip is to the Shekou Industrial Zone, just over the border in **Shenzhen** (to visit industrial sites and a small museum) and then onto **Guangzhou** (formerly known as Canton), the province's capital. It's a bustling city of motorcycles, miniskirts, billboards, and superb expense-account, gourmet Cantonese restaurants that will recall the Hong Kong left behind. The day trips include guided tours to the Sun Yat-Sen Memorial, Guangzhou Zoo, Six Baiyan Temple, and other sites that begin to give visitors a glimpse of the PRC. Most tours use the hydrofoil to reach Shekou and return to Hong Kong via the Kowloon Railway; costs average HK$850 ($109) for adults, HK$635 ($81.50) for children, including visas, transportation, and lunch.

Another popular day trip is to **Zhongshan,** the birthplace of Dr. Sun Yat-Sen. This tour uses the hydrofoil to **Macau,** pauses for a brief tour of the Portuguese colony, and proceeds overland to the rural district of Zhongshan, where various landmarks from Sun Yat-Sen's life and local villages are visited. (When we took this tour in 1980 there was a restaurant that displayed dried cat and dog skins outside to prove to clients that their meat was fresh!) This tour costs from HK$540 ($62.75) to HK$600 ($77), depending on transportation and day of departure, about one-third less for children.

The **Gray Line of Hong Kong Ltd.** (tel. 3-687-111) is one of many companies offering day trips and two- through six-day packages to China; contact your hotel concierge or a local travel agent for more information.

Full Tours to China

Visitors who are using Hong Kong as a springboard for a full-fledged China tour can obtain visas for independent travel to dozens of cities with little problem. The official PRC travel bureau is the **China International Travel Service,** on the sixth floor, Tower II, of the South Seas Centre, 75 Mody Rd., Tsimshatsui East (tel. 3-721-5317), or in Room 809-809B of Swire House, 11 Chater Rd., Central (tel. 5-810-4282). Their Hong Kong affiliate is the **China Travel Service (HK) Ltd.,** with offices on the fourth floor of CTS House, 78-83 Connaught Rd., Central (tel. 5-853-3888), or on the first floor of Alpha House, 27 Nathan Rd., Kowloon (tel. 3-667-201).

Other travel agents who can expedite the issuance of China visas are **Lap Ming International Travel Services,** at the East Ocean Centre, Room 601, 98 Granville Rd., Tsimshatsui (tel. 3-723-8803); **EBM Tours Ltd.,** in the Four Seas Building, Room 802B, 208-212 Nathan Rd., Kowloon (tel. 3-721-2259); or the budget-oriented **Time Travel Services,** Block A, 16th floor, Chungking Mansion, 40 Nathan Rd., Kowloon (tel. 3-723-9993). The **Hong Kong Student Travel Bureau Ltd.,** Star House, Room 1024, Tsimshatsui (tel. 5-414-841 or 3-721-3269), is an excellent agency that can arrange for visas and issue fair-priced air tickets to China. Prices range from HK$90 ($11.50) to HK$250 ($32) for visa processing, which takes about three days.

8. EXPLORING MACAU

It seems rather anomalous that in the latter half of the 20th century there should exist a country on the Asian coastline that still looks to Portugal, a colonial power of the 16th century, for administration and protection. Yet that is the status of Macau, a 15-square-kilometer country founded in 1557 as "Cidade do Nome de Deus de Macau, Não Há Outra Mais Leal" (City of the Name of God, Macau, There is None More Loyal).

Today Macau's 350,000 residents (95% Chinese with only 3% European) host over five million tourists annually, most of whom are drawn by its casinos, although a few visit its beaches on two outer islands, Taipa and Coloane. An increasing amount of the country's real estate is dedicated to industry, but the still-rich legacy of colonial and art deco architecture makes Macau's streets a joy to explore. Macau also has its own cuisine, with a melding of Chinese and Portuguese tastes and ingredients.

HISTORY: Early 16th-century Portuguese explorers were the first Europeans to sail into the South China Sea after the voyages of Vasco da Gama. By the mid-16th century they had established a territory, under the protection of the King of Portugal, that would ultimately become the Western foothold for all trading with China and Japan. As colonists spread the gospel of commerce with the West, Portuguese missionaries began to disseminate Christian dogma into the greater part of East Asia.

Important links were made in Macau, including the United States' first Treaty of Trade and Friendship with China (supposedly, the tea dumped into Boston's harbor during the Tea Party was loaded in Macau). After these agreements were formed (creating "treaty ports" such as Canton), Macau became a less important center of exchange. It was soon transformed into a lavish summer residence for the taipans who, by agreement with the Chinese, were allowed to winter only in nearby Canton.

Macau's influence declined precipitously after the mid-19th century, when the British established a foothold in nearby Hong Kong. Since then Macau has become a secondary manufacturing zone that, like Hong Kong, will soon break free of its European ties and become one of China's special autonomous regions. The current plan is to return Macau to Chinese control in 1999; until then it remains a Chinese territory under the administration of the Portuguese.

A trip to Macau can be treated either as a day excursion or an extended visit, with fine accommodations in Macau and on Taipa. If, as we suggest, you plan on a one-day outing, including a visit to the major sites with a trip to Taipa (for lunch) and a visit to a casino, plan on leaving in the morning and returning at about 8 p.m.

ORIENTATION: The tiny peninsula of Macau juts out from the western bank of the Pearl River estuary. Hong Kong is located about 64 km (38 miles) away on the eastern bank and Canton is approximately 113 km (68 miles) upriver, to the north, in mainland China. The city of Macau is located on a land mass that is joined by a series of bridges and causeways to two outer islands, Taipa and, farther south, Coloane.

All boats dock at the ferry terminal on the east coast along Avenida Amizade. Continuing south on the same thoroughfare are the Mandarin Oriental Hotel, the casino at the Hotel Lisboa, and nearby on the southern tip of the peninsula, the statue of Governor Amaral and the entrance to the Macau-Taipa Bridge. Most of the tourist sites are in the center of the town, generally atop the city's low hills. The city is quite small by Asian standards, but is still best navigated by taxi or private car. Walking is a must in the old section of town, particularly along the main street, Avenida do Conselherio Ferreira da Almeida, which runs north-south through the middle of Macau and terminates at the entrance to the Taipa bridge. Off the main street, but running east-west, is Rua Tomás Viera, which leads south to the ruins of St. Paul's Cathedral and the Monte Fort, and north to the lovely Camões Garden and the old Protestant cemetery. The other area of interest is the southeastern tip of land, overlooking tiny Praia Grande Bay. Here one finds the 13th-century A-Ma temple (on the east coast road, Rua do Almirante Sérgio), the Governor's Residence, and the Pousada de São Tiago Hotel on Avenida da República.

Although Portuguese is the official language of Macau, it is Cantonese that is mostly heard on the street. In the tourist trade English is the lingua franca.

Useful Information

There are two **Department of Tourism information offices:** a counter at the ferry terminal (tel. 853/555-424), open daily when the boats operate, and an office at 1 Travessa do Paiva (tel. 853-77-218), open Monday through Friday. Try to pick up a copy of the Macau guidebook and the "Macau Is Waiting for You" map; both are excellent, free of charge, and published by the Department of Tourism.

You need a passport to enter Macau, but unless you plan on staying longer than 90 days, you won't need a visa. *Note:* The Macanese monetary instrument is called the **pataca** (1 pataca = 100 avos). If you're coming from Hong Kong you won't have to worry, because the pataca is roughly equal to the Hong Kong dollar (with a possible variation of up to 10%). Vendors commonly call it the **Macau dollar (M$).** There are change booths and banks all over the island, including the ferry terminal. The General Post Office is located on Senate Square along Avenida Almeida Riverio near the public library. If you call Hong Kong, the **country code is 852.**

GETTING THERE: Most tourists to Macau arrive from Hong Kong or Kowloon by all manner of seagoing vessel (there is no airport): jetfoils (tel. 852/5-457-021 in Hong Kong for reservations and information), hydrofoils and jet catamarans (tel. 852/5-218-302), Hovercraft ferries (tel. 852/5-423-081), high-speed ferries (tel. 852/5-815-2299), and slow-boat ferries (tel. 852/5-457-021) ply the waters of the South China Sea every day, day and night. Most boats depart from the main terminal in Central, the ultramodern Macau Ferry Terminal in the Shun Tak Centre, on Connaught Road west of the Star Ferry. On the Kowloon side, Macau-bound boats call at the Shamshuipo pier, near the MTR station. The fastest boat is the jetfoil, which takes about 55 minutes; hydrofoils and jet-catamaran journeys run 75 minutes; high-speed ferries make the commute in 90 minutes, while the slow boat takes a leisurely 2½ hours. Check the schedule for current operating hours, but count on boats leaving every half hour; one-way fares range from an average of HK$80 ($10.25) for a jetfoil (you are allowed to carry hand-luggage only) to HK$34 ($4.50) for the regular ferry. There is a Hong Kong government tax of HK$15 ($2) on all fares. Tickets can be purchased at the ferry terminals, Ticketmate outlets, and at the major MTR stations in Hong Kong and Kowloon. On Macau, tickets are sold at the ferry terminal, S.T.D.M. ticket outlets, and in the lobby of the Hotel Lisboa.

GETTING AROUND: There are many options available, though if you are short on time, consider renting a **taxi.** Rates are low with an average crosstown fare equalling M$7.80 ($1); if you plan on visiting the islands by car, there are surcharges of M$5.50 (70¢) for trips to Taipa, M$11 ($1.50) to Coloane. **Pedicabs** can be rented by the hour for about M$35 ($4.50), although many drivers will not climb the city's hills. For M$25 ($3.25) an hour you can rent a **bicycle,** an ideal way of seeing the city (you are not allowed to cross any of the bridges by bike). Rental outlets are centered around the entrance to St. Joseph's College at the corner of Rua da Praia Grande and Rua do Campo and also next to the São Francisco Barracks and Garden. We like the local **bus system,** which costs a mere M$.85 (10¢) and runs in town and on the islands. On arrival, you can pick up the no. 3 bus, which runs south along Avenida da Amizade and into the main section of town. Self-drive locomation is usually by **Mini-Moke,** an open-air Jeep. The Macau Mokes' office is located in the ferry terminal on Macau (tel. 78-851); plan on spending M$340 ($43.50) per day, including insurance. Avis also rents Mokes at similar rates from their office in Macau's Mandarin Oriental Hotel (tel. 555-686).

ACCOMMODATIONS: If you choose to stay overnight in Macau, there is a range of lodging options from the luxurious, starting at HK$825 ($105), for the casino crowd, to the simple at HK$185 ($23) that will barely bite into your budget. Most hotels charge an extra 10% for service, while all charge 5% tax; the international hotels tend to quote rates in Hong Kong dollars.

The paragon of luxury in Macau is the Mandarin Oriental, located on Avenida da Amizade (tel. 853/567-888), a short distance south of the ferry terminal. This bright white high-rise was built in 1984 and is so well maintained that it still looks brand new. The elegant lobby combines Portuguese décor with Oriental motifs. Guest rooms are trimmed in dark hardwood and have all modern amenities. The hotel complex includes a pool, a 24-hour casino, and a sophisticated Grill restaurant. Single or double standard rooms face the mountains and cost HK$825 ($105.75), while the HK$1,050 ($134.50) deluxe rooms have views over the harbor.

Pousada de São Tiago, on Avenida da República, Fortaleza de São Tiago da Barra (tel. 853/78111), is the name of a 23-room, romantic hideaway that was built in 1629 as a fortress overlooking Macau's Praia Grande Bay. It was converted to a hotel built on five levels in 1981, and climbs up a bluff that is home to Macau's elite residents, including the Portuguese governor. The grounds are planted with gorgeous age-old trees and lined with flowers, with a small, inviting pool overlooking the harbor and nearby islands. Our favorite part of the hotel is the entrance: a cave-like, barrel-vaulted stairway leading directly into the lobby (you'll understand if you visit!). There is even an 18th-century chapel within the hotel complex. The interior of the Pousada de São Tiago is decorated with European tiles and Portuguese furnishings, though all is not traditional: rooms are equipped with television and mini-bar, and air-conditioned. All rooms face the harbor, with rates ranging from HK$900 ($115.50) to HK$1,050 ($134.50), depending on size and location. If you eat at the hotel's fine Fortaleza Grill, make sure to sample the African chicken, a Macanese specialty. From the port, take a taxi or the hotel limo (HK$40, $5) to get to the Pousada de São Tiago as it's on the extreme southwest tip of the peninsula.

Among the better in-town alternatives is the 380-room **Hotel Royal,** at 2,4 Estrada da Vitória (tel. 853/552-222), where standard double rooms rent for HK$700 ($89.75). The Royal is particularly popular with Japanese tourists; it's well run and relatively quiet for its center-city location.

The colonia-era **Hotel Bela Vista,** at 8 Rua Comendador Kou Ho Neng (tel. 853/573-821), overlooking Praia Grande Bay, was built in 1875 as a private house, later converted to a sanitorium and hospital and still later to a hotel. Today it retains its character, with high ceilings, art deco furniture, and lovely balconies and terraces, but it is definitely old, worn, and in a state of disrepair. If restored, as the government promises in the near future, it would be fabulous. As is, it is a richly atmospheric inn that is clean enough and relatively inexpensive: single rooms are M$185 ($23.75) while a standard double runs M$265 ($34).

DINING: Macanese food is a complex combination of colonial cooking styles. Most of the dishes combine ingredients and techniques from Portugal, southern Africa, India (especially Portuguese Goa), Malacca (in Malaysia), and of course, China. Although the Portuguese cultural influence in Macau is waning, Macanese food is in no danger of extinction, for it represents a long history of Asian and European intermingling and is a gustatory delight.

Our favorite dining in Macau is south in Taipa (bus no. 11 will take you there), where one can still find authentic Portuguese and Macanese cuisine. One of the best eateries is the **Galo Restaurante** at 47 Rua do Cunha (tel. 27-318). Linda Mota, cook, hostess, and owner, turns out delicious specialties such as caldo verde, a Portuguese green vegetable soup, carangueijos a Macau (Macau crabs), rancho Portuguese beans in a slightly piquant sauce with potatoes, carrots, and smokey Portuguese-style sausage, and homemade ice cream and cake. A complete meal for two, including a bottle of Portuguese wine, will cost approximately M$280 ($36). Open daily for lunch and dinner.

Just down the street and around the corner from Galo is the excellent **Cozinha Pinocchio,** 4 Rua do So (tel. 27-128), a garden restaurant that also specializes in Macanese food. Among the specialties are back-opened hot prawns, roast pigeon and quail, cod stew, African chicken, and hot prawns with garlic and salt. Like Galo, the ingredients are locally harvested, such as prawns, or imported from Portugal, such as sparkling vinho verde. Pinocchio's is more expensive than the Galo, with a meal for two running about M$335 ($43). Closed Monday; reservations are suggested.

Also on Taipa is **Panda,** 4-8 Rua Carlos Eugénio (tel. 27-338). Here one finds similar Portuguese-style preparations with such dishes as curry crab, spicy giant prawns, and Macau sole at prices that are similar to Galo. Panda is open daily for lunch and dinner; they offer free car service in the evenings to the Hotel Lisboa.

Traveling farther south to Coloane Island, just north of Coloane town, is **Pirão** (tel. 28-189) where two can dine on Portuguese and Macanese specialties for even less; expect to pay M$225 ($28.75) for lunch or dinner for two.

In-town dining is a more formal affair at such restaurants as **Fat Siu Lau,** 64 Rua da Felicidade (tel. 573-585), established in 1903, and **Fook Lam Moon,** 57 Avenue da Amizade (tel. 86-883). The former is a palace of Macanese specialties such as roast pigeon and quail and various styles of prawns and crabs, while the latter is Macau's best Chinese outlet, specializing in Cantonese cuisine, such as shark's fin and roast squab, with a daytime emphasis on dim sum. Expect to pay upward of M$465 ($59.50) for two for dinner or lunch.

Tung Hoi East Ocean Seafood Restaurant, 35A-B Rua da Praia Grande (tel. 562-313), on the southern waterfront, serves delicious Cantonese seafood entrees from a large menu. The slick interior is home to many in the commercial and diplomatic community, especially at lunch time. A meal for two should run about $375 ($48).

Budget Macanese dining is best done at **Riquexo,** also known as Pak Kai, at 69 Avenue Sidónio Pais (tel. 76-294). Most entrees, such as a Portuguese beef stew and rice, cost about M$20 ($2.50), and are served cafeteria style in a cramped dining room inside a modest shopping arcade. Riquexo is open daily for lunch only.

WHAT TO SEE AND DO: The sights in Macau relate mostly to the territory's colonial past, such as the eloquent ruins of St. Paul's cathedral (the largest in Asia), with just a few Chinese highlights, including the A-Ma temple; however, we're more intrigued by the early-20th-century architecture now being recognized for its marvelous originality.

Walking Tour of Central Macau

To simplify your orientation, start your tour on top of a hill (getting there by taxi), at the **Monte Fort** atop the Citadel of São Paulo, right in the middle of the city. This fortress was built between 1617 and 1626 by the Jesuits of Chunambo as part of a complex containing a college and the monumental St. Paul's Cathedral. The fort served its best purpose during the resistance against the invading Dutch forces in 1622, when cannon fire destroyed their armory and left a peaceful city to the Jesuits. The fort is open daily from dawn to dusk, and is a wonderful spot for a city view.

Just across the street from the fort are the ruins of **St. Paul's (São Paulo),** an early-17th-century church that was destroyed by a fire in 1835. The remaining stone façade and grand staircase date to 1602. St. Paul's was designed by an Italian Jesuit and built by Japanese Christian refugees. To the right of the church was a Jesuit college, the first such European institution in East Asia, where such missionaries as Matteo Ricci studied Chinese prior to his posting to Peking's Royal Ming Court. In its day St. Paul's was the most ornate and highly revered Christian church in East Asia and crowned the island of Macau. Today it's the city's favorite photo spot and on Sunday, from 10:30 a.m. to noon, traditional Portuguese folk dances are performed for visitors.

The next stop on the walking tour is a cluster of three sites: the old Protestant Cemetery, the Luís de Camões Museum, and the Camões Garden. To get there, walk down (west) Rua Horta da Companhia until you reach St. Anthony's Church. Turn right on Rua Coelho do Amaral and to your left will be the gate leading into the **Protestant Cemetery.** This quiet spot in Macau was established by the East India Company in 1814 and primarily holds the remains of English, Dutch, and American traders and sailors who died while working on the China trade routes. To the left of the gate is an Anglican church where there are English-language services every Sunday. It is fascinating history to read the inscriptions on the tombstones.

Next door is the **Luís de Camões Museum,** which once was the Macau headquarters for the East India Company Select Committee. Today it houses a fine collection of colonial-era paintings, including Chinese coastal landscapes by the 18th-century artist George Chinnery (who is buried next door), exquisite portraits of Mandarins, and other superb traditional Chinese brush paintings. The museum is open daily except Wednesday from 11 a.m. to 5 p.m.; admission is M$1.50 (20¢).

Continue north to **Camões Garden,** an 18th-century park that was once connected to the house of the chairman of the British East India Company. It is now a lively meeting place for Macanese of all ages who gather in the shade of the huge banyan trees.

Other Macau Sights

Among the many Chinese temples, the complex devoted to the goddess of seafarers and fishermen, **A-Ma,** is both the oldest and most important. The Portuguese cited this 13th-century shrine when they landed, giving rise to the name "A-Ma-gao" (Bay of A-Ma), which became "Macau." Our favorite image in the temple is the polychrome carved-stone Chinese junk in bas-relief, which is supposed to be the ship that transported the goddess from China to Heaven by way of Macau. The Temple of A-Ma is on the western coast road (Rua do Almirante Sérgio) at the base of Barra Hill.

The other Chinese temple of note is at the opposite end of the city, just off Avenida do Coronel Mesquita. The **Temple of Kun Iam** is also dedicated to a woman, the Queen of Heaven and the Goddess of Mercy. This complex is interesting for many reasons, paramount for Americans is that the "most favored nation" treaty with China was signed here by Chinese Viceroy Yi and Ambassador Caleb Cushing in 1844. Another important Western visitor represented here in typical Chinese fashion is Marco Polo (with lots of facial hair and big, round eyes) in a case of the 18 wise men of China. As for the temple itself, it is thought to date from the 15th century, during the period of the Ming Dynasty, and is the most elegant of all Macau's Buddhist shrines. As you enter, you'll pass two stone lions with stone balls in their mouths. It is considered good luck to turn these to the left three times. After entering the main temple, the third altar is devoted to Kun Iam, with the goddess attired as a bride. Local Buddhist devotees come to the temple for fortune-telling; you can read the future by shaking joss sticks or buying fortune cards.

The last sight on this tour of Macau is the central city itself, from the **art deco houses** in the São Lázaro quarter down to the earlier 20th-century structures along Avenida Feriera de Almeida. To fully appreciate the architectural diversity here, one has to walk up and down the side streets. One such Moorish deco abode, on Avenida Sidónio Pais, is the **Sun Yat-Sen Memorial Home,** commemorating the time when the founder of modern China practiced medicine in Macau (the house is open for tours daily except Tuesday from 10 a.m. to 1 p.m.). The buildings on Avenida Feriera de Almeida are reminiscent of 18th-century colonial India, and after their final restoration, are slated to be occupied by government offices. Among the best examples of classical Macanese architecture is the **Leal Senado,** or Loyal Senate building, across from the post office on Avenida Almeida Riviero.

Gambling

The activity that interests many visitors to Macau is gambling, presented here in huge variety. The **Hotel Lisboa** has a 24-hour, twin-story casino; there is a 24-hour casino at the **Mandarin Oriental Hotel.** At the **Jai-lai Casino** across from the ferry terminal, games are played weeknights and during the afternoon on the weekend (admission is M$1.50, 20¢) and there is gambling on the west side of town, on Rua das Lorchas in the **Macau Palace Floating Casino.**

In addition, there is greyhound and harness racing, respectively, at the **Canidrome** on Avenida General Castelo Branco every Thursday through Sunday from 8 p.m. and on Sunday at the **Macau Trotting Club** on Taipa.

CHAPTER VI

INTRODUCING
INDONESIA

□ □ □

1. INTRODUCTION
2. INDONESIAN CULTURE
3. SUGGESTED ITINERARIES
4. GETTING THERE AND GETTING AROUND
5. THE ABC'S OF INDONESIA
6. RECOMMENDED READING

The varied people and cultures that welcome visitors with a warm *Selamat Datang* ("Welcome to Indonesia") make Indonesia one of Southeast Asia's most fascinating destinations. Miles of rice paddies tilled by water buffalo; gold, silk, and batik fabrics; ornate architecture of Javanese sultans' palaces; hibiscus and coconut palms fringing Bali's white sand beaches; orangutans hurtling through the dense Sumatran jungle; New Guinea's highlands farmed by bare-breasted Dani women—all are images of this most exotic place. The state motto "Bhinneka Tunggal Ika" (Unity in Diversity) neatly sums up the 13,677 islands that make up the young Republic of Indonesia. Go now and experience the authentic, unique, traditional life that still exists in a nation undergoing rapid modernization.

1. INTRODUCTION

The vast majority of Westerners know nothing about Indonesia's geography. The five main islands of Sumatra, Java, Kalimantan (Borneo), Sulawesi (Celebes), and Irian Jaya (western New Guinea) and 30 smaller archipelagos form the largest archipelago in the world, spread over 5,193,460 km² (1,870,000 square miles). Approximately 12,700 of these islands are uninhabited, and 7,600 are not even named! From Sumatra in the Indian Ocean, at the western border, to Papua New Guinea in the east, Indonesia extends for 5,100 km (3,060 miles), and from north to south it covers 2,000 km (1,200 miles). Less than 100 miles separates Sumatra from Malaysia and Irian Jaya from Australia.

The majority of land consists of rugged volcanic islands blanketed in rain forest. Heavy rainfall and a tropical climate (Sumatra straddles the equator) dictate its use: 90% of the arable land is devoted to rice cultivation, and 6% is pasture. Indonesia has a tremendous range of flora and fauna including the world's largest flower, the *Rafflesia arnoldi* (unique to Sumatra) and the last extant mem-

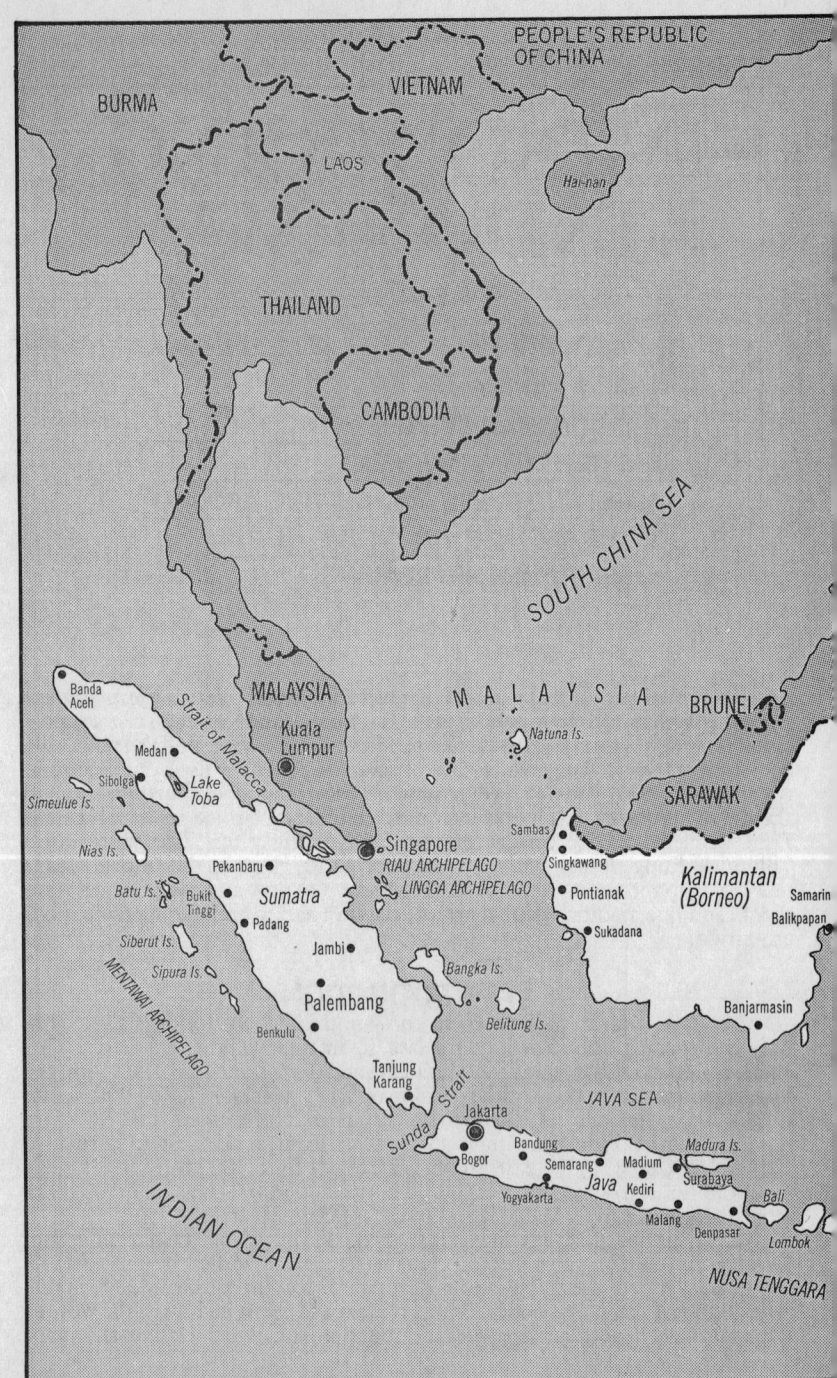

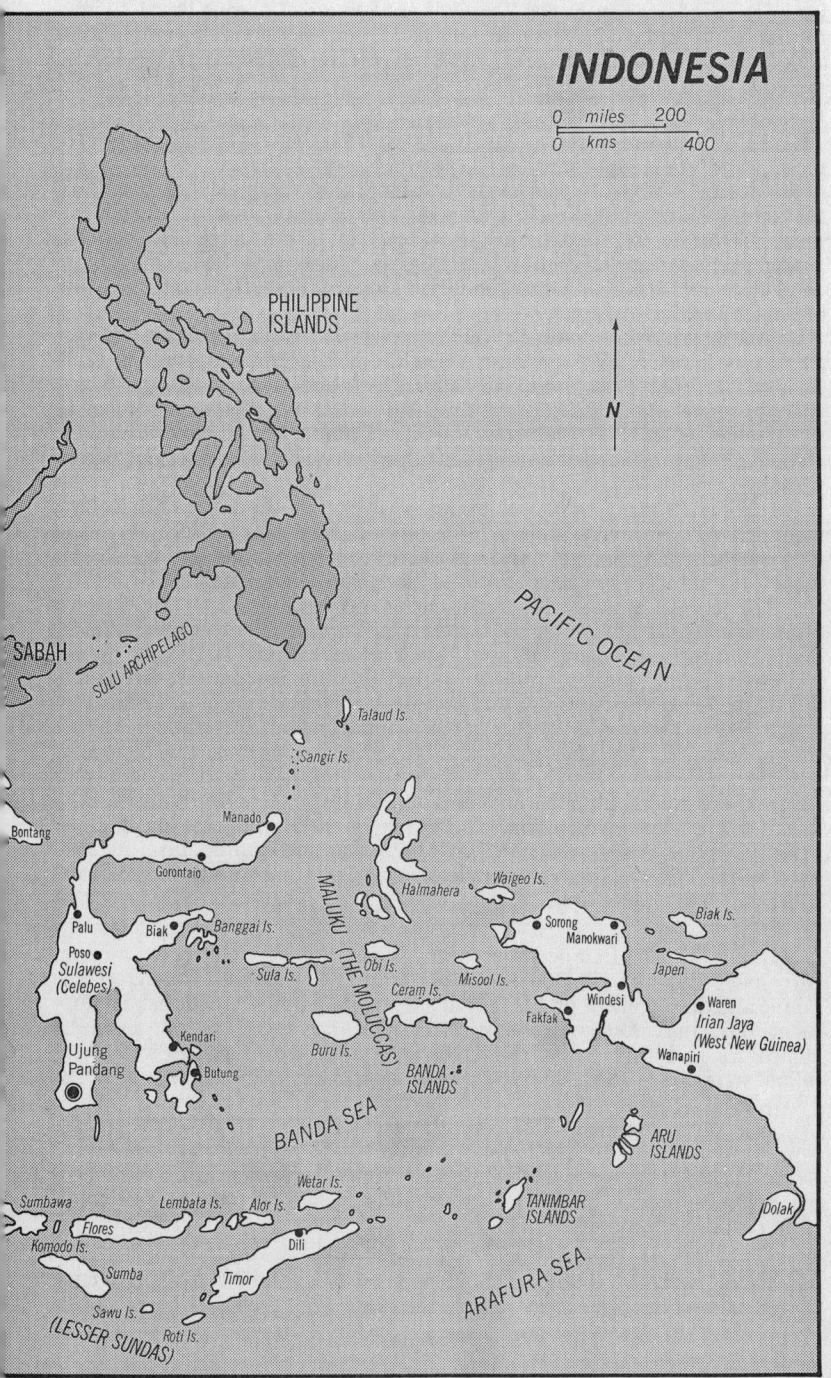

INDONESIA

0 miles 200
0 kms 400

N

PHILIPPINE
ISLANDS

PACIFIC OCEAN

SABAH

SULU ARCHIPELAGO

Talaud Is.

Sangir Is.

Bontang

Manado

Gorontalo

MALUKU (THE MOLUCCAS)

Halmahera

Waigeo Is.

Sorong
Manokwari

Biak Is.

Palu
Biak
Banggai Is.

Obi Is.

Japen

Poso
Sulawesi
(Celebes)

Sula Is.

Misool Is.

Ceram Is.

Windesi

Irian Jaya
(West New Guinea)

Kendari

Buru Is.

Fakfak

Waren

Ujung
Pandang

Butung

BANDA
ISLANDS

Wanapiri

BANDA SEA

ARU
ISLANDS

Wetar Is.

Sumbawa

Lembata Is.

Alor Is.

TANIMBAR
ISLANDS

Dolak

Flores

Dili

Komodo Is.

Sumba

Timor

Sawu Is.

Roti Is.

(LESSER SUNDAS)

ARAFURA SEA

ber of the dinosaur family, the *Varanus komodoensis* or Komodo lizard, unique to that island in the Nusa Tenggara chain. The archipelago is also rich in minerals, with petroleum, natural gas, uranium, nickel, tin, and copper currently mined.

THE PEOPLE: Indonesia's population, estimated to be 175 million in 1988, makes it the fifth-largest country in the world. However, the uneven distribution of population is more of a problem here than overpopulation. Java, only 6.9% of the country's land mass, currently supports 61% of the population. The government's Transmigrasi programs, begun 50 years ago by the Dutch, have been extended to encourage people to relocate from the heavily populated islands of Java and Bali to Sulawesi, Kalimantan, and Irian Jaya, lesser-populated ones with arable land or natural resources.

Indonesia's ethnic diversity, which appeals so to Western scholars and visitors, has been one of the major obstacles in uniting the Republic. There are three basic ethnic groups: the Hindu rice farmers of inland Java and Bali, the Malay coastal peoples who practice Islam, the tribal peoples who follow myriad traditional religions, and 366 other subgroups. The Chinese, brought in by European colonists to farm the plantations in the 16th century, are the largest foreign population.

Indonesia's many ethnic subgroups speak nearly 300 different languages, most derived from an Austronesian base and still commonly in use. Several have their own script and literature, and some have caste distinctions, so that different words are used according to the status of the person being addressed.

The national language, Bahasa Indonesia, was developed from an early form of Malay influenced by Arabic and Sanskrit and contains words from several Indonesian languages, Portuguese, and Dutch. It was adopted in 1928 by the All Indonesia Youth Congress, promoted in the fight for independence, particularly during the Japanese occupation, and became the official language in 1945.

Religious diversity is another of the country's hallmarks, although 85% of the population follow Islam, which was introduced to western coastal regions by traders from India and Persia in the 12th century. Freedom of worship is guaranteed as the first principle (Belief in God) of the state philosophy, Pancasila. Hinduism is prevalent on Bali, Christianity (about 60% Protestant and the rest mainly Catholic) is widely scattered, and Buddhism and Confucianism are practiced by the Chinese. Several tribal religions based on animism and ancestor worship flourish in isolated areas.

ECONOMY: The Indonesian economy is based on agriculture and mining. After independence from Dutch colonial rule in 1945 Indonesia faced great economic and development problems. Outside capital from international development programs, foreign investment by Japanese and U.S. multinational companies, and increased oil revenues have contributed to growth in the economic sector since 1967. In 1980 the average per capita income was $430; in 1987, $600.

Agriculture represents 25% of GNP and employs almost 60% of the population. Most are independent farmers, but the estate plantations begun by the Dutch have contributed to a lucrative export of rubber, coffee, tea, tobacco, copra, spices, and palm products. Timber is fast becoming Indonesia's second-largest export commodity.

TRANSMIGRASI: Residents of overpopulated Java and Bali have been transported to lesser-developed regions since the 1930s when the Dutch began a reset-

tlement program to match the archipelago's natural wealth with manpower. At
first the indigent, the unemployed, ex-convicts, and others who didn't succeed in
their home environment were forcibly shipped to the hinterlands to establish agricultural communities. After many years the Transmigrasi program has gained
in sophistication; training, counseling, and the simultaneous development of local infrastructure are supposedly provided to support all new settlements in
prime target areas such as Sulawesi and Irian Jaya.

HISTORY: The earliest record of the area's human life is Java Man, dating back
four million years to the Pleistocene era. In the Paleolithic era Negroid tribes migrated from Asia, most of them settling on New Guinea. Later these groups were
joined by Proto-Malay peoples and in the Bronze and Iron Age by Mongol
tribes.

Although Hindu traders from India had arrived on Sumatra and Java centuries before Christ, their greatest influence extended from the 5th through the
9th centuries when the Hindu kingdom of Srivijaya ruled Sumatra and the Malay
Peninsula from its capital in Palembang. On Java it later became the powerful
Mataram Kingdom. From the 10th to the 16th century the Buddhist Cailendra
Dynasties and the Majapahit Kingdom ruled central and east Java during a gold-
en age of art and architecture that produced such monuments as the Hindu complex at Pramabanan and the Buddhist sanctuary Borobudur.

After the 12th century Islam was also introduced and quickly accepted in
Java, and Muslim sultanates became part of the great Hindu kingdoms. Rivalries
developed and after many battles in the 17th century the Mataram Kingdom
emerged victorious in central and eastern Java, the reign of Mataram Sultan
Agung (1613–1645) being considered the Islamic golden age in literature arts
and crafts in this area, although the artistic influence of Hindu India remained
strong.

During the early 16th century a Portuguese explorer discovered the Spice
Islands (Moluccas), but it was the United Dutch East India Company who developed a lucrative trade, establishing their capital at Batavia (Jakarta) in 1619. For
340 years the Netherlands East Indies was part of the Dutch Empire, except for a
brief interlude during the Napoleonic wars from 1811 to 1815 when British
Lieutenant Governor Sir Thomas Stamford Raffles ruled. The annexation by the
Dutch was not easy and during the 19th century the complicated history of the
area reflected the rivalries between the colonial powers.

During World War II the Netherlands East Indies was occupied by the Japanese. After Japan's surrender, Nationalist forces proclaimed a new nation on August 17, 1945. The Dutch tried to reclaim their colony, but five years later peace
was negotiated through the United Nations Security Council. On August 17,
1950, it became the Republic of Indonesia, led by President Soekarno. During
the early years of independence political strife and instability and a crumbling
economy culminated in 1965 when a group of army conspirators captured and
murdered six army generals who they said were planning a coup against the president. A military general, Soeharto, seized the opportunity to consolidate his
own power, blaming the consipiracy not on the army but on the national Communist party, the PKI. A wave of anti-Communist violence followed and eventually in 1968 Soeharto was appointed president. Former President Soekarno was
kept under house arrest until his death in 1970.

The first Five-Year Plan to achieve self-sufficiency in rice production was im-
plemented and inflation brought under control by the new military government.
General elections were finally held in 1977 and although the results were ques-
tioned by analysts and still are at every subsequent election most of the opposition has been restrained in recent years. After being elected to a fifth term in

March 1988 President Soeharto appointed a new vice-president, Soedharmono, along with 19 new cabinet members in what was hailed as an effort to rejuvenate his government.

2. INDONESIAN CULTURE

One of Indonesia's primary attractions is the incredible diversity of traditional cultures in each region. Although immigrants, invaders, and colonists have left their mark over the centuries, the family unit and personal and religious rituals are still remarkably traditional due to the guiding force of *adat* (custom).

ADAT: Societies as different as that of the highly sophisticated Javanese court or the Stone Age Asmat tribes guide themselves by *adat,* loosely translated as the customary laws or local traditions that govern daily life. Adat dictates customs such as the usage of high Javanese when speaking to elders, clan relationships among the Bataks of North Sumatra, buffalo worship ceremonies in Torajaland, the caste society of Bali, the matrilineal inheritance system of the Minangkabau, and most other facets of regional culture. Although most visitors will observe Indonesia's traditional cultures without fully comprehending their adat, an effort to follow the accepted etiquette will be rewarded.

ETIQUETTE: Indonesian culture puts great emphasis on small indications of mutual respect and courteous behavior. Following some simple rules will avoid offense. For instance, Indonesians consider the soles of the feet unclean; pointing your toes or feet at someone is considered impolite. Do not sit cross-legged, especially during an official government visit. In most Muslim cultures the left hand is considered unclean, so use only the right hand for eating or passing objects to other people. The head and back are considered sensitive; it is an insult to touch someone on the head, and you should avoid the Western pat on the back.

If you are making an official or business call, coffee or tea will be served usually just before the visit is about to end. You should wait to drink until your host invites you and then take only small sips.

Indonesians are very careful not to offend or disturb other people, so they will rarely bring up unpleasant or disagreeable things or directly say "no." Anger is rarely displayed; it is very rude, offensive, and ineffective for Westerners to respond with anger or raised voices to public or private problems. Always act in such a way that the person you are dealing with may save face and you'll find that most problems are easily resolved.

THE ARTS: Many of the arts popularly thought of as Indonesian come from the cultures of Java and Bali and spread to the other islands through trade and tourism. The best known of these are the music of the *gamelan* orchestra, the drama of the *wayang* shadow play, Javanese classical dance, the intricate paintings of Hindu mythology, and the floral print of batik fabrics.

The Music of the Gamelan

The gamelan is an orchestra of mainly percussion instruments (metal and wooden gongs, xylophones, and drums) which are accompanied by lutes, flutes, and often a solo voice. An orchestra of up to 80 musicians, sitting cross-legged opposite one another, is divided into two sections, one tuned to the ancient *pelog* five-tone scale and one to the *slendro* seven-tone scale. Gamelan perform concerts or as accompaniment to dance performances or puppet shows, adapting the blend of tone scales to create appropriate harmonies and melodies for each.

Although the artistry of the gamelan reached its peak under the patronage of Javanese sultans, it is believed to be the root of pre-Hindu music throughout much of the archipelago. Today the sounds created by costumed musicians differ in each region. The slower, more restful and melodic Javanese gamelan has been described as "liquid moonbeams," while the quick, brilliant, and powerful Balinese gamelan is used to drive away demons in trance dances.

Travelers will find many opportunities to hear gamelan in Yogyakarta and Bali. The *angklung,* a reed orchestra made up of bamboo pipes tuned to different notes, is a special feature of Bandung (see Chapter VIII, "Overland Across West Java"), and can also be heard in Bali. The Bataks of North Sumatra are noted for their lively "mariachi"-style singing and guitar playing, yet another of the many musical styles found in every province.

Wayang Theater

The traditional Wayang theater is a drama performed by dancers (*wayang wong*), leather puppets (*wayang kulit*), or wooden puppets (*wayang golek*). The best-known form is wayang kulit, still widely performed on Java and Bali. Wayang kulit, literally "shadow leather," dates back to the earliest Javanese culture; the *dalang* (master puppeteer) was considered the medium between the living and the spirits of the dead, which he lured into each leather puppet. The earliest figures were primitive carvings of deceased ancestors or village elders who could bring wisdom in times of crisis and good fortune to major family events.

With the arrival of the Hinduism in the archipelago in the 5th century, the wayang kulit theater began to draw on the classic Indian epics for inspiration. Eventually, the epic poems *Mahabharata* and *Ramayana* became the most popular sources of moral tales and wayang kulit evolved from its original religious function into popular entertainment.

The dalang plays a dual role as conductor of the gamelan orchestra which accompanies each performance and as narrator of the story. He illustrates his tales with a lineup of incised, painted leather figures, uses small hammers and rattles for sound effects, and modulates his voice for every character. Puppets stand upright in the soft trunk of a banana tree that frames the bottom of a taut white sheet. When the dalang lights an overhead lantern, the shadows of the good characters (to his right) and the bad (to his left) become apparent to the audience on the other side of the screen. Each show is opened and closed with the *gunungan,* a spade-shaped puppet representing a mountain (perhaps the gods' home, Mount Meru), which the dalang holds up for blessing, a ritual carried over from wayang kulit's religious origins.

Wayang golek is a lesser-known but equally entrancing puppet show. The wooden puppets' three-dimensional, carved, and painted heads crown costumed stick-figure bodies. Wayang golek was introduced later to Java by Muslims trying to convert the "heathen" Hindus to the Islamic faith; most tales are based on the Islamic stories of Amir Hamzatt. Both forms of puppet theater are still extremely popular to celebrate family events, commemorate national festivals and holidays, air political ideas, or communicate social issues to villagers.

Classical Dance

On Java, classical dance developed at the sultan's court and was performed only by the descendants of royalty for their own entertainment. Only recently have classic and traditional folk dances been taught and performed outside the *kraton* (palace) walls. *Wayang orang* (dance drama), based on tales of love and war from the Indian epics, is the most entertaining for Westerners because of its comprehensible storyline. In Yogyakarta the best example is the *Ramayana* ballet, fragments of the Hindu epic performed by up to 20 dancers in ornate traditional costumes of batik, gold, and jewels. Often a dalang narrates the legend of King Rama, his kidnapped wife, Sinta, the heroic monkey, Hanuman, and a host of demons and heroes. The dancers' slow, subtle finger movements, tiny footsteps, and flashing eyes are accompanied by a classical singer and a gamelan orchestra.

Wayang topenq (masked dance) often tells folk tales to the accompaniment of drums or a simple ensemble. On Bali (see Chapter IX) the increasing number of visitors has encouraged a tremendous range of dances, both new and traditional. In every region there are a great number of local dances performed at family or religious events, and occasionally staged for tourist groups or arts festivals.

Painting

Indonesia's damp climate has eradicated most traces of early painting, but examples in the form of painted bark, resist-dyeing on long cotton scrolls, painted illustrations, and frescoes depicting heroes from the Indian epic poems have been found on Java and Bali. Raden Saleh (1816–1880) is considered one of the first modern masters, although some critics contend that his landscapes and portraits were too heavily influenced by European techniques.

These techniques included an academic approach, fine brushes, watercolors, tempera paints, and paper. In the 1930s Balinese artists inspired by European settlers (see Chapter IX) began painting themes from daily life and using brighter colors. Typical Balinese paintings fill the entire canvas with images that disregard a realistic perspective; galleries filled with modern paintings and traditional Hindu themes can be found in the village of Ubud. Javanese artists rejected the Europeans' influence and their taste for scenic landscapes. Since the 1940s S. Sudjoyono of Jakarta and Affandi of Bandung (still working in Yogyakarta) sought to encourage Indonesian artists to use local themes and revolutionary politics as the basis for abstract expressionist art.

The Batik Arts

Batik fabric is Indonesia's most recognizable product, although the special patterned cloth was originally brought to Java by Egyptian traders. Today's batik artists use the same techniques: the desired pattern is drawn in pencil on fabric; each part that's not to be dyed in the first color bath is protected by wax applied with a *canting,* or bamboo pen. This hand-application of wax layers is redone for every color, producing the finest quality and most expensive batik (*tulis*). Fine batik tulis worn by royalty often took months to make.

The cap, or carved copper block, is a faster method of application and covers large areas of fabric at each application. Mechanical printing made batik affordable for all Indonesians, and the process can be considered the national craft. Shoppers will find that cap-printed batiks are more expensive than the silkscreen machine-printed fabrics used in cheaper garments. Yogyakarta, Java's batik center, is known for its intricately patterned, somber-hued batik. Traditional patterns (many developed especially for the kraton) were derived from nature and indicated a person's social rank or profession. Elsewhere the patterns differ; for example, in Cirebon batik designs with cloud and rock patterns indicate a Chinese influence.

ARTS AND CRAFTS: There is a wide range of handcrafts produced throughout Indonesia. Although batik dominates the treatment of fabric in Java, *ikat* (tie-dyed) cloth is most common in Sumba and Flores in the Nusa Tenggara islands and excellent *songkhet* (gold and silver thread) weaving is seen in Sumatra. Woodcarving for architectural ornamentation and religious rituals differs in each region as prescribed by adat, but modern craftsmen make decorative wooden sculpture using age-old techniques. Metalwork is commonly used for ornaments, household items, and weapons. Stone sculpture, still crafted in the volcanic rock used for Borobudur; bamboo, reed, and rattan plaiting; and pottery are some of the many other crafts still practiced.

Ikat and Songkhet Weaving

Ikat (meaning to tie or bind) is another resist-dyeing technique where prewoven warp thread is tied in patterns and then dip-dyed to produce colors in specific patterns. Usually a plain weft thread is then interwoven but often in silk fabrics the weft thread is also dyed. A rich indigo and earthy red are the most common colors. Patterns vary from the primitive imagery of animals and people popular in Nusa Tenggara to extremely sophisticated and complex geometric work. The village of Tenganan Pageringsingan on Bali is famed for its unique double ikat (warp and weft dyed) or *grinseng* cloth. Songkhet weaving is embroidered with cotton, silk, or metallic threads. The most common form creates a motif on one side of woven cloth, but more complex techniques are used to create patterns in reverse on the other side of the fabric.

Woodcarving

Much of Indonesia's earliest woodcarving has been lost over generations due to a damp climate, but traces exist in every village. Wooden ornamentation on temples, and finely wrought signs and architectural details, ornately carved and painted doors grace many buildings. Craftsmen still use wood for functional elements, household items, and masks worn in topeng dances, but many create figurative sculpture popular with tourists. Artworks such as religious icons, natural figurines, and animals are carved from ebony, hibiscus, cypress, or satin wood imported from Kalimantan and Irian Jaya. Extremely realistic, sophisticated works can be bought on Java or Bali, and charming folk art is easily found in small villages or the outer islands.

Metalwork

The most interesting example of Indonesian metalwork is the mysteriously powerful *kris* (*keris*), a talisman or weapon according to its owner's desire. The first kris dates to 13th-century Java, when the Majapahit Kingdom used this special dagger as its national weapon. The kris is usually made of meteoric metal shaped into a wavy blade of 5 to 45 ripples; the number of ripples, the carving or inlay work on the hilt, and the sacrifices or rituals the kris maker suffered during its creation all imbue each kris with unique powers. Krises vary in length from 5 to 12 inches, with sheaths of ornately carved wood or metal, depending on their use. Although contemporary krises are sold for decorative men's wear, Indonesians treasure old krises thought to have magical power as family heirlooms.

Today metalsmiths work more in silver, producing silverware in traditional Javanese court designs, ornamental jewelry, and classic European silver services for the tourist trade.

CUISINE: For such a varied culture and mixture of peoples, the cuisine is surprisingly homogenous. The foreign palate will find it difficult to discern the subtleties between Javanese, Sundanese, Balinese, and other regional cuisines, although each area does have local specialties. The exception is West Sumatra's wildly spiced Padang food, remarkable for its use of coconut and chiles.

Rice is the main staple, though on some islands only corn, sweet potatoes, or sago are cultivated as the basic foodstuff. *Nasi goreng* is the country's most popular dish and can be found in any restaurant at any time of the day. This fried-rice meal is served with a few skewers of barbecued chicken or pork (*sate ayam* or *sate babi*), a piece of fried chicken (*ayam goreng*), or a spicy hard-boiled egg (*telor*). Well-cooked meat, vegetable, fish, or fowl entrees are usually served with boiled rice (*nasi putih*) and a tasty but *hot* chile sauce (*sambal*). *Sate* (pronounced "sahtay"), chicken, lamb, or fish grilled on a skewer, is also a popular entree, eaten with rice and a selection of soy bean dishes (*tahu* or *tempe*), boiled vegetables (*sayur*), or soup (*soto*). *Gado-gado* (written as gado²) is a salad of blanched vegetables served with a delicious peanut sauce that's also widely available. The standard and wholesome breakfast or late-night snack is known as *bubur ayam,* a rice porridge served with many side dishes such as shredded chicken, pickled vegetables, and piquant condiments.

Chinese food is the most common "foreign" cuisine, although American fast-food outlets are cropping up. In the cities you'll find fancier, air-conditioned eateries classified as *restoran,* more casual places with limited menus as *rumah makan* (food house), and open-air storefronts or street stalls as *warung.*

Indonesia's tropical climate nurtures a tremendous selection of fruit all year round; don't miss a chance to sample some from our glossary:

Apple or Rose Apple (*jambu air*)—deep-red skin and crispy flesh.

Banana (*pisang*)—vary from yellow to green to brown, but the small *pisang mas* are best for eating uncooked.

Citrus fruits (*jeruk*)—usually served as delicious chilled juices (*jeruk es*); the tangerine (*jeruk garut*) is best to eat.

Durian—large, greenish, hard-spined skin with foul-smelling, juicy white flesh adored by many in Asia. Try sampling it first as ice cream or fruit juice before attempting the real thing.

Jackfruit (*nangka*)—greenish, football-shaped, prickly skinned fruit with tasty, firm yellow flesh sectioned around large pits.

Lichee (*rambutan*)—large red berries with soft spines sold in clusters with delicious, sweet white flesh.

Mango (*mangga*)—thick glossy orange skin with sweet, juicy fruit.

Mangosteen (*manggis*)—brownish purple, hard-skinned fruit with six-pointed knob at one end and excellent white flesh in segments.

Papaya (*pawpaw*)—long or pear-shaped, soft-skinned fruit with delicious yellow or orange flesh.

Passion fruit (*markisa*)—purple red, smooth-skinned fruit made into an excellent juice.

Pineapple (*nanas*)—small and gold colored with very juicy flesh.

Snakeskin fruit (*salak*)—brown scaled skin with tasty, crisp white flesh in segments.

Starfruit (*belimbing*)—pale greenish plastic-like skin shaped like elongated star with crisp flesh used in cooking.

Watermelon (*semangka*)—round green melons have pink flesh; striped melons have juicy yellow flesh.

Currency

Rp	$U.S.	Rp	$U.S.
100	0.06	15,000	9.38
200	0.13	20,000	12.50
300	0.19	25,000	15.63
400	0.25	30,000	18.75
500	0.31	35,000	21.88
1,000	0.63	40,000	25.00
1,500	0.94	45,000	28.13
2,000	1.25	50,000	31.25
2,500	1.56	75,000	46.88
3,000	1.88	100,000	62.50
3,500	2.19	125,000	78.13
4,000	2.50	150,000	93.75
4,500	2.81	175,000	109.38
5,000	3.13	200,000	125.00
7,500	4.69	225,000	140.63
10,000	6.25	250,000	156.25

3. SUGGESTED ITINERARIES

Indonesia is a huge island country most easily linked by air. Any itinerary professing to offer just a taste of the country would have to include forays into lesser-developed provinces where diverse ethnic groups with unique cultures are the allure. We suggest reading Chapter X, "Indonesia Off the Beaten Path," before you make a final decision on your destination.

ONE MONTH: Days 1–3: Jakarta. **Day 4:** Overland by train to Yogyakarta. **Days 5–10:** Yogyakarta, with day trips to the Borobudur and Prambanan temples and to Solo. **Days 11–18:** Fly to Bali, spending five nights at a beach resort and two nights in the hill village of Ubud. **Days 19–24:** Fly to Ujung Pandang and continue overland to central Sulawesi to see the buffalo cult worship practiced by the people of Tana Toraja. **Days 24–30:** Fly to Jayapura and then to the Baliem Valley or Merauke to trek through the villages of Stone Age tribesmen; *or* fly to Medan or Padang in Sumatra and explore the Batak and Minangkabau cultures by traversing Sumatra overland.

TWO WEEKS: Days 1–2: Jakarta. **Day 3:** Overland by train to Yogyakarta. **Days 4–7:** Yogyakarta, with day trips to the Borobudur and Prambanan temples and to Solo. **Days 9–14:** Fly to Bali, spending four nights at a beach resort and two nights in the hill village of Ubud.

ONE WEEK: Day 1: Jakarta. **Days 2–3:** Fly to Yogyakarta; see the palace, the museum; shop; see a *Ramayana* ballet performance; and take half-day trips to the Borobudur and Prambanan temples. **Days 4–7:** Fly to Bali, spending four nights at a beach resort and touring the island's sights by day.

4. GETTING THERE AND GETTING AROUND

There are now seven international gateways to Indonesia, though most travelers still enter the country by air through Jakarta or Denpasar, Bali.

GETTING THERE: The national airline, **Garuda Indonesia,** flies three times weekly from Los Angeles to Bali or Jakarta via Honolulu and Biak. The 1988 super-APEX fare was $1,176, including two free stopovers. Travelers who fly from Australia, Japan, Europe, or the U.S. on Garuda Indonesia are eligible to purchase domestic tickets to destinations east of Bali at a 50% discount and west of Bali at a 25% discount, but they must be purchased in your country of origin. Contact your travel agent for current fares on **Japan Airlines, British Airways,** or **Qantas Airways** to Indonesia.

Within Southeast Asia, **Thai International Airways** flies from Bangkok to Jakarta or Bali, **MAS** flies from Kuala Lumpur to Medan or Jakarta, **Singapore Airlines** flies to Medan or Jakarta, and **Cathay Pacific** flies from Hong Kong to Bali.

A few companies offer cruises from Penang, Malaysia, to Medan, North Sumatra. In Medan, contact **Eka Sukma Wisata Tour and Travel** (tel. 061/41275); their overnight cruise cost $110 in 1988. For information about boats to Singapore, see "Getting There" in Chapter XIV.

GETTING AROUND:
Traveling through Indonesia can be simple or wildly adventurous, but in any case it must be looked upon as part of your travel experience. Nothing is as simple, efficient, or timely as you'd like it to be. Because of the great distances between tourist destinations, we recommend flying wherever possible. Flights are also relatively inexpensive (although trains, ferries, and buses are dirt cheap).

By Guided Tour
Those with a tight schedule or limited capacity for patience should consider having a travel agent make transportation, hotel, and sightseeing arrangements on a group or individual basis. Two recommended tour operators with offices in the U.S. are **P.T. Vayatour,** 3440 Wilshire Blvd., Los Angeles, CA 90010 (tel. 213/655-3851), and **Natrabu Indonesian Travels and Tours,** 323 Geary St., Suite 318, San Francisco, CA 94102 (tel. 415/362-2540, or toll free 800/628-7228). An American tour operator specializing in adventure travel to Indonesia is **Sobek Expeditions,** P.O. Box 1089, Angel's Camp, CA 95222 (tel. 209/736-4524).

By Air
Garuda Indonesia is the largest and best-run of the domestic airlines, and offers frequent and efficient service to many destinations. In 1988, travelers planning to tour Indonesia while still outside the ASEAN region were eligible to purchase a **Visit Indonesia Air Pass** (this program may be discontinued by the time this guidebook appears). Garuda's **Five-City Airpass** cost $300 in 1989 and included Medan (North Sumatra), Padang (West Sumatra), Jakarta (Java), Biak (Irian Jaya), Ujung Pandang (South Sulawesi), and Denpasar (Bali). For $400 you could get a **Ten-City Airpass,** and for $500 one to 35 cities. The Airpass must be purchased outside of Indonesia and Southeast Asian countries, and there are other restrictions. Contact Garuda Indonesia Airways, Indonesian Consulate General Building, 3457 Wilshire Blvd., Los Angeles, CA 90010 (tel. 213/386-3323 or 213/387-0651), or your travel agent for more information.

Sample one-way air fares on Garuda Indonesia in 1988: Jakarta–Yogyakarta, $56.50; Jakarta–Jayapura, $325.25; Jakarta–Denpasar, $96.50; and Jakarta–Medan, $141.75.

Always remember to confirm your reservation within 72 hours of departure, if possible in the city from which you will be departing (overbooking is common). Communication is not always easy and reserving a seat between Jakarta and Medan, North Sumatra, from Denpasar, Bali, probably will not work.

Merpati Nusantara is the next largest airline, primarily servicing lesser-used routes, although when they fly the same routes as Garuda Indonesia, their prices are usually at least 10% cheaper.

By Train

Java is the only island with enough of a rail network to make train travel practical. Central Java's extraordinary landscape also makes this a particularly rewarding, if not fast or efficient experience. The few first-class trains are air-conditioned with comfortable, cushioned seats; second-class cars are fan-cooled with cushioned seats, and third-class cars are window-cooled with wooden seats. Fares for overnight trips are about 16,000 Rp ($10); most routes are under 3,200 Rp ($2). See "Getting There" in Chapter VIII for some suggested train trips.

By Bus

Indonesia has a tremendous network of long-distance buses that extends to the smallest town and runs around the clock. You can ride in some "comfort" (see "Trans-Sumatra Overland" in Chapter X) from Medan to Jakarta (72 hours, $25), from Jakarta to Bali (24 hours, $10) or any other distance in between. Longer trips are quite an adventure and a unique way to see every local bus stop. The safety record of long-distance buses on Java is particularly abominable, although the national government claims to be reducing overcrowding and improving driving skills and road conditions.

By Boat

The government-owned **Pelayaran Nasional Indonesia (PELNI)** line is the only ferry transport between the island groups, but its routes are so inconvenient and its schedule so erratic that it's hard to recommend this as a mode of transport. Contact their Jakarta sales office at Jl. Pintu Air 1 (tel. 021/358-398) for more information. **P.T. Lumba Lumba Permai** operates the luxury cruiser *Island Explorer*, a 133-foot catamaran with 18 staterooms and extensive recreational facilities. Contact their office at Jl. Let. Jen. S. Parman 78 Slipi, Jakarta Barat (tel. 021/593-401; Telex 46683 SA IA/46081 MENDUT), for more information about their cruises through the archipelago.

Local Transportation

Within each city you'll have a broad range of transportation. Taxis are usually inexpensive and reliable, and although fares are fixed outside of Jakarta, a taxi rented by the hour is usually the best way to sightsee.

Bicycle-powered *becaks* (rickshaws), three-wheeled *bajaj* (motorscooters with a passenger seat in front), *helicaks* (motorcycles with a sidecar), and horse-drawn *andong* (covered carts) are only some of the other options for shorter distances. Fares must always be negotiated before boarding; check what the approximate rates should be with your hotel concierge, and then stand firm.

5. THE ABC'S OF INDONESIA

A first-time visitor arriving in Jakarta may be somewhat overwhelmed. The heat and humidity greets you, hugs you like a long-lost friend, and just won't let go. While the language is written in Latin letters and some words have some affinity with English, you can't escape the fact that this is a Third World country, though with many modern elements. It takes some getting used to and some guidance to know how to behave, how to eat, how to travel, and how to enjoy it.

This section deals with the broad questions of travel in Indonesia. "The ABCs of Jakarta" and the "Useful Information" sections of other chapters will supplement this general information for specific locales. This section cannot answer all your questions, and the most timely information will come from the concierge or manager of your hotel, who will be generally very helpful and eager to please. If you have major problems, health or otherwise, call the consulate of your country.

BANKS AND MONEY EXCHANGE: The major cities in each province have foreign-exchange banks and authorized moneychangers, though travelers should carry an ample supply of rupiah when traveling to the smaller towns. Most hotels will also change foreign currency, but at lesser rates.

BATHROOMS: Many restaurants and all hotels above the budget level have Western-style toilets. However, in the smaller towns, shops, and budget hotels, rest rooms will have an Asian toilet, a hole in the ground with "launching pads" on either side. The good news is that they are usually quite clean. The water bucket or sink with a small ladle found next to the toilet is for flushing and cleaning. Always carry your own supply of toilet paper. In budget hotels, you'll also find the Asian shower or *mandi,* a deep square well with a large ladle. Take the ladle and pour the water over you, soap up, and do the same to rinse, being careful not to soil the communal well. The water's cold, but in the heat, you won't mind.

BUSINESS HOURS: Government offices are open from 8 a.m. to 3 p.m. Monday through Thursday, from 8 to 11:30 a.m. on Friday, and from 8 a.m. to 2 p.m. on Saturday—although this varies in every province. **Businesses** are generally open from 8 a.m. to 4 p.m. or from 9 a.m. to 5 p.m.
    Shops often stay open until 7 p.m., although some open for a half day only on Saturday or Sunday, and some close for siesta and reopen from 5 to 9 p.m.
    Banks are open from 8 a.m. to 4 p.m. Monday through Friday, to 11 a.m. on Saturday, but often exchange traveler's checks only until noon. Bank branches in the urban hotels stay open later.

CLIMATE: Let's be very clear: it's hot—very hot. Most of the country is south of the equator, which runs through the middle of Sumatra. There are two seasons: rainy and dry. The dry season runs from April through October and the rainy season from November through March, with December and January the wettest months. The temperature in the coastal areas varies from 23° to 33°C (74° to 92°F); it's somewhat cooler in the highland areas. If you do travel during the rainy season, it will rain some part of every day. Bring an umbrella and you'll be fine.

CLOTHING: Cool, light clothing is the only solution to the heat. This is a predominantly Muslim country, so modest styles are in order for both men and women. Men should generally wear slacks, though long shorts are acceptable in a few places like Bali. A jacket and tie are definitely in order for business and government meetings, although the long-sleeved, formal batik shirt, as acceptable as a jacket and tie, is a much more comfortable choice. Women should not wear shorts or revealing blouses. Even in Hindu Bali, where rules are less rigid, revealing outfits are proper only on the beach. Indonesians are very embarrassed by immodesty, so please abide by their sense of decorum.

CREDIT CARDS: Most international hotels and larger businesses on Java, Bali, and in provincial capitals accept major credit cards, but none will accept personal checks. Traveler's checks are negotiable (with your passport) in most banks, hotels, restaurants, and tourist-oriented shops. In smaller towns and outer provinces, rupiah will be the only acceptable form of currency.

CURRENCY: The Indonesian currency is the **rupiah (Rp).** Banknotes come in denominations of 100, 500, 1,000, 5,000, and 10,000 rupiah. Coins come in Rp 100, Rp 50, and Rp 10 denominations. Note that the Rp symbol precedes the number. The exchange rate at the time of publication was about Rp 1,600 = $1 U.S.

CUSTOMS: Tourists are allowed to enter the country with a maximum of two liters of alcoholic beverages, 200 cigarettes or 50 cigars, and a reasonable amount of perfume per adult. Cars, photographic equipment, and typewriters are allowed provided they are re-exported, and must be declared as you enter. There are no restrictions on the import of foreign currencies or traveler's checks; however, you cannot import or export Indonesian currency in excess of Rp 50,000.

DOCUMENTS FOR ENTRY: All visitors to Indonesia must be in possession of passports valid for at least six months, with proof of onward passage (either a return or through ticket). Visas are required except for nationals of Australia, Canada, Ireland, New Zealand, Great Britain, and the United States. There are other countries exempted as well.

The visa-free entry is valid for a maximum of two months and is not extendable. Entry and departure must be through one of the major ports of entry, such as Jakarata, Biak, Medan, Bali, Batam, Pekanbaru, Manado, Ambon, Benoa, and Surabaya. For any other port of arrival, a visa is required. Check with the Indonesian Consulate or Embassy in your country for more information.

If a tourist visa is needed, a visa valid for 30 days can be obtained from any overseas Indonesian Embassy or Consulate. Two passport-size photographs are required and a small fee is charged.

Visa-free entry is granted to business people visiting Indonesia to conduct business, but not for purposes of employment. You cannot perform a job without a visa, and should allow two months or more for processing.

DRINKING WATER: *Never drink the tap water,* unless there is a sign to the contrary. Drink lots of bottled water to combat the effects of the heat. You'll always find a container or bottle of boiled water in your hotel room, and all food shops sell it. Most restaurants will serve boiled water and ice made from boiled water, but always ask in a smaller restaurant if the water is boiled or *air putih* (pronounced *"Ay-*eer poo-*tee"*). Even the local Indonesians drink boiled or bottled water.

ELECTRICAL APPLIANCES: Most hotels use 220 volts A.C., 50 cycles. In the larger urban hotels, bathrooms usually have a 110-volt outlet for electric shavers or hairdryers.

EMBASSIES: Embassies for many countries are located in Jakarta. The **U.S. Embassy and Consulate,** are located at Jl. Merdeka Selatan 5, on the south side of Merdeka Square (tel. 340-001); they're open weekdays from 8 to 11:30 a.m. and 1 to 3 p.m. The **British Embassy and Consulate** are at Jl. Thamrin 75 (tel. 330-904); the **Canadian Embassy** is in the Wisma Metropolitan Building, Jl. Jend. Sudirman Kav. 29 (tel. 510-709); and the **Australian Embassy and Consulate** are at Jl. Thamrin 15 (tel. 323-109).

There are also American Consulates in Medan, North Sumatra, Surabaya, and Sanur Beach, Bali. There is an Australian Consulate in Bali.

EMERGENCIES: Throughout the country, the emergency numbers are 110 for **police** and 118 or 119 for **ambulance.**

FESTIVALS AND HOLIDAYS: There are several Indonesian national holidays with fixed dates, and several Muslim, Hindu/Balinese, Buddhist, and Chinese holidays whose dates vary annually according to their calendar system. Contact the nearest Tourist Information Office for more information.

National Holidays
January 1: New Year's Day, or Tahun Baru.
April: Good Friday and Easter (celebrated in Christian communities nationwide).
April 21: Kartini Day (celebrates the birth of Raden Ajeng Kartini, founder of the women's emancipation movement).
May 20: Hari Siliwangi (celebrated in West Java to commemorate the founding of the Siliwangi army division).
June 22: Jakarta Anniversary (celebrates the city's founding in 1527).
August 17: Independence Day (celebrated nationwide).
October 1: Hari Pancasila (celebrates the adoption of the state philosophy).
October 5: Armed Forces Day (celebrated with parades).
November 10: Heroes' Day (commemorates the battle against the Dutch and the Allies at Surabaya in 1945; celebrated at cemeteries).
December 25: Christmas (a general holiday).
December 31: New Year's Eve (celebrated nationwide).

Muslim Holidays
Idul Fitri or Lebaran: Feast marking the end of the fasting month of Ramadan (Puasa).
Idul Adha, Feast of Sacrifice.
Satu Muharam, Islamic New Year

Hindu/Balinese Holidays
Nyepi/Caka, a day of silent retreat in honor of the Hindu New Year.

Chinese Holidays
Imlek (Chinese New Year), usually celebrated in January or February.

Balinese Festivals
Bali, being predominantly Hindu, has a dense calendar of holidays and temple festivals which are held almost daily.
Garebeg Maulud is celebrated annually in Yogyakarta in honor of the birthday of the Prophet Muhammad. Huge mounds of food are brought from the kraton (sultan's palace) to the Grand Mosque to be distributed to poor.
Bull races are held once or twice a month in the major towns on the island of Madura (off the east coast of Java) to determine the finalists for the anual championship races held in Pamekasan, the capital.
The *Ramayana* **ballet,** a full night of dance and drama based on the Hindu epic, is presented each full moon from June to October for four consecutive nights at the Prambanan temples, near Yogyakarta.
Waisak, celebrating the day of the birth, death, and enlightenment of the Lord Buddha, is celebrated annually during the full moon at the Borobudur temple, near Yogyakarta.

FILM AND CAMERA: You should bring your camera, but buy your film in Indonesia. Kodak has a manufacturing plant here and the price of both Kodak and Fuji film is often less than in the U.S. One-hour photo processing has swept the country by storm and they've shaved the time in some provinces to 45 and even 27 minutes. We can't vouch for the longevity of these prints, but found the quality acceptable.

HEALTH AND VACCINATIONS: If you're careful, staying healthy will not be a problem. The Indonesian government does not require any vaccinations, but if you are traveling from an infected area, you must have proof of smallpox and cholera inoculations. For up-to-date information, contact your local or state health department or the U.S. Public Health quarantine station nearest you (tel. 718/917-1685 in New York).

Prevention is the best approach to health. We repeat: **Do not drink tap water.** Make sure water is boiled or bottled. Don't eat unpeeled fruit or vegetables. Street food is generally questionable; examine each vendor's cart and use common sense. Fully cooked or fried foods—nasi goreng (fried rice), pisang goreng (fried bananas), and countless other snacks—are usually fine and delicious.

Don't swim in freshwater streams or pools, as they are probably contaminated. Avoid the ocean wherever freshwater streams empty into it, thus avoiding contaminated waters and the poisonous sea snakes that inhabit these areas. Be careful of coral reefs and treat all cuts immediately, by washing and applying an antibiotic cream.

Be careful of sunstroke or heat exhaustion. Take it easy on the early days of your visit. Drink lots of bottled water. Avoid long periods of exposure to the sun and wear a hat for protection. We found that restricting alcohol consumption and eating lightly helped to acclimate to the heat and sun.

Diarrhea is to be expected in the adjustment to a new cuisine and climate. If it persists beyond 48 hours or is accompanied by fever or dehydration, consult a doctor.

HITCHHIKING: There are no laws prohibiting it, but we saw no hitchhikers. Use the inexpensive public transportation instead.

LANGUAGE: The official language is **Bahasa Indonesia,** which was adopted in 1928 to help bring a national identity to the diverse ethnic groups that make up the country. Bahasa Indonesia is written in the Roman script and is simple to learn. English is spoken in the major cities and by workers in most hotels, restaurants, and shops.

LAUNDRY: Almost every hotel has laundry service and at refreshingly reasonable prices. There are no public coin-operated laundries, but you occasionally find dry cleaners who offer one-day service.

LIQUOR LAWS: Because Indonesia is a predominantly Muslim country, liquor is not widely available, though alcoholic beverages are available in the bars of every major hotel. There is no Indonesian wine, except for the red and white Balinese rice wine. The red rice wine is extremely sweet, but the white, found almost exclusively in Ubud, is quite delicious.

METRIC MEASURES: Indonesia uses the metric system. For a table of metric conversions, see "The ABCs of Burma" in Chapter II.

NEWSPAPERS AND PERIODICALS: The major English-language dailies are the *Jakarta Post* and the *Indonesian Times.* Most hotels carry the *Asian Wall Street Journal* and the *International Herald Tribune,* along with the international editions of *Time* and *Newsweek.* Weekly editions of *Asiaweek* and the *Far Eastern Economic Review* are also available.

POLITICS: Most Indonesians don't like to discuss the politics of their own country, though you'll find many conversant in current world affairs. The present government is a republic, based on the 1945 Constitution, headed by a president who is elected every five years by the MPR (People's Consultative Assembly), which meets once every five years to establish overall policy. The DPR (House of the People's Representatives) holds legislative powers; one-fourth of its members are appointed by the president and three-fourths are elected. The Sekber Golkar is a joint secretariat of 61 non-affiliated groups representing farmers' associations, school groups, military organizations, and other civilians who want to make known their point of view. The Supreme Court is the highest court of law.

POSTAL SERVICE: Post offices and their hours are listed in each chapter. Poste restante is an excellent way to receive mail anywhere in the country, if you don't have a specific address. Poste restante is found at the main or general post office in each city.

If you are thinking of shipping your purchases home, check the rates before you buy. Air freight is quite expensive, and sea mail, about 50% less, is very slow. Ask your hotel to recommend a reputable, insured shipping company. DHL, the international delivery service, has offices in several of the major cities and promises the fastest shipping. DHL also offers a special rate to Texas, a spinoff of the local oil business.

SAFETY: The rate of personal crime in Indonesia is quite low. We heard no reports of mugging or burglary anywhere except in Kuta Beach, Bali, and Jakarta, but take the usual precautions of leaving valuables and passports in hotel safes. Carry a photocopy of your passport so that you can cash traveler's checks. On public buses and trains, be watchful of your purse, camera, and bags.

TAXES AND SERVICE CHARGES: Hotels charge a basic tax and service charge that averages 15%, though smaller hotels will often quote the price inclusive of these charges. Always ask to be sure. The new 10% VAT and 10% to 20% luxury sales tax will be collected on certain purchases, although not on services.

TELEPHONE, TELEGRAPH, AND TELEX: Major hotels on Java, Bali, and in provincial capitals have international long-distance **telephone service,** either direct dial or through a Jakarta international operator. Hotels charge a surcharge on local and long-distance calls that can add up to 50% in some cases. There are Kantor Telepon offices open 24 hours throughout the country where long-distance domestic and international calls can be booked. International calls often take up to an hour to place; in 1988 a station-to-station call to the United States cost Rp 14,400 ($9) for three minutes, person-to-person calls cost an additional Rp 9,500 ($6). Credit card and collect calls can easily be placed from Java or Bali, but using rupiahs in cash is the policy almost everywhere else. Pay telephones are rare outside Jakarta, but if found, require a rarely seen Rp-50 coin.

Every Kantor Telepon has a **telegraph office** (usually open from 8 a.m. to 3 p.m. daily except Sunday), but no one ever received any telegrams we sent.

Large hotels and Kantor Telepon offices in the major cities also provide **Telex services.**

TIME: Indonesia is divided into three time zones: Western Indonesia Standard Time covers Sumatra, Java, and Madura and is Greenwich Mean Time (GMT) plus seven hours. Central Indonesia Standard Time covers Bali, Kalimantan, Sulawesi, and West and East Nusa Tenggara and is GMT plus eight hours. Eastern Indonesia Standard Time covers the Moluccas and Irian Jaya and is GMT plus nine hours. See "Useful Information" sections for time differences from New York and Los Angeles.

TIPPING: In restaurants where a service charge is not added, a tip of 5% to 10% is appropriate, for acceptable service. Airport or hotel porters expect tips of Rp

500 (30¢) per bag. Tipping taxi drivers is not mandatory, but a few hundred rupiah or rounding the bill to the nearest Rp 500 is appreciated.

TOURIST INFORMATION: In each section, we note the local tourist information offices by city and province. They are often very helpful and should be consulted on travel plans.

Overseas, you'll find offices of the **Indonesian Tourist Promotion Office** at 3457 Wilshire Blvd., Los Angeles, CA 90010 (tel. 213/387-2078); c/o Geoffrey Gray-Forton Association Ltd., 16 Hanover Square, London WIR OAU, England (tel. 01/629-4917); c/o Garuda Indonesian Airways, 4 Bligh St., Capel Court Bligh House, Sydney, NSW 2000, Australia (tel. 232-6044); and 10 Collyer Quay, no. 1203 Ocean Building, Singapore 0104 (tel. 585-3588).

You can also contact the **Indonesian Consulate General** at 5 E. 68th St., New York, NY 10021 (tel. 212/879-0600); 1990 Post Oak Rd. South, Suite 1900, Houston, TX 77056 (tel. 713/626-3291); 351 California St., Suite 700, San Francisco, CA 94104 (tel. 415/892-8966); or in Canada at 470 Granville, Vancouver, BC V6C 1V5 (tel. 604/669-0574).

If you're in Bangkok, Kuala Lampur, Rangoon, Penang, or Hong Kong, contact the local Indonesian Embassy or Consulate or the Garuda Indonesian Airlines office for information.

6. RECOMMENDED READING AND USEFUL PHRASES

If you are planning an extensive tour of the country, we recommend the *APA Insight Guides* (New York: Prentice Hall Press) on Indonesia, Bali, or Java for in-depth historical and cultural background. The low-budget tourist on an extended tour would do well to purchase either Lonely Planet's *Indonesia: A Travel Survival Kit* (Victoria, Australia: Lonely Planet Publications, 1986) or Bill Dalton's *Indonesia Handbook* (Chico, Calif.: Moon Publications, 1985).

For a historical overview, D. G. E. Hall's *A History of Southeast Asia* (London: Macmillan, 1977), or more specifically, Wilfred Neill's *Twentieth Century Indonesia* (New York: Columbia University Press, 1973) are recommended. One of the best works on art is Claire Holt's *Art in Indonesia: Continuities and Change* (Ithaca, N.Y.: Cornell University Press, 1967); on music, Judith Becker's *Traditional Music in Modern Java, Gamelan in a Changing Society* (Honolulu: University of Hawaii Press, 1980) or Colin McPhee's *Music in Bali* (New Haven, Conn.: Yale University Press, 1966); on batik, Inger McCabe Elliot's *Batik, Fabled Cloth of Java* (New York Clarkson Potter, 1984). Literary works in English include Joseph Conrad's *Almayer's Folly: A Story of an Eastern River and Tales of Unrest*, about Kalimantan; Eduard Douwes Dekker's *Max Havelaar, or the Coffee Auctions of the Dutch Trading Company*, an 1860 work about the exploitation of the Javanese (reprinted by the University of Massachusetts Press, Amherst, 1982); Raden Kartini's *Letters of a Javanese Princess* (New York: Alfred Knopf, 1920), about court life and the early Nationalist movement by Indonesia's first feminist; or Peter Matthiessen's *Under the Mountain Wall* (New York: Penguin Books, 1987), about Stone Age New Guinea.

For movie buffs, Peter Weir's *The Year of Living Dangerously*, based on the last years of the Soekarno era and partially shot in Jakarta, is one of the few widely released films ever made about the country.

USEFUL PHRASES: Bahasa Indonesia is written in the Latin alphabet, using an orthography similar to that of English and Dutch (note the exceptions: c = *ch* as in "church" and au = *ou* as in "ouch").

Indonesian grammar has no articles and there is no difference between singular and plural. To indicate plural nouns just double them; i.e.: anak = child, anak-anak = children.

COMMONLY USED PHRASES:

Selamat pagi	Good morning
Selamat siang	(11 a.m. to 3 p.m.) Good afternoon
Selamat sore	(3 p.m. to sunset) Good afternoon
Selamat malam	Good evening/night
Selamat tinggal	(if you're going) Good-bye
Selamat jalan	(if you're staying) Good-bye
Selamat datang	Welcome
Apa kabar? Kabar baik.	How are you? Fine.
ya/tidak	yes/no
Silahkan/Terima kasih	Please/Thank you
Terimakasih kembali	You're welcome
Maafkanlah saya, Ma'af	I'm sorry/Excuse me
Saya tidak tahu/paham.	I don't know/understand.
Saya mau pergi ke . . .	I want to go to . . .
Di mana ada . . .	Where is . . .
Kantor Penerangan Wisata	Visitor Info. Office
toko/kantor	shop/office
Pasar Malam	Night Market
kereta api/terminal bis	train station/bus station
Kantor Pos Pusat	General Post Office
Kantor Telepon	Telephone Office
Kapan kereta api itu berangkat?	When does the train leave?
Jam berapa sekarang?	What time is it?
Berapa jam perjalanan ini?	How many hours does the trip take?
Berapa harganya?	How much does this cost?
Saya mau menukar uang saya.	I want to change money.
Di mana hotel yang paling dekat?	Where is the nearest hotel?
Satu kamar/Dua orang	One room/Two people
Beri saya se daftar.	Please bring a menu.
Saya mau makan pagi.	I want to eat breakfast.
Saya mau minum air dingin.	I want to drink cold water.
makan siang/makan malam	lunch/dinner
bir/minuman ringan	beer/soft drink
kopi/teh es/teh panas	coffee/ice tea/hot tea
kopi susu/teh jeruk	coffee with milk/tea with lemon
gula/manis	sugar/sweet
Tolong, rekening saya.	The bill, please.

For an in-depth phrasebook, try Lonely Planet's *Indonesia Phrasebook* (Victoria, Australia: Lonely Planet Publications, 1986).

CHAPTER VII

JAKARTA, THE NATION'S CAPITAL

□ □ □

1. ORIENTATION

2. THE ABC'S OF JAKARTA

3. ACCOMMODATIONS

4. DINING

5. SIGHTS, SHOPPING, AND NIGHTLIFE

Jakarta, the national capital on the island of Java, has survived so many names and incarnations in the last 1,500 years that it should come as no surprise that the city today reflects this mixture of past and present. If you arrive at the ultramodern Soekarno-Hatta International Airport, you can take an air-conditioned Mercedes Benz up the new toll highway to town, along 15 miles of freeway that initially cuts through rice paddies tended by water buffalo. You'll pass bicycle-powered becaks (pedicabs) loaded with a hundred pounds of cabbage, horse-drawn andong bringing shrouded devotees to the mosque, huge painted billboards advertising appliances and cosmetics, mini-skirted executives on motorbikes, office towers with corporate logos emblazoned in neon, bumper-to-bumper Japanese cars, and a thousand food stalls offering fried rice and noodles to passersby.

Jakarta was never a visually enchanting city. Its original canal network, extensive enough to rival Bangkok's, became so noxious and malaria-ridden by the 18th century that under Dutch rule most of it was paved over. The few urban parks and gardens that remained were incorporated after independence into massive civil monuments commemorating Indonesia's independence struggle. The '70s oil boom brought more changes to the face of the capital. The newfound funds that restored Fatahillah Square, center of the Dutch colonial city, also fueled a wave of modern development that has left parts of the city looking like Houston.

Yet Jakarta, *ibu kota* (mother city) of the archipelago, still thrives at center stage of a rapidly developing nation. Its seven million plus residents, representing ethnic groups from every far-flung province, live 25,000 per square kilometer, but have achieved peaceful coexistence. As for the future, planners envision a 21st-century megalopolis extending 7,500 km² with a population of 25 million, a possibility in just 25 years.

HISTORY: Today's Jakarta is the world's sixth-largest city on the site of one of its most ancient settlements. Archeological evidence indicates that the Java Sea coast has been inhabited since prehistoric times, although little is known about early settlements or the appearance of Indian culture on Java until the 5th century A.D., the date of Sanskrit tablets found inscribed with the name Purnawarman.

An Asian Entrepôt

The huge boulders described the Hindu settlements around Jakarta Bay, which were united under King Purnawarman into the Taruma Negara kingdom. Its port was known as Sunda Kelapa (Coconut Coast). In 1292 Marco Polo was the first European to visit Java. Soon after, the Hindu kingdom of Majapahit took control of East Java and successfully thwarted the advances of Moghul Emperor Kubilai Khan. The mightiest Majapahit ruler, Raja Hayam Wuruk, and his deputy Gajah Mada have their names on the modern-day avenues that bisect Jakarta's Chinese quarter.

The Portuguese arrived in Java in 1513 and found Sunda Kelapa under the control of the Hindu King Pajajaran. They tried for years to secure their place in the spice trade, and in 1522 Pajajaran, to gain allies against the invading Muslim forces from the Kingdom of Demak (near Cirebon, East Java), signed a friendship treaty with Portugal. The Portuguese fortified the Kasteel Jakarta at the harbor, but after several battles, in 1527 the city finally fell to the Muslim Prince Fatahillah. He ousted the Portuguese and renamed it Jayakarta, or Great Victory. Under Prince Fatahillah's rule Sunda Kelapa remained a key Asian entrepôt.

Under Dutch Rule

The first Dutch trading vessels arrived in 1598 and in just four years the Dutch East Indies Company (VOC or Verenigde Ooost-Indische Compagnie) had set up shop. The Dutch and other Europeans moved in quickly, changing the name of the city to Jacatra and installing a resident governor-general. In 1621, under Jan Pieterzoon Coen, the city that had been taken from Fatahillah was renamed Batavia. Batavia's commercial center remained at the port on the Java Sea, but the Dutch fortress built inland along the Ci Haliwung River became the center of the European residential community. By the 17th century Batavia was a powerful international center of trade known as the Queen of the East. The Dutch expanded their city (Kota) south along the Ci Haliwung, but growing malaria problems posed by the old canal network forced them to move farther south to Weltevreden, near the present-day Gambir Railroad station. Under the Batavian leader Daendels, government offices and official residences were moved out to Waterlooplein, today the park behind the Borobudur Inter-Continental Hotel.

By the mid-17th century the central Javanese kingdom of Mataram and other Muslim groups began to rebel against Dutch rule. In 1740 Batavia's Chinese population, formerly engaged as intermediaries between the Dutch and Indonesians, rebelled and were violently repressed. During the Napoleonic Wars, Dutch holdings reverted to the British East India Company (1811–1816) and Lt.-Gov. Sir Thomas Stamford Raffles found Batavia plagued by overcrowding and poor sanitation. The Dutch Batavian Republic reclaimed its territories from the British, and for the next century a wave of rebellions led by Diponegoro, Imam Bonjol, Teuku Umar, Sisingamangaraja, and others continued throughout the islands.

The Dutch prospered in Batavia until March 9, 1942, when the city fell to the Japanese and was renamed Jakaruta Tokubetsu Shi. Three days after the Japanese surrender on August 14, 1945, Nationalist movement leaders Soekarno and Hatta proclaimed Indonesia's independence. The seat of government was briefly moved from Jakarta to Yogyakarta when fighting broke out between the Dutch, who were trying to regain their former colonies, and Indonesian National Army troops. Finally, on December 27, 1949, Jakarta became the capital of the new republic.

1. ORIENTATION

The Jakarta most travelers will visit is bounded on the north by the Sunda Kelapa Harbor on the Java Sea, and on the south by the ritzy suburb of Kebayoran Baru. Monas, the white obelisk of the National Monument, stands proudly above Merdeka Square at the city's center.

LANDMARKS AND NEIGHBORHOODS: From **Sunda Kelapa Harbor** stretch narrow streets which parallel Jakarta's few remaining canals. A short drive east of Sunda Kelapa is the modern Jaya Ancol Dreamland amusement park. Due south are the winding streets of **Kota,** the center of the city under Dutch rule and still a hub for bus and train transport. In the heart of Kota is the restored **Taman Fatahillah,** a square enclosed by Dutch-era buildings (now history, ceramics, and puppet museums) and other sights of tourist interest. A half-hour walk south through narrow backstreets or along Jl. Gajah Mada and Jl. Hayam Wuruk (broad avenues lined with shopping malls) leads to **Glodok,** the center of the Chinese community and a teeming commercial area.

From Glodok it is a ten-minute taxi ride to **Merdeka Square.** The National Monument, the National Museum, the Jakarta Fairgrounds, and most of the government offices are along the four streets that enclose this square: Jl. Medan Merdeka Utara, Selatan, Timur, and Barat (literally Merdeka Square Street North, South, East, and West). From here, most street names breed confusion; broad one-way avenues built since liberation fan out from the city's center in an irregular pattern, changing names almost every mile to honor a different hero of the independence movement.

From the southwestern corner of the square Jl. Medan Merdeka Barat becomes **Jl. M.H. Thamrin,** or Hotel Row as far as most visitors are concerned. The Hotels Sari Pacific, President, Indonesia, and the Jakarta Mandarin line both sides of Jl. Thamrin south to the Welcome Monument traffic circle. The Sarinah Department Store, two offices of the Visitor Information Service, and the Garuda Indonesia airlines office are also along this stretch. Jl. Imam Bonjol, the avenue that begins on the southeast side of the traffic circle, becomes Jl. Diponegoro and leads into the older, elegant residential suburb of **Menteng.** Menteng has a few hotels, some guesthouses, and several good shops and restaurants, and is generally a pleasant place to walk around.

At the Welcome Monument traffic circle, Jl. Thamrin becomes **Jl. Jend. Sudirman,** a broad, modern six-lane drive lined with office towers, banks, foreign firms, international restaurants, and construction sites. On Jl. Jend. Sudirman, between the Welcome Monument and the traffic cloverleaf at Jl. Gatot Subroto (a similarly modern drive that's lined with construction), are the Kartika Plaza, Sahid Jaya, and the Jakarta Hilton Hotels, whose park grounds form the intersection with **Jl. Gatot Subroto.** From the intersection, Jl. Sudirman curves southwest to the more elegant, nouveau-ritzy suburb of Kebayoran Baru, and Jl. Gatot Subroto runs east to the Soekarno-Hatta International Airport, about 45 minutes away. **Kebayoran Baru** offers all the latest shops in Blok M, a fashionable new commercial district, as well as several good restaurants and services catering to the local expatriate community. For most visitors staying along Jl. Thamrin, the half-hour taxi ride to Kebayoran Baru will not be necessary, unless you're doing business along Jl. Sudirman or Gatot Subroto.

ARRIVING IN AND LEAVING JAKARTA: Most of Jakarta's transportation hubs are centrally located. Many of the 12 bus stations (for city or for long-distance buses) and four railway stations are located within a five-mile radius of the city's central Merdeka Square. The Soekarno-Hatta International Airport

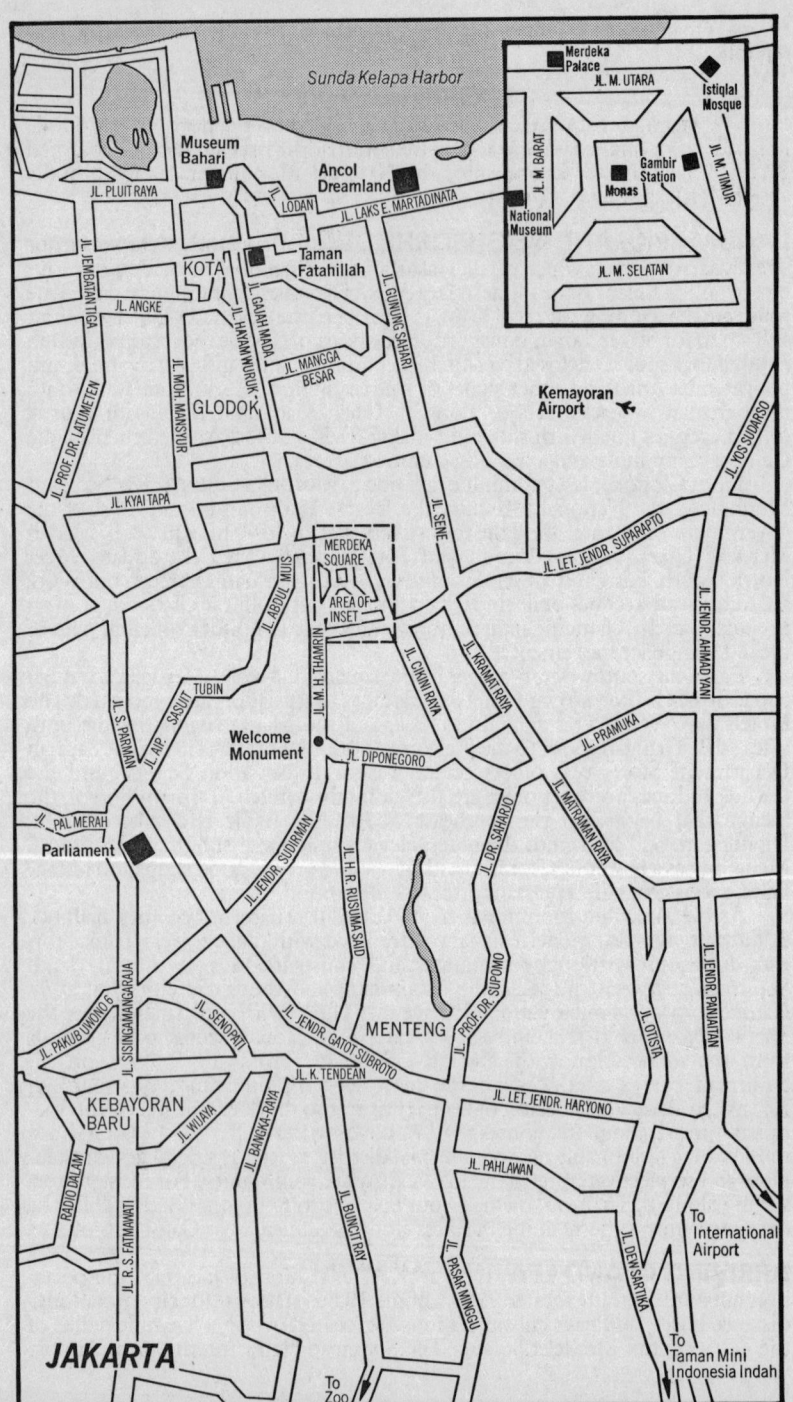

Sunda Kelapa Harbor

Merdeka Palace

JL. M. UTARA

Istiqlal Mosque

JL. M. BARAT

Gambir Station

JL. M. TIMUR

Monas

National Museum

JL. M. SELATAN

Museum Bahari

Ancol Dreamland

JL. PLUIT RAYA

JL. LODAN

JL. LAKS E. MARTADINATA

JL. JEMBATAN TIGA

KOTA

Taman Fatahillah

JL. ANGKE

JL. GAJAH MADA

JL. HAYAM WURUK

JL. MANGGA BESAR

JL. GUNUNG SAHARI

Kemayoran Airport

JL. MOH. MANSYUR

GLODOK

JL. PROF. DR. LATUMETEEN

JL. KYAI TAPA

JL. SENE

JL. YOS SUDARSO

JL. LET. JENDR. SUPRAPTO

MERDEKA SQUARE

AREA OF INSET

JL. ABDUL MUIS

JL. JENDR. AHMAD YANI

JL. S. PARMAN

JL. AIP

SASUIT TUBIN

Welcome Monument

JL. M. H. THAMRIN

JL. CIKINI RAYA

JL. KRAMAT RAYA

JL. PRAMUKA

JL. DIPONEGORO

JL. MATRAMAN RAYA

JL. PAL MERAH

Parliament

JL. JENDR. SUDIRMAN

JL. H. R. RUSUNA SAID

JL. DR. SAHARDO

JL. PROF. DR. SUPOMO

JL. OTISTA

JL. JENDR. PANJAITAN

JL. PAKUBUWONO 6

JL. SISINGAMANGARAJA

JL. SENOPATI

MENTENG

JL. JENDR. GATOT SUBROTO

RADIO DALAM

KEBAYORAN BARU

JL. WIJAYA

JL. BANGKA RAYA

JL. K. TENDEAN

JL. LET. JENDR. HARYONO

JL. PAHLAWAN

JL. R. S. FATMAWATI

JL. BUNCIT RAY

JL. PASAR MINGGU

JL. DEWI SARTIKA

To International Airport

To Zoo

To Taman Mini Indonesia Indah

JAKARTA

(used also for domestic flights) is inconvenient, lying about 26 km (16 miles) from the city. Jakarta's traffic jams can be endless, and because air-conditioned taxis are so inexpensive and reliable, we recommend that you take them everywhere within the city. For overland travel across Java, we prefer trains to the long-distance buses and suggest at least one train ride to view the lush scenery and village life. If you're under time constraints, Garuda Indonesia, the national airline, makes it simple, pleasant, and inexpensive to province-hop throughout Indonesia. See the ABCs section for ticket information and sample fares, but always refer to the Visitor Information Centre (tel. 364-093) for current information.

The Airport

All air travelers arrive at the **Soekarno-Hatta International Airport,** the most beautiful in Southeast Asia. (Jakarta's Kemayoran Airport is used only by charters and private planes.) The trip into town will take one to two hours, depending on traffic and which part of the city you're going to. The extremely helpful **Welcome and Information Centers** (tel. 550-5307) located in every terminal can help arrange transportation by limousine, taxi, or private bus.

Some of the luxury hotels provide private **limousines** at the airport to meet guests, but anyone can book an unclaimed car to another destination. These cars will seat four comfortably and charge Rp 28,800 ($18), plus the Rp-3,650 ($2.50) toll to central Jakarta. Large, imported air-conditioned **sedans** operate in the netherworld between these "official" limousines and licensed taxis. Their entrepreneurial drivers will solicit passengers and bargain to a rate somewhere in between.

Taxis (*taksi*) are the best buy in the city. There are usually several of the sky-blue Blue Bird Taxis or bright-yellow Sri Medali taxis at the airport. These drivers can be counted on to use their meters, and including any airport surcharge and toll (a card given out at the taxi stand explains the current fare), a ride into town should cost Rp 15,000 ($8) to Rp 18,000 ($10). Jakarta's cabbies, in contrast to those in most cities, are generally literate, speak some English, and are polite, safe, reliable drivers.

Local tour operators often have **minibuses** at the airport to transport individual travelers to the major hotels in town. The Visitor Welcome or Information Centers know which bus service is currently available and can arrange for you to be taken to your hotel for Rp 5,000 ($3) per person, although you may have to wait for other passengers.

The Railroad Stations

We prefer trains for traveling overland through Java because they're more comfortable and usually faster than Indonesian long-distance buses. Trains south and west to Bogor, Bandung, Yogyakarta, Solo, and Surabaya leave from the convenient Kota or Gambir Railroad Stations. The **Stasiun Kerata Api Gambir** is on the east side of Merdeka Square at Jl. Medan Merdeka Timur and has several local and express trains leaving daily. Contact the Visitor Information Center (tel. 364-093) for current schedule information. At Gambir, the stationmaster's office (*stasiun kepala*) provides information, tickets, and sleeper or first-class reservations; follow the signs marked "Special Reservation for Tourism." Tickets for the evening trains are sold after 10 a.m., and all others two hours before departure.

The older, colonial-style **Stasiun Kereta Api Kota** is on Jl. Mangga Dua just east of Fatahillah Square. The **Stasiun Kepala** is rarely manned by someone speaking English and most of the train service is local. Unless you're taking the overnight *Bima Express* sleeper train to Yogyakarta which leaves from this station, use the Gambir station.

The **Stasiun Kereta Api Tanah Abang,** west of the Hotel Indonesia near the Textile Museum, is the departure point for trains to Palembang and destinations in Sumatra.

If you don't mind the minimal service fee, you can avoid a lot of aggravation by letting **P.T. Carnation Tours** at Jl. Menteng Raya 24 (tel. 344-027) make all your train travel arrangements.

The Bus Stations

In Indonesia, long-distance bus travel can be thrilling or terrifying, cozy or cramped, leisurely or excruciatingly slow, depending on your point of view and threshold of pain. In any case, it's always cheap, and you can still travel three days between Sumatra and Java for $25. Since Java has the best railway network of all the islands, we recommend taking trains here and saving your bus-trip stamina for places where you'll have no choice.

The **Terminal Bis Pulo Gadung** is on Jl. Perintis Kemerdekaan, on the eastern edge of town and surrounded by rice paddies. Buses leave daily from here heading east to Semarang, Yogyakarta, Solo, Surabaya, and Denpasar (Bali). For much closer West Java destinations like Bogor or Bandung, buses depart from the **Terminal Bis Cililitan** on the southeastern edge of the city near the airport. Buses north toward Sumatra leave from the **Terminal Bis Grogol** on Jl. Kiyai Tapa, a few miles west of Merdeka Square.

For current schedule and fare information, contact the Visitor Information Center in town (tel. 364-093). They can recommend the best long-distance bus company servicing your destination; some buses originate at their company's ticket office in the center of town before heading out to the central terminal. ALS, Big Bird (tel. 325-607), and Pluit Jaya (tel. 629-1937) are just a few of the many companies operating in Jakarta.

Ferry Service

We've listed ferry service from Jakarta last because it has the reputation for being the least pleasant, educational, reliable, or efficient way to travel through the 13,677 islands of the Indonesian archipelago. Pelayaran Nasional Indonesia, the government-owned ferry company known as PELNI, has erratic, once- or twice-a-month departures from Tanjung Priok Harbor, a modern harbor several miles east of Sunda Kelapa on the Java Sea. Call their main office at Jl. Angkasa 18 (tel. 416-262) for information about their scheduled routing to 30 ports in 20 provinces.

GETTING AROUND THE CITY: Jakarta is so large and spread out that it's reminiscent of a freeway-less Los Angeles. Fortunately, most sights and services are clustered around Merdeka Square and easily visited by taxi. Although there is a public bus system, it can be extremely confusing and crowded at rush hour. It's cheap, but so are the taxis, and in Jakarta's tropical climate they are infinitely more comfortable. The average visitor is not likely to spend more than a half hour or Rp 4,800 ($3) on any one fare.

By Taxi

Clean, air-conditioned, and comfortable taxis can be found at hotels. Most drivers speak some English or at least understand your pronunciation of common sights, and restaurant and hotel names. The taxis all have meters and you should insist on using them. The first flagfall is Rp 600 (40¢), and it's only Rp 300 (20¢) per kilometer thereafter; no one offers a better price off the meter. Tipping is not customary with the locals, although drivers have come to expect 5% to 10%, or rounding off the meter to the nearest Rp 500, from foreigners. Taxis are readily available and can be hailed on the street. If you've got a number of errands to run, you might prefer to rent a taxi by the hour (see "By Rental Car").

By Rental Car

The best value can be found at **Blue Bird Taxi** (tel. 325-607), where an air-conditioned car with driver starts at Rp 9,000 ($5.50) per hour, two-hour minimum. Day rates range from Rp 95,000 ($59.50) for a compact to Rp 225,000 ($140.50) for a Mercedes. They also rent minibuses at the same rate as compact cars.

Although we would advise against it, self-drive cars are available from about $88 daily and $490 weekly for an air-conditioned compact with unlimited mileage. **Avis** has an office at Jl. Diponegoro 25 (tel. 349-206), **Hertz** is at Jl. Maluku 13 (tel. 336-942), and **National** is at the Kartika Plaza Hotel on Jl. Sudirman (tel. 333-423). These companies offer chauffeur-driven cars from $14 per hour or $99 for an eight-hour day. Cars can be hired for out-of-town touring, though the driver's overnight costs would be added on. The major hotels also offer chauffeured cars on an hourly or daily rate.

By Bus

Jakarta does have extensive, frequent bus service to most areas. Stops are clearly signposted on the main avenues, although circuitous routes are employed because of the many one-way streets. If you're one of those travelers who is trying to make it around the world on a very strict budget, then use the public bus system. Otherwise, *don't.* If you do, stop at the Visitor Information Center at Jl. Thamrin 9 across from Sarinah and pick up their brochure entitled "Jakarta: See for Yourself." It lists all the route numbers for buses servicing the principal tourist destinations. The public bus costs only Rp 200 (12¢); the conductor will even make change for you. Don't forget to watch your valuables while riding the buses.

By Unique Asian Transportation

Jakarta offers choices among *bajaj, bemo, helicak,* and *becak:* four forms of incredibly efficient, noisy, cheap, and compact local transportation. Because the distances between tourist destinations are relatively long (a ten-minute taxi ride would take twice that in a bajaj), most visitors probably won't experience one of these amazing gizmos until they travel outside the city. Try one for a short ride; the noise, heat, and exhaust from the surrounding traffic is usually overwhelming after about ten minutes.

The most common mode of local transportation is the bright-orange **bajaj,** an enclosed three-wheeled motorized scooter that seats two skinny passengers behind the driver. Negotiate the fee before you climb in; Rp 300 (20¢) is the minimum and most rides should only cost Rp 500 (30¢) or Rp 600 (35¢).

In Jakarta there are small motorcycles with sidecars holding up to six skinny people that are called **bemos.** (In most other Indonesian cities a bemo is a small mini-van charging about Rp 300, or 20¢, per passenger for any destination along a fixed route.) The sidecar bemos are usually seen in the older residential sections of town because their use is restricted on the main avenues.

It's said that there are still **helicak** in Jakarta, but we've only seen them in North Sumatra. The helicak is a brightly painted bulbous vehicle where two very skinny passengers ride in a covered bucket in front of the driver, who guides this motorized cycle from behind.

The **becak** is a tricycle with a covered cart that can seat two slender people. Muscular-calved drivers pedal from the front. As with the bajaj, bemo, or helicak, negotiate the price to your destination before you climb into a becak. Alas, the becak, workhorse of almost every other Indonesian city, is banned from much of central Jakarta, although becak drivers still cluster on small backstreets looking for customers.

2. THE ABC'S OF JAKARTA
Here is a brief look at the essential city services for travelers.

AIRLINES: The most convenient office of **Garuda Indonesia Airlines,** the Indonesian national airlines with the major domestic and international routes, is in the BDN Building at Jl. Thamrin 5, near the Sari Pacific Hotel (tel. 334-425). There is also a Garuda office in the second-floor arcade of the Hotel Borobudur (tel. 359-901). The main Garuda sales office is in the Wisma Dharmala Sakti Building at Jl. Sudirman 32 (tel. 588-707) and there is also an office in the Hotel Indonesia (tel. 325-288). **United Airlines** has its office on the ground floor of the Hotel Borobudur, Jl. Lampangan Banteng (tel. 361-707). **Merpati Nusantara Airlines** flies some of the less-frequented domestic routes and has offices at Jl. Angkasa 2 (tel. 417-404).

AIRPORTS: Most airlines require you to check in one hour before domestic flights and 2½ hours before international flights. There is an airport tax of Rp 9,000 ($5.50) for international flights and between Rp 2,500 ($1.50) and Rp 4,000 ($2.50) for domestic flights. For more information on airport services and transportation, see "Arriving In and Leaving Jakarta."

AMERICAN EXPRESS: The most convenient **American Express Bank** office is in the Arthakola Building on Jl. Sudirman, near the Sahid Jaya Hotel (tel. 587-401); the office for cashing traveler's checks or credit-card advances is on the second floor. It's open from 8:15 a.m. to 2 p.m. weekdays and 8:15 a.m. to 1 p.m. on Saturday. Don't forget to bring your passport or a photocopy.

The same services are available from the American Express agent, **Pacto Ltd.** at Jl. Surabaya 8 (tel. 347-416). Pacto's hours are 8 a.m. to 5 p.m. Monday through Friday and 8 a.m. to 1 p.m. on Saturday.

For **lost traveler's checks,** call 587-512 or Pacto.

BANKS: There are domestic banks everywhere, including in the lobbies or arcades of many hotels. Most have foreign-exchange services, at rates generally better than hotel cashier rates. On Jl. Thamrin, you can find **Bank Dagang Negara** at no. 5, and **Bank Indonesia** at no. 2. Banking hours are 8 a.m. to 3 p.m. Monday through Thursday, and until 1 p.m. on Friday. Several hotel branches keep later hours.

Citibank is in the Landmark Building on Jl. Sudirman (tel. 578-007), and **Chase Manhattan Bank** is in the Chase Plaza Building at Jl. Sudirman kav 21 (tel. 578-2213). **Bank of America** is located in the Wisma Antara Building at Jl. Merdeka Selatan 17 (tel. 348-031). While these American banks have foreign-exchange and traveler's check services, don't expect to walk in and cash your personal Citibank check. Special arrangements for fund transfers have to be made before leaving the U.S.

BEAUTY PARLORS/BARBERSHOPS: Major hotels have at least one barbershop and beauty shop in their shopping arcades. In addition, the **House of Revlon** has a "Beauty Center for Men and Women" at Jl. H.R. Rasuna Said kav 10 in the southern suburb of Kuningan (tel. 512-013). For traditional Indonesian cosmetics and hair care, try **Martha Griya,** at several locations, including Jl. Wahid Hasyim 19 (tel. 325-921). **Rudy Hadisuwarno** is a well-known hairdresser with "unisex" salons at a number of locations around town.

BOOKSTORES: Seasoned Jakarta hands recommend Singapore as the best source of English-language books, but some closer choices include **Pt. Gunung Agung** at Jl. Kwitang 6 (tel. 683-649), **Pt. Gramedia** at Jl. Gaja Mada 109 (tel.

627-809), and the book departments of the **Sarinah** department stores. There is also a reasonably good bookstore in the lobby of the **American Express Bank building** on Jl. Sudirman.

BUSINESS HOURS: Government offices are open from 8 a.m. to 3 p.m. Monday through Thursday, 8 to 11:30 a.m. on Friday, and 8 a.m. to 2 p.m. on Saturday. Businesses are generally open weekdays from 8 a.m. to 4 p.m.; shops often stay open until 7 p.m., though some open for only half a day on Saturday.

BUSINESS SERVICES: Many of the major hotels have business centers offering services to the business traveler, including secretarial, Telex, and photocopy assistance. Among these are the Executive Business Center at the Hilton (tel. 578-981), the Business Centre at the Borobudur (tel. 370-108), the Business Services at the Mandarin (tel. 321-308), and Carlos' Secretarial Services at the Sari Pacific (tel. 323-707).

CAMERA REPAIR AND FILM: There are many small photo-developing stores, but the major camera stores include **Hawii Photo** at Jl. Kebon Jati 13 (tel. 322-781) and **Merdeka Photo** at Jl. Merdeka 49 (tel. 57780).

Both Kodak and Fuji film are widely available and reasonably priced. Short-term processing (27-minute) shops abound at low prices but only average quality.

CREDIT CARDS: American Express, VISA, and MasterCard are widely accepted in deluxe and first-class hotels, many international restaurants, and large shops.

CRIME: Jakarta is a fairly safe city. There have been occasional reports of thefts or muggings. We would advise normal precautions while riding public buses or visiting the night markets. As always, leave valuables, air tickets, and passports in the hotel safe. Carry only a photocopy of your passport with you.

DENTISTS/DOCTORS: If you have a major medical problem, call the **U.S. Consulate** (tel. 340-001, ext. 260, 262, or 339), or your own consulate, for 24-hour assistance. For minor problems, try the **SOS Medika,** located at Jl. Prapanca Raya 32 in the southern suburb of Kebayoran Baru (tel. 733-014), or the **Metropolitan Medical Center,** located in the Wisata Office Tower next to the Hotel Indonesia on Jl. Thamrin (tel. 324-408). These are group clinics offering a wide range of medical and dental services with English-speaking personnel. Most hotels also have a doctor or nurse on call.

DRUGSTORES: Most major hotels have a pharmacy in their lobby. The *Jakarta Post* publishes a daily list of the drugstores in town that stay open past normal business hours.

EMBASSIES: The **U.S. Embassy and Consulate** are located on the south side of Merdeka Square at Jl. Merdeka Selatan 5 (tel. 340-001); they're open weekdays from 8 to 11:30 a.m. and 1 to 3 p.m. The **British Embassy and Consulate** are at Jl. Thamrin 75 (tel. 330-904), the **Canadian Embassy** is at Jl. Jend. Sudirman kav. 29 (tel. 510-709), and the **Australian Embassy and Consulate** are at Jl. Thamrin 15 (tel. 323-109).

EMERGENCIES: For **police emergencies,** call 110; for an **ambulance,** call 118; for a **fire,** call 371-109.

HOSPITALS: These are called *Rumah Sakit.* You must bring money to pay for your care. Hospital personnel may not speak English if you call, but there will probably be someone there who does. **St. Carolus Hospital,** at Jl. Salemba Raya 41 (tel. 883-091), is a private hospital with a critical care unit. The **Pertamina Hospital** is at Jl. Kyai Maja 29 (tel. 787-279), in Kebayoran Baru, and is a private hospital with an emergency room and burn unit. If you are ill enough to be in the hospital, call your consulate for assistance.

NEWSPAPERS: The daily English-language newspaper, the *Jakarta Post,* is sold in hotels and large office buildings, along with the *International Herald Tribune* and the *Asian Wall Street Journal.*

POST OFFICE: The **General Post Office** (Kantor Pos Pusat) is located at Jl. Pos Utara 2 (tel. 350-004), northeast of Merdeka Square and the Istikal Mosque. It is open from 8 a.m. to 3 p.m. Monday through Saturday for most services. Most hotels offer basic postal services, so you can save yourself a trip.

The only **poste restante** service is at the General Post Office. This window is not marked, but is at the left rear of the service area. It's only open until 2 p.m. Monday through Friday. You must present your passport and pay a small fee for mail received, but they'll forward mail when you leave Jakarta.

RAILWAY INFORMATION: The **Visitor Information Center** (tel. 364-093) can provide current train schedules and departure locations. **PT. Carnation Tours,** at Jl. Menteng Raya 24 (tel. 344-027), is the best travel agent for train tickets.

RELIGIOUS SERVICES: For English-language church services, try the **Anglican/Episcopal All Saints Church** at Jl. Arif Rahman Hakim 5 (tel. 345-508), opposite the Hyatt Hotel; the **Kebayoran Baptist Church** at Jl. Tirtayasa Raya 1 (tel. 711-799), in Kebayaron Baru; the **Roman Catholic St. Canisius College Chapel** at Jl. Menteng Raya 64 (tel. 365-682); and the beautiful 19th-century **Protestant Gereja Immanual** at Jl. Medan Merdeka Timur 10 (tel. 342-895).

SHOE REPAIR: If you don't walk past hundreds of other repairmen in every neighborhood, try **Laba-laba Toko** at Jl. Cikini Raya (tel. 337-587), or **Buana Terang Toko** at Jl. Kebon Jati 20 (tel. 321-423).

TELEPHONE/TELEGRAPH: The **area code** of Jakarta is 021. Most hotels have direct-dial international service, but the hotel surcharges add up to 50% to the cost of the call. Even collect calls carry a surcharge in some hotels.

The **Kantor Telepon** (public telephone offices) offer international and domestic telephone service, as well as telegraph and Telex services. The most convenient office is in the lobby of the Skyline Building at Jl. Thamrin 9, across the street from Sarinah department store. There is another office on the second floor of the building next to the Jayakarta Tower Hotel on Jl. Hayam Wuruk, where collect or credit-card calls can be made at cheaper rates, and a Kantor Telepon at the domestic terminal at Soekarno-Hatto International Airport. Most parts of Indonesia have direct-dial service. Telegrams can also be sent from the General Post Office.

TIME: In Jakarta, as in all of Java, the time is GMT plus seven hours, with no seasonal changes. This is 12 hours ahead of New York and 15 hours ahead of Los Angeles, plus one hour during Daylight Savings time.

TOURIST INFORMATION: There is a **Tourist Information Center** outside the arrival area at the airport. The most convenient Tourist Information Center is in the Skyline Building at Jl. Thamrin 9 (tel. 354-094), near the Kantor Telepon and across the street from the Sarinah Department Store. There is also an office in the Oriental Building at Jl. Thamrin 51 (tel. 332-067). Hours are 8 a.m. to 3 p.m. Monday through Thursday, until 11 a.m. on Friday, and until 1 p.m. on Saturday. The staff is very friendly, speaks English, and can provide information and maps for Jakarta and other destinations in Indonesia. Inquire here for transportation schedules, route maps, and information.

TRAVEL AGENTS: There are many travel agents in Jakarta offering both local and country tours. **Vayatours** is located just north of Merdeka Square on Jl. Batu Tulis (tel. 365-008). Manager Eddie Jaya is very helpful and knowledgeable and Vayatours has offices in many other parts of Indonesia. **Pacto Tours** the American Express agent throughout Indonesia, has its office at Jl. Surabaya 8 (tel. 347-447). They offer a wide variety of tours as well as complete travel services.

3. ACCOMMODATIONS

Indonesia offers some fine Western-style hotels in almost every tourist destination, but only Jakarta and Bali have truly deluxe accommodations. Although the archipelago was colonized 340 years ago, there are few Raffles or Orientals left to display the grace and grandeur of bygone days. The vast majority of luxury, first-class, and moderately priced hotels are recently built and offer air conditioning, full baths or showers, TVs, phones, in-house restaurants, and swimming pools. Since Jakarta's hotel market caters mainly to international business people and is not seasonal, travelers may be able to get 10% to 30% discounts on stays of several days at some of the first-class and moderately priced hotels.

Advance reservations are recommended, but not necessary except at the best hotels; you can write or call yourself or contact the nationwide **Indotel Reservations Service,** Nugra Santana Building, Jl. S. Parman 75, Jakarta 11410 (tel. 021/548-2335), with a specific request or general price range. It's not necessary to send a deposit.

READERS' TRAVEL TIP: "We negotiated our hotel rates in Indonesia from the tourist bureaus at the airport on our arrival. This will save 15% to 50%, sometimes more" (Tony and Jean Triumpho, Canajoharie, N.Y.).

LUXURY CHOICES: Jakarta boasts several luxury-class hotels (rates from $120 and up, plus 15% to 21% in taxes and service charges), all built in the heyday of the oil boom when visiting sheiks and Texans demanded only the best. Travelers can take advantage of these currently underutilized facilities and enjoy a very luxurious holiday, but you'll find their orientation to the business traveler and expatriate community brings high service charges and a somewhat formal atmosphere. All hotels in the luxury and first-class categories quote room prices only in dollars.

The best of the best in this competitive market is the **Jakarta Hilton International,** located at Jl. Gatot Subroto (tel. 021/583-051), 15 minutes south of the city center by cab, but that much closer to the newer office towers and international airport. From any angle, the tall white towers isolated in 80 acres of dense foliage and flowering plants are an impressive sight on Jakarta's rapidly changing skyline. A gold-and-red lacquer replica of the Sultan of Yogyakarta's palace encloses a huge lobby where antique gamelan instruments are played daily. From Hindu temple guardians at the gate to an open-air Balinese theater, the Hilton has translated all aspects of Indonesia's rich culture into world-class luxury and comfort. Rooms in the main hotel, decorated with contemporary batiks, ornate Javanese wicker, and plush furniture, are priced from $120 to $135 single, $140 to $150 double, depending on view.

Recently 213 more rooms were added in the 17-story Garden Tower. Decorated in a subtle international style using cool pastel batiks and furnishings, these rooms are more spacious and feature luxurious marble bathrooms. In the Garden Tower, with an exclusive ladies' floor and no-smoking rooms, double-room rates range from $160 to $180. Sheiks will enjoy the two-bedroom, duplex penthouse with private pool and helipad ($1,800 a night).

Jakartaites proudly claim the Hilton as a "Diamond Five-Star" hotel, and the city's expatriates and elite fill its seven restaurants and Oriental Disco. Business travelers will appreciate the full-service Business Center, Executive Health Club, and elegant Taman Sari restaurant. Families will enjoy the ten tennis courts, poolside barbecue, extensive grounds, and a lakeside pizzeria where live bands play nightly.

The recently completed 30-story Hilton Residence has tasteful, fully furnished two- and three-bedroom apartments with some hotel services, which rent for $3,900 and up per month, with a six-month minimum.

The **Hotel Borobudur Inter-Continental** is uniquely situated on 23 handsomely landscaped acres on Jl. Lapangan Bantang Selatan (tel. 021/370-108), near Merdeka Square. It's within walking distance of many government offices and the Istiqlal Mosque, and a short cab ride away from the National Monument and Museum. The Borobudur's palatial tropical grounds with tennis courts, half-mile jogging track and 150-foot swimming pool surround a large-scale model of its namesake, the Buddhist temple complex of Borobudur. The remodeled granite lobby filled with Balinese sculpture and elegant shops; many fine, comfortable restaurants and the gracious, friendly service all belie the Borobudur's huge capacity. There are 1,172 rooms, but it never feels crowded! Recently renovated rooms, priced at $120 single, $135 double, and $195 and up for a suite, are luxuriously appointed in Javanese style, with carved teak moldings and batik wall hangings.

The Borobudur offers a business center, popular disco, and complete health club (recently chosen by the *Wall Street Journal* as one of the best sports facilities in Asia!). There is also the modern Garden Wing, where newly transplanted business people and short-term visitors can rent one- or two-bedroom residential units for $2,500 or $3,400 a month respectively, plus 15% tax and service.

The super-elegant **Mandarin Oriental Jakarta,** on Jl. M. H. Thamrin (tel. 021/321-307), doesn't offer a tranquil park setting but few can match the sophisticated style and service of the Bangkok Oriental's younger sister. Its white, 25-story tower overlooks the city's Welcome Monument, a traffic circle central to Jakarta's business community and within walking distance of many shops and restaurants. The Mandarin Oriental's 455 rooms are very spacious and elegantly decorated. Batik fabrics designed by the noted Iwan Tirta are hand-sewn into wall panels and quilted bedspreads. Teak furniture, embroidered cushions, Indonesian artifacts, and marble bathrooms with twin sinks are just some of the luxurious touches in their single ($112) and double ($125) rooms. Even larger, more glamorous suites start at $240 per night.

The Mandarin Oriental has some of Jakarta's finest restaurants (see "Dining") and a comfortable balcony (overlooking Javanese sculpture in the lobby) where tea is served so properly that we interrupted a shopping spree to attend. Services include an impressive Executive Center, beauty salon and barbershop (open from 9 a.m. to 6 p.m.), meeting rooms, and a fitness center with daily aerobics classes and squash courts. Their fifth-floor pool deck, high enough above traffic to be tranquil, features a Friday-night Indonesian buffet and outdoor screenings of American and European films every Sunday.

Aryaduta is Indonesian for "ambassador," and the **Hyatt Aryaduta Jakarta,** at Jl. Prapatan 44/48, not far from Merdeka Square (tel. 021/376-008), is the chain's deluxe representative. The totally renovated Hyatt has expanded to 340 rooms, and boasts an airy mocha granite lobby, a new pool and Balinese garden sundeck, and fitness and business centers. Redecorated, spacious double rooms, furnished in bleached teak, Javanese rattan with mauve silk upholstery, and large bathrooms, are excellent value at $110. Even larger, Ambassador Wing rooms with desks, a full marble bath with separate shower stall, king-size beds, and fully planted verandas off the pool (on the third floor only) rent for $135 per night; plush suites decorated with provincial wood sculpture start at $165. The Hyatt's Regency Club level offers a common lounge for complimentary, buffet-style continental breakfast, cocktails, newspaper delivery, and a more luxuriously appointed room for a $20-per-night premium. The facelift has given the Hyatt a new Japanese restaurant, French bistro, the Tavern Pub, and a piano in its popular lobby lounge, now sheltered from the bustling lobby by wood screens carved with lotus flowers.

One four-star hotel that offers a deluxe but comfortable ambience and stands out from the many along Jl. M. H. Thamrin is the ten-year-old **Hotel Sari Pacific** (tel. 021/323-707). Since it's long been a favorite of frequent visitors to Jakarta, most guests treat the Sari Pacific's piano bar and coffeeshop (especially their lunch buffets) as a second home. Evenings are spent at the quiet, tasteful Jayakarta Grill, known for excellent continental cuisine and attentive service. Bamboo furniture, louvered window shades, and native fabrics give the guest rooms a warm, luxurious Oriental feeling. Rates run $120 for singles and $125 for doubles, though their four "super executive" floors, with complimentary breakfast, cocktails, newspaper delivery, and other amenities, are a bargain for only $8 more.

FIRST-CLASS HOTELS: Jakarta's first-class hotels (rates from $60 to $110 per night, quoted in dollars, plus 15% to 21% tax and service charges) are primarily the older international-style ones that have been maintained well enough to fetch international rates. Most are conveniently located along Jl. M. H. Thamrin, the business and tourist boulevard that runs north-south through the city.

The **Sahid Jaya Hotel** is at the southern end of the hub at Jl. Jend. Sudirman 86 (tel. 021/587-031). A fine teak-and-marble lobby, the large pool terrace where a new wing is being constructed, and some good dining are all first-class here. Spacious rooms with Indonesian décor are well kept and rent for $92 single or $102 double.

Another choice with more modest facilities is the nearby **Kartika Plaza Hotel**, at Jl. M. H. Thamrin 10 (tel. 021/321-008). Bright décor, comfortable furnishings, and a separate seating area make its renovated rooms, priced at $70, a good value. The older rooms, spartan and rather drab with age, rent for $50 to $60 for two (15% less for singles), but the $58 rooms have balconies overlooking a large pool and pleasant garden area.

The 354-room **President Hotel** is centrally located at Jl. M. H. Thamrin 59 (tel. 021/320-508). Evidence of its ownership by Japanese Nikko Hotels International can be found everywhere. The staff is attentive and extremely polite. Rooms are neat, small, but very compact, and offer first-class amenities (such as a seating area, workspace, complimentary toiletries) for $75 single, $90 double, or $110 and up for suites. The President has two popular Japanese restaurants, two penthouse sky-view restaurants atop their 28-story office tower, and an arcade with a jeweler, hair salon (open from 8 a.m. to 7:30 p.m.), bakery, dry cleaners, batik shop, and the Japan Airlines office. By the time of your arrival the President's management hopes to have completed construction on a pool and fitness center for its guests.

The huge **Hotel Indonesia,** a concrete megablock at the central Welcome Monument traffic circle on Jl. M. H. Thamrin (tel. 021/320-008), is charming in its own peculiar way. Built as Jakarta's first international hotel for the 1962 Asian Games, it is finally undergoing a facelift. An $8-million renovation has turned the cavernous lobby (stage for much intrigue in *The Year of Living Dan-*

gerously) into a glass-and-chrome atrium. All 599 rooms are being renovated in stages. Rooms in the Ramayana Wing open off long, tiled, open-air corridors and have been redone to compete with those at other first-class hotels; rates are $95 single, $110 double, and $275 for a two-bedroom suite. The Indonesia's large pool is at the center of a lush garden with a grass sunbathing area (remember Sigourney Weaver in a bathing suit?), tennis courts, and shops. The enormous Ramayana Terrace coffeeshop has been rebuilt with sweeping columns, tiered seating areas, and a delightful aviary.

The **Hotel Horison,** at Taman Impian Jaya Ancol (tel. 021/680-008), in the heart of the Ancol Dreamland amusement park, overlooks Jakarta Bay and a palm-fringed beach. Modern, airy rooms with views over the bay or nearby golf course, a large pool and sunbathing area, several restaurants, and the Disneyland-like surroundings create a resort atmosphere within a half hour of the city's center. Rooms cost $45 for a single and $60 for a double room (more for a bay view); it's good value if you and your family want to enjoy Ancol Dreamland or the Thousand Islands resort, but considering Jakarta's maddening traffic, too far away if you intend to explore the rest of the city.

THE MODERATELY PRICED RANGE: Luckily for the traveler, Jakarta has some excellent hotels in the moderate price range—between Rp 40,000 ($25) and Rp 96,000 ($60) per night, plus 12% to 16% tax and service charges. They are generally locally managed, and offer the traveler a neighborhood feeling, friendly staff, and clean comfortable rooms with good amenities. Our selections are conveniently located in the residential areas that surround the city's central business core, but only one has a swimming pool. Don't forget that a bit of bargaining is in order at these smaller hotels; you can expect a 10% to 40% discount or at least an upgrade to a better room if they're not fully booked. Unlike the luxury and first-class hotels, room rates are quoted in rupiah and may fluctuate with the current exchange rate.

The best value in this price range is the **Cikini Sofyan Hotel,** at Jl. Cikini Raya 79 near the T.I.M. Arts Center in the posh Menteng area (tel. 021/320-695). A glitzy lobby displays the carved-wood and marble décor of Sumatra. Modern rooms are spotless, carpeted, and trimmed in batik, with built-in desk units or, in junior suites, a built-in breakfast nook. Want to phone home? Private phones all offer IDD (a new, money-saving intercontinental direct-dial service). Doubles range from Rp 61,400 ($38.50) to Rp 69,100 ($43.25) for standard, larger "executive" rooms, junior suites, or suites. The Cikini Sofyan has a lovely garden outside its 24-hour coffeeshop.

The government-owned **Wisata International,** on Jl. M. H. Thamrin (tel. 021/320-308), another fine choice with 165 rooms, was created from the former staff quarters of its neighbor, the Hotel Indonesia. Although it doesn't boast its own luxurious grounds, in five minutes you can stroll over to the Hotel Indonesia's gardens and jump into their huge pool ($3 admission fee). Recently modernized rooms in one wing of the Wisata are bright and stylishly decorated in rose and burgundy hues. Singles at Rp 73,600 ($46) and doubles at Rp 89,440 ($56) run 20% higher than in the unrenovated wing, but are worthwhile because of their freshness and first-class feel. Each room also offers a copy of the Koran, the Bible, and the Teachings of Buddha, in keeping with the country's policy of religious diversity.

The next two choices are located in Glodok, Jakarta's Chinatown and heart of the old city. The **Hotel Chitra** is one block off the main street, Jl. Medan Glodok, at Jl. Toko Tiga 23 (tel. 021/629-1213). The Chitra's décor—marble with paper lanterns and other Chinese accents—reflects its environment. Yet once you step in out of this densely populated, narrow-laned quarter, the halls and rooms are surprisingly bright, clean, and spacious. Front rooms on the bustling Jl. Toka Tiga (potentially noisy, so check first) overlook the canal, a vestige from the Dutch colonial period when this area was known as Kota ("city"). Singles or doubles cost Rp 40,000 ($22.50) to Rp 49,500 ($31), depending on floor (the Chinese don't like high floors) and view. The larger **City Hotel** is around the corner on Jl. Medan Glodok, at the corner of the busy Jl. Gajah Mada (tel. 021/629-7008). Take an elevator to the bright, cheerful lobby, a refreshingly peaceful sanctuary on the third floor above several stories of shops, Chinese fast-food stalls, jewelers, and other vendors. Pleasant rooms are simply furnished in rattan with Chinese motifs, and offer small refrigerators. Third-floor "deluxe" rooms, with balconies overlooking the red-tiled roofs of Chinatown, cost Rp 57,600 ($36) for singles, Rp 67,200 ($42) for doubles. We preferred the top-floor, back-facing rooms, and they even cost $1 less! If you must, you can save another 15% in an inside, windowless room. Both hotels share a great location for walkers, within minutes of the colonial Kota Railroad Station, Fatamillah Square, old Batavia, and the colorful produce and flower markets of Chinatown. Since Jakarta has a 25% ethnic Chinese population, in the weeks around Chinese New Year (generally late January to early February) it will be virtually impossible to get a room.

The classiest moderately priced hotel and a comfortable place to call home, the **Hotel Kemang,** on Jl. Kemang Jaya (tel. 021/799-3208) is in Kebayoran Baru, an exclusive suburb. It's a great location if you're in Jakarta to do business, visit friends, or stay a while, but you'll be about a half-hour cab ride south of the National Monument and at least an hour away from the port. Across the quiet street is a mini-mall with a Dunkin' Donuts, pizzeria, laundry and dry cleaners, and a gourmet supermarket with an Indonesian take-out deli. Many European guests favor the Kemang because of the large pool area, lawns, and small yet comfortable rooms. They are spotless, have the usual amenities, and cost Rp 76,800 ($48) for two, with negotiable long-term rates. There is a friendly bar/coffeeshop, open from 6 a.m. to 11 p.m., which does not serve alcohol in deference to the owners' religious (Muslim) beliefs. However, guests are free to buy their own and stock the refrigerators that are in every room.

BUDGET CHOICES: Jakarta's hotels generally are more expensive and of lesser quality than those in most other Southeast Asian capitals, and nowhere is this more evident than in the budget range (rates below $20, usually including tax and service charges, and somewhat negotiable). Recommended hotels offer air conditioning (or fan, as noted), private attached toilets and hot-water showers, and basic furnishings. These hotels all have laundry service and breakfast facilities, and some have pools, private phones, or TVs. Although we considered all hotels under $20 per night for this category, we cannot recommend any we saw in the below-$10 range.

The best of the budget rooms are the clean, comfortable accommodations at the **Menteng I** and **Menteng II Hotels** in the fashionable residential district of the same name. The Menteng II, a 78-room facility at Jl. Cikini Raya 105 (tel. 021/325-543), is the newer and more appealing of the two. Standard rooms are Rp 38,000 ($23.75) single, Rp 44,000 ($27.50) double. The hotel has a small pool, coffeeshop, and 24-hour room service. Although the Menteng II is built on a quiet lane away from the busy street, choose a back-facing room. If it's fully booked, another 71 clean but worn rooms are nearby at the Menteng I, at Jl. Gondangdia Lama 28 (tel. 021/325-208). For Rp 6,000 ($3.75) less per night, similar but older rooms also have their own TV and phone. We welcome readers' comments on the Menteng I's intriguing Hot Men Bar.

A perennial favorite of budget globetrotters is Jakarta's answer to Motel 6. The **Marco Polo Hotel** is at Jl. Cikditiro 19 in Menteng (tel. 021/325-409), about a 15-minute walk from the Welcome Monument. Their large pool, bordered by lush plantings and a gold mermaid, is a welcome sight on a hot day. The spacious, comfortable lobby features a good, cheap coffeeshop. Rooms are spartan, worn, relatively clean, and all one price—Rp 32,000 ($20)—although outer rooms have small balconies and inner ones only offset the lack of windows with a color TV!

Guesthouses and Hostels

Jakarta's best buy in lodgings are the unregistered "guesthouses" in Menteng that were converted from private Dutch-owned residences and usually cater only to former colonials. These large mansions offer travelers four to eight rooms with high ceilings, traditional Dutch architecture, and green lawns in a quiet neighborhood. If your budget is below $10 per night, rock-bottom accommodations can be found along Jl. Jaksa, about five minutes south of Merdeka Square, off Jl. Kebon Sirih. There are many hostels where two will find cots for less than $4 a night, but *caveat emptor!*

The best of those guesthouses open to the public is the **Guest House P.G.I.**, at Jl. Teuku Umar 17 (tel. 021/342-896). Managed by Dr. Tanamal for the Communion of Churches in Indonesia (P.G.I.), this charming guesthouse has 14 rooms ranging from Rp 18,000 ($11.25) to Rp 21,300 ($13.25) for a single and Rp 26,250 ($16.50) to Rp 29,500 ($18.50) for a double. In the one family room, four can sleep in old-fashioned simplicity for Rp 39,500 ($24.75). Rates vary if rooms have air conditioning, hot water, or a private bathroom, but all are spotless and have ceiling fans, screened windows, towels, and sinks. The missionaries serve simple meals, do laundry at modest prices, and are friendly, though few speak English. Call or write for reservations here; in the busy year-end holiday season and during the summer Guest House P.G.I. is often booked two weeks in advance.

The **Teuku Umar Guest House** is down the street at Jl. Teuku Umar 66 (tel. 021/310-0599). The huge sculpted white horse in front distinguishes this three-story stucco home and lovely gardens from its neighbors. Inside, 15 guest rooms —most large with attached bath, some with air conditioning, none with hot water—surround an open, central courtyard. Rates run Rp 18,500 ($11.50) to Rp 29,000 ($18).

Among Jl. Jaksa's numerous hostels we found the **Djody Hostel and Hotel** (tel. 021/346-600) to be the cleanest. Very basic rooms are arranged around a courtyard with common toilet and cold-water shower at one end. Most have fans but no windows, and cost Rp 11,000 ($7) for two, although the eclectic variety of rooms includes some with antique, carved-wood marriage beds, small windows, and even private baths for up to Rp 22,400 ($14). Their hostel two doors away has dormitory accommodations at Rp 3,500 ($2.25) per bed.

4. DINING

The recent influx of foreign businesses to Jakarta has brought with it a dramatic increase in the number of fine restaurants serving Indonesian, Asian, and European cuisines. A number of the finer establishments are in the hotels, but we encourage travelers to try independent restaurants, where a special meal may be more authentically prepared. Bottled or boiled water (*air putih*) is served everywhere and the strict standards of hygiene enforced by government licenses usually ensure a safe meal.

After "Culinary Highlights" (our choice of unforgettable meals), this section is divided by the ethnic cuisines available. Whether you're looking for a lunch break while sightseeing or a gourmet dinner, select the cuisine and flag a taxi. Most of our recommendations are centrally located within 20 minutes of Merdeka Square and are well worth the journey.

Unless otherwise noted, Jakarta's restaurants invite casual dress (but not tank tops or shorts) and are open daily for lunch (11:30 a.m. or noon to 2:30 or 3 p.m.) and dinner (6:30 or 7 p.m. to 10 or 11 p.m.).

You'll find that fine dining is a real bargain here, but don't be put off by menus that rarely list prices. Restaurateurs cite two factors: (1) the seasonal variation in wholesale prices, and (2) the possible discount when large portions are ordered. So rather than charge top dollar, they pass their savings on to customers. Waiters are happy to tell you before ordering what your choices will cost; *the price estimates we quote are the cost of average meals for one person.*

Many of the restaurants listed require reservations only for weekend evenings and accept credit cards, although call ahead if this is a prerequisite.

CULINARY HIGHLIGHTS: To our palates, Jakarta's three musts in dining each promise a night to remember. All are open for lunch, accept credit cards, request reservations at any meal, and suggest dressy or festive attire.

If you've got only one night, spend it at **Oasis,** Jl. Raden Saleh Raya 47 (tel. 326-397). From the tree-shaded, classic white façade it's difficult to tell that this 1928 mansion was originally the estate of Dutch tea and rubber magnate F. Brandenburg van Oltsende, and was later occupied by the governor-general of the Dutch East Indies and the U.S. naval attaché. In 1970 the house was converted into the present-day Oasis Restaurant, known for its fine European food. Each parlor and living space has been decorated with the arts or handcrafts of a particular region of the archipelago, lending the place a decidedly colonial grandeur even today. Guests are greeted by costumed attendants who strike an 18th-century Javanese gong to announce your arrival.

You can still select excellent entrees such as lobster thermidor, escalopes of veal Sorrento, or chateaubriand with herbs. But Oasis is unique for its preparation and service of the traditional Indonesian rijsttafel. Legend has it that under the Dutch plantation owners, rijsttafel (from the Dutch "rice table") evolved from the typical Indonesian meal of steamed rice, a meat, chicken, or fish dish, vegetables, and chili sambal into a feast of several exotically spiced, varied dishes. At Oasis 12 graceful waitresses in typical Javanese costumes parade out to your table, each proudly bearing a separate dish. After the sop telur puyuh (quail egg soup) arrives in antique bowls, the women begin to ladle specialties like sweet-and-sour gurame fish, shrimp and chicken satay, dried beef, fried grated coconut with peanuts, and assorted condiments around the perimeter of a large Javanese ceramic platter filled with rice. Their timing and precision is impeccable; the service, ceremonial but not at all stuffy. Take your time sampling each new flavor and the servers will still be waiting in the wings to refill your plate. An exotically delicious makanan penutup (pudding) follows for dessert, with rich Java kopi or teh.

By this time the lively orchestra has usually coaxed dancers onto the checkered marble floors or the lush Italianate garden off the back parlor. More sedate guests can stroll through the first floor admiring the fine collection of Sumatran weavings and primitive Asmat woodcarvings. This unforgettable evening of feasting and theater can be yours for Rp 32,000 ($20) per person. Oasis is open daily except Sunday.

The finest in European and Indonesian nouvelle cuisine is found at **Taman Sari,** the super-elegant restaurant at the plush Jakarta Hilton International Hotel (tel. 583-051). Carved-teak and gilt-coffered ceilings, a tuxedoed trio playing romantic standards, fountains, an open kitchen, and fresh orchids provide the backdrop for European cuisine and Indonesian nouvelle cuisine, a creative blend of Indonesian spices and ingredients with a light but deft touch. Small, delicately ornate portions of the freshest vegetables and herbs accompany chicken, fish, and meat entrees laced with newly interpreted, classic Indonesian sauces. The range and depth of flavors of the daily foods of the local people is astonishing, and totally enlightening to those accustomed only to nasi goreng, sate ayam, and gado-gado.

The delicious taste and uniqueness of this dining event make Taman Sari a must. The restaurant is open daily except Sunday. Indonesian nouvelle cuisine is served evenings only, although at lunch there are excellent prix-fixe European meals. At supper, the set Indonesian nouvelle menu costs Rp 38,400 ($24) and the set gourmet menu, Rp 51,200 ($32), both a worthy gastronomic experience.

The exquisite imperial-style Chinese cuisine and fine service at **The Summer Palace,** on the seventh floor atop the Tedja Buana Building, Jl. Menteng Raya 29 (tel. 332-969), makes this one of Jakarta's culinary highlights. Excellent Szechuan and Cantonese food is presented in their spacious, elegantly traditional premises. A bevy of formally dressed servers appear with silver, porcelain, ceramic, and ornate wood platters heaped with gourmet fare. Each dish is decorated in edible art worthy of a Ming emperor. For instance, the superb combination roast duck and pressed chicken appetizer arrives on a wooden ship draped in papaya fishing nets; the piquant, tender squid with chiles comes in a bird's nest of fried taro. Radish and ginger flowers or cucumber and melon fans garnish the likes of crisp Peking duck, shark's fin, or abalone (these gourmet entrees are priced from $25, depending on availability). The desserts are novel, refreshing, and very satisfying.

The Summer Palace is open daily. In addition to the extensive à la carte menu, they offer prix-fixe banquet menus (for a party of ten or more) and dim sum brunch on Sunday from 10 a.m. to 2:30 p.m. Two can revel in an afternoon or evening of memorable food and impeccable service for Rp 45,000 ($28) to Rp 76,800 ($48).

INDONESIAN CUISINE: Most Jakartaites won't recommend an Indonesian restaurant unless the chili sambal is so spicy that you leave with a numb tongue! The truth is, Indonesians don't even like restaurants; everyone prefers to eat at a favorite *warung,* those tiny roadside stalls that announce their specialty on banners and are set up on folding tables along the busiest avenues. For health safety reasons we can't really recommend the Jakarta warungs to tourists, so instead try any of the restaurants throughout the city. What they serve is, if not completely authentic, at least quite delicious. Only gourmands will catch the subtle differences between Javanese, Sundanese, Maduran, and the regional cuisines from each province; we're going to consider them all equally Indonesian.

A new option for street-food aficionados that replicates the pleasures of warung dining without the health risks is **Puja Sera 4,** independent warungs given a group home at Jl. Kebun Sirih 63, off Jl. Thamrin near the Sari Pacific Hotel (tel. 322-487). You can travel the culinary archipelago of Indonesia and sample regional cuisines from over two dozen stalls. Try the spicy dishes of Padang food from West Sumatra, a nasi gudeg complet (fried rice with chicken and jackfruit) from Yogyakarta, a martabak, the flavorful omelet/pancake found everywhere, gado-gado, Chinese food, and even cheeseburgers. The food is cheap—two can eat for Rp 6,500 ($4)—delicious, and prepared and presented in hygienic surroundings open 24 hours a day. What more could you want?

Atithya Loka, on Jl. Gatot Subroto next to the Satriamandala Military Museum (tel. 516-102), is one of the city's most dramatic venues for local cuisine. Fish ponds and footbridges under towering palm trees define a dining area decorated with carved, life-size banana trees from Bali and primitive statuary from Irian Jaya. Traditional favorites such as sate ayam (skewered chicken with peanut sauce), ikan bakar (crisp, broiled carp), or ayam goreng Bogor (moist fried chicken with local spices) are served by a staff eager to offer suggestions and make their guests feel at home. Athithya Loka is open for lunch and dinner, for about Rp 13,600 ($8.50) per person; reservations are recommended.

This one is simply decorated, just a big yellow hall with multilevel seating and plastic tablecloths. Yet **Sari Kuring,** in the shadow of Monas at the Jakarta Fairgrounds on Jl. Silang Monas Timur (tel. 352-972), comes up on everyone's list of the best Sundanese cuisine. Even Jakartaites approve of their keredok (local vegetables in a peanut sauce) and many fish dishes. Spices are fresh and liberally used. We'd recommend a visit to this or their other restaurant, at Jl. Batu Ceper 55A (tel. 341-542), after you've acclimated to Indonesian food in milder, tourist-oriented restaurants. Both locations are very casual, authentic, and cost less than Rp 6,800 ($4.25) per person.

Another casual choice for indoor and outdoor dining is **Mira Sari** Jl. Patiunis 13, in Kebayoran (tel. 771-621), a ritzy suburb in south Jakarta. Tall philodendron and arica palms surround the patio tables with their red-checkered cloths, while the interior's blond-wood paneling makes it a bit better dressed. Mira Sari serves interesting variations on standard Javanese fare. Nasi goreng kepiting is their fried rice with crabmeat; their martabak is a particularly light, tasty vegetable omelet. Every dish is well cooked, moderately spiced or with killer chiles on the side, and the generous portions are fairly priced. Expect to pay less than Rp 8,800 ($5.50) per person. Mira Sari is open nightly for dinner only; closed Friday.

Sari Nusantara, on Jl. Silang Monas Tenggara (tel. 352-972), is the dressed up, air-conditioned companion of Sari Kuring, nearby at the Jakarta Fairgrounds. An excellent ayam gulung saus (rolled chicken) and tumis kangkung trasi tauco (sautéed vegetables with shrimp) are typical of their well-flavored, not-too-spicy entrees. Sari Nusantara's framed batiks, traditional music, linens, and uniformed waiters add about $2 per person to the bill you'd pay next door, but it's conveniently located and a good introduction to the cuisine.

If you've begun to appreciate Indonesian food and are feeling adventurous, move on to Padang food, the spicy cuisine from West Sumatra that has migrated to the farthest reaches of the archipelago. Intricately flavored curries; crisply fried meat, fowl, and fish; smooth sauces of turmeric, coconut milk, and cayenne add a variety of accents to the usual Indonesian ingredients for those saturated with satay. At **Sari Ratu Padang Restaurant** you'll be served ten or more dishes from the ones stacked like pyramids in the front window; each will have a few portions, in the true Padang style. Knoshers will love the chance to sample a bit, or share a portion, of the curried hard-boiled egg, cold-potato vegetable pancake, pickled greens, fried quail breast, curried beef liver, or fiery randang dishes because you only pay for what you eat. Never mind that your entrees were served earlier to someone else; the food is so well cured, stewed, and spiced that no bacteria could ever survive it. At Padang restaurants you can count on eating a unique meal in less than a half hour and for less than Rp 6,000 ($3.75) each. Sari Ratu Padang Restaurant has two locations: in the basement of the Ratu Plaza Shopping Center on Jl. Jend. Sudirman near the Jakarta Hilton (tel. 712-209), or on the ground floor of Gajah Mada Plaza on Jl. Gajah Mada in Glodok (tel. 366-070). Both are open from 9:30 a.m. to 8 p.m. Monday through Friday and 9:30 a.m. to 5 p.m. on Saturday and Sunday.

One of Indonesia's best-known culinary delights is satay, a skewer full of chicken (sate ayam), beef (sate sapi or daging), lamb (sate domba), pork (sate babi), or goat (sate kambing) that's covered with a lightly spiced peanut sauce. Jakarta's popular chain **Satay House Senayan** has four locations open daily. Guests dine family style at long picnic tables under an intricately carved Javanese wood canopy. Try soto Madura (hearty beef soup from Madura Island) and lontong cap go meh (rice cooked in coconut sauce) with your choice of satay. All dishes, priced at Rp 1,620 ($1) to Rp 3,400 ($2) should be washed down with an es kopior, the juice of a green coconut served in its shell. A centrally located Satay House Senayan is at Jl. HOS Cokroaminoto, 78 in Menteng (tel. 334-243), but check with your hotel to see if one of their other branches is more convenient.

A more upscale, European-style restaurant serving Indonesian fare to the business and expatriate crowd is **Restoran Indonesia,** in the Panin Bank Center, Jl. Jend. Sudirman 1 (tel. 739-5904). It is stylishly decorated with marble floors, wood and glass walls, and lush plants. Violin and piano music is played at each meal. Their eclectic menu features provincial favorites like ayam goreng Bogor (fried chicken), ikan bakar Ujung Pandang (baked fish), and rendang Padang (spicy pot roast). The daily luncheon is a carvery and rijsttafel buffet and on Sunday it's Chinese dim sum from 7 a.m. to 2 p.m. Dinner for two will run Rp 25,600 ($16) to Rp 40,000 ($25); lunch, 20% less.

CHINESE CUISINE: More than 25% of Jakarta's residents are of Chinese origin. Although the government strives to integrate the Chinese by slowly eradicating signs of their language and culture, Chinese cuisine has been fully embraced by the Indonesian community. So much so that most Indonesian restaurants claim some Chinese dishes on their menu and so-called Chinese restaurants serve nasi goreng. If you're craving the taste of oyster sauce or bamboo shoots, and aren't expecting the gourmet purity of the Summer Palace (see "Culinary Highlights"), we can recommend a few establishments.

Our first choice is the **Spice Garden,** in the Mandarin Oriental Hotel on Jl. Thamrin (tel. 321-307), a contemporary pavilion in cream, red, and gold tones. The hotel's enterprising management imported a chef from China's Szechuan province who has trained his staff in the fiery-hot cuisine from that region and gourmet Cantonese fare. Novices should try a set menu for about Rp 38,000 ($23.75) at lunch or dinner, a six-course feast that includes three entrees. Beancurd rolls filled with sprouts and Szechuan sauce, stir-fried beef with bamboo and mushrooms, and crispy double-steamed duckling with chicken and shrimp are properly piquant and decoratively presented. Two ordering from the à la carte menu should expect to pay Rp 56,000 ($35) and up.

Local gourmands concur with the choice of **Yun Njan,** Jl. Batu Ceper 69 (tel. 364-063), for the best seafood, prepared in a Chinese fashion, in town. It's an unprepossessing place: a large neon sign is over a plain storefront with some Chinese décor, and inside there are Formica tables and folding chairs. Don't be fooled—the seafood that streams out of the kitchen is anything but plain. Favorites include shark's-fin soup with crabs and prawn, fresh boiled shrimp, steamed fish with black mushrooms, and fried squid with oyster sauce. A rich, seafood feast for two (it's cheaper by the dozen!) should average Rp 22,400 ($14). Yun Njan is open daily for lunch and dinner except on Monday when they serve dinner only.

If you crave dim sum, those tiny plates of assorted hors d'oeuvres, the Chinese quarter's biggest tea hall is the **Palace Restaurant,** on the fifth floor of Gajah Mada Plaza, at Jl. Gajah Mada 19-26 in Glodok (tel. 356-252). This 2,000-seat gold-and-red ballroom, replete with stage and dance floor, does a booming dim sum lunch trade between 7 a.m. and 3 p.m. daily. Each dim sum dish costs less than Rp 1,500 (90¢); the six Hong Kong chefs turn out Cantonese favorites at dinner for Rp 8,800 ($5.50) and up per person.

OTHER ASIAN CUISINES: One of the treats of being in a cosmopolitan Asian capital is the range of other Asian cuisines that are readily available. Jakarta boasts at least one fine restaurant from every region, including **Maharajah** (Indian), Jl. Agus Salim 52 (tel. 337-142); **Paregu** (Vietnamese), at Jl. Sunan Kalijaga 64 in Blok M (tel. 717-114); and **Sri Thai** (Thai), in the Setia Budi Building on Jl. Rasuna Said (tel. 515-124). Since the business people demand to be fed, it's the city's Korean and Japanese restaurants that stand out.

The **Korea Garden** at Jl. Teluk Betung 33 (tel. 322-544), is only a five-minute walk from the Hotel Indonesia but several countries away from Jakarta. The décor is classically Korean, with wood trellis and paper screens, ornately carved furnishings, fine Korean paintings, prayer fans, and bronze wall hangings. After you're seated by the costumed hostess, a uniformed waitress will arrive with a full white apron for each guest. A traditional Korean barbecue includes a variety of delicious appetizers and the classic kimchee, a spicy pickled cabbage. Sliced beef, ribs, or chunks of sirloin are cooked on a sunken grill right at your table, followed by a refreshing, light soup. Two can enjoy an afternoon or evening in old Seoul for Rp 23,000 ($14.50) to Rp 40,000 ($25). Larger parties wanting to dine in one of Korea Garden's elegant private rooms should contact the charming owner, Mr. Kim, for reservations; open daily.

The recent influx of Japanese capital into Indonesia has spawned a number of luxury restaurants catering to the local and visiting business community, and some are as authentic and expensive as any you'll find in Tokyo. **Tokyo Garden,** located in the Lippo Life Building at Jl. Rasuna Said kav. B 10-11 (tel. 517-828), stands out in the crowd. The décor is quietly and thoroughly Japanese, with teak and sandalwood teppanyaki tables looking out over graceful Japanese gardens. The busy businessman usually orders one of the lunch specials, ranging in price from Rp 6,500 ($4) to Rp 13,350 ($8.25). Evening diners prefer the theatrically cooked teppanyaki dishes, Tokyo Garden's specialty. Grilled chicken and salmon meals, or imported beef, also served with fresh, grilled vegetables, cost from Rp 8,800 ($5.50) to Rp 10,000 ($6.25) per person.

Of the many Japanese restaurants found in the deluxe hotels, **Keio,** in the Borobudur Inter-Continental, on Jl. Lapangan Bantang Selatan (tel. 370-108), is recommended. Food preparation and presentation are supervised by chefs brought over from the Tokyo Inter-Continental. Their traditional tatami rooms can accommodate Westerners who prefer to sit on the floor, with sunken wells under each table in which to extend your legs. Favorites among their authentic entrees are the teriyaki grill, Yakimono broiled salmon with grated radish, and sashimi moriawase. Every business day Keio Japanese Restaurant offers a choice of eight set luncheons for Rp 8,500 ($5.25) to Rp 13,500 ($8.50) that are paid for (in true Japan, Inc., style) with coupon books bought by companies for their employees. Travelers with rupiah and credit cards are also welcome. Complete six-course dinners cost Rp 18,000 ($11.25) to Rp 34,000 ($21.25) and the superb fresh sushi is Rp 16,000 ($10) for a deluxe assortment. Keio's lunch and dinner crowd are a bit dressy; reservations are recommended.

The most elegant of the new crop of Japanese restaurants, **Chikuyo-Tei,** on the ground floor of the modern Summitmas Tower at Jl. Jend. Sudirman 61 (tel. 520-0880), is the tenth in a chain that's grown from this hundred-year-old Tokyo restaurant. At Chikuyo-Tei, kimono-clad waitresses pad softly across polished black-tile floors bearing lacquer baskets and artistic dishware. The best buy here is at lunch, when you can sample their pricey entrees in set menus. Deep-fried oysters or seafood with mixed vegetables, soup, rice, and dessert cost Rp 8,000 ($5) to Rp 15,000 ($9.50). In the evening, well-dressed Europeans and Japanese crowd the tatami rooms to feast on unagi kabayaki teishoku, a complete traditional meal including sashimi and their celebrated boiled eel, which costs Rp 46,000 ($28.75). Reservations, and jacket or batik shirt for men, are recommended.

WESTERN DINING: Centuries of colonization, an international business community, and the once-flourishing oil industry have graced Jakarta with a number of elegant continental and steak restaurants, and a surprising array of fast-food favorites.

Continental Cuisine

As you might expect, many of the best continental restaurants are found in the luxury hotels. Most are open daily for lunch and dinner, reservations are recommended, particularly on weekends, and casual but neat attire is accepted. Prices are steep by Indonesian standards, a 16% to 21% tax and service charge will be added to your bill, and an additional 5% to 10% tip will be expected. Credit cards are accepted by all.

After the Hilton's Taman Sari (See "Culinary Highlights"), our first choice is the **Jayakarta Grill,** on the second floor in the Hotel Sari Pacific, on Jl.

Thamrin (tel. 323-707), a restaurant whose grace is reminiscent of New York's Russian Tea Room. Named for Glorious Victory, the 16th-century capital of the Muslim kingdom of Prince Fatahillah, the Jayakarta Grill reflects a past glory in its huge brass garuda-shaped chandeliers and collection of antique Javanese porcelains. The menu reflects a sophisticated continental and Asian taste: braised duck in burgundy, red mullet with ginger sauce, and rack of lamb in green peppercorns are some specialties. A romantic evening at the Jayakarta Grill will run upward of Rp 64,000 ($40) per person, although a prix-fixe lunch is a bargain at Rp 31,000 ($19.50).

The **Toba Rotisserie** is the pricey, dark velour and lace restaurant at the Hotel Borobudur Inter-Continental on Jl. Lapangan Bantang Selatan. Nightly, classical music soothes diners who are paying upward of Rp 48,000 ($30) for fine French fare. We preferred the more casual dining experience offered by the Borobudur's **Nelayan Seafood Restaurant** (tel. 370-108). Guests can survey the display of fresh seafood and choose the catch they prefer. Chefs will prepare any fish grilled, fried, broiled, or cooked with Indonesian spices. The Nelayan's large seafood salads are a refreshing choice for those who like the raw vegetables and lettuce that visitors shouldn't eat outside the better hotels. The daily buffet costs Rp 10,200 ($6.50), and their big-enough-for-two seafood basket is Rp 25,000 ($15.50).

Memories, on the ground floor of Wisma Indocement, an office tower at Jl. Jend. Sudirman kav. 70-71 (tel. 578-1008), evokes the bygone grandeur of Dutch colonial rule and is the specialty of this new restaurant. Classic ceramic tiles, pottery, Indo-European brassware, and wonderful documentary photographs from the Dutch era provide the décor. The menu offers Dutch specialties and staples like matjes herring, beef rolled and cooked in coconut sauce, Belgian endive with ham, and cheeses and poffertjes (sugar pancakes) for dessert. The business community entertains here for about Rp 19,500 ($12.25) and up per person. In the evening the pianist entertains a bubbly expatriate and Indonesian crowd who favor Memories' interpretations of Indonesian food. Meals begin at Rp 33,000 ($20.50). Memories is open daily except Sunday.

Casual and Fast Food

Casual ethnic restaurants are so popular with Jakartaites that a bistro, steakhouse, pizzeria, Mexican cantina, English pub, snackbars, and coffeeshops make up our list of informal, inexpensive eateries. Most are open for lunch and dinner daily, and request reservations for Saturday night, if at all; some take credit cards; all would be suitable for children.

A popular French bistro that opened in 1986 is **Le Coq Hardi,** Jl. Jaksa 8 (tel. 336-376). Dark-red brick wallpaper and rust-colored tablecloths establish a cozy venue for tasting leek soup, filet of pomfret, stewed veal, bouillabaise asiatique, or leg of lamb. Prix-fixe lunches range from Rp 9,200 ($5.75) to Rp 13,600 ($8.50), including a glass of wine; an à la carte supper will cost from Rp 20,000 ($12.50).

You can avoid the hefty prices of the five-star hotel grill rooms at **House of Gandy Steak House,** at Jl. HOS Cockroaminoto 90, in Menteng (tel. 333-292), or their two other locations. Chandeliers and rattan jazz up an otherwise fast-food anonymity, but House of Gandy serves a fine T-bone steak, New Zealand filet mignon, or plump "Down Under" lamb chops. Families like their good Junior Menu and wide selection of desserts; adults should plan to spend about Rp 17,920 ($11.25) each for a complete meal, and children pay less than half that amount.

For a refreshingly different change of pace, try **Pizzaria,** the outdoor Italian café run by the Jakarta Hilton on its lush grounds on Jl. Gatot Subroto (tel. 583-051). Pizzaria's red-and-white checkered tables fill a terrace hanging over a duck-filled pond in their Indonesian Bazaar. In view of an ornate Balinese temple and theater, arched bridges, and insistent ducks, an imported pop music band plays top-40 and Indonesian love songs. Local students, expatriates, and the young at heart flock to have pizza exotica (curried chicken, bamboo shoots, and mushrooms), pizza rustica (feta, garlic, and olives), one of their many other combo pizzas, or traditional pasta dishes. Two can have a lot of fun and a great meal for less than Rp 24,000 ($15)! The Pizzaria is open daily from 11:30 a.m. to 12:30 a.m. Sorry, no delivery.

You're in a dark cantina where Indonesian waiters wear blue jeans, snap-closed shirts, and black Stetsons, where the Amri Pulau band plays Willie Nelson tunes, where the passing combination taco plates, chips, and salsa waft heavenly scents of Acapulco your way. Welcome to the **Green Pub,** on the ground floor of the Djakarta Theatre building on Jl. Thamrin, across from the Sarinah department store (tel. 359-332). This is Jakarta's best Mexican restaurant and a favorite haunt of expatriate Americans nostalgic for the sounds and tastes of home. The food is respectable, all ingredients are local except the tortillas, the salsa has bite, and entrees cost about Rp 7,500 ($4.75).

Anglos and Anglophiles will find a bit of home at the **George and Dragon Pub,** at Jl. Teluk Betung 32 off Jl. Thamrin (tel. 325-625), behind the Hotel Indonesia. Dark-wood booths, checkered tablecloths, the long, low bar, and British flags leave no doubt as to the owner's birthplace. Some of the more tempting selections are fish and chips, steak-and-kidney pie, chef's salad, pizza, and banana splits—all costing between Rp 4,800 ($3) and Rp 6,400 ($6) at lunch and about double that at dinner.

The best round-the-clock eatery in town is the **Fiesta Coffee Shop,** in the Hotel Sari Pacific on Jl. Thamrin (tel. 323-707). Try to catch their tasty Indonesian buffet, served daily from noon to 3 p.m., a varied, well-prepared introduction to the local cuisine for just Rp 13,600 ($8.50). If you miss it, their moderately priced menu runs the gamut from chicken salad sandwiches to nasi goreng. Night owls should note that the bubur ayam buffet (chicken or beef slices with rice porridge) runs from 11 p.m. to 4 a.m.

The local breakfast or late-night haunt in town is the new **Ramayana Terrace Coffee Shop,** in the Hotel Indonesia, nearby on Jl. Thamrin (tel. 332-008). Budget prices, in or outdoor dining, a fascinating aviary against one wall, and the fine staff have made this long-popular meeting spot better than ever, *and* it's open 24 hours. The extensive European and Indonesian food buffets served at lunch for Rp 9,700 ($6) and at dinner for Rp 11,400 ($7) are another popular bargain.

Fast-food junkies will not have any problem getting a fix in Jakarta, where the local ayam goreng fans now patronize the many outlets of **El Pollo Loco, Texas Fried Chicken, Pizza Hut,** and **Kentucky Fried Chicken.** There are also several **Dunkin' Donuts,** local pastry shops, **A&W** outlets, **Burger King,** and even a **Bob's Big Boy.** Fast-food chain restaurants can be found in all the shopping malls and along the main business streets like Jl. Gajah Mada in Glodok or Jl. HOS Cockroaminoto in Menteng. Check a local telephone directory to find those nearest you. Most stay open all day between 7 a.m. and 11 p.m. and are as good and cheap as you'd expect back home.

5. SIGHTS, SHOPPING, AND NIGHTLIFE

Present-day Jakarta, the sixth-largest city in the world and one of the most rapidly changing cities in Southeast Asia, will fascinate both newcomers and old Asia hands alike. Huge concrete monuments, high-rise shopping malls to rival Hong Kong's, and the international discos in this predominantly Muslim culture never fail to surprise visitors. In 48 hours you can glimpse the new and the old, the traditional past and the contemporary Western, as well as the harmony and the chaos that engulf and enliven the nation's capital.

THE SIGHTS: Jakarta has a surprising number of museums dedicated to the arts, crafts, history, revolutionary heroes, and other aspects of Indonesian culture. The **Visitor Information Offices** (tel. 354-094 or 332-067 in town, 550-7088 at the airport) publish an excellent city map and brochure called "Jakarta: See for Yourself" which describes 32 museums and sights, and best yet, how to get there by public bus. Several travel agents offer bus tours of the city, yet taxis are so plentiful and inexpensive that we'd recommend using them for sightseeing.

Although Jakarta has museums, monuments, and neighborhoods displaying a legacy dating to prehistoric times, those constructed in the last 30 years reveal the most about Indonesia today. A cab ride through town past mammoth sculptures, large urban parks, monumental traffic circles, and new office towers is a good introduction to this impressive city. Yet behind most of the 20-story office towers and Dutch-colonial mansions are the narrow, twisting *kampungs* (neighborhoods) of the poor who make up most of Jakarta's estimated 7.5 million inhabitants. That the city functions as well as it does under the constant strains of overpopulation, unemployment, and demand for public services indicates just how effective the centralized government (not always a model democracy) has been in keeping things together.

The Soekarno Monuments

Public monuments from the Soekarno era (1945–1962) were built to commemorate the centuries of struggle against colonial rule and to celebrate the country's newfound power. The two figures waving from a pedestal above the busy traffic circle in front of the Hotel Indonesia are atop what is known as the **Welcome Monument,** built in 1962 to welcome international visitors to the Asian Games. Just south of the Welcome Monument on Jl. Imam Bonjol is a monument given by a Japanese sculptor to honor **Raden Kartini,** a Javanese princess who led Indonesia's women's emancipation movement. Across town, an abstract figure casting off chains stands atop the **Irian Jaya Liberty Monument,** honoring the province liberated from the Dutch in 1961. In the fashionable Menteng district, on the site where the Independence Declaration was first read, is **The Proklamator,** dedicated to Soekarno and Hatta, first president and vice president of the Indonesian Republic. In 1965 seven revolutionary heroes were killed in an attempted Communist coup ten miles southeast of the city at Lobang Buaya, Pondok Gede. The **Monumen Pancasila Cakti,** a complex that includes statues of each man, the house where they were tortured, and the well where their bodies were dumped, can be seen in this village near the Taman Mini cultural park.

The best way to appreciate Jakarta's reincarnation as the center of the struggle to achieve and maintain independence for the whole republic is to visit the greatest monument of them all—

The National Monument

The **Monumen Nasional** (known as **Monas**), a 137-meter- (445-foot-) tall white marble obelisk dominating central Jakarta's Merdeka Square, was built in 1961 in honor of the national spirit that helped Indonesia gain independence on August 17, 1945. This date is commemorated architecturally in an 8-meter- (26-foot-) wide central column set on a base 17 meters (55 feet) high and 45 meters (146 feet) wide. A rooftop **viewing gallery** offering an excellent panorama over the city is capped by the "Eternal Flame of Independence," 77 pounds of gold foil.

The ground level of the monument is occupied by the dramatically lit, all-marble **Hall of Independence.** Take a seat and a guide will explain the four national treasures housed within. On one wall hangs the Sang Saka Merah Putih flag, the red (for bravery) and white (for holiness) banner sewn by Mrs. Soekarno for the independence ceremony in 1945. The original text of the Declaration of

Independence is mounted on another marble façade. As carved gold doors slowly open, the solemn voice of President Soekarno, declaring independence to the nation in his original 1945 speech, fills the hall. The guide will lead you around past a 22-karat-gold map of the Republic of Indonesia's 13,677 islands and toward the national coat-of-arms. This shield features a golden mythical garuda bird whose eight tails, 17 wings, and 45 neck feathers are symbolic of the date of independence (8-17-45). The five governing principles of the Republic (the Pancasila) are also symbolized on the shield. Ten feet below ground is a fascinating **Museum of Natural History,** a display of 48 dioramas depicting the development of the archipelago and the many battles fought to unite it. Here the heroes commemorated in Jakarta's street names come to life.

The immense symbolic power of Monas makes it a compelling and worthwhile experience for any visitor to the nation's capital. The National Monument is open daily from 9 a.m. to 5 p.m. except the last Monday of every month. General admission is Rp 600 (40¢); another Rp 1,600 ($1) is charged to visit the viewing gallery.

Merdeka Square

Medan Merdeka (Freedom Square) became the center of the new Jakarta developed by Soekarno, and remains the largest open space and has the tallest single structure (the Monas) in the city. Most of the government ministries and the headquarters of the Pertamina Oil Company are here; the National Parliament on Jl. Gatot Subroto is the only notable exception. South of the fountain at the entrance to the National Monument is the **Statue of Prince Diponegoro** on horseback. Because he led the Javanese in an unsuccessful war against the Dutch from 1825 to 1830, Diponegoro was later exiled to South Sulawesi (his prison cell can be seen today in Ujung Pandang). On the north side is the **Istana Merdeka** or Presidential Palace, known as the Konigsplein when it was built for the Dutch governor-general in 1879. Behind it on Jl. Veteran is the smaller **Istana Negara,** an older palace built for a Dutch businessman and currently used for special state functions and to house visiting dignitaries. On the west side of Merdeka Square is the neoclassic **National Museum.**

Opposite the museum is **Taman Ria,** the Jakarta Fairgrounds. Every year between June and August a trade fair, displaying products from all over Indonesia, is held here. At other times a nightly amusement park, with a roller coaster, rides, and games, several restaurants, and frequent popular concerts keep the fairgrounds busy. Taman Ria is open Monday through Saturday from 5 p.m. to midnight.

There are three houses of worship worth noting on or near Merdeka Square. At Jl. Medan Merdeka Timur 10 is the charming **Dutch Protestant Immanuel Church,** dating from 1835. Nearby is Jakarta's largest Christian church, the impressive **Roman Catholic cathedral** on Jl. Gereja Katedral, built in 1829. It can be photographed from Jl. Medan Merdeka Timur with Jakarta's **Mesjid Istiqlal** in the foreground—the perfect illustration of the country's practice of religious tolerance.

The Istiqlal Mosque

More than 90% of the Indonesian people are Muslims and the gleaming white dome of one of the world's largest mosques stands northeast of Merdeka Square on Jl. Veteran. Mesjid Istiqlal (Freedom Mosque), completed after ten years of work in 1978, is so graceful in its simple lines and white marble interior that it, too, can be considered one of Jakarta's greatest monuments. As at the National Monument, Monas, the numerology symbolic of Indonesia's revolution was used as the architectural measure. The main hall is 45 meters (146 feet) square for the year of independence, by 27 meters (87 feet) high for the number of provinces, and the mosque is built on five levels (for the five principles,

Pancasila). Properly dressed visitors (no shorts or bare arms) are welcome to enter after removing their shoes, but may be shown to the balcony if worshippers are praying in the great hall below. This a good vantage point from which to admire the contemporary, yet traditionally Islamic, architecture. Prayer begins at 4:30 a.m. and then at four other times (approximately three to four hours apart) each day, with devotees summoned by the amplified wailing of the muezzin's call to prayer. On Friday, the Muslim holy day, you'll find the field of carpeting filled with Jakartaites stopping to pray on their way to and from work.

The National Museum

Indonesia's National Museum on Merdeka Square was founded in 1778 by the Batavian Society of Arts and Sciences. It's poorly lit, and unlabeled items are often difficult to date or place, but even the faint-hearted museum buff can absorb some of the varied wonders of the country's 27 provinces. There are hourlong gallery tours in English every Tuesday, Wednesday, and Thursday at 9:30 a.m., and help immeasurably in enjoying this museum.

The country's startling diversity is effectively conveyed by the huge ethnographic map on the rear wall, surrounded by portraits of each of the country's ethnic groups. Galleries to the right of the entrance display carved wooden models of traditional homes, village squares, boats, and tools used in Sumatra, Sulawesi (the Celebes), Kalimantan (Borneo), Irian Jaya (New Guinea), and other regions. The accompanying display of musical instruments, jewelry, primitive art, and local crafts is particularly interesting.

Another gallery displays export porcelain from China, Annam (Vietnam), and Thailand, some dating as far back as the Han Dynasty (206 B.C. to A.D. 220), which was brought to Indonesia by traders and has been found intact on many islands.

The central galleries and courtyard are devoted to sculpture, including temple remnants from the Hindu-Javanese period. Stone reliefs and roof ornaments from the Siva temples of the Dieng Plateau, and 8th- and 9th-century sculptures from the Buddhist temple of Borobudur and Hindu temple of Prambanan (both in central Java) are also displayed. The excellent guidebook *Djakarta Museum Art Treasures,* prepared by Endang Sulbi and sold at the museum's small gift shop for Rp 3,200 ($2) is crucial if you're interested in sculpture.

Other galleries include a numismatics exhibit, assorted bronze work and sculpture, contemporary Indonesian painting, and upstairs, the Treasure Room, a collection of gold, silver, and precious jewels. Votive objects, the jewelry of sultans, kings, and their courtesans, pearl- and ruby-encrusted *kris* (the short Javanese swords with mystical powers), primitive utensils, hairpins, and other items in metalwork display the diverse styles and uniform skill of Indonesian craftsmen over the centuries.

The National Museum is centrally located at Jl. Merdeka Barat, on the west side of Merdeka Square. It's open Tuesday through Thursday from 8:30 a.m. to 2 p.m., on Friday till 11 a.m., on Saturday till 1 p.m., and on Sunday till 2 p.m. Admission is Rp 150 (10¢), and photography is not permitted. Group tours are organized as half- or full-day coach packages and can be booked through Vayatours (tel. 365-008), Panorama Tours (tel. 350-438), or through your hotel concierge. A five-hour tour including a visit to the National Monument and Old Batavia costs Rp 15,000 ($9.50).

Taman Mini Indonesia Indah

Taman Mini Indonesia Indah is one of the most intriguing monuments commemorating the unification of Indonesia. Taman Mini (short for Beautiful Indonesia in Miniature Park) is a cultural theme park built by the government, about 20 km (12½ miles) southeast of the city. The landscaped 250 acres includes the Museum Indonesia, an IMAX movie theater, swimming and recreation area, orchid garden and aviary, and most important, 27 pavilions representing the architecture and culture of each province in Indonesia. The pavilions are set around a huge lake filled with sculpted grass islands representing the Indonesian archipelago, a sight best viewed from the aerial tramway that traverses the park. A religious exhibit includes a mosque, Catholic church, Hindu temple, Buddhist temple (all offering services), and a replica of the Buddhist shrine at Borobudur. Taman Mini can be an educational experience absorbed over several days (especially if you're traveling with children), a cultural sampler tasted in a half-day coach tour, or a self-guided introduction or summary to touring the rest of the country.

Start your visit at the **Teater Keong Emas,** viewing the two movies, *Indonesia Indah I* and *II;* both are photographed in the awesome IMAX wide-screen format and are excellent introductions to the country's beauties. Showings are weekdays from noon to 4 p.m., on Saturday from 11 a.m. to 7 p.m., and on Sunday from 10 a.m. to 5 p.m. Call 840-1021 for further information. Admission is Rp 2,600 ($1.50).

It's a ten-minute walk from the theater to the brick- and carved-stone Balinese palace housing the **Museum Indonesia** and the best collection of costumes, arts, household artifacts, and regional crafts in the country. Don't miss the seven-ton engraved copper Balinese Tree of Life on the top floor! Informed guides can be hired at the museum entrance for Rp 3,200 ($2) per hour; it's open daily from 8 a.m. to 6 p.m.

Once you've learned about the ways of life throughout Indonesia's 27 provinces, you can explore the many pavilions, all built to resemble traditional houses and containing exhibits of local crafts. There are round thatch *honay* from Irian Jaya, carved wood Batak houses from North and Central Sumatra, peak-roofed, brightly painted Toraja homes from South Sulawesi, and many others. You can enter each (many by stairs or ladder because they're built on stilts) and a guide, dressed in the traditional provincial costume, will give you a tour. Several provinces offer music and dance performances on Friday, Saturday, and Sunday (call 849-022 for information).

If your kids begin to suffer from cultural overload, there's a large **recreation area and swimming pool.** Two indoor restaurants (one air-conditioned) serve Indonesian and some continental fare. There are also several typical warung (outdoor foodstalls) serving fried rice, noodle dishes, satay, and snack food.

Taman Mini Indonesia Indah is open daily from 8 a.m. to 5 p.m., and is crowded with local tourists on Friday afternoons and weekends. Admission is Rp 500 (30¢), twice that for automobiles. For a private tour you can rent a taxi through your hotel (or call Blue Bird at 325-607) and book a Taman Mini guide (call 849-525); rates are Rp 5,600 ($3.50) per hour. Private cars can drive through most of the exhibition areas. Group tours are organized as half- or full-day coach packages and can be booked through Vayatours (tel. 365-008), Panorama Tours (tel. 350-438), or through your hotel concierge. A six-hour tour, including a visit to the National and Pancasila Monuments, costs Rp 15,000 ($9.50). To see Taman Mini on your own, take a taxi from the city to the park, for about Rp 13,000 ($8) each way for the 30-minute ride. You can explore it by foot, or rent a bicycle or horse-drawn cart once inside the gates.

Sunda Kelapa and Pasar Ikan

Sunda Kelapa, the natural harbor formed by the Java Sea on Jakarta's north shore, has been a center of trade for centuries. In the early 1500s the Portuguese were the first Europeans to discover Java's riches and sign a trade treaty with the Kingdom of Pajajaran. **Pelabuhan Sunda Kelapa,** or Harbor of Coconut Palms, still welcomes more than 70 ships a day via the Ciliwung River. An early-morning visit to the harbor is most enjoyable. The inlet is filled with sampans manned by craggy-faced oarsmen, fishing or transporting crew to the shore from ships moored farther out in the channel. If you stand still long enough, one will glide up to the pier and offer a round-trip tour of the harbor for about Rp 4,000 ($2.50). It's a great way to admire the *phinisi*, the brightly painted mahogany cargo ships built by the Bugis of South Sulawesi.

The seven-sailed phinisi were honored in 1986 when the *Phinisi Nusantara*, specially built for the voyage, sailed from Jakarta to the World's Fair in Vancouver, Canada. Just 10 to 15 crew man the average ship. Although the engines are typically less than 200 hp, phinisi can haul 100 to 150 tons of cargo under sail. Renting for about Rp 1,000,000 ($6,600) per day, most make the four-day sail between Kalimantan and Jakarta loaded with teak, ironwood, and other lumber, and return with manufactured goods. If you ask permission from the sailors, tourists are welcome to go aboard. We were told that you could hitch a ride to the outer islands on a phinisi by bringing gifts of cigarettes or alcohol to the captain. Since women passengers are thought to bring bad luck, the sacrifice of one chicken is usually necessary before departure.

Sunda Kelapa can be reached from the head of Jl. Lodan or by walking up the picturesque Jl. Pasar Ikan, then taking a boat. This twisting lane is named after the fish market, **Pasar Ikan**, housed in a warehouse at the end of the lane. Between 4 and 6 a.m. it's literally hopping with the day's catch, a market of exotic seashells, lounging fishermen, women cleaning fish, and eager buyers. The **Museum Bahari** is at Jl. Pasar Ikan 1 in the red-tile-roofed warehouses of the old Dutch East India Company, diagonally across from the original harbormaster's tower. Inside is a collection of nautical history, memorabilia, old maps, and some fine wooden models of Indonesian sailing ships. The Bahari Marine Museum is open Tuesday through Thursday from 9 a.m. to 2 p.m., on Friday till 11 a.m., on Saturday till 1 p.m., and on Sunday till 2 p.m. Admission is Rp 150 (10¢).

The city tours, which include a visit to Sunda Kelapa and Pasar Ikan, probably won't satisfy maritime buffs, but the harbor is easily reached by taxi in about a half hour in traffic north of Merdeka Square, for Rp 4,800 ($3).

Old Batavia, Taman Fatahillah, and the Fatahillah Square Museums

In 1527 Prince Fatahillah of the Muslim Kingdom of Demak invaded Sunda Kelapa and on June 22 defeated the Sundanese Kingdom of Pajajaran and its Portuguese allies. Fatahillah renamed the bustling port Jayakarta (City of Victory) and Islam began to replace Hinduism across the archipelago. Today the religion of over 90% of the population, Islam is one of the few vestiges from this period of Muslim rule.

Jayakarta's success as a trading port soon attracted European merchants. In 1602 the Dutch East India Company (Verenigde Ooost-Indische Compagnie or VOC) was founded on Java, and Western interests became quickly entrenched. After several attempts, the Dutch forces under Jan Pieterzoon Coen seized Jayakarta in 1619. Two years later the newly fortified city was named Batavia.

Taman Fatahillah, the tranquil square between Jl. Pintu Besar Selatan and the Kota Railway Station railyards a mile or two north of Merdeka Square, is the heart of Old Batavia. The original Dutch Stadhuis (City Hall) still stands in the center of the square. Built and renovated between 1627 and 1710 for VOC and government offices, including Batavia's court and prison, it was restored as the **Museum Sejarah Jakarta,** exhibiting a collection of maps, Dutch period furnishings and ceramic ware, European paintings, and some antiques that will interest visitors with a penchant for Jakarta's colonial history. Hours are Tuesday through Thursday from 9 a.m. to 2 p.m.; on Friday till 11 a.m.; on Saturday till 1 p.m., and on Sunday till 2 p.m. Admission is Rp 150 (10¢). In the center of Fatahillah Square is **Si Jagur,** a bronze cannon from Macao, once worshipped for its mystical powers to grant fertility and prosperity, particularly to those who sat upon it. Behind it is the traditionally Dutch, tan-stucco and green-trim Fatahillah Restaurant, an open-air café that's convenient for sodas, snacks, or a light Indonesian meal.

Just west of the square is the **Museum Wayang,** a marvelous collection of puppets housed in a colonial-era residence at Jl. Pintu Besar Utara. The earliest reference to *wayang purwa* (literally "ancient shadows") comes from an 11th-century poem, but by then the teaching of ethics, history, and cultural traditions through puppet performances was already well established. Shadow plays and puppet performances are still privately sponsored to celebrate personal events such as a youth's tooth-filing, a circumcision, birthday, or wedding. The government also stages public performances to convey information or air political issues. If you've ever enjoyed an Indonesian puppet show and hungered for a look behind the scenes, this is the place for you. If you haven't experienced this unique cultural performance, try to arrange your visit for a Sunday morning, when *wayang kulit* demonstrations are given.

The museum's ground floor has well-labeled display cases filled with the good (white-faced) and evil (black-faced) characters from the Hindu epics, the *Mahabharata* and the *Ramayana,* the traditional moral tales told by the *dalang* (master puppeteer) in his performance. There is also a display of contemporary puppets carved to resemble government officials and professional figures; they're used for contemporary stories that often deal with family planning, military service, and political issues such as transmigration. The collection includes *wayang kulit,* the flat, painted-leather puppets used behind an illuminated screen in shadow plays; *wayang golek,* the painted and costumed wooden puppets that are manipulated on a stage; and *wayang orang,* the wooden masks used by dancers in theatrical shows. Upstairs you'll find a wax-figure display of a dalang manipulating wayang kulit puppets to the accompaniment of a gamelan orchestra. There are also cases of puppets from India, Sri Lanka, China, Cambodia, and other Asian countries.

Hours are Tuesday through Thursday from 9 a.m. to 2 p.m.; on Friday till 11 a.m., on Saturday till 1 p.m., and on Sunday till 2 p.m. Admission is Rp 150 (10¢).

The **Balai Seni Rupa Jakarta** (the Jakarta Museum of Fine Arts) and **Museum Keramik** (the Ceramics Museum) share a classic building north of Fatahillah Square. The first has a poorly displayed collection of contemporary Indonesian paintings and a gallery for temporary exhibition of new artists. The second is also poorly lit and organized, but the collection of imported porcelains from China and Annam (Vietnam), the Thai celadons, and the variety of ceramic wares acquired by trade throughout Southeast Asia is so impressive that it warrants a visit by anyone with an interest in ceramics. The museums are open Tuesday through Thursday from 9 a.m. to 2 p.m., on Friday till 11 a.m., on Saturday till 1 p.m., and on Sunday till 2 p.m. Admission is Rp 150 (10¢).

The Ceramics Museum houses some of the late Adam Malik's collection of Sung and Ming ware, but aficionados should visit the fine ceramics in the odd, eclectic collection at the **Adam Malik Museum,** Jl. Diponegoro 29, in Menteng. The former vice president's home is open Tuesday through Saturday from 9:30 a.m. to 3 p.m., until 4 p.m. on Sunday. Admission is Rp 1,200 (75¢).

There are few tangible traces of **Old Batavia.** If you continue to walk north along Jl. Pintu Besar Utara, take a left at the first junction to the bridge over Kali Besar. The Great Canal marks the site of the early-17th-century **Kasteel Batavia,** the fortress built by Jan Pieterzoon Coen at the mouth of the Ciliwung River. In the 19th century, poor sanitation, odors, and the mosquito-infested waters from Batavia's many canals, which spread malaria, had become such a health problem that most were filled in and the city center moved south to Weltevreden. The Kasteel was torn down and its bricks used to construct the new residential areas. South of Fatahillah Square, the Dutch-era Kota Railway Station and the huge

Bank Exspor Impor Indonesia across from it are two impressive structures from the colonial period. Nearby on Jl. Pangeran Jayakarta is the **Gereja Sion,** a lovely church built by Portuguese traders who'd settled in Jayakarta in 1693. If you knock on the caretaker's door he'll let you visit the vaulted, columned interior and see the huge, hand-driven organ located on the balcony.

Other Museums

The **Museum Textil,** at Jl. Satsuit Tubun 4, is one of the more popular small museums, displaying over 327 varieties of batik and weaving from throughout Indonesia. It's open Tuesday through Thursday from 9 a.m. to 2 p.m., on Friday till 11 a.m., on Saturday till 1 p.m., and on Sunday till 2 p.m. Admission is Rp 150 (10¢).

The **Museum Abri Satriamandala,** Indonesia's armed forces museum, contains dioramas and displays of the battles for independence and developments in military history since 1945. It's on Jl. Gatot Subroto and is open daily except Monday from 9 a.m. to 4 p.m.; admission is Rp 150 (10¢).

Ancol Dreamland

The newest addition to Jakarta's tourist scene is **Taman Impian Jaya Ancol,** or Ancol Dreamland, a 500-acre recreational resort built on reclaimed land in the bay featuring the Horison Hotel, rental cottages, a youth hostel, water sports (though the bay is polluted), a giant swimming pool complex, a golf course, an oceanarium with dolphin shows, and cultural performances (call 683-843 for information about dance and puppet performance schedules).

Ancol Dreamland is also referred to as Jakarta's Disneyland because of **Dunia Fantasi,** its children's Fantasy Land amusement park. Dunia Fantasi includes replica buildings from the city of Old Batavia, from several Asian countries, from Timbuktu in Africa, and an American Wild West town. There's a miniature Indonesia and a fairytale castle, amusement rides, bumper cars, a Ferris wheel, and more. Dunia Fantasi is open from 2 to 9 p.m. Monday through Saturday and 10 a.m. to 9 p.m. on Sunday and holidays. Admission is Rp 5,100 ($3.25) weekdays, Rp 5,800 ($3.50) on Saturday, and Rp 7,500 ($4.75) on Sunday.

The **Pasar Seni,** or Art Market, offers a wide cross section of the arts and crafts from all provinces, with many high-quality items. When your kids tire of playing at Fantasy Land, they'll enjoy watching the metalsmiths, woodcarvers, and painters creating the utensils and decorative objects on sale. The Art Market is open daily from 10 a.m. to 9 p.m.

The whole Ancol Dreamland complex is 20 to 30 minutes north from Merdeka Square, and is most easily reached by taxi. If you prefer to take a group tour, weekday coach packages can be booked through Vayatours (tel. 365-008) or Panorama Tours (tel. 350-438). A 3½-hour evening tour including Ancol Dreamland, Dunia Fantasi, supper, and Pasar Seni costs Rp 25,000 ($15.50) for children, Rp 30,000 ($18.75) for adults.

The Ragunan Zoo and the Bird Market

Another sight that children in particular will enjoy is **Kebon Binatang Ragunan,** the zoological park ten miles south of the city in Pasar Minggu. The animal enclosures attempt to replicate natural habitats, making a tour through the zoo an introduction to Indonesia's varied flora and fauna. Rare species such as the world's only extant prehistoric creature, the Komodo lizard (*Komodovaranus komodoensis*) from Komodo Island, orangutans from Sumatra, and birds of paradise from Irian Jaya are featured. The zoo is open daily from 9 a.m. to 6 p.m., and admission is Rp 400 (25¢).

A totally different experience featuring animals is a visit to the **Pasar Burung,** the daily outdoor bird market on Jl. Pramuka, northeast of Medan Merdeka. Cages strung one atop the other up tall bamboo poles contain mynahs, lovebirds, cockatoos, parakeets, and other songbirds. At ground level are the chickens, turkeys, pigeons, and other birds prized for their eggs and meat. Early morning and at sunset are particularly boisterous times to visit, but to savor the locals swooning to these tunes, Sunday is the best.

SHOPPING: Jakarta has become such a cosmopolitan city in the last five years that you can shop just as easily for Charles Jourdan shoes from Paris or Revlon cosmetics as you can for silk batik scarves or lifesize carved wood banana trees. There are typically Third World outdoor markets filled with new and recycled paraphernalia, Singapore-style chrome-and-glass indoor malls, a flea market where you can still find an undiscovered bargain, and a marvelous department store that has everything. If you're interested in things Indonesian, then the best buys are the locally produced batik cloth, woven fabrics, and woodcarvings.

Batiks and Woven Fabrics

Intricately patterned, brightly colored batik fabric is Indonesia's best-known commodity. The traditional patterns derived from nature are applied by the resist-dyeing method. First the design is drawn in pencil on fabric and then each portion of it that's not to be dyed in the first color bath is protected by wax applied with a canting, or bamboo pen. This hand-application of wax layers is redone for every color, producing the finest-quality and most expensive batik (tulis). A faster method of applying the wax by hand is using a cap, or carved copper block, which can cover larger areas of fabric at each application. Cap-printed batiks are also of excellent quality and fetch a higher price than the silkscreen-printed fabrics used in low-cost garments. Behind Jakarta's **Government Batik Outlet (GKBI,** a batik products cooperative with a variety of merchandise) at Jl. Agus Salim 39, in Menteng, is the Toko Ibu Bintang Negara, a batik factory where you can watch the fabric being made. Even the lowest-grade, factory-produced batiks delight visitors with their ornate floral and animal images and rich tropical colors.

Men take note: Long-sleeved batik shirts are accepted formalwear at the best restaurants and functions. They're cut full and not tucked into slacks, much cooler for those hot, humid tropical nights than a jacket and tie.

The best-known name in batik artistry is **Iwan Tirta,** a designer who specializes in the highest-quality handmade batik in traditional Indonesian colors, patterns, and styles. Mr. Tirta's many admirers include Nancy Reagan; he designed a dress for her during President Reagan's Indonesian visit in 1986. Women's conservatively stylish cotton dresses start at Rp 160,000 ($100). Iwan Tirta's darker colors and somber patterns are perfectly suitable for any event; cotton and silk shirts range from Rp 64,000 ($40) to Rp 144,000 ($90). Their in-house tailor and upholsterer will cover you or your home in any of their large selection of cotton and silk fabrics. They cost Rp 80,000 ($50) to Rp 180,000 ($112.50) for approximately 12-foot by 44-inch lengths. The two shops also offer a wide variety of clothes and gift items made in batik such as tablecloths and silk scarves at Rp 65,000 ($40.50), women's cotton T-shirts at Rp 15,000 ($9.50), men's sport shirts at Rp 45,000 ($28), and UNICEF greeting cards at Rp 5,600 ($3.50). Mr. Tirta, a noted historian and collector of textiles, sells beautiful samples of *ikat* cloth (hand-woven from predyed threads) and other hand-spun fabrics from the provinces.

The Iwan Tirta boutique in the Hotel Borobudur Continental, at Jl. Lapangan Banteng Selatan, is open from 9 a.m. to 9 p.m. Monday through Saturday and 9 a.m. to 1 p.m. on Sunday. His shop in Menteng, at Jl. Panarukan 25 (tel. 354-267), open from 9 a.m. to 6 p.m. Monday through Saturday, whose displays are worthy of a visit from anyone interested in textiles, traditional jewelry, and Indonesian chic, offers a much wider selection of merchandise.

Another shop with a wide selection of high-quality batik is **Danar Hadi Batik,** at Jl. Raden Saleh 2 (tel. 323-663), part of a chain throughout Java. It's open Monday through Saturday from 9 a.m. to 6 p.m. Here you'll find casual sportswear and clothing that's more youthful, stylish, and oriented to Western taste. Danar Hadi also offers machine-printed batik at popular prices: shirts from Rp 14,000 ($8.75) and up. It may be a better bet if you're not shopping for a connoisseur of batik fabrics.

Batik Keris, with boutiques in Menteng, in the Sarinah department store, and at Ratu Plaza on Jl. Jend. Sudirman, is another shop with a selection of stylish, high-quality merchandise, particularly silk and cotton *ikat* fabrics.

Excellent hand-painted batik is also widely available in Yogyakarta and Solo, the cities of central Java, where this art form originated.

Woodcarving

The ornamental use of wood to decorate homes, temples, and public buildings is common throughout Indonesia and skilled woodcarvers have been prized for centuries. The Balinese in particular use teak, ebony, and local woods to create wonderful works that range from playfully painted fruit trees to artistic, sculpted portraits in natural wood.

Though many gift shops offer a few pieces of decorative carving, none match the variety, price and quality of the shops at **Pasar Seni,** the Indonesian Art Market at the Taman Impian Jaya Ancol, the resort complex on the bayshore at Jakarta's northern edge. At the large arts and crafts shopping bazaar where workmen create out in the open, you can buy reasonably priced woodcarvings, woven items, metalwork, and other crafts representative of all the provinces. It's true that a two-foot-tall carved banana tree that costs Rp 32,000 ($20) in Bali may cost twice that at Pasar Seni, but you would have spent the difference buying a suitcase to bring it back in! Some bargaining is possible, and most of the shops don't accept credit cards or handle shipping. However, shopping in Pasar Seni can be as educational as it is fun.

Department Stores and Malls

If you have the energy for only one store in Jakarta it should be **Sarinah,** a department store to rival Bloomingdale's (in fact, there's a branch at 54th Street and Fifth Avenue in New York). If the Sarinah on Jl. Thamrin near the President Hotel (tel. 327-147) doesn't have what you want, then their glitzy new store, Sarinah Jaya at Jl. Iskadarsyah 11/2 in Blok M, in the southern suburb of Kebayoran Baru (tel. 347-528), certainly will. Both are open seven days a week from 9 a.m. to 10 p.m., accept credit cards and traveler's checks, and even change foreign currency (not traveler's checks). Pasaraya is an entire floor in each store and is dedicated to Indonesian handcrafts, clothing, souvenirs, and gifts. Sarinah imports the best batiks from Solo and Yogyakarta, woodcarvings from Bali, weavings from Sumatra, model houses from Tana Toraja, and almost anything else an avid shopper would have purchased on travels throughout the archipelago. Many items are made exclusively for Sarinah and the selection and quality are impeccable. Tablecloth-and-napkin sets are under Rp 16,000 ($10) and a two-week supply of herbal Young Lasting pills from the Jamu traditional medicine counter is only Rp 3,000 ($2); all their prices are reasonable.

The **Indonesia Bazaar** at the Jakarta Hilton International on Jl. Gatot Subroto is another fun place for shopping. Here, several batik, souvenir, and crafts boutiques housed in traditional red brick, carved-stone Balinese cottages are grouped around a lovely lake. If you're there at lunch don't miss the al fresco Pizzaria.

Jakarta's most elegant stores and exclusive European merchandise can be found at **Ratu Plaza,** one of the newest malls on Jl. Raya Jend. Sudirman, about 15 minutes by taxi south of Merdeka Square. Ratu Plaza has a Matahari department store, an Étienne Aigner leather boutique, a Charles Jourdan clothing shop, and many other high-fashion, and equally high-priced, shops. There is also an excellent Padang-style restaurant on the ground floor.

Other fashionable new shops have opened in **Blok M,** a recently developed commercial area along Jl. Melawai in the exclusive suburb of Kebayoran Baru.

BARGAIN SHOPPING. The real bargains found in Asia are in ready-to-wear clothes, small appliances, toys, and other manufactured goods. The older indoor shopping complexes are downtown around the **Glodok** area south of Fatahillah Square, along Jl. Gajah Mada and Jl. Hayam Wuruk. Plazas named after both avenues, the Duta Merlin Shopping Centre and Glodok Plaza are a few that offer inexpensive sportswear, jewelry shops, grocery markets, and shoe stores. About 15 minutes' north of the Borobudur Inter-Continental Hotel is Jakarta's **Pasar Baru,** off Jl. Samanhudi and Jl. Pasar Baru. As it does in all Indonesian towns, the New Market has several shop-lined streets, hawkers of every imaginable type of merchandise, an indoor/outdoor produce market, and street food and trinket vendors.

Jewelry

Indonesia is not the bargain place for jewelry that Bangkok or Hong Kong is, but items made with certain traditional techniques can be good buys. Repoussé, a technique that produces a decorative relief on metal by hammering it from behind and is often used for silver set with local semiprecious stones. Skilled local craftsmen can produce repoussé jewelry better and less expensively than in other countries where this is not a traditional craft. Cheaper labor rates usually mean better buys on gold too, but it takes an astute shopper to know quality versus price. Stick to the jewelers in the major hotels for your purchases. The Indonesian Opal and Jewellery Centre at the Jakarta Hilton International's Indonesian Bazaar, Jay's Jewelry at the Jakarta Mandarin, Joyce Spiro Jewelry at the Hotel Sari Pacific, and Linda Spiro Jewelry at the Hotel Borobudur-Inter-Continental are all recommended.

Antiques and Curios

Jakarta's antique (*antik*) hunters shop primarily for colonial-era imported furnishings, Southeast Asian and Chinese export ceramics, foreign coins, religious sculpture and art, and Javanese ceremonial objects from the sultans' courts. There are several well-established shops on Jl. Palatehan I in Blok M, Kebayoran Baru, and others along Jl. Majapahit in Kota and along Jl. Kebon Sirih Timur Dalam in Menteng. Most shops are open from 9 a.m. to 6 p.m. Monday through Saturday. Some knowledge of antiques and a good bargaining ability are highly recommended.

Jakarta's famous antique, flea, or thieves market is along **Jl. Surabaya,** between Jl. Diponegoro and Jl. Cikini Raya, southeast of Merdeka Square in Menteng. Dozens of stalls selling reproductions of bronze busts of Indonesian royalty, European commemorative plates, used manual typewriters, worn Dutch coins, and hundreds of other items line the quiet street. Shops are open daily from 10 a.m. to 5 p.m. (or until sundown if busy); expect to bargain down to about 40% of the tagged price. We wouldn't even think of telling you there are any authentic antique items here, but others claim there are.

If you've got a huge suitcase, colonial rattan furniture and typical Indonesian carved-wood pieces can be purchased along Jl. Bogor Raya, the old scenic route to Bogor on the southeast edge of town. Anyone considering shipping purchases home should investigate the Kantor Pos charges for air freight and seamail before they buy. Shipping is much more expensive than you'd imagine. Also ask your hotel or the Tourist Information Center to recommend private shipping agents, and compare prices.

NIGHTLIFE: In the last few years Jakarta's nightlife scene has begun to catch up with some of its Asian neighbors. The bars long favored by expatriates now bring in musicians from Singapore and the Philippines, new supper clubs with live music and dancing have opened, and a few discothèques, with video and lighting systems to rival Europe's best, are luring locals with their Western sounds.

Pubs and Bars

Favored pubs include **The Tavern,** a comfortable new pub in the basement of the Hyatt Aryaduta Hotel at Jl. Prapatan 44/48, near Merdeka Square (tel. 376-008), with none of the "hotel bar" feel that sometimes intimidates travelers. There are good local pop and jazz bands every night (until 12:30 a.m. weeknights, until 2 a.m. on Saturday) and respectable burgers and snack food served at lunch.

The **Jaya Pub,** on Jl. Thamrin opposite the Sari Pacific Hotel, is the spot favored by the raucous "Down Under" crowd.

The **George and Dragon Pub,** at Jl. Teluk Betung 32 (tel. 325-625), behind the Hotel Indonesia, is Jakarta's original watering hole. Evenings, you'll find Aussies, Brits, and assorted Anglophiles sipping mugs of beer and munching on fish 'n' chips. The conservative lunchtime expatriate crowd loosens their ties about 6 p.m., a good time to make friends there. A more eclectic crowd, some Americans and Indonesian movie buffs, gather at **The Green Pub,** a Mexican food cantina on the ground floor of the Djakarta Theatre Building on Jl. Thamrin (tel. 359-332). An original frozen margarita, chips, and salsa will be served by an Indonesian cowboy or cowgirl in full regalia. They have a great country-western and and nightly entertainers; there's no cover charge.

The luxury hotels all offer a variety of places to meet and drink. Although drinks are obviously higher priced at all the five-star hotels, their nightspots are more luxurious than most Jakarta bars. Some impose a cover charge if there's live entertainment. Every afternoon from 4 to 6 p.m. a full gamelan orchestra plays the antique *cakra dalam raya gamelan* in the lobby of the Jakarta Hilton on Jl. Gatot Subroto. On a quiet day the ethereal strains of this classical percussion music waft over into the dark, rattan-furnished **Kudus Bar** (tel. 583-051).

For cocktails or late-night socializing in a sophisticated environment, try the **Captain's Bar** in the Mandarin Hotel on Jl. Thamrin (tel. 321-307). Low, comfortable seating complements the intimate ambience created by the nightly jazz performances.

Single women who prefer less intimate situations will like the quiet lobby bar in the **Hotel Borobudur Inter-Continental** on Jl. Lapangan Bantang Selatan (tel. 370-108), which overlooks the beautifully landscaped grounds below and their poolside outdoor café. The **Hotel Sari Pacific,** on Jl. M. H. Thamrin (tel. 323-707), also has a comfortable lobby bar with live piano music, and a more elegant one outside their Jayakarta Grill. The Hilton's **Garden Tower Lounge,** a pastel tea room, also serves cocktails.

Nightclubs and Discos

The most popular of Jakarta's nightclubs is the **Blue Ocean Nightclub** at Jl. Hayam Wuruk 5 (tel. 366-650), in the Glodok section of town. Behind that grim, neon-lit façade are more than 300 hostesses, at Rp 9,600 ($6) per hour, waiting in a huge, ornate ballroom. When Chinese acrobats, Javanese crooners, or Singapore cabaret acts appear at two shows nightly, the 2,000 seats fill up quickly. The Blue Ocean serves good Cantonese food.

A far more subdued, upscale crowd can be found lounging at the Jakarta

Hilton's **Oriental Club** (tel. 583-051). The Oriental is a private disco club that admits the hotel's guests free of charge and the city's elite for a Rp 20,000 ($12.50) cover charge.

If you're looking to dance those socks off, try **The Pitstop,** the early-30s to mid-40s expatriate favorite at the Sari Pacific Hotel on Jl. Thamrin (tel. 323-707).

Ebony, in the Kuningan Plaza Building, Jl. Rasuna Said (tel. 513-700), is the choice of Jakarta's yuppies. A well-dressed late 20s to mid-30s crowd pays Rp 22,000 ($13.75) cover, including the first drink. The splashy two-story "videothèque" shows rock videos on a large screen.

The casual student crowd heads for **Stardust,** a wildly lit, very loud club in the Jayakarta Tower Hotel on Jl. Hayam Wuruk in Glodok (tel. 624-408). At Stardust, admission is Rp 6,000 ($3.75) weeknights and double that on Saturday night, but on Thursday, Sunglasses Night, single women in "groovy shades" are admitted free.

The older fringe, some casual, part local/expatriate crowd gravitates to **Tanamur,** at Jl. Tanah Abang Timur 14 (tel. 535-947). International top-40 music, professional escorts, and a less formal atmosphere keep this place hopping.

A safer choice may be the new **Music Room,** the pride of the Hotel Borobudur Inter-Continental (tel. 370-108), modeled after the glitzy Bacchus of London. It starts hopping after 10 p.m., as do most of the clubs.

For **adult entertainment,** head to Jl. Mangga Besar, behind the Hotel Metropol downtown. You'll find several bars, nightclubs, and massage parlors. *Be warned:* this scene is not as accepted as it is in Bangkok, so watch your wallet, stay alert, and stick to well-lit sidewalks.

Theater, Cultural Performances, and Cinemas

The city's only live theater is found at **Taman Ismail Marzuki** (tel. 337-357), or **TIM,** a cultural center at Jl. Cikini Raya 73. TIM has an indoor and outdoor stage, two movie theaters, a planetarium (shows only in Bahasa Indonesia), an astronomy museum, and an art school. During our visit the Australian Song Company was playing alternate nights with Shakespeare's *Macbeth* and a Minangkabau troupe from West Sumatra. Their schedule changes monthly, and sometimes features traditional Indonesian dance performances or concerts.

Movies are extremely popular with Jakartaites, who seem to prefer Chinese, Indian, locally produced, and American "B" pictures to anything that might be considered an "art film." Ask your hotel to check whether the film that interests you is dubbed or subtitled. The best new screens in town with full Dolby stereo are the **Studio 21 Multiplex Cinema** and the **Galaxy Century Jakarta,** charging Rp 7,500 ($4.75) for admission. The **Djakarta Theatre,** on Jl. Thamrin next to Sarinah, has two screens, and the **Gajah Mada Plaza,** downtown in Glodok, has four; admission here should be $1 less.

CHAPTER VIII

EXPLORING JAVA

□ □ □

1. ORIENTATION

2. EXCURSIONS FROM JAKARTA: PULAU SERIBU
   AND KRAKATOA

3. OVERLAND ACROSS WEST JAVA: BOGOR AND BANDUNG

4. JAVA'S CULTURAL CAPITAL: YOGYAKARTA

5. TEMPLES OF CENTRAL JAVA: BOROBUDUR,
   PRAMBANAN, AND OTHERS

6. EASTERN JAVA: SOLO, MOUNT BROMO, TRANSPORTATION
   TO BALI

The island of Java, about 500 miles long by 100 miles wide, is officially divided into the provinces of West, Central, and East Java, and the special territories of Jakarta and Yogyakarta. West Java offers many beaches and weekend resorts catering to well-to-do Jakartaites and expatriates. The infamous volcanic island of Krakatau, immortalized in popular history by the film *Krakatoa, East of Java,* is west across the Sunda Strait. Off the north coast in the Java Sea is Pulau Ceribu, a popular diving resort known as the Thousand Islands. The former colonial "hill station" at Bogor and the prosperous commercial city of Bandung are two possible stopovers on the scenic overland journey to Yogyakarta.

Yogyakarta is the center of Javanese culture: gamelan music, shadow puppets, batik cloth making, classical Javanese dance, Islamic Kingdom period architecture, and modern painting. Once the seat of Java's most powerful Muslim sultans, it is today a special territory whose titular sultan, Sri Hamengku Buwono IX, remains politically active as the governor. Yogyakarta, the largest city in Central Java, is a must-see for anyone interested in Indonesian arts.

Indonesia's religious diversity is vividly illustrated in Central Java. In the last millennium the Buddhist monuments of Kalasan and Borobudur (the largest Buddhist temple complex in the world and now fully restored), the Siva temples at Prambanan and the Hindu temples on the Dieng Plateau were built by successive kingdoms who reigned in Central Java. The arts patronage and royal architecture of the sultan's courts are vestiges of the Islamic golden age. Fortunately, all these sites can be visited on organized day trips from Yogyakarta and should not be missed.

Solo, also called Surakarta, is the most interesting tourist destination east of Yogyakarta. Once the seat of a powerful sultanate rivaling Yogyakarta, Solo is also the birthplace of batik art. In a day you can visit the *kraton* (palace) of Sultan Pakubuwono VIII and the *puro* (royal home) of Prince Mangkunegaran (both are closed Friday) and shop in many fine batik shops. Travelers continuing overland to Bali will cross into East Java. Surabaya is East Java's capital and a huge industrial and commercial city, of little interest to tourists. From here, an overnight excursion can be made to the volcanic Mount Bromo for views of the spectacular sunrise over the Java Sea (best done in the dry season between April and November). From Ketapang, on Java's east coast on the Bali Strait, there are regular ferries to Gilimanuk, on the island of Bali.

HISTORY: One of the earliest references to Java comes from Ptolemy, the Alexandrian geographer and astronomer, who wrote that Labadiou (then Java) was an advanced agricultural country learned in navigation, astronomy, the making of batik cloth (an ancient Egyptian technique originally brought by traders), and the minting of coins. Indian traders, who arrived in the centuries before Christ and brought their religion, named the island Java Dwipa or Rice Island.

The Middle Kingdoms

The period of the Hindu Kingdoms, when Java and many of the Indonesian islands were ruled by rajas who fostered the Hindu and Buddhist religions and culture, lasted in some parts from the 5th to the 16th century. Performing arts, the social caste system (still used in Bali), government by monarchy, and the epics, the *Ramayana* and the *Mahabharata*, were all introduced during this period. The Hindu sanctuary at Prambanan, a complex of impressive Siva temples, was constructed in the late 9th century by the Mataram Kingdom, which later merged with stronger East Javanese kingdoms.

After the 6th century the Srivijaya Kingdom in Sumatra, a noted center of Buddhist learning, spread its religion east across Java. The Buddhist Çailendra Kingdom emerged in Central Java fueled by commerce and maritime trade. The rajas of the Çailendra Dynasty (A.D. 750–850) fostered local culture and arts and were responsible for the building of Borobudur, Mendut, Kalasan, and other Buddhist monuments in the area around present-day Yogyakarta.

Over the next 200 years, the Central Javanese kingdoms declined and many lesser-known kingdoms like the Singasari emerged in East Java. The Singasari raja, Dharmawangsa, codified Javanese laws and had the Hindu epics, the *Mahabharata* and the *Bhagavad Gita,* the key section distilling Hindu philosophy and practice, translated from Sanskrit into Javanese. Many literary works, including the Indonesian Panji novels, date from this period. By the 13th century the once-mighty Srivijaya Empire of Sumatra, after constant attack from the Chola Kingdom in South India and under pressure from the Javanese Majapahit Kingdom, began to decline. The Javanese kingdoms were finally united by the Majapahits under Raja Hayam Wuruk and Gadja Mada, who also consolidated their acquisitions beyond the archipelago to Cambodia, Vietnam, and the Philippines.

A Stronghold of Islam

Islam took root on Java in the western Kingdom of Demak, then spread east. In 1527 Sunda Kelapa, the present-day Jakarta, was converted to the Muslim faith. Muslim sultans eventually vanquished the Majapahit Kingdom and continued east to Sulawesi and the Moluccas. Hindu religious scholars, practitioners, and former rulers retreated to the islands of Bali and Lombok.

The Dutch began to take over Java after the founding of the Dutch East India Company (the VOC), but not until 1775 did they split the last great kingdom of Central Java into the sultanates of Yogyakarta and Surakarta (Solo). The legacy of 340 years of Dutch colonial rule is relatively minor. In contrast, the influence of Sultan Agung and others from the second Mataram Kingdom, who fostered the performing arts and culture that are considered traditional to Java, is strongly felt today.

1. ORIENTATION

Java is a large and scenically beautiful island; overland travel is the best way to appreciate its villages, rolling hills, and verdant rice paddies. If your time is limited, consider visiting Java's sights in day excursions from Yogyakarta, stronghold of Javanese culture.

Central Java has the greatest number of historical sights. Visitors should allow at least two days to sample some of Yogyakarta's offerings, plus time for day trips to Borobudur, Prambanan, or any of the marvelous holy shrines nearby. Few travelers will take the time to explore East Java, most preferring to fly directly to the island paradise of Bali, next door.

GETTING AROUND JAVA: The island of Java, home to 61% of the nation's population and its center of government, has the most advanced infrastructure in Indonesia. A wide range of accommodations; good roads; regular but not always safe long-distance bus service; a convenient, cautious but slow train network; and frequent moderately priced air transport between several widely dispersed airports.

By Car

Because most of the tourist destinations discussed in this chapter can be visited as excursions from a base in Jakarta or Yogyakarta, a private car or taxi is usually the most convenient and efficient method of getting around. Travel agents can arrange for a car and driver and an English-speaking guide; rates will vary from about $50 to $80 per day (quoted only in U.S. dollars), depending on the mileage covered and the number of hours. Both cities have car-rental/taxi services on an hourly basis, for about Rp 6,400 ($4) to Rp 8,000 ($5) per hour, that can be reserved through the hotels; detailed information and prices are provided in each section.

By Train

To cover longer distances, such as the Jakarta–Yogyakarta axis, we'd recommend Java's comfortable trains. A day among local travelers and other tourists, a nasi goreng lunch in the dining car, and the brief contact with village life at each station make it a worthwhile trip for those with the time to travel overland. From Jakarta's Gambir Railroad Station, two morning trains leave daily for the 11-hour trip to Yogyakarta. Tickets in the fan-cooled, second-class section, at Rp 12,000 ($7.50), provide a rolling aisle seat to some of the most dramatic scenery in the country. If you don't care to see the natural beauty of the surrounding countryside, a night train with sleeper cars leaves daily from the Kota Railway Station at 4 p.m., making the trip in ten hours. There are several trains daily between Jakarta's Gambir Station and Bogor or Bandung, at Rp 5,200 ($3.25) in second class; if you choose to stop over, it's easy to catch a train from either town heading east to Yogyakarta. More specific travel information is provided in each section.

By Air

If you're pressed for time, Garuda Indonesia has four flights weekdays and five on Saturday and Sunday between Jakarta and Yogyakarta. The 1988 one-way fare was $56.50. There are three flights a week to Yogyakarta from Bandung ($88), daily service from Surabaya ($28), and three flights daily from Denpasar, Bali ($97). **Garuda Indonesia** has offices in Jakarta at the Hotel Borobudur Inter-Continental on Jl. Lapangan Selatan (tel. 359-901), plus two others; in Bandung, at Jl. Asia Afrika 73 (tel. 4023), and in Yogyakarta at Jl. P. Mangkubumi 56 (tel. 4400).

By Bus or Coach Tour

The safety record of Java's public buses as reported by the daily *Indonesia Times* or *Jakarta Post* is so poor that it's impossible to recommend traveling overland this way (though many budget-conscious travelers use them for the economy and the experience). Of course, there are also daily reports on the government's efforts to improve safety standards. Police roadblocks to inspect paperwork, spotchecks of loaded buses to reduce overcrowding, and stiffer enforcement of traffic laws have all been imposed; we'll wait until the next edition to check on their results. Unfortunately, there are areas where the public buses are most convenient and economical for short excursions; we have included information about them in these specific sections.

Several tour operators offer daily coach tours led by English-speaking guides from Jakarta or Yogyakarta to nearby sites. **P.T. Vayatour,** with offices in Jakarta at the President Hotel, Jl. Thamrin (tel. 336-640), in Bandung at the Panghegar Hotel, Jl. Merdeka 2 (tel. 57239), and in Yogyakarta at the Amburrukmo Palace Hotel, Jl. Adisucipto (tel. 88488), is one of the best; daily coach tours cost Rp 19,200 ($12) to Rp 48,000 ($30) per person. Vayatours also operates a well-guided nine-day coach tour called "Exotic Java Bali Overland." There's a great deal of sightseeing and shopping between Jakarta and Bali, with overnights in Bandung, Yogyakarta, Tretes, and Sanur Beach. Double-occupancy rates start at $435 per person.

2. EXCURSIONS FROM JAKARTA: PULAU SERIBU AND KRAKATOA

Pulau Seribu (literally, Thousand Islands) is to Jakarta's expatriate community what Fire Island is to New Yorkers. Every Friday afternoon at the Jaya Ancol marina, families who've reserved a hotel room weeks in advance join the fortunate few with second homes for the two-hour ferry ride. The four islands that have been developed with overnight facilities are extremely popular with Japanese travelers and rank as sumptuous, luxury resort living. The more adventuresome head south by land to Carita Beach, the coastal resort opposite the volcanic remains of Krakatoa. Carita Beach has its own devotees among the expatriate crowd. The sandy beach and calm waters (from May to October) can't touch the palm-fringed tropical paradise you'll find on Bali but like the Jersey shore, Carita has a charm all its own and it's a much cheaper weekend getaway.

PULAU SERIBU: The Thousand Islands are actually 112 small coral atolls snaking along the horizon about 40 miles off Jakarta's coast. Of the seven inhabited islands, four have so far been developed for tourism: Pulau Pelangi, Putri, Ayer, and Petondan Timur. Recent Japanese investment indicates that the islands will soon become much more developed. The resorts provide room and board; travel agents usually make reservations so that water sports, scuba-diving or snorkeling, boat transportation for sightseeing, and ferry service can be prearranged. We recommend an excursion to Pulau Seribu only to those who are based in Jakarta; most of you will be glad you saved your money for Bali.

Getting to Pulau Seribu

All boats to Pulau Seribu leave from the Jaya Ancol Pier at Jaya Ancol Dreamland in Jakarta and, for some bureaucratic reason, anyone using the pier must first pay the $2 admission to the amusement park. The one-way fare to any of the above islands can range from $50 to $5 to gratis if it's included in the price of your room reservation. You may find private boats that offer transportation for

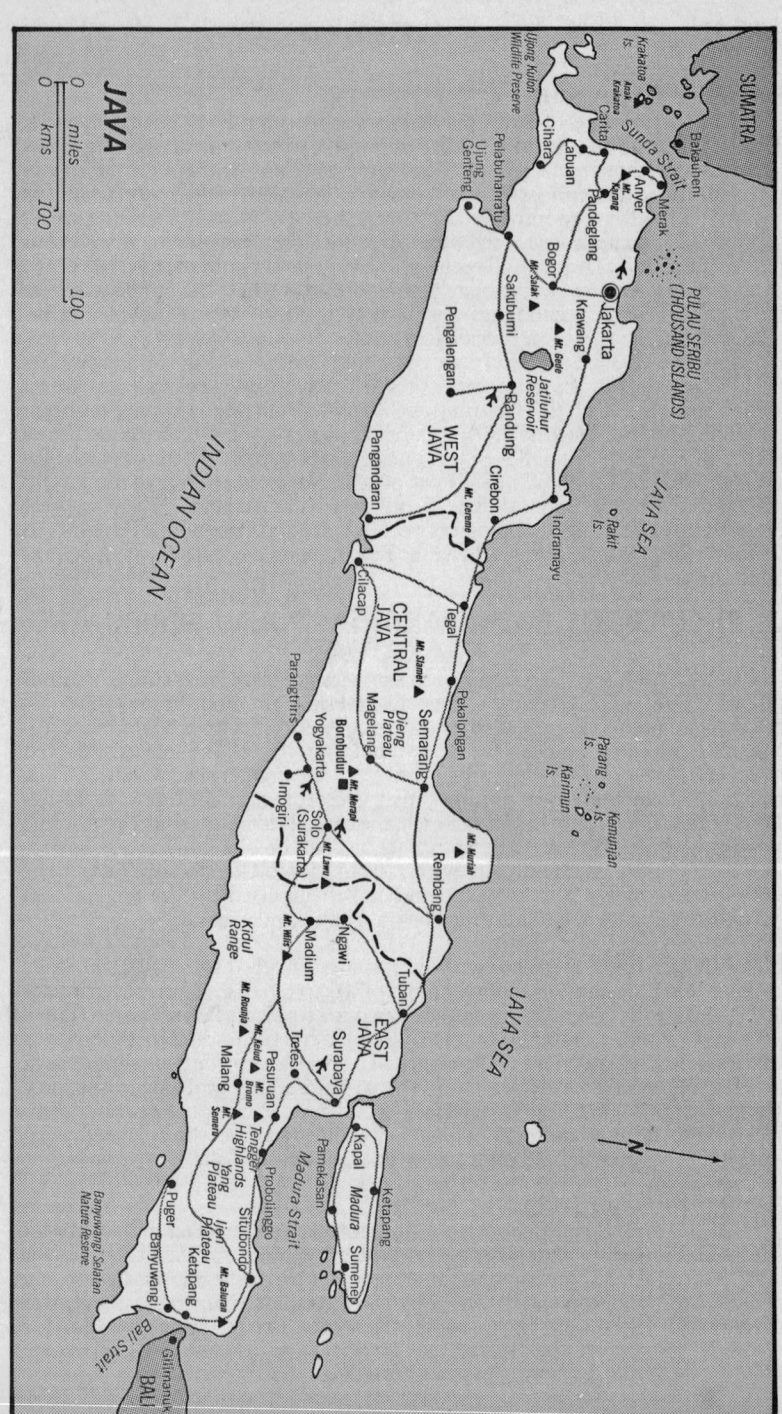

the one- to three-hour ride, but negotiating a fare and arranging a pickup at the island for your return can be tricky. Instead, contact one of the travel agents who specialize in this resort, such as **PT Pulau Seribu Paradise,** in the Setia Budi Building I in Block C1 (tel. 515-884); **PT Batemuri Tours,** in the Wisata International Hotel on Jl. Thamrin (tel. 320-807); **Vayatours,** in the President Hotel on Jl. Thamrin (tel. 365-008); or the private **Pulau Burung Indah** office (tel. 489-8092). **Panorama Tours** (tel. 350-438) offer day trips by motor boat to Pulau Bidadari. The five-hour excursion costs Rp 20,000 ($12.50).

Accommodations and Dining

Here's a brief look at the accommodations available on each island. Note that these resorts can only be booked through travel agents, and paid for in U.S. dollars.

At the **Pulau Pelangi,** 27 wooden bungalows with large porches and thatch roofs contain spacious rooms with air conditioning, a private bathroom, and a mini-bar; they run about $90 per person in a twin room, including breakfast, for a two-night weekend. Pulau Pelangi (Rainbow Island) is noted for its good, clean beaches and snorkeling, plus an attractive and popular floating restaurant.

Pulau Putri (Princess Island) has 25 varied bungalows and cottages shaded by trees, in groupings around its perimeter. All rooms have air conditioning, private bathroom, and a terrace. A weekend cottage or bungalow (bedroom plus kitchen facility) will run $70 to $110 per person.

At **Pulau Ayer,** several slat-wood huts are built on stilts off the coast. Each has a kitchen, TV, and attached bath; boats pull up to the small porches off the living room. Two nights cost $60 to $105 per person including breakfast, depending on type of cottage.

Pulau Petondan Timur (or Pulau Papa Theo) has simple thatch hut housing, some with private toilets and showers, that cost about $30 per day. It's convenient to the excellent nearby diving.

The Japanese-financed **Pulau Seribu Marine Resort** (tel. 370-108 at the Hotel Borobudur, Room 6/7) is a super-deluxe, all-inclusive resort spread across three islands, with weekday bungalow rates starting at $152 for two, including full board and water sports.

The Pulau Seribu coral reefs, indigenous underwater species, and clear water lure many scuba-divers from Jakarta. Pulau Burung Indah (Beautiful Bird Island) is now being packaged just for divers, who can dive for two days, including overnight accommodation and meals, for about $85 per person.

KRAKATOA: For thousands of years the wooded island of Krakatau sat 30 miles off the coast of West Java, uninhabited and ignored. Then about 100 years ago Krakatoa became famous for an intensely violent volcanic eruption that wiped the island off the face of the earth. Recently, a small resort has sprung up at Carita Beach to capitalize on the mystical attraction the island still exerts over visitors. Pulau Krakatau (the Javanese name) was originally five miles long and one to three miles wide, made up of three volcanic cones: Rakata, Danan, and Perboewatan. After several months of minimal volcanic activity, Krakatoa exploded on August 26, 1883, with the force of 100,000 hydrogen bombs. For 19 hours smoke, flames, ash, and pumice spewed forth from within the island until three-quarters of its surface collapsed. Inhabitants of coastal areas in West Java and southern Sumatra saw their sea sucked up by the huge underwater caldera that was formed. When the sea water came into contact with molten magma and rocky debris under the island, it caused gas explosions that sent out tidal waves traveling at 350 mph. Coastal villages were devastated by waves up to 135 feet high; rocky debris blown 25 miles into the atmosphere circled the globe and darkened the area for three days. Krakatoa's fury was evident everywhere. Residents of Sri Lanka, Australia, and the Philippines heard her roar; tidal waves from the Java Sea were felt in the English Channel, 11,000 miles away. Some 36,000 deaths were recorded.

When the dust settled three months later, all that was visibly left of the island was the 2,500-foot cone of Rakata. Then 44 years later a new island began to rise out of the sea to claim Krakatoa's place. Volcanic activity below the water's surface was pushing up what would soon be known as Anak Krakatoa ("son of . . ."). In 25 years it rose to 200 feet above sea level. Now, a barren cinder block 600 feet above sea level and billowing smoke, Anak Krakatoa has risen to claim its parent's legacy. Today's adventurers can quench their curiosity at its shore.

Getting to Krakatoa

Jakarta travel agents such as **Pacto Ltd.**, at the Hotel Borobudur Inter-Continental on Jl. Lapangan Banteng Selatan (tel. 370-108), or **Natrabu,** at Jl. H. Agus Salim 29A (tel. 331-728), can help you reserve a tour to Krakatoa which often includes stops at the traditional villages of the Badui people and the Ujong Kulon Wildlife Preserve, making it an overnight excursion via the mainland Pantai Carita (Carita Beach). Prices will be quite high if you cannot put together a group of at least four people.

The Carita Krakatau Beach Hotel offers transportation to individual travelers and will help group guests together for the eight-hour boat trip. You can start out from your seaside bungalow early in the morning and head to nearby Labuan. Local fishermen charter their boats for about Rp 144,000 ($90) to Rp 240,000 ($150) per day. Bring food, a parka, rugged nonslip shoes, Dramamine, and sun block; up to ten people can share most of the boats. Sea excursions are not recommended during the rainy season of November to March.

The most relaxed and luxurious way to see Krakatoa is on a Spice Island Cruises tour of West Java and the Sunda Strait. **P.T. Lumba Lumba Permai,** at Jl. S. Parman 78 (tel. 593-401), runs the luxury catamaran *Island Explorer,* a two-deck vessel with 12 cabins, six suites, first-class amenities, and modern safety equipment. Their seven-day tours run $1,400 to $2,700 per person, including meals, water sports equipment, and hotels on land.

Accommodations and Dining

An enterprising German named Alex Ridder, owner of the Carita Krakatau Beach Hotel, is almost singlehandedly responsible for creating the new awareness of Pantai Carita as a tourist destination. His *Krakatau Newsletter* and many brochures crop up everywhere so that newcomers to Jakarta often find themselves asking "What is Carita Beach and how do I see Krakatoa?"

The **Carita Krakatau Beach Hotel,** Pantai Carita (tel. 330-846), has a Jakarta office in the Hotel Wisata International on Jl. Thamrin (tel. 320-252) which accepts reservations for rooms and bus transportation. The hotel has 150 simple wooden cottages, those with private toilets and cold-water showers cost Rp 38,400 ($24) for a double on weeknights and Rp 75,000 ($47) on weekends, including tax and service. The deluxe cottages are wood and concrete with modern hot-water plumbing and a kitchen; these cost Rp 72,000 ($45) on the weeknights, Rp 112,000 ($70) on weekends. All are scattered along the beachfront and water sports facilities are provided.

Another choice is the two-star **Anyer Beach Hotel,** on Jl. Raya Karangbolong (tel. 381-382), the coast road through Banten. Nearby is the 230-foot-tall Anyer lighthouse, built in 1855 to commemorate the construction of the Trans-Java Highway which begins here and traverses the island. Cottages with similar amenities run $40 to $86, depending on the day of the week and facilities; reservations can be made in Jakarta at Gedung Patra, Jl. Jend. Gatot Subroto, kav. 32-34 (tel. 510-322).

Budget-watchers should check out Alex Ridder's hostel, the **Hostel Rakata,** about 50 yards from the beach at Carita. Large, simple, clean rooms rent for Rp 4,500 ($2.75) single, Rp 6,500 ($4) double, with fancier rooms available from Rp 8,000 ($5) to Rp 28,000 ($17.50). There are several small *losmen* (guest-houses) and local hotels along the coast road, but the Carita Krakatau Beach complex, with its expatriate flair, has a unique appeal.

When it comes to dining at Carita Beach, there is the Carita Krakatau Beach Hotel's restaurant with a standard European/Indonesian menu and their special lobster dishes. Several warung, small Indonesian restaurants with some seafood dishes, nasi goreng and sayur (vegetables) are great for lunch.

Getting to Carita Beach

To make the most out of your 2½-hour trip to Carita Beach, rent a Blue Bird taxi (tel. 325-607) so that you can stop, shop, and take pictures along the way. A taxi should cost about $60, although you'll have to negotiate the return fare.

The Carita Krakatau Beach Hotel offers private bus service, with a one-way fare of Rp 19,200 ($12); check their office for current information and seat reservations (tel. 320-252).

For the brave and adventurous there is a public bus leaving from the Terminal Bis Kalideres almost hourly throughout the day to Labuan. From the Labuan terminal you can catch a minibus to Pantai Carita. The total fare should be about Rp 3,500 ($2.25) one way; contact Jakarta's Visitor Information Centre for schedule information (tel. 364-093).

3. OVERLAND ACROSS WEST JAVA: BOGOR AND BANDUNG

The former hill station of Bogor, the scenic Puncak Pass, and the province's capital city of Bandung are representative of the varied scenery, village and town life encountered in West Java. If you're traveling overland and have the time to stop, each offers small pleasures to the visitor curious about contemporary Javanese life.

BOGOR: Once a Dutch hill station and popular weekend resort, Bogor is fast becoming one of Jakarta's bedroom communities. The village, situated at the foothills of the Salak, Pangrango, and Gede mountains enjoys a cooler climate and more daily rainfall than much of West Java because of its altitude of 942 feet. Bogor's Kebun Raya (Botanical Gardens) is a popular destination for day trips from Jakarta, particularly on the weekends.

Leave Jakarta by the Old Bogor Road (Jl. Bogor Raya) and you'll drive through Ciputan, a suburb known for its many art, antique, and ceramics shops. Most express buses will use the faster toll road, the Jagorawi highway; avoid it if you can, and see Java's natural beauties sooner. The blacktop Bogor Road undulates next to cultivated rolling hills, less than a half hour from Merdeka Square, along with flooded rice paddies tended by women in sarongs, heads shaded by woven reed caping. Papaya, coconut, mango, banana, and durian trees flank the busy two-lane thoroughfare. Every few miles a small fruit stand offers freshly picked produce to passersby. Suddenly, the roadside fruit stands appear closer together and the shoulders of the road become crowded with becak drivers; you've reached Bogor.

Kebun Raya (The Bogor Botanical Gardens)

Kebun Raya, a 272-acre botanical garden, dominates the colonial town of Bogor. The garden has more than 15,000 species of tropical plants, and an orchid garden (closed for renovation during our visit) with more than 3,000 varieties. Many Indonesian couples and families come to picnic and fill the miles of pathways, enjoying the park that Sir Thomas Stamford Raffles built in 1861, before founding Singapore.

North of the Botanical Gardens stands the **President's Palace,** built by the Dutch in 1745 as a retreat for their governors-general. The palace, which houses the late President Soekarno's art collection, is used for state functions and is rarely open to the public. Visitors can admire the imported deer from Bengal, India, that roam the lawns. Down the street from Kebun Raya is the **Zoological Museum,** containing many indigenous species of wildlife displayed in a natural setting. Since the town is built up around the Botanical Gardens, the main gate is a good starting point for exploration. At lunch, you can cross Jl. Kebun Raya to **Pasar Baru,** a lively market filled with small restaurants. If you don't want to eat here you can buy a picnic, or follow the stream of vacationing Jakartaites into their favorite warung.

The Puncak Pass

As the road rises from Bogor, there is a choice between mountain and sea, a fork in the road for Bandung and Sukabumi. The Bandung road weaves through mist-shrouded mountains and manicured hillsides blanketed in tea plantations. It peaks at the 5,525-foot Puncak Pass, a scenic spot best appreciated by stopping at the **Puncak Pass Hotel** (tel. 0255/2503). The restaurant overlooks a verdant valley and serves a standard Indonesian buffet for Rp 7,000 ($4.50). On a clear day, the view is worth the price of a meal. To explore the area and breathe deeply of the crisp mountain air, spend the afternoon hiking or riding a pony, which you can rent for Rp 3,000 ($2) per hour at the hotel's entrance. Those continuing east to Bandung have two more hours of scenic driving.

Horticultural buffs with their own transportation should try to stop at the **Cibodas Botanical Garden,** about ten minutes past Puncak on the Bandung road. Cibodas was established on 198 acres of hillside to grow flora that required an alpine climate and conditions. It lies 4,500 feet above sea level on the slopes of Mount Pangrango and Gede.

Getting to Bogor and Puncak

If you're planning a day trip from Jakarta, your hotel can arrange for a private car or **Blue Bird taxi** for about Rp 100,000 ($62.50) per day. Several tour companies, including **Vayatours** (tel. 365-008), offer a guided eight-hour bus tour to Bogor and Puncak Pass at Rp 50,000 ($34.50) for adults, Rp 33,000 ($20.50) for children, as well as longer day trips that include Bandung. Tours run daily except weekends.

If this marks the beginning of your personal Java overland expedition you can take a long-distance **bus** or a train to Bogor. Buses leave from Jakarta's Terminal Bis Cililitan for the 1½- to 2-hour ride several times daily; the fare is Rp 1,000 (60¢). From the Bogor bus terminal, you'll have to take a local taxi to Kebun Raya. **Trains** leave from Jakarta's Gambir Station hourly between 6:30 a.m. and 8:30 p.m.; the two-hour ride will cost Rp 300 (20¢) in third class.

Visitors arriving at Bogor's railroad station can hire a becak or walk for about 15 minutes to the gardens. Local buses leave Bogor frequently for the hour ride to Puncak Pass (there is no train service). From Puncak you can continue on to Bandung by public bus, or return to Bogor to catch a train.

BANDUNG: Bandung is a prosperous center of commerce and trade once known to the Dutch as "Paris van Java" because of its graceful colonial architecture and broad, landscaped avenues. Thousands of students inhabit this city of almost two million, attending the 27 universities and technical colleges that flourish here. Their youthful vitality is part of Bandung's appeal. The aspect of Bandung's culture that lures most tourists is the opportunity to attend an *angklung* concert, performed by locally trained musicians on the traditional bamboo percussion instruments. If this is why you want to stop in Bandung, make sure to call ahead to the local Tourist Information Center (tel. 022/56644 or 71724) to confirm the concert schedule as it's often geared to the arrival of tour groups. Without the allure of an anklung performance, Bandung is primarily a stop of architectural and historical interest.

Orientation and Sightseeing

Today, Bandung's charm comes from the few remaining colonial and art deco structures in the city's center that survived a citywide fire in 1946. **Gedung Sate** on Jl. Diponegoro is a huge white stucco, green-roofed edifice that's named after the decorative meat skewer at its peak. This impressive building was built in 1920 by the Dutch to house their Ministry of Transportation and Irrigation, and is now the seat of the provincial government (offices are open from 8:30 a.m. to 1 p.m. Monday through Thursday, till 11 a.m. on Friday, if you want to peek inside). The **Isola Villa** is a five-story nautical-style deco building constructed for an Italian aristocrat. It's now the Teachers' Training College (also known as Bumi Siliwangi) about five miles north of the city. The **Bandung Zoo** and **Babakan Siliwangi** (a touristy complex with shops, restaurants, and occasional cultural shows) are along Jl. Siliwangi on the way to the Isola Villa.

Gedung Merdeka, restored as the Independence Building in 1955 for the first Afro-Asian Conference, is located at the heart of Bandung on Jl. Asia Afrika, at Alun-Alun, the main town square. It was designed in 1879 by Van Gallen and Wolff Schoemaker as a meeting hall for the Dutch Societeit Concordia. It has a monumentality reminiscent of fascist architecture in Europe, but with a deco flair; bronze lamps and lettering decorate the façade. In fact, Jl. Asia Afrika is dotted with shops and small office buildings with subtle details such as pressed-tin ceilings and mosaic floors, all reminders of Bandung before the fire.

Across the street from Gedung Merdeka on Alun-Alun Square is the helpful **Tourist Information Center** (tel. 022/56644 or 71724), or Dinas Pariwisata Kotamadya. It has a good selection of maps and brochures, can find local students to guide you, and stays open daily from 9 a.m. to 5 p.m. if volunteer staff is available. The post office, most tourist services, and hotels are located along Jl. Asia Afrika in this area. The **Savoy Homann Hotel,** within walking distance of the square, is another architectural treat in the Indo-European deco style.

Getting to and Getting Around Bandung

Bandung is the third-largest city on Java and is easily reached by bus, train, or plane. **Panorama Tours** (tel. 350-438) runs daily coach tours from Jakarta; the 12-hour guided round-trip excursion costs Rp 88,000 ($55) for adults, Rp 78,000 ($48.75) for children. Long-distance **buses** leave regularly from Jakarta's Terminal Bis Cililitan for the 115-mile (four-hour) bus trip. Bandung's Terminal Bis is located about ten minutes by taxi northwest of Alun-Alun Square, off Jl. Sunia Raja. From here, overlanders can catch the Bandung Express (tel. 58312) or another long-distance bus company's transport to Yogyakarta (about 300 miles, ten hours, $3).

Trains leave Jakarta's Gambir Station five times daily for the 3½-hour trip to Bandung and costs about Rp 5,000 ($3). The Stasiun Kereta Api Bandung is near the bus terminal, off Jl. Oto Iskandardinata. Two trains daily continue east on the ten-hour journey to Yogyakarta. Air-conditioned, soft-seat first-class cars at Rp 12,000 ($7.50), or fan-cooled, soft-seat second-class cars at Rp 7,000 ($4.75), will make the incredibly scenic trip much more bearable than the fan-cooled but hard-seat third-class cars at Rp 3,200 ($2).

The city and its architectural sights are spread out. To sightsee, get a **taxi** for at least two hours, which happens to be the minimum. In many Indonesian cities the tourist office and taxi drivers have agreed to a flat drop-off rate to any city destination of Rp 4,000 ($2.50) or a two-hour minimum for sightseeing of Rp

12,000 ($7.50) to start and Rp 5,000 ($3) per hour thereafter. If you plan to spend a lot of time in Bandung, ask the Tourist Information Office in Alun-Alun Square to help you rent a bicycle.

Angklung

The *angklung* is a traditional instrument formed of one long and one short bamboo pipe, notched to create an eight-note scale and held upright in a wooden frame. When shaken, the angklung creates a xylophone-like sound, and several played together can form intricate, delicate melodies. The Badui tribes of West Java originally used the four-tone bass angklung to inspire soldiers marching to battle. Today nine instruments, with a *dogdog* (small drum), *bedug* (large drum), and *terompet* (a small horn) comprise the traditional angklung orchestra that performs for weddings, family ceremonies, harvests, and other festivals held in the Sundanese communities of Java and on the island of Bali.

The angklung enjoyed a revival in the 1930s and is now found in most West Javanese households. Mr. Ujo, a master performer and founder of the Saung Angklung Padesuka, began a **training school** for children to study the angklung instruments, Sundanese dance, and other arts. The school, which is about two miles east of the city, offers the opportunity to watch an angklung performance (often an orchestra of 74 instruments) once weekly (usually Saturday) during the summer months. Call the Tourist Information Office (tel. 022/71724) for schedule information, because more performances are added on request from group tours. During the summer months the **Hotel Panghegar,** Jl. Merdeka 2 (tel. 022/57584), also offers once-weekly (usually Wednesday) cultural performances, including angklung music.

Accommodations and Dining

If you're fortunate enough to catch an angklung performance, you'll need a place to stay. The best deluxe rooms can be found at the **Hotel Panghegar,** in the heart of town at Jl. Merdeka 2 (tel. 022/57584), where executive services, inter-city direct-dial phones, and a large swimming pool cater to many business people. Rooms are spacious, simply decorated, and each has a *kendi*, a West Javanese terracotta jug that keeps drinking water cool. Double rooms range from Rp 82,500 ($51.50) to Rp 98,000 ($61.25), depending on size and view, and singles will pay 10% less; all rates include taxes.

Architecture and art deco buffs should head straight to the **Savoy Homann Hotel,** at Jl. Asia Afrika 112 (tel. 022/58091), within walking distance of the Gedung Merdeka and Visitor Information Center. The Savoy, renovated by the Dutch architect Albers and once host to world leaders at the first Asia-Africa Conference in 1955, has achieved a new landmark status. Its nautical deco façade and vertical marquee date from 1938, when the original 1888 structure was expanded. The lobby opens onto a bar decorated in murals, and the dining room has chrome banisters and stepped ceiling lights. Hallways with stained-glass panels and lead window mullions lead to good-sized, clean rooms that cost Rp 82,500 ($51.50) for two. Around the tropical garden are vast "superior" rooms, where two can lounge in an enclosed patio or amble through quarters divided by stained-glass panels for Rp 98,000 ($61.25) per night. Budget travelers can pay $30 for their two "economy" rooms, similar to these but without air conditioning, phone, or TV.

More conventional three-star facilities can be found nearby at the **Hotel Kumala Panghegar,** at Jl. Asia Afrika 140 (tel. 022/52141). Clean and pleasant rooms run Rp 55,000 ($34.50) for a single, Rp 64,000 ($40) for a double, including breakfast.

Low-budget travelers will have a hard time staying in Bandung since inexpensive accommodations are hard to come by. A Rp-4,000 ($2.50) taxi ride from the train station, the attractive colonial-style **Hotel Braga,** Jl. Braga 8 (tel.

022/51685), is on what was formerly Bandung's most elegant street. The two-story white lodge features worn but clean, high-ceilinged rooms for Rp 25,000 ($15.50) including a fan, hot water and private shower, and breakfast in the sunny courtyard.

4. JAVA'S CULTURAL CAPITAL: YOGYAKARTA

The images that most of us associate with Indonesia—the bold floral prints of batik cotton, the intricately carved and painted pointy-nose leather puppets, the formality and grace of a sultan's court—are visions of a unique and exotic society from Java's cultural capital, Yogyakarta. Its crowded and seemingly bland urban façade houses a fascinating world of dance, drama, and music.

Almost 20% of the inhabitants are students at the Republic's esteemed Gajah Mada University or one of the many arts academies, where learning is based on a respect for tradition and spiritual values. Today Yogyakarta thrives on intellectual and artistic commerce. The artistry in batik fabrics and paintings, the superb wayang puppetry that entertains locals and visitors, and the exquisitely disciplined classical dance that flourishes here can be traced back to the sultanate's support.

A BRIEF HISTORY: Yogyakarta (pronounced "*Joeg*-ja-kar-ta" and called "Yogya" for short) was officially founded in 1755 but its importance as a cultural and artistic center dates back much earlier. The Hindu culture of central Java, based south of Yogyakarta, spawned monuments such as the Pramabanan temples and fostered the development of wayang, the shadow puppet theater. The Buddhist culture imported from Sumatra during the Çailendra Dynasty left its mark north of the city with several monuments including Borobudur.

In the 1500s Islam swept into central Java. Hinduism remained very strong in East Java. Senopati (1584–1601) is credited with founding the new Islamic Mataram Kingdom; he conquered Pajang (the present-day Solo) in 1587 and brought their *pusaka,* or sacred regalia, to his new capital at Kota Gede. He was assisted by the Goddess of the South Sea, Kanjeng Ratu Kidul; the court's gratitude is shown annually at Labuhan, when offerings of food, silks, gifts, and clippings of the current sultan's fingernails and hair are thrown into the sea.

Sultan Agung (1613–1646) is the best known of the Mataram rulers. He attempted to unite Java under the Islamic faith and in 1640, after moving all the Hindus to the island of Bali, took the Islamic title of sultan.

After his death the Mataram Kingdom was torn by political rivalries. Agung's grandson was implicated in a political scandal, and with the help of the Dutch East India Company (VOC) eventually moved his rival court to Solo. His brother, Puger, consolidated forces in Mataram but eventually fell in with the VOC and was rewarded with the title of Susuhunan (emperor) Paku Buwono I. The royal relatives fought three Javanese Wars of Succession until Prince Mangkubumi (Puger's nephew) was declared susuhunan and set up court in Yogyakarta in 1749. Meanwhile the VOC had installed another susuhunan in Solo, Paku Buwono III. Under pressure, Mangkubumi gave up his title and became the Sultan of Mataram, Hamengku Buwono I. Under the treaty signed by both rulers and the VOC in 1755, the Mataram Kingdom was divided in two.

The sultans' courts at Yogyakarta and Solo developed separately. For the next half century there was intermittent resistance to established Dutch rule and then to the British, who took over Java in 1811. When Lt. Gov. Stamford Raffles discovered a conspiracy between the courts of Yogya and Solo in June of 1812, his troops marched on Yogyakarta, attacked and looted the kraton, and greatly humiliated the Mataram court. In 1825 the Mataram Prince Diponegoro led another rebellion against Dutch rule. His five-year Java War ended in negotiations, but Diponegoro was exiled, and both sultanates of Yogya and Solo began to decline in autonomy and power.

During the next century of relative peace, the sultans devoted their resources to cultivating traditional Javanese arts and culture. Both kratons became centers of dance and music, with training sponsored by the courts' resources.

After World War II the Dutch returned to reoccupy Jakarta and the newly formed Republic of Indonesia moved its capital to Yogyakarta. On December 18, 1948, the Dutch marched on Yogya and imprisoned the new republic's leaders. Soekarno and his cabinet's weak resistance began alienating the republic's military. The national army declared martial rule over Java and, led by Lt.-Col. Soeharto (the current president), retook Yogyakarta the following year. The Dutch retreated under international pressure and at the end of 1949 granted sovereignty to Indonesia.

Sultan Hamengku Buwono IX gave his territory to the republic, served as vice-president for many years, remained in the cabinet from 1946 to 1953, and currently serves as governor of the Special Territory of Yogyakarta. The peoples' warm affection and respect for him is still evident; his patronage has made the kraton (named Ngayogyakarta Hadiningrat Palace after the city's original name) the center of Yogyakarta's cultural life and a stronghold of Javanese traditions, beliefs, and social customs.

GETTING THERE: You can take almost any vehicle to Yogya; only the rough Indian Ocean on central Java's south coast prevents ferries from reaching this popular destination. **Garuda Indonesia** flies direct from Jakarta four times daily, five times on weekends; from Denpasar, Bali, twice daily; and from Surabaya, once a day. From Adisucipto National Airport you can walk to the main road (300 yards) and take a public minibus (every 20 minutes between 6 a.m. and 6 p.m.) for 20¢ into the inconveniently located bus terminal, or take a taxi directly from the terminal for Rp 7,000 ($4.50) for the 5½-mile ride.

Buses run regularly around the clock from almost every Javanese city to Yogyakarta. Check the local Tourist Information Office or the Terminal Bis for schedule information. Several **trains** make the 11-hour trip from Jakarta's Gambir Stasiun daily; the luxury-class afternoon *Bima Express* can make it in 9½ hours from the Kota Stasiun, but you miss lots of fine scenery. Call the Tourist Information Center or the Yogyakarta Stasiun (tel. 4270 or 2870) for schedule information and fares.

ORIENTATION: The Special Territory of Yogyakarta consists of 31,000 km² (11,150 square miles) of richly planted, densely populated farmland. Fortunately for the visitor, almost everything of interest is within three miles of the **kraton,** the sultan's palace and the city's political and cultural center. The inner kraton, still used by Sultan Hamengku Buwono IX, is surrounded by an outer kraton filled with the ruins of the 18th-century water castle **Taman Sari,** an active bird market, and several batik factories and art galleries. The 2½ miles of outer wall that still stand are lined with local housing.

Perpendicular to the north end of the kraton, across Senopati Medan (Square), is **Malioboro Street,** the city's commercial center. Around or near the square are the Sonobudoyo Museum, the Seni Bono National Gallery, a Bank Negara Indonesia, the post office, and a central taxi stand. One block north along Malioboro (also named Jl. Achmed Yani here) is the minibus terminal to Prambanan or the airport and the daily Beringharjo Market, filled with produce, spice, batik, woven-reed bags, and other dealers. This is one of the few neighborhoods where you need to safeguard your wallet from pickpockets. One block north of the market, on Malioboro, is the **Tourist Information Center** (tel. 0274/2812, ext. 30, or 0274/3543). Hotels, restaurants, and shops (most of which are open from 9 a.m. to 1:30 p.m. and 5 to 9 p.m. six days, half days on

Sunday) line the mile to the railroad tracks. The Kerata Api Stasiun is just west of Malioboro Street. At about 10 p.m. each night this stretch of Malioboro becomes the Pasar Malam, or Night Market. Throngs of people take over the street and straw mats and serving dishes take over the sidewalks, creating a huge outdoor café.

Five hundred yards north of the railroad tracks, Malioboro (here also called Jl. Mangkubumi) intersects Jl. Diponegoro (to the west) and Jl. Jend. Sudirman (east). East along **Jl. Jend. Sudirman,** which soon becomes Jl. Adisucipto, are some of the newer restaurants, the sultan's former summer retreat that became the Ambarrukmo Palace Hotel, the painter Affandi's Museum, and 5½ miles out, the **Adisucipto National Airport.** Jl. Jend. Sudirman eventually becomes the Yogya–Solo highway and runs past the Prambanan temple complex.

About 500 yards southwest of the kraton, off Jl. Bantul, is the AGASTYA, a wayang puppetry school where performances are given daily. About 500 yards southeast are the **galleries and batik shops** of Jl. Tirtodipuran, and just east of it, the **guesthouses** and budget hostels of Jl. Prawirotaman. The Terminal Bis Umbulharjo is about 2½ miles west of the kraton at Jl. Veteran and Jl. Kemerdakaan. The silversmiths and shops of **Kota Gede** are 15 minutes by cab southeast of here; the sultans' burial ground at **Imogiri** is equidistant, due south.

GETTING AROUND: Getting around Yogyakarta can be a bit frustrating. Although most sights are within a 20-minute walk of the Tourist Information Center on Malioboro, the traffic is so noisy and the weather so hot that a short walk can become unpleasant.

Bicycle-powered becaks and taxis (best for longer distances) are two alternatives. The narrow two-seater becaks cluster at every intersection and their drivers are tough bargainers when it comes to giving two hefty foreigners a ride. Nevertheless you can get around the core of town in about 15 minutes for about Rp 1,500 (95¢).

Taxis are available at the train station, the Tourist Information Center, the kraton, and in front of the larger hotels. They cost a flat Rp 4,500 ($2.75) per in-town fare, or Rp 8,000 ($5) for a two-hour minimum, plus Rp 4,000 ($2.50) per hour thereafter; taxis are good value to see the sights if you get them by the hour.

The bold and fit can rent a **bicycle** (95¢ a day) or **motorbike** ($5.50 a day) from several shops opposite the railroad station; be sure to check on insurance and helmet rental.

Yogya Rentals and other travel agents on this street rent **chauffeured minibuses,** great if you've come with your own group (one way to Surabaya will cost about $64). Don't even consider trying to drive yourself around Yogyakarta.

USEFUL INFORMATION: The **Tourist Information Center,** at Jl. Malioboro 16 (tel. 0274/3543), is open daily except Sunday from 8 a.m. to 8:30 p.m. Make sure to get a city map and a current schedule of cultural performances. There is also an Information Desk at the airport.

The **police** are on Jl. Reksobayan (tel. 2487). . . . The **Bethesda Hospital** is on Jl. Jend. Sudirman (tel. 2281). . . . The **telephone area code** for Yogyakarta is 0274.

The **Garuda Indonesia** office is at Jl. Mangkubumi 56 (tel. 5184). The **Merpati Nusantara** (tel. 4272) and **Bouraq** (tel. 86-664) offices are nearby on Jl. Jend. Sudirman.

Outside regular banking hours, try the **Bank Niaga** in the Garuda Hotel, open Monday through Saturday from 7 a.m. to 7 p.m. The **C.V. Alif International Moneychanger** at Jl. Pasar Kembang 19 (opposite the railroad station) is open daily from 6 a.m. to 10 p.m.

Pacto Travel Ltd., at Jl. P. Mangkubumi 5 (tel. 2740), is the local American Express representative. They're open from 7:30 a.m. to 4 p.m. and handle lost credit cards or traveler's checks, and sell new traveler's checks.

The **post office** (Kantor Pos) is on Senopati Medan; it's open daily except Sunday and receives poste restante. If you're shipping purchases overseas the Customs agent will have to inspect them, so don't seal your packages until your paperwork's complete. **Intras Travel** (tel. 2846) is recommended as a sea or air cargo-shipping agent; call for information before packing your parcel.

The **Kantor Telepon** is on a traffic circle called Yos. Sudarso, about 15 minutes by becak from the tourist office, and is open 24 hours. . . . The local chain of **Duta Foto** is incredibly cheap—when we were there they had a special on 35-mm film, including processing, for $3.50 a roll!

Shop for local guidebooks on the Borobudur and Prambanan temples at Gunung Agung or any of the **bookshops** off Malioboro Street because they'll have a bigger selection and better prices than those at the sites. Michael Smithies' book *Yogyakarta, Cultural Heart of Indonesia,* published by Oxford University Press, is one of the best about the region and is available for sale here.

ACCOMMODATIONS:
Yogyakarta has a mixed bag of hotel choices; there are no luxury rooms and only a few strong recommendations in other price ranges. However, the city becomes so crowded between June and September that we wanted to offer the largest selection possible without compromising quality. Since you've come this far, try to book one of the more special hotels at least two weeks in advance. Note that most of the smaller hotels do not accept credit cards, and all the hotels except those in the budget category quote their room rates in U.S. dollars.

First-Class Choices
There are three special hotels in this category, where prices range from $35 to $76 per double room, including tax and service charges.

Yogyakarta's finest rooms are in its most stylish hotel, the newly restored **Hotel Garuda,** Malioboro Street 60/72 (tel. 0274/86353). The Garuda was opened in 1911 as a bungalow complex in the heart of the city; the wings that frame its grand driveway in an Indo-European deco style were added in a 1930 renovation. Stained-glass panels, deco wall sconces, and a batik mural commemorating the liberation of Indonesia decorate the grand lobby. The 120 rooms are large, furnished in local batiks, and offer air conditioning, TV, and mini-bar—ask for one overlooking the pool terrace. Rooms in the central seven-story tower run $55 double, $46 single, but if you want to spring for $90, book a junior suite in one of the original wings. These restored, high-ceilinged bungalows, rich in carved wood and batik, have patios facing the main courtyard. The Garuda has an attractive restaurant offering European cuisine and a coffeeshop off the lobby.

The only hotel within royal grounds is the **Ambarrukmo Palace Hotel,** on Jl. Laksda Adisucipto (tel. 0274/88488), about 2½ miles from the city's center. Its six floors of rooms are built on parkland next to the country retreat of Sultan Hamengku Buwono III. The Ambarrukmo Palace was Yogya's first international hotel and, though aging, still boasts comfortable, old-fashioned rooms with air conditioning, TVs, mini-bars, and balconies. The pool is huge and sits in landscaped splendor among tropical plants, songbirds in cages, with the rice fields beyond. There is a bar, coffeeshop, shopping arcade, and a very fine Indonesian restaurant, the Bale Kambang, in the old palace compound. Nightly performances of classical dance or wayang kulit puppetry, and afternoon gamelan concerts, are given by resident performers. Double rooms run $66 to $76 (singles are $10 less); the rooms with pool views are infinitely more preferable although the rooftop supper club's orchestra can be boisterous.

To live like a sultan and no. 1 wife in the most romantic accommodations, try the **Puri Artha Cottages,** tucked away at the north end of town at Jl. Cendrawasih 9 (tel. 0274/5934). There are four rooms off the main garden with gold-and-red carved-wood doors, lavish palace décor, and canopied bridal beds. Totally classic in décor, yet featuring all the modern amenities, these uniquely Indonesian sleeping quarters cost only $39 for two. The Puri Artha offers 60 others, less extraordinary rooms grouped around landscaped gardens or goldfish ponds on both sides of this quiet lane. All have tiled private baths, attractive rattan furniture, and phones; some have TVs and mini-bars as well. Each room opens onto its own furnished patio, some with a view of the private pool. These rooms cost $35 for a twin-bedded room or $66 for a suite. Another treat here is the restaurant, known as one of the best Indonesian eateries in town.

The **Yogya International Hotel** opened in 1988 at Jl. Adisucipto 48 (tel. 0274/2327), a convenient location on the busy, noisy Solo road. It's built in a contemporary Javanese style with acres of tan and brown tiles, a long beige granite lobby, and large rooms with dark-wood furniture and trim. Each has a seating area, attached tile bathroom, and full first-class amenities. The large, round pool is set in a nicely landscaped lawn and can be admired from the deluxe room balconies. A Chinese restaurant and a shopping arcade are planned to benefit the 51 rooms already completed. Deluxe rooms at Rp 77,000 ($48) for two are much better value than the interior-facing standard rooms for Rp 70,000 ($43.75). All rates include breakfast.

In the summer months, when other first-class hotels are fully booked, you'll find large, modern, and comfortable rooms at the less conveniently located **Sahid Garden Hotel,** on Jl. Babarsari, about 5 minutes from the airport or 15 minutes from town (tel. 0274/3697). A white, glazed-brick eight-story building, 40 semi-attached cottages, and an older motel offer three separate lodgings in a well-landscaped park. Modern tower rooms cost $65 double, private six-sided cottages are $55 for two, and the worn, but clean, HoJo-style motel rooms are $35 for a sole traveler, $43 for two. The Sahid Garden's bar and restaurant are located in the reception pavilion next to the new tower.

Our next two choices have all the amenities (pool, air conditioning, TV, phone, private bath) but are older hotels that aren't quite as well maintained. In most cases we'd opt for one of the newer, full-service guesthouses whose personalized management offers hospitality that larger hotels can't match. The **Sri Wedari Hotel,** on Jl. Adisucipto (tel. 0274/88288), is also on the airport road, but its standard rooms are cozily grouped in cottages spread throughout a landscaped garden. Two caged peacocks add to the ambience; rooms rent at $37 for two. The Sri Wedari's dining room, a free-standing pendopo with bamboo shades, is a pleasing Indonesian touch. The most centrally located of all these hotels is the **Hotel Mutiara,** at Jl. Malioboro 18 (tel. 0274/4531), next to the Tourist Information Center. The newer section, a six-floor tower with clean, modern, but slightly worn rooms, rents for $54 for two, a much better deal than their aging original wing. The glitzy new lobby has a comfortable bar and coffeeshop.

Moderately Priced Accommodations

Yogyakarta's newer guesthouses are centrally located, offer bright new rooms with attached baths and air conditioning (rarely phones or TVs), and usually have a friendly and helpful staff. Hotels and guesthouses in the moderately priced group charge Rp 22,400 ($14) to Rp 35,200 ($22) for two, including tax and service, but often quote prices only in U.S. dollars.

Ranking with the best of the town's hotels, the **Peti Mas Guesthouse,** centrally located near Malioboro at Jl. Dagen 39 (tel. 0274/2896), is built around a lush, beautiful garden with a charming pendopo in the center, which serves as the dining room. Cages full of songbirds dot the garden, and in this quiet sanctuary provide accompaniment to the gentle breezes. A clean, bright pool adjoins the pavilion; most rooms have porches with rattan furniture. Clean, simple rooms run Rp 39,000 ($24.50) for two, Rp 27,200 ($17) with a fan only, Rp 4,800 ($3) less with cold water only. Economy rooms with shared bath cost only Rp 15,200 ($9.50) for two. The second-floor rooms are preferable, but Room 28 is our favorite in town. It's a solitary room on the third floor with its own roof garden and a thrilling view of Mount Merapi looming above the roofs of Yogya, and costs only Rp 27,200 ($17) because it's fan-cooled!

Close behind the Peti Mas are the **Wisma Gajah Guesthouse** (tel. 0274/2479) and the **Airlangga Guesthouse** (tel. 0274/3344). Both are located south of the kraton on Jl. Prawirotaman, at no. 2a and 4 respectively, but are of much better quality than most of the neighboring guesthouses. The Wisma Gajah is built around nicely landscaped, spacious courtyards enclosing a clean good-sized pool. The open porches are tiled and wood-paneled, with rattan chairs for lounging. It's a light, bright place with simple, but homey, décor. Spotless rooms run Rp 22,000 ($13.75) to Rp 26,000 ($16.25) with air conditioning, Rp 14,500 ($9) to Rp 20,000 ($12.50) with fan, including breakfast and evening snack; singles are $2 less. The Airlangga has recently added a pool, dining hall, and fully tiled second-story rooms to its range of accommodations. We preferred the larger ground-floor rooms, with small patios opening onto their densely planted gardens and collection of primitive Irian Jaya sculpture. The 31 new rooms cost Rp 34,000 ($21.25) for two, including breakfast, $3 more if you turn on your air conditioner. The fan-cooled older rooms have a ladle-water-over-your-head-mandi and cost only Rp 23,000 ($14.50). Guests can avail themselves of a lobby TV, phone, laundry service, and front-desk information counter.

Our last moderately priced choice is conveniently near the railroad station, handy if you arrive late at night but not really the nicest area to stay in this small, easy-to-get-around city. Surprisingly attractive for a cheaper hotel, the **Batik Palace Hotel**, at Jl. Pasar Kembang 29 (tel. 0274/2149), is built around a pavilion with gardens. Rooms are plain and fairly clean, and the staff is friendly. Air-conditioned doubles are Rp 32,000 ($20), singles run Rp 23,000 ($14.50), including breakfast; $4 less with fan only. The Batik Palace has another, slightly fancier branch, with a pool, more expensive, and about half a mile north at Jl. Mangkubumi 46 (tel. 0274/2229).

The Budget Range

Jl. Pasar Kembang, the busy avenue across from the train station, is Yogya's center for cheap, truly spartan, cold-water/shared-mandi losmen, the mainstay of the Around-the-World-for-$500 crowd. Yes, you can find a cot for $2 a night, but if you leave the train station and accept a becak as daily transport, Jl. Prawirotaman (ten minutes by becak south of the kraton) offers several better choices in the budget guesthouse category. Three stand out, in order of quality: the **Duta Guesthouse** at no. 20 (tel. 0274/5219), the **Rose Guesthouse** at no. 22 (tel. 0274/87991), and the **Metro Guesthouse** at no. 7/71 (tel. 0274/3982). All are built in the open-courtyard style with pools, and all offer a range of simple comforts and low prices. Economy rooms, some with cold-water private bath, some with common bath, range from Rp 6,500 ($4) for one to Rp 15,000 ($9.50) for two. With fan, single rooms range from Rp 10,000 ($6.25) to Rp 24,000 ($15); doubles, from Rp 12,000 ($7.50) to Rp 29,000 ($18). Add $3 to $4 at most for larger, more comfortable, air-conditioned rooms. All prices include breakfast and afternoon tea. If these are fully booked, continue walking down either of Jl. Prawirotaman's two parallel lanes and inspect what's available.

There are two budget choices that are less convenient, but much cleaner and more clean-cut than those above. Although it doesn't have a pool and is a bit out of town, the small **Wisma Prambanan Guesthouse**, on Jl. Solo (tel. 0274/4709), across from the Ambarrukmo Palace Hotel, deserves mention. The manicured gardens, pet ducks, and homey, lace-covered dining table overlooking the central lawn all reflect the family-style management. Rooms with fan and private mandi or shared full bath start at Rp 12,500 ($7.75) and range to air conditioning and private bath for Rp 19,500 ($12.25), including breakfast. For an extra $1.50 per day you can use the plush grounds, pool, and towels at the Ambarrukmo across the street. The 26-room **Pura Jenggala Guesthouse,** located opposite the Puri Artha Cottages on a small lane at Demengan Baru 11–13, off busy Jl. Jend. Sudirman (tel. 0274/2283), is both quiet and pleasantly suburban. Clean, neatly kept simple rooms for two with air conditioning, shower, and private toilet are Rp 23,000 ($14.50), including breakfast, but the price drops down to Rp 16,000 ($10) for two in simpler lodgings. The friendly staff encourages use of the large back lawn and seating area for sunning and relaxation.

BUDGET TIP: "The **Losmen Indonesia,** near the Superman Restaurant by the train station, was very clean and safe. An old woman ran it and charged Rp 3,500 ($2.25) for a bed." (Stan Mendoza, New York, N.Y.).

DINING: Yogyakarta's large student population and steady stream of budget travelers have spawned a number of cheap, mediocre Indonesian-cum-Chinese-cum-continental eateries with little to offer except cleanliness and a fast-food approach. Most are centered on Malioboro Street, which in the evenings becomes the city's Pasar Malam, a Night Market of food vendors. Fortunately, if you're willing to spend a bit more money (rarely more than $5 per person), there's some excellent food to be had in the cultural capital. All restaurants are open for lunch (usually from noon until 2:30 p.m.) and dinner (usually 6 to 10 p.m.) daily unless otherwise noted. During the evening we'd suggest hiring a taxi round trip, since most of our recommendations are somewhat off the taxi circuit.

Indonesian Cuisine

Yogya's culinary and aesthetic dining treat is the **Bale Kambang,** the floating royal pavilion at the Ambarrukmo Palace Hotel, on Jl. Adisucipto, the airport road (tel. 88488). In a graceful two-story, octagonal pavilion built for Sultan Hamengku Buwono III's country palace, guests sit on woven mats at low tables and enjoy the view the sultan once had of his wives bathing in the pools below him (the pools are still there—the wives are not!). The Indonesian buffet is excellent and varied, the gamelan music sweet, the atmosphere exotic and romantic. Prices start at Rp 12,500 ($7.75) per person and reservations are necessary, often a few days in advance. Bale Kambang is open daily, for dinner only. Many evenings there is a free wayang kulit performance given at 8 p.m.

Another attractive outdoor setting for an evening out is the **Chandra Room** at the Puri Artha Cottages, Jl. Cendrawasih 9 (tel. 5934). You can dine on well-prepared Indonesian specialties under a carved wooden canopy, surrounded by batiks, rattan, and tropical palms. The chef's specialties include the spiced chicken and coconut nasi gudeg (to be ordered an hour in advance), sayur lodeh (eggplant, green beans, and peppers in a coconut-milk broth), and tender sate babi (grilled pork on skewers). Many evenings, a buffet of regional foods is offered for Rp 12,800 ($8) per person, and two can dine à la carte for about Rp 28,000 ($17.50). Reservations are recommended in the June to September high season.

When you've had your fill of local ambience, head straight to **Pesta Perak** (known to locals and cabbies as "Yogya Food") at Jl. Tentara Rakyat Mataram 8 (tel. 86255), near the road to Borobudur. The attractive, tiled dining room is sided by a rough-stone wall bathed in cool water that feeds a goldfish pond below. The special buffet provides some of the best Indonesian food in town, with a wide selection of local dishes, all typical Yogya food, and Indonesian desserts. The price is a bargain at Rp 6,000 ($3.75) and lures as many locals as visitors.

If you ask Indonesians about Yogya food, they'll reply "nasi gudeg." This local specialty, greatly resembling pot roast, is actually a sweet and spicy blend of

218 □ EXPLORING JAVA

jackfruit, chicken, nuts, and coconut. The gudeg is served with nasi (white rice), telor (hard-boiled egg), and krecak (fried cow's skin, which is much tastier than shoe leather). It makes a filling, if somewhat odd, meal. **Andra Wina Loka**, at Km. 9 on Jl. Adisucipto (tel. 87662), on the way out of town, serves the best gudeg in Yogya. In a two-story, brightly painted pavilion, locals argue about the merits of each gudeg entree. When you can experiment with a new dish, do it in a pleasant outdoor café, and spend less than $1, why not try it?

The next most popular meal in town is fried chicken and there's even a branch of Kentucky Fried Chicken to prove it. However, locals drive right past it out to **NY Suharti** (it means Mrs. Suharti), Km. 7 on Jl. Adisucipto (tel. 5522). Ayam goreng is a Javanese favorite and few do it better than Mom Suharti. In her bird-filled garden you can try a half or a whole bird, with rice and a cold Bintang, for less than Rp 5,500 ($3.50) per person.

Other Cuisines

There are many Chinese and Western restaurants that cater to the local market, particularly on Saturday evenings when students are out in full force for "Date Night." Since Yogyakarta is only 17 miles from the sea, you can expect excellent seafood, and on the Borobudur road is **Sintawang Seafood**, Jl. Magelang 9 (tel. 2901). It's a light, bright place with big round tables and Asian muzak. The menu is huge—42 seafood entrees, 39 Chinese dishes, an assortment of European specialties, Indonesian standards, and even pizza—but seafood is their strength. Two can dine for Rp 15,000 ($9.50), although special choices like sea slugs run higher.

The recently opened **Korean Ginseng House**, at Jl. Solo 33 (tel. 86955), serves (what else?) Korean food, a large selection of teas including ginseng, and a few Japanese standards such as sushi, sukiyaki, and udong noodles. A "complete" Korean meal of barbecued beef ribs starts with kimchee (a spicy pickled cabbage) and relishes of mixed vegetables and bean sprouts, followed by steamed rice, soup, and fresh papaya. Other good choices are the broiled tuna and the shellfish in pot soup, a spicy Korean bouillabaise. Two can dine for Rp 20,000 ($12.50).

A casual, convenient midday stop near the Tourist Information Center is on a second-floor balcony above Jl. Perwakian 3. The **Legian Restaurant** (tel. 87985), where rattan chairs are grouped under straw huts and large plants provide diners with privacy, has long been a hangout for budget travelers of all ages. Backpackers splurge on a meal of Legian's special deep-fried seafood combo; families share dishes from a varied European and Chinese menu; all enjoy the travel tales swapped over entrees, which only cost Rp 2,800 ($1.75) to Rp 5,600 ($3.50) each.

Western food eateries are clustered in the north end of the city, closer to the university and its hungry student body. **Gita Buana**, at Jl. Adisucipto 169 (tel. 87164), is typical with its comfortable booths, rather bland décor, and extensive menu of steak, sandwiches, pasta dishes, burgers, Chinese favorites, and ice cream. Entrees average Rp 3,500 ($2.25). The young at heart will have much more fun at **Valentino**, Jl. Magelang 57 (tel. 88824), a lively white-tiled establishment up a flight of neon-rimmed steps from the busy street. Asian rock videos dominate one corner of this large place, a live band occasionally takes over another, or you can curl up in an isolated booth and watch Yogya's young elite file by. The menu favors Cantonese seafood dishes, but steaks, pork chops, and continental favorites are easily had. Two can have a night on the town (it's more fun than at lunch) for Rp 13,000 ($8) to Rp 20,000 ($12.50). After dinner, head across the street to Borobudur Plaza, a jazzy mall with an ice-cream parlor, bakery, popular coffeeshop, and movie-hall complex.

For a quick lunch or refreshing fruit juice at midday, try the **Helen Café**, at Malioboro 44 (tel. 88242), a few minutes' walk from the Hotel Mutiara. The

Helen Café is open daily from 7 a.m. to 10 p.m. to serve an inexpensive breakfast or Chinese, European, or Indonesian fast food. The dullness of their clean, modern cafeteria environment is relieved by turtles that swim lazily in a tank at the back.

CULTURAL ACTIVITIES:

First-time visitors sometimes find Indonesia so exotic and unfathomable that throughout their stay they remain passive spectators of its culture. Yogyakarta rewards the active by providing several opportunities for participation in Javanese cultural life. You can see wayang kulit, a shadow puppet performance, from the traditional audience point of view or from backstage, over the puppeteer's shoulders. The classical dance once performed only for the sultans is presented nightly as the *Ramayana* ballet, short dance segments based on stories from the Indian epic, the *Ramayana*.

Batik fabric, Indonesia's best-known export, was originally developed here and in nearby Solo. In several small cottage factories (*fabriks*) you can watch gifted artisans hand-painting the cotton in patterns that emerge after resist-dyeing. Yogya's artists are also using these age-old techniques to "paint" images, some abstract and some realistic, on framed pieces of fabric. Window-shoppers and collectors are welcomed at dozens of galleries found in the outer kraton.

Wayang Kulit Puppet Performances

Wayang kulit (literally "shadow leather") is a play narrated by a dalang (master puppeteer) and acted by puppets who cast their shadows on a backlit screen. Performed for religious ceremonies in the earliest Javanese culture, wayang kulit was greatly influenced by the Indians who brought Hinduism to Java in the 5th century. Puppet shows accompanied by vibrant gamelan music continued to entertain and educate the Javanese during later Buddhist and Islamic eras. The artistry of dalangs and musicians and the craftsmanship of the puppet makers reached its peak in the 18th century at the great sultans' courts.

The postwar disintegration of the sultanates and the ensuing decline in their patronage threatened the study and presentation of wayang kulit. Today organizations like Yayasan Kesenian Agastya (Agastya Art Institute) train the young to be puppet makers and dalangs, and give regular performances.

If you've come to Yogya just for its masterful wayang kulit, you must arrange to be here over the second Saturday of the month. On this night each month the traditional full-length wayang kulit is performed outdoors from 9 p.m. to 5 a.m., under the auspices of the kraton. Contact the Tourist Information Center, on Jl. Malioboro (tel. 0274/2812, ext. 30) for information.

If this isn't possible, for Rp 2,400 ($1.50) every day except Saturday from 3 to 5 p.m. you can watch an excerpt from the classic shadow play at **Agastya Art Institute,** Jl. Gedongkiwo MD III/237, just southwest of the kraton. At Agastya visitors are seated backstage, behind the screen, the better to view the dalang and gamelan orchestra. They also sell a small selection of new and used puppets from their workshops. Each Monday, Wednesday, and Saturday evening from 9:30 to 10:30 p.m. you can experience a small wayang kulit show from the audience's point of view at the **Ambar Budaya Yogyakarta Craft Center,** on Jl. Adisucipto opposite the Ambarrukmo Palace Hotel. Contact the Tourist Information Center (tel. 0274/2812, ext. 30) for details on both performances.

A lesser-known but equally entrancing puppet show is **wayang golek,** performed by wooden puppets. The best local wayang golek performance is given at the Agastya Art Institute every Saturday from 3 to 5 p.m. Tickets cost Rp 2,400 ($1.50).

If you're interested in purchasing old or new wayang kulit puppets, wayang golek, or wayang topeng (carved-wood masks), try **Meoljo Soehardjo** or **Hadi Sukirno,** two large shops next door to each other on Jl. S. Parman, due west of Taman Sari. Bargaining is expected when negotiating for the "antique" pieces; a new wayang golek character that costs Rp 8,000 ($5) can cost more than Rp 32,000 ($20) if used.

Ramayana Ballet Classical Dance

Don't miss the *Ramayana* ballet, short segments from the nightlong dance drama inspired by the Indian epic *Ramayana*. The classical dances (ballet) are performed by up to 20 dancers in ornate court costumes of batik, gold, and jewels.

Every full moon from May to October the traditional *Ramayana* ballet is performed over four evenings at the Prambanan temple outside of Yogya. If you've missed this moonlit spectacle, don't pass up a performance at Yogya's premier training academy. The **Dalem Pujokusuman,** on Jl. Katamso, presents fragments of the *Ramayana* ballet or Javanese classical dance every Monday, Wednesday, and Friday evening from 8 to 10 p.m. Tickets cost Rp 4,000 ($2.50). Their students rehearse classical dance at the kraton every Sunday from 10:30 a.m. to noon, and the royal gamelan orchestra also rehearses without dancers on Monday and Wednesday from 10:30 a.m. to noon. Contact the Tourist Information Center (tel. 0274/2812, ext. 30) for further details.

The Batik Arts

Yogyakarta is known for its intricately patterned, somber-hued batik fabric. Traditional patterns (many developed especially for the kraton) were derived from nature and signaled a person's social rank or profession. Vegetable dyes, primarily in indigo blue or warm earth tones, were combined with the naturally white fabric by the resist-dying method.

Local artists making batik "paintings" use several methods to create imagery that's often derived from the Hindu legends or from abstract ideas.

There are dozens of batik galleries and workshops in the narrow lanes surrounding Taman Sari in the outer kraton. Most are open from 8 a.m. to 8 p.m. daily, with the artists on hand to display and discuss their work. Shoppers should feel free to bargain; expect to pay about 30% less than the originally quoted price. South of the kraton on Jl. Tirtodipuran are several batik fabriks where you can watch skillful artisans hand-painting the fabric. At **Batik Winotosastro,** Jl. Tirtodipuran 34 (tel. 2218), craftsmen work all day (with a noon to 1 p.m. lunch break) to produce goods for their retail shop at Jl. Laks. Adisucipto 21, and their shops in Bali, Jakarta, and Surabaya.

For moderately priced (no bargaining) gifts and garments, shop at **Terangbulan,** a small department store of batik items that's centrally located on Malioboro Street. For the highest-quality artistry (and décor to rival a sultan's) visit the **Sapto Hoedojo (Hudoyo) Art Batik Gallery** at Jl. Solo Km. 9 Meguwo (tel. 87443), almost opposite the gates to the airport. Sapto Hoedojo features a large variety of men's and women's clothing, a wealth of batik art, and antiquities and sculpture from throughout the archipelago. They're open 8 a.m. to 4 p.m. daily, and accept American Express and other credit cards.

WHAT TO SEE AND DO IN THE CITY: The kraton is only one of the many sites that recall the sultanate's glorious past. The ruins of Taman Sari, the so-called water palace recreation area, the cemetery at Imogiri, and the remnants of royal housing in the silversmith's village of Kota Gede are others. Yogyakarta, cultural capital of Java, also has an impressive number of small museums.

The Sultan's Palace (Kraton)

The royal palace of the sultans, or the **Kraton Ngayogyakarta Hadiningrat,** was begun in 1756 by Sultan Hamengku Buwono I in the Garjitawati Forest (now dusty, downtown Yogya). To create enough space for later expansion, the sultan diverted the Winanga River westward so that it could flow alongside the palace-to-be and the Code River eastward (to eventually feed his Water Castle). It took 36 years to complete the compound, which now covers 14 km² (5 square miles), and it's one of the most fascinating sights in Yogya.

The architectural style and number of structures was based on numerology and mystical and philosophical beliefs. Five gates pierce the thick outer walls; the Nirbaya gate led to the Alun-alun, a large grassy square planted with gayam trees, whose fragrant flowers were said to lull anyone resting under them right to sleep. The nine entrances to the kraton symbolized the nine orifices of the body. The central courtyard is planted with 64 trees to commemorate the year of the Prophet Mohammed's death. Details like the dragon-head bannisters, the number of ripples in their tail and every color (for example, green meant peace), were of mystical import. At the south end of the Alun-alun was the main entrance where two *gopalas* (giant guardians who warded off evil) protected the *proboyesko,* the personal quarters of the sultan and his family. Sultan Hamengku Buwono IX, governor of Yogyakarta, still occupies the area marked by a yellow (color of royalty) door.

Excellent tour guides accompany every visitor to point out the royal collection of ancient gamelan instruments, the ornately painted and carved wooden pendopo known as the Golden Pavilion (used for state receptions), and the small, carved-teak Sarong Boyo pavilion ("Nest of Danger") where alcohol was kept.

The kraton is open Sunday through Thursday from 8:30 a.m. to 12:30 p.m., on Friday and Saturday from 8:30 to 11:30 a.m., and costs Rp 500 (30¢). Guides are provided free of charge; proper dress is requested. On Monday and Wednesday the royal gamelan orchestra rehearses, and on Sunday the *Ramayana* ballet troupe rehearses, from 10:30 to 12:30. There are frequent ceremonies at the kraton to celebrate the sultan's family events and Muslim or national holidays; check with the Tourist Information Center for schedules as dates change each year.

The Water Castle (Taman Sari)

After a visit to the kraton or Museum Sonobudoyo, wander into the cool labyrinth of the water castle and bird market, located west and south of the inner kraton. **Taman Sari,** meaning "Park of Beauty," was a private pleasure palace for the first sultan. He built it after a long war with the Dutch and surrounded it with a large moat. Only moss-covered fragments of the original remain, but they make for a fascinating ramble through the ruins of the old city and the homes of the modern-day Javanese who live there.

At the Jl. Taman entrance are the renovated pavilions (once housing the royal gamelan) and the outer gates with their guardian icons, which watched over the Ladies' Pool. It's said that the sultan used to stand on the ornate balcony and enjoy watching the bathing rituals of his harem. Now, local children cavort there gleefully. If you wander out and around to the left, you'll find the dank and musty sultan's bedroom, marked by a large stone platform bed. Taman Sari is open daily from 8 a.m. to 5:30 p.m. Admission is Rp 350 (20¢). The local guides who hang around by the ticket booth can be helpful in your explorations.

The unrenovated part of Taman Sari is north of the pool by the high, crumbling walls; it can also be reached by exiting the kraton at the fifth courtyard. The blistering-white stucco remains are intriguing. At the ruins of an underground mosque are tunnels thought to have led several miles from the kraton through Taman Sari and out past the city walls, although not out to sea as many enthusiastic guides will claim.

Wander farther north and you'll be in the **Pasar Burung,** or Bird Market, where both poultry and songbirds are traded. The Javanese love the musical birds and have been known to pay as much as Rp 2,000,000 ($12,500) for a particularly gifted one. From the Pasar Burung it's a short walk to the many nearby batik galleries.

Museum Sonobudoyo (Palace Museum)

The Museum Sonobudoyo, located on the northwest side of Senopati Square, was founded in 1935 and has one of Indonesia's best collections of cultural artifacts. The traditional Javanese pavilions contain several rooms of household items from past sultanates, including a superb carved-wood bed belonging to Sultan Hamengku Buwono I. There are prehistoric stone carvings, fine wooden Hindu bronzes, and a wonderful 9th-century Hindu temple bell in silver with a fierce Bhinari spirit on top. There are wayang and topeng, batik, and artwork from Lombok, including paintings and wooden sculptures. The Balinese-style garden is guarded by two gopala, and also contains many fine pieces. Unfortunately, few objects are labeled in English, but an English-speaking guide is often available at the door. The museum is open Tuesday through Thursday from 8 a.m. to 1:30 p.m., on Friday till 11 a.m., on Saturday and Sunday until noon; closed Monday. Admission is Rp 150 (10¢).

Other Sights

Not far from the main kraton is **Puro Paku Alaman,** a smaller palace restored after an earthquake in 1867 to house Paku Alaman I, a prince brought from Solo by Sir Thomas Stamford Raffles to supervise Yogya's turbulent, feuding sultanate. Puro Paku Alaman is another fine example of traditional Javanese architecture; four front rooms comprise a museum of ceremonial artifacts, royal weaponry, uniforms, and other items of historical interest. Currently the residence and offices of Sri Paku Alaman VIII, vice-governor of Yogyakarta, are located here, so it's only open to the public from 9 a.m. to 1 p.m. on Monday and Thursday.

About 12 miles south of Yogya is the small town of **Imogiri,** beyond which is the original site of the royal cemetery, where almost every sultan from the courts at Yogyakarta and Surakarta (Solo) is buried. Go through the pendopo and up 345 shallow stone steps to the bluff containing their tombs. The graves of the sultans of Solo are to the left, of Yogya to the right, and of Mataram in the center.

To visit the holiest shrine, Sultan Agung's, go up the central steps and don the Javanese court wardrobe offered by the shrine elders: a sarong to be worn without shirt for men and a sarong and sleeveless batik top for women. A fee of Rp 800 (50¢) each is required for the clothing, but admission is free. Leave all your worldly possessions (including cameras) behind and ascend barefoot to the tomb, where you'll be shown inside to make an offering and be blessed by an ancient Javanese priest. Bring about Rp 1,000 (65¢) in coins or small bills to make donations at each step of this fascinating, mystical journey. The Filling of the Vases Ceremony is held annually in the Javanese month of Suro (September 9 in 1988), a day when four bronze water jars are refilled at the cemetery in thanks to God, but any day is worth a visit to this important shrine.

Penembahan Senopati, founder of the Mataram Kingdom, is buried at **Kota Gede,** the Mataram capital, about three miles southeast of the city, where there is a small royal cemetery.

Both Imogiri and Kota Gede are open only on Monday from 11 a.m. to 1 p.m. and on Friday from 11 a.m. to 4 p.m. to visitors in traditional Javanese court dress, which is available for rent at the gates.

Kota Gede is much better known as a silversmith's village. Tucked in among the fading colonial mansions and Indo-deco residences of former jewelers are small factories and shops. Sri Moeljo (tel. 88042) and Tom's (tel. 2818) are typical of many where you can watch repoussé work being done and purchase samples. Javanese silver and gold pieces were created for the court, and traditional patterns are usually ornate and derived from nature. Silverwork is sold by the gram, priced according to workmanship and purity. Most shops are open daily from 8 a.m. to 6 p.m.; rent a taxi by the hour so you can comparison-shop. In some shops you can bargain. *Note:* If you're continuing onto Bali, we'd recommend that you do your silver shopping there.

The **Affandi Museum,** a unique structure designed to resemble a watermelon on the Gajah Wong River, houses the paintings of Affandi, best known of the modern Indonesian painters, plus works by his daughter and her collection of primitive New Guinean art. The Affandi Museum is on Jl. Adisucipto, on the way to the airport, and is open daily from 9 a.m. to 4 p.m. Admission is Rp 150 (10¢).

Those staying in Yogyakarta more than four days should contact the Tourist Information Center for information on the city's other small museums and sights.

5. TEMPLES OF CENTRAL JAVA: BOROBUDUR, PRAMBANAN, AND OTHERS

Central Java is sometimes referred to as the province of Historic Middle Kingdoms because of its role during the Hindu, Buddhist, and Muslim eras. Between the 8th and 10th centuries it was the most powerful region in Java, until some unknown event (perhaps a natural disaster or invasion) caused a sudden shift of wealth and power to East Java. Not until the founding of the sultanate of Demak in 1511, when Islam began its conquest of the island, did Central Java again assume the importance it had once commanded.

From the 7th century on, the Hindu-influenced Mataram Kingdom controlled south-central Java, and the Buddhist Cailendra Dynasties controlled the north, although each region is dotted with candi that reflect both religions. Candi (pronounced "chandy" and meaning "temple") were monuments built as memorials or offerings by royalty and were used for ceremonial reasons rather than ordinary religious functions. Scholars date the Siva temple complex at Prambanan to the period of Sanjaya rule, thought to be about the mid-9th century, when the Buddhist candi at Borobudur was built. By that time, both religions had coexisted peacefully in Central Java for generations, having united in the 8th century by intermarriage between the two royal families. The Buddhist and Hindu candi that remain in central Java are the tremendous legacy of this golden age.

BOROBUDUR: The largest Buddhist sanctuary in the world, considered one of the Seven Wonders of the Modern World, is located just 42 km (25 miles) west of Yogyakarta. Borobudur, derived from the Sanskrit "vihara Buddha uhr" (Buddhist monastery on the hill) is a massive gray volcanic stone monument towering 103 feet above the plain of Kedu. Scholars believe that Candi Borobudur was built between A.D. 780 and 825 during the Çailendra Dynasty by one of the Srivijaya kings from Sumatra. Soon after the fall of the local Mataram Kingdom in 920 it fell into disuse, gradually disappearing under dense tropical foliage and volcanic ash from nearby Mount Merapi and Mount Sumbing. When the British took over Java, Lt.-Gov. Thomas Stamford Raffles, an avid student of local culture, commissioned a study of the legendary Temple of a Thousand Buddhas. It took 200 of his laborers nearly eight weeks to clear enough trees, soil, and underbrush from the site to distinguish Borobudur's profile. Since his efforts in 1815, scholars have attempted to decipher its famous carved-stone reliefs and the mystical significance of its design. After the Indonesian government discovered that some of Borobudur's outer walls were collapsing, several governments and UNESCO joined in an international preservation effort. Borobudur's total restoration was completed in 1983.

This magnificent Buddhist monument, dating two centuries earlier than Cambodia's Angkor Wat, was designed according to the principles of what scholars term Buddhist Tantrism. The local religion was partially derived from the Mahayana (or Large Vehicle) sect which encouraged enlightenment through teaching by Bodhisatvas, disciples of the Buddha who relinquished their chance for Nirvana (eternal peace) to remain on earth and teach others. This school of Buddhism was combined with the prevalent Java-Hindu Tantrism practiced earlier by the Javanese. The 504 Buddha sculptures that decorate Borobudur are extremely traditional; the finely wrought faces, the *usnisha* (flame of enlightenment) swelling above the snail-shaped ringlets of hair, the *urna* (the symbolic third eye) of wisdom in the middle of the forehead, and the elongated earlobes of the former prince make these among the most beautiful and sophisticated sculpture found on Java.

Borobudur's architecture is also very sophisticated. The monument was designed in three levels to symbolize different aspects of Buddhism. The base and first four terraces are built in the shape of a mandala, symbolic of the universe. The broad base, the sphere of desire, has bas-reliefs (only revealed on the south side) depicting heaven and hell. Restorers discovered the carvings behind stone slabs that were installed centuries before, perhaps to support the sinking base or to mask the imagery for symbolic reasons.

If religious pilgrims ascend the monument clockwise starting on the east side, they pass events in the life of Siddhartha Gautama, continue up past depictions of his enlightenment, see the miracles that were performed, and eventually see carvings of Buddha Maitreya, the future incarnation. This ascent through the sphere of form, designed to replicate the profile of the cosmic Mount Meru, covers almost a mile. The seated Buddhas on the eastern side, right hand pointing down in the bhumisparca mudra (hand posture), are calling upon the earth to witness enlightenment. To the south they express the mudra of charity; to the west, meditation; and to the north with a raised right hand, the mudra of fearlessness.

The fifth level begins the sphere of formlessness, the immaterial world achieved by the most devout. There are three small, circular terraces covered with 72 Buddhas under trellised stone stupas. In this symbolically spiritual and immaterial world the Buddha's presence is indicated, yet simply disguised under the stone canopies. Above all is the huge solid stupa thought to contain an incomplete statue of the Buddha. It is said that Buddha created the stupa shape when his followers asked for something they could worship. He folded his robes, set his food bowl down in the middle, and then placed his walking stick on top. Capping this gigantic monument with the slender peak of the uppermost stupa makes it extremely graceful for a temple of such size.

Don't miss the lone Buddha seated on the ground below, under the shade of a huge Bodhi tree planted in 1934. This tree has grown from a cutting sent by a Sri Lankan temple, which raised its Bodhi since 234 B.C. from a cutting of the Indian tree under which the Buddha sat when he achieved enlightenment.

Borobudur's is a world-class site that shouldn't be missed by anyone visiting Southeast Asia. It is open from 7 a.m. to 5:30 p.m. daily, and admission is Rp 150 (10¢). For children, *Borobudur, An Open Book of Stories* by Soewito Santoso is an excellent explanation of the site and its reliefs. It's on sale at the site for Rp 800 (50¢). The brown-covered *Borobudur* by Yazir Marzuki and Toeti Heraty, Rp 6,400 ($4), is the best in-depth guide about the site.

Getting There

The **Yogyakarta Tourist Information Service** (tel. 3543) arranges popular daily minibus transport to the site for Rp 7,500 ($4.75); after a two-hour wait they continue on to the Dieng Plateau (see below). For less than 50¢ you can take the public bus from Yogya to Muntilan and change for Borobudur, but the limited schedule and two-hour travel time make it a dubious choice.

Several travel companies also offer tours to Borobudur, alone or in combination with city tours or other sites. **P.T. Vayatours,** in the Ambarrukmo Palace Hotel (tel. 88488, ext. 121), and **Pacto Tours,** on Jl. Malioboro (tel. 2740), offer daily guided tours in a more comfortable, air-conditioned bus for about Rp 12,800 ($8) to Rp 19,200 ($12) per person, depending on the number of people in the group.

If you're very interested in this site and its sculpture, we'd recommend reserving your own **taxi** from one of Yogya's hotels for about Rp 32,000 ($20), or a driver and guide from one of the travel agencies for about Rp 80,000 ($50), so that you can spend as much time as you want. Borobudur should not be rushed through.

Food and Lodging
A welcome new addition to Borobudur's facilities is the nearby **Saraswati Restaurant and Lodging,** at Jl. Bala Putera 10, a short walk from the main gate. Saraswati serves some Indonesian and Chinese dishes, and even hamburgers are freshly cooked, very tasty, and less than Rp 2,100 ($1.25). Fan-cooled rooms with common bath rent for Rp 16,500 ($10.25) for two.

CANDI MENDUT AND PAWON: Two smaller candi within two miles of Borobudur and built on a straight line leading to it are thought by many to have been part of the original complex. The oldest, Mendut, faces toward Varanasi, India, and the site of Sarnath, where Buddha first preached to his disciples. Within this tall, pyramid-roofed temple is a ten-foot-tall Buddha, carved from one stone, which many art historians consider to be the finest-known sculpted Buddha. He sits, hands in the teaching mudra, with Lokesvara and Vajrapani, two Bodhisatvas, by his side. Some scholars speculate that Mendut was where pilgrims stopped to purify their minds before ascending Borobudur. Others think it was built in tribute by King Indra, who is thought to be buried in the nearby candi Pawon. The smaller Pawon is a beautiful architectural work that was restored in 1903; little is known about its religious function. Only a few tours stop at either temple, so double-check before you sign up. You can enter Mendut from 7 a.m. to 5:15 p.m. daily. Admission costs Rp 150 (10¢). Pawon can only be seen from the outside.

The annual Waicak Ceremony (held on May 2 in 1988) is a religious procession in which Bikhus (ascetic monks) carry Buddhist icons from Mendut to Borobudur to celebrate the moment when Siddhartha Gautama achieved enlightenment.

THE PRAMBANAN TEMPLES: The Hindu temples known as Candi Larad Jonggrang are in Prambanan, about 17 km (10½ miles) east of Yogyakarta on the road to Solo. The Prambanan complex, which once included 240 temples, was built in the 9th and 10th centuries and then gradually buried under the mounting ash from the eruptions of nearby Mount Merapi. The main temple, 47 meters (153 feet) of sculpted stone, has been restored and now towers above the excavated site in much of its former glory.

The temple complex dedicated to Siva consisted of three courtyards, the outer (390 yards square), middle (222 yards square), and inner (110 yards square) court; the outer courts enclosed hundreds of small perwara temples, and the inner court held the main sanctuary, three temples each dedicated to one of the Hindu trinity—Siva the Destroyer in the center, Vishnu the Creator to the north, and Brahma the Protector to the south. All face to the east. Opposite each of these larger candi are three smaller Candi Vahara, once thought to contain the vehicles of each god. The central shrine does contain a nandi, a beautifully carved bull used by Siva, but more recent studies indicate that the other two shrines probably housed different manifestations of the god.

Each temple was built in three parts, representing the stages of the Hindu cosmos. The base was the underworld for common men, the body was the middle world for those who'd renounced the worldly life, and the slender summit represented the upper world inhabited by the gods. Steps ascending the main temple were built at the four compass points, the eastern steps leading to the Siva statue being the widest. The ten-foot-tall Siva statue stands proudly in the eastern niche of the temple, on a three-foot-high base shaped like a *yoni,* the female symbol. The imposing, four-armed Siva is carrying a rosary, trident, and flywhisk, his symbols of power, and wears a skull and lunar crescent in his headdress. Opposite him in the western cella is his charming, elephant-headed son, Ganesha, for Indonesian Hindus, the god of wisdom. In the south cella is Bhatara Guru, a god depicted as a pot-bellied priest, and in the north is Dewi Durga (the wife or shakti of Siva), an eight-armed figure in the posture of killing a demon bull. Locals claim that this is Rara Jonggrang (thus the name of the candi), daughter of King Boko. According to legend, long ago an ugly giant named Bandung Bandawesa proposed to the princess. To avoid his advances, she insisted that he build 1,000 statues for the Prambanan temples in one night. With his powers he was able to enlist spirits who carved stone throughout the night. After several hours, Rara Jonggrang realized that he might succeed and so began burning hay and pounding rice in mortars until she aroused all the chickens. When they started crowing, the spirits were fooled into thinking it was dawn and they ceased work—only one statue short of their goal. Bandung Bandawesa was so furious that he turned Rara Jonggrang into stone, placing her in the north cella to complete his task.

The ornately carved stone reliefs of Prambanan are justly famed as some of the most beautiful Hindu sculpture in the world. Typical Prambanan motifs include statues of lions in niches, kalamakara mythical figures posed on both sides of a tree of heaven, and peculiar kinnaras, half-human/half-bird figures. The outer balustrade of the main temple has 62 panels depicting Bidadari, heavenly creatures, musicians, and dancers doing a dance in honor of Siva. The inner balustrade tells tales from the *Ramayana,* the Indian epic that is also performed outdoors here in dance (over four nights every full moon from May to October). The upper base is sheathed in 24 panels representing the four Lokopala, gods of the winds, and their followers.

The smaller candi Vishnu to the north features a four-armed god holding a *cakra* (discus) and winged conch. The inner balustrade here recounts stories of the youthful Krishna and his brother, Balarama. At the southern candi Brahma, the four-headed and four-armed Protector god stands in a niche surrounded by more reliefs based on the *Ramayana.*

The Prambanan temple complex is open daily from 6 a.m. to 6 p.m., for a Rp-150 (10¢) admission fee and evenings during the *Ramayana* ballet performances. Check the Yogyakarta Tourist Information Center (tel. 2812, ext. 30) for the current schedule. Prambanan can be easily reached by the Solo minibus (45 minutes; 20¢) which departs from Yogya's Jl. Simanjuntak Terminal every 25 minutes between 5 a.m. and 5 p.m., or by renting a taxi for about Rp 12,000 ($7.50) for two hours from any of Yogya's hotels.

OTHER TEMPLES: There are several lesser sites near Prambanan that are best seen on a taxi tour of the area. The site of **King Boko's Palace** (known as Kraton Ratubaka), about 1½ miles south of Prambanan atop the Sorogedug Plateau, offers views of Prambanan and Candi Kalasan. Remains of the auditorium and the princess's bathing pool have been excavated. Just 1½ miles southeast of here is the small, curved-roofed **Candi Banyu Nibo,** built in the 12th century and recently renovated. **Candi Sewu,** 500 yards northeast of Prambanan, are just the remains of another huge complex thought to date from A.D. 850, where 250 shrines once surrounded a main temple. Within half a mile east of Candi Sewu are the two remaining temples of **Plaosan** standing side by side, one decorated with reliefs of men, the other of women. What makes Plaosan special is that it was a Buddhist sanctuary, and one that existed freely in such proximity to a Hindu complex. Nearby is the Buddhist **Candi Kalasan,** built 78 feet tall in the shape of a cross to commemorate the marriage of the Hindu Sanjaya king to the Buddhist Çailendra princess in A.D. 778. The Candi Sari is just northeast of Kalasan; the candi at Sambi Sari (now partially buried by volcanic ash) and Gebang (an earlier shrine of a *lingga,* the male symbol) are about three miles west, closer to Yogyakarta.

THE DIENG PLATEAU: The Dieng Plateau is nestled at the foot of the Sindoro and Sumbing mountains, 26 km (15½ miles) north of Wonosobo, and a three- to five-hour drive from Yogyakarta. The site is known for its early Hindu temples—the Semar, Arjuna, Bima, and Gatotkaca candi—all dedicated to Siva. Although somewhat reconstructed, the bas-reliefs that once covered each temple are so eroded that you shouldn't make the trip for its Hindu sculptures. Go instead for the scenic countryside, tumbling rice paddies, and dramatic, thrilling ascent to the plateau. Once there, the tranquility of this serene setting is sure to erase the travel pains many experience from the heat and narrow, twisting roads. You can get to Dieng on the Borobudur coach tour organized through the Yogyakarta Tourist Information Service, on Jl. Malioboro (tel. 3543), for Rp 7,500 ($4.75), or take a taxi from any hotel for Rp 75,600 ($47.25) for ten hours.

CANDI SUKUH—THE EROTIC TEMPLE: The so-called Erotic Temple is set on a slope of Mount Lawu, about 35 km (21 miles) east of Solo. Architecturally, Sukuh is closer to the Mayan pyramids of Mexico than the Hindu candi at Prambanan, particularly because of the *gapura* (gateway) styled like an Egyptian pylon. Its sculpted reliefs are more primitive than most on central Javanese candi, but those over its gapura, which tell tales of men, beasts, and giants, have a numerological significance indicating to historians that Sukuh was built in 1359 by the Javanese lunar calendar, or in 1437 by ours. The carvings depicting the lingga (male symbol) and yoni (female symbol) have earned Sukuh a reputation for eroticism. Locals consider the stones a fertility symbol; it's said that if a virgin jumps over these carved stones before her wedding day her sarong will come loose! Visitors who've seen the temples at Khajuraho, India, will find Sukuh extremely tame. Candi Sukuh can be reached by public bus or taxi from Solo, or by several coach tours operating from Yogyakarta.

6. EASTERN JAVA: SOLO, MOUNT BROMO, TRANSPORTATION TO BALI

Most tourists continuing east fly from Yogyakarta directly to Denpasar, Bali. However, fans of batik and traditional architecture will enjoy a visit to Solo, an easy day trip from Yogyakarta when combined with a stop at Prambanan. Those traveling overland to Bali can detour north through the unappealing industrial city of Surabaya (Indonesia's third largest) to Mount Bromo, one of East Java's most active volcanoes and an area of great scenic beauty. From Yogya or Surabaya trains and slow express buses go to Ketapang, port city for the ferries to Bali.

SOLO (SURAKARTA): For nearly 200 years the sultanate of Solo rivaled the sultanate of Yogyakarta for prominence in the political and cultural life of Central Java. Because Solo had sided with the Dutch during the colonial period, after the establishment of a republic in Indonesia its political clout declined. Yogyakarta, heralded as the last bastion of Javanese culture, developed the visual and performing arts into a major industry, while in Solo they remain the curious vestiges of a once-powerful court.

The people of Solo believe that their kingdom was ordained by Allah about 1744. King Pakubuwono II (who had set up court in Kartasura originally with the help of the VOC) asked his advisors to seek another base for his kingdom. They heard Allah proclaim that Sala would be the new capital and arranged with the village's elders to relocate there. Unsuccessful efforts to fill nearby swampland succeeded after 10,000 ringgits were paid to the village's chief storyteller and rhubarb leaves and pomegranate flowers were thrown in the water. When the kraton was finally completed, the king renamed his kingdom Surakarta, in the village of Sala (Solo).

Useful Information

The helpful **Tourist Information Office** is on Jl. Slamet Riyadi (the Yogya–Solo highway) at no. 235 (tel. 0271/6508) in the center of town. It's open Monday through Saturday from 8 a.m. to 5 p.m. and offers a large variety of brochures and a good city map. . . . The Tourist Information Office forms the western tip of a triangle with the Puro Mangkunegaran (the prince's palace) on Jl. Sraten at its north tip and the Kraton Surakarta (the recently reopened king's palace) on Jl. Jend. Sudirman at the southeast. Either is a 15- to 20-minute becak ride away.

Garuda Indonesia has two flights daily from Jakarta and one flight from Surabaya; its office is in the Kusuma Said Prince Hotel at Jl. Asrama 22 (tel. 6846). The **Adi Soemarmo Airport** is 4½ miles northwest of town.

A **minibus to Solo** leaves from Yogyakarta's Terminal Bis Simanjuntak every half hour between 5 a.m. and 5 p.m. daily; the Solo coach returns every 15 minutes between 4 a.m. and 8 p.m. The ride takes 1½ to 2 hours and costs less than $1. . . . **Trains to Surabaya** leave from the Stasiun Kereta Api Balapan, north of the Puro at Jl. Gajah Mada and Jl. Monginsidi. . . . The **bus station** for long-distance buses is just north of it; contact the Tourist Information Office for schedule information. . . . **Taxis between Yogya and Solo** can be rented for Rp 30,000 ($18.75) one way, or Rp 38,000 ($23.75) round trip, including about two hours of sightseeing time.

Accommodations

During the rebuilding of the Kraton Surakarta, which was destroyed in a disastrous fire in 1984, Solo's King Pakubuwono VIII chose the **Kusuma Sahid Prince Hotel,** at Jl. Sugiyopranoto 22 (tel. 0271/6356), a long walk or becak ride from the former kraton, but a short walk away from the lovely Puro Mangkunegaran, home of the prince. Any king would feel right at home having tea under the ornate private *pendopo* (open-air pavilion), lounging around the huge pool, or enjoying a drink with gamelan accompaniment (from 5 to 8 p.m. nightly). The superior rooms are just that, with rattan furnishings, canopy bed, and a carved-wood room divider that creates a private seating area. Deluxe rooms are grouped in two stories around the gardens, double room rates, (quoted in U.S. dollars) run $58. The smaller moderate rooms are finely appointed, and the poolside cabaña wing is the nicest. Singles are $42; doubles, $48. Budget travelers can enjoy the Kusuma Sahid Prince's amenities for just $21 by taking an economy room with shared bath.

If this hotel is full, the **Hotel Chakra,** centrally located on the main highway at Jl. Slamet Riyadi 171 (tel. 0271/5847), is a slightly less expensive choice. The Chakra is set up like an American motel. Behind the fancy new, classical façade are deluxe rooms that face onto a back parking lot (there is no pool). These comfortable rooms with seating area cost $38 for two; for $3 less you can get a smaller room overlooking the private garden.

BUDGET TIP: "A becak driver took me from the Solo train station to the **Westerners Losmen,** on Kemlayan Kidul II (tel. 3106). The people were nice, and good cooks. The dorm room was cheap and clean" (Stan Mendoza, New York, N.Y.).

Dining

For an elegant, old-world luncheon, try the **Gambir Seketi Coffee Shop** in the Kusuma Sahid Prince Hotel (tel. 6356). The cool, formal dining room with an ornately painted ceiling overlooks the pool area. Specialties include nasi liwet Sala, the local coconut-flavored rice which goes well with rawon sapi, an East Javanese dish of cubed beef spiced with an indigenous black curry. The restaurant's large menu includes a variety of European entrees, salads, and steaks; Indonesian dishes will cost Rp 2,400 ($1.50) to Rp 6,400 ($4); continental dishes, Rp 4,800 ($3) to Rp 16,000 ($10). Finish your meal with one of their special spiced coffee, hot ginger, or hot lemon drinks. Open daily from 11 a.m. to 11 p.m.

Adventurous eaters should try **Timlo Solo,** at Jl. Jend. Urip Sumoharjo/ Mesen 106 (tel. 6180), about a five-minute drive from the Kusuma Sahid Prince Hotel. Hailed by Soloites as the best place for local cuisine, this casual, well-lit eatery is crowded with locals craving nasi Timlo Solo ayam, a tasty chicken-rice soup filled with bean curd, a boiled egg, noodles, and spices that's a full meal, for only Rp 1,200 (75¢). Be sure to sample the kopi susu—hot, spiced coconut milk with coffee. It's open daily except Sunday from 8 a.m. to 9 p.m.

If this sounds too exotic, head for the **Holland Bakery,** on the same street at no. 135 (tel. 2452), halfway between the Kraton and the Puro. The Holland's mirrored walls, leatherette booths, air conditioning, and extensive pastry display are perfectly familiar. Mocha cream cakes, pound cake, fruit tarts, ice cream, and juices start at Rp 720 (45¢). They also serve a variety of Western dishes ranging in price from Rp 1,600 ($1) to Rp 6,000 ($3.75). Popular local bands play nightly and they're open daily from 9 a.m. to 9 p.m.

What to See and Do in Solo

The ornate 18th-century pendopo and gingerbread-trimmed offices of the **Kasunanan Palace,** also known as the **Kraton Surakarta,** seat of Solo's sultanate, reigned as the city's best-known attraction until fire razed the site in January 1984. Reconstruction was completed in December 1987, but less than half of the original buildings remain. The Kasunanan Palace was built by Pakubuwono II in 1745 after his decision to move the royal court to Solo from nearby Kartasura. The large outer court contains the pendopo (traditional Javanese open-sided pavilion) where the king's advisors would receive the public. In the court beyond it is a smaller teak pendopo where the king would greet important guests. Visible above all the courtyards is the **Panggung Songgo Buwono,** the Tower of the Universe, built by Pakubuwono III in 1782 for meditation. The three-tiered white and blue-trimmed structure is octagonal and topped by a sculpted compass which resembles a dragon. Both shapes and symbols relate to the numerology of the building date, A.D. 1708 by the Javanese calendar.

The Tower of the Universe borders the inner court containing the main ceremonial pendopo, now rebuilt, where each March the coronation of the present King Pakubuwono XII is celebrated. The metal Ionic columns and the many black and white painted statues are original; the teak-tile roof, marble floors, chandeliers, and furnishings are all skillful Indonesian replicas. The ceremonial pendopo faces east to the sun goddess, and the open courtyard where 77 trees planted in memory of Pakubuwono IV in 1877 are tended with care and replanted to maintain that mystical number.

The small **Suaba Budaya Museum** around the corner from the kraton houses King Pakubuwono VIII's art and kris (Indonesian knife) collection. The selection is limited and poorly labeled, but the last room has some fine Buddhist sculptures and stone reliefs from the Prambanan temples. The kraton and museum are open six days from 9 a.m. to noon; closed Friday. Admission is Rp 600 (40¢), plus a Rp-1,000 (65¢) fee to permit photography.

Solo's real highlight, one of the finest examples of royal Javanese architecture, is the palace of the prince, **Puro Mangkunegaran.** This palace faces south to the kraton of the king. The Mangkunegaran court was established in 1757, after a long and complicated power struggle that divided Central Java into several dominions. The puro was begun in the late 18th century by Prince Mangkunegaran II, and completed in 1866. Inside the large courtyard sits the massive (200 by 160 feet) pendopo, an open pavilion whose peaked roof is supported by four pillars. The ceiling is batik painted on wood, with Javanese astrological symbols on the border. Behind the pendopo is the *dalem,* a ceremonial hall with an outer porch to receive guests. The dalem is an elegant space, now used for displays of princely heirlooms, but occasionally the site of weddings, funerals, and family functions, including the 1988 coronation of the new Prince Mangkunegora. Special dances are performed at these ceremonies in which female dancers must be virgins and male dancers, the offspring of royalty. When the ladies of the court are not in residence, their outer quarters can be viewed also. Don't miss the palace tours led by informative, English-speaking guides. Puro Mangkunegaran is open daily from 9 a.m. to noon, closed on Friday. Admission is 500 Rp (30¢), including the guide fee. If you visit this court on a Wednesday you can watch a classical dance performance accompanied by a full gamelan orchestra.

Solo is the home of batik, and if you haven't explored this art form in Yogya, Solo is the place to do it. The **Batik Shop Semar,** Jl. Raden Mas Said 132 (tel. 2937), opens its doors to visitors from 9 a.m. to noon daily to watch the canting process, the laborious application of wax to fabric which is then "resist-dyed." Seeing the natural cotton decorated with pale wax lines evolve into a multicolored dress shirt can inspire even the most jaded shopper. The Semar retail shop is open daily except Sunday from 8 a.m. to 4 p.m. **Danar Hadi Batik,** one of the best-known batik manufacturers, keeps the same hours at the main store at Jl. Dr. Rajiman 8 (tel. 4126). Both manufacturers have smaller stores on Jl. Slamet Riyadi, open from 8 a.m. to 2 p.m. and 5 to 7 p.m. Pick up the Tourist Information Office's latest map and it will list many other batik fabriks and shops, where you can compare price and quality. Shoppers enjoy an array of purses ($4 and up), casual sports shirts ($6 and up), fashionably styled dresses ($8 and up), hand-painted silk shirts ($30 and up), and an assortment of inexpensive, though typical, souvenirs.

If you're a seamstress or an upholsterer, look for bargain batik by the bolt at **Pasar Klewer,** located near the Kasunanan Palace. This two-story, block-long market arcade feels like New York's Seventh Avenue at rush hour. Daily between 8 a.m. and 4 p.m., fabric stalls, itinerant vendors, hucksters, and established retail outlets sell their wares to savvy locals. Be prepared to bargain down the asking price by 20% to 30%, and watch out for damaged, irregular, or poorly dyed goods.

From Yogyakarta or Solo, your next stop in Java might be Mount Bromo.

MOUNT BROMO: Mount Bromo, home of the Fire God Betoro Bromo, is a still-active volcano which last erupted in 1930. Bromo towers 2,382 meters (7,742 feet) above a six-mile stretch of sand, the caldera left by the eruption of ancient Mount Tennger. Four newer volcanoes and craters have risen from the caldera, including one of Indonesia's highest mountains, Mount Semeru (also known as Mahameru, or Meru, the abode of the gods, at 3,676 meters, or 11,947 feet). Mount Bromo, the nearby perfectly conical Mount Batok, and the Sand Sea are part of a national park preserve including the Bromo-Semeru massif covering 800 km² (290 square miles) of East Java.

The local Tenggerese people visit Bromo's crater at several annual festivals making offerings to the gods to secure a good harvest. They're thought to be descendants of the Islamic Majapahit rulers, but practice a combination of ancestor worship and Hinduism. Rituals are usually held at midnight, but the best time to appreciate this region's spectacular scenic beauty is at dawn. As the sun rises and the mists evaporate a gentle light illuminates the bubbling crater of Bromo, the steep green-clad walls of Batok, the golden dunes of the Sand Sea, and the puffs of smoke emerging from Mount Semeru's cone. *Note:* This only applies to the dry season, from April to November, when you can actually appreciate the sunrise. Other months of the year, the ascent to Mount Bromo will be unrewarding, if not dangerous.

Getting to Mount Bromo is half the fun. From the nearest town, **Ngadisari,** it's a four-mile, two-hour walk across the Sand Sea. Ngadisari has several guesthouses with extremely simple accommodations and shared bath facilities for Rp 3,800 ($3) to Rp 6,400 ($4) per person. All are accustomed to sending their guests out at 2 a.m., and can arrange for ponies to take you up to the crater rim for Rp 4,800 ($3) one way. At Cemaralawang, about halfway from Ngadisari, there's the small **Bromo Permai Hotel** (tel. 0335/10335 or 21510) with slightly better facilities and an hour's less walk. To reach Ngadisari, you can take a second-class train to Surabaya for Rp 19,200 ($12) and change trains for Probolinggo (a 22-hour journey), or a third-class train direct from Yogya to Probolinggo for Rp 4,800 ($3) for the ten-hour trip. From Probolinggo several minibuses leave every half hour for the one-hour-plus trip to Ngadisari for 80¢.

If you prefer a more luxurious outing, several travel agents in Surabaya, such as **Pacto Ltd.,** Jl. Pemuda 78 (tel. 031/472-706), offer air-conditioned night buses that leave Surabaya after midnight for the three-hour ride to Ngadisari, and then organize walkers and pony riders from there to the crater's rim. Estimate the time of sunrise during the dry season at about 5 a.m., and bring a sweater, scarf, and gloves for the ascent.

For more information about Bromo or about climbing Mount Semeru, contact the **Surabaya National Tourist Information Office** at Jl. A. Yani 242 (tel. 031/815-312), or the **East Java Regional Tourist Information Office** at Jl. Pemuda 118, Surabaya (tel. 031/472-503).

READERS' TRAVEL TIPS: "We flew to Surabaya, checked in at the Hotel Simpany ($50) and rested until 11:30 p.m. when a tour bus called for a tour to the volcano Mount Bromo, which is a must. We drove to the foot of Mount Bromo, had a 1:30 a.m. breakfast, then mounted horses for a 2½-hour ride in the dark over winding trails. We arrived at Mount Bromo to watch the sunrise over the volcano—a stirring adventure!" (Jean and Tony Triumpho, Canajoharie, N.Y.). [*Authors' Note:* We were told by other travelers that getting to Probolinggo by changing bemos was a lot cheaper than taking the express bus from Bali. Others complained that guides led some travelers up Mount Batok in the middle of the night, saying they'd have a good view of Bromo, but that the climb was very difficult through the soft, volcanic ash.]

TRANSPORTATION TO BALI: Those continuing overland to Bali can leave from Yogyakarta, Surabaya, or more locally, from Ngadisari. **From Yogyakarta** there are several express buses daily which usually leave in the afternoon and arrive in Denpasar, the southern capital, about 15 hours later. Check with the Yogyakarta Tourist Information Office (tel. 0271/2812, ext. 30) or the bus ticket agents on Jl. Sosrowijayan in Yogya for schedule information. A non-air-conditioned bus will cost about Rp 11,200 ($7) one way.

From Surabaya, travelers can take the **train** to Banyuwangi (about $2.50) and then change for a local bus to the port of Ketapang, which meets the ferry and then continues onto Denpasar (another $2). This route will also take about 15 hours.

From Ngadisari or Tosari (another access point for Bromo) travelers can catch local buses to Ketapang (about six hours, 50¢).

Ferries to Bali leave Ketapang almost every hour, 24 hours a day. The 40-minute ride to Gilimanuk, on the northwest coast, costs Rp 480 (30¢).

And now, Bali high!

CHAPTER IX

BALI, ISLAND OF THE GODS

□ □ □

1. ORIENTATION

2. BALINESE CULTURE

3. THE BEACH RESORTS: SANUR, KUTA BEACH, AND NUSA DUA

4. VILLAGE LIFE: UBUD

5. EXPLORING THE ISLAND

6. BEYOND BALI: LOMBOK AND KOMODO ISLAND

Since the 1920s the name Bali has evoked fantasies of an isolated tropical paradise. Many Westerners are surprised to find that it is, in fact, a province of Indonesia, the first island west of Java in the Nusa Tenggara archipelago. It's a land where 2.5 million people share verdant valleys and volcanic peaks with more than 20,000 temples dedicated to the Hindu gods.

Honoring the gods is such a longstanding tradition that the island was named after the native word for "offering," *bebali.* For the Balinese, to make the material world as beautiful as possible ensures a safe journey to the afterlife and a better reincarnation. We've simply never seen such a gorgeous place. And though 500,000 tourists clog its beach resorts each year, most visitors will still find in Bali a vision of paradise.

1. ORIENTATION

Bali is shaped somewhat like an elongated diamond, extending east to west about 145 km (87 miles) and north to south about 95 km (57 miles). The vast majority of tourist development is in the south, along both coasts and on the small peninsula south of the capital, **Denpasar.** Most visitors arrive at Ngurah Rai International Airport on the southwest coast; most popular beach resorts are located nearby. Our favorite for its superb beach, quiet sophistication, and tasteful commercial development is **Sanur,** the oldest resort community on the island. Sanur is about 20 minutes by car north of the airport on the east coast, where a calm surf and broad sand bar make for shallow water and easy swimming. **Kuta Beach** is the playground of Australians from every walk of life; the Kuta strip which extends north to Legian is lined with so many bars, restaurants, mopeds, and din that it's hard to identify it as Bali (traffic jams, petty crime, and rock music are not our idea of paradise). Kuta is about ten minutes north of the airport on the windier west coast, creating better surfing conditions off its broad but often poorly maintained beach. Bali's newest resort, one envisioned by the Indonesians and their French planners to handle future waves of tourists without adversely affecting the local culture, is at **Nusa Dua.** This development is tucked away on the east coast of the peninsula, about ten minutes south of the airport. Nusa Dua has indeed had little impact on the local culture, but its isolation guarantees that the local culture has no impact on its four hotels. Guests at these huge resort compounds who come for the exquisite, pristine beaches and gentle surf often miss experiencing the island.

The inland village of **Ubud** is typical of hundreds in the interior. Just 60 minutes north of Denpasar, it is a community of thatch-roofed homes of both farmers and artisans without such modern conveniences as telephones. Unlike most villages, Ubud has a thriving tourist industry that may threaten to choke it. Ubud has drawn European tourists since the 1930s when its enlightened king began inviting noted artists and writers to visit him at his palace. A large but low-profile expatriate community still flourishes on the fringes of the village. Although Ubud is popular as a cultural and shopping day trip, a number of tourists are charmed into spending the night discovering the serene underside of this sand-and-sea tropical paradise.

Temples, craftsmen, scenic wonders, idyllic beaches, cultural performances, wildlife, and rice paddies are scattered throughout the island. All can be visited by public transportation, a rental car, moped (*not advised*), or by several guided tours. Bali's mountainous interior and narrow curving roads can make short expeditions into long ones, but make sure to get off that beach towel and explore the special Balinese universe.

Bali has something for everyone; to leave Southeast Asia without experiencing its pleasures is to miss one of the gods' gifts to mortals.

USEFUL INFORMATION: The main **Bali Government Tourism Office** is in the Niti Mandala Civic Centre, Jl. Raya Puputan, in Denpasar (tel. 0361/22387). There are also very helpful regional offices in Denpasar, Sanur, Kuta Beach, Ubud (tel. 0361/23062), (see those sections) and at Ngurah Rai International Airport in both the International and Domestic Terminals (tel. 51011 or 25081). . . . *Bali Plus,* a manual published by the Bali Tourism Promotion Board and available at local tourist offices, is an excellent source of information about the island's history, religion, and cultural attractions.

For **emergency or police assistance** throughout the island, call 110; for an **ambulance,** dial 118. The **R.S.U.P. Sanglah Hospital** is on Jl. Bali in Denpasar (tel. 27911). Your hotel can recommend a doctor for minor illness, but if you are in an accident or become seriously ill, call your consulate for medical advice. Sophisticated medical care can only be found in Jakarta or Singapore.

Note that in the beach resorts, streets are named after the closest hotels.

Pay **telephones** require a 50-Rp coin for local calls. Dial 108 for local information, or 102 for an international operator. For long-distance service outside your hotel, you'll have to go to one of the Kantor Telepons: on Jl. Kaliasem in Denpasar (open 24 hours), on Jl. Legian in Kuta Beach (open 24 hours), on Jl. Br. Sindhu in Sanur (open from 8 a.m. to 6 p.m. six days; closed Sunday), or at the airport. It takes about an hour to make an international call but AT&T credit cards are accepted. The **telephone area code** for the entire island is 0361.

Bali's time zone is GMT plus eight hours, one hour later than Java.

Bali is 13 hours ahead of New York and 16 hours ahead of Los Angeles; add one hour during Daylight Savings.

Most major villages and larger hotels offer postal services. The main Bali **post office** is Kantor Pos Pusat Renon, on Jl. Raya Puputan in Denpasar. This is the island's only poste restante branch (open Monday through Thursday from 8 a.m. to 2 p.m., to 11 a.m. on Friday, and to noon on Saturday; closed Sunday) if the sender hasn't specified which community you'll be in.

Both certified **packing and shipping** companies and Indonesian **air freight** (reliable) and seamail (not reliable) are extremely expensive. The minimum crating charge for up to 25 kgs (55 pounds) per box is $25; private air cargo costs $8 per kilo (2.2 pounds) to New York City, but is held at the airport; the national postal service charges $11 per kilo sent direct to your home. Seamail takes from two months to forever and costs $25 per 10-kilo (22-pound) package (the maximum weight allowed). Two reliable shipping companies are **Alpha Sigma,** Jl. Imam Bonjol 98 (tel. 24864), and **Pacific Express,** Jl. Arjuna 21 (tel. 26221), both in Denpasar.

American Express cash advances and traveler's check or credit-card replacement services are handled by **Pacto Ltd.,** at the Bali Beach Hotel, Jl. Bali Beach, in Sanur (tel. 8449). They're open from 8 a.m. to 4 p.m. weekdays, till noon on Saturday; closed Sunday. . . . Cash advances for VISA cardholders can be obtained only at **Bank Duta,** Jl. Raya Hayam Wuruk 165 in Denpasar (tel. 35140), open Monday through Friday from 8 a.m. to 2 p.m. and on Saturday until 11 a.m. For lost credit cards or checks, first obtain a police report and then report the loss to Bank Duta. . . . There are **moneychangers** with extended hours throughout the resort communities; for travel to smaller villages it is advisable to have rupiahs.

Garuda Indonesia has offices in Denpasar at Jl. Melati 61 (tel. 27825 or 22788), in Sanur at the Bali Beach Hotel, Jl. Bali Beach (tel. 8243), in Kuta at the Kuta Beach Hotel, Jl. Pantai Kuta 1 (tel. 51179), and in Nusa Dua at the Nusa Dua Beach Hotel, Jl. Nusa Dua Beach (tel. 971-444). **Merpati Nusantara** has an office in Denpasar at Jl. Melati 57 (tel. 22864).

Two of the many good travel agents are **Pacto Ltd.,** Jl. Tanjung Sari in Sanur (tel. 8247), with other branches at several hotels, and **Tunas Indonesia,** at the Bali Beach Hotel arcade in Sanur (tel. 8511) or at the Pertamina Cottages arcade in Kuta.

There is an **American Consular Agent** at Jl. Segara Ayu 5 in Sanur (tel. 8478), open from 8 a.m. to 4 p.m. Monday through Friday; and an **Australian Consulate,** which handles all Commonwealth citizens, at Jl. Raya Sanur 146, Tanjung Bungkak, Denpasar (tel. 25997).

For simple camera repairs, try the **Fuji Photo** on Jl. Imam Bonjol in Kuta Beach.

There are English-language **Roman Catholic** services in Sanur at the Bali Beach and Bali Hyatt Hotels on Saturday afternoon, at the Church of St. Francis Xavier in Kuta on Sunday morning, and at the Bali Sol Hotel in Nusa Dua on Sunday afternoon. . . . **Baptist services** are held at the Bali Beach Hotel in Sanur on Sunday morning and nondenominational Protestant services in the evening.

The **Family Bookshop,** opposite the Bali Hyatt in Sanur, has an excellent collection of international newspapers and magazines, and fiction and nonfiction books about Bali. It's open from 8 a.m. to 8 p.m. every day. . . . Those interested in studying Balinese dance or music can apply to the **national dance academy,** ASTI, c/o Werdhi Budaya Art Centre, Jl. Nusa Indah, Denpasar (tel. 0361/ 22776).

We are sad to report a **crime alert for Kuta Beach hotels.** There have been an increasing number of incidents of thefts from hotel rooms, some occurring while guests were asleep. There have also been incidents of tourists boarding unlicensed bemos (public minibuses) in Denpasar and finding themselves robbed and abandoned on deserted roads. See the Kuta Beach section and the "Getting Around" section for details.

GETTING THERE: Denpasar, Bali, is one of Indonesia's six international gateways and one of its busiest. **Garuda Indonesia** flies twice a week from Los Angeles via Biak; three times a week from Bangkok via Jakarta; twice a week from

Darwin, twice a week from Perth, and five times a week from Sydney or Melbourne; daily from Hong Kong, Singapore, and Tokyo; twice a week from Manila or Taipei; and three times a week from Kuala Lumpur, Malaysia. **Singapore Airlines** flies nonstop twice a week from Singapore; **Cathay Pacific** flies nonstop three times a week from Hong Kong; **Qantas** flies twice a week from Sydney, Darwin, Melbourne, and Perth; and **MAS (Malaysian Airlines System)** flies nonstop twice a week from Kuala Lumpur.

Merpati Nusantara handles some domestic routings to Bali (including five flights daily to and from Lombok) and Garuda Indonesia offers six flights daily to Denpasar from Jakarta, three flights daily from Yogyakarta, and one flight daily from Ujung Pandang and several other Indonesian cities.

Several luxury **cruise ships** call on Bali annually, but their routings change often; the Indonesian-owned *Island Explorer* sails from Jakarta regularly. Check with your travel agent for the latest information.

GETTING AROUND: Even though Bali is a small island, its mountainous interior and curving narrow roads make most expeditions into day-long adventures. Long-distance buses operate out of Denpasar, but those wanting to explore the island themselves will be better off renting a car or chartering a taxi. Local transport or bemos (mini-vans traveling on fixed routes) are the cheapest way to travel between the beach resorts and Denpasar, but incidents of robbery on these vehicles have become more common. Motorcycles, mopeds, and bicycles are readily available for rent in each resort (including liability insurance), but poorly paved, often wet roads, erratic drivers, and general pedestrian and animal cart traffic make motorcycle driving extremely hazardous. Only *experienced* motorcycle riders should attempt day trips into the mountainous north, and in any vehicle, *tourists should not drive after dark.*

From the Airport

Ngurah Rai International Airport (named for a general in the Independence Army) is within a half hour of most resort hotels; taxi fares are fixed according to destination. An air-conditioned taxi seating three or four will cost Rp 14,000 ($8.75) to Sanur, Rp 5,000 ($3) to Kuta Beach, Rp 14,000 ($8.75) to Nusa Dua, Rp 30,000 ($18.75) to Ubud, and Rp 10,000 ($6.25) to Denpasar. Several of the larger resort hotels have mini-vans which provide an airport shuttle service at nominal cost for their guests. There is no practical public transportation to or from the airport.

By Bus

Long-distance buses traverse the island from terminals in central Denpasar. The Terminal Bis Ubung on Jl. Cokroaminoto has routes running north and west; the Terminal Bis Tegehe on Jl. Gianyar has routes running east and west; and the Terminal Bis Teggal on Jl. Imam Bonjol handles routes running south. Contact the Denpasar Tourist Information Office, in the Niti Mandala Civic Centre, Jl. Raya Puputan (tel. 22387 or 23602) for schedule information. Long-distance buses stick to the main roads and don't pass directly through the beach resorts, so your excursions must originate from Denpasar. *Note:* Property theft and pickpocketing are common on long-distance buses.

By Bemo/Mini-Van

The three main beach communities are serviced by public bemos, or shared taxis, which look like mini-vans. Each bemo plies a set route; locals hail them, jump off at their destination, and pay a fixed fare, regardless of distance. For example, bemos run along Sanur's beachfront main street, down the main route, and into the heart of Denpasar for a fare of Rp 800 (50¢) compared with Rp 4,000 ($2.50) for a taxi. Enterprising bemo drivers will offer to abandon their regular route and charter their mini-van to a particular destination (especially in the evening). Ask your hotel receptionist what the price to your destination should be and then bargain that down 10% to 20% (most drivers start out asking at least double the standard fare). Since most bemo drivers speak some English, sightseeing with them can be fun and economical. Expect to pay about Rp 27,000 ($17) a day for bemo tours originating from Sanur or Kuta Beach.

Warning: When using shared bemos in the beach resorts or between Denpasar and anywhere else, always watch your valuables. There have been alarming reports that tourists taking bemos from the Denpasar bemo station have found themselves driven to a deserted road where they were robbed and left stranded. Always write down the license plate number of the bemo in an obvious way.

By Taxi

The major hotels can arrange chauffeured cars or taxis for sightseeing at rates ranging from Rp 8,000 ($5) to Rp 18,000 ($11.25) per hour, and most drivers speak English. However, at the front gate of these hotels you'll usually find a bemo willing to negotiate an hourly price (for up to eight people) at 50% less than the taxi rate.

By Rental Car, Moped, or Bicycle

Rental cars (usually Jeep clones) are widely available on Bali and are popular with long-staying tourists, particularly families, who are exploring the island in depth. Although there isn't much traffic, road conditions can be poor (particularly in the rainy season) and hazardous: don't be surprised to find stray water buffalo, temple processions with gamelan orchestras, dogs, and women laden down with thatch all claiming right of way.

Avis Rent a Car has offices in Denpasar (tel. 24233), in Sanur at the Bali Hyatt (tel. 8271, ext. 85023) and Sanur Beach (tel. 8011, ext. 7) hotels, and in Nusa Dua at the Bali Sol (tel. 71510, ext. 88018) and Nusa Dua Beach Hotels (tel. 71210, ext. 739). Self-drive Suzuki Jeeps run about Rp 88,000 ($55) per day including insurance. Many other resort hotels, travel agents, and small businesses rent out cars by the day or week at a lesser rate, Rp 25,000 ($25) to Rp 56,000 ($35) per day, depending on season, though bargaining is in order and insurance provisions should be examined closely. An International Driver's License is a requisite for renting any vehicle. If you didn't bring one, apply at the Traffic Police Department, Jl. Seruni in Denpasar (tel. 22828), where a license valid for one month, for motorcycles and mopeds *only,* can be obtained in a couple of hours, for about Rp 6,000 ($3.75).

Motorcycles and mopeds are also widely available for rent, but are most competitively priced along the Kuta Beach strip for about Rp 8,000 ($5) per day. Insurance must be purchased separately and is sold by the Timur Jao office in Kuta and by other government-owned agencies; medical and accidental death coverage costs less than $1 a week. **Bicycles** (often very poorly maintained Chinese one-speeds) can be rented through many hotels and run Rp 1,000 (60¢) to Rp 3,500 ($2.25) an hour. *Caution:* Riding a moped or motorcycle in Bali can be extremely hazardous. Accidents are all too common among tourists.

2. BALINESE CULTURE

The Balinese have maintained their unique culture for centuries despite many outside influences: the fervor of Islam in the 16th century, the arrival of the Dutch in the 17th century, and the modern waves of Dutch, Japanese, and Europeans each trying to adopt the island as their own.

HISTORY: Before the 10th century the Balinese prospered in small communal villages in the interior agricultural regions. Religion was based on a pantheon of gods who influenced the workings of nature; mountains, rivers, trees, and animals exercised control over the agricultural landscape. Ancestors were worshipped through ritual dances, funerary rites, and frequent offerings, and gifted villagers would communicate with them during spiritually induced trances.

On neighboring Java the Hindu Majapahit Kingdom (13th to 16th centuries) and the Buddhist Çailendra dynasties (10th to 12th centuries) ruled the central and eastern regions. In the 10th century a Javanese priest named Danghyang Markandeya and his pilgrims traveled to Bali to spread Hinduism. They built several temples, including Besakih, Bali's Mother Temple, on the slopes of Mount Agung, and began settlements.

At the same time the Warmedewa Dynasty united Bali administratively and developed an advanced irrigation system. The marriage of the fourth Warmadewa king to an East Javanese princess in A.D. 1011 reaffirmed Bali's autonomy. Their sons inherited different parts of the kingdom; Anak Wungsu, who inherited Bali, invited the Javanese priest Empu Kuturan to teach the principles of the Hindu trinity (Brahma the Creator, Vishnu the Preserver, and Siva the Destroyer) to the Balinese. Soon after, the Majapahit Kingdom centered around Yogyakarta sent its foremost priests to Bali to teach traditional Javanese arts (especially refining wayang kulit) and the ancient Indian epic texts, the *Ramayana* and the *Mahabharata*. As Hinduism became more firmly entrenched on the island many traditional Balinese rituals and gods representing the natural elements were incorporated into a new religion.

In the 14th century the new Muslim faith spread so quickly through Java that almost all signs of Hinduism and Buddhism vanished. Conquest of the Majapahit Kingdom by the Islamic forces from West Java caused thousands of Hindus to flee for Bali. Finally Sultan Agung (1613–1646), leader of the Islamic Mataram Kingdom in central and eastern Java, exiled all the remaining Hindu nobility and priests to Bali. Java's most gifted scholars, artists, performers, writers, and religious leaders brought a new level of sophistication and artistry to the already well-developed Balinese culture.

The deposed Majapahit emperor established a new court near Klungkung. Over time the island evolved into eight kingdoms ruled by rajas. The Dutch, who had colonized Java much earlier, didn't attempt to take Bali for nearly 300 years. On September 14, 1906, Dutch troops landed on Sanur Beach and marched on Bali's capital, Denpasar. When they arrived at the Puri Pemecutan, the raja emerged with his retinue and the palace guards. Rather than be taken captive, he asked his guards to kill him, thus beginning a chain of suicides among his retinue, the ladies of the court, and the nobility. This mass suicide, the Balinese tradition of *puputan,* soon became a conventional massacre by the foreign troops. It took 60 years and many puputan massacres in each court before the Dutch could claim Bali.

The Dutch steamship line, K.P.M., began organized tourism in the 1920s, and by the 1930s more than 100 travelers per month were visiting Bali. Tjokorde Gde Agung Sukawati, King of Ubud, began inviting foreign guests to stay at his Puri Saren Palace in the 1930s. European artists, writers, and scholars came and kept returning with new friends, spreading news of this tropical paradise. The rapid growth in tourism was suddenly stifled by World War II and the Japanese invasion. The Japanese Occupation (1942–1945) brought famine and hardship, encouraging the soldier Gusti Ngurah Rai to begin training volunteers for a freedom army. After the Japanese surrender and the Declaration of Independence of the new Republic of Indonesia in 1945, the Dutch returned to reoccupy Bali, crushing the brave resistance of Ngurah Rai's forces. The Dutch ceded most of Indonesia in late 1949, but Bali remained an administrative district in the Dutch Republic of East Indonesia, finally joining the Republic of Indonesia in 1956.

RELIGION AND RITUAL: The Hindu-Dharma religion (known as Agama

Tirta, the religion of holy water) is currently practiced by 95% of the population. This uniquely Balinese combination of Hinduism, Buddhism, and ancestor worship is basically a monotheistic religion, with one Supreme Being, Sang Hyang Widhi. All other deities are different manifestations. Trisakti, the holy Hindu trinity of Brahma in the creative mode, Vishnu as the preserver, and Siva as the destroyer of the material world, embodies all aspects of the one Supreme Being. The Balinese have adapted their own Five Religious Principles: (1) Brahman, belief in One Supreme Being; (2) Atman, belief in the souls and spirits; (3) Samsara, or reincarnation; (4) Karma, that action and practice is appropriately rewarded, that is, good rewards good and evil, evil; and (5) Moksha, the possibility of unity with the divine.

Other aspects of Indian Hinduism are interwoven in the Balinese faith. A four-tiered caste system, much looser and less pervasive than in India, regulates society and religious rituals. The Brahmanas are the holy caste, the Ksatriyas are royalty, the Wesya are merchants, and the Sudra caste is made up of farmers and workers. The Balinese eat meat, except for the cattle raised in the village of Taro —these special albino cattle are bred to wander around as sacred creatures.

The average Balinese takes part daily in offerings to the traditional gods of wealth, health, and good fortune. Lavish sculptural offerings of food and gifts are created for *odalan,* regular temple festivities. A person's life is marked by rituals: beginning in pregnancy with the seventh-month ritual, and continuing with a birth ritual, the sixth-month "baby touching the ground" ceremony, the teenager's toothfiling ceremony, wedding and birthday celebrations, and clan gatherings at temple anniversary ceremonies. The ultimate ritual, Pitra Yodnya, is the elaborate cremation of the dead, to speed their souls to heaven so they can return for an even happier existence in another physical form.

Rituals are scheduled by the complex Saki lunar calendar of 12 or 13 months of 29 or 30 days each. Within this calendar weeks can vary from one to ten days. The commonly used Pawukon calendar is a combination of the Javanese lunar calendar and the more complicated Balinese one; temple festivities are scheduled on auspicious days that coincide in both calendars. The Pawukon seven-day week occurs 30 times each half year, so that "annual" festivities occur every 210 days. Balinese New Year or Nyepi (usually in March) is a day of total silence, when work, cooking, and all activity ceases and all tourists are asked to remain in their hotels. It follows many days of merrymaking with fireworks, in an effort to flush out the evil spirits. When the first day of the New Years arrives and all is quiet, the Balinese believe that the evil spirits will bypass the island, thinking that everyone has left. Anyone hoping to attend an "annual" festival should consult with the nearest Indonesian tourist office before scheduling a visit.

PERFORMING ARTS:
The religious rituals of Balinese daily life are a continuous performance, often combined with traditional music, dance, theater, and the arts to give pleasure to the gods. The careful attention lavished on every banana-leaf offering covered with rice and marigolds, on every *penjor* (coconut-palm flag) are as acutely creative as the organized arts that flourish throughout the island.

One of Bali's earliest art forms was *wayang kulit,* the shadow play acted out by leather hand puppets, but it evolved to a more sophisticated form after the 11th-century influx of Javanese. The original Balinese *wayang lemah* was a puppet show performed in front of an audience in daylight; the *wayang peteng* is closer to the Javanese tradition of manipulating puppets behind an illuminated screen while the audience watches in darkness. Most Balinese dalangs narrate stories from the *Gambuh,* East Javanese tales of Prince Panji, as well as from the classic Indian epics, but wayang kulit is not performed as regularly as dance.

Most of the larger hotels have evenings of classical Javanese dance and music made up of several dance fragments, accompanied by a gamelan orchestra. The

Pendet or Panyembrama is a welcoming dance performed by young girls who carry trays of marigolds, which they sprinkle over the audience. The simplest dance steps to a lilting gamelan melody are used to introduce the audience to this style; the boys' Baris dance uses equally rudimentary steps to tell of a noble warrior on his way to battle. The Legong Kraton, so called because the village girls used to live in the kraton (palace) while training in this court dance, are quick-paced fragments of much longer, classic Gambuh dances.

The Kechak, or Monkey Dance, is one of the most popular with visitors. On an open-air stage, a 100-man chorus dressed in checkered sarongs chants and sways in concentric circles. In their midst, costumed and masked Wayang Wong dancers perform excerpts from the *Ramayana* legend. The flickering torchlight, gracefully slow dance, and the rhythmic "chak . . . kechak . . . chak . . . chak" accompaniment create a hypnotic effect. Today's modern Kechak is said to have been devised in the 1930s by Walter Spies, the German artist working in Ubud, who combined the *Ramayana* ballet form with the original Sanghyang trance dance (used to communicate with deceased ancestors) to create this exciting performance.

Children love the Barong dance, a moral tale in the Wayang Wong style that tells of the struggle between the good Barong monster (a manifestation of Vishnu) and Rangda, an evil witch. The Barong's huge, hairy, and glittering costume is supported by two grown men, and his actions, the obvious plot, and the pulsing gamelan music are delightful. Check the local Tourist Information Office for the schedule of nightly performances at the beach resorts or in the villages, and try to see at least one during your stay.

In Bali's many temples several classic dances are performed for the temple anniversary, and for other important events. Visitors wearing the traditional sarong (wrap-around skirt) and saput (sacred waist sash) are welcomed to watch and discreetly photograph the festivities.

VISUAL ARTS: The oldest-known sculpture on Bali is the solid-bronze drum displayed in the Pejeng temple, known as the "Moon of Pejeng." Scholars date the drum to 300 B.C. and credit its decoration to the Dong San culture from Vietnam. Most early sculpture was in wood, but little has survived in Indonesia's humid climate. Generations of carvers who made dance masks, architectural ornaments, or musical instruments have passed their skills on to the woodworkers of Mas. Bali's stone sculpture, most influenced by Hinduism between the 11th and 14th centuries, is more fully described in "Exploring the Island."

Architecture is dictated by *desa adat,* the traditional Balinese village plans prescribed by a Javanese Hindu priest in the 11th century, which required each community to have three temples. The Pura Pusa, for Brahma the Creator, was to be in the north; the Pura Desa Adat, for Vishnu the Preserver, was in the middle; and the Pura Dalem, for Siva the Destroyer, was in the south. The temples came to be thought of as representing birth, life, and death in each village, which also had to have its own graveyard outside the common walls. Every Balinese home had to have four pavilions (for men, women, dance/gamelan performances, and religious rituals) enclosed by a wall and gate to foil demons, as well as a temple in the northeast corner. Today classic family compounds enclosed by tall red-brick walls line every road.

The earliest references to painting come from manuscripts produced by the court of King Anak Wungsu in the 11th century and from *lontar* (palm-leaf books) illustrated with figures resembling the wayang puppets. This rigid, one-dimensional imagery was used until the 17th century, when King Dalem asked a painter from the village of Kamasan in central Bali to decorate some government buildings. His frescoes (like the one still visible at Kerta Gosa in Klungkung) came to be known as the Kamasan school. Lively wayang figures in warm natural colors depict moral tales from the Indian epics on the pavilions, shrines, temples, and official calendars of Bali.

In the 1930s the German artist Walter Spies and the Dutchman Rudolf Bonnet came to Bali as guests of the King of Ubud. They introduced artificial pigments and free-hand drawing from nature or live subjects to local artists who'd only painted for religious purposes, and according to strict rules of style. Spies founded the Pita Maha School in Ubud and neighboring Batuan in 1935; after Spies's death in Japanese internment Rudolf Bonnet (who later founded the Puri Lukisan Museum in Ubud) continued to work with many local artists. In the 1960s a Dutch artist, Arnie Smit, organized the Young Artists group, bringing in schoolboys and farmhands to draw and experiment. Later work came to be known as the Academic School because many of these artists continued to receive formal training. Contemporary artists have taken from all these movements, improvised their own themes or revitalized traditional Hindu ones. The tremendous growth in tourism has generated demand for the work of all Balinese artists and craftsmen, revived their traditional skills, and fostered a thriving new industry.

3. THE BEACH RESORTS: SANUR, KUTA BEACH, AND NUSA DUA

Bali is such an exquisite combination of visual, physical, and intellectual pleasures that visitors will enjoy their stay in any of the resort areas. The three main beach resorts—the elegant Sanur, the party-mad Kuta, and the isolated compounds at Nusa Dua—provide a variety of accommodations in every price range so anyone can afford to stay right on the shores of Paradise. Where you sleep will influence where you dine in the evening (the resorts are about 20 minutes apart), but to a much lesser extent, where you spend your days. Our first choice: Stay in Sanur, shop in Kuta, surf in Nusa Dua.

SANUR: When the Dutch-built Bali Hotel opened in Denpasar in 1929 its guests used to take carriages out to the nearby beach at Sanur. Since that time tourists have come in steady streams to enjoy this utopia, and because development was kept back from the shore behind dense landscaping, Sanur's beachfront has retained much of its natural beauty. Daily offerings of rice, marigolds, and incense are still left on banana-leaf dishes at every beach path and in front of every *prahu* (fishing boat) pulled up on shore. At dawn and sunset the local women stroll down to bathe in the warm, shallow sea or collect fish for supper. Only one or two markets dot the 1½-mile stretch between the Bali Beach Hotel (on the north end) and the Sanur Beach Hotel (on the south). Skillful women offer massage and hair-braiding to indolent sun worshippers along this stretch as well.

Useful Information

Sanur is basically a one-street town; the road running parallel to the coast is known as **Jl. Sanur Beach** or **Jl. Hotel Hyatt,** and the small lanes that run perpendicular from it toward the beach are usually called by the name of a hotel on their length. . . . A privately run **Tourist Information Office** is at Jl. Hotel Hyatt 129 (tel. 8451), opposite the Ramayana Hotel. It's manned by a helpful staff from 8 a.m. to 5 p.m. Monday through Friday. . . . Several **moneychangers** on the main street stay open until 8 p.m. to change traveler's checks. . . . Sanur's **post office,** Permutel Kantor Telepon, inland on Jl. Br. Sindhu, is only open from 8 a.m. to 6 p.m. Monday through Saturday; closed Sunday. . . . Bemos (group mini-van taxis) ply Jl. Sanur all day and night and charge up to Rp 500 (30¢) to travel within Sanur. Check with your hotel desk for rates for chartered bemos.

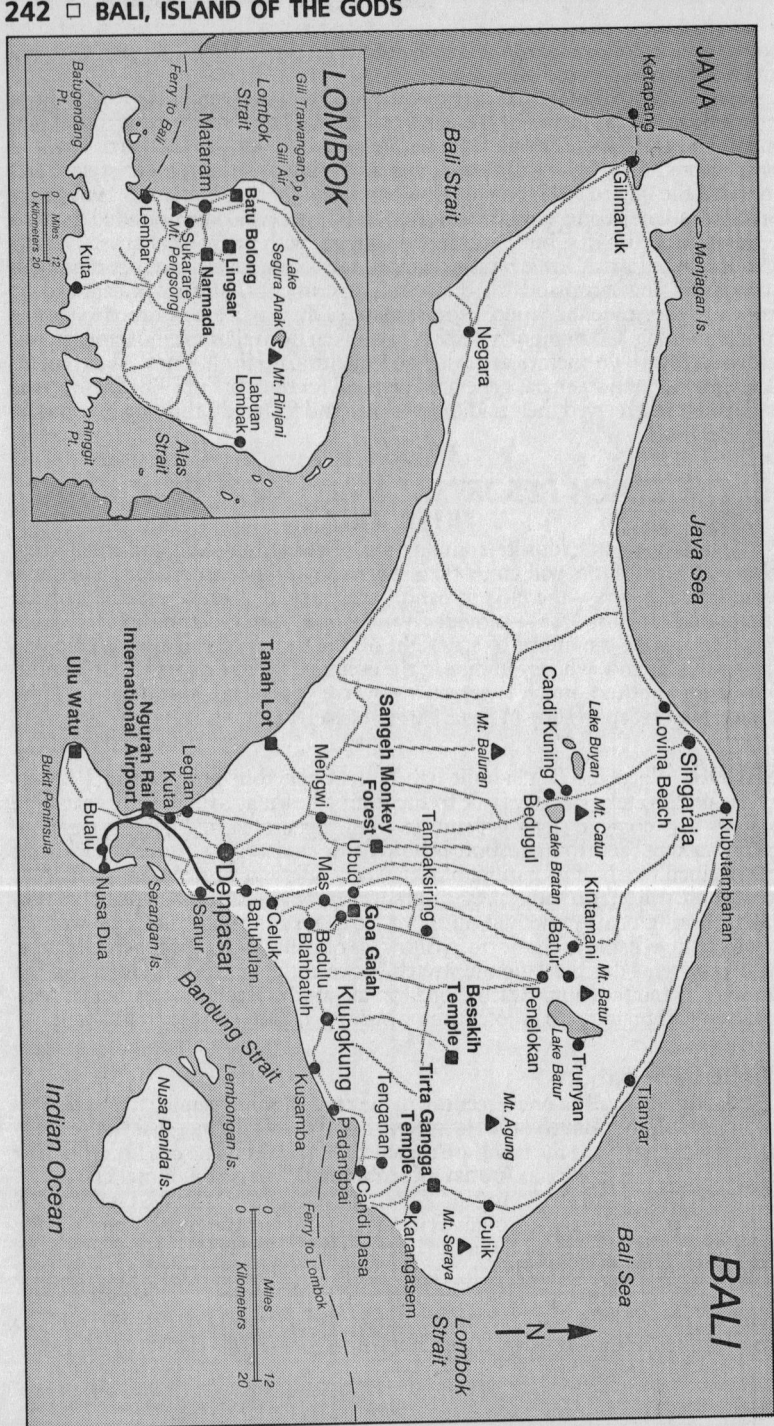

Accommodations

Sanur boasts some of the island's best five-star hotels and the widest selection of moderately priced ones. We've tried to recommend only those directly on the beach, but so many are listed because from mid-July to mid-September and mid-December to mid-January it's often impossible to find a room. Note that addresses, if any, are streets named after the hotels on them. Any bemo or taxi driver will know how to get to your hotel. Reservations addressed to a hotel's Denpasar post office box a month in advance will ensure rooms during the summer and winter holiday high seasons. Most hotels discount their rates (always quoted in U.S. dollars) by 15% to 50% the rest of the year if you ask when you reserve a room.

FIRST CLASS HOTELS. Sanur's three five-star hotels rank with any listed in Jakarta's luxury category, yet rates, quoted in U.S. dollars, run only $80 to $140, plus 16% to 21% tax and service charges for a double room.

The **Bali Beach Hotel,** on Jl. Bali Beach (tel. 0361/8511), was the first of Bali's "international" resorts, a ten-story white tower built in 1966 over one of the nicest parts of Sanur beach. Since then, the two-level garden wings and a collection of traditional stone Balinese cottages have been added to create a total of 605 luxurious rooms. The Bali Beach has a nine-hole golf course, a bowling alley, tennis courts, three swimming pools, several restaurants, and landscaped grounds, which extend farther than many villages (and eliminate crowding). Despite its size it's an excellent, well-run hotel where guests can lounge casually or dress for the nightclub. The tower rooms have been renovated recently to deluxe standards, and the modern garden rooms and native bungalows are sparkling, tasteful, and neatly kept. Whatever your taste, for the amenities of a large hotel with true Balinese hospitality, the Bali Beach is still the best at Sanur. Plush suites start at $110, double rooms cost $92, and singles run about $10 less.

The overwhelmingly tall, chandeliered pendopo that greets guests at the **Bali Hyatt,** P.O. Box 392, Denpasar (tel. 0361/8271), leads to gilt, red, and purple armchairs, wings named after hibiscus and frangipani, and elevators plying four concrete stories. Balconied rooms are large, extremely tasteful, and superbly maintained by an army of smiling staff. The rich décor, deluxe amenities (but no TV!) and complimentary toiletries are identical in all 387 rooms; high-season doubles range from $130 to $145, depending on the view, with a sea view commanding a $20 premium. The Bali Hyatt's junior suite with a two-sided terrace, beach views, and large seating area (which can sleep one) is truly sumptuous at $250 a night. The ground floor offers a glamorous shopping arcade, the Ming Tea Room, a pretty restaurant, and gamelan-accompanied access to the huge, fountain-fed pool, and beyond it, a well-kept beach.

The third five-star lodging is the **Hotel Sanur Beach,** P.O. Box 279, Denpasar (tel. 0361/8011), on the southern end of Sanur Beach. It was built in 1974 and remodeled in '84; now its 310 rooms and public spaces have an elegant Hong Kong slickness about them. This property is beautifully landscaped and filled with songbirds, but the beachfront has been bulkheaded to prevent erosion and is tiered in concrete slabs. The most attractive rooms are in the Sanur Beach's new wing, overhanging a courtyard dominated by a huge Vishnu statue and gurgling fountains. Large doubles with all the amenities and a terrace overlooking the garden or beach cost $86. Rooms in the four-story main building cost $80, more private bungalows rent for $92, and ten suites start at $115. The Sanur Beach has a large pool and sunning area, tennis court, water sports, bike rental, three restaurants, and a bar operating from a schooner moored in the pool. The friendly staff and warm feeling of the hotel make it a good value for those who don't mind the narrow beach.

The **Hotel Tandjung Sari,** P.O. Box 25, Denpasar (tel. 0361/8441), located midway down Sanur Beach, is included in the first-class category because of its pricey rates, although its simple accommodations have become very fashionable. A variety of free-standing bungalows range from $100 to $135 for two, plus a $20-per-night high-season supplement. Here, stylish primitivism and a smattering of Indonesian antiques disguise modern amenities. One- and two-story cottages are screened in on all sides and cooled by overhead fans or air conditioning contained by drawing fabric curtains. Bungalows in the interior without sea views feature a comfortable seating area and large bed. The bathrooms have a bidet and sculpted bathtub, both of which open onto a private garden. The Tandjung Sari offers an elegant exoticism, a restaurant with a good Indonesian buffet, and grounds that include a small pool and bar next to the pristine beach.

MODERATELY PRICED RANGE. Sanur excels in the quality of moderate-priced lodging. Because most small hotels are built in the traditional red-brick and carved-stone Balinese style they have a sense of indigenous charm; their personal service adds to an ambience rivaling that of more expensive hotels. Some rooms have phones or TVs, and all are air-conditioned. Our choices, priced in U.S. dollars, range from $40 to $75, including tax and service for two (bargain rates down 15% to 50% in the low season), and are noted in order of preference. Advance reservations will ensure a room during the summer- and winter-holiday high seasons.

One of the Sanur's best values is the **Santrian Beach Cottages,** P.O. Box 55, Denpasar (tel. 0361/8181), located midway on Sanur beach. One hundred modern rooms tucked in traditional Balinese bungalows are scattered throughout the large, lush grounds. Balinese sculpture appears everywhere among the flowers, pools, and footpaths. The facilities and attentive service are embellished with fine detail; guests will find flowers and rice wine in their rooms and soft wicker furniture on their private porches. The Santrian has two restaurants (one on the beach) and a good pool. Garden- or sea-view rooms are a reasonable $45 to $52 single, $52 to $57 double. The same fine host, Mr. Tjethana Putra, has built new accommodations at the south end of Sanur Beach, the **Santrian Bali Beach Bungalows,** P.O. Box 55, Denpasar (tel. 0361/4009), known locally as Santrian II. Two-story, traditional bungalows dot the smaller but beautifully landscaped gardens. The white sand beach is easily accessible from the warm tile-and-wood rooms ($45 a single, $52 a double), which are grouped around a large pool that has a bar set into its shallow end. Breakfast is served in a decorative, fan-cooled pavilion or at poolside.

La Taverna Bali Hotel, south of Jl. Sanur Beach Village (P.O. Box 40, Denpasar, tel. 0361/8497), is an 84-room hotel that maintains a small, intimate atmosphere. Its white stucco bungalows have a lot of local style, with petite, carved-wood doors, dark bamboo furniture, and sunken baths. Some feel a little worn but the hotel's thoughtful staff, large pool, and inviting beachside bar make up for it. Rooms near the beach are the best value and run $70 for a single, $78 for a double, and $110 for a family suite.

If you're traveling with children, the family-run **Segara Village,** on Jl. Segara (P.O. Box 91, Denpasar, tel. 0361/8407), can't be beat. The rooms are clustered in Balinese village style among shrines, flowers, and fountains on 11 beachfront acres. Individual and two-story bungalows or attached units range from $48 to $75, depending on view and style. For $75 you can rent a "rice storage" bungalow: upstairs a thatch roof, air-conditioned master bedroom, dressing area, and master bath; downstairs a living area or child's room ($11 extra per bed). All have small patios with comfortable chairs overlooking the heavily planted grounds. Membership in the Leisure Club (at a cost of $100 per week for a family of four) includes a playgroup, water sports, tennis, bicycling, flower arranging, traditional Balinese dance, woodcarving, batik, and gamelan lessons. Two pools, fed by spouting carved-stone frogs and other sport facilities are always open to guests, and single classes can be taken for a nominal fee. There is also babysitting available for $2 an hour.

The **Bali Sanur Bungalows,** P.O. Box 306, Denpasar (tel. 0361/8421), are grouped in four separate locations, with 180 units at different price ranges spread mid-beach in Sanur. The B.S.B. Besakih Beach unit north of the Santrian I Hotel is a rather drab collection of simple bungalows that are clean, but plain. The B.S.B. Penida View, south of the Santrian I, offers classier rooms with batik and bentwood; both units have pools and pleasant restaurants, and are priced at $42 single, $48 double.

The **Baruna Beach Inn,** at Jl. Pantai Sindhu 17 (tel. 0361/8546), has seven typically Balinese bungalows on the beach that rent for $32 single or $40 double, including continental breakfast and afternoon tea. Intimate woven bamboo bungalows with ornately carved wood and batik-covered rattan furniture feel totally authentic while offering the modern conveniences of air conditioning, screened windows, mini-fridge, and large, all-tile bathroom. The Baruna Beach has no pool, but you can walk down the beach for five minutes to the plush Bali Beach or Bali Hyatt Hotels and swim for a nominal charge.

The **Sindhu Beach Hotel,** P.O. Box 181, Denpasar (tel. 0361/8351), has a beautiful beachfront and pleasant pool nearby in the mid-beach stretch. Their 50 bungalow rooms feature phones, TVs, and mini-bars, but are showing signs of wear and tear. If all else is booked, rooms here are well priced at $42 to $46, including breakfast for two. Another alternative is the **Gazebo Beach Cottages Hotel,** Jl. Hotel Hyatt (tel. 0361/8300), also midway down the beach, with 60 stylish, tastefully decorated bungalows and attached standard rooms that are well kept, if slapdash in construction. Large duplex thatch-roofed cottages are $35; standard doubles are $30.

If there's absolutely no room in the beachfront inns, drop back to Jl. Sanur Beach, just north of the Bali Hyatt, to the **Swastika Bungalows** (tel. 0361/8693). (Forgive the name—the swastika symbol has been used by the Hindus for centuries to represent the Wheel of Life and has no relationship to Nazism.) The Swastika Bungalows complex has a nice pool and 40 rooms in garden bungalows set well back from the road, it's about 500 yards from the beach. Rooms are plain, clean, and comfortable with screened-in porches, but second-floor rooms have better ventilation. Rates vary according to amenities: hot showers and air conditioning cost $35 for two, rooms with fans only cost $29 for two, including breakfast. The **Laghawa Beach Inn** is also set back from the beach on Jl. Tandung Sari (tel. 0361/8494). Its 12 simple rooms are well tended and trimmed in typically Balinese woven bamboo; air-conditioned doubles cost $35, $23 with fan only. Although the Laghawa Beach doesn't have a pool, the Santrian Beach Cottages' nearby pool is accessible for a fee of Rp 3,600 ($1.50) a day.

BUDGET CHOICES. Low-budget accommodations are more common in Kuta Beach and the more recently developed beach communities, such as Lovina or Candi Dasa (see "Exploring the Island"), than in Sanur, but we found three choices where doubles rent for under Rp 40,000 ($25), plus 5½% to 15½% tax and service charges.

The best value in these simple accommodations is the **Werdha Pura Cottages,** P.O. Box 24, Denpasar (tel. 0361/8171), complex on the beach next to the Santrian I. There are 56 *wisma wisata pantai* (tourist cottages) built by the national government in 1970 as prototypes for Bali's future development. Facing the beautiful surf are 16 bungalows, each with a small patio, comfortable simple furnishings, a fan, phone, and spotless private bathroom. Rates are Rp 15,000 ($9.50) for one or Rp 23,000 ($14.50) for two, including breakfast served in a small pavilion on the grounds. If you're with family or friends, rent one of their simply furnished, concrete two-bedroom bungalows with kitchen, living room, and private bath. They're fan-cooled, clean, and farther back from the beach, but only cost Rp 46,400 ($29) a night for four, including breakfast! The Werdha Pura serves only breakfast and drinks at its bar, but Sanur has ample dining possibilities within walking distance. If you miss having a pool, try the Santrian I's next door ($1.50 a day).

Simple rooms with some Balinese décor, private bath, phone, and air conditioning are offered at the **Bali Sanur Bungalow**, P.O. Box 306, Denpasar (tel. 0361/8421), Respati Beach unit. A narrow, landscaped corridor of attached bungalows leads to a small dining pavilion and pool, and a great stretch of cream-colored sand. Functional lodging costs Rp 43,200 ($27) for single travelers, Rp 56,000 ($35) for two.

Another budget choice, but one off the beach, is the ten-room **Hotel Ramayana**, at Jl. Sanur Beach, Batujimbar (P.O. Box 66, Denpasar) (tel. 0361/8429), opposite the Bali Hyatt. Rooms are plain but clean, with some care taken in the furnishings. Air-conditioned hot-water doubles cost Rp 36,800 ($23), air-conditioned cold-water rooms are Rp 32,000 ($20), and cold-water fan-cooled rooms cost Rp 22,400 ($14).

Restaurants

The restaurants along Jl. Sanur Beach and the narrow lanes that run from it toward the beach represent some of the best food on Bali. You can dine on Indonesian specialties while admiring a classical dance performance, listening to gamelan, or seeing shadow puppet theater. Evenings are usually casual but your spiffy new resortwear would be suitable for our first three recommendations.

The **Bali Beach Hotel** (tel. 8511) offers assorted classical and folk dances with a large buffet of Indonesian and European specialties at the Pendawa pool every Monday, Wednesday, and Friday evening for Rp 30,400 ($19) per person. On Sunday, cultural performances move to the more intimate Rama Stage or outdoors in front of their garden wing. Classical Balinese dance accompanied by an angklung orchestra follows a luxurious meat, chicken, and lobster barbecue for Rp 30,400 ($19) per person. The Indonesian buffet and barbecue begin at 7 p.m. so that the audience can dine before the performance. Excellently prepared food, an informative narrator, and the respectful atmosphere make this an educational as well as thoroughly enjoyable night out.

The thatch-roofed dining pavilion of the **Tandjung Sari Hotel** (tel. 8441) is in a dramatic setting, facing an elevated cut stone bar that overlooks the sea. Their large menu has Balinese and European offerings, all carefully prepared with Western tastes in mind. The sate ikan (barbecued fish on a skewer) is moist and mildly spiced, a perfect complement to urap urap (steamed local vegetables with a piquant coconut chili sauce). Vegetarians can sample the nasi goreng sayuran; those seeking more familiar fare can have a peanut butter 'n' jam sandwich or hamburger. All of Tandjung Sari's fare is tasty, and the beachside setting feels totally Balinese. Diners will pay upward of Rp 16,000 ($10) each; reservations recommended Saturday night for the special rijsttafel (classic Dutch version of an Indonesian buffet), which costs Rp 25,000 ($15.75).

Telaga Naga (tel. 8271) is an elegant, upscale setting for Chinese cuisine owned by the Bali Hyatt and directly across from the hotel on the main road. A central pavilion with two wings perched over lotus ponds is thatch-roofed and supported by rough-hewn coral walls. A gamelan quartet serenades European diners as they sample Szechuan classics such as fried prawns in chili tomato sauce, Szechuan smoked duck, fried beef with green peppers, or braised bean curd with hot bean sauce. There's an Indonesian air to all the spices, but the food is excellently prepared and presented. Portions are large, service is rude but prompt, and the prices are "international hotel" high. Two can splurge in the quietly luxe ambience for about Rp 56,000 ($35), but it takes four or more to sample the varied fare. Telaga Naga is open nightly from 6 to 10:30 p.m. and reservations are recommended, particularly to avoid the management's policy of seating small parties at less desirable tables.

Sanur offers several good, moderately priced restaurants not affiliated with the deluxe hotels. Our favorite restaurant in Sanur, and one of the island's best, is **Kul Kul Restaurant,** located opposite the Hyatt on Jl. Sanur Beach (tel. 8038). It's a thatch-roofed pendopo set in a lush outdoor garden, with flowers and elegant wooden temple bells hanging everywhere. For intimate dining in a reclining position, there's a small pavilion with a Balinese bed (groups of two or more, please!). The setting is very special, as is the food. If you order a day ahead or the morning of the same day, and can muster at least four hungry eaters, you can enjoy the Balinese babi guling (roast suckling pig) for Rp 40,000 ($25). If there are only two of you, order ahead for the bebek tutu (smoked duck) or ayam tutu (smoked chicken), a duo of taste treats for a reasonable Rp 8,500 ($5.25) each. Seafood is delicately prepared on the grill as a seafood platter (fish, crab, turtle, lobster) or Balinese-style ikan pepes, wrapped in banana leaf with coconut milk. There is also a rijsttafel at Rp 16,000 ($10) for two. Need we say more to praise this best of Balinese cuisine. Open daily for dinner only. Call for a reservation and free pickup from your hotel.

For the best casual lunch (swimsuits and bare feet okay) or dinner (shorts or resortwear) right on the beach, try the **Sanur Beach Market Bar and Restaurant,** just south of the Bali Beach Hotel at the end of Jl. Segara (tel. 8574). Bamboo tables shaded by a thatch pendopo are set near a small stage where charming children's classic legong dances are performed on Wednesday and Saturday evenings. The menu includes a variety of grilled fish entrees for Rp 4,200 ($2.50) to Rp 14,000 ($8.75), sandwiches and salads that are so fresh and flavorful they could only come from a tropical isle. Their specialties, which must be ordered a day before, are juicy babi guling (the local special roast pig) for Rp 12,000 ($7.50), and bebe tutuk (roast duck) for Rp 10,000 ($6.25). Sanur Beach Market, a cooperative venture whose profits support the local Sanur Village Foundation, will provide free pickup at any of the Sanur hotels if diners call ahead. They also have a smaller café, the **Chemara Beach Market Restaurant,** located at the south end of the beach next to the Sanur Beach Hotel.

Trattoria Da Marco, a longtime favorite Italian ristorante, recently moved to larger quarters on main street, Jl. Sanur Beach, about 500 yards north of the Sanur Beach Hotel (no phone number as of this writing; ask your concierge). Italian tourists, as well as travelers of other nationalities and local Indonesians fill the tables in this contemporary-styled pendopo to order bruschetta, their three varieties of delicious and relatively authentic pizza or six different spaghettis. Specials include the tender bistecca alla pizzaiola (steak in a tomato-and-cheese sauce), gamberoni jumbo alla griglia (grilled Bali prawns), and fagioli secchilessati con cipolla (dry beans with onions and a vinaigrette sauce). A good hearty meal, some swaying and singing along with the excellent Italo-Balinese crooner, and a carafe of wine should run Rp 40,000 ($25) per couple. Open from 7 p.m. to midnight; closed Thursday.

A popular bar and restaurant in Batu Jimbar, the heart of Jl. Sanur Beach, is **Penjor** (tel. 8226), open daily for lunch and dinner, with three weekly cultural shows. Penjor's menu offers Balinese, Indonesian, Chinese, Korean, Japanese, and seafood entrees, and six daily set menus. The grilled-seafood menu costs Rp 12,000 ($7.50) and includes crabmeat soup, a banana-leaf platter filled with lobster, ginger crab, shrimp and fish sate, and an exotic fruit salad. Penjor, the Indonesian name for the tall coconut tree banners that fly outside homes or temples during a festival, will provide free transportation in Sanur to diners who call ahead.

Some totally unpretentious choices for a good, casual meal include **Ronny's,** Jl. Sanur Beach (tel. 8370), an outdoor pub with a large menu and live band or, next to it, **Oka's Coffee Shop**, a bright fast-food eatery with a simple, but varied Western menu. The **Swastika I and II Restaurants** (tel. 8693) are operated by the hotel of that name and are also midway on Jl. Sanur Beach. Both offer basic Indonesian fare and local seafood. **Sri Dewi** is a small typical restaurant north of the Ramayana Hotel on Jl. Sanur Beach, with a simple menu of Indonesian, European, and seafood dishes. At all these restaurants you can eat well for less than Rp 6,400 ($4). Be sure that the water's been boiled, and make certain that the salad produce has been thoroughly cleaned.

What to See and Do in Sanur

Tucked away under the palms at the north end of Sanur Beach near the Bali Beach Hotel is Sanur's only cultural sight, the tiny **Le Mayeur Museum.** The traditional Balinese beachside home of Beligian artist A. J. Le Mayeur de Merprés (1880–1958) was built in 1932 and is still occupied by his descendants. You visit more for its sculpture garden, carved-wood architectural embellishments, and Balinese furnishings than for the small Le Mayeur oils on canvas and murals that are displayed. In the gift shop you'll find fascinating photo albums of Le Mayeur with his Balinese wife, Ni Pollok, taken during a time when the island was still new to tourism. The museum is open Tuesday through Thursday and Sunday from noon to 2 p.m., from 8 to 11 a.m. on Friday and till 12:30 p.m. on Saturday; admission is Rp 250 (15¢).

Snorkeling and scuba-diving are offered by **Bali Marine Sports** (tel. 8776), whose Sanur office is in a tiny building off the sand about midway down the beach. Snorkeling costs Rp 16,000 ($10) a session and scuba and gear runs Rp 88,000 ($55) a session, including a diving guide and transportation. Windsurfing ($6 per hour) and parasailing ($10 per trip) equipment is also available. Bali Marine Sports also offers excursions to Nusa Lembongan, an islet next to Nusa Penida (a large, little-developed island off Sanur's coast) that's popular for day trips.

Bali Water Tours offers morning or afternoon half-day sailing tours along the coast of Sanur or Nusa Dua on their 70-foot yacht the *Sri Dewi*, for $23 per person, half price for children under 12. Call 8086 for information and reservations.

After you've had a suntan-lotion-lubricated massage on the beach for about Rp 5,000 ($3) or had those salt-soaked locks turned into a dozen tiny braids (corn rows to some of us, "plaits" to the Balinese, and only Rp 100 or 15¢ per), it's time to go shopping!

SHOPPING. Fashionable resort clothes for men and women can be found in the **arcade shops** at the Bali Beach or Bali Hyatt Hotels. At both, style-conscious designers have turned indigenous batiks and painted fabrics into harem pants, long tunic tops, and sophisticated, broad-shouldered citywear. Batiks, woodcarvings, and better souvenirs can be bought at the **Sanur Beach Market,** a community cooperative venture on the beach at the end of Jl. Segara. At all the markets, the rule is to bargain prices down at least 35%. There are many **gift and crafts shops** along Jl. Sanur Beach, most on the south end between the Bali Hyatt and Sanur Beach hotels. If you're tempted by one of those gorgeous life-size wooden banana trees, count on dismantling it and carrying it as hand luggage (see "Useful Information" for shipping costs).

Sanur's **Pasar Seni,** the art market on Jl. Sanur, offers little more than the same batik rayon shirts and hokey woodcarvings seen in every moneychanger's stall. If you go before 10 a.m., though, you'll be able to bargain with the locals over the day's choice of produce and cut flowers.

The **Family Bookstore,** on Jl. Sanur Beach opposite the Bali Hyatt (open daily from 8 a.m. to 8 p.m.), is sure to have that magazine, trashy novel, or great literary work you've been dying to read. They also have an excellent collection of books on Bali and Indonesia (at fair prices). The **drugstore** in the lower level arcade of the Bali Hyatt also has a wide selection of books on Southeast Asia's history, ethnography, and culture.

KUTA BEACH: Kuta Beach is so raucous, crowded, and commercialized that it's hard to say anything nice about it. In its favor, Kuta has the Bali Oberoi, the most beautiful hotel on the entire island, some of the finest restaurants, and the best-looking, least-expensive resortwear we saw in Indonesia. If you can afford to stay at the Bali Oberoi then you can afford a car and driver to avoid Kuta in the evenings. If you're staying in Sanur, come for the day to shop and have an excellent lunch, then return to the natural beauty and tranquility of your hotel before sunset. If you're on the $500-around-the-world circuit, plan on staying here because it's got the largest selection of rock-bottom-priced budget lodgings.

Orientation

The Kuta Beach coast is about four miles long and crisscrossed with narrow lanes and *gangs* (alleys) filled with shops, bars, restaurants, and pensions. The developed beach area extends from the isolated Pertamina Cottages resort near the airport (south) as far as the isolated Bali Oberoi resort (north). The main north-south street is called Jl. Ngurah Rai Airport until it meets Jl. Bakung Sari about midway, where it becomes Jl. Legian; the central Jl. Bakung Sari, and Jl. Pantai Kuta just north of it, run west to the beach. The northern part of the Kuta area is called Legian. Most addresses are given in relation to the Tourist Office, the main beach (Jl. Pantai Kuta), or the larger hotels, so it may take a day or two to get oriented. The in-town bemo, for Rp 2,400 ($1.50), north to south, is the best transportation if you don't like long walks or mopeds.

Useful Information

The local **Tourist Information Office** is on Jl. Bakung Sari (tel. 0361/ 51419), in the heart of town. They're open from 8 a.m. to 4 p.m. Monday through Saturday, and offer a helpful Hotel Reservations Service that's also open on Sunday. . . . Several local **moneychangers** are open daily from 7 a.m. to 7 p.m. daily, but require a passport. (*Note:* Some won't change American Express traveler's checks because of the high incidence of forgery, though the Tourist Information Office can send you to a moneychanger who will.) . . . The **postal agent** in the tourist office will pack your souvenirs for shipping, help with Customs forms, and speed things out of the country for a nominal charge.

The **Easy Rider Travel Service** at Loji Garden, Legian (tel. 51746), offers the largest variety of group tours, rents a car and driver with guide for about Rp 40,000 ($25) a day, and books air tickets, etc. . . . The Bali Oberoi Hotel is reputed to have the best **hair salon** on Bali. . . . **Mudy's Laundry and Ironing,** on Gang Poppies off Jl. Legian, will launder all those batik shirts. . . . **St. Francis Xavier Roman Catholic Church** has services every Sunday morning. . . . The **post office** (Kantor Telepon), on Jl. Legian, is open 24 hours. Keep an eye on handbags and wallets, on the beach and particularly on the Jl. Legian strip at night. . . . If you are staying in budget accommodations without safety deposit boxes, you should stow your passport, air tickets, and extra funds or traveler's checks in safety boxes available at **Bank Panin** on Jl. Legian or at one of several moneychangers. Cost should be around Rp 500 (30¢) per day.

Accommodations

Kuta Beach is lined with such a tremendous number of lodgings that we've tried to sort out a few quiet and special ones in each price range. Since tour operators (usually from Australia) tend to book the larger hotels a year ahead, we'd recommend making a reservation at the preferred hotel's Denpasar P.O. box or street address as far in advance of the high season (mid-July to mid-September and mid-December to mid-January) as possible.

FIRST CLASS HOTELS. Our first choice is one of the world's great hotels; the others are luxury accommodations that range in price from $60 to $100, plus 16% to 21% tax and service charges. Rates are always quoted in U.S. dollars.

The **Bali Oberoi,** P.O. Box 351, Denpasar (tel. 0361/51061), has a motto —"This is how you want Bali to be"—and we couldn't agree more. It's a superbly designed hotel located about 2½ miles north of Kuta's center and a world apart from that crowded, noisy former village. Its 60 standard rooms are found in Balinese-style stone-walled, thatch-roofed lanai cottages, widely scattered across the 17 acres of landscaped grounds. Each has a queen-size four-poster bed, covered in fine Balinese batik. The spacious bath has a lovely sunken tub installed against a wall of light. The lanai porches, many facing the sea, are well furnished and designed for lounging. These rooms cost $115 for two ($92 for one), but have a quality of luxury that elevates them above any other hotel room on the island. Honeymooners and hedonists should spend $220 on one of the 13 private villas, an even more exquisite environment. Each is a stone-wall-enclosed Balinese cottage with a lush, private garden enlivened by a goldfish pond and dining terrace. The tastefully traditional room has two queen-size four-poster beds, an elegant seating area, and a heavenly bathroom. Its sunken tub sits in a private garden open to the sky; the rough-hewn stones that border it are shaded with delicate ferns.

The entire hotel, once a private club, has taken the best of indigenous and international styles and created a perfect harmony. The Bali Oberoi's pool, fed by spouting statues, sits grandly above the wide and immaculately maintained beach. A fine restaurant looks out to the sea and offers a gourmet selection of Balinese, Indonesian, and European specialties. The Oberoi has chauffeured cars and shuttle buses that wend through the rice fields back into bustling Kuta when you're ready to cope with the outside world; most guests quickly return to how they want Bali to be. However, we should point out that the ocean here is not always hospitable, with tricky currents making swimming a sometimes-risky enterprise.

The southern tip of Kuta is dominated by the 25-acre complex of **Pertamina Cottages,** P.O. Box 121, Denpasar (tel. 0361/51161): 178 deluxe rooms and eight presidential suites built in 1975 by the government-owned Pertamina Oil company. It's a deluxe resort with so little Balinese décor that it could be on Waikiki. Standard rooms with silver or gold wallpaper, velour furniture, and wall-to-wall carpeting offer all the first-class amenities and a mini-bar for just $105 per double. The executive cottages are much larger private bungalows, with separate dressing and seating areas and a pastel color scheme—good value in a suburban home away from home at $115. The Pertamina does have a great pool (though a badly eroded beach studded with concrete bulkheads), tennis and water sports facilities, Japanese and formal continental restaurants, and Kuta's only upscale disco. Although its brochure lists such past guests as Prince Gholam Reza Pahlevi of Iran, Prince Charles, and Ferdinand Marcos, the hotel's draw is frequent guest President Soeharto and Pertamina's fellow OPEC members.

More deluxe cottages in a "Holiday Inn meets Bali" style have recently been built along Legian Beach where the surfside road into downtown Kuta begins. The **Bali Intan Cottages,** at Jl. Melasti 1 (P.O. Box 1002, Legian) (tel. 0361/51770), offer first-class amenities in simple, motel-like, balconied double rooms for $63, or in larger cottages with private, planted, open-air bathing facilities for $75. A glass-sided breakfast pavilion and the Mina Seafood Restaurant are located near the large pool in dramatically planted, tropically lush grounds.

MODERATELY PRICED CHOICES. Kuta's dozens of moderately priced accommodations tend to be clustered around the central beach, the bars, clubs, and clutter. Unfortunately, the heavily trafficked beach is not cleaned often enough to keep up with its frantic sun worshippers, so we've tried to recommend some hotels a bit out of the maelstrom. Kuta's moderate hotels range in price from $25 to $45, including tax and service charges. Rates are usually quoted in U.S. dollars.

The best value of these, and a close competitor to the Bali Intan, is its neighbor, the **Legian Beach Hotel,** also on Jl. Melasti in the upper part of the strip (P.O. Box 308, Kuta) (tel. 0361/51711). Red-brick bungalows spread over a large park containing gardens and a pool; the Legian Beach's wide beach out front is equally well maintained. Standard rooms ($52 for two) are plain but comfortable, with some detailing and cool porches. Superior rooms ($58 for two, including breakfast), many with sea views, have canopied beds and feel more luxurious. Budget watchers can even enjoy the facilities by booking one of their 20 fan-cooled rooms. They're plain but have private hot-water showers and rent for $20 a single, $25 a double.

The **Natour Kuta Beach Hotel,** at Jl. Pantai Kuta 1 (P.O. Box 393, Denpasar) (tel. 0361/51361), has 36 ornately detailed brick-and-stone cottages. This is right off the central beach, but the friendly staff keep their sand broom-clean, and the spacious grounds and pleasant pool warrant mention. Through the glass-pane front walls of the sea-view bungalows you can watch fishermen in outrigger canoes transporting surfers to the far-off reef. Large bungalow rooms have first-class amenities and rent for $60 double, including a full breakfast.

The **Bali Mandira Cottages,** P.O. Box 1003, Denpasar (tel. 0361/51381), are another choice. Their 96 rooms are sheathed in typical bungalows and clustered behind a large pool and well swept beach on Jl. Padma, the north end of the Kuta strip. Plain, comfortable rooms feature a stone garden in the open-air bathroom, but many ground-floor sea-view rooms don't have windows. Check before you commit to rates of $42 to $48 for two.

Poppies Cottages, P.O. Box 378, Denpasar (tel. 0361/51059), are in the heart of Kuta madness on Gang Poppies, near the justly celebrated restaurant of the same name and a short walk to the beach. Each stylish room is an individual white stucco cottage with local furnishings and an open-air, tiled-tub bathroom/ garden. Five of their 20 cottages are air-conditioned ($43 per double) and the rest have ceiling fans that stir up a breeze from the screened windows on every side ($33 per double). Poppies Cottages also offers a densely flowering courtyard and pool, room service from their noted restaurant, and a gracious staff.

BUDGET RANGE. Kuta Beach has been on the $500-around-the-world circuit for so long that its losmen, homestays, and unregistered hostels defy census. In examining hotels priced at under Rp 35,000 ($22), including tax and service, we concentrated on the best-value beachside choices and then the cleanest of the rock-bottom hostels. If you've arrived without a reservation, it's best to check with the Kuta Tourist Information Office (tel. 51419) anyway to see if there are newer and better lodgings in town.

A Warning: We find it necessary to issue a warning to travelers staying in budget accommodations. There have been increasing numbers of reports of guests being robbed while they sleep by stealthy intruders. If there is no chain or double lock on the door, you are vulnerable. Check your valuables at the desk, if there are lock boxes, and if not, at the safety-deposit vaults of Bank Panin on Jl. Legian or at one of the moneychangers offering this service.

Set back from the south end of Jl. Bakung Sari are the pleasant and quiet **Bakung Sari Cottages,** P.O. Box 1044, Kuta Beach (tel. 0361/51868). Well-manicured grounds, neat bungalow accommodations, and a large pool with a dining pavilion form attractive budget housing. Very simple rooms with private bath and fan cost Rp 33,600 ($21) double, including breakfast. Air conditioning will cost you an additional Rp 11,200 ($7). More bungalows close to the beach are gathered at Kuta's north end.

The **Three Brothers Bungalows** are on Jl. Legian, just north of Jl. Padma (tel. 0361/22949). Bungalow rooms range from Rp 11,200 ($7) to Rp 22,400 ($14) for loft beds, cold-water showers in a private garden setting, and unscreened windows with fans. Exotic top-rupiah rooms have an upstairs bedroom with a four-poster bed draped in mosquito netting, and a garden, large bath, and white-tile living area downstairs—great value at this price.

Just south of the deluxe Bali Oberoi are clusters of spartan, private, woven-palm-leaf cottages. It's an area where rice paddies, water buffalo, and local farmers outnumber boutiques and music shops, yet it's close enough so that a 20-minute surfside walk can bring you back to Gang Poppies. The **Legian Sunset Beach Cottages,** P.O. Box 335, Denpasar (tel. 0361/51060), are typical. Clean concrete floors, thatch walls and roof, unscreened windows, private cold-water shower, and two clean sheets are yours at Rp 22,400 ($14) to Rp 12,000 ($7.50) for two. Rates depend on having a fan, proximity to the local soiled beach, and toilet facilities.

Cheaper rooms, on the main road with shared toilet facilities and sometimes no windows, can be found north along the coast.

Restaurants and Nightlife

Some of Kuta's restaurants are known for their bars, some bars for their fish and chips, most places for their clientele. Any evening out in Kuta should be preceded by a stroll down the strip to check out the latest in local nightlife. Since most restaurants have outdoor cafés and pervasive popular music, a simple dinner can evolve into a night to remember. Unless otherwise noted, restaurants mentioned are open for lunch and dinner daily.

The most luxuriously exotic evening in Kuta is one spent at the Bali Oberoi Hotel's **Kura Kura Restaurant** (tel. 51061). This dining pavilion sits in the middle of a frangipani grove just 30 feet from the pounding surf of Kuta Bay. Perimeter tables are set with china and batik under hand-painted silk parasols; inside tables overlook a carved-stone fish pond and fountain. Three evenings a week Balinese classical dance and music are performed outdoors, accompanied by an Indonesian rijsttafel for Rp 32,000 ($20) or grilled seafood buffet for Rp 28,800 ($18). The fold-out à la carte menu resembles a Sanskrit prayerbook. A meal of sop kaki (chicken and herb bouillon), ikan pappas (red snapper en papillote), or babi kecap (pork casserole with rice) and a passion-fruit parfait will run Rp 11,200 ($7) per person. Specialties include bebek betutu (whole duck steamed in banana leaf for two, to be ordered eight hours in advance) at Rp 25,000 ($15.50), keema aloo (minced curried lamb and potatoes), bouillabaisse for two, or roast quail.

The best restaurant outside the hotels is **Poppies,** on Gang Poppies off Jl. Legian (tel. 51059). It's a soothing and comfortable spot in the eye of the storm; tables are grouped under trellises draped with morning glory, and the patio is shaped into intimate dining areas by tall fruit trees. Poppies's small menu is perfectly suited to Western taste: mixed tropical drinks and imported wines; guacamole, pâté, and a variety of cold salads; shish kebab, barbecued tuna, or vegetable curry; crisp gado-gado, hamburgers, or grilled cheese and tomato on garlic bread. The dessert menu includes Balinese black-rice pudding (made with dark sticky rice, and delicious), chocolate cake, and mango pie (in season). If you have only one meal in Kuta, this should be it. A gracious mid-shopping-spree lunch should run about Rp 15,000 ($9.50); a romantic dinner with drinks starts at Rp 20,000 ($12.50). Open for breakfast at 8 a.m., and closes at 11 p.m. daily.

Another hot spot, a good bar and a spicy Mex meal is yours at **T.J.'s Restaurant** (tel. 51093), a lively Mexican restaurant located on Poppies Lane beyond the cottages and restaurant of that name. In a quiet Balinese garden with a pendopo-style seating area you can wolf down delicious back-home combo plates, chicken mole, mushroom enchiladas, nachos, or lunch specials of flautas, chimichangas, quesadillas, or tamales. The food is surprisingly authentic and quite reasonable at about Rp 13,000 ($8) for a dinner for two or a bargain Rp 1,000 (65¢) for the lunch special. When in London, try T.J.'s on Fulham High Street. Open daily for lunch, dinner, or drinks.

Among the flood of Kuta restaurants catering to strictly Western tastes, we've singled out a few for more ethnic cuisine. Few have phone numbers, so just drop in between noon and 10 p.m. The **Do Drop In** is in the northern half of the Jl. Legian strip; warm lighting, rattan, and the quietly intense crowd draw clients more than its moderately priced continental fare. One of the better Chinese restaurants in Kuta (well-to-do locals actually eat there) is **Lenny Seafood,** on Jl. Pantai Kuta. Its interesting menu features spicy shrimp with green chili, crab with black-bean sauce, or squid with sweet corn. A seafood feast for two will cost a reasonable Rp 22,400 ($14). The **Bali Indah** (tel. 51937) is another Chinese place that's less expensive than Lenny's, but on the very moped-noisy Jl. Buni Sari. Their kolo shrimp is very popular; count on paying about Rp 8,000 ($5) per person.

Kuta's super-casual day-and-night hangout in mid strip is **Warung Made,** meaning "Foodstall of No. 2 Son." This large, tiered café opens out onto Jl. Pantai Kuta for the constant show of colorful passersby. Both customers and pedestrians bring Haight Street in San Francisco to mind, but you can't beat Made's prices; most entrees are less than Rp 1,200 (75¢). Breakfast choices are the **Sri Nadi,** on Jl. Padma, where coffee and fresh croissants are ready after 7 a.m., and the **Yudit Bakery,** a much larger place on Jl. Legian, near Jl. Melasti, that serves hot meals.

When it comes to bars, Kuta's Aussie contingent dominates the scene with **Waltzing Matilda's,** on Jl. Legian Klod, and **The Anchorage,** on the same busy strip. **The Pub** is a popular multinational drinking spot on the south end of Jl. Legian at Jl. Buni Sari. It's neatly modern, tiled, and sleek, with an active bar serving burgers and snack food up front and intimate tables for getting to know new friends in back. The Pub gets going after 7 p.m. nightly except Monday. **Goa** is an Indian restaurant on the northern half of the strip where batiks, rattan, stuffed floor pillows, and a mixture of Indian and Indonesian music create a spiritual setting that lures traveling youth to congregate over beer, appetizers, and the available chess boards.

Popular discothèques spring up and close more frequently than the seasons, so just ask around when you land in town. The Pertamina Cottage's **Ayodya,** at Kuta's south end (tel. 51161), is certain to continue as Kuta's chicest for at least this generation. It's open nightly except Tuesday from about 9 p.m. to midnight, proper dress is required, and the Rp-6,400 ($4) cover charge includes one drink.

What to See and Do in Kuta Beach

The singular attraction that warrants a trip to Kuta is the film *Lempad of Bali,* shown daily at 4 p.m. at the Bali Oberoi Hotel; admission Rp 32,000 ($2). This hour-long documentary produced for the Australian Broadcasting Corporation profiles the life and work of I Gusti Nyoman Lempad, Bali's most respected artist. His death in 1978 at the age of 116 years and the subsequent cremation rituals were chronicled by filmmakers Lorne Blair and John Darling. They do an extraordinary job of educating us in the ways of the Balinese, their religion, arts, family, village life, and social customs. Lempad is seen before his last vigil waiting for the sun to rise in the northeast, the auspicious moment in life's cycle when he'd chosen to die. The fervent planning and building for his journey to heaven and the construction of a seven-roofed tower to transport his body to the cremation site are fascinating, particularly to those who've had the luck to witness one of these ceremonies during their stay. If you've never seen *Lempad of Bali*, go before you explore the rest of the island.

SHOPPING. Once you've seen the film, worked on your tan, and surfed off Ulu Watu, it's time to go shopping. Kuta's main streets, Jl. Legian and Jl. Bakung Sari, have dozens of souvenir shops that feature T-shirts with off-color messages printed on them (very popular with the Aussies at $5), but you can do better elsewhere.

The **Pasar Seni** is more a clothes than an art market and has many stalls filled with cotton batik shirts, shorts, dresses, and skirts. At Pasar Seni you can complete your summer wardrobe for about Rp 48,000 ($30), as long as you bargain things down by 35% to 50%.

On Jl. Pantai and north on Jl. Legian in Kuta, you'll find very fashionable shops where the taste of expatriate designers is behind the padded shoulder or Big Look creations. Avant-garde batik patterns on cotton and rayon, stylish fall or spring outerwear, and evening resortwear can be paid for by major credit cards, but don't let that keep you from bargaining. **Mr. T-Shirt** on Jl. Pantai Kuta sells great shirts in both long and short sleeves, starting at Rp 4,800 ($3). The Black Roots label shirts, widely available at many shops, are of particularly fine design, and cost Rp 12,800 ($8) to Rp 28,800 ($18). Naturally tanned leather handbags, summer shoes and sandals, and woven reed bags from Borneo (Kalimantan) are also good purchases.

Indonesia's bargain-priced (often pirated) tape cassettes at Rp 1,600 ($1) to Rp 4,000 ($2.50) are rampant on Bali, particularly Kuta, and free headsets are set up along the sidewalk like Sirens to lure passersby.

Ikat Art, near the tourist office on Jl. Bakung Sari (tel. 51051), sells native textiles from the entire Indonesian archipelago, but prices run dear, so bargain hard.

NUSA DUA: Nusa Dua is Bali's newest and most complete resort, one developed by the Bali Tourism Development Corporation and French consultants to handle future tourism on the island. The 2.5 million Balinese currently receive almost 300,000 visitors a year, and are planning to welcome 500,000 a year in the near future. With Sanur well developed and Kuta Beach overdeveloped, the national government decided in 1980 to plan and contain future facilities. Their strategy was to limit tourist resources to the southern tip of the island to protect the traditional culture of the Balinese. The result is the four hotels (1,200 rooms) of Nusa Dua and the cleared land and infrastructure to handle six more in a compound on the eastern coast of the Bukit Peninsula. While we applaud their motivation, they've created a truly dull place that is so removed from the local culture that you're not sure what island you're on. Suffice to say that when President Reagan agreed to attend the ASEAN summit a few years ago, this complex on Bali was chosen because its isolation made it the easiest to secure.

Useful Information

Nusa Dua is a broad roadway that winds between the four hotels that have been constructed on the Bukit Peninsula. The village of Bualu outside the main gates is the nearest sign of Balinese life. A wildly painted Jungle Bus shuttles constantly between the hotels for a fare of Rp 200 (15¢). This is the only cheap thing in Nusa Dua. Although Nusa Dua is only a few miles from Ngurah Rai Airport, the fixed taxi price is Rp 10,000 ($6.25) for an airport taxi, Rp 13,000 ($8) for an air-conditioned one. Chauffeured cars can be rented for sightseeing at $100 per day through your hotel reception. Bicycles can be rented from the hotels for Rp 2,400 ($1.50) an hour, although you're too far from anywhere to bike. The hotels have their own moneychangers, doctors on call, pharmacies, postal agents, travel agents, and hair salons.

Accommodations

All of Nusa Dua's hotels are rated five stars except for the small Hotel Bualu, originally a hotel training school that's been opened to guests interested in a water sports and diving package holiday. Rates, quoted in U.S. dollars, range from $75 to $175 for two, plus 15.5% tax and service charges. Because of their isolation guests tend to dine at the hotels, which charge considerably more than private restaurants at Sanur or Kuta Beach. However, the Nusa Dua hotels host many tour groups, and travel agents can sometimes book individual rooms at substantial discounts, particularly in the low season.

The most dramatic, and probably the best, of the four hotels is the **Nusa Dua Beach Hotel,** P.O. Box 1028, Denpasar (tel. 0361/71210), a staggering homage to Balinese style and aesthetic. There are tiered meru towers and split gates to honor the gods, pendopos, and thatch roofs, features borrowed from homes and temples throughout the island and all gathered here in rococo frenzy. Large rooms with brand-new first-class amenities each have a balcony facing the sea or the beautifully landscaped gardens. There is a sprawling pool, one of Bali's prettiest beaches, several good restaurants, tennis courts, a health center, and most persuasively, some feeling for Bali. Double rooms rent for $92 to $98 a night; singles are $10 less. The Executive Club is a special floor of larger rooms ($135 for two), with a private lounge, extra amenities, and complimentary breakfast and cocktails. The bulletproof suite modified for President Reagan rents for $1,400 a night.

At the **Bali Sol Hotel,** P.O. Box 1048, Tuban (tel. 0361/71510), elements of Balinese décor are mixed with Spanish, the influence of this flagship from Spain's Hoteles Sol International chain. The towering white pendopo lobby has a neo-Balinese mural on the ceiling; from here the sleeping wings radiate around lushly planted inner courtyards. The 490 spacious rooms are refreshingly decorated in pastels and rattan with balconies overlooking the sea and gardens; rates run $92 to $88 for two. The Bali Sol's attractive junior suites have a well-designed sleeping loft for two floating above a living room that also sleeps two; they rent for $150. Other guest comforts include a lending library, gymnasium, squash and tennis courts, and a bar beside the rambling pool.

The hotel with the least Balinese flavor is, ironically, the government-owned **Hotel Putri Bali,** P.O. Box 1, Nusa Dua (tel. 0361/71020). This large, sprawling stucco structure has little cohesive character, but rooms with first-class amenities and balconies are comfortable. The pool is quite large and it's situated on a lovely beach cove. The Putri Bali's accommodations rent for $80 to $90 for single guests, $92 to $100 for two, or $115 to $160 for the small bungalows that are spread among the gardens leading to the beach.

The 50-room **Hotel Bualu,** P.O. Box 6, Nusa Dua (tel. 0361/71310), is the smallest of Nusa Dua's hotels and one that's rarely mentioned. It's set about half a mile from the beach behind the Hotel Putri Bali, but offers all-inclusive water sports packages and horse-and-buggy transportation to the nearby waves. This former hotel training school has a young and friendly staff. Rooms are comfortable and much more casual than its neighbors; the focus here is on training in their pool for a dive, or practicing your windsurfing at the beach. The excellent in-house Bali Marine Sports offers day excursions to all the major dive spots off Bali. Room rates of $80 for two, $75 for one, include most of the gear for windsurfing, snorkeling, sailing, or surfing, with some specialized equipment and diving gear at a nominal extra charge.

Restaurants

Nusa Dua's restaurants, all in hotels, are briefly listed here. None warrants a trip to Nusa Dua from any of Bali's other communities, though hotel guests often pool cabs to try local nightspots in Sanur and Kuta Beach.

Kerta Gosa, the elegant continental cuisine restaurant at the Nusa Dua Beach Hotel (tel. 71210), is the area's prettiest choice. Cream-and-gold walls rise to a majestic frescoed ceiling inspired by the 18th-century courthouse in Klungkung in east-central Bali. Nightly except Monday from 7 to 11 p.m. Kerta Gosa offers baked Balinese lobster, king prawns in green lime sauce, or the classic Indonesian rijsttafel plus many familiar European entrees. After dining, you can work off that cream sauce by dancing to the international standards performed by their popular house band. Two can expect to pay upward of Rp 64,000 ($40); jackets or batik shirts for men are requested, and reservations are recommended.

The **Lotus Restaurant,** on the ground floor of the Bali Sol Hotel (tel. 71510), is an oasis of black bamboo furniture, reed screens, and terracotta tiles hovering over still pools of water. Cantonese seafood, meat, and poultry specialties, priced about Rp 9,600 ($6) per entree, are gracefully served in this tranquil setting. It's open nightly from 6:30 to 10:30 p.m. and reservations are recommended. The Bali Sol's French restaurant, **Pavilion** (tel. 71510), will be moved to new, more luxurious quarters by the time you arrive, but their food remains highly praised. The entrecôte of sirloin, cotelette d'agneau, or veal escalope are popular choices, all finely cooked and elegantly presented to coddled diners. Couples can dine in style for Rp 80,000 ($50) and up; Pavilion is open nightly from 6:30 to 11:30 p.m.

For casual, open-air dining on fresh seafood, try **Lumba Lumba,** by the pool at the Nusa Dua Beach Hotel (tel. 71210). Their seafood basket filled with lobster, squid, crab, shark, and shellfish is quite a feast for Rp 12,800 ($8). Lumba Lumba also has a large salad bar and a small, but good, wine list. Plan to spend Rp 20,000 ($12.50) per person and up; it's open nightly from 7 to 10:30 p.m.

4. VILLAGE LIFE: UBUD

The village of Ubud is known as an artistic community where generations of painters have lived and worked. Today the once-secret destination of world travelers has come to epitomize the True Bali Experience for tourists interested in the local culture and arts of Bali. Although thousands come on bus tours and hundreds fill the homestays (family-run guesthouses), away from its main street Ubud continues to delight with its charm. We'd urge you to allot two nights of your visit (assuming you have a week) to a quiet sojourn in this tranquil and timeless environment. Far from the waves and the sand, far from the TVs and bemos, surrounded by rice paddies and mountains, you'll be closest to the soul of Bali.

HISTORY: It is thought that Ubud was founded in the 8th century by the itinerant Hindu priest from Java, Rsi Markandeya. He erected a temple across the river from Ubud at Campuhan and then asked pilgrims to settle in neighboring Ubud. This agricultural village nestled in the fertile hills and valleys of central Bali flourished on crops of white rice, glutinous rice, and thatch grass. Ubud became the center of a prosperous kingdom bearing that name and fostered architectural, sculptural, and painted works in the region.

Tjokorde Gde Agung Sukawati (1910–1978) is the best known of Ubud's kings and the one who introduced tourism to Bali in the 1920s by inviting European artists and writers to visit his palace. Many eventually settled in Ubud and changed the face of Balinese art forever. As they spread news of this tropical paradise in Europe, interest in Bali grew enormously, but it wasn't until after World War II and the expulsion of the Japanese and Dutch that tourism finally took hold. The gentle ways of Ubud remained the choice of many expatriate settlers. Electricity arrived in 1974, the postal system in 1978, and a public telephone exchange in 1984. When the benevolent and deeply loved Tjokorde Gde Agung Sukawati died in 1978, villages throughout Bali spent one year creating art, music, dance, and ritual sculptures for a grand cremation ceremony. Today the changes that the sudden tourist boom have wrought would sadden the king responsible for it all.

ORIENTATION: Ubud has spread from a cluster of farmhouses to a bustling, commercial village stretching for several miles east west along Jl. Raya Ubud, or Main Street as it's usually called. South from the mid-section of the village near the market, runs Jl. Monkey Forest, a one-mile-long road spotted with boutiques, homestays, and cafés that ends in a not-so-interesting nutmeg grove inhabited by monkeys. At Ubud's western end is a small bridge high above a narrow ravine. On the other side, the road veers sharply north and begins the village of Campuhan (pronounced like "*Chomp*-one," but also written Tjampuhan), the rural outskirts of town and an area of many homestays and the Neka Museum.

Useful Information

Note: As of this writing, there was only one telephone in all of Ubud, hence the lack of telephone numbers in this section. Although service was said to be on the way for the entire town, we're not holding our breath.

The **Bina Wisata (Ubud Tourist Information Office)** is in the center of Main Street and is open Monday through Saturday from 8 a.m. to 7 p.m. Their volunteer staff is extremely helpful and sells the *Bali Pathfinder,* a map of the area that's very useful for walkers; it's Rp 2,000 ($1.25) and also sold at Warung Sayan on Main Street. The Tourist Office will reserve tickets for cultural performances, and help organize group transportation or book taxis for round-the-island tours for about Rp 50,000 ($31.25) per day, plus gas. They will even hold your luggage until you find a room!

Several Main Street shops rent **bicycles** for Rp 1,500 (95¢) to Rp 3,000 ($2) per day. . . . Ubud's **bemo station** is across from the Pasar (market); bemos to Denpasar run from 6 a.m. to 4 p.m. and cost Rp 600 (40¢) plus Rp 100 (7¢) per bag. . . . There are many **moneychangers** along Main Street, open from 8 a.m. to 6 p.m. daily, but no banks.

The **post office** (Kantor Pos) is on the west side of Main Street and the Perumtel Kantor Telepon in the middle. The Permutel Telephone Office on Main Street is open from 8 a.m. to 3 p.m. daily, but will not place collect calls; a new Kantor Telepon will soon open in Andong, half a mile east, and will be open 24 hours.

Ubud's **Pasar** is most active every three days when villagers from the area come in with their straw weavings, paintings, and ikat work.

By the way, it's refreshingly cool year round in Ubud, but between June and August it can drop to 55° Fahrenheit, so bring a sweater.

Getting There and Getting Around

Ubud is in south-central Bali, about an hour by bemo or taxi north of Denpasar. An air-conditioned taxi direct to Ubud from Nugurah Rai International Airport will cost Rp 30,000 ($18.75). A privately chartered bemo (organized by your hotel) from the resorts at Kuta or Sanur will cost about Rp 24,000 ($15). Public bemos depart from the Terminal Bis Ubung on Jl. Cokroaminoto in Denpasar regularly. Contact the Denpasar Tourist Information Office in the Niti Mandala Civic Centre, Jl. Raya Puputan (tel. 22387 or 23602) for schedule information; the fare is Rp 3,000 ($2).

Within Ubud, most hotels offer bemos that will take visitors up and down the two-mile-long Main Street for a minimal fee. The most pleasant way to get around the village is by foot.

ACCOMMODATIONS: Ubud's hotels are simple and rustic by demand; foreigners who sleep here want to get as far away as possible from the modern amenities they have at home. Rates are quoted in U.S. dollars unless noted in rupiah; they run from Rp 80,000 ($50) for a palace chamber to Rp 12,800 ($8) for a rice-paddy hut, all including tax and service, and most including breakfast for two as well. Our recommendations are divided by those in a more rural, quiet setting on the edge of town and by the livelier selections just off Main Street.

On the Edge of Town

A recently built complex on a hillside in Sanggingan features the best-value accommodations in Ubud. The **Ulun Ubud Cottages** P.O. Box 333, Denpasar (tel. 0361/26414, at the Tilem Gallery in Mas for reservations), are two- and three-tiered stone, thatch-roofed bungalows that march down a verdant ravine just two miles north of Ubud's Main Street. Large, Balinese-style rooms are tiled, are furnished in rattan and bamboo, and have modern attached bathrooms and porches with spectacular vistas over rice fields and the Campuhan River. At the bottom of the hillside complex is a large pool and sundeck; at the top, the reception lounge and restaurant. Ulun Ubud's isolation makes it ideal for hikers, if somewhat inconvenient for shoppers, but bemos into town are easily arranged, so don't be intimidated by the distance. Enjoy it for the views, the serenity, and the reasonable rates: $35 for a single, $50 for a double, $85 for a triple, and $110 for an entire two-story bungalow—all inclusive of breakfast brought by a "roomboy" to your veranda.

The **Ananda Cottages,** P.O. Box 205, Denpasar, are about 1¼ miles north of Ubud in Campuhan, but they are well worth the walk. Set in the middle of rice fields are some of the nicest bungalows in this area. The view from the second-floor rear rooms to Sanur and the sea more than 30 km (18 miles) away, is breathtaking. Large, open rooms of woven rattan, batik, and simple bamboo furniture renting for $40 for two, or entire two-story bungalows for families, at $65, to sleep four, are available. The Ananda has a lovely pool in its garden, hot water and modern plumbing, and a friendly, attentive staff. They are indeed very luxurious accommodations for these parts in an utterly unspoiled, natural setting.

The **Hotel Tjampuhan,** P.O. Box 15, Denpasar (tel. 0361/28871), is legendary in Ubud, being the second-oldest hotel (after the Puri Saren palace) and occupying one of the most dramatic sites in the area. The classic older thatch cottages have a faded tropical aura about them and perch on the steep side of a gorge over a rushing river, just north of the Campuhan bridge. Bedrooms and porches look out across a beautiful valley to coconut palms silhouetted on a ridge. It's a gorgeous spot and loyal guests have enjoyed the view and the sounds since after the war, when Ubud's royal family built the hotel to accommodate the overflow of foreign guests to their palace. The artist Walter Spies, a prime mover in Ubud's artistic renaissance, built a studio on the site in the early 1930s. Heiress Barbara Hutton built her friend Spies a swimming pool later in the decade and guests can still enjoy its spring-fed waters. The old-fashioned quality of the rooms—their rattan walls, sloped wood floors, ceiling fans, screened no-glass windows—ensures that regulars keep returning despite wear, tear, and minimal maintenance. Mad protests from purists accompanied the introduction of electricity in 1984, but some upkeep is due the old part of the hotel. A score of newly built rooms have the same stunning river views, but boast modern bathrooms with enclosed rock gardens, and traditional batik and bamboo décor. We would steer most travelers toward these rooms. An excellent breakfast is served by your "roomboy" on a private porch; full board is available for an additional $12 per couple. The Tjampuhan's original rooms cost $32 for a single, $42 for a double. The new larger "Agung" rooms cost $60, and the top-floor, deluxe "Raja" rooms cost $80 for one, $100 for two.

Another fine choice among recently built country lodgings is the **Ubud Inn,** located on Jl. Monkey Forest about a half mile from the center of town. Their nine tastefully appointed rooms of thatch, bamboo, and batik face rolling rice paddies or the dense Monkey Forest. Spacious accommodations with private showers and hot water between 6 a.m. and 5 p.m. rent at $29 for an upstairs double room, $23 for a ground-floor double.

Back on the road north to Campuhan, on a hill that's a few hundred yards closer than the Ananda Cottages, are the **Wisata Cottages.** This is a group of ten small bungalows in a pastoral setting, but each is clean, modern, and well maintained. Simple rooms overlook a valley of thatch grass fields and coconut trees at Rp 28,500 ($17.75) for two.

READER'S ACCOMMODATION SELECTION: "A clean losmen in Ubud was the **Happy Inn,** on Monkey Forest Road. My room had a fan, window screens, and a clean bath outside. The rate for one bed and breakfast, but no soap or towels, was Rp 4,000 ($2.50)" (Stan Mendoza, New York, N.Y.).

In Town

City living is hard to recommend in Ubud because it belies much of the charm of a Balinese life—the sounds and smells of the land, its rice paddies, fruit trees, and animals. Because the daytime bus tours, bemos, mopeds, and hawker action along Main Street can become tiresome and the nighttime motorbike parade may inhibit sound sleep, we prefer rooms a little off the beaten path. **Hans Snel's Siti Bungalows** are up on Ubud's Avenue of the Stars, a poured-concrete path opposite the Tourist Office engraved with the hands, feet, hearts, and signatures of locals and foreigners between 1979 and 1985. Five bungalows (at $35 to $45 for two) with modern, cold-water baths are very stylishly decorated with batik, terracotta, local paintings, and thatch. The bungalows are spread out on the attractive grounds, adding privacy and quiet.

Tjokorde Gde Agung Sukawati, patron of the arts and munificent "Umbrella to the Village," opened his palace to foreign guests in 1930. **Puri Saren Agung,** an unmarked classic Balinese structure opposite the Tourist office on Main Street, now has eight separate cottages with antique furnishings, excellent stone and wood-carved ornamentation, and hot-water plumbing. Two can sleep in regal comfort and be brought breakfast on a private veranda for $35 a night. The situation and the grounds are wonderful, the execution and upkeep somewhat haphazard. Room 1, nearest to the current Prince Putra Sukawati's residence, is sumptuous. Inspect other rooms before you commit to them or any of the six additional rooms in their outer court. The **Puri Saraswati,** on Main Street next to the Lotus Café, also looks like the palace it once was, but is signposted. Simple, worn bungalows on the noisier side street run $23 for two, including breakfast in their beautiful central dining pendopo. In the inner court gardens are more luxurious bungalows with décor in the palace style and newer plumbing, for $25 and $30. Here again, see a selection of rooms before you settle on one.

One of the attractions of **Kampung Ama** is living near the land, even though it's on a hill right above Main Street at the west end of town. This hotel is a collection of five bungalows surrounded by rice paddies, with views to coconut groves and the sea in the distance. Each evening kerosene lamps and candles are lit, even though electricity is available. Each bungalow is furnished with great individual style, with paintings and even dance costumes on the walls. The drinking water is from a spring, and each bath is clean and has a modern Asian toilet. Prices are a modest $15 single, $20 double, including breakfast.

The **Oka Wati Guesthouse** offers similar, simple accommodations in brick-and-stone bungalows. Head down Jl. Monkey Forest, about 300 yards off Main Street, and at the Oka Wati sign, turn right into the rice paddies. You'll find Oka Wati and much smaller homestays like **The Eustace** or **Warji Homestay.** Homestays in Ubud spring up every week and are usually two to four new rooms (with private cold-water Asian baths and clean beds) that have been built on family property. A room for two, including breakfast, usually costs Rp 15,000 ($9.50).

RESTAURANTS: One of the highlights of Ubud living is the food at **Murni's Warung,** a small restaurant perched high above the river on the bridge to Campuhan. The menu ranges from an Upper Elk Valley burger to a special Balinese feast for two that features bebek tutu (smoked duck), saffron rice, and Balinese vegetables. Walk by Murni's and order it early in the day so they'll have time to cook the duck; two can gorge themselves on the best in Bali for Rp 12,000 ($7.50). Desserts are equally fine, but don't leave the island without sampling a bottle of Murni's homemade white rice wine. The white rice wine (found only in Ubud) is less sweet than the red that's bottled commercially, and is superb with Balinese cuisine. Murni's is open six days from 8 a.m. to 10 p.m.; closed Wednesday.

    Café Lotus, a small oasis beside a flowering lotus pond on Main Street, also offers an appealing array of Western and Asian dishes. It's run by an Australian with great taste in health food, fresh salads, and ethnic favorites like chicken Kiev or samosas. Her Balinese husband has supplied the expertise in local cuisine (a fine bebek tutu if ordered in advance) and attentive service. Café Lotus's outdoor terrace, candlelit tables, mellow Muzak, white rice wine, exotic menu, and Earl Grey tea may justify prices higher than Murni's. Two can dine splendidly here for about Rp 17,600 ($11). Café Lotus is open daily except Monday from 9 a.m. to 11 p.m.

    In Kedewatan, just two miles north of Ubud (your bemo driver will know it), a new restaurant called **Kupu-Kupu Barong** is perched atop one of the most scenic ravines in Bali. Diners look out over steeply terraced rice fields and the roaring Ayung River several hundred feet below. Kupu-Kupu Barong serves Indonesian and Western dishes; the rich Balinese pumpkin soup is excellent with the teriyaki chicken, spinach and cheese crêpes, or nasi campur, a fried rice dish served with vegetables, a boiled egg and grated coconut. Kupu-Kupu is best at lunch, because of its stunning views, and will cost about Rp 18,000 ($11.25) for two. If you can't tear yourself away, the six fancy bungalows built nearby have deluxe amenities and Western prices at $115 for two. If that's too high for you (and it should be), get a taxi from Ubud to take you out, wait while you eat, and bring you back to town.

    Ubud has dozens of other dining possibilities. Dutchman Hans Snel runs the pleasant outdoor **Hans Snel Café** and bar at his Siti Bungalows off Main Street. It draws an older, more sophisticated crowd to its European cuisine. The **Beggar's Bush,** just over the Campuhan bridge, is another expatriate-owned bar and grill that's a popular hangout. On Jl. Monkey Forest we liked the casual **Bendi.** And the **Puri Snack Bar,** on Main Street near the Pasar, is a good juice stand and snackbar that serves white rice wine until 9 p.m.

CULTURAL ACTIVITIES: Ubud is a center for visual arts and its Main Street is lined with galleries. Contemporary and traditional art can be seen at two museums. The **Museum Puri Lukisan,** on Main Street west of the Tourist Office, was founded in 1953 by the artist Rudolf Bonnet and Tjokorde Gde Agung Sukawati to display the work of Balinese artists. Each of its three buildings covers a different period. Paintings executed between 1932 and World War II were influenced by Walter Spies, a German realist painter who lived and taught in Ubud. A few works by I Gusti Nyoman Lempad, considered Bali's most gifted artist, are included in the collection. Later work done under the training of Rudolf Bonnet and the more recent Academic School fills the other galleries. Open daily from 8 a.m. to 4 p.m. Admission is Rp 200 (15¢).

    The **Neka Museum** was founded by local artist Suteja Neka to exhibit the work of any artist whose subject was Bali. Located about 1¼ miles north of town on the main road of Campuhan, the collection is very well displayed in four traditional pendopos and includes six paintings by I Gusti Nyoman Lempad, several by Affandi (the celebrated modern painter from Yogyakarta), some by Walter Spies, Rudolf Bonnet, and Arnie Smit (all of whom taught in Ubud), and paintings by others including W. K. Hoefner and Antonio Blanco. Open daily from 8 a.m. to 4 p.m. Admission, Rp 200 (15¢).

The **House and Museum of Antonio Blanco** belongs to this European artist and his Balinese wife. Mr. Blanco is an extremely affable and eccentric charmer who gladly opens his home just above the Campuhan bridge to both art connoisseurs and the curious alike. He's usually home; just knock for admission.

Ubud's royal family long supported the performing arts, and the nearby village of Peliatan is famous for its **Legon Kraton Dance** group. The Tourist Office has a current schedule of almost nightly performances, but the classic legong dances and a 27-piece gamelan orchestra performing *tingklik* music usually appear on Saturday evening at 7:30 p.m. Unreserved seats in the village's theater cost Rp 3,500 ($2.25) each; it's about a 10-minute walk from the center of town, about 20 minutes from Campuhan. The entrancing Kecak (pronounced "ke-*chak*") dance is performed by 100 chanting dancers in black-and-white-checkered sarongs. Rattan chairs facing an outdoor stage lit by oil lamps fill up quickly for the Sunday-night performance, usually given at 7 p.m. by the town's farmers and merchants, in nearby Padang Tegal.

The **Mekar Sari of the Puri Kalaren Peliatan,** or Ladies Gamelan Orchestra and Dance Troup of Peliatan, is a wonderful ensemble of local women who play traditional and original gamelan music for a performance of legong dance by the village children. This is a unique show and not to be missed, every Sunday at 7:30 p.m. in the Jaba Puri Peliatan, about two miles from Ubud; admission is Rp 3,500 ($2.25). Buy tickets in Ubud at the Tourist Office or make arrangements at your hotel. Tickets include round-trip transportation from Ubud.

SHOPPING: Ubud is filled with shopping opportunities. For high-quality sarongs and *saputs* (waist scarves), necessary wear for temple ceremonies, cremations, or other traditional rituals, try Ubud's **Pasar,** a two-story collection of stalls on Main Street. Be prepared to bargain or look elsewhere, as many of the vendors have similar merchandise. Shops along Main Street or Jl. Monkey Forest offer a selection of woven goods, straw handbags, and weavings. **Jani's Place** has an excellent collection of the navy and maroon-hued double ikat weavings from Sumba and other Nusa Tenggara islands, but prices are very high. Many shops nearby sell single-weave ikat sarong fabric that is handmade in Bali and a better value.

Modern Balinese painting and new paintings of traditional subjects such as wayang figures or ancient calendars are sold widely, and are a good value. We've been assured that there are no "antique" or Lempad paintings on the market today. Other souvenirs like decorative carved-wood pieces or silver jewelry are usually cheaper at the more competitive resorts of Sanur or Kuta Beach.

5. EXPLORING THE ISLAND

The island's rich history is reflected in several temples, royal buildings, museums, and ruins that peek through the dense tropical growth, but a chance to witness the daily rhythms of life on Bali is the best excuse for any excursion to the island's interior. The elderly herding ducks to pasture, the young balancing on the steeply tiered paddy to plant rice, brightly clad women with temple offerings stacked on their heads, villages decorated with fine bamboo *penjor* banners to welcome ancestral spirits—all delight visitors with their uniquely Balinese purity.

Shoppers should look for resortwear in Kuta Beach (see Section 3), stone carving in Batubulan, silverware and jewelry in Celuk, woodcarving in Mas, and painting in Ubud, all districts discussed under the heading "Exploring South-Central Bali."

GETTING AROUND: There are so many sights that it's impossible to list them all in these pages, and equally impossible to see them all on your first trip. The island's interior mountain ranges effectively limit how much you can see in one day, so most travel agents have packaged Bali's better-known sights into several day trips. Organized tours booked by every hotel, though usually diluted by a fair amount of shopping and coffee-break time, are an effective way to see the sights. **Pacto Tours,** on Jl. Tanjung Sari, Sanur (tel. 8247), and **Nitour,** at Jl. Veteran 5 in Denpasar (tel. 24233), are reliable operators with a variety of daily guided tours by air-conditioned bus which range in cost from Rp 12,800 ($8) to Rp 16,000 ($20).

If you prefer the flexibility of a personalized itinerary, **rent a bemo** with an English-speaking driver through your hotel or a travel agent for about Rp 40,000 ($25) per day (on succeeding days you can negotiate your own "special fare" with the driver). We've organized the sights by location and proximity to the major roads, and recommend that you purchase the excellent *APA Indonesia No. 3 Bali* map. Try to group those that interest you into day trips; if you're heading out of South-Central Bali, count on about four to six sights per day. Verify the practicality of your plans with a hotel concierge or the local Tourist Information Office, and check on any special temple festivals or cremation ceremonies scheduled during your stay. Bring bottled water, cash in rupiah, a traditional waist sash and sarong if you have one, a hat, comfortable nonskid sandals or shoes, and a taste for the unexpected. But first, a word about. . . .

BALINESE ETIQUETTE: Just as their world is uniquely Balinese, so are some of the customs and rules that visitors are requested to follow. The Balinese are friendly and courteous, and welcome visitors to share in the most holy temple festivals, family events, and even cremation ceremonies. Foreign guests are expected to be unobtrusive and quiet: to watch from the sidelines and not impede the progress of a procession. At all festivities there are temple guardians dressed in white; their instructions should be followed graciously. According to custom, it is wrong to hold your head higher than a priest or a village headman; therefore, don't climb on temple walls, and stand away from (rather than in front of or over) someone kneeling in prayer. Discreet photographers are welcome to record public events, but ask first or avoid photographing someone bathing or dressed casually in their own home. The Balinese ask that women who are menstruating not enter their temples (this is at your own discretion) and that visitors wear the traditional sash or *saput* when visiting any place of worship. These beautiful batik or woven lengths of cloth are sold at every market and at many sites for only a few dollars. Those who wear sarongs to temple festivals and cremations are particularly appreciated. In general, shorts, tank tops, and revealing clothing should be confined to your hotel or the beach. Think about it: we would dress respectably while visiting a church.

EXPLORING SOUTH-CENTRAL BALI: The South and Central Bali section covers the most densely populated part of the island and will give the first-time visitor a thorough sampling of museums, shopping opportunities, colorful villages, and religious shrines. It begins at any of the south-coast hotels and heads north to the middle of the island.

Denpasar

Denpasar is Bali's crowded, urban capital and one that reflects little of the island's ubiquitous beauty. The **Pasar Raya** (main market) is at Jl. Gajah Mada and Jl. Thamrin in the center of town. In the early morning it's filled with locals vying for the best produce and flowers. Romantics can rent a *dokar* (a rustic horse-drawn cart) to sightsee in the quieter backstreets for about Rp 320 (20¢) per kilometer (30¢ a mile).

The **Museum Bali** on Jl. May Wisnu is very educational about the thriving Balinese culture and is the perfect primer for anyone heading out to explore the island as it is today. The buildings themselves are part of the collection; some, recently built red-brick galleries; others, ancient structures. The 20th-century paintings collection illustrates a wide range of indigenous styles and the influence of European artists who came in the 1930s. One of the most fascinating exhibits is the collection of household items made and decorated in extraordinary ways. Art is such an integral part of Balinese daily life that it even finds expression in such everyday items as a carved spinning wheel, intricately styled nutcrackers, even a spool for yarn carved in a figure with four arms holding the thread. Bali's carved doors are famous, but notice the carpenter's wooden tools with figurative handles and delicate cricket cages. Other rooms are devoted to cremation ceremony artifacts and another to a wonderful collection of Barong dance masks and costumes. The Museum Bali is open Tuesday through Thursday and Sunday from 8 a.m. to 2 p.m., till 11 a.m. on Friday, till 12:30 p.m. on Saturday; closed Monday. Admission is Rp 250 (15¢).

A ten-minute walk from the museum is the **Puri Pemecutan,** at Jl. Thamrin 2 (tel. 23491), palace of the late King of Badung, now a hostel for domestic tourists. It is of some interest if you want to see a typical Balinese compound. The king's family still uses the men's and women's living pavilions, saving the ceremonial and dance/gamelan pavilions for special festivities. After the hostel rooms (not worth a look, though very cheap), which enclose the first courtyard, are the clan houses for the royal family and beyond, off-limits to the public, the royal temple.

The **Werdhi Budaya Art Centre,** on Jl. Nusa Indah (tel. 22776), is a complex of open-air stages, art galleries, and parkland which opened in 1976. It is currently the home of the ASTI dance academy, the Bali conservatory, an art school, a school of traditional dance and drama, and the annual Bali Festival of Art, a celebration of Indonesian performing arts which runs from June to July (call the Tourist Information Office at 22367 or their office for schedule information).

If business makes it necessary to stay in Denpasar, overnighting at the grand **Bali Hotel,** at Jl. Veteran 3 in the heart of town (P.O. Box 3), Denpasar (tel. 0361/25681), will make it better. Built in 1929 the Bali retains a nostalgic grandeur in its huge fan-cooled lobby furnished in velvet and rattan. Huge rooms are built bungalow style around heavily planted, fragrant courtyards. Rates are in U.S. dollars: doubles with air conditioning cost $50 per night; with fan and Asian mandi, $38 a night—including breakfast and tax.

At lunch, stop for the islander's favorite, babi guling: a suckling pig cooked over coconut charcoals. Babi guling is the crisp, tasty skin, fat and tender roast pork. Babi gorengan is a combination plate of fried intestines, sliced liver, pork chitlins, and freshly ground sausage. Babi sate are moist, tender chunks of pork barbecued on a skewer. It's eaten with lombok, a green chili that's not as hot as sambal, plus nasi, sayur, and telor (rice, vegetables, and hard-boiled eggs). At **Rebo,** a tiny, casual eatery on Jl. Sesatan about ten minutes from Denpasar on the road to Kuta, a babi guling feast with a choice of beverage and fresh fruit will cost Rp 7,200 ($4.50) for two.

Batubulan

The village of Batubulan, about 4½ miles north of Denpasar, is known for its **stone carving.** Dark lava rock and limestone sculptures of temple guardians, demons, mythical animals, and local heroes line the narrow roads that lead into it. Batubulan, which means moonstone, is better known by tourists for its daily performance of the **Barong dance.** This colorful masked and costumed dance drama of good demons and evil witches will delight everyone and shouldn't be missed. Performances are given daily at the outdoor stages in the heart of town from 9 to 10 a.m.; admission is Rp 4,000 ($2.50) with first-come seating.

Celuk

Celuk, a few miles north of Batubulan, is the village known for its **silver and goldsmiths.** Since the days of the rajas, craftsmen have created ornate filigree jewelry and dishware in the traditional royal patterns, once influenced by Hindu motifs but now typically Balinese. Most goods are in silver or a combination of both metals; individual pieces sold by weight range from Rp 2,400 ($1.50) for a small ring to Rp 4,800,000 ($3,000) for a classic tea service, said to be made from a 90% silver, 10% copper alloy mined in Kalimantan.

Two paths to the left of the main road as you enter Celuk are lined with small workshops and residences where you can watch the smithing. Wayan S. is typical of many small shops, the Sura Art Shop is the oldest in town and has a large selection; most shops are open daily from 7 a.m. to 6 p.m. and will bargain down their quoted prices by about 20%.

If you're going on to Yogyakarta, you'll see a wider variety of silverwork at higher prices at Kota Gede.

Mas

Bali's center of woodcarving is Mas, a small village about six miles north of Celuk. Although there are many noted woodcarvers around the island, over generations most have congregated here. Fine artworks include religious icons, mythical beasts, natural figurines, and animals carved out of black ebony, brown hibiscus wood, or tawny cypress or satin wood. Decorative sculptures of fruit trees, flowers, animals, and household items are usually made from hibiscus and then brightly painted. At the residential compounds and workshops you can watch apprentices learn from masters how to sculpt to enhance the natural wood grain. Prices range from Rp 9,600 ($6) for a six-inch-tall meditating priest to Rp 12,000,000 ($7,500) for a four-foot-tall Rama and Sinta sculpture (bargaining is expected). Shipping to the U.S. runs about $300 per cubic yard.

The **Tantra Gallery,** open from 7 a.m. to 4 p.m., is both home and workshop, typical of many; the gallery of Ida Bagus Tilem and his father Ida Bagus Nyana, renowned local artists, features their work. The dramatic and decorative masks used in topeng dance are also made in Mas; Ida Bagus Anom is well known for this specialty, though prices can be quite high. These workshops have no formal addresses, but bemo and taxi drivers will know how to take you there.

Goa Gajah, the Elephant Cave

Traveling east from Mas to the popular elephant cave, named for the beautiful Ganesh (elephant-headed god) statue inside, you'll pass through **Bedulu,** a small town whose daily market is famous for woven straw products. Handbags, baskets made with coconut palm leaves, leather purses, and bamboo goods are displayed outdoors and sold at bargain prices. **Goa Gajah** is just half a mile west of Bedulu, and though this cave complex was built to be a religious hermitage, it was not discovered until 1923. A huge stone *kala* (demon's mouth) forms the entrance to the cave. A short tunnel lined with niches (thought to be storage space for monks' possessions while they prayed) leads to a chamber with Ganesh and three stone linggam (phallic symbols). Stone sculpture from the 9th to the 14th centuries decorates the exterior and six larger-than-life maidens spout water into the purifying bathing pools in the outer court. Open daily from 8 a.m. to 5 p.m.; admission is Rp 250 (15¢). The village of **Blahbatuh,** nearby, is noted today for its metalsmiths who turn out gamelan instruments for the island's many orchestras.

Ubud

The village of Ubud is famed for its painters. As other craftsmen have gathered in Celuk or Mas, generations of native and foreign painters have chosen to live and work in Ubud (the village and its museums are more fully described in Section 4). Just a mile from Jl. Raya Ubud (the main street) down Jl. Monkey Forest is the **Monkey Forest.** Peanuts can be purchased for about Rp 1,200 (75¢) at the gate, and as you wander in to look at the small temple in the forest, monkeys may swoop down on you to collect their lunch. This monkey forest is much tamer than the better-known one at Sangeh; it's open from 8 a.m. to 4 p.m. daily.

Tampaksiring

Tirta Empul, the temple of holy springs that draws tourists and pilgrims to this site, is 1¼ miles outside the village of Tampaksiring. Local legend tells of an evil demon king who forbade the Balinese to worship their Hindu deity. The god Indra and a troop of holy warriors were sent to earth to punish him, but the demon poisoned the well where they were drinking. Indra shot an arrow into the ground and a spring of pure water poured forth; this spring is the focus of a lovely temple thought to have been built by King Chandrabhayasingha in A.D. 960. Outside the temple are pools of sacred water fed by rows of five carved-stone spouts, and at the entrance to the complex are two larger pools of the healing waters for the local men and women to bathe in. Tirta Empul is open daily from 7 a.m. to 5 p.m., and a contribution of Rp 250 (15¢) is requested.

Above the temple is the **Presidential Summer Palace,** remodeled by the late President Soekarno from a former Dutch controller's mansion. Nearby Tampaksiring is a collection of cut-rock Buddhist tombs built by King Anak Wungsu for his concubines and his family.

EXPLORING NORTHERN BALI: Traversing the island to explore Bali's

wilder northern half is one of the most scenic trips. This route follows the eastern north-south road up to the coast, heads west to the rustic beach resort of Lovina, then comes back south on the western north-south road. Kintamani is the focus of many organized day tours, which include Penelokan, Batur, and often Celuk, Mas, and Tampaksiring on the itinerary.

Penelokan

One of Bali's most **spectacular vistas** is from Penelokan or "place for looking," about 75 km (45 miles) north of the beach resorts. From the top of a hill lined with small cafés you'll have a stunning 180° view, west across a once-verdant valley, now blanketed in lava from Mount Batur's last eruption in 1926. Due north, the light changes over the crest of **Mount Batur,** whose still-smoking summit is often shrouded in clouds. To the east, sheer cliffs frame the huge **Lake Batur** in a tremendous caldera created by volcanic activity.

On the far shore of Lake Batur is the small village of **Trunyan,** a Bali Aga settlement inhabited by an original Balinese people. Their customs predate the 9th-century arrival of Hinduism and include the display of their dead above ground, to be reclaimed by the elements. A bemo and boat trip to the shore of Trunyan can be negotiated at the Penelokan cafés for about Rp 14,400 ($9) per person round trip for the three- to four-hour excursion by adventurous travelers with their own bemo transport.

Penelokan, one of our favorite spots on the island, is at least worthy of a tea break to watch the chiaroscuro dramatics.

Batur

The mountaintop village of Batur was settled after the 1926 eruption of Mount Batur washed over its original valley homes with a wave of lava. The new and still-growing **Pura Ulun Danu Batur** temple has tall, very ornate carved gates to keep out demons, three courtyards, and an 11-roofed *meru* (tower) dedicated to the destructive mountain.

Kintamani

The nearby village of Kintamani, 1,500 meters (4,950 feet) above sea level, draws Balinese from throughout the region on market day, held every three days. Specialties from this agricultural region are the sweet oranges and passion fruit.

Singaraja

Singaraja, 80 km (50 miles) north of Denpasar, was the former capital of Bali and is still a bustling city and commercial port. The resident Dutch colonial governor's house on the central square (marked by a winged golden lion sculpture) is now used as a government building. Singaraja is known by locals for its historical library, which houses a large collection of rare Balinese manuscripts. Public bemos from the Terminal Bis Ubung on Jl. Cokroaminoto in Denpasar make the two-hour trip for Rp 1,600 ($1).

Lovina

On Bali's rugged north coast, about six miles west of Singaraja, is the village of **Kalibuk-buk** and the popular rustic resort of **Lovina Beach.** At tranquil Lovina, Bali's usual stunning landscape is reversed; the sea and Java's profile are north on the horizon while to the south are the interior mountains the Balinese revere. Lovina's white sand beach, calm sea, verdant farmland, and easy village life draw visitors who've sampled the bigger resorts and are seeking a back-to-nature holiday. You can rent a bicycle for Rp 2,400 ($1.50) a day or swim out 200 yards and snorkel ($1.50 a day for gear) at the coral reef.

The tiny homestays (the quaint name of unregistered hotels and unlicensed guesthouses) that dot the coast road have no phones or TVs, few have hot water, but most have fan-cooled private cabañas facing the sand and simple mandi bathing facilities. Thatch-roofed pavilions serve as dining room, library, and social center in the evening. The **Permata Sea View Cottages** is the local Tourist Information Office and booking central for other homestay rooms. Their beachfront bungalows rent for Rp 16,000 ($10) for two, while the ones with no views are only Rp 9,600 ($6). Other popular homestays include the Banyualit Cottages, Lila Cita Cottages, Kalibuk-buk Cottages, and Sri Homestay. Popular restaurants are the Manggala and the Harmoni.

The cheapest way to reach the village is by bemo from Denpasar to Singaraja (two hours for about $1), then by bemo to Lovina.

READER'S ACCOMMODATION SELECTION: "I rented snorkel gear and a boat for a three-hour trip to the reef for Rp 2,000 ($1.25) from my losmen, the **Susila Inn**. It was near the beach and was simple, but all set up to do your laundry outdoors, and they had a really good breakfast included for only Rp 4,000 ($2.50)" (Stanley Mendoza, New York, N.Y.).

Bali's Golf Resort

Golf spouses beware! The **Bali Handara Kosaido Country Club,** P.O. Box 324, Denpasar (tel. 0361/28866), course in Pancasari was designed by Peter Thompson Associates and claims itself "one of the world's 50 greatest." Pancasari is about an hour north of Denpasar; steep, twisting lanes, tropical jungle, and clove orchards reveal a modern hotel with panoramic views over a lake, mountains, and healthy, manicured greens. The Bali Handara Golf Course, opened by Indonesian entrepreneur Ibnu Sutowo in 1970, charges $35 (in U.S. dollars) for greens fees, $4 for the caddy's fee, and $25 for a golf cart per 18 holes; a full set of clubs and shoes can be rented for $20. Large, simple balconied rooms with all the amenities start at $75; cozy but worn cottages with a small fireplace and kitchenette cost $55 per night.

If you want to warm up first, try the nine-hole course with greens fees of Rp 19,200 ($12) at the Bali Beach Hotel in Sanur (tel. 0361/8511).

A private taxi can be rented from your south-coast hotel to Bali Handara for about $35 for six hours.

Lake Bratan

In the vicinity of beautiful Lake Bratan is Bali's small **Kebun Raya,** a botanical garden opened in 1955. Almost 322 acres of land on slopes rising to 1,450 meters (4,775 feet) have been designated for the gardens, but little except a small orchid collection (*koleksi anngrek*) is organized or labeled. It's open daily from 8 a.m. to 4:30 p.m. for an admission of Rp 200 (15¢), and is popular on weekends for local picnickers. Just north of this road is the flower market at **Candi Kuning,** a village whose central market boasts a huge assortment of flowers bought for homes, offerings, and temple shrines.

In nearby **Bedugul** is the picturesque lakeside temple known as **Pura Ulun Danu Bratan.** The temple, dedicated to Chudamani, has multiroofed meru for Brahma, Vishnu, and Siva, which are reflected in the lake's still water, but it's considered more of a resort for Indonesian tourists and Balinese students (there are several cheap losmen nearby) than a holy shrine. Along its banks are several *jukung,* outrigger canoes used for fishing. Pura Ulun Danu Bratan is open daily from 7 a.m. to 4 p.m., with a suggested contribution of Rp 250 (15¢). Several organized day tours include Bedugul on their itinerary with the Sangeh Monkey Forest and Tanah Lot.

EXPLORING EASTERN BALI: The foothills of Mount Agung descend to the shores of eastern Bali, limiting road access through this less populated area. Our mini-tour is a circular one which begins just beyond the provincial capital of Gianyar and runs counterclockwise north to Bali's greatest temple, Besakih. Klungkung and Besakih are included on many organized day tours. The other sites are most easily reached by privately chartered bemo, but are of less interest to most visitors.

Klungkung

The village of Klungkung, once the seat of a mighty Hindu kingdom, is known for the Royal Courthouse, **Kerta Gosa,** whose frescoed ceiling is one of the oldest examples of the original Balinese style of painting. Bali's original Kamasan school of painting was based on the traditional wayang theater; its rich, warm colors and elaborate religious imagery evoke the detailed painting of leather shadow puppets. Kerta Gosa's ceiling, dating from the 18th century, depicts the punishments that a criminal will undergo in hell and the rewards the innocent will receive in heaven. This painful fresco was meant to be contemplated by those awaiting trial. Besides the court, open daily from 8 a.m. to 4 p.m. for an admission of Rp 250 (15¢), there are remains of a moat and the gate of the former palace at the site. It was occupied by the Klungkung royal family until they committed suicide in the puputan massacres started by the Dutch invasion in 1908.

Nusa Penida

Off Bali's east coast in full sight of Sanur is the island where the rajas used to exile their enemies. **Nusa Penida** now welcomes skillful surfers and tourists in self-exile from modern ways. Small boats from **Kusamba,** north of Sanur, make the two-hour crossing to Nusa Penida for about Rp 3,200 ($2) per person. The island's tranquility can occasionally be sampled by private day trips leaving from Sanur, but there are rooms for rent for those who want to stay longer.

Padangbai: Ferries to Lombok

The tiny port of Padangbai (written as Padang Bay but pronounced "buy") is also simply called Padang. Padangbai is the departure point for ferries to Lombok, Bali's eastern neighbor and the beginning of the West Nusa Tenggara province. During our visit car-ferries left daily at 8 a.m. and 2 p.m. for the 3½-hour voyage to the port of Lembar. Tickets, bought at the port, cost Rp 5,000 ($3) in first class and Rp 3,600 ($2.25) in second class. Padangbai is 60 km (36 miles) east of Sanur and can be reached by public bemos from Sanur or Denpasar.

Candi Dasa

This is another coastal area that tourism officials would like to see developed as an alternative (read: budget, rustic) beach resort. **Candi Dasa,** 38 km (23 miles) east of Klungkung or 15 minutes' drive past Padangbai on the east coast, is an enclave of "Me Tarzan, You Jane" bungalows uncomfortably crowded between steep cliffs, the coast road, a picturesque lake, and the narrow beach. Its coarse-sand beach and rough surf do have devotees. The Ayuduta, Wiratha, Candi Dasa Beach Bungalows, and Ida Homestay are just a few of the many phoneless lodgings, shops, and restaurants in the area.

Balina Beach is another tiny tourist cove south of the better-developed Candi Dasa. Some 40 bungalow homestays, with rates ranging from Rp 19,200 ($12) to Rp 48,000 ($30) for a simple room, cluster along Manggis Beach, the home of the Bali Diving Center (tel. 8777 in Sanur or 021/310-3589 in Jakarta). From this beach, one-day snorkel trips at Rp 12,800 ($8) or scuba expeditions at Rp 56,000 ($35) depart for nearby reefs or Kambing Island.

Candi Dasa can be reached by public bemos from Denpasar, or by privately chartered bemos from Sanur or Kuta.

Bali Aga Villages

This area of eastern Bali has three interesting Bali Aga ("traditional Bali") villages. **Tenganan,** a few miles inland of Candi Dasa, has retained customs not practiced in other villages since the 15th-century arrival of the exiled Javanese Hindus. High walls enclose a village of weavers who turn out the famous double ikat gringseng cloth (pattern-dyed on both warp and woof threads) believed to magically protect its wearer from harm. Young boys still practice ritual dances and ceremonial battles with pandanus-leaf swords. In **Asak,** near Karangasem, the capital of this district, the rare Rejang dance and temple ceremonies are carried out in full antique regalia, including headdresses. The Bali Aga village of **Bungaya** is known for its skilled stone carvers, fabric weavers, and basket makers. These villages can be visited by privately chartered bemos or by private guided tours organized by local travel agents or through your hotel.

The Royal Bathing Pools at Tirta Gangga

North of Karangasem are the remains of a royal water palace and a temple called **Tirta Gangga,** built over holy waters said to flow from the Ganges. The lotus-filled pools can be seen daily from 8 a.m. to 5 p.m., for an admission of Rp 250 (15¢). It is most easily reached by privately chartered bemo.

Desa Besakih

The **Besakih Temple** is Bali's holiest shrine, one dedicated to Mount Agung, the island's highest at 3,142 meters (10,210 feet), and the site of pilgrimage by hundreds of thousands during the centenary Eka Dasa Rudra Festival held in 1979. Besakih is thought to have been built on the site of a rice temple dating from pre-Hindu times by Dang Hyang Markandya, a Hindu priest, in 1007. A central open court enclosed by stone walls was the holiest place, and other courtyards for various religious functions surrounded it. Of Besakih's seven compounds, the most sacred is the one housing three temples: the eastern one dedicated to Brahma, the central one to Siva, and the western one to Vishnu.

Worshippers follow ritual steps at each temple festival. After entering the split gate guarded by raksasa demons, families continued through a single gate to the inner court. East of the main temple are clan temples where members of the extended family gathered to be blessed. After taking a purifying bath, each clan brought offerings of rice cakes decorated with young coconut and flowers to the main temple, prayed, and then returned to the outer courtyards to eat.

Even when there are no specific festivals, Besakih is imposing and gives visitors a chance to observe Balinese spiritual rituals. Returning south to the coastal resorts from Desa Besakih, there is a scenic vantage point at Bukit Jambul, which means "cockscomb hill."

Besakih is one of Bali's most important sites. Several organized full-day tours depart from Sanur, Kuta, or Nusa Dua. Travelers who prefer more serendipitous outings should hire a bemo through their hotel.

EXPLORING WESTERN BALI: Bali's west coast may be the least developed for tourism but its temples at Tanah Lot and Ulu Watu, standing alone on seabound rocks off the coast, are some of the island's most unforgettable attractions.

Ulu Watu

The temple of **Pura Luhur Ulu Watu** sits on a promontory 200 meters (650 feet) tall over the Bukit peninsula, about 12 km (7¼ miles) southwest of Nusa Dua. The views south off the island's rocky coastline to the Indian Ocean are breathtaking, as is the surfing along the promontory. Legends claim that Ulu Watu's perch is the petrified ship of Dewi Danu, goddess of the sea. Others say the spot is sacred because the Hindu saint Sang Hyang Nirartha came here to achieve unity with the Supreme Being, and died peacefully. Open daily from 8 a.m. to 7 p.m.; sarongs are available at the door for those in shorts for a donation of Rp 250 (15¢).

Ulu Watu is about 45 minutes by private bemo south of Denpasar. It's most easily reached from Kuta, where a steady stream of surfers seeking its turbulent waters helps keep bemo prices competitive.

Tanah Lot

The island temple at Tanah Lot is most lovely at sunset, but dawn or midday are equally fine times to appreciate one of Bali's most beautiful sights. Tanah Lot means "hard earth" and it's said that the site was discovered in the 10th century by priests who would come to this promontory to meditate. They built a temple dedicated to the sea on a huge boulder that rises 30 yards offshore. Watersnakes that are believed to guard the temple are rumored to live in big caves below sea level. Visitors can scramble across the tide-washed rocks daily between 6 a.m. and 5 p.m.; admission is Rp 2,400 ($1.50). Go to the temple's gate at sea level for a somewhat closer view, but Tanah Lot is truly remarkable seen as a whole from the dry distance of one of the cliffside cafés.

Tanah Lot is about one hour by private bemo northwest of Kuta or Sanur, and there are several organized half-day tours there from both resorts.

Taman Ayun

The Temple of Taman Ayun is in the village of **Mengwi,** 15 km (nine miles) northwest of Denpasar. Beyond its moat is the *wantilan,* a ceremonial pendopo in the outer courtyard where cockfights (to represent a blood sacrifice to the gods) were held. Clans worshipping at Taman Ayun bring offerings of gas lamps or roast pigs to fulfill the *kaul* (pledge of giving) if prayers are answered.

The many meru (towers) here are all dedicated to the various mountains on Bali: the thatched 11-roofed meru is for Mount Agung, the tallest; then there are 9-, 7-, 5-, 3-, and 2-roofed meru for smaller mountains. Taman Ayun, one of Bali's most intriguing temples because of its architecture, faces south to the sea, rather than to the mountains, the more traditional orientation. It can be reached by private bemo or as part of a half-day tour including Tanah Lot.

Sangeh, the Monkey Forest
The Monkey Forest at Sangeh has been a stop on the tourist itinerary for so long that the monkeys have become more and more demanding, daring, and obnoxious. An otherwise attractive nutmeg forest is filled with yelping nasty critters that steal glasses, handbags, and Nikons. If your tour bus stops here, avoid it and take a beverage break.

Gilimanuk: Ferries to Java
Gilimanuk is on Bali's west coast about 135 km (80 miles) west of Denpasar. Other than a few homestay opportunities, you'll probably only pass through if you're catching a ferry to Java. Ferries to Java leave this port hourly, 24 hours a day. The 40-minute ride across the Bali Strait to Ketapang on Java's northeast coast costs Rp 400 (25¢).

6. BEYOND BALI: LOMBOK AND KOMODO ISLAND
From Denpasar you can head in almost any direction and enter a new world, the world of yet another island in the Indonesian archipelago. More adventurous travelers sometimes head east into the Nusa Tenggara chain: for the nearby island of Lombok, or for a tour to Komodo Island, home of the famous lizard of the same name. The other islands of Sumba, Sumbawa, and Flores are of lesser tourist interest, but are sometimes included on tours to Komodo Island.

LOMBOK: Lying 80 km (50 miles), just 20 minutes by air, east of Bali, Lombok has been touted in recent years as "Bali like it used to be"—without tourists, tour buses, or the hawkers who are drawn to both. We wish it were so, but alas, Lombok lacks the pleasures and cultural sights of its justly loved neighbor, Bali. It does have some fine beaches, some idyllic satellite islands, and a high mountain range popular with trekkers. There are, in fact, few tourists (26,000 in 1987), only a handful of tour buses, and a smattering of hungry hawkers.

The island is slightly smaller than Bali, with a population of over two million, most of whom are Muslims, descended from the indigenous Sasak tribe. Hindus, who emigrated from Bali 250 years ago, live in the western part of the island. Besides these two religious groups there's a category of Muslims known as "Three Times Muslims," who pray only three times a day rather than the traditional five.

Orientation
Mataram, the capital and main city, lies near the west coast in plains that quickly rise into the foothills of Mount Rinjani. **Mount Rinjani** dominates the northern part of the island and shapes the weather patterns: the western part is moist and tropical; the eastern part is dry and arid. The major points of tourist interest are within a three-hour drive of Mataram; the airport is located on the edge of town.

Useful Information
There are tourist information counters at the airport and ferry port. The main **Tourist Information Office** is located at Jl. Langko 70 (tel. 21866), in the

eastern part of the city. . . . The only places to change money are the **Bank Negara Indonesia,** on Jl. Langko (tel. 21964), near the Tourist Office, and **Bank Export-Import,** in the western Cakranegara Shopping Center on Jl. Pejanggik (tel. 21240).

Garuda Indonesia Airways is located on Jl. Langko (tel. 23762), near the Tourist Office, as is the head office of **Merpati Nusantara Airlines** (tel. 21757).

The **police station** is on Jl. Selaparang on the eastern side of town. . . . The **post office** is located at the intersection of Jl. Mayasari and Jl. Langko.

The time zone is GMT plus eight hours.

Lombok is 13 hours ahead of New York and 16 hours ahead of Los Angeles; add one hour during Daylight Savings.

The **telephone area code** for Lombok is 0364. The Kantor Telepon is in the Cakranegara Shopping Center on Jl. Selabarang, open 24 hours daily for international calls. The other telephone office is for domestic calls only.

Local travel agencies include **Satriavi Tours** at the Senggigi Beach Hotel (tel. 23883); **Swastika Tours,** on Jl. Langko (tel. 21037); and **Lombok Independent Tours,** at Jl. Bunung Kerinci 4 (tel. 23241).

The **dress code** for Lombok, like that for most of Indonesia, is more conservative than for Bali. Shorts, halter tops, or suggestive clothing are discouraged anywhere but the beach. Both men and women should wear long pants, again except at the beach.

Getting There and Getting Around

You can fly to Lombok from Bali in 20 minutes or take the ferry for 3½ hours. **Merpati Nusantara Airways** offers seven flights daily to and from Denpasar at a fare of Rp 43,000 ($27). **Garuda Indonesia** has one flight daily to and from Surabaya with a round-trip fare of $103. Merpati also flies east from Lombok, with daily flights to Bima on the island of Sumbawa, one of the points of departure for Komodo Island, and to Ende on Flores.

There are two **boats** daily from Padangbai on the east coast of Bali (about an hour north of Sanur) to Lengar, the port for Mataram, 26 km (15½ miles) west of that city. Fare is Rp 3,600 ($2.75) in second class, Rp 5,000 ($3) in first class. The journey takes 3½ hours.

A bus from the ferry into Mataram costs Rp 100 (40¢) to Rp 600 (65¢). Call the Tourist Office in Denpasar or Kuta for current schedules.

Accommodations and Dining

The best hostelry in Mataram is the **Granada Hotel,** located on Jl. Bung Karno (tel. 0364/22275), in the eastern part of the city on lushly landscaped grounds with a pool. Plain but comfortable rooms run Rp 38,000 ($23.75). The only tourist-class beach resort is the **Senggigi Beach Hotel,** on Senggigi Beach (tel. 0364/23430), on the west coast about five miles north of Mataram. Comfortable bungalows facing the beach range from $52 to $75 (quoted in U.S. dollars only) per night for a double. Water sports, a large pool, and the view of Mount Agung in distant Bali round out the resort package that attract people to this spot. More adventuresome travelers can choose among several simple losmen (guesthouses) within half a mile of the Senggigi Beach, the best of which is the **Mascot Cottages,** charging Rp 12,000 ($7.50) per night for a double. However, cases of malaria, of a strain resistant to the traditional chloroquinine treatment, have been reported here.

Lombok's cuisine is based on typical Indonesian staples of chicken and vegetables but is flavored with chiles more fiery than any others we tasted in Southeast Asia (and that places it in the nuclear chili category). The best place to sample this Sasak fare (named after the island's main ethnic group) is at **Denny Bersaudara Restaurant,** located at Jl. Pelikan 6, a ten-minute walk from the Granada Hotel. Ayam taliwang is grilled or fried chicken with local spices, and a chili sambal (hot sauce) on the side; its cousin ayam pelicing comes doused with a ground chili sauce so spicy that even a seasoned Tex-Mex veteran can't handle it. Both dishes are served with steamed rice and pecel, the local gado-gado. Milder dishes are available in the form of sates or simple ayam goreng (fried chicken). Two can feast for Rp 12,000 ($7.50).

What to See and Do

The best thing about Lombok are its **beaches.** Kuta Beach, on the south coast 54 km (33 miles) from Mataram, is a gorgeous, gracefully curving, white sand beach with rocky promontories on each end and a reef creating good surfing waves. Accommodations here consist of a few simple losmen and a *warung* (café). Rumbles of tourist development suggest some major hotels planned here, but until further notice, stay in Mataram and make a day trip.

For those seeking to get even farther away, there are three small islands on the northwest coast, **Gili Air, Gili Meno,** and **Gili Trawangan,** which offer splendid isolation with very simple accommodations. There are a few small bungalows on Gili Air, available for very little money but without modern facilities. Ask the Tourist Office in Mataram for information about visiting these islands. Local travel agents can also arrange trips, which involve a cab or bus ride, then a short boat trip to the islands.

Most day tours of Lombok cover the west coast and **Mataram** area, populated mainly by Balinese Hindus who migrated here in the 17th and 18th centuries. Any tourist would enjoy beginning the tour at the local **museum,** located on Jl. Panji Telare Negara (tel. 22159), open daily except Monday from 8 a.m. to 2 p.m. Admission is Rp 150 (10¢). Interesting displays of local handcrafts, especially the weaving of both Lombok and neighboring Sumbawa, are particularly worthwhile.

Near Mataram there are tours to the remains of the Old Hindu Kingdom, beginning with **Mayura,** a Hindu temple and "floating palace" in a small lake dating from 1744, when Lombok was a colony of the Balinese kingdom. **Narmada** is a temple and water palace complex six miles east of Mataram, dating from the same period. **Lingsar** is northwest of Narmada and has both a Hindu temple and a Muslim mosque, an accommodation to the "Three Times Muslims." Built in 1714, it is the most sacred of the Hindu temples on Lombok. **Batu Bolong** is a small temple built on the rocky coast south of Senggigi, a special place to watch the sun set over Mount Agung on Bali, visible across the straits on a clear day.

The other, and less satisfying, tours cover the south and south-central coast, with a visit to **Sukarare,** a weaving village with shops selling sarongs and ikat cloth; **Rambitan,** a traditional Sasak village; and to Lombok's **Kuta Beach.** A tour can be arranged through one of the travel agencies listed in "Useful Information."

Trekkers come to Lombok for five- or seven-day hiking tours to the peak of **Mount Rinjani,** 3,726 meters (12,200 feet) high. It's best done in the dry season (March to October) and booked through a travel agent in Mataram. Costs range from Rp 48,000 ($30) to Rp 80,000 ($50) per day.

KOMODO ISLAND: *Varanus komodensis,* once thought to be a mythical creature, is the last lizard belonging to the dinosaur family left on earth today. The Komodo dragon (as it's popularly called) is found only on Komodo, this barren 280-km² (101-square-mile) isle tucked between Sumbawa and Flores in the Nusa Tenggara island group. The green creatures grow to ten feet long and resemble alligators with bright-red, forked tongues. They are carnivorous, even eating their own kind, but are not likely to attack humans. On Komodo they are kept in a preserve; visitors are led by their tour group guides to a feeding ground where goat meat is used to draw them out.

Komodo Island can only be reached by boat and offers only primitive ac-commodations. It's advisable to make your dragon safari by guided tour, and many leave on three-day packages from Denpasar. On Bali, both **Natrabu,** at Jl. Seruni 21 (tel. 5448), and **Tunas Indonesia,** at the Hotel Bali Beach (tel. 8511) or at Pertamina Cottages (tel. 6961), offer adventure tours to Komodo Island. **Garuda Indonesia Airlines** (tel. 27825 in Denpasar) offers a four-day package from Bima, Sumbawa, for $295.

CHAPTER X

INDONESIA OFF THE BEATEN PATH

□ □ □

1. NORTH SUMATRA AND LAKE TOBA
2. WEST SUMATRA, LAND OF THE MINANGKABAU
3. SOUTH SULAWESI: TANA TORAJA
4. IRIAN JAYA, STONE AGE TRIBES OF THE BALIEM VALLEY

In Indonesia, traveling "off the beaten path" through *any* province is an opportunity to meet its indigenous peoples, each with their own language, art, religion, and culture. Here, we've focused on four ethnic groups whose homelands are accessible by guided tour or, for the spirited traveler with time and patience, by independent means. The once-fierce Bataks around North Sumatra's scenic Lake Toba, the Minangkabau's matriarchal society in West Sumatra, the buffalo-worshipping Torajanese in South Sulawesi, and the primitive tribes settled in the highlands of Irian Jaya represent citizens of a country encompassing 13,677 islands. That they are unified politically, socially, and by a second, common language is one of the greatest achievements of the new Republic.

You'll be exploring provinces outside of Java and Bali, where the tourist infrastructure is not as well established. Transportation to the hinterlands can be unreliable, slow, and difficult. Overland transportation is usually by bus, Jeep, or private plane, and weather delays are common. Less developed communications systems mean that long-distance telephone and telegraph services are often difficult, though rarely impossible. Tourist accommodations may be limited and with a few exceptions are very basic. Credit cards are almost unheard-of.

But it's everything that's not there that makes traveling off the beaten path an adventure. Removing the safety net of service developed for mass tourism makes the modern-day explorer more self-reliant, and usually brings him or her into closer contact with the local populace. To us, all this adds up to a more genuine and culturally interesting journey. Travel in Indonesia is, after all, a cultural adventure, and if you're willing to put up with a little hardship you'll find Indonesians, in their all their diversity, ready to welcome you.

1. NORTH SUMATRA AND LAKE TOBA

The prosperous and fertile province of North Sumatra (Sumatera Utara) has a population of 9,500,000 spread over 70,000 km² (25,000 square miles). Ironically, the standard of living seems markedly lower than on overcrowded Java, seat

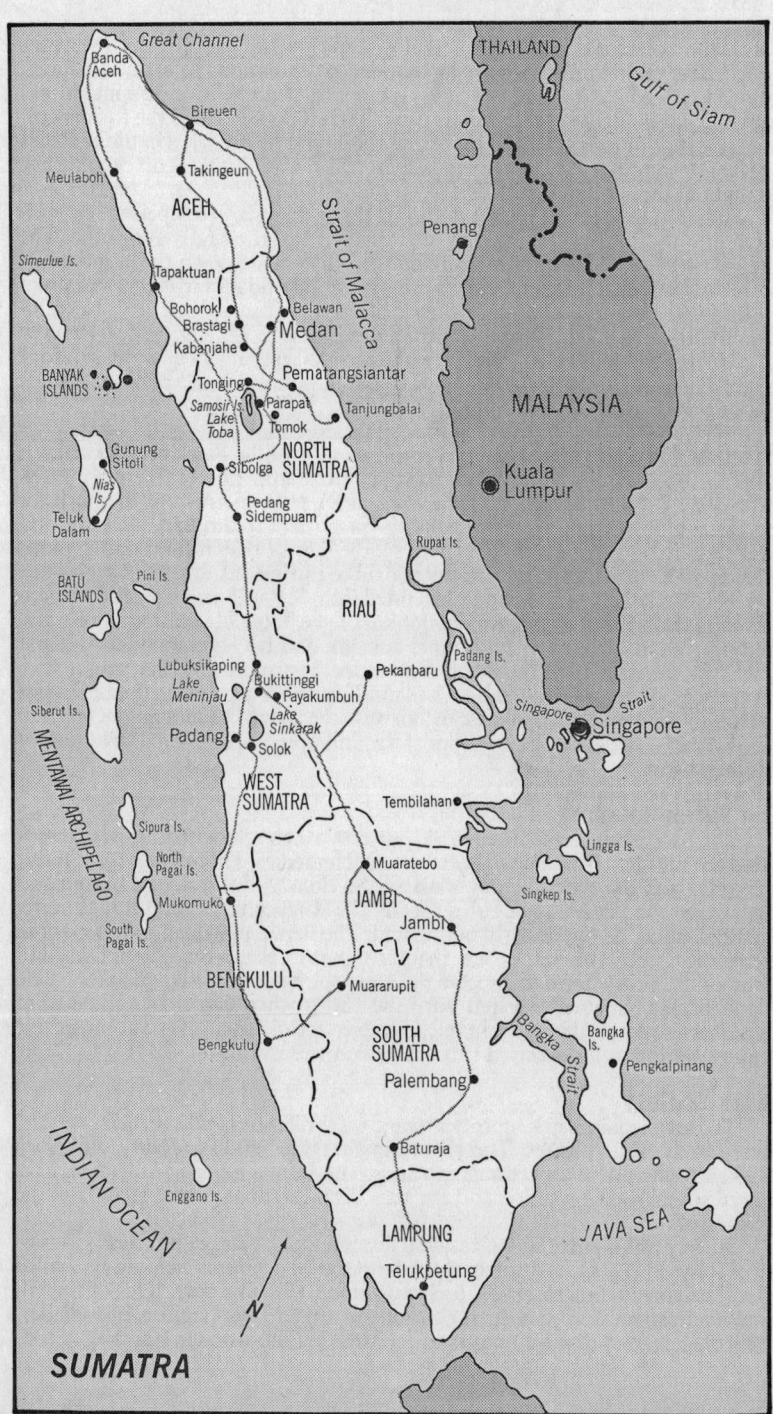

SUMATRA

of the central government. The complaint since independence has been that Sumatra, the country's breadbasket, shares disproportionately in the country's wealth. The capital city, Medan, surrounded by thousands of acres of rubber, palm, and cocoa plantations, is a busy commercial center with a thriving port at nearby Belawan, 26 km (15½ miles) away. In the hills beyond is the former colonial resort of Brastagi. Lake Toba, one of the largest inland lakes in the world, is a lovely, tranquil resort area inhabited by the native Batak peoples who live throughout the central highlands.

Sumatra, the second-largest island in the Indonesian archipelago, extends north into the Indian Ocean, west of and parallel to the Malay Peninsula. The Bukit Barisan or "Marching Mountains" literally parade down the island creating heavily wooded jungles, verdant rain forests, abundant birdlife, a variety of wildlife, and great scenic beauty in their trail. Sumatra's varied terrain causes temperatures to range from 70° to 90° Fahrenheit (21° to 33° Centigrade). December to March are the wettest months, while June to September constitutes the dry season. The cool climate at Lake Toba makes it popular with vacationers from Malaysia and Singapore year round.

THE BATAK CULTURE: *"Horas"* is the greeting of the Batak peoples in Tano Batak, or Batakland, the most interesting cultural attraction of the region. Unfortunately for the traveler, centuries of zealous missionaries and the push for modernization have almost eliminated the practice of traditional Batak arts and rituals. Only odd wooden houses with saddle-shaped thatch roofs and copious legends of the Batak warriors' cruelty remain to intrigue us.

The Bataks believe they were descended from Si Raja Batak, a legendary hero born on Pusuk Buhit mountain overlooking Lake Toba. He created the Bataks' guiding system of *adat,* or traditional custom, and his sons founded the first clans. Scholars think that the Bataks descended from a proto-Malay people who left the region around the present Thailand-Burma border during the onslaught of Mongol raiders. The Torajanese in Sulawesi, the Dayak in Kalimantan, tribes in the Moluccas, and even certain tribes of the Philippines are believed to be part of this migration.

The Batak Religion

The Batak script is recorded in old *pustaha,* bark books with intricate carved-wood covers, filled with magic rites and herbal remedies. The *tarombo* is the Batak holy book and describes Debata Mulajadi Na Bolon, the creator of heaven and earth. As Silaon Na Bolon he ruled the middle kingdom of man and as Pane Na Bolon he ruled the underworld of the dead. The Bataks practiced animism (note the reptile, insect, and bird images that recur in the designs on their houses) and many of the rituals were to appease the *begu,* spirits of deceased ancestors. The inland Bataks remained isolated until the 1800s when Christian and Muslim missionaries ventured into the jungle to convert them. Their efforts among these democratic and well-organized tribes were very successful.

Batak Society

The seven main Batak subtribes have great similarities yet have their own dialects, rituals, and cultures. The Karo, Simalungan, Pak-Pak (Dairi), and Toba Bataks settled around the central highlands. The Mandailing and Angkola Bataks moved south in the province, and the Nias Bataks settled on Nias Island, off the west coast.

Society was divided into clans who lived in *hutas,* village units with kings or tribal chiefs in charge. To protect against other tribes, villages were always walled in and usually had ramparts or ditches around them. On both sides of the village's main street were *jabu* (peaked-roof houses) and *sopo* (similar, but smaller, rice-storage barns) that are unique to the Bataks. Each wooden building is constructed without nails and is ornately carved with red, black, and white reliefs. Houses are windowless, raised on stilts, and entrance is through a trapdoor; this protected them from enemy attack, provided a waste outlet in case of danger outside, and created a sheltered area to raise chickens and pigs. Inside, the open space was divided by mats and woven curtains into private "rooms."

Each village had a communal hall where social and political problems could be aired before the chief. Adat dictated severe punishment for certain crimes, thus the Bataks' reputation for cruelty. A conviction for incest condemned practitioners to be eaten by their fellow villagers, although only small amounts of flesh were consumed out of wrath, not hunger. Captors often ate certain body parts and drank the blood of prisoners of war, particularly the fiercest fighters, whose blood was thought to impart bravery. This treatment was also accorded to traitors, but while they were still alive. Grave offenses such as adultery with the king's wife would garner the dreaded *di siraasoman,* the rite of pouring lime and salt into a victim's wounds and leaving him in the sun to die.

The earliest missionaries were astonished to find such a codified adat, an organized agricultural industry, and a democracy among people still practicing ritual cannibalism. Batak arts were also well developed; the region's males are still noted singers and musicians throughout Indonesia. Unfortunately, unlike South Sulawesi, where the Toranjanese continue to build unique homes and practice traditional rituals, the culture of Batakland is seen only in museums, occasional performances for tour groups, and ornately carved houses. Our tour of North Sumatra includes a few Batak villages and a brief respite from the heat of travel on Samosir Island in Lake Toba.

EXPLORING NORTH SUMATRA: Medan, the provincial capital, is a necessary stop on the way south to the resort of Lake Toba. Animal lovers should make a day trip north to the Bohorok Orang Utan Preserve, world famous for its work in repatriating orangutans to their native habitat. The Batak culture, its tribes spread through the central highlands and clustered around Lake Toba, can best be studied on the journey south from Medan to Parapat, the port from which boats sail to Lake Toba.

Getting There

Medan's **Polonia Airport** is a bustling international gateway. The Medan to Kuala Lumpur route is serviced daily by MAS and twice weekly by Garuda; to Amsterdam, twice weekly by KLM; and to Singapore, four times weekly by Singapore Airlines or daily by Garuda. Garuda Indonesia flies domestically to Padang (West Sumatra) or Ujung Pandang (South Sulawesi) daily, twice daily to Denpasar via Jakarta, and five times daily to Jakarta. Porters in bright-yellow coveralls buzz around both terminals waiting to pounce on your luggage (tip about Rp 300, or 20¢, per bag).

There is also regular **ferry service** from Belawan, the port of Medan, to Penang, Malaysia. Call **Eka Sukma Wisata Tour and Travel** (tel. 51562) for information about their cruise ships; the overnight journey costs about Rp 160,000 ($100).

From Medan, there are several long-distance **bus** companies that traverse the island and head for Jakarta (see "Trans-Sumatra Overland"). **ALS** (tel. 22014) was one of the better ones at our visit; check the Tourist Information Office for their current recommendation or ask your hotel concierge. The buses meet the hourly car-ferry from Bakauheni to Merak on Java; the 72-hour expedition will cost about Rp 46,000 ($28.75), plus much wear and tear on your body.

Getting Around

The closer you are to Medan, the easier the transportation. The hinterlands are best served by local buses, but their difficult-to-determine and infrequent schedules make planning your trip rather difficult. Between major tourist destinations there are frequent, reliable, but slow, long-distance buses. The train line running from Medan through the eastern part of North Sumatra goes as far as Pematangsiantar (P. Siantar) on the way to Lake Toba. Since you have to catch a local bus from there, it makes more sense to make the entire journey to Lake Toba by bus.

BY PRIVATE TOUR. Several Indonesian tour operators offer four- or five-day North Sumatra–Batak Tours that stop in Medan, Brastagi, and Parapat. Contact **Pacto Ltd.**, at Jl. Palang Merah 26F, Medan (tel. 061/513-669); or **Garuda Indonesia Holidays,** c/o Nitour Inc., Jl. H. M. Yamin SH21-E, Medan (tel. 061/513-074). Packages range from Rp 208,000 ($130) to Rp 320,000 ($200) per person on a twin sharing basis.

BY TAXI OR CHAUFFEURED CAR. If you arrive at Medan's Polonia Airport you can catch a fixed-fee taxi into Medan for Rp 4,000 ($2.50), drive two hours to Brastagi for Rp 32,000 ($20), or three hours direct to Parapat on the Toba shore for Rp 56,000 ($35). **Pacto Ltd. Tour and Travel Service** (tel. 513-669) is one of many that can arrange a car and driver (with or without guide) for any of these journeys, although a taxi is usually cheaper.

BY BUS. The **Sutra Bus Company** on Jl. Iskandar Muda in Pasar Pringgan has buses to Brastagi every hour between 8 a.m. and 7 p.m. The scenic three-hour ride will cost Rp 1,150 (70¢). To Parapat and Lake Toba there are several options. The **Bintang Utara** and **Medan Raya** bus companies, both on Jl. Sisingamangaraja near the Great Mosque, have hourly departures between 7 a.m. and 6:30 p.m. daily. The four-hour ride costs about Rp 22,000 ($1.50). Only public buses go to the Bohorok Orang Utan Preserve. Two buses leave the Terminal Bis Sei Wampu daily for the five-hour trip, at Rp 1,280 (80¢), but taking either requires an overnight at the reserve. An exciting alternative is a bus and river-rafting day trip offered by **Sobek Expeditions** with Pacto Ltd. Tours (tel. 510-081); these trips run once a week and cost Rp 120,000 ($75) including transportation, guide services, lunch, and admission fees.

MEDAN: Before heading out to explore North Sumatra, most travelers will have to pass through Medan. North Sumatra's capital city is a thriving commercial center with a negligible tourism industry. The brusqueness of its inhabitants and the difficulty of making travel plans ensure that it will remain that way. Visitors interested in the Batak culture should pay a brief visit to the Museum Sumatera Utara and then catch the next bus (or preferably rent a chauffeured car) out of town.

Orientation

The city was founded in 1590 on a low, broad plain cut by the Deli River, which still snakes through the central part of this urban sprawl. Medan (named after the holy city of Medina) was the battleground of sultans until the Deli sultanate was subjugated by the Emperor of Aceh. Its **Great Mosque (Mesjid Raya),** built in 1906 on Jl. Sisingamangaraja, is an elegant reminder of its former power. The mosque's keyhole arches are derived from Turkish Islamic style, its ornate carving from India, and its stained glass and marble columns from the Middle East. Across from it on Jl. Brigjend. Katamso is the landmark **Maimoon Palace,** a Victorian Arabic-style wooden palace painted yellow and gray. Both restored buildings (open from 9 a.m. to 5 p.m. six days, until 1 p.m. on Friday) were built in the late 1800s by Sultan Makmun Alrasyid Perkasa Alamsyah and form the core of the older city.

In 1870 the Dutch designated Medan the capital of Sumatra Oostkust and installed hand-picked local officials to manage their nearby plantations. The city hall (ca. 1908) and tile-roofed post office (dating from 1911) on Jl. Balai Kota are on the eastern side of the city at the manicured **Merdeka Square.** With the imposing Bank Exspor Impor across the square they form the core of the business and government area. The daily **Pasar** (market) is on Jl. Perniagaan, off the square; it becomes a festival of foodstalls after 7 p.m., as does the **Pasar Malam.**

The **Museum Sumatra Utara** is at Jl. H. M. Joni 51, north of city hall between the two forks of the river. The displays on the Batak tribes include *pustaha,* books in bark about the tribes' magic and herbal medicine rites; ornately carved-wood housewares; musical instruments; costumes for the *hoda-hoda* dance; and a representative collection of local weaving. The museum is open Tuesday through Thursday and Sunday from 9 a.m. to 2:30 p.m., till 11 a.m. on Friday, and till 1:30 p.m. on Saturday; closed Monday. Admission is Rp 150 (10¢).

Several hotels are located in this area but transportation is widely scattered. The bus station north to the Orang Utan Preserve at Bohorok is at the north end of the city on Jl. Sei Wampu; the bus terminal to Parapat and Lake Toba is on the south end of town and Polonia International Airport is only 1¼ miles west of the city. The **Medan Trade Fair** is held annually at the Taman Ria fairgrounds on Jl. Gatot Subroto in the northeast part of the city. During the trade fair from March to May, cultural performances are held at traditionally designed pavilions next to the fairgrounds; the rest of the year this area becomes an after-dark amusement park.

Useful Information

The **Medan Dinas Pariwisata (Tourist Office)** is at Jl. Palang Merah 66 (tel. 061/511-101), open Sunday through Thursday from 8 a.m. to 2:30 p.m., till noon on Friday, and till 2 p.m. on Saturday. At Polonia Airport there is a Hotel Desk in the Domestic Terminal and a Tourist Information Office in the International Terminal nearby (but it's only open to meet international arrivals).

In case of **emergency,** call 110 or the **police** at 521-379. The **telephone area code** for Medan is 061; for Lake Toba, it's 0664.

The office of the **U.S. Consul General** is located at Jl. Imam Bonjol 13 (tel. 061/322-200).

The **Garuda Indonesia** office is at Jl. Lt. Jend. Suprapto 2 N/O (tel. 25700). . . . **Pacto Ltd. Tours,** Jl. Palang Merch 26F (tel. 513-669), offer one- to eight-day river-rafting trips, with the American Sobek Expeditions, along the Alas and Wampu Rivers ($75 to $975) through North Sumatra. All the larger hotels will store your luggage while you venture out into the jungles.

The **Bank Exspor Impor,** off Merdeka Square, is open till 5 p.m. . . . The **Kantor Pos** is opposite it and the **Kantor Telepon** is on Jl. Printis Kemerdekan (open 24 hours).

Sumatra time is Greenwich Mean Time plus seven hours.

Sumatra is 12 hours ahead of New York and 15 hours ahead of Los Angeles; add one hour during Daylight Savings.

Getting Around Medan

Within Medan you'll need wheels for sightseeing. Pedal becaks average Rp 500 (30¢) a trip and motorized ones about twice that. One-way taxi fares are fixed at Rp 4,000 ($2.50), but you can rent a car for sightseeing by the hour—at Rp 6,000 ($3.75) per hour with a two-hour minimum—and tour the city in about three hours.

Accommodations

Overall, North Sumatra hotels are inexpensive (our selections range from $74 to $10 for two; prices for first-class hotels are quoted in U.S. dollars and include tax and service charges) and fairly well maintained. Vinyl-covered, flower-print headboards, little décor, and tubs with Danish showers are common. To the ire of single travelers, many hotels charge the same rate (including breakfast) for one or two people in the room. The only high season is late January or early February, during the Chinese New Year, when tourists from Singapore and Malaysia come in droves. At any other time of year you can just call ahead or show up, although you may be out of luck at the deluxe hotels if one of the "Sumatra Overland" tours from Holland has arrived.

The top hotel in town is the **Hotel Tiara Medan,** on Jl. C. Mutiah (tel. 061/516-000), not far from the Great Mosque. Rooms are modern with Sumatran décor; there's a nice swimming pool, Medan's best European restaurant, and a capable and eager staff. Double rooms cost $74, but there are two tiny "economy" studios per floor where a full-size bed, sleeping one or two, rents for $29.

Families would have more fun at the **Hotel Danau Toba Internasional,** located near the mosque at Jl. Imam Bonjol 17 (tel. 061/327-000). The hotel is older than the Tiara, but the pool is large and lively, and a mini-golf course is next door. Rooms are modern though showing their age; doubles range from $58 to $75, depending on floor and level of luxury.

Another good choice in the heart of town is the **Hotel Dharma Deli Natour,** at Jl. Balai Kota 2 (tel. 061/327-011). The lobby and older wing were once the Dutch-style Hotel De Boer, recently renovated but still retaining a charming old-world feel. Attached motel rooms with large verandas next to the pool cost $24. The newer eight-story wing offers good rooms for $55 (a better value) to $60 for two. The Dharma Deli's restaurant serves an authentic Melayu buffet of very spicy Indonesian food with local chile sauces at lunch (daily except Sunday) for only Rp 4,000 ($2.50).

The **Polonia Hotel,** at Jl. Sudirman 14 (tel. 061/325-300), is another modern choice with large, comfortable, though worn rooms from $29 to $34. The best value are the corner rooms in the B wing: half moon in shape, a round double bed, brightly decorated, and windows on every side for $29.

The best budget accommodation is the **Hotel Sumatra,** located at Jl. Sisingamangaraja 21 (tel. 061/24973), near the long-distance bus company offices. The Sumatra's 56 worn but friendly rooms, each with cold-water mandi and Asian toilet, open onto a cool dark courtyard. Air-conditioned quarters cost Rp 25,000 ($15.50) for two; fan-cooled rooms with common bath range from Rp 15,000 ($9.50) to Rp 24,000 ($15). The rooms on the higher floors help dull the street roar below.

Dining

Indonesia's third-largest city hosts business people and expatriates year round, so international-style restaurants are the norm.

The **Tip Top Café,** at Jl. Jend A. Yani 92 (tel. 24442), is an old-fashioned luncheonette that's very popular for its inexpensive Dutch, continental, Chinese, and Indonesian meals. A varied menu of steaks, salads, noodle and rice dishes, and scrumptious ice-cream extravaganzas will cost about Rp 5,400 ($3.50) per person.

The Tip Top is open daily from 11 a.m. to 2 p.m. and 5 to 10 p.m. A dressed-up version is **Lyn's Café,** down the block at no. 98 (tel. 518-367). Locals and Westerners huddle together over Chinese chicken with sweet corn, and T-bone steaks and belimbing (star fruit) juice, while the sound system pumps out kitschy 1950s music at a discreet volume. Lyn's corn ice cream was a new one to us, and quite tasty! It's open from 11 a.m. to 11 p.m. daily.

A Day Trip to Visit Orangutans

The **Orang Utan Rehabilitation Center** opened in 1976 in the wilds at Bukit Lawang, Bohorok, and has since returned more than 100 *orang utans* (an

Indonesian word meaning "people of the forest") to the wild. About 150 orang-utans from around the world are currently in residence.

The rehabilitation program works in stages. Orangutans spend their first six months at the center being cared for and trained in cages, then roam free for two to three years in the preserve where they are fed bananas and milk twice daily. When the gamekeepers feel they're ready for independence, they are taken in backpacks and released several days' walk away. Our guide, who once accompanied them, claimed the freed orangutans started wailing like children in an attempt to rejoin their keepers.

Visitors can watch the feeding at 8 a.m. and 3 p.m. after obtaining a permit from the Bohorok office (passport required). A preserve guide will lead you on a challenging 1½-mile hike into the jungle and over a river to the treehouse feeding station. The preserve's lush setting, myriad birds, and other monkeys create a dramatic backdrop for camping. A campground by the roaring Bohorok River is free of charge with tents and mattresses available from the park office for Rp 6,500 ($4) per day; simple bungalows with shared cold-water facilities are also available for the same price. From Bohorok, visitors can hire local guides, for about Rp 20,000 ($12.50) per day plus expenses, to backpack into the jungle, or even hike to Brastagi in three days for about Rp 20,800 ($13) per person, including all provisions.

BRASTAGI AND THE BATAK HIGHLANDS: The road south from
Medan provides a firsthand look at the region's agricultural wealth. The blacktop winds through thousands of acres of sugar palms, cultivated for cane sugar and palm oil. Goodyear logos announce thousands more acres of rubber plantations, producing one of the province's biggest exports since colonial times. Papaya groves, vegetable farms, and coffee and tea plantations provide shade and interest along the drive. On the way to Brastagi, check out the many roadside stalls selling dodol, a locally made sweetcake of rice and red-palm sugar.

Brastagi
The former Dutch hill station of Brastagi has become modernized in recent years by the influx of weekend Medanites. From the scenic overlook called Gundaling the burgeoning village of 5,000 is surrounded by the spires of Christian churches. Although in the midst of the Karo Batak highlands, most Brastagi residents were long ago converted to Christianity by missionaries. We mention Brastagi because group tours usually stop there overnight on the way to Lake Toba, and hikers sometimes enjoy a night or two in this tranquil setting.

Brastagi Cottages, located on the hill above town (tel. 061/526-876 in Medan or 76 in Brastagi), is one of the many newer, simple resort complexes that dot the hillsides.

The restored colonial-era **Bukit Kubu Hotel** is in the heart of the village at Jl. Sempurna 2 (tel. 061/519-636 in Medan or 0628/20832 in Brastagi). Its manicured lawns, golf course, and fields of flowers have been held in high regard since 1939. Rooms have simple décor but very high ceilings, verandas, and rattan; Room 10, with a shared bath and a fabulous view over the valley, was our favorite. Rates range from Rp 22,000 ($13.75) to Rp 35,000 ($22), depending on facilities. The Bukit Kubu, fully booked most weekends, also arranges horseback riding, tennis, and hiking. If you don't have the time to stay overnight, stop for tea in front of their fireplace.

READERS' ACCOMMODATIONS SELECTION: "On the way back to Medan by tour bus, we spent a night at Brastagi at the **Danau Toba Cottage** hotel—lovely, good food, traditional dancing. We viewed two volcanoes from the hotel, Sinabung and Sibayah" (Jean and Tony Triumpho, Canajoharie, N.Y.).

The Batak Highlands

South of Brastagi, 2¾ miles from Kabanjahe, is the Karo village of **Lingga.** In the center of this tiny village of modern-day shanties is a towering peaked-roof Batak house belonging to the late King Simulingga. The house, thought to date from the 1500s, is built entirely of peg-and-beam construction. The geometric black, white, yellow, and red matting that decorates the building is detailed with an abstract reptile pattern in woven rope, a typical Karo Batak motif.

If you're not traveling with a guide, villagers will show you around inside. Up to ten families, the relatives of royalty, once lived here. The smaller green-and-white house nearby was used by the village's young men to keep them separated from unmarried women, who moved to their husbands' homes after marriage. In the front of the village is a *geriten,* a "skeleton place," where the bodies of the village wise men were kept in a coffin for up to three years after death. When their flesh deteriorated, the bones were cleaned off, packed in small boxes, and stored in the top floor of this structure in reverence.

The vistas of dense rain forests and broad valleys and hills unfolds as you approach Lake Toba. Above Tonging on the north shore of the lake is **Si Piso Piso,** a 370-foot-tall waterfall that crashes down from the altitude of the main road and wends its way to the lake. From Tonging there is a local ferryboat that makes the two-hour trip to Samosir island, seen in the lake to the southwest.

The traditional Batak rumah bolon, or long house, is a restored 350-year-old palace of the Simalungun Batak King Pangultapultap. The **Istana Rajah Pematang Purba,** as it's officially known, is the last of 22 buildings that formed the royal compound; the others were destroyed in a local antifeudal movement in 1947. The son of the last Simalungun king (in full Batak regalia typical of court costume for ceremonial occasions) now guides tourists through the house.

His father, 12th king in this dynasty, was known to have 27 wives and reportedly used herbal potency drugs. When you visit the rumah bolon, make sure to spend some time with its fascinating keeper! It's open daily from 8 a.m. to 7 p.m.; a donation of Rp 600 (35¢) is appropriate. If your visit coincides with that of a large tour group you may see the *torta sumba* performed. Dancers in woven blue sarongs with jackets and chest sashes, all in peaked pirate-like Batak hats, bow to the king and then perform a classical Batak dance.

The bustling city of Pematangsiantar (or P. Siantar to the locals) is the last major town and the end of the train line on the road to Parapat, gateway to Lake Toba.

LAKE TOBA AND SAMOSIR ISLAND:

Ferries ply the still waters of Lake Toba from the resort village of Parapat to Samosir Island, bringing Batak women carrying vegetables and supplies, old men delivering motorbikes, and foreigners in hiking boots. Toba has long been popular, particularly with Europeans, for its scenic beauty, excellent swimming, cool climate, and tranquil ambience. However, the area's scenic beauty has recently been marred by the construction of the Asahan Hydroelectric Plant downstream, which has caused the lake level to sink by six feet, leaving many once "lakeside" hotels with a beach of mud. It's still a dramatic setting with cheap accommodations, few phones, and plenty of hiking, but if you're looking for swimming and sun, you'll do better in Bali.

Danau Toba is one of the largest and highest lakes in the world (it's 52 miles long by 18½ miles wide, and almost 2,800 feet above sea level), bordered by the dense pine and tropical forest at the foothills of the Bukit Barisan range. Scientists believe that it's the caldera formed by a prehistoric volcanic eruption, and that the 627 km² (225 square miles) of Samosir, a scrubby isle covered in pampas grass, is the peak of the former volcano. Visitors looking for more modern amenities may prefer to stay in Parapat on the shore, and see Samosir and its Batak villages on a day trip.

Parapat

The little traffic, narrow streets, and souvenir shops of Parapat reminded us of a small Mediterranean port town. Since Samosir Island offers very few services, most travelers will find themselves returning to Parapat for more information, cash, toiletries, phone calls, etc.

USEFUL INFORMATION. The main business street, **Jl. Sisingamangaraja** (S.M. Raja for short), runs roughly along the Toba shore. A pharmacy, hospital (the Rumah Sakit, about 1½ miles from town), most restaurants, the Kantor Pos, police, and several travel agents are on this street. Inland, the small Parapat peninsula forms a cove encircled by the hotel strip, **Jl. Pulau Samosir.** At its end is the Market Tigaraja ferryboat pier.

The helpful **Tourist Information Office** is at Jl. Pulau Samosir 1, under the Batak welcome Gate at the intersection. They're open daily from 8 a.m. to 8:30 p.m. and have good maps. . . . The **telephone area code** for Parapat and Samosir Island is 0664, and the only **Kantor Telepon** is inland on Jl. Josep Sinaga. . . . There are no banks in Parapat, but the **post office** (open from 8 a.m. to 2 p.m. Monday through Thursday, till 11 a.m. on Friday, and till noon on Saturday) and travel agents (open from 8 a.m. to 5 p.m. daily) will change traveler's checks.

GETTING TO SAMOSIR. If you've taken the **bus** from Medan to Parapat, it will stop first in town at the Welcome Gate by the Tourist Information Office, and then continue on to the ferryboat pier (almost a 1¼-mile walk). **Public ferries** leave from Market Tigaraja every hour between 9 a.m. and 6 p.m.; the 30-minute ride to Tomok costs Rp 800 (50¢). The car-ferry leaves from Ajibata, about 1½ miles farther south, every three hours between 8:30 a.m. and 8:30 p.m. It lands at Tc ok, and the fare is Rp 6,000 ($3.75) per car plus Rp 500 (30¢) per passenger. Once you land at Tomok you can take the public bus or bemo to Tuk Tuk (four miles) or elsewhere for Rp 650 (40¢); a private bemo on Samosir will cost Rp 11,50) ($7.25).

L)cal travel agents offer day trips to the Batak villages on Samosir; a car with driver, guide, and room for two passengers costs about Rp 104,000 ($65). You can charter your own ferry seating 40 or a five-man speedboat to Tomok for Rp 28,000 ($17.50) round trip, including an hour's waiting time, from the ferryboat pier off Jl. Pulau Samosir opposite the Atsari Hotel. Two-man paddleboats can be rented for Rp 1,000 (65¢) per hour too, but it's a long, long paddle to Samosir.

ACCOMMODATIONS AND DINING. The Chinese New Year (late January or February) is the only time when hotels are fully booked, with vacationing families from Jakarta, Medan, Malaysia, and Singapore. The best rooms and scenic views are offered by the **Hotel Natour Parapat,** located on the slopes of the Parapat cove at Jl. Marihat 1 (tel. 0664/41012), on the site of a 1919 Dutch-owned inn. The Parapat's 33 superior rooms have outdoor verandas within steps of the lake and have private baths, TVs, and phones at Rp 61,000 ($38) for two. Rates range down to Rp 40,800 ($25.50) for a roadside room without a view, but all include breakfast and service charges for two. The Parapat's manicured, blooming grounds, small sandy beach, water sports facilities, and fine dining room make it a true vacation spot and better than any facility on Samosir.

Facilities, maintenance, and location decline rapidly as you look elsewhere. The **Hotel Danau Toba Internasional** is in the center of town at Jl. Pulau Samosir 19 (tel. 0664/41583). Here the best rooms are Rp 51,200 ($32) and, though simple in décor, have an outdoor seating area on a ledge above the lake that's a perfect spot to have breakfast. If a grand view is more important than the patio, ask for Room 506.

If the first two choices are booked, try the **Hotel Tarabunga,** on the main street at no. 20 (tel. 0664/41089). Moderate rooms cost Rp 35,200 ($22), but they're clean and comfortable, and have scenic overlooks from their small balconies. The companion hotel, **Tarabunga Sibigo** (tel. 0664/41800), is up the hill with newer doubles at the same price, or just Rp 32,000 ($20) without a lake view.

Parapat's budget hotels are removed a bit from the shoreline, although most are on Jl. Samosir. The **Budi Mulya** (tel. 0664/41216) has worn but clean, spartan rooms with private hot-water mandi, ranging in price from Rp 16,000 ($10) to Rp 20,800 ($13). Several Batak-style houses have become losmen on Samosir Island, and offer better facilities, face the water, and cost only Rp 5,500 ($3.50) to Rp 18,000 ($11.25) for two.

Every Parapat hotel has its own restaurant and all offer adequate, simple Indonesian and Western fare. The **Hotel Parapat** will prepare (with two hours' notice) an ikan mas panggang, a grilled fish with local Batak spices. The **Berastagi Restaurant** is one of several on Jl. S.M. Raja, along with the **Paten** and **Sehat** restaurants. They serve Indonesian favorites and very similar food prepared in a "Chinese" fashion. Two can eat heartily almost anywhere for under Rp 8,000 ($5).

Samosir Island

Barren, scrubby Samosir first drew the Bataks because its impressive rocky presence suggested their mythical homeland. A 2,882-foot-tall mountain range forms the island's interior. One narrow road encircles Samosir, with only one lane crossing the interior. Limited transportation confines sightseers to the east side of the island where the ferries arrive. Although ferryboats land at Tomok, many visitors prefer the rustic accommodations available north or south of the tiny port.

ACCOMMODATIONS. The first-class hotels on Samosir set its Mediterranean style: white stucco, lots of tile, picture windows, and tiers of bougainvillea-draped concrete steps. None offers air conditioning, pools, phones, or TVs. All have a touch of the Batak about them in the occasional swayback roof, and red, black, and white trim. In contrast, low-budget losmen are often created from unused Batak housing.

The 120-room **Toledo Inn** in Tuk-Tuk (tel. 0664/41181) has one of the best-landscaped grounds and the nicest of the man-made sandy beaches. Most rooms are attached motel style with neat verandas offering views across the lake. The best rooms are on the top floor of their few Batak houses, where modern comforts cost Rp 37,000 ($23) for two.

The **Toba Beach Hotel** (tel. 0664/41275) hugs a long sandy strip in Tomok, about 1½ miles south of the ferryboat landing. The 62 rooms are large, clean, and comfortable, and the friendly staff and cozy atmosphere encourage lounging at Batak-style dining and bar pavilions. Rates are Rp 24,000 ($15) for a single traveler or Rp 29,000 ($18) for two, and Rp 45,000 ($28) for their uniquely regal Batak bungalow.

The 14 white Batak-roofed bungalows of the new **Sopo Toba Hotel** (tel. 0664/41616) are stacked on a hillside just north of Ambarita, about four miles from the ferryboat pier. Bright, parquet-floored rooms have tile baths and porches with rattan furniture; one or two will pay Rp 42,000 ($26.25) a night.

Most young people come to Lake Toba to hang out, hike, and live cheaply. Dozens of losmen (usually a few Batak houses with twin beds and cold-water mandis) are owned by the restaurants that line the 2½-mile coastal drive between the Wisma Duma Sari and Toledo Hotels. The **Carolina Hotel,** on Tuk-Tuk's southernmost point about 1½ miles north of Tomok (tel. 0664/41920), is the best of them. The English-speaking staff, good cheap Western and Indonesian food, and a lobby bulletin board with hiking-trail maps and traveler's mail add up to the casual and comfortable surroundings. Their best rooms, in new Batak-style houses on the rocky ledge above the lake, equal those at the big hotels with the exception of hot water and Western plumbing (the management says they will be "modernized" in 1989). Rooms cost Rp 23,500 ($14.75); the 40 simpler rooms range in price down to Rp 6,400 ($4) per double, with a rustic, thatch-roofed cottage, attached rooms with verandas, and very spartan bungalows in between.

Our next choice after Carolina's is **Bernard's,** an excellent neo-Greco columned restaurant with cottages less than a half mile north in Tuk-Tuk. Bernard and his lovely wife keep eight simple Batak-style A-frames perched on the rocks above the lake; they rent for Rp 7,000 ($4.50) for two.

DINING. Sumatrans cite a distinct difference between the slightly sweeter northern Melayu food and the western fiery, hot Padang food. Actually, in any *rumah makan* (local restaurant) where dishes filled with spicy beef, fried chicken, baked fish, boiled vegetables, and chili sambal line the windows, you're in for a treat. In authentic Padang restaurants (from the capital of West Sumatra) every customer is served a plate of steamed rice, then platters with two or three portions of each entree are placed on the table. You only pay for what you eat. Padang food is very piquant and the Melayus claim that their dishes are much more subtly flavored with local spices. The distinction escapes us, but we liked what we ate, particularly the local gado-gado with a coarse ground-peanut dressing.

Ironically, the best food is found in restaurants where tourists have contributed their touch to the menu and to the preparation of local staples. **Bernard's,** on the pedestrian coast route in Tuk-Tuk, serves great fried chicken or fish with french fries. The vegetable taco, a huge spring roll (a rice-flour wrapper stuffed with grated cabbage, carrots, greens, tomatoes, and chilis), is imaginative and wonderful. It also has lace tablecloths, the nicest young waitresses, a quiet crowd, and freshly made salads and juices. It's open daily from breakfast till 10 p.m., and two can feast for under Rp 6,400 ($4).

The **Hotel Carolina** also has an excellent "crossover" restaurant. Here you can dine on fresh papaya juice, toast, and an omelet for Rp 2,000 ($1.25), at a comfortable rattan table overlooking the lake.

If you're in Tomok at lunch, try the **Islam Hidangan Restoran** near the ferry landing. They serve good Melayu food, particularly grilled fish steaks, in Padang fashion on picnic tables in the front room. A filling repast can be enjoyed for under Rp 6,000 ($3.75) for two.

BATAK SITES ON SAMOSIR. The east coast of Samosir, in sight of the sacred Pusuk Bukit mountains, mythical birthplace of the Batak people, has three villages with remains of traditional Toba Batak culture. All are open daily and can be easily visited by foot (within an hour's hike of Tuk-Tuk) or by the coast road bemo that circles the island throughout the day. The small guidebook *Primitive Art of the Ancient Batak* by Dr. Jamaludin S. Hasibuan is quite interesting and one of the few guides available ($2, for sale in Parapat and Tomok at our visit).

Makam Raja, three tombs built for kings of the Sidabutar Dynasty, are located on a hillside above the village of Tomok. The Tomok kings, famed for their military prowess, even ruled the region of Tuk-Tuk at the height of their power. The oldest tomb (on the right) is thought to be about 350 years old. Although kings were left buried, royal relatives buried with them were later disinterred so their bones could be preserved in ceremonial boxes. The center tomb resembles a sarcophagus and contains Raja Opu Sulabatu, King Sidabutar II, whose likeness is carved on the front of the tomb. King Sidabutar III, buried in 1929, lies in the more simple Christian tomb. Nearby is the village of Sigale Gale, where four traditional Batak homes housed the Sidabutar clan.

Shoppers should check out the little **market** that's sprung up at this tourist site. A large selection of *mangiring* (hand-woven womens' shawls, for about $5 to $8), *pussar* (the men's shawls, for $20 to $35), lesser-priced *kepala pussar* to cover the head, *sadum* (black shawls with colorful wool embroidery, for $15), wooden icons, cylindrical Batak calendars, and newly carved wood book covers (from $2 up) are available. Bargain prices down to 60% of the original quote.

The traditional **Siallagan Village** of the Siallagan ruling clan is outside the modern-day Ambarita, about four miles north of Tomok. Stone walls once topped with bamboo blinds kept enemies and animals away. The focus of the site is six carved-stone straightback chairs and three benches grouped around a table. A seated stone figure on the "throne" bench was modeled after the first raja of the clan; this area was used by the *datus* (medicine men) and by the king's court to discuss political or social issues or make offerings. The large *rumah bolon* (king's house), thought to be about 200 years old, is still there. Just west of this area are the execution ground and five stone benches. Villagers could watch criminals being punished as decreed by adat.

The **Museum Huta Bolon** of the Sidarok rajas is in the town of Simanindo, 21 km (12½ miles) north of Tomok. The main street has five large *jabu*, or houses (the second from the left was the king's rumah bolon) on the left and five smaller *sopo*, rice-storage barns used as sleeping quarters for the village's young men, on the right. The 11 buffalo horns mounted on the rumah bolon indicate that 11 generations of Sidarok kings lived here. Inside the rumah bolon is a small, well-labeled display of household artifacts, traditional costumes, and weaponry. A pavilion for the *solu bolon* (royal barges) and a pavilion of royal graves is at the entrance to the village. The museum is open daily from 8 a.m. to 5 p.m. Admission is Rp 500 (30¢).

Hiking is the best way to see the island; the more adventurous and physically fit traveler can see small family compounds of traditional Batak houses with new peaked tin roofs around every bend. One popular walk is over the central mountain from Tomok to Pangururan; from here there is a land bridge to Harianboho on the western shore of Lake Toba. Halfway through this 12-hour hike on a stone-and-paved road is the traditional village of Rong Gurriuhuta. The Hotel Carolina in Tuk-Tuk is the best local source for hiking and trail information.

TRANS-SUMATRA OVERLAND: Most travelers heading from Lake Toba to Padang, West Sumatra, return to Medan to catch Garuda Indonesia's daily flight (70 minutes, $65). However, going trans-Sumatra overland by bus is a much easier and more comfortable journey than it used to be. Now several buses ply the scenic two-lane blacktop via Parapat, Sibolga, and Bukittingi for 26 hours and charge less than Rp 12,000 ($7.50). Two factors contribute to the recent ease of this once-legendary expedition: the national government allotted funds for the constant paving and maintenance of this flood- and landslide-prone network, and police checkpoints (established after several fatal accidents on Java) control the speed and overloading of buses on this route.

From Medan to Padang or vice versa, the trip takes 24 to 30 hours, depending on the weather, current bridge conditions (usually washed out or under repair), and whether it's market day in any of the hundreds of villages along the route. The route from Medan south to Parapat is lined with shady plantations and large modern towns. The eight-hour stretch between Parapat and Padang Sidempuan, 88 km (53 miles) south of Sibolga, circling the coast of Lake Toba, is particularly breathtaking, veering through the jungle-clad mountains and descending to the coast at Sibolga where you can catch a spectacular sunset over the Indian Ocean. The last leg between Lubuksikaping and Padang winds through more dense rain forest, past the tiniest villages, and weaves through the Bukit Barisan foothills to plains dotted with peak-roofed Minangkabau villages.

For reasons of sanity, hygiene, or cultural interest you may want to break up the trip over two days (this will also give you a chance to switch bus companies, although you probably won't find wider or softer seats). Sibolga, 388 km (233 miles) from Medan or 489 km (293 miles) from Padang, is a port town that's more appealing as a scenic vista from the mountain highway than it is at sea level. However, it's the place to stop if you're planning to catch a ferryboat to Nias Island.

Choosing Your Bus

Several bus companies ply the route between Medan and Padang, the north-bound ones often going as far as Banda Aceh (12 hours north of Medan) and the southbound ones sometimes heading for Jakarta (72 hours from Medan). Check with the **Tourist Information Office,** at Jl. Palang Merah 66 in Medan (tel. 511-101), to determine which company currently has the best buses and fares, then go to their offices. You can usually find a bus to inspect, and can reserve your seat. The front bench behind the driver has the most legroom and best vantage going southbound. The front seats on the door side have better northbound viewing, but this area gets loaded with mounds of luggage, produce, and even the conductor when the bus gets crowded.

A reminder: this is adventurous travel! Our first bus caught on fire, but the conductor just threw some water on the engine and we kept going. Our second bus was delayed when a drunken man fell out of his seat, hit his head, and couldn't be roused for treatment at the next town. We were moved to a third bus when our conductor decided to cut short the journey at his village. That third bus stopped only once—to pick up passengers stranded when *their* bus had broken down. Each bus was not (despite claims) air-conditioned, but all were window-cooled, cramped but bearable, and the scenic beauty unfolding before us was worth every minute of the ride.

Nias Island

Nias Island is of great ethnological interest because its isolation in the Indian Ocean—125 km (75 miles) west of the mainland—has helped preserve the traditional Nias Batak adat and ceremonies. Ferries make the 16-hour journey daily to Teluk Dalam, a port that's 120 km (72 miles) away from the better tourist facilities in the large town of Gunung Sitoli. (Merpati Nusantara has flights from Medan to Gunung Sitoli.) About 14 km (8½ miles) from Teluk Dalam are the traditional villages of Bawomataluo (where a classic Nias palace is decorated with the jaws of sacrificed pigs and has an executioners' block on display) and Hilisimaetano (a traditional settlement with unique Nias Batak houses). At Gomo, 80 km (50 miles) away from the port, there's a rock garden filled with primitive rock carvings. If you happen to be there when an organized group tour is going through, you can witness the Nias stone jumpers, youths practicing the sport of leaping over six-foot-tall rocks to prepare for battle.

Accommodations in Sibolga or Padang Sidempuan

Sibolga is big and rather drab, but the **Hotel Nauli,** in the town's center (tel. 061/327-896 in Medan for reservations) is probably the town's best offering, with double rooms with private hot-water facilities under Rp 25,000 ($15.50).

A better overnight if you're not going to Nias Island is south at Padang Sidempuan, 476 km (286 miles) from Medan or 401 km (241 miles) from Padang. It's a much smaller city with a lively Pasar Malam and a less jaded approach to tourists. The **Hotel Samudera** has neat, clean rooms from Rp 8,000 ($5) to Rp 22,500 ($14) depending on availability of air conditioning and hot water. Let the bus driver know where you want to go before you reach either city and he'll drop you off at your hotel! If the hotel desk can't help you find a bus for your onward journey the next morning (they start running about 5 a.m. and stop in early afternoon), you can take a becak to the bus terminal and inquire there.

2. WEST SUMATRA, LAND OF THE MINANGKABAU

Padang is the capital of West Sumatra (Sumatera Barat), a lesser-known but prosperous and culturally rich province. Its 50,000 km² (18,000 square miles), with a population density of only 74 people per square kilometer, is more open and densely green than the north; the cool blue mountain lakes that dot the hills are delightful. The coal mined inland and the produce from cinnamon, timber, coffee, tea, and nutmeg plantations are exported throughout Asia. The original Minangkabau peoples who settled here are still the dominant political, economic, and cultural force. Although converted to Islam, the Minangkabau, particularly in the central hills around the village of Bukittingi, follow their adat in all social behavior—housing, family rituals, and the arts. The primitive, near Stone Age Orang Mentawai who inhabit the difficult-to-reach Mentawai Islands are another fascinating ethnic group who secretly follow an ancient religion and customs outlawed by the government. West Sumatra is actually best known for its food—various fiery-hot meat and vegetable dishes seen everywhere in Indonesia as "Padang food." The combination of culture, natural beauty, and good food makes it well worth a visit.

THE MINANGKABAU CULTURE: According to Minangkabau legend, these tribes were originally descended from the Greek conqueror Alexander the Great. "Before my father's father's time" (as they would say), Alexander and his three sons were traveling after a great flood, and parted ways to find dry land. The youngest son, Maharaja di Raja, sailed south and anchored his boat on a small island. When the waters receded he found himself atop Mount Merapi (near Bukittingi), so he and his followers descended to Pariangan, spread out, and founded several clans. In this, legend has it, was the origin of the four different clans of West Sumatra—the Piliang, Bodi, Caniago, and Koto.

Legend also tells about the origin of this tribal name. In ancient times there was a rivalry between the tribes on Java and the tribes on Sumatra. Unsure of military victory, the Sumatrans challenged the Javanese to a bullfight. The clever Sumatrans had starved a young calf beforehand and sent it into the ring with knives strapped to its horns. When the hungry calf tried to suckle the huge Javanese bull, it cut its stomach open and won the fight. The word *minangkabau* means "victory buffalo."

Minangkabau Society

The Minangkabau are unique for their matrilineal social system in which inheritance is passed from mother to daughter. A single woman chooses her husband and then brings gifts or money (these days, even a car) to his family as a dowry. Teenage boys leave their mother's home to sleep at the local prayer house, but once married, move into their wife's home. Children are raised by their mother's brothers and uncles, but the eldest daughter inherits the family property. In the Minangkabau genealogy, the descendants of the mother are called *saparuik,* meaning "from one womb." The descendants from the father's side are called *anak pisang,* "sprouts of the banana," and are considered part of their mothers' clans. Although the eldest woman is the strict leader of family affairs, women are not allowed to be on the village council. Instead, men and women from each clan choose their *penghulu,* or leader, and he represents them in village matters.

Minangkabau Adat

The Minangkabau have an extremely strong adat (traditional law) based on logic and inevitability. Written adat such as "what is round will roll, what is flat will float" or "what seems good to oneself should be agreed upon by others" form the basis for social custom, religious rituals, and a democratic government. The local religion was strongly based on Hinduism until the arrival of Islam in the 12th century. Today more than 200 Minangkabau dialects are based on Arabic script and the Arabic greeting "Assalamu-alaikum" is used when meeting someone, who replies "Alaikum-salam."

The Minangkabau continue to build rumah adat. These traditional peaked-roof houses (with points emanating from the sides of the house, as well as in front and back like those of the Bataks) are covered in brightly painted woodcarvings. The common houses with four-peak roofs representing buffalo horns equalled the number of Minangkabau clans; only the homes of penghulu or other chieftains could have more peaks. This status system has died out, but new homes are still built with graceful peaks and generous decoration.

Whereas West Sumatra embraces the Minangkabau, another offshore culture, the Orang Mentawai, still survives in obscurity.

THE ORANG MENTAWAI: The 44,000 Mentawai tribesmen live on four islands 200 km (120 miles) west of Padang; Siberut is the largest and most commonly visited. Orang Mentawai follow an adat based on Arat Sabulungan, a religious system that imbues all things, animate and inanimate, with their own spirit. Because these spirits live outside their physical being, the world of mortals often causes them conflict. Ceremonies to appease the spirits and restore harmony with humans must be performed; nightlong dancing, drumming, bell ringing, trances, and communal feasting are some of the ways.

Each Mentawai prizes his individuality. If a conflict cannot be resolved by the *rimata*, or tribe leader of the communal *uma* (their long house), the individual moves on to another tribe. When the Indonesian government outlawed loincloths, bare breasts, tatoos, and the Mentawai religion in 1954 (and forced them to choose an accepted national religion), many tribes went into hiding. The Mentawai, terrified of government raids searching for ceremonial items, avoid the large towns for fear of *Orang Tepi*, the "peripheral people" that they believe everyone else to be.

GETTING THERE: Garuda Indonesia flies to Padang from Singapore three times weekly, from Jakarta four times daily ($102), and once a day from Medan ($65). **Merpati Nusantara** flies once daily from Jakarta (about 20% to 40% cheaper), as does the difficult-to-keep-track-of **Mandala Airways.** The **train** tracks that circle through the area handle cargo trains only, usually shuttling coal from Sawalunto to Telukbayur Harbor. However, the Tourist Information Office in Padang can arrange private passenger-train tours through the hill country upon request. Several long-distance **bus** companies (see "Trans-Sumatra Overland" in Section 1) service Padang via the Terminal Bis on Jl. Pemuda. The 40-hour bus ride to Jakarta costs Rp 34,000 ($21.25); the 1½-hour ride to Bukittingi (several departures hourly) costs Rp 1,250 (80¢). The national **PELNI cruise lines** (tel. 22109) run ships once every two weeks between Jakarta and Padang; the 36-hour cruise costs Rp 45,000 ($28) to Rp 84,000 ($52.50), including meals and a bunk.

The national **Kanwill Deparpostel Tourist Information office** in Padang will provide the little information available on the Mentawai, and can help arrange permits and a guided foray into their world. Siberut, Sipura, and North and South Pagai are crisscrossed with swamps and canals that the Mentawai use to get around, making a knowledgeable guide critical. The PELNI lines has one ship

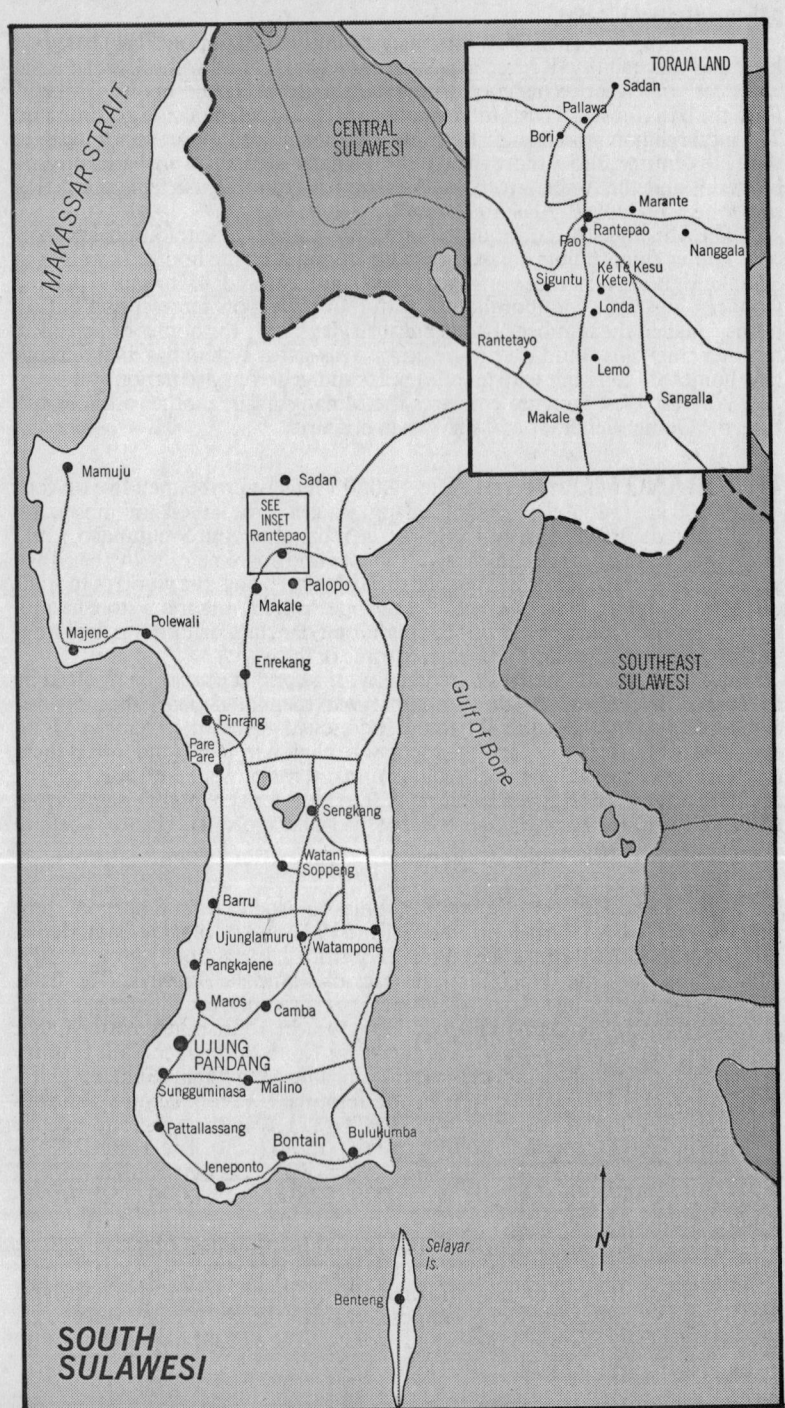

SOUTH
SULAWESI

every two weeks going to Siberut, then the other Mentawai Islands (14 hours, for Rp 4,500 or $2.75). You can sometimes charter a local boat for about Rp 6,500 ($4) per person. Merpati Nusantara flies to Sipura, an island about four hours from Siberut by charter boat.

GETTING AROUND: Transportation in West Sumatra is good enough to make independent travel throughout the region practical. In Bukittingi, a local *opelet* (the Sumatran name for bemo or mini-van) can be rented for sightseeing for about Rp 24,000 ($15) per day, but prearranged guided tours can be much more efficient.

Several Indonesian tour operators offer two- or three-day "Minangkabau Culture" guided packages to Padang and Bukittingi. Contact **Tunas Indonesia Tours and Travel,** Jl. Pondok 86, Padang (tel. 0751/22920), for more information. Prices range from $120 to $175 per person on a twin sharing basis.

PADANG: The capital of West Sumatra is a clean and quiet city of 500,000 with a lot of restaurants and a small museum. All travelers will pass through this transportation hub to gain access to the Minangkabau villages in the countryside or before making the difficult passage to the Mentawai Islands.

Orientation

Padang's commercial district is centered between forks of the Muara River; its busy harbor at Teluk Bayur is four miles south and Tabing Airport is five miles southeast. The city's heart is at **Jl. Pasar Raya,** the market filled with new shops and restaurants, and the intersection of Jl. M. Yamin, site of the opelet (mini-van) terminal. **Jl. Jend. Sudirman,** a broad, landscaped avenue draped with bougainvillea and studded with Minang-style government buildings, runs parallel to Jl. Pasar Raya. Hotels and the Terminal Bis are within half a mile of here.

The **Adityawarman Museum** (open daily except Monday from 8 a.m. to 5 p.m.), nearby at the Jl. Yani and Jl. Diponegoro square, is a traditional Minangkabau rumah gadang filled with such cultural artifacts as costumes, tools, household items, and weavings. There is a fascinating section devoted to the Mentawai Islands people.

Useful Information

The **Dinas Pariwisata Tourist Information Office** is north at Jl. Sudirman 43 (tel. 21716), and is open from 7:30 a.m. to 2 p.m. Monday through Thursday, till 11 a.m. on Friday, and till 1 p.m. on Saturday. There is also a branch at Tabing Airport, open daily except Sunday from 8 a.m. to 4 p.m. Travelers interested in the primitive Orang Mentawai on the Mentawai Islands should contact the national **Kanwil Deparpostel Information Office,** on Jl. Khatib Sulaiman (tel. 22118) open the same hours as the local tourist office.

Dial the **police** at 110 in case of emergency; the Kantor Polisi is on Jl. M. Yamin. . . . The missionary **Yos. Sudarso Hospital** is on Jl. Situjuh (tel. 22091).

Several **banks** on Jl. Sudirman are open from 7:45 a.m. to noon and 1 to 2 p.m. Monday through Friday and 7:45 to 11 a.m. on Saturday; the **Cv. Eka Jasa Utama Moneychanger** on Jl. Niaga is open daily from 8 a.m. to 4 p.m. Take cash rupiah if you're traveling out to the countryside.

The **Kantor Pos** and the **Kantor Telepon** are on Jl. Bed. Aziz Chan, one block west of the market. The **telephone area code** for Padang, Bukittingi, and environs is 0751.

Happy World Photo, at Jl. Karya 12, has film and photo supplies.

Garuda Indonesia is at Jl. Sudirman 2 (tel. 23823), and **Merpati Nusantara** is at Jl. Pemuda 45A (tel. 21303). . . . **Natrabu Tours and Travel,** at Jl. Pemuda 29B (tel. 23410), and **Tunas Indonesia,** at Jl. Pondok 86C (tel.

22920), are reliable tour operators and can handle flight reservations and travel planning. Try **Mariani Tours and Travel,** at Jl. Bundo Kandung 35 (tel. 25446), for guided tours of the Minangkabau villages.

Getting Around

Within the Padang area there are opelets (mini-vans, called bemos elsewhere) that ply a set route from the terminal at Jl. M. Yamin for Rp 200 (10¢). The Padang municipality voted to outlaw becaks, declaring the work "inhumane" to drivers, and this has fostered a thriving *bendi* system. These simple horse-drawn carts charge about Rp 650 (40¢) for short trips.

READERS' TOURING SUGGESTION: "In Padang and some other places we used a hotel employee as a local guide. We found that this method of local travel gives us a personal and more local flavor, as they often take us around their neighborhoods and to their homes. We give our guides small American flags as a token of goodwill and appreciation" (Jean and Tony Triumpho, Canajoharie, N.Y.).

Accommodations

Padang's small collection of hotels cater mostly to business people and are usually well kept, always available, centrally located, and moderately priced from Rp 11,200 ($7) to Rp 60,800 ($38) for two, including tax and service charges.

The **Mariani International Hotel,** near the Pasar at Jl. Bundo Kandung 35 (tel. 0751/25446), is one whose charming owner, Mrs. Mariani, fills the inviting place with her energy and cheer. She has shopped in Java, Japan, and the States to furnish her 30 rooms in a unique way. The ten deluxe rooms, at Rp 74,000 ($46.25), are done in baroque Oriental with gilded carved Javanese furnishings, a wild array of floral prints, and modern amentities. First-class and standard rooms are smaller, though some are done in lesser Java baroque and some in "nouvelle American motel"; they are Rp 60,800 ($38) for two. Mrs. Mariani's infectious warmth and lavish taste overrun the cozy lobby and early Victorian dining area as well; a night here is a night to remember.

If the Hotel Mariani is full, try **Pangeran's Hotel,** located a short walk from the museum at Jl. Dobi 3-5 (tel. 0751/26233). It's a straightforward choice, with clean, slightly worn rooms and modern amenities. Larger, first-class rooms run Rp 72,000 ($45) for two; standard doubles cost Rp 32,000 ($20).

A good budget choice at Jl. Pemuda 31 opposite the Terminal Bis is the **Tiga-Tiga Hotel** (tel. 0751/22633). This older building has graceful seating areas throughout. VIP rooms, plain but clean with cold-water private bath, rent for Rp 17,600 ($11) for two, including breakfast. Smaller rooms with shared facilities cost Rp 10,400 ($6.50) for two, Rp 5,400 ($3.50) for a single.

Dining

Padang food is as ubiquitous in Indonesia as Mexican food is in the U.S., and it's hot! You can sample it throughout your Indonesian journey, but it's most refined at the source. Instead of ordering, diners are presented with up to 15 different dishes, most guaranteed to reduce a chili aficionado to tears, and a large platter of rice. Favorites include randang daging (buffalo or beef cooked in coconut milk and spices until black), dendeng (beef cooked until hard and dry), gulai kambing (goat curry), ayam (chicken), and sayur (vegetables) cooked several (often not-too-spicy) ways, and exotic ones like tambonsu (cow's stomach), krupuk (cow's skin), liver, and other organs. You can't go wrong choosing what looks good, because you only pay for the amount you eat. Order a jeruk es (lemonade) to cool you down and another to keep you cool. Although Padang food is displayed pyramid style in shop windows all day, the spices seem to preserve it.

One of the local favorites is **Restoran Tanpa Nama,** at Jl. Rohana Kudus 87 (tel. 26687), one block west of the Pasar Raya. You can sit outdoors and enjoy

Padang specialties, geared to a palate preferring milder foods. It's open daily except Friday for lunch and dinner (from 11 a.m. to 9 p.m.). **Rumah Makan Roda Baru,** on the second floor of the Pasar Raya (tel. 22814), is wide open, all white, clean, and refreshingly breezy with views out to the bustling street. The food is very well seasoned here—dare to weep. The friendly staff will bring out more and more devilish concoctions if you show your appreciation. Roda Baru is open daily from 8 a.m. to 9 p.m.; expect to spend about Rp 5,400 ($3.50) per person at either place.

The martabak is a highly prized, utterly delicious genus of street food, resembling an omelet in a turnover, with scallions, onion, daging (Padang beef, which is optional), and chopped fiery green peppers in an egg batter. Spiced ginger soy sauce is served with this delectable item, which costs Rp 500 (30¢) to Rp 900 (55¢), depending on size. Although martabak is sold on street corners, savvy locals head to **Restoran Kubang,** on Jl. M. Yamin (tel. 28143), around the corner from the Terminal Bis. You can watch their graceful assembly line satisfy the queue of take-out customers or dine casually inside. Don't miss it.

BUKITTINGGI: To venture into Minangkabau country, most visitors prefer to base themselves at Bukittingi, 91 km (55 miles) north of Padang. This simple hill town is 3,000 feet above sea level with a cool, pleasant climate year round. Narrow roads course through terraced rice paddy and pink- and green-leafed cinnamon groves, past peak-roofed houses, mosques, and big, shallow goldfish ponds. The surrounding Sing galang, Sago, and Merapi volcanoes (the latter two are still active) create a dramatic backdrop from the town's central Panorama Park.

Orientation

Bukittinggi is a very small town, with most guesthouses and restaurants around the main street, **Jl. A. Yani.** Cross streets are marked in relation to **Jam Gadang** or Big Ben, the 1898 clock tower that dominates the center of the village near the Pasar, and **Fort de Kock,** the remnants of a Dutch fortress built in 1830 that once guarded the east end of town. From here or Jl. Panorama there is a wonderful vista over **Sianok Canyon,** a verdant limestone valley that's great for hiking. In just a mile you can reach the silversmiths' village of Kota Gadang.

Useful Information

The local **Kantor Penerangan Pariwisata Information Office** is at Jl. A. Yani 107 (tel. 22403), and is open daily except Sunday from 8 a.m. to 4 p.m., although office hours are very casual in this sleepy place. In fact the whole town is very pleasantly disorganized. If you haven't arrived from Padang with your own car and guide (about $50 to $70 per day through travel agents), the tourist office will help organize a group to charter an opelet seating eight for day trips in the region for about Rp 4,000 ($25). This is also the source for local schedules of events like the bull versus bull fight in Kota Baru, Market Day, or the Pacu Kuda horse races in Solok. Traditional dances are put on sporadically for tourists.

Hikers interested in climbing Mount Merapi (9,540 feet) or Mount Singgalang, both believed by locals to be the home of sacred spirits, should register with the Kantor Polisi in Kota Baru, east of town on Lake Maninjau. The police can usually provide a guide, at about Rp 14,000 ($8.75), for the nighttime ascent when the mist has lifted. Merapi is said to be easier and cooler, but protection against leeches is recommended for either climb, as is a guide.

In case of an **emergency,** contact the local **police,** on Jl. Agus Salim (tel. 110). . . . The **Kantor Telepon** and **Kantor Pos** are on Jl. Jend. Sudirman. . . . The **Dymen's Tours** office is the agent for Garuda Indonesia air tickets. . . . Bendi horse carts are the best transportation if you're tired of walking, and cost about Rp 600 (40¢) anywhere in town.

The Muslim Minangkabau are devout and modest folk—revealing clothing or public displays of affection are frowned upon. . . . Don't forget a sweater and rain parka for the cool, often misty nights.

Accommodations

Lodgings in Bukittinggi are generally of good quality and several offer clean rooms, attached baths with hot water, TVs, and small balconies for under Rp 40,000 ($25) for two, including tax and service charges.

The most homey one, the **Minang Hotel,** is a ten-room hotel located at Jl. Panorama 20A (tel. 0751/21120). As the address suggests, the view is splendid, overlooking the Sianok Valley. Rooms are large and cozy, many opening onto a common lounge area. Front rooms are favorites because when you awake the view of the valley shrouded in mist is memorable. Rates range from Rp 24,800 ($15.50) to Rp 51,000 ($32) for one guest to Rp 32,000 ($20) to Rp 56,000 ($35) for two guests, depending on size and vista.

The larger **Denai Hotel** is at Jl. Dr. Rivai 26 (tel. 0751/21460), about 15 minutes' walk from Big Ben. It has an elegant lobby decorated with dark woods and handsome local embroideries, and is built in grand Minangkabau style. The soaring pointed roofs shade less grand, plain rooms with modern amenities, though there are two cottages that emulate the Minang style, are larger, and have balconies with valley views. Double rooms are Rp 42,000 ($26.25); cottages for one or two are Rp 55,000 ($34.50).

The best value in Bukittinggi is **Lima's Hotel,** near the Denai at Jl. Kesehatan 34 (tel. 0751/22641). Perched on the hillside below Fort de Kock, each floor has a spacious sun room with splendid views where guests can enjoy breakfast. Rooms are simple and small, with a hot-water mandi (Asian water well) and detachable Danish spray shower, but it's spotless and a friendly place. Bathless economy rooms cost only Rp 10,000 ($6.25), standard doubles run Rp 22,400 ($14), and doubles with TVs are Rp 46,000 ($28.75).

The $500-around-the-world crowd ("Ten-Dollar Snails" as locals call budget hikers with backpacks) has a very large selection of losmen known as "guesthouses." The best is the **Singgalang Inn** on Jl. A. Yani (tel. 0751/21576), opposite the tourist office. Spartan rooms with camp beds and shared cold-water mandi cost Rp 3,600 ($2.25) per person.

Dining

There are a number of restaurants in Bukittinggi, including several coffeehouses reflecting its European tourist tradition. Most of the coffeehouses are on Jl. A. Yani, and we found **The Three Tables** to be the best. Travelers in town for more than two days will settle into their own favorite.

For Padang food, locals scorch their tongues at **A.C.C.** or **Simpang Raya,** both opposite the clock tower on Jl. Muka Rama. Dressed-up ambience, pop music, and a great view supplement the Padang food found at **Famili Ruman Makan,** on the Fort de Kock hillside.

For a local and unusual breakfast treat, try the **Kedai Kopi Sianok,** a fast-food coffeeshop at the edge of the Pasar Atas near Big Ben. Kampiun is the breakfast of Minangkabau champions, a bowl of sticky rice mixed with shredded coconut, served with a fried banana and palm-cane sugar. Add a cup of the intense kopi susu (rich, locally grown coffee with condensed milk) and you're sure to start your day better.

EXPLORING THE MINANGKABAU CULTURE: The best place to begin your appreciation for this colorful society is at the **Taman Bundo Kanduang Museum,** a cluster of traditional houses in town. Two *rang kiang,* or rice houses, greet visitors who proceed to the *rumah gadang,* the communal living house where exhibits of kitchen items, tools, musical instruments, model houses, bronzework, and family rituals are well displayed. The rumah gadang itself is beautifully decorated with painted carved-wood reliefs in Islamic floral patterns. A collection of headdresses, each in a different cloth to indicate position in society or occupation, are as revealing as the costumed mannequins are about Minangkabau culture. You must take off your shoes to enter the museum. It's open daily from 7:15 a.m. to 5 p.m. and the admission is Rp 250 (15¢). On Saturday, Sunday, and Wednesday there is a performance of *saluang,* classical flute music, at 11 a.m., and a show of *pandai,* traditional dances, at noon. For another Rp 500 (30¢) you can visit the **Kebun Binatang,** a small local zoo that's behind the museum.

Efficient sightseeing outside Bukittinggi is hampered by infrequent public transportation, so visitors are strongly advised to rent a car and hire a driver and guide, or join a guided tour. The first stop might be six miles away in **Pantai Sikat.** The name means "skilled weaving," and nothing could better describe the principal product made in this tiny village: traditional songkhet cloth, hand-woven and embroidered with silver or gold thread. The charming *rumah adat* (traditional house) of **Mrs. H. Sanuar** sells some of the finest shawls, purses, sarong fabrics, and traditional ornaments for wedding tents.

This area is filled with nature's beauties. The **Lembah Harau** (Harau Valley) is about 30 minutes by car from Bukittinggi. The 778 acres of protected parkland is outside the basket weavers' village of **Payakumbuh,** also the site of a bat-filled cave, 260 feet deep, that didn't interest us in the least. From the main car road you can walk along a broad path 2½ miles into the Harau park past swollen rivers and crashing waterfalls, then pass through a game preserve of tapir, wild goats, monkeys, and the occasional tiger. A narrow hiking trail leads another two miles to the village of Harau. Geologists speculate that this area used to be the ocean floor, although the Indian Ocean is now 60 miles away. Contact the Resort PPA Harau at the park's entrance for camping information; admission is Rp 250 (15¢).

From the scenic lookout at **Embun Pagi,** a short drive from Harau Park, you have a wonderful view of **Lake Maninjau,** six miles away. It takes 44 sharp curves to descend to the sapphire-blue lake almost 70 km (42 miles) in circumference. Onion-domed mosques with buffalo-horn roof trim, women harvesting rice with their heads covered, and the wailing call of the muezzin indicate how thoroughly the Minangkabau adopted Islam.

Heading south, 65 km (40 miles) from Bukittinggi is the village of **Balimbing,** a traditional settlement with many Minang houses almost 200 years old. **Lake Singkarak** is another beautiful inland lake, smaller than Maninjau. On the road to the hot springs at **Sulit Air** are many rumah bolon, long houses with as many as 20 families in each. **Solok** is a wealthy agricultural village with many finely decorated rumah adat.

One of the oldest Minang villages where sacred tablets are stored is **Batu Sangkar.** On the way you'll pass **Tabek Patah,** a scenic overlook with views to the Harau Valley. **Rao Rao** is three miles farther south, another very old settlement, and nearby is the **Al Huda Mosque.** The mosque dates from 1917 and is built in a blend of Minangkabau and Muslim styles. Its peaked roof caps a central minaret that is used by the village's muezzin five times daily to call the faithful to prayer. A few miles farther is the lovely **Pondok Flora Restoran,** a Padang eatery with cane chairs and rattan tables on covered decks above a goldfish pond.

From Batu Sangkar, opelets, usually filled with schoolchildren, run regularly to the **Istana Pagarruyung,** a palace with a 12-peaked roof that was restored by the government in 1976. The original palace was built for the Sultan Bagagarsah, who died in 1889; his family continued to live there until the palace accidentally burned down. It was rebuilt as a grand museum. Scholars have tracked past generations of the sultan's family to Brunei and Malaysia, where they established

Minangkabau enclaves that flourish today. The tremendous space is divided into rooms for the king's seven daughters and their families. To the left of the entrance are two rooms kept for the *bundo kanduang,* the clan's eldest stateswoman. Behind the beautifully decorated main building, through the unused kitchen, is a smaller pavilion used for prayers and religious study. The palace's second floor was the room for unmarried princesses, and the third floor (now a library) was their very ornate playroom. The Istana Pagarruyung is a testament to the Minang artistry. It's open daily from 8 a.m. to 5 p.m. for an admission of Rp 200 (10¢).

North of Bukittinggi in the village of **Palupuh** grows the unique *Rafflesia arnoldi* (yes, Raffles was here too!), the largest flower in the world. It blooms for a short time only, once a year during the rainy season (November to March), but if you're set on planning your trip around it, contact the tourist office for predictions. The merely curious should try to obtain their brochure with a photograph of the ugly thing.

The **Rimba Panti Nature Preserve,** 61 miles north of Bukittinggi, is another popular hiking area filled with flora and fauna from the Sumatran highlands and coastal plains.

3. SOUTH SULAWESI: TANA TORAJA

Tana Toraja, northeast of Sumatra and Java, is the land of the Torajanese people (also called Torajaland) in the province of Sulawesi Selatan. The unique Toraja culture is centered around the worship of the water buffalo and manifests itself in ornate peaked-roof houses, visual arts, funerary rites, and burial practices, making this the prime tourist destination on the island of Sulawesi. Formerly known as the Celebes, Sulawesi is a two-hour flight northeast of Java and is politically divided into the provinces of North, Central, Southeast, and South Sulawesi. The north-coast capital, Manado, is frequented by diving enthusiasts, who compare local coral reefs to the more celebrated underwater preserves off the nearby Philippines.

South Sulawesi has a population of 6,600,000, primarily of Bugi, Makassar, and Toraja descent. Although each group retains its own language and culture, that of the Torajanese has remained the most visible. The Buginese from the Capital, Ujung Pandang ("Cape of Pandanus Leaves"), are framed for their sailing and boat-building skills. Their broad-beamed sailing craft known as *pinisi,* once the terror of traders passing through on the way to the Spice Islands (the present-day Moluccas), are a lifeline to every harbor. The Makassar tribes, who long ruled the southern kingdoms of Goa and Bone, are now farmers and fishermen with a special weaving tradition. The coveted Makassar cotton, usually a cool green color, like their landscape, is naturally dyed and hand-woven into plaid or striped lengths, then polished to a rich sheen with a conch shell. The houses of the south-central plains have rattan walls, louvered windows, small porches, and roofs rising to an "X" in front and back, typical of Makassar architecture.

THE TORAJA CULTURE: According to Toraja legends, the first settlers arrived by boat from the far south, sailed toward the mountains, and ran aground near Bamba Puang in the central highlands. They spread out to establish villages and, having no resources, transformed their ships into houses. To avoid clashes with other tribes, they moved north into the forests (the present Tana Toraja) and built houses with roofs shaped like boat prows in memory of their first homes.

Scholars believe that the Torajanese are descended from a proto-Malay people who left the region between Assam in northeastern India and the present Thailand/Burma border during the onslaught of Mongol raiders. The Batak tribes in North Sumatra, the Dayak in Kalimantan, and some tribes in the Moluccas and Philippines are thought to have emigrated at the same time.

Toraja Society

Toraja house-building is governed by an adat which dictates that the traditional bamboo roof have squared off, horn-like peaks over the front and back. Most *tongkonan* (original family houses) are still built of wood and roofed in bamboo, but even modern concrete buildings have painted sheet-metal roofs in the traditional swayback shape. The house frame is ornately carved with floral and geometric patterns, and painted in the traditional Toraja colors: white representing the flesh of human existence, red for blood, yellow for God's glory, and black for death. To indicate status, the horns of buffalo sacrificed in ancestral burial ceremonies are mounted on a pillar in front of each house. Toraja society is governed by a noble class, with *topakenge* or spiritual leaders reporting to noble tribal chieftains. Commons are divided into a four-tier caste system that dictates little more than the level of funeral ceremony accorded the deceased.

Toraja Religion and Funeral Ceremonies

Even after widespread conversion to Christianity, the Torajanese follow *aluk todolo,* or the teachings of the ancestors, an adat that was passed on orally. It teaches a belief in Puang Matua, one creator who is worshipped as three deities; as god of the heavens, earth, and underworld. The adat of ancestor worship, particularly funeral ceremonies, is based on the belief that the souls of every animal sacrificed will accompany the deceased to heaven and serve him. Inheritance is meted out according to the devotion accorded one's elders. Men or women can be rewarded by a family's fortune if they provide regular offerings and a fine funeral; families must keep their deceased in a coffin in their home until such time (often several years) as they can afford a proper burial ceremony.

Rambu solo, the burial ceremonies, are meant to provide for the soul of the dead in *puya* (the afterlife), but also indicate social status, provide an opportunity to repay gifts from other families, and determine the allocation of family inheritance. Codified ceremonies are as simple as the *dibai a'pa',* when just four pigs are sacrificed the night before a burial, to the overwhelming *dipapitung bongi,* a seven-day and -night ceremony when a number of water buffalo are sacrificed and an exact carved wooden effigy of the deceased is honored. If the person was of noble caste, this ceremony is always required. Torajanese believe that the ancestors' souls will become demi-gods after so much worship. Typical ceremonies, usually held between July and September when the harvest is in and the cash flow most secure, last up to four days. On the first day the village priest would come to the deceased's home to give a sermon before the body departs for its journey to the burial site (nobles would be carried in a peaked-roof bier). The next day guests are greeted as they arrive at the burial site with gifts for the hosts, or pigs and buffaloes to contribute to the ceremony. (It is recommended that tourists bring cigarettes or food items.) Guests are led to *lantang,* ornately painted, temporary thatch pavilions constructed at the site to house visitors. The corpse remains in richly carved and painted coffin at the top level of the *lakkean,* a small thatch building sometimes decorated in fine beadwork.

After this, the animals are quickly but ritually slaughtered, after the guests have admired them (buffaloes painted in many colors are particularly prized and equal in value to seven plain animals). The least costly ceremonies (each plain buffalo is worth over $300) require the sacrifice of four to seven buffaloes. If there are many guests and many animals this phase can take several days. Although the family keeps the buffalo hides, the meat of the sacrificed animals is divided up among the guests to take home. Buffalo horns will be saved to mount on a post outside the central tongkonan. On the last day, the burial itself takes place, in one of the traditional ways.

The Toraja adat prescribes four types of *liang,* or graves: families buried together "underground" with a typical peaked-roof tomb; a "hanging" grave or coffin placed in a natural cave; a "stone" or "rock-cut tomb" cut into the cliffs to hold a corpse and subsequent family members; and coffins buried underground in the Christian tradition. Hanging graves and rock-cut tombs of the nobility are marked by carved wooden effigies of the deceased within.

Visitors to Tana Toraja often witness some or all of the stages of a burial ceremony, and can always tour the region to see grave sites and many traditional villages. A full slaughter ceremony is quite dramatic and gory—the faint-hearted be forewarned. In the July-to-September high season it becomes almost impossible to find a hotel, or a car and driver, or even a local guide in Rantepao, so we'd urge you to plan your trip through a local travel agent, or avoid coming in these months. We felt a guide was essential to our understanding of this fascinating culture, but if you're an anthropologist or speak good Bahasa Indonesia, you can see and learn a lot with just a car and driver.

GETTING TO TANA TORAJA: It's impossible to reach Tana Toraja without connecting through Ujung Pandang (UJPG). **Garuda Indonesia** flies there three times daily from Jakarta, twice daily from Surabaya, and once daily from Biak (Irian Jaya), Denpasar, Medan, and Menado. **Bouraq Airways** flies weekly from Balikpapan, Kalimantan. The modern **Hasanuddin Airport** (where you may spend *lots* of time) has a telephone and Telex office (open daily from 8 a.m. to 6 p.m.), a postal agent, moneychanger, gift shop, Information (Penerangan) Desk with luggage deposit, and the excellent Mandai restaurant in the departures terminal. The arrivals terminal next door has a helpful Tourism Information Desk, another luggage deposit, and a regulated yellow taxi service that charges Rp 8,000 ($5) to any destination in the city, 23 km (14 miles) and about 20 minutes away. If this strains your budget, walk outside the airport entrance for about 500 yards and hail a bemo, which charges Rp 1,200 (75¢) per person into town.

From here, it's relatively simple, though time-consuming, to reach Tana Toraja. The 320,000 Torajanese are spread in villages around the small commercial center of Rantepao, situated in the highlands 328 km (200 miles) north of Ujung Pandang—ten hours away by bus, seven hours by car, or 45 minutes by plane.

By Air

The most expedient way is to arrange your flight to UJPG to make a direct connection to the **Merpati Nusantara** flight to "Tator" (Tana Toraja). Merpati currently flies three days a week: on Tuesday at 10:30 a.m. and on Thursday and Saturday at 9 a.m., returning to UJPG from Tana Toraja at 10:15 or 11:15 a.m. the same day. At the time of writing, the fare was Rp 40,300 ($25.25) each way. Flights land at Pongtiku airport in Rantetayo, 12 km (7¼ miles) west of Makale and 30 km (18 miles) south of Rantepao; taxis and bemos into the cities are available. If you're flying to Tator or elsewhere from UJPG, get to the airport at least one hour in advance so that your seats aren't given away on the often overbooked flights. Have an alternative travel plan if time is critical as flights are sometimes cancelled because of bad weather in Toraja (often in the rainy season) or in UJPG. If you prefer to drive one way, count on flying up and driving back.

By Private Car

Several travel agents in UJPG, such as **Limbunan Tours and Travel** (tel. 0411/5010), **Pacto Ltd.** (tel. 0411/83208), or **Ramayana Tours,** at Jl. Bawakaraeng 121 (tel. 0411/4153), are recommended for tour packages, car rentals, and other travel services. They charter Jeeps (to explore the widest range of sites if you have more than two days) seating four for about Rp 56,000 ($35) a day with a three-day minimum, which includes gas and the driver's expenses. A larger group can charter a minibus seating six for about Rp 53,000 ($33) a day with a three-day minimum. A private Jeep affords the luxury of stopping at will, continuing on, or tracking down a far-off burial ceremony. Daily guides cost about Rp 18,000 ($11.25) to Rp 25,000 ($15.50) per day, and can be arranged through the Rantepao Tourist Information Office (no phone) on Jl. Jend. Yani or at the Toraja Cottages Hotel, two miles south of the central market. In the hectic July-to-September burial season arrangements should be made as far in advance as possible.

By Bus

The budget alternative is provided by the **Liman Express Bus Company,** at Jl. Laiya 25 (tel. 5851), or contact the Marlin Hotel (tel. 5542), opposite the Ramayana Hotel, for tickets; or the newer **Alam Indah** company, at Jl. Agus Salim 28 (tel. 4937). Both are local buses that run twice a day to Tana Toraja, at 7 a.m. and at 7 p.m. Large buses are not air-conditioned but are fairly comfortable; for Rp 6,000 ($3.75) a ticket you can survive ten hours in a narrow seat. Buses stop at the district capital of Makale (with limited tourist services) and continue on to the main market of Rantepao. All companies claim to provide free transportation from your hotel to the UJPG Terminal Bis. Check with the airport's Tourist Information Desk or the office at Jl. Jend. Yani (tel. 7128) for the current bus company favorite. Once in Rantepao you'll have to rent a bemo for sightseeing from the central station at the Pasar; with bargaining you'll pay about Rp 40,000 ($25) per day. Other travelers assured us that it was impossible to rent a motorbike.

By Tour

An all-inclusive land package, with car and driver, English-speaking guide, hotels in UJPG and Tana Toraja, and meals cost $190 to $285 (in 1988) per person for a four-day (two days of travel, one day in UJPG, one day in Toraja) trip. We recommend the five-day version, that allows for some serendipity in your sightseeing. Contact **Pacto Ltd.,** at Jl. Jend. Sudirman 56, UJPG (tel. 0411/83208), or **Limbunan Tours and Travel,** at Jl. Bawakaraeng 40, UJPG (tel. 0411/21710), for information.

READERS' TOURING SUGGESTION: "We arranged a three-day tour of the land of the Torajas. Tour cost for the two of us was $250, including driver, guide, hotel, breakfast, and dinner. It was a super tour and our base hotel in Rantepao, the Missiliana, is very lovely, new, and built like Toraja houses. This area is new and just opening up to tourism. It's a must!" (Jean and Tony Triumpho, Canajoharie, N.Y.).

UJUNG PANDANG: Since many visitors spend at least a night in UJPG on
either their way to or from Tana Toraja, we provide a brief look at the city.

This city of 700,000 near the southwestern tip of the island, formerly known as Makassar, is rapidly maturing from an overgrown port town to a bustling Third World metropolis. Half-completed roads, expanding services, constant construction, and the din of progress startle the first-time visitor. Most arrange their Tana Toraja itineraries as quickly as possible and leave.

Orientation

The most pleasant part of Ujung Pandang (or UJPG to the locals) is its port. The city's westernmost street, **Jl. Pasar Ikan,** on the Makassar Strait, is a lively promenade lined with seafood restaurants and the city's **Pasar Malam** (night market). The harbor, **Pelabuhan Paotere,** is most beautiful around dawn (6 a.m.) or sunset (6 to 7 p.m.) when hundreds of pinisi schooners are being loaded. Out in the strait are dozens of *bagang,* bamboo fishing platforms that sit above the water like daddy longlegs, illuminated by kerosene lanterns to attract fish.

On the north shore, at the site of the 16th-century Fort Makassar built by the King of Goa, is **Fort Rotterdam.** This collection of Dutch colonial buildings houses government offices, the interesting **Lagaligo Museum** of regional culture, open daily except Monday from 8 a.m. to 2 p.m. for an admission of Rp 150 (10¢), and the prison that held the Indonesian hero of independence, Prince Diponegoro. South of the port is Taman Anggrek, the orchid garden better known as the **House of Clara Bundt.** The daughter of a German expatriate and Ambonese mother, Clara began a collection of seashells that has become its own tourist attraction. Her father collects, raises, and sells orchids from the house, shipping them as far as Europe. This eccentric establishment will delight you daily from 9 a.m. to 5 p.m.

Unfortunately, this rapidly expanded city and its services are very spread out; Hasanuddin Airport is 23 km (14 miles) east of here. The Terminal Bis is also to the east on Jl. Urif Sumoharjo, although most overland travelers to Rantepao (the center of Tana Toraja) catch an express bus from agents' offices a bit closer in. Most of the city's major avenues are named after islands, and its minor cross streets after fish.

Useful Information

A **Tourist Information Office** is in the transit hall of Hasanuddin Airport; it's open daily from 8 a.m. until the last flight has arrived, and has the only maps of the city and of Tana Toraja. The inconvenient government Tourist Information Office is a taxi ride away from the port at Jl. Andi Pangerang Petta Rani (tel. 21142). It's open from 8 a.m. to 2 p.m. Monday through Thursday, to 11 a.m. on Friday, and till 12:30 p.m. on Saturday; closed Sunday.

Dial 110 in case of **police emergency,** or 118 for an **ambulance**. . . . There is a Rumah Sakit **public hospital** (tel. 82122) and the Pelamonia **military hospital** (tel. 4710) in the city.

The **telephone area code** for Ujung Pandang is 0441; the **Kantor Telepon** is Jl. Balai Kota 4 and the **Kantor Pos** is at Jl. Slamet Riyadhi 10, both near the port.

The time in Sulawesi is Greenwich Mean Time plus eight hours.

Sulawesi is 13 hours ahead of New York and 16 hours ahead of Los Angeles; add one hour during Daylight Savings.

The **Bank Indonesia** and **Bank Rakyat** near the Raodah Hotel are open from 8 a.m. to 4 p.m. weekdays; the **moneychanger** at the airport is open for all flights. . . . There is a left-luggage office at the airport departures terminal. It's open daily to meet all flights and charges Rp 600 (35¢) per piece per day. . . . There is a **Fujicolor** shop on Jl. Riburana and a **Kodak** shop on Jl. Irian.

Getting Around Ujung Pandang

Within the city you can rent a taxi for Rp 4,500 ($2.75) per hour (two-hour minimum) for sightseeing. To sun and swim at Samalona Island, just a few miles east of UJPG, rent a boat from behind the Golden Makassar Hotel for the half-hour trip. Bring a picnic or sample the local warung; boats rent for Rp 3,500 ($2.25) per person round trip with a prearranged pickup time, or for Rp 35,000 ($22) for the day. There are bemos running from the central market on Jl. Jend. Sudirman costing Rp 350 (20¢), and clusters of hungry becaks at every corner.

Accommodations

With the exception of our first choice, all of Ujung Pandang's accommodations range in price from $5 to $30 for two, including tax and service charges. Most are used by business people so rooms are available year round, but you should book ahead during the July-to-September tourist rush for the funeral season in Tana Toraja.

The best in town is the **Makassar Golden Hotel,** located at Jl. Pasar Ikan 52 (tel. 0411/22208). It has an international flavor, with huge, modern carpeted rooms, batik hangings, TVs, mini-bars, and other first-class amenities. All rooms face the strait and offshore islands, fishing platforms, and the setting sun. There is a French restaurant, a great terrace coffeeshop with harbor views, and a nice swimming pool. You'll pay for all the comforts; doubles are $67 and singles are $58, but well worth it.

The city's largest hostelry, with 206 rooms, a large pool, and a 24-hour coffeeshop, the **Marannu City Hotel** is conveniently located two blocks from the port at Jl. Sultan Hasanuddin 3-5 (tel. 0441/21470). Pleasant and clean doubles, well kept though undistinguished, have a TV, mini-bar, and seating area, and rent for Rp 64,000 ($40).

An excellent value across the street is the **Pondok Suada Indah,** at Jl. Sultan Hasanuddin 14 (tel. 0441/7179). The guesthouse consists of two charming Dutch-era houses divided into large, comfortably appointed rooms furnished like a European pension. Rooms are air-conditioned, with spotless, modern private bathrooms. In the more luxurious front house doubles cost Rp 43,500 ($27.25) and singles are Rp 38,500 ($24); in the simpler rear house they are Rp 10,000 ($6.25) cheaper. The Pondok's staff are very gracious but speak little English; many visitors will find its charm worth this inconvenience.

Generations of low-budget travelers have stopped at the **Hotel Ramayana,** located at Jl. Bawakaraeng 121 (tel. 0411/22165), next to the pickup point for buses to Tana Toraja in the east-central part of the city. Its convenient location and price are the only things worth recommending, as its three classes of rooms start at shabby and go down from there. "First-class" rooms fetch Rp 28,800 ($18) for two; rates range down to double "economy" rooms for Rp 12,800 ($8), still the best budget deal in town.

Dining

Dining fits in well with one of UJPG's best activities, a stroll along The Strand, Jl. Pasar Ikan. It's billed as "The Longest Table in the World" because at night locals gather along the concrete balustrade and dine from tiny pushcart warungs that crowd the sidewalk. Although surrounded by water and a thriving fishing industry, the warung all compete for the best nasi goreng! A small café mid-Strand, the **Kios Semarang** offers an excellent vantage to the harbor from its third-floor roof. Over a beer, some tasty jalan kote (a meat and vegetable turnover), and lemper (steamed rice and beef wrapped in a banana leaf), you can watch the parade below. It's best at sunset, from 6 to 7 p.m.

Since the Bugis are seafaring folk you can expect terrific, fresh fish in Ujung Pandang. One of the better seafood cafés is the **Losari Beach Restaurant,** on the waterfront just south of the Golden Makassar Hotel (tel. 6309). The dining area is Indonesian-modern with ceiling fans, batik, and clean tiles, and the fish is delicious. An appetizer of otak otak ikan (fish cake wrapped in banana leaves) followed by grilled baronang, papakulu, titang, or bandeng (all local fish), and stir-fried greens makes a great meal for two for about Rp 13,500 ($8.50).

The **Anging Mammiri Terrace,** at the Makassar Golden Hotel (tel. 22208), is the port's prettiest venue for seafood or any other treat. It hangs over the water's edge with an unrivaled view that should whet your appetite for ikan bakar, a variety of grilled fish, or salads, omelets, or hamburgers. A full meal can be had for under Rp 18,000 ($11.25), and the many snacks, desserts, and famed locally grown rogusta coffee (boiled with cardamom) for under Rp 9,000 ($6.50). Open daily from 7 a.m. to 2 a.m.

If you want more formal fare or an air-conditioned, elegant environment, try the same hotel's waterside **Losari Room,** open at 7 p.m. nightly to serve French cuisine.

Excellent seafood inland with a funky Sulawesi décor is found at **Restaurant Asia Baru,** at Jl. Salahulu 2 (tel. 3659), a 15-minute cab ride from the port.

Your choice of local fish, squid, or prawns is grilled at their outdoor barbecue; two will pay a reasonable Rp 11,200 ($7).

For seafood prepared in a Chinese style, try **Setia,** one of the local favorites in UJPG's Chinatown section at Jl. Bacan 1A (tel. 4587). The Setia has a tasty fried whole fish in sweet-and-sour sauce and fried crabs with oyster sauce; two can dine for about Rp 22,000 ($13.75).

RANTEPAO—THE CENTER OF TANA TORAJA: Rantepao is the region's commercial center and the easiest base from which to explore the Toraja villages, burial sites, and crafts center. Makale, about 20 km (12 miles) south, is the capital of the Regency of Tana Toraja, and offers a few tourist services, government offices, and some losmen, in case you're stuck without a room in the busy season.

Orientation

Most of the Toraja cultural sites are within 30 km (18 miles) of Rantepao. This area, about 2,650 feet above sea level, is verdant, crisscrossed with streams, and refreshingly undeveloped. Though the government has installed paved roads to some backwoods sites, others require a short hike, a climb, or a slosh through mud.

Rantepao reminds us of a Wild West town. The central **Pasar** dominates the intersection of the few major streets with the bustle of hawkers, villagers from the hinterlands, merchants pushing cheap souvenirs, and vendors of piping, rubber, wire, tools, and other implements of the new development. The north-south street that crosses Pasar square is called **Jl. Jend. Yani** south to Makale and **Jl. Pahlawa** north to the village of Sadan, but it's been newly renamed Jl. Mappanyuki (although most locals don't know it). The main east-west street is **Jl. Diponegoro.** Rantepao is still small enough that there are no street signs, traffic lights, or formal use of street names.

Useful Information

The **Tourist Information Office** (no phone) is on Jl. Pontigu (or Jl. Jend. Yani) about half a mile south of the market. They're open daily from 7 a.m. to 4 p.m., are very helpful when someone who speaks English is on duty, have the only maps (hand-drawn) of the area, and are a clearinghouse for day guides and charter bemos. (The Toraja Cottages Hotel also sends its staff as day guides, when available, at the same rates.)

South of here you'll find the small local **Rumah Sakit Hospital. . . .** The **Merpati Nusantara** office is on Jl. Pontigu/Yani (tel. 97), near the tourist office, and is open daily except Sunday from 7 a.m. to 2 p.m. . . . The **Liman and Alam Indah bus company offices** are on Jl. Diponegoro off the square.

There is a **Bank Rakyat** off the square open Monday through Friday from 7:30 a.m. to noon, on Saturday till 11 a.m. A **moneychanger** cum "antiques" dealer is on the square and changes traveler's checks at usurious rates from 8 a.m. to 5 p.m. six days and noon to 5 p.m. on Sunday. (We suggest that you use the bank.)

There is a **Kantor Pos** south of the square. . . . The new **Perumtel Telepon** office next door is open 24 hours to make long-distance calls, but all calls must be paid for in cash. The few local phones in use talk only to other local numbers.

Tana Toraja can be muggy and hot during the day and cool in the evening; a sweater, rain gear, closed walking shoes or hiking boots, and mosquito repellent are essential. . . . The **Pasar** is a fun place to browse, particularly on market day which occurs once every six days. That's a good time to buy Toraja crafts or ceremonial objects from eager out-of-town villagers; otherwise, quality and prices are better in the few Toraja crafts villages.

The book *Toraja, An Introduction to a Unique Culture,* by L. T. Tangdilintin and M. Syafei, is available in most hotels and shops and will interest ethnography buffs.

Adventure Travelers Note: Overnight hikes and treks are very popular from Rantepao. If you bring your own gear, the tourist office in Rantepao can help you find a local guide for Rp 30,000 ($18.75) per day, who can lead you on a three- to seven-day trek through the forest and jungle to neighboring villages.

Accommodations

After the first two hotels listed below, the quality, comfort, and cleanliness of sleeping quarters declines rapidly. Room and board, though not expensive by our standards, are high priced by Indonesia's. However, in the July-to-September high season (when rooms are sold out six months in advance) travelers are at the mercy of an underdeveloped tourism infrastructure controlled by new tour operators from UJPG. Note that none of the hotels has phones that connect to long-distance lines, and most have no telephones at all.

Tana Toraja's best accommodations are at **Toraja Cottages,** a complex of 63 attached rooms and bungalows about 1½ miles east of Pasar Square (tel. 220); reservations can be made in Jakarta at Jl. Johor 17 (tel. 0221/340-122), or by writing to Toraja Cottages, Rantepao, Sulawesi Selatan. All rooms have carpeting, modern baths, and a veranda facing the surrounding hills and lushly planted grounds. Rooms 429 to 440 of the attached blocks are bigger and include a work space; all rooms are Rp 58,000 ($36.25) for two. Three hillside bungalows contain several rooms at the same rate with a better view, but are smaller, and there are two deluxe VIP suites at Rp 164,800 ($103) a night. There is a small pool, two dining rooms with carved-wood décor, and a bar serving fresh-squeezed tarong juice, a unique local treat.

The **Misiliana Hotel** (tel. 56; can be only called locally. Telex: 71476), has another 63 rooms with full amenities out on the main road to Makale in Pao, about 1½ miles south of Rantepao. Economy rooms in their original wing are worn but have Toraja carving, small modern baths, and verandas facing the garden and rent for Rp 51,200 ($28) for two. Rooms in the new addition are larger, with an inside seating area and views over the surrounding rice paddies, and cost Rp 58,000 ($36.25) for two. A new wing, five minutes' walk down the road, also offers a new pool and large sundeck on the roof of the dining hall. The new rooms are the best in town but are right on the main road.

Rooms in Torajaland drop from moderate to low-budget very quickly. Most of the town's small hotels are kept fairly clean, have private bathrooms with Asian toilets and mandi tubs, are a short walk to the few restaurants and Pasar, but have few or no English-speaking staff. The two-story **Wisma Maria** is at Jl. Ratulangi 27 off the main street, a quiet location but for the cacophony of neighboring farmyards. There is a pleasant courtyard for reading and a breakfast hall with a small collection of Toraja artifacts. Very simple, poured-concrete rooms are worn but clean: for Rp 9,200 ($5.75) single or Rp 15,500 ($9.75) double you get a hot-water mandi; for cold water only, Rp 3,200 ($2) less. The nearby **Hotel Indra** is at Jl. Landorundun 63 (tel. 97). The planted courtyard and open lobby are built around an *alang*, a Toraja rice house. Spartan rooms with a private mandi and toilet cost Rp 15,500 ($9.75) for one or two. The **Hotel Marlin**, at Jl. Mappanyuki/Pahlawa next to the Liman bus office, has second-floor rooms with simple, cold-water facilities, but is often packed with university students from UJPG who are taking a school trip to Tana Toraja. Across the street is the small, new **Wisma Indo Grace** with more rooms.

There are other budget lodgings, less convenient because of their out-of-town locations. The **Wisma Maria II** is a friendly collection of 16 attached rooms on a hillside above Pao, a district about 1½ miles south of Rantepao. Small rooms are shabby but have a hot-water private mandi and rent for Rp 18,000 ($11.25) for two. The government-run **Batapupan Hostel,** on the main road between Rantepao and Makale, has 19 clean rooms with a view over the neighboring hills. Three doubles with hot water cost Rp 11,600 ($7.25) each, and the 16 rooms with private cold-water mandi cost Rp 3,000 ($2) per bed. Up the road is the **Wisma Puri Artha,** with very simple accommodations for a bit more. These hotels are excellent value, but only if you're touring with a car and driver or need a base from which to trek to remote villages.

Dining

Tana Toraja imports a limited range of foods; consider this an opportunity to try some local dishes unavailable elsewhere. The specialty is papiong: buffalo meat, local spices, and coconut milk steamed in a bamboo shoot. Papiong can be sampled at Toraja Cottages or the Misiliana if ordered in advance. Coconut is used in the preparation of bage kotu, a local candy, and to make gula mena, a sweet palm-sugar wine that is collected from tree tops with long bamboo pipelines. The tarong, a dark-red, oval fruit grown only in this area, has a kiwi-like texture and refreshing, sweet taste. It's best sampled as fresh-squeezed juice but is made into a wonderful jam and sauce for rice pudding. The seeds of the tarong, ground with clove and local spices, flavor the excellent pararan, a blackened pork cutlet that's a favorite with Torajanese. Finish your meal with the refreshment taken by rice farmers each afternoon—a strong cup of rogusta (boiled with cardamom) or first quality arabica coffee.

One of the few restaurants outside the hotels, **Rachmat** is on the Pasar square and perfect for lunch. Some 38 choices of Indonesian, Chinese, and quasi-Western entrees appear in an Indonesian, English, French, German, and Italian menu. Rachmat's folding bridge chairs and Formica tables are jammed with tourists of every persuasion, giving Rantepao an unusually cosmopolitan air. It's a friendly place to swap stories and meet others; all the food is tasty if not gourmet, and entrees run Rp 1,750 ($1) to Rp 6,000 ($3.75). Try the steak of buffalo tongue or their filling nasi campur (rice with vegetables), and accompany it with a fresh tarong or marquisa juice. Tarajaland is famous for the nectar of these fruits, found only here. Don't miss them.

Sightseers can stop for a fancier meal at the **Misiliana Hotel,** 1½ miles south of Rantepao. Their restaurant, decorated with Toraja motifs, offers a set menu of Indonesian food daily; lunch is Rp 8,000 ($5) and dinner costs Rp 11,000 ($7) per person.

EXPLORING TANA TORAJA: The landscapes of Tana Toraja are surprisingly dramatic and graceful, but it is the Toraja burial ceremonies that are the prime attraction for most visitors. The Tourist Offices in Ujung Pandang (tel. 0411/7128) and in Rantepao are kept informed of upcoming ceremonies, and in the case of rare, elaborate rites for noblemen, may know several months in advance. However, there are common ceremonies frequently, and upon arrival, you can check with your hotel reception to see if any are occurring in nearby villages. Don't miss several of the other sites in the region. We're listing only the best-known and most accessible ones that can be seen in one or two days; the locally produced maps note almost 50 places of interest.

The hanging graves at **Lemo,** 6½ miles south of Rantepao, are one of the best-known sites. The graves are cut out of a rock cliff and sealed with a wooden door. Standing along roughly sculpted balconies are a number of wooden effigies, carved, painted, and clothed to resemble the deceased hidden inside. Unfortunately, in recent years several have been stolen and more removed by families fearing theft. The choir of solemn figures that once lined the cliffs has been reduced to fewer than a dozen, standing on the highest tiers. The Indonesian government claims to have found several in European collections; for the Torajanese who have relatives buried, it is better to leave the grave unmarked than to have the personification of a deceased's soul taken away from Torajaland.

The oldest site of hanging graves is at **Marante,** four miles east of Rantepao. The earliest Torajanese buried their dead in wooden coffins shaped like buffalo or pigs and placed the coffins in shallow pits. To prevent theft of the relics buried with them, they began putting the coffins up in the cliffs, high off the ground. Here, a collection of biers, skulls, and bones, some 500 years old, are tucked into nooks and crevices. A new, small house tomb with a Christian cross marks the recent grave of a nobleman.

There are natural caves or hanging graves at **Londa,** four miles southwest of Rantepao. Local guides—tip them Rp 2,000 ($1.25)—at the site will take you into the cave with a lantern to see the new coffins. **Pallawa,** six miles north of Rantepao, is a traditional village of Toraja homes with moss growing from the original bamboo roofs. Opposite the tongkonan are smaller alang, rice houses with sheltered platforms where farmers rest, play cards, and drink coffee after a long day in the fields. The weaving village of **Sadan** is 1½ miles to the north, and is a collection of typical houses by a tranquil river. The chieftain's house by the water's edge has 57 buffalo horns and a necklace of pig's jawbones displayed out front. Women weave in the village shop, making new sarongs (from Rp 6,400 or $4, and up), decorative fabrics, and scarves (from Rp 2,500, or $1.50). These items are sold at reasonable prices, but woven blankets from Sumba and Timor are quite expensive. The village chief has given into demand and now welcomes travelers who want to spend the night. Mats, floor space, use of the outhouse, and a simple breakfast cost Rp 6,000 ($3.75) per person.

Ke'te' Kesu is another village of traditional houses south of Rantepao, built around a plaza and intermingled with new lantang constructed for the huge funeral ceremony of King Ne'Raba in January 1987. Beadwork and handcrafts are for sale outside many of the tongkonan. If you follow the footpath back toward the woods you'll find the tomb and effigy of King Ne'Raba, which cost over Rp 17,000,000 ($10,625) to build. During our visit, villagers were still cleaning the 40 sets of buffalo horns from his burial ceremony. There are hanging graves in the rocky hillside, with remnants of coffins shaped like pigs or buffalo and tongkonan-shaped biers.

The large tongkonan of wealthy officials can be seen in **Siguntu,** a hill village 4¼ miles southwest of Rantepao across the river. The largest one was the seat of local government, but all display rich carving and coloration. In **Sangalla,** about 7½ miles east of Makale, there are the royal houses of the last Sangalla king and effigies of the royal family. The 14 alang, or rice barns, of a wealthy landowner are lined up at **Nanggala,** nine miles east of Rantepao. He and his wife lived in the original small house with a carved buffalo head and portrait of President Soeharto under the eaves. It's thought to be 300 years old and is simply maintained by changing the bamboo roofing every 30 years. The landowner's widow now lives in the fancier, gingerbread-trimmed house next to it and opens the traditional buildings to visitors after every harvest.

The burial ceremony site at **Bori,** three miles north of Rantepao, has several *simbuang* or chiseled stones, but we found the megalithic stones at **Karassi,** on a hillside only 1½ miles south of Rantepao, used since the 1700s to tie up buffalo before the sacrifice, to be more interesting. It's now a permanent burial site for use by any villager; the many lantang were built in the late '70s.

From Sulawesi we fly east to Jayapura, our final foray off the beaten path.

4. IRIAN JAYA, STONE AGE TRIBES OF THE BALIEM VALLEY

The simplicity and beauty of the peoples who inhabit Irian Jaya is difficult to convey. Their warmth and childlike innocence took us completely by surprise and left an indelible impression. The primitive cultures of these Stone Age tribes have remained intact precisely because they live so far off the beaten path. Irian

Jaya's gateway, Jayapura, is over 3,500 km (2,175 miles) and seven hours by plane from Jakarta. And the Dani tribes of the Baliem Valley, like others settled in the impenetrable jungles, who live at a pace that has been unchanged for centuries, can be reached only by foot. To meet them is to come face to face with our own primordial selves, and to see the future—a travel experience that pales all others.

ORIENTATION: Irian Jaya, the western half of the island of New Guinea, is Indonesia's largest province. Its 422,000 km² (152,000 square miles) comprise 21% of the country's land mass, yet its 1,325,000 inhabitants give it a population density of only 3.2 people per square kilometer. The island stretches like a grounded bird with its head poking out into the Pacific, almost 1,200 km (725 miles) from the west coast to its border with Papua New Guinea.

The climate ranges from the humid and tropical coastal areas with temperatures between 20°C and 30°C (68°F and 86°F) to the central highland plateaus where temperatures drop below 10°C (50°F) in the evening. Inland waterways fed by heavy rains cut through the mangrove swamps, rain forest, and thick jungle of the south. The island's central mountain range has snow-covered peaks crowned by Indonesia's highest peak, Mount Jayawijaya, at 5,500 meters (17,875 feet). The mountains cause great weather shifts: in the north part of the island the rainy season is from October to March; in the south part, from March to October; in the central highlands, the rains shift from valley to valley. From September to February it rains almost every day somewhere in the Baliem Valley.

About one-third of the Irianese land is protected by the government. The island's wildlife is varied and exotic—kangaroos and kus-kus like Australia, several species of cendrawasih or birds of paradise, cockatoos, casuarius, parrots, and crocodiles. Unfortunately, Irian Jaya is also blessed with huge mineral deposits, oil and timber reserves that are being exploited at an alarming rate. Nickel is mined in Waegeo, copper at Kokonao, oil at Mamberamo and Sorong, and hard woods, especially the local ironwood, from many areas.

The only thing that has slowed the total despoliation of the island is the difficulty of traversing it. Sorong, on the "bird's head" (northwest corner of the island), is the biggest commercial port. The interior has no through roads, but 52 government-owned and 207 missionary-owned airfields provide access to inland villages and transmigration settlements. As part of an effort to modernize the most "backward" province, the national government has begun construction on a Trans-Irian Highway, which will link Jayapura on the north coast to Merauke, 1,500 km (900 miles) away on the south coast. Construction at each coast and in the middle at Wamena signals the change and possible demise of one of the most fascinating cultures on earth.

HISTORY: Scholars believe that New Guinea was joined to the Australian land mass in the Pleistocene epoch. Negroids related to the aboriginal tribes were the first settlers, about 50,000 years ago. Melanesian Neolithic tribes came in a later migration from the east, settling in the coastal regions and mingling with Micronesian and Polynesian tribes. They brought tools, weapons, skills in woodcarving, outrigger canoes, and cowrie shells as currency. The island's interior remained inhabited primarily by Papuan tribes. The northwestern bird's head was later settled by Asian ancestors from the present-day Moluccas Islands. Hunting and gathering dominated until about 6,000 years ago, when the first signs of cultivation appeared. The indigenous Irianese now number hundreds of tribes with racial, social, and cultural differences and over 250 separate spoken languages.

The Spanish explorer Ortis de Retes discovered the northern islands of Biak and Yapen and the Irian land mass in June 1545 and named it Nova Guinea after another Spanish colony in Africa. In the 16th century many European traders from the nearby Spice Islands (the Moluccas) tried to establish colonies. Under Dutch colonization in 1848 the island's name was changed to New Guinea. The Dutch founded their capital at Manokwari in 1898 and founded Holandia, modern-day Jayapura, the present capital, in 1910 to affirm their presence during German occupation of neighboring Papua New Guinea.

The first two missionaries came from Europe in 1855, but it wasn't until 1933 that several representatives of different Christian faiths arrived. Today the majority in the northern, eastern, and western regions have been converted from their primitive belief in animism to Protestant Christianity, in the south and inland villages, to Catholicism, and in a few communities to Islam. In 1944 Irian Jaya put up little resistance to another set of invaders, the Allied Pacific fleet under Gen. Douglas MacArthur. More than 500 ships were moored in the harbor at Jayapura until the end of World War II.

After World War II the Dutch were forced out of the new Republic of Indonesia but annexed Irian Barat (West Irian) and eventually set up a State of Papua, causing tremendous friction with Indonesia. In 1962 a caretaker agreement was signed with the help of the United Nations that gave West Irian to the Republic of Indonesia with the provision that elections be held to determine the wish of the Irianese. The contested outcome gave the Indonesians supremacy, but not without controversy. Dissident factions such as the OPM guerillas from the Free Papua Movement have been much less active since that time, but almost every election has brought death and rioting to many towns.

THE BALIEM VALLEY: The Grand Valley of New Guinea, 72 km (43 miles) long and from 16 to 32 km (9½ to 19 miles) wide sweeps up from the banks of the rushing Baliem River at over 5,200 feet above sea level. The Baliem Valley was discovered from the air only in 1938 by an American explorer, Richard Archbold, who marveled at the stone walls that surrounded neatly planted, well-irrigated fields. He landed his seaplane on a nearby lake and discovered a Stone Age culture of primitive warriors and an agricultural society.

The valley is populated by more than 100,000 Dani tribesmen who have retained many of their traditional ways in a changing environment. Long hikes from the town of Wamena into the countryside, far from the first link in the Trans-Irian Highway, are the only way to meet the Dani and observe their primitive ways.

The Dani, a Stone Age Tribe

Dani men will always greet you with "*Nyack*" (the male greeting for other men) or "*Lauk*" (the greeting for women and by women) or with a "*Nyack Lak*" (to a mixed group). The smiling Dani have the whitest teeth and the warmest, gentlest handshakes. If asked, they enjoy being photographed, and a Polaroid picture or an offer of cigarettes or candy can bring exclamations of "Wawawawawa!" The Dani have seen most of our modern ways; they realize city life in Wamena means needing money for the shelter, food, and firewood they now provide for themselves. Those you meet trekking through the wild countryside have chosen to remain with the land that supports them.

The proud Dani men have the lean, muscular bodies of hunters and warriors and beautiful, serene faces with broad aborigine-like features. The male role in this agricultural society is to lead the rituals of animism, wielding *ye* (carved ceremonial stones), bows and arrows decorated with feathers. By day they sharpen stones, make jewelry, sit around the fire, smoke, and socialize or walk into Wamena with an extra ceremonial object or tobacco to trade. They have the vanity of birds of paradise, wearing only a *holim* (*koteka* in Bahasa Indonesia) or penis gourd (short and thick, or long and curled up, depending on the tribe), and maybe a pig's-tooth necklace, tin earring, nosering, headband of cassuary feathers, or perhaps tufts of white egret feathers placed behind their ears. For ceremonial occasions, several layers of pig's-tooth jewelry, woven armbands, *walimo* (the breast plate of cowry shells), and ankle bracelets may be added. The men wear their naturally kinky hair short and greased with pig fat or in long Rastafarian-like strands; elders mix ashes with pig fat to cover the gray. When it's cold, many wear crocheted berets or wool caps acquired in the market, rub on pig fat, and stand with their long arms wrapped around their upper bodies.

The lithe Dani women are in constant motion: cooking, cleaning, nursing their children, harvesting crops, carrying bales of firewood, taking produce to market, trading for tobacco or beads. They are customarily bare-breasted (though some sport wild secondhand T-shirts) and wear *sali,* long grass skirts, until marriage. After marriage the village women make them a *jokal,* strands of seeds worn draped in layers around their hips. Their hair is worn short and natural, and they usually don't adorn themselves, although occasionally you'll find a woman wearing a single strand of colored beads or a braided ankle bracelet. *Noken,* large woven bark bags, are used to carry children, produce, or merchandise from the market in Wamena. They're hung one on top of another from the forehead and provide shade by day or warmth at night.

The Dani Culture and Community

The strong social adat of the Dani has remained intact despite their conversion to Christianity. Their belief in the spirits of nature and of the deceased, and rituals of magic and cult initiation, still persist. Centuries of fierce tribal territorial battles and ritual warfare, long practiced as a social rite to avenge the ghosts of the dead, have been ended by the government. The circular, thatch-roofed *honay,* with earthen floors but without windows to keep in the warmth, is the basic housing unit in the valley; in many other areas a wood-and-thatch long house sleeping several families is common. Village compounds surrounded by thatch fencing consist of honay for the men on one side and a long hut for the women and children on the other side; in the center there is a common cooking area and a central honay for the village chieftain.

Water is carried in *isoak,* dried gourds decorated with carved patterns. The *hipere* (sweet potato) is the staple food, and *hipere ka* (the leaves) are steamed and eaten or fed to the pigs. Cassava, cabbage, red and white onions, and tomatoes are also cultivated, but not eaten as often. Pigs serve as dowries, sacrificial animals, and currency between tribes; a large one fetches $300 to $400 in the market, so they are only eaten when sacrificed for weddings or special rituals.

The village chieftain is not a hereditary position; the bravest and strongest in each tribe vie for the chance to lead their village and its council of elders. Men take as many wives as they can afford, usually offering a few pigs as payment, though special wives may cost up to ten pigs. Some anthropologists believe that polygamy stems from the Dani taboo against intercourse with a mother who's still nursing her child (as long as five years, in their culture), but since women do all the farming and harvesting, it's practical to have enough wives to cultivate your land.

Cannibalism was practiced for centuries and has been outlawed, although it still surfaces occasionally as an expression of revenge. Locals say that a missionary plane downed in a remote area less than ten years ago was found without its passengers, whom local tribesmen had eaten.

One of the Baliem Valley's better-known "sights" is the 300-year-old mummy of a chieftain in the village of Aikima. All the dead are now cremated and their ashes buried outside the village with great ceremony. Traditionally, the women relatives of the deceased would cut off two to four fingers or a piece of their ear in mourning, and close male relatives would cut off two fingers to the first joint. The Indonesian government has outlawed this practice, so women now cover their bodies in caked mud as a sign of mourning, though we saw many women bearing the marks of the old custom.

The Dani peoples have been in direct contact with Westerners since 1954, when missionaries established their first permanent settlements. To get schooling or medical supplies, villagers don secondhand clothes supplied by the missionaries and use the Bahasa Indonesia they have learned. Back in their villages they shed modern garments and stiff-soled shoes and return to the natural state.

Getting to the Baliem Valley

Garuda Indonesia flies thrice weekly from Los Angeles to Biak, daily from Jakarta and several other cities via Ujung Pandang to Jayapura, and five times a week from Bali to Jayapura. Garuda flights to Sorong, Wamena, and other destinations within Irian Jaya are often handled by Merpati Nusantara. **Air Niugini** is supposed to fly once weekly from Port Moresby, Papua New Guinea, Wewak, and Vanimo to Jayapura, but missionaries we met told us that these flights were often cancelled because of political problems.

Merpati Nusantara (or their subsidiary, **Airfast**) flies at least twice daily (if the weather's good) from Jayapura to Wamena, for Rp 36,000 ($22.50); daily to Biak, for Rp 52,500 ($32.75); three times weekly to Manokwari, for Rp 96,400 ($60.25); three times weekly to Nabire, for Rp 73,900 ($46.25) and FakFak; and less frequently to Merauke, for Rp 91,500 ($57.25), and several other destinations.

Everyone visiting Irian Jaya who plans to travel beyond the city of Jayapura must have a **Surat Jalan,** or Visitors Permit, specifying the region they are permitted to visit. *Importation of alcohol is strictly prohibited,* and your Surat Jalan and luggage will be thoroughly checked before boarding flights to Wamena or other inland destinations.

Obtaining a Surat Jalan

The Surat Jalan is normally issued by POLRI, the police in Jayapura, but may be issued in Jakarta (for special cases only). You'll need to give them your passport, four passport-size photographs, and a specific list of areas you want to travel in. Wamena and the Baliem Valley are the easiest areas to obtain permission for. Climbers were allowed at Mount Trikora, 4,750 meters (15,437 feet), during our visit only with a special permit from Jakarta, and the south-coast areas around Agats and Merauke, home of the Asmat tribes, were totally closed. If you're set on seeing the Asmat villages, source of most of the primitive art that explorer Michael Rockefeller introduced to the U.S., you should contact one of the travel agents listed below to determine if these areas are open.

If you need more information, contact the government's **Dinas Pariwisata Daeran Propinsi Irian Jaya (Tourist Information Office),** at Jl. Soa Siu Dok II (tel. 0967/21381, ext. 263), about ten minutes by taxi outside central Jayapura. The **Jayapura Kantor Polisi (POLRI)** is on the main street, Jl. A. Yani, and is open Monday through Saturday from 8 a.m. to 2 p.m. and on Sunday from 10 a.m. to 1 p.m. to issue Surat Jalans. Dress neatly and ask at the gate for a Surat Jalan. The policeman on duty will type up an application form that will be stamped in a few hours and returned free of charge.

Once issued, take it to a local photocopy shop; you'll need your Surat Jalan to check in for any inland flights, and extra copies for the police and your hotel in Wamena. You must check in with the Wamena police on arrival, but can request permission to visit regions outside the area or the Baliem Valley from them. On your hike you're expected to check in (for your own safety) with every local police station you pass, and all will ask to see your Surat Jalan. Even if you're going to Irian Jaya with a fully inclusive tour, the agent will wait to apply for a Surat Jalan until your arrival in Jayapura.

Getting Around the Baliem Valley

Travelers with four or five days to spend in the Baliem Valley can make day trips or overnight forays to many villages and scenic spots within 20 miles of Wamena, by bemo for the length of the Trans-Irian Highway (about five miles at the time of our visit), and by foot the rest of the way. To stray farther, you'll need to fly to another missionary outpost and continue hiking from there.

BY AIR. Your only chance of seeing a number of tribes is to fly on one of the missionary airlines. Tiom, at 8,500 feet, is a mountain village surrounded by very different terrain that's a good two-day hike from Wamena, where you land. Piramid, at 5,740 feet, is a three-day trek north of Wamena. **Note:** *You must have your Surat Jalan amended* by the Wamena police to include these destinations if you want to go and can get on a flight. If the south coastal areas reopen to travelers, the missionary airlines provide the only service to them from Wamena, saving you a return trip to Jayapura.

Mission Aviation Fellowship (MAF) is by far the largest, and welcomes tourists who reserve at least one week in advance through their Jakarta office, Yayasan MAF Indonesia, P.O. Box 29, Grogol, Jakarta Barat; or their Jayapura office, Naftali, Flight Operations, MAF Sentani, P.O. Box 239, Sentani, Irian Jaya (tel. 0967/10 or 38), open weekdays from 7:30 a.m. to 4:30 p.m. However, their schedule changes according to the needs of each missionary station served and your reservations depend on how much cargo or priority passengers (religious, governmental, or medical personnel) must be carried.

It takes five passengers to charter your own plane; 1988 rates are based on Rp 39,000 ($24.50) per 100 kms (60 miles), with a 20-kg (44-pound) baggage limit per passenger. Paying five times that amount will take you to your destination, if planes are available and not tied up with emergency runs or mechanical problems, or stranded by weather. The charming Elsie, who runs their Wamena office from the black tin shed next to the Wamena airfield (open from 5:30 a.m. to 5:30 p.m. daily except Sunday, with weekly schedules posted outside), will try her hardest to get you on flights to missionary stations in the Baliem Valley or elsewhere, but it's definitely a standby proposition. From Wamena to Tiom there's one scheduled flight per week for Rp 24,000 ($15) one way; charter seats on periodic flights to Piramid cost Rp 12,800 ($8) each way. From Wamena, a MAF pilot recommended a flight excursion to the mountaintop, Soba, at 13,000 feet, an extremely scenic route southeast of Wamena that crosses the Baliem Gorge, plus several waterfalls and canyons. A plane seating the pilot plus five would cost about Rp 142,000 ($88.75).

AMA is another, much smaller, missionary airline whose office is the brick house at the south end of the Wamena runway. They also have flights from Wamena to other Irian destinations, but their office is only open when their planes are coming in or out of Wamena.

BY ORGANIZED TOUR. Many travelers, especially those with limited time, would prefer to have their visit to Irian Jaya prearranged by a tour operator. We found that even the largest Indonesian or foreign travel agents offering tours to Irian Jaya all eventually went to a local tour operator to arrange their trips. Reliable tour operators (in order of reputation) include **P.T. Indonesia Safari,** Jl. Kemiri (P.O. Box 211), Sentani (tel. 0967/94); **P.T. Bawa Makmur,** Jl. Koti 72, Jayapura (tel. 0967/22180); **P.T. Dani Sangrila Tours,** Jl. Matahari 11, Jayapura (tel. 0967/22666; Telex 76122 Airfast IA); and **P.T. Natrabu,** Jl. Pembangunan 26, Jayapura (tel. 0967/22689). All their trips are custom-tailored, but prices for a fully inclusive tour (flights within Irian Jaya, an English-speaking guide and/or

Papua translator, porters, tents and camping gear, food supplies and a cook, and hotels where there are any) range from $315 for four days to $570 for seven days per person, sharing twin accommodations. To go on your own and hire a local guide in Wamena, porters for day trips, and pay for meals, Wamena hotels or overnight accommodations in missionary homes or honay, will cost about $45 per person per day. Because it's often difficult to contact these tour operators, begin your correspondence early, and be flexible. We met other hikers who just flew to Jayapura, walked into a tour office, and left two days later on a fully organized expedition.

BIAK: Travelers coming from the east or west on Garuda are likely to fly through Biak on their way to Jayapura, so let's take a brief look.

The **Frans Kaisiepo Airport,** the refueling stop for Garuda's trans-Pacific flights, is the only place you need to see on the island. As of this writing, Garuda Indonesia's new service from Los Angeles is three times a week; Immigration officials were only on duty to handle those flights. The airport has a moneychanger, snack shop, gift shop, and information officer who can help you get on the next plane out to Jayapura. If you have a long layover and want to sightsee, leave your luggage at Information and head to the **Japanese Caves** (Gua Jepang) in a mountainside about 12 miles away, where Japanese soldiers hid during World War II. There are mineral springs at **Air Biru** with strange stalactites, and an acceptable beach at **Bosnik.** From the airport, a taxi should cost between Rp 13,000 ($8) and Rp 17,500 ($11) per day.

If you're stuck overnight, the simple **Hotel Irian,** charging Rp 27,000 ($17) for two, is across the street from the runway, and the somewhat fancier **Hotel Titikawa** is a short taxi ride away.

JAYAPURA: The city of Jayapura, built amphitheatrically around a cove on the Pacific Ocean, is a surprisingly cosmopolitan outpost. Expatriates and foreign workers from the U.N., several development agencies, mining and oil companies, religious leaders, missionaries from dozens of faiths, Indonesian government officials, and representatives from every expatriate's government fly in and out of the city constantly. See "Getting to the Baliem Valley" for transportation details.

Getting Around Jayapura

From **Sentani Airport** you can take a taxi mini-van into Jayapura for a fixed rate of Rp 17,500 ($11), or change three times for bemos that cost Rp 400 (25¢) each. The taxi ride takes about 45 minutes in midday. (Be sure to arrive one hour before flight time for security checks at the Jayapura airport if you're flying anywhere within Irian Jaya.) Getting around the city is easy; you can walk almost anywhere you need to go in Jayapura.

Orientation

Sentani Airport, on the shore of this beautiful inland lake, is scenic but isolated—46 km (27½ miles) from the city. Once your bemo descends into the post-prefab, not-quite-urban sprawl, go straight to the port. **Jl. Koti** is the harbor street, with **Jl. Percetakan** and **Jl. Jend. A. Yani** running inland from it on the northwest side, forming the core of tourist services. To the southwest, past the post and telephone offices, the road runs right next to the water and a civic promenade. Inland from here are the central bemo station and taxi stand, the Pasar Malam, and the market and commercial center.

Useful Information

The regional office for **Tourism Development and Information** is five minutes by taxi out of the city in a new development at Jl. Soa Siu Dok II (tel.

0967/21381, ext. 263). It's open Monday through Thursday from 8 a.m. to 2:30 p.m., and on Friday and Saturday till 12:30 p.m. If Hans Menanti, our skillful English-speaking guide, is there, you'll have no problem. Otherwise, there will be few brochures or maps available due to their limited budget.

The **Kantor Polisi (POLRI),** which also issues the Surat Jalan (Visitors Permit) necessary for touring the island, is on Jl. A. Yani one block in from the port. In case of any **emergency,** dial 110. . . . The **Rumah Sakit Umum public hospital** is in Dok II.

The **telephone area code** for Jayapura is 0967 and the Time Zone is Greenwich Mean Time plus nine hours.

Irian Jaya is 14 hours ahead of New York and 17 hours ahead of Los Angeles; add one hour during Daylight Savings.

The **Garuda Indonesia** office is next to the Hotel Dafonsoro on Jl. Percetakan (tel. 21220), and is open weekdays from 8 a.m. to 4 p.m. (with a lunch break), till 1 p.m. on Saturday; closed Sunday. . . . The **Merpati Nusantara** office is at Jl. A. Yani 15 (tel. 21111), next to POLRI, and is open six days from 8 a.m. to 2 p.m. and on Sunday from 10 a.m. to 1 p.m. They only accept cash rupiah in payment for tickets.

The only bank for currency exchange is the **Bank Ekspor Impor Indonesia,** on Jl. A. Yani, open six days from 8 a.m. to 4 p.m. (you can only change money until noon), on Saturday till 11 a.m. If you're stuck, the Hotel Danfonsoro, on Jl. Percetakan, will change *cash* foreign currency into rupiah, but at a bad rate. Those going to Wamena should allow about Rp 2,000 ($1.25) per person per day, in the red 100-rupiah notes that are used to thank tribesmen posing for pictures, to tip local porters, etc. It's hard to spend Rp 80,000 ($50) per person daily unless you're investing in tribal art; 5,000-rupiah notes or smaller are the easiest to do business with.

The **Kantor Pos** (open Monday through Thursday from 8 a.m. to 2:30 p.m., and on Friday and Saturday until 12:30 p.m.) and the **Kantor Telepon** (open 24 hours) are on Jl. Koti at its southeastern port side. National and international communication is possible from Jayapura; no credit-card or collect calls are accepted. The **Telegraph and Telex Office** next door is open Monday through Thursday and Saturday from 8 a.m. to 2 p.m., on Friday from 8 to 11 a.m. and 1 to 6 p.m., and on Sunday from 10 a.m. to noon. Telephone service was out of order in Wamena when we visited, although telegraph service was operational.

Variant Photo, next to the Triton Hotel at Jl. A. Yani 58, will do four instant black-and-white photos for Rp 5,000 ($3). They're open from 8 a.m. to 3 p.m. and again from 5 to 9 p.m. Monday through Saturday, from 5 to 9 p.m. only on Sunday. Most Jayapura stores keep these hours, though ones with Muslim owners close early on Friday instead of Sunday.

If you're planning long hikes in the Baliem Valley, stock up on imported canned goods and toiletries in the **market** at the harbor, or at the **supermarkets** on Jl. A. Yani, a block inland from POLRI.

Accommodations

If Jayapura is your first stop in Indonesia, let us say that the hotel standards you've come to expect in European countries or more advanced Southeast Asian nations will not be met. The national Indonesian Hotel and Restaurant Association (PHRI) does an excellent job of maintaining fair prices, safe accommodations, and a welcoming atmosphere among its member hotels. However, an extremely damp climate (and shortage of funds for maintenance) usually means worn, less-than-spotless accommodations.

The majority of Jayapura's visitors are domestic travelers connected to the government, development agencies, or church-related organizations. It's usually easy to find a room, but August, September, and December are the busiest months due to visiting relatives and international conferences. Tourism is such a recent and limited phenomenon in this part of the world that you can count on one hand the number of hotels with hot water. This is a list of the best that's available; all rates include breakfast, tax, and service charges.

The **Irian Plaza Hotel,** centrally located at Jl. Setaipura 11 (P.O. Box 40) (tel. 0967/21575), opened in late 1986. Rooms are simple but much fresher and cleaner than the competition, plus they distribute the only printed map of Jayapura in town, gratis! Deluxe rooms at Rp 45,000 ($28), are carpeted and air-conditioned, with TV (reception from 7 p.m. to 2 a.m.), phone, and hot-water bath and shower. For another Rp 6,500 ($4) larger rooms also have a mini-bar. Good standard rooms with air-conditioning, phone, and cold-water mandi (the Asian well with a scooper) cost Rp 27,000 ($17) single, Rp 34,000 ($21.25) double.

The **Hotel Triton,** located around the corner at Jl. A. Yani 52 (P.O. Box 33) (tel. 0967/21218) is the next best bet. The VIP rooms, renting for Rp 58,000 ($36.25) double, are neat, clean, and air-conditioned, with TV, video, and hot water. Economy rooms without any of the above frills cost Rp 13,000 ($8) less.

The **Hotel Dafonsoro,** at Jl. Percetakan 22-24 (tel. 0967/22285), Jayapura's first modern hotel, charges top prices for very simple, weary-looking rooms with hot-water Danish shower. There are 28 rooms with TV, phone, and air conditioning, overlooking the busy main street. Larger, deluxe doubles cost Rp 58,000 ($36.25), standard doubles are Rp 38,400 ($24), and singles are Rp 28,000 ($17.50).

The **Numbai Hotel,** on Jl. Trikora Dok V Alas (P.O. Box 22) (tel. 0967/22185) is a motel-block compound located on a hilltop about ten minutes by taxi ($3.50) west of town. The view is great, and simple rooms have air conditioning and hot water. The location is inconvenient, but it's good value: double rooms cost Rp 38,400 ($24), and fan-cooled rooms cost Rp 5,000 ($3) less.

Heading the list of cold-water lodgings is **Wisma Mess G.K.I.,** conveniently located at Jl. Sam Ratulangi 6, P.O. Box 222 (tel. 0967/21574), about two blocks west of Jl. Percetakan, and run by the friendly Meity Gaspersz for the Christian Church. Simple fan-cooled rooms with a shared mandi cost Rp 14,800 ($9.25) for one, Rp 28,000 ($17.50) for two, including breakfast. For Rp 6,500 ($4) more per person you can have a hearty lunch and dinner. Less appealing, but reputedly one of the better losmen in town, is **Losmen Sederhana,** at Jl. Halmahera 2 (P.O. Box 45) (tel. 0967/21291). Second-story rooms overlook the bustling food stalls of the Pasar Malam. Spartan doubles with shared cold-water facilities cost Rp 21,000 ($13) to Rp 37,500 ($23.50), depending on whether the room is window, fan, or machine-cooled. If this is fully booked, there are several other losmen nearby.

Dining

Jayapura's fanciest restaurant is right on the water, offering a fine view of the harbor and refreshing breezes. The **Jaya Grill,** at Jl. Koti 5 (tel. 22783), serves a wide range of Chinese and seafood dishes in a pleasant, batik-trimmed dining room. All the food in Jayapura is more expensive than elsewhere in Indonesia, and the Jaya Grill is no exception. Grilled fish, abalone, frog, and crab entrees cost Rp 7,500 ($4.75) to Rp 25,000 ($15.50); steak, spaghetti, burgers, and European entrees cost about the same. To keep up with the development and the demands of the expatriate clientele that passes through this Christian town, they also offer 73 mixed drinks. The Jaya Grill is open for lunch and dinner daily.

As expatriates prefer the Jaya Grill, locals eat heartily at **Rasa Sayang,** at Jl. A. Yani 54 (tel. 21171), next to the Triton Hotel. Its popular for an extensive seafood and continental menu, air conditioning, small dance floor, and disco Muzak. From 10 a.m. to 3 p.m. the metallic party decorations add a festive spirit, but at night (6 to 11 p.m.) the place is hopping. Adventuresome diners will appreciate the wide range of pigeon and frog dishes; there's a good tuna salad with french fries or a curried chicken salad. Two should spend about Rp 19,500 ($12), Rasa Sayang is closed Sunday.

Budget-watchers can try the Padang-style food at **Restaurant Nirwana** at no. 40, down the street from Rasa Sayang. Soup and a selection of spicy beef and chicken dishes are served; you'll only pay for what you eat.

Cheaper still, and often the best meal in town, is found at the **Pasar Malam,** near the port on Jl. Irian. After 7 p.m., several warung hang up banners proclaiming Ikan bakar (baked fish), gado² (gado gado, or mixed vegetables with peanut sauce), nasi goreng (fried rice), es cendol (a drink of coconut milk and palm sugar), and other regional specialties. Inspect the cooking and washing facilities before you dine and then take a seat. Remember, fully cooked foods are much safer to eat.

What to See and Do in Jayapura

Once you've taken care of your Surat Jalan, changed money, acquired small bills, and purchased Merpati tickets, you may have time to kill in Jayapura. Your first stop should be at the wonderful, simply displayed collection of tribal art and artifacts at the **Cenderwasih University Museum (Museum UNCEN)** in Abepura. This small museum, located on the main road between Jayapura and Sentani Airport, is a real gem. The collection is small but contains choice pieces of art from the many tribes of Irian Jaya. Many items were donated by the John D. Rockefeller Fund or Michael Rockefeller, who disappeared while doing anthropological research near the south coast. The Asmat pieces are particularly fine and well displayed, but surprising and new are works from the tribes of Jayapura, Sentani, and the Baliem Valley. The museum with its small art shop selling locally produced artifacts, is open Monday through Thursday from 7:30 a.m. to 2:30 p.m., on Friday till 11 a.m., and on Saturday till 1:30 p.m.; closed Sunday. Bargain-rate bemos run regularly from the central *stasiun* to Abepura.

Base G Beach (formerly Tanjung Ria) is the only nearby spot for recreational swimming, located 12 km (7½ miles) west of the city. So called from its days as a staging ground for the Allied forces, Base G is a narrow, undeveloped white sand and driftwood strip leading to a gentle, shallow surf. The beach should be avoided weekends when all the Jayapurites are out in full force. Base G can be reached by local minibus for Rp 450 (30¢) from the Jayapura *stasiun bemo* to the Base G Kantor Polisi. The bus stop is the nearest warung, and the beach is a ten-minute walk down hill. *Warning:* Buses stop running at 2 p.m. A charter taxi will cost Rp 4,500 ($2.75) per hour.

During the final years of World War II, Irian Jaya was used by General MacArthur and the Allied forces as a base of operations in the Pacific. The **General Douglas MacArthur Column** is a 6½-foot-tall monument marking the spot on Ifar Hill (8½ miles west of Jayapura) where he devised the "leapfrog strategy" that was so successful against the Japanese. This scenic spot overlooking Sentani Lake can only be reached by four-wheel-drive vehicles. About a half mile from Jayapura is **Hamadi Beach,** site of the Japanese landing in New Guinea. A half-sunk personnel carrier and some rusted, destroyed Allied tanks mark the spot.

If you still have time to kill, ask a local to help you rent a boat, for about Rp 6,500 ($4) per hour, in Yoka, 21 km (12½ miles) west of Jayapura, or from the tiny inlet of Telaga Maya to sightsee on beautiful **Sentani Lake.** You can visit fishing villages on the islands offshore that form such a wonderful vista on the drive from the airport.

SENTANI: If you're in transit from Wamena to another inland destination, you don't need to spend the hour and $12 each way to take a bemo into Jayapura. The small town of Sentani lies just outside the airport and has all a traveler needs for an overnight stay. On the first left outside the gates is the MAF Airways office and nearby, the Kantor Telepon. The main street of Sentani is about 500 yards up and left at the intersection. You'll find a Kantor Pos, some shops, warung, and a few losmen, as well as a helpful travel agent, Indonesia Safari Tours.

The closest losmen to the airport lies 200 yards to the right, just outside the gates. **Losmen Mansapur Rani,** on Jl. Yabaso Sentani, has five simple rooms with screened windows and common cold-water mandi. The rent for two is Rp 8,000 ($5) per night; it's certainly ample for an overnight stay if you have (what always seems to be) an early flight.

WAMENA AND THE BALIEM VALLEY: The new, tin-roofed town of Wamena, stretched over dusty, broad, unpaved streets in neat squares, is the only "civilization" known for hundreds of miles around and the only practical base for exploring the Baliem Valley.

Useful Information

Wamena is spread out over streets that look remarkably similar; spend some time walking around and your confusion will disappear. The town seems to radiate right from the domed red-and-tan airport building. The tarmac **runway** serves as a thoroughfare and busy, sun-heated path for neighboring tribes and cows; when the bellowing warning siren announces the next plane, everyone moves into the fields. Wamena's other landmark is the **Pasar Raya,** the large, fascinating central market a block from the airport, which draws villagers to trade and shop.

Your first stop should be the **Kantor Polisi (POLRI),** half a block from the airport, where you *must* file your Surat Jalan obtained in Jayapura. The local police are very helpful and may even put you up in their barracks if no rooms are available.

There is a **Bank Rakyat** about one block west of the airport; it's open six days from 8 a.m. to 12:30 p.m., on Saturday till 11 a.m. . . . . The **Kantor Pos** is about two blocks west of the market, but never ship art or souvenirs you've purchased from here. It's said that nothing ever arrives. . . . The **Kantor Telepon** (if its transmission tower has been repaired) is up the street and also sends telegrams. . . . The **Merpati Nusantara/Airfast** office is one block up from the airport; it opens at 7 a.m. daily and closes after the last flight arrives.

Accommodations and Dining

Accommodations are very limited in Wamena, but fortunately the wave of government officials and trekkers seems to move through in such a way that there's always room at an inn. Communication is so difficult that it may not be possible to make an advance reservation, but if adventure is what you came for. . . . All rates include breakfast, tax, and service charges.

Tops on our list is the **Baliem Cottages,** Jl. Thamrin 1 (P.O. Box 32), Wamena, a collection of 15 round, thatch-roofed cottages that look like the Dani honay. The interiors are carpeted, dim, and very cozy; mattresses are sunken into low platforms and the seating area is stepped down to imitate the Dani's style of sleeping and eating on the floor. The attached full bathroom is set in an enclosed rock garden open to the sky, but the hot-water heaters were never connected while we were there and that luxurious tub became a cold-water mandi. Since life in Wamena itself is an adventure, ask Gim (Jimmy), the excellent manager, for candles or a kerosene lamp, mosquito coils, toilet paper, soap, and boiled drinking water. He'll even find someone to do one-day laundry service (although no matter how much laundry we gave the friendly laundry man he always charged Rp 4,000!). Singles cost Rp 28,800 ($18), doubles are Rp 40,000 Rp ($25), and an extra bed is Rp 10,000 ($6.25) more. Baliem Cottages also turns out an excellent supper for Rp 8,000 ($5) per person, most welcome after a long day of hiking.

Baliem Cottages is a ten-minute walk from the airport, which may seem like a long way when you arrive with your luggage. The only way to avoid it is to stay at the **Nayak Wamena Hotel,** Jl. Gatot Subroto 1 (P.O. Box 57, Jayapura), directly opposite the airport entrance. It's not worth it. Not-too-clean, concrete boxes with a private cold-water mandi cost Rp 18,000 ($11.25) single, Rp 32,000 ($20) double. With lunch and dinner, add Rp 16,000 ($10) per person.

The third hotel in Wamena is the **Losmen Syahrial Jaya,** Jl. Gatot Subroto, about ten minutes along the airport road to the left as you exit. Equally simple, clean rooms with private cold-water mandi cost Rp 9,000 ($7.50) for two. (At these prices, you can justify walking into the Pasar for dinner.)

Since there are no other official accommodations in Wamena, check with the police if you find yourself roomless.

At lunch, dine at one of the warung next to the Pasar Raya. **Warung Gembira** serves an excellent ikan bakar, a fish steak barbecued on their grill at the back. Everyone is served sayur (vegetables), nasi (rice), and some excellent ground peanut and chili sambal; two can sate themselves for about Rp 8,000 ($5). **Masakan Padang,** a warung serving the spicy, crisp-fried beef and chicken dishes from West Sumatra, is another good choice. They also make tasty leaf packets of steamed rice, good picnic food for hikers, and only Rp 200 (10¢) each. Both warung are open daily from 9 a.m. to 9 p.m.

Across the way at the intriguing **Pasar,** local women fry up a variety of banana-batter doughnuts, thick crêpes filled with ground peanuts, and round vegetable patties, all good eating and picnic food at 15¢ each.

Exploring the Baliem Valley

Wamena's **Pasar Raya** is one of the most fascinating sights in the valley. Transmigrant merchants from Java and Bali, donning the latest Western sports clothes, haggle over the price of rope or other supplies with tribesmen who've walked for days to get here. Most of the covered shops belong to the newcomers, but the action is in the open courtyard of the market, where seated women sell their produce while piglets and children swirl around them. One area of the market is relegated to Dani handcrafts like woven bags ($3.50 to $12) and beaded necklaces ($1 to $20). However, if you deal directly with the tribes people on the road, you will find better workmanship and lower prices. There is a new market, the **Pusat Perbelanjaan Wamena,** opposite the Pasar Raya, which has a tribal art shop with Dani and Asmat tribal works. They're open daily from 7 a.m. to 6 p.m. (closed on Friday from 11 a.m. to 2 p.m.) and sell single-strand beads for Rp 5,000 ($3) and up and small men's woven bags from Rp 3,500 ($2.25) and up. Their Asmat sculpture, imported from the south-coast villages, is much more expensive.

GUIDES. Once you're ready to walk out of the village you need to have a guide. The closest trails are easily followed, but within an hour of the town you could be lost for days. We were lucky enough to hire **Justinus Daby,** a security guard at the airport who was raised in Jiwika as a chieftain's son. Daby is an extremely intelligent and thoughtful man who was educated by missionaries. (Daby can be reached at P.O. Box 50, Wamena Airport.) **Gim,** the manager at the Baliem Cottages, also knows several local guides who speak some Papuan, Bahasa Indonesia, and some English. Day guides are paid about Rp 30,000 ($18.75), and the porters they hire will charge Rp 5,000 ($3) to Rp 8,000 ($5) per day. For longer trips, add in the cost of their meals and lodging.

NORTH OF WAMENA. The Trans-Irian Highway is being built north from Wamena, so the first three destinations can be reached by car, although that's not nearly as interesting as walking along the road's shoulder and meeting the Dani. At **Pikhe,** an hour's walk or Rp 600 (35¢) by public bemo, there's an original Dani footbridge over the Baliem river, and beyond it, a new one-lane car bridge. The famous 300-year-old **mummy at Aikima** is in this village off the unpaved roadway, about 1½ to 2 hours' walk beyond Pikhe and Rp 30,000 ($18.75) by private bemo charter. Hulolik Elosak, the village headman, is a descendant of the mummy. Upon payment, he and his cronies will carry the black, seated figure from a honay into the sunlight and prop it up in a chair. The mummified village chieftain was smoked for several weeks, thus preserving him in this ebony-like state. Let your guide negotiate the fee to see it; cigarettes and candy sweeten any deal, but it cost the two of us Rp 10,000 ($6.25) plus Rp 100 (5¢) for each photograph after the first three. We heard they charged some tour groups over Rp 100,000!

Jiwike is a lovely village farther north in the valley, and when we visited, was where road work on the Trans-Irian Highway ceased. It's about a 3- to 4-hour walk north of Aikima, or 22 km (13½ miles) and a 5½- to 7-hour walk north of Wamena. A chartered bemo will make the rough trip for Rp 65,000 ($40.50). It's a tranquil crossroads in the valley, with many other small sites within a few hours' walk. Accommodations in Jiwika include rooms with the village schoolteacher or a primitive honay lit by candlelight, where you sleep on reed mats. Each costs about Rp 7,000 ($4.50) per person.

From Jiwika, walk north (about an hour) over many narrow foot bridges, and west through the village of Wagalala. After passing Waga Wagh, you'll come to **Taman Ria Remaja**, a fenced-in garden landscaped by transmigrants and used as picnic grounds by the local Dani children. Continue through the dense underbrush and scenic mountain terrain as the path narrows (about an hour) and you'll cross many more handmade bridges until you come across a sign on the right for the **Goa Konti Lola**, a natural cave filled with thousands of bats. You can walk deep into the cave and down toward a small pool, where the Dani launch their boats to go bat hunting.

East of Jiwika is **Ilueagamo** or the **Salt Pool**, known as Air Garam in Bahasa Indonesia. It's a tougher walk, an uphill climb about 1½ hours east of the village, but the jungle scenery is very different from other walks. The Dani consider Ilueagamo a "present from god to the Dani people"; the stalk of a banana tree soaked and squeezed out repeatedly in this natural mineral spring will give out salt when dried over a fire.

From Jiwika, the nearest village to spend the night in is Piramid, another six hours to the northeast and across the river.

WEST OF WAMENA. The foothills to the west of Wamena are rapidly being developed, yet **Sinatma** (a 45-minute walk), site of a new small-scale hydroelectric plant, has two marvelous, primitive suspension bridges over the rushing Uwe River. Farther west (about two hours) on the hill is **Walesi**, one of the few Muslim tribal villages. Circling back east toward Wamena from Sinatma, you can take narrow paths through the woods to the collection of tribal honay at **Boma** (about 30 minutes). Across a modern footbridge is **Mapi 5**, a new transmigrant community whose neat lawns and flower beds belong to former residents of Ujung Pandang and Java.

EAST OF WAMENA. To exit Wamena from the east, cross the runway and hike through potato fields. The first village is **Wesaput**, where many Dani people who work in the town live. Turn south along the Baliem River and continue along the bank until you reach the Kupelago Manuggal XIII Bridge, built by soldiers and villagers together to ford the broad Baliem. After the crossing, head up a gentle rise (30 minutes); from the top you'll have a wonderful view of the neighboring valley. **Pugima** is the most scenic destination in this area, about an hour away. It takes about 30 minutes to descend into the valley; turn east at the fork in the road, work your way through rice paddies, clusters of honay, and cultivated fields of sweet potatoes, and you're on your way back to Wamena.

CHAPTER XI

INTRODUCING MALAYSIA

◻ ◻ ◻

1. INTRODUCTION

2. SUGGESTED ITINERARIES

3. GETTING THERE AND GETTING AROUND

4. THE ABC'S OF MALAYSIA

5. RECOMMENDED READING

Entering Malaysia is as pleasant as slipping into a warm bath: you feel embraced by the gentleness and generosity of the people, awed by the wild, mostly untouched beauty of the land. Underlying this serene setting is a strong element of spirituality created by the blending of three distinct religious philosophies: Islam, Hinduism, and Buddhism. Contributing to this unique Malaysian mélange is the still-visible presence of past foreign occupation. Visitors will recognize vestiges of British, Dutch, and Portuguese colonialism in Malaysian customs, government, and architecture, albeit slightly skewed with equatorial influences serving to tint the familiar with riotous Technicolor hues.

After leaving Kuala Lumpur, the nation's capital—a gleaming ultra-modern city along the lines of a mini-Singapore, complete with skyscrapers, throngs of pedestrians, cacaphonous traffic, and shopping malls—excursions to the countryside provide a disconcerting contrast revealing a life of utmost simplicity, and in a few locations, true enchantment. In those special places, such as Borneo, you'll be lulled to sleep by the rustlings of the jungles and rain forests, home to innumerable varieties of flora and fauna. Wild elephants and orangutan roam the forests instead of deer and mountain lion; monkeys, hornbills, and parrots perch in the trees instead of squirrels and owls.

Life in Malaysia—relaxed, prosperous, generous, and unhurried—owes much to the tropical climate and abundance of resources. It's hot as blazes, and humid; the weather can be a humbling experience for the first-time Western visitor. Come in late January, or whenever winter at its most ruthless arrives in your corner of the globe, in order to truly enjoy life in the tropics. Once here, temper your forays in the jungles and coastal areas with trips to the hill stations, such as the Cameron Highlands, plateaus boasting cooler air and a more moderate climate.

With everything it has to offer, the best news about vacationing in Malaysia may be no news at all. Compared to traditional Southeast Asian tourist destinations such as Hong Kong, Singapore, and Thailand, Malaysia is not overrun by visitors and the accompanying pandemonium. The rugged beaches of eastern peninsular Malaysia, for example, are among the most pristine on earth, with nary a resort or tourist to be seen for miles.

Come to Malaysia to relax. The climate, the landscape, the sea, and the food (Malaysian food deserves a book of its own, one we'd be only too honored to research and write) combine to form the perfect setting for indulging in creature comforts. There are no jarring realities to jangle the senses upon arrival. There is no desperate poverty or misery, no rude awakening to inflationary spiraling prices. In fact, if this is your first trip to Southeast Asia, consider making Malaysia your first stop. Its charm and ease are for the American traveler perhaps most reminiscent of California—an evocative yet reassuring introduction to the mysterious Orient.

Last, Malaysia is perhaps the single best travel value in Southeast Asia. Cuisine, transportation, and accommodations are among the most sophisticated anywhere and at prices that make nearby Singapore feel pricey.

1. INTRODUCTION

Malaysia is a fascinating blend of old and new; established as a nation less than a generation ago, in 1963, the country is considered one of the oldest sites of human settlement in the world—archeologists date evidence of man on Borneo to 40,000 years ago. Malaysia is also one of the oldest sites in the world of natural development, with the country's 150 million-year-old tropical rain forests predating the Ice Age.

Chinese and Sanskrit records note Malaysian kingdoms from the 7th and 8th centuries, offering glimpses of the indigenous culture and history of a land subsequently under the rule and influence of nearly half a dozen successive foreign powers, ranging from the Chinese to the British. The emerging nation today is an intriguing palette of languages, peoples, resources, customs, and geography, forging one of the strongest nations in Southeast Asia, empowered by diversity.

THE LAND: Malaysia is a remarkable marriage of two lands separated by 640 km (400 miles) of the South China Sea. West Malaysia, the mainland, occupies the southern half of peninsular Malaysia, bordered on the north by Thailand and regional neighbor to Burma, Laos, and Vietnam. The total land area of West and East Malaysia is 330,000 km² (127,000 square miles), its size further validating a comparison with California, which is slightly larger. East Malaysia, composed of the states of Sabah and Sarawak, occupies most of northern Borneo and straddles tiny (but exceedingly rich) Brunei. The island republic of Singapore, connected to the peninsula by causeways, was one of the four original states incorporated as Malaya when independence was granted by the British in 1957, but it left the nation of Malaysia in 1965. Malaysia's strategic location in central Southeast Asia, coupled with its command of the Straits of Malacca, have ensured its continued dominance of the region.

The peninsula is defined by a mountainous core giving way to coastal plains. Nearly three-fourths of the country is covered by rain forest (some predating the Ice Age) and jungle, irrigated by a complex system of truncated rivers and streams. The eastern coast of the peninsula is rocky and discontinuous, largely uninhabited, but punctuated by long beaches. The land in the west once yielded rich deposits of tin, now mined to the brink of depletion, yet tin mines still provide a major export for the country and employment for a large portion of the rural population. Although the soil quality is poor, robbed of nutrients by the equatorial sun, nearly 70% of the Malaysian people, most of them native Malays, are farmers. Rice is the main food crop, but the country is most known as a leading exporter of pepper, palm oil, and rubber.

Eastern Malaysia, Sabah and Sarawak, is similarly blessed in natural resources, similarly deficient in arable land. Again, mountain ranges form the backbones of the states, giving way to rain forests, which comprise most of the land area, before ending in the coastal plains home to most of the population. Sarawak's oil fields are being developed in a time when the country's other major exports of tin and rubber find an ever-smaller world market. Mount Kinabalu is eastern Malaysia's most striking geographical feature: at 13,455 feet, it's the highest point in central Indochina, and site of Malaysia's most magnificent national park.

THE PEOPLE: The population of Malaysia in mid-1988 approached 16 million. The makeup of the nation's population profile reflects a true melting pot. Malays, known as *bumiputras* (literally, "native sons"), number half of the population. The Chinese comprise a third, Indians make up 10%, and indigenous peoples the remainder, including the Orang Asli, the peninsula's aborigines, as well as the many tribes that occupy Sabah and Sarawak.

Nearly 70% of the population lives in rural areas. Most of the rural dwellers are Malay, while the Chinese and Indians dominate the cities. Some 13.5 million live in West Malaysia; the rest are settled in the sparsely populated states of Sabah and Sarawak on northern Borneo. Kuala Lumpur, the nation's capital, is also Malaysia's largest city, home to one million. The city was founded in 1864 by Chinese, who remain the largest segment of its population.

Little is known about Malaysia's earliest inhabitants. Archeologists cite evidence of humans in the caves of northern Borneo 40,000 years ago. West Malaysia saw a steady trickle of emigration from the north, mostly southern China, beginning perhaps 7,000 years ago with the Orang Asli. Today the fate of the aborigines can be compared to that of the American Indian: both peoples' governments have established land reservations for their populations. The Orang Asli live as they have for centuries, hunting and fishing with traditional implements fashioned centuries ago. (Their woodcarvings are on display in handcrafts shops in Kuala Lumpur and Malacca's antique shops.)

Indians and Chinese began making their way into Malaysia approximately 4,000 years ago. These arrivals were infrequent and discontinuous and did not comprise a genuine wave of settlement until the 19th century, when their appearance en masse was engineered by the British, who imported large numbers of Chinese and Indians to work in the tin mines and rubber plantations as well as to modernize the colony's infrastructure.

Native Malays are a rural people, mostly engaged in farming. The Chinese are the urban dwellers, comprising a large faction of the business community. The Indians, who as a group are perhaps the best educated, tend to dominate the professions of medicine, law, and engineering.

The peoples of Sabah and Sarawak are even more diversified. Sarawak is dominated by the Chinese, who make up one-third of that state's population. Other groups include the tribal cultures of Iban and the Land Dayak, Malays (less than 20%), and various smaller, indigenous groups.

Kadazan are Sabah's native people and comprise about one-fourth of its population. They are a friendly, welcoming people, engaged mostly in fishing and farming. Other groups include Chinese, Bajau, Murut, Malay, and smaller tribal groups. Most of the indigenous tribes in Sabah have retained their ancestral customs, with the important and reassuring exception of headhunting and warfare conducted with blowpipes and poison darts. A few others have adopted aspects of Islam and Christianity but mostly adhere to the traditional faiths they have professed for centuries.

The Muruts share with the Ibans and Land Dayaks of Sarawak a communal living arrangement in "longhouses," one-story structures built of connecting rooms sharing a common veranda.

LANGUAGE: Bahasa Malay is the official language of Malaysia and is essentially the same as Indonesian. The language is quite simple, relying on repetition of nouns for emphasis and amplification, as opposed to adverbs and adjectives, and involving no changes in tense. The Malay script, called Jawui, traces its beginnings to ancient Sanskrit.

English is still widely spoken in all but the most rural areas, but is no longer used as the first language in education and government. Most businesses, especially those involving tourists, rely on English as their main language. Different groups of Chinese often speak English to communicate with each other. The tribesman of Sabah and Sarawak have been the most successful in preserving their traditional customs and native dialects. The Indian minority speak Tamil, as well as Bahasa, and in most cases, English.

ECONOMICS: Malaysia's commodity-driven economy has relied on its domination of the world markets of rubber, tin, and palm oil in establishing its profile as an emerging power in Southeast Asia. The collapse of the world tin and rubber markets a few years ago has precipitated a change of emphasis in shaping Malaysian economic policy, with the safest course of action seen as a beefing up manufacturing. Prime examples of this new strategy are the Proton automobile and the semiconductor industry established in Penang's free-trade zone.

Internal economics in Malaysia still closely adhere to ethnic stratifications. The Chinese control a disproportionate amount of commerce and business, despite enactment in 1970 of the New Economic Policy (NEP). The NEP's ambitious goal was, within 20 years, to place at least 30% of business and trade in the hands of the bumiputra who, although outnumbering every other ethnic group, controlled only about 4% of the nation's economy. Today that figure is 18%, still woefully shy of the NEP's 1990 deadline.

Reaction to the NEP has been mixed. Ostensibly founded on good intentions, to better the dismal economic lot of native Malays, its real effect has been a reverse of affirmative action: discrimination against Malaysian Chinese and Indians and the spread of increasing resentment and ethnic division.

The Malaysian economy has a projected inflation rate of 4%.

RELIGION: Islam is the state religion of Malaysia, but Malaysia is not an Islamic state. In other words, the goals of the state are not necessarily the advancement of Islam, as is true in the Islamic nation of Iran. In recent years, however, Malaysia has seen an emerging Islamic fundamentalist movement, largely concentrated in the predominantly Malay east coast. Even with this trend, Malaysia's constitution still guarantees freedom of religion for all faiths. Malaysia's tolerance of all religions practiced by its citizens can be seen in the national holiday status accorded many religious observances; this is a country that, for example, celebrates three distinct New Years. Malaysia's various faiths have contributed much to the country's art and culture: temples, shrines, and pagodas are among its most stunning displays of craftsmanship and architecture.

Ever since its introduction in Malacca in the 15th century, Islam has been the predominant faith of West Malaysia, with a smaller impact in Sabah and Sarawak. Buddhism unites Malaysia's Chinese while Malaysians of Indian descent by and large are practicing Hindus.

The indigenous tribes maintain their traditional faiths, based on pantheistic and animistic precepts, with some nodding toward Islam and Christianity, the latter seen mostly in Sabah and Sarawak. The Portuguese, Dutch, and British (with a few stray American missionaries) all tried to bring Christianity to the peninsula, and particularly in recent years to Borneo, all with negligible results.

HISTORY: Malaysia's history is an odd combination with the most important events either occurring thousands of years ago or only a few hundred years ago.

West Malaysia

Nearly 7,000 years ago Malaysia's aboriginal Orang Asli arrived on the peninsula, believed to have migrated from southern China. They roamed as hunters and food gatherers, primarily on the west coast, a trend in settlement that continues to this day, with the east coast still sparsely populated and not easily accessible overland through the jungles of central Malaysia.

The people known as Malays share roots with the earliest inhabitants of Indonesia. Some archeologists maintain that their appearance on the peninsula occurred 4,000 years after the arrival of the Orang Asli. Over the centuries various Javanese and Sumatran rulers established vaguely defined kingdoms whose boundaries and very existence surged and ebbed like the tides; none achieved sustained domination and there is little evidence of their presence.

By the 14th century Malacca, on the southwestern coast, was known to traders throughout the world as an important and bustling port. Ships arrived from China, India, and Indonesia, as well as Europe. In 1405 Islam was introduced to the peninsula's peoples by the Chinese admiral Cheng Ho, who landed in Malacca and soon named himself ruler.

In 1511 the Portuguese, who had visited two years earlier, returned to capture the city, covetous of its strategic command of the Straits of Malacca. In 1641 the Portuguese gave way to the Dutch, who had enlisted the men of Johor, to the south, in their seizure of the city. The Johor men, with a score to settle, were descendants of the Malaccans displaced by the Portuguese over a century earlier.

British rule of Malacca was established in 1824 with the enactment of the Anglo-Dutch treaty, in which the Dutch relinquished control of Malacca in exchange for England's Bencoolen territory in Sumatra. With this move the Dutch consolidated their holdings in Indonesia and the stage was set for British development of the peninsula, a period lasting from that time until independence.

During Malacca's Dutch and Portuguese years the British, in the person of Capt. Francis Light, arrived in Penang in 1786. Light established the island city as a free-trade zone, spurring its rapid growth as an important port.

With the acquisition of Malacca and Singapore and with Penang serving as a base, Britain proceeded to move inland and north on the peninsula, negotiating land treaties with the Thais as it approached that country's borders. Britain's next move shaped the future of Malaysia's economy and cultural makeup. By establishing tin mines and rubber plantations, the British set Malaysia squarely on the path that in this century has seen the country's emergence as a powerful entity among Southeast Asian nations, third only to Japan and Hong Kong in growth and prosperity. Homogenization of Malaysian society was achieved with the large-scale importation of Chinese and Indians to work in the tin mines and rubber plantations.

Tin and rubber remain among Malaysia's chief exports today; the Chinese and Indians have endured and prospered, and to the dismay of the Malay bumiputra, dominated commerce and the professions.

East Malaysia

The history of the island of Borneo, where the Malaysian states of Sabah and Sarawak lie separated by the tiny kingdom of Brunei, is the history of earliest man.

Archeologists have uncovered evidence of primitive man in the caves of Gomantong (Sabah) and Niah (Sarawak) dating to 40,000 years ago. Western influence plays a much smaller role in the history of East Malaysia than that of the peninsula. Separated by 640 km (400 miles) of South China Sea from the mainland, East Malaysia's relative isolation coupled with the sheer impenetrability of much of the land have served to ensure that the native peoples live lives virtually unchanged from those lived by their ancestors thousands of years ago.

A British explorer named James Brooke embodies one of the more interesting developments in modern Sarawak history. Arriving in the capital city of Kuching in 1838, Brooke, perhaps the first practitioner of shuttle diplomacy, immediately helped quell incipient native rebellions and was rewarded by the Brunei rulers with land that today comprises most of Sarawak. Known as the "White Raja," Brooke founded a family dynasty that continued to rule the country until the Japanese invasion in World War II. Following the war the restored Brooke family rulers turned the territory over to the British government.

Meanwhile, in Sabah, Malaysia's largest and most sparsely populated state, the British were successful in the 19th century in establishing the domination of the British North Borneo Company, paving the way for annexation and eventual inclusion in the federation.

Modern History

After World War II and the Japanese seizure of the peninsula and northern Borneo, Britain began the laborious task of reweaving the Malaysian territories ravaged by war. Nationalist sentiment grew more pronounced and was acknowledged by Britain in its attempts to establish a unified nation among the disparate Malayan and Borneo territories.

An uprising by the Malaysian Communist Party in 1948 caused Britain to declare a state of emergency, the beginning of a 12-year period pocked by violence and guerrilla warfare.

On August 31, 1957, Britain granted independence to Malaya. Over the next six years negotiations proceeded fitfully to include Singapore, Brunei, Sabah, and Sarawak in the new nation.

The nation of Malaysia was formed in September 1963, its new name acknowledging inclusion of Sabah and Sarawak. Brunei was not among the original states—and remains independent today—while continued differences with Singapore led to that state's seccession in 1965.

The modern state was founded on the basis of religious and ethnic tolerance, allowing all citizens to express their beliefs and customs in a manner of their choice. Today this doctrine is still in force, but the tensions of diverse interests constantly test the country's political mettle, often with discordant effects.

MODERN POLITICS: Malaysia is a constitutional monarchy. Its nine royal rulers meet every five years to elect a king from their ranks. The birthday of King Tuanku Ahmad Shah al Mu'adzam Billah, like those of many Malaysian rulers, is celebrated as a national holiday, but his authority is far more than ceremonial. He appoints the prime minister and cabinet from among members of the legislature, as well as the leaders of four states and members of the Malaysian judiciary. Nine of Malaysia's 13 states are feudal monarchies, ruled by hereditary sultans. The states of Malacca, Penang, Sabah, and Sarawak are ruled by governors appointed to four-year terms by the king.

Malaysia's working government is headed by the prime minister. Dr. Mahathir Mohammed has held the post since 1981 and is the nation's fourth prime minister since its founding in 1963. He is perhaps the country's most conservative ruler to date—under his rule a new wave of fundamentalism has gathered momentum—and the first to have received a Western education. He presides over a two-house legislature: the Dewan Rakgat and the Dewan Negara, modeled after Britain's Houses of Lords and Commons.

The third branch of government is the judiciary, composed of the High Courts of East and West Malaysia, which administer the law of the land. High Court decisions may be appealed to the Federal Court.

The bumiputra, or native Malays, through undisputed control of national politics, have established a formidable system of cronyism, strengthened under the rule of Dr. Mahathir. The bumiputra continue to enjoy educational, vocational, and economic advantages over other Malaysians. Government, their uncontested arena, is closely linked to commerce and industry by the strategic placement of former civil servants in key public-sector positions in transportation, service industries, and communications.

However, the collapse of the market for Malaysia's chief exports, tin and rubber, have forced the government to adopt a somewhat more pragmatic, bottom-line approach: less coddling of the native sons and greater concentration on long-term strategies for the country's growth. Still, despite these considerations, Malaysian politics is largely reminiscent of a private men's club. Deals and agreements are by and large the products of "mutual self interest" and "pull."

Thus far this system seems not so much a corrosive as it is a leveler in assuring the country's continued political stability and economic prosperity. But minority groups, namely Chinese and Indian, who seem to have a keener appreciation of the rewards of business and commerce than do the chiefly agrarian Malays, are justifiably resentful of the socioeconomic advantages enjoyed by the bumiputra. Quite simply, the Chinese and Indians are Malaysia's most ambitious and hard-working citizens, yet they are treated in a second-class manner. They are most comfortable with the prospect of guiding Malaysia into the 21st century, yet the least equipped, on the political front, to effect change.

M$	$ U.S.	M$	$ U.S.
0.25	0.10	50.00	19.23
0.50	0.19	75.00	28.85
0.75	0.29	100.00	38.46
1.00	0.38	125.00	48.08
2.00	0.77	150.00	57.69
3.00	1.15	175.00	67.31
4.00	1.54	200.00	76.92
5.00	1.92	225.00	86.54
6.00	2.31	250.00	96.15
7.00	2.69	275.00	105.77
8.00	3.08	300.00	115.38
9.00	3.46	325.00	125.00
10.00	3.85	350.00	134.62
15.00	5.77	375.00	144.23
20.00	7.69	400.00	153.85
25.00	9.62	425.00	163.46

2. SUGGESTED ITINERARIES

The description of Malaysia in this book covers only the highlights of the country. The following itineraries are based on selected destinations and are geared for the general-interest traveler. Those who have special interests should modify these basic plans.

ONE MONTH: Days 1-3: Begin with Kuala Lumpur (KL), taking day trips to the Batu Caves and Fraser's Hill. **Days 4-6:** Drive to the Cameron Highlands and take a jungle walk. **Days 7-10:** Drive through Ipoh on the way to Penang; tour the island, including visits to Penang Hill, Batu Ferrenghi, and Georgetown. **Days 11-15:** Fly or drive to Kota Bahru and continue down the coast through Kuala Terengganu to Kuantan, with a five-day stay on the beach. **Days 16-17:** Fly to KL and drive (or drive directly) to Malacca. **Days 18-24:** Fly to Kuching or Miri on Borneo for a week-long river trip/jungle trek through Sarawak, including visits to Gunung Mulu and/or Niah National Parks. **Days 24-29:** Fly to Kota Kinabalu for a climb up Mount Kinabalu, a day-long boat tour of the outer islands, and a Sabah jungle walk. **Day 30:** Return to Kuala Lumpur.

TWO WEEKS: We would either spend the two-week period touring peninsular Malaysia or East Malaysia, but not both. In other words, divide the above month-long itinerary into two halves, both beginning in Kuala Lumpur and choose either one, depending on your interests. Our inclination is to spend the two weeks in Sarawak and Sabah.

ONE WEEK: Days 1-2: Begin with Kuala Lumpur, taking day trips to the Batu Caves and Malacca. **Days 3-4:** Drive to the Cameron Highlands and take a jungle walk. **Days 5-6:** Drive through Ipoh on the way to Penang; tour the island, including visits to Penang Hill, Batu Ferrenghi, and Georgetown. **Day 7:** Return to KL.

3. GETTING THERE AND GETTING AROUND

Malaysia is not as easy to get to as the nearby hub cities of Singapore and Bangkok; however, it is connected by train and air to both Singapore and Thailand, and is well served by the national air carrier, Malaysian Airline Systems.

GETTING THERE: Many international air carriers fly to Kuala Lumpur, although at this point there are no American carriers that travel directly to Malaysia. In addition, there is train service from Singapore and Thailand, and freighter service from miscellaneous Asian ports.

By Air

The most convenient way to reach Malaysia from the United States is on **Malaysian Airline System** (MAS; tel. toll free 800/421-8641), which flies three times weekly (on Monday, Thursday, and Saturday) to Kuala Lumpur from Los Angeles, via Honolulu or Tokyo. The 1989 round-trip APEX fare was $1,049, with one stopover allowed. For another $25 you can make an additional stopover (perfect for those on an extended tour of Southeast Asia) in another Asian capital via **Northwest Airlines.** Business Class (called Golden Club Class) tickets run about $1,200 more, while first-class transportation runs $3,999, with unlimited stopovers from any Northwest Airlines or MAS city in the United States. MAS also offers a large selection of air/land packages on their **Malaysia Stopover** program; the prices on hotels are really outstanding (with discounts up to 50%), so contact their sales office for more information.

MAS has flights from other Southeast Asian cities to Kuala Lumpur (KL) including Bangkok, M$404 ($161), daily; Denpasar, M$559 ($223), twice weekly; Hat Yai, Thailand, M$178 ($71), daily; Hong Kong, M$821 ($320), daily; Jakarta, M$426 ($170), four times weekly; and many daily flights to Singapore for M$130 ($52). They also have international connections to Penang from Bangkok daily for M$312 ($125); Hat Yai, daily, for M$86 ($34); Phuket, once a week, M$117 ($47); and Singapore, daily, for M$150 ($60). MAS has some direct connections from Southeast Asian cities to East Malaysia, including flights from Kuching for M$170 ($68); and daily flights from Singapore to Kota Kinabalu (K.K.), for M$346 ($138.50); as well as twice-weekly flights from Hong Kong to K.K.

Thai Airways International (tel. toll free 800/426-5204) flies daily from Bangkok to KL for 4295 baht ($172).

One of the best ways to travel in Southeast Asia is via the so-called ASEAN Promotional Fare that includes 6 stopovers in Singapore, Thailand, Malaysia, Philippines, Indonesia, and Brunei from KL for M$1,300 ($520). There are restrictions on this fare, so check with your travel agent or MAS before departing.

By Train

There is train service, organized by **Malayan Railways,** that originates in Singapore, passes through Malaysia (making a stop in Kuala Lumpur), and terminates in Butterworth (Penang); the train then joins the Thai rail system and runs up to Bangkok. The fare from Singapore to KL runs M$74 ($29.50) for a first-class, air-conditioned seat. The trip takes about 6½ hours. The 30-hour trip from Bangkok to KL costs approximately $100.

By Boat

Feri Malaysia operates a cruise ship that travels from Kuantan to Kuching and Kota Kinabalu via Singapore once a week. The ferry departs on Saturday from Kuantan and takes about 36 hours to reach Kuching. Cabin-class fares range from $40 to $120; deluxe class, from $55 to $172; and suites, from $80 to $240 —depending on size and location. For more information, contact the Malaysian Tourist Development Corporation in Kuantan, Singapore, Kuching, or Kota Kinabalu.

GETTING AROUND: Travel within Malaysia is extremely efficient and inexpensive, perhaps cheaper than in any other country in Southeast Asia. If you are on a limited time schedule, by all means fly; but if you have the time and want to take in the countryside, either take the train or rent a car.

By Air

All domestic flights are on **MAS,** with Kuala Lumpur serving as its hub city. There are connecting flights between KL and Penang, Kota Bahru, Kuala Terengganu, Kuantan, Kuching, and Kota Kinabalu. There are also connecting flights from Penang to Kota Bahru, Kuala Terengganu, and Ipoh. Typical one-way fares and flights (as of 1989) to these destinations are shown in the table.

Route	One-Way Fare	Flights
KL to Penang	M$86 ($34.50)	daily
KL to Kota Bahru	M$86 ($34.50)	daily
KL to Kuching	M$231 ($92.50)	daily
Kuching to Kota Kinabalu	M$198 ($79.25)	daily

Children under the age of 12 travel at half the posted rate; infants travel at 10% of the normal fare.

By Train

Train service around the country is excellent and comfortable, with a full range of service available. **Malayan Railways** organizes its routes along two separate lines. The first is the west-coast line from Singapore up to Butterworth near the Thai border. The other line runs from the west-coast city of Gemas and continues northeast up to the Thai border above Kota Bahru. For typical rates, see "By Train" in the "Getting There" section.

Children between the ages of 3 and 12 travel at half the posted rate.

By Rental Car

Renting a car is a particularly good option in Malaysia as the roads are good and getting better. If you feel so inclined, it is inexpensive to hire a driver to guide you along the way. Most of the international rental-car companies are represented in Malaysia, some with branches outside KL in Penang and on the east coast.

Unlimited-mileage rates range from M$88 ($35.25) to M$240 ($96) daily for a locally produced Proton Saga up to a Mercedes; expect to pay M$300 ($120) to M$800 ($320) for a weekly rate. **Avis** (tel. 242-3500 in KL; or toll free 800/331-1212 in the U.S.), **Hertz** (tel. 243-3014 in KL; or toll free 800/654-3131, in the U.S.), **Thrifty** (tel. 248-2388 in KL), and **Mayflower Acme** (tel. 261-1136 in KL) all operate agencies around the country.

Most of the rental-car agencies will allow you to drop off a car at their other stations (typically, Penang or Singapore) for an additional charge ranging from M$85 ($34) to M$165 ($66).

Chauffeur-driven cars may be rented from any of the major chains with typical daily rates from M$200 ($80) to M$460 ($184), including insurance and fuel.

By Bus

Travel by bus is the cheapest mode of transportation in Malaysia. Options abound, but the major choices break down to non-air-conditioned interstate or intrastate and air-conditioned interstate coach. Most foreign travelers (and those locals who can afford it) take air-conditioned buses.

We suggest taking trains along the west coast, but buses are the ideal mode for journeying along the less-well-served east coast. From Kota Bahru, for example, there are frequent daily buses to Kuala Terengganu and Kuantan, with fares of M$8 ($3.25) and M$17 ($6.75) respectively.

Outstation Taxis

A form of travel that we find delightful is the so-called outstation taxi, a long-haul private car that is shared among four people. All you pay for is your seat, not the charter price for the entire car. This substantially reduces the cost of travel, while providing you, the comfort-seeking tourist, with many of the advantages of a private car. A typical outstation taxi route is from KL to Malacca; on that well-traveled route, expect to pay M$20 ($8) each way.

Local Transportation

As with the rest of Southeast Asia, local transport in Malaysia offers several categories of private and public transportation, ranging from taxis to trishaws, some motorized and a few bicycle (human) powered. Most taxis and private cars (such as those arranged by luxury hotels) have posted rates or use meters; however, in the smaller cities you'll likely have to negotiate your fare. If you don't know the correct fare, inquire of a shop owner, hotelier, or restaurateur as to what you should pay given your destination, and negotiate accordingly with the driver. Most taxi fares will average about M$5 ($2) in the cities, a little less in the provincial towns. Most around-the-town trishaws charge about M$3 ($1.25) for a 15-minute ride. Tipping is not expected.

It's generally quite safe to travel by local bus in the cities, and you'll have a hard time beating the price. The fare in KL, for example, averages only M$1 (40¢) for a long city ride.

4. THE ABC'S OF MALAYSIA

This section is intended as a quick reference for the traveler, listing services and practical information applicable to Malaysia as a whole and supplementing the "Useful Information" sections for each city.

AIRPORTS: Malaysia is served by nine domestic and two international airports. The largest and most important is the **Subang International Airport,** approximately 45 minutes southwest of Kuala Lumpur, the nation's capital, in the western state of Selangor.

All international travelers must pay an **airport tax** of M$15 ($6); the fee for Singapore-bound passengers is M$5 ($2), and on domestic flights, M$3 ($1.25).

When flying from West Malaysia to the states of Sabah and Sarawak on northern Borneo you must once again clear Customs.

AIRLINES: Nearly two dozen foreign carriers fly to Malaysia. In addition, the national airline, **Malaysian Airline Systems** (MAS), flies to dozens of foreign cities and maintains an extensive domestic network. MAS offices in the United States are located at 420 Lexington Ave., Suite 2044, New York, NY 10170 (tel. 212/697-8994); at 919 N. Michigan Ave., Suite 1900, Chicago, IL 60611 (tel. 312/943-0925); 5933 W. Century Blvd., Room 56, Los Angeles, CA 90045 (tel. toll free 800/421-8641); and at 360 Post Rd., Suite 603, San Francisco, CA 94108 (tel. 415/788-0555).

Once in Malaysia, you'll find MAS offices for information on domestic flights in Kuala Lumpur, on the 33rd floor, Bangunan MAS Jalan Sultan (tel. 774-7000); in Penang, in the Kompleks Tun Abdul Rasak, Penang Road (tel. 620-011); in Kota Kinabalu, on the 10th floor, Kompleks Karamunsing Jalan Tuaran, Selantan (tel. 88-300); and in Kuching, Bangunan MAS, Lot 215, Tong Thian Cheak Road (tel. 93-100).

BANKS: It may be more convenient to change your currency in hotels, department stores, or supermarkets, but banks, followed by licensed moneychangers, offer the best exchange rate.

Official **banking hours** throughout most of Malaysia are Monday through Friday from 10 a.m. to 3 p.m., on Saturday from 9:30 to 11:30 a.m. The exceptions are the states of Kedah, Perlis, Kelantan, and Terrengganu, where hours are limited on Thursday to 9:30 to 11:30 a.m. Banks in these states are also closed on Friday, the state holiday, as opposed to Sunday everywhere else.

BATHROOMS: Hotels, larger restaurants, department stores, museums, and the ubiquitous shopping malls all offer clean, well-maintained facilities styled in the comforting tradition of Western self-flushing porcelain. Once you leave Kuala Lumpur, or Penang, or Malacca, forewarned is forearmed. Carry your own toilet paper, and otherwise be prepared for the rustic simplicity of Asian toilets, identified by the accompanying water pail and ladle, to be used for flushing by hand.

BUSINESS HOURS: In general, supermarkets and department stores are open daily from 10 a.m. to 10 p.m.; smaller shops, from 9:30 a.m. to 7 p.m. Offices are open longer than in the West, from 8 a.m. to 5 p.m. Monday through Friday, with many offices open in the mornings on Saturdays.; the pace is set by the indefatigable Chinese. Twenty-four-hour gas stations are fairly easy to find in most larger cities, and in Kuala Lumpur some stores are also open around the clock.

CLIMATE: The climate in Malaysia, which lies just north of the equator, is sunny, hot, and humid year round, with the temperature rarely varying from the 70° to 90°F range and humidity averaging 90%. Short, sudden mid-afternoon thunderstorms are common and rarely disruptive. The rainy season runs from September through December on the west coast, November through February on the east. The hill stations, Malaysia's mountain settlements, offer a cooling refuge from the tropical weather and in the evenings often dictate a sweater.

Extra precautions and common sense will protect you from dehydration and the heat, especially when you first arrive and are not yet acclimated. Drink plenty of water (boiled or bottled in rural areas), take it easy on alcohol, and enjoy a slower pace.

CLOTHING: Fabrics that breathe, such as cotton, linen, raw silk, and even ramie, will help you weather the sun and humidity. Loose, comfortable, lightweight, and light-colored clothing is appropriate and practical for the tropical climate. Colorful batiks are worn by everyone, everywhere. Men generally wear long trousers, particularly in the cities. Jackets and ties for men, and dresses for women, fill the bill for the most formal occasions and business meetings. Malaysia is predominantly Muslim, and women dress modestly. Short-shorts, miniskirts, halters, and clinging tops can, and do, offend Malaysian sensibilities.

Consider bringing a wide-brimmed straw hat, or buy an inexpensive, locally made one once you arrive, especially if you are fair-skinned or thinning on top. Shoes should be comfortable and easy to remove, which you will have to do upon entering a Muslim or Hindu home or any religious temple.

Long-sleeve shirts and high socks will help protect you from mosquitos and other insects in the jungles and rain forests. Bring a sweater if you are venturing to the hill stations. Remember to bring an umbrella if you are traveling in the rainy season, and at least one bathing suit, whenever you come.

COMMONLY USED BAHASA MALAYSIA WORDS AND EXPRESSIONS: Bahasa Malaysia isn't a language that most Westerners speak, but if in your travels you pepper your English with a few key words, it's bound to bring a smile to the faces of the local populace. The following list should be useful both for the description of sights within this book as well as for the pleasantries of everyday travel.

Bahasa Malaysia	English
selamat pagi	good morning
selamat petang	good evening
selamat malam	good night
selamat tinggal	good-bye
ya	yes
tidak	no
terima kasih	thank you
sama sama	you're welcome
apa khabar	how are you?
farang	foreigner

teksi	taxi
bandar	city
jalan	road or street
pantai	beach
wisma	building
lapangan terbang	airport
pasar	market
pejabat pos	post office

CREDIT CARDS: Most larger businesses in Malaysia accept all major credit cards, and the larger hotels prefer them, often requiring a large deposit when you propose paying in cash. Traveler's checks are accepted at most hotels, banks, larger restaurants, and shopping malls. Upon venturing to the countryside and *kampongs,* as local villages are known, you'll find that the Malaysian dollar, called a ringgit, is almost always the only language spoken. To report lost or stolen credit cards, call the following numbers, all in Kuala Lumpur: American Express (tel. 261-4000), VISA (tel. 238-3270), Diner s Club (tel. 261-1322), and Carte Blanche (tel. 261-1211).

CUISINE: Be prepared to enjoy some of the most delicious food in the region! The three dominant cultures in Malaysia—Indian, Chinese, and Malay—make possible a national cuisine virtually endless in variety and gustatorial pleasures. Whatever your budget or taste (and we hope the latter is eclectic and adventurous), Malaysia offers something for everyone, from the thousands of roadside stalls and open-air bazaars to fine continental dining in the larger hotels. If you insist, you can even find a Big Mac or a leg of Kentucky Fried, or something dubiously similar in the Western-style regional fast-food chains.

You can dine deliciously, for pennies, on peanut-flavored *satay* (a national snack made of barbecued meat on a skewer dipped in a sauce of coconut or curry) and noodles at a hawker's stall. In fact, **hawker's stalls** are the closest you may come to a ubiquitously Malaysian dining experience. These are clusters of food vendors, each family operated and offering one or two specialty dishes. Food is one of Malaysia's best bargains, and a feast al fresco will rarely cost you more than M$10 ($4) per person. Hawkers are rather nomadic, and what's good today may be gone tomorrow. Consult your concierge for the best stalls operating during your visit, or follow the natives to the ones found in local neighborhoods. Stalls concentrated in traditional tourist areas are usually more expensive and not as good.

From hawker's stalls, which are as unfettered a dining experience as you'll find save for preparing your own meals, we move up one rung in formality to **banana-leaf restaurants,** storefront establishments offering Indian specialties. Upon taking your seat at one of the long cafeteria-style tables, you will soon find placed in front of you a large banana leaf, which serves as placemat and plate combined. First you are served a ladle of rice and samplings of various curries. A traditional Indian bread such as a chapati is used to soak up the curry. The key here is that you are encouraged to eat with your hands (there is always a sink in the back to wash up after the meal is over).

Treat yourself to at least one **"steamboat" meal** during your stay in Malaysia. The "steamboat" is a large bowl of bubbling broth set in the center of your table, surrounded by dishes filled with skewers of meat and vegetables you order and pay for by the piece. In effect you cook your own meal, dipping each skewer into the broth for a minute or two. The caliber of a steam boat restaurant is determined by the variables possible in broth and skewer inventions. The broth—be it a sauce of vegetables, curry, sweet and sour, or good old hot water—is always a secret family recipe plainly prized by your hosts.

Skewers can be made of beef, chicken, mutton, pork, seafood, or vegetables. The vegetarian selections identify the staples to be found in a Malaysian greengrocer: spinach, okra, cabbages, snowpeas, bamboo shoots, various peppers, and unique to Malaysia, a small black mushroom that grows wild called oyster mushroom—sublime!

We found Malaysian **fruits** to be more interesting and infinitely more varied than vegetables. There are 26 varieties of bananas alone, some with seeds! Crushed with ice (be careful) in thirst-quenching drinks, or diced and chilled for snacks, Malaysian fruits are plentiful, and to the Western palate, exotically refreshing. Popular varieties include ciku, brown and egg-shaped, with sweet white meat; mangosteens, dark purple (it stains!) on the outside, inside white and tasty; rambutans, red and furry; star fruit, long, yellow-green and in star shaped cross-section succulent, and enhanced with a sprinkling of salt; and durians, a native delight (pungent, to put it mildly, which they ain't) that perhaps only a native can love. There will also be many fruits you'll recognize on sight, including watermelons, papayas, mangos, pineapples, and yes, bananas.

Seafood is most plentiful in coastal towns and larger cities, and we think best prepared by the Chinese. You will find more about our favorites in the local area chapters, especially those in Penang (we have named this city the unofficial culinary capital of Malaysia). Other cities will offer many of the traditional Malaysian foods we've discussed in this section, but only in Penang is there a perfect balance of cuisine and culture.

CURRENCY: The Malaysian unit of currency is the **ringgit,** nearly always referred to as the **Malaysian dollar (M$),** divided into 100 sen. Malaysian paper notes are denominated in M$1,000, 500, 100, 50, 20, 10, 5, and 1. Coins are multiples of the sen: 50, 20, 10, 5, and 1. There are no restrictions on the amount of Malaysian currency you may bring in or take out of the country.

As of early 1989, the rate of exchange was M$2.6 = $1 U.S.

CUSTOMS: Visitors to Malaysia are not required to pay duty on personal items such as cameras, watches, portable cassette players, perfumes, cosmetics, or lighters. Dutiable goods, such as video equipment, may dictate a deposit for temporary importation, normally 50% of value, redeemable upon departure. Carry the receipt of purchase for these items, and make sure you get an official receipt for any tax or deposit paid, to be refunded when you leave the country. Duty-free allowances are given to travelers carrying up to 200 cigarettes and one liter of spirits or wine.

DOCTORS AND DENTISTS: Malaysia's medical professionals are able and well educated. All major hotels have doctors on call. Private doctors and clinics are easy to find throughout the country, and offer good, inexpensive care. Your embassy or a local Tourist Development Corporation (TDC) office should be able to provide the names of recommended physicians.

DOCUMENTS FOR ENTRY: You must be in possession of a valid passport or other internationally recognized document of identification, current at least six months beyond the date of your arrival, to enter Malaysia. United States citizens are granted visa-free entry for social, business, and student trips not to exceed three months. Extensions are rarely problematic provided you allow sufficient time for processing. Visas are not required for Commonwealth citizens (except Indian nationals), British Protected Persons, or citizens of the Republic of Ireland.

Once you enter the country, you are free to travel as you please. The eastern states of Sabah and Sarawak, on the northern part of Borneo, accessible from the mainland via commuter flight, are the exceptions in entry requirements. Your passport will be checked upon entry to both states; however, no such procedures are conducted in either when you return directly to peninsular Malaysia.

DRINKING WATER: Although water is reputedly safe to drink straight from the tap in most hotels in Kuala Lumpur and major hotels in most larger cities, we suggest sticking to bottled water. In the countryside, make sure that all water used for drinking or cooking has been either boiled or bottled. Fruits and vegetables should be peeled and washed before eating.

DRUGSTORES: Drugstores in Malaysia are numerous and generally open longer than other stores. Ask your concierge for the one nearest your lodgings. Most Western palliatives are stocked, as well as some traditional Chinese medicines.
   Warning: While we're in this section we might as well address controlled substances. In a word, death—that's the penalty for dealing in illegal drugs.

ELECTRICAL APPLIANCES: The electrical supply is standardized throughout Malaysia at 220 volts, 50 cycles, A.C. You will need an adapter if you are traveling with a hairdryer, battery charger, or converter for a miniature cassette player, radio, computer, contact lens sterilizer, travel iron, etc.

EMBASSIES AND CONSULATES: There are 77 countries with diplomatic missions in Malaysia, headquartered in Kuala Lumpur. Consult a telephone directory or your own government for those not listed below: **Australia,** at 6 Jalan Yap Kwan Seng (tel. 242-3122), with hours Monday through Friday from 8:30 a.m. to noon and 1:30 to 4 p.m.; **Canada,** at MBF Plaza, 7th floor, Jalan Ampang (tel. 261-2000); **United Kingdom,** at Wisma Damansara, 13th floor, Jalan Semantan (tel. 254-1533), with hours Monday through Friday from 8:15 a.m. to 4 p.m. (closed from 12:30 to 1:30 p.m. for lunch); and the **United States,** at 376 Jalan Tun Razak (tel. 248-9011), with hours Monday through Friday from 7:45 a.m. to 4:30 p.m.

EMERGENCIES: Malaysia's **national telephone number** for police and emergencies is 999.

ETIQUETTE: In Malaysia, a country with so many cultural and social legacies, you might get dizzy from the effort expended to avoid giving offense to any of your hosts, be they Chinese (Buddhist), Indian (Hindu or Muslim), or Malay (also practicing Muslim). Relax! The country is deeply rooted on foundations of racial tolerance, cooperation, and respect. Malaysians are warm and welcoming, easygoing and hospitable. A respectful attitude toward local customs guarantees pleasant encounters with just about everyone, provided you are conversant with a few rules of order, such as the following practical do's and don'ts:

Malaysians, despite their friendliness, are much more reserved than Westerners in demonstrating affection. Be careful not to touch a Chinese friend on the head or shoulders; indeed, any greeting more intimate than a handshake may be disconcerting to your host. A Buddhist's spiritual center of being is perceived to be at the top of his head, closest to heaven. Babies and children are for looking, not petting. Among Hindus and Muslims, the best thing to do with your left hand is to sit on it. That way you won't be tempted to eat with it. The left hand is considered unclean, and is best employed at the more prosaic tasks in grooming and upkeep.

You should remove your shoes upon entering someone's home, or any religious temple or shrine. The soles of the feet are considered unclean. Pointing your toes or the bottoms of your feet at someone is unthinkable. It is safest to sit with your legs uncrossed.

Once you know what to do with your hands and feet, the rest is simple common sense. Politeness, self-deprecation, and modesty are character traits indigenous to the population. Face, or public standing, can be irreparably damaged by displays of aggression or anger. Do not run the risk, in confrontations, of publicly insulting someone, lest you cause him to lose face. No matter how exasperated you may be, adopt a conciliatory tone and manner.

Islam, state religion of Malaysia, places restrictions on the movement and behavior of Malaysian women, and its traditions can be perceived to a lesser degree by Western female visitors, although the business and tourist climates are somewhat more relaxed. Discretion is probably the better part of valor. Save the wet T-shirt contests for Fort Lauderdale.

FESTIVALS AND HOLIDAYS: Given Malaysia's diverse cultural history and the country's advantages in climate, natural resources, relative prosperity, and stability, it should come as no surprise that the calendar includes plenty of occasions considered worth celebrating. Exact dates, based on the lunar calendar, vary from year to year for many religious observances and festivals. Consult a local Travel Development Corporation (TDC—its logo is a jolly green frog) office for schedules of events and holidays during your stay.

National Holidays
In addition to many local observances, the 12 national holidays celebrated throughout Malaysia are as follows:

Late January/February	Chinese New Year
May 1	Labour Day
Mid- to late May	Wesak Day
May, June, or July	Hari Raya Puasa
June 3	The King's Birthday
August, Sept., or Oct.	Hari Raya Haji
August	Muslim New Year
August 31	National Day
October/November	Deepavali
November/December	Muhammad's Birthday
December 25	Christmas Day

Muslim Holidays

The most holy period of the year for Muslims, who make up over half of the Malaysian population, is **Ramadan,** (in April, May, or June depending on the religious calendar) a month of fasting and prayer. The end of Ramadan is celebrated on **Hari Raya Puasa,** a day devoted to family and prayer, feasting, and friends.

Chinese Holidays

Chinese New Year in Malaysia is ushered in by street parades and traditional dancing, the exchange of gifts, entertaining friends and family during open house, and, a special treat for children, gifts of money in bright-red envelopes called *ang pows.* Buddha's birth is celebrated on **Wesak Day,** when many rituals illustrating his teachings are performed.

Indian Holidays

Deepavali is an Indian word meaning "Festival of Lights." Homes are decorated with candles and small lamps to celebrate the victory in Hindu mythology of Rama over King Ravana. The other major Hindu festival is **Thaipusam,** literally, the Milk Festival. This is one of the most extraordinary ceremonies seen anywhere in the world with devout worshippers in trances placing hooks and spears through their skin while walking under the tremendous weight of milk buckets.

Christian Holidays

Traces of Christianity's influence are seen mainly in the city of Malacca, once ruled by the Portuguese, and in the states of Sabah and Sarawak on northern Borneo. **Christmas** in Malaysia is celebrated with singing and gifts.

FILM AND CAMERA: By all means bring your camera! Malaysia offers plenty of scenic backdrops and stunning sunsets to show the folks back home. Film is readily available in many shops, usually at prices lower than those in the United States. It's probably a good idea to have film developed as soon as you've exposed it—otherwise it just might melt like candy left on the dashboard. One-hour photo shops are easy to find and are reasonably priced.

HEALTH AND VACCINATIONS: Vaccinations are not required for entry to Malaysia unless you have been in a yellow-fever-infected country within the six days prior to your arrival. Standards of living are high throughout Malaysia, posing few health problems for the traveler. The heat is a force to be reckoned with, deceptively enervating and potentially dangerous if you don't give yourself time to adjust and slow your pace. Alcohol packs quite a pistol in the tropical climate, so go easy. Plenty of water (bottled or boiled in rural areas) and fruit juices will protect you from dehydration.

Your body may have strong opinions about its new diet, which is to be expected, but if diarrhea persists more than a day or two, or is accompanied by fever or other symptoms, seek treatment. Your embassy can suggest a doctor or clinic or offer advice on local health nuisances. Carry insect repellent and know how to use it, as mosquitos can be more than an irritation. (It is laughingly said that they abduct children and small farm animals in some parts of Malaysia, especially in rural areas.)

As in all travel throughout the region, we recommend that you ask your doctor whether you should receive cholera, typhoid, and/or polio inoculations before your arrival. We also recommend ongoing use (starting one month before you leave home) of an antimalarial drug (such as Aralen), especially if you plan to travel in Sarawak and Sabah and jungle regions.

LANGUAGE: Bahasa Malay is the official language of Malaysia, but English is widely spoken, especially among older people who grew up during the British colonial period when public education was still conveyed in English.

LAUNDRY: Nearly all the larger hotels provide dependable, inexpensive laundry and dry-cleaning services, generally on a same-day basis. Local establishments can be found in all but the tiniest kampong, again very affordable but with a longer turnaround time.

MEASURES: Malaysia's weights and measures adhere to the metric system. For a table of the most common metric equivalents to U.S. measures, see "The ABC's of Burma," in Chapter II.

NEWSPAPERS AND PERIODICALS: English-language local newspapers and magazines include the following: *New Straits Times,* a daily newspaper publishing general local and world news; *Business Times,* a daily newspaper reporting economics and trade; and *Selamat Datang,* an independent, colorful monthly magazine geared to tourists, with extensive listings of important addresses, telephone numbers, dates, events, and religious services.

In addition, the *International Herald Tribune* and *Asian Wall Street Journal* are available in the larger cities, along with several Western news and general-interest magazines.

POSTAL AND GENERAL DELIVERY: Local post offices are listed in each city chapter. Throughout the country, hours are 8 a.m. to 6 p.m. Monday through Friday and 8 a.m. to noon on Saturday. The cost of sending an aerogram anywhere in the world is 40 sen (15¢). The price of a postcard depends on its destination: to Europe the cost is 40 sen (15¢); to America, 55 sen (20¢).

Shipping packages overseas by air can be enormously expensive, so consider sea mail for less urgent deliveries (a package sent to the United States via sea can take anywhere from two to four months to arrive).

Electronic mail service has arrived in Malaysia. Facsimile facilities are available at the Subang International Airport in Kuala Lumpur, in the capital's larger hotels, and at the official Kedai Telekom and Telegraph offices.

Several international overnight delivery services land in Kuala Lumpur and other Malaysian cities. Some of those with offices at Subang International Airport include **Federal Express,** represented locally by Nationwide Express Courier Services, 9 Jalan 215 Petaling Jaya (tel. 03/792-8566); **DHL International,** Wisma DHL, 116 Jalan Loke Yew (tel. 03/221-2044); and **Flying Tigers,** Kida 47200 Subang Selangor, West Malaysia (tel. 03/746-4423).

SAFETY: Malaysia is a safe country, and crime against foreign visitors is rare. The larger cities are well lighted, and the police are easy to find and quite forthcoming when approached for assistance or information. About the scariest experience you'll have will be your first encounter with an Asian toilet.

TAXES AND SERVICE CHARGES: The last tax you will pay in Malaysia is the exit tax at the airport: M$15 ($6) on international flights, M$5 ($2) when arriving from Singapore or Brunei, M$3 ($1.25) on domestic flights.

A 5% government tax is automatically added to hotel and restaurant bills, while a 10% service charge is commonly added to hotel telephone charges, pricier meals, and intangibles. Before agreeing to a hotel room rate, make sure that it includes tax.

TELEPHONE: The Malaysian telephone system is efficient and accessible. Larger hotels offer direct dialing for both local and international calls. They are your best best when placing an overseas call. Coin-operated telephones are found in supermarkets, post offices, and shopping malls.

Long-distance rates are lower on nights and weekends, although if you are charging the call to your home number, the rate applied does not vary. A ten-minute call made from Malaysia to the U.S. cost about $20 in mid-1988 when charged to the American party.

In **international dialing,** Malaysia's country code is 60; the **telephone area code** for Kuala Lumpur is 03.

TELEVISION AND RADIO: Television is a big leisure-time activity in Malaysia. It is even responsible for the national fascination with American-style professional wrestling. Consider packing a few Hulk Hogan T-shirts, especially if you're traveling to Sabah and Sarawak, where Hogan rivals local religious figures in the all-important image recognition factor.

Three television stations, two run by the government, broadcast English-language programming, often featuring British and American imports. Most luxury hotels offer in-house video programming, featuring relatively recent American films.

In addition, the government maintains a network of radio stations throughout the country, offering native and classical music as well as news and commentary in all major languages. The Voice of America and the BBC World Service both broadcast daily throughout the country.

TIME: All of Malaysia lies in one time zone, eight hours ahead of Greenwich Mean Time. The country is 16 hours ahead of Los Angeles, 13 hours ahead of New York, and 7 hours ahead of London.

TIPPING: An automatic service charge of 10% is added to hotel and restaurant bills. Otherwise, tipping in Malaysia is generally discouraged, although Kuala Lumpur is growing more tolerant of the practice.

In order to help eliminate extortionary and inflationary practices among taxi drivers, the government has instituted a standardized pricing system for riders, with fares established at the outset of a trip and payable with vouchers purchased from the TDC.

It is not inappropriate to acknowledge exceptional service by adding your own gratuity to the bill.

TOURIST INFORMATION: The **Tourist Development Corporation (TDC)** of Malaysia operates offices throughout the world and its own territories. In the United States the TDC is headquartered at 818 W. 7th St., Los Angeles, CA 90017 (tel. 213/689-9702). In England, the TDC is found at 57 Trafalgar Square, London WC2N 5DU (tel. 01/930-7932); in Australia, on the 7th Floor, R & W House, 92 Pitt St., Sydney, N.S.W. 2000 (tel. 232-3751).

All TDC offices provide detailed literature, maps, guides, and information. They can arrange tours, issue taxi vouchers, cash traveler's checks, and offer suggestions for finding accommodations, services, shopping, dining, and information. Your embassy is also a good source of information about local customs, medical facilities, and other services.

The **Malaysian Airline System (MAS)** maintains offices throughout the country and the world. Their telephone operators can even help you plot your course through the country. MAS has offices at 420 Lexington Ave., Suite 2148, New York, NY 10017 (tel. 212/697-8994), and at 510 W. 6th St., Los Angeles, CA 90014 (tel. 213/627-1301).

The **Malaysian Consulate in the United States** is headquartered at 140 E. 45th St., New York, NY 10017 (tel. 212/490-2722).

5. RECOMMENDED READING

Many studies, novels, and guidebooks have been written about Malaysia, ranging from historical tracts on the "White Rajas" to terrifying tales of treks in the jungles. The following recommendations are some books we feel will heighten your awareness and appreciation of the multifaceted splendor that was, and is, Malaysia.

Our first two choices offer intimate glimpses into early 1900s Malaysia by two well-known British authors who recount their adventures in the guise of fiction. *The Collected Short Stories of Somerset Maugham,* vol. 4 (London: Penguin Books, 1951), presents several stories set in British colonial Malaya in the 1920s and 1930s; if you're a Maugham fan, or just interested in getting a feeling for Malaysia, then these stories are a must-read. Equally rewarding is Anthony Burgess's *Malayan Trilogy* (London: Harmondsworth, 1981), set in post–World War II Malaysia. We were astonished to find some hotels and bars in Kuala Lumpur that he describes in the trilogy, which is an autobiographical account loosely veiled as fiction. (This work stands with Lawrence Durrell's *Alexandria Quartet* as a classic in the travelogue-as-memoir genre.) If you're in the mood to tackle Joseph Conrad's thick, late-19th-century prose (we love it!), try *Almayer's Folly* (London: Penguin Books, 1936) or his *An Outcast of the Islands* (London: Penguin Books, 1975), two dark morality tales set in the "Malayan islands."

Paul Theroux, author of *The Mosquito Coast,* utilized Johore as the backdrop for *The Consul's File* (London: Harmondsworth, 1977), a novel depicting life in Malaysia for a group of American diplomats.

John's favorite book of 1988 was *Stranger in the Forest* (Boston: Houghton Mifflin Co., 1988), an account by Eric Hansen of his journey on foot across Borneo. This is a fantastic story, bordering on the edge of credulity (if not sanity), about one man's attempt to reach the inner recesses of deepest Borneo. We give it our highest recommendation, even if you're not going to Sarawak or Sabah.

The classic book detailing the history of the British in Malaysia and profiling the different ethnic groups at that time is Steven Runciman's *The White Rajahs—A History of Sarawak from 1841 to 1946* (Cambridge: Cambridge University Press, 1960), a voluminous and fascinating study of how present-day Malaysia came to be under the auspices (read: dynasty) of the Brooke family, who resided in what was then called Borneo. If it's a straightforward rendering of the history of Malaysia from its inception down to the present day that you're looking for, then Harry Miller's *The Story of Malaysia* (London: Faber & Faber Ltd., 1965) will bring you up-to-date easily and pleasantly; Miller is a British journalist who has written extensively on Malaysia.

Those of you who like your historical background with as much adventure as possible should look for F. Spencer Chapman's *The Jungle Is Neutral* (London: Corgi Books, 1949), an engrossing and harrowing account of jungle warfare in World War II, told by a British officer who was lost in the wilderness for three years and survived to tell the story. Malcolm MacDonald's *Borneo People* (London: Jonathan Cape, 1956) is a gripping account of life in Sarawak in the 1940s and 1950s, as told by an officer who was with the British colonial service at that time.

If flora and fauna are part of your agenda, then *The Malay Archipelago—The Land of the Orangutan and the Bird of Paradise* (New York: Dover Books, 1962), by the great English naturalist Alfred Russel Wallace, is just the ticket; he spent many years traveling the mainland and islands categorizing and notating the various facets of nature that surrounded him everywhere he went.

Charles Shuttleworth has written two well-known and witty accounts of his activities as a guide and nature lover, both very entertaining reading: *Malayan Safari* (London: Dent, 1965), in which he recounts his various and sundry activities as a guide; and *Malaysia's Green and Timeless World* (published in Kuala Lumpur in 1981), his panoramic view of the jungles and wilderness, both in photos and reportage.

The best assemblage of books and periodicals about Malaysia that we found was invariably in the lobbies of the big hotels, where the resident book-and-tobacco shops carried entire sections proudly devoted to local and famous international literature about Malaysia's past and future.

CHAPTER XII

KUALA LUMPUR

□ □ □

1. ORIENTATION

2. THE ABC'S OF KUALA LUMPUR

3. ACCOMMODATIONS

4. DINING

5. WHAT TO SEE AND DO IN THE CITY

6. SHOPPING

7. NIGHTLIFE

Kuala Lumpur is Malaysia's capital and its most visible symbol of the future, a future in which Malaysia hopes to achieve parity with Japan and Korea as a major industrial and economic competitor in Southeast Asian market warfare.

KL, as nearly all residents refer to it, isn't the most fascinating city for tourists, but it is a vital and exciting place. One of the most striking aspects of the city is the confluence of races and ethnic groups, mirrored in the names, streets, and architecture of the city: Malay, Chinese, and Indian side by side, casually and routinely. Muslim mosques and Hindu temples, Chinese pagodas and Christian churches all share the modern skyline. The mixture results in some decidedly urbane ideas on urban coexistence, and because of its status as the flagship city everything is constantly and well maintained, from the parks to public-access areas such as train and bus stations, clean, well-lighted places where anyone can feel secure at all times. And how can you not love a city that celebrates New Year's four times a year?

HISTORY: The name Kuala Lumpur loosely translates as "muddy river mouth (or confluence)," an apt name given it by the traders and miners who came here searching for tin, and who settled where the Gombak and Klang Rivers converge because the estuary was the highest upstream point where they could land their supplies. By the 1860s this landing spot had become a trading village along the lines of California's gold-rush hamlets, with constant clashes over mining claims and a high incidence of theft and murder. At the beginning KL was predominantly Chinese, run under the watchful eye of Yap Ah Loy, the Kapitan China, who was in charge until his death in 1885. Due to continuous warring among its constituency, KL was little more than a random collection of huts at the time of Loy's death. Then the British stepped into the picture in the person of Frank Swettenham, the Resident of Selangor, who reconstructed the town with wider streets, brick and stone houses instead of wood huts, and made Kuala Lumpur the capital of Selangor, thus assuring the city of a growing population and industry. By the end of the century it was the capital of the Federated Malay States, which in 1946 became the Federation of Malaya. After independence was declared in 1957, KL grew at an even faster rate, so much so that on February 1, 1974, it was formally detached from the state of Selangor and made its own Federal Territory, the seat of government for all Malaysia.

1. ORIENTATION

One of the nicest aspects of the city is its size and scale—this is not one of the region's mega-metropolises. In fact, for a capital city in Southeast Asia, it is remarkably compact and easy to navigate.

KUALA LUMPUR'S LANDMARKS AND NEIGHBORHOODS: Most of the tourist destinations within Kuala Lumpur are centered in the old section of town, radiating from the confluence of the Klang and Gombak Rivers, near **Jalan Raja.** A mosque, Masjid Jame, marks the spot where boats from the Ampang tin mines used to offload their cargo. Nearby is the State Secretariat (now referred to as the Sultan Abdul Samad Building), one of the city's finest examples of Moorish Victorian architecture. Following the road south, it merges into **Jala Sultan Hishamuddin,** which leads to one of the main bus stations (at the intersection with Jalan Kinabalu) and the wildly ornate Railway Station and the Malayan Railway Administration building. The **Kuala Lumpur Visitors Centre** is located here. A short distance to the east are the Indian and Chinese neighborhoods with their colorful shops and jam-packed streets. **Jalan Petaling** and **Jalan Bandar** are the major arteries of Chinatown.

Most of the luxury and first-class hotels are conveniently located east of the center, only a 15-minute drive from downtown, in an area referred to as the "golden triangle" (not because of drug traffic, as in Thailand, but because of the high cost of real estate; remember, drug dealing carries the death penalty in Malaysia). **Jalan Sultan Ismail** and **Jalan Imbi,** streets where you will find several fine restaurants are the major thoroughfares in this part of the city.

GETTING TO AND LEAVING KUALA LUMPUR: Kuala Lumpur is a well-organized city and its accessways into and out of town are similarly efficient. The airport is located about a 45-minute ride from the center, and the bus and train stations are within a short distance from each other in the downtown section. The city has no shortage of inexpensive taxis and buses, both for city travel as well as "outstation" touring. The Malaysian train system is highly modernized and will take you on the popular north-south axis in comfort. As for long-distance travel, MAS offers flights to nearly all areas of the country, including Sarawak and Sabah, from the KL airport; domestic transportation prices are extremely reasonable and the air fleet is modern. (See the ABCs section for ticket information and sample fares.)

The Airport

All visitors flying domestically or internationally arrive at the **Kuala Lumpur (Subang) International Airport,** south of the city, about 45 minutes away by car. The airport is adjacent to Petaling Jaya, one of KL's largest suburbs.

The **TDC** and the **Malaysian Tourist Information Centre** run a booth (tel. 03/775-5707) in the terminal; they are open daily from 10 a.m. to 6 p.m. daily in Arrival Hall No. 1; in addition, there are general information booths in the terminal, open 24 hours.

The major luxury and first-class hotels in Kuala Lumpur and the Genting Highlands are represented by **Tina Travel Counter** (tel. 03/746-2436), located at the Hotel Reservations Desk downstairs. They're open from 8:30 a.m. to 9:30 p.m. daily except for holidays. There are rooms at the Subang Airport Hotel (see "Accommodations") and a good Indian restaurant (see "Dining") located a

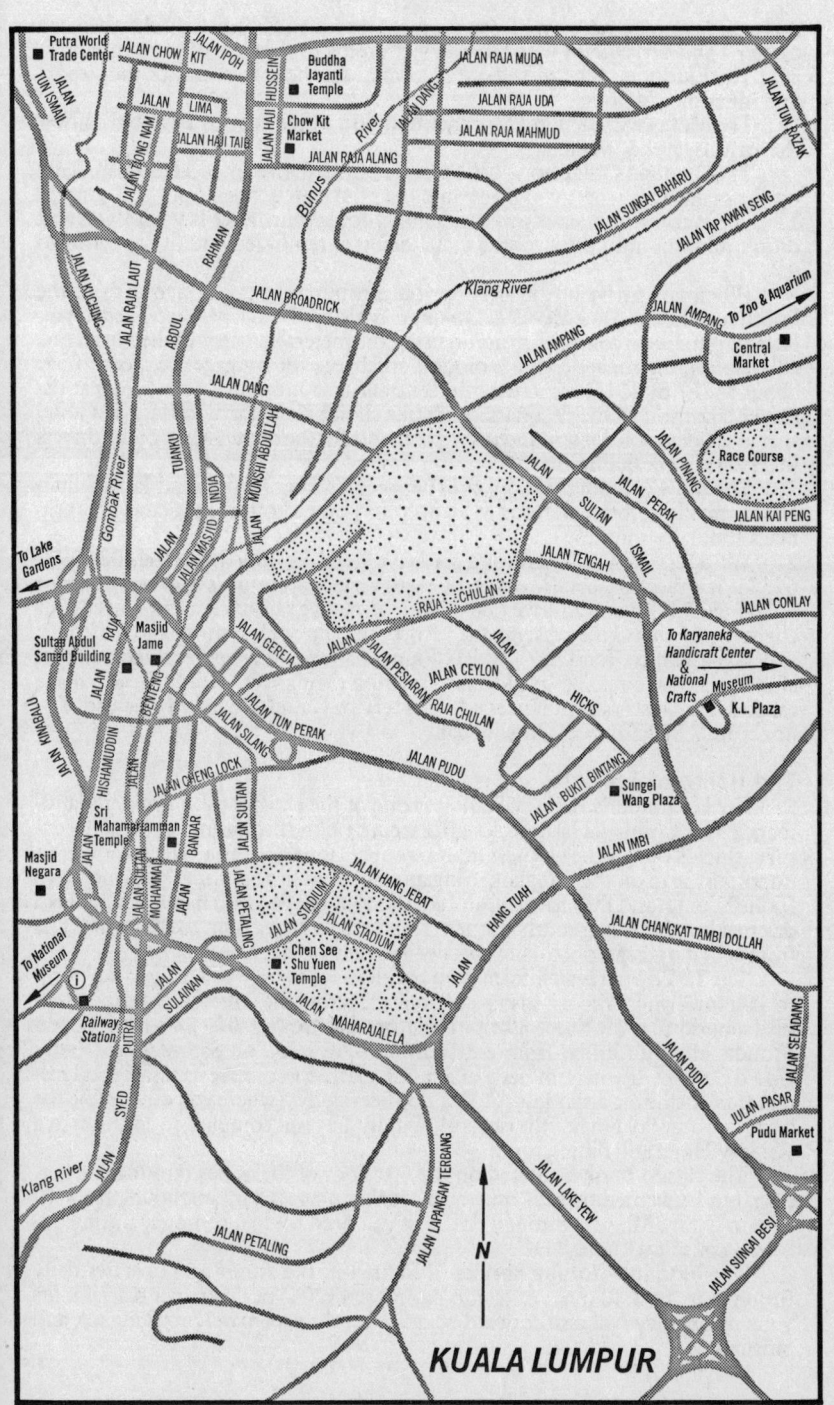

KUALA LUMPUR

mere three-minute walk away from the main terminal; for quick snacks, there is a cafeteria and a restaurant with table service on the upper floor of the terminal.

The **luggage-storage service** is located on the lower level of the airport and functions 24 hours.

The **Malaysian Banking Money Changing office** is open 24 hours daily at the arrivals level downstairs.

The **Overseas Telephone office** is open from 8:45 a.m. to 11:30 p.m. daily on the main level, where you'll also find the **post office,** open from 7:30 a.m. to 11 p.m. every day, in case you accidentally took your hotel key with you and didn't find out until the airport's metal detector reminded you (it happened to us).

When you arrive at the airport, you can purchase taxi coupons from the booths on the concourse level. All **taxis** are registered and fares are posted; if you haven't purchased coupons, insist on using the meters that are installed in all cars (drivers can legitimately levy a modest surcharge for baggage). Expect to pay about M$37.50 ($15) for a ride into central Kuala Lumpur. Make sure that the driver takes you to the destination of your choice or you may end up at a hotel that is less desirable for you and more profitable for the driver. Most of the drivers in legal taxis speak English.

The no. 47 **airport bus** operates between Subang Airport and Jalan Sultan Mohammad, in the center, for M$1.50 (60¢) every hour from 6 a.m.; the trip takes about 45 minutes.

We discovered an interesting service offered by **TravTrade** (tel. 03/293-6233). It's their airport "Meet and Greet" service and this is how it works: for M$44 ($17.50) you can have one of their attractive saronged agents meet your client (or friend) as they disembark, escort them through security and Customs, and take them to TravTrade's V.I.P. lounge, a luxurious and exclusive airport club where you could be comfortably awaiting their arrival. They will also make car and hotel reservations if needed. This service is available for groups also. The hours are 7:30 a.m. to 11:30 p.m. daily.

The Railroad Station

Kuala Lumpur's Railway Station is one of the city's most prominent landmarks. This whimsical Islamic design, executed at the beginning of the 20th century, shields one of the cleanest train terminals found in Asia. The station is an important stop on the Bangkok–Singapore line, with additional stops north to Ipoh, Taiping, and Butterworth, and south to Johore Bharu. There are six trains a day making this north-south journey. You can also take a train to the Batu Caves from KL; it operates once daily, usually in the morning.

The **TDC** operates an information booth in the foyer, open daily from 7 a.m. to 10 p.m. (where there is also a post office); across the street, at 3 Jalan Sultan Hishamuddin, is the **Kuala Lumpur Visitors Centre** (tel. 03/230-1369), open Monday through Friday from 8:30 a.m. to 4:45 p.m., on Saturday to 1 p.m.; closed Sunday. If you're in need of a quick snack, there are several fast-food restaurants, including a spotless A&W Root Beer outlet (where you can sample the best root beer float in Southeast Asia), within the train complex, in addition to a Railway Hotel and dining room.

The closest **bank** is located on the first floor of the annex (around the corner), but be warned that it's only open during normal banking hours, from 10 a.m. to 3 p.m. Monday through Friday; if you need to change money during off-hours, consult with the TDC.

The **luggage-storage service** is located in the annex and operates daily from 6 a.m. to 8:30 p.m.; expect to pay 55 sen (20¢) per piece per day (if it fits your plans, they will also forward baggage very inexpensively to Bangkok and Singapore).

If you do visit the train station, be sure to take in the Malayan Railway Administration Headquarters, located across the street. Like the station itself, this sprawling structure is a fine example of Malaysia's unique blend of Colonial Victoriana and Moorish design.

The Bus Station

Travel by bus and minibus in Kuala Lumpur is well organized, comfortable, and inexpensive. There are seven major bus terminals and ten major minibus routes; try to get a free copy of "Lani's Kuala Lumpur Discovery Map" from the TDC office. It has a listing of all the bus/minibus stations and routes, each cross-referenced on a map for your convenience.

GETTING AROUND THE CITY: As with most aspects of life in Kuala Lumpur, transportation within the city is comfortable, well organized, and inexpensive. From renting a private car to taking a public bus, you can efficiently move around the city for a fraction of what you'd pay back home. Again, consult your TDC KL brochure or "Discovery" map for your transportation options and prices.

By Taxi

Malaysia has a two-tier taxi system. The **yellow-and-black cars** generally operate within the city area, cruising the hotel, business, and shopping areas, and are reasonably priced. The vast majority of these cars are air-conditioned and most drivers speak English. Taxi fares start at M$1.10 (40¢) for the first 1.6 km and 33 sen (10¢) for each additional .8 km. Taxis can also be rented by the day for approximately M$14 ($5.50) per hour. Be sure to use the meter for all trips, including the airport. Many of the top hotels operate their own fleet of private cars for hire; however, the rates are often two to three times the regular taxi fare. In some cases you'll have to walk to the perimeter road of the hotel to find a regular taxi, as some hotels discourage the use of any but their own cars and drivers. KL also offers fleets of radio cabs, such as **Comfort Radio Taxi Service** (tel. 733-0507) and **Radio Teksi** (tel. 221-7600), both of which can be called on a 24-hour basis; they charge from the nearest dispatching station to the ultimate destination.

The other category of car operates on **outstation,** or interstate, journeys. The fare is calculated by the number of passengers, with most cars offering room for four passengers. If you wish you can rent the entire car, but be prepared to pay for the pleasure. Remember always to negotiate your fare prior to engaging a driver or you'll almost certainly overpay. Tipping is not expected.

By Bus

Kuala Lumpur has an extensive and inexpensive bus system with a combination of public and private bus companies. Bus fares are low, with prices ranging from 30 sen (10¢) to M$1.65 (65¢). The main stations for both in-town and outstation travel are: the S. J. Kendraan bus at Jalan Sultan Mohammed (at the multistory parking lot) to the Lake Gardens, Parliament House, International Airport, Petaling Jaya, and Port Kelang; either the Len or S. J. Kendraan buses at Hentian Pudu Raya on Jalan Pudu to Templer Park, the Lake Gardens, Batu Caves, and all interstate areas including Port Dickson and Fraser's Hill; Jalan Ampang, to the National Zoo and Aquarium and Mimaland; Jalan Leboh Ampang, across from the AIA building, to the Batu Caves; Mara Station on Jalan Medan Tuanku, to Kuantan on Malaysia's east coast; Budaya Ekspres Station at Lorong Medan Tuanku, to Kota Bahru.

Minibuses supplement the public buses and charge a flat fee of 65 sen (20¢). For the most popular tourist destinations, minibuses run on the following routes: bus 17 along Jalan Silang to the Selangor Pewter Factory, Zoo, and Aquarium; bus 41 along Jalan Bukit Bintang to the Batu Caves; and buses 22, 30, 35, and 46 along Jalan Tauanku Abdul Rahman to Petaling Jaya Old Town.

By Rental Car

Unlike other countries that we've visited in the region, Malaysia is relatively safe for driving. If you feel the need, be assured that there are many rental-car agencies (see "Car Rental" in the following section). Remember to wear a seatbelt: it's the law in Malaysia.

If you do rent a car, we recommend engaging a driver as well for all city and day-trip touring around KL. The price is so reasonable, the service convenient, and the drivers knowledgeable of the roads, and all important, finding parking is usually so exhausting that it more than compensates for the freedom of having your own car.

2. THE ABC'S OF KUALA LUMPUR

The following directory is a summary of services available in the city and where to find them.

AIRPLANE TICKETS: Most international carriers have offices in Kuala Lumpur where you can make reservations or confirm flights. Within Malaysia, **MAS** is the only carrier. For information on schedules and fares, visit the main MAS office on Jalan Sultan Ismail (tel. 03/200-011), across from the Hilton. Airplane tickets can also be purchased at one of the city's many travel agencies or bucket shops (see "Travel Agents").

AIRPORT: Kuala Lumpur's Subang International Airport is a modern, full-service facility with information, banking, postal, restaurant, hotel, and other tourist services all within its bounds (see "Getting To and Leaving KL" for more information). For general **airport information,** call 746-5707. For information about flights on **MAS,** call 03/768-555 at their airport counter or 206-633 at their offices in 4 Jalan Sulaiman in town.

All international travelers must pay an airport tax of M$15 ($6); the fee for Singapore-bound passengers is M$5 ($2), and on domestic flights, M$3 ($1.25).

AMERICAN EXPRESS: The American Express office is located in the MAS building, Bang MAS, on Jalan Sultan Ismail (tel. 261-0000); normal service hours are 8:30 a.m. to 5:30 p.m. Monday through Friday. If you need to report lost credit cards and traveler's checks, you can do so by calling 261-4000 at all other hours. Remember to bring your passport for all transactions.

Note: This office does not cash traveler's checks; you'll have to go to a bank or change booth.

BANKS: Kuala Lumpur has bank branches all over the city, many with automated teller machines that dispense cash to cardholders. Nearly every bank exchanges foreign currency during regular hours, which are 10 a.m. to 3 p.m. Monday through Friday and 9:30 to 11:30 a.m. on Saturday. Change booths, which are also scattered throughout the city, charge rates similar to banks (many of them are actually owned and operated by banks) and generally keep much longer hours. It is essential to bring your passport for changing money.

Many American banks maintain offices in Kuala Lumpur, including Bank of America, Citibank, and Chase Manhattan.

BEAUTY PARLORS/BARBERSHOPS: Most establishments in this category are unisex. Among the locally recommended salons are: **Louise Clerk,** on the fourth floor at the KL Hilton; **Michael Choi,** at his shop near the Le Coq d'Or Restaurant on Jalan Ampang; and the Japanese-trained haircutters at **Kenji,** at the upstairs arcade in the Shangri-la Hotel (tel. 230-6202). A full cut and dry will range from M$28 ($11.25) to M$40 ($16).

BOOKSTORES: Almost every international-class hotel has a bookstore in its shopping arcade; most of these offer a small selection of publications. There are some terrific bookstores around the city and in the many malls. Two of the better ones are the **Berita Book Centre,** located on the first floor of Bukit Bintang Plaza on, you guessed it, Jln Bukit Bintang (tel. 241-6071), and **Guardian Books and Stationery,** located just across the floor from Berita (tel. 242-8231). Both feature large Western bestseller sections, many coffee table books on Malaysia, and large sections of professional journals and reference books.

BUS TERMINALS: The main bus terminals are listed above in "Getting Around" for both in-town and outstation travel. If you need additional information, call the TDC at 293-5188 or contact a travel agent.

BUSINESS HOURS: Most shops, and especially those catering to tourists, are open daily from 9:30 a.m. to 7 p.m. The major department stores found in the shopping malls are generally open from 10 a.m. to 10 p.m. Government hours are 8 a.m. to 12:45 p.m. and 2 to 4:15 p.m. Monday through Thursday, on Friday from 8 a.m. to 12:15 p.m. and 2:30 to 4:15 p.m., and on Saturday morning from 8 a.m. to 12:45 p.m. Banking hours are listed above (see "Banks").

BUSINESS SERVICES: Most business services, such as secretarial work, photocopying, word processing, facsimile and Telex, computer and database time are available on a per-use basis in the business centers of the major international hotels. The Hilton and the Shangri-la have particularly well-equipped and comfortable facilities.

CAMERA EQUIPMENT/REPAIR AND FILM: Although cameras and accessories aren't quite the bargain they may be in Hong Kong, many people still find prices lower in Kuala Lumpur than in the United States. Film is about on a par with most American camera stores, if not a shade cheaper. A full range of Fuji and Kodak film is available around Kuala Lumpur. If you need your camera repaired it's best to inquire at the concierge's desk in your hotel for a reputable shop. Fast photo-processing labs are proliferating throughout the city and offer generally good results at low prices.

CAR RENTAL: Avis and Hertz are both represented in Kuala Lumpur. **Hertz** has two branches: the first is at Lot 11, Kuala Lumpur Hilton (tel. 243-3014); the other is at Subang International Airport (tel. 746-2091). Unlimited-mileage rates range from M$88 ($35.25) to M$240 ($96) daily for a locally produced Proton Saga up to a Mercedes; expect to pay M$300 ($120) to M$800 ($320) for a weekly rate. **Avis** operates three branches: their headquarters and central reservations is at 40 Sultan Jalan Ismail (tel. 242-3500); they are also at the Hilton Hotel (tel. 241-7144) and at Subang International Airport (tel. 746-3950). Their rates are comparable with those at Hertz. **Thrifty** (tel. 248-2388) maintains offices at the Holiday Inn on the Park, and **Mayflower Acme,** in the Angkasa Raya building at 123 Jalan Ampang (tel. 261-1136), the largest tour company in Malaysia, offers cars at a slight discount. Most of the rental-car agencies will allow you to drop off a car at their other stations (typically, Penang or Singapore) for an additional charge ranging between M$85 ($34) and M$165 ($66).

Chauffeur-driven cars may be rented from any of the major chains with typical daily rates from M$200 ($80) to M$460 ($184), including insurance and fuel.

CREDIT CARDS: All major cards are accepted in the luxury and first-class hotels and restaurants and in most upmarket shops. If you lose your credit card call one of the following telephone numbers: **American Express** (tel. 261-4000), **Diners Club** (tel. 261-1322), **Carte Blanche** (tel. 261-1211). For VISA or MasterCard holders, the fastest refund procedure is to make an international collect call (tel. 415/574-7111 for VISA, and 314/275-6100 for MasterCard) to the United States (they're open 24 hours a day), after which they will authorize a refund at the nearest local branch.

CRIME: Kuala Lumpur is a safe city, although there is the occasional incidence of petty crime, including bag snatching, pickpocketing, and credit-card and traveler's check fraud. As with other Southeast Asian cities, much of the security problem is concentrated on public buses. Pay close attention to your belongings at all times, keeping valuable possessions in front of you (don't keep a wallet, for example, in a back pocket). As you would anywhere, keep all important documents and jewelry in your hotel's safe-deposit box. Be careful with credit cards, in particular making sure that you tear up carbons and keep all receipts. Be suspicious of any prolonged period of time when your credit card is away from you, such as stores that take your card for a credit check. It is also suggested that you exercise caution about strangers who approach you, offering to be your guide or to buy you a drink or food.

DENTISTS AND DOCTORS: Malaysia has good medical care and many fine doctors and dentists. The U.S. Embassy publishes a listing of recommended physicians and dentists, both generalists and specialists. Telephone the embassy (tel. 248-1702) for specific names. In addition, some of the better hotels have doctors and/or nurses on their staff who can treat minor maladies. If there is a particularly serious problem, patients can also be taken to Singapore.

DRUGSTORES: Kuala Lumpur has many drugstores, dispensing both American and foreign-made pharmaceuticals. For specific recommendations of dispensaries, call the American Embassy (tel. 248-1702) or ask the concierge at your hotel. Some hotels maintain a limited supply of medication.

EMBASSIES: The **U.S. Embassy** is located at 376 Jin Tun Razak (tel. 03/248-9011), and is open Monday through Friday from 7:45 a.m. to 4:30 p.m. The **British Embassy,** at 186 Jin Ampang and Wisma Damansara (tel. 03/245-1533), is open Monday through Friday from 8:15 a.m. to 4 p.m. (closed from 12:30 to 1:30 p.m. for lunch). The **Canadian Embassy** is located on the seventh floor of the MBF Plaza (tel. 03/261-2000). The **Australian Embassy** is at 6 Jin Yap Kwan Seng (tel. 03/242-3122), and has hours from 8:30 a.m. to noon and 1:30 to 4 p.m. Monday through Friday.

EMERGENCY: If you find yourself in need of the police, the fire department, or an ambulance, dial **999.**

HOSPITALS: The **General Hospital** is between Jalan Tun Abdul Razak and Jalan Pahang. It's relatively new and clean, the doctors speak English, and there are labs and dispensaries on the premises. Dial 999 to reach the hospital.

INFORMATION: Dial 03/293-5188 for information from the **Tourist De-**

velopment Corporation (TDC) located on the 24th floor of the Putra World Trade Centre and open Monday through Friday from 8:30 a.m. to 4:45 p.m., to 1 p.m. on Saturday; closed Sunday. The **Kuala Lumpur Visitors Centre** is located near the train station at 3 Jalan Hishamuddin (tel. 03/230-1369), and keeps the same hours as the TDC. You can also receive reliable information from **Mayflower Acme Tours** at their travel office in the Angkasa Raya building at 123 Jalan Ampang (tel. 03/248-6023). Their rental car division is at the same location (tel. 03/261-1136).

LAUNDRY AND DRY CLEANING: Most hotels offer laundry and dry-cleaning services, and the work is usually fast and excellent.

LIBRARIES: The U.S. Embassy runs the **Lincoln Resource Center,** a free public library at 376 Jalan Tun Razak, available for both foreigners and residents.

LOCKSMITHS: Soon Kee Locksmith at 49 Jalan Jejaka 9 Taman Maluri can be of great help for everything from locking your keys in your car to repairing small locks for luggage. Otherwise, consult with the concierge at your hotel.

MAPS: The TDC publishes two fine maps that are sure to please the most demanding of visitors. **"Lani's Kuala Lumpur Discovery Map"** is of the same style as Nancy Chandler's excellent maps of Bangkok and Chiang Mai and the "Secret" map of Singapore—that is, a hand-drawn, personal guide to the city that highlights good food, shopping, tourist sites, markets, and other useful services. The other, more general map, is the **"Kuala Lumpur Map and Guide,"** which is really no more than a brochure, but it contains a wealth of information and tips for the first-time visitor to KL. Both maps are available free from the TDC.

NEWSPAPERS AND PERIODICALS: The issue of newspapers and periodicals is a touchy one in Malaysia. As of our last visit, only the *Malay Mail* and the *New Straits Times* (our favorite) were still allowed to publish. (The other publications were closed down by the government for political reasons.) Both the *Asian Wall Street Journal* and *International Herald Tribune* are available Monday through Friday and can be purchased on their day of publication. The TDC publishes *Selamat Datang,* a slick English-language magazine that is published monthly and available in nearly every hotel. All of these newspapers and periodicals are sold in newsstands and bookstores in the international hotels and in tourist areas, particularly around Jalan Sultan Ismail and Jalan Ampang.

POLICE: Dial 999 for any and all police matters.

POST OFFICE: The **Central Post Office** is located on Jalan Sultan Hishamuddin near the intersection with Jalan Kinabalu in the Dayabumi Complex. The postal service counters, telegraph offices, and telephone services are all on the same level. There is an English-language counter on the second floor.

    Poste Restante is located in the GPO. You can receive mail at Poste Restante with proper identification, either a valid passport or ID card. Upon receiving mail you must sign a receipt; hours of operation are the same as the post office.

RAILROAD INFORMATION: Train tickets can be purchased directly at the station. Reservations may be made by telephone: for southern routes, call 274-7443; for northern routes, call 274-7442. The **general information** telephone number is 238-4132 or 274-7434. If you plan on taking a sleeping berth train to Bangkok, try to make your reservation as early as possible; reservations are taken

30 days in advance of the trip for a night sleeper, 10 days in advance for an express train. (For more information about the rail system, see "Getting Around").

RELIGIOUS SERVICES: For Anglican and Episcopalian services, contact the **Anglican Church Diocese of West Malaysia** at 9 Jln Tengah (tel. 242-7303). The **Church of St. Mary,** on Jalan Raja Laut (tel. 293-5702), is a fine example of 19th-century colonial-era construction. Catholic services are held at the **Church of the Holy Redeemer** at Psiarn Rajawali (tel. 341-6812). The **Zion Church** is located at 21 Jalan Abdul Samad, and **St. Andrew's Presbyterian Church** is at 31 Jalan Raja Chulan. For information regarding **Methodist** churches, call 243-2872.

SHOE REPAIR: Most of the shopping malls have shoe-repair shops or stands. You can also find shoe stores and repair shops along Jalan Tuanku Abdul Rahman, as well as Jalan Petaling, in the older section of town. For the closest shoe repair, contact your concierge or ask the hotel to arrange for the work.

TAILORS: Again, consult with your concierge; many hotels have tailors on the premises and can make repairs very quickly.

If you're looking for made-to-order clothing, consider a visit to perhaps the most famous tailor in Kuala Lumpur, **Groovy Apparel,** known for making a safari suit for Muhammad Ali! You'll find Groovy at 77 Jalan Alor (tel. 242-7863).

TAXIS: Consult the section on "Getting Around." Remember that there are taxis that will take you around the town and its environs, and those that will literally drive you all the way to Singapore if you like.

TELEGRAMS: The office is in the GPO and is open 24 hours a day, every day, and also offers telegram restante service.

TELEPHONE: For international calls you can dial the U.S. directly from any of the major hotels, for which you pay a surcharge ranging from nominal to pricey. Or you can make your way to the GPO on Bukit Mahkamah off Jalan Raja Chulan, which is open always, as is the airport phone office.

The procedure for making a call is as follows: Book your call by filling out a form at one of the desks, specifying the telephone number you wish to call; take the form to the cashier and wait until you are called to a booth. For international information, dial 108. Collect or credit-card calls can be made without an extra fee.

The **telephone area code** for Kuala Lumpur is 03.

Local calls can be made from any red pay telephone. Calls cost 10 sen (5¢).

TOURIST INFORMATION: Information can be obtained during business hours from the **Tourist Development Corporation (TDC),** Putra World Trade Centre, 24th Floor (tel. 03/293-5188); information offices are open from 8:30 a.m. to 4:45 p.m. Monday through Friday, to 1 p.m. on Saturday; closed Sunday.

Inquiries may also be made at the **Kuala Lumpur Visitors Centre,** located at 3 Jalan Hishamuddin (tel. 03/230-1369), which is open from 8:30 a.m. to 4:45 p.m. Monday through Friday and 8:30 a.m. to 1 p.m. on Saturday.

The **Malaysian Tourist Information Centre,** at the Subang International Airport (tel. 03/775-5707), operates from 8 a.m. to 11:30 p.m. daily.

TRAVEL AGENTS: The top agency for local excursions is **Mayflower Acme Tours,** in the Angkasa Raya building at 123 Jalan Ampang (tel. 03/248-6023). They have programs that vary from daily local bus tours to custom, fully escorted tours of the country. Mayflower can arrange to pick you up at nearly any of the major hotels. Typical local tours visit Chinatown, the National Museum, the Karyaneka Handicraft Center, Masjid Jame, Kampang Bharu night market, Batu Caves, Selangor Pewter and Batik "factories," and the Lake Gardens. Mayflower offers a range of all-inclusive peninsular Malaysia tours from a three-day KL, Cameron Highlands, and Penang excursion for M$325 ($130), to a ten-day romp including Malacca, Kuantan, Genting Highlands, Cameron Highlands, Penang, and the east coast for M$1,100 ($440).

3. ACCOMMODATIONS

Kuala Lumpur is a buyer's market for luxury and first-class hotel accommodations. Fueled by the enormous expansion of the economy during the late '70s and early '80s, and virtually abandoned after the price collapse of tin, rubber, and oil in the late '80s, KL sustains a surplus of glitzy, Hong Kong–style hotels that, like Singapore, are only ever half filled.

With such a market, it's natural that hoteliers would offer steep discounts during periods of low occupancy. The rates listed below are those published by the hotels. If you were to make a reservation directly from the United States you'd likely pay those rates; however, if you make the same reservation through an agent or merely ask the front desk for a discount, you are likely to receive up to a 50% reduction in the quoted price. The best method is to telephone ahead, inquiring if such a discount is available. Most hotels will be happy to accommodate any reasonable offer. Unless otherwise stated, all listed hotels have air conditioning and swimming pools. With that in mind, we begin our tour of Southeast Asia's best lodging market.

A LUXURY CHOICE: The 722-room high-rise **Shangri-la** at 11 Jalan Sultan Ismail (tel. 03/232-2388), is the epitome of Kuala Lumpur's hotel extravagance. The handsome lobby is sheathed in a quarry full of white and green marble. Outdoor waterfalls and palms soften the expanse of stone, polished brass, and dark wood. Guests rooms, and in particular deluxe accommodations, are surprisingly spacious and equipped with all of the latest amenities. The marble décor, so evident in the hotel's public spaces, is restated in the bathrooms. Since opening in 1985 the Shangri-la has gained a fine reputation for its restaurants (eight in all!), especially Lafite, the continental outlet, Shang Palace for Cantonese cuisine, and Nadaman, its Japanese eatery. As with all Shangri-la hotels in the region, the KL branch is run by a courteous and helpful staff. Rates are M$180 ($72) for a superior single, M$200 ($80) for double occupancy; deluxe rooms run M$205 ($82) for a single and M$225 ($90) for two.

FIRST-CLASS HOTELS: The city's best-established hotel, and still one of its finest, is the **Kuala Lumpur Hilton,** located on Jalan Sultan Ismail (tel. 03/242-2122). The Hilton has long served as the premier venue for government and high-level business functions and dignitaries (when we last stayed here we shared the floor with the Sultan of Brunei's brother!). Each of the hotel's 589 rooms includes the latest amenities and most have fine views overlooking the nearby Turf Club or downtown. We especially enjoy the Aviary Bar, the Hilton's lobby pub which must have the most active social scene of any public building in KL. Just relax, order a drink, listen to some fine jazz, and watch the KL glitterati embark on their nightly parade. Not to be overlooked are the many restaurants at the Hilton. We especially enjoyed a fine lunch in the elegant Malaka Grill. The Hilton also has excellent business services and a full complement of sports facilities. All in all, the Hilton is one of KL's best lodgings. Room rates run M$155 ($62) for a deluxe single and M$175 ($70) for a similarly appointed double.

The **Regent,** starring on Jalan Sultan Ismail (tel. 03/242-8845), is a genuine jewel on the KL hotel scene (as is every Regent we've seen in Southeast Asia).

The décor is chic and warm, the service first-rate, and with only a M$10 ($4) difference between standard and deluxe accommodations, you can go first-cabin and find your windows shuttered with sliding teak shades and your room as comfortable as you'd ever hope for. The Regent also houses several first-class restaurants, among them the Sausa Brasserie, probably the best-known continental restaurant in the city; the Regent Court (gourmet Chinese); and the Ranch Grill, famed for its Western-style steaks and salads. The Regent is also within wallet-range of the upscale Sunge Yang shopping plaza. Luxury, convenience, and great meals, and all of it for two for M$165 ($66).

The **Ming Court,** on Jalan Ampang (tel. 03/261-8888), is an elegant and excellent hotel. While not as flashy as the Regent or the Hilton, it is well appointed and comfortable, so much so that its lobby has become the preferred power lunch rendezvous spot for young KL execs. The décor is warm and rich and, like the Regent, the Ming Court boasts several very good restaurants: Japanese, Szechuan, French, and American fare are all well served here. The rooms are all the same size: what differentiates a deluxe double from its superior counterpart are balconies overlooking the swimming pool. We thought the deluxe cabaña, at M$180 ($72), the best overall value.

In the same price range as the Ming Court is the **Merlin,** located at 2 Jalan Sultan Ismail (tel. 03/248-0033). Everywhere you go in Malaysia you see a Merlin hotel; and this is one of the nicest, with dark peacock-style furnishings, large dressing mirrors (for you peacocks), and views of downtown KL for M$175 ($70). The Merlin also has a shopping arcade replete with a travel agent, hairdresser/barber, florist, and camera repair shop.

If you're visiting Kuala Lumpur as part of a delegation to a convention, you'll likely stay at the sparkling **Pan Pacific,** adjacent to the Putra World Trade Center and the Mall (tel. 03/442-5555), one of Southeast Asia's largest shopping centers. What you can expect is excellent service and some of the most pristinely maintained accommodations in the city. From the slick atrium-style lobby with its bank of glass elevators to the pastel-colored guest rooms with writing desks, sofas, optional waterbeds(!), and bathrooms that are equipped with separate bath and shower, the Pan Pacific presents a very attractive lodging alternative for those who want to be out of the busy downtown area, but on the edge of the action. Superior-room rates are M$165 ($66) for a single, M$185 ($74) for a double. Deluxe accommodations run M$25 ($10) additional.

As you drive up Jalan Imbi and approach the **Prince Hotel** (tel. 03/243-8388), a 305-room, starkly modern high-rise structure, you are surprised to be greeted by doormen attired in traditional Malaysian costumes. Although the hotel offers all the modern amenities, its traditional attitude toward hospitality and service make it evident that this is one hotel that hasn't forgotten its local heritage. Even the spacious rooms, with their high ceilings (for a newly constructed building), evince this gracious style (not to mention the largest "selamat datang" fruit basket we've ever seen). Room rates run M$160 ($64) for a standard single, M$185 ($74) for a double. Superior-category rooms run M$25 ($10) higher, while deluxe accommodations are an additional M$30 ($12).

The **Holiday Inn City Center,** on Jalan Raya Laut (tel. 03/293-9233), is an 18-story, 250-room inn that was built in 1986 to complement its companion hotel, the **Holiday Inn on the Park,** a very homey 200-bed hotel on Jalan Pinang (tel. 3/248-1066), that boasts, among other attributes, a perfect panorama of the KL racetrack directly across the park. This version of "no surprises" is a very acceptable lodging in a convenient location overlooking the Gombak River. We particularly appreciate the three full floors of no-smoking rooms. This Holiday Inn is a fair departure from the chain's norm, if only for its decorative lobby with Islamic motifs. A standard room, single or double, rents for M$130 ($52). The Inn on the Park, priced similarly, is a tad nicer due to its décor and locale.

What can you say about a hotel with a 1960s Aeroflot poster in the lobby?

Welcome to the **Federal Hotel,** at 35 Jalan Bukit Bintang (tel. 03/248-9166), a 450-room modern inn that wins points if only for its revolving Bintang Lounge on the 18th floor with the best views of KL. Though the public spaces and guest rooms are perfectly clean, they are showing signs of wear. A single standard room runs M$130 ($52), M$155 ($62) for a double—not bad if you're in a pinch.

THE MODERATE CLASS: The **Hotel Equatorial,** several doors north of the Hilton on Jalan Sultan Ismail (tel. 03/261-7777), opened in 1973 and is in the process of upgrading an already fine moderately priced hotel into a more elegant moderately priced hotel. Although the rooms are of better quality than similarly priced hotels, the Equatorial is known to locals for its fine dining rooms serving Chinese and continental fare (see "Dining"), and for its Blue Moon Bar, specializing in '60s and early '70s music, which enjoys a popular local following. It's the kind of dark, plush piano bar that inspires late-night revelry and illicit romance. Our only gripe with the Equatorial is its indifferent service. If you can see your way past that, then this is one of the city's better mid-price buys. A superior single costs M$100 ($40); a twin, M$110 ($44). Deluxe singles run M$120 ($48) while a double sells for M$135 ($54). Note: Most deluxe rooms are attached to a superior room, making this a fine place for families.

The **Plaza Hotel,** on Jalan Raja Laut (tel. 03/298-2255), is another good choice and, though slightly more costly than the Equatorial, the staff is more courteous and expert. We found the deluxe doubles here much nicer than their superior counterparts (deluxe means a refrigerator and deep tub), and at M$165 ($66), they are only M$10 ($4) more in price—and worth it.

The **Mandarin Hotel** is situated at 2 Jalan Sultan (tel. 03/230-3000), in the heart of KL, so much so in fact that we were told this was the hotel of choice for American sailors on shore leave! All we can add to that recommendation is to make sure that you ask for an outward facing room: they're a bit nicer. A deluxe double here runs M$125 ($50), though they had a promotional rate of M$80 ($32) when we were there.

For you party animals looking for a Bruce Willis–style hotel, welcome to the **Hotel Malaya,** on Jalan Bandar and Hang Lekir (tel. 03/232-7722). The City Palace Club on the second floor, in cahoots with the Malaya's health club, has video games rooms, 15 slot machines, three pool tables, a card room with two tables, and a bar lounge with dart boards—if this is your idea of health, then you'll feel just fine here. The rooms are comfortably nice, and at M$90 ($36) for a deluxe double or twin, it's a happening place. We recommend that you go for the deluxe twin: it's bigger and nicer than the double. The Malaya also has family rooms (interconnecting single rooms, one with a king-size bed and one with two twins and a futon sofa) that are a good buy.

Some hotels opened just in time for the local economy to crash. When you enter such an establishment, it seems as if things just haven't started, as if the hotel was in a pre-opening phase. Such is the case with the **Hotel Grand Continental,** on Jalan Belia/Raja Laut, near Jalan Sultan Ismail (tel. 03/293-9333), a plain, no-frills inn that is clean, modern, and manned by a staff that's eager to please. The polished granite lobby sparkles, as do the 328 rooms. The hotel has complete facilities and is very reasonably priced (including aggressive promotions): twin rooms cost M$80 ($32); deluxe suites run M$100 ($40).

For those who see merit in staying in the heart of Chinatown, the 15-story **Hotel Furama,** on Jalan Sultan (tel. 03/230-1777)—not associated with the hotel of the same name in Hong Kong—is just the place. Medium clean and a bit worn, the Furama is literally in the thick of KL's busiest shopping zone. A double room runs M$60 ($24); singles are M$10 ($4) less.

One of our favorite hotels is also one of the least expensive: the **KL Station Hotel,** located at the KL Railway Station on Jalan Sultan Hishamuddin (tel.

03/274-7433). The Moorish architecture of the station is mirrored in the hotel's 30 rooms, all of which are huge: 16-foot ceilings look down on Colonial-style cream and green rooms that are twice the size of any other in the city, and each has an old air conditioner or overhead fan, private bathroom with shower/tub, writing desk with two chairs, and a large balcony looking out over KL. The only small thing here is the price: a double is M$45 ($18)! You've got to love a place whose brochure, after listing the prices, checkout time, etc., says "Guest with Light Luggage are requested to pay in advance." There's a dining room in the hotel, and downstairs in the station building there is everything else, including a great A&W! Budget pilgrim, your search has ended.

THE BUDGET RANGE: When you need a room that is truly budget priced, you can always depend on your friendly local **YMCA Hostel,** fairly out of the way at 95 Jalan Padang Belia (tel. 03/274-1439), a substantial taxi or bus ride into the center of town. The Y complex includes a low-cost restaurant, launderette, and tennis courts. Both men and women are welcome to stay in the private rooms, though only men may stay in the dorms. The best values are the dorm and non-air-conditioned rooms. The third-floor dorms, with four people to a room, run M$12 ($4.75) per bed. Single fan-cooled rooms are M$20 ($8); double rooms cost M$30 ($12).

AT THE AIRPORT: Those who have an early-morning flight might consider a night at the **Subang Airport Hotel** (tel. 03/746-2122), just a three-minute stroll across a covered walkway from the main terminal of Kuala Lumpur's international airport. Both standard and superior rooms are small but clean and efficiently laid out. All rooms receive televised flight information from the airport, so you can't fault the hotel for missing a flight! Standard singles cost M$105 ($42), with a room for two renting at M$120 ($48); there are "family rooms" in the hotel for M$175 ($70).

4. DINING

Our personal suggestion, other than the specific recommendations below, is to tell you to head straight for the street food stalls, known locally as **hawker stalls.** With food this good, why not dine alfresco à la Malaysian? Kuala Lumpur has hundreds of hawker stalls, and they're by far the best dining value. There's also fine Indian food (mostly southern), and you can find good Indian fare in the food stalls. For meat eaters, finding a steak (from New Zealand cattle) or hamburger is a cinch in KL: Kentucky Fried Chicken, A&W Root Beer, and McDonalds have hit KL in a big, big way, especially Kentucky Fried, which was celebrating its 14th anniversary when we were there, with banners at every intersection. One of their franchises inhabits a large Colonial-style mansion downtown!

CULINARY HIGHLIGHTS: If this is your first time in Malaysia and you're looking for a special meal "offering authentic Malay cuisine amid a scenario of cultural performances," then head straight to **Yasmin,** at 6 Jalan Kia Peng (tel. 241-5655), where a large terraced restaurant resides in a distinctive colonial-era house. You can lunch here, but it's the buffet dinner and floor show (beginning at 8:30 p.m.) that sets Yasmin apart from every place else: it's almost impossible to describe the breadth of the buffet selection, other than to say that it's an extraordinary display of regional cuisines. The cultural show is similarly eclectic, with all manner of regional dance, music, and theater presented with tremendous immediacy (you dine about ten feet away from the stage). Yasmin is the favored place for locals to bring out-of-town guests, in addition to being on the tourist beat, but don't let that dissuade you from experiencing a wonderful evening of Malay food and entertainment. Yasmin is open Monday through Saturday from noon to 10 p.m. An intimate evening for two (we saw a navy couple necking at the next table) costs about M$35 ($14), including the show.

MALAY CUISINE: Another Malay buffet option is the **Cempaka Restaurant,** in the Holiday Inn on the Park, at 130 Jalan Selar Cheras (tel. 930-2789). Here you'll find a cornucopia of local dishes and regional specialties. Cempaka is open daily for lunch and dinner; expect to pay M$20 ($8) per person.

The breakfast of Malaysian champions in KL is served at the **Hilton Hotel** from 6:30 to 10 a.m. For M$18 ($7.25) you can sample several traditional Malay/Chinese/Indian dishes, all you can eat buffet style, or have bacon-and-eggs with sautéed mushrooms and a croissant. We urge you to try such local specialties as the traditional Malay eye-opener nasi lemak (rice steamed in coconut milk with chicken curry, egg, meat, and fried peanuts), yong tau fu (a Chinese morning soup similar to Thai congee, with large noodles, stuffed chiles, fish, tofu, and sesame seeds), and chicken porridge (like you'd imagine, with chives and onions). All of these are absolutely delicious and not to be missed. This breakfast will make a champion out of anybody and set you up for a full day of sightseeing.

Our favorite way to sample Malay food is, as we'd already said, at the hawker stalls. We suggest you take the opportunity to explore the city and venture to some of KL's ethnic neighborhoods. One excellent area for this style of eating is **Kampung Baharu,** northeast of city center. Although there are street stalls on various corners in this residential neighborhood, there are a greater concentrations of stalls in the markets; ask your concierge or taxi driver to direct you to the best stalls. Our suggestions are **Pasar Minggu,** the site of the Sunday market located on the city's north side, and the **Chow Kit** market, near the intersection of Jalan Dang Wangi and Jalan Batu on Jalan Haji Hussein, where the evening dining is excellent. You'll find it difficult to spend more than a few Malaysian dollars for anything.

Nyona cooking is an adaptation of Malay recipes for the Chinese and Indian population. The area to visit for Nyona food is Damansara in Petaling Jaya to the South of KL about 30 minutes by taxi, particularly **Medan Ria,** where there are a multiplicity of stalls.

CHINESE CUISINE: At the top end of the market, the **Golden Phoenix Restaurant,** in the Equatorial Hotel on Jalan Sultan Ismail (tel. 261-3608), will satisfy those in search of finely created Chinese specialties. This dining room, long popular with business people in the "Golden Triangle" area, specializes in shark's fin, suckling pig, spareribs, roast chicken with onion sauce, and deep-fried pomfret. A typical banquet for two should run M$100 ($40). Open every day for lunch and dinner; all credit cards accepted.

Another upscale Chinese dining room is **Marco Polo,** located at Wisma Lim Foo Yong on Jalan Raja Chulan (tel. 292-5595). Marco Polo's Hong Kong chef specializes in the preparation of Cantonese barbecue dishes, especially duck and suckling pig. We particularly liked the Szechuan prawns, sweet-and-sour fish, and chicken with dried chile. Marco Polo is open every day for lunch and dinner. Two people can dine for M$55 ($22).

If you really want to experience the local scene, head for **Tai Thong,** off Medan Imbi and Jalan Barat (no telephone). This extremely informal stand is wildly popular with wealthy Chinese who've made their fortune gambling, either on the street or at the racetrack. Tai Thong serves exotic Chinese fare with specialties, including such delicacies as bear paw, cockerel testicles, and bird's nest. If you do it as the locals do, with full exotica, a banquet for ten can run as much as M$4,000 ($1,600), but you needn't indulge yourself to that degree; more mundane dishes are available for significantly less money.

Another outdoor stand-style establishment, near Tai Thong, is the **Imbi Bharu Restaurant,** just off Jalan Imbi (no telephone). This decidedly informal eatery has great Chinese food, with emphasis on beef noodles and many prawn dishes. Dining here is inexpensive, with the average entree running M$12 ($4.75) for a large portion. The Imbi Bharu is open for dinner only.

In the same area is the Jalan Imbi branch (no. 88) of the **Overseas Restoran** (tel. 248-7567), a "steamboat" diner. Now this is eating well and on the cheap. Imagine plate after plate of skewered vegetables, meat, fish, and seafood; you choose what you want, then immerse it in bubbling vats of clear or curried broth (Mongolian hotpot style) for a mere M$6 ($2.50) per person—that's "steamboat," a popular local way to dine. The other branch of the Overseas is set in the Central Market (tel. 274-6406). Open daily.

Among the best places for Chinese seafood are the **Chun Kee stalls** located along Old Klang Road. These stalls, about 12 in all, are renowned for preparing crab in every conceivable fashion.

One of our favorite Chinese seafood eateries is **Garden Seafood,** at 8 Jalan Ulu Klang (no telephone). This outdoor, very informal restaurant features a large fish tank with fresh prawns. The chef is incredibly accommodating and will cook to your specifications, and will be happy to also make recommendations. Our suggestion is to eat whatever is fresh—usually crab, prawns, eel, and native fish—and let the chef choose the appropriate sauce; you won't ever go wrong. If it's in season, the green Malay-style asparagus is a must. Two can dine here for under M$55 ($22).

Nearby in the Ulu Klang area are yet more Chinese stalls that are reputed to serve the best beggar's chicken in Kuala Lumpur.

One of our absolute favorite steamboat-style restaurants in KL, if not all of Malaysia, is the **Restoran Lee Wong Kee** at 239 Jalan Tuanku Abdul Rahman (tel. 292-6285), to the north of the center city. This particular dining spot was introduced to us by several local friends who, we had the sneaking suspicion, were a little reluctant to share their "secret" food spot with us. Not wanting to hold anything back, we share this gem with you in hopes that you enjoy their Chinese-influenced steamboat cuisine. As with most such eateries, the cost of a meal for two is quite reasonable, with a full meal for two averaging about M$35 ($14); open daily.

INDIAN CUISINE: Once again, head for the stalls for the best Indian food. Perhaps the best area to begin your quest for the most delicious dosai or chapati is the area around Jalan Masjid India and, in particular, **Jalan Leboh Ampang** (and the many side streets and alleyways), off Jalan Gareja, a bit north of center city. Here you'll find rows of Indian restaurants, mostly of the southern variety, punctuated by jewelry shops. These "banana-leaf" restaurants serve delicious dosai (an Indian crêpe), idli (a fritter), curry, and fish dishes of various flavors with chapati, nan, and paratha (breads), all served on a large banana leaf. It's proper form to eat with your fingers (right hand only) and wash up after you're finished. What a treat! And all for under M$11 ($4.50) for two.

The less atmospheric and more upscale version of this type of eating can be experienced nearby at the **Bilal Restaurant,** 33 Jalan Ampang (tel. 232-0804). You can sample the very same menu for about twice the price. Open daily for lunch and dinner.

A similar establishment is **Shiraz,** located at Tuanku 3 Jalan Medan (tel. 292-2625), attached to the Shiraz Hotel. This is an older establishment that turns out very good northern Indian cuisine. Tandoori chicken, chicken tikka, and steamed prawns are all specialties of the house; plan on spending approximately M$40 ($16) for two. Shiraz is open for lunch and dinner, and they accept all major credit cards. There is a branch of Shiraz in the Subang Airport Hotel complex.

On the other side of Jalan Masjid India are more stalls and restaurants, specifically on Jalan Tuanki Abdul Rahman, otherwise known as Batu Road. The most notable of the restaurants is **Bangles**, at 60A Jalan Tuanki Abdul Rahman (tel. 298-3789). It also has a branch in Petaling Jaya. The food can be characterized as Malay Indian, with a typical dish such as mutton with dried fried chile serving as an example. One can also sample such northern Indian dishes as chicken tandoori, tikka, and nan, but we go for the cross-breed cuisine. Bangles is on the high side for prices, with dinner for two running about M$65 ($26), but it's still a very fine value. Open daily for lunch and dinner; all major credit cards accepted. Don't overlook the stalls, just down the street. The food is simple, inexpensive, and delicious.

The other major neighborhood for excellent Indian food is Jalan Brickfields, so named for the Indian brickmakers who lived and worked in the area and helped to build much of colonial Kuala Lumpur. Here you'll find another klatch of banana-leaf restaurants, such as **Vijay Ranai's** (no telephone) and **Devi** (no telephone). Jalan Brickfields is a bit out of the way, to the southwest of the train station.

WESTERN/CONTINENTAL CUISINE: Most of the continental restaurants are located in the international hotels. Our favorite, however, **La Terrase,** is set in a lovely private house near the Royal Selangor Golf Club at 388 Jalan Tun Razak (tel. 248-4243), directly across the street from the American Embassy. The wonderful proprietor, Susan Lim, opened this casually elegant dining room in 1985, and when we last visited it still only had seven tables. As you enter you see the bar, with its cane chairs and café tables, beckoning you to share its cozy ambience. The food, as prepared by Ms. Lim and her capable staff, is exquisite. The menu tilts toward Mediterranean recipes with such entrees as stuffed duck, moussaka, and lasagne; we loved the rack of lamb and pepper steak, as well as a delicious assortment of locally grown vegetables (including a local wild black oyster mushroom that's fantastic). Make sure you leave enough room for dessert, especially La Terrase's profiteroles and crêpes. A complete meal for two, including wine, should run about M$80 ($32), which we judge to be an excellent value. The service is extraordinary, replete with waiters hovering observantly in the background profferring fresh silver for each course. La Terrase is open for lunch and dinner Monday through Saturday, and for dinner only on Sunday; they accept major credit cards. Reservations are recommended.

Among the best continental restaurants in the hotels is the **Chalet** located in the Equatorial Hotel (tel. 261-7777). Not only is the food sumptuously prepared, but we like the cozy, chic ambience of the main dining room. The best value is the fixed-price lunch, which is offered Monday through Friday for M$35 ($14). Dinner is entirely à la carte, with a typical meal running about twice the lunch tariff.

The **Malakka Grill,** located in the Hilton Hotel on Jalan Sultan Ismail (tel. 242-2222), is an excellent continental restaurant with a large comfortable dining room. The service here is prompt, attentive, and friendly. Their prix-fixe lunch is M$35 ($14); dinner, M$45 ($18). The tender beef and roast fish meals are superb, as are the "tiger" prawns, so named because of the distinctive black banding on their back. The back wall of the Malakka is glass, and looks out on the Hilton's pool and garden, making for a romantic dinner à deux. You should figure on M$110 ($44) per person without wine. Open Monday through Friday for lunch and dinner, dinner only on Saturday, and all day on Sunday.

The Shangri-la Hotel's **Lafite** (tel. 232-2388) wins hands down for the most lavish dining room in KL. It's decorated in an omni-European style (in Thailand, it would be referred to as "Louis"). By far the best value here is the set-price menu, which combines a wonderful buffet with a selection of first-rate entrees. At lunch such a meal runs M$35 ($14); dinner costs a very reasonable M$50 ($20). If you opt for the à la carte menu, expect to pay approximately M$175 ($70), including wine. It's a good idea to make a reservation during the prime dinner hours; Lafite takes all credit cards.

Feel like visiting an American-style steakhouse? Look no farther than the **Ranch,** located in the downstairs of the Regent Hotel, on Jalan Sultan Ismail (tel. 242-5588). In addition to an excellent salad bar, they serve up juicy steaks, including porterhouse cuts, sirloins, and filet mignon. A typical meal, including the salad bar and an eight-ounce porterhouse steak, runs M$48 ($19.25); if you opt for the salad bar only, the price is M$12 ($4.75). The Ranch is open for lunch and dinner Monday through Friday; closed Saturday and Sunday during lunch. They take all major credit cards.

Another good chop house is the **Dallas Grill & Texas Bar,** on Damansara Jaya in Petaling Jaya (tel. 719-3848).

One of the more elegant, if slightly faded, settings for a Western restaurant is **Le Coq d'Or,** at 121 Jalan Ampang (tel. 242-9732). The restaurant is housed in a grand Colonial mansion with soaring ceilings and ornate architectural elements. As for the food, we suggest that you skip the fixed-price lunch—as much of a bargain as it is—and opt for the à la carte menu. We enjoyed a fabulous sizzling tenderloin steak preceded by a fine okra-crab soup. Expect to pay about M$66 ($26.50) for two from the à la carte menu. Le Coq d'Or is open for lunch and dinner.

The Ship, at 1222 Jalan Dang Wangi (tel. 291-3373), is a steak-and-brew chain restaurant that is good value for the money. Steaks, both of New Zealand and American variety, plus a salad run about M$35 ($14). Open daily for lunch and dinner.

FAST FOOD: It would be impossible to review KL's many eating options without making significant reference to fast food, for this category seems to be overrunning the city to a far greater degree than anywhere else in Southeast Asia. We speculated that with the amount of exposure he receives, the ghost of Colonel Sanders could easily be elected to office in nearly any major Malaysian city. Not to slight the others, but Kentucky Fried Chicken seems to be everywhere.

As one might imagine, the city's many shopping malls are home to most fast-food outlets. Our short list of familiar chains includes Kentucky Fried Chicken, McDonalds, Burger King, Pizza Hut, A&W Root Beer, Dunkin' Donuts, and Foremost. Prices are amazingly low, with a typical burger and fries running about M$6 ($2.50).

5. WHAT TO SEE AND DO IN THE CITY

Most of the sights in and around Kuala Lumpur can be seen in a day or two, including excursions to the nearby Batu Caves and visiting the rubber plantations and tin mines. If you intend to visit Fraser's Hill or the Genting Hillands, plan on a full day trip.

For those with just a day to see the highlights, we suggest visiting the National Museum, taking a drive around the city to see the distinctive Malaysian architecture (such as the Railway Station, Masjid Jame, and some of the residential neighborhoods), visiting one of the outdoor markets (such as Pudu), and climbing up to the dramatic Batu Caves. During the evening, consider a visit to Chinatown and the Indian neighborhoods for a taste of the street life and hawker food.

MASJID JAME: About the best place to begin a tour of Kuala Lumpur is at the meeting point of the Gombak and Klang Rivers, the literal "Muddy Confluence" that gives the city its name. This attractive spot, in the center of the city, is marked by a distinctive red-and-white striped pavilion-style mosque with double minarets and a walled courtyard. The coconut palms and waterways provide an oasis in the middle of KL's older downtown. Where the mosque stands now (it was built at the turn of the century) was once home to a shantytown of stores, bars, and makeshift houses, that is, the original Kuala Lumpur.

SULTAN ABDUL SAMAD BUILDING: Today this remarkable example of Moorish-influenced Victorian architecture houses the Malaysian Courts, but originally it served as the State Secretariat. It was from here, formally, and across the street, informally, on the Padang cricket fields and in the parlors of the Selangor Club, that the British exercised their rule over Malaya. The building itself was constructed during 1894–1897 and is most noted for its 135-foot clock tower.

THE RAILWAY STATION: You might have arrived here, but if you didn't, at least drive by this Disneyland version of Moorish architecture, designed and built under the aegis of the British in 1911 to house a very European-looking glass-and-iron train shed. The interior was recently renovated and presents a remarkable contrast to the exterior structure. Across the street is a more sedate example of the same style, this time housing the administrative offices of the Malayan Railway.

LAKE GARDENS: Lake Gardens is KL's answer to New York City's Central Park, a giant sprawling landscape designed to coax relaxation and encourage abandon. In 1888 the architect A. R. Venning set to work and put a 160-acre park together that includes **Lake Club,** a private club in the park plus jogging tracks, a roller-skating area, and a wonderful **boating pond** (open from 2 to 6:30 p.m. weekdays, plus 10:30 a.m. to 12:30 p.m. on weekends) that will only cost you M$1.20 (50¢) an hour to rock and row on the water. Truly this is a spectacular park, the more so because it's absolutely pristine, like the shore around Lake Geneva in Switzerland. We're talking fairybook gorgeous here, folks. As if this weren't enough, in the middle of the park there are the **Orchid Gardens** (open from 9 a.m. to 6:30 p.m. daily), where you'll find dozens of different orchids growing side by side, and there's a nursery where you can purchase any of the various varieties for a fraction of what you'd pay back home, the difference being you couldn't find these flowers anywhere else but here and in Thailand. If you want a romantic rendezvous, a place to cool off on a hot day, or just your regular cheap thrill, Lake Gardens is a must-see in KL! No kidding, don't miss it.

MASJID NEGARA (NATIONAL MOSQUE): Farther south, on Jalan Sultan Hishamuddin, is Masjid Negara, Malaysia's national mosque and one of the largest in Southeast Asia. The religious complex is central to the country's predominantly Muslim population; it houses a Great Hall, a 245-foot-tall minaret and a cluster of buildings including a library, mausoleum, and other administrative and meeting halls. Though the mosque is of recent vintage it is undergoing significant renovation, and when we were last there it wasn't open to the public; however, when the upgrading process is complete visitors will once again be welcome. Visitors are required to dress modestly and remove their shoes upon entering the mosque; there are separate entrances for men and women. The mosque is open daily from 8 a.m. to 6 p.m. (on Friday from 2 to 6 p.m.).

NATIONAL ART GALLERY: Housed in the former Hotel Majestic, at 1 Jalan Sultan Hishamuddin, the National Art Gallery presents a survey of modern painting and sculpture created by Malaysian artists from the 1950s to the present. We enjoyed the tremendous diversity of the collection, much of which echoes Western art trends but has a distinctly Malaysian spirit. The museum regularly sponsors exhibitions and sales of contemporary art. The museum is open daily from 10 a.m. to 6 p.m. (closed from 12:15 to 2:45 p.m. on Friday for prayers); admission is free.

THE NATIONAL MUSEUM: The National Museum contains two fine collections, cultural and historical, that provide visitors with an excellent introduction to the country. The highlights of the cultural section include shadow puppets from around Asia, Banjarmasin hobby horses, exhibits on the Baba or Peranakan people, and the toys, costumes, hats, and jewelry seen throughout Malaysia. The historical half features archeological finds and other historical relics from Malaysia's rich past. The museum is open daily from 9 a.m. to 6 p.m. (closed Friday between 12:15 and 2:45 p.m.); admission is free.

NATIONAL CRAFTS MUSEUM: This compact collection of traditional and contemporary crafts is an excellent display of the varied styles of work found throughout Malaysia, including tribal decorative articles from Sarawak and Sabah. The museum often holds exhibitions of fine contemporary craftsmanship. The museum is open on Monday from 9:30 a.m. to 5 p.m. and Tuesday through Sunday from 9:30 a.m. to 6 p.m. It's located in the Ethnographic Botanical Garden, adjacent to the Karyaneka Handicraft Centre (see "Shopping") on Jala Raja Chulan and just a few minutes' walk from the Hilton Hotel. The garden itself, open from 9 a.m. to 7 p.m. every day, is a beautifully landscaped small-scale botanical garden, with a nursery in the back from which you can purchase several varieties of local flora.

Also on the grounds is the **International Crafts Museum** (same hours as the National Crafts Museum), which houses examples of indigenous folk art from other countries around the world, all of it sent as a gift to the people of Malaysia by their foreign friends.

THE BUDDHA JAYANTI TEMPLE: This octagonal, trilevel temple features a small Buddha with neon halos(!) with a grandfather clock to his left. There's a huge bronze tureen outside for incense, and crossed banana trees form the arch that's the doorway to the temple. Though not the most gorgeous temple we've ever seen, it's certainly interesting to contemplate a neon-haloed Buddha when life gets you down.

SRI MAHAMARIAMMAN TEMPLE: This Hindu temple, one of the oldest (built in 1873 and subsequently rebuilt in the 1960s) and most ornate in the country, is the starting point for the celebration of Thaipusam and is a center of KL's Hindu community.

CHAN SEE SHU YUEN TEMPLE: This is one of KL's most elaborate Chinese temples. Built in 1906, it features elegant woodcarvings, wall paintings, and ceramic tiles and figures, most of which were brought from China. The temple not only has religious significance for the Buddhist community, but it also serves as a shrine for Kuala Lumpur's Chan clan.

BATU CAVES: One of the most impressive sites in the Kuala Lumpur area, or any other area in the world for that matter, are the Batu Caves, located about eight miles north from the city on Jalan Ipoh, about a M$7 ($2.75) cab ride. This 350-foot cavern is reached after climbing 272 stairs. Inside the cave is a small Hindu temple that is the focal point of the annual milk festival known as Thaipusam. During the balance of the year Hindus visit the shrine to make offerings, so the temple is in constant use. The cave itself, and surrounding caverns, are part of a huge limestone deposit that has been quarried over the last 100 years and extends north toward Ipoh. The interior of the caves are breathtaking, with trees growing out the sides of solid rock walls; it looks like the perfect place for

James Bond to miraculously escape from, though once there you don't feel like leaving. The Batu Caves are also accessible by public bus. The caves are a must-see for any visitor to KL; don't miss them.

NATIONAL ZOO AND AQUARIUM: Situated about 7½ miles northeast from the city center, the National Zoo encompasses 65 acres of shady forestland and lake that is home to over a thousand different species of Malaysian flora and fauna, as well as to a collection of animal species from all over the world—the orangutan, the Gir lion (from western India), and rare mammals, birds, and reptiles (such as the dwarf crocodile). You can see them all via elephant, camel, donkey cart, and boat rides. The aquarium boasts 82 different species of marine life, all housed in darkness. And did we forget to mention that seemingly every single kind of monkey in the world is here, as well as a pair of trained dolphins named Hawkeye and Trapper that dance to "Party All the Time" and execute backflips while balancing things on their noses? The zoo has three shows (elephant/bird/sea lion), starting at 10 a.m., 2:15 p.m., and 4:30 p.m. daily. The shows are great, and we guarantee you'll find yourself contemplating adopting an animal by the end of them. The complex also has a restaurant. Everything is open daily from 9 a.m. to 6 p.m., though tickets aren't sold past 5 p.m. Admission is M$3.50 ($1.50) for adults, M$1.25 (50¢) for children, and M$.35 (15¢) for students.

RUBBER PLANTATIONS: Malaysia is the world's chief producer of natural rubber. On the outskirts of Kuala Lumpur you will frequently see rubber plantations lining the highways. Visits to the plantations to observe the collection and processing of latex can be arranged through local tour operators such as Mayflower Acme Tours (tel. 248-6023). Many city tours include a stop at a rubber plantation in their day trips.

6. SHOPPING

Kuala Lumpur is not a shopper's paradise like Hong Kong, Bangkok, or nearby Singapore; KL does, however, have some intriguing shopping possibilities.

As elsewhere in Asia, bargaining is the norm (except in shopping malls). If you plan on purchasing expensive items like jewelry, shop around to get a feel for prices and quality.

WHERE TO SHOP: Most major hotels have **shopping arcades** on the grounds. In many cases these are quality shops with respectable reputations, though prices are often higher than in middle-class neighborhoods around the city. The best arcades we found are connected to the Shangri-la Hotel, the Hilton, and the Regent.

Batu Road (also known as Jalan Tuanku Abdul Rahman, or Jalan TAR, a north-south running street on the north side of town, is the paradigm of shopping in KL. Not only can you find everything there, but there are many food stalls where you can take a break in between bargains. And running parallel one street over is **Jalan Masjid India,** the "Little India" of KL, where we recommend that you go when your feet fail you for banana-leaf food and beverage.

Some interesting shopping also takes place in the city's markets and ethnic neighborhoods. Let's take a look at the most popular locations:

The **Central Market** (tel. 274-6542) in the downtown area, is an indoor market with more than 80 shops, where the wares range from framed butterflies, restaurants, and tile paintings to pet shops and tailors.

Yuan Chow, located across the street from the Ampang Park Shopping Plaza, a M$2.50 ($1) cab ride away from your hotel, is a modern six-level plaza with such chic international shops as Piaget, Crabtree & Evelyn, Bally, and Rolex, situated among jewelry stores, tailors, and (surprise!) a Kentucky Fried Chicken outlet.

Ampang Park Shopping Plaza / Sungei Wang Plaza (both interconnected), located on the east side of the street, Jalan Bukit Bintang, has four levels and 500 shops, open from 10 a.m. to 10 p.m., spanning the gamut from all-cotton socks to zebra-style home furnishings, Sungei Plaza boasts an excellent restaurant, the Chicago Smokehouse, where you can get some very fine ribs, and you'll also find many computer shops with prices well below those at American shops.

Yoahan (The Mall) is the most popular mall and a landmark in KL. It's located one block south of Putra World Trade Center on the north side of the city. Special events such as Tai Chi demonstrations and Chinese New Year's festivities are often sponsored on the main floor, and around the mall's perimeter roost McDonald's, Pizza Hut, and other American food chains. Inside, the shops are much like your local mall, with record shops, shoe stores, and clothing and snack shops dominating the floor space. The shops range in taste from Alexander's to Saks, and every day large, eager crowds of Malaysians valiantly vie for Western-style bargains.

Pudu Market, bordered by Jalan Yew, Jalan Pasar, and Jalan Pudu, open from 7 a.m. to noon, is predominantly a "wet" market, meaning it's mostly food and produce. The fruit and vegetable stands are outdoors, while the spice, fish, meat, and poultry stands are inside the concrete building. The flavor of Pudu Market is nominally Chinese, and even if you're not in the market for fresh produce, Pudu makes for a great visit, what with its stationery, bicycle repair, and Chinese orthopedic shoe stalls. Make sure to visit early (7 to 9 a.m.) for maximum shopping pleasure.

Chow Kit Market, located on Jalan Haji Hussein in the city center, is the "Malay" market in town, where you'll see older women dressed in native garb cruising the wedding shops for their daughters. There is a covered area in the market where you'll see a red sandal shop surrounded by shutterbugs; nearby there's a curry-powder factory! The market closes at 6 p.m., then the eating stalls open up full blast and go until 2 a.m. At night Chow Kit becomes the Times Square of KL with as much sleaze as this clean city can muster.

KL Plaza, on Jalan Bukit Bintang, is five levels of middle- and upper-middle-class shopping from 10 a.m. to 9:30 p.m. daily. This plaza is a smaller version of Yoahan Plaza, but has some very nice shops, including **Mun Loong** (check out its bathing accessories department, chock full of various salts, soaps, and sudsy items to immerse yourself in) and **Jim's Shop** (tel. 241-9718), a custom tailoring and men's wear store where you can be fitted for a shirt (make an appointment) and receive a sartorial signet for a bit less than in Hong Kong. Ladies, if you're looking for some jewelry buys, stop by at **Kelvin Gems** while your husband's at Jim's Shop. Book mavens will want to head to **Kancilmas Bookmart** to catch up on their reading.

Chinatown

For the casual shopper the center city district is a fun place to start. The action is best at night in the triangle formed by the three main streets: Jalan Petaling, Jalan Sultan, and Jalan Bandar. In the evening, the roads are closed off and the streets are clogged with food vendors, local and visiting shoppers, textile jobbers, herbalists, luggage salesmen, T-shirt racks, and every manner of fruit and vegetable stand, forming a *pasar malam,* or outdoor night bazaar. You'll also find many watch vendors, selling absolutely perfect replicas of Rolex, Piaget, Gucci, and Cartier watches, so perfect you can't tell the difference from the real thing. The most honest and best-supplied vendor we found was **T. K. Chong,** at 96 Petaling St., open from 11 a.m. to 5 p.m. Spending between $12 and $40, you can own a gorgeous facsimile whose interior is made in Japan, exterior in Malaysia. They make the perfect gift and are built to last. Outdoor Chinatown calms down around 11 p.m., so don't wait too long or you might find the area deserted.

Kampung Bharu
This pasar malam is a ten-minute taxi ride north from KL center in the neighborhood of the same name. The best time to visit Kampung Bharu is at night, especially on Saturday when the market really comes to life. Not only can one pick up all manner of Malaysian souvenirs (remember to bargain), but there are terrific hawker stalls for sampling delicious local delicacies.

HANDCRAFTS: The **Karyaneka Handicraft Center,** on Jalan Raja Chulan, close to most international hotels (tel. 243-1686), is definitely on the tourist bus trail, and the merchandise is correspondingly less interesting than what one finds in the markets, but the layout and design of this complex make it a good introduction to the various regional contemporary crafts in Malaysia. Each of the 14 Malaysian states is represented by its own A-frame wooden house in which objects from that region are on display (and for sale). There are frequent craftmaking displays, and on Saturday from 4:30 to 6:30 p.m. there is a cultural show. On the same grounds is the National Crafts Museum, devoted to the best traditional and contemporary crafts in the country; we loved it and recommend a visit, especially for those who will be traveling to other parts of the country.

Batik making in Malaysia isn't up to the best Indonesian standard, but there is still very good-quality material available, particularly in the outdoor markets. For those who'd like to see how batik is made, there are demonstrations at the **Selayang Batik Factory** Monday through Friday from 9 a.m. to 5 p.m. and on Saturday from 9 a.m. to 1 p.m. You can also visit the **Syarikat Batik Factory** in Selangor (tel. 689-1948), on the way to the Batu Caves, for a similar demonstration and sale; they also have a showroom in the Malaysian Arts and Crafts shop in the Regent Hotel shopping arcade.

PEWTER: Perhaps the most sought-after souvenir of Malaysia is pewter, its manufacture owing to the country's rich tin deposits (pewter is an alloy of refined tin, copper, and antimony). The nation's no. 1 manufacturer is **Selangor Pewter,** 4 Jalan Usahawan Enam (tel. 422-1000), a company that exports high-quality objects to the United States and Europe. Although there are Selangor Pewter outlets all over the city, you can arrange to take an interesting tour of the main factory and visit its largest showroom. (Some city tours of Kuala Lumpur include this as part of their one-day package.) Hours are 8:30 a.m. to 4:45 p.m. Monday through Saturday, and 9 a.m. to 4 p.m. on Sunday and holidays. Selangor Pewter ships to all parts of the world.

ANTIQUES: Before trying to find those Asian treasures in Kuala Lumpur, where they're relatively scarce, consider a trip to nearby Malacca where the choice is definitely more plentiful and interesting.

With that in mind, our only recommendation in KL is **Peiping Lace,** 223 Jalan Abdul Rahman (tel. 298-3184), where you'll find furniture and objets d'art, most dating from the 20th century.

JEWELRY: The only local stones mined in Malaysia for jewelry are semiprecious gems such as blackstone, agate, and onyx (most precious stones come from Sri Lanka, Thailand, and Burma). Nevertheless, Malaysian workmanship is quite good and the gold prices are about equal to those in Hong Kong.

Most knowledgeable locals we canvassed agreed that nearly all the jewelers located in the very best hotel shopping arcades produce fine-quality work at fair prices, though higher than in such places as Chinatown. We particularly admired the work at **H. Sena,** in the Shangri-la Hotel arcade (tel. 230-2848); **P. H. Hendry,** at 4 Jalan Tuanku Abdul Rahman (tel. 292-6537); and **Storch Brothers,** in the Yow Chuan Plaza (tel. 243-7192).

Our local experts recommended shopping the stores along **Jalan Bandar** in Chinatown, as well as those along **Jalan Leboh Ampang** in the Indian section of KL.

7. NIGHTLIFE

Malaysian nightlife is considerably more conservative than that of its Asian neighbors, like Bangkok and Singapore. There are cafés, clubs, and discos in nearly every large city, but the preferred evening out is a great meal in a nice restaurant, with a stroll through a night market afterward to browse and be seen. The younger generation boogies like everywhere else, though without the alcohol apocalypse that accompanies so many Western forays into fun. Rest assured that there are bars and watering holes throughout the city; it's just that you'll see mostly foreigners imbibing. Most of the hotels also have lounges featuring live Filipino cover bands, considered the finest in Southeast Asia, maybe the world. American Top-Ten hits are handled expertly by these bands, almost none of whom have a drummer (drum machines are standard issue) and all of whom have one or more cute female singers/instrumentalists to help take the sting out of unrequited love. To find out what's going on in KL on a given night, pick up a copy of *Out Time,* a monthly city guide that carries comprehensive listings for nightowls and diehard party animals.

TRADITIONAL CULTURE: Traditional music and dances are a major part of Malaysian life, though today they are most often performed at special ceremonies like weddings, official functions, and holiday celebrations. A gamelan orchestra consisting of brass and wood percussion instruments, with an accordionist and/or violinist, provides the backdrop and beat as elaborately clad dancers weave their spell with their hands and hips, performing dances from the various Malaysian states like Timang Burung, a Kelantan court dance imitating the flight of birds, or Kudu Kepang from Johor, a stately dance filled with joy. Tourists can get a taste of these arts along with a fine meal in a special dinner/theater package at **Yasmin** at 6 Jalan Kia Peng (tel. 241-5655), and the **Dayang Hotel,** on Jalan Barat in Petaling Jaya (tel. 755-5011). The shows at both places feature a mock Bersanding, or Malay wedding ceremony in which the audience participates by blessing the union of the couple with scented flower petals, yellow rice, and rose water. A buffet dinner of Malaysian fare plus show will run you about M$35 ($14), and the show runs about an hour.

MOVIE THEATERS: There are movie theaters at nearly all the shopping centers and malls in the city. Most cinemas show English-language films, some dubbed, others with subtitles. Ask your concierge to call the theater to determine whether the film is being shown in English. Also scan the *New Straits Times* for movie advertisements; they usually list all films shown in English.

DISCOS AND NIGHTCLUBS: When we were in KL the hottest discos were **Faces,** at Ampang Plaza, (tel. 261-2562); ensconced in an old colonial house at 103 Jalan Ampang, home to students and young professionals; **Hollywood East,** at Ampang Plaza (tel. 261-2562); **Sapphire,** at Yow Chuan Plaza (tel. 243-0043); and **Rumours,** in the Merlin Hotel and **The Tin Mine,** located in the Hilton Hotel, both filled with a slightly older (30 to 40 years old), more successful, but no less enthusiastic crowd. Cover prices are no more than M$10 ($4) for any of the discos and clubs.

The Hilton also boasts a very fine jazz lounge, **The Aviary,** where on different nights you can groove to a fusion band or a late bop group. At Yow Chuan

Plaza, the **Cotton Club** features older jazz stylings in a relaxed environment, while KL Plaza has an old-style English pub called **The Hop Sack,** which has music nightly. **Dinty's,** on Jalan Tun Sambanthan, was the only club we found that had country, blues, and rock 'n' roll, all performed by the same band!

BARS: Our favorite bar in KL is the **Coliseum Café and Hotel,** on Jalan Tuanku Abdul Rahman (tel. 292-6270). Slow overhead fans dictate the pace of life in this, KL's most atmospheric watering hole, redolent like old Humphrey Bogart–style bars. The Coliseum opened in the 1920s and some of the furniture has more or less survived since then. Along the way it took on a 1950s-looking bar ensemble and some 1960s artwork. 'Round about happy hour the locals start arriving in search of a good time à la Nashville, lower Manhattan, or Southside Chicago bars. 'Nuff said.

All the major hotels have elegant bars, but our favorite is the **Blue Moon Bar** in the Equatorial.

SEX CLUBS AND MASSAGE PARLORS: Oddly enough, while we were driving around KL and Penang we kept noticing that barbershop poles, the old-style electric red-and-white-striped ones, kept popping up in bunches, usually a group of them bunched on the same street. When we asked the driver about them, he smiled and told us we could get more than a haircut or manicure in these places for a negotiated price. Subsequently, in other towns we noticed that these establishments tended to be on the second floor and that business seemed to pick up later in the evenings; you learn something new everywhere you go in this world.

CHAPTER XIII

PENINSULAR MALAYSIA

□ □ □

1. CAMERON HIGHLANDS
2. PENANG
3. THE EAST COAST
4. MALACCA (MELAKA)

If you have only a week and want to see the most of Malaysia, a trip around the peninsula is a must. Our suggestion is to travel clockwise, from KL north to the Cameron Highlands, a British hill station dating from the 1930s, to the island of Penang, across to the east coast with its excellent beaches and back to KL with a day's foray to colonial Malacca, Malaysia's most fascinating historical city.

1. CAMERON HIGHLANDS

During the colonial period the ruling British had an uncanny knack for discovering the most sublime spots in their Asian territories and developing them into hill stations, cool retreats from the heat and humidity of the lower climes. The so-called Cameron Highlands is just such a place: nestled in the Pahang countryside are verdant valleys, terraced tea plantations, pristine waterways, and fog-shrouded hills. By the 1930s there were magnificent private estates, golf courses, and country inns, most of which survive as today's tourist infrastructure.

The Cameron Highlands is also home to the Orang Asli aborigines, a hunting-and-gathering nomadic tribe that inhabit the deep interior jungle. Occasionally they come down to the developed areas, but they tend to eschew modern tourist culture, preferring the traditional life.

HISTORY: The area known as the Cameron Highlands was named for a surveyor, William Cameron, who in 1885 found "a plateau with gentle slopes shut in by loftier mountains, which from the plateau's elevation of 4,500 to 4,600 feet above sea level, appear comparatively low." As early as the late 19th century there was an effort to develop the area into a "sanitorium," but it wasn't until the mid-1920s that Sir George Maxwell formally committed to establishing the area as a hill station. Between 1926 and the middle 1930s Cameron Highlands enjoyed its most extensive building boom with the creation of roads, townships, residential land tracts, parks, and recreational areas. It was also during this period that the first tea estates were planted. The Cameron Highlands was in the news in the

1960s when the American-born Thai silk king, Jim Thompson, mysteriously disappeared in the jungle, never to be seen again.

ORIENTATION: There are actually three towns that comprise the Cameron Highlands. **Ringlet** is the first town one enters and is most distinguished for the lake, and the Sultan Abu Bakar Dam and nearby power station. The middle village, which is the central town for most services and hotels, is **Tanah Rata.** The town farthest north is **Brinchang,** the gateway to the largest tea estates and vegetable farms as well as the highest peak in the area, Gunong (Mountain) Brinchang, at 6,666 feet.

On the way up to the Cameron Highlands you'll reach a bend in the road where, on your left you'll see **Lata Iskendar,** a series of waterfalls that plunge into an inviting swimming hole. There are food stalls and souvenir stands at this delightful resting point halfway on the curving mountainous road.

USEFUL INFORMATION: The **Museum and Tourist Information Centre** is located on the main street of Tanah Rata (tel. 941-266), and is open from 9 a.m. to 5 p.m. Monday through Friday, to 1 p.m. on Saturday. This small collection displays items of historical interest about the discovery and development of the Highlands.

There is a **taxi station** in Tanah Rata (tel. 941-234 or 941-555); taxis can be called from any hotel for local travel. The **bus** stops in all the towns, upon request; for the current schedule, call 941-485.

In case of a medical emergency, call the **hospital** at 941-966; for all other emergencies, contact the **police** station at 941-2222.

Tanah Rata has a **post office** from where you can make telephone calls and two **banks,** both of which exchange foreign currency.

The local **telephone area code** is 05.

GETTING THERE: The only way to get to the Cameron Highlands, 140 miles north of KL, is by road, either by car or bus. There is direct **bus** service between KL and Tanah Rata once daily for M$14 ($5.50); expect to pay M$27.50 ($11) for an **outstation taxi.** The actual climb up to the Highlands begins at the Tapah turnoff on the road between Kuala Lumpur and Ipoh. There are buses every hour for the two-hour trip between Tapah and Tanah Rata for M$4.50 ($1.75). For about twice the price, you can take a taxi.

By bus or car from Kuala Lumpur, count on spending between three and four hours, depending on traffic and the number of stops; from Penang, it takes approximately 4½ hours. The nearest **train station and airport** is in the town of Ipoh, located about two hours away.

GETTING AROUND: There is a **local bus** that travels between the towns on a regular basis. In addition there is a **local taxi service** (tel. 941-234 or 941-555) that will pick up passengers at all hotels; a typical fare between Strawberry Park and Tanah Rata is M$4.50 ($1.75).

ACCOMMODATIONS: There are few more evocative venues in Asia of English country architecture than the 20-room inn known as **Ye Olde Smokehouse,** set overlooking the hills and golf course of Tanah Rata (tel. 05/941-2145). This split-beam Tudor-style hostel is designed to make its guests nostalgic for Olde England, even if they've never been there. You don't have to spend the night in one of the delightfully decorated rooms, replete with four-poster beds and antiques, to enjoy afternoon tea with freshly made scones and locally grown tea for M$9 ($3.50). Room rates are fairly steep, ranging from M$95 ($38) to M$300 ($120) for a double, depending on size and view, but this truly is a unique pleasure. Ye Olde Smokehouse serves lunches and dinners that are equal-

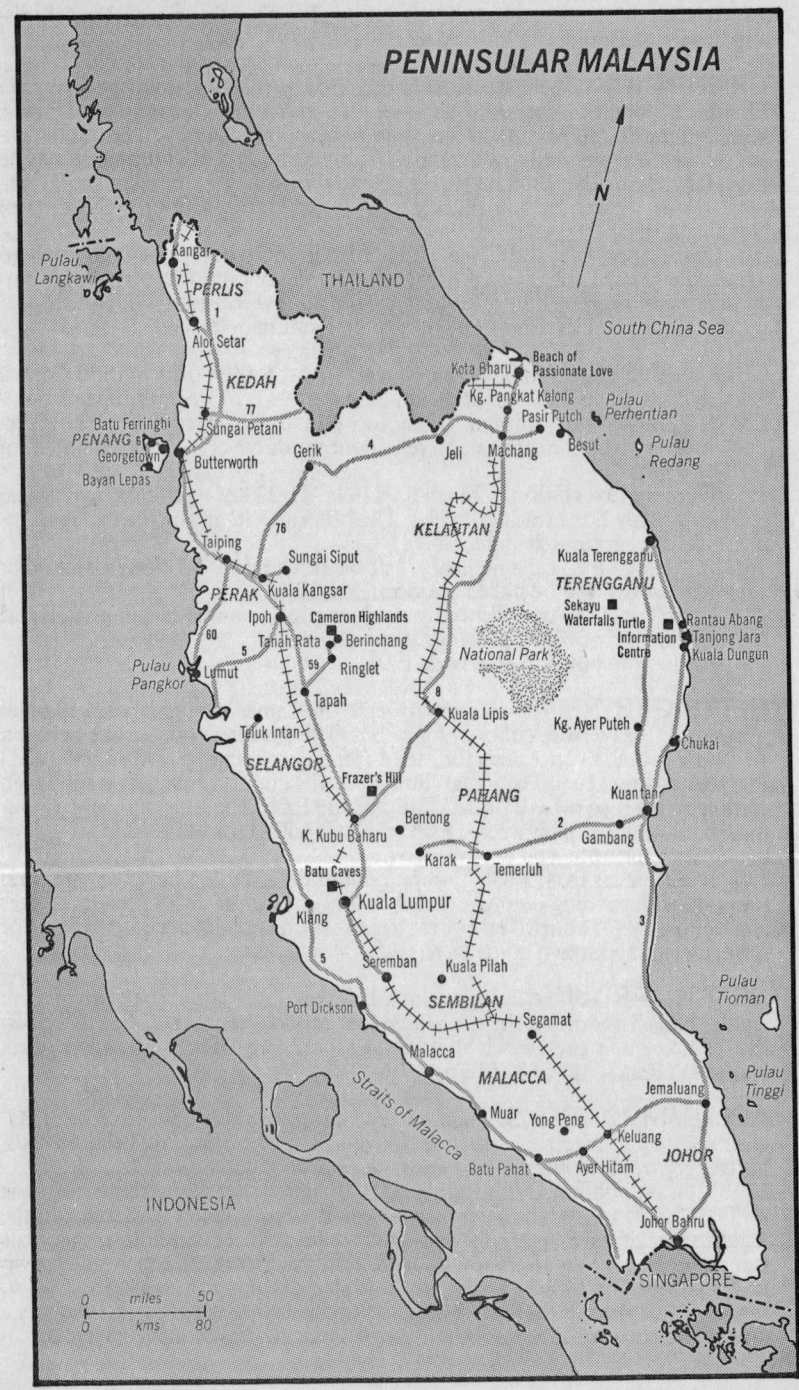

PENINSULAR MALAYSIA

N

THAILAND

South China Sea

Pulau
Langkawi

Kangar
7
PERLIS
1
Alor Setar

KEDAH

Beach of
Kota Bharu   Passionate Love
Kg. Pangkat Kalong
Pasir Puteh   Pulau
Perhentian

77

Batu Ferringhi
PENANG
Georgetown   Sungai Petani   Gerik   4   Jeli   Machang   Besut   Pulau
Butterworth   Redang
Bayan Lepas

76

Kuala Terengganu
Taiping   Sungai Siput
TERENGGANU
Kuala Kangsar
PERAK   Cameron Highlands   Sekayu   Rantau Abang
Ipoh   Tanah Rata   Berinchang   Waterfalls   Turtle   Tanjong Jara
60   National Park   Information   Kuala Dungun
Pulau   5   59   Ringlet   Centre
Pangkor   Lumut   Tapah
8   Kuala Lipis
Teluk Intan
SELANGOR   Kg. Ayer Puteh   Chukai

Frazer's Hill
PAHANG   Kuantan
Bentong   2   Gambang
K. Kubu Baharu
Batu Caves   Karak   Temerluh   3
Kuala Lumpur
Klang   Pulau
5   Seremban   Kuala Pilah   Tioman
Port Dickson   SEMBILAN   Segamat   Pulau
Tinggi
Malacca   Jemaluang
MALACCA
Straits of Malacca   Muar   Yong Peng   Keluang
Batu Pahat   Ayer Hitam   JOHOR

INDONESIA   Johor Bahru

SINGAPORE

0   miles   50
0   kms   80

ly evocative of Britain with such specialties as roast ribs, brown stews and dumplings, steak-and-kidney puddings, grilled fish, and fresh strawberries. It's a good idea to make a reservation both for accommodations and meals.

One of the best values in the Cameron Highlands is the **Merlin Inn Resort,** which, like Ye Olde Smokehouse, overlooks the golf course and hills of Tanah Rata (tel. 05/941-211). All rooms have attractive views and, though sparsely furnished, are of ample size and include modern amenities. Standard singles run M$90 ($36) and doubles cost M$100 ($40).

We were confused when we pulled into **Strawberry Park,** Tanah Rata, Cameron Highlands (tel. 05/941-166). This complex of luxury apartments, tennis courts, swimming pool, and squash courts looked more like private homes than a hotel. Our confusion was well founded, for Strawberry Park began as a condominium project for KL weekenders, but with slack demand the project was converted into a hotel. Although the facility is well equipped, the location is a bit distant from central Tanah Rata; you'll have to take a five-minute taxi ride down the hill. The price for a standard room is M$155 ($62), a one-room apartment runs M$185 ($74), and M$230 ($92) gets you a two-room apartment. If you eat at the hotel, we suggest trying the steamboat menu.

The best accommodations in Ringlet are found at **Fosters Lakehouse,** overlooking Sultan Abu Bakar Lake (tel. 05/996-152). We were shocked to learn that this Tudor-style stone and wood-beamed inn was only constructed in 1977, for the look is decidedly antique. The Lakehouse has a very attractive bar and restaurant that serves the guests who stay in the 12 bedrooms. Room rates are M$165 ($66) for a double, M$145 ($58) for a single, with deluxe rooms M$55 ($22) additional.

Less expensive rooms can be found at the **Golf Course Inn,** back in Tanah Ratah (tel. 05/941-411), for M$90 ($36) single and M$100 ($40) double. Deluxe rooms face the golf course and have large balconies; otherwise the rooms are furnished simply.

The **Garden Inn** (tel. 05/941-911) offers slightly less luxurious accommodations than the nearby Golf Course Inn, though these 46 motel-style rooms are a fine value. Standard doubles run M$75 ($30), while singles cost M$65 ($26).

For those of you on a backpacker budget, head straight to **Holiday Chalets,** up the hill from the other hotels, near Ye Olde Smokehouse, where a room for the night will set you back M$22 ($8.75), for which you'll get a clean, well-lighted place run by friendly folks.

DINING: Other than the English country menu at Ye Olde Smokehouse (see "Accommodations"), eating in Cameron Highlands isn't a very distinctive experience. We recommend trying the steamboat restaurant in the **Garden Inn** (tel. 941-911), as well as the **Hong Kong Restaurant** and the **Hollywood Restaurant,** both Chinese food outlets on the main strip in Tanah Rata.

There is a row of Indian and Malay **food stands** next to the Esso station in Tanah Rata where you can sup on inexpensive fare; we had a breakfast of roti and tea for about M$2.50 ($1) for two.

Brinchang has two good steamboat diners, the **Brinchang Restaurant** and the **Kowloon.**

WHAT TO SEE AND DO: The most fascinating activity in the Cameron Highlands is taking **walks into the jungle,** preferably on a marked trail (lest you meet the fate of Jim Thompson). The first piece of equipment you need is a good map, and fortunately the "Cameron Highlands Guide Map" is just the ticket; this indispensable guide is available in nearly all hotels and souvenir shops. On it you'll find trail descriptions and walks by the number, so if you wish to visit Robinson Waterfall for a refreshing swim (the most popular route), for example, just say that you wish to take path no. 9. Plan on wearing good walking shoes and consider bringing a raincoat; other than that you need enthusiasm and two legs. There are a wide variety of premarked walks in the area, so if you wish to visit a waterfall, search out exotic flora, or just take a casual stroll through the jungle, know that there is a trail for you; most walks take between 45 minutes and three hours. It's wise to consult your concierge, after studying the Guide Map, for the best route. If you do take a jungle walk, keep your eye trained for wild orchids, the very occasional horn bill, and the more ubiquitous butterflies.

If you feel like driving with a walk at the end, you might consider visiting **Gunong Brinchang,** at 6,666 feet, the highest peak in the area. There is a transmitting station on top from which there are excellent views of the Highlands. There are no food stands there, so plan on bringing your own food for a picnic (see "Tea Plantations and Vegetable Farms," below).

Tea Plantations and Vegetable Farms

If you've never driven or wandered through a tea estate, by all means take the opportunity to do so in one of the many in the Cameron Highlands. The rolling hills, thickly carpeted with low, deep-green tea shrubs are truly a breathtaking sight. Several local tea plantations offer tours of the estate including: **Blue Valley Tea Estate,** about 18 miles northeast of Tanah Rata (tel. 05/991-302); **Boh Tea Estate,** which is 9½ miles southeast of Tanah Rata (tel. 05/996-032); **Gunong Emas Tea Estate,** 7 miles southwest of Tanah Rata (tel. 05/996-108); and **Sungei Palace Tea Estate,** about 7 miles north of Tanah Rata, closed on Monday.

The **vegetable farms** in the Cameron Highlands are remarkable for the way they are built into the hills as terraces. The vegetables and fruit grown in the area are highly prized and especially delicious. To see such a farm (you can also buy produce there for a picnic) you can visit the **Kea Farm,** about five miles north of Tanah Rata; Trinkap village farms are located three miles farther north.

Fishing

There is fishing at the Sultan Abu Bakar (the former Sultan of Pahang) Dam and Lake, down toward Ringlet around the 32nd milestone on the main road, near Foster's Lakehouse.

Golf

This is one of the Cameron Highlands' original pastimes, and with Ye Olde Smokehouse as a backdrop, it all seems to make sense. There is a golf club and they allow visitors to play on the course. It's best to arrange this with your concierge, or you may contact the golf club directly at 05/941-126. We've been told by some pretty fair golfers that this is a challenging course. The club has golf gear for rent and can provide caddies as well.

2. PENANG

The popular image of Penang, an island located directly across from Butterworth on the northwestern corner of the Malaysian peninsula, is that of a developed tourist resort, replete with a panoply of high-rise hotels, long sandy beaches, and day-long diversions. Though this image of the island is familiar to many Europeans on group tours (as well as ex-GIs dating from R&R visits during the Vietnam War), Penang has an entirely different persona for those who wish to delve deeper into the local culture.

We think Penang offers the best of Malaysia with a rich melding of Chinese, Malay, and Indian cultures. Various ethnic cuisines, ornate Colonial architecture, Buddhist, Hindu, and Muslim religious shrines, and street and village life are aspects of these cultures that are to be discovered around the island.

HISTORY: The English explorer Francis Light sailed into Penang's harbor in

1768, when the native population of the entire island numbered less than a thousand. Light's arrival marked the first British presence in Malaysia, soon to be followed by the establishment of Fort Cornwallis in 1810. Within ten years, thanks to Light's shrewd decision to establish free-trade zones, the population swelled to 10,000. Eager Chinese, Indians, and British arrived to contribute to the bustling trade and commerce, which continues to characterize Penang to this day.

ORIENTATION: The heart of the island is **Georgetown,** a rich and energetic city of over a half million citizens composed of the usual Malaysian mix, but in this case with a larger proportion of Chinese and Indians. The structure of the city is quintessentially Malaysian. Its core is found along the northern waterfront, the colonial military, administrative, and mercantile center, built largely by the British (with imported Indian labor) during the 19th century. In this area are well-established neighborhoods with impressive mansions, upcountry bungalows, and private clubs, most in a state of excellent repair and populated by Malaysians of all ethnic groups. To the southeast, in the center of modern Georgetown, are the newer Chinese, Indian, and Malay communities. Here one finds shops and markets, twisting lanes leading to sumptuously decorated Chinese and Hindu shrines, moneychangers, and craftsmen, as well as some of the finest hawker stands found anywhere in the country.

Outside Georgetown, the majority of the island is richly agricultural, peopled largely by Malay peasants who follow a traditional pattern of agrarian life. In stark contrast is the **industrial zone,** located on the southeastern quarter of Penang, which looks distinctly like Silicon Valley in California, with whom it shares many tenants, companies such as Intel, Advanced Micro System, and National Semiconducter. Finally, there is **Batu Ferringhi** ("Foreigner's Rock") on the north coast, where the majority of tourist groups base themselves to take advantage of the sandy beaches. If you plan on serious sunbathing, remember that the rainy season extends from April to May and August to November, with only occasional showers throughout the remainder of the year. The best (that is, driest) months are January to March. If you plan on visiting in December, inquire as to the date of the Dragon Head Boat Race, held annually on the island.

USEFUL INFORMATION: The **TDC office** is located in Georgetown between the ferry pier and Fort Cornwallis at 10 Jalan Tun Syed Sheh Barakbah (tel. 04/619-067); hours are 8 a.m. to 4:15 p.m. Monday through Friday and 8 a.m. to 12:45 p.m. on Saturday; closed Sunday. There is also a branch at the airport. Just a few doors down from TDC is the helpful **Penang Tourist Association** (tel. 04/614-461), which dispenses excellent brochures and maps of the island, especially its "Penang Island and City Map," in addition to a walking map of Georgetown.

The **PTT** is next to the Old Post Building on Leboh Downing, near the ferry pier (tel. 04/627-848); the telephone and telegram office is open 24 hours. The **General Post Office** is next door.

For medical emergencies, contact the **Penang Adventist Hospital** (tel. 04/373-344) or **St. John's Ambulance Service** (tel. 04/685-972).

There is a **British Representative** in Penang at Birch House, 73 Jalan Dato Keramat (tel. 04/27-166), in addition to a branch of the **British Council** (tel. 04/611-152).

Penang has a plethora of financial institutions, including a branch of **Citibank,** on Jalan Sultan Ahmad Shah (tel. 04/363-222). All local commercial banks, such as those along Beach Street, keep regular banking hours (Monday through Friday from 10 a.m. to 3 p.m. and on Saturday from 9:30 to 11 a.m.), but licensed **moneychangers** are located throughout the city who keep more flexible hours while, in most cases, offering a higher rate of exchange. The largest concentration of moneychangers is found in the Indian areas, especially on Pitt Street. The **American Express** representative is located on the third floor of the Green Hall Building (tel. 04/368-317).

The **telephone area code** for all of Penang is 04.

GETTING THERE: Penang is easy to get to: it's well connected to peninsular Malaysia by its international airport; several trains daily link it with Bangkok and Singapore; and there is a good network of roads to Kuala Lumpur and Kota Bharu.

By Air

The **Penang International Airport** is located 16 km (10 miles) south of Georgetown at Bayan Lepas (tel. 831-373). **Malaysian Airline System** (tel. 620-011) has daily flights to Penang from KL for M$88 ($35.25) one way, Kota Bharu for M$80 ($32), and Kuala Terengganu for M$80 ($32); the MAS office is located in the Tun Abdul Razak Compleks. Most of the major airlines have offices in Penang, including **Cathay Pacific Airways** (tel. 620-411), **MAS** (tel. 621-403), **Northwest** (tel. 619-487), **Singapore Airlines** (tel. 363-201), and **Thai Airways International** (tel. 23-484). Remember that there is an airport tax: M$3 ($1.25) for domestic destinations, M$5 ($2) for Singapore-bound flights, and M$15 ($6) for all other international flights.

The TDC operates an **information booth** in the arrival hall, open from 8:30 a.m. to 5 p.m. Monday through Friday, to 1 p.m. on Saturday; closed Sunday. Upstairs is an official moneychanger with daily hours from 8:30 a.m. to 6:30 p.m.; there is a bank downstairs that keeps normal banking hours.

Plan on a 20- to 30-minute trip from the airport by **taxi** with the fare to Georgetown at M$17 ($6.75) and M$24 ($9.50) to the beach; call 834-181 for taxi service. The **public bus** operates hourly between the airport and the Georgetown ferry pier from 7 a.m. to 10 p.m. for M$1.50 (60¢). **Thrifty, Budget, Avis,** and **Hertz** all have counters on the upstairs floor of the terminal. MAS runs a **luggage-storage service** charging M$3.50 ($1.50) per day per piece; they are open whenever there is a flight. Forget to buy stamps? The airport **post office** is open from 8 a.m. to 10 p.m. Monday through Saturday and 9 a.m. to 6 p.m. on Sunday.

By Train

There is train service between Penang (via Butterworth on the mainland and the ferry to Georgetown) and Thailand to the north, Kuala Lumpur and Singapore to the south. The Butterworth–Bangkok shuttle operates once a day on Monday, Wednesday, and Friday: a first-class double berth is M$25 ($10), and that's for an air-conditioned double! The trip takes almost a day, so make sure you buy some books. There are two (express) trains daily from Butterworth to Kuala Lumpur, and one that stops in KL for a half hour before pulling out for Singapore. The Butterworth–KL ride takes 6½ hours and costs M$34 ($13.50), and the Butterworth–Singapore trek takes 12½ hours and is M$60 ($24). This is the time to catch up on your reading.

Train tickets within Georgetown can be purchased at the ferry terminal (tel. 610-290), the **Butterworth Train Station** (tel. 347-962), or by a travel agent. It's crucial to make reservations in advance (you can make them up to 90 days prior to departure), especially if you wish to reserve an air-conditioned sleeper or first-class seat.

By Ferry

There is 24-hour ferry service for both passengers and vehicles between Butterworth and Georgetown. The two-mile journey takes a scant 15 minutes, with ferries departing every 20 minutes (every half hour after midnight). You need only purchase a ticket on the Butterworth side as the return trip is free. Round-trip fares are 45 sen (20¢) for adults, half price for children under 12, and M$4.50 ($1.75) to M$6.50 ($2.50) for vehicle and driver.

By Road

With the completion of the Korean-built, billion-dollar **Penang Bridge**, driving to Penang is now possible, though you'll pay for the pleasure. The M$8 ($3.25) levy is paid in Prai on the mainland side. As with the ferry, there is no return toll. Penang can be reached by either the north-south highway from Kuala Lumpur or the east-west highway from Kota Bharu.

GETTING AROUND: Penang offers several options for local travel, including very inexpensive taxis.

By Taxi

If you arrive at the airport, the taxi fare to your destination will be fixed (see "Getting There") and is normally paid for with coupons purchased in front of the terminal.

Taxis cruise the streets in Georgetown and other tourist areas and charge according to the meter within that area (fixed-price fares cover inter-island travel). Fares are calculated by time and distance: an average ten-minute ride costs about M$6.50 ($2.50). If you need to reserve a taxi by telephone, try **Syarikat Georgetown Taxi and Tour** (tel. 613-853) or contact the concierge at your hotel.

Want to book a car and driver to take you around, show you the sights, and act as a guide? Call the best, **Mayflower Acme Tours** (tel. 628-196). Their drivers live locally and really know the terrain: our driver was a Mr. T. F. Yang, and he introduced us to many of his favorite haunts and sights that quickly became our favorites. Since there are so many different choices, call them and describe what you're looking for and ask them how much it will cost you: we think you'll be surprised at how affordable touring can be.

By Bus

Buses in Penang are color-coded for specific routes, making it easy to identify the correct coach for your destination. The two most prominent routes are the blue and yellow lines. **Blue line buses** begin in Georgetown along Jalan Maxwell and run along the northern coast to Batu Ferringhi, while the **yellow line bus** begins on the same road then runs to the southern and western perimeters of Penang. An **around-the-island bus tour,** on a combination of the blue and yellow lines, takes about five hours with stops.

The **local MPPP buses** are extremely inexpensive and operate throughout the entire city, leaving frequently from the main terminal at Leboh Victoria. The route number and destination are shown above the windshield on each bus, including buses nos. 1 and 8 that, by connection, stop at the Penang Hill Railway and the Kek Lok Si Temple via Ayer Itam. For a current schedule of the buses, contact the TDC or the Penang Tourist Association.

By Trishaw

There's no better way to travel within the city than by a human-powered trishaw. This symbol of Asia past is still very much in evidence in Georgetown, where trishaw drivers will seek you out, especially if you reside at a first-class hotel. You'll have to negotiate your fare (don't rely on the so-called published fares); expect to pay between M$1.50 (60¢) and M$3 ($1.25) for most rides in the city. Trishaws can be rented by the hour for about M$8 ($3.25).

Rental Cars

Avis operates from the E&O Hotel (tel. 373-964) and at their affiliate at Bunga Raya Travel (tel. 365-212). You can also try **Hertz** (tel. 375-914) and **National Car Rental** (tel. 372-424), both with rental facilities in Georgetown. All major rental-car companies maintain counters at the airport. The daily rates, for unlimited-mileage vehicles, vary from M$140 ($56) for economy cars to M$330 ($132) for a Mercedes.

ACCOMMODATIONS: Accommodations in Georgetown are of good quality and reasonably priced. We prefer to base ourselves in Georgetown, with its more interesting ambience and sights, and then take the bus or taxi to the beach by day. Confirmed beachaholics will find good facilities along the northern coast between Georgetown and the Batu Ferringhi resort village.

First-Class and Moderately Priced Accommodations

Georgetown's premier hotel is the centrally located **Shangri-la Inn,** an imposing high-rise structure next to the domed convention center on Jalan Magazine (tel. 04/622-622). The Shangri-la is the town's newest hotel and, as such, sparkles with all of the latest amenities. The swimming pool and gym, in addition to the tennis and squash courts, are especially welcome as a retreat from Georgetown's noisy and hectic street life, and the hotel's business center is fully staffed and equipped. The dining rooms and bars offer a full complement of Asian and continental specialties and are often filled with locals. As for service, we found the staff at the Shangri-la hospitable, knowledgeable, and helpful, reflecting the chain's very high standards. Room rates are M$125 ($50) for a standard single and M$145 ($58) for a double.

The **Eastern and Oriental Hotel,** 10 Leboh Farquhar (tel. 04/375-322), also known as the E&O, is the grande dame of Penang's hotel set. Built in 1885 on a seafront garden, the E&O is distinguished by its tasteful Colonial architecture and setting. The dome lobby, mohair furnishings, and cage elevator are all excellent examples of period design. Although there is much to admire about the E&O, the upkeep and modernization of the rooms detracts from the other more carefully restored aspects of the building. Nevertheless, this is a unique building, actually an institution in Penang, and is a fascinating lodging alternative. Superior singles cost M$140 ($56) and doubles run M$160 ($64); add M$25 ($10) for deluxe accommodations.

The **Merlin,** located at 3 Jalan Larut/Burmah (tel. 04/376-166), is near the Penang Plaza Complex and across the street from the Kentucky Fried Chicken-in-a-Mansion, a local landmark. The Merlin, like the Shangri-la, boasts luxury amenities and restaurants, a spa, and entertainment facilities. Though a bit older and worn, the Merlin is a well-located alternative. A deluxe double here is M$150 ($60). Make sure you ask for a sea-view room.

The 323-room **Orchid Hotel** is set away from the hotel strip near a fairly quiet residential area on Tanjung Bungah (tel. 04/803-333). This recently built inn has the advantage of having all its spacious and brightly furnished rooms facing the sea as well as having spotlessly maintained public spaces. Though the Orchid is a bit out of the center, the hotel provides a shuttle to the nearby northern beaches, making this an excellent choice for those who want to straddle Georgetown and Batu Ferringhi. Deluxe singles run M$135 ($54); doubles are M$160 ($64).

The **City Bayview Hotel,** located at 25A Farquhar St. (tel. 04/363-161), is a ten-minute walk from the financial and business center of Georgetown. It has all the luxury amenities sans spa, and one of our favorite hotel inspirations: a revolving rooftop restaurant! The Bayview is a favorite of traveling Asian businessmen. A deluxe sea-view double is M$145 ($58), and a junior suite costs only M$35 ($14) more. We say go for it and feel like a big wheel.

Budget Hotels

One of the better budget values in central Georgetown is the **Hotel Oriental,** at 105 Penang Rd. (tel. 04/24-211). Given the central shopping-street location, the guest rooms are reasonably quiet in addition to being well maintained and air-conditioned. The staff is friendly and accommodating, and room rates are reasonable: singles cost M$66 ($26.50), and doubles run M$72 ($28.75). Nearby are banks, airline offices, and restaurants, making this a convenient low-budget alternative.

Nearby is the **Towne House Hotel,** at 70 Penang Rd. (tel. 04/368-621), with characteristics similar to those of the Oriental. All rooms are clean, well kept, and air-conditioned, and for a quiet night's sleep we suggest requesting a high floor (good views), back-facing room. Room rates are M$72 ($28.75) for a single and M$76 ($30.50) for a double, though during holidays they rise to what the market will bear.

Penang's **YMCA,** at 211 Jalan MacAlister (tel. 04/362-211), is a fairly institutional place on a somewhat noisy road, but it does have the advantage of providing clean, air-conditioned double rooms for M$28 ($11.25) per night for both men and women. You'll do better with a back-facing room as modest insulation from the street noise.

Lodging at Batu Ferringhi

There are several very good hotels along the beach that differ primarily in their landscaping, choice of coloring, and age (read: amenities). They all share the same gorgeous strip of coastline.

Our favorite is the **Golden Sands,** on Batu Ferringhi (tel. 04/811-911), located right on the beach. We found this place, well, simply sandsational. For starters it has a wonderful landscaped pool/bar/restaurant complex: three pools, including one with a Jacuzzi and one with a waterslide, each with a thatched-hut poolside bar. The lawn extends right onto the beach, where you can waterski-glide, windsurf, you name it—the hotel has it all. They also have a guided two-hour jungle trek organized just for guests. All the rooms have natural-wood-style décor, rattan furniture, and beach-motif wallpaper and prints, as well as hairdryers and in-house video. There's a small shopping arcade along the outside of the hotel, and the area between the pools and beach houses the Sea Pavilion, an open-air surf-and-turf restaurant with large ceiling fans that has a grill and an orchestra at night so you can work off some calories after dessert. The tariff for all this pampering is M$250 ($100) for a deluxe double, a deal as far as we're concerned.

The **Ferringhi Beach Hotel** (tel. 04/805-999) is one of the northern coast's most attractively built lodgings. The hotel is located midway between Georgetown and the resort village, but it does have its own modest beachfront: unfortunately, it's literally across the street, so that you have to cross the highway to get there! From there it's an easy commute to the longer stretches of sand farther north. The lobby is the white-marble and rattan-furniture variety, lending an open, airy ambience. All rooms have balconies and fine sea views. With superior singles running M$145 ($58) and doubles at M$165 ($66), the Ferringhi Beach is a fine value.

Here you are in faraway Penang and what do you see? The familiar green-and-white logo of the **Holiday Inn** (tel. 04/811-601). The company's anonymous design motif extends throughout the lobby and public spaces, but the new wing offers a step up in taste and luxury. The outdoor dining area, oversize pool, and beach are the highlights here. Superior (ocean-view) singles cost M$175 ($70), while doubles run M$200 ($80).

Two of the most favored European tourist-group hotels are the **Rasa Sayang** (tel. 04/811-811)—with a name that translates as "the feeling of love," who can doubt its popularity?—and the **Casuarina** (tel. 04/811-711). The beachfront location and backyard lawn of the Rasa's pool are suburban comfortable. The only drawback of the Rasa Sayang is that it isn't as well maintained as other beach hotels. Guest rooms are small, with unexceptional views, but if you've come here for the beach (which is the only reason to stay at Batu Ferringhi) it's still a good alternative. Don't miss the palm reader in the upstairs shopping arcade! Mountain-view doubles rent for M$170 ($68); those with ocean/pool/garden views run M$220 ($88). The Casuarina is similar, but better maintained; the big drawback here is that it's predominantly a tour-group hotel, with all that that implies. A deluxe double is M$210 ($84); we liked it more than the Rasa.

One of our favorite hotels falls into the niche between luxury and budget. The **Palm Beach Hotel** (tel. 04/811-833), also located on the short beachfront strip is aptly named; your first impression is of a southern California beach condo. The rooms are homey, with large, clean bathrooms, and they have family-size rooms that comfortably sleep five (spend the extra $5 for a superior room; they're slightly bigger and have balconies facing the sea). The décor is natural wood and peach (sound familiar?). The Palm Beach is casual-cool, the kind of beach place where you figure Tom Waits would run into Robin Williams if they'd strayed over from their respective hotels. A superior double here is only M$155 ($62). Just think of it as low-end luxury.

Back in 1948, when the **Lone Pine Hotel** (tel. 04/811-511) was built, Batu Ferringhi must have been an exotic beach retreat. Now this simple lodging seems lost among the international-style behemoths, yet the allure is still here. The Lone Pine's 54 rooms aren't fancy, but there is still an excellent beachfront and ocean view, as well as a hint of Colonial bungalow architecture, particularly evident in the high-ceilinged dining room. The prices at this casual, quiet inn are M$75 ($30) for a sea-facing double, M$55 ($22) for a single.

DINING: The best dining (by far) in Penang is done at the hawker stands and informal restaurant stalls in the city's ethnic neighborhoods. If you do venture to these places, you'll be rewarded with some of the best food Malaysia has to offer, and at modest prices. Those of you staying at the beach will find inexpensive coffeeshops and restaurants in all the beach hotels, and small stalls in the stretches in between; ask the concierge where the best hawker stands are.

Hawker Cuisine

Among our favorite central Georgetown stalls are those off **Jalan Dato Keramat,** where you may sample truly excellent and inventive steamboat and hawker fare for a pittance; expect to pay about M$10 ($4) per person for a feast. These stalls are open daily from 3 to 9 p.m. The majority of the evening stalls are located on the north side of town, either on Pesiaran Gurney (the waterfront road) or Jalan Sultan Ahmad Shah. One of the less commercial group of stalls is located off Jalan Bagan Jermal. We suggest taking a taxi to the waterfront road and walking from one food market to another, sampling Chinese, Indian, and Malay food along the way.

If you wish to try steamboat dining in a restaurant setting, consider a visit to the **Hollywood Restaurant** in Tanjung Bunga (about a ten-minute ride from Georgetown) on the coast road towards Batu Ferringhi.

Near the Shangri-la Hotel is **Jalan McAlister,** where hawker stands crowd each other to please patrons deep into the night (this is a favorite dinner stop for trishaw drivers, so it's got to be good).

Indian Cuisine

Most of the Indian food is of the southern variety and can be found in both hawker stands and in informal eateries, known as banana-leaf restaurants. Several of these can be found on **Leboh** and **Penang** streets. One of the better ones is the **Shan Villas**, at 34 Ah Quee St. (tel. 29-532), where two can sup for M$6.50 ($2.50) for a complete banana-leaf lunch including various curries, rice, and appetizers.

Another fine example (one of our favorites, in fact) of Indian cooking can be found at the **Hamieediyah Restaurant,** 164-A Campbell St. (tel. 611-095), where the specialty is nasi kandar (a curry-and-rice concoction) and murtabah (wrapped in crepe) chicken, beef, lamb, and veal. There is no alcohol here, so try some local soft drinks. Again the price is low; expect to pay about M$12 ($4.75) for two.

Nearby is the **Dawood Restaurant,** at 63 Leboh Queen (tel. 611-633). Suggested entrees include chicken biryani, chicken kapitan, roast duck, and their assorted vegetable dishes; a meal for two should run about M$12 ($4.75).

Chinese Cuisine

Penang has a large and ethnically varied Chinese population and its restaurants reflect that diversity. Among the top Chinese restaurants are the **Dragon King Restaurant,** on Bishop Street, for Nyonya food (a Chinese/Malay melding of cooking styles); **Chuan Lok Hooi Restaurant,** on McAlister Road, for Hokkien food; and the **Prosperous Restaurant,** on Jalan Gottlieb, for Hainanese specialties. These are relatively inexpensive eateries, not running more than M$35 ($14) for two for a large meal.

If you want to splurge, consider the **Shang Palace** at the Shangri-la Inn on Jalan Magazine. For lunch they have a dim sum menu, while the dinner menu features Cantonese and Peking dishes such as shark's-fin soup, roast pork, and Peking duck.

Western and Fast Food

As you can imagine, Penang is not the place for top-of-the-line continental dining. However, if you crave a steak you can always rely on **The Ship,** 46 Sri Bahari Rd. (tel. 29-532). Like its cousins in Kuala Lumpur, this branch serves eight- to ten-ounce New Zealand/American beef for approximately M$40 ($16) per person, including unlimited visits to the salad bar.

For more upscale dining, consider a meal at the **Shangri-la Inn** dining rooms, where you'll find a large offering of Western entrees.

As with all of Malaysia, Penang is littered with fast-food joints, especially the ubiquitous Kentucky Fried Chicken (they have actually retrofitted a K.F.C. in a colonial mansion, making this the fanciest fast-food outlet we've ever seen).

Dining at Batu Ferringhi

There aren't many choices outside the hotels; however, there is a modest cluster of **hawker stalls** opposite the beachfront strip with acceptable food.

The splashiest restaurant on the strip is **Eden's Seafood Village** (tel. 811-852), which advertises: "Anything That Swims We Have It!" They combine an actual acrobatic show with a showy meal that's fun though not haute cuisine. Expect to pay approximately M$33 ($13.25) per person for a full-course meal.

WHAT TO SEE AND DO: Because of Georgetown's colonial history and ethnically diverse neighborhoods the city has several compelling sights, perhaps none more so than Penang Hill. If you have the time, an around-the-island day tour is also worth taking, if only for the varied scenery and glimpses of rural Malay life.

Georgetown

The following tour begins with several sights on the outskirts of the city and works its way back into the central area. All these sights are a quick taxi ride from the center of Georgetown.

PENANG HILL. An excellent way to start your tour of the Georgetown area is to take the 30-minute **funicular railway** to the cool plateau atop Penang Hill. This approximately 2,000-foot-high hill station offers an extraordinary vista of Georgetown, Butterworth, and to the west, Penang's interior. This railway to Penang Hill was built by the British in the days of their colonial settlement and is a wonderful engineering achievement, not unlike Victoria Peak in Hong Kong. On your ride up you won't fail to notice the monkeys that hang out alongside the track.

Once on top you'll walk around and discover that there's an entire village there. You can also take a ten-minute walk to the **Penang Hill Hotel** (tel. 04/892-256) where there is a lovely dining room, terrace, and back garden. As you approach the hotel you will hear the **Bellevue Aviary Gardens,** open from 9 a.m. to 6 p.m. daily. For the M$1.25 (50¢) admission you can parrot the parrots and commune with some gorgeous (and loud) feathered friends. This hotel and aviary were a favorite haunt of Buckminster Fuller, of geodesic dome fame, who was a personal friend and mentor of the hotel's owner/designer, and the hotel's bookstore has posters and books by and about this noteworthy American architect. If you decide to stay at this delightful 12-room inn, expect to pay M$90 ($36) for a double room. The rooms are cozy and spacious, with large bathrooms and tiny windows. The back garden has an old viewscope, singing birds, and a special serenity that's quite lovely.

Among the other facilities on the hill are a children's playground, tea kiosk, police station, and post office.

The railway operates from 6:30 a.m. to 9:30 p.m., with departures every 30 minutes. The cost of a round-trip ticket is M$3.50 ($1.50). If in doubt about the weather, take a sweater; it can be quite cool up top.

KEK LOK SI TEMPLE. By far the most imposing Buddhist temple in Malaysia is Kek Lok Si, located on a bluff near the Ayer Itam region. This 19th-century complex combines Chinese, Thai, and Burmese architectural elements, particularly in its centerpiece, the multitiered Ban Po Thar pagoda. The base, with its unique ornamentation, is of Chinese design, while the middle section is Thai motifs, and the upper third is Burmese. In addition to the main pagoda there are several lesser pavilions as well as a turtle pool where one can feed the turtles and, according to Buddhist beliefs, gain merit.

COLONIAL GEORGETOWN. Perhaps our favorite sight within the city is the colonial mansions, clubs, and administrative buildings that line the city's northern streets. If you rent a car, drive along **Jalan Sultan Ahmad Shah,** past the E&O Hotel and to the original center of British presence, **Fort Cornwallis.** This will give you a sense of Georgetown's colonial occupation and the grandeur that was its hallmark.

WAT CHAYAMANGKALARM. This Thai-style Buddhist temple of recent vintage in the Lonron Burmah area is a giant quonset hut containing what is asserted to be the world's third-largest reclining Buddha (108 feet). Much more interesting are the fortune-telling wheels and many niches containing photographs and remains of the dead.

Around the Island

The stretch between Georgetown and Batu Ferringhi is about all that most visitors see of the island. That's unfortunate, because the majority of this varied and agriculturally rich island is scenically fascinating. From rice paddies to Malay *kampongs* (villages) to nutmeg and clove gardens and exotic fruit estates, the interior of Penang deserves at least a half-day tour. Such a tour can be taken either by private taxi or by the yellow and blue buses.

Other than the highlights listed below, be sure to stop at one of the **fruit stands** near Pantai Acheh and Sungei Pinang, where you can sample durian, betel nut, mangosteen, coconut, cocoa, and a variety of herbal oils and spices. If you have a private car, don't hesitate to stop in one of the **kampongs** on the western plain where you'll find traditional stilt houses side by side with modern trailer homes. The houses are built on stilts to avoid floods, insects (the exterior siding is oiled, not painted, to repel termites), and snakes, as well as to provide insulation from the warm earth. Kampongs are typically dominated by a headman and the local spirits are appeased by a witch doctor, who also tends to the physical maladies of the inhabitants.

If you follow the route to the southeast corner of the island, at Bayan Lepas (near the airport), you'll see Malaysia's Silicon Valley, a high-technology industrial park with American, Japanese, and German factories.

SNAKE TEMPLE. Known formally as the Pure Cloud Temple and dedicated to Chor Soo Kong, a local deity associated with healing, the Snake Temple (as it's more popularly called) is unusual for the proliferation of live poisonous vipers that are wound around the trees in the first pavilion. The temple was built in 1873 by the good graces of David Brown, an ailing Englishman who suffered from an "incurable" disease. After making his offerings to the local deity, Brown miraculously regained his health and constructed the Pure Cloud Temple as a gesture of thanks. Soon after the building opened, highly poisonous Wagler's pit vipers crawled down into the temple from the surrounding hills. They clung to the plants and were lulled into a quiescent state by the thick smoke of the votive incense. The surprising aspect of this story is that only one species of snake inhabits the temple. Today, as in the 19th century, there are still many snakes living in the front hall. If you feel so inclined, you may handle defanged vipers in the adjoining room for a small fee. For M$2.50 ($1) the handlers will drape three or four of the snakes over your head, arms, neck, and chest—remember to bring your camera to immortalize the moment. Alternatively, for M$9 ($3.50) the handlers will take snapshots of you with your favorite creeper. The Snake Temple is located south of Georgetown in Bayan Lepas, in the heart of Penang's high-technology industrial zone.

BOTANICAL GARDENS. The ostensible reason to visit this 75-acre tropical park is to meander through its cool, sprawling grounds as a respite from an overheated day of sightseeing. The planted trees and flowers, in addition to hothouses and ponds, make a sumptuous backdrop for a picnic. You'll definitely have to contend with the wild Rhesus monkeys that roam the park and follow you in search of a few hundred peanuts, a banana, or your lunch! The Botanical Gardens are open daily and are located to the west of Georgetown on Botanical Gardens Road.

BUTTERFLY FARM. Just west of Batu Ferringhi, in Teluk Bahang, 22 km (14 miles) from Georgetown, is one of the island's most enchanting tourist stops, the Penang Butterfly Farm (tel. 811-253). This center, which is on a conservation, education, and profit-making mission, is devoted to the over 95 separate species of butterflies found in Malaysia. The farm has more than 4,000 butterflies dancing in a controlled landscape that approximates a natural habitat. The best time to visit is in the early morning when it's possible to watch the butterflies emerge from their pupae.

In addition to the butterfly exhibit there are several related side shows, including a scorpion pit, frog pond, and an amazing display of live insects that blend in perfectly with their environment. For the inveterate shopper, there is a unique gift shop that sells all manner of mounted and framed bugs at reasonable prices.

The Penang Butterfly Farm is open from 9 a.m. to 5 p.m. Monday through Friday and 8 a.m. to 6 p.m. on Saturday and Sunday; admission is M$2.50 ($1) for adults, half price for children. The butterfly farm should be a must-see on your Penang itinerary.

Kongsi Temple

Located at 18 Cannon Square, just a short walk from the Shangri-la Hotel, is the Kongsi Temple, the richest single clan house in Malaysia. What this means is that a single family built their own temple, and succeeding generations of the clan kept building onto it until today this temple is an incredible example of Chinese architecture, with its intricate work and extremely fine ornamentation. Kongsi is open from 9 a.m. to 5 p.m. Monday through Friday, until 1 p.m. on Saturday; closed Sunday.

SHOPPING: Although Penang is a duty-free port, it doesn't present the kind of shopping opportunities found in Singapore or Hong Kong. There are modestly intriguing shops along Penang Road and in the Indian and Chinese neighborhoods. Two of the more interesting shops are **Oriental Curios and Jewelry,** at 84 Penang Rd. (tel. 310-861), and **Hong Giap,** at 308-310 Penang Rd. (tel. 25-092). Both stock Malaysian souvenirs, Kelantan masks, and a very few, expensive (but highly negotiable) Chinese and Thai antiques.

The area bounded by King, Queen, and Market Streets is known as **"Little India,"** and we found many antique furniture shops here, with pieces ranging from old Colonial to heavy mahogony. Across the street from the Eastern and Oriental Hotel on Penang Road there are antique shops dealing in old jewelry and family keepsakes.

For more mundane goods, the best shopping is in the rotating **night market** (ask your concierge where the market is held during your visit). There is a fine market in the city center near Jalan Magazine and Penang Road selling clothing, suitcases, and odd objects. In the modern complex at the same intersection is the city's largest **shopping mall,** with all manner of locally produced and imported goods. **Bookstores** are grouped together on Penang Road and Long Beach Street.

NIGHTLIFE: The best night scene is found at the hawker stands on the north side of town. However, if you are in quest of other activities, Penang will do its best to satisfy every taste.

Bars

It would be difficult to find a better watering hole in Penang than the **Hong Kong Bar** at 371 Chulia St. (tel. 619-796). Long a favorite of the British (it was established in 1920), then American, now Australian expatriate and military community, the Hong Kong has the kind of forbidding façade and comforting interior that marks a true hangout. Ask to sign the guestbook. Better yet, ask to read the guestbook from your favorite year—they've kept every book since they opened! This place is truly a gem.

Disco and Nightclubs

The places that were hot when we were there were **Penny Lane,** located in the basement of the City Bayview Hotel (tel. 04/363-161), featuring music from the '60s, and the second-floor club in the Shangri-la Hotel.

There are two popular cabarets in town, **Tucson** and the **Latin Quarter,** and the Penang equivalent of a hostess club, **Toki,** located on the ground floor of the Hotel Malaysia. Check with your concierge for rates and show times.

Other Night Activities

You can find traditional adult evening entertainment at such establishments as Tiffany or the Pink Carnation along Jalan Sri Bahari. Many such venues are advertised as barbershops (as in Taiwan) and haircuts are actually available for about M$12 ($4.75), but for an additional fee you can arrange for more personal service. You'll know you're there if there's a barberpole outside the shop. Most of these businesses operate from 10:30 a.m. to 8 p.m.

3. THE EAST COAST

Malaysia's lesser-developed east coast, including the states of Kelantan, Terengganu, and Pahang, is treated like the "ugly stepchild" region of the country, though it's blessed with some of the finest beaches in all of Southeast Asia. Imagine hundreds of miles of unspoiled, sandy stretches, with rice paddies, coves, and islands punctuating the landscape. Most towns, from Kota Bharu through Terengganu and Kuantan, are being built up as metropolitan districts, mostly due to profitable oil facilities that have been constructed in the past 20 years. Aside from these, the majority of east-coast towns are Malay kampongs, where the inhabitants live a more "traditional" life than in the rest of peninsular Malaysia. For this reason the east coast is an important bastion of fundamentalist Islamic belief—it's not surprising to see veiled women in black fundamentalist clothing.

The east coast has a distinctive culture from the rest of Malaysia, with its own games, crafts, and theater, all on display in the main cities. But for most visitors the main attraction here is the miles and miles of beaches. If you really want to escape the hordes, you won't have to search far on the east coast. If you do go, try to visit from June to August when the giant leatherback turtles lay their eggs on the beach at Ranau Abang. It's best to avoid visiting from November to February when the weather and sea are quite rough.

ORIENTATION: Kota Bharu is located in the northeast corner of the peninsula, close to the Thai border. In fact, locals in search of a less restricted good time often head up to Thailand for a quick sin fix and Thai meal. The coast road leads down to Kuala Terengganu, Rantau Abang, Tanjong Jara, and ultimately to Kuantan. The entire trip, from Kota Bharu to Kuantan, can easily be done in one day by private car or bus with stops in each town.

USEFUL INFORMATION: The three major towns on the east coast are well organized for tourists and easily connected to each other and the rest of Malaysia by road and air traffic.

The **telephone area code** for the east coast is 09.

Kota Bharu

The **Tourist Information Centre** is located on Jalan Sultan Ibrahim (tel. 09/785-543), near the Kelantan Royal Club; hours are 8:30 a.m. to 4:30 p.m. Saturday through Wednesday, to 1:15 p.m. on Thursday; closed Friday. The **police station** and **post office** are also located on Jalan Sultan Ibrahim, just down from the Tourist Information Centre.

The best way to get around Kota Bharu is by **trishaw**. Again, you'll have to negotiate the fare, but expect to pay about M$3.50 ($1.50) for most rides within the town. For longer journeys, travel by **taxi** is recommended. The taxi and **Central Bus Station** is located just off Jalan Padang Garong on Jalan Masjid Abidin. There are frequent daily buses to Kuala Terengganu and Kuantan, with fares of M$8 ($3.25) and M$17 ($6.75) respectively. There is also daily overnight bus service to Kuala Lumpur and Penang. Call 09/621-581 for taxi information; a **city tour** should run M$5.50 ($2.25) and the 20-minute airport commute costs about M$12 ($4.75). There is a **car-rental agency** in Kota Bharu organized by Mars Kelantan International Travel (tel. 09/744-737). **MAS** (tel. 09/747-000) offers daily air service to Kota Bharu from Kuala Lumpur for M$86 ($34.50) and Penang for M$72 ($28.75); they have an office in the Kompleks Yakin on Jalan Gajah Mati.

Kuala Terengganu

The **TDC** maintains an office in Kuala Terengganu at 2243 (ground floor) Wisma MCIS on Jalan Sultan Zainal Abidin (tel. 09/621-433). The **police station** is on the corner of Jalan Masjid and Jalan Sultan Ismail. The **post office** is located near the jetty around the corner from the Maziah Palace.

As in Kota Bharu, there are **trishaws and taxis** for hire for local and outstation travel; call 621-581 for a taxi. Express **buses** to Kuala Lumpur, Kota Bharu, and Kuantan leave from the Central Bus Station on Jalan Masjid Abidin.

MAS has an office on Jalan Sultan Ismail at Lot 6, Wisma Maju (tel. 09/621-415); they offer daily connections with Kuala Lumpur, Penang, and Johore Bharu for M$86 ($34.50), M$80 ($32), and M$163 ($65.25) respectively. **Sultan Mahmud Airport** is located about 30 minutes north of the city; a taxi costs about M$17 ($6.75) for the excursion.

ACCOMMODATIONS AND DINING: The lodgings along the east coast range from luxurious seaside resorts to primitive beach bungalows. *One word of warning:* Many of the moderate and budget rooms in the east-coast cities tend not to be as clean and well maintained as in the rest of Malaysia. Be sure to check your room thoroughly before agreeing to stay.

As for food, we found lesser-quality fare than in other parts of Malaysia at the hawker stalls and restaurants, but there are still a few scattered eateries that are recommended.

Kota Bharu

The best facility in town is the **Hotel Perdana,** located across from the Kelantan Cultural Center on Jalan Mahmud (tel. 09/785-000). The rooms are plain and clean, and the hotel offers good sports options including a swimming pool, squash courts, and playground. A standard single rents for M$85 ($34), with a double running M$110 ($44).

The **Temenggong Hotel,** on Jalan Tok Hakim (tel. 09/783-130), is a small hotel (36 rooms) where all the rooms have air conditioning, private bath, and shower for M$60 ($24), making it a good deal for a quick night in the capital.

Opened in 1987, the **Tokyo Baru Hotel,** at 3945/46 Jalan Tok Hakim (tel. 09/749-488), is a 22-room, reasonably clean lodging with basic amenities. Room rates run M$45 ($18) for a double and M$40 ($16) for a single.

The Beach of Passionate Love isn't a great beach but it has a million-dollar name, and there is a modest resort of the same name (at least in Bahasa Malaysia), called **Resort Pantai Chinta Berahi** (tel. 09/781-307). For M$65 ($26) a couple can rent an air-conditioned bungalow complete with mini-refrigerator; a fancooled facility is only M$5 ($2) less. The lobby and dining room are open breezeways and lead to the wide sandy beach with that great name. Just down the way is a cluster of no-name, fan-cooled "chalets" for M$35 ($14) a night for two.

You will probably have better luck with Thai food in Kota Bharu than with most other alternatives. A delicious suggestion is the **Restoran Syam,** at Lot 594, Jalan Hospital (tel. 784-713). Don't let the address put you off, for the food is both clean and savory, with such suggested highlights as udang bakar ("burnt" prawns) and tong yam ikan (spicy fish soup). A meal for two runs about M$33 ($13.25). Restoran Syam is open daily for lunch and dinner.

The best **hawker food** we found is at Merdeka Square (open day and night) and the Central Market.

Terengganu

The international-style luxury hotel in Kuala Terengganu, if not in the entire state, is the **Pantaj Primula,** strategically built half a mile north of the town on a fine sandy beach (tel. 09/622-100). This is really more of a resort than a hotel, offering an incredible array of outdoor-sports options, including excursions to nearby islands. The design of the complex is almost monumental in scale, with waterfalls and huge wooden structures gracing the oversize lobby. Even the swimming pool is dramatic: a bridge, boat/bar, and diving rocks make it seem like something from Disneyworld. All 264 rooms are decked out with a full complement of modern amenities, and most rooms have a view of the sea. Room rates are M$155 ($62) for a deluxe single and M$25 ($10) additional for a double. We particularly enjoyed the food at the Pantai Primula, especially the local and regional specialties. The hotel provides a free shuttle service to and from the airport, about 20 minutes north.

Two of our favorite hotels are located on the east coast, between Kuala Terengganu and Kuantan: the **Rantau Abang Visitor Centre** (tel. 09/841-533), and five miles south, the **Tanjong Jara Beach Hotel** (tel. 09/841-801). It's possible to write about them together, because both are constructed in a similar manner and operated by the same company. What differentiates these two lodgings from nearly anything else in the country is that they incorporate traditional Malaysian motifs and materials to such superb effect that both were recipients of international awards for architectural excellence. Not only are the buildings so tastefully designed, but the landscaping superbly enhances the entire complex. The rooms are built with locally grown hardwoods and are graciously large, all with balconies. Most of the guest facilities are organized as individual chalets or bungalows at the Rantau Abang, the lodging closest to the beach where the leatherback turtles lay their eggs. Each chalet is equipped with a hot-water shower and fan, and can accommodate up to 4 people. The cost for a chalet is M$100 ($40) from June to August (turtle season) and M$65 ($26) from September to May.

The rooms at the slightly more sophisticated Tanjong Jara are built in clusters in small wooden pavilions; they differ from the Rantau Abang's in size (they're larger) and have the option of air conditioning. The upper-floor rooms command the best views. Deluxe air-conditioned rooms run M$130 ($52), with lower rates during the monsoon season from October to February. The Tanjong Jara also has complete sports facilities, such as tennis and squash courts, a pool, a sauna, and windsurfing gear. We can't fail to mention the Tanjong Jara's exquisite dining room and bar, which to our tastes is like supping in paradise.

Our only reservation about these lodgings is that though they were built in the early 1980s, they are not especially well maintained. Everything is clean, but beginning to show signs of wear. Aside from that, these are two first-class establishments.

Nearby is the **Merantau Inn** (tel. 09/841-131), which is a 23-room motel-style lodging. Each single room or chalet has one double and one single bed for a cost of M$42 ($16.75); a double (two single beds) runs M$66 ($26.50). All rooms are fan cooled and are equipped with a shower.

For budget accommodations there is the remote **Cotton Island Bungalows** (no telephone), with a M$33 ($13.25) tariff per night. Although the facilities are primitive—shared bath, no fan, and only very simple food—the beach is superb (great for snorkeling and diving). The catch is that you have to take a fishing trawler to get there, as the lodging is on Pulau Kapas (Cotton Island); a round trip costs M$17 ($6.75). The trawler leaves from Marang, a fishing village, located about ten miles south of Kuala Terengganu.

Kuantan

The night we arrived at the **Ramada Beach Resort**, located on the north side of Kuantan (tel. 09/587-544) we didn't know what to expect: we'd heard about a freak flash flood, the first in many years, that ate the hotel's computers just a couple of weeks before the hotel's opening. As it turned out, we arrived the very day of the reopening, and the hotel manager, Frank Liepmann, joked that it was the first time he had ever opened the same hotel twice! We have no doubt that the Ramada will recover very nicely from its initial setback, for the hotel bears little resemblance to its American cousin (it's much more luxurious and attractive) and is blessed with maybe the finest single strip of beach on the entire east coast, which borders a huge lawn area. The landscaping and layout of the hotel were well planned, with swimming pools and dining rooms working in tandem to maintain each guest's optimum level of comfort. For joggers the Ramada has provided a 1.6-mile track with intentional minor obstacles to keep runs interesting, and a playground for children complete with swings and an indoor video room. The Japanese and Chinese restaurants are both very good, and beautifully appointed. We liked the Ramada very much, especially for M$120 ($48) double for the night.

Superficially similar in style to the Tanjong Jara, but definitely in the Western mode, is the **Hyatt Kuantan**, a short seven-minute ride from the town on Telok Chempedak beach (tel. 09/525-211). The rooms and public spaces are luxurious, the pool and courtyards are sensationally well landscaped, and the restaurants that we sampled were very good indeed. Other facilities of the hotel include tennis and squash courts, windsurfers, and the availability of snorkeling and sailing gear. The only minor drawback at the Hyatt is access to the beach (it's built somewhat above it), but that's but a minor concern; other than that, the Hyatt is an excellent option. Standard room rates are M$140 ($56) for single or double occupancy.

It's hard not to like the unpretentious **Cherating Holiday Villa** located 40 minutes north of Kuantan airport at Lot 1303, Mukim Sungai (tel. 09/243-4693), with its seemingly endless beach, casual atmosphere, and reasonable price. Even its 1987 motel-style layout and décor, with two-story guest quarters built in a horseshoe shape around an oversize suburban-looking pool (which is connected to the beach by, you guessed it, a huge backyard lawn!), doesn't detract from its basic appeal. And it has a staff that is wildly enthusiastic, assuring guests that a good time will be had by all. If you aren't yet convinced that this is the place for you, let's mention that they rent horses for M$25 ($10) per hour for that storybook ride on the beach. All of this can be yours (with air conditioning too) for M$90 ($36) single or M$100 ($40) double. Two-bedroom family apartments cost M$175 ($70). The staff will gladly pick you up at the airport in the hotel van.

Nearby in Cherating there is a series of **chalet villages** with bungalows on the beach for rents ranging from M$15 ($6) to M$50 ($20). There is a lovely long beach which, other than the Club Med just up the road about a mile or so, is relatively devoid of commercial interruption. The recommended eatery is the **Cherating Bay Restaurant.**

We found a delightful southern Indian restaurant in Kuantan called the **Parvathy Restoran,** at 75 Jalan Bukit Ubi (tel. 513-140). Among the items we sampled, the best was a slightly spicy masala dosai (a pancake stuffed with spiced vegetables); with a cold beer and appetizers, a dinner for two will cost about M$22 ($8.75). Open daily for lunch and dinner.

Recommended by locals as excellent restaurants were two seafood establishments, **Malaysian Sea Food** and **FPC,** and two Chinese places, **Chu San** and **Kum Leng.** Though we didn't try them, they were endorsed by cab drivers and hotel personnel, two sure signposts of excellence as far as we're concerned.

WHAT TO SEE AND DO ON THE EAST COAST: The main point about
the east coast of Malaysia is to spend time on the beach. Most of the urban life is generally uninteresting, with only an occasional opportunity to take in the compelling aspects of the local culture. As a natural setting there are a few genuine destinations of interest, especially during June to August when the giant leatherback turtles lay their eggs. There are also many opportunities to take jungle walks, explore nearby islands, and go snorkeling.

From Kota Bharu to Terengganu
The town of Kota Bharu isn't of tremendous interest for most tourists, but there are some interesting craft and cultural performances open to the public. The major venue for these performances is the **Kelantan Cultural Centre,** across the street from the Hotel Perdana, where every Wednesday and Saturday are shows highlighting local talent. Among the arts on display are *gasping* (top-spinning), *wayang kulit* (shadow puppets), *silat* (the local art of self-defense), and traditional dances and performance art. On Saturday afternoons there is a *wau-* (kite-) flying demonstration and competition with highly decorative Moon Kites on display. Check with the Tourist Information Office or your hotel for the current schedule.

Aside from a quick walk through the **Central Market** for a whiff of fresh produce, spices, and meat, and a short tour of the **Istana Jahar Museum** (a fine example of late-19th-century Islamic architecture), we suggest that you head toward the **Beach of Passionate Love.** Along the road, called Jalan PCB, is a good selection of shops producing local handcrafts. Among the shops that we found are **Ismail Hasan's brassware shop** (tel. 791-236), where you can find well-crafted brasswork, such as a betelnut set for M$36 ($14.50); **Tuan Haji Yaacob's silverware shop** (tel. 783-079), where they make finely spun filigree pins for about M$17.50 ($7) and wonderful bangles for approximately M$45 ($18); the **Handicraft Centre** (tel. 741-345), where we admired Kelantan kites and locally produced batik; and **Pantas** (tel. 22-687), for batik, brocade, and *songket* (woven cloth with gold and silver threads) at very good prices.

As you're cruising this route keep a lookout for trained monkeys harvesting coconuts. They climb the trees and toss the coconuts down to their handlers (if you've been to Thailand, this is the same routine as described in the section on Koh Samui). For snorkeling, consider a day trip (or longer) to tropical **Pulau Perhentian,** off the coast of Besut. It's a short excursion to the island, and once there, you'll discover very inexpensive bungalows for rent. Contact the District Office in Besut (tel. 09/972-328) for a current listing of available accommodations; expect to pay about M$35 ($14) per night for a chalet.

From Terengganu to Kuantan
Along the east coast are several islands with nary a resort or disco but miles of empty beach and lovely clear water for snorkeling.

One of the more serene interior spots is around the **Seyaku Waterfalls,** located about 35 miles southwest of Kuala Terengganu, a series of modest cascades that are nestled in a shaded rain forest. Locals visit for a picnic, but there are several simple guesthouses for those who want to explore the area. For information concerning lodging, contact Jabatan Perhutanan Daerah, Kuala Berang, Terengganu (tel. 09/811-259).

Naturalists from around the world arrive annually to watch the giant **leath-erback turtles** slowly crawl up the beach to bury their eggs in the sand. These magnificent reptiles, some thought to be hundreds of years old, are protected and studied by the Sea Turtle Research and Conservation Project, which counts the eggs and tries to track the young turtles as they emerge from their shells. The mature females are quite enormous, with an average length of 4½ feet, weighing some 750 pounds; each lays about 85 eggs per year. Most of the nesting activity takes place at night, and the **Turtle Information Centre** at Rantau Abang, about 37 miles south of Kuala Terengganu, conducts programs for those who want to learn about and observe the process. Several beaches in the area are run as private, profit-making hatcheries (most of the turtle eggs are harvested and sold in the local markets), but we liked the educational aspect of the centre; don't miss their excellent videotape about the nesting process. The hours of the centre vary, but generally you can count on its being open during the season, Wednesday through Monday from 8 a.m. to 4 p.m., with extra hours on Thursday and Saturday when they stay open until 10 p.m. During the off-season they are open five days from 8 a.m. to 4 p.m.; closed Friday and Tuesday.

4. MALACCA (MELAKA)

The city of Malacca is located on the western coast of peninsular Malaysia, almost halfway between Kuala Lumpur and Singapore in the state of Malacca. Malacca state covers 658 km² (257 square miles) and borders Negeri Sembilan to the north and, to the south, Johor. The state is divided into three districts, Alor Gajah, Melaka Tengah (Malacca Town), and Jasin, and is bordered on the west by the Straits of Malacca.

Malacca is a modern city with tangible ties to its long past; you can see them in the city's architecture, its streets and shops, and in the life alongside the Melaka River as it winds through the city to merge with the Straits of Malacca. In the center of the city the river takes on the air of a canal, and you think you've discov-ered the Venice of Malaysia: small boats moored to the banks beckon you to hop in and be transported back in time, restaurants along the quays offer relaxed and romantic dining, and it all seems like long ago. The Chinese temples, Indian an-tique shops (Malacca is Mecca for antiquers), Dutch churches, and Portuguese homes all attest to Malacca's having played host to various nations searching for a rich port to conquer, as we shall see.

HISTORY: Malacca was founded around A.D. 1400 by Prince Paremeswara, a Hindu prince from Palembang, Sumatra, who sought refuge from an invasion of his country in a fishing village he later decreed was to be called Melaka, from the melaka tree. In 1409 a Chinese trade ambassador, Yen Ho, paid a visit to the new-ly established port and showed interest in establishing trade. In exchange for pro-tection against the Siamese army and offering a lucrative source of commodities, the Chinese aided Malacca's growth as an important trading center in Southeast Asia.

Chinese, Indian, Siamese, and Arab traders frequented Malacca's port, mak-ing it a center of barter and newly created wealth. By the early 16th century Euro-pean traders tried to enter the Malacca trade, particularly for the valuable spice market; in 1509 the Portuguese navy arrived, determined to capture a portion of the market in what had become one of Asia's most lucrative trading centers. They were attacked and captured by locals, yet their admiral managed to escape and report back to his superiors in the nearby Portuguese outpost of Goa, in western India. This resulted in the invasion and conquest of Malacca in 1511 by Admiral Alfonso d'Alburquerque, giving Portugal control of the much sought-after spice trade in Malacca for the next 130 years. During this time the Portuguese built fortifications and introduced Catholicism to the populace at large.

In 1640 the Dutch attacked the Portuguese, and it took the better part of a year before they seized control in June 1641, while also establishing a trading port in Jakarta, Indonesia. They in turn introduced Protestantism, and controlled trade for the next 150 years until the British seized the port in 1795. The occupation changed hands several times until 1824, with the acceptance of the Treaty of London (the Anglo-Dutch Treaty), whereby the Dutch received British-occupied territories in Indonesia in exchange for England's securing Holland's Malayan colonies. For the next 133 years England enjoyed the profits of the spice trade and other valuable commodities, until August 31, 1957, when Malacca gained its independence.

Each foreign power left behind its mark, and today every street, house, and edifice in Malacca bears witness to its "melting pot" past, reflected in the city's mosques, temples, churches, and fortresses, as well as her inhabitants, who speak English, Arabic, Portuguese, Dutch, Malay, Chinese, Tamil, Hindi, and Urdu.

ORIENTATION: The center of town is located on the eastern bank of the **Melaka River,** and is bounded by three main streets: **Jalan Laksamana** (Jalan Quayside), **Jalan Temenggong,** and **Jalan Kota.** There is a bridge at the intersection of these thoroughfares where you'll find the **Malacca Tourist Centre.** Most of the historic sights in town are within eyesight, or a short walk away.

From the front door of the tourist centre you can see the Dutch-era pink-colored **Christ Church** and the **Stadthuys** across from each other, and behind the church, the post office.

Looking northeast you see **Bukit China,** a hill housing one of the largest Chinese cemeteries outside China, and once the home of a Chinese princess and her retinue of 500 ladies-in-waiting.

South from here you can see **Bukit St. John,** and beyond, the **Portuguese Settlements.**

If you cross the bridge in the opposite direction (heading northwest) you'll join **Jalan Hang Jebat,** the main artery of Old Malacca, with its Baba and Nyonya homes and Buddhist temples. This side of the river is mostly residential and historical, and it's here that you'll find the many Chinese and Indian antique shops that are unique to Malacca, as well as the old medicine shops with their patent remedies.

USEFUL INFORMATION: Head straight to the **Malacca Tourist Information Centre** at the bridge on Jalan Quayside (tel. 06/225-895), for help with anything from accommodations to getting the schedule and rates for boat trips up and down the river (a great way to see the historic and romantic side of the city). The centre is open from 8:45 a.m. to 5 p.m. weekdays, 8:30 a.m. to 1:30 p.m. on Saturday, and 9 a.m. to 12:30 p.m. on Sunday; call beforehand just to make sure they're open. While you're there, make sure you pick up a copy of *The Cultural Melting Pot,* written and published by Robert Tan Sin Nyen, an excellent guide to historic Malacca by the city's resident expert. We happened to be there when Robert was autographing copies, and we're pleased to report that we've included some of his (and now, our) favorite restaurant and shopping tips. Thank you, Robert.

There are many banks and some moneychangers in town, but the most conveniently located are **Bank Bumiputra Malaysia Bhd.,** located on Jalan Kota, and **Public Bank Berhad,** on Jalan Laksamana; hours for both are 10 a.m. to 3 p.m. weekdays and 9:30 to 11:30 a.m. on Saturday.

The **post office** is behind Christ Church on Jalan Laksamana (tel. 233-846); you can also send telegrams from here. Contact the tourist information office for current hours of operation. The **PTT** (tel. 239-492) is found next door to the post office. The local **telephone area code** is 06.

The **taxi station** is in Kampong Morten between Jalans Kilang and Hang (tel. 223-630). One caveat: Most of the taxis in town are not metered, making negotiation for each trip a must before you get under way. If the taxi has to come from the station, the rate is double; after 1 a.m. there is a 50% surcharge. Obviously, try to get a cruising cab. All of this said, cabs here are still a very good deal: you can rent one to take you all the way to Kuala Lumpur for M$20 ($8) per person.

The **Tourist Police** are just off Jalan Kota, behind the Tourist Information Centre (tel. 222-222); call them if you have a medical emergency. The **People's Pharmacy,** at 59 Jalan Bendahara (tel. 223-975), has a 24-hour line.

The **MAS** reservation office is at 238 Taman Melaka Jaya (tel. 235-722); the telephone number for general **airport information** is 224-637. The **Express Bus Terminal,** located on Jalan Kilang (tel. 224-470), is where you find buses to Johore Bahru and Singapore; the **Melaka Bus Terminal** (tel. 229-956) is the center for local bus routes.

GETTING THERE: Unfortunately there is no direct train service to Malacca, nor is there regular or reasonable air service from Kuala Lumpur. That said, it's still a snap to get to Malacca, either from Kuala Lumpur or Singapore.

The easiest and quickest way to traverse the 148 km (92 miles) to Malacca from Kuala Lumpur and points north is to drive the brand-new, and sinfully smooth, **North-South Highway.** We did it in five extremely leisurely hours, but it can be accomplished in about half the time. For M$70 ($28) you can hire your own taxi to take you the distance!

There is an **Express Bus** (tel. 06/222-503) between the two cities that costs a mere M$7.50 ($3). Express buses connect Malacca to nearly every other major Malaysian metropolis: Butterworth and Ipoh to the north, Kota Bahru and Kuantan to the east, and Johore Bahru and Singapore to the south. The most expensive bus (from Kota Bahru) is just M$30 ($12), thus making a visit to Malacca painless and inviting.

There is **ferry** and **plane** service between Malacca and Sumatra, Indonesia. The ferry crosses the Straits of Malacca thrice weekly during a four-hour ride: the current schedule includes sailings on Tuesday, Thursday, and Saturday; tickets may be purchased from **Madai Shipping,** at 320 Jalan Kilang (tel. 06/240-671). There is a once-a-week flight that is M$150 ($60) one way; we say skip it and make the drive. The North-South Hwy. is the Malaysian equivalent of Rte. 66 and, after all, does adventure traveling get any better than cruising for kicks on Rte. 66?

GETTING AROUND: Before discussing the mechanized modes of transportation, we heartily suggest taking to Malacca's attractive lanes on foot. The scale of the town is such that you can walk nearly anywhere you might want to go. This is especially true in the old Chinese quarter of the city, where you'll want to savor the flavor of the town.

The fun way to see Old Malacca is by **riverboat** (tel. 236-538). The 45-minute trip passes upriver through the major areas of historical interest, and the cost is just M$5 ($2). There is also a 90-minute trip down the coast to the old Portuguese Settlement; the cost is M$10 ($4). Both boats leave four times daily—at 10 a.m., noon, 2 p.m., and 4:30 p.m.—and you catch them right behind the Tourist Information Centre on Jalan Quayside.

Taxis are the most comfortable and convenient way to get around the city; expect to pay about M$3 ($1.25) per person for a drive across town. The other alternative is a **trishaw** which, if you're not in a hurry, is a lovely mode of transportation; it's a good idea to hire a trishaw at least a short distance from your hotel, especially for those who stay at the large, luxury inns, as we've heard about price-gouging by unscrupulous drivers.

ACCOMMODATIONS: As with the rest of Malaysia, Malacca has experienced a recent wave of hotel building, perhaps adding more rooms than the market justifies. This situation can only benefit the tourist, so don't be shy about asking for a "special" or promotional price. A typical example that we encountered was at one of the new high-rise hotels that listed the cost of a deluxe room for M$160 ($64), but we were offered that same room for 50% of the price.

Most of the town's inns are located in not very interesting neighborhoods to the east of the city center, within a walk (or a quick trishaw ride) of the old city and most of the tourist sights.

First-Class Accommodations

The 24-story **Ramada Renaissance Hotel,** on Jalan Bendahara (tel. 06/248-888), is the most expensive and luxurious hotel in town. The first thing you notice when you arrive is the Famosa Lounge to your right, with its tropical décor and Filipino cover band ready to soothe you after a long day of sightseeing. The rooms are attractive and roomy (many have fine town views), the service attentive, and the atmosphere relaxed. As with most hotels in this category, one finds the usual list of endless amenities, including a swimming pool and numerous restaurants. A deluxe double here lists for M$180 ($72); singles run M$160 ($64), although we'd suggest inquiring about promotional discount rates.

Along the same lines of the Ramada is the 181-room **City Bayview Hotel,** on Jalan Bendahara (tel. 06/239-888). The hotel opened in 1987, and it still sparkled like new when we visited recently. The clean, salmon-colored rooms command fine views of Malacca and the Bayview offers all the modern conveniences one expects at the best hotels. All this and a discount too: the posted room rate is M$160 ($64) for a double, but they often run special promotions which can bring the price down substantially.

The **Merlin Melaka** (not part of the chain), on Jalan Munshi Abdullah (tel. 06/240-777), has views their brochure describes as follows: "every day you'll see 500 ships channeling their way to East and West." The Merlin is a great value, with more recreational and culinary facilities than the other hotels and an attractive tariff of M$90 ($36) for a deluxe double (our recommendation here, as the standard rooms have no fridge or mini-bar). Their two swimming pools and pool tables, their excellent Chinese restaurant (the Golden Dragon), Camelot Disco, and (yes!) bowling alleys, all, well, bowled us over.

Moderate and Budget Accommodations

In the lower budget range there are two hotels we can recommend. The **Palace Hotel,** down the street from the Merlin at 201 Jalan Munshi Abdullah (tel. 06/225-355), offers small, comfortable doubles for M$60 ($24) without television, M$75 ($30) with. The **Hotel Wisma,** just down the street from the Palace at no. 114A (tel. 06/228-311), has plain-Jane doubles for M$35 ($14). We spoke with the manager, who told us that Chinese families visiting relatives were his regular clientele. Both hotels have air conditioning, but no recreational facilities or other amenities.

DINING: We rank Malacca just after Penang for its delicious cuisine. Not only can you find excellent hawker fare, but Malacca offers Nonya restaurants serving their unique Malaccan blend of Chinese and Malay recipes, a special treat for those who savor esoteric styles of Chinese food. There are several small restaurants throughout the city serving Indian and Malay meals where you can go during the daytime hours.

After 4 p.m., the best places to go are outdoors and generally along the banks of the Melaka River. Here, at **Jalans Bandar Hilir** and **Taman** you'll find food stalls, steamboat restaurants, and the water's edge all vying for your attention. This area is locally known as "The Glutton's Corner"; we did our bit to justify the name and tried between seven and a dozen of the various stalls. The steamboat-style stall called **Prince Satay Chelop,** at 16 Jalan Bandar Hilir (no telephone), was our favorite, in no small part due to the personality of its owner, Winnie Lim, and her family. Winnie would appear from the kitchen periodically to inform us that the sauce/broth she was cooking our dinner in was made from a secret recipe (16 ingredients!) her grandmother brought over from mainland China. Or that there wasn't any chicken that night due to an abundance of ugly chickens. Well, with quality commentary like that, how can you fail to find everything delicious and the ambience convivial? Two hungry travelers can gorge themselves here for about $5 and sit outside basking in the breeze off the water. Rest assured that if you're not in the mood for steamboat, that you'll find a myriad of other, equally tempting tastes at the Glutton's Corner hawker stall market. Don't miss it.

As for restaurants, you can have a holiday here sampling the city's supply of Malay, Chinese, Indian, Portuguese, American, and Japanese restaurants. Here are some of the best:

For Malay meals try the **Restoran Seleranika,** on Jalan Kota (tel. 234-679), or the **Mini Restaurant,** on Jalan Taman (tel. 229-413); they're both inexpensive and very good.

If you're in the mood for Chinese, get yourself to the **Hi Keng Restaurant,** at 112 Taman Melaka Jaya (tel. 233-292), for low-priced and excellent Cantonese food, or to **Lim Tian Puan,** 251 Jalan Tun Sri Lanang (tel. 222-727), for a taste of the real thing: spicy, pungent versions of what you don't get at home, at a fraction of the price.

Since Malacca is home for the Nonyas and Babas (the Malaccan ethnic mix of Malay and Chinese dating from the earliest Chinese settlements in the area) only here can you sample their cuisine, an exquisite blend of Chinese and Malay customs and tastes with a strong use of shrimp paste, curry, and other strong spices. There are two very good places to try: **Nyonya Makko Restaurant,** at 123 Taman Melaka Jaya (tel. 240-737), and **Ole Sayang Restaurant,** up the street at no. 192 (tel. 231-966).

Two well-known and much frequented Portuguese places are the **Restoran De Lisbon** (tel. 248-067) and the **Restoran De Portugis** (tel. 243-156), both located in the main square at the Portuguese Settlement to the south of the main town (you'll have to take a taxi). Two can dine at these places for a bit more (due to its tourist status), roughly M$50 ($20).

There's a Japanese restaurant in town that was recommended to us by our MAS stewardess: **Kiraku,** part of the Ayer Keroh Country Resort (tel. 323-600).

Finally, if like us you've become dependent on Indian banana-leaf food, rest easy; the **Banana Leaf Restaurant,** on Jalan Munshi Abdullah (no phone), the **Sri Lakshmi Villas Restaurant,** at 2 Jalan Bendahara (tel. 224-926), and its next-door neighbor, the **Sri Krishna Bhavan Restaurant** (tel. 229-206), await your Madras and Bangalore cravings. The Banana Leaf is the least expensive and most "local"; the two Sri's are good, so choose by judging that day's menu and the décor!

WHAT TO SEE AND DO: Malacca has a ripe mercantile, religious, and military history, remainders of which pepper the city. From a Portuguese Settlement to Chinese apothecaries, Malay mosques to Indian moneychangers, Malacca makes for fascinating exploration with its myriad monasteries, forts, shops, and houses all densely concentrated into old neighborhoods, which haven't changed for generations. Other than a visit to the Portuguese Settlement, all of the most interesting places to visit are within fairly easy walking of each other, and the following listings are arranged as a guided walking tour.

As a supplement to walking Malacca's streets, we again make a pitch for the boat tour of the town (see "Getting Around" for details).

Our walking tour begins at the bridge next to the Tourist Information Centre, on the so-called Dutch Square, south of the Melaka River in the old administrative zone.

Christ Church

This distinctive, pink structure is the oldest functioning Protestant (originally Dutch Reform, now Anglican) church in Malaysia, and an excellent example of traditional Dutch architecture. Completed in 1753, Christ Church has handmade pews, a glazed tile frieze of the Last Supper, and several fine construction details, including 16 beams that support the ceiling (each is a single log, with no joints). Masses are given in English, Mandarin, and Tamil (check the current schedule on the board outside the church).

The Stadthuys Building (Malacca Historical Museum)

Today the salmon-colored Stadthuys, located in the Dutch Square just up from the tourist information kiosk, houses a historical museum and is admired chiefly for its clean Dutch design, masonry, and woodworking, reflected in the heavy doors, wrought-iron hardware, and its fine hand-carved ceiling. It is said to have been completed in 1650 and was home to the Dutch governors and their aides during the Dutch colonization of Malacca. The museum has been closed since 1986 for renovation, but is expected to reopen in 1989. Its collection includes many objects from the colonial period as well as items illustrating aspects of Chinese, Indian, and Malay cultural styles and tastes from the 15th to the 19th century.

Porta de Santiago (La Famosa) and St. Paul's Church

If you proceed west, toward the straits, along Jalan Kota, you'll come to a ruined gateway at the foot of St. Paul's Hill that is the last testament to the 16th-century Portuguese fortification known as La Famosa. This fragment of the once-mighty laterite structure protected the Portuguese hold on Malacca's port; it was built by Alfonso de Alburquerque, the Portuguese conquerer of Malacca, in 1512. The Dutch rebuilt the gateway after their successful attack against the Portuguese in the 17th century (thus the "Anno 1670" above the gate and the reference to the Dutch East India Company, referred to as VOC, the Dutch initials), and the fortress itself was largely pulled down by the British during the early years of the 19th century. What remains is attributed to the preservation efforts of Stamford Raffles, of Singapore fame.

You'll have to climb to the top of the hill, via a set of stairs, to reach the remaining shell of St. Paul's Church. Founded in 1521 by the Portuguese as Duarte Coelho, the structure was completed in 1590 by the Jesuits; St. Paul's was until 1753 a leading Catholic house of prayer and was given its name by the Dutch. St. Francis Xavier first preached here in 1545, using it as his base to introduce Christianity to Indonesia, the Philippines, Japan, and China over the course of just seven years, and he was buried near the church (his body was later moved to Goa). After the Dutch built the Christ Church down in the town, St. Paul's fell into disuse and was largely abandoned by the Dutch, other than to bury their dead in the nearby cemetery. What we love about the church is its site, high on a hill overlooking the port and old Malacca, with great views of the city; we also enjoy reading the giant old tombstones, with inscriptions from the 11th century!

Cheng Hoon Teng (Green Cloud Temple)

The remainder of the sights are located north of the river, in what is referred to as Old Malacca or Chinatown. To reach there from atop St. Paul's Hill, take the stairs leading back into town (not the one leading back down to the Porta de Santiago) and cross the bridge adjacent to the Tourist Information Centre in the Dutch Square. Although we describe several sights of interest, don't limit yourself to those few destinations, instead wander aimlessly through Old Malacca's lanes. You're bound to discover treasures at nearly every turn.

If you turn right after coming off the bridge and make a left on Jalan Tukang Emas (which becomes Jalan To Kong), continuing up 2½ blocks, you'll find yourself at Cheng Hoon Teng Temple, founded in 1645 and the oldest functioning Chinese temple in Malaysia. All the materials and labor to construct this complex were imported from southern China, and though the temple was established in 1645, it wasn't until the early part of the 19th century that it was completed. This gorgeous temple, easily our favorite Chinese shrine in Malaysia, has excellent carved 18th-century wood and lacquerwork depicting the life of Buddha, spread across its three altars. Here the three doctrinal systems of Taoism, Confucianism, and Buddhism meld together into *San E Chiao,* a Chinese system of ethics, morality, and religion derived from the above-named disciplines. Cheng Hoon Teng Temple is the ongoing repository for the spiritual, intellectual, and cultural heritage of Chinese Malacca, as well as a must-see on your trip.

Kampong Keling Mosque

If you double-back on Jalan To Kong, you'll come to the Mosque of Kampong Keling, on Jalan Tukang Emas (an extension of Jalan To Kong). This mosque was completed in 1868, and it's a masterful mix of Western and Eastern influences and a perfect example of Malacca's cultural synthesis. A hand-carved pulpit that reveals both Indian and Chinese influence, Corinthian pillars in the main prayer hall and veranda, Portuguese and English glazed tiles on the walls of the main hall, and a Victorian chandelier, all housed in an Islamic religious building designed in the Sumatran style—no doubt about it, this is an interesting place. The Keling also boasts a three-tiered roof that is pyramidal in shape, with a carved-wood ceiling underneath it that perfectly caps this Islamic house of prayer. Since this is a mosque, take note that you must remove your shoes before entering, and women should cover their heads and wear a dress.

Sri Poyyatha Vinayagar Moorthi

If you continue in the same direction you'll arrive at the Temple of Sri Poyyatha Vinayagar Moorthi. This Hindu temple was constructed in the late 18th century to honor Vinayagar, the deity possessed of a human body (with four hands) with an elephant's head, and a rat forever at his feet. There is a superb black stone statue of him (Malaysians relate black stone with good fortune) and several side altars.

The Baba and Nyonya Heritage Museum

Our last stop on this brief walking tour is to the Baba and Nyonya Heritage Museum, located at 52 Jalan Tun Tan Cheng Lock (tel. 222-065), two blocks west of the previous three stops. The origin of those who are known as Baba (male) and Nonya (female) is that they are the descendants of the first Chinese South Sea traders who, in the 1400s, intermarried with the indigenous Malay. Over the centuries they have managed to maintain their unique Chinese/Malay society with its own distinct customs. We delighted in the recreation of a typical Straits-Chinese ("Peranakan" as they are also called) home in the Kuala Lumpur Museum, but to tour the real thing is a much better treat; these homes are part of a private museum owned and operated by the Peranakan themselves. From front to back the house is about 150 feet long, replete with a bridal chamber, two function halls, a veranda, and an exquisite display of all matters Peranakan.

The Baba and Nyonya Heritage Museum is open from 10 a.m. to 12:30 p.m. and 2 to 4:30 p.m. weekdays. There is a M$7 ($2.75) admission charge, worth every sen.

The Portuguese Settlement

This settlement, in Jalan Ujong Pasir (about a 15-minute taxi ride south of Malacca; you can also take a boat), was created in the late 1920s by two Jesuit priests, one Portuguese, the other French, to immortalize the Portuguese involvement in Malacca; and within ten years Eurasian descendants of the original settlers started to move in to preserve their heritage by actually living it. When the Treaty of London was signed in 1824, the Dutch nationals who chose not to relocate in Batavia (today's Jakarta, Indonesia) stayed in Malacca, converted to Catholicism, and married the Eurasians of Portuguese descent. All this mixing of bloodlines also yielded a dialect of its own, still spoken in this community today —Cristão (pronounced "chris-tang"), a mixture of Portuguese, Dutch, Chinese, and Iberian! There isn't really much to see here other than a few buildings (and two decent Portuguese restaurant, which we noted in the "Dining" section), but if you have the time, it's interesting to see yet another of Malacca's confluence of cultures.

SHOPPING: When in Florence, buy leather. If it's perfume, then go to Paris. But if it's colonial Dutch, English, and Chinese antiques you seek, look no further than Malacca, for here all is to be found.

Jalan Hang Jebat, commonly known as Jonker Street, is the street that consists of practically nothing but antique shops. Victorian brass beds, Chinese porcelain, 18th-century Japanese art, mother-of-pearl, and English colonial furniture—you name it and you can find it here, ranging from bargain to expensive. Of all the shops we saw, three stood out as being well-stocked, -run, and -priced.

Keris Woodworks at 25 Jonker St. (tel. 236-113), specializes in Straits Chinese ware, antique porcelain, and furniture (with some high-quality reproductions) of various styles. Their inventory is impressive and the quality appears to be on a very high level.

The **Royal Antiques House,** farther up the street at no. 86 (tel. 220-097), has a business card that folds out like a screen, with a sketch of *all* the Chinese dynasties on the inside. They specialize in pottery arts from Asia, with magnificent bronze and porcelain pieces scattered among the ceramics and old coins. Mr. Chee runs the place and is happy to promote his wares as the finest available.

The **Kowloon Antique Shop,** at 38 Jonker St. (tel. 223-433), carries only Chinese antiques, ranging from furniture to porcelain to jewelry. Everything here is gorgeous: we wanted to make him an offer for the entire store!

Just across the street is an exquisite small Chinese temple, **Hikkien Huay Kuan,** with wonderful hand-carved and -painted doors and windows looking out on the street.

There are three other streets that boast specialized services and shops. On **Jalan Tukang Besi** you'll find blacksmiths and metalworkers; on **Jalan Hang Kasturi** you can watch tinsmiths and woodworkers create everything from portable altars to Latex bins to bathtubs; and on **Jalan To Kong** you'll find dozens of religious paraphernalia shops, as well as old Chinese apothecary/medicine shops.

Again, we suggest walking as the best means of transportation, as the entire antique/temple/shop area is about ten square blocks, and makes for an easy and fascinating walk. Go before dusk so you can end your shopping day by having a drink while you watch the sunset; this is when the colors of Malacca really shine.

CHAPTER XIV

EXPLORING BORNEO: SARAWAK AND SABAH

□ □ □

1. SARAWAK
2. SABAH

Most visitors to Malaysia, and many of the country's citizens, tend to forget about the two distant states of Sarawak and Sabah, known as East Malaysia. Separated from the peninsula by 500 miles of the South China Sea, Sarawak and Sabah occupy the northern coast of Borneo with a brief punctuation by Brunei, the oil-rich sultanate, and border the Indonesian territory of Kalimantan to the south. Though few bother to make the long journey—a two-hour flight from Kuala Lumpur, via Singapore—we found this region the most fascinating in the entire country. When we travel to Malaysia, this is the area that we most look forward to visiting.

In case Borneo hasn't figured in your travel imagination thus far, try to picture a land of 150-million-year-old tropical rain forests that predate the Ice Age, a breeding ground for exotic animals—including the Orang Utan ("Man of the Forest," but also known as "the Wild Man of Borneo"), the region's renowned primate—and a place where tribal people still forage in the dense jungle for food and live communally in delicately constructed longhouses. Other than in the sparsely settled towns, the whole territory is as wild as any on earth. This makes Borneo an area with vast potential for adventure travel. You can visit the world's largest cave, navigate an underground river, shoot the rapids on little-explored waterways, climb the highest peak in Southeast Asia, or just take a casual stroll through the jungle, all within a few hours of the area's two main cities, Kuching and Kota Kinabalu. Borneo also offers the traditional diversions for pleasure seekers: fine beaches, a few luxury hotels, and interesting dining and shopping venues.

If you plan on spending time on the beach, remember that there is a monsoon (rainy season) from November to March.

There are many fine books about Sarawak and Sabah (see "Recommended

Reading" in Chapter XI), most of which were written during the British rule; however, in 1988 an extraordinary book appeared, written by Eric Hansen and entitled **Stranger in the Forest** (Boston: Houghton Mifflin Co., 1988). A paperback edition is available as well from Penguin Books. This is a contemporary account of an American who walked across Borneo and made contact with the island's most remote jungle tribes. If you want to get excited about your visit to East Malaysia, we know no better way than to pick up a copy of this exceptional account.

1. SARAWAK

Sarawak, Malaysia's largest state, occupies 46,000 square miles on the northwest coast of Borneo, covering over 700 km (440 miles) of coastline, and is inhabited by an ethnically diverse population of Malay, Chinese, Iban, Bidayuh, Melanau, Kayan, and Kenyah people, comprising a total of less than 1.4 million people. The main city and capital, Kuching, is set on the banks of the Sarawak River, with its many forts and administrative buildings dating from the 19th century, during the reign of the so-called White Rajas. The vast majority of Sarawak, over three-quarters of the land mass, is tropical rain forest, home to most of the tribal people and a rich blend of exotic flora and fauna. The coastal waters, especially near Brunei, are scattered with oil derricks, pointing the way to Sarawak's future as a petroleum power.

We suggest making the capital your base of operations for forays into wildly exotic, unspoiled Sarawak, where you can visit the Niah Caves, home to earliest man; Gunung Mulu National Park, with the world's largest cave; Dayak and Iban settlements, the tiny villages of local tribesmen, who live as they have for centuries; the white-water rapids of the Skrang River; and the many coastal fishing and resort towns easily reached by bus and ferry.

Before setting off to visit Sarawak's tribal villages, make sure to stop by the Sarawak Museum in Kuching, one of the most interesting ethnographic collections in Southeast Asia. The museum has an extensive collection of ancient Borneo artifacts, including masks, early weapons and jewelry, costumes, and a complete reconstruction of a longhouse, the 30 to 40 family structures housing a "village under one roof."

HISTORY: Sarawak's recorded history seems to begin in the 16th century when the area was referred to as Cerava, and was visited by pirates and traders from China and surrounding countries. It wasn't until the late 1830s that Sarawak achieved its greatest historical notoriety, that being the beginning of the 100-year reign of the Brooke family, known as the White Raj. Prior to that time the area of Sarawak (the original name of Kuching) was under the control of Brunei, whose foremost nemeses were the Bidayuh and Iban people as well as the ethnic Malays. James Brooke, an English officer in the East India Company, arrived on Borneo in 1839 and within two years quelled a Bidayuh rebellion; as an expression of gratitude (and compensation) from the Sultan of Brunei, Brooke was established as the Raja of Sarawak and given control of the territory. Brooke completed the transfer of influence (as well as the capital) from the Malay-dominated town of Lidah Tanah to Sarawak. It was Charles Brooke, the second in the family line, who officially changed the name of the town to Kuching, a name thought to have been derived from the Sungei Kuching (Cat River). One Brooke was followed by another, each ruling with considerable success. The chief accomplishments were establishing a formal government for the territory, building a network of fortifications to defend the area from pirates and raiding tribal groups, and expanding commerce and the area's economy; in short, it was during the reign of the White Raj that Sarawak emerged into the modern era. One of the major changes that occurred during the rule of the White Raj was the invasion of Christian mission-

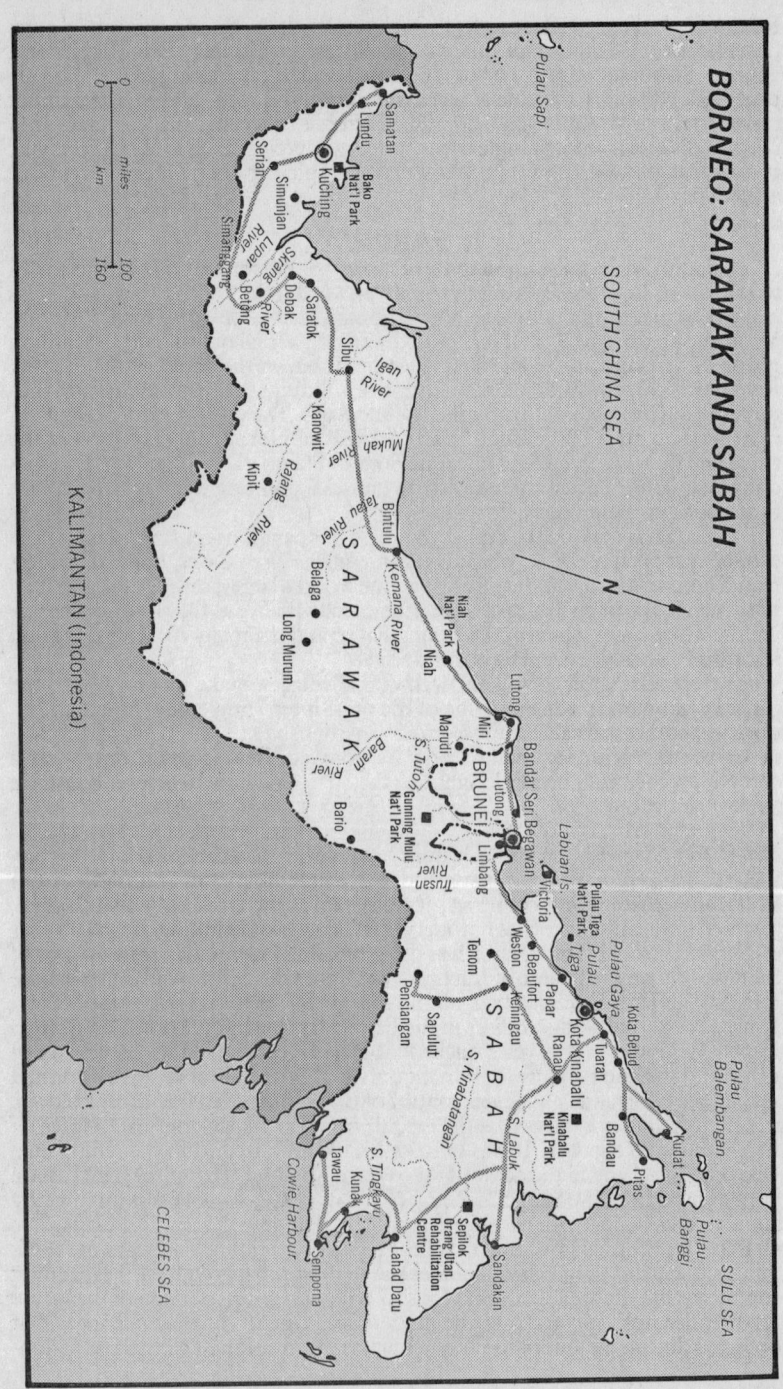

ary troops into Sarawak's interior to convert native animist headhunters into Christians. They were at least partially successful: Sarawak has few, if any, native headhunters.

The last of the so-called White Rajas, Vyner Brooke, ruled until 1941 when the Japanese invaded and took control of Sarawak. Brooke returned to power after the war, under the auspices of the Australian Military Administration, and in 1946 placed Sarawak under the aegis of the British, bringing the Brooke family rule to its conclusion.

After several near misses at full independence in the late 1950s, Sarawak allied itself with Malaya and Sabah in 1963 to form the Federation of Malaysia.

ORIENTATION: Kuching is small and compact, an elegantly landscaped city of some 150,000 inhabitants, divided by the River Sarawak and located in the far-western corner of the state. The city is clean, well kept, and quite pleasant, even as its skyline is edging upward into modernity. There are still many fine examples of 19th-century architecture dating from the early Brooke era; among these, and most intriguing, is the glorious Istana (Palace) built in 1870 by Charles Brooke, second of Sarawak's dynastic White Rajas.

Kuching International Airport is likely to be your point of entry to Sarawak; it's a 15-minute drive from there to central Kuching. Most of tourist Kuching is concentrated in a five-square-block area from the river and can be navigated by foot.

In the southern section of town, on **Jalan Tunku Abdul Rahman** (the waterfront street) are the first-class hotels, most of the airlines, and some good restaurants. Nearby is the **Sarawak Tourist Association,** also on Jalan Tunku Abdul Rahman (tel. 82/20-620), next to the Holiday Inn complex, and at their new office (same telephone) on Main Bazaar Road in a renovated shipping building; the **TDC** office is on Jalan Song Thian Cheok, on the second floor of the A.I.A. building (tel. 82/56-775), near the intersection with Jalan Pandungan, just one block from the river.

On the northern end are the historical sights, including the Brooke Memorial, the Clock Tower, and the departure point for many river cruises; the main thoroughfares are **Leboh Carpenter, Leboh India,** and running perpendicular to the river, **Jalan Tun Haji Openg,** leading to the Sarawak Museum.

Nearly all the most important sights are located on the "town" or west side; the two important exceptions are the Istana (closed to the public) and Kuching's most significant stronghold, **Fort Margherita.**

The other important town in Sarawak for tourists is **Miri,** located 842 km (522 miles) from Kuching in the northeastern section of the state, near the border with Brunei. Miri is not only a major petroleum center, but is also the jumping-off point for visits to the Niah and Mulu caves, as well as many jungle walks and river trips.

USEFUL INFORMATION: Visitors bound for Sarawak are required to carry a valid passport as they must go through Immigration and Customs inspection procedures, even if they have done so upon entering another Malaysian city. Nearly all travelers from English-speaking countries, including the U.S., the Commonwealth, and British-protected citizens, aren't required to apply for a visa. There is an **Honorary British Representative** (tel. 23-616) as well an office of the **British Council** (tel. 56-044), located on the first floor of the Ang Cheng Ho Building on Jalan Tunku Abdul Rahman. The nearest American, Australian, and Canadian representatives are in Kuala Lumpur.

No special vaccinations are required for entry to Sarawak, except for those coming from yellow-fever-infected areas. The government recommends that people planning to spend time in the jungle take antimalarial pills as a precaution (see "Health and Vaccinations," in "The ABCs of Malaysia" in Chapter XI).

There are branches of the **TDC** as well as the **Sarawak Tourist Association** in Kuching (see "Orientation" for details); in addition, there is a Sarawak Tourist Association stand at the airport (tel. 82/456-266). Both organizations publish an enormous amount of literature about Sarawak, including several brochures that are very useful; among them is the excellent booklet, "Sarawak: The Window to Nature's Treasure," as well as some fine maps and descriptions of the national parks. There is an office of the Sarawak Tourist Association in Miri (tel. 85/32-804).

The **telephone area code** for Kuching is 82; Miri's code is 85.

The **Kuching General Post Office** is located on the corner of Leboh Carpenter and Jalan Tun Haji Openg (tel. 21-311).

The telephone number for **Kuching General Hospital** is 57-555; other medical services, such as dentistry, can be found by calling the local TDC office (tel. 56-775) or inquiring of your concierge.

If there is an **emergency,** dial 999. Otherwise the **police** can be reached by calling 21-222.

There are three local **English-language newspapers,** the *Sarawak Tribune,* the *Borneo Post,* and the *People's Mirror,* in addition to Malay and Chinese-language editions. All first-class hotels carry the *International Herald Tribune* and *USA Today* as well. There is a small but excellent bookstall in the shopping arcade (no. 3) at the Holiday Inn called **Mohamed Yahia & Sons** (tel. 54-282); they specialize in books about Borneo.

Kuching has a large number of **banks,** especially concentrated around the first-class hotels; the Standard Charter Bank, for example, is located across the street from the Holiday Inn in the Wisma Bukit Mata Kuching.

GETTING THERE: There are international flights to both Kuching and Miri, though the majority of planes land at the former, with far fewer extensions to the latter. **Malaysian Airline System (MAS)** has a sales office at Lot 215, Cong Thian Cheok Road (tel. 246-622), and at the airport (tel. 454-255, ext. 218). MAS flies several times daily between KL, Kuching, and Miri, in addition to flying other inter-Sarawak and Sabah routes to Bintulu, Sibu, Kapit, Kota Kinabalu, Kudat, and Sandakan, among others. Expect to pay M$231 ($92.50) for a one-way ticket from KL to Kuching, M$136 ($54.50) from Kuching to Miri. MAS also maintains an office in Miri, at Lot 239, Beautiful Jade Center on the New Town Extension (tel. 85/34-407).

Other airlines that have offices in Kuching are: **Royal Brunei Airlines** (tel. 21-082), **Singapore Airlines** (tel. 20-266), **British Airways** (tel. 20-977), and **KLM Royal Dutch Airlines** (tel. 35-413).

If you're traveling from Kuantan, on Malaysia's east coast, or from Singapore, there is a weekly **cruise ferry** that stops in Kuching and Kota Kinabalu (Sabah). The ferry departs on Saturday from Kuantan and takes about 36 hours to reach Kuching. Depending on size and location, cabin-class fares range from $40 to $120; deluxe class, from $55 to $172; and suites, from $80 to $240. We haven't taken this trip, but have heard that the schedule can change during rough weather; otherwise it sounds like an ideal way to cozy up to a Conrad novel while sailing toward Borneo. For more information, contact the TDC in Kuantan, Singapore, Kuching, or Kota Kinabalu.

GETTING AROUND: Taxis are available in Kuching, Miri, and other main towns, and comfortable tour coaches operate in Kuching, as do **express boat services** linking the towns. Contact the TDC or the Sarawak Tourist Association for the current schedule of buses.

For those who intend to explore inland (remote) Sarawak, the principal mode of travel often involves the area's complex network of navigable waterways, the details of which can be gleaned from your hotel, local travel agency, or the sailing schedule listed in the *Borneo Post*. MAS flies regularly between major cities (daily between Kuching and Miri) and several rural areas, while smaller towns are served by Fokker Friendship, Twin Otter, and Britten Norman Islander charter aircraft.

Sarawak's interior regions are accessible only on an infrequent (and often unpredictable) basis by air. **Hornbill Skyways,** at 440 Jalan Kubber in Kuching (tel. 411-737), can arrange everything from an aerial tour of the jungle to a quick flight to an exotic outpost; they have a hangar in North Pan at the Kuching Airport. **Sea Helicopters,** located on Pejabat Hangar Lapangan Terbang in Kuching (tel. 81-107), has the choppers.

ACCOMMODATIONS: Kuching has fewer hotel options than Malaysia's other major cities. Not for long. When we last visited, a brand-new Hilton had just gone into operation and some of the other top hotels were expanding or being renovated. By the time you arrive in Kuching the selection will be greater than what we found.

First-Class Accommodations

The plushest accommodations in town are to be found at the recently built **Kuching Hilton,** on Jalan Tunku Abdul Rahman (tel. 82/248-200). All 318 pastel-colored rooms and suites are decorated and equipped with all the amenities you'd expect of a deluxe luxury hotel: air conditioning, mini-bar, television with in-house video and international 24-hour news Telex channel, direct-dial telephone, and the ubiquitous taped music channels. Their Executive Business Centre offers secretarial, Telex, fax and copying services; computers; a reference library; and access to an international courier service. Not only is the facility first-rate, but the level of service is very high. The rates are M$170 ($68) for a standard single and M$190 ($76) for a double; the deluxe versions go for M$20 ($8) more each.

The **Holiday Inn,** Kuching's first international-style hotel, is also on Jalan Tunku Abdul Rahman (tel. 82/423-111). Its rooms have the same basic amenities as the Hilton (though at a lower pitch), with the addition of the Rajang Bar, their swinging nightspot that features an ever-present Filipino cover band. The Holiday Inn has a breakfast café (the Orchid Garden) on the main floor and the Meisan Szechuan, a very fine Chinese restaurant, upstairs. There's also an in-house club, the Aquarius Disco, which rocks from 9 p.m. to 2 a.m. weekdays, and to 3 a.m. weekends. The room rates here are M$135 ($54) for a standard single, M$155 ($62) for a double, with the deluxe versions of each going for an additional M$20 ($8).

There is also the **Holiday Inn at Damai Beach,** situated on Teluk Bandung Beach (tel. 82/411-777), which is linked to Kuching by ferry, a half hour and 12 miles outside the city. The hotel is a top-notch resort, with tennis courts, water sports, and a golf course that was under construction when we were there. Joggers will be overjoyed to know that an extensive jogging track has been designed to take them from the beach up through the rain forest at Mount Santubong and back, with exercise stations located at appropriate intervals along the way. Rooms here, half of which face the South China Sea, cost about 15% more than in the city, but rates seem to be subject to fluctuation varying with demand and season; call before you arrive to confirm the rate.

Moderately Priced and Budget Accommodations

The **Ferritel,** located on Kuching Bypass (tel. 82/484-799), is just outside town (about a ten-minute ride by taxi). Its 54 chalet and terrace rooms have the regular amenities, plus sports facilities including two squash courts and a jogging track. The chalets (our pick here) are M$80 ($32) for a double, while the terrace rooms are M$60 ($24) for a triple. They also have a five-bed room that rents for

M$90 ($36), if you're traveling in a group. Though it's not terribly convenient, the Ferritel offers very good value.

Back in town is the **Liwah Hotel,** on Jalan Song Thian Cheok (tel. 82/249-222), a Chinese inn, very decorative (especially on Chinese New Year) and very worn. A standard room with TV and fridge goes for M$108 ($43.25) single, M$118 ($47.25) double.

The **Aurora Hotel,** on Jalan McDougall (tel. 82/240-281), features strictly institutional décor in its 86 air-conditioned rooms; the rates here are M$95 ($38) single, M$115 ($46) double. The Aurora is located next door to Kuching Plaza, the town's main shopping mall.

The **City Inn,** at Lot 275, Abell Road, near the Holiday Inn (tel. 82/414-866), has a clean, simple lobby and rooms to match that contain air conditioning, TV, and wall-to-wall carpeting. A single deluxe (our recommendation) room runs M$55 ($22); a double, M$68 ($27.25) — a good budget alternative.

One promising budget alternative is the 12-room **Government Guest House,** located in a quiet neighborhood on Jalan Crookshank (tel. 82/24-2042). When we visited they were renovating this very basic inn, but we liked the simple 1950s colonial ambience and hope that they've preserved some of its original character. Rates are extremely reasonable: doubles rent for M$44 ($17.50) while singles run M$33 ($13.25).

DINING: Dining in Kuching is not nearly the sublime experience of, say, Penang, but still an endeavor offering more than a few memorable experiences. Among them we found some terrific Chinese and Indian restaurants and a fantastic fish eatery. The hawkers' stalls are of interest as well, though the selection is less interesting than in KL or Penang.

The **KTS Seafood Canteen,** at 157 Jalan Chan Chin (tel. 426-528), is simply *the* great place to eat in Kuching. Sweet-and-sour fish, jungle ferns (that's right) with shrimp paste and chile, vegetables with sea cucumbers . . . the list of goodies is practically endless, more so if you have a Chinese cabbie who knows the place and what to ask for (don't worry if you don't — the staff is extremely helpful). We had our finest meal here, and it was just a quick lunch! As for décor, KTS is little more than an extended diner, but the food is great, and a meal for two hungry people runs a mere M$35 ($14). Not to be missed!

As mentioned above, we very much enjoyed the **Mesian Szechuan Restaurant** in the Holiday Inn (tel. 423-111). The setting is quite formal and the service very attentive, but the star here is the food. We especially liked the fish and seafood dishes. A typical meal for two costs M$50 ($20).

Other restaurants that were recommended to us by locals are: in the center, the **Malaya Restaurant,** at 53 Leboh India (tel. 22-842), for both Malay and Indian cuisine; west of the museum, the **Rock Road Seafood Restaurant,** at Mile 2, Jalan Tun Haji Obeng (tel. 21-575), on the way to the airport, for excellent Chinese seafood; and in the southern part of Kuching, the **Bangkok Thai Seafood Restaurant,** off Jalan Padungan; **Duffy Banana Leaf Restaurant,** on Jalan Ban Hock (no telephone); and the fine **Tsui Hua Lau,** at 22 Jalan Ban Hock (tel. 427-408), for Mandarin Chinese food.

For good-value dining, try the **Fima Rantai Restaurant,** on Crookshank Road (tel. 57-886), just below the Government Guest House, featuring Western, Malaysian, Chinese, and Japanese cuisine. They have a cheap "Express" set lunch for M$5 ($2), served Monday through Saturday from 11:30 a.m. to 2:30 p.m.

Perhaps the two best hawker venues to recommend are the **Open Air Market** (with a roof!), located across the street from the bus station bordered by Jalan Mosque, Market, and Khoo Hun Yeang, for late-night dining; and the **Rex Cinema Hawker Centre,** at the intersection of Leboh Temple and Jalan Tunku Abdul Rahman, for good early-evening satay grazing. In both locations you'll find a great many stands serving a variety of dishes. Recommending any one is impossible, so you'll just have to sample them all!

At the other end of town, off Jalan Padungan, is the **Permata Food Centre,** a collection of hawker stalls that are slightly more upscale (and slightly more expensive) than the street stalls. This is the antiseptic version of the Open Air Market stalls, so take your pick.

WHAT TO SEE AND DO: The basic appeal of Sarawak is not to be discovered in the cities—as pleasant as Kuching is—and it requires a certain amount of planning, energy, and resources (read: money) in order to encounter the real Borneo. One of the best starting points for your tour of Borneo is to find a tour company or guide who can make your arrangements as well as offer advice about an appropriate itinerary.

To begin, we recommend a great guide: **Thomas Goh** (tel. 82/423-620), a Kuching resident and a TDC registered guide (no. 0782). Thomas is Chinese, speaks English (plus several local dialects), and is familiar with an incredible variety of flora and fauna; most important, he knows the geography and ethnicity of a vast area in Borneo, especially around Sarawak. Consult with the regional TDC office for other recommended guides if Thomas isn't available.

Another recommendation is a fairly new touring outfit, **Borneo Adventure,** located on the first floor of the Padungan Arcade on Jalan Song Thian Cheok in Kuching (tel. 82/245-175). This operation is run by Philip Yong and Robert Basiuk, who both know Borneo well and came highly recommended by various people we met on our journeys.

To begin our tour of Sarawak we'll start in Kuching, as that's where most travelers to Borneo arrive.

Kuching

If you have only a day in Kuching, try to visit the Sarawak Museum, which houses an excellent collection of Borneo artifacts. After that, consider taking a walk around the old center of Kuching, tracking the development of the city under the rule of the Brooke family.

SARAWAK MUSEUM. Two sections comprise the Sarawak Museum. The original collection was opened in 1891 by Alfred Wallace, a local naturalist. This building, executed in a classical Western style, houses collections of wildlife and everyday objects used by the tribes of Borneo (don't fail to notice the bizarre sexual contraptions); it also has informative historical exhibitions about Sarawak. As fascinating as this is, it's the ethnographic display in the newer building that merits such high praise and consideration, for here you will find an elaborate array of objects, costumes, vehicles, and in some cases, housing (including a reconstruction of a longhouse) of Borneo's tribal people. Not to be overlooked is the museum shop, with a fine selection of books and crafts. There is a videotape about the development of Kuching shown every other hour, beginning at 10 a.m., in the small theater attached to the museum's offices. Museum hours are 9:15 a.m. to 5:30 p.m.; closed Friday and public holidays. The museum is located on Tun Haji Openg and admission is free.

ISTANA (PALACE). Although it's not open to the public and can only be appreciated from the outside, the Istana, located across the river from central Kuching, is one of the most elegant buildings in all of Kuching. The Colonial-style palace, now the official residence of Sarawak's head of state, was built in 1870 by Charles Brooke, the second of the White Rajas, as a bridal gift. The building has been used to house rajas, Japanese war prisoners, and state visitors.

FORT MARGHERITA. It's either ironic or a testament to the military prowess of the

Brooke family that, since its opening in 1879, Kuching's most famous fort has never been attacked. Located on the same side of the river as the Istana, it was originally built to protect the city against tribal attacks from upriver, Fort Margherita has been looked on by locals and visitors as a very attractive, three-story English Renaissance-style structure that, even in its day, was designed for Charles Brooke "to enhance the beauty of the town" (perhaps that's why it was named for Charles's wife, Ranee Margaret, who, based on the photos we've un-earthed, was built like a fortress). The only real threat the fort ever suffered was during the 1941 bombing of Kuching by the Japanese—they missed.

Today the fort is the home of the **police museum,** with all manner of history and tools of the trade on display; the cell for condemned prisoners is open for touring.

To reach Fort Margherita, take the very short (and frequent) river cruise from Pangkalan Batu, in the downtown section.

"LEGACY WALK." The Sarawak Tourist Association has organized a 30-minute walk in the colonial section of Kuching that provides a fine introduction to the town. We suggest procuring a copy of the Sarawak map published by the Sarawak Ministry of Environment and Tourism (try the STA or TDC office); they have conveniently marked the route and added small descriptions along the way.

A good place to begin is the so-called **Bishop's House,** on Jalan McDougall, thought to be the oldest extant residence in Sarawak. The house, built in 1849, was originally occupied by a Dr. McDougall, a year after he arrived in Kuching to be installed as the first Anglican bishop of Borneo. If you continue up Jalan McDougall you'll pass the Anglican church. Make a left on Jalan Tun Haji Obeng, past the War Memorial, coming out on Jalan Mosque. If you continue toward the bus station, you'll arrive at the Open Market (see "Dining"), not a bad spot for a snack.

Make a right on Jalan Market, which becomes Jalan India. Here, at no. 37, you'll find an **Indian mosque,** originally built in 1850 but rebuilt some 30 years later for Kuching's Indian Muslim community.

Continuing on Jalan India, you'll come to the center of old Kuching with the Court House, Clock Tower, Square Tower, Brooke Memorial, Round Tower, and the post office, all structures that were constructed during the reign of the White Raj. The **Court House,** with its Colonial Romanesque façade, was built as the administrative hall in 1874 for the White Rajas. It continued to house the main offices of government until 1973; today it serves as the magistrate's court. The **Clock Tower** and the **Brooke Memorial** are landmarks in Kuching, the former built by a Brooke and the latter honoring one. The memorial was erected in 1924 and includes figures of Sarawak's tribal people as well as a heartfelt description of Charles Brooke, the Raja of Sarawak for 49 years. The **Square Tower** (octagonal, actually) was built in 1879 both as an extension of the Fort Margherita complex—it housed prisoners—and as a fortress across the way from the Istana. We like the fact that, when not under attack, it was used as a dance hall. The **Round Tower,** on Jalan Carpenter, remains an enigma. Built in 1886, its purpose isn't known to this day. Yes, it occupies a strategic spot, but with so many other forts in the area, who needs it? Apparently the Brookes felt that this particular fort would serve them well in an emergency, but even that explanation draws blanks from local historians. Its use today is generally better understood; it houses the Labor Department. We mention the **post office** as a sight worth noticing because the locals love to show it off, perhaps because of its dominating neoclassical design. After all, where else in Borneo will you find Corinthian columns and 10¢ stamps?

TUA PEK KONG (GRAND UNCLE). Centrally located at the junction of Padungan Road and Jalan Tunku Abdul Rahman, at the end of Jalan Carpenter, Tua Pek Kong is the oldest Chinese temple in Sarawak, having been built in 1876. It is also known as the Siew San Teng Temple and is dedicated to the Cantonese deity Loh Hong Pek, whose job it is to protect the people of the surrounding area. Although the temple is dedicated to old Loh, the current vogue is for a "vegetarian" deity who commands a strong following in contemporary Kuching.

Day Trips from Kuching

One of the best places to see examples of Borneo's exotic animal life is a visit to the **Wildlife Rehabilitation Centre,** located 22 km (13 miles) from Kuching in Semonggok (tel. 44-2081); after getting to the entrance, you must walk about 25 minutes to reach the centre. The sanctuary is operated under the auspices of the Forestry Department. Here you'll find a fantastic variety of fauna, including the Orang Utan, hornbills, and honey bears, all of which have been placed in the centre for rehabilitation or protection. As a precaution, plan on wearing good walking shoes and bringing rain gear and insect repellent.

In order to visit, you must apply for a permit from the Forestry Department at the STIDC Building in Kuching. Operating hours at the centre are 8 a.m. to 4:15 p.m. Monday through Friday and 8 a.m. to 12:45 p.m. on Saturday; closed Sunday. Admission is M$25 ($10) per person.

BAKO NATIONAL PARK. Only 37 km (23 miles) from Kuching, an escape to Bako National Park transports you quickly into the wilds of Borneo's rugged coast. Not only is there a range of vegetation from desert scrub to verdant forests with rare ferns, but Bako is home to Borneo's uncommon and endangered proboscis monkey, as well as monitor lizards and bearded pigs. Bako is also an ideal park for those who like to boat and hike to isolated beaches and swimming coves.

There are a few primitive hostels and resthouses in the park for those who wish to stay overnight; expect to pay M$2 ($1) per person in a hostel and M$21 ($8.50) for a resthouse that accommodates six people.

Visitors must arrange permits and accommodations with the National Parks and Wildlife Office on Jalan Gartak in Kuching (tel. 82/24-474).

There are frequent buses from Kuching to Kampong Bako via the Matang Transport Co., running from 7 a.m. to 4 p.m. along the Kuching–Bako road; in Kampong Bako you can rent a longboat for the 25-minute ride to the park for about M$25 ($10) per boat. During the monsoon, from November to March, the schedule is dependent on the weather.

LONGHOUSE TOURS. There are a wide variety of tours to Sarawak's many tribal longhouses offered out of Kuching, some organized as day trips while others require an overnight stay. **Interworld Travel Service,** on Jalan Song Thian Cheok in Kuching (tel. 82/24-873), offers a one-day visit to a Land Dayak longhouse near Kampong Gayu. Aside from touring the actual tribal village, most tours transport you through the wondrous Sarawak jungle, with pitcher plants, pepper groves, and wild orchids, all growing amid one of the world's oldest landscapes. Note that most day-trip longhouse tours visit kampongs that are frequented by tourists, and thus may lack some of the "authenticity" seen in the remote villages. If you hire your own guide, ask to visit longhouses that are off the tourist beat and you'll be well rewarded. Otherwise plan on taking an overnight trip to more remote locations. One such trip, offered by **Borneo Adventure** (tel. 245-175), is the four-day Longhouse Adventure with a visit to the Iban village of Ulu Ai; expect to pay $390 per person, including transportation and accommodations.

Touring Sarawak

If we were to advise would-be Sarawak travelers how best to spend their time, we'd suggest taking a week or two of trekking, rafting, and climbing through Borneo's remote interior. Again, you can hire a private guide to arrange and accompany you on such a trip or reserve a tour with a travel company. **Borneo Adventure** (tel. 82/245-175) offers such trips either as the "Borneo Heartland" seven-day expedition or the ten-day "Borneo Highland" trek. Both visit sections of Sarawak that are far off the tourist beat, but they require a spirit of adventure and physical fitness; expect to pay $740 per person for the former and $940 for the latter.

The most frequently advertised "off the beaten track" tour is the so-called Skrang River package, combining a river float trip with an overnight visit to an Iban longhouse; **Interworld Travel Service** (tel. 82/24-873) has both two-day and three-day versions of this trip.

The other must-do activity is to visit Gunung Mulu National Park, 120 km (75 miles) east of Miri, one of the great undiscovered natural settings on earth, as we shall soon see.

GUNUNG MULU NATIONAL PARK. Established in 1974 as a national park, Mulu has quickly become the preeminent natural site in Malaysia, if not all of Southeast Asia. Since the early 1960s there have been numerous international expeditions to Mulu, and yet the mapping and exploration of its vast network of underground caverns is only beginning. To date, explorers have discovered a 150-km (93-mile) cave passage (Deer Cave, the world's longest) and the world's largest natural chamber (Sarawak Chamber). It's almost impossible to comprehend the magnificence of the Sarawak Chamber; even the scale of it, accommodating the equivalent of 40 Boeing 747s, doesn't convey the grandeur of one of the world's most extraordinary natural sights. But Mulu National Park is not only a superb series of caverns; it contains within its 200 square miles the country's second-highest peak, all eight variety of hornbills, 170 species of orchid, 8,000 types of fungi, 20,000 separate animal species (the majority of which are insects), and a formation of 125-foot-tall limestone pinnacles that rivals the stone forest of Kuching in southern China. What is equally astonishing is that Mulu National Park is as undiscovered as it is unexplored: you might find yourself alone (or nearly so) in even the most renowned sites.

What's the rub, you ask? Well, first you have to get to Borneo (Kuching or Kota Kinabalu, Sabah); then you have to travel to Miri (one hour by air, a lot longer by bus); after that it's either a 12-minute flight or a three-hour boat ride to Marudi; then it's on to an express boat to Kuala Apoh on the Tutoh River for another three-hour journey with 14 rapids and shallow water that often requires portaging (carrying the boat over land); finally you approach the park entrance, after which it's another hour or so by foot to reach the entrance to Deer Cave, much farther to ascend Gunung Mulu at 2,376 meters (7,795 feet)—three days, on average.

Obviously this isn't a trip for everyone, but there are ways to make it easier. One such alternative is to take an organized tour, out of either Kuching, Miri, or Marudi. **Borneo Adventure** has a seven-day trip starting in Kuching or Miri, including river rafting, cave exploring, and trekking up peaks to view pinnacles for $640. Another company, **Gua Mulu Tours and Travel Services,** located at 31-G Park Arcade in Miri (tel. 85/37-278), offers four-, seven-, and eight-day excursions into the park and environs.

Alternatively, if you can get yourself to and from Marudi, the Park Service has five-day group tours (minimum of seven people) for M$280 ($112); for additional information, contact the **National Parks and Wildlife Office,** Jalan Gartak, 93000, Kuching (tel. 82/244-474), or the **Section Forest Office,** 98000, Miri (tel. 85/36-637).

If you decide to arrange the trip yourself, remember that you must make a reservation and confirm it five days before making the visit; no visitors will be allowed in the park without a permit, which must be applied for at the National

Parks office. Finally, you'll have to bring all your supplies with you, including food, raingear, drinks, etc. The park bungalows, renting for M$5 ($2) per night, offer beds, blankets, cooking facilities, water, and electricity.

For an excellent description of the geology of the area, read *Caves of Mulu,* published by the Royal Geographic Society (London, 1981), one of the many groups to sponsor an expedition to the caverns.

NIAH NATIONAL PARK. The discovery of a 40,000-year-old skull and prehistoric cave paintings led explorers (and later, tourists) to visit the 7,756-acre Niah National Park, located 108 km (67 miles) south of Miri. Yet it's the Great Cave, a 27-acre limestone cavern, that today attracts most visitors. Archeological excavation, under the auspices of the Sarawak Museum in Kuching, continues to unearth tools, ornaments, and stone pottery from both the old and new Stone Age, at the same time that geologists proceed to explore Niah's massive natural underground formations. Like Mulu, the center of the park is dominated by a peak; in this case it is the 1,294-foot-high Gunung Subis mountain.

To reach the **Great Cave** and the **Painted Cave,** you'll have to walk 2½ miles on a plank walk from the park entrance through gorgeous lowland rain forests. You are certain to see a large variety of butterflies and birds, if not hornbills and small mammals. In order to enter the Painted Cave, you'll have to present a letter of permission from the director of the Sarawak Museum in Kuching and arrange for a local guide; this is done in order to protect it from the traveling hordes. Permits can be forwarded to the Park Ranger, Niah National Park, Batu Niah; allow six to eight weeks for delivery. Local guides charge M$25 ($10) for the journey through the Painted Cave and can be arranged through the Park Ranger's office.

Although a trip to Niah can be done as a day trip from Miri, the Park Service operates a **Visitors Bungalow** at Pangkalan Lobang, near the beginning of the plank walk. There are complete facilities here for cooking, sleeping, and bathing, all for a modest M$5 ($2) per person. Reservations can be made by contacting the Section Forest Office in Miri.

You can take either a bus or a taxi from Miri or Bintulu to Batu Niah. From Batu Niah you can reach the Visitors Bungalow and trailhead either by renting a local longboat, following the footpath from Batu Niah along the Niah River (45 minutes), or by driving on the Sim Kheng Hong Road. Most travel companies in Kuching offer excursions to the Niah Caves as a two- or three-day journey.

SHOPPING: Kuching is the best serious shopping center in East Malaysia. We found interesting antiques, locally made tribal handcrafts, and high-quality Sarawak pottery scattered in shops and markets throughout the city.

For antiques and *ikat* (woven fabric that has a "bleeded" pattern) textiles, try the **Sarawak House,** at 39 Jalan Wayang (tel. 52-531). **Thian Seng,** at 48 Main Bazaar (tel. 22-918), carries both fine antiques and gold jewelry. On the same subject, remember that no antiques (any object dated before 1850) can be exported without obtaining a permit from the curator of the Sarawak Museum.

Quality handcrafts are for sale at the **Sarawak Art Shop,** in the new wing of the Sarawak Museum (tel. 25-716). Similar goods can be found at **Syarikat Pemasaran Karyaneka,** at Lot 87, Jalan Rubber (tel. 41-5761).

The **Sunday Open Market,** on Jalan Satok, offers everything from tribal artifacts to local produce at very negotiable prices.

We were taken by our guide to the **Sarawak Pottery Center,** along the Kuching Bypass (tel. 451-709), which boasts the finest pottery in Sarawak, as well as the finest potter, Goh Teck Yuong, a young artist who learned his craft as it was passed on to him through his family. The work here is well crafted and festive, resembling the very colorful ceramic work seen in Mexico. The huge inventory ranges from tiny espresso-size cups to decorative plates to giant frieze-enveloped vases that sell for M$3,000 ($1,200).

NIGHTLIFE: Due to the smallness of the city center, nightlife in Kuching belongs to the lounges, restaurants, and clubs in the hotels, primarily the Holiday Inn and the Hilton. During our visit the local hangout was the **Rajang Bar** in the lobby of the Holiday Inn; here the Filipino cover band not only entertained, but served as the go-between for the single males and females by dedicating songs all night to various objects of affection. Oh l'amour, l'amour. . . .

For confirmed filmaholics, there are English-language films at the **Rex Cinema.** Check the local newspapers for other listings.

2. SABAH

Sabah is located on the other side, that is, to the east of Brunei, on Borneo's northwestern coast. The state is perhaps even less known than Sarawak, and for all but a few tourists and oil drillers, remains completely unexplored. Like Sarawak, it has ancient jungles and remote rivers, huge caves and underground streams, as well Mount Kinabalu, at 13,455 feet above sea-level, the tallest peak in Southeast Asia. Sabah hosts another world size site: the world's largest Orang Utan sanctuary, created to protect the "Wild Man" from the ravages of human development.

Sabah's largest town and capital is **Kota Kinabalu,** known by locals as KK, located midway on the northwest coast between Brunei and the Balabac Strait, on the northern tip of Borneo. Most likely, Kota Kinabalu will appear on your Malaysian itinerary as not much more than a point of entry to deepest Sabah, a region of truly spectacular scenic splendor, wherein lies the real appeal of that state for the visitor.

ORIENTATION: Kota Kinabalu is a new, fast-growing city risen from the ashes of World War II. Known as Jesselton during British rule, Sabah's capital was intentionally destroyed by its people in order to prevent the Japanese from using it as a base during the war. Their efforts, heroic and dramatic as they may have been, were for naught: Japan rolled through Borneo with even more ruthless efficiency than it displayed in its one-month campaign to seize control of the Malaysian peninsula.

The city limits extend for miles along the coast of North Borneo and its inhabitants number nearly a quarter of a million. The city center, however, is quite compact and easily seen on foot. Upon arriving, your strongest impression of Kota Kinabalu may be its evocation of a South American concrete boomtown, perhaps a Brazilian port hacked out of the Amazon jungle. The city's paved streets rapidly give way to mud tracks woven through the surrounding rain forests. Kota Kinabalu's strategic command of the Gaya Bay on North Borneo has caught the roving eye of many an acquisitionally minded explorer; from the colonial British to the relentless Japanese to, most recently, the Filipinos and Indonesians.

KK's layout is fairly simple, with the **fish, central, and night markets** on the quayside, roughly bisecting the town. There is a walkway from the central market to the **bus station.** To the west are the **TDC** and the **Sabah Tourist Association** offices, in and around the **Sinsurin** complex; the Sinsurin Plaza is the main shopping mall in town, with Hong Kong–style overhead walkways leading to it in all directions. To the west, still on the coastline, is **Tanjung Aru,** a resort center with a luxury hotel of the same name. Farther west and inland is the **international airport,** about 15 minutes from the city. To the east of the markets is the business center of KK, around **Segama,** with a small concentration of hotels, foreign banks, and airline offices. Along the waterfront in this part of the town is the **boat dock** for service to the outlying islands.

Outside the city, the main destinations of interest to travelers are **Mount Kinabalu National Park,** located 113 km (70 miles) to the east of KK; **Sepilok Sanctuary,** the Orang Utan reserve located 24 km (15 miles) from Sandakan on Borneo's east coast and 386 km (240 miles) from KK on the opposite side of the state; and the **offshore islands** of Pulau Gaya, Pulau Sapi, and Pulau Manukan, all within a short ride from KK.

USEFUL INFORMATION: Like Sarawak, visitors to Sabah must be in possession of a valid passport to go through Immigration and Customs, even if they have already entered another Malaysian city. Nearly all travelers from English-speaking countries, including the U.S., the Commonwealth, and British-protected citizens, aren't required to apply for a visa. Remember that most businesses and government agencies in KK keep hours according to the Muslim schedule, so that many offices close in the afternoon or all day on Friday with a half day on Saturday.

The main Sabah branch of the **TDC** is located in the Sinsurin Plaza in Kota Kinabalu (tel. 88/211-732); their hours are 8 a.m. to 12:30 p.m. and 2 to 4 p.m. Sunday through Thursday and on Saturday to 1 p.m. The **Sabah Tourist Association (STA)** operates an information counter at the airport on Level 1. Their main office is located in Block 1, Lot 6, on Bandaran Sinsurin (tel. 88/211-484), with similar hours to the TDC.

The **telephone area code** for KK is 88.

The **General Post Office** is located on Jalan Gaya, near Australia Place.

For **medical emergencies,** dial 999 or contact the STA or TDC.

As a largely commercial city, KK has a large number of **banks,** especially concentrated around the eastern half of town. There you'll find the Charter Bank as well as the Sabah Bank. The **Rahmat Bookstore,** in the arcade at the Hyatt Hotel, has a good selection of paperback books about Malaysia.

GETTING THERE: Malaysian Airline System has daily flights to KK's international airport from Kuala Lumpur, with connections to/from Singapore and Penang; a one-way ticket costs M$380 ($152). MAS also has service four times weekly between KK and Jakarta via KL. You can even fly nonstop from Hong Kong (twice weekly) to KK on MAS, or via Brunei on Cathay Pacific. There are daily flights between Kuching and Kota Kinabalu on MAS for M$198 ($79.25) each way, as well as Twin Otter commuter flights from Miri for M$82 ($32.75). The MAS office is located on the tenth floor of the Kompleks Karamunsing on Jalan Tuaran (tel. 88/51-455); call 52-553 for airport information.

Sabah's major towns are served by daily air service on MAS; a 40-minute flight from KK to Sandakan (near the Orang Utan sanctuary), for example, runs M$69 ($27.50). **Sabah State Railway** has regular service between Tanjung Aru, Tenom (via Papar), and Beaufort, down the coast from KK, covering a distance of 154 km (96 miles).

There is a weekly **ferry** running from Kuantan on the east coast of peninsular Malaysia to Singapore, Kuching, and KK. For further information, see "Getting There" in the preceding section on Sarawak. Contact the STA or TDC for the current schedule and prices.

GETTING AROUND: In and around KK, trips are easily done by **taxis;** they're not metered, so find out in advance what the fare will be. A trip across town should run no more than M$5 ($2). Journeys to the interior can also be made by taxi, though Jeeps or land cruisers are a better option.

Kinabalu Rent A Car has two offices in KK's top hotels, in the Hyatt Kinabalu International (tel. 219-888) and in the Tanjung Aru Beach Hotel (tel. 58-711). A Toyota Corona rents for M$185 ($74) daily, M$1120 ($448) weekly, including unlimited mileage and insurance; with a driver, the same car rents for

M$230 ($92) daily. There are also Isuzu Troopers and Toyota Land Cruisers available for about M$100 ($40) more per day, and cassette decks are standard on these babies.

ACCOMMODATIONS: Kota Kinabalu isn't a major tourist center and its hotel scene reflects that reality; however, it does have enough choices to satisfy even the fussiest guest and those in search of a luxurious resort. Because KK is a commercial town that, like much of Malaysia, has been experiencing an economic slowdown, there are often "promotions"—discounts—available in many of the hotels. Don't be shy about asking for a "special price."

First-Class and Moderately Priced Accommodations

Without question the finest hotel in Kota Kinabalu, perhaps in all Borneo, is the **Tanjung Aru Beach Hotel,** just a ten-minute drive from Kota Kinabalu Airport and only a short distance to central KK (tel. 88/58-711). The finely landscaped grounds, all 23 acres of garden, are immaculately maintained and command a great patch of real estate where the bay and ocean meet. The Tanjung Aru is so well equipped and serviced that, though we don't suggest it, it's the kind of resort that one could imagine never leaving on a holiday: there are three restaurants on the premises, and the sports facilities include tennis courts, three swimming pools, a fully equipped and staffed gym/spa, and an entire spectrum of lawn and watersports, from croquet and badminton to windsurfing, waterskiing, and scuba-diving in the South China Sea. The rooms are comfortable, with all the usual amenities plus a balcony overlooking the sea and outer islands. (We thought that the whole complex had a feeling of Hollywood glitz, and in fact when we mentioned that to the friendly staff, they told us that Gene Hackman and Danny Glover had stayed at the hotel for months while on location for the filming of *Bat 21.*) The single and double rooms here fall into three categories: medium, superior, and suites. A superior double (the best value) is M$275 ($110), and the suites start at M$850 ($340). The Tanjung Aru is an M$8 ($3.25) cab ride from downtown KK, and the hotel provides its own shuttle service to and from downtown.

The 14-story **Hyatt Kinabalu International** is located in the heart of the city on Jalan Datuk Salleh Sulong (tel. 88/219-888), overlooking the waterfront. This luxury hotel's 345 good-size, well-appointed rooms and suites were renovated in 1979; the tone here is understated elegance wrapped in peach and beige. As with other Hyatts, the hotel's architectural signature is a four-story moss-covered atrium that opens out toward the reception area on one side and to the swimming pool on the other—the effect is quite lovely. As for food, the Hyatt comes through with a good range of alternatives. There's the Semporna Grill on the premises that serves both hawker and Western-style food, a 24-hour coffeeshop in the atrium, and a Chinese restaurant (the Phoenix Court) that serves Cantonese-style cooking and dim sum (our guide told us that it was the best place in town and popular with locals). A deluxe double goes for M$240 ($96), but make sure you ask for a room above the eighth floor, with a sea view—the lower rooms overlook the pool.

Behind the Hyatt and down the road at 75 Bandaran Berjaya is the **Hotel Shangri-La** (tel. 88/212-800), but unlike others in Asia with the same name, the hotel is *not* a part of the Shangri-La International chain. Most of the clients here are Chinese businessmen and families visiting relatives. Each of its 122 rooms has wall-to-wall carpeting and fairly basic amenities. On the plus side, the hotel has a small gym and two restaurants, and is conveniently located adjacent to the local night market and cinemas. A standard double is M$130 ($52), with a superior double M$20 ($8) additional.

The **Palace Hotel,** at 1 Jalan Tangki, Karamunsing (tel. 88/211-911), bills itself as "the Budget Luxury Hotel" and to a great extent it's just that. Located about half a mile from the center of town on a hillock, its brochure claims that it has the "kind of peace and tranquility that Kings and Queens expect" (we like their style!). More to the point is the Palace's castle-like exterior, which is illuminated at night. Its 160 rooms are decorated in a simple fashion and, though a bit small, are good value for M$120 ($48) double. When we were there they had a special promotional rate of M$85 ($34) for a standard double, so make sure you ask when you arrive if they're having any "promotions."

Budget Accommodations

First and foremost at the lowest end of the price spectrum is Jon Reese's **Travellers Rest Hostel,** on the third floor of the S.T.P.C. Building in the Sinsurin Shopping Plaza in Block L (tel. 88/231-892). Mr. Rees has a tour company called White Water Adventures (see "Exploring Sabah" section), and he runs this small hostel out of his office. The place is clean and friendly, and seems to be the focal meeting place for international backpackers passing through Borneo. A standard dormitory (each room houses six to ten people) bed with fan goes for M$17 ($6.75), and the deluxe version with air conditioning is M$27 ($10.75). A double room runs M$46 ($18.50). Nearby are open-air markets, restaurants, stores, and stalls; it's also close to the bus station. The people we talked to who were staying there liked it a lot, a good recommendation.

Down the block from the hostel is the TDC-suggested **Hotel Rakyat** (tel. 88/211-100), whose nine rooms are simple to the point of being drab and run between M$35 ($14) and M$55 ($22), depending on size.

Another inexpensive and simple lodging is the **New Capital,** at 7 Jalan Laiman Diki (tel. 88/53-011), whose 15 rooms range between M$27 ($10.75) and M$40 ($16).

DINING: Three excellent restaurants we found are the **Seri Sempelang,** an open-air eatery near the Sabah Museum serving authentic Malay specialties; **Yong Moh,** a Chinese dim sum restaurant; and for Indian/Malay cuisine, **Sri Melaka.**

Downtown Kota Kinabalu has a local shopping plaza, **Sinsurin Plaza** (open until 10 p.m. daily), which is bordered by hawker stands offering everything from bird's-nest soup (gathered from nearby caves—it's fresh nest!) to jungle greens and rice. We had some great hawker meals walking through the stands on the trail of scents unknown, tastes untried.

WHAT TO SEE AND DO: As with Sarawak, the main attractions of Sabah are to be found outside the main city, in this case, KK. And like its neighbor, it will take some effort to get to the destinations of interest, such as Mount Kinabalu, the outer islands, and the Orang Utan Sanctuary. Unless you just feel like relaxing at the beach (Tanjung Aru Beach Hotel, for example), we suggest moving on from KK as soon as possible and starting your adventure into Borneo's interior. If you do stay in the city there are only a few sights worth seeing, and those can easily be visited in a day.

Kota Kinabalu

Although not on the level of the Sarawak Museum in Kuching, the **Sabah Museum** definitely merits a visit. The building itself is modern and spacious, giving ample room for exhibitions of Borneo artifacts, religious statues, and dugout canoes. There is a good historical display about Borneo and a small bookstall that sells many specialized publications about the region and its ethnicity. The museum is located on Jalan Tunku Abdul Rahman, on the road to the State Mosque; hours are 10 a.m. to 6 p.m. daily except Friday. Admission is free.

One of the oft-mentioned stops on the Sabah itinerary is a visit to the ultra-modern gold-domed **State Mosque** on Jalan Tunku Abdul Rahman, cited as a magnificent example of contemporary Islamic architecture and craftsmanship. When we visited, non-Muslim visitors were not allowed into the main sanctuary. Although the most interesting time to visit is probably during Friday noontime prayers, you are even less likely to be invited into the inner chambers of the mosque at that time. If you do intend to visit, remember to wear clothing that is modest and respectful.

Day Trips from Kota Kinabalu

Pulau Gaya, Sapi, and Manukan are collectively referred to by locals as the "offshore islands," located off the coast of Kota Kinabalu in the Gaya Bay. These islands are but a few miles from Kota Kinabalu, within an area bracketed as the **Tunku Abdul Rahman National Park,** a protected zone for a wide variety of coral and marine life. The islands are popular with KK-er's in search of a beach less crowded than Tanjung Aru, especially on busy weekends. There are both fishing and tour boats making the short commute from the pier in central KK; contact the TDC for the schedule.

For those in search of a more adventurous outing, we suggest a full-day tour to the more remote islands, including **Pulau Tiga National Park** and Snake Island. Pulau Tiga National Park is an island/park that is ostensibly 1,500 acres of jungle ringed by a beach, located offshore from Papar, a small kampong south of KK. There are four trails carved out of the wilderness Tiga that make exploration possible for those with a strong heart and good shoes. The trails are outlined and timed, with the longest walk being about 1½ hours each way; start by going to the Mud Volcano, just a 20-minute walk from the trailhead. Monkeys, birds, creatures moving under your feet, and practically no sunlight—that's the world of the jungle and its inhabitants, and it is in places like this that you get a taste of the real Borneo.

Not for the faint-of-heart is a visit to **Snake Island,** so named because the island is literally crawling with poisonous vipers; there is a prominent wooden sign with a warning not to set foot on shore unless accompanied by a warden. Our guide thought we'd find it interesting and assured us that the notice was alarmist; however, within minutes of stepping off the boat we saw snakes slithering through the rocks on the shore and, to the accompaniment of laughter from our guide, quickly got back on the boat!

To get to Pulau Tiga and Snake Island from Kota Kinabalu, you'll have to take a 1¼-hour train ride south, down to Papar and, from there, a boat to the two islands. The train ride is one of the secret pleasures of Sabah; it leaves from the Tanjung Aru station at 8 a.m. (check with the TDC for the current schedule), with a one-way fare of M$5 ($2). The powder-blue trains are ancient, almost Mexican in style, with small wooden shutters over each window. The cars are impeccably clean, and leave *exactly* on time, so don't be late! The train pokes along, making it ideal for a leisurely bit of sightseeing-by-rail. The train is bound to stop from time to time for lackadaisical water buffaloes to find more congenial spots to slumber. While waiting for the tracks to clear, you'll see farmers fishing in their rice paddies for frogs, crayfish, and large worms that are a Chinese delicacy.

Upon arrival in **Papar,** head for the docks where tour and fishing boats bound for the islands are moored. As you head upriver toward the South China Sea you'll see open beaches, festooned with palm trees, that are completely devoid of commercial development. Where the river meets the sea there's a beach on the left-hand side where wild ponies graze along the shore and gallop down the beach. When you reach the breakwater you're at **Kimanis Bay;** from there, you can make a diversion down the **Mambakut River,** about two hours away. At the mouth of the Mambakut are prawn beds, marked by buoyed red plastic bags; fishermen attract the prawns by feeding a mixture of chicken remains and edible clay overboard at the buoys. The houses along the shore are made from dried pandanas leaves, giant reeds that grow along the riverbanks; water buffaloes graze while herons and kingfishers glide overhead searching for seafood below. The next stop, about an hour away, is Pulau Tiga, and from there it's on to Snake Island.

If you haven't figured it out by now, visiting these villages and islands in one extended (as much as ten hours) excursion means a lot of boat travel across open and sometimes choppy waters. If you're prone to seasickness, this may not be the trip for you.

We arranged our jaunt to the islands with **Marina Tours,** located adjacent to the Tanjung Aru Beach Hotel (tel. 88/58-711). Their director and guide, Eric Chien, offers nine sea and land excursions to other far-flung locations from the KK area.

Exploring Sabah

In comparison to neighboring Sarawak, adventure trips in Sabah represent the avant garde of off-the-beaten-track travel in Malaysia. It's only in the last few years that local travel companies, specializing in deep-jungle outdoor adventures, have offered their trips to individual tourists.

Some of the expeditions include destinations in Sarawak, such as Mulu or Niah (see the preceding section about Sarawak for a description), while most include a climb up Mount Kinabalu, but we like the trips that take you into territory little explored by Westerners.

For those in search of that kind of high-voltage adventure, **Jon Rees** is your man. He is extremely knowledgeable about Borneo, and he is highly recommended by people who have taken his trips. His company, **White Water Adventures** offers a range of tours for those in search of deepest Borneo, from a standard 3-day trip that runs about $400 to his 15-day Niah/Mulu/Kota Kinabalu extravaganza ($1,200), which promises to convert you completely. But it is his private tours that we found the most interesting, those that will transport you to the truly remote sections of the state by four-wheel drive, foot, and waterway. You'll need to plan this sort of trip well in advance of your arrival, but it's almost certain to be worth the effort. For more information, contact the White Water Adventures office at P.O. Box 13076, Kota Kinabalu 88834 (tel. 88/231-892). He also runs a hostel—see "Budget Accommodations."

KINABALU NATIONAL PARK. The climb up 13,445-foot-high **Mount Kinabalu** is bound to be one of the highlights of any trip to Borneo, if not all of Southeast Asia. The mountain and its slopes boast an incredibly rich ecology, ranging from giant moss-covered trees at the base of the trail to almost microscopic rhododendrons that cling to fissure walls in the exposed expanse of gray granite on the top. Climbing up the well-marked trails, you're bound to find wild orchids, edible berries, and the famed pitcher plant, a medium-small shrub with large ewer-like sacks that catch water and insects. Less shy animals such as mouse deer, tree shrews, and red-leaf monkeys make their home on Mount Kinabalu and are found in the middle elevations.

The mountain itself, called Aki Nabalu by the Kadazans (local tribal people), is considered sacred as the "home of the Spirits of the Departed." When you're on the summit in the early morning and you can hear the glaciers cracking and moaning, there is a strong inclination to believe that the mountain is home to some pretty powerful deities.

Kinabalu Park lies 83 km (51 miles) from KK, a comfortable two-hour bus ride away; a ticket runs about M$9 ($3.50). The **park headquarters** is located about a third of the way up the mountain at 5,000 feet. The administration building is a modern structure with exhibits, a restaurant, and an information counter (next door) which also serves as the center for organized tours in the park. The park officers will arrange a guide for you (if desired), as well as make reservations at the Laban Rata Resthouse located at 11,000 feet. Behind the headquarters is a mountain garden, a well-marked and -maintained collection of plants that are typically found at various elevations on the peak; the garden is open from 8 a.m. to 1:30 p.m. Monday through Friday and 8 a.m. to 4 p.m. on Saturday and Sunday. Admission is free. There is a free 1¾-hour guided walk conducted by local rangers beginning daily at 11:15 a.m. A slide-and-film show is presented every evening at 7:30 p.m.; admission is free.

If you do plan on ascending Mount Kinabalu (and we encourage you to join the 15,000 rough-and-ready souls a year who do), you'll have to register with the parks office; if you want a guide (we suggest it), the cost is about M$50 ($20) for a group of one to three people (slightly higher for larger groups). The trailhead is located at 6,000 feet, a ten-minute ride from the headquarters, along Kamborongoh Road to the power station; the park service can arrange for your transportation. The hike takes two days: on the first day you should leave in the leisurely morning hours and plan on climbing for three to six hours up to the Panar Laban stop. The **Laban Rata Resthouse** is an extremely comfortable mountainside inn with hot-water showers, an overpriced restaurant, and warm bedrooms; all this high-altitude luxury costs a mere M$25 ($10) per person. Spend the night, rising in time to reach the summit at 6 a.m. for a gorgeous sunrise; plan on a 1½- to 3-hour hike in the dark to the top from the hut. The hike down the mountain takes between 2 and 5 hours.

As for practical hints based on our ascent, we suggest the following: Wear shoes with a textured sole, as the trail is likely to be wet, slippery, and muddy. Don't bring a sleeping bag or other bed linen as the resthouse has sufficient gear and lots of heaters. Bring a rain shell or poncho—it will almost certainly rain— as well as gloves (canvas or leather for holding onto the occasional rope), a working flashlight (with extra batteries), and a sweater (not only is it lonely, but it's cold at the top). Don't shlep a heavy backpack if you can help it, as most of the gear you need can be stuffed into a daypack ("the lighter and smaller, the better" is our one contribution to universal truth). Take lots of snack food for energy; there's water to drink along the way. And finally, if you want to save your knees from two weeks of pain, take the descent very slowly—we did it in less than two hours and regretted it for days. Most of the guides are really friendly and helpful, but they can almost run up the mountain. Don't be shy about asking them to stay with you.

For more information about reservations and guides, contact the **Sabah Parks Office,** P.O. Box 10626, Kota Kinanbalu (tel. 88/211-585).

SEPILOK ORANG UTAN REHABILITATION CENTRE. The Sepilok Orang Utan Rehabilitation Centre, situated on Sabah's east coast, 24 km (15 miles) from Sandakan, is the world's most important refuge for Borneo's legendary (and endangered) "man of the forest." The majority of orangutans in the sanctuary were either confiscated from poachers who captured babies (usually by killing the mother) in the wild, or those that are found orphaned in nearby logging areas. The young primates are carefully nurtured, so they can ultimately be reintroduced into the forest. The Sepilok Rehabilitation Centre is set just within the boundary of the **Sepilok Forest Reserve,** a virgin woodland that not only provides a suitable setting for orangutans, but is an example of the fast-disappearing Sabah lowland rain forest. You can wander along well-marked trails through the jungle, coming to waterfalls, natural pools, and out to the coast along Sandakan Bay.

If you come here to see orangutans in a natural setting, plan on being in the park by 10 a.m. when the wild primates are fed. Although there are normally quite a few in the park, there is no guarantee that you'll actually spot one. You can usually find caged orangutans in the centre itself; those are often the most recently captured primates, which are being monitored for disease. The Rehabilitation Centre is open daily from 9 a.m. to 4 p.m.

Near the Rehab Centre is the **Sepilok Nature Education Centre,** with an excellent display, media presentation, library, and other resources for those interested in forest ecology. The centre is open daily from 9 a.m. until 4 p.m.

To get to Sepilok, you'll have to fly to Sandakan (see "Getting There") and from there either take a taxi the seven miles from the airport, or take a bus. There is a bus marked "Sepilok Batu 14" that runs four times a day directly to the reserve; otherwise you can take any bus that stops at the Sepilok junction, after which you must walk the 1½ miles to the centre. For further information, contact the Labuk Road Bus Company in Sandakan (tel. 215-106).

While in **Sandakan,** you may also visit the Sandakan Orchid House as well as the Gomantong Caves; contact the TDC for more details.

SHOPPING: Other than what one finds in the city's ordinary central market, the best shopping venue by far is the much-ballyhooed **Sunday Market,** or *tamu,* in the village of Kota Belud, located 77 km (47 miles) north of KK. Trading commences in the very early-morning hours and is over by noon. What can you buy? Other than Kadazan, Bajaus, and assorted Sabah tribal handcrafts of a good standard, one can haul away an ox or a bushel of tobacco or some bird's nest. Anybody want a used blowpipe?

NIGHTLIFE: KK isn't exactly a hip town, and its ultra-tame nighttime scene reflects that sobriety. There are nightclubs and discothèques in the **Tanjung Aru Beach Hotel** and the **Hyatt** with local entertainers and Filipino cover bands. When we stayed at the Tanjung Aru Beach Hotel they had a trio (two guitars and a bass) called "The Strollers," whose repertory ranged from Django Reinhardt to Jimmie Rogers to jazz, swing style; if these guys are playing anywhere during your stay, by all means see them.

Otherwise there are two movie halls in Kota Kinabalu, the **Twin Cinema** and the **Capitol**; both feature English-language films.

CHAPTER XV

SINGAPORE

□ □ □

1. AN INTRODUCTION TO DIVERSE CULTURES
2. THE ABC'S OF SINGAPORE
3. ACCOMMODATIONS
4. DINING
5. SIGHTS, SHOPPING, AND NIGHTLIFE

The three terms that most often come to mind when we think of modern-day Singapore are "clean," "shopping," and "modern." The Republic of Singapore is all that—and much more. It is an introduction to three of the most fascinating cultures in this part of the world—Chinese, Malay, and Indian. Singapore, a tiny nation, known in the business world as one of the "Four Tigers," along with Hong Kong, Korea, and Taiwan, enjoys one of the highest standards of living in Asia. In just three decades since its independence Singapore has become a major player in finance and world trade.

Singapore *is* astonishingly clean, a consumer's paradise, and an all-new, fully functioning system that balances the community needs and their environmental concerns. Those troubled by life in the oldest and largest cities of the West will find tremendous accomplishments in transportation, communication, civil service, housing, and medical care.

Both critics and supporters cite the 30 years of rule by President Lee Kuan Yew (fondly known as a benevolent dictator) for such stunning achievements and racial harmony. In 1988, Singaporean students and others, content with their country's material progress, announced they were ready for more democratic rule. Lee's government was criticized for stifling the press and for the imprisonment of opposition party members and suspected dissidents. Ironically, this admirable citystate functions so efficiently precisely because of a strictly disciplined, centralized leadership which discourages independent thinking.

Among travelers, Singapore prompts a rivalry with Hong Kong that parallels that of New York and Los Angeles. Devotees of Singapore cite its relaxed pace, the eternal sunshine, the efficiency of a newly constructed city, the obvious affluence, a respect for immaculately kept parks and gardens, and the plethora of dining experiences. Singaporeans have eschewed their colonial heritage for an American-style pop culture whose familiarity never fails to startle the Western visitor. Yet beneath the superficial "international" façade there is a respect for multicultural traditions. As the Singaporeans say, "Never judge a man by his flip flops."

1. AN INTRODUCTION TO DIVERSE CULTURES

Singapore's 2.6 million residents are approximately 76% Chinese, 15% Malay, and 7% Indian. Although the Chinese presence and influence clearly dominates daily life, the minority citizens of Malay and Indian descent have retained their own cultural traditions and religion. The republic ensured their cultural autonomy by designating four official languages: Mandarin, Malay, Tamil, and English. That these diverse and potentially conflicting groups coexist harmoniously can be ascribed to the common benefits each group derives from its adopted homeland. To quote Prime Minister Lee: "Singapore is an immigrant society. Our values are those which ensure survival, security, and success." We call it "Unity in Prosperity."

A BRIEF HISTORY: Since the 4th century, Indian, Arab, and Chinese traders visited the island of Temasek, strategically located at the Straits of Malacca joining the Bay of Bengal with the South China Sea. Temasek, or Sea Town, was part of the Buddhist Sri Vijaya Kingdom based in Sumatra. In the 13th century the Raja of Palembang, titled Sri Tri Buana, named it Singhapura (Sanskrit for "Lion City") after spotting a lion roaming the site he'd designated for his new capital. Less than a century later it was sacked by troops from Java's Hindu Majapahit Kingdom. Little was heard from Singhapura but tales of its pirating natives, feared by Chinese mariners trying to ford Lung Ya Men (the Dragon's Teeth Gate) between Singapore and Sentosa islands, were told throughout Asia. The island fell into obscurity, overshadowed by the antics of the Malay sultanates. During the 18th century Singapore reverted to the fiefdom of Temenggong, a minister of the Riau-Lingga Kingdom.

In 1818 Thomas Stamford Raffles and Maj. William Farquhar eyed Singapore (a fishing village of 120 Malays and 30 Chinese) as "one of the most safe and extensive harbors in these seas." Raffles, a colonial secretary in the Straits Settlement of Penang who was fluent in Malay, had been designated lieutenant governor of Java (Indonesia) in 1811. The British had managed the lucrative Dutch colony during the Franco-Dutch Wars, and when the war ended in 1816 Raffles was determined to secure a British trading post in the region. The Dutch, already established in neighboring Riau (islands off Sumatra) and Melaka (Malacca in Malaysia), strongly objected to the British move. But Raffles prevailed, and in 1819 he signed a treaty for Singapore with the Temenggong Abdul Rahman, sultan of Riau. Raffles gave Abdul's elder brother the sultanship of neighboring Johore on the Malaya peninsula and granted them both pensions in exchange for creating a settlement on the island.

In 1824 the brothers ceded the island to the East India Company and it became a model duty-free port, with no taxes, wharf fees, port dues, or import restrictions to stifle expanding trade. Soon porcelain, elephant tusks, gold, spices, and plantation crops from throughout the region flowed through Singapore's harbor in exchange for fabrics and manufactured goods from Europe. The Singapore River, clogged with lighters shuttling cargo from large ships moored in the outer harbor to the inland *godowns* (warehouses), became the center of commercial activity and the residential quarters for waves of Indian, Chinese, and Malay migrant workers.

By the 1830s Singapore was the center of commercial activity and the political heart of the Straits Settlements, colonies in Malaya jointly ruled by the Indian government and the East India Company. Orchard Road, spine of the present shopping district, was shaded by nutmeg, pepper, and fruit plantations; the new road bisecting it was named for Capt. William Scott, the harbormaster. Singapore became a British Crown Colony in 1867, and by 1880 its business community was handling £90 million sterling worth of merchandise. In 1900 Keppel Harbour was opened to new steamships that required a deeper draft than the older vessels. The new docks and traffic generated by the opening of the Suez Canal were handled by the next wave of immigrants, many of whom were women. Traders who had prospered in the colony took responsibility for improving the lot of their fellow countrymen by initiating reforms in education, housing, and medical care.

The Immigrants

The first Chinese who came after colonization were coolies (unskilled laborers) on their way to the plantations of Sumatra and Malaya who stayed to work on the docks of Singapore's bustling harbor. The Straits Chinese who emigrated from the British Straits Settlements prospered because they spoke English. They lent money and organized other Chinese settlers who came from the regions of Hokkien and Teochwew. Triads, or secret societies similar to the social organizations they had left behind, controlled the tightly knit Chinese community and its businesses. Disruptive Triad wars broke out several times in the mid-1800s, and in the 1870s the legitimate China Protectorate took over labor management, regulated prostitution, and controlled the Triads. Then more Chinese immigrants began to establish families and settle permanently in Singapore.

Malays were the island's earliest inhabitants, having moved south from the Malaya peninsula and west from the islands of Riau and Sumatra. Their kinship to the Bugis people of the Celebes (Sulawesi), their common language, and their shared Islamic beliefs created strong ties to neighboring islanders in Indonesia. The intermarriage of Malay women with the Straits Chinese (already influenced by European ways) created the unique Peranakan culture. The Straits Chinese and Peranakans remained loyal to the colonists and raised money to support British troops in World War I. Their quick assimilation and generally higher standard of living also made them politically influential.

The Indians who settled in Singapore were brought from that vast British colony to manage the construction of roads, bridges, and government buildings. Raffles initially imported a great number of Indian prisoners to build up the settlement, and when their sentences were up, many chose to stay on the tropical island. Those who immigrated later to Singapore came from the agricultural regions of the south, primarily from what is now Tamil Nadu.

The Modern Republic

World War II changed the face of Singapore—its river and godowns, street merchants and rural *kampongs* (villages)—forever. Although the British had fortified the colony with seapower, in 1941 the Japanese began their assault on land, via the Malaya peninsula. On February 8, 1942, Japanese troops under General Yamashita invaded the island; one week later British General Percival surrendered the burning, bombed-out city. After three years of harsh Japanese rule, on September 12, 1945, Lord Louis Mountbatten accepted the Japanese surrender in City Hall. Singapore remained a British colony until 1959, although other European powers that tried to reestablish former colonies had little success against growing nationalist movements.

In 1954 Lee Kuan Yew, an active Singaporean lawyer trained at Cambridge, founded the People's Action Party (PAP), a liberal coalition of trade activists and pro-Communist organizations. In the late '50s PAP's pro-Communist faction began to grow rapidly, diminishing the power of the more conservative Lee. After the abrupt arrest of party "extremists" by colonial officials, Lee was elected prime minister in 1959. The threat of the newly formed opposition party, the Barisan Socialis (Socialist Front), forced Lee in 1963 to support the proposal of Malaya's president Tunku Abdul Rahman to unite Singapore, Malaya, Brunei, North Borneo (now Sabah), and Sarawak into the Federation of Malaysia. Brunei declined and in 1965 Singapore, troubled by economic and racial differences with federation members, left and declared total independence.

Prime Minister Lee Kuan Yew and the conservative PAP are still in power. Strictly enforced policies include a belief in state capitalism and foreign investment to fuel economic growth, an emphasis on discipline, English-language education, government-funded public housing and medical care, and central intervention in social areas ranging from legalized prostitution to film censorship, to hefty fines for littering or disobeying traffic regulations. The results Lee has obtained in the last 30 years are what most impress visitors today.

S$	$ U.S.	S$	$ U.S.
0.25	0.13	60.00	30.00
0.50	0.25	70.00	35.00
0.75	0.38	80.00	40.00
1.00	0.50	90.00	45.00
2.00	1.00	100.00	50.00
3.00	1.50	110.00	55.00
4.00	2.00	120.00	60.00
5.00	2.50	130.00	65.00
10.00	5.00	140.00	70.00
15.00	7.50	150.00	75.00
20.00	10.00	175.00	87.50
25.00	12.50	200.00	100.00
30.00	15.00	225.00	112.50
35.00	17.50	250.00	125.00
40.00	20.00	275.00	137.50
45.00	22.50	300.00	150.00
50.00	25.00	325.00	162.50

ORIENTATION: The Republic of Singapore consists of 58 small islands; the largest named Singapore is 585 square kilometers, just twice the size of Rhode Island. Although the northern portion of the island displays the tropical foliage and hilly terrain typical of its Malaysian and Indonesian neighbors, most visitors confine their stay to a highly developed 30-km (18-mile) stretch along the south coast, between the airport and the suburb of Jurong. The taxi ride from the ultra modern **Changi International Airport** on the southeast tip to **Orchard Road,** the tourist hub in the south central part of the island, takes less than half an hour.

All the hotels and most of the restaurants and shopping areas listed are on, or within walking distance of, the main intersection of Orchard and **Scotts Road.** The 2½-mile belt of contemporary malls, imaginative high-rise hotels, and modern office buildings rivals Tokyo's Ginza for commercial density. Due east of Orchard Road is the modern landfill development known as **Marina Square.** These are the closest hotel and shopping facilities for visitors doing business downtown in the **Center City** or **Shenton Way** area. Here older government buildings and colonial-era greens vie with the futuristic towers of the financial district in a scenic area abutting the Singapore River. Due west and inland from Center City are the narrow, congested lanes and two-story shophouses of **Chinatown.** North of Orchard Road, tucked in among public housing developments, are the long, low blocks of **Little India** and **Arab Street,** the two other ethnic neighborhoods of tourist interest.

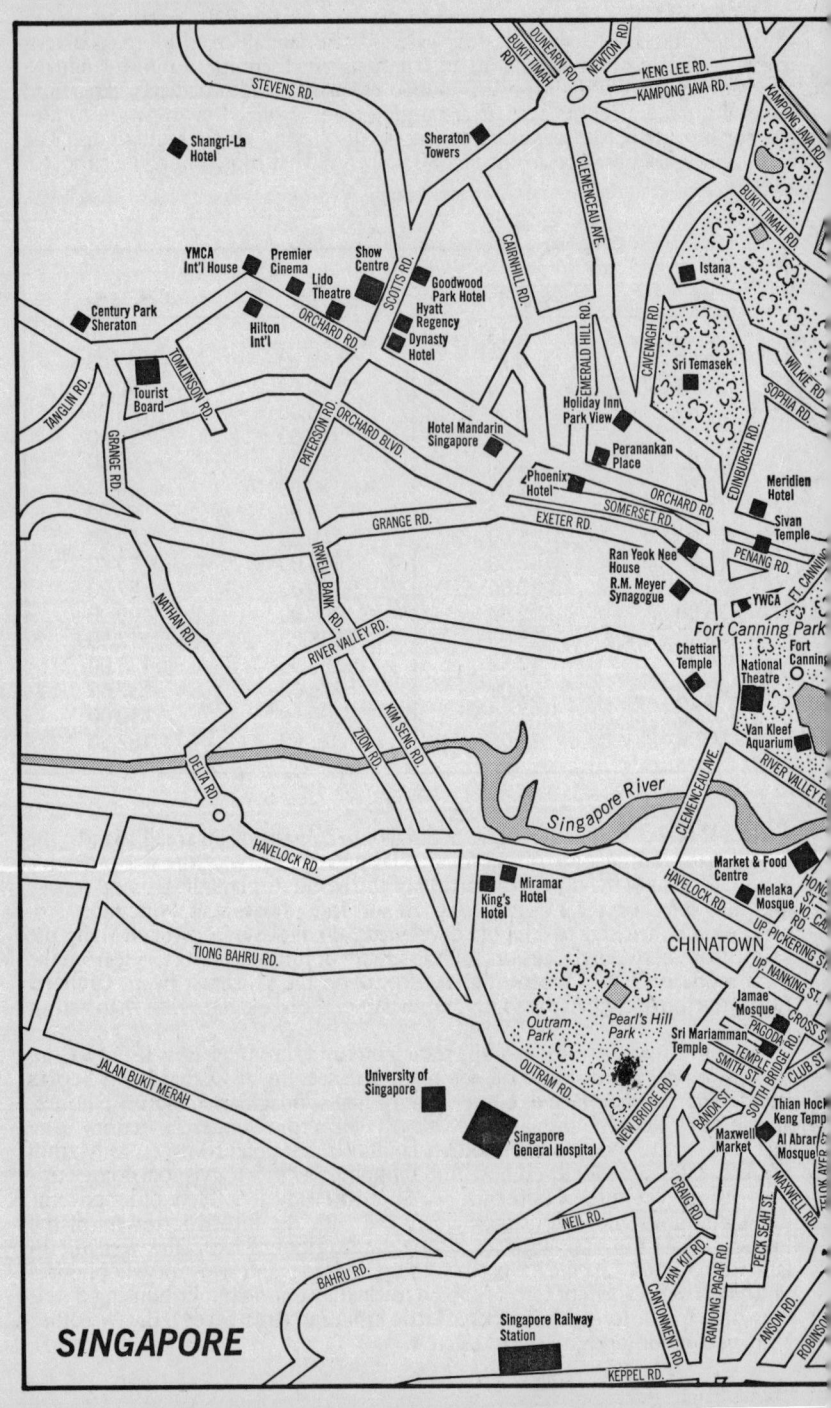

SINGAPORE

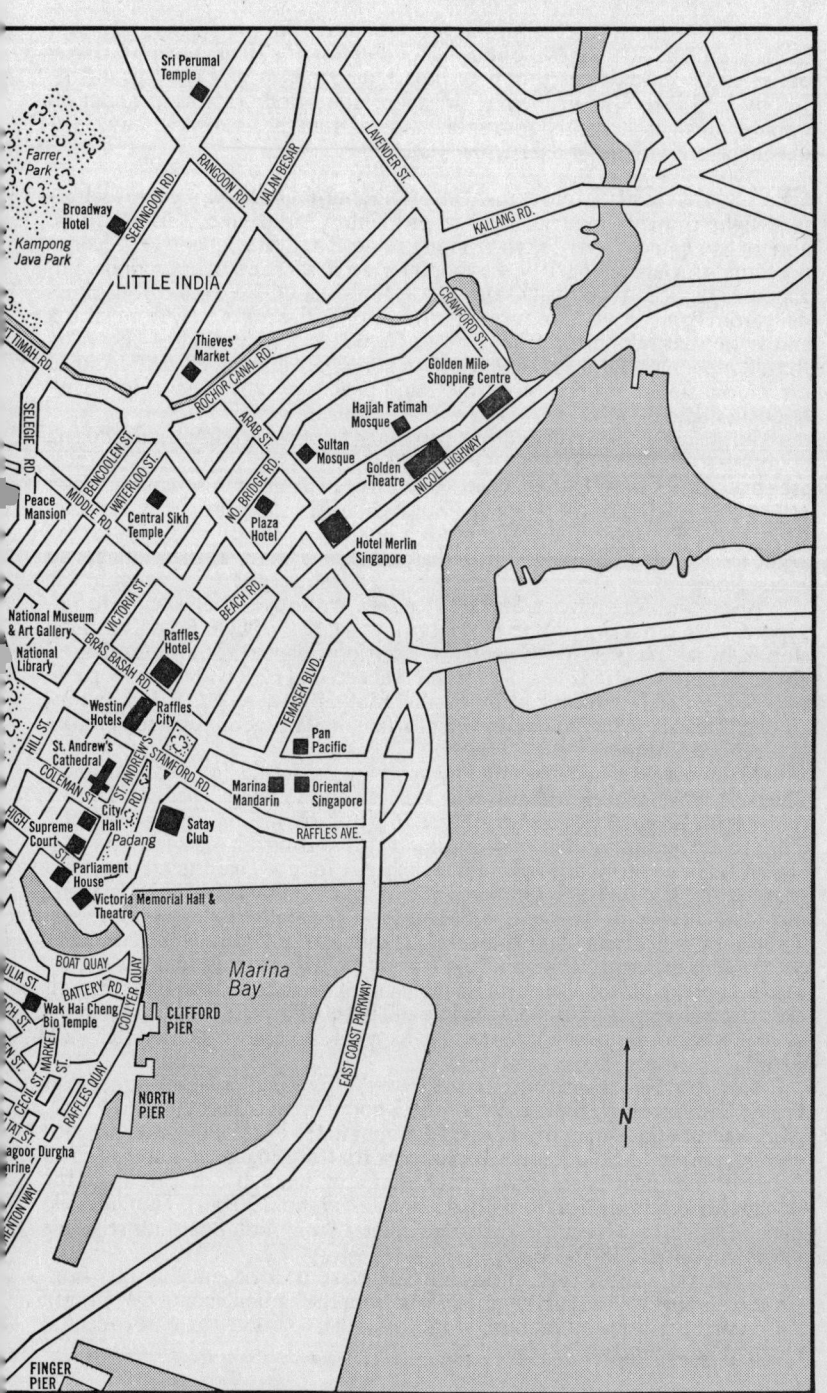

Sri Perumal Temple

Farrer Park

Broadway Hotel

Kampong Java Park

SERANGOON RD.

RANGOON RD.

JALAN BESAR

LAVENDER ST.

KALLANG RD.

LITTLE INDIA

TIMAH RD.

CRAWFORD ST.

Thieves' Market

ROCHOR CANAL RD.

Golden Mile Shopping Centre

SELEGIE RD.

ARAB ST.

Hajjah Fatimah Mosque

Sultan Mosque

Peace Mansion

BENCOOLEN ST.

WATERLOO ST.

MIDDLE RD.

Central Sikh Temple

NO. BRIDGE RD.

Golden Theatre

Plaza Hotel

NICOLL HIGHWAY

Hotel Merlin Singapore

VICTORIA ST.

BEACH RD.

National Museum & Art Gallery

National Library

BRAS BASAH RD.

Raffles Hotel

HILL ST.

Westin Hotels

Raffles City

TEMASEK BLVD.

St. Andrew's Cathedral

ST. ANDREW'S RD.

STAMFORD RD.

Pan Pacific

COLEMAN ST.

City Hall

Marina Mandarin

Oriental Singapore

HIGH ST.

Supreme Court

Padang

Satay Club

RAFFLES AVE.

Parliament House

Victoria Memorial Hall & Theatre

BOAT QUAY

JULIA ST.

BATTERY RD.

Marina Bay

COLLYER QUAY

EAST COAST PARKWAY

Wak Hai Cheng Bio Temple

CLIFFORD PIER

CH ST.

N ST.

MARKET ST.

RAFFLES QUAY

NORTH PIER

CECIL ST.

TAT ST.

agoor Durgha nrine

ANTON WAY

N

FINGER PIER

The industrial district of **Jurong** was reclaimed from swampland and prawn farms in the late '50s to provide housing for the poor. It's 20 minutes by taxi west of Orchard Road and houses the beautiful Chinese and Japanese Gardens and the Jurong Bird Park. The marvelous Singapore Zoological Gardens lie about 30 minutes north of the central tourist belt, not far from the narrow causeway linking Singapore with Johor Bahru, Malaysia.

GETTING THERE: More than 40 **international airlines** have regularly scheduled flights from 50 countries to Singapore. United Airlines flies daily from New York or San Francisco via Tokyo or Hong Kong. The 1988 Super-APEX economy round-trip fare was $1,199; see your travel agent for relevant restrictions. Singapore is serviced twice daily from Hong Kong via Cathay Pacific, four times daily from Bangkok via Thai Airways International, five times daily from Jakarta and twice weekly nonstop from Bali via Garuda Indonesia, and twice weekly from Rangoon via Burma Airways Corporation. The extremely efficient national carrier, Singapore Airlines, serves these and dozens of other destinations with frequent flights.

Surprisingly, there is no direct passenger ferry service from neighboring countries to the port of Singapore, one of the busiest in the world, although there are small ferries from Changi Point to Desaru, Malaysia. However, five major **cruise lines** (including the celebrated Royal Orchid Lines) call at the new harbor. Contact the Singapore Tourist Promotion Board (tel. 235-5433) or your travel agent for information about cruises that call at Singapore, Thailand, Bali, and Hong Kong.

An adventurous traveler, Stanley Mendoza, wrote us about his cruise to Singapore: "You can take a boat to Singapore if you take the **PELNI Boat Company** ship from Jakarta [see the "Orientation" section Chapter VII for information about PELNI] to islands near Sumatra. I went second class with four people in my bunk-bedded room. It cost Rp 63,000 ($39.50) and took 2½ days, but included all meals. From Jakarta we went to Tanjung Pinang on Riau, then took a hydrofoil to Singapore."

Many travelers enjoy leaving Singapore by the scenic **"express" train** to Bangkok, which makes many stops in Malaysia and southern Thailand. During our visit the Bangkok express left daily at 10 p.m., arriving in Kuala Lumpur at 7 a.m. the next morning. Travelers continuing on to Bangkok must leave the Malaysian Railways at Bukit Merkayam and change for the Thai International Express; arrival in Bangkok is estimated at 8:35 a.m. on Day 2. The first-class fare, including sleeper to Bangkok, is S$160 ($80); second class is S$120 ($60). There are also five trains daily to Kuala Lumpur, for S$60 ($30) in first class and S$30 ($15) in second class, and the *Rakyat Express* morning train to Butterworth, the stop for the Malaysian island resort of Penang, for which the second-class fare is S$55 ($27.50). For schedule and ticket information (reserve sleepers as far in advance as possible), contact the Keppel Road Railway Station (tel. 222-5165).

Comfortable long-distance **buses** leave the Terminus at New Bridge Road Fringe Car Park seven times daily for the 5-hour trip to Malacca for S$12 ($6), twice daily for the 8-hour trip to Kuala Lumpur for S$19 ($9.50), and once each evening for the 14-hour journey to Butterworth (for Penang), at a cost of S$33 ($16.50). Frequent buses to the beach at nearby Johor Bahru leave from the Rochor Road Terminus or from Bukit Timah Road (no. 170 bus). The fare is less than S$1 (50¢). Contact the Singapore Tourist Promotion Board for schedule information (tel. 235-5433).

Taxis are plentiful and inexpensive at every port of entry. A taxi from Changi Airport will cost about S$12 ($6); from the harbor, about S$9 ($4.50); and from the train station, about S$7 ($3.50). All fares quoted here are to central Orchard Road hotels.

GETTING AROUND: Singapore has a public transportation system that equals any other in the world. In fact, private automobiles are taxed with a 200% import duty to encourage the use of public transportation. Traffic is checked during rush hour by the imposition of fines for vehicles carrying fewer than four passengers in the Central Business District (or CBD, the area you're most likely to stay in). Between 7:30 and 10:15 a.m. a S$5 ($2.50) fee is imposed on private cars (half price for taxis) in the CBD and between 4 and 7 p.m. a S$1 (50¢) surcharge is imposed on taxis leaving the CBD with passengers. Despite tourists' confusion regarding fares, taxis are abundant and cheap. Public buses are modern and clean, and the new subway system is a model of luxury and efficiency. The compact geographical layout of the city makes the age-old system of walking an easy option, though the heat may discourage all but the hardy.

By Rental Car

Driving is quite easy, but take note of restrictions on access to the Central Business District during the morning rush hour. A self-drive car might be handy for exploring the island, or for overland travel to Malaysia, but within the city a chauffeur-driven car is advised. Rates for a self-drive car start at S$100 ($50) per day or S$600 ($300) per week. Rates for chauffeur-driven cars start at S$40 ($20) per hour with a three-hour minimum, or S$270 ($135) daily for eight hours. There are premiums for night work and for round trips to Malaysia. **Avis Rent-A-Car** has an office conveniently located on the ground floor of the Liat Towers, on Orchard Road near the Hilton (tel. 737-9477). Your hotel can also arrange car-rental services.

By Taxi

There is no shortage of taxis except at the end of a shopping day on Orchard Road. All are metered and charge S$1.75 (90¢) for the first 1½ km and S$.50 (25¢) for every kilometer after that. There's a S$3 ($1.50) surcharge for taxis taken from Changi Airport, but no surcharge going to the airport. There are also surcharges for each passenger in excess of two, at S$.50 (25¢) per person; for luggage, at S$1 (50¢) per bag; and for trips between midnight and 6 a.m. (50% of the metered fare).

You can order a **taxi by phone** (tel. 452-5555 or 250-0700) with a surcharge of S$1 (50¢) for immediate booking and S$3 ($1.50) for advance booking.

If you have **complaints** about specific taxi service, call 459-4222.

By Bus

The **Singapore Bus Service (SBS)** is very good and easy to navigate. The *SBS Bus Guide* can be purchased for S$.70 (35¢) from any bookstore or you can pick up a handy brochure at one of the STPB Tourist Information counters. Regular service on the scenic double-decker buses operates from 6 a.m. to 11:30 p.m. daily. Fares range from S$.40 (20¢) to S$1.20 (60¢), and exact change is required.

For sightseeing and exploring, the best deal around is the One-Day or Three-Day **Explorer Bus Ticket,** allowing unlimited travel on the red-and-white SBS buses or the orange-and-yellow Trans Island Bus Service buses. The fare is S$5 ($2.50) for the one-day ticket and S$12 ($6) for the three-day ticket. With your ticket comes an "Explorer Bus Map" guiding you to major points of interest on the island. Explorer tickets can be purchased at most moderate and first-class hotels. Call the SBS (tel. 287-2727) for information.

By Subway

Singapore's **Mass Rapid Transit (MRT) system** is a model of speed, comfort, cleanliness, and design. The system was constructed between 1982 and 1987 at a cost of S$5 billion ($2.5 billion), and to a couple of New Yorkers it's one of the wonders of the modern world. Ride it to witness the achievement and to savor the ease of negotiating the system. There is a north-south line running from Yishun in the north to Marina Bay in the south, intersecting with the east-west line, which runs from Boon Lay in the west to Pasir Ris in the east. Fares range from S$.60 (30¢) to S$1.20 (60¢). Single-trip tickets are purchased from vending machines in each station, but you can also buy S$10 ($5) tickets for multiple trips.

Most tourists will start with either the Orchard Road station, located opposite the Dynasty Hotel at the intersection of Orchard and Scott Roads, or the City Hall station, located just opposite the Raffles City Towers. Pick up an MRT guidebook at the station or at a Tourist Information Counter, or call 732-4411 for information.

By Pedicab

In areas frequented by tourists, such as around the Raffles Hotel and Chinatown, you'll find clusters of pedicabs or trishaws (bicycle-powered two-person carts) that provide a leisurely method of transportation. The pedicabs, so common in other ASEAN capitals, cater only to curious tourists in Singapore. Pedicab tours of Chinatown, the waterfront, or Little India average about S$18 ($9) for a half-hour spin through the district.

By Ferry

Regular ferry service to Singapore's Southern Islands and Sentosa departs from the World Trade Centre pier downtown. Boats to the beaches at Kusu Island and St. John's Island depart twice daily Monday through Saturday, and up to ten times daily on Sunday and holidays. The trips take 45 minutes and one hour respectively. Ferries to Sentosa depart every 15 minutes between 7:30 a.m. and 11 p.m. daily, until midnight on weekends, for the six-minute trip. Contact the Singapore Tourist Promotion Board for schedule information (tel. 235-5433).

2. THE ABC'S OF SINGAPORE

In contrast to some Southeast Asian countries, Singapore is a thoroughly modern, efficient, and well-organized city/country. Printed information is readily available to the traveler. English is spoken everywhere and Singaporeans, from the hotel concierge to a passing stranger, are always ready to answer the questions of a perplexed tourist. This section outlines many areas of travelers' concerns; we urge you to call or write the Singapore Tourist Promotion Board (see "Tourist Information" below for the address) with any questions not answered here.

AIRLINES: Singapore is a major transportation hub for Southeast Asia, served by over 40 airlines. The **United Airlines** office is located downtown at 16 Raffles Quay, no. 01-03 (tel. 220-0083). The main ticket office of **Singapore Airlines** is located at 77 Robinson Rd. (tel. 223-8888), with branch offices in the Mandarin Hotel on Orchard Road and in the Raffles City Shopping Center at 252 North Bridge Rd. Other international airlines landing here are Air France, Alitalia, British Airways, Pan Am, Lufthansa, Sabena, Swiss Air, and a host of others.

AIRPORT: Singapore's **Changi Airport** (tel. 542-1122) is located about 30 km east of the city. It is a very modern airport with extensive facilities. Some of the world's best duty-free shopping, several displays of free tourist brochures, a hotel reservations desk offering current bargain rates, and free city tours for transit passengers are only some of its merits.

Travelers are required to pay a Passenger Service Charge (PSC) of S$12 ($6) when departing for all countries except Malaysia and Brunei, for which the fee is S$5 ($2.50). You may purchase the PSC coupon at most hotels, travel agents, or airline ticket offices and save time at the airport.

AMERICAN EXPRESS: There are two American Express offices, both in the Orchard Road area. One is located on the ground floor of the Lucky Plaza Building at 304 Orchard Rd. (tel. 235-8133), near the intersection of Scotts Road. The other office is on the second floor of the UOL Building at 96 Somerset Rd. Both are open weekdays from 8:30 a.m. to 5 p.m. and on Saturday until noon.

BANKS AND MONEY EXCHANGE: Few cities in Southeast Asia offer the range of financial services available in Singapore. Money can be changed and traveler's checks cashed at a wide variety of **banks,** beginning at the airport and continuing down Orchard Road to the Raffles Square area. Banks are open from 10 a.m. to 3 p.m. weekdays and 9:30 to 11:30 a.m. on Saturday, although the Development Bank is open on Saturday until 3 p.m.

Licensed moneychangers are found in most shopping malls on Orchard Road and in the downtown area (many are open till 9 p.m.) and offer rates roughly comparable to bank rates. Tourists are warned to avoid unlicensed moneychangers. As always, hotel cashiers offer the same services, though generally at less favorable rates.

BEAUTY PARLORS/BARBERSHOPS: Every major hotel and most shopping malls have beauty parlors and barbershops. Manicures and pedicures are widely available and a real bargain.

BOOKSTORES: One of the best English-language bookstores is the **Sogo Book Shop,** part of the sprawling Sogo Department Store, located on the ground floor of Raffles City, 250 Bridge Rd. (tel. 339-1100).

BUSINESS HOURS: Government and private offices have staggered opening hours, varying between 7:30 a.m. and 9:30 a.m. and closing between 4 and 6 p.m., Monday through Friday, and closing between 11:30 a.m. and 1 p.m. on Saturday. Many private business firms are closed on Saturday. Most shops are open from 9 a.m. to 6 p.m. daily, although department stores and tourist shops close as late as 10 p.m.

CLIMATE: Singapore is located very near the Equator and that means it's hot and humid. Temperatures range from 75°F to 84°F (23.8°C to 29°C). Heaviest rainfall months are November to January, although light daily rainfall is common.

CLOTHING: Light, casual clothing beats the heat for sightseeing and is acceptable at most restaurants. "Smart Casual" is requisite at most restaurants and nightclubs—meaning no jeans, no sneakers. For fancier restaurants and clubs, jackets (ties are sometimes worn) for men are in order. Women should dress accordingly. Local businessmen favor short-sleeve shirts with ties and no jacket during the day.

CREDIT CARDS: Major credit cards are accepted at most shops and restaurants, and at all hotels. Some establishments may insist on adding a surcharge for credit-card purchases. You should refuse to do this but if a merchant persists, report it to the credit-card company for a refund. For any credit-card problems, including lost cards, call American Express (tel. 235-8133), VISA (tel. 532-3577), or MasterCard (tel. 224-0444). VISA has recently negotiated to allow cardholders to withdraw cash in Singapore currency from 60 bank cash machines. Call them toll free in the U.S. (tel. 800/227-6811) for information before your departure.

CRIME: Of all the major cities in Southeast Asia, Singapore has the lowest crime rate. You can safely walk in almost any area, even at night. However, we recommend that you leave valuables, airline tickets, and passports in the hotel safe. Carry a photocopy of your passport with you. In case of crime, contact the Singapore Tourist Promotion Board for assistance.

CURRENCY: The local currency is the **Singapore dollar (S$),** which comes in almost the same denominations as the U.S. dollar. The exchange rate fluctuates, but averages about S$1 = 50¢ U.S., which is the rate used throughout these pages.

CUSTOMS: Visitors over the age of 18 to Singapore are allowed to bring in duty free (except when coming from Malaysia) one bottle of alcohol, wine, and beer and up to 250 cigarettes, 50 cigars, or eight ounces of tobacco. Vaccines and controlled drugs require special authorization for import. There are no restrictions on the import or export of foreign currency, but import and export of gold must be declared to the Trade Development Board.

DENTISTS/DOCTORS: Singapore is world famous for its high standard of medical care. Most hotels have a doctor on call or can refer you to a qualified doctor or dentist. You can also confer with the embassy of your country for advice.

DOCUMENTS FOR ENTRY: Valid passports are required of everyone entering Singapore. Visas are not required for social visits of up to three months for U.S. and Western European citizens; 14 days for citizens of most other countries. British and Commonwealth citizens do not require visas. For employment purposes or residence, special visas are required.

DRINKING WATER: Tap water is clean and safe to drink. Medical wisdom says to drink lots of it.

DRUGSTORES: Pharmaceutical supplies are readily available in drug departments of supermarkets, department stores, and shopping centers. Most are open from 9 a.m. to 6 p.m. Your hotel concierge can advise you on locations of drugstores with extended hours.

ELECTRICAL APPLIANCES: Local voltage is 220-240 volts, 50 cycles, A.C. Most hotels have built-in transformers in bathroom outlets to reduce voltage to 110-120 volts, 60 cycles.

EMBASSIES: The **U.S. Embassy and Consulate** is located at 30 Hill St. (tel. 338-0251), and is open weekdays from 8:30 a.m. to noon. The **British High Commission** is on Tanglin Road, near the corner of Napier Road (tel. 473-9333). The **Canadian High Commission** is located in Faber House, 230 Orchard Rd. (tel. 737-1322). The **Australian High Commission** is at 25 Napier Rd. (tel. 737-9311). Hours vary widely, so call before you go.

EMERGENCIES: For **police** emergencies, dial 999; for **ambulance or fire** emergencies, call 995.

FESTIVALS AND HOLIDAYS: The ethnic diversity of Singapore is reflected in the rich calendar of festivals throughout the year.

January	**New Year's Day,** a public holiday
	Thaipusam Festival, a Hindu celebration where penitents with skewers and hooks piercing their bodies walk in a trance-like state between two temples, carrying decorated metal arches
February	**Chinese New Year,** when Chinatown is festively decorated and full of shoppers
April	**Good Friday and Easter,** celebrated by Christians
May	**Festival of Arts**
	Hari Raya Pusada, the end of Muslim Ramadan
June	**Dragon Boat Festival,** with boat races and feasting
July	**Bird Song Festival**
Aug.-Sept.	**Market Festival**
November	**Thimithi Festival,** a Hindu festival in which devotees of the goddess Draupadi walk across burning coals
	Deepavali, the Hindu Festival of Lights
December	**Christmas**

FILM AND CAMERAS: Good bargains abound in cameras (see "Shopping"). Film is cheap and readily available. Processing is a very good bargain and available as quickly as 27 minutes. Orchard Road offers a wide variety of camera shops and processing labs.

HEALTH AND VACCINATIONS: No immunizations are required for entry, with the exception of yellow fever vaccinations, required of persons who have visited countries where yellow fever is endemic. This currently includes certain African and South American countries. Call the Singapore Embassy in your country for more information.

HOSPITALS: Ask the concierge of your hotel for guidance on medical care, if needed. **Mount Elizabeth Hospital,** on Mount Elizabeth Road, off Orchard Road, is highly respected among Western medical authorities.

LANGUAGE: English is so widely spoken that it is considered the first language of Singapore. The four official languages, however, are Mandarin, Malay, Tamil, and English.

LAWS: Singapore's reputation for cleanliness is well deserved and strictly enforced with S$500 ($250) fines for littering. Jaywalking is also strictly prohibited. Pedestrians crossing a road within 150 feet of a crosswalk, pedestrian bridge, or underpass are fined S$50 ($25). Drug laws are severe and rigorously enforced.

MAPS: *The Map of Singapore,* published by American Express in conjunction with the Singapore Tourist Promotion Board (STPB), includes the names of major office buildings and is indexed, a necessity to get around the city. It's distributed free at the STPB office and at many hotels.

METRIC MEASURES: Singapore uses the metric system. A compendium of metric measures conversion tables is in "The ABCs of Burma," Chapter II.

NEWSPAPERS: The local English-language newspaper is the *Straits Times.* The local business daily is the *Business Times.* The *International Herald Tribune* and international news magazines are widely available. Political controversy has at different times led to governmental restrictions on the distribution of certain publications, such as the *Asian Wall Street Journal* and the *Far Eastern Economic Review.*

POSTAL SERVICE: Visiting a post office in Singapore may be the highlight of your stay! Courteous, smiling, well-dressed staff seated at large desks amid carpeting, marble, and comfortable seating areas manage to assist everyone quickly and efficiently. Don't miss it! The **General Post Office** is located on Fullerton Road south of Marina Center, near Victoria Hall (tel. 533-6234), and is open 24 hours daily for limited services. For most services, the GPO is open from 8 a.m. to 6 p.m. weekdays (on Wednesday until 8 p.m.) and on Saturday until 4 p.m.; closed Sunday and holidays. Branch offices are located throughout the city and are open weekdays from 8:30 a.m. to 5 p.m. (on Wednesday until 8 p.m.) and on Saturday until 1 p.m.; closed Sunday. Call the GPO for exact locations.

Express mail service called **Speedpac** is available to the U.S. and many European countries. Nifty parcel-packing cartons called **Postpacs** are available at reasonable prices. However, be advised of U.S. Customs regulations regarding shipping of textiles or clothing. Call the U.S. Embassy for more information on import quotas.

The only **poste restante** service is at the General Post Office on Fullerton Road. Hours are 8 a.m. to 6 p.m. weekdays, to 4 p.m. on Saturday; closed Sunday. As always, you must present your passport for identification.

RAILWAY INFORMATION: The main railroad station (tel. 222-5165) is located in the western part of the city. Trains leave here regularly for Malaysia and Thailand.

RELIGIOUS SERVICES: In this country of diverse ethnic groups, you can find almost any kind of religious service. For English-language services, try the **Roman Catholic Cathedral of the Good Shepherd,** on Queen Street (tel. 337-2036); the **Orchard Road Presbyterian Church,** at 3 Orchard Rd. (tel. 222-2651); the **Wesley Methodist Church,** 5 Fort Canning (tel. 336-1433); the **Jewish Synagogue,** on Waterloo Street (tel. 336-0692); or the **Anglican St. Andrew's Cathedral,** on Coleman Street (tel. 337-6104).

SMOKING: Smoking is prohibited in public buses, elevators, government offices, cinemas, and theaters. Fines range up to S$500 ($250) for each offense.

TELEPHONE/TELEGRAPH: Most hotels offer direct-dial international service, but with the usual usurious surcharges. However, international telephone rates are the cheapest in Asia, so save up your calls.

The main public telephone office, **Comcentre,** is located at 31 Exeter Rd. (tel. 734-3344), parallel to Orchard Road and southeast of the Mandarin Hotel. It is open 24 hours daily. Other branches are located in the General Post Office on

Fullerton Road and at Changi Airport, both open 24 hours, and in the Handicraft Center on Tanglin Road, open from 8 a.m. to 6 p.m. weekdays, until 2 p.m. on Saturday, and closed Sunday.

The country code for Singapore is 65.

TIPPING: The government is trying to curb the spread of tipping, never a tradition in Singapore. It is prohibited at the airport and discouraged in hotels and restaurants that have a 10% service charge.

TIME: The time is Greenwich Mean Time plus 8 hours, with no seasonal changes, making it 13 hours ahead of New York, 16 hours ahead of Los Angeles. For Daylight Saving Time adjustments in the U.S., subtract 1 hour.

TOURIST INFORMATION: The main office of the **Singapore Tourist Promotion Board (STPB),** on the 36th floor of Raffles City Towers, 250 North Bridge Rd. (tel. 339-6622), is very well organized and prints a wide range of helpful brochures. All are available at the information booth at the airport or at their Tourist Information Centres in the Singapore Handicraft Centre at 163 Tanglin Rd. (tel. 235-5433), or at shop 19 on the first floor of the Raffles City Shopping complex at 250 Northbridge Rd. (tel. 330-0431). Office hours are 8 a.m. to 5 p.m. weekdays, until 1 p.m. on Saturday.

Overseas, the STPB has offices in **New York** at 590 Fifth Ave., 12th floor, New York, NY 10036 (tel. 212/302-4861); in **Los Angeles** at 8484 Wilshire Blvd., Suite 510, Beverly Hills, CA 90212 (tel. 213/852-1901); in **London** at Carrington House, 1st Floor, 126-130 Regent St., London W1R 5FE, England (tel. 01/437-0033); in **Sydney** at Goldfields House, Eighth Floor, 1 Alfred St., Circular Quay, Sydney, NSW 2000, Australia (tel. 02/241-3771). An office is planned for Toronto.

3. ACCOMMODATIONS

Finding a place to sleep is one of Singapore's pleasures—accommodations in this buyer's market are usually quite luxurious and an excellent value. Overbuilding in the mid-'80s created a hotel glut, and only tremendous price reductions kept the international hotels competitive. Today, advertised "Executive Plans," "Singapore Getaways," "Shopper's Specials," and "travel agent rates" are common modes of discounting at all the hotels.

Competition has improved the quality of most facilities, encouraging hotels in every price range to adopt the luxuries once found only at the most expensive hotels. First-class hotels routinely offer such extras as a mini-bar, private coffee/tea setup, hairdryer, toiletries, bathrobes, and newspaper delivery. Almost every moderately priced hotel boasts a Business Center with secretarial, translation, computer rental, Telex, and fax services, and a Fitness Center with sauna, steambath, massage, and exercise equipment. Even budget hotels provide full air conditioning, attractive pools, room service, choice of restaurants, and shopping arcades. It's difficult to distinguish between the dozens of high-quality hotels, so our selections favor hotels closest to Orchard Road, the lifeline of international shoppers.

In this section we've noted the "list" prices for each hotel as a reference point, although these rates are never charged in Singapore itself. One exception —if you reserve an international chain hotel's room through another of the chain's hotels or reservations services, you'll be quoted only "list" price. (We have heard of travelers checking out the morning after their arrival and making a new reservation for the same room at 50% less.) Instead, book your hotel room through a travel agent, or better yet, check with the **Hotel Reservations Desk** at Changi International Airport when you arrive (there are always rooms available if you're a bit flexible). The Changi desk and local travel agents offer the best rates and the latest "specials"—you can get 30% to 50% or more off the rates quoted below, but not every week at every hotel (occasionally a group of conventioneers will come to town and make the market more competitive).

Contact the **Singapore Tourist Promotion Board (STPB),** Raffles City Tower No 36-04, 250 Northbridge Rd., Singapore 0617 (tel. 339-6622), for more information about advertised special rates.

Now, for a look at the best of the best. . . .

LUXURY CHOICES: Singapore offers lots of luxury at very affordable prices, with choices ranging from S$150 ($75) to S$250 ($125) per night for a double room, plus 13% tax and service.

High on everyone's list of the world's great hotels is the **Shangri-La Hotel,** at 22 Orange Grove Rd. (tel. 737-3644), five minutes by taxi east of Orchard Road. Calm, quiet, and confident elegance draw visitors into the expansive marble-and-glass lobby. Three wings, on 15 stunningly landscaped acres far from the madding crowd, house 800 rooms varying from the super-luxe to the sublime. The original main tower has that Shangri-La trademark, an imperial Chinese feel. Deep blues, red, and gold decorate large, comfortable rooms with full amenities, imported toiletries, marble baths, and city views; they're well priced at S$175 ($87.50) to S$195 ($97.50) for two, S$25 ($12.50) less for singles. The newer Garden Wing is built courtyard style around a lush tropical garden, with bougainvillea spilling from every balcony railing. Rooms are richly colored in pale green and yellow with fine Japanese straw matting on the walls and Philippine cane furniture. Views over the pool and garden and a more spacious, sumptuous setting command S$270 ($135) for two. The ultimate Valley Wing offers its own lobby for private check-in, personal butler service, and fresh flowers daily. Larger, more luxuriously appointed rooms in the European style, with muted pastel colors and a full seating area, rent for S$315 ($157.50).

Guests in any wing can sample the Shangri-La's gourmet Chinese, Japanese, and European restaurants, enjoy its well-trained and gracious staff, or make use of the 24-hour Business Centre that's tuned round the clock to the world markets.

The **Sheraton Towers Singapore,** at 39 Scotts Rd. (tel. 737-6868), five minutes by taxi north of the Scotts and Orchard Roads intersection, is a newly built hotel offering stiff competition. Plush Oriental carpets, a soaring marble lobby with fountains and a sweeping staircase, and hundreds of smartly uniformed staff exemplifies the tasteful opulence that touches every aspect of the hotel's operation. Spacious rooms with cool, modern décor (many are cabañas overlooking manicured gardens and a large pool) feature plump rose upholstery, deluxe European furnishings such as a traditional men's coat stand, fresh flowers, marble bathrooms with twin sinks and a separate shower stall, and a selection of video movies. Rates of S$170 ($85) to S$210 ($105) for tower rooms or S$200 ($100) to S$250 ($125) for cabaña or terraced rooms include 24-hour butler service, valets to press out clothing on arrival and present a pot of coffee or tea with your morning paper, and a full breakfast served in your room or in the pretty Terazza Café. The Sheraton Tower has the requisite business and fitness facilities, plus indulgences like the renowned Domus Restaurant with its daily selection of gourmet French and continental fare, and Li Bai, Singapore's most sumptuous venue for Cantonese fare.

The **Goodwood Park Hotel,** at 22 Scotts Rd. (tel. 737-7411), is one of Singapore's most distinguished hotels and as much an institution with knowledgeable travelers as the more heralded Raffles. It was built at the turn of the century for the Teutonia Club, a German social organization, but evolved through the years into an elegant and luxurious hostelry, a brief walk from the favorite shopping district at Orchard Road. The Goodwood Park's original wing and tower, renovated in 1985, resemble a Teutonic castle, now flanked by two modern wings, apartments, and two pools.

The Goodwood Park is known for impeccable service and fine restaurants, yet its unique tranquility and old-world grandeur are what's worth paying for. However, the loyalty of past guests means that room rates are less negotiable than at other, less popular establishments. Almost half of the 235 rooms are suites, and each wing has its own elegant style. Spacious, deluxe double rooms in the original wing, which rent for S$220 ($110, $15 less for single occupants), are furnished in chintz and plush like an English drawing room, and in an opulent, modern international style in the newer wings. Junior suites with a separate seating area cost S$280 ($140), larger poolside cabañas with a sitting room run S$410 ($205), and the fancy, neoclassic Brunei Suite (designed for His Highness's frequent shopping sprees) costs S$3,000 ($1,500).

The **Oriental Singapore,** at 5 Raffles Ave. (tel. 338-0066), is the most luxurious of the three starkly modern 500+-room hotels opened in 1987 at the new Marina Square development. As one of the Mandarin Oriental chain, the Oriental prides itself on superb service, the best of Asian hospitality, and the resourcefulness to satisfy every guest's whims. A posh lobby of black granite, marble, and gold sits at the base of a startling triangular atrium, the focal point for cafés, lounges, and a piano bar. The Oriental's Cherry Garden Restaurant, a replica of a Ming nobleman's courtyard, serves Cantonese dishes family style.

Very contemporary rooms detailed in teak wood with peach and lime silk furnishings, full marble baths, and state-of-the-art media overlook the Singapore River or the gardens of Marina Square. Double room rates range from S$150 ($75) to S$230 ($115); many suites, starting at S$300 ($150), include kitchenettes and balconies.

The **Marina Mandarin** at 6 Raffles Ave. (tel. 338-3388), is the other Mandarin Oriental property in Marina Square, with an emphasis on a more casual and visually pleasing atmosphere. Designed in the familiar John Portman atrium fashion, the Marina Mandarin's cream marble lobby comes alive with tinkling wind chimes and the muted patter of guests and staff. Beautifully decorated rooms in teal blue, with canopied beds and teak and burlwood furnishings, contain full-size desks, a seating area with tea service, large marble baths with twin sinks and separate shower, and full balconies with views of the huge pool, Singapore harbor, or the city skyline. Several restaurants include the stylish Ristorante Bologna, where fine northern Italian dishes are served in- or outdoors; the House of Blossoms, which specializes in the spicy Chinese cuisine from the Teochew region; and the rollicking Cricketer bar. Room rates are S$150 ($75) to S$170 ($85), depending on floor; the Marina Club floor, with rooms at S$190 ($95), includes concierge service, complimentary full breakfast, and a private lounge for tea or cocktails—one of the city's best values in "executive" floors.

A SENTIMENTAL FAVORITE: If there is any institution that is synonymous with Singapore it must be the legendary **Raffles Hotel** located at 1-7 Beach Rd. (tel. 337-8041), at the edge of the business district. This venerable inn has been around since the early 1800s, evolving from a beachfront bungalow into a "Tiffin House" (a dining room within a private home), then into a full-fledged hotel built in 1896 by the Armenian Sarkie brothers as the classiest venue in the colony. It became just that, attracting a stellar list of world travelers and Singapore's smart set for dining and dancing. Writers always congregated there, drawn by the cavernous rooms with shaded porches, the leisurely colonial style of luxury, and the Long Bar, source of the Singapore Sling. Rudyard Kipling graced it with praise, Somerset Maugham and Noël Coward touted it, and one wag in the 1920s called it "the Savoy of the East."

Just as we went to press, the Raffles management announced that the hotel will be closed till sometime in 1991 for extensive renovation and expansion. Check with the Singapore Tourist Promotion Board or your travel agent before you plan a visit to the Long Bar or the Palm Court.

FIRST-CLASS HOTELS: The first-class category denotes hotels that are often on a par with luxury-class lodgings but are priced somewhat less, from S$130 ($65) to S$220 ($110), plus 13% tax and service charges. Several of our choices also readily sell discounted rooms through reservations services; for example, one of our favorites rented its S$210 rooms for S$88 to celebrate 1988, the Year of the Dragon.

The **Hilton International Singapore** is at the heart of the shopping district at 581 Orchard Rd. (tel. 737-2233). Its ideal, walk-to-anywhere location, efficient staff, excellent Harbour Grill Restaurant, and complete executive facilities make it popular with business travelers. The understated elegance of a gray- and red-veined marble lobby is picked up in the muted earth tones of 435 large, well-kept guest rooms, renting for S$170 ($85) to S$210 ($105). A dozen suites on the 22nd floor, designed by Hubert de Givenchy with a Chinoise flair, treat guests to private maid and butler service, a personal steam shower, whirlpool, and large private balcony; these cost S$450 ($225) per night, with smaller suites starting at S$320 ($165). The Hilton has a rooftop pool, big enough for real swimmers, enveloped by panoramic city views; the health club's complete facilities are frequented by local members as well as hotel guests.

The **Hyatt Regency,** at 10-12 Scotts Rd. (tel. 733-1188), off the corner of Orchard Road, retains a sense of intimacy despite being one of Singapore's largest (1,120 rooms) hotels. Across a cool, quiet marble lobby is the older wing, with pleasant but undistinguished rooms running S$180 ($90) for two. Beyond it past a dramatic waterfall is the newer Regency Terrace Wing, which opens onto a verdant pool terrace. Rooms are radically more luxurious; marble baths, breakfast alcoves with garden views, and sophisticated gray décor make the S$200 ($100) price seem like a steal. Both wings offer extra amenities (breakfast/cocktail lounge, newspaper delivery, etc.) on the Regency Club floor for an additional S$50 ($25) per night.

The newly built **Pan Pacific Singapore Hotel,** at 7 Raffles Ave., Marina Square (tel. 336-8111), radiates from a graceful 36-story marble-clad atrium the largest in Southeast Asia, ribbed with futuristic glass-bullet elevators. Spacious rooms paneled in rich woods are luxuriously furnished in pastel fabrics. Marble bathrooms with imported amenities and a separate toilet complete a well-priced package that ranges from S$155 ($77.50) to S$225 ($112.50), depending on floor and view; harbor views cost S$20 ($10) additional. For a splash of luxury, go straight up to the Kingfisher floor, where rates of S$295 ($147.50) include breakfast, a private lounge for complimentary cocktails and tea, and butler, laundry, and dry-cleaning service. For more splash, head to the pool terrace and lyrical Japanese Gardens, or sample one of the Pan Pacific's many fine restaurants.

The **Century Park Sheraton,** at 15 Nassim Hill (tel. 732-1222), is located in a park-like setting a 15-minute walk from Orchard Road. The reception, paneled in dark wood with fluted Cornithian columns and rich tapestries, reminds guests more of an English manor house than a hotel. Newly renovated deluxe rooms at S$220 ($110) are comfortably furnished in moss-green and tan fabrics, with built-in seating and work areas. Standard rooms at S$160 ($80) are more commonplace, but the hotel's large pool, garden, and the excellent Hubertus Grill and Unkai restaurants make it a good value.

The **Holiday Inn Park View,** at 11 Cavenagh Rd. (tel. 733-8333), one block behind Orchard Road, is that chain's entry into the deluxe/businessmen's market. The Park View's 320 rooms have a low-key international style derived from bentwood furniture, tan marble, beige fabric wall coverings, and sky-blue upholstery. Standard doubles renting for S$160 ($80) to S$200 ($100) include private safe, work area, seating lounge, and marble bathrooms. The Executive Floor has a private lounge with complimentary breakfast buffet, tea, cocktails, and newspaper delivery for an additional S$50 ($25) daily. The Park View has the amenities of all its competitors, plus a quiet yet very convenient location, an excellent Indian restaurant, and a bake shop.

The 40-story twin towers perched over the shopping district at 333 Orchard Rd. belong to the **Mandarin Singapore** (tel. 737-4411), a locally owned deluxe hotel that was one of the republic's first. The Mandarin is currently undergoing a renovation that will equip its 1,200 guest rooms with whirlpool baths, a televised phone-message system, and new Oriental furnishings. Rates for spacious rooms with well-lit makeup tables, work desks, and lots of turquoise silk run S$135 ($67.50) to S$175 ($87.50). There are five beautifully decorated Presidential suites whose modern, Japanese, Persian, Asian, and Mandarin (our favorite) styles rival the best suites anywhere at only S$1,200 ($600) per night. The Mandarin's classically glitzy lobby with a towering crystal chandelier from Venini is a popular meeting spot for locals heading to the 24-hour Chatterbox Coffee Shop.

Le Meridien Singapore is tucked in behind a row of designer boutiques at 100 Orchard Rd. (tel. 733-8855). The six-story atrium lobby is lined with pure-white Italian marble, accented by colorful orchids and ivy which trail from each landing. Pleasant "superior" rooms with all the amenities and tasteful pastel décor fetch S$170 ($85) for two, similar "deluxe" rooms with views of the fifth-floor pool terrace run S$200 ($100), and single occupants pay S$30 ($15) less. As expected from this French chain, Le Meridien serves up superb cuisine française in the resident, casual Brasserie and the more formal Restaurant de France.

The facilities of the new **Westin Plaza** and **Westin Stamford Hotels,** at 2 Stamford Rd. (tel. 338-8585), in the heart of the Raffles City complex belong in the *Guinness Book of World Records.* The Stamford is the tallest hotel in the world at 73 stories, with rooms overlooking Singapore, Malaysia, and Indonesia. The two Westins share 17 bars and restaurants, a jazz club and disco, two swimming pools, six tennis and four squash courts, health and business centers with the latest technology, a surrounding 75-shop mall with a Sogo Department Store, and a 6,000-seat convention center.

If record-breaking is not what you want from a hotel, you'll prefer the cool sophistication of the Westin Plaza. It has 796 large rooms with balconies and all amenities, tastefully furnished in Oriental shades of umber and jade. The well-trained staff manage to keep its 23 stories rather calm and businesslike although the crucial front desk is shared by both hotels. Rates at the more exclusive Westin Plaza run S$160 ($80) to S$200 ($100) for single occupants, S$30 ($15) more for doubles (although children up to 18 years can share the room free with their parents), and S$460 ($230) and up for suites, all depending on view.

At the Westin Stamford 1,253 smaller but very gracious guest rooms fill an adjoining tower. These rent for S$140 ($70) to S$180 ($90) for singles, S$30 ($15) more for doubles, and upward of S$460 ($230) for suites. All rooms have balconies, including the usually sold-out 73rd floor! Although the tremendous capacity of the Westin Stamford makes personalized service impossible, its novelty appeals to many travelers.

The **Dynasty Hotel,** 320 Orchard Rd. (tel. 734-9900), is one of Singapore's most dramatic and distinctively Chinese hotels, its pagoda-style octagonal tower rising 33 stories above the intersection of Scotts and Orchard Roads. The tower's gold-tiled base houses a stunning lobby framed on two sides by enormous, exquisite Chinese woodcarvings. The 24 teak panels, each 48 feet by 4 feet, depict scenes of Chinese wars, legendary historical personages, and illustrations of myths. Shanghai woodcarvers labored for almost two years to complete the work commissioned by C. K. Tang, one of Singapore's wealthiest men and the owner of the Dynasty and the Tang's department store at its base. Chinese modern décor dominates the 378 spacious and comfortable rooms; doubles cost S$185 ($92.50) to S$195 ($97.50).

THE BUDGET RANGE: Most of Singapore's moderately priced hotels are a bit away from the expensive Orchard Road real estate belt but still just a short walk from the shops. Our selections are new or recently renovated and well maintained, and offer so many attractive amenities (such as pools, personal coffee/tea setup, mini-bar, color TV with in-house movies, choice of restaurants, complimentary toiletries) that most travelers, especially those in groups or with families, will find them very good value. List prices range from S$105 ($52.50) to S$160 ($80) for two, plus 13% tax and service charges, but with typical discounts of 20% to 40% they can be considered budget hotels.

The best of these is the **Ming Court Hotel,** at 1 Tanglin Rd. (tel. 737-1133), just off Orchard Road, where guests are greeted by a hefty doorman in a silver-studded Ming warrior's costume. The Chinese atmosphere created by courteous service, jade-green rugs, skillfully carved teak furnishings, and the enclosed lobby courtyard becomes more international in the pastel fabrics and contemporary furnishings of 300 newly renovated rooms. Spacious living quarters, including rooms on two no-smoking floors, run S$120 ($60) to S$160 ($80), depending on view. The Ming Court has a popular coffeeshop with an ethnic buffet and international food, a good Szechuan restaurant, and a Singapore rarity—a pleasant sidewalk café on bustling Orchard Road.

The **Crown Prince Hotel,** at 270 Orchard Rd. (tel. 732-1111), is a white edifice with black-glass windows that match the wildly popular fashions of its ground-floor Esprit clothing shop. This well-run, Japanese-owned hotel has 300 rooms decorated in a soothing light oak, coral, and jade color scheme. The Crown Prince has a lively coffeeshop, Japanese and Szechuan restaurants, and a comfortable cocktail lounge; doubles run S$160 ($80) to S$180 ($90) and suites start at S$350 ($175).

The **Royal Holiday Inn,** 25 Scotts Rd. (tel. 737-7966), will make many travelers feel right at home. The bustling lobby is filled with children in bathing suits, moms with shopping bags, and business people with newspapers. Spacious rooms eschew marble tiles for carpeting and molded-plastic bathrooms, all spotlessly clean. Pastel colors and trendy décor, laundry rooms with dryers and ironing boards, and soda machines abound in a comfortable, homey atmosphere. Rates range from S$145 ($72.50) to S$175 ($87.50), S$15 ($7.50) less for singles and S$350 ($175) and up for suites, with pricier rooms offering king-size beds, bathrobes, and slippers. The Royal Holiday Inn has a lobby pastry shop, a popular smörgåsbord served at the Baron's Table, a good Szechuan restaurant, and a pool and sundeck level with a snackbar, miniature golf course, and a small Fitness Centre.

The **Boulevard Hotel** is at 200 Orchard Blvd. (tel. 737-2911), a block behind Orchard Road off Cuscaden Road. It offers many of the amenities of its more expensive neighbors, but on a smaller scale. Single travelers will find the best rate in this neighborhood, with compact, well-furnished rooms starting at S$115 ($57.50). Twin rooms, a bit larger with a seating area, start at S$155 ($77.50) and range to S$175 ($87.50), roomier still with a small kitchenette. The Boulevard's atrium lobby, accented by a 15-story-tall aluminum sculpture, lends a classy air.

The **Plaza Hotel,** at 7500A Beach Rd. (tel. 298-0011), opposite the traditional markets of Arab Street, is less convenient but provides regular shuttle service to shopping and business areas. Excellent-value rooms are large and newly furnished in bleached woods and pastels, with marble bathrooms and deluxe amenities; they rent for S$120 ($60) to S$140 ($70), S$20 ($10) less for singles. The seventh-floor "Penthouse" has 28 lovely rooms with private terraces, a lounge for complimentary breakfast and cocktails, valet service, and newspaper delivery for S$30 ($15) more per day. The Plaza has a new fitness center, squash and tennis courts, a large pool, the Streets of London pub, and the Club 5 dance lounge (very popular with locals).

The **Peninsula Hotel,** at 3 Coleman St. (tel. 337-2200), off North Bridge Road, is an older choice, located in a small shopping mall about a ten-minute walk from Raffles City. The facilities and rooms are worn but clean, and the group tours that frequent it and the adjoining Excelsior Hotel make it a lively place. Large rooms (particularly the corner ones with harbor views) rent for S$95 ($47.50) to S$115 ($57.50) single, S$105 ($52.50) to S$130 ($65) double.

Another good choice is the **York Hotel,** directly behind Goodwood Park at 21 Mount Elizabeth Rd. (tel. 737-0511), a budget member of the posh Goodwood Park Hotels chain. Recently refurbished, the York offers clean, comfortable double rooms for S$115 ($57.50) to S$155 ($77.50), depending on size and view. The York has a nice outdoor pool and easy access to the Goodwood Park's marvelous coffeeshop for high tea, and is a short walk from the Orchard Road shops.

The **Tai-Pan Ramada Hotel,** at 101 Victoria St., off Bras Besah Road (tel. 336-0811), is a ten-minute walk from the Raffles City complex. After a recent renovation and expansion, the hotel has 500 full-amenity rooms decorated in rosewood furniture with an Oriental flair. Singles run S$125 ($62.50) to S$180 ($90), and doubles are S$15 ($7.50) more, depending on floor. The Tai-Pan also has one- and two-bedroom suites with kitchenettes for long-term guests which start at S$2,500 ($1,250) per month, a rate that includes a 50% discount on laundry and dry cleaning. The hotel has a small pool, disco, Chinese and Japanese restaurants, and a café popular for its inexpensive Indian curry, Indonesian rijsttafel, or Thai buffet meals.

READERS' HOTEL SELECTION: "We have been in Singapore ten times and have stayed at the Ladyhill Hotel—it was good and inexpensive. We stayed at Raffles—very old, very British, very nice, and expensive. The Orchard Hotel has an excellent buffet breakfast of American and Chinese food. We prefer to stay at the **Asia Hotel** (tel. 737-8388) so that we can treat ourselves to one night in Raffles. This fine hotel is ideally located on Scotts Road (next to the American Club) and three blocks off Orchard Road, and has all the amenities except a swimming pool. It cost only S$50 ($25)" (Jean and Tony Triumpho, Canajoharie, N.Y.).

HOSTELS: Singapore's tourism industry is so strongly oriented to the international shopper who comes to spend money that few inexpensive hostels exist in the republic. Most of our selections are student facilities that welcome travelers of any age; rates run S$30 ($15) to S$80 ($40) for two, plus 13% tax and service charges.

Ironically, the best bargain is ideal for budget watchers who want to shop. The **YMCA International House,** at 1 Orchard Rd. (tel. 337-3444), is conveniently located near the National Museum and a short walk from the Orchard Road shops. Air-conditioned rooms are clean and comfortable, with plain but tasteful furnishings. They rent for S$45 ($22.50), S$55 ($27.50), and S$70 ($35) for one, two, or three occupants; the triple is a small suite with a separate sitting room. Dormitory rooms with four bunks each cost S$20 ($10) per bed, but all rooms have private shower and TV. There is a small canteen serving cheap, tasty food and a McDonald's on the ground floor which will deliver a Big Mac to your door! The YMCA's gym, Olympic-size pool, and squash courts are available to guests at certain hours.

The **RELC International House,** at 30 Orange Grove Rd. (tel. 737-9044), is part of the Regional Education Language Centre located next door to the opulent Shangri-La Hotel. The centre provides its students with 128 hotel rooms, which are open to travelers when available. They are large, comfortable, and tasteful, and many have balconies overlooking the Shangri-La's gardens. Prices range from S$52 ($26) for a twin-bedded room, or S$58 ($29) for a queen-size bed, to S$65 ($32.50) for a suite with sitting area. A small restaurant offers reasonably priced meals. The RELC's exceptional facilities make it a good value, despite its inconvenient location.

The English Tudor-style **Sloane Court Hotel,** at 17 Balmoral Rd. (tel. 235-3311), is one block from the public buses of Stevens Road or a 15-minute taxi ride from the shopping area on Orchard Road. Although somewhat inconvenient, this budget lodging has a hotel rather than a youth hostel feel. There are 32 worn but cozy rooms with twin beds, a seating area, phone, TV, and attached bath. Rooms rent for S$45 ($22.50) to S$75 ($37.50) for singles, or S$10 ($5) more for doubles; for another S$5 ($2.50) you can have a full, fairly authentic English breakfast. The Sloane Court's quiet residential neighborhood, bargain prices, and home-like Berkely Pub make it very popular with travelers from the former colonial powers.

The **Fort Canning Center YWCA Hostel** is a prim and proper, no-frills lodging just one block from Orchard Road (tel. 336-3150) behind the Supreme House shopping complex. Simple, worn, but clean twin-bedded rooms with ceiling fans and a shared bathroom rent for S$24 ($12) for one, S$30 ($15) for two, but are available to women only. Newer, air-conditioned rooms with private shower are also available to married couples and families for S$28 ($14) for one, S$35 ($17.50) for two. Rates include continental breakfast, and the cafeteria serves inexpensive lunch and dinners. Each floor of the YWCA has a common refrigerator, laundry sinks with ironing facilities, and payphones.

READER'S GUESTHOUSE SELECTION: "There weren't too many cheap places, but I found **Sim's Guest House,** where a bed (four to a room) cost S$5 ($2.50). It was a nice place at 114A Mackenzie Rd., near Bukit Timah and Serangoon Rd. (tel. 336-4957)" (Stan Mendoza, New York, N.Y.).

4. DINING

It's no surprise that the four tapered white columns of the War Memorial are nicknamed the "Four Chopsticks." Food—its ingredients, preparation, and presentation—is an all-consuming pastime with Singaporeans. Typically, locals will arise early to have a full breakfast of *congee* (Chinese rice porridge), *bubur* (Malay rice porridge) or *dosai* (Indian rice flour pancakes) before work. At lunch, lines form at the best *dian xin* (dim sum or Chinese dumplings) restaurants, at hawker's centers (outdoor ethnic food malls), or at the international buffets served at most hotels. In the late afternoon, those who can get away plan high tea with their friends. After work, fresh ingredients are picked up for the evening meal, usually eaten at home with the many generations of family who live together. After supper, the young meet up with their friends to listen to music or see a movie, and often end their evening at one of the popular Orchard Road coffeeshops that specialize in bubur ayam (rice porridge with chicken) or Hainanese chicken rice. Every ethnic food is served by variety fast-food outlets that feed those who grab a croissant and coffee on the way to work, wolf down pizza or hamburgers at their desk, and buy take-out meals for supper; but if time allows, most Singaporeans will opt for more leisurely and social dining.

It's no wonder then that Singapore rivals Hong Kong in its choice of cuisines and excellence of preparation. Singaporeans will go anywhere for a good meal, and every international hotel competes for this lucrative local market with a variety of high-quality restaurants. So don't be surprised when we urge you to leave your hotel to sample fare at the one next door; it's one of the few cities in the world where "hotel food" usually is better, and where reasonable prices, buffets, and fixed-price menus make even gourmet meals affordable.

The section following "Culinary Highlights" (our selection of the best in each category), is divided into the ethnic cuisines available. Most visitors don't have time to sample everything, but you should try at least one ethnic Chinese, Malay or Peranakan, and Indian meal, and one from the Singapore-style mélange served in hawker's centers.

Most of our recommendations are centrally located near the Orchard Road shops and hotels; larger facilities and hotel restaurants all accept credit cards. Unless otherwise noted, restaurants request "smart casual" dress (not tank tops or shorts). They are open daily for lunch (from 11:30 a.m. to 3 p.m. six days, from 10:30 a.m. on Sunday) and dinner (from 6 to 10:30 or 11 p.m.), and prefer reservations for supper.

CULINARY HIGHLIGHTS: A continental and a Chinese restaurant in two of Singapore's finest hotels offer such excellent fare in so beautiful an atmosphere that dining at these two places can be a memorable experience of your stay. On the opposite end of the scale in terms of expense and formality are the hawker's centers, multi-ethnic food malls where dining is a distinctly Singaporean adventure that's not to be missed.

D.O.M.U.S., in the ultra-luxurious Sheraton Towers at 39 Scotts Rd. (tel. 737-6868), is a dining room of quiet elegance, a restaurant whose ambience, excellent continental and French cuisine, and impeccable service are truly memorable. D.O.M.U.S. sparkles among the best internationally distinguished restaurants; gold silk banquettes and tables set with crystal, porcelain, and silver glow in candlelight reflected by bronze mirrors. Broad marble columns provide an intimacy that is discreetly romantic. A gourmet feast is delivered with the smoothest of service: smoked goose breast or pigeon bouillon with zucchini to start, a crayfish cassolette trailed by a palate-cleansing sorbet, pan-fried beef with cabernet sauce or a navarin of lobster and spring vegetables, followed by a platter of cheeses and grapes and a selection from their heavenly dessert menu. Consistently excellent and creative fare is complemented by an extensive wine cellar, encouraging those accustomed to the best at home to sample the best here. Two should count on spending S$160 ($80) to S$210 ($105) with wine; dressy attire and reservations are requested.

Some of the finest Cantonese cooking and most extravagant Chinese décor is found at the **Shang Palace,** on the second floor of the opulent Shangri-La Hotel, 22 Orange Grove Rd. (tel. 737-3644). The Shang Palace replicates a Shang Dynasty courtyard, with enormous red Chinese lanterns, rich wood paneling, and ornately carved screens. The preparation of ancient Chinese recipes with remedial and spiritual benefits is a specialty that lures gourmands and tradition-minded locals. Seafood is one more common specialty; chili crabs, steamed Soon Hock fish, and pan-fried scallops in black-bean sauce, served in a basket of woven yam slices, are favorites. The crispy, deep-fried duck stuffed with water chestnuts and mushrooms is also excellent. A wide variety of unusual and well-prepared dim sum is served at lunch and makes a filling, satisfying meal for S$16 ($8) to S$25 ($12.50) per person, although the more numerous your party, the cheaper sampling many dishes will be. Dining from the regular menu runs upward of S$32 ($16) per person.

After you've tired of sophisticated hotel restaurants, spend a relaxed afternoon or evening at a hawker's center, where dozens of foodstalls hawking every variety of local and ethnic fare allow you to explore new tastes with ease.

SINGAPORE-STYLE DINING / THE HAWKER'S CENTRES: Don't leave Singapore without a visit to the **Newton Circus Hawker Centre** at the north end of Scotts Road at the Newton Circus traffic circle. It's an open-air bazaar of 50 foodstalls whose proximity to the Orchard Road hotels makes it the ultimate venue for Singapore's favorite sport.

To eat Singapore style, select a numbered table and plant one of your companions at it, then take turns shopping at each foodstall. You can watch the Chinese, Malay (Muslim), and Indian cooks concoct their specialty; to order, indicate the dish you want and the size of the portion. Prices are posted, but check what your order will cost and give the hawker your table number. (The busboy/attendants in marked T-shirts are very helpful if the aromas disorient you.) Continue strolling and choose soups, vegetable dishes, appetizers, noodles, fruits, desserts, or fresh-squeezed fruit drinks. Most items cost less than S$3 ($1.50) a portion, with Chinese dumplings, Indian pakoras, or Malay fish balls less than S$.50 (25¢) each. Pay for each dish when it's brought to your table and you can feast with friends for less than S$10 ($5) each.

Our favorite grazing items include popiah (a delicate rice-flour crêpe filled with chopped steamed vegetables, peanuts, and a sweet bean sauce), Hainan chicken rice (a plate of rice with side orders of moist, sliced chicken and chicken broth that's flavored with chili sambal), murtabak (an exquisite pancake filled with egg, ground meat or chicken, green chiles, and onions), chay tow kueh or carrot cake (a Chinese treat of fried radish cakes scrambled with eggs, turnips, garlic, and chile), mee Siam, Thai style (flavorful glass noodles with condiments), satay ayam (grilled chicken on skewers doused in a Malay sweet peanut sauce), rojak (a piquant salad of fresh guava, orange, cucumber, pineapple, bean sprouts, and sliced Chinese cruller in peanut sauce), and kutu piring (rice cakes drowned in dark sago palm syrup with grated coconut). The gourmet will enjoy *The Guide to Singapore Hawker Food,* a delightful encyclopedia of edibles by James Hooi that's sold in most bookstores.

The Newton Circus Hawker Centre is a nighttime affair, best visited from 6 to 11 p.m.

Rasa Singapura, or "Taste of Singapore," is an excellent choice for lunch, remaining open from about 9 a.m. to 7 p.m. It's located at the Singapore Handicrafts Centre on Tanglin Road, next to the Singapore Tourist Promotion Board office and opposite the Marco Polo Hotel.

The **Cuppage Plaza Hawker Centre** is a small, more comfortable enclave of foodstalls behind the Centrepoint shopping complex at Cuppage and Orchard Roads (opposite the Mandarin Hotel). Tiny stalls and a few coffeeshops serve shoppers indoors or out on the promenade, between 10 a.m. and 7 or 8 p.m.

Travelers with more time or the will to explore should try the **UDMC East Coast Seafood Centre,** located next to the modern sports facility on East Coast Parkway, about 25 minutes' drive from Orchard Road. The indoor and outdoor restaurant are competitively priced, offer the freshest seafood around, and are packed on weekends. Chilli crab (Singapore spelling) is the national favorite—chunks of fresh crab fried with chile, ginger, and tomato, and coated with a bright-red, not-too-spicy sauce. Chinese prawns steamed in black-bean sauce, crisp fried squid, and steamed pomfret and garoupa (similar to carp) are also delicious.

The **Ocean Park Seafood Restaurant,** at no. 01-02 (tel. 448-1895), is one of the many excellent restaurants. Expect to pay about S$30 ($15) per person in a group of four. The East Coast Seafood Centre is open daily from 5 p.m. to about midnight, from 11 a.m. on weekends.

CHINESE CUISINE: Mandarin-speaking Chinese make up 76% of the republic's population, a majority that controls business, commerce, and some of the best restaurants around. Although most families emigrated from the Fukien province, Cantonese fare is the best represented of China's regional cuisines, with dim sum (dian xin in the Mandarin dialect) served at lunch almost everywhere. The spicy cuisine from Szechuan province is also available and specific dishes from Hokkien, Hainan, Teochew, and other provinces are sold at the hawker's centers. Local Chinese favor independent restaurants and the small coffeeshops of Chinatown, where old ways and old prices still prevail.

To get the most from your meal, dine with at least four people so you can sample the most dishes, be open to new tastes, and in the Chinese manner, follow your waiter's suggestions to balance the yin (coolness) and yang (warmth) of your entrees.

Diners looking for a splurge and a superb Cantonese meal should dress up and head for **Li Bai,** the restaurant named for the 8th-century Tang Dynasty poet in the Sheraton Towers Hotel at 39 Scotts Rd. (tel. 737-6888). The décor and table furnishings are exquisite; deep-red walls, ebony wood trim, and glass screens separate tables set with jade chopstick rests and silver and ivory chopsticks. Li Bai's specialties include suckling pig, grilled boneless breast of duck with mango, and a variety of abalone, whelk, and other seafood dishes. The service is both refined and attentive, with staff eager to help create your banquet, but jade, ivory, and service have their price. Couples will probably spend about S$150 ($75) for a memorable meal; reservations recommended.

A more modest but attractive and very popular spot for gourmet Cantonese fare is the **Tung Lok Shark's Fin Restaurant,** 177 River Valley Rd. (tel. 336-6022), on the fourth floor of Liang Court, an office-and-shopping complex next to the New Otani Hotel. Tung Lok and its guests are elegant in a distinctly Chinese fashion; clients savor pricey shark's-fin dishes ("superior" shark's fin can cost $150 a portion), abalone, and bird's nest. We liked the Beijing dry-fried mutton with leek, and sea scallops in a batter of mashed yams; average meals run about S$30 ($15) per person. Lunch is a good time to experiment with more exotic fare via dim sum. Feather-light steamed dumplings filled with shark's-fin soup, turnip cakes with Chinese sausage, and daily specials are delicious and affordable, costing S$30 ($15) to S$50 ($25) for two.

Dim sum or dian xin, which translates as "to touch the heart," is a selection of freshly steamed morsels eaten with tea. It's as much a morning and midday social gathering as a meal. Delicate dumplings, spring rolls, steamed buns, and bean, rice, or noodle dishes are served in small portions and shared by the table. **Fook Yuen,** in the prestigious Paragon shopping center at 290 Orchard Rd. (tel. 235-2211), is considered one of Singapore's best dim sum restaurants. Favorites such as minced-pork dumplings, deep-fried prawns with mashed yam, green leek dumplings, and banana and prawn rolls are served daily from 11 a.m. to 3 p.m. Expect to pay S$55 ($27.50) for two at lunch; reservations recommended.

Another popular venue for dim sum is the **Seafood Garden Restaurant,** in the Goodwood Park Hotel, 22 Scotts Rd. (tel. 737-7411). In a bright-white lively grotto, aquariums display dining possibilities to seafood lovers. But the crowds come every Sunday from 11 a.m. to 2:30 p.m. when the restaurant has an "all you can eat" brunch for S$15 ($7.50) where more than 50 different kinds of dim sum are featured.

Another local favorite is the **Ming Palace,** in the Ming Court Hotel at 1 Tanglin Rd. (tel. 737-1133). Every day between 11:30 a.m. and 2:30 p.m. a huge buffet is laid out for S$13 ($6.50), a better value for those who sample everything than for the gourmand who prefers freshly steamed dim sum. At night the Ming Palace features a steamboat buffet for S$16 ($8), where diners can choose sliced seafood or meat and cook it fondue style over a steaming cauldron at their table.

The well-spiced meats and chile-laced dishes prepared in the Szechuan style have become very popular. The **Min Jiang Sichuan Restaurant,** in the gracious Goodwood Park Hotel at 22 Scotts Rd. (tel. 737-7411), is the powerbroker's choice for Szechuan cuisine. Gilt-coffered ceilings overhang large tables, many of which are set aside behind screens for private parties, at S$500 ($250) minimum of ten people. In the main dining room parties of four or more can savor spring-onion dumplings, whole roast duck, sautéed king prawns with dried chile, and many other flavorful specialties. Min Jiang's menu also includes Cantonese items such as shark's fin and bird's nest, but the salty, spicy foods from Szechuan, best consumed with a cold beer, are our choice. Four will feast for S$160 ($80) to S$210 ($105). It's open daily from noon to 2:30 p.m. and 6:30 to 10:30 p.m., and reservations are recommended.

Mei San, in the Royal Holiday Inn at 25 Scotts Rd. (tel. 737-7966), was Singapore's first Szechuan restaurant and remains very popular. In typical Ming Dynasty surroundings diners can examine fresh seafood in a wall of aquariums and order it in a variety of styles, or enjoy camphor-smoked duck, Szechuan pan-cakes filled with red-bean paste, or red-chile chicken with cashew nuts. Dinner for two averages S$85 ($42.50) to S$110 ($55), including beer.

MALAY AND NONYA CUISINE: Singapore's Malay population is pre-dominantly Muslim, with strong ties to its neighbors in Indonesia and Malaysia. The local Malay cuisine uses rich sauces of coconut milk, fresh seasonings, and herbs to create exotic meat, fish, and poultry stews, and mixed-vegetable dishes that are always spicy but not necessarily hot. The most popular Malay dish is satay, skewers of meat, seafood, or chicken that are grilled over coals and served with a sweet peanut sauce. The Peranakan culture (also known as the Straits Chi-nese) derived from the intermarriage of local Malays with immigrant Chinese. It produced a rich blend of Oriental and tropical island cuisine that is called Nonya cuisine, after the Peranakan word for "woman." Visitors interested in sampling Malay and Nonya cooking will find many vendors in hawker's centers, but only a few authentic restaurants.

Gunong Sayang, is on the third floor of 15 Scotts Rd. (tel. 235-4848), next to the Royal Holiday Inn. It's a simple place with plastic-covered batik table-cloths and overhead fluorescent lighting, but its Nonya cuisine is rich and com-plex. Vegetables, curries, spices, coconut, and fruits are blended into exotic sauces. Try the udang kuah nanas (prawns with pineapple), otah otah (fish paste steamed in banana leaves), kachang titek (green beans), buah keluak (chicken cur-ry with nuts), or hati babi bungkus (spicy pork livers). The friendly staff is eager to help you order, and most dishes are S$5.50 ($2.75) or less. Gunong Sayang is open daily from 11:30 a.m. to 10 p.m.

Aziza's Restaurant is housed in a traditional two-story shop/house at 36 Emerald Hill Rd. (tel. 235-1130), off Orchard Road in Peranakan Place. The dark interior, decorated in batik and rattan, is in keeping with the Malay heritage of its cuisine. Specialties such as ayam pudima Asmara (mint and almonds with chicken) and terutop (fish stuffed with chile and onions) are typically Malaysian. Many chicken, pork, and fish entrees that sound Indonesian are cooked a bit dif-ferently, using a variety of spices. Aziza is a good starting point on an odyssey through Singapore's many cuisines and is good value at S$35 ($17.50) for two. Open daily for lunch and dinner, except Sunday when it's open from 7 to 11 p.m. only.

INDIAN CUISINE: Most of Singapore's Indian population derive from trad-ers who came from what is now Tamil Nadu, in the south. Their neighborhood around Serangoon Road, northeast of Orchard Road, has several restaurants spe-cializing in southern Indian cuisine, mostly spicy vegetarian foods eaten by the Tamil Hindus. Outside this area are several fine restaurants that serve the mutton curries and biryani dishes of the Muslim north and the saffron-laced dishes from Kashmir. Hawker's centers usually have several Indian foodstalls that sell typical Indian dishes or the Indian interpretation of popular Malay and Nonya dishes.

The most elegant of these many establishments is **Tandoor,** the northern Indian restaurant in the Holiday Inn Park View at 11 Cavenagh Rd. (tel. 733-8333). Tandoor's fragrant aroma, deep cinnabar coloring, its still pool around which tables are placed, and the soothing ragas of the nightly sitar player transport diners to a maharaja's court. If you're unsure whether to order the moist tandoori chicken (baked with lemon in a clay oven), prawns in masala (spiced) curry, Kashmiri pillau (saffron rice with dried fruit and nuts), or saag paneer (cheese cooked in the creamiest spinach), walk over to the glass-enclosed kitchen to see what the chefs are up to. Be sure to order some naan or roti (Indian breads) with any meal. Fully satisfied guests of the maharaja should pay about S$36 ($18) per person and daily luncheon specials are S$19 ($9.50); reservations are recommended at dinner.

Banana-leaf restaurants are a true Singapore specialty, casual places where a placemat-size banana leaf is used instead of plates. The best of these is **Banana Leaf Apollo** at 56 Race Course Rd. (tel. 293-5054), in Little India. Locals line up for authentic fish-head curry, but you can request that only the okra cooked with the fish head in a delicious curry sauce be served over your mound of rice. Food is displayed in serving dishes at the rear; check out the vegetable curry, mutton Mysore, cuttlefish curry, and piquant side orders of cabbage and green beans served to every diner. Two will spend about S$22 ($11).

Noncarnivores will find an Indian home at **Komala Vilas Vegetarian Restaurant,** at 76-78 Serangoon Rd. (tel. 293-6980), in Little India. It's a plain coffeeshop serving southern Indian staples such as vegetable biryani (a rice casserole), dosai (thin crêpes with various fillings), and thali (sectioned metal platters with several dips and curries to flavor your chapati bread). Vadai is a breakfast snack/dessert shaped like a small doughnut that's made with ground lentil flour and onions and served with a chutney. Komala Vilas is popular at breakfast and for a coffee break; two can sample many items for about S$10 ($5).

Visitors fond of Indian cuisine should try **Annalakshmi,** located on the second floor of the Excelsior Hotel shopping complex at 5 Coleman St. (tel. 339-9993). Delicious southern Indian vegetarian dishes are served amid bold Indian woodcarvings and delicate homespun fabrics. The surrounding décor of art, sculpture, and music seems to add flavor to the food. Annalakshmi presents a lavish buffet for lunch and dinner at S$16 ($8), and is open daily from 7:30 a.m. to 9:30 p.m. except Thursday, when it closes after lunch at 2:30 p.m. A fascinating store for Indian arts and crafts, and a cultural association, located next door, are funded by the restaurant's profits.

OTHER ASIAN CUISINES:

As in every other ASEAN capital, a recent wave of Japanese investment has given this cuisine a large presence on the dining scene, although prices are generally too high for the local market. Thai, Korean, and Taiwanese restaurants can be found in much smaller numbers.

Sitting high atop the Shangri-La Hotel at 22 Orange Grove Rd. is the **Nadaman Japanese Restaurant** (tel. 737-3644), one of Singapore's best. Select your favorite dishes—sushi, tempura, teppan yaki (honored by its own menu), or a combination—and enjoy them at specially designed tables which overlook a Japanese garden and beyond, the Singapore skyline. Nadaman excels at Kansairyori cuisine from southwestern Japan, with many dishes to please its varied clientele, producing the freshest sushi, the most expertly cooked teppan yaki (prepared by a private chef on a grill in front of you), and the lightest tempura-battered seafood. Nadaman's ultimate meal is the ten-course Kaiseki banquet, described as the "transformation of nature's blessings into food." The Kaiseki Omakase (chef's choice), S$155 ($77.50), should be savored sitting on reed mats in the shoji-screened tatami rooms. If you don't have the ultimate feast you can spend up to S$110 ($55) per head, or try a set luncheon at S$30 ($15) or a set dinner at S$70 ($35).

Unkai, on the second floor of the Century Park Sheraton at 16 Nassim Hill (tel. 732-1222), is another fine choice. Unkai's classic Japanese design separates the sushi bar, a popular venue for what's rumored to be the best raw fish in town, from the tables adjoining teppan yaki grills and the private tatami rooms. Unkai's special Omakase banquet, a multicourse feast of ornately presented meat, fish, and vegetable specialties costs S$110 ($55) and up. Set lunches range from S$12 ($6) to S$35 ($17.50), a moderately priced way to sample fine food.

For a taste of Thailand, try the **Her Restaurant,** on the first floor of the Forum Galleria (tel. 732-5688), next to the Hilton Hotel off Orchard Road. Her is warm and casual, with umber tones, rattan furnishings, and Thai antiques on display. An enticing array of Thai dishes (many of which have a Chinese flair) include fish maw soup, mei krob (crispy Thai noodles), fried beef with kale, and an assorted dessert tray with tapioca and shredded coconut pastries. Two can dine in style for about S$50 ($25); reservations are recommended at lunch.

For a complete change of pace, transport yourself to the South Seas via **Tiki,** the colorful Polynesian hideaway in the Pan Pacific Hotel at Marina Square (tel. 336-8111). In surroundings of thatch and primitive Melanesian masks and serenaded by a Hawaiian band, you can idly feast on conch chowder, Roratonga wonton (chopped fish, prawns, and chicken in a fried pancake wrapper), and a wiki wiki hot plate (seafood, chicken, pork, beef, and vegetables for two, cooked in a tropical style at your table), or roast duckling with macadamia nuts. Tiki has set luncheons featuring their most popular dishes for S$24 ($12), but the evening entertainment makes dinner a more magical event at S$38 ($19) and up per person. Each Sunday at 11:45 a.m. there is a special children's brunch; reservations recommended for weekend evenings.

WESTERN DINING: Western influences from every continent have had an effect on Singapore's eating habits, but none more so than fast-food fever. The young who won't take the time to prepare traditional ethnic cuisine prefer to consume burgers, fries, and pizza, and dine at restaurants when they get nostalgic for mom's cooking. Several outlets of McDonald's, Dunkin' Donuts, Denny's, Pizza Hut, and Burger King fill the most expensive storefronts in the classiest shopping centers, and all are standing room only at lunch.

Fortunately for the visitor, the hotels have once again provided gourmet alternatives for those ready to lay down their chopsticks. There is excellent continental cuisine to be had at prices less than those in major American cities. Singapore has recently been swept by a passion for high tea, and as expected, locals are very opinionated about the various venues. We'll take a brief look at those and at a few very casual places.

Continental Cuisine

To enter the renowned **Hubertus Grill,** off the Old English lobby of the Century Park Sheraton Hotel at 16 Nassim Hill (tel. 732-1222), is to step into the rich world of the German hunting lodge, with exposed wood beams and brick walls decorated with beer steins and classic hunting scenes. The weekday luncheon buffet at S$28 ($14) is legendary for its range and quality, with appetizers galore and entrees such as perfectly cooked prime rib, grilled meats, and delectable fresh seafood. The evening menu features wild-game dishes like venison St. Hubertus, roast pheasant, and wild hare filet in red currants. An evening meal for two will average S$125 ($62.50); proper attire and reservations are recommended.

A longtime favorite for freshly prepared, "clean" continental cuisine is the **Harbour Grill,** on the fourth floor of the Singapore Hilton International at 581 Orchard Rd. (tel. 732-2197). A vendor's cart piled high with the day's fresh produce greets guests as they enter. Seating is at comfortable tables in front of the copper-trimmed, open kitchen or in cozy banquettes. The chef's emphasis is on fresh ingredients, simply prepared to enhance natural flavors. Prime rib, roast venison, rack of lamb, and steak are specialties, but regulars often opt for the Surprise Gourmet Dinner at S$80 ($40), by tradition a five-course meal of the chef's choosing that changes daily—even the waiters won't reveal its contents till served. The Harbour Grill is a comfortable and solid choice for home-cooking where you'll pay S$75 ($37.50) and up per person with wine; reservations are recommended.

A contender for top honors as Singapore's leading French restaurant is **Le Restaurant de France,** in the elegant, French-run Le Meridien Singapour Hotel on Orchard Road (tel. 733-8855). Le Restaurant is a beaux arts fantasy in pink with Corinthian columns, plush Chinese carpets, and table settings in shades of rose. The expert staff, under the supervision of master chef Louis Outhier, serves up a daily menu de degustation, the chef's recommendation, at S$80 ($40). The menu might include steamed filet of pomfret in cardamom butter or veal loin with morel gravy; a local favorite is escargots with artichoke hearts followed by salmon en croûte with champagne sauce. Dinner for two ranges upward of S$110 ($55), not including a selection from their fine wine list. Dressy attire and reservations are recommended weekend evenings.

The **Ristorante Bologna,** located off the main lobby of the Marina Mandarin Hotel at 6 Raffles Ave. (tel. 338-3388), is a picturesque setting for northern Italian cuisine. In trattoria style, diners can choose tables set indoors on black and white tiles or eat al fresco beside a cascading waterfall. A tempting Italian buffet at S$28 ($14) is good value at lunch; at dinner the special osso bucco (veal stew), crayfish with parsley and garlic, and many pasta dishes will cost about S$85 ($42.50) for two.

Supper at the **Palm Court,** in the Raffles Hotel, 1-7 Beach Rd. (tel. 337-8041), is the quintessential Singapore experience, one that epitomizes the elegance and leisure of the bygone colonial era. Marble and wrought-iron tables are set under green broad-striped awnings; overhead fans stir nearby palms as a tuxedoed musical ensemble plays such classics as "Begin the Beguine"; a bevy of waiters silently deliver Singapore Slings, prawn cocktails, a rich curried mulligatawny soup cooked just the way the colonists liked it, and tasty beef or lobster entrees. The ambience that transcends anything on the menu to create a very special evening. A full meal with wine will cost S$55 ($27.50) to S$80 ($40) per person; reservations are recommended. The Palm Court is open daily from 7:30 a.m. to 11:30 p.m. and is a wonderful spot to relax and have a drink. **See page 427 for press-time addition.**

High Tea

One of the most elegant high teas in town can be had in **L'Espresso,** in the Goodwood Park Hotel, 22 Scotts Rd. (tel. 737-7411), a pretty, sun-filled lounge which overlooks the courtyard. The array of finger sandwiches (without crusts, of course), pastries, and cakes is splendid, the assortment of fresh ground coffees and teas is impressive, and the orchestra is most soothing. High tea is impeccably served from 2:30 to 6:30 p.m. daily and costs S$10 ($5) weekdays, S$12 ($6) weekends.

The highest of high teas is served at the **Compass Rose Lounge,** on the 70th floor of the world's tallest hotel, the Westin Plaza in Raffles City (tel. 338-2862). The Compass Rose is stunning; classical columns link the modern blue gray décor to soaring ceilings and frame the spectacular harbor views. From 3 to 5:30 p.m. daily a huge buffet of sandwiches, snacks, and fine pastries is yours for the taking for S$15 ($7.50). The Compass Rose Lounge also serves a high-quality seafood buffet for S$38 ($19) at lunch, and is open until 1 a.m. for drinks and hors d'oeuvres. *Note:* A "smart casual" dress code here means no collarless T-shirts or jeans.

If you're in the midst of shopping and you just have to take your shoes off, wander over to the huge, opulently decorated lobby of the **Dynasty Singapore Hotel,** at the corner of Orchard and Scotts Roads (tel. 734-9900). You can relax in plush upholstered chairs and relish the moist scones and fresh fruit jams served at high tea. Daily from 3 to 6 p.m. sandwiches, scones, and pastries are served for S$10 ($5) per person.

The pianist who accompanies the clinking of silver on porcelain makes high tea at the **Oriental Singapore,** 5 Raffles Ave. (tel. 224-3450), a pleasant and relaxing occasion. The fresh tea sandwiches are particularly good; tea is served daily from 3 to 6 p.m. and costs S$12.50 ($6.25).

The best value in high tea, as well as a quiet, relaxing place for lunch or a respite from shopping, is **La Boulangerie de Paris,** on the ground floor rear of the Far East Shopping Center on Orchard Road (tel. 734-1576). The tiny bistro serves cappuccino, tea, or coffee, and a buffet of good pastries and scones for only S$5 ($2.50) per person, daily from 3 to 6 p.m. Their small luncheon menu includes quasi-French fare like Caesar salad, fish'n'chips, and deep-fried Camembert with cranberry jam; full meals cost less than S$11 ($5.50). La Boulangerie is closed Sunday.

Casual and Fast Food

An excellent and very traditional choice for lunch is the **Tiffin Room,** in the Raffles Hotel at 1-3 Beach Rd. (tel. 337-8041). The Colonial Tiffin Curry buffet was originated by the British in India to denote a light lunch of assorted, not-too-spicy curries and a variety of condiments. The buffet includes curries of lamb, prawn, and chicken (traditionally without the skin), plus chile, chutney, lemon pickles, coconut, and other sambals (sauces) to add flavor. The Tiffin Room's lofty ceilings, whirring fans, and swaying palms recall an ambience appropriate for tiffin lunch at the turn of the century. Although the meal typically starts with a fresh lime drink, a Singapore Sling can be ordered. The buffet is served daily from 12:30 to 3 p.m. at S$17 ($8.50); reservations are recommended. **See page 427 for press-time addition.**

The **Chatterbox Coffee Shop,** at the Mandarin Hotel on Orchard Road (tel. 737-4411), is one of this neighborhood's most popular hangouts. From an early breakfast of ham and eggs to a Hainan chicken rice snack in the wee hours, young Singaporeans fill the comfortable booths to chat and visit. The Chatterbox has a large menu with continental, Chinese, fast-food, and ASEAN favorites that are reasonably priced; lunch can be had for under S$12 ($6).

A popular alternative to the hawker's centers is the **Scotts Picnic Food Court,** an indoor food mall at the corner of Scotts and Orchard Roads, which is open from 10 a.m. to 10:30 p.m. daily. Small, fast-food counters serve a Western and Oriental mix: everything from fried chicken, sushi, fresh baked cookies, frozen yogurt, Tandoori Indian food, beef noodle dishes, vegetarian items, a deli counter, or seafood stand to a Mövenpick (Swiss fast-food) outlet. The Scotts Food Court also has the most convenient supermarket for those Orchard Road hotel guests who have mini-refrigerators in their rooms.

If you long for a casual Italian meal or pizza, walk over to the Hyatt Regency Hotel on Scotts Road and downstairs to **Pete's Place** (tel. 733-1188). This cozy cellar has exposed brick walls, checkered tablecloths, and a friendly crew. Italian favorites include veal Florentine, cioppino (seafood stew), cannelloni, rigatoni, and fettuccine Alfredo. Pizza gourmands should order pizza malesia (tomato, lamb, green peas, and chiles). Add the extensive salad bar and a bottle of chianti and two can get away for less than S$65 ($32.50).

5. SIGHTS, SHOPPING, AND NIGHTLIFE

First-time visitors to this reputed consumer capital may be surprised to learn that there's more to do than shop in Singapore. In fact, the republic is an interesting composite of cultures represented in Arab, Chinese, and Indian neighborhoods that are well worth a visit. Then, after a day of sightseeing and shopping, don your new clothes and head out to one of the music bars or hostess clubs that have taken the town by storm.

SIGHTS: Although many Singaporeans have assimilated Western ways and appear so "international" in public, the traditional customs practiced at home can be examined in several museums. Vestiges of a long colonial heritage can be seen among the glass-and-concrete high-rises, and there are delightful zoos and parks to relieve the cityscape. The harbor and nearby Sentosa Island to the south are other sightseeing options for those with more than three days to spend.

Singapore is so small and well organized that sightseeing on your own by taxi and the marvelous MRT subway system is convenient and inexpensive. Budget watchers can take advantage of the "Singapore Explorer" bus ticket, which allows unlimited use of the public buses for one day for S$5 ($2.50) or three days for S$12 ($6). Just put on good walking shoes and pick up the STPB's brochure "Singapore, Tour It Yourself" from your hotel or the nearest STPB office. There are also several companies offering air-conditioned coach tours, which we have noted where relevant.

Cultural Activities

Just as New York City's ethnic blend has been called a "melting pot," Singapore's has been called a "salad." It's not surprising to see an Indian woman in a sari, a veiled Muslim woman in a baju kurong, and a Chinese woman in a cheongsam standing next to each other at a crosswalk.

When Sir Thomas Stamford Raffles founded this trading post in 1819, he established specific districts where each ethnic group could reside. The Chinese majority and Malay and Indian minorities live throughout the republic now, but have maintained quarters where traditional foodstuffs, clothing, religious, or cultural artifacts can be bought.

ARAB STREET. Singapore's Malay neighborhood, popularly called Arab Street, is the part of town where Javanese, Buginese, and Arab traders settled as immigrants. It is named Kampong Glam (village of eucalyptus) after the tree bark and oil that were used in boat building. The gold-domed **Sultan Mosque** at its center was rebuilt in 1928 on the site of the 1820s Masjid Sultan built by the Sultan of Singapore with a grant from Raffles. It is on Bussorah Street off North Bridge Road and remains the city's largest. The Sultan Mosque is very stately, with inscriptions from the Koran decorating the inner walls; visitors are welcome if modestly dressed (no shorts for men or women) and must remove their shoes at the entrance. During the fasting month of Ramadan (generally in the spring), when Muslims cannot eat between sunrise and sunset, temporary foodstalls open along Bussorah Street in the late afternoon to sell specially prepared foods to break the daily fast.

The few blocks of Arab Street between North Bridge and Beach Roads feature **shophouses** filled with baskets and household goods in rattan, Indonesian and domestically produced batik fabric for clothes, fabric and notions shops with the fineries befitting Malay bridal costumes, prayer rugs, spices, herbal medicines, and even a Muslim undertaker. On North Bridge Road are stalls selling the skull caps, prayer shawls, and religious literature used by the devout preparing for the *haj*, the pilgrimage to Mecca. Opposite the mosque are several Indian foodstalls where northern Indian snacks are served, and tiny shops filled with essences and oils to create perfumes.

The popular walking tour booklet of Arab Street described by the STPB originates at Arab and Beach Streets (about a 15-minute taxi ride from Orchard Road) and can be done in about one hour with breaks.

CHINATOWN. The huge area south of the Singapore River that Raffles gave the Chinese has been diminished over the years by urban renewal, but Chinatown is still well worth a visit. The oldest settlements were along the shores of the **Singapore River.** Small vessels called lighters ferried in cargo from large ships moored out in the harbor, and colonial traders relied on Chinese labor to unload them. Barges and bumboats clogged the river with activity until 1983, when the government decided to clean up the area. The decrepit *godowns* (warehouses) and colonial shophouses that can be seen on Boat Quay are a poignant reminder of this once-vital area.

A good place to start a morning tour of Chinatown (before 9:30 a.m.) is at the intersection of Mosque Street and South Bridge Road, just south of Cross Street. Several small coffeeshops serve dim sum (dian xian), the delicious steamed and fried dumplings and spring rolls served with tea for breakfast. From here, walk down Cross Street to China Street, which comes alive in the early morning with vendors preparing the basic foodstuffs, sauces, and spices of Chinese cooking. Continue back to Cross Street and make the second right onto Telok Ayer Street. At the intersection of Boon Tat Street you'll see the ornate **Nagoor Durgha Shrine,** built by Tamil Indians in 1830.

Mid-block is the **Temple of Heavenly Happiness,** or **Thian Hock Keng** (also called Tian Fu Gong in the Mandarin dialect), an ornate red-and-gold Hokkien temple built during the Portuguese colonization (1840) to honor the goddess of seafarers, Ma Cho Po. Two stone lions guard the door to Singapore's oldest Chinese temple, decorated with dragons and phoenixes for luck. Worshippers burn incense and joss sticks to safeguard relatives, or give cigarettes for luck to the Taoist figures who preside over the temple to the Gambling Gods. The **Al Abrar Mosque,** at the corner of McCallum Street, was built between 1850 and 1855 by Muslim Indians.

Retrace your steps to Cross Street, turn left, and take the first left down **Club Street,** a lane of craftsmen, woodcarvers, creators of religious icons, small social clubs, and pagoda-roofed buildings. At the end of Club Street, a right turn will bring you back to South Bridge Road. To the right is the **Sri Mariamman Temple,** the oldest (1827) and largest Hindu temple in Singapore. Its multicolored spires carved vividly with beasts and gods beckon visitors to enter (take off your shoes in the courtyard). During Thimithi (the fire-walking ceremony in October) the Hindus who crowd the streets around Sri Mariamman will make you forget you're in Chinatown.

Walk from here down Pagoda Street to Trengganu Street. These backstreets are the heart of the **Chinese market.** Singaporeans distinguish between a dry market, where appliances, notions, and clothes are sold, and a wet market, where selling meat, poultry, and produce necessitates washing down carts, stalls, and streets regularly. The wet market opens about 6 a.m. daily; early risers can look over the pythons, bats, iguanas, mice, and other special ingredients used for Chinese cooking and herbal medicine. Shophouses sell paper and silk flowers, stationery, religious items, hand-painted kites, and herbs till late in the evening. At **Kwong Onn Tong,** 16 Trengganu St. (tel. 223-8975), a variety of aphrodisiacs, potions to increase concentration and stamina, or capsules promoting youthfulness and bodily functions are custom-made or pre-packaged and sold for cures or unique gifts. The **Chinatown Centre** on Trengganu and Smith Streets is a modern version of these markets; the second-floor Food Hall, filled with fishball and noodle hawkers, is particularly fun to wander through.

Chinatown is best explored on foot; a taxi from the Orchard Road hotels downtown to South Bridge Road and Cross Street should take about 15 minutes. The route suggested above will give you a taste of the neighborhood in about 1½ hours. The STPB's brochure "Singapore, Tour It Yourself" has an excellent in-depth tour which will take two to three hours. Many visitors enjoy touring by pedicab, a bicycle-powered rickshaw seating two; a 40-minute spin through Chinatown should cost S$30 ($15) after bargaining. And only in Singapore could this price actually include medical and liability insurance!

LITTLE INDIA (SERANGOON ROAD). When Raffles founded the colony in 1819 he brought Indian convicts over to work the port and build roads, bridges, sewers, and public works. When their sentences were served, Raffles allowed them to remain in Singapore. These immigrants settled in the Arab Street quarter, but soon outgrew it and established their own neighborhood northeast around Serangoon Road. The southern Indian enclave known as Little India is spread along Serangoon Road and its cross streets for several miles, making it a somewhat amorphous neighborhood to explore.

The large field and parking lot at Rochor Canal and Serangoon Road known as **Kandang Kerbau** was once a cattle and dairy market run by Muslim Indians who would milk cows in front of their customers to prove the milk's freshness. On the Serangoon Road side is the new Zhu Jiao Centre, a food hall with fresh and cooked foods, baked goods, and Indian snacks, and upstairs, a dry market. Opposite Zhu Jiao is Campbell Lane, and at its intersection with Clive Street you'll find the traditional shophouses where pots and pans, spices, rice, dried beans, and herbs are sold by men in *dhotis* (the typical sarong-like Indian garment worn by men). Here and on Buffalo Road are storefronts festooned with orchid garlands, sari shops where eager brides try on embroidered silks (sold in six-yard lengths at bargain prices), and suppliers of Indian cosmetics. Most shops are open daily from 10 a.m. to 8:30 p.m.

Singaporeans who long ago moved from this area to outlying estate developments return to the vegetarian coffeeshops for dosai and idli (savory pancakes and steamed buns) and the Indian sweet shops for pastel-colored treats wrapped in gold and silver foil. At Serangoon and Kerbau Roads is a fortune teller who will examine shells, drop a deck of colored cards, or have his parakeet pick out a card and so read your fortune for only S$1 (50¢), although a Tamil interpreter is useful.

Hail a pedicab on Serangoon Road to take you to the **Sri Perumal Temple** at Serangoon and Perumal Roads. The fantastic carvings on the *gopuram* (gateway) are reminiscent of those at the Sri Mariamman Temple in Chinatown. This gate is the starting point for festivities at Thaipusam (a day of penitence when devotees in makeup and costumes pierce their bodies), usually held in February.

The STPB's brochure "Singapore, Tour It Yourself" has an in-depth tour of shops and temples which will take about 1½ hours. A taxi from the Orchard Road hotels to Serangoon and Buffalo Roads will take about 20 minutes. If sightseeing and the many aromas make you hungry, walk north on Kerbau Road a few blocks to Race Course Road, which parallels Serangoon Road. You'll find our favorite restaurant in the area, Banana Leaf Apollo (see "Dining") at no. 56, and nearby the Success Vegetarian and Muthu's Curry Restaurants.

THE NATIONAL MUSEUM AND ART GALLERY. The National Museum, on Stamford Road at the east end of Orchard Road (tel. 337-7355), has an excellent collection of cultural artifacts in the **Straits Chinese Gallery** and Oriental arts and crafts acquired locally. The Peranakan or Straits Chinese culture, which originated in Malacca and Penang, derived from the intermarriage of local Malays with immigrant Chinese merchants and seamen in the 1800s. The conservative Peranakans, usually well-to-do and British-educated, developed a visual style combining Victorian and Imperial Chinese influences. The ground-floor exhibit devoted to household items, art, furniture, and clothing is fascinating and worthy of close study. The elegantly carved, teak opium bed draped in lace covers, a four-poster with classic canopy, epitomizes this peculiar blend of cultures.

On the second floor is the **Haw Par Jade Collection** contributed by Aw Boon Par and his younger brother, Aw Boon Haw. The introduction of a salve to cure physical and spiritual ailments in the 1930s enabled the Aw brothers to amass the Tiger Balm fortune. Their collection of jade, jasper, lapis, rose quartz, and agate statuary, boxes, religious figures, and other exquisitely carved items by Chinese artists is one of the largest in the world.

The second floor has a cultural section with displays of Hindu and Indian Muslim artifacts and religious icons, old ship models, marionettes, and a gallery of ceramic ware brought to Singapore by traders. The first-floor gallery teaches the republic's history in dioramas.

The Art Gallery contains historical paintings of Singapore notables and is used for temporary exhibitions.

The National Museum is visited too briefly by many day tours but is easily absorbed by individual visitors with an hour to spend. It's open daily except Monday from 9 a.m. to 4:30 p.m., and English-language guided tours are offered free at 11 a.m. Admission for adults S$1.25 (65¢), half price for children. The nearest MRT subway stop to the museum is Dhoby Ghaut.

PERANAKAN PLACE. Peranakan Place is a small mall and pedestrian thoroughfare of restored Peranakan shophouses that extend up Emerald Hill Road from Orchard Road, near the Centrepoint shopping complex. Emerald Hill was originally deeded to William Cuppage in 1845 for a nutmeg plantation, but the land was divided and developed after 1900. The Chinese baroque two-story houses were used as commercial storefronts with residences on the upper floor, and many still serve that purpose. Small galleries, restaurants, and boutiques fill the pastel-stucco buildings whose ceramic tile roofs and carved wooden shutters kept the interior refreshingly cool. The model **Peranakan House** at no. 2 (no telephone) is furnished in traditional fashion with carved-wood and wicker furniture, teak ceiling beams, tile floors, and a wooden canopy bed. Several typical Peranakan outfits help re-create a vision of daily life circa Singapore 1910. The outdoor café in Peranakan Place serves beverages and snacks daily. The house is open daily from 11 a.m. to 6 p.m. with tours given on the half hour; admission is S$2.50 ($1.25).

CULTURAL PERFORMANCES. If Singapore's "salad" of Asian cultures intrigues you, seek out a capsulized, miniaturized, easy-to-photograph cultural feast called the **Instant Asia Cultural Show.** Dances from the Malay, Chinese, and Indian traditions are performed in traditional costumes to live music. After a selection of classic and folk dances, an Indian snake charmer and his charmed snakes perform. The 45-minute show is currently presented at the Raffles Hotel, 1-3 Beach Rd., at 11:45 a.m. daily; admission is S$5.50 ($2.75).

Check with the STPB (tel. 339-6622) for reservations and information and for the schedule of other cultural shows.

At the **Mandarin Singapore Hotel** (tel. 737-4411) the regular "ASEAN Night" by the pool celebrates the foods, songs, and dances of Singapore, Malaysia, the Philippines, Brunei, Indonesia, and Thailand. The **Hyatt Regency** (tel. 733-1188) also presents an al fresco meal and performance called "Malam Singapura"; both cultural show and dinner events cost S$40 ($20) for adults, S$24 ($12) for children, or half price for the show only.

Singapore's Colonial Heritage

Sir Thomas Stamford Raffles founded a trading post for the British East India Company in Singapore in 1819 that was so successful that it became a colony of the British Empire 48 years later. Raffles's name has come to symbolize the entire colonial period, and no tour would be complete without a stop at the Raffles Hotel.

The history of the **Raffles Hotel,** 1-3 Beach Rd. (tel. 337-8041), began in

1886 when three Armenians, the Sarkies brothers who owned the Eastern and Oriental Hotel (E&O) in Penang, bought a beach house on Beach Road. Within a year the waterfront property was converted to a 20-room inn that became popular with resident British. In 1899, concurrent with the opening of the Sarkies' Strand Hotel in Rangoon, the Raffles Hotel was expanded in its present French Renaissance style to accommodate 100 guests in a grand fashion. Complained one regular then: "Did we come to Asia to spend our time in clamouring for a miserable mimicry of metropolitan luxury?"

Raffles became the centerpiece of the colonial community and attracted writers and celebrities from around the world. Rudyard Kipling, Noël Coward, Herman Hesse, the Sultan of Johor, Malaya, Mary Pickford and Douglas Fairbanks, Haile Selassie, Charlie Chaplin, and John Lennon are only some of the notables who stayed here; Somerset Maugham praised his stay, saying, "Raffles stands for all the fables of the exotic East." In 1933 the hotel went public after a lavish expansion brought it to the brink of bankruptcy. During World War II the Raffles ballroom was the scene of the colonists' last party before the hotel was occupied by the Japanese. The staff buried the silver collection, including a silver art nouveau roast beef trolley, under the lawn of the Palm Court, where it remained until 1945. In 1950 air conditioning was installed and the hotel was refurbished.

The current general manager, Roberto Pregarz, restored the Raffles's high ceilings, overhead fans, and original tiled Tiffin Room restaurant in the 1970s. Preservationists claim the beautiful white structure as one of the few victories in Singapore's relentless modernization, and plans to fully restore the hotel are now in effect at presstime. **See page 427.** The Tiffin curry luncheon, a favorite of colonists, is often sold out and the classic Palm Court requires reservations in the evening (see "Dining"). More than 1,000 Singapore Slings, the famous gin-and-fruit drink first served at the Long Bar in 1915, are consumed daily.

Most other colonial-era structures are near the Singapore River. At North Boat Quay a bronze replica statue marks **Sir Thomas Stamford Raffles Landing Site,** where Raffles is thought to have first touched land. Nearby, a narrow lane stretching from Collyer Quay to De Souza Street is called **Change Alley,** since colonial times the venue for foreign traders to exchange their money and still an intriguing backstreet. Just inland is **Parliament House,** built around an 1827 mansion that was converted to a courthouse. Across St. Andrew Road is the **Victoria Theatre,** built in 1862 as the Town Hall. The original bronze statue of Raffles is across the square in front of the **Victoria Memorial Hall,** the home of the Singapore Symphony, which was built in 1905. Behind the hall on **Empress Place** is a former East India Company courthouse that now houses government offices. If you walk parallel to the **Padang,** a field once used by the Singapore Cricket Club for games, you'll come to the **Supreme Court** and **City Hall.** One block up at St. Andrew's and Coleman Streets is **St. Andrew's Cathedral,** a Gothic cathedral completed in 1861 to replace an earlier church that had been struck twice by lightning. If you walk east across the Padang you'll come to the nighttime hawker's center known as the **Singapore Satay Club,** an open-air collection of foodstalls offering Malay, Indian, Chinese, and Western foods, but specializing in satay (barbecued beef, mutton, or chicken served on skewers with a heavenly peanut sauce). One block north is the **Raffles City Shopping Complex.**

The STPB publishes a detailed walking tour of the "Colonial Heart" of Singapore that will take about two hours. It begins at the General Post Office, on Fullerton Road, a 15-minute taxi ride from Orchard Road or a brief walk from the Raffles Place MRT station. The Raffles Hotel is always open for a visit, a drink, or a meal and is a short walk from the MRT station at Raffles City.

Singapore's Zoos, Parks, and Gardens

For an island that's only 42 km (26 miles) long by 23 km (14 miles) wide, Singapore has a surprisingly large number of public parks and gardens containing animals, birds, and plants.

SINGAPORE ZOOLOGICAL GARDENS. A half day spent at the Singapore Zoological Gardens, at 80 Mandai Lake Rd., about 30 minutes' drive from the Orchard Road hotels (tel. 269-3411), is a treat. The 235-acre zoo is a beautifully landscaped, well-maintained garden of "open zoo" design with enclosures made naturally of rocks, lakes, and vegetation. The animal collection is diverse (1,600 animals of 17 different species) and includes many endangered Southeast Asian species. The zoo also offers several imaginative animal shows designed to delight kids of all ages, even adults. You can share a very tasty breakfast buffet (9 a.m. daily except Sunday and holidays) or high tea (3 p.m. on Monday, Wednesday, or Friday) with an orangutan. The handler feeds the lovely Ah Meng at the next table; you can sit beside her and she'll put her arm around you for a photograph. There are two staged animal shows, each presented twice daily, and all tickets are S$1.50 (75¢); the orangutan/chimp/reptile show and elephant/sea lion/otter show are both fun and informative. You can wander around the park or ride the tram that snakes through it for a quick tour. Children have a "hands-on" baby zoo of chimps, orangutans, gibbons, pythons, and an elephant to play with, as well as pony and elephant rides.

The Singapore Zoological Garden is open daily from 8:30 a.m. to 6:30 p.m.; admission is S$4 ($2) for adults, S$1.75 (90¢) for children, plus a S$.50 (25¢) fee for still cameras and S$2 ($1) for movie cameras. Holders of the Singapore Explorer bus ticket can take bus 171 from Orchard Road or bus 137 from Upper Thompson Road and should allow about one hour. The zoo runs a twice-daily "Zoo Express" bus service that picks up at the Orchard Road hotels and Mandai Orchid Garden; the fare is S$16 ($8), S$10 ($5) for children under 12, and includes zoo admission; arrangements should be made through your hotel concierge.

To enjoy breakfast or high tea at the zoo, it's best to join a group tour that also stops at the nearby Mandai Orchid Gardens. **Elpin Tours** (tel. 235-3111) operates a daily breakfast tour at S$32 ($16) for adults, S$20 ($10) for children; or a zoo, animal show, and orchid garden tour at S$22 ($11) for adults, S$12 ($6) for children.

THE JURONG BIRD PARK. The obvious fascination throughout Southeast Asia with the training of songbirds dates back centuries. If you noticed the absence of these all-important birds at the zoo, it's because they're all across the island at the Jurong Bird Park, on Jl. Ahmad Ibrahim in the industrial suburb of Jurong, about 30 minutes by car from Orchard Road (tel. 265-0022). The bird park's collection of caged songbirds is well labeled and provides a melodious introduction to this delightful pastime. This vocal group will serenade guests who come early enough for the breakfast buffet held by the park's main pond. Romantics may enjoy the World of Darkness, the bird park's recently opened display of nocturnal birds, which features owls, bats, and other creatures. It's a brief walk or tram ride to the park's centerpiece, a five-acre (the world's largest) walk-in aviary where over 2,000 birds from more than 60 species strut and fly freely. The place is lushly landscaped; footpaths and a suspension bridge provide roosts to admire birds flying over a roaring waterfall and verdant ravine. There are two trained-bird shows daily (at 10:30 a.m. and 3:30 p.m.) with talking macaws, smart cockatoos, and eagles.

The park is open daily from 9 a.m. to 6 p.m.; admission is S$4 ($2) for adults, S$1.75 (90¢) for children, plus a S$.50 (25¢) fee for still cameras. There is a special Road Runner Express Bus to the bird park from the Orchard Road hotels; contact **Journey Express** (tel. 339-7738) for schedule information. A taxi from Orchard Road should cost about S$15 ($7.50).

CENTRAL PARKS AND GARDENS. Beneath the Singaporean's seeming obsession with concrete and steel you'll find a deep devotion to the center city's parks and gardens. Near the commercial hum of Orchard Road is the century-old **Botanic Gardens,** acres of manicured lawns, a quiet lake, palms, and countless tranquil nooks for relaxing. Locals frequent the park early in the morning to practice Tai Chi and late in the evening to enjoy the cool breezes. The Botanic Gardens have been scientifically tended to develop orchids and other hybrids. Here the British botanist Henry Ridley nurtured the rubber tree seedlings that began the rubber plantation business in Southeast Asia. The gardens are at the intersection of Cluny and Holland Roads, a 5-minute taxi ride or a 15-minute walk from the Orchard Road hotels; they're open daily from 5 a.m. to 11 p.m.

    Fort Canning Park is located in the heart of the city on a hill that was the site of the first government house. An old colonial cemetery, outdoor squash courts, foodstalls, the Fort Canning Reservoir, the remains of a British fort, and the small Van Cleef Aquarium are here. The park is liveliest at lunch; it's located behind the National Museum, off Clemenceau Avenue, a five-minute taxi from the Orchard Road hotels, or across from the Dhoby Ghaut MRT station.

    If you long for an Asian garden, take a stroll through the **Chinese Gardens (Yu Hwa Yuan)** in the suburb of Jurong. The 34-acre garden is built on an island within a pond, and re-creates the landscaping of Beijing's Summer Palace. Among the twin pagodas, giant Chinese fans, weeping willows, and graceful knolls you'll spy a remarkable number of brides and grooms in wedding regalia, out for photo sessions.

    Adjacent to the Chinese Gardens is the **Japanese Garden (Seiwaen),** which means the Garden of Tranquility. A full-size teahouse is included in the simple plantings, manicured shrubbery, and rock formations of what is one of the world's largest Japanese gardens. Both gardens are at Yuan Ching Road in the industrial suburb of Jurong and can be combined with a visit to the Jurong Bird Park. They're open Monday through Saturday from 9 a.m. to 7 p.m.; on Sunday and holidays, from 8:30 a.m. Admission to both is S$3 ($1.50), half price for children. The Jurong Bird Park's Road Runner Express Bus stops here regularly; call Journey Express (tel. 339-7738) for details.

    The **Mandai Orchid Gardens** is a commercial orchid farm with many varieties of the national flower, seen in a kaleidoscope of colors that blanket a hillside. Real and risis orchids (picked flowers dipped in gold) are for sale here. The gardens are on Mandai Lake Road close to the Singapore Zoological Gardens (see above for Zoo Express bus transport), and are open daily from 9 a.m. to 6 p.m. Admission is S$1 (50¢).

    For a more eccentric experience with nature, visit the **Tiger Balm Gardens** at Haw Par Villa, at 423 Pasir Panjang Rd., a 25-minute taxi ride from Orchard Road. Visitors to Hong Kong may remember the house and garden there built by the Aw Brothers, originators of the popular eucalyptus ointment. This hillside garden populated with stone sculptures depicting heroes of Chinese legend and mythology is in the midst of becoming the "world's first mythological theme park." The STPB is redeveloping it into 20 acres of special effects, amusement rides (such as a boat trip through the spirit world), and performances. The new Haw Par Villa should be opened in 1989–1990. The gardens are open daily from 8 a.m. to 6 p.m.

    Golf is a favorite pastime of Singaporeans; a rolling green with skyline views may be just the parkland you're looking for. The best golf course is at Bukit Timah, site of the Singapore leg of the Asian Circuit and host to many international pros. It's one of four 18-hole, par-71 courses at the **Singapore Island**

Country Club, on Upper Thomson Road (tel. 459-2222). Reservations are accepted weekdays only, with a greens fee of S$100 ($50) per player. There are 12 other courses besides Sentosa Island (see below), plus the **Parkland Driving Range,** on East Coast Pkwy. (tel. 440-6726), which remains open from 7:30 a.m. to 10 p.m. daily. Check with your home club first to see whether they have reciprocal membership with any of the Singapore clubs so you can save on greens fees, then contact the STPB (tel. 339-6622) for more information.

City Tours

A half-day coach tour called "Contrasting Cultures," run by **Singapore Sightseeing** (tel. 737-8778), includes stops in Little India, the Kwong Min San Temple, and Peranakan Place; it costs S$32 ($16) for adults, half price for children.

A popular "Footsteps of Raffles" half-day coach tour run by **Tour East** (tel. 220-2200) includes stops at the National Museum, Little India, a Chinatown temple, the Raffles Hotel (where a historical film is shown), Raffles Landing Site, Mount Faber, and the Botanical Gardens; it costs S$28 ($14) for adults, half price for children.

Activities for Children

Singapore is at once exotic and familiar enough to appeal to most children. It's compact and easy to get around; taxis are inexpensive and plentiful, buses are not too crowded and run frequently, and the MRT subway is a delightful attraction on its own. There are fast-food restaurants everywhere, and myriad public toilets that are well maintained. Once you get out of the shopping crush on Orchard Road you'll find that Singaporeans love kids and are very good with them.

Of the attractions listed above, we'd recommend the Singapore Zoological Gardens, the Jurong Bird Park, an Asian Cultural Show, and the Tiger Balm Gardens as fun and easy to be in with children. Children also like the Van Cleef Aquarium in Fort Canning Park, but we'd recommend a day trip to the Marine Museum and other attractions on Sentosa Island (see below).

One of the most fascinating attractions for children between 6 and 18 years of age is the **Singapore Science Centre,** on Jurong Town Hall Road (tel. 560-3316), about 40 minutes by taxi from Orchard Road hotels to Jurong. There are interactive educational exhibits devoted to the physical, life, computer, and aviation sciences, as well as an Omni, super-large theater. The Omnitheater and Planetarium offer star shows, Omnimax films such as the American-produced *To Fly* and an ode to Singapore called *Time Concerto,* an audio-visual feast for visitors.

The Science Center is open daily except Monday from 10 a.m. to 6 p.m.; admission is S$2.50 ($1.25) for adults and S$.75 (40¢) for children. The Omnitheater is open Tuesday through Friday from 10 a.m. to 10 p.m. and on weekends and holidays from 9 a.m.; admission is S$4 ($2) for adults and S$3 ($1.50) for children, for planetarium shows, and S$7 ($3.50) for adults, S$4.50 ($2.25) for children, to the Omnimax films. The easiest way to reach the Science Center is by taxi; it should cost about S$10 ($5) from the Orchard Road hotels, plus S$16 ($8) per hour waiting time, a necessity because of the scarcity of taxis in this area.

The Harbor and the Islands

Singapore's harbor is one of the busiest in the world and at any time of day you can see the state-of-the-art container cranes gracefully unloading huge international freighters from Southeast Asian ports. Visitors with high-rise hotel rooms in Marina Square have a bird's-eye view of the western end of the port, but to really appreciate the magnitude of Singapore's shipping industry you have to get out into deeper water.

Harbor cruises on motorized but otherwise traditional Chinese junks depart from Clifford Pier, off Fullerton Road, three times daily. As you pass the entrance to the Singapore River, note the 25-foot-tall Merlion (half merman, half lion) that is the symbol of Singapore. Morning and afternoon cruises navigate around Pulau Brani, a former British base, Sentosa Island, and Pulau Kusu, where a stop is made to see a Chinese temple. Every nautical mile reveals boats from far-off ports; *phinisi* schooners from Indonesia, Chinese bumboats with eyes on the bow to indicate the waterline for overloads and to act as the spiritual "eyes" of the vessel, supertankers from Eastern Europe, and container vessels from the Middle East. The afternoon and evening cruises offer cooling breezes and a sunset view of the skyline, surprisingly large and spread out when seen from the sea.

Tours are given daily by **Eastwind Tours,** at 1A Clifford Pier, Collyer Quay (tel. 533-3432). You can make reservations through your hotel or directly with them; 2½-hour cruises cost S$22 ($11) for adults, half price for children, during the day. An evening cruise, including a generous buffet dinner of local and western foods and dance music, departs daily at 6 p.m. and costs S$40 ($20) for adults, half price for children. Several other tour operators have announced plans to introduce "business lunch" cruises, luxury ships with sundecks, a catamaran cruise with dinner and dancing, and cruise/picnic combinations stopping at several islands. Contact the STPB for more information.

The financial, shipping, and trade capital we call "the city" is the largest of the 58 islands that make up the Republic of Singapore. **Sentosa Island,** the second largest, has been developed as a tourist resort and is just a short ferry or cable-car ride across from the main harbor.

The British used Sentosa as a military base (their abandoned Fort Silosa can be visited) until 1970 and two years later a plan to attract tourists was developed for the island. Sentosa has been shaped and built up to provide a swimming beach and lagoon, golfing at the **Sentosa Golf Club** (tel. 472-2722), bicycling, hiking, and dining at **Rasa Sentosa,** an outdoor hawkers' center. Attractions include the **Rare Stone Museum,** the **Coralarium** with a seashell and coral reef exhibit and an aquarium, an **insectarium** with 3,000 butterflies and another 1,000 insects on display, and a **Maritime Museum** with a history of the port and seagoing vessels. We most enjoyed the **Sentosa Wax Museum,** with several tableaux depicting the history of Singapore—its most notable citizens and events frozen in time. Next door are documents, photographs, and wax displays illustrating the Japanese occupation and surrender in 1945.

The STPB is planning more development on Sentosa, including Underwater World, a huge underwater cave of glass, a large hotel, and a butterfly park. At present there is camping at the island's **youth hostel** at S$6 ($3) per bed; call the STPB (tel. 339-6622) for information.

To reach Sentosa, you can take a **ferry** from the World Trade Centre ferry terminal, about 10 minutes by taxi from downtown. Ferries leave every 15 minutes from 7 a.m. to 11 p.m. daily; fare is S$4 ($2). You can also take a **cable car** from the top of Mount Faber or the PSA Tower adjacent to the World Trade Centre for S$5.50 ($2.75). A package price ticket including one-way travel on both the ferry and cable car and entrance to the Coralarium and Sentosa Wax Museum is S$13 ($6.50). Once you've reached Sentosa, a public bus or the island's picturesque monorail will transport you between major sites.

SHOPPING: Singapore has long been touted as a "Shopper's Paradise" because of the tremendous variety of goods sold at moderate prices. Air-conditioned malls, with haute couture designer boutiques and gourmet stores, compete with the quaint two-story shop/houses, filled with ethnic products, for tourist dollars. Unlike other ASEAN countries, whose economies are based on manufacturing, Singapore's business is the *importation* of handcrafts, arts, clothing, and accessories manufactured by other countries. Low prices are the result of international trade, and shopping is more of a sport than a contest. Shoppers will be pleased to learn that fixed-price goods can be as much a bargain as the bargained-for goods from countries where haggling is the norm.

Singapore is a duty-free port, which means that most goods and luxury items are not subject to a duty tax when imported; a complete list can be obtained from the Trade Development Board, 1 Maritime Square (no. 03-01) World Trade Centre, or by calling 271-9388. Duty-free goods include cameras, most electronic equipment, appliances, carpets, fabrics (but not readymade clothing), most jewelry, antiques more than 100 years old, sporting goods, optical goods, musical instruments, and leather goods. *Note:* Though buying antiques is strictly regulated in neighboring Southeast Asian countries, it is easy in Singapore. If you're going to another Asian country from here, be sure to have all your import papers in order so as not to have difficulty when you exit another country.

What to Shop For

Dutiable items like clothing are a good buy because there's no sales tax, and fashions made in Singapore are often cheaper even than in Hong Kong. Most products from Southeast Asia are good value because of the cheaper cost of materials and labor, making Oriental carpets and jewelry from the region other good buys. Luxury items produced in Japan and Europe (particularly watches, perfumes, and some designer clothing) can be better buys than in their country of origin because of fluctuating exchange rates, the volume of goods imported and the absence of sales tax or VAT commonly imposed in Europe. Of these, watches are most heavily discounted although fraudulent merchandise is very common too.

The **Singapore Tourist Promotion Board (STPB)** (tel. 339-6622) produces several shopping brochures for those searching out particular items. Since you can buy most things in any shopping area, this section is organized by shopping districts and their good buys. Professional shoppers and the curious should buy the excellent *Secret Map of Singapore* published in Singapore in 1986 by Ropion, Hunt, and Mowe, available for S$5 ($2.50) in most bookshops, a picturesque and practical guide to the ethnic esoterica of Chinatown, Little India, Arab Street, and the international fare along Orchard Road.

Shopping Tips

Everybody loves a bargain and Singapore abounds with merchandise that seems dirt cheap by our Western standards. The informed shopper who has comparison-shopped is the best judge—six yards of embroidered silk (a sari) bought in Little India for $30 is a more likely bargain than a "genuine" gold Rolex watch bought from a sidewalk vendor for $500. We recommend that you clip advertisements for "special sales" of equipment, watches, or any other item you could buy back home (the Sunday *New York Times* is filled with them) and bring them with you. You'll often find that the stereo store on New York's Canal Street that ships tax free to out-of-state buyers can beat the prices you'd pay for goods that may be dutiable when you reach U.S. or your national Customs.

The easiest way to ensure the quality of the merchandise you buy is to shop at stores with the decal of the Singapore Tourist Promotion Board Associate Member program in their window. The red square with the gold merlion symbol indicates that the store has been inspected for quality, price, fairness, and service by the STPB. More than 150 stores selling a wide variety of goods participate in this program and have assumed an extra responsibility to shoppers, although there are hundreds of trustworthy merchants who have chosen not to join.

Always be sure to get an International Guarantee card (when you purchase camera, audio, computer, or other electronic goods) that has been filled out by the vendor and is good for one year. You can find steep discounts on "gray market" goods (goods that are manufactured in Asia for domestic use only and do not have international warranties), but they're no bargain when you get home and they don't work.

Make sure to get an official receipt for all your purchases and duplicates of paperwork for merchandise that is being shipped. Most larger stores will pack and ship merchandise for a nominal fee; see "The ABCs of Singapore" for more information on postal regulations. Duty-free goods from Singapore are not necessarily free of Customs duties in your own country, and receipts will verify an item's true cost. Contact your embassy in Singapore for more information on Customs duties, import taxes, and conservation laws that may prohibit the importation of items made of endangered species skins (such as reptile products).

Most shops and all department stores take major credit cards such as American Express, Diners, VISA, Carte Blanche, and MasterCard. It is illegal for a store to add a surcharge for use of a credit card, although paying "cash" will often get you a better price when bargaining. Make sure to put a capital "S" in front of the $ sign on your charge slips (indicating "Singapore dollars") to avoid confusion when your credit-card bills come in. Traveler's checks are widely accepted, and authorized moneychangers are found in almost every shopping complex and hotel. Department store prices are fixed, but bargaining is the rule at most smaller shops and a necessity in the shops of Chinatown, Arab Street, and Little India. If you've comparison-shopped you'll be the strongest bargainer; the meek should start out offering about 60% of what's quoted on the price tag. Most of the larger stores will allow you to exchange items if the price tag and label are still intact and you have a receipt, although refund policies differ from shop to shop.

Any complaints from clients who are dissatisfied with merchandise purchased or shipped from any store (not only the Associate Member stores) will be handled by the STPB (write to them at Raffles City Tower, 250 North Bridge Rd., no. 36-04, Singapore 0617).

Singapore is well organized and an easy place to shop; avoid the persistent touts who hover along Orchard Road offering to take you to "bargain" shops elsewhere. Department stores open daily from 10:30 a.m. along Orchard Road because of traffic regulations on taxis entering or leaving the Central Business District (CBD) during peak rush hours (see "Getting Around" for more information), but they usually stay open until 9:30 p.m. Smaller shops and department stores in other districts are usually open from 9:30 or 10 a.m. to 6 p.m. daily, though some Muslim shops close on Friday and some shops close on Sunday. Taxis are convenient and inexpensive, but the taxi stand lines can be very long at rush hour; the efficient public buses are a good alternative. Orchard Road, Marina Square, and Raffles City are conveniently serviced by the MRT subway system.

Orchard Road: High Fashion and Department Stores

Most visitors will want to get started on Orchard Road, the most posh, varied, and impressive shopping district. At least ten major indoor malls and hundreds of shops line both sides of Orchard Road between Tanglin Road (the Ming Court Hotel) and Clemenceau Avenue (Le Meridien Singapor Hotel), and both sides of Scotts Road, which intersects with Orchard at the Dynasty Hotel.

Starting from the east end are some new malls with more varied stores, including health food and gourmet delis, athletic supply stores, greeting card shops, and appliance outlets. The **Meridien Shopping Centre** in the hotel of the same name features the French Au Printemps department store, **Orchard Plaza** has a Burger King and several beauty parlors, **Orchard Point** has a Denny's and many sneaker stores, and **Cuppage Plaza** has several foodstalls and one-hour photo-processing outlets (note how prices drop 20% to 50% if you wait two or three hours for your photos!). **Centrepoint,** across Cuppage Road, is the most upscale of these, with Benetton and Charles Jourdan boutiques, Italian shoe stores, French clothes and accessory shops, and the local, high-quality

Robinson's Department Store. Prices for designer clothes and accessories imported from Europe are comparable to those at New York boutiques, but you can save on the sales tax. Centrepoint also has a new supermarket and a McDonalds.

Next door is the pedestrian mall at **Peranakan Place,** with a pleasant café to relax in, the fine **Aziza's** restaurant for a spicy lunch of local Nonya cuisine, and some art galleries. If you cross the street you'll come to the **Specialists Centre,** an older shopping mall with many local shops selling casual clothes, toiletries, sporting goods, jewelry, and leather goods at good prices.

A few minutes' walk from Centrepoint is the huge **Esprit** store in the Crown Prince Hotel mall. On two floors hung with stylish, casual, and fun clothing for the young and the young-at-heart, shoppers can buy the latest Esprit designs at prices that are 10% to 40% lower than in major American cities. Across narrow Bideford Road is the **Paragon** complex. At Gucci, long leather wallets with the status stirrup clasp start at S$230 ($115); the Laura Biagotti, Emanuel Ungaro, and Emporio Armani boutiques rival the inventory and prices found on Milan's Via Montenapoleone. Paragon also has a Metro Department Store, a good stop for inexpensive, locally made sportswear such as men's polo shirts from S$18 ($9), accessories, and gift items. Relax outside at the pleasant but pricey **Trumps Café,** a good vantage point over Orchard Road's colorful parade. **The Promenade,** next door, is just that, and a stroll here is much quieter. A sloping ramp leads past displays of the latest Ralph Lauren Polo, Issey Miyake, Gianni Versace, and other international finery. The elegance for sale, from Dickson's to Master Penguin's Dry Cleaners (a budget alternative to your hotel) to Abraxas' moderne furniture, does not depend on volume generated by discount prices; it's very low-key.

The opposite is true at **Lucky Plaza,** a boisterous jumble of small shops spread over seven stories. Electronics, mid-priced clothing, dozens of watch stores, cameras, and shoes vie for your interest. We priced a stainless-steel Rolex watch here at S$2,000 ($1,000), about what you'd pay in the U.S. or Canada from a jewelry wholesaler before sales tax.

Across the street is the latest mall replete with glass elevators and splashing fountains, the blue-tiled **Wisma Atria.** Expensive, super-couture, international designers such as Ermengildo Zegna (men's linen shirts from S$380, or $190), Georg Jensen, Christian Dior, Gianni Versace, and Ralph Lauren crowd the ground-floor storefronts (most close at 7 p.m.). Four more stories contain a mix of small local shops for fashion, novelties, and accessories. The moderately priced and high-end Japanese department store, Isetan, is fun to explore.

Tangs is at the corner of Scotts and Orchard Roads, known in Singapore since the '50s for its high-class Asian curios, arts and crafts, Chinese products, and colorful souvenirs. Tangs sells cooking implements (best buy: ten pairs of ornately enameled chopsticks for S$10, or $5), international cosmetics and toiletries (many discounted up to 35% less than U.S. prices), and better clothing and jewelry (great silver and shell earrings from S$30, or $15) from the ASEAN countries. Next door is the bright **Scotts Center,** a three-story mall with a Metro department store and a St. Michael's (a bargain clothing shop affiliated with England's Marks and Spencer). Upstairs is Cost Plus, one of the best local shops for fixed-price, discounted camera, stereo, and electronics merchandise. The bustling **Scotts Picnic Food Court** in the basement is a New Wave hawkers' center. The 800 shops next door in **Far East Plaza** present every imaginable item sold in the republic at reasonable prices—too much for us to handle.

Back up on Orchard Road next to the Lido Cinema is the International Building, which houses the second-floor **Chinese Emporium,** stocked with good buys in fabric, brocade, Oriental china, and myriad inexpensive gifts and souvenirs. Across the street is **Galeries Lafayette,** a mens/womens' high-fashion French department store where we picked up a fashionable linen blazer for S$220 ($105). The merchandise is 20% to 40% less than you'd find it in Paris. Behind it at the rear of the **Far East Shopping Centre** (another crowded mall geared to local shoppers) is the soothing **Boulangerie de Paris**, a tiny bistro for espresso and a pastry. Down the block next to the Hilton Hotel is the new **Forum Galleria**, popular for its Toys "R" Us and an entire floor filled with hawker foodstalls.

Downtown: The District for Electronics

The streets between Fort Canning Park and City Hall are known for the many older, low-rent malls packed with camera, stereo, computer, appliance, and electronics stores. North Bridge Road, Coleman Street, and High Street are the best places to begin.

The **Funan Centre**, located behind the Excelsior and Peninsula Hotels off North Bridge Road, is one of the most competitive places to shop for computers. Several shops offer state-of-the-art, name-brand hardware (not any cheaper than what you'd pay at a U.S. discount store), but software and Asian-produced clones and PC copies are true bargains. Start at the top and bargain your way down until you've found the best price.

The **Excelsior Hotel Mall** has some small camera and watch shops, as well as a few stores of Indian handcrafts and curios, and an excellent lunchtime buffet of southern Indian cuisine at **Annalakshmi**.

At **Peninsula Plaza**, across Coleman Street, there are more camera shops and a moderately priced Klasse department store selling international and locally produced casual wear.

Up the block along **Stamford Street** there are several small shops specializing in reptile handbags, starting at S$90 ($45) and going way up, and accessories; comparison-shop with prices in the shopping malls and try to verify what skin you're buying.

At the **South Bridge Centre** a number of Singapore's longtime jewelers have moved into a mall that dazzles with gold and gems. Gems from Burma and Thailand that are set in 22-karat gold by local craftsmen can be a good value, but be sure to bring an expert with you to verify quality.

The New Malls: Marina Square and Raffles City

Marina Square is a huge, three-story shopping complex built on landfill overlooking the east side of Singapore harbor. The Marina Mandarin, Mandarin Oriental, and Pan Pacific luxury hotels that are part of the development pour customers into the 200-shop mall at an alarming rate. The exciting **Tokyu Department Store** from Japan draws in locals, but the Metro department store and other camera, clothing, food, electronics, jewelry, optical, and arts shops similar to those in the Orchard Road malls pay too much rent to be competitive. If you're in the neighborhood, it's worth a visit to catch the occasional strolling musician or magic act hired to entertain window-shoppers.

The complex at the foot of the Westin Stamford and Westin Plaza hotels known as **Raffles City** is one of the most pleasant shopping malls in town. An open, airy atrium with casual seating around a fountain has become a meeting spot for workers in the adjoining office tower; international visitors from the hotels; locals using the post office, dental clinic, banks, or beauty parlors; and shoppers combing the 80 shops filled with cameras, watches, electronics, sporting goods, clothes, sunglasses, shoes, and souvenirs. The Japanese Sogo department store sells locally made separates and resort wear, including colorful, stylish Aloha shirts for S$25 ($12.50). A sprinkling of high-fashion boutiques among practical outlets with moderately priced merchandise, some music and bookstores, tailors, a dry cleaners, and a travel agent give Raffles City a broad-based appeal. Remember to dress well so they'll let you into the 69th floor **Compass Rose Restaurant** when you need a pick-me-up at high tea.

The Ethnic Neighborhoods: Asian Handcrafts and Curios

You can shop for antiques and curios in the expatriate's favored **Holland Village,** an area of shops and restaurants at the intersection of Holland Road and Holland Avenue, just west of the city's center. Otherwise, head directly to the more ethnic fare of Chinatown, Arab Street, and Little India.

The neighborhoods of two-story shophouses that were spared from the wrecker's ball are part of Singapore's charm. Shopping in the crowded lanes of **Chinatown** means rising early to pick the best produce on Tenggaru Street or catch the craftsmen before the noonday sun. Around the corner on Temple Street are small wood-trimmed shophouses filled with generations of curios, Chinese handcrafts, souvenirs, and sometimes, antiques. General stores sell inexpensive dishware with colorful mythological symbols, carved wooden icons, and collapsible red lanterns. The **Thong Chai Medical Institution (Tong Ji Yi Yuan)** is a 19th-century, stucco-and-tile, pagoda-roofed building on Wayang Street (behind Outram Park) originally built as a medical clinic. It's been converted to a store of Chinese handcrafts, embroidery, lacquerware, and dishware, and also sells knick-knacks from Indonesia, Thailand, Malaysia, and the Philippines. The **People's Park Complex** at New Bridge and Upper Cross Streets is a modern shopping mall frequented by locals and reputed to have the best prices on fabric, cameras, computers, appliances, and goods from China. Bargaining here for those not conversant in Chinese may prove a problem.

Serangoon Road is the central shopping street for Indian goods, though they are spread out through Little India. One of the best buys is fabric (sold in the sari shops in traditional six-meter lengths), especially hand-woven cottons, silk, and the embroidered silks used to make classic wedding saris. Window-shop in the **Zhujiao Centre** on Buffalo and Serangoon Roads or on Dunlop and Clive Streets. Notions stores and a few gift shops sell tie-dyed scarves for as little as S$5 ($2.50), thin, brightly colored bangles worn in bunches and ornate, filigreed silverwork, at moderate cost. Dried spices and exotically packaged incense (sold in the open-front provisions shops on Hasting and Campbell Streets) make good, inexpensive gifts, for as little as S$2 ($1), but make sure they are well-labeled for Customs.

Arab Street, between Beach and North Bridge Roads, is the area for Malay, Indian, Muslim, and Indonesian goods from throughout the region. Pilgrims on their way to Mecca and housewives looking for lightweight dresses comb through the shophouses overhung with woven baskets, wicker chests, and whisk brooms. Woven wicker chickens make great bread baskets and sell for S$14 ($7). Cheap, machine-printed (*cap*) and finer, hand-drawn (*tulis*) batik is sewn into clothing, tablecloths, handbags, and gift items. Search the **Textile Centre** on Jalan Sultan for batiks, cottons, synthetics, trimmings, and sequins at the lowest prices. *Caveat Emptor!* to those lured in by the precious and semiprecious stones sold in these narrow lanes. Inexpensive leather bags and belts are very good buys for those who bargain, although it isn't first-quality leather.

The **Singapore Handicraft Centre,** on Tanglin Road off Orchard Road (open daily from 10 a.m. to 6:30 p.m.), is a mini-mall of shops selling the arts, crafts, fabric, and jewelry of 16 Asian countries. There are several stores of Chinese souvenirs, curios, and contemporary artwork; boutiques with handmade gift items, sculpture, woodcarving, and jewelry from Indonesia and Malaysia; woven fabrics, statuary, metalware, and lacquerware from India; gold-dipped orchids known as *risis* and Selangor pewterware from Singapore; silk and gemstones from Thailand; and a variety of dishware, clothing, ceremonial masks, accessories, and souvenirs from Taiwan, Korea, the Philippines, China, Sri Lanka, Pakistan, Bangladesh, Borneo, and other countries. Prices are reasonable and it's an easy place to shop if you're looking for a regional souvenir. Some shops have workmen demonstrating their crafts periodically; Wednesday, Saturday, and Sunday evenings a sleepy Pasar Malam (Night Market) is held after closing hours.

Rasa Singapura, a hawkers' center open from 11:30 a.m. to 10 p.m., offers a wonderful array of local foods that are the center's real bargain. There is an **Information Office** of the STPB in shop no. 167 (tel. 235-5433) that's open from 8 a.m. to 5 p.m. weekdays, until 1 p.m. on Saturday, for brochures and information.

NIGHTLIFE: Singapore's nightlife is as varied as the city itself, offering private tours by trishaw in the old neighborhoods, multi-ethnic entertainment at the top hotels, jazz clubs, international discothèques, and very Asian hostess clubs.

The Cultural Scene

A **trishaw tour** is one of the most pleasant ways to explore the city; group or private tours are organized through hotels and travel agents, for about S$40 ($20) per person for two hours. Participants get in the mood for a bicycle view of the Raffles Hotel, with a Singapore Sling (or a Virgin Sling for children) served outdoors in the Palm Court. From there, two (or three skinny) passengers mount the narrow, canopied bench seat behind a powerful cyclist who pedals smoothly past City Hall, along the harbor, and into Chinatown, where you can alight for a pedestrian tour. At night, the Singapore harbor is alive with freighters, supertankers, sailing ships, and Chinese junks giving **harbor tours.** See "The Harbor and the Islands" section for more information about waterborne entertainment.

At Empress Place, the **Victoria Concert Hall** (tel. 338-1230) and **Victoria Theatre** (tel. 337-7490 between noon and 8 p.m.) are venues for the Singapore Symphony Orchestra and Chinese opera, Western musicals, or visiting ballet companies. In fact these groups often perform Sunday evening or weekday lunchtimes in the Botanical Garden. Contact the box office or check the daily *Straits Times* for schedule information.

Bibi's Restaurant, in the restored Peranakan Place off Orchard Road (tel. 732-6966), has regular cultural shows. The spicy Nonya cuisine of the Straits Chinese culture is served while traditional dances and a typical Peranakan wedding ceremony are staged. Other **cultural programs,** which include a dance and music performance and dinner, are offered at Raffles, the Singapore Mandarin, and the Hyatt Regency hotels; see "Cultural Performances" for information.

And in a city of such cultural diversity, every day seems to be either a Buddhist, Hindu, Muslim, or Christian holiday, each celebrated to the fullest. The STPB (tel. 235-6611) keeps a current schedule of **festivals and special events,** and of regular activities such as wayang, the popular Chinese opera performed on makeshift stages in the streets.

There are more than 50 **movie theaters** showing a wide variety of American, European, Chinese, and Indian fare, the latter three often dubbed in English. The Republic of Singapore has strict censorship laws regarding pornography, sex, and violence, and seeing an old favorite here can be a real eye-opener! The Lido Cinema at Orchard and Scotts Roads features Western films at six showings daily; tickets are S$4 ($2). Check the *Straits Times* for listings of other theaters.

Bars, Clubs, and Discos

Singapore nightlife usually consists of a meal out, drinks afterward at a music club or disco, and a late-night snack. The bar scene, like the dining scene, relies heavily on the facilities of top hotels. Visitors can choose from dozens of pleasant bars and lounges with live entertainment, and will find that locals drawn by the music or ambience occupy half the seats. The **Cricketer Club** in the Marina Mandarin, 6 Raffles Ave. (tel. 338-3388), has Olde English sporting prints and a genteel atmosphere appealing to expatriates and locals looking for a more sophisticated, quieter crowd. The Mandarin Hotel's mezzanine-level lounge and the Westin's Somerset are other popular, high-class watering holes. **Jimm's Pub** in the Negara Hotel, 15 Claymore Dr., near Orchard Road (tel. 737-0811), is popular with locals, mostly male, who enjoy the nightly guitarist, casual atmosphere, and inexpensive drinks. **Brannigan's Bar** at the Hyatt Regency, 10-12 Scotts Rd. (tel. 733-1188), is popular with Singaporean yuppies and tourists for its ever-changing rock, country-western, and jazz bands who keep this small club hopping. The **Saxophone Bar and Restaurant** in Cuppage Plaza is one of the better clubs to hear quality jazz in a relaxed, comfortable setting. **Club 392,** at 01-21 Orchard Towers, first floor (tel. 737-7334), is another plush jazz club frequented by a well-dressed, white-collar elite. It's open daily from 4 p.m. to midnight.

The Orchard Towers complex has some of the city's most popular nightspots. **Top Ten,** at no. 04/35-36 (tel. 732-3077), is the hottest club in town, a four-story kaleidoscope of lights, wild dancing, the newest fashions, crowded bars, and some terrific DJ work that alternates with live rock bands. This place is always packed after 10 p.m. with a nice local/foreign, late-20s to mid-40s mix of foot stompers. Cover charge weeknights is S$18 ($9), and weekends, S$28 ($14). Open daily from 8 p.m. to 3 a.m. **Celebrities,** in the basement at no. B1-41 (tel. 734-5221), is into mystery lighting and pin spots, enabling you to evaluate your escort only at proscribed intervals. Solid, imported live bands draw a late-20s crowd, often the overflow from Top Ten upstairs. The cover charge ranges from S$14 ($7) to S$22 ($11) depending on the weeknight. Open daily from 8 p.m. to 1 a.m. **Ceasar's,** upstairs at no. 02-36 (tel. 235-2840) uses some classic columns, Roman statues, and toga-clad waitresses to full effect; decadence and easy-to-find company are the draw. Weekend cover charge is S$22 ($11), plus one drink. Open daily from 8 p.m. to 3 a.m.

If you've tired of ballroom dancing at the Raffles Hotel, **Rumours Disco,** on the third floor of the Forum Galleria (tel. 732-8181), considered the tops by locals, may be the answer. Other discos in order of popularity (a peculiarly transient phenomenon) are: **Scandals,** at the Westin Plaza Hotel, 2 Stamford Rd. (tel. 338-8585), is the posh and elaborately lit space; **Xanadu,** at the ritzy Shangri-La Hotel, 22 Orange Grove Rd. (tel. 737-3644), has the wealthiest clients and draws a lot of beautiful Singaporean women; **The Warehouse,** a converted go-down on the Singapore River at 332 Havelock Rd. (tel. 732-9922), is favored by the young 20s crowd for its laser light show. The **Reading Room** at the Marina Mandarin Hotel, 6 Raffles Ave. (tel. 338-3388), has an upscale crowd and opens to the public after 9 p.m. The Plaza Westin Hotel's **Studio M,** at 2 Stamford Rd. (tel. 298-0011), specializes in '50s music, and the Century Park Sheraton's **Black Velvet,** at 15 Nassim Hill (tel. 732-1222), with a smokey black-and-gold interior, makes less than pro dancers feel very comfortable. Most of these discos are open till 2 a.m. weeknights and 3 a.m. weekends, and have a cover charge ranging from S$15 ($7.50) to S$25 ($12.50); smart casual dress is a must.

Hostess clubs—an Asian phenomenon for pairing single men with attractive young "public relations officers" for an evening of drinking and dancing—have found a small niche in the Singapore nightlife scene. Favorites are the **Golden Million,** in the Peninsula Hotel at 3 Coleman St. (tel. 336-6993); the **Grand Palace,** in the Orchard Building at 1 Grange Rd. (tel. 737-8922); and the **Lido Palace,** in the Glass Hotel at 317 Outram Rd. (tel. 732-8855). All serve supper (mainly Chinese cuisine), have floor shows of costumed chorines and singers imported from Hong Kong, Taiwan, or Europe, and start hopping after 10 p.m. (until about 2 a.m.). Hostesses charge from S$30 ($15) to S$50 ($25) per hour, but drinks can run as high as S$200 ($100) per bottle. Intimacy is officially discouraged here but after-hours escorts are reputedly available.

CHAPTER XVI

INTRODUCING THAILAND

□ □ □

1. INTRODUCTION
2. SUGGESTED ITINERARIES
3. GETTING THERE AND GETTING AROUND
4. THE ABC'S OF THAILAND
5. RECOMMENDED READING

When Thailand was known as Siam in the Western world, the land of golden temples, royal white elephants, and dense teak forests figured only in the imagination of adventurers and poets. The impression of Thailand that the majority of Westerners had was gleaned from the story of Anna Leonowens, a tutor at the strict and formal court of the 19th king, who served as the inspiration for the story *Anna and the King of Siam*. This story that has so captured the imagination of Westerners falsely portrays Thailand from a typical Eurocentric viewpoint. According to historians, Anna's influence was vastly exaggerated and her story largely fictional. It's a story that the Thais prefer to ignore. In reality, 19th-century travel to the distant kingdom was arduous, making it difficult and forbidding. Few could reliably report on conditions found there, and so the legends multiplied.

Yet, even then, foreign dignitaries and writers would return with tales of the Land of Smiles, marveling at the country's serene, gracious people. They remarked always on the Thais' combination of enduring independence ("Thailand" means Land of the Free) and their ancient Buddhist culture, which gave them a strong identity that enabled them to extend a deeply gracious hospitality to the *farang* (foreigner) without being subservient or obsequious. And travelers today are still similarly impressed. Even with all its natural and cultural wonders, that wonderfully amiable hospitality survives, causing many a modern traveler to fall in love with both the country and its cordial hosts.

1. INTRODUCTION

Thailand is roughly equidistant between China and India, in the center of Southeast Asia, and is bordered by Burma to the north and west, Laos to the northeast, Cambodia to the east, and Malaysia to the south. The southwestern coast stretches along the Andaman Sea, while the southern and southeastern coastline borders the Gulf of Thailand. The country has an area of approximately 180,000 square miles making it roughly the size of France. Because of its geographical location within the region, Thailand has often acted as a magnet for refugees from China, Tibet, Burma, Laos, Cambodia, Vietnam, Malaysia, and India, as well as hosting a myriad of nomadic hill-tribe people. Even today many Vietnamese and Cambodians continue to pour into the country—the legacy of the Vietnam War and the upheaval that followed afterward. With such an ethnic diversity, an enviable geographic position within the region, and a wealth of natural resources, the country has a rich cultural and trading tradition.

THE LAND: The land mass of Thailand can be divided into six major geographic zones. The north, really the foothills of the Himalayas, is a mountainous belt where elephants have traditionally provided the heavy labor needed to harvest teak and other hardwood forests. As with much of the rest of the country, there is a tremendous amount of agricultural farming in the cool hills, where strawberries, peaches, lychees, and other fruits are grown. At the higher elevations many hill-tribe farmers cultivate poppies for the production of opium. Fluorite, wolfram, and tungsten are mined in this region. The main cities in the north are Chiang Rai, Chiang Mai, Lamphun, Lampang, and Mae Hong Son.

The northeast plateau, perhaps the least developed of any region in Thailand, is bordered by the Mekong River—one of the country's four great rivers—and is home to the most ancient Bronze Age village in the country (if not the world), at Ban Chiang, dating back more than 5,600 years. There are also Khmer ruins in the area, principally at Phimai and Surin. The region has little economic development other than potash mining. In contrast, Thailand's central plain is a fantastically fertile region, providing the country with its massive rice crop. The main city is Phitsanulok, and nearby is the ancient city of Si Satchanalai and Thailand's first capital, Sukhothai. South of these Thai cities is Lopburi, an ancient Mon settlement.

The southeastern coast is lined with seaside resorts, such as Pattaya and the island of Koh Samet. Farther east, in the mountains, is the greatest concentration of Thailand's sapphire mines. Recently natural gas deposits were discovered off the southeastern coast, and they are beginning to be developed. On the opposite side of the country, west of Bangkok, are a series of mountains and valleys that were carved by the Kwai River, made famous during World War II by the "Death Railway" and the famous bridge over the river near Kanchanaburi immortalized by the film *Bridge on the River Kwai*. Just to the north of Bangkok, which is in the center of the country (built along the banks of the Chao Phrya River), is Ayutthaya, Thailand's second capital.

The long, skinny southern peninsula extends to the Malaysian border bisecting the Andaman Sea and the Gulf of Thailand. The coastline along the Gulf of Thailand extends over 1,125 miles, while the opposite shoreline, on the Andaman Sea, runs 445 miles. This region is the most tropical zone in the country and experiences heavy rainfall during the monsoon. Here there are glamorous beach resorts, such as the western islands of Phuket and nearby Koh Pipi, as well as Koh Samui on the eastern shore. The primary industries in this region are tin mining, rubber production, and fishing.

THE PEOPLE: As of 1983, Thailand's population was estimated at 50 million, ranking as the 20th most populous country in the world. Before World War II, population growth was only 1.9%, but from the '50s to the '70s it jumped to over 3.5%, partly due to a decrease in infant mortality and the control or eradication of several fatal diseases (such as malaria). Life expectancy climbed to over 60 years for both males and females, placing huge new strains on the society.

Although recent very creative and effective birth-control programs have reduced the growth rate to under 2% again, there continues to be an increasing demand for arable land (almost 70% of the population is engaged in some form

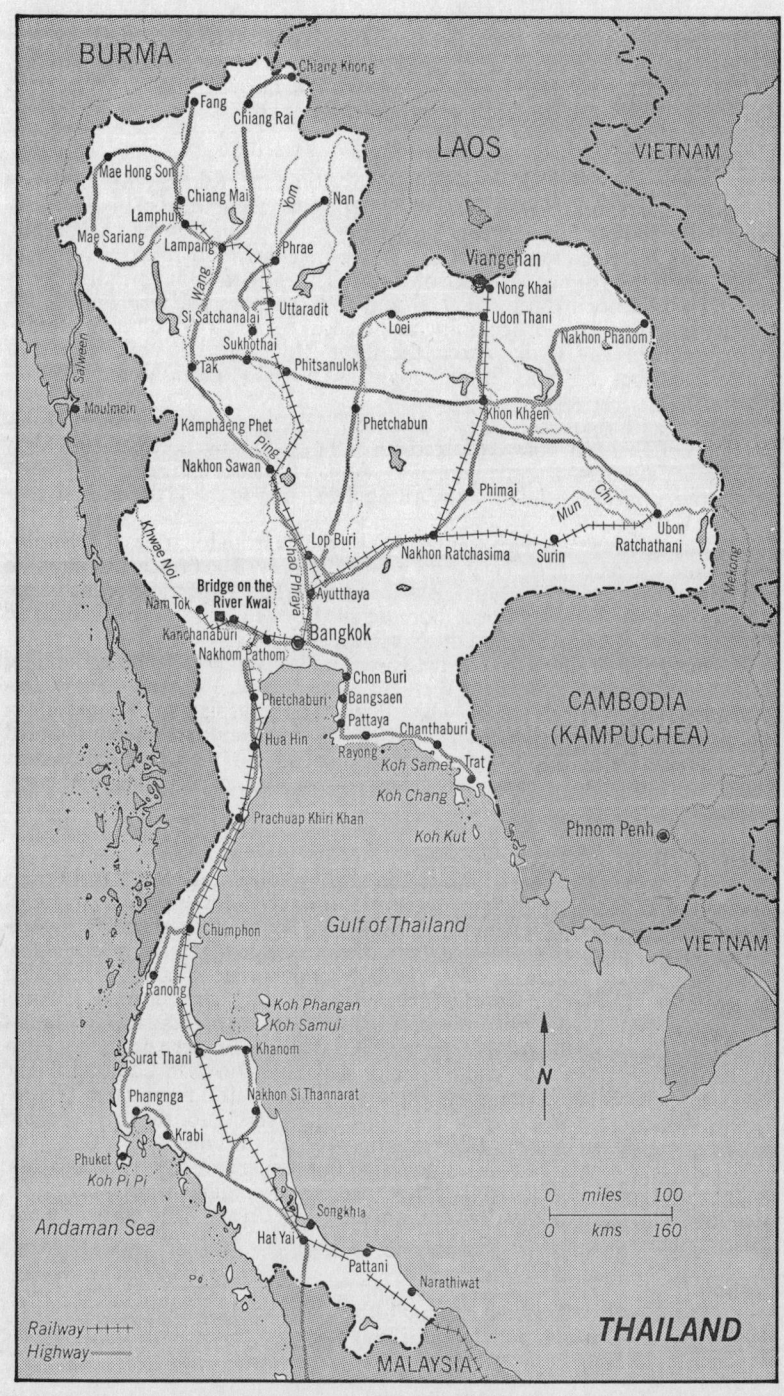

BURMA

Chiang Khong

Fang

Chiang Rai

LAOS

VIETNAM

Mae Hong Son

Chiang Mai

Nan

Lamphun

Yom

Mae Sariang

Lampang

Phrae

Si Satchanalai

Wang

Uttaradit

Viangchan

Nong Khai

Sukhothai

Loei

Udon Thani

Phitsanulok

Nakhon Phanom

Tak

Kamphaeng Phet

Phetchabun

Khon Khaen

Ping

Nakhon Sawan

Phimai

Mun

Chi

Lop Buri

Nakhon Ratchasima

Surin

Ubon
Ratchathani

Chao Phraya

Ayutthaya

Bridge on the
River Kwai

Nam Tok

Khwae Noi

Mekong

Kanchanaburi

Bangkok

Nakhom Pathom

Chon Buri

CAMBODIA
(KAMPUCHEA)

Phetchaburi

Bangsaen

Pattaya

Chanthaburi

Hua Hin

Rayong

Koh Samet

Trat

Koh Chang

Prachuap Khiri Khan

Koh Kut

Phnom Penh

Salween

Moulmein

VIETNAM

Gulf of Thailand

Chumphon

Ranong

Koh Phangan

Koh Samui

Surat Thani

Khanom

Phangnga

Nakhon Si Thannarat

Krabi

Phuket

Koh Pi Pi

Songkhla

Andaman Sea

Hat Yai

Pattani

Narathiwat

| 0 | miles | 100 |
| 0 | kms | 160 |

N

Railway ++++
Highway ——

MALAYSIA

THAILAND

of agriculture) and other natural assets, placing pressure on the government to adopt some kind of land-reform program. One in ten Thais lives in the country's capital, Bangkok, a city whose population has swollen because of urban migration. It has experienced a population growth rate of over 5% since 1961. It is significant that half of these people are under the age of 30.

Ethnicity

Approximately 90% of the population is ethnically Thai, 9% is of Chinese or Indian ancestry, and 1% of various hill-tribe origins. The lineage of the Thai people is still a matter of dispute. The prevailing theory posits that the Thai people, who were a unified culture by the 7th century, migrated south from the Nanchao Kingdom in the Yunnan Province of China. They settled in independent states throughout the north during the 11th and 12th centuries, and were united during the Sukhothai Period, beginning in the 13th century. Thai culture was influenced primarily by settlers from the great Mon and Khmer civilizations. Individual tribes of Tibeto-Burman origin also played a role in shaping Thai culture.

Other anthropologists believe that the Thai people were the indigenous inhabitants of Thailand, but were forced out of the country by more powerful Mon and Khmer invaders. They fled north to Yunnan Province and returned to their homeland, under pressure from the Mongolians, during the 11th and 12th centuries.

Although they number a scant 416,000, the six main hill tribes of the north contribute a great deal to Thailand's ethnic diversity. The principal groups are the Karen, Hmong, Lahu, Mien, Akha, and Lisu, and all of them reside in the hills around Chiang Mai. For a more detailed description of these tribes, see Chapter XIX, "Chiang Mai and the Northern Hills."

Since 1975 Thailand has accepted over a million refugees from surrounding Indochinese countries. Since the Vietnam War, Laotians, Vietnamese, and Cambodians have flocked to Thailand where many of these displaced persons reside in camps along the eastern border. The Thai government and various international aid organizations have provided temporary provisions for these people; however, their tenure in Thailand hangs precariously on the vagaries of regional and international politics.

Language

The basics of the Thai language were codified during the Sukhothai Period during the reign of King Ramkhamhaeng. During the 13th century, elements of Mon and Khmer script, themselves derived from South Indian script, were combined by the king with traditional Thai forms to create the modern Thai alphabet. The spoken language was similarly influenced, though it reflected contributions from other Buddhist cultures. Specifically, Sanskrit and Pali words were integrated into the four levels of language common to this day. The highest level is *rachasap,* or the royal language. This dialect's Khmer vocabulary most closely corresponds to the contemporary spoken language in Cambodia. The other three levels are ecclesiastic, formal, and slang, all differentiated by pronouns. Today most people speak a fairly standard version of the language, but even a foreigner can hear the differences between regional dialects.

Language scholars are most interested in the many dialects spoken by the tribespeople in the northern hills, where there is a far-ranging diversity of linguistic roots, with the majority derived from Sino-Tibetan and Tibeto-Burman language systems.

Religion

On the surface Thailand appears to be a religiously homogenous country where over 95% of the population follow the precepts of Buddhism. Yet the

Thai people have traditionally accepted other rituals and religious dogmas, as long as they can coexist with the dominant thread of Theravada Buddhism, itself a very tolerant philosophy. Much of Thai ritual is derived from Chinese and Indian traditions, such as ancestor worship, Confucianism, and Brahmanism, and all find expression in contemporary Thai life. In addition, there are other philosophical accretions: animism, Islam, Christianity, Hinduism, and Sikhism can all be found throughout the country.

Buddhism first came to Thailand in the 3rd century B.C. when missionaries sent by King Asoka of India arrived at Suvannabhumi, near present-day Nakhon Pathom. Other schools of Buddhist thought from Sri Lanka and India, such as Mahayana Buddhism, influenced the country's religious thinkers and royal rulers, culminating in the writing of the *Tribhumikatha*. This 14th-century treatise, summarized by King Li Thai, incorporated ideas about the Buddhist cosmology from many schools of thought, making it the central text taught in the country's monasteries; even today Buddhist monasteries continue to study this work. Buddhist ideas also influenced music, art, theater, and architecture, all quite apparent as one travels around the country.

Chinese and Vietnamese comprise the majority who follow the tenets of Mahayana Buddhism, a philosophy that derives from ancient Indian teachings. There are 34 Mahayana Buddhist monasteries operating within the country.

Islam, of the Sunni variety, is followed by over two million Thai citizens and is largely concentrated in the south. The vast majority are of Malay origin and are descendants of the Muslim traders and missionaries who spread their teachings in the southern peninsula in the early 13th century. There are approximately 2,000 mosques in Thailand.

Although the Christian church has been represented in Thailand since the 16th century by generations of Jesuit, Dominican, and Franciscan missionaries from Europe and America, there are only a quarter of a million converts who live in the country. Thais have learned and accepted much from Christian representatives, particularly in the fields of education, health, and science, and are deeply appreciative of their efforts, but it is not in the Thai inner spirit to accept such a limited or exclusive dogma. Indeed, one of our favorite stories about King Mongkut (the king in *Anna and the King of Siam*) is his remark to a group of visiting missionaries: "What you teach us to do is admirable, but what you teach us to believe is foolish."

The king is dubbed "Upholder of All Religions" and, though he is a Buddhist, it is a testament to the Thai sense of tolerance and diversity that the nation's leader is charged with the responsibility of protecting all beliefs. Still, it is the network of over 27,000 Buddhist monasteries that most occupies the attention of the king and government.

ECONOMY: Ever since the Thais settled the country in the 12th century, the dominant aspect of their economy has been agriculture; today nearly 70% of the population is engaged in some aspect of agriculture. With huge tracts of fertile land, fed by a series of rivers and dikes, the country is not only a self-sufficient producer of food, but it is also one of the developing world's largest agricultural exporters. Its main farm or food export products range from tapioca—exported by Thailand at a greater rate than any other country in the world—to rice (second-largest exporter), pineapple, shrimp, sugar, maize, a cornucopia of exotic fruit and flowers, and tobacco. The waters surrounding Thailand abound with many species of fish and shellfish, ranking the country behind Japan and China as Asia's largest fish exporter and tenth overall in the world. In addition the country is also rich in other commodities including natural rubber, tin, fine hardwoods (including teak), a range of minerals (among them manganese, barite, tin, fluorite, gypsum, and wolfram), and colored gems such as sapphires and rubies, all of which are exported. The variety of locally processed and consumed minerals and agricultural products is far greater, adding diversity to a largely self-sufficient economy.

Oil and gas deposits, found in the Gulf of Thailand, are the most recently discovered resources. Although the country has been a net importer of these commodities, the future development of its stores promises to decrease its dependence on foreign sources of energy. In addition to its bountiful commodities, Thailand is expanding its manufacturing base to include clothing, electronics, heavy equipment, and chemical and petrochemical products. Even Japanese multinationals, faced with rising domestic labor costs, have turned to the Thai labor pool to retain their manufacturing cost advantage.

Tourism has become an enormous revenue source. In 1987 tourism overtook rice production as the number one revenue earner. The effects of mass-scale tourism is still left to be seen in the decades ahead.

Still, with all Thailand's advances, the disparity between rich and poor remains an ever-present problem. Population growth also inhibits a rising standard of living, as well as placing pressure on heavily farmed land. These imbalances, and a reduction of trade deficits, are the major challenges to be faced by the government in the next decade.

HISTORY: Although their origin is debated, the history of the Thai people is very much a source of national pride, for Thailand, as is often pointed out, is one of the few Asian countries never to have been occupied by a Western power. In fact the country has never been completely overrun by any foreign power since its formal establishment as a unified nation during the Sukhothai Period in the 13th century. The continuing theme of independence explains much about the development of the Thai nation.

Neolithic Period

While there are remains of Neolithic villages around the country, those that have attracted particular attention are at Ban Chiang, in the northeast of Thailand. Evidence of a highly evolved civilization, dating back to 4,000 B.C., has been found at this site. One aspect of this agrarian culture that has fascinated archeologists is the sophistication of its metallurgy, predating similar examples found in China by hundreds of years. The Ban Chiang villagers are thought to have migrated to this fertile region from Vietnam and their enigmatic disappearance is linked to an ecological disaster, possibly related to their slash-and-burn agricultural methods.

Other tribes coexisted with the Ban Chiang people, though none left such a lasting legacy. Among the people who may have lived in the verdant Chao Phrya River basin were the predecessors of the ethnic Malays as well as various tribes that migrated south from China.

Of particular importance to the spiritual development of Thailand was the spreading of Buddhist precepts by missionaries sent by the Indian Emperor Asoka, who reigned during the 3rd century B.C. Small, politically independent states were formed and ruled by these Buddhist leaders, though none had any degree of permanency.

Dvaravati Period

Among the tribal people who were to directly affect the early development of Thailand, the most significant were the Khmer and the Mon. Both groups originally lived in southern China and migrated south during the 1st century B.C. The Khmer ultimately settled in the northeastern section of Thailand; the majority of them built villages in what is now Cambodia, where they constructed their magnificent capital at Angkor. The Mon concentrated their colonization along the Chao Phrya River valley; they built their capital near Nakhon Pathom, which was already a major Buddhist center. Both the Khmer and the Mon influenced much of what would later become Thai culture. Their art forms, language, religious rituals, and architectural ideas all influenced later Thai culture.

During the height of the Mon Empire in the so-called Dvaravati Period (6th to 11th centuries), the first Tibeto-Burman people settled in the northern hills. These people were the original hill-tribe dwellers and roamed for centuries throughout the northern part of Indochina.

It was also during the Dvaravati Period, during the 7th century, that inhabitants of the Nanchao Kingdom in southern China banded together to live as a common Thai people. However, because of the economically oppressive policies of the Chinese rulers, it wasn't long before the Thais began the long process of migrating south to the Indochinese peninsula. Over a period of 200 years (beginning in the 11th century) these pioneers established small, independent states in the north. The settlers brought with them improved methods of irrigation and rice cultivation; they also had a ready trading network with Chinese merchants from Yunnan Province. It wasn't long before these northern dominions grew affluent and influential. By the 13th century the final wave of immigrants moved south. The Mon Empire was already in decline, but it was the imminent assault by Kublai Khan, in nearby Burma, that finally moved the Thai states together to form three great 13th-century kingdoms: Lanna Thai (based in Chiang Mai), Phayao, and Sukhothai. Of these, Sukhothai was the most powerful military state and was expected to protect the other kingdoms from attack.

Sukhothai Period

At the outset of the Sukhothai Period (13th to 14th centuries) the Khmer kings, based in Angkor, controlled much of Thailand. No single Thai state could defeat the Khmer armies, but in 1238 two local headmen combined forces to expel a Khmer division. This allied victory led to the founding of the Kingdom of Sukhothai, or in Pali, "Dawn of Happiness." One of these leaders, Khun Bang Klang, was named the first King of Sukhothai and was called by the title "Sri Inthrathit."

The apex of the Sukhothai Period was reached during the reign of the third ruler, King Ramkhamhaeng (1275–1317). After the military expulsion of Khmer forces, the remaining independent Thai kingdoms made alliances with Sukhothai, leading to the birth of a unified Thai state. In addition to his military conquests, during his 42 years as king, Ramkhamhaeng made remarkable progress on political, economic, cultural, and religious fronts. He was responsible for creating the Thai alphabet, establishing Theravada Buddhism as the dominant religious belief (and at the same time, creating a religious connection with Sri Lanka), and promoting the growth of the Sangkalok ceramics industry, expanding trade throughout all of Asia (especially with Burma and India, with whom he concluded separate treaties), as well as sending ambassadors to the Chinese court. All of these actions were to have far-reaching implications for the destiny of the country, with effects felt to the present day.

One of the most lasting legacies of the Sukhothai Period is the art that was created at that time. The most characteristic image is that of the parrot-nose Buddha, either sitting, or more characteristically, walking. These images are considered the greatest of all Buddha figures, and the period is regarded as the zenith of Thai culture.

After Ramkhamhaeng's reign there followed a series of kings with diminishing influence, leading Sukhothai to become a vassal state to the rising power of the 14th century, Ayutthaya. The last Sukhothai king, Phra Ramesuan, was actually an Ayutthaya prince.

Ayutthaya Period

Ayutthaya, set 400 km (240 miles) south of Sukhothai along the Chao Phrya valley, was the capital of Thailand from 1350 until 1767. At its height, during the 17th century, the city's population was greater than that of contemporary London. Not only was Ayutthaya populous but it was also cosmopolitan, with citizens hailing from as far away as England, Holland, France, Spain, Portugal, Japan, China, and Persia. So deeply were these outsiders involved in local life that a Japanese merchant was actually promoted to the post of commander of the King's Cavalry.

It was during this period that Thailand enacted its first set of civil laws. The kingdom also greatly expanded its boundaries, under the strong hand of King Naresuan, to Angkor in nearby Cambodia. Naresuan not only made the country larger, but he also neutralized what was considered the greatest remaining military threat to Thailand. (From 1569 to 1584 Thailand was ruled by the Burmese; however, King Naresuan defeated the Burmese crown prince and repulsed five subsequent invasions.)

Perhaps of equal importance was King Ekathotsarot's (Naresuan's successor) and King Narai's opening to the Western powers in the 17th century. In consecutive reigns they sent and received ambassadors to the Dutch and French courts, in addition to establishing relations with Portugal. Even though Ayutthaya was open to European traders, the Ayutthaya government was wary of Western colonial designs and kept a check on their influence. After the suspicious death of King Narai, nearly all Europeans were expelled from the country and trade with the Western world all but ceased for 200 years.

One of the legacies of the Ayutthaya Period was the changing attitude or posture of the king. During the Sukhothai Period, the king lived by the principles of Buddhism and was called "King of Righteousness," as he was expected to embody the basic tenets of Buddhist faith. During the Ayutthaya Period the king was regarded as divinely appointed and followed Brahman or Hindu rituals. They lived above the people in a god-like glow; their palaces were decorated with corresponding opulence. The kings took names from the Hindu epic, *Ramayana,* and gave themselves derivative appellations such as King Ramathibodi I. This change in custom or attitude concentrated power on the throne and led to a series of corrupt and dictatorial rulers, who often failed their basic responsibilities. Ultimately this weakness contributed to Ayutthaya's final destruction by the Burmese in the 18th century.

Bangkok Period

Before Burma destroyed Ayutthaya, the city had more than a million inhabitants. After the invasion only a few thousand were left in the ancient capital. The social order was thrown into chaos, with nearly every institution, including the royal line, in a shambles.

King Taksin, last of the great Ayutthaya rulers, moved the capital to safer ground, south to Thonburi. For the next 15 years he fought the Burmese and reformed the country's political and social system. As a final death knell to the Ayutthaya Period, Taksin proclaimed a new royal line, with his most powerful general, Chao Phrya Chakri, crowned Rama I in 1782.

During that year Rama I relocated the capital across the Chao Phrya River in the trading village of Bangkok ("Village of the Wild Plums"). For the next 27 years Rama I laid the groundwork for a city intended to surpass the grandeur of Ayutthaya. At the same time he enacted a series of laws that were designed to correct the underlying weaknesses of the previous empire, thus beginning a new administrative and economic order.

By the 18th century Thailand felt secure enough to reopen its doors to the outside world. Christian missionaries from England and America brought modern methods of medicine, education, and agriculture, helping to move the nation forward into the modern era. King Mongkut (Rama IV) and his son, King Chulalongkorn (Rama V), were the 19th-century architects of Thailand's full-scale entrance into the modern world as a completely independent nation. Both kings were social reformers and brilliant diplomats. During their reigns slavery was abolished, a technologically modern infrastructure was established, civil laws were reformed, trade treaties were concluded with nearly every significant power of the time, and the nation's security was guaranteed by a strong army (and the clever manipulation of playing one international alliance against another).

The next two reigns led to a decline in the power of the throne and coincided with rising expectations of the military, government officials, and a growing merchant class. All three factions banded together to topple the king in 1932, leading to the creation of a democratic, parliamentary form of government with the king as the nominal head of state.

MODERN POLITICS: With the ascension of a civil/military coalition government, the country attempted to establish a firm political base. This agenda was set back by the occupation by the Japanese during World War II.

The Pacific war broke out on December 8, 1941, and, faced with the overwhelming power of the Japanese, the Thais gave up resistance quickly, entering into an alliance with Japan on December 21. When British and American planes bombed Bangkok, Thailand declared war against the Allies on January 25, 1942, but at the end of the war no punitive treaties were imposed on Thailand, thanks to the Free Thai Movement that had been organized abroad by M. R. Seni Pramoj, then Thai consul in Washington, and the underground resistance led by Dr. Pridi Panomyong.

After the end of the war, parliamentary democracy, with changes brought about by socially active students, reasserted itself as the dominant and accepted political form. Since the late 1940s the government has been led by a series of military field marshals and generals (brought to power through coups), with short intervening periods of civilian control. Thailand managed to stay out of the Vietnam War (though it felt, and continues to feel, the repercussions of that war), and was largely responsible for the formation of the Association of Southeast Asian Nations (ASEAN). During the mid-1970s, as a result of another period of student uprisings, the country was led by academic and political figures not associated with the military. Since 1977, with the coup engineered by Gen. Kriengsak Chammanand and the subsequent administration of General Prem, the country has been ruled by military leaders.

Baht	$ U.S.	Baht	$ U.S.
1	0.04	500	20.00
5	0.20	750	30.00
10	0.40	1,000	40.00
15	0.60	1,250	50.00
20	0.80	1,500	60.00
25	1.00	1,750	70.00
50	2.00	2,000	80.00
75	3.00	2,250	90.00
100	4.00	2,500	100.00
125	5.00	2,750	110.00
150	6.00	3,000	120.00
175	7.00	3,250	130.00
200	8.00	3,500	140.00
225	9.00	3,750	150.00
250	10.00	4,000	160.00

2. SUGGESTED ITINERARIES

The description of Thailand in this book covers only the highlights of the country. The following itineraries are based on these destinations and are geared for the general-interest traveler. Those who have special interests should modify these basic plans.

ONE MONTH: Days 1-7: Begin with Bangkok, taking day trips to Ayutthaya, Kanchanaburi, and perhaps Hua Hin; the highlights in the capital are the Floating Market, Temple of the Emerald Buddha and the Grand Palace, Wat Po, Wat Arun, Jim Thompson's House, Wang Suan Pakkard, the Golden Buddha, the National Museum, and the various markets throughout the city. **Days 8-13:** Fly or go by train to Chiang Mai, with day trips to Lamphun, Lampang, and Chiang Rai. **Days 14-18:** Trek through the northern hills, either toward Mae Hong Son to the west or Chiang Rai and the Golden Triangle to the north. **Days 19-20:** Fly or go by train to Phitsanulok, with day trips to Sukhothai and Si Satchanalai. **Days 20-24:** Fly, via Bangkok, to Phuket, with side trips to Koh Pipi, Krabi, or Phang Nga. **Days 25-27:** Fly or go overland by bus or car to Surat Thani and take the ferry to Koh Samui, with a side trip to Phang Nga. **Days 28-30:** Return to Bangkok. One can substitute an optional trip to Pattaya and Koh Samet in place of Koh Samui or Phuket.

TWO WEEKS: Days 1-4: Begin with Bangkok, taking a day trip to Ayutthaya or Kanchanaburi. **Days 5-8:** Fly to Chiang Mai, with day trips to Lamphun, Lampang, or Chiang Rai. **Days 9-10:** Fly to Phitsanulok, with day trips to Sukhothai and Si Satchanalai. **Days 11-13:** Fly, via Bangkok, to Phuket, or to Surat Thani and take the ferry to Koh Samui. **Day 14:** Return to Bangkok.

ONE WEEK: Days 1-3: Begin with Bangkok, taking a day trip to Ayutthaya or Kanchanaburi. **Days 4-5:** Fly to Chiang Mai, with day trips to Lamphun, Lampang, and Chiang Rai. **Days 6-7:** Fly to Phitsanulok, with day trips to Sukhothai and Si Satchanalai or, after returning to Bangkok, fly to Phuket. **Day 7:** Return to Bangkok.

3. GETTING THERE AND GETTING AROUND

Thailand is centrally located in Southeast Asia and functions as a hub city for many international carriers, making it exceptionally easy to reach.

GETTING THERE: Nearly all international air carriers fly to Bangkok. In addition, there is train service from Singapore and Malaysia, and freighter service from various Asian ports. At this point, only private cars (not rented autos) can be driven into the country along the Malaysian frontier.

By Air

One of the most convenient ways to reach Thailand is on **United Airlines** (tel. toll free 800/538-2929), which flies three times weekly (on Tuesday, Friday, and Sunday) to Bangkok from San Francisco, via Hong Kong or Tokyo. There are additional routings to Bangkok from New York, via Tokyo. The 1988 weekday APEX fare was $1,249 round trip, with no stopovers allowed. For an additional $120 you can take their weekend flight and make two stopovers (perfect for those on an extended tour of Southeast Asia). Business-class tickets run $2,462, with a $25 levy for each stopover; first-class tickets cost $4,528, with unlimited stopovers. United also offers a Bangkok air-and-land package combined with their flight to Hong Kong: air transportation to Bangkok from Hong Kong, plus transfers, four nights at the Dusit Thani or Indra Regent Hotel, and a sightseeing tour runs $485 per person, double occupancy. For information about United's land packages call toll free 800/328-6877.

Thai Airways International (tel. toll free 800/426-5204), the country's international airline, flies four times weekly from Dallas–Fort Worth and daily from Seattle to Tokyo and Bangkok. Beginning in 1988 Thai Airways International began flying from Toronto three times weekly. In 1988 the Seattle originating Super APEX fare was $1,120, round trip. The midweek Super Saver fare was $1,050; no stopovers are allowed. Business-class tickets run $2,088, with unlimited stopovers; first-class seats cost $3,828, also with unlimited stopovers. If you intend to visit Chiang Mai you're better off to add the trip to your international ticket. Ditto for Phuket and Pattaya, as well as Hong Kong, Kathmandu, Singapore, Burma, India, and Tokyo. Thai Airways International also offers air/land packages that are worth investigating.

Within Southeast Asia, Thai Airways International has direct flights from Bangkok to Jakarta, Rangoon, Manila, Hong Kong, Singapore, Kuala Lumpur, and Penang. Garuda International flies from Jakarta to Bangkok; MAS flies from Kuala Lumpur to Bangkok; Singapore Airlines flies to Bangkok and Phuket; Dragon Air flies from Hong Kong to Phuket; and Philippine Airlines flies from Manila to Bangkok.

By Train

There is train service, organized by the **State Railway of Thailand,** that originates in Singapore, passes through Malaysia (making a stop in Kuala Lumpur), and terminates in Bangkok. The fare runs 2,315 baht ($92.50) for a first-class, air-conditioned sleeping berth. The entire trip takes 30 hours, not including a 10-hour layover in Kuala Lumpur, for the 1,160 miles journey.

By Boat

Several international cruise companies have cruises that travel to Thailand, docking near Pattaya. More frequent service is via freighters that ply the waters between Japan, Hong Kong, Singapore, and south to Indonesia. Because these schedules change so frequently, you'll have to consult your travel agent or procure an up-to-date shipping manual with current times and prices.

GETTING AROUND: Travel within Thailand is extremely efficient and inexpensive. If you have limited time, by all means fly, but if you have the time and want to take in the countryside, either take the train or rent a car.

By Air

Other than to Koh Samui, all domestic flights are on **Thai Airways** (which recently became part of Thai Airways International), with Bangkok serving as its hub city. There are connecting flights between Bangkok and Chiang Mai, Chiang Rai, Mae Hong Son, Phitsanulok, Surat Thani, and Phuket. There are also connecting flights from Phuket to Surat Thani and from Chiang Mai to Phitsanulok. Maximum flight time from Bangkok to any location within Thailand is no more than one hour. Typical one-way fares and number of daily flights (as of 1988) to these destinations are shown in the table.

Route	One-Way Fare	Daily Flights
Bangkok to Chiang Mai	1,275 baht ($51)	2–4
Chiang Mai to Phitsanulok	505 baht ($20.25)	1
Bangkok to Surat Thani	1,380 baht ($55.25)	1
Bangkok to Phuket	1,545 baht ($61.75)	3

In 1988, **Sahaon Air** began flying to Koh Samui from Bangkok once daily. Children under the age of 12 years old travel at half the posted rate; infants travel at 10% of the normal fare.

By Train

Train service around the country is excellent and comfortable, with a full range of service available. The **State Railway of Thailand** organizes its routes along four separate lines, all with their terminus in Bangkok: the Southern Line, which makes stops at Kanchanaburi, the River Kwai Bridge, Hua Hin, and Surat Thani (Koh Samui stop), with international service continuing to Kuala Lumpur and Singapore; the Northern Line, which makes stops at Don Muang, Bang Pa-In, Ayutthaya, Lopburi, Phitsanulok, Lampang, Lamphun, and Chiang Mai; the Northeastern Line, which makes stops at Don Muang (the airport), Ayutthaya, Surin, and ultimately, Non Khai, near the Laotian border; and the Eastern Line, which continues to Aranyaprathet, near the Cambodian border.

Typical one-way, second-class fares (as of January 1988) and average hours of travel time to these destinations are shown in the table.

Route	One-Way Fare (Second class)	Time
Bangkok to Chiang Mai	255 baht ($10.25)	14 hours
Bangkok to Phitsanulok	143 baht ($5.75)	7 hours
Chiang Mai to Phitsanulok	112 baht ($4.50)	8 hours
Bangkok to Surat Thani	224 baht ($9)	12 hours

There are three categories of trains (in order of speed and comfort): express, rapid, and ordinary. In most cases, only rapid and express trains have sleeping berths, and express trains also offer first-class compartments. The surcharge (to the above rates) for traveling on an express train is 30 baht ($1.25), 20 baht (80¢) for a rapid, and 50 baht ($2) for a second-class air-conditioned coach. The first-class air-conditioned single-cabin sleeping-berth surcharge runs 350 baht ($14) per person; a double costs 500 baht ($20). The second-class surcharge for an air-conditioned berth runs 200 baht ($8) in a lower berth, 170 baht ($6.75) for an upper berth, per person.

Children between the ages of 3 and 12 travel at half the posted rate.

By Rental Car

Renting a car is a snap in Thailand, though you might choose to hire a driver to guide you along the way and to minimize the aggravation of driving in sometimes chaotic traffic conditions. Among the many rental-car agencies, **Avis** (tel. 233-0397 in Bangkok, or toll free 800/331-1212 in the U.S.) and **Hertz** (tel. 253-6251 in Bangkok, or toll free 800/654-3131 in the U.S.) have offices around the country with representatives in Bangkok, as well as Pattaya, Phuket, Koh Samui, and Chiang Mai. There are many smaller, local agencies that rent cars for less than the international firms, though not all have full insurance coverage and chauffeur service. Typical rates for a Toyota Corona from one of the major firms are 1,440 baht ($57.50) per day with unlimited mileage or 930 baht ($37.25) plus 3 baht (12¢) per kilometer. The collision damage waiver is 120 baht ($4.75) per day. Chauffeur-driven rates for a similar car are 1,500 baht ($60) per day with an out-of-town surcharge of 3 baht (12¢) per kilometer. Gasoline costs about 10 baht (40¢) per liter ($1.60 per gallon). If you rent a chauffeured car for overnight trips, the average cost per hour for a driver is 150 baht ($6) and 300 baht ($12) for lodging and food per night.

By Bus

Buses are the cheapest mode of transportation in Thailand, and they travel to the farthest and most remote destinations in the country. Options abound, but the major choices range from public or private buses, and air-conditioned or non-air-conditioned coaches. Most foreign travelers (and those locals who can afford it) use the private air-conditioned buses.

Ideally, buses are best taken on short excursions—for example, a day trip from Bangkok to Pattaya or Ayutthaya or from Phitsanulok to Sukhothai. One can expect to pay a minimum, for example, of 50 baht ($2) for a one-way ticket on an air-conditioned bus from Bangkok to Pattaya. Longer-haul buses are excellent values—for example, a ticket to Phuket runs 320 baht ($12.75)—but their lack of speed is a real liability.

Unfortunately, we need to issue a warning, particularly for those who do take long-haul bus trips: some tourists have had their luggage and other personal possessions stolen on bus trips. Though travel on private air-conditioned buses is considerably less risky than, for example, riding on the public bus in Bangkok, you should still exercise caution and keep an eye on all your valuables.

Local Transportation

There are several categories of private and public transportation, ranging from private cars (such as those operated by Thai Airways and individual hotels) to the ubiquitous *samlor* or, as this motorized bicycle rickshaw is onomatopoetically called, the *tuk-tuk*. With taxis and tuk-tuks you'll have to negotiate; more expensive private cars have posted rates. If you don't know the correct fare, ask a shop owner, hotelier, or restaurateur what you should pay given your destination, and negotiate accordingly with the driver. Most taxi fares will average between 10 baht (40¢) in the provincial towns, to 75 baht ($3) within Bangkok, depending on route, distance, condition of the car, and mood of the driver. With taxis or tuk-tuks, always remember to agree on your fare before engaging a driver or you will almost certainly overpay. Tipping is not expected.

Zippy little tuk-tuks resemble souped-up golf carts but are propelled by gasoline engines. Expect a fairly noisy, windy ride, with an occasional daring driver darting in between buses, trucks, water buffalos, and motorcycles. As with taxis, you'll have to negotiate your fare, but expect to pay a few baht less.

Except for Bangkok, we recommend traveling by local bus. (For our description of the hazards of busing in Bangkok, see "Getting Around" in Chapter XVII). The fare averages only a few baht, and it's a safe and dependable option.

4. THE ABC'S OF THAILAND

Most travelers who arrive in Thailand for the first time are struck with how such a traditionally oriented culture presents such a modern, efficient façade. This is one of the many paradoxes and joys of life in Thailand: there is enough of the familiar to bridge what is utterly foreign. As modern as some aspects of the country may be, it's best if you think of it as a developing Third World culture; you'll be better prepared to deal with those parts of life that are maddeningly slow if not impossible, and you'll be pleasantly surprised if things work out the way you want!

Even though many aspects of life in Thailand are so familiar, it's a good idea to review such issues as appropriate behavior, dining customs, modes of travel, and how to have fun in the process. The following section is designed to help you through some of the broad questions of travel in Thailand. "The ABCs of Bangkok" and the "Useful Information" sections of other chapters will supplement this chapter for specific locales.

BANKS AND CURRENCY EXCHANGE: Nearly all hotels will change foreign currency, but banks and moneychangers offer better rates. Official **bank-**

ing hours are 8:30 a.m. to 3:30 p.m. Monday through Friday. All major cities in each province have foreign-exchange banks and moneychangers, many of which keep special extended hours for exchange, typically open as late as 10 p.m. Always ask for a receipt; it's useful if you wish to repurchase foreign currency. After many unfortunate experiences, we also suggest that travelers carry an ample supply of baht as well as dollars when traveling to more remote areas.

BATHROOMS: Unlike many other parts of Asia, Thailand does not uniformly use the Asian toilet (the hole in the ground with foot pads on either side). Many restaurants and all hotels above the budget level will have Western toilets. However, in the smaller towns, the rest rooms of shops, restaurants, and budget hotels will have an Asian toilet. They are usually quite clean, but most difficult to use for anyone who is physically handicapped. Near the toilet will be a water bucket or sink with a small ladle. The water is for flushing and cleaning the toilet. There may be some toilet paper, but it's best to carry your own supply.

In some lodgings you may find an Asian shower. What you get is a square sink in the bath with the same kind of ladle as in the toilet. You take the ladle and pour water (cold) over yourself, soap up, and do the same to rinse.

BUSINESS HOURS: All **government offices** are open from 8:30 a.m. to 4:30 p.m. Monday through Friday, with a lunch break between noon and 1 p.m. **Businesses** are generally open from 8 a.m. to 5 p.m. **Shops** often stay open from 8 a.m. until 7 p.m. or even later, seven days a week. **Department stores** generally open at 10 a.m. and close at 7 p.m. For banking hours, see "Banks and Currency Exchange."

CLIMATE: Thailand has two distinct climates, though both are always humid. The south is tropical, dominated by the annual monsoon, while the north is a tropical savannah environment. Except in the more temperate south there are three distinct seasons. The hot season lasts from March to May, with temperatures averaging in the upper 90s Fahrenheit (mid-30s Celsius). The rainy season begins in June and extends into October; the average temperature is 84°F (29°C) with 90% humidity. The cool season, from November through February, has temperatures averaging in the high 70s to low 80s Fahrenheit (26°C). In the north, particularly in the hills around Chiang Mai, temperatures can go down to the low 60s (16°C); don't forget a sweater. The southern half of the country, below Bangkok, is nearly always rainy (though with intermittent showers except during the monsoon); temperatures average in the low 80s (30°C). Unlike other Asian countries such as India, the monsoon isn't nearly as monolithic; you can actually travel around the country in comfort.

CLOTHING: Light, casual clothing is de rigueur in this part of the world as your best defense against the heat. Breathable cotton or linen is far preferable to synthetics, although keeping your clothing pressed is problematic (hotels usually offer prompt laundry service). Thailand is a relatively formal country, so count on wearing modest styles (no strapless blouses, for example), especially if you are touring *wats* (temples) or other religious monuments. Since you are often required to remove your shoes in religious buildings, we suggest wearing easy-to-remove footwear, such as sandals or slip-on shoes. At the beaches, nudity is illegal and is considered offensive by local residents; if you absolutely have to undress at the beach, do so only at a completely deserted location, otherwise you'll risk offending Thai residents.

Men should generally wear long pants, though longer shorts are acceptable in beach communities. Pressed cotton pants, shirt, and tie (a jacket is optional, depending on the formality of the meeting) are definitely in order for business and government meetings. A coat and tie is proper for evening engagements. Women should refrain from wearing shorts or revealing blouses; dresses are the conservative choice. During the monsoon, remember to bring an umbrella. If you plan on visiting the north during the cool season, bring a light sweater.

As for colors, try to avoid wearing too much black; it's considered, at least among the more traditional Thais, an unlucky color.

COMMONLY USED THAI WORDS AND EXPRESSIONS: It isn't likely that you'll end up speaking fluent Thai by the end of your trip, but you'll probably find yourself picking up a few key words. The following list should be useful both for the description of sights within this book as well as for the pleasantries of everyday travel.

Thai	English
sawatdee	hello
lakon	good-bye
cha	yes
mai	no
khob khun	thank you
samlor (tuk-tuk)	motorized tricycle
my pet	not hot
Geography:	
ban	village
doi	mountain
hat	beach
klong	canal
koh	island
mae nam	river
muang	city
soi	lane
thanon	road
Architecture:	
bot	central shrine in a Buddhist temple
chedi	a pointed, domed structure housing the relics of the Buddha; also called a stupa
mondop	square-shaped structure containing a Buddha
naga	dragon-like snake figure
prang	Khmer-inspired cactus-shaped tower
viharn	large hall in a Buddhist temple used for daily rituals
wat	temple or monastery complex

For Thai words relating to food, please refer to the "Cuisine" section in this chapter. For those who would like a phrasebook, we suggest a guide called *Practical Thai* (APA Productions, Hong Kong, 1982; distributed in the U.S. and Canada by Prentice Hall).

CREDIT CARDS: Nearly all international hotels and larger businesses accept major credit cards, but few accept personal checks. Traveler's checks are negotiable in most banks, hotels, restaurants, and tourist-oriented shops, though you'll receive the best rate at commercial banks. In smaller towns and provinces, baht will be the only acceptable form of currency.

CUISINE: This is one of the true joys of travel in Thailand. If you aren't familiar with Thai cooking, imagine taking the best of Chinese-style preparation and combining it with the sophistication of Indian spices and you'll have some idea of what to expect. The basic ingredients include an enormous variety of shellfish, fresh fruits and vegetables—lime, asparagus, tamarind, bean sprouts, carrots, mushrooms (many different kinds), morning glory, spinach, and bamboo shoots—and spices, including basil, lemon grass, mint, chili, garlic, and coriander. Thai cooking also uses coconut milk, curry paste, peanuts, and a huge variety of noodles and rice.

Among the dishes you'll probably find throughout the country are: *tom yum goong,* a Thai hot-and-sour shrimp soup; *satay,* charcoal-broiled chicken, beef, or pork strips skewered on a bamboo stick, dipped in a peanut-coconut curry sauce; *spring rolls,* similiar to eggrolls but thinner and usually containing only vegetables; *larb,* a spicy chicken or ground-beef concoction with mint and lime flavoring; *salads,* made with nearly any ingredient as the prime flavor, but most have a dressing made with onion, chili pepper, lime juice, and fish sauce; *pad Thai,* literally "Thai noodles" (this is one of our favorites and you can find it everywhere), it includes rice noodles, large shrimp, eggs, peanuts, fresh bean sprouts, lime, and a delicious sauce; *khao soi,* a northern curried soup served at small food stalls; a wide range of *curries,* flavored with coriander, chili, garlic, and fish sauce or coconut milk; *tod man pla,* one of many preparations of fish, this one is spicy; *sticky rice,* served in the north and made from glutinous rice, prepared with vegetables and wrapped in a banana leaf; and *Thai fried rice,* a simple rice dish made with whatever the kitchen has on hand.

As a word of caution, the Thai palate relishes incredibly spicy food, normally much hotter than is tolerated in even the most piquant Western cuisine. Most restaurants will oblige if you ask for the dish to be prepared without such hot spices (in Thai you can request, *mai pet,* meaning "not spicy").

Traditional Thai cuisine does not deliver super-fancy desserts—the most you'll find on any menu are a variety of fruit-flavored custards—but there's no need to, because the local fruit is so luscious and makes a perfect dessert. Among the many familiar fruits are the following: pineapple, which is so sweet and eaten with salt by the Thais to bring out even more flavor, plus mangoes, bananas, guava, papaya, coconut, and watermelon. Less familiar is *durian,* a legendary fruit, in season in June and July, that by many accounts tastes wonderful but smells odious; *mangosteen,* a purplish, hard-skinned fruit with delicate, whitish-pink segments that melt in the mouth, available April to September; *jackfruit,* which is large, yellow-brown with a thick, thorned skin enveloping tangy-flavored flesh, available year round; *lychee; longan,* a small, brown-skinned fruit with very sweet white flesh available July to October; *tamarind,* a spicy little fruit in a bean-type pod that you can eat fresh (it's also used to make a delicious spicy sweet-and-sour sauce); *rambutan,* which is small, red, and hairy, with transparent sweet flesh clustered round a woody seed, available May to July; *pomelo,* similar to a grapefruit, but less juicy, available October to December—and that's not all of them! By the way, some of these fruits are served as salads—the raw green papaya, for example, is particularly delicious.

If you begin to suffer from Thai burn-out, we suggest visiting a Chinese restaurant. Most of the Chinese cuisine served in Thailand is from Yunnan Province or Canton, meaning that the spices are restrained and the food delicious.

Thailand also offers a large number of Indian restaurants, many of which have a wide variety of vegetarian dishes. We've found that most of the Indian restaurants serve northern, cooler cuisine than the fiery dishes that one finds in the south.

With such an international community in the country, it's not surprising that Thailand has a large assortment of European-style restaurants. Don't be surprised if your Thai host suggests visiting a French or Italian restaurant. They are extremely popular, and in our experience, are often quite good. If you do visit a Western-style restaurant, experiment and try those dishes that combine traditional European recipes with native Thai ingredients. They are particularly delicious.

CURRENCY: The Thai unit of currency is the **baht.** The baht is divided into 100 **satang,** though you'll rarely see a satang coin. Copper-colored coins represent 25 and 50 satang, while silver-colored coins represent 1, 2, and 5 baht. Baht notes come in denominations of 10 baht (brown), 20 baht (green), 100 baht (red), and 500 baht (purple). The exchange rate at the time of publication was 25 baht = $1 U.S., making 1 baht equal to 4¢.

CUSTOMS: Tourists are allowed to enter the country with a maximum of one liter of alcoholic beverages and 200 cigarettes (or 250 grams of cigars or smoking tobacco) per adult free of duty. Cars (with a cash or bank guarantee, vehicle registration, and proper driver's license), photographic equipment (one still or movie camera, plus five rolls of still film or three rolls of 8-mm or 16-mm motion-picture film) and professional instruments are allowed provided they are taken out on departure. (The number of rolls of film is not strictly enforced and exceeding the stated amount is not a problem.) They must be declared as you enter. Firearms and ammunition can only be brought in with a permit from the Police Department or local Registration Office. Animals brought by air are allowed with a permit for entry, which can be obtained at the airport. If pets are brought in by boat, one must apply in advance to the Department of Livestock Development (tel. 251-5136) in Bangkok. In any case, all animals must have proper vaccination certificates. Certain plants are restricted for import; contact the Department of Agriculture (tel. 579-0151) in Bangkok for particulars.

There are no restrictions on the import of foreign currencies or traveler's checks; however, you cannot export foreign currency in excess of $10,000. Individuals may bring a maximum of 2,000 baht (4,000 baht per family) into the country; individuals may take out not more than 500 baht (1,000 baht per family) upon exit.

DOCUMENTS FOR ENTRY: All visitors to Thailand must carry a valid passport, with proof of onward passage (either a return or through ticket). Visas are not required if you are staying only a maximum of 15 days and are a national of Argentina, Australia, Austria, Belgium, Brazil, Brunei, Burma, Canada, Denmark, Finland, France, Greece, Iceland, Indonesia, Ireland, Israel, Italy, Japan, Luxembourg, Malaysia, Mexico, Netherlands, New Zealand, Norway, Philippines, Saudi Arabia, Singapore, South Korea, Spain, Sweden, Switzerland, Turkey, United Kingdom, United States, or West Germany.

This visa-free entry cannot be extended. Entry and departure must be through the airport or one of the major ports of entry, such as Bangkok, Phuket, or Chiang Mai. Check with the Thai consulate or embassy in your country if you plan to enter Thailand via an exotic port. If you wish to stay longer than 15 days, then you need to obtain a 60-day tourist visa or 30-day transit visa from any foreign Thai embassy or consulate. Three photographs and $10 are required for a transit visa, $15 for a tourist visa, and $20 for a non-immigrant (business) visa. If you have a question as to which type of visa is required (if any), call or write to the nearest Thai embassy or consulate. If you apply in person, the entire process takes only one business day.

Business people require a visa for purposes of business contacts, calls, or meetings, as well as employment. A non-immigrant visa can be obtained for a period up to 90 days with an accompanying letter from the employer of the applicant stating the period and purpose of stay in Thailand. The visa must be used within 90 days of issue.

If you enter the country on a non-immigrant business visa or have earned income while in the kingdom, you must go through tax clearance prior to exiting. Contact the Tax Clearance Sub-Division (tel. 281-5777), Central Operation Division of the Revenue Department in Bangkok at Building 1 on Chakrapongse Road, or any District Revenue Office.

Check for information at the consulate or embassy for up-to-date information about possible health certificates that may be required for entry into Thailand. As of this writing, there were no required inoculations, other than for tourists coming from an infected zone.

DRINKING WATER: Even though there has been a campaign to clean up tap water in the country, we strongly recommend that you *never drink the tap water*. Nearly all hotels will include bottled water in the bathroom; use this for brushing your teeth as well as drinking. Most restaurants will serve bottled or boiled water and ice made from boiled water, but always ask to be sure. Even the Thais drink bottled or boiled water. Drink lots of it—it's the best antidote to the heat.

ELECTRICAL APPLIANCES: All outlets in the country, with the exception of some luxury hotels, are 220 volts, 50 cycles, A.C. If you use a 110-volt hairdryer, electric shaver, or battery charger for a computer, bring a transformer and adapter.

EMBASSIES AND CONSULATES: All embassies are located in Bangkok. The **U.S. Embassy** is located at 95 Wireless Rd. (tel. 252-5040), and is open Monday through Friday from 7:30 a.m. to noon and 1 to 4:30 p.m. The **British Embassy,** at 1031 Wireless Rd. off Ploenchit Road (tel. 253-0191), is open from 8 a.m. to 1 p.m. on Monday and Tuesday, 8 a.m. to 2 p.m. on Wednesday, and 2 to 4:30 p.m. on Thursday and Friday. The **Canadian Embassy** is in the Boonmitr Building, at 138 Silom Rd. (tel. 234-1561), and is open from 8 a.m. to 12:30 p.m. and 1:30 to 4:30 p.m. Monday through Friday. The **Australian Embassy** is at 37 S. Sathorn Rd. (tel. 286-0411), and keeps hours from 9:30 a.m. to 12:30 p.m. and 2 to 3:30 p.m., Monday through Friday.

There are also **U.S. Consulates** in Chiang Mai, Songkhla, and Udorn.

EMERGENCIES: Throughout the country, the emergency number is **191** for police or medical assistance. You should also contact your embassy or consulate, or the local Tourist Authority of Thailand (TAT) office (see "Tourist Information").

ETIQUETTE: Although life in Thailand is fairly casual, don't mistake this easygoing manner for an acceptance of "anything goes" behavior. For example, Thais have a great reverence for the royal family and never make jokes or disparaging comments at their expense. Similarly, there is great respect for religious figures. It is particularly important for women not to touch a monk. If a woman wishes to give something to a monk, she must put the object down somewhere near him and let him pick it up. Great respect is also shown for parents and elders.

The Thai people have very specific ideas about the head and feet. Thais consider the soles of the feet unclean; pointing your toes or the soles of your feet at someone is considered impolite. When you enter a temple, be sure not to point your toes at the Buddha. Sit down and fold your legs to the side. Be careful not to cross your legs, especially during an official government visit, for fear you may accidentally insult your host. Do not climb on or pose in front of a Buddhist figure. Shoes should be removed when entering a private home, or any Buddhist or Islamic shrines.

At the other end of the body, the head is considered the highest spiritual point, and it is an insult to touch someone on the head; avoid the Western custom of patting on the head or back.

If you are making an official or business call, coffee or tea will be served. You should wait until your host invites you to drink before touching your cup or glass. This will usually occur just before the visit is about to end. When you eat in the communal style, do not fill your plate with food. Only take a small amount (a few bites at most) or your host may think you a glutton.

Thais rarely offend or disturb other people. A public display of anger is absolutely taboo and will be considered extremely embarrassing. At all times, the sense of maintaining "face" must be observed, allowing individuals the opportunity to save their dignity. Although it may be hard to resist at times (and this may be the most difficult of all Asian skills to master), it is very rude and ineffective for Westerners to respond with anger and raised voices to private problems. You should always find a way to allow the person you are dealing with to save face. Smile, be calm but insistent, and if you're patient, things will work out to everyone's satisfaction.

Public displays of affection, with the possible exception of hand-holding, is considered in questionable taste and should be kept to a minimum.

One of the lovely Thai gestures is the *wai* (pronounced "why"), a form of greeting, which consists of placing the palms of the hands together, with the tips of the index fingers raised to eye level and a subtle bowing from the waist and bending of the knees. This is the accepted way of honoring someone's presence and is done with all people other than children and service people. Don't be surprised if you are addressed by your first name, such as Mr. John or Ms. Kyle; this is normal etiquette and doesn't imply a slight or a lack of formality.

FESTIVALS AND HOLIDAYS: Many holidays are celebrated based on the Thai lunar calendar; check with TAT for the current year's schedule. The **national holidays,** besides Christmas, Easter, and New Year's (Western New Year on January 1, as well as the water-throwing festival of Songkran in April, marking the beginning of the Buddhist year, and Chinese New Year), are: Magha Puja, in February, celebrating the day the Buddha preached his doctrines; Chakri Day, in April, commemorating the founding of the Chakri Dynasty (the reigning dynasty); Coronation Day, on May 5, honoring the coronation of His Majesty King Bhumibol in 1950; Visakha Puja, in mid-May, marking the birth, enlightenment, and death of the Buddha; Asalha Puja, in July, signaling the beginning of the Rains' Retreat and the three-month period of meditation for all Buddhist monks; August 12, marking the birthday of Her Majesty the Queen and also Mothers' Day; Thot Kathin, from October to November, during which monks are presented with new robes; Chulalongkorn Day, on October 23, honoring the country's favorite king; Loi Krathong, in early November, one of Thailand's greatest holidays, honoring the water spirit and serving as a day to wash away sins committed during the previous year; December 5, marking His Majesty the King's birthday and Fathers' Day; and December 10, Constitution Day, recognizing Thailand's first constitution in 1932. There are many more holidays celebrated by the hill-tribe people in the northern hills of Thailand; check with TAT in Chiang Mai or Chiang Rai for the local schedule.

Thailand has a great many **festivals.** Among the most widely recognized are: in early February, Chiang Mai's fabulous Flower Festival; in April, the Ayutthaya Festival with an elaborate sound-and-light show; in April, the Pattaya Festival and the International Kite Festival; in early May, the Royal Ploughing Festival, marking the commencement of the annual rice-planting cycle; September, the Phichit Boat Races; in late September, the Vegetarian Festival on Phuket, with special food and incredible athletic displays; and in mid-November, the Elephant Round-Up in Surin, Northeast Thailand. As with holidays, there are many festivals celebrated by the hill-tribe people; check with TAT for the latest schedule of events.

FILM AND CAMERA: You should definitely bring your camera, but if you need to, you can buy your film here. Kodak has a manufacturing plant in the region and the prices of both Kodak and Fuji film are often less than in the U.S. One-hour photo-processing centers are nearly everywhere with prices less than in the States.

HEALTH AND VACCINATIONS: There are no inoculations or vaccinations required to enter Thailand, except for travelers coming from contaminated regions. Malaria prophylaxis is advised for travelers outside the major cities, particularly in the north. Check with your doctor or health clinic as there are exotic varieties of malaria in some places that do not respond to the traditional malaria medicines.

You shouldn't have any health problems, other than the normal maladies associated with relocating in a different environment; however, it's best to be sensitive to potential problems. Above all, *do not drink tap water.* Make sure water is boiled or, more likely, bottled. Avoid salads and dairy products, including ice cream. Don't eat unpeeled fruit or vegetables, except at the larger hotels and restaurants, and even then, inquire whether fresh food is washed with bottled water. We eat street food, but exercise caution; check to see if oil and ingredients look fresh, and never eat anything raw prepared at a street stand, especially seafood.

Don't swim in freshwater streams or pools (other than chlorinated hotel pools), as they are probably contaminated. Avoid the ocean near the outlets of freshwater streams, to avoid contaminated waters (especially around Pattaya) and the poisonous sea snakes that inhabit these areas. Be especially careful of coral reefs (such as those along Phuket), jellyfish, and sea urchins, and treat all cuts or stings immediately by washing and applying an antibiotic cream. Ear infections are a problem, so make sure you dry your ears thoroughly.

Exercise caution about physical activity, with the idea of avoiding sunstroke or heat exhaustion. Don't try to run around in the first few days of your visit; the slower pace of life here is dictated by the hot and humid weather, not the absence of Western values. Above all, be sure to drink lots of liquid to avoid dehydration; we consumed huge amounts of bottled water. Avoid long periods of exposure to the sun (you can burn in less than 15 minutes under the hot Thai sun), use a strong sun screen, and wear a hat for protection. We found that restricting alcohol consumption and eating lightly helped our acclimatization to the heat and sun.

Diarrhea is to be expected in the adjustment to a new cuisine and climate. If it persists beyond 48 hours or is accompanied by fever or dehydration, consult a doctor.

The Medical Service (tel. 252-5040) at the American Embassy is extremely knowledgeable about local maladies and can refer you to local physicians or hospitals for appropriate treatment.

HITCHHIKING: Public transportation by air, train, and bus is so reasonably priced and convenient that there really is no need for hitchhiking; we never saw any hitchhikers during our travels around the country, though it isn't prohibited.

LANGUAGE: Thai is the official language of the country, which was derived from such diverse linguistic sources as Mon, Khmer, Sanskrit, and Pali—not the stuff of tenth-grade language classes. Hill-tribe people speak many different dialects with linguistic roots spreading as far as Tibet, China, Laos, and Burma.

The Thai script is written in a modified form of Mon and Khmer, which in turn was influenced by Sri Lankan writing styles—the bottom line is that you can't read it! Fortunately, English is spoken in the major cities and by workers in most hotels, restaurants, and shops, and is considered the second language among the professional class.

LAUNDRY: Almost every hotel in the country has laundry service, and compared to what we pay in New York, prices are reasonable. You'll find a laundry, and in most cases, a dry cleaner in nearly every town in the country. There are a few public coin-operated laundries only in the main cities, such as Bangkok and Chiang Mai.

LIQUOR LAWS: Thailand has a huge number of bars, and liquor and beer are widely available in stores, restaurants, and hotels. There are several fine varieties of beer brewed in the country; the best known are Singha and a locally brewed German beer, Kloster. There isn't much in the way of Thai wine. Most wine is imported, and while it is readily available in Bangkok, it's not found in the countryside, except at Western restaurants and then often so aged as to be undrinkable! Locally produced whisky is very popular, and Johnnie Walker Red is still one of the most highly prized gifts one can give.

METRIC MEASURES: Thailand uses the metric system. For metric conversion tables, see "The ABCs of Burma" in Chapter II.

NEWSPAPERS AND PERIODICALS: The *Bangkok Post* and *The Nation* are daily papers that are distributed in the morning in the capital and later in the day around the country. The *Bangkok World* is an afternoon publication. All three are in English, carry decent coverage of international news from AP and UPI, and cost 10 baht (40¢). Both the *Asian Wall Street Journal* and *International Herald Tribune* are available Monday through Friday and can be purchased on their day of publication in Bangkok; they seem to reach the provinces two or three days later. *Where, Look East,* and *Saen Sanuk* are slick English-language magazines that are published monthly and cost 25 baht ($1). All three magazines emphasize events and features concerning Bangkok, with lesser emphasis on other Thai cities and provinces. All of these periodicals, as well as *Time, Newsweek, The Economist,* and the *Far Eastern Economic Review* are sold at newsstands and bookstores in the international hotels and in tourist areas.

POLITICS: It is a tribute to the Thai people that the nation has never been ruled by a foreign power. One of the reasons for this is the interest that the Thai citizenry have in protecting their political structure and freedom under the central triad of nation, king, and religion. Another factor supporting their independence is that the political system is relatively fluid, responding to the changing needs of the times. Since abandoning the absolute monarchy in 1932, the government has gone through many different transformations between democratically elected regimes, military coups, and authoritarian domination. Even during periods of open government, the military has played an influential role, as has the royal family (often steering in different directions from each other), in maintaining a semblance of stability.

As for its formal structure, the government is a constitutional monarchy with King Bhumibol Adulyadej serving as the head of state and chief of staff of the armed forces, as well as the protector of religion (including Buddhism). The administrative, judicial, and ministerial bodies all operate semi-autonomously, under the king's nominal supervision. Bangkok is the capital city, while the rest of the country is organized into 73 provinces (*changwat*). These geographic regions are further organized into districts (*amphoe*) and villages (*muban*).

POSTAL AND INTERNATIONAL DELIVERY SERVICES: In each chapter, we list the local post offices with their operating hours. If you don't know what your address will be, consider using Poste Restante (followed by the name of the town) as an address, anywhere in the country. A Poste Restante window will be found at the main or general post office of each city. A first-class letter to the United States costs 11.50 baht (45¢) per 5 grams. A postcard costs 9 baht (35¢). An air parcel costs 356 baht ($14.25) per kilo ($6.50 per pound) and a sea parcel costs 135 baht ($5.50) per kilo ($2.50 per pound).

If you are thinking of shipping purchases by freight, check the rates, as it can get quite expensive by air. **DHL Thailand** with offices at 501/111 Nang Linchee Rd., Ratchada-Pisek Intersection, Yannawa, Bangkok (tel. 286-7209), and **Federal Express,** which ships through Transport and Freight Forwarding International Co., C.C.T. Building, 10th Floor, 109 Surawong Rd., Bangkok (tel. 235-8602), the major international delivery services, have their main dispatching offices in Bangkok, though they deliver throughout the country.

SAFETY: The rate of serious crime in Thailand is quite low; however, unfortunately there is a high risk of petty crime, such as purse-snatching or pickpocketing. Particular care should be taken for those traveling overland in remote parts of the country, as pirates frequently rob tourists.

Also, there is a scam involving credit cards, for those who leave their cards with other individuals for safekeeping (such as during a trek). *Do not, under any circumstance, allow anyone to hold onto your credit cards; if you do not want to carry them, place them in the hotel safe.*

Be sure to place all other valuables in the hotel safe. Pay particular attention to your possessions, especially purses and wallets, on all forms of public transportation, with extra caution on buses and trains.

TAXES AND SERVICE CHARGES: Hotels charge a government tax of 11% and typically add a service charge of 10%; hotel restaurants charge an 8½%

tax. Smaller hotels will often quote the price inclusive of these charges, but be sure to ask before agreeing to a room and price.

TELEPHONE/TELEGRAPH/TELEX: Major hotels in Bangkok, Pattaya, Phuket, Chiang Mai, and the provincial capitals have international direct-dial long-distance telephone service. Hotels charge a surcharge on local and long-distance calls, which can add up to 50% in some cases. A better bet is usually to make credit-card or collect calls. Most hotels also levy a service charge for credit-card and collect calls. There are Overseas Telegraph and Telephone offices (also called **PTT,** for Post, Telephone, and Telegraph) open 24 hours throughout the country where long-distance domestic and international calls can be booked. International calls can take up to an hour to place, but normally it's only a few minutes before your connection is made; in 1988 a station-to-station call to the United States cost 210 baht ($8.50) for three minutes, person-to-person calls cost an additional 280 baht ($11.25). Credit-card and collect calls can be easily placed from most hotels and PTT offices, but cash-only is the policy for all other categories of calls. Pay telephones (red) are fairly common in most parts of the country, and cost 1 baht (4¢) on the street for local calls and up to 5 baht (20¢) in hotel lobbies. Nearly every hotel also offers Telex and telegram service, and an increasing number are offering facsimile service from their business centers. Every PTT has a telegram office.

TELEVISION AND RADIO: American and British television shows are broadcast in Thai, but local FM stations sometimes simulcast English-language soundtracks for selected programs, such as English-language news. In addition, large hotels often show fairly recent films on their own video systems. If you have access to a video recorder, there are video rental shops all over the country.

There is English-language programming on certain AM and FM radio stations throughout the country with American, British, and Thai disk jockeys playing good pop music. Foreign radio networks, such as American Armed Forces Radio and the BBC, can be received in Thailand. Check the local newspaper for station frequencies.

TIME: Thailand has one time zone which is Greenwich Mean Time (GMT) plus 7 hours, making it 12 hours ahead of New York and 15 hours ahead of Los Angeles. If you intend to make an overseas call, check to see whether Daylight Savings Time is observed in the country you wish to telephone.

TIPPING: In restaurants where a service charge is not added, a tip of 10% to 15% is appropriate, if the service was acceptable. In the small noodle shops, a 10-baht (40¢) tip may be added if the service is particularly good. Airport or hotel porters expect tips of 10 baht (40¢) per bag. Since fares are negotiable, tipping taxi drivers is not expected. It's a good idea to carry small bills, as many cab drivers either don't have (or won't admit to having) small change.

TOURIST INFORMATION: Your major source of information is the **Tourist Authority of Thailand (TAT),** with offices throughout the country and abroad. The TAT is often very helpful and should be consulted on travel plans, hotels, restaurant suggestions, and current schedules for festivals and holidays. A bilingual (English and Thai) **Tourist Police** force is part of the TAT in all major tourist areas. They can be helpful in emergencies such as filing police reports for theft of personal property and of travel documents.

We will note the address and telephone number of local TAT offices in the appropriate sections of the following chapters. Overseas, you'll find TAT offices at 3440 Wilshire Blvd., Suite 1101, Los Angeles, CA 90010 (tel. 213/

382-2352); 5 World Trade Center, Suite 2449, New York, NY (tel. 212/432-0433); 9 Stafford St., London WIX 3FE, United Kingdom (tel. 01/499-7670); Royal Exchange Bldg., 12th Floor, 56 Pitt St., Sydney 2000, Australia (tel. 02/277-549); 702B Admiralty Center, Tower 1, Harcourt Road, Hong Kong (tel. 5-286-763); c/o Royal Thai Embassy, 206, Jalan Ampang, Kuala Lumpur, Malaysia (tel. 248-0958); and c/o Royal Thai Embassy, 370 Orchard Rd., Singapore 0923 (tel. 235-7694).

You can also contact the **Royal Thai Consulate General** at 53 Park Pl., New York, NY 10007 (tel. 212/732-8166); 35 E. Wacker Dr., Suite 1834, Chicago, IL 60601 (tel. 312/236-2447); 801 N. La Brea Ave., Los Angeles, CA 90038 (tel. 213/937-1894); and the **Royal Thai Embassy** at 2300 Kalorama Rd. NW, Washington, DC 20008 (tel. 202/483-7200), or the Royal Thai Embassy in your home country.

If you're in Jakarta, Kuala Lumpur, Manila, Rangoon, Penang, or Hong Kong, you can contact the local **Thai Airways International** for additional information.

5. RECOMMENDED READING

If you're planning an extensive tour of the country, we recommend the *APA Insight Guide* on Thailand (published in the U.S. and Canada by Prentice Hall Press) for in-depth historical and cultural background. The low-budget tourist on an extended tour of off-the-beaten-track destinations would do well to purchase Lonely Planet's *Thailand: A Travel Survival Kit,* by Joe Cummings. If you plan to travel to out-of-the-way upcountry villages, try John Hoskin's *Guide to Chiang Mai & Northern Thailand* (Hong Kong: Hong Kong Publishing Co., 1986).

For an overview of the hill tribes in Thailand we recommend Paul and Elaine Lewis's excellent *Peoples of the Golden Triangle* (London and New York: Thames and Hudson, 1984) in addition to George Young's *The Hill Tribes of Northern Thailand* (Bangkok: Siam Society, 1966) and the Technical Service Club's *The Hill Tribes of Thailand* (Thailand, 1986). For a historical overview of the region, try D. G. E. Hall's *A History of Southeast Asia* (London: Macmillan, 1977) or more specifically, M. L. Jumsai's *Popular History of Thailand* (Bangkok: Chalermnit, 1970) or W. A. R. Wood's *A History of Siam* (London: Unwin, 1979). For a 19th-century description of travel in Thailand, we recommend *Temples and Elephants* (Oxford: Oxford University Press), a delightful account written during King Chulalongkorn's reign by Carl Bock. For an entertaining and well-written history of Bangkok, read Alec Waugh's *Bangkok, Story of a City* (Boston: Little Brown, 1971). Among the best works on art and sculpture are Piriya Krairiksh's *The Sacred Image* and *Art in Thailand Since 1932* (Bangkok: White Lotus, 1980), as well as Reginald LeMay's *The Culture of Southeast Asia* (London: Unwin, 1954). Literary works in English include *Anna and the King of Siam* by Margaret Landon and the related *The English Governess at the Siamese Court* by Anna Leonowens; William Warren's *Jim Thompson: The Legendary American* (Boston: Houghton Mifflin; now out-of-print but available in libraries), Reginald Campbell's *Teak-Wallah* (Oxford: Oxford University Press), and Ernest Young's *The Kingdom of the Yellow Robe* (Oxford: Oxford University Press). Many of these books can be ordered from Paragon Book Gallery Ltd., 2130 Broadway, Mezzanine, New York, NY 10023 (tel. 212/496-2378), or Traveller's Bookstore, 22 W. 52nd St., New York, NY 10019 (tel. 212/664-0995).

Thai literary suggestions include translations of the epic Sanskrit work, *Ramakien,* based on the *Ramayana; Four Reigns* and *Red Bamboo* by Kukrit Pramoj (Bangkok: D. K. Books), a contemporary novelist; and *A Man Called Karn,* by Suwanee Sukonta (Bangkok: Bannakarn).

A good introduction for business people who intend to work in the country and need a comprehensive understanding of the culture is *Conflict or Communication,* reprinted from "Business in Thailand" (Business Information and Research Co., Petchburi Road, Bangkok). If you plan on living in Thailand, and in particular Bangkok, for an extended amount of time, the *Bangkok Guide* (compiled by the Australian–New Zealand Women's Group, Bangkok, 1986) is an excellent reference handbook that will ease your move.

Few films have been made about Thailand. Recently a spate of Vietnam War pictures have been shot in the country to replicate other Southeast Asian zones, and you might be interested to see how the terrain and people are depicted. *The Killing Fields* concerns the mass murder of Cambodians during the Pol Pot regime and takes place along the Thai-Cambodian border. Monologist Spalding Gray describes his experiences in Thailand on the production of the same film in *Swimming to Cambodia.* Robert De Niro starred in the Academy Award–winning *The Deer Hunter,* which was shot in Thailand. Robin Williams played a disk jockey during the war in *Good Morning Vietnam,* another feature shot in Thailand. On a more classical note, the Rex Harrison and Linda Darnell version of *Anna and the King of Siam,* followed by the musical version with Yul Brynner and Deborah Kerr, *The King and I,* were both shot in Hollywood on a sound stage.

CHAPTER XVII

BANGKOK

□ □ □

1. ORIENTATION

2. THE ABC'S OF BANGKOK

3. ACCOMMODATIONS

4. DINING

5. WHAT TO SEE AND DO IN THE CITY

6. SHOPPING

7. NIGHTLIFE

8. DAY TRIPS FROM BANGKOK

Most people who visit Asia for the first time include Bangkok (along with Tokyo and Hong Kong) as a must-see destination on their Grand Tour. What these eager travelers often envision is a microcosm of all of Southeast Asia, conveniently wrapped up in one city. Although the expectation may be extravagant, Bangkok does lay claim to being the region's most exotic capital city. The ancient city, including the network of *klongs* (canals) and the Floating Market, has all the romance and wonder of any Asian city. Here is the Temple of the Emerald Buddha and the Grand Palace, as well as a concentration of golden *wats* (temples), museums, and regal monuments. Surrounding the ancient city are legendary markets of Thai, Chinese, and Indian origin that rival anything on the Asian continent. In the outer sections of the city are new neighborhoods where the majority of the six million inhabitants reside, making it the base for one of the fastest-growing economies in the region.

Although all the major Asian capitals have first-rate accommodations to offer tourists, Bangkok arguably has the greatest concentration of moderately priced luxury-class accommodations of any city in the world, not to mention that it serves as the capital of sumptuous Thai cuisine.

In addition to the city itself, Bangkok is located in the center of the country, making day trips and extended tours a short commute. And with the possible exception of Chiang Mai, Bangkok offers unrivaled shopping opportunities for Southeast Asian handcrafts, antiques, silk, and jewels. For the nightlife crowd, One Night in Bangkok still delivers.

HISTORY: To understand Bangkok's origins you must realize the historical context—the central Thai city and long-time capital, Ayutthaya, with more than a million inhabitants, had been totally destroyed by the Burmese in 1767.

King Taksin retreated, moving the capital south to Thonburi, where he spent the next 15 years rebuilding the capital as well as repelling the Burmese. To complete the rejuvenation process, Taksin handed the royal reins to his most powerful general, Chao Phrya Chakri, thus beginning the Chakri Dynasty. General Chakri was crowned Rama I, and one of his first acts in 1782 was to move the capital across the river to the quiet trading village of Bangkok ("Village of the Wild Plums"). It was Rama I who dug the first canal or *klong* in Bangkok to make his new capital a more defensible island. In an effort to provide a sense of continuity between the ancient capital and Bangkok, Rama I embarked on a building program to create a city that surpassed, but recognized the legacy of Ayutthaya. He also enacted a series of laws, called the *Tra Sam Duang* or Law of the Three Seals, which incorporated aspects of administrative and economic order from the guiding principles of both the Sukhothai and Ayutthaya empires.

1. ORIENTATION

Vintage 19th-century photographs of Bangkok show vivid images of the bustling life on the Chao Phrya River, bobbing with boats that ranged from the humblest rowboat to the regal royal barge. The city, built along the banks of the S-shaped river, spread inland through a network of klongs that rivaled the intricacy, though not the elegance, of Venice. After the destruction of Ayutthaya in 1767 by the Burmese, the capital was moved by General Phrya Tak to the more secure south, centered in Thonburi, on the western side of the river from what is now Bangkok. Only 15 years later was the capital moved across river to its present site.

Since that time the city has become more densely developed and populated, extending its boundaries in all directions. Sadly, as it does so, it is filling in more and more of the klongs that originally defined the character of the city. As more klongs are filled in, cars, buses, motorcycles, and *tuk-tuks* (motorized three-wheeler rickshaws) follow and the resultant rush-hour traffic jams are so horrendous that the best way to travel around the city is still via the river. In short, much of historic Bangkok is retreating, making it almost impossible to find, other than in carefully preserved pockets. Yet the spirit of the city lives on — the temples and shrines remain in all their splendid, exaggerated opulence and mystery, and the people retain an incredible grace and charm that is fast becoming rare in the world.

BANGKOK'S LANDMARKS AND NEIGHBORHOODS: The most significant axis in Bangkok is the **Chao Phrya River.** Along the banks of this busy thoroughfare are most of the major tourist sites including, from north to south, the National Museum and National Theater, the Grand Palace and Wat Phra Keo (repository of the Emerald Buddha), the Reclining Buddha at Wat Po, the Khmer-style complex of Wat Arun, the city's historic Chinatown, and the trio of luxury and first-class hotels, the Oriental, Shangri-la, and Royal Orchid (and the River City mall).

The river is spanned by four major bridges. The **Krung Thon Bridge** crosses at the northern end of the city, with its access road, **Ratchawithi,** leading east to the Dusit Zoo, Wat Benjamabophit (the Marble Temple) off Rama V, Chitralada Royal Palace, the Victory Monument, and off Sri Ayutthaya, Suan Pakkard Palace. Off the Thonburi side of the **Phra Pinklao Bridge,** along Klong Bangkok Noi, are the Royal Barges. The bridge crosses close to the National Museum and Theater on the Bangkok side and becomes Ratchadamnoen Klang, continuing east past the Democracy Monument and becoming Phetchaburi (and later New Phetchaburi) Road. Running parallel to Phetchaburi Road is one of the most important avenues, **Rama I,** which farther on becomes Phloenchit Road and, ultimately, Sukhumvit Road. Jim Thompson's House is located off Rama I, along Klang Mahanak. Siam Square and Mah Boon Krong Center, two of the city's

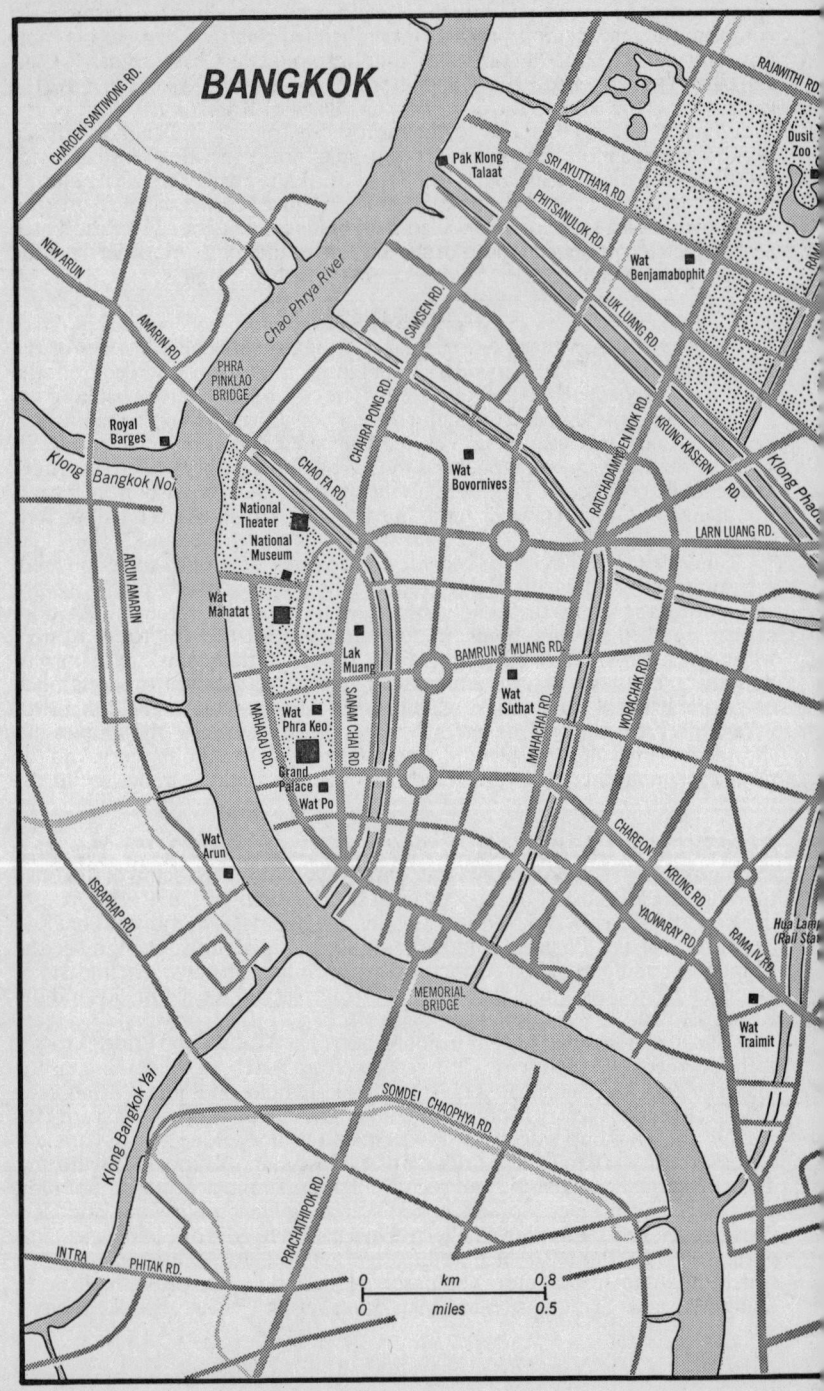

BANGKOK

RAJAWITHI RD.

CHAROEN SANTIWONG RD.

Dusit
Zoo

Pak Klong
Talaat

SRI AYUTTHAYA RD.

NEW ARUN

PHITSANULOK RD.

AMARIN RD.

Chao Phrya River

Wat
Benjamabophit

SAMSEN RD.

PHRA
PINKLAO
BRIDGE

LUK LUANG RD.

KRUNG KASERN RD.

Royal
Barges

Klong Bangkok Noi

CHAO FA RD.

CHAKRA PONG RD.

Wat
Bovornives

RATCHADAMNOEN NOK RD.

Klong Phao

ARUN AMARIN

National
Theater

National
Museum

LARN LUANG RD.

Wat
Mahatat

Lak
Muang

BAMRUNG MUANG RD.

SANAM CHAI RD.

Wat
Suthat

WORACHAK RD.

MAHARAJ RD.

Wat
Phra Keo

MAHACHAI RD.

Grand
Palace

Wat Po

CHAREON

Wat
Arun

KRUNG RD.

ISRAPHAP RD.

YAOWARAY RD.

RAMA IV RD.

Hua Lam
(Rail Sta

MEMORIAL
BRIDGE

Wat
Traimit

SOMDEI CHAOPHYA RD.

Klong Bangkok Yai

PRACHATHIPOK RD.

INTRA

PHITAK RD.

0   km   0.8
0   miles   0.5

largest shopping malls, are located along Rama I, as are the Royal Bangkok Sports Club (and race track), embassies, the city's largest office buildings, and some of Bangkok's best hotels including the Hilton (off Wireless Road) and the Regent (off Ratchadamri). Sukhumvit Road is home to many excellent restaurants and shopping arcades.

The **Memorial Bridge** leads directly into Chinatown, Sampeng Lane, and many specialized markets, one of the most richly ethnic of neighborhoods in Bangkok. The southernmost of the major crossings is **Taksin** (or Sathorn) **Bridge,** crossing from Thonburi over to the Bangkok side just below the Shangri-la Hotel. The street becomes Sathorn Road and intersects with Rama IV at Lumpini Park. Running parallel, to the north of Sathorn, are Silom Road and Surawong Road, both important shopping, restaurant, hotel, and evening entertainment (including notorious Patpong, home to Bangkok's wild sex-club scene) thoroughfares. **Rama IV,** which begins as Charoen Krung in Chinatown, leads past the Golden Buddha at Wat Traimit, Hua Lampong (the main train station), the Snake Farm, and such hotels as the Dusit Thani, ending at Lumpini Park.

GETTING TO AND LEAVING BANGKOK: Because of Bangkok's central

location within Thailand, it is the country's most important transportation hub, although the facilities are very spread out. The city has three bus stations, a very convenient train station, and a huge, modernized airport that is maddeningly close in distance but seemingly as far as Tibet in traffic. Plan on an hour's ride and you should make your flight (unless your hotel happens to be near the airport highway or you're leaving very early in the morning). Once in the city, taxis and *samlors* (tuk-tuks) cruise the broad avenues and are inexpensive and reliable; we recommend that you take them everywhere within the city.

The Airport

All visitors flying domestically or internationally will arrive at **Don Muang Airport,** north of the city, about 45 minutes (depending on the traffic and the hour) away by car. The airport has a domestic and an international terminal. There is a shuttle bus, for 55 baht ($2.25) that connects the two every 10 minutes; however, if you have light luggage, it's often faster to walk the 1,000 yards than to wait for the bus. There is a plan to build a moving sidewalk. The helpful **TAT** has a booth in the international terminal, open daily from 8 a.m. to 11 p.m. There are also general **information booths,** open 24 hours, in both depots. The Hotel Association operates a booth from 7 a.m. to 9 p.m. daily.

GETTING TO AND FROM THE AIRPORT. Most of the luxury and first-class hotels either send their own cars to pick up guests or use the Thai Airways **limousine service** to and from the airport, but passengers can reserve them for any other destination. These sedan cars will seat four comfortably and charge 400 baht ($16). You can also take the Thai Airways mini-van that makes regular stops at the major hotels for 140 baht ($5.50) per person.

Taxis are a better value, though in the past some drivers unscrupulously charged unknowing riders inflated prices. Now all taxis are registered and fares are posted, as well as monitored by meters. These reformed drivers actually do use their meters; expect to pay between 150 baht ($6) and 300 baht ($12) for a ride into central Bangkok. Be sure to get a legal taxi (not through touts but from the taxi desk) and take the card that the dispatcher hands you; it's your precaution over possible price gouging. Also make sure that the driver takes you to your chosen destination. Don't let him take you to another hotel, for example, where he very well may get a kickback. Most of the drivers in legal taxis speak some English.

The Thai **airport bus** runs between Don Muang and 485 Silom Rd. for 100 baht ($4). The public buses 4 and 13 run between Bangkok's main streets and the airport for 20 baht (80¢).

The Railroad Station

The Thai train network is extremely well organized and connects Bangkok with nearly any destination you might wish to visit. All trains to and from the capital stop at **Hua Lampong station,** located at the intersection of Rama IV and Krung Kasem. Contact the reservation and information office (tel. 223-3777) for the current schedule and fares. Reservations can be made up to 30 days in advance of traveling; during the peak season, plan on making arrangements at least one week before departure (more like three weeks ahead for a sleeper on the overnight train to Chiang Mai). For information regarding the various classes of trains and service, see "Getting Around" in Chapter XVI.

The system for **buying a ticket** is a bit Byzantine, but the following should guide you through the process. First, you have to request your ticket at the appropriate counter—there are three, each corresponding to a specific line. When you enter the reservations hall and request a particular destination, you'll be handed either a red, green, or white slip indicating the particular line. Take the colored slip to a desk to make the actual reservation. Take the reservation slip that you will be given to the pay desk; there you will get a number which will be called out in Thai, so keep close and follow the numbers being called. Wait for a few minutes and pick up your ticket. On most days this process takes about ten minutes, largely due to the helpful, friendly staff, but we've been there when it has taken an hour.

If you're arriving in Bangkok, perhaps from Malaysia or points south, know that the train station has a **money-exchange booth** open daily from 6:30 a.m. to 6 p.m. There is a luggage storage room, open daily from 4 a.m. to 10:30 p.m.; rates are 6 baht (25¢) for each piece of luggage. A **hotel-booking office** is open Monday through Friday from 8:30 a.m. to 6 p.m., and on Saturday, Sunday, and holidays from 8:30 a.m. to noon.

The Bus Stations

Travel by bus in Thailand is well organized, comfortable, and inexpensive. There are three bus stations in Bangkok; if you make reservations for your journey through a travel agent, you can often make things easier by arranging a transfer from your hotel to the appropriate terminal. Buses leaving for northern and northeastern points including Aranyaprathet, Ayutthaya, Bang Pa-In, Chiang Mai, Chiang Rai, Lamphun, Lop Buri, Phitsanulok, Sukhothai, Tak, and Uthai Thani depart from the **Northern Bus Terminal,** on Phahonyothin Road (tel. 279-4484). Those going to Chanthaburi, Pattaya, and Rayong depart from the **Eastern Bus Terminal,** on Sukhumvit Road, near Soi 63 (tel. 392-9227). For points south such as Hua Hin, Kanchanaburi, Krabi, Nakhon Pathom, Phang Nga, Phetburi, Phuket, and Surat Thani (including Koh Samui), buses leave from the **Southern Bus Terminal,** on Charansanitwong Road (tel. 411-4978). If you need additional information, call the TAT at 282-1143 or contact a travel agent.

GETTING AROUND THE CITY: Like some of Asia's other mushrooming capitals, Bangkok's layout is part archaic and impossible and part modern and efficient. In the downtown area around Chinatown you can forget about driving (in fact, whole sections are off-limits to cars) because of the density of street life and the narrow, twisting lanes. Other sections, particularly in the area from Rama IV to Sukhumvit Road, Bangkok's wide avenues are reminiscent of southern California. Almost all sites and tourist services are located near enough to any of the major hotels to visit by taxi or tuk-tuk, both of which are inexpensive.

If you plot an itinerary with a map you might be lulled into thinking that crossing from one section of the city to another is a short, 15-minute ride. Unfortunately, it's not, because most of the main streets are one way and traffic can best be described as horrendous. Count on spending between 30 and 45 minutes, for example, to cover the distance between lower Sukhumvit Road in the east and the Oriental Hotel to the south. The good news is that you'll only spend 110 baht ($4.50) to travel from the farthest parts of the city to nearly anywhere else in metropolitan Bangkok.

Wherever you can, we suggest using boats rather than surface roads to get around the city. This network is efficient, inexpensive, and remarkably serene in comparison to all other options; they are particularly convenient for those people staying at one of the hotels along the river.

Unfortunately, the very cheap, convenient, and fairly fast (thanks to bus-only lanes) public bus system should be used with care because of the problem of pickpockets, purse slashers, and other petty criminals who take advantage of the densely crowded conditions aboard. Use the air-conditioned buses, if you do use buses, for a few baht extra.

By Boat

There are many ways to see the Chao Phrya river and its miles of klongs. The best way is to use the river as an avenue to the tourist sites along the river traveling aboard the express boats operated by the **Chao Phrya Express Company** (tel. 222-5330) and the ferries that cross the river connecting Thonburi and Bangkok.

Board the express boats near the Oriental Hotel, at the pier just south of the hotel or directly behind the River City Shopping Center. Other docks for express boats are not always easy to find, but a good street map and friendly advice from locals can guide you. Some docks are used by both express and ferry boats. Express boats are larger boats with bench seats and open sides. There is a large number on the side and often the Chao Phrya Express logo. (Don't confuse these with the smaller, unmarked cross-river ferries.) Boats pull up and pause for a fleeting moment and passengers must step lively to board. Fares are based on distance. The ticket taker will ask you for your destination and charge between 4 baht (15¢) and 9 baht (35¢) for the trip, the best deal in town. To exit, you must move to the back of the boat and be ready to hop off. As on any public conveyance in Bangkok, keep a close hand on your purse, wallet, or camera.

Navigating the express boat system can be tricky, since the names of the docks give little hint of the tourist sites near them. However, most ticket takers speak English and will guide you to your destination. The major docks nearest the main attractions are: for Chinatown, the Memorial Bridge or Rajinee Piers; for Wat Po, Tha Thien Pier; for the Grand Palace, Tha Chang Pier; for the National Museum, Maharaj Pier; for Wat Arun, Tha Thien Pier, where you transfer to the cross-river ferry.

By Taxi or Tuk-Tuk

There are several categories of taxis ranging from private cars (such as those run by Thai Airways and individual hotels) to extremely modest cars that seem to hang together with paper clips and glue. The best method of private travel for those with limited time? Hiring a car and driver for the day. For 140 baht ($5.50) an hour, or about 1,100 baht ($44) a day, you have the assurance of knowing that there is a car always waiting for you, able to transport you anywhere at a moment's notice. Most cars for hire with drivers are available at the major hotels; however, if you walk to the main road at the entrance to the hotel you'll be able to negotiate rather than pay the "official" rate. You'll also have to negotiate with regular taxi drivers. The best method, assuming that you don't know the local fare, is to ask a shop owner, hotelier, or restaurateur what you should pay to a given destination and negotiate accordingly. Most taxi fares will range between

55 baht ($2.25) and 100 baht ($4) within the city, depending on route, distance, condition of the car, and mood of the driver.

Tuk-tuks, known formally as samlors, derive from the days of bicycle rick-shaws; however, nowadays these speedy three-wheeled covered carts are pro-pelled by gasoline engines. The ride can be wild (and we're from New York!), as daring drivers dart in between buses, trucks, water buffalo, and motorcycles. As with taxis, you'll have to negotiate your fare. Expect to pay 15 baht (6¢) to 25 baht ($1) less than a taxi fare over a similar distance.

Remember always to negotiate your fare before engaging a driver or you'll almost certainly overpay. Tipping is not expected.

By Bus

We feel ambivalent about Bangkok's excellent bus system. On the one hand the city supports incredibly cheap—3 baht (12¢)—extensive, and frequent pub-lic bus service to nearly all areas. If you're traveling on the cheap, by all means consider the bus. But we need to issue a **warning,** loud and clear: most petty crime, such as robbery, against tourists reported to the local police takes place on the public bus, so ride at your own risk. We can't help feeling paranoid, especially since Kyle lost her passport, credit cards, checks, cash, and visa on a bus during her first visit to Bangkok a few years ago. Terribly sad stories tacked up on guest-house bulletin boards speak eloquently of the dangers of bus travel. If you can afford it, take another form of transportation. If you do take the bus, keep all of your possessions in front of you, carry only what you can afford to lose, and stay away from the back door where most thieves operate.

By Rental Car

Of course, you can drive yourself around Bangkok, but we're not sure why you'd want to. If you feel the need, there are many rental-car agencies (see "Get-ting Around" in Chapter XVI).

2. THE ABC'S OF BANGKOK

Here are some answers to some commonly asked questions.

AIRPORT: Metropolitan Bangkok's **Don Muang Airport** is undergoing a ma-jor renovation and expansion program that will make it the largest in Southeast Asia. The airport is organized into two parts, the domestic and international ter-minals.

The **domestic terminal** offers a wide range of services. Luggage storage, for 25 baht ($1) a day, is open from 7 a.m. to 10 p.m. The post office, which can also book international phone calls, is open daily from 9 a.m. to 4:30 p.m. A bank is open daily from 6 a.m. to 10 p.m. There are two information booths that are quite helpful. There is a 24-hour booth manned by airport personnel who can point you in the right direction and offer reliable information. The Hotel Associ-ation, open daily from 7 a.m. to 9 p.m., will advise you on vacancies and can reserve hotel rooms in the Bangkok area. There is a cafeteria-style coffeeshop open from 7 a.m. to 10 p.m.

The airport has a **shuttle service** between the domestic and international terminals for 55 baht ($2.25), which operates approximately every ten minutes. For information about getting into Bangkok, see "Getting to and Leaving Bang-kok."

The **international terminal,** some 1,000 yards away, has similar services with the addition of a TAT booth that usually stocks a full range of travel bro-chures and up-to-date schedules.

For **general airport information,** call 531-0022. For information about flights on **Thai Airways,** call 523-8271 at their Don Muang counter.

Passengers on domestic flights pay 25 baht ($1) **departure tax,** while those on international flights pay 200 baht ($8).

AIRPLANE TICKETS: Most international carriers have offices in Bangkok where you can make reservations or confirm flights. Within Thailand, Thai Airways and Bangkok Air (serving only local commuter routes), are the only carriers. For information on schedules and fares, visit the **Thai Airways** (domestic tickets) office at 6 Larnluang (tel. 280-0090). For reservations, call 280-0070. **United Airlines** has offices on the 16th floor of the Regent House at 183 Ratchadamri Rd. (tel. 253-0558). **Thai Airways International** (tel. 233-3810) has offices at Vipavadi Rangsit Road and at 485 Silom Rd. Airplane tickets can also be purchased at one of the city's many travel agencies or bucket shops (see "Travel Agents").

AMERICAN EXPRESS: American Express doesn't have its own office. Instead, **Sea Tours,** located on the fourth floor in the Siam Center at no. 414 (tel. 251-4862), acts as its agent in Thailand. There you can receive mail, buy traveler's checks with cash or against an American Express card, or arrange for a refund on lost credit cards and traveler's checks. Office hours are 8:30 a.m. to 4:30 p.m. Monday through Friday and 8:30 a.m. to 11:30 a.m. on Saturday; closed Sunday. American Express operates a 24-hour telephone service for lost cards and checks; call 235-0090 or 253-8377. You should bring your passport for all transactions.

Note: This office does not cash traveler's checks; you'll have to go to a bank or change booth.

BANKS: Bangkok has bank branches all over the city, many with automated teller machines that dispense cash to cardholders. Nearly every bank will exchange foreign currency between 8:30 a.m. and 3:30 p.m. Monday through Friday. Change booths, which are also heavily scattered throughout the city, charge similar rates to banks (many of them are actually owned and operated by banks) and generally keep much longer hours. It's essential to bring your passport for changing money.

Among the major Thai banks are **Bangkok Bank,** with its main office at 333 Silom Rd. (tel. 234-3333); **Bank of Ayutthaya,** at 550 Ploenchit Rd. (tel. 253-8676); and the **Thai Farmers Bank,** at 400 Phaholyothin Rd. (tel. 270-1122).

Many American banks maintain offices in Bangkok, including **Bank of America,** next door to the Hilton at 2/2 Wireless Rd. (tel. 251-6333); **Chase Manhattan,** at 965 Rama I Rd. in the Siam Center (tel. 252-1141); **Citibank,** at 127 S. Sathorn Rd. (tel. 286-3392); and **Chemical Bank,** at 183 Ratchadamri Rd. on the 13th floor of the Regent House (tel. 251-1752).

BEAUTY PARLORS/BARBERSHOPS: Most establishments in this category are unisex. Among the locally recommended salons are: **The Best,** in the Nai Lert Park Building at 87 Sukhumvit Rd., Soi 5 (tel. 251-1358), as well as locations in the Oriental Plaza and at Sukhumvit Road, Soi 21; **Michael John,** on Sukhumvit Road, Soi 20 (tel. 258-1291); **Khun Choom/Ginger Group,** on the third floor of the Peninsular Plaza (tel. 252-3421). Most of the international hotels also have haircutting services.

BOOKSTORES: You'll find the best selection of English-language paperbacks at **D. K. Bookshops,** at 244-6 Siam Square (tel. 251-6335). The **Bookseller Co. Ltd.,** at 81 Patpong Rd. (tel. 233-1717), off Silom Road, also has a fine selection of English-language books, magazines, and cards; it's open from 9 a.m. to midnight daily. **D.D. Books,** on Sukhumvit Road, 32/9-10 off Soi 21 (tel. 258-3703), is particularly good for books on Asian subjects. **Bangkok Books,** at 302-304 Siam Square (tel. 251-6348), in the shopping arcade opposite Siam Center, has a good variety of English-language books and magazines. They have another outlet at 544/3-4 Ploenchit Rd. (tel. 250-1367). Last, almost every international-class hotel has a bookstore in its shopping arcade; however, most of these offer only a small selection of publications.

BUS TERMINALS: See "Getting To and Leaving Bangkok."

BUSINESS HOURS: Business hours are 8:30 a.m. to 5 p.m. Monday through Friday, with a half day on Saturday. Offices are generally closed on Sunday and holidays. Shops that cater to the tourist trade are often open daily from 8:30 a.m. to evening, often closing at 7 p.m. or 8 p.m. Government agencies operate Monday through Friday from 8:30 a.m. to noon and 1 to 4:30 p.m.

BUSINESS SERVICES: Most business services, such as secretarial work, copying, word processing, facsimile and Telex transmission and receival, and computer and database time are available on a per-use basis in the business centers of the major international hotels. The Hilton has a particularly well-equipped and comfortable office.

CAMERA EQUIPMENT / REPAIR AND FILM: The price of film is about on a par with most American camera stores. A full range of Fuji and Kodak film is available around Bangkok. The light is very bright and an ultraviolet or sky-light filter and low-speed film (ASA-25 or ASA-64) are advisable. Don't forget to try to keep your film, both exposed and unexposed, out of the light and in a cool place. It's also a good idea to carry all film in your hand luggage on the plane and to have it inspected by hand rather than passing it through an x-ray machine.

If you need your camera repaired, it's best to inquire at the concierge's desk in your hotel for a reputable shop. Fast photo-processing labs are proliferating throughout the city and offer generally good results at low prices. **Fast Foto,** at 38 Surawong Rd. (two blocks from the Jim Thompson Silk Co.), open daily from 9 a.m. to 9 p.m., processes film in three hours for 250 baht ($10) for 36 exposures and 175 baht ($7) for 24 exposures. Fast Foto has many more branches around the city.

CAR RENTAL: See "Getting Around" in Chapter XVI.

CREDIT CARDS: If you lose your credit card, call one of the following telephone numbers: **American Express** (tel. 02/235-0090), **Diners Club** (tel. 02/233-5644), **MasterCard** or **VISA** (tel. 02/252-2212).

CRIME: Bangkok is quite a safe city, although there is a large incidence of petty crime, including bag snatching, pickpocketing, cutting of purses and wallets with razors, and credit card and traveler's check fraud. Much of the security problem is concentrated on public buses. We advise you to avoid them altogether, but if you insist, pay very close attention to your belongings at all times, keeping valuable possessions in front of you (don't keep a wallet, for example, in a back pocket). It's advisable to keep all important documents and jewelry in your hotel's safe-deposit box. Be careful with credit cards, in particular making sure that you tear up carbons and keep all receipts. As well, be suspicious of any prolonged period of time when your credit card is away from you, such as stores that take your card for a credit check. It is also suggested that you exercise caution about strangers who approach you, offering to be your guide or to buy you a drink or food.

DENTISTS AND DOCTORS: Thailand has excellent medical care and many fine doctors and dentists. Most medical personnel speak English and many of them were trained in the United States. The U.S. Embassy publishes a listing of recommended physicians and dentists, both generalists and specialists. Telephone the Embassy Medical Unit (tel. 252-5040) for specific names. In addition, some of the better hotels have doctors and/or nurses on their staff who can treat minor maladies.

DRUGSTORES: Bangkok has a great many drugstores, many dispensing drugs of differing quality. Among the better outlets are the **British Dispensary,** 109 Sukhumvit Rd., near Soi 5 (tel. 252-8056), and on the corner of New Road and Oriental Lane (tel. 234-1881); and the **Phuket Dispensary,** at 383 Sukhumvit Rd., Soi 21 (tel. 298-3749). For additional recommendations, call the American Embassy Medical Unit (tel. 252-5040) or ask the concierge at your hotel. Many hotels actually have their own doctors and a limited supply of medication.

EMBASSIES: The **U.S. Embassy** is located at 95 Wireless Rd. (tel. 252-5040), and is open Monday through Friday from 7:30 a.m. to noon and 1 to 4:30 p.m. The **British Embassy,** at 1031 Wireless Rd., off Ploenchit Road (tel. 253-0191), is open from 8 a.m. to 1 p.m. on Monday and Tuesday, 8 a.m. to 2 p.m. on Wednesday, and 2 to 4:30 p.m. on Thursday and Friday. The **Canadian Embassy** is in the Boonmitr Building at 138 Silom Rd. (tel. 234-1561) and is open from 8 a.m. to 12:30 p.m. and 1:30 to 4:30 p.m. Monday through Friday. The **Australian Embassy** is at 37 S. Sathorn Rd. (tel. 286-0411) and keeps hours from 9:30 a.m. to 12:30 p.m. and 2 to 3:30 p.m.

EMERGENCY: The general emergency line is 191; however, this is for locals as well and the operator may not speak English. The **Tourist Police** number is 281-5051 and they do speak English. If there is a **fire,** call 199 or 281-1544. The central emergency number for the police **hospital,** in the event of an accident, is 252-8111. Call 251-0415 for **ambulance** service.

HOSPITALS: There are many in the Bangkok area. In an emergency, call 281-5051 or 191 for the location of the nearest infirmary. Both **Chulalongkorn University Hospital** (tel. 252-8181) and **Ramathibodi University Hospital** (tel. 245-5708) are leading teaching and research facilities and are located on Rama IV Road. The **Bangkok General Hospital** is off New Petchburi Road, at 2 Soi Soonvijai 7 (tel. 318-0066).

INFORMATION: Dial 282-1143 for information from the **Tourist Authority of Thailand (TAT)** located on Ratchadamnoen Nok Avenue and open Monday through Friday from 8:30 a.m. to 4:30 p.m. The TAT also has an office at the airport. You can also receive reliable information from **Sea Tours,** located at 965 Rama I Rd. on the fourth floor of Siam Center (tel. 251-4862); or **World Travel Service,** at 1053 Charoen Krung Rd. (tel. 233-5900). Both are experienced and reputable travel agencies.

LAUNDRY AND DRY CLEANING: Most hotels offer laundry and dry-cleaning services, and the work is usually very good. Locals recommend the **dry cleaners** at the Dusit Thani Hotel, Erawan Dry Cleaners, and Sukhumvit Dry Cleaners, at 929 Sukhumvit Rd., near Soi 51.

There are also an enormous number of **laundries** throughout the city. Those recommended are Laundromat at 18/6 Soi 23 Sukhumvit Rd. (about $1.25 per load) and Laundry at the intersection of Rama IV and Sukhumvit, Soi 42.

LIBRARIES: The American University Alumni (A.U.A.) runs a free **public li-**

brary at 179 Ratchadamri Rd. (tel. 252-4021), open to foreigners and residents from 8:30 a.m. to 8 p.m. Monday through Friday and 10 a.m. to 3 p.m. on Saturday. The **National Library,** on Samsen Road (tel. 281-5212), is open Monday through Friday; admission is free. The **Siam Society** at 131 Soi 21 off Sukhumvit Road (tel. 391-4401), operates a library concentrating on history, art, and culture that is open to members only. The **Neilson Hays Library,** at 195 Suriwongse Rd. (tel. 233-1731), is a private lending institution that has a good selection of English-language books.

MAPS: Of the three excellent maps of Bangkok, we recommend that you carry two. The first is affectionately called "The Bus Map" by many, but is formally known as **"Latest Tour's Guide to Bangkok and Thailand."** It costs 50 baht ($2) and is in its 22nd edition. The **"Bangkok Thailand Guide Map,"** by Discovery Map, is a slightly more up-to-date version of the Bus Map and also runs 50 baht ($2). Either one is acceptable for an authoritative street guide. The other map that we enthusiastically suggest you carry is Nancy Chandler's "Map of Bangkok" alias **"The Market Map and Much More."** Nancy has a keen eye for quality, taste, value, and the bizarre. She is a graphic designer by training who has lived in Thailand for the last 19 years and knows the city exceedingly well. Nancy has fashioned a delightful guide to the city with special attention to Bangkok's rich markets, shopping opportunities, and sightseeing highlights. The map costs 80 baht ($3.25) and is available at most of the bookstores listed above.

NEWSPAPERS AND PERIODICALS: See "The ABCs of Thailand" in Chapter XVI.

POLICE: The **Tourist Police** (tel. 281-5051) speak English and are open 24 hours. The **Police Emergency** number is 123 or 191, though they do not always have operators who speak English.

POST OFFICE: The **General Post Office (GPO)** is located on New Road (tel. 233-1050), between the Oriental and Sheraton Royal Orchid hotels. A large institutional building behind a black iron fence, it contains postal service and telegraph offices, with telephone service just north on the same grounds. Airmail postcards to the U.S. cost 9 baht (35¢), first-class letters cost 11.50 baht (45¢) per 5 grams (rates to Europe are about the same). The postal service claims four-day delivery to the U.S.—and that's usually the case. Air parcel post costs: 356 baht ($14.25) per kilogram ($6.50 per pound). Surface or sea parcel post costs: 135 baht ($5.50) for one kilogram ($2.50 per pound). GPO hours are 8 a.m. to 8 p.m. Monday through Friday and 8 a.m. to 1 p.m. on Saturday and Sunday. Express mail hours are 8:30 a.m. to 3:30 p.m. Monday through Friday and 9 a.m. to noon on Saturday.

    Poste Restante is located in the GPO on the left as you enter. You can receive mail at Poste Restante with proper identification, either a valid passport or ID card. Upon receiving mail you must sign a receipt and pay 2 baht (8¢). Hours of operation are the same as the post office.

RAILROAD INFORMATION: The main terminus is **Hua Lampong Train Station,** on Krung Kasem Road at the intersection with Rama IV Road (tel. 233-0341 or 223-3777). It is advisable to book rail tickets a week in advance, particularly if you desire a sleeper berth. Reservations can be made at the train station (for more information about the rail system, see "Getting Around").

RELIGIOUS SERVICES: For Catholic services, contact the **Holy Redeemer Roman Catholic Church,** at 123/19 Soi Ruam Rudee, off Wireless Road (tel. 253-0305). For interdenominational English-language services, contact the **In-**

ternational Church, at 67 Soi 19, off Sukhumvit Road (tel. 253-2205). Anglican and Episcopalian services are held at **Christ Church,** at 11 Convent Rd. (tel. 234-3634). There are Jewish services at the **Jewish Center,** on Soi 22, off Sukhumvit Road (tel. 252-6598). For those who are kosher, contact the Jewish Center for food recommendations.

SHOE REPAIR: Break that heel descending Wat Arun? There are many shoe-repair shops along New Road and lower Silom Road, near the Oriental, and along Sukhumvit Road. Almost any shoe store will repair shoes, often in a matter of hours. Among many, try **Siam Bootery,** at 292-4 Sukhumvit Rd. (tel. 251-6862) and its other store on Soi 3 (off Silom Road); or **Tony Leather,** up the street at 300-302 Sukhumvit Rd. (tel. 251-6861), for repairs and good custom work.

TAXIS: See "Getting Around."

TELEGRAMS: The telegraph office is on the north end of the GPO where there is a separate entrance. The office is open 24 hours a day, every day, and also offers telegram restante service.

TELEPHONE: The government telephone office is housed in a separate building on the grounds of the GPO and is open 24 hours, seven days a week. The procedure for making a call is as follows: book your call by filling out a form at one of the desks, specifying the telephone number you wish to call and an approximate length of your call; take the form to the cashier and pay; wait until you are called to a booth. The cost of a person-to-person call to the U.S. is 280 baht ($11.25) for three minutes; station-to-station calls are 210 baht ($8.50) for three minutes. Collect or credit-card calls can be made without an extra fee.

If you make international long-distance calls from most hotels, there is a surcharge, usually 25% (but occasionally much higher; check with the hotel operator before dialing) of total costs at official government rates. A credit-card or collect call carries a service charge, typically 160 baht ($6.50), but again, check before booking.

Local calls can be made from any red pay telephone. Calls cost one baht (4¢) for several minutes, with additional 1-baht coins required after hearing multiple beeps on the line. There are also blue long-distance telephones in strategic places throughout Bangkok, such as at the airport.

Private telephones in hotel lobbies, that look very much like public phones, often cost as much as 5 baht (20¢) for a local call.

For **Information** within the Bangkok metropolitan area, dial 13; for the provinces, 183.

The **telephone area code** for Bangkok and vicinity is 02.

TOURIST INFORMATION: Information can be obtained during business hours from the **Tourist Authority of Thailand (TAT),** located on Ratchadamnoen Nok Avenue (tel. 282-1143). There you'll find a wealth of brochures, maps, listings, schedules, and advice from the normally helpful, English-speaking staff. Hours are 8:30 a.m. to 4:30 p.m. Monday through Friday. Recently, some of Bangkok's major banks have started to stock TAT brochures in their branch offices.

TRAVEL AGENTS: Bangkok has an array of travel agencies providing everything from local tours to bucket-shop, cut-rate international airline tickets. The two top agencies for local excursions are **Sea Tours** (tel. 251-4862) and **World Travel Service** (tel. 233-5900). Both agencies have branch offices in nearly every international hotel and can arrange to pick you up at any of these spots. Typical tours and rates include: Grand Palace and Emerald Buddha Temple Tour, 340 baht ($13.50); Floating Market Tour, 290 baht ($11.50); Rice Barge Cruise, 300 baht ($12); Jim Thompson House and Wang Suan Pakkard, 350 baht ($14); River Kwai Tour, 550 baht ($22); and the Oriental Queen Ayutthaya Tour, 550 baht ($22). **Where Travel Service** at 27 Ngam Dupli Rd. (tel. 286-8556), opposite the Malaysia Hotel, is a bucket shop that we have used for the last eight years and have found reputable. With any bucket shop, remember to check the airline's reservation roster to confirm your seat before handing over money to your travel agent; otherwise you might find that your ticket is worthless.

3. ACCOMMODATIONS

Perhaps in no other city in the world are the moderate, first-class, and luxury hotels as handsome and attractively priced as Bangkok. The battle for guests at the city's major hostelries is so intense that it places great competitive pressure upon hoteliers to maintain high standards of service, amenities, and maintenance while keeping a clamp on prices. Most of the lesser hotels will offer air conditioning, television, and mini-bars in guest rooms, at least one swimming pool, and a full complement of restaurants. The first-class and luxury hotels offer the same amenities plus a full range of business services (exceeding those typically found in the best Western hotels) and an unparalleled level of service. We marveled at finding 350-room hotels with a staff in excess of 800. Staying in one of Bangkok's finer hotels is truly a delight.

Even though prices are relatively reasonable, it's possible to improve upon the published rates by reserving through a local travel agent, combining your hotel reservation with your air ticket (through Thai Airways packages, for example) or just plain bargaining at the front desk. It might seem a tad odd to haggle in the lobby of a superior hotel, but don't discount the possibility of reducing your room rate by as much as 20% to 30%. It is done.

We advise that you read the Orientation section carefully before selecting a hotel, given the size of the city. Strangely, few of Bangkok's upper-crust hotels are located in the heart of the sightseeing zone, that is, near the Royal Palace. With that in mind, we've listed luxury and first-class hotels according to our evaluation of quality and value. Moderately priced and budget hotels are organized by quality within areas of the city.

As we go to press in early 1989, the following hotels opened for business. In 1988-89: **Royal River Hotel,** Charansanitwong Road; **Thara Hotel** (The Imperial Hotel Group), Soi 26, Sukhumvit Road; **Holiday Inn Bangkok,** 981 Silom Road; **Novotel Bangkok,** Siam Square; **Pansea Bangkok Resort,** Near Bangkok Bridge; **Siam Thani,** 477 Sri Ayutthaya Road.

In 1990, the Grand Hyatt will reopen a newly furbished **Grand Hyatt Erawan** at 494 Rajdamri Road. The old Erawan was the hotel of choice for most travelers in the 1950s and 1960s.

LUXURY CHOICES: Bangkok presents an embarrassment of riches when it comes to selecting its finest hotels. Many experienced travelers only (and often religiously) invoke the name "The Oriental" as first among the best. Not wanting to be intentionally iconoclastic, we think that the top has become a bit more crowded than before, a situation that especially benefits the buyer.

Part legend, part reality, **The Oriental** (tel. 02/236-0400) stands tall on the banks of the Chao Phrya River as queen of Bangkok's finest hotels. The legend goes back to the 1860s when the original hotel, no longer standing, was established by two Danish sea captains soon after King Rama IV (Mongkut) reopened Siam to world trade. Since that time the hotel has built three new buildings (the first in 1876, the more modern and larger pair in 1958 and 1976), withstood occupation by Japanese and American troops, and played host to a glittering roster of Thai and international dignitaries, celebrities, and malcontents (chiefly, writers). Joseph Conrad, Somerset Maugham, and Noël Coward spent time at the hotel on numerous occasions. Even Jim Thompson, of Thai silk trade fame, served for a brief period as the hotel's proprietor. Since then the hotel has garnered as many accolades as famous guests. Thus the legend.

In reality, the Oriental is a fine and elegant hotel that fits in the pantheon of Bangkok's best, although we feel that its reputation as the world's best must surely rest on its service and not on the quality of its restaurants. The hotel is best understood as a complex, comprising the rather small 19th-century building that contains the four Author's Residences; two modern high-rises (where most guests stay); a shopping arcade offering high-quality goods; a disco, and swimming and sports facilities (across the river); two good Western-style restaurants and a Thai restaurant (also across the river); and a Thai cooking school. Add to that list the various and sundry public spaces (like its famed lobby), and a sleek touring boat that makes daily excursions to Ayutthaya and the Summer Palace, and you'll understand how some visitors to Bangkok never leave the comfortable confines of the hotel. All 398 rooms overlook the river.

Single occupancy ranges from 4,000 baht ($160) to 5,625 baht ($225), depending on location and room size; doubles run 4,375 baht ($175) to 6,125 baht ($245). Suites in the Author's Residence cost 11,500 baht ($460) to 14,400 baht ($576), and go as high as 45,000 baht ($1,800)—no charge for cots. The Oriental maintains a 99% occupancy rate, so we strongly suggest that you make a reservation as far in advance as possible.

While the riverfront hotel is the classic hotel of Bangkok-style glitz, the **Hilton International,** at 2 Wireless Rd. in Nai Lert Park (tel. 02/253-0123), offers an equally fine, alternative experience of luxury. Set in a lush, finely landscaped park near the British and American embassies, the Hilton is as close to a tropical paradise in a noisy, polluted teeming Asian capital as one can imagine. Its distance from shopping centers, nightlife, and sights may be an occasional inconvenience, but its relative isolation in the more serene diplomatic sector is a blessing in disguise, especially for those who intend to stay in Bangkok longer than two or three days. It's a 20-minute taxi ride to center city, for 60 baht ($2.50) to 80 baht ($3.25). After a long day of meetings or sightseeing, returning to the Hilton has the very comfortable feeling of returning home.

The feeling of both public spaces and rooms is distinctly Thai modern, from the atrium lobby with a teak Thai pavilion to the rooms with fine Thai-style furniture and fresh orchids. The Hilton is extremely elegant but not austere: the grounds are positively lush, guest rooms are homey but luxurious, and the staff is friendly and extremely capable. The "coffeeshop," really a grand dining area overlooking the garden, is first rate, offering both Thai and Western cuisine. Ma Maison, the Hilton's best dining room, offers excellent French cuisine (using fresh Thai ingredients) at reasonable prices and ranks among the top Western restaurants in the city. A Japanese restaurant and an evening poolside grill complete the food service.

A world-class pool and fitness center with tennis and squash courts are also on the grounds, where many a guest jogs in tropical splendor. Room rates run 3,625 baht ($145) for a single, 3,875 baht ($155) for a double, with suites going for 7,500 baht ($300) and up. Garden-facing rooms are a definite recommendation for a 625-baht ($25) premium.

The very glitzy **Shangri-la Hotel,** on the banks of the Chao Phrya at 89 Soi Wat Suan Plu (tel. 02/236-0280), opened in March 1986. Cast in the mold of this chain's other prestigious Asian hotels, the Shangri-la boasts acres of polished marble, a jungle of tropical plants and flowers, and 25 floors (697 rooms) offering a breathtaking view of the river. The opulence of the Shangri-la, though distinctly modern, harkens back to the august hotel palaces of the late 19th century —this isn't a subtle place.

Lush carpeting, slippers, a safe, marble bathtubs, bidets, and elegant Thai-style décor and flowers grace the rooms, rivaling those at the nearby Oriental. River- and city-view rooms are well priced at 3,750 baht ($150) for a single, 4,125 baht ($165) for a double. For 750 baht ($30) additional, your double room will overlook the river and pool, with a small balcony from which to admire the spectacular sunsets. Many of the hotel's 47 ultra-plush suites, starting at 5,750 baht ($230), open onto larger terraces. The Shangri-la's extravagant facilities include the riverside Coffee Garden and Maenam Terrace restaurants, the two-story Palm Court bar, a chandeliered French restaurant La Tache, the popular Shang Palace for Chinese food, and one of Bangkok's prettiest settings for Thai cuisine, Sala Thip, housed in two teakwood pavilions sitting tight by the active riverside.

The starkly modern **Regent of Bangkok,** 155 Ratchadamri Rd. (tel. 02/ 251-6127), opened in 1983, will feel like home to all who have sampled this chain's deluxe accommodations in the U.S. or Asia. Provided in 400 spacious rooms are such thoughtful items as cotton robes, slippers, a scale, and an umbrella tucked in a plush carpeted dressing area off the tiled bath. Cool gray uphol-stered couches and armchairs invite windowside seating, especially appealing if your room overlooks the verdant turf of the nearby Royal Bangkok Sport Club and Race Track. The cavernous lobby boasts ceiling frescoes and a mural depicting 200 years of Bangkok history.

We found the lobby dining area a bit too exposed for casual supping, but it's great for tea, when you can sample for a mere 140 baht ($5.50) dainty smoked salmon and roast beef tea sandwiches, scones with jam and cream and cream-filled cakes accompanied by a pot of real tea, chosen from a tray offering many different kinds. This afternoon ritual seems to belong to another, earlier, more elegant era and is made even more so by the sounds of a quartet wafting from the musicians' balcony above. The Brasserie's booths are popular for relaxed eating, while the Spice Market is reputed to be one of the finest Thai restaurants in the city with an informal décor of Thai staples and herbs that tempts guests to sample local cuisine. Le Cristal is the Regent's premier spot for continental fare, in a serene Thai setting. Fitness buffs will appreciate the large pool and the hotel's health club (open from 7 a.m. to 9 p.m. daily) with weight machines, aerobics classes, and instructors who keep a computerized record of your health statistics.

Single- or double-occupancy rooms run 3,950 baht ($158); suites start at 7,500 baht ($300).

The urbane 525-room **Dusit Thani,** conveniently located on Rama IV Road near the Silom Road intersection (tel. 233-1130), offers understated Thai-style hospitality as fine as any hotel in the city. Gurgling lobby fountains, exotic flower displays everywhere, and a poolside waterfall cascading through dense foliage make this hotel a welcome retreat at the end of a day's sightseeing. The service throughout is gracious, while among the seven restaurants there are a few real high spots, most notably the Mayflower, which has to be one of the finest Chinese restaurants in the city. The top-floor Tiara Restaurant has a sensational view over the city; in the Pavilion Café, each Sunday the Family Buffet luncheon, at 190 baht ($7.50) for adults and 80 baht ($3.25) for children, includes all the tempura, pizza, or kua tiew rua ("boat noodles" or noodle soup) you can eat. The Bussaracum Thai Restaurant (an offshoot of the original on Soi Pipat) is considered among the best in Bangkok, although there are those who feel that it panders to Western tastes too much. Bubbles Disco tops our dance-fever list.

The luxurious, well-lit rooms are adorned with Thai arts and architectural details, and use traditional materials such as silk and teakwood. The Landmark Tower rooms are extremely large and include some extra luxuries—

complimentary fresh fruit and flowers daily, English-language newspapers, bathrooms with bathrobes, hairdryers, slippers, and massage showers, and complimentary breakfast and drinks in the Landmark Lounge are just a few.

Facilities include a business center, a fitness center with gymnasium, tennis and squash courts, and a swimming pool that is very attractively landscaped. Singles run 3,250 baht ($130) to 3,700 baht ($150) and doubles cost 3,575 baht ($143) to 4,875 baht ($195), depending on size and whether they're located in the Landmark Tower.

FIRST-CLASS HOTELS: Bangkok is one of the few cities in the world that boasts a wide selection of luxury and first-class hotels that range from $84 to $170 for a double room. Although the first-class hotels listed below are a quantum notch below those listed above, all are high-quality establishments. The hotels are, like the luxury inns, listed in order of quality and price—in other words, value.

The **Royal Orchid Sheraton,** conveniently located at 2 Captain Bush Lane, off Siphya Road, adjacent to the River City Antique Center (tel. 02/234-5599), like its downriver neighbors the Oriental and Shangri-la, overlooks the magnificent Chao Phrya from all of its 758 rooms. River City is a major stop for the water ferries that ply Bangkok's many routes. The Sheraton and Oriental also run a complimentary shuttle boat that motors back and forth between the two hotels every 15 minutes or so.

A golden spirit house forms the focus of the marble, brass, and glass lobby, which is surprisingly intimate for such a monumental hotel. As with Bangkok's other mega-hotels, the Royal Orchid Sheraton (as distinguished from the Tawana Sheraton; very different) has five restaurants, mostly on the lobby and mezzanine level. An enormous pool lies on the terrace built above the riverbank. The atmosphere is lavish with breathtaking views and rooms paneled in dark teak. Single rooms run 2,250 baht ($90) to 2,875 baht ($115), doubles are 2,625 baht ($105) to 3,250 baht ($130), and suites start at 5,300 baht ($212). The Sheraton Towers, a hotel within a hotel located on the 26th through 28th floors, offers more ornate décor and private clubs for a premium.

The deluxe **Indra Regent,** on Rajaprarob Road (tel. 02/251-1111), is in the heart of the Pratunam shopping district. Built 15 years ago by the Regent International chain, it maintains the luxurious Oriental elegance of a bygone era. The grand staircase leading into the lobby is carpeted with a floral Chinese runner; two tall elephant tusks flank a Thai bronze gong on the landing. The 500 spacious rooms are well appointed and protected from street noise by the cushion of five floors of restaurants and lounges below. The Indra Regent's pool, sheltered by a huge white spirit house and the carved teak Sala Thai restaurant, is one of the most appealing in Bangkok. Single travelers will pay 2,125 baht ($85) and two can expect to pay 2,250 baht ($90) for standard rooms; rates vary 10% on either end for other accommodations. Among first-class hotels, the Indra Regent represents fine value.

The popular **Narai Hotel,** located in the heart of the shopping and financial district at 222 Silom Rd., off Decho Road (tel. 02/233-3350), is 20 years old and excellently maintained. Off the welcoming lobby, on the right, is a homey pizzeria and bakery, and on the left, the pagoda-roofed Don Juan lounge. Waist-high carved-wood animals stand amid comfortable armchairs. The 500 rooms are of medium size and offer all first-class amenities at a reasonable price: 1,750 baht ($70) single, plus suites from 3,325 baht ($133) to 7,500 baht ($300). Lunch can be served at their rattan-furnished pool terrace or in the Laksmi Restaurant, where full-scale royal Thai barges display Thai, Japanese, and European specialties in a tempting buffet that's only 160 baht ($6.50) per person.

Set in 26 acres of parkland off Rama I Road (and immediately adjacent to the Siam Center shopping arcade), the **Siam Intercontinental** (tel. 02/253-0365), like the Hilton, is an island of calm in sometimes frenetic Bangkok. This is especially true if you stay in the hotel's low-rise Garden Wing. Many of these rooms have sliding glass doors that lead directly to the lawn and pool. The six-story high-rise is far less appealing, though the amenities are the same. All rooms are furnished with full-size desks, a plus for those who feel cramped doing work at normally diminutive hotel desks. Like many of Bangkok's top hotels, the Siam Intercontinental has recently been expanded and renovated with the construction of an enormous marble lobby with a towering vaulted ceiling. Doubles range from 4,235 baht ($169) to 4,800 baht ($192). Singles rent for 3,900 baht ($156) to 4,500 baht ($180), depending on size and location.

The all-you-can-eat buffet lunch at Talay Thong, the Intercontinental's Thai and seafood restaurant, is an unusually good value at 135 baht ($5.50). As with other first-class hotels, the Intercontinental offers all the necessary business services and seems to maintain a laudable service level.

Since the Meridien Hotel chain took over the 400-room **President,** 135-26 Gaysorn Rd. (tel. 02/253-0444), in late 1986, renaming it the Meridien President, it has undergone extensive renovation. The hotel is divided into two wings, east and west. The west-wing rooms are more sumptuously appointed with dark-wood paneling, tasteful furnishings, and the usual panoply of luxury amenities. The east wing, older of the two, is less attractive, particularly at the same nightly rate of 3,325 baht ($133) for a standard double and 3,600 baht ($144) for a deluxe room; singles run 2,600 baht ($104). Like most of Meridien's other hotels, many of the guests are French, adding a bit to the ambience. Nowhere is this more apparent than poolside, especially along the spacious sundeck. Cappuccino, the President's coffeeshop, is considered one of Bangkok's best; their desserts are excellent.

Completely renovated in 1985, the **Mandarin,** 662 Rama IV Rd., near Suriwongse (tel. 02/233-4980), is a glitzy full-service hotel that is perhaps better known for its nightclub (wildly popular on weekends with locals) than for its rooms. Actually, the accommodations are quite satisfactory: clean, modern, and spacious. The color scheme is white and light gray, creating a luminous effect. Combine that with velvet upholstered reproductions of Asian and European antiques in the public spaces, accented with polished-brass doors and glittering chandeliers and that pretty much sums up the lively lobby. The Mandarin is located directly on Rama IV Road (down from the train station), but management had the good sense to install double-pane windows to cut down on street noise. The pool is small, often shrouded in shade, and noisy from the nearby traffic. Superior singles and doubles run 2,100 baht ($84), while deluxe accommodations cost 2,400 baht ($96) to 2,700 baht ($108).

As mentioned above, the Mandarin is home to the widely regarded king of the Bangkok cocktail lounge, the Mandarina, where Thai crooners belt out popular Thai and international tunes. Next door is the Nile Night Club, a disco with live music that handles much of the overflow from the Mandarina. Both clubs are open nightly, but the real action takes place on the weekends.

The **Tawana Sheraton,** at 80 Surawong Rd. (tel. 02/236-0361), is centrally located, about a five-minute walk from sleazy Patpong and the more upscale shopping district. For mid-range rooms prices run 3,000 baht ($120) to 3,500 baht ($140) single and 3,250 baht ($130) to 3,600 baht ($144) for a double, depending on size and view. The Tawana Sheraton offers a few luxury-class touches: daily newspapers are delivered to the rooms in the morning; there are safety boxes in all rooms; and the bright, clean bathrooms are fully stocked with the usual toiletries. The Bon Vivant restaurant serves continental food poolside, an area pleasantly engulfed in orchids and hanging vines. The Port of Call Bar and Cavern Nightclub (featuring a British DJ and live bands after midnight) are popular hotel attractions. The Tawana is a typical Sheraton-quality hotel, although for location and value it's been surpassed by that chain's newer Royal Orchid.

Just around the corner from the Tawana Sheraton is the similarly classed **Montien,** at 54 Surawong Rd., near Rama IV Road (tel. 02/233-7060). The marble-and-glass lobby yields to dark-teak-paneled hallways with 500 bright, pleasant rooms. The clientele is often made up of tour groups from Australia, Europe, and Hong Kong, who enjoy the Montien's central location near bawdy Patpong. The Montien, like its other first-class cousins, has a full selection of in-house American, Chinese, and continental cuisine. The basic charge for a single or double is 2,375 baht ($95), with deluxe doubles up to 4,500 baht ($180).

Next door to the U.S. Embassy, the **Imperial Hotel,** on Wireless Road (tel. 02/254-0111), is a favorite of visiting business people and U.S. government employees. The landscaped garden setting and large pool area provide a respite from Bangkok's bustle. The decorative, cavernous teak lobby, competent staff, and excellent Tai Pan Chinese restaurant (one of the city's best) rate better than the small, though comfortable, rooms. Standard rates are 3,300 baht ($132) for a double, though many of the Imperial's guests are associated with Thai or U.S.-based businesses that take advantage of the much lower commercial rate. If this applies to you, the Imperial is a score. (As of our last visit in 1988, the guest-room quarters were in the process of renovation; we expect that room quality will improve after this upgrade is complete.)

The **Regal Landmark Hotel,** 138 Sukhumvit Rd. (tel. 02/254-0404), an ultramodern 31-story, 415-room hotel that opened in late 1987, is conveniently located in the embassy district with easy access to the Airport Expressway. It's not a super-luxury hotel, but it offers a full range of services. Rooms are decorated in a typical Western style in gray and jade florals, with modern furnishings including brass floor lamps. Apart from a few Thai pictures, you'd never know you were in Thailand. Rooms have modern desks, mini-bar, safe-deposit box, color television with in-house movies, and full amenities in the bathrooms. Superior rooms contain a sofa and an extra telephone in the bathroom. In a bid to attract business people the hotel offers a 24-hour business center that's able to answer all secretarial needs and is equipped with Telex and personal computers. In-room videotext computers provide a direct connection to this center. The videotext also supplies daily updated information about stock market data, weather, airline schedules, and much other very useful information. Guests can also use the system to send and receive Telex and fax, draft their correspondence on screen and send it electronically to the business center for final typing, and even review their hotel bill and check out of the hotel, if they signed a credit-card voucher when checking in.

Other facilities include an open-air pool with a bar and a sundeck above, health club, squash court, and Jacuzzi. Seven restaurants are planned, including a rooftop dining room, a steakhouse, and others specializing in Japanese, Chinese, Burmese, and other cuisines. When we visited, only the Atrium Café, just off the lobby, was open. It serves a good luncheon buffet for 220 baht ($8.75). Among the spread you might find roast duck and pork, barracuda, beef with peppers, and chicken in wine, as well as dozens of luscious desserts.

Singles range from 2,250 baht ($90) to 2,750 baht ($110); doubles, from 2,500 baht ($100) to 3,000 baht ($120); suites begin at 3,750 baht ($150).

THE MODERATELY PRICED RANGE: Bangkok's reputation for fine lodgings extends beyond the bounds of luxury and first-class hotels. Its many moderately priced accommodations, with rooms renting for $28 to $84 a night, represent very good value, though the level of service in particular is not up to the extraordinary standards of the higher-priced establishments. However, one should expect most, if not all, of the below-listed hotels (organized by quality within districts of the city) to include such first-class amenities as swimming pools, air conditioning, and in-house food and beverage facilities.

Around the Oriental

Just a five-minute walk from the allure of the Oriental Hotel and Chao Phrya river is the bright, new **Manohra Hotel,** at 412 Surawong Rd. (tel. 02/234-5070). Its modern, white-tiled lobby (which has a view of the Manohra's indoor pool) is a quiet oasis from the busy street. The Buttercup Coffee Shop is popular with *farangs* (foreigners) in search of a more familiar cuisine. When we visited, the carpeted, spotless rooms with white-tile baths had fresh pink roses placed in vases around the room. The guest rooms are smaller than those in some first-class hotels, but they feel just as luxurious and cost only 1,625 baht ($65) single, 1,750 ($70) double, and 5,200 ($208) for a suite. Many European travelers have discovered that the Manohra and its 250 rooms fill up early, so reserve ahead.

Another less expensive choice in the downtown area near the Oriental is the **New Fuji,** at 299-301 Surawong Rd. (tel. 234-5364). It was refurbished in 1983 and now has 66 small, neat rooms with new bathrooms and a seating area. The rooms are clean, surprisingly quiet, and like the Manohra, had fresh flowers on the night table. The New Fuji attracts many Japanese and budget business travelers, and offers secretarial services, a barbershop, and closed-circuit video security. Single rooms run 830 baht ($33) and doubles are 960 baht ($38). Down the block at 295/3 Surawong is the **New Peninsula Hotel** (tel. 02/234-3910), owned by the same company that owns the New Fuji. This hotel was renovated in the late 1970s and has similar accommodations, with much simpler décor, for 830 baht ($33) single and 900 baht ($36) double. Nearby, the historic Trocadero Hotel (Bangkok's oldest after the Oriental) has, unfortunately, been neglected by the same management. Perhaps it, too, will be upgraded in the near future.

The 150-room **Victory Hotel,** located on busy (and noisy) Silom Road just off New Road (tel. 02/233-9060), is another popular spot for Japanese businessmen on a budget. Very simple décor, less than modern furnishing, but clean accommodations mark the Victory as an acceptable alternative. All rooms are air-conditioned but are not equipped with television. The Victory doesn't have a pool (a real liability in Thailand), but its guests are granted swimming privileges at the nearby Narai, a sister hotel. The downstairs coffeeshop, specializing in Japanese cuisine, is quite popular. At 1,000 baht ($40) for a double or 725 baht ($29) for a single, the Victory merits consideration.

Around the Royal Palace

If you've come to Bangkok for touring only, you'll find it difficult to locate an acceptable hotel near the center of this city's legendary sights, unless you're willing to stay at a guesthouse for those on a very low budget. One curious exception is the **Royal Hotel,** which occupies a noisy but enviable location across from Thommasart University and close to the Royal Palace (tel. 02/222-9111). The lobby of the Royal, with polished marble floors and massive modern white Corinthian columns and chandeliers, buzzes with activity as guests from around the world relax after a hot day of sightseeing. Leading up from the reception area is a staircase of regal proportions that appears to date from the art deco era. Other aspects of the Royal harken back to the 1950s, so that the overall effect is an architectural pastiche that would make Robert Venturi proud. Doubles in the old wing are quite spacious and are equipped with air conditioning, color TV, and mini-bars. Twins are 810 baht ($32) and singles are 700 baht ($28), making the Royal a very good value in one of the city's best locations. A word to the wise: Before accepting your room, make sure that it faces away from the street or the noise could disturb your sleep.

Not quite as good, but nearby, is the **Thai Hotel,** centrally located at 78 Prajathipatai Rd. (tel. 02/282-2831), set back from the street by a small pool and lawn. If you've traveled the region, then calling this a "typical Indian businessman's hotel" will have meaning. If not, you'll find that for 650 baht ($26) single or 775 baht ($31) double you'll have a large, simple, cleanly scrubbed (though not spotless) room with bath, air conditioning, and your own phone and TV. The Thai hosts businessmen from all over Asia; single women may not be comfortable here, although budget-minded couples may enjoy its international flavor.

Around Sukhumvit Road

Sukhumvit Road is a bustling shopping, eating, bar-hopping strip that offers many fascinating diversions for tourists. It is also where many businesses, once firmly entrenched downtown, have moved within the last few years.

Just off the busy main street on a quiet lane, at 6 Sukhumvit, Soi 7 (opposite the German beer garden) is the **Park Hotel** (tel. 02/252-5110), boasting an airy, comfortable lobby, a pleasant pool and garden, and clean, bright, unadorned rooms. At 625 baht ($25) for a single and 750 baht ($30) for a double, the Park represents good value, especially for those who insist on a quiet sleeping chamber.

Another suitable choice is the **Nana Hotel,** at 4 Nana Tai (tel. 252-0121), one block off Sukhumvit. You'll know you've arrived at the Nana when you spot their banner proclaiming "Luxury but Economy" (not quite "Taxation Without Representation," but it will do). Facilities and quality are similar to the Park Hotel, but the rooms, though pleasant, are less richly appointed. We'd recommend the larger rooms in the new wing. Still, at 888 baht ($35) double and 815 baht ($32) single, the Nana is a pretty fair value. Reservations are recommended as European tour groups grab the majority of rooms.

Around the Railroad Station

As with most cities, the area around the train station is not idyllic, and if you don't have a place to stay, it's best to take a tuk-tuk or taxi to another part of town where the hotels are certain to be better, or contact the Thai Hotel Association's booth, which is located in the terminal and open from 8:30 a.m. to 6 p.m. Monday through Friday, and 8:30 a.m. to noon all other days and holidays. However, if you really need to stay in the station area, there is one moderately priced alternative, the 228-room **Bangkok Centre Hotel,** opposite the train station at 328 Rama IV Rd. (tel. 02/235-1780), a plain, functional hotel set back from the busy, clamorous thoroughfare. It's a basic businessman's hotel—not fancy, but convenient for anyone making an off-hour train connection. Singles go for 1,250 baht ($50); doubles, 1,375 baht ($55).

The Best of the Rest

Although most of the hotels are built in clusters, Bangkok has a scattering of attractive lodgings in other parts of the city, often in extremely convenient locations. Among our favorites is something of a surprise. Imagine a modern nine-story hotel with sparkling-clean, homey rooms, a 75-foot swimming pool, and multi-ethnic restaurant service, all tucked into a quiet lane off Sathorn Road, near the luxurious Dusit Thani Hotel in the embassy district. On top of that, the staff is extremely friendly and prices are a magnet to budget-minded tourists or business people. All of this may not sound like the YMCA, but that's exactly what the new **Collins House YMCA,** 27 South Sathorn Rd. (tel. 02/287-1900), is: the best low-priced hotel in Bangkok with no compromise in comfort. All rooms are equipped with air conditioning and private shower. The business center (whoever heard of a Y with a business center?) offers copy, Telex, and secretarial services. They even have suites! Doubles run 875 baht ($35); singles, 750 baht ($30); and suites, 1,750 baht ($84). The older Sathorn Wing has more spartan décor, but is equally clean and costs 20% less than the new wing. A Bangkok best buy!

We found the **Century Hotel**, at 9 Rajaprarob Rd., off Din Daeng Road (tel. 02/245-3271), a good value despite its location, about a 20-minute ride from the central shopping district. The Century is an older Thai-style hotel that's a bit worn, but it's the only hotel we found that comes with copies of *The Teachings of Buddha* in the rooms. Of course it has the more ubiquitous amenities such as TV, telephone, spotless private bath, and contrasting flower-print bedspreads that lend a certain coziness to the place. Floor waiters on call for 24 hours and a congenial staff make the Century a good choice for families. Single travelers stay in double rooms for 830 baht ($33), while two can share for 990 baht ($39.50). We prefer the cheerful rooms in the back that overlook the neighborhood's Wat Ta Pan.

The **Florida Hotel**, at 43 Phyathai Square (tel. 02/245-3221), is newly painted, refurbished, and carpeted in such a bright red that it's hard to imagine it's almost 20 years old. Their Orlando dining lounge, overlooking the pool, has white linen tablecloths and the Tampa Coffee Shop is open 24 hours. The spirit temple in their parking lot strives to ward off the sounds and smells of crowded Sri Ayutthaya Road. The Florida's management recommends street-facing rooms to those overlooking the much-used railroad tracks. Guest rooms have very simple décor but are spacious and well air-conditioned. The Florida's a 20-minute ($4 for a taxi) ride from the city's old section, but is a good bet for families on a budget. Room rates run 750 baht ($30) for a single or double, 1,250 baht ($50) for a simple suite that sleeps three, and 1,510 baht ($60.50) for a two-room suite.

The **Siam** (pronounced "see-ahm") **Hotel,** on New Petchburi Road (tel. 02/252-5081), is not to be confused with the first-class Siam Intercontinental Hotel. This Siam is certainly not the most convenient lodging, but it's fine in a pinch. Set back from busy New Petchburi Road, the Siam is an aging though well-preserved alternative. Its dark-teak-paneled hallways open to stucco rooms, some of which face open fields and railroad tracks in the back. A pleasant pool and decent coffeeshop add to its virtues. The trip to town is a minimum 75-baht ($3) ride, making the Siam a slightly less desirable choice. Though its clientele is largely Middle Eastern, it shouldn't pose a problem for couples; however, single women beware! Singles run 830 baht ($33) and doubles are 960 baht ($38).

BUDGET CHOICES: For the truly budget-conscious traveler, Bangkok has a good selection of acceptable low-cost lodgings. Expect to pay from $12.50 to $25 a night for a double room. In addition, Bangkok possesses a huge inventory of extremely inexpensive guesthouses or travel halts, mostly run by Chinese families. These accommodations are popular with backpackers, especially Europeans, and those traveling "on the circuit" throughout Asia.

One of the most interesting aspects of staying in a travel halt is to plug into the information network for Thailand, and often for all of Southeast Asia. If you stay in such a place there is bound to be a bulletin board that notifies other tourists of potential ripoffs, recommendations of restaurants and other inexpensive guesthouses throughout the region, and just sage advice. Many people rely on these bulletin boards to leave and pick up messages. The greatest concentration of guesthouses is on Kao-Sarn Road, near the Royal Hotel and the Royal Palace. Most of these establishments charge about $3 to $8 a night per person.

Around the Oriental

Many a budget traveler, one economic notch up from the guesthouse bracket, has discovered the **Swan Hotel** (tel. 02/234-8594). The location is great—almost in the shadow of the aristocratic Oriental. The pool is large, and nearly all rooms are air-conditioned (16 have fans only). And yes, the price is right: air-conditioned doubles run 475 baht ($19); with, fan 325 baht ($13). Air-conditioned singles are 400 baht ($16), while singles with fan are 250 baht

($10). Our only gripe with the Swan is that many of the rooms are clean but terribly shabby. Be advised to look first before committing to a room. If it meets your standard, then you've found about the only acceptable low-cost accommodations smack in the middle of Bangkok's Gold Coast.

The Best of the Rest

Kyle stayed at the **Bangkok YWCA,** 13 Sathorn Tai Rd. (tel. 02/286-1936), in 1981, and when we came back to review it she couldn't believe the change. Yes, the venerable YWCA has come of age. Not only catering to women, it also offers its clean, spartan rooms to men (and of course, couples). It would be hard, if not impossible, to top the Y for value. Where else can you find quiet accommodations for two, with air conditioning, private bath, phone in the room, and a pool for 500 baht ($20) a night. Singles run 360 baht ($14). Maintaining their tradition of serving women, the Y does offer terrifically clean dormitory facilities for a mere 125 baht ($5) per bed. To top it off there's a canteen/snackbar and a full-service restaurant where two can dine for less than 145 baht ($5.75). Did we forget to mention the Thai Language School? A solid value!

The **Malaysia Hotel,** at 54 Soi Ngam Duplee, off Rama IV Road (tel. 02/286-3582), has been Bangkok's best-known budget halt for years. Immortalized in Tony Wheeler's *Southeast Asia on a Shoestring,* it still hosts round-the-world travelers and now boasts "Malaysia's World Famous Bulletin Board" (their own designation; T-shirts are available for $3.75). The Malaysia has settled on maintaining its reputation. Just as hippies have evolved into budget yuppies, the Malaysia has adopted a uniformed, courteous lobby staff, soap and towels in its shabby air-conditioned rooms, and a small fleet of taxis at its door. Double rooms at 460 baht ($18.50) and the Malai Coffee Shop's 31-baht ($1.25) continental breakfast have shoved real budgeteers out to the $3 beds in slummy guesthouses. Yet those with a little more to spend on simple amenities can still swap stories with fellow adventurers in the lobby of the world-famous Malaysia Hotel.

The **Bangkok Budget Hotel** (no phone) is a popular 12-room lodging on Soi 11 off Sukhumvit Road. This little hotel is a bit difficult to find: though the address is Soi 11, it's better to take Soi 3 and turn right at Bumrungrad Hospital, and turn right again onto Soi 3. There you'll find a very quiet hotel that's really more like a bed-and-breakfast inn than a guesthouse. During the past few years the Bangkok Budget Hotel has proved popular with American and European volunteers working at the refugee camps along the Cambodian border. Needless to say, this is an interesting place for stories. Doubles range from 280 baht ($11) to 420 baht ($17), depending on the size and location of rooms.

READER'S HOTEL SELECTION: "I left the Hotel Malaysia for a cheaper place and liked the **Boston Inn,** near it. Two of us paid 200 baht ($8) for a room with a fan. The place was once a hospital and is rundown, but has a pool" (Stan Mendoza, New York, N.Y.).

Guesthouses

The **Lek Guest House,** located at 125-127 Khao San Rd. (tel. 02/281-2775), is set among a row of fairly indistinguishable travel halts. What distinguishes the Lek from the others is that it seems to be a tad cleaner, a bit fresher than its neighbors. Though the accommodations are as basic as can be, most of the guests we spoke to felt that the proprietor and family work hard to keep the standard high. Accordingly, they offer a safe for storing valuables; free luggage storage for past guests; clothes-washing/drying facilities on the roof; and a very economical restaurant on the street-level floor. Single rooms for 100 baht ($4) and doubles for 125 baht ($5.75) all have fans and fluorescent lights. If you desire a quieter night's sleep, request a room away from the hubbub of the street below.

Similar accommodations are available at the **Sawatdee Guest House,** 71

Sri Ayutthaya Rd. (tel. 02/281-0757). The location, between Samsen Road and the wat (close to the National Library) near the river, in the middle of a real Thai neighborhood rich with the sounds and images of local life, is a real plus. A two-story rooming house, the Sawatdee has an upstairs porch and first-floor living room full of young travelers swapping road yarns. Rooms lie off narrow dark halls, but are clean and light. The innkeeper charges 50 baht ($2) for a dormitory bed, 75 baht ($3) for a single room, and 125 baht ($5) for a double. Showers and Asian-style toilets are on the first floor. The hostess serves good, inexpensive food and there are several rice shops on the street. The Sawatdee is close to the ferry dock where you can conveniently catch a boat to another part of town.

Around the Railroad Station

The super-convenient **Sri Krung Hotel**, at 1860 Krung Kasem Rd. across the river from Hua Lampong (tel. 02/223-1901), is a good budget choice for cross-country train travelers. Back-facing rooms (quieter) have small balconies and a city view, air conditioning, private toilet, and Asian shower, as well as a high standard of cleanliness. Each of its seven floors has a pay telephone and luggage locker, a very handy way to leave extra luggage during an upcountry expedition. The Sri Krung caters to Thai business travelers, as evidenced by the local specialties on the menu of its Valentine Coffee Shop. Tourists, too, can find comfortable and convenient rooms at only 375 baht ($15) for two.

4. DINING

Among the cuisines of Southeast Asia, Thai ranks in the highest echelon. Within the general category of Thai cooking are regional specialties as well as classes of food, ranging from simple noodle or rice-shop fare to the elegant dishes served in restaurants specializing in "royal" or "palace" cuisine. One of the particular joys of sampling Thai fare in Bangkok is that you'll have a hard time spending more than $20 for two people, even at the top Thai restaurants.

And when your stomach needs a break from the spicy flavors of Thai food—as it inevitably will unless you're very unusual—the city also offers a spectacular array of fine European, Chinese, and Japanese dining spots. As might be expected, those restaurants that cater to a more international crowd charge correspondingly higher prices than those that cater to locals. Still, restaurant prices are an absolute bargain compared to their Western counterparts.

TWO CULINARY HIGHLIGHTS: The **Lemongrass Restaurant**, 5/1 Soi 24, off Sukhumvit Road (tel. 258-8637), just may be the best introduction to Thai cooking in all of Bangkok. Here, in a converted Thai house decorated in a homey pastiche of Asian styles, is a kitchen that turns out consistently delicious Thai food. (Its certificate awarded by a local Bangkok gourmand society, Shell Chuan Chim, attests to its standing as one of the city's finest eateries.) The staff is helpful and knowledgeable, and speaks enough English to guide you through the menu. Among our favorite dishes are kai yang pak panang (a richly sauced grilled chicken on coconut sticks), a sumptuous lemongrass chicken, Burmese-style pork curry, and tom yang kung (a spicy sweet-and-sour broth flavored with large fresh shrimp and ginger shoots). None of the many dishes we sampled was mouth-numbingly hot, and yet the spices and ingredients were absolutely authentic and fresh. The Lemongrass is open daily for lunch (11 a.m. to 2 p.m.) and dinner (6 to 11 p.m.). A large meal for two will run about 460 baht ($18).

Among Bangkok's finest Chinese restaurants is **Edith Tai's Silver Palace**, located at the corner of Silom Road and 5 Soi Pipat (tel. 235-5118). You enter a warm and elegant dining room furnished with lovely Chinese bentwood chairs. It is clear that Mrs. Tai cares deeply about her restaurant, as she scours her native Hong Kong for new recipes several times a year. Her work has paid off, for the menu is both diverse and imaginative. The duck, seafood, and shark-fin choices are extensive and delicious. Favorites include braised duck with eight-jewel rice, large and truly succulent whole roast pig (sometimes devoured by as few as three diners), subtly flavorful prawns in garlic-and-soy sauce, shark fin with crabmeat in a brown sauce, and of course, Peking duck of a very high order. Some complex dishes require advance notice, such as the Peking duck, phu thew chang, and other shark-fin specialties. Mrs. Tai is often around lending a gracious touch to the service. Prices are remarkably reasonable: dinner for two should be about 575 baht ($23). A dim sum lunch is served from 11 a.m. to 2 p.m. Daily dinner hours are 6 to 10 p.m. Reservations are suggested.

THAI CUISINE: For the real McCoy, as they say, try any of the following.

Moderately Priced Dining

Long the choice of locals, **My Choice Restaurant,** situated just off Sukhumvit Road on Soi 33 (tel. 258-5726), is an excellent suggestion for travelers in search of fine Thai food served in a totally casual environment. My Choice is filled with Thai diners who enjoy their garden tables and fairly unusual menu. The owner, Tienjai, will recommend dishes suited to your taste thermometer (the food can be, if so ordered, very hot). In the mid-range piquant, roast duck with vegetables was mild and flavorful. Thai watercress salad and escargot curry were deliciously novel to our farang tastebuds. Seafood in coconut milk carried a gentle "kick," but didn't cause pain. My Choice is an altogether excellent value, with an average meal running 345 baht ($13.75) for two.

In an unassuming two-story white house at 10 Pramun St., a side lane near the Oriental Hotel, sits **Thanying Restaurant** (tel. 236-4361), one of Bangkok's best downtown eateries. The menu at Thanying is of the royal school, owing its specific recipes to the mother of one of the owners, Princess Sulap Walleng, sister of and head chef to Queen Rambhai Bhanee, wife of King Rama VII. Thanying is a delight for the eye and palate. Cream-white walls and pink tablecloths are set off by delicate orchids and many pictures of ancient royalty. We enjoyed appetizers of savory with spring greens, chicken wings stuffed with pork, chicken and bamboo shoots, and stuffed fried crab (with pork and crab filling) cooked in a delicate egg batter. Southern-style curried vegetable soup was dangerously hot (but we like to live dangerously); cooler alternatives can be ordered. Luscious entrees filled out the meal. Among the best are duck braised in coconut and broad beans with whole shrimp. Dinner or lunch for two should be about $17.50 to $23. Private rooms are available for parties.

Although according to locals the **Toll Gate** (tel. 391-3947) is not what it used to be, it's still an unusual place. The restaurant is set in the ground floor of a private home at 245/2 Soi 31, a narrow street off frenetic Sukhumvit Road. When you see the dark-wood gate and twin Chinese lanterns, you'll know you're there. The food is rich and sophisticated, prepared in palace style under the supervision of Mom Taw Kritikara. Palace style (recipes prepared for the royal families of Thailand) refers to a highly refined method of cooking, largely forgotten (or ignored) because of the exotic ingredients and labor-intensive manner of presentation. The menu is strictly fixed price at 215 baht ($8.50) and determined by the whimsical taste of the proprietress. It's pointless to make specific recommendations, because each night's menu is different, though one normally is served a soup, three entrees, and dessert. As for ambience, it's virtually nonexistent other than a modest orchid collection growing behind a pane of glass. Never mind the asceticism, the Toll Gate serves some of the most elegant cuisine in Bangkok. Make sure to have your hotel concierge write out the address in Thai because it isn't an easy place to find. Open Monday through Saturday for lunch and dinner. Given the quirky nature of this place, you'd be well advised to call ahead for reservations.

AT THE HOTELS. Arguably Bangkok's most romantic Thai restaurant is the new **Sala Thip,** on the river terrace at the Shangri-la Hotel (tel. 236-0280). Diners can feast on superbly presented classic Thai cuisine in one of two carved-teak pavilions perched over a lotus pond, or at tables on the terrace overlooking the Chao Phrya River. Of their many fine dishes, we enjoyed the airy spring rolls, kuey-tiew phad thai (noodles), and roast duck with vegetables. Sala Thip is open daily for lunch and dinner; a meal for two will cost about 700 baht ($28).

Many contend that the **Spice Market,** downstairs at the Regent of Bangkok (tel. 251-6127), is the city's best Thai restaurant (at least in a hotel). The tasteful décor reflects the name with sacks and jars of spices set in dark-wood built-in cabinets around the dining area. Hanging from the ceiling are colorful hand-painted umbrellas, like those made in Chiang Mai. The food is artfully presented and, though authentically spiced, can be modified to suit your taste. Among the better dishes are khao tang na tung (deep-fried crispy rice with minced pork dip), kaeng kiew-warn (green curry with chicken), kai hor bai-toey (deep-fried chicken), pla dook thord foo (deep-fried catfish), and pla jaramet sarm rod (a whole pomfret in a spicy sweet-and-sour sauce). The Spice Market is open daily for lunch (11:30 a.m. to 2:30 p.m.) and dinner (6:30 to 11 p.m.). Expect to pay about 575 baht ($23) for a complete dinner for two.

The traditional favorite for Thais hosting foreigners is **Bussaracum.** The classical royal décor of the original at 35 Soi Pipat 2, off Silom Road (tel. 235-8915), is now rivaled by the recently opened branch in the Dusit Thani Hotel on Rama IV Road (tel. 233-1130). At this tranquil teak-paneled sanctuary with linen tablecloths the Thai menu is changed every month. Their rhoom (minced pork and shrimp in eggnet wrapping) was the favorite appetizer of King Rama II. The saengwa (cold shrimp salad served in a squash gourd) is an unusual dish that complements gaeng kari gai hang (special chicken curry). Allow the helpful staff to make suggestions and then finish the meal with bauloy sarm see, a dessert of taro and pumpkin in coconut milk. A full meal for two will cost 575 baht ($23) to 700 baht ($28). Reservations are recommended; Bussaracum is open from 11:30 a.m. to 2 p.m. and 5 to 10:30 p.m. daily.

The Budget Range

If you find yourself on upper Sukhumvit Road, around Soi 49 at 11/1 Soi Apichart, and are looking for a fine Thai meal, try **Lai Cram** (tel. 258-9616). The wood and wrought-iron furnishings hardly suggest Thailand, but the extensive menu will more than compensate for the boring surroundings. As at other Thai restaurants mentioned above, you might want to tone down the spices here at Lai Cram. A full meal for two is a reasonable 345 baht ($13.75) to 460 baht ($18.50). One of Lai Cram's virtues is that it remains open every day throughout the day (most restaurants close from 2 to 6 p.m.) and takes all major credit cards. Lai Cram is located off Soi 49-4, opposite the large hospital building.

K.C. Place (tel. 221-9073) is a comfortable and informal half-open-air restaurant on a pier alongside the Chao Phrya River. Located behind Wat Mahatat, it's a scenic ten-minute walk through a fascinating series of lively backstreets and impromptu markets from either the Royal Palace or the National Museum. In either case, its river-perch location provides midday relief from heat and sun. The menu offers mostly Thai specialties, with a few Indian and Chinese dishes for cosmopolitan flavor; most entrees are a very reasonable 35 baht ($1.50) to 70 baht ($2.75). We enjoyed an especially flavorful chicken larb, ground chicken mixed with mint leaves and lime juice served on a bed of raw cabbage, and a cooling plate of pad thai noodles. One of the pleasures of eating at K.C. Place is that it adjoins a very active ferry landing with its busy river traffic. Open daily for lunch and dinner.

At the Democracy Monument on Rajdamnern Avenue, **Sorndaeng Res-**

taurant (tel. 224-3088) is one of the city's oldest restaurants, filled with local people dining on very reasonably priced food. Of the two dining rooms, opt for the one that is cooled by fans or air conditioning and furnished with simple white bentwood chairs set at tables. Among our favorite dishes are the papaya salad, beef with basil leaves and chili, hot-and-sour chicken, and fried morning glory in oyster sauce (in particular do try this fresh green water plant). Prices range from 25 baht ($1) to 50 baht ($2), so expect to pay a very low 200 baht ($8) for a full meal for two, including beer. Open daily for lunch and dinner from 10 a.m. to 10 p.m.

At the huge, open-air **Koom Luang** on far-off (20-minute taxi ride) Asoke Din Daeng Road (tel. 246-3273), hundreds of dining tables stand in the dark-wood pavilions above lily-filled ponds. Fountains lit from below the water change from red to green to gold like Bangkok's few traffic signals. And young Thai crooners sing love songs to the accompaniment of an electric piano. In case this sounds like dinner for 2,000, rest assured that this is the latest in Bangkok's fast-changing restaurant scene; Koom Luang ranks among the best of Bangkok's splashy, very "in" football-field-size garden eateries. Let your costumed waiter (one or two speak halting English) help you choose from more than 100 varieties of Thai appetizers and entrees. The excellent four hot hors d'oeuvres platter is really four plates of crispy spring rolls, broad rice noodle rolls filled with mushrooms, slices of fried minced prawn stuffed in chicken skin, and a fried-egg and vegetable dish. We gasped over the fiery-hot seafood curry soup but were comforted by a lightly steamed Siam gobi fish and fresh, slim asparagus stalks. Koom Luang is open daily for lunch and dinner; expect to pay 350 baht ($14) for two.

Off noisy, jammed Silom Road, the weary traveler can find a convenient and quiet sanctuary in the Silom Village Trade Center, at 286 Silom Rd., south of the Narai Hotel. Set in the mall, the **Silom Village Restaurant** (tel. 234-4448) offers basic Thai fare, reasonably priced but fairly undistinguished, in a lovely garden atmosphere among the tree-lined shops. This café is an offspring of the fancier Ruen Thep, located in the same mall where, at night, Thai classical dancers perform on the open-air stage. Dinner for two should run $14 to $18.

Thai Cuisine and Traditional Dance

These establishments really merit a separate category, for in most cases their format is quite similar. Generally, the restaurants offer a package, where for one price you are served a fixed-menu dinner and, after dining, are entertained by a demonstration of Thai classical dancing. Unlike most of the above recommendations, these restaurants are almost exclusively the domain of tourists, a less discriminating culinary clientele than native Thais; the quality of food suffers in comparison. As compensation, visitors don't have to choose from an often discouragingly alien menu and have the opportunity to see a fine sampling of various Thai dancing styles. Many packaged tours include at least one meal in this category of restaurant, and we encourage you to try one, if only to view the incredibly graceful and exquisite Thai dancing.

One of the prettiest settings for a classic Thai meal and dance performance is the poolside **Sala Thai,** at the Indra Regent Hotel on Rajaprorob Road (tel. 251-1111). This stunning carved-teak pavilion is a detailed replica of a 13th-century Thai nobleman's hall. Banquette seating frames a space where women perform the hill tribes' folk *serng,* the royal *rum sat cha-tri,* and other examples of classical dance. The richly festooned traditional costumes complement the beautifully presented Thai specialties. An evening's introduction to regal cuisine and dance costs 325 baht ($13) per person; nightly seating is at 7:30 p.m. and the performance begins at 8:30 p.m. Reservations are suggested.

For a traditional Thai dinner with classical dancing, the Oriental's **Sala Rim Naan** (tel. 437-6211) is another luxurious option, and the trip across the river from the hotel a nighttime treat. In the glittering teak-and-marble main hall finished with bronze trim, guests sit at low tables on comfortable pillow sofas and dine on unremarkable Thai dishes. Classical dancers from Bangkok's Department of Fine Arts perform royal dances of the Sukhothai and Ayutthaya Periods, as well as various folk dances, during the one-hour show. Sala Rim Naan offers several options, including a prix-fixe meal plus dance demonstration for 600 baht ($24), and dance only with no food service for 200 baht ($8). Sala Rim Naan is also open for a buffet lunch for 225 baht ($9).

Ferry pickups can be arranged from other hotels. Reservations are required. (For those who have visited before, Sala Rim Naan is no longer operated by the excellent D'Jit Pochana kitchen.)

Another fine choice for dinner with Thai dance is **Ruen Thep Restaurant,** located in the Silom Village Trade Center, 286 Silom Rd., near the Narai Hotel (tel. 235-8760). Diners sit on the floor of a banquet hall and sample a traditional Thai meal, followed by a demonstration of Thai classical dance. The prix-fixe dinner is served at 7 p.m., with dancing at 8:30 p.m. Ruen Thep offers a lunch buffet for a fixed price. Reservations are suggested for dinner and dance.

Our final dance-restaurant recommendation is something quite different from those already mentioned. **Tumpnakthai,** at 131 Ratchadapisek Rd. (tel. 276-1810), bills itself as the largest restaurant in the world, with tables enough for 3,000—we would be foolish to disagree. Waiters on roller skates deliver food from the kitchen to one of 33 far-flung dining pavilions. (We heard a story from a fellow traveler about trying to meet a friend at Tumpnakthai and never finding him!) There is a party atmosphere every night with a good mixture of tourists and locals. The food is good, though hardly Bangkok's best. However, we very much enjoyed the traditional Thai dancing, judging it one of the finest presentations in the city. For the serious gourmand the ideal way to enjoy the Tumpnakthai experience is to treat it as a drinks-and-appetizer extravaganza and then move on to more serious dining at another venue. If you do go to see the dancing exhibition, make sure to tell your host that you want a table near the stage, otherwise you might as well try to see it from two miles away. Tumpnakthai has a huge menu with specialties from the major regions of Thailand; a sampling of hor d'oeuvres and beer will run 280 baht ($11.25) for two. Open daily from 11 a.m. to 11 p.m.; show time is 8 to 9:30 p.m.

Thai Fast Food

The Thai-style food hall is meant to serve much the same function as any Western-style fast-food chain, like McDonald's.

Our favorite Thai fast-food outlet is the **Mah Boon Krong Food Center,** located on the sixth floor of the M.B.K. Shopping Center, near Siam Center, a vast treasure trove of Thai and Chinese specialties, all at astonishingly low prices: $2 to $3 is a princely sum to spend here. The food is served from modern, clean booths. Most of it is take-out, but there are tables for those who want to eat here. Because one can order small amounts of food, the M.B.K. is an ideal place for the single traveler to sample a wide variety of tastes without grossly overordering. The system of buying food is rather unusual: first, purchase food coupons from vendors with baht; second, select food on trays and pay with coupons, cafeteria style; and third, cash in excess coupons for change. Why they do this I don't know, but perhaps it makes the whole system work faster. In any event, visiting the M.B.K. Food Center, open daily for lunch and dinner, gives you a glimpse of how contemporary Thai families are combining local style with Western methods.

More conventional is the **See Fah Restaurant,** at 434 Siam Square, across from Siam Center (tel. 251-5517), a wildly popular Thai-style "coffeeshop," with the vast majority of menu items of Thai or Chinese origin. Among the better dishes that we sampled were stuffed chopped shrimp and coconut meat in a thin crispy crêpe, emee (egg noodles steamed in a clay pot with white-meat chicken and ham), roast duck, and rajavong (a special variety of noodle). Many locals dine at See Fah because of its quick service and low prices. A large meal for two will run about 230 baht ($9.25). There are two other See Fah restaurants, at 47/19-22 Ratchadamri Rd. and at 942/31 Rama IV Rd. Though the restaurants have changing operating hours, the See Fah chain often stays open until very late at night.

CHINESE CUISINE: One of Bangkok's best-kept culinary secrets is the excellent quality of its many Chinese restaurants.

Some of the best are found at the city's fine hotels. Current favorite is the **Mayflower** at the Dusit Thani (tel. 233-1130), a cool, elegant pastel-decorated room. If you've never tasted some of China's more exotic delicacies then this is the place to try them. The menu lists nine varieties of sharks-fin soup and more than half a dozen each of abalone dishes and swallow's nest items. The shark fin in brown sauce is particularly flavorsome. The Peking duck, served in several courses, is also outstanding—really crisp skin followed by rich, moist meat wrapped in thin, toothsome pancakes. Beef, prawn, pork, crab, bean curd, noodle, chicken, and more exotic pigeon and turtle dishes round out the menu, with most priced from 200 baht ($8) to 325 baht ($13). Dinner for two will run about 2,500 ($100), including some of the more exotic higher-priced dishes, but it will be well worth it.

Another of our favorites is **Tai Pan** at the Imperial Hotel (tel. 254-0111), just a short walk from the U.S. Embassy. Highest kudos go to their kitchen for the Cantonese-style roast duck. Unlike Thai-style duck, this delectable dish has a very crispy skin and juicy meat with a micro-thin layer of fat. Also excellent are sautéed crystal prawns, shark-fin soup (they serve nine varieties), an assortment of dim sum dishes, and deep-fried pancakes stuffed with Chinese plum (or the evil-smelling durian, if in season). Dinner for two, including some of the more exotic entrees, runs 700 baht ($28) to 900 baht ($36). Tai Pan is open daily: lunch hours are 11:30 a.m. to 2 p.m.; dinner hours are 6 to 10 p.m.

One of Bangkok's oldest Chinese palaces is **Hoi Tien Lao**, in the heart of Chinatown at 308 Sua Pha Rd. (tel. 221-1685). It's a traditional-style restaurant with wonderful food and the atmosphere is pure Chinese (noisy and exciting). Like the many gargantuan establishments in Hong Kong, Hoi Tien Lao is a multistory affair with a nightclub on the top. The dishes are well prepared and reasonably priced; expect to pay 460 baht ($18.50) for two. Hoi Tien Lao opened a second restaurant in the last year, near the Oriental Hotel. Though we didn't have an opportunity to eat there, longtime Bangkok residents prefer the older Chinatown location. Open daily for lunch and dinner.

Shangarila is a glitzy, crowded, Shanghai-style restaurant, on Silom Road's busy strip, at no. 154/4-7 (tel. 234-5588). The décor is bright and splashy, with a carp pond occupying part of the downstairs dining room. Upstairs rooms are quieter and have more subdued furnishings. One of the fun "show" dishes is handmade noodles; the chef, who performs this bit of magic at your table, methodically pulls dough, doubling it each time to create noodles out of what appears to be thin air. Beggar's chicken is stuffed with mushrooms and baked in a thick clay coating. Peking duck, pig's leg in brown dumpling, and many seafood dishes are among the favorites. Dinner should be about $11.50 to $14 for two. The Grand Shangarila is a larger version of the original restaurant, with the same menu, at 58/4-7 Thaniya Rd. (tel. 234-2045). Both restaurants are open daily for lunch and dinner.

A fat, smiling gold Buddha presides over the colorfully decorated **Shang Palace,** the popular Chinese restaurant in the riverside Shangri-la Hotel (tel. 236-0280). At dinner an elegant Thai and tourist crowd enjoys the wide range of Cantonese specialties. At lunch the Shang Palace concentrates on its dim sum menu, that wonderful display of noodle- and pastry-wrapped appetizers that allows even the novice to sample an extensive range of Chinese tastes. Steamed pork dumplings, shrimp balls, and spring rolls are served by the plate, with three to six pieces per portion. Prices average 230 baht ($9.25) per person at lunch and approximately 460 baht ($18.50) per head for dinner. Reservations are recommended for evening and weekend meals.

For a super bargain, stop at local favorite **Maria Restaurant,** Chalerm Thai Theater Building, Rajdamnern Avenue, near Wat Saket (tel. 221-5211), and select some of the dim sum that will be brought to your table on a rolling cart and served in bamboo steamers. Try the pork or mung bean, or else order à la carte from the selections of Szechuan, Cantonese, Japanese, and Thai dishes. It's a large and noisy restaurant—an authentic Chinese Bangkok experience. A full meal for two will cost about 200 baht ($8). Open for lunch only, daily from 11 a.m. to 2 p.m.

OTHER ASIAN CUISINES: As we said, there's plenty of choices to soothe the troubled tastebuds. Here's a sample.

Japanese

Since the explosion of Japanese business and tourism within Thailand, there has been a simultaneous increase in the number of Japanese restaurants. In nearly every international-class hotel you can find a sushi bar and full Japanese restaurant, such as the attractive **Genji Restaurant** at the Hilton. Few are regarded as anything particularly special, though all have access to Bangkok's ready supply of fresh fish and are generally of good quality.

One Japanese restaurant that is often commended by local residents for its fine cuisine and elegant surroundings is **Daikoku,** located opposite Lumpini Park at 960/1 Rama IV Rd. (tel. 233-1495). There you can sample a full range of Japanese specialties in a comfortable, though rather formal, setting. We particularly enjoyed the sushi, and the bill for a complete meal came to about $29. Daikoku is open daily.

Indian

There are also a fair number of Indian restaurants in Bangkok due to the influx of Indians during the last two decades. Most of the restaurants are located downtown and in particular there is a concentration of places on New Road near Silom. Of this group we enjoyed **Himali Cha Cha,** at 1229/11 New Rd. (tel. 235-1569); it's actually 50 yards off New Road on a small lane (look for the sign). Cha Cha, the graying chef and proprietor, was on Mountbatten's staff in India. He then cooked for the diplomatic corps in Laos, and after the fall of that country, came to Bangkok where he opened his restaurant in 1980. Specialties include three darbesh curry, vegetable kofta curry, and palak paneer, all extremely flavorful and well prepared. For a full course meal, two should expect to pay 400 baht ($16). Though reservations aren't strictly required, Himali Cha Cha fills up during prime dining hours. Open daily for lunch and dinner.

If Himali Cha Cha is filled, you might want to take a short walk around the corner to 460/8 Suriwongse Rd. to the **Café India** (tel. 233-0419). It's a perfectly acceptable alternative, also specializing in northern Indian cuisine. If you crave a soothing curry and are up in the Sukhumvit area, you might want to visit the **Moghul Room,** on a small soi off Soi 11 (tel. 251-0645). As with the other two Indian restaurants mentioned, the Moghul Room specializes in mild, northern cooking styles.

Vietnamese

We were surprised at how few Vietnamese restaurants existed in Bangkok given the number of refugees who fled to Thailand (especially in contrast to Hong Kong, which has a great diversity of Vietnamese establishments). One place that we appreciate both for the food and its lovely garden setting is **Le Dalat,** located across from the Indian Embassy at 51 Sukhumvit on Soi 23 (tel. 258-9298). The restaurant is quite casual with most tables placed in a reed-and-bamboo garden. The food is prepared by Vietnamese-trained Thai chefs and the dishes they turn out are fine. Le Dalat has a lot of understated style, perfectly suited to the taste of its proprietress who also runs Asian Heritage, a refined little antique store down the street. Le Dalat is open daily for lunch and dinner. A dinner for two should run about 290 baht ($11.50).

HEALTH FOOD: We didn't find a single vegetarian-only restaurant in Bangkok (if you find one, please write to us), but vegetarians take heart: in nearly all Thai, Chinese, Indian, and Japanese restaurants there is a full complement of nonmeat appetizers and entrees.

A handy lunch spot that's very popular with health-conscious locals and tourists is the **Whole Earth Restaurant,** conveniently located at 93/3 Soi Langsuan (tel. 252-5574), a few minutes' tuk-tuk ride off Ploenchit Road. It's easily identified by a globe-and-graphic logo very reminiscent of the Hard Rock Café of New York and London fame. The atmosphere is decidedly casual and comfortable. The large menu, a mix of Thai, Indian, and Western entrees, features some meat dishes in Thai style, like charcoal-broiled pork (see what we mean about the lack of vegetarian places) with honey sauce served with vegetables, but shines in the vegetarian department with 26 dishes. Favorites include vegetable curry in a banana-leaf bowl, a thick seasonal vegetable soup, and charcoal-broiled eggplant. End the meal with homemade fruit ice cream and you'll leave with a smile. A complete meal for two is a reasonable 230 baht ($9.25). The Whole Earth Restaurant is open daily from 11:30 a.m. to 2:30 p.m. for lunch and 5:30 p.m. to midnight for dinner.

SEAFOOD: Thailand has plenty of fish and seafood, coming from the gulf, the Andaman Sea, and the country's many rivers and lakes. Most restaurants feature a wide array of saltwater and freshwater entrees, but several spots in Bangkok specialize in seafood only.

Most famous, if (we feel) somewhat overpriced, is **Lord Jim's** at the Oriental Hotel (tel. 236-0400). The elegant room overlooks the famous hotel terrace and the river that glides along beside it. Among the appetizers are several famous selections: Lord Jim's seafood tartare, warm lobster salad with abalone mushrooms and mint vinaigrette, or the characteristic and subtly flavored deep-fried lobster roll with coriander and chili-butter sauce. The main courses, priced from 325 baht ($13) to 600 baht ($24), range from a simple steak and baked potato and the renowned Lord Jim's seafood basket for two to dishes that combine meat and fish like the veal medallions filled with scallops and served with a crab sauce, as well as a variety of Thai, Japanese, Indian, and Chinese items. For a delightful shock to the senses, try the black-peppered pineapple for dessert, served with cacão sauce and vanilla ice cream. Dinner for two without wine will cost about $125. The wine list is extensive, but very expensive.

Run like a fish-and-vegetable mart, the **Seafood Restaurant,** at 388 Sukhumvit Rd., opposite Soi Asoke (tel. 258-0218), is a cross between the consummate tourist restaurant and an American-style supermarket replete with low ceilings, long, cool fluorescent lighting, shopping carts, and checkout lines. A waterfall, "Tavern on the Green"–style lights, and '50s American jukebox tunes complete the picture. As you enter you'll find a team of chefs stationed over a panoply of cooking devices: woks, grills, ovens. The action in this open kitchen appears reckless and wild; these folks are cooking your food, but the "show" rivals Benihana. Walk to the rear of the dining room and choose from the awesome selection of fish, seafood, and vegetables on display (their ruby-colored neon sign advertises, "If it swims, we have it"!). Food consultants (not waiters) will assist you as to how a particular item should be cooked: broiled, steamed in a pot, deep-fried, grilled, sautéed, boiled, or made into one of several soup concoctions. Though the spices are distinctly Thai, the Seafood Restaurant is really more of a crossover establishment that will especially please those who are befuddled by often-difficult Thai menus. Prices are determined by the food selected and how it is to be prepared. The formula is fairly arcane but the net result is a medium-priced meal; dinner for two should run about 575 baht ($23). The Seafood Restaurant is open daily from 1 p.m. to midnight.

WESTERN CUISINES: Bangkok has plenty of choices for those times when your stomach just can't manage the range of spicy local cuisine.

French

There has long been an association between French and Southeast Asian cooking, primarily because of the French occupation of Indochina during the first half of this century. However, in the case of Thailand, a country that hasn't been occupied since the days of the Burmese Empire, the connection between these two divergent cuisines is one of fashion, not of imperialism. Nouvelle cuisine, with its reliance on intricate preparation, is a perfect partner for the exotic spices, fruit, and vegetables of fine Thai food. Most of the restaurants cited below create dishes that are prepared in the French style, but use the bounty of the local harvest to produce imaginative and delicious results.

Nearly every international hotel lays claim to its French restaurant as the tops, so the competition within the city is intense. Each hotel tries to woo this year's Chef of the Year from France, thereby increasing its standing both in Bangkok and around the world.

One of the most elegant dining experiences in Bangkok is found at the Hilton's **Ma Maison** restaurant (tel. 253-0123). The food is superb, the service graciously attentive but comfortably unpretentious, and the pastel-and-peach décor restful. Diners can feast on an interesting array of French classics, ranging from succulent canard à l'orange to fresh snapper in a light cream sauce. Vegetables from upriver farms are delicately prepared and served on the side. Guests can also choose more nouvelle fare from the prix-fixe menu. Traditional French desserts and inventive fruit pastries that take advantage of Thailand's bounty are delightful, and followed by rich chocolates. A fine wine list complements this culinary experience, though as always in Southeast Asia, the French wines are quite expensive. The prix-fixe price is an excellent value at 500 baht ($20) for lunch, 750 baht ($30) for dinner. Neat attire and reservations are recommended.

The **Normandie,** at the Oriental Hotel (tel. 236-0400), is Bangkok's most formal and most expensive French restaurant, and commands a fine view of the river from its lofty location on the upper floors of the hotel. The dining room is intimate and sumptuously appointed. Gault Millau Chef of the Year in 1985, Jean Bardet presides over the kitchen (he actually is there on only limited occasions, residing in his native France but making journeys to Bangkok) and what an interesting array of dishes he concocts. His philosophy is to create dishes that are inspired by French cuisine but adapted to Thai produce, such as warm prawn salad with almonds and yellow mushrooms, chilled cream of Surat Thani oysters with caviar, blue river lobster wrapped in green cabbage, and pan-fried tiger prawns with fresh tomatoes and basil. The menu is prix fixe at 2,000 baht ($80) per person, not including wine (they have an extensive selection from France). Normandie is open daily for lunch and dinner. Reservations are required, as are jacket and tie.

Le Bistrot, nestled in a fancy shopping arcade behind Embassy Row, at 20/18 Ruam Rudee Village (tel. 251-2523), is Bangkok's best independent (not part of a hotel) French restaurant. People who are tired of gilt and colored mirrors will be soothed by Le Bistrot's pale-gray and pink décor, intimate booth seating, and sparkling-crystal and linen table settings. Thai waitresses in black uniforms with white lace trim serve salad niçoise, a choice of seven pâtés, steaming gratinée onion soup, pigeon rôti, tournedos madère, and mousse au chocolat, among other authentically prepared French specialties. An average-priced meal will cost 360 baht ($14.50) per person, without wine. Le Bistrot serves lunch only Monday through Friday; dinner is served seven days a week. Reservations are recommended for dinner.

Bangkok's only revolving restaurant is **La Rotonde,** on the 15th floor of the Narai Hotel on Silom Road (tel. 233-3350). Casual dress and an appetite for French, seafood, or continental favorites are all that's required. Dinner for two averages 600 baht ($24) to 825 baht ($33). Reservations are suggested for weekend evenings.

Among other well-regarded establishments is **La Paloma Restaurant Français,** located at 26/2 Mahesak (tel. 233-3853), serving continental and French fare at prices a bit less than the more upscale hotel restaurants. A favorite of local residents.

American

For 18 years the expatriate community has relied on casual **Neil's Tavern** (tel. 251-5644) for steak and seafood prepared American style. Located on narrow Soi Ruam Rudee at 58/4, behind the line of embassies on Wireless Road, Neil's cool, red-brick interior with cowhides and piped-in Muzak make many feel right at home. Neil's serves its American, Japanese, and European guests such thoroughly American standards as surf and turf, charcoal-broiled filet (with burgundy sauce), and lobster (in this case, it's the cobalt-blue Phuket lobster, the closest thing this side of Tongo to a Maine snapper). For dessert, don't pass up the Venice chocolate cake. Salad, potato, garlic bread, and vegetable are included with all dinners. A filling dinner for two should run about $23. Neil's Tavern is open for lunch Monday through Saturday from 11:30 a.m. to 2 p.m., and for dinner nightly from 5:30 to 10:30 p.m. Reservations are necessary on weekends. Dress is casual, although business people often dine in jacket and tie.

Italian

Why? Perhaps because there are throngs of Italian visitors who travel through Thailand each year and every so often one of them decides to stick around and open a trattoria. Before you dismiss this category, know that the food is really quite good.

On the corner of Sukhumvit Road and Soi 33 is Bangkok's favorite Italian eatery, **Pan Pan** (tel. 258-9304), with a second branch at 45 Soi Langsuan, just a short walk from Ploenchit Road (tel. 252-7104). Pan Pan's white pagoda-style pavilion hides a cozy bistro where good pasta dishes, creamy desserts, and Italian coffees are served. Dinner for two will cost about 460 baht ($18.50). Both locations are open daily for lunch and dinner.

At **L'Opera,** 55 Soi 39, off Sukhumvit Road (tel. 258-5605), one is struck with a curious sense of familiarity: red-and-white checkered tablecloths, empty bottles of chianti displayed on the shelves, framed photographs of famed Italian sites, and a menu resplendent with Italian regional favorites. In fact everything is so similar to an average American-style neighborhood trattoria that it's sometimes easy to forget you're in Thailand (which might be why it's so popular with Westerners, particularly visiting Italians). What might bring you back to a sense of place are the low prices, with most dishes running 115 baht ($4.50), and the wonderful combination of Thai seafood with Italian recipes. We particularly enjoyed mixed seafood with olive oil and garlic for 185 baht ($7.50). L'Opera is open daily for lunch and dinner.

If you're in the Patpong area, you might want to try **Trattoria da Roberto,** in the Plaza Arcade, Patpong 11 (tel. 233-6851). The cuisine and prices are similar to Pan Pan and L'Opera, and locals claim that Roberto serves the best pizza in town.

Fast Food

Bangkok, like most other cities in the world, has experienced the fast-food explosion. McDonald's, Kentucky Fried Chicken, Pizza Hut, et al. have all made inroads in Bangkok and will probably spread into the outer lying regions in the not too distant future.

Tired of surprises? At Soi Surawong Plaza, opposite the P.I.A. ticket office, is a classic **Pizza Hut.** It's open seven days from 10 a.m. to 11 p.m. and features the familiar super-supreme pizza, salad bar, and a choice of sodas. There's also a Pizza Hut in Siam Square and on Soi 51 Sukhumvit.

If it's ice cream you're craving, you can visit **Swensen's,** in the same building as the Sukhumvit Pizza Hut.

Kentucky Fried Chicken, of course, has several branches in Bangkok. Right now they're located in Siam Square, on Ratchadamri Road in the Mall, and at Central Plaza.

A & W, of root beer fame, has fast-food outlets on Silom Road and in Siam Square.

There's a **Dairy Queen** on the corner of Rama IV and Silom Roads.

And, finally, **McDonald's** is on Ploenchit Road, on the ground floor of the Amarin Plaza.

5. WHAT TO SEE AND DO IN THE CITY

Few capitals in Southeast Asia have as much to see as Bangkok. From its fascinating klongs to its incredible Buddhist wats, or temples, from its wide range of sports activities (kick boxing, kite fighting, and cock fighting are only a few) to exciting day trips, Bangkok demands three or four days of solid sightseeing just to visit the most important monuments.

If you only have a short time in the city, be sure to visit the klongs (canals) on a boat tour, the Grand Palace and Wat Phra Keo (the Emerald Buddha), Wat Po, and across the river, Wat Arun. If you can squeeze them in, two of our favorite special sites, Wang Suan Pakkard and Jim Thompson's House, should also be on the travel agenda.

The best introduction to the city is certainly via boat, and that's our favored mode of transportation to reacquaint ourselves with the city whenever we visit.

EXPLORING BANGKOK'S WATERWAYS: A large part of Bangkok's magic must be ascribed to its waterways, which were once so extensive that early admirers dubbed the city the "Venice of the East." Sadly, many of the canals (klongs) have been paved over in the last decade or so and the heart of the city is now filled with traffic-clogged streets. Still, Bangkok does retain much of its magic and the broad and magnificent Chao Phrya River is very much part of that magic. It cuts through the heart of the city, separating the early capital of Thonburi from the later one, Bangkok, and branches off into a myriad network of klongs on the Thonburi side.

The Chao Phrya is the major thoroughfare for people and commerce, with boats of all sizes and shapes plying the river day and night. Ferries run up and down and across the river, carrying commuters to work, kids to school, and saffron-robed monks to temple. The huge but strangely elegant rice barges lumber up and down, towed by tugs whose taut ropes pull mountains of rice, gravel, lumber, vegetables, and countless families who make their homes on the barges.

The strangest, most frequently seen boat on the river is the *prahu,* or long-tailed boat. It is a long, thin, graceful vessel, powered by an automobile engine connected by a long, exposed shaft (tail) to the propeller. The engine assembly is totally exposed and finely balanced on a fulcrum mount. The muscular boatmen move the entire motor and shaft assembly to steer the boat, an amazing feat of strength and balance, executed with surgical precision at 30 knots. The boats are brightly painted and swift as the wind, their unmuffled roars echoing across the river day and night. These water taxis carry passengers throughout the maze of klongs and are a vital element in supplying fresh food from upriver farms and fresh fish from coastal villages to Bangkok.

Any visitor coveting an intimate glimpse into the textures and rhythms of local life should explore the waterways. You'll see people bathing in the river, washing clothes, even brushing their teeth at its edge (a habit not recommended to Westerners); floating kitchens in sampans serving rice and noodles to customers in other boats and on the docks; men dancing across carpets of logs floating to lumber mills; the unending cycle of loading and unloading. Wooden houses on stilts spread back from the banks of the river and klongs, each with its own spirit house decked with flowers and other offerings and perfumed with incense. A river or klong trip provides a rich panoply of life and color, not the least of which is the forever downstream flow of hyacinths drifting to the sea.

The best view of Bangkok's floating life can be had by chartering a long-tailed boat for 230 baht ($9.25) per hour and touring the klongs of Thonburi. Be prepared to negotiate the price. The Tha Chang pier, close to Wat Phra Keo, is a good place to charter a boat, although prahu drivers also hover around most of the piers near the hotels, waiting for less frugal tourists. The concierge at your hotel can probably arrange one for you.

Among the many tours, the "Floating Market" tour is the most popular, but we feel it's too touristy and you're better to go to the floating market about 65 miles outside Bangkok at Damnoen Saduak, if you have time. If you don't have time, the Floating Market Tour departs from the River City or hotel docks at about 7:30 a.m. every day to explore the Floating Market of Thonburi near Wat Sai, across the river from Bangkok. In the narrow klong, women in woven bamboo hats sell fruit, vegetables, chili paste, rice, and noodles from their small canoe-like boats. The tour boats stop at a large souvenir market catering strictly to the tourist trade, then pause for half an hour at a snake farm. It's a wildly entertaining show, after which the boats stop at the remarkable Wat Arun before returning to the pier. It's a fun and colorful half-day tour, recommended for anyone, but as we mentioned above, it's on the touristy side and the klong is incredibly crowded with other tour boats. This tour can be booked through tour operators in most hotels.

A day trip to the more authentic Damnoen Saduak floating market in Ratchaburi, about 109 km (65 miles) south of Bangkok, is well worth the effort (see "Day Trips from the City").

THE ROYAL BARGES: While you're cruising the Chao Phrya, stop by a unique museum housing a collection of royal barges. These elaborately decorated sailing vessels are used by the royal family on state occasions or for high religious ceremonies. In 1987 these barges, each rowed by 60 or so oarsmen, were featured in a procession honoring the king's 60th birthday. The king's barge, the *Suphanahong,* is marvelously decorated with red-and-gold carvings; the prows and sterns are magnificent too, usually featuring fearsome or awesome mythological beasts, like the Garuda or the dragon. The museum, in an oversize shed, is located on Klong Bangkok Noi, near the Phra Pinklao Bridge. Hours are 8:30 a.m. to 4:30 p.m. daily; admission is 15 baht (60¢). For more information, call 282-7966. If you can't make it to the royal barges, there is a smaller display of barges at the National Museum, near Wat Phra Keo.

WAT PHRA KEO (THE EMERALD BUDDHA) AND THE GRAND PALACE:

Perhaps no other shrine in Thailand is as revered as Wat Phra Keo, or as it is commonly known, the Temple of the Emerald Buddha. Within the grounds of this sacred complex, surrounded by walls over a mile long, are some of the finest examples of Buddhist sculpture, architecture, painting, and decorative craft to be found in the country, making it a must-see for all visitors to Bangkok. Admission is 100 baht ($4), which includes admission to the Grand Palace.

Wat Phra Keo (The Emerald Buddha)

Central to the wat is the **Emerald Buddha** itself, a rather small, dark statue, a little over two feet high, made of green jade (the translation of the word "emerald" in Thai refers to something of intense green color only, not to the specific stone) that sits atop a huge gold altar. This very revered image was first discovered inside a *chedi* (a pointed dome-shaped stupa with a relic of the Buddha) in Chiang Rai when a bolt of lightning struck the monument in 1434. (Some historians believe that the Buddha was sculpted around that time, attributing it to the Chiangsaen school; others believe that it was produced in Sri Lanka, also around the same time.) The reigning king of Chiang Mai (at that time the most powerful state in the north) attempted to bring the Buddha to his city, but on three separate occasions the elephant that was to transport the statue halted in the village of Lampang. Never one to cross the determined spirit of the Buddha, the king installed the statue in a monumental wat in Lampang, where it remained for 32 years. A more dogged monarch, King Tiloka, insisted that the Emerald Buddha be brought to Chiang Mai. There it was placed in a chedi at Wat Chedi Luang, but not for long. In 1552 the new ruler of Chiang Mai, King Chaichettha (of Laotian descent), moved back to his native country and took the peripatetic Buddha with him to Luang Prabang. Some 12 years later, the statue was moved again, this time to Vientiane, where it stayed for 214 years, until Rama I brought it back to his capital at Thonburi after his successful campaign in Laos. A few years later, in 1784, when the capital was moved across the river to Bangkok, Rama I installed the precious figure in its present shrine where it has been on display ever since.

The Buddha is covered in a seasonal cloak, changed three times a year to correspond to the summer, winter, and rainy months. The changing of the robes is an important ritual that is performed by the king, who also sprinkles water over the monks and other well-wishers attending the ceremony to bring good fortune during the upcoming season.

The Emerald Buddha is housed in an equally magnificent **ubosoth,** a hall, like a *viharn,* used by monks to perform important religious rituals. The interior walls are decorated with late-Ayutthaya-style murals depicting the life of the Buddha, steps to enlightenment, and the Buddhist cosmology of the Worlds of Desire, Form, and Nonform. The cycle begins with the birth of the Buddha, which can be seen in the middle of the left wall as you enter the sanctuary. The story continues in a counterclockwise direction, illustrating the Buddha in meditation in the forest; the confusion of the world; Buddha achieving enlightenment; and disciples studying the philosophy of the Buddha. Note also the exquisite inlaid mother-of-pearl work on the door panels.

The surrounding portico of the ubosoth is an example of masterful Thai craftsmanship; walk around the building and notice the extraordinary carving, inlaid doors, and stucco work. On the perimeter of the ubosoth are 12 open pavilions, built during the reign of Rama I. The portico galleries across from the ubosoth, which defined the original boundary of the wat, contain painted murals depicting stories from the *Ramakien,* the Thai version of the Hindu epic *Ramayana.* The painting media are pastel and gold leaf, requiring artisans to repaint the vast mural every five years or so; it's likely you'll see a restorer working somewhere in the galleries.

Subsequent kings built more monuments and restored or embellished existing structures. Among the most interesting of these are the three pagodas to the immediate north of the ubosoth, representing the changing centers of Buddhist influence: the first, to the west, is **Phra Si Ratana Chedi,** a 19th-century Sri Lankan–style stupa housing ashes of the Buddha; in the middle is the library, or **Phra Mondop,** built in Thai style by Rama I, famous for its excellently crafted Ayutthaya-style mother-of-pearl doors, and inside, bookcases containing the *Tripitaka* (sacred Buddhist manuscripts), human- and dragon-headed nagas (snakes) and, surrounding the building, statues of Rama kings; and to the east is the **Royal Pantheon,** built in Khmer style during the 19th century, where the Emerald Buddha was to be moved (but the building was deemed too small for the honor) and is open to the public in October for one day to commemorate the dynasty of the first Rama kings. To the immediate north of the library is a model of Angkor Wat, the most sacred of all Cambodian shrines, constructed by King Mongkut as a reminder that the neighboring state was under the dominion of Thailand. To the west of the ubosoth, near the entry gate, is a black stone statue of a hermit, considered a patron of medicine, before whom relatives of the ill and infirm pay homage and make offerings of joss sticks, fruit, flowers, and candles.

Scattered around the complex are statues of elephants, considered by Thais to represent independence and power. Thai kings fought on elephants, and it is customary for parents to walk their children around an elephant three times to bring them strength. We enjoyed participating in a uniquely Thai custom of rubbing the head of elephant statues, considered a good luck ritual; notice how shiny the heads are from polishing by millions of superstitious palms!

Wat Phra Keo is open daily from 8:30 to 11:30 a.m. and 1 to 3:30 p.m.; admission is 125 baht ($5) and includes the Vivanmek Palace.

The Grand Palace

One of King Rama I's earliest accomplishments was to begin the process of rebuilding the capital in the image of Ayutthaya. The construction of the Grand Palace and Wat Phra Keo was the first phase of his grand goal, though both were added to and rebuilt in subsequent reigns. The palace, as it appears today, is greatly influenced by Western architectural styles, including colonial and Victorian motifs, dating from the regimes of Rama III, Rama IV, and Rama V. Perhaps the best-known Western figure to have lived in the royal complex was Anna, tutor to the son of Rama IV, who became the central figure in the story *The King and I* (which, by the way, is mostly fiction and not exactly a favorite topic of conversation among Thais; the film is in fact not shown in Thailand). Though the royal family moved to Chitrlada Palace after the death of King Ananda in 1946, the Grand Palace continues to hold its place in contemporary Thai life. It was here, in 1981, that General Chitpatima attempted to overthrow the government in an unsuccessful coup.

As you enter the gate, built in the 1780s, you'll come to the **Pavilion for Holy Water,** where priests purified themselves and swore loyalty to the royal family with the water from Thailand's four main rivers. Nearby is a lacquered-wood structure called the **Arporn Phimok Prasad** (Disrobing Pavilion), which was built for the king to conveniently mount his palanquin for royal elephant processions; most of the time it served as a kind of elephant parking lot. Nearby is the **Chakri Maha Prasad,** designed as a royal residence for Rama V by Western architects, to commemorate the centenary of the Chakri Dynasty. The king's advisors urged him to use Thai motifs to demonstrate his independence from growing Western influence, so the Thai temple-style roof rests physically and symbolically on top of an Imperial Victorian building. This Thai-Victorian building contains the ashes of members of the royal family on the third floor, the throne room and reception hall on the main floor, and a collection of weapons on the ground floor.

The whitewashed stone building nearby now serves as the **Funeral Hall,** though it originally was the residence of Rama I and Rama II. The corpse of the deceased royal figure is kept in this building for a year before it is cremated in a nearby field. On the four corners of the roof are garuda figures ("vehicles" for the Hindu God Rama), symbolizing the king, who is thought to be a reincarnation of Rama. The garden was rebuilt under Rama IV in the 1860s; the highlight here is a section that reproduces the landscape of a Thai mountain-and-woods fable. This structure was used as a ceremonial place for Thai princes to cut the top knot of their hair as a coming-of-age ritual.

The Grand Palace also has a harem building, or the **Forbidden Quarters** (no one other than the king was allowed to enter), where the king's wives lived. Close by is the Amarin Vinichai Prasad or the **Coronation Hall,** built by Rama I and added to by subsequent kings. Today this building is used, like the palace in general, for royal coronations, weddings, and state events only, and it is here that the king makes his most grand appearance.

The grounds of the Grand Palace are open daily from 8:30 to 11:30 a.m. and 1 to 3:30 p.m.; however, most of the individual buildings are closed to the public except for special days, proclaimed by the king, throughout the year. Admission is 125 baht ($5) Monday through Friday, and free on Saturday, Sunday, and Buddhist holidays.

WAT MAHATAT: This temple, still much in use, is a center of Buddhist meditation and study and is mostly known for its overwhelming amulet, talisman, and traditional medicine market on the periphery of the temple grounds. Each day hundreds of worshippers squat on the ground, magnifying glasses in hand, to study tiny images of the Buddha, hoping to find the one that will bring good fortune. (The other, newer amulet market is attached to Wat Rachanada, off the intersection of Mahachai Road and Rajadamnoen Klang, across from the Golden Mount at Wat Sakhet.) Inside the wat is a center for Vipassana meditation at the Buddhist University, with access for English-speaking guests to various programs. Inquire at Section 5 office for more information. Wat Mahatat itself is one of Bangkok's oldest shrines, built to house a relic of the Buddha.

The wat is open daily from 9 a.m. to 5 p.m. and is located on Na Phrathat Road, near Sanam Luang Park (in between Wat Phra Keo and the National Museum).

THE NATIONAL MUSEUM: The National Museum, a short walk north of the Temple of the Emerald Buddha, is the country's central treasury of art and archeology; 32 branches are located throughout the provinces. Here in Bangkok, some of the buildings themselves are works of art.

When the capital of Siam was moved from Thonburi to Bangkok in 1782, the Grand Palace was constructed on its present site on the banks of the Chao Phrya River. The current museum was built at that time as Wat Na or the Palace to the Front, the home of the princely successor to the king, often, though not always, a brother. The position of princely successor was eventually abolished and the Wang Na buildings came to house the museum. Thammasart University, the College of Dramatic Arts, and the National Theater were also built on the royal grounds, along with additional museum buildings.

If you want to see the entire collection (which we'd recommend), plan on spending about three hours, starting with the Thai History and the Prehistoric Galleries in the first building. If you're rushed, skip these and go straight to the **Red House** behind it, a traditional 18th-century Thai building that was originally the living quarters of Princess Sri Sudarak, sister of King Rama I. It is furnished in period style, with many pieces that were owned by the princess.

Another essential stop is the **Phutthaisawan Chapel,** built in 1787 to house the Buddhist figure Phra Buddhasihing, brought here from its original home in Chiang Mai. It is an exquisite example of Buddhist temple architecture decorated with beautiful murals, mosaics, and carvings.

From the chapel, work your way back through the **main building** of the royal palace and an eclectic collection from Thailand's splendid past. The precious objects room contains gold jewelry, some from the royal collections. There is a fine collection of Thai ceramics, including many pieces in the five-color Bencharong style. There is a room of ivory carvings, the "Old Transportation Room" with its elephant chairs and royal palanquins, rooms of royal emblems and insignia, stone carvings, woodcarvings, costumes, textiles, musical instruments, and Buddhist religious artifacts.

We loved the collection of royal funeral chariots, but the connoisseurs of fine art and sculpture will spend most of their time in the newer galleries at the rear of the museum compound. Here, gallery after gallery are filled with both Thai and pre-Thai sculpture (including some excellent Mon work), and Hindu and Buddhist images from the provinces.

The museum is open from 9 a.m. to noon and 1 to 5 p.m. daily except Monday and Friday. English-language tours are offered at 9:30 a.m. on Tuesday, Wednesday, and Thursday (call 224-1333 or check with the newspaper or TAT for the current schedule) and are worth the trip. Admission is 25 baht ($1). It is located about a 15-minute walk north of the Grand Palace, on Na Phra That Road, opposite the colorful Pramane Grounds, used for sports and kite-flying by locals.

LAK MUANG (CITY PILLAR): Northeast of the Grand Palace complex, appropriately near the Defense Department Building on Sanam Chai Road, is a delightful, diminutive shrine said to be inhabited by the spirit that protects the city of Bangkok. Rama I placed a stone pillar, perhaps harkening back to the Hindu custom of installing a lingam (phallic symbol) at the center of its Shiva temples, to mark the site of the city's guardian soul. Lak Muang was recently renovated, and though it isn't on most tourist itineraries, many locals pay tribute to this shrine and there is often Thai classical dancing performed (a little before noon) to amuse the spirit.

WAT PO (TEMPLE OF THE RECLINING BUDDHA): Wat Po, also called Wat Phra Chetuphon, was built by Rama I and is the oldest (originally built in the 16th century) and largest Buddhist temple in Bangkok. The compound is divided into two sections by Chetuphon Road (a 15-minute walk south of the Grand Palace): the northern area contains the most important monuments and southern portion serves as the living quarters for resident monks. Most people go straight to the enormous Reclining Buddha (in the northern section), built during the reign of Rama III in the middle of the 19th century and measuring over 140 feet in length and 50 feet high. The statue is built of brick and covered with layers of lacquer, plaster, and always-flaking gold leaf. It was being regilded and restored when we visited in 1988. As impressive as the body of the recumbent figure is, we suggest that you head for the feet, which are inlaid with mother-of-pearl illustrations of 108 "auspicious" signs of the Buddha. Be sure to notice the traces of the well-painted murals representing scenes of Thai life from past centuries.

Outside, the grounds contain 91 chedis, four viharns (halls), and a bot (the central shrine in a Buddhist temple), with the most impressive (aside from the Reclining Buddha) being the four main chedis dedicated to the first four Rama kings and, nearby, the library. (We found Wat Po among the most photogenic of all the wats in Bangkok, so don't forget your camera and film.)

Of all of the major temples in Bangkok, Wat Po is one of the most active, with monks living and studying Buddhism as well as running a school for traditional massage in the compound. In fact, the temple is considered the first public university in Thailand, with many of the monuments explaining principles of art, religion, science, and literature. In the past, visitors entered the grounds to study the inscriptions and illustrations. They also dropped (and still drop) 1-satong pieces in 108 bronze bowls, corresponding to the 108 auspicious signs of the Buddha, to bring them good fortune and to make a contribution to the upkeep of the wat and its monks. Today visitors are encouraged to learn about traditional Thai massage and medicine at the Traditional Medical Practitioners Association center. Although we enjoyed a fabulously restorative Thai medical massage here—80 baht ($3.25) for 30 minutes, 120 baht ($4.75) for an hour—those with sensitive muscles may prefer to abstain and watch instead.

The grounds are open daily from 8 a.m. to 5 p.m.; admission is 15 baht (60¢). Generally, massages are offered in the late afternoon; for more information, call 222-0933.

WAT ARUN (TEMPLE OF DAWN): The 260-foot-high, Khmer-inspired prang (Khmer-style cactus-shaped tower) majestically rises on the western banks of the Chao Phrya, across from Wat Po. This ribbed, cactus-shaped tower, Phra Prang, forms the centerpiece of a religious complex that served as the royal chapel during King Taksin's reign, when Thonburi was the capital of Thailand. The original tower measured only 50 feet high, but was greatly expanded during Taksin's rule. The exterior, which from a distance takes on a Sangkalok green cast, is decorated with shards of tiles, plates, cups, saucers, and other ceramics formed into the shape of flowers and other decorative motifs. At the base of the complex are Chinese stone statues, gifts from Chinese merchants; like the Chinese statues in Wat Phra Keo, these stone images were used as ballast in trading ships. Nearby there are also small statues of King Taksin.

You can ascend the central prang. However, be warned that the steps are treacherously large and steep, and are even more precarious on the descent. As you go up, notice the caryatids as well as the Hindu deities atop the three-headed elephants. The view of the river, Wat Po, and the Grand Palace is inspiring and well worth the climb.

For those who stay below, be sure to walk around the back of the tower to the monastic living quarters where the quiet is broken only by the tinkling sound of bells. Even during the height of the season, a walk to the rear of Wat Arun will lead you into a tranquil world where the gentle breezes floating in from the river will give you, for a moment, that sense of inner peace that many of the saffron-robed monks seek.

Although it's called the Temple of Dawn, we suggest visiting in the late afternoon for the best light and marvelous vistas over Bangkok. The temple is open daily from 8:30 a.m. to 5:30 p.m.; admission is 10 baht (40¢). To get to Wat Arun, take a water taxi from Tha Tien pier (at Wat Po) or cross the Phra Pinklao Bridge and follow the river south on Arun Amarin Road.

WANG SUAN PAKKARD: One of our favorite places in all of Bangkok is Wang Suan Pakkard, or the Palace of the Cabbage Garden. This off-the-beaten-path site was the home of Princess Chumbhot of Nagara Svarga, located behind a tall wooden fence at 352 Sri Ayutthaya Rd., near Phaya Thai Road (tel. 245-4934). Five elegant 19th-century teak houses were moved in 1952 from Chiang Mai and reconstructed in a tranquil garden on a private klong, seemingly a thousand miles from the tumult of Bangkok. In addition to the teak houses there is a Lacquer Pavilion, actually an Ayutthaya house moved here in 1958, that was given as a birthday present from the prince to the princess; it was originally the king's library.

The princess was an avid art collector and one of the country's most dedicated connoisseurs. In fact, she is credited with having partly financed the excavations at Ban Chiang in 1967, which led to the discovery of an agricultural society dating from 5,000 to 7,000 years ago. There is an entire room of objects from that site, including pottery and jewelry, surpassing what's on display in the National Museum.

The balance of the collection is fairly diverse, with items ranging from Khmer sculpture to ivory boxes, perfume bottles, Niello ware, and wonderful prints made by European artists of their image of Siamese people before the days of Prince Narai's opening to the Western world. There is a fabulous Buddha head from Ayutthaya on display in the garden, as well as a royal barge, ready to float up to Chiang Mai, in the klong. Be sure to ask to see the pavilion housing the princess's collection of Thai and Chinese ceramics—it's exquisite.

The gift shop at Wang Suan Pakkard has some fine pieces of Thai ceramics at very fair prices. Many collectors bring items to the museum that are ultimately bought but not put on display. Some of these are sold to other collectors or the public.

Wang Suan Pakkard is open Monday through Saturday from 9 a.m. to 4 p.m.; admission is 100 baht ($4), and for the price there is an excellent tour of the grounds and collections.

JIM THOMPSON'S HOUSE:

Jim Thompson was an architect from New York City who served in the OSS in Thailand during World War II and afterward settled in Bangkok. He single-handedly revived Thailand's silk industry, employing Thai Muslims who were skilled silk weavers and building a manufacturing industry around this cottage industry. After establishing the industry and gaining access to international markets, Mr. Thompson mysteriously disappeared in the Cameron Highlands in Malaysia in 1967. His body has never been recovered, and despite extensive investigations, the case has never been resolved.

His legacy is substantial, both as an entrepreneur and as a collector. Mr. Thompson's traditional Thai wooden house, located at the end of Soi Kasemsan 2, off Rama I, contains a sumptuous display of Khmer sculpture (some of the best we've ever seen), Chinese porcelain, wooden Burmese carving (in particular, a 17th-century teak Buddha), and antique Thai scroll paintings.

Thompson's training as an architect paid off handsomely if his house is any measure of his skill. It comprises six linked teak and theng (harder than teak) wood houses from northern Thailand that were rebuilt according to Thai architectural principles, but with Western ideas (such as a staircase). In some rooms the floor is made of Italian marble, but the panels are pegged teak. The house slopes toward the center to help stabilize the structure (the originals were built on stilts and had no foundation). Upstairs is a wonderful sitting room and balcony with a view of the garden. The house overlooks a klong that was once home to Mr. Thompson's first weavers (long since gone). Still, the densely landscaped garden is a lovely spot, especially on a hot day.

Jim Thompson's House is open every day, except Sunday, from 9 a.m. to 4:30 p.m.; admission is 125 baht ($5), 30 baht ($1.25) for students. All profits support several local charities. Call 215-0122 for more information.

If you wish to purchase silk from the Jim Thompson Company retail shop, head for the intersection of Surawong and Rama IV. There you'll find a busy, high-priced shop with finely made material, although we found the clothes somewhat old-fashioned.

WAT BENJAMABOPHIT (THE MARBLE WAT):

This early-20th-century temple was designed by the half-brother of Rama V, King Chulalongkorn, and is the most modern of Bangkok's royal wats. The current king was a monk at this wat, conveniently located around the corner on Sri Ayutthaya between the Chitrlada Palace and the Government House.

Unlike the older complexes, there is no truly monumental viharn or chedi dominating the grounds. In its place are many smaller buildings reflecting a melding of European materials and design motifs with traditional Thai religious architecture. The courtyards are made of polished Carrera marble. Be sure to walk inside the compound, beyond the main bot, to view the many Buddhas—ancient and modern, standing, sitting, and walking—that represent various regional styles. During the early-morning hours, monks chant in the main chapel. On our last trip, we visited on a day when there was a conclave of monks from around the country, and they chanted so intensely that we thought the temple was going to lift off!

The wat is open daily until 5 p.m.; admission is 15 baht (60¢).

WAT BOVORNIVES: Although few visitors bother to come to this temple, we find it one of the most rewarding. Located on Phra Sumein Road opposite the old town wall, it's a quiet retreat and you can wander along the pathways that lead between the monks' quarters and over the waterways that are occupied by many a sun-basking turtle. Many kings have served as monks here, including Prince Mongkut (later King Rama IV), who served as abbot here for 14 years. The two buddhas inside the bot are particularly impressive. The smaller one in front comes from Sukhothai and was cast in bronze there in 1257 to celebrate the country's liberation from Khmer rule. Note also the murals, several of which depict farangs in Thailand—the English at a horse race, American missionaries disembarking, and Germans prospecting for minerals.

WAT SUTHAT: This temple, located near the intersection of Bumrung Muang and Ti Thong Road, at Sao Chingcha square, is immediately identifiable by the giant teak arch in front, all that remains of an original giant swing. Until 1932 this swing was used in a ceremony to thank Shiva for the bountiful rice harvest and to ask for the god's blessing on the next. The minister of rice, accompanied by hundreds of Brahman court astrologers, would parade around the city walls to the temple precinct. At the giant swing he would observe several teams of men riding the swing as high as 82 feet into the air and attempting to grab a bag of silver coins between their teeth. Although the swing ceremony has been discontinued, the festival of thanksgiving is still celebrated in mid-December after the rice harvest.

The temple is among the oldest and largest in Bangkok. It was built by Rama I, and one of the viharn's doors was in fact carved by him. It houses a beautiful 14th-century Phra Buddha Shayamuni that was brought from Sukhothai. The wall paintings for which it is well known were done during Rama III's reign; note also the frescoes on the pillars. Outside the viharn stand many Chinese pagodas, bronze horses, and figures of Chinese soldiers. Well worth visiting.

Open daily from 9 a.m. to 5 p.m.

VIVANMEK MANSION: Built in 1901 by King Chulalongkorn the Great (Rama V), this large teakwood building was only recently restored and reopened by Her Majesty Queen Sirikit as a private museum displaying a fascinating collection of the royal family's memorabilia. The hour-long tour will take you through a series of apartments and rooms. Among the highlights are the Trophy Room, the king's working room, the library with ivory items, and in a series of other rooms, displays of blue and white china, tortoiseshell boxes, enamels, musical instruments, thrones, weapons, portraits, and old photographs. The building itself is quite beautiful.

Admission is 50 baht ($2); less if you combine it with a visit to the Grand Palace and Wat Phra Keo. Open daily from 9:30 a.m. to 3 p.m.

KAMTHIENG HOUSE (THE SIAM SOCIETY): Like Wang Suan Pakkard, the Kamthieng House, on the grounds of the Siam Society Headquarters at 131 Soi Asoke, off Sukhumvit 21 (tel. 258-3491), is a transplanted teak house from Chiang Mai in the north. Unlike the Pakkard palace, this 19th-century house is home to a collection of ethnographic objects illustrating the culture of everyday life. The house was moved from Chiang Mai in the 1960s and the museum was organized with financial help from the Asia Foundation and the Rockefeller Foundation. There are many agricultural and domestic items on display in this fine collection, but we were most drawn to the exhibits concerning the hill tribes of the north. If you plan to trek through this area, you would particularly enjoy this small but informative collection.

In addition to the teak buildings and the museum, we enjoyed walking through the grounds, which are landscaped like a northern Thai garden, with representative flora.

The Siam Society supports an excellent library and gallery, at the same location, concentrating on regional culture. They also publish scholarly texts on Thai culture. The museum is open Tuesday through Saturday from 9 a.m. to noon and 1 to 5 p.m.; admission is 25 baht ($1), free for students.

WAT TRAIMIT (TEMPLE OF THE GOLDEN BUDDHA): One of the

most astonishing Buddhas, said to be cast of solid gold, is housed in a most unpretentious viharn near the train station, on Traimit Road. Ten feet high and weighing over five tons, this powerful image has such a reflective, polished finish that its edges seem to disappear. The seated statue was supposed to have been cast during the Sukhothai period, though it has a strangely robotic appearance to us.

The story of this Buddha is as fantastic as its appearance. Not long ago, a large stucco Buddha, believed to be from Ayutthaya, was being temporarily stored, and during a storm, water poured onto the statue, creating cracks in the stucco. Some pieces fell off, revealing a gold surface underneath. The stucco was removed and the Golden Buddha revealed. Pieces of its protective exterior, thought to have been applied to disguise this valuable image during the Burmese invasions in the 18th century, are on display in a case to the left of the Buddha.

To find Wat Traimit, go to the intersection of Krung Kasem and Charoen Krung (a continuation of Rama IV, at the train station end of the road), walk southwest on Traimit Road, and look for a school with a playground. The wat is located up a flight of stairs overlooking the school. If you're in need of a snack there's a pretty good place right below the wat for a quick bite.

The wat is open from 9 a.m. to 5 p.m. daily; there is no admission fee.

MARKETS: If you're there on a weekend, don't miss the **Weekend Market.** It

covers a vast area with rows and rows of stalls selling everything you could possibly dream of—fresh crabs and seafood, dried seafood, chilis piled high in great baskets and other vegetables, blue vases and other pottery, live fish that are scooped from tanks, live chicks, orchids, clothes, foods of all sorts, and a host of strange exotic items that you won't know what to call. It's a great way to introduce yourself to the exotic sights, flavors, and colors of Thai life. Located at Chatuchak Park, off the Airport Highway. Open on Saturday and Sunday.

Pak Klong Talaat (also called the Talaat Taywait) is home to Bangkok's **cut-flower market** and one of the city's inspiring sites. Located along the Chao Phyra on Luk Luang, it's open 24 hours. Huge bushels of cut flowers and vegetables arrive at the market every night and buyers from all around the city do their shopping in the very early morning hours. If you're wandering around the city after midnight and are looking for an offbeat attraction, shop at the Flower Market, selecting from baskets or orchids, lotus, jasmine, marigolds, and many more. You'll pay about 50 baht ($2) for a lovely bunch of orchids. You can also watch the flower vendors threading leis and assembling the huge, colorful, intricately patterned funeral wreaths.

For additional markets, see "Shopping."

RED CROSS SNAKE FARM: If you missed the Thonburi Snake Farm on the Floating Market tour, you might want to stop by the Thai Red Cross Snake Farm in the heart of Bangkok on the Red Cross grounds on Rama IV, east of Surawong Road, near the Montien Hotel (tel. 252-0161). This center was established in 1923 and was only the second such facility in the world (the first was in Brazil). There is a half-hour snake-handling demonstration weekdays at 11 a.m. and 2:30 p.m., on weekends and holidays at 11 a.m. only. In an attraction exhibition area you can watch the handlers work with deadly cobras, and you'll cringe (we did) when they pick up a handful of equally menacing banded kraits, as well as a green pit viper. They also demonstrate venom milking to stockpile antidote for those who're snapped at by ominous serpents. Admission is 50 baht ($2).

In case you want a souvenir, the Thai Red Cross will also inoculate you against other maladies, such as typhoid, cholera, and smallpox.

KITE FIGHTING: One of Bangkok's favorite sport is kite fighting, a team event with sponsors and prizes. The sport is seasonal, extending from February through April, and is held in the city's main parks. The two major sites are Sanam Luang (Pramane Grounds) just north of Wat Phra Keo, and Lumpini Park, near the Snake Farm. Even if you aren't part of a team, you can buy a colorful "male" or "female" kite here and just send it flying into the sky.

COCK, BEETLE, AND FISH FIGHTING: These three spectator sports are largely held in marketplaces, such as the Weekend Market, and are betting vehicles for the gambling Thai. In addition to pugnacious cocks, Siamese fighting fish and large-horned beetles are the favored participants in these bouts. Some markets offer these animals for sale with the average price of a fighting fish at 180 baht ($7.25). Children train crickets for fighting and arrange bets on these battles.

TAI CHI: Though Tai Chi is of Chinese descent, this Asian stretching exercise regimen is practiced in Thailand by Chinese and Thai alike. As usual, you'll have to get up early in the morning to witness (or participate in) this ritual. Lumpini Park, at the intersection of Rama IV and Wireless Road, is a center of Tai Chi.

DUSIT ZOO AND THE CELESTIAL RESIDENCE: The **Dusit Zoo** (also called Khao Din Wana) is set in a lovely park, between the Chitrlada Royal Palace and the National Assembly, at Rama V and Ratwithi Road. In addition to the gardens and many indigenous Asian animals (including royal white elephants), you can rent paddleboats and float on the pond. Children love riding the elephants, while tired parents are often seen sitting at one of the zoo's cafés under broad shade trees. The Dusit Zoo is open daily from 7 a.m. to 6 p.m.; admission is 6 baht (25¢).

Behind the National Assembly is the **Phra Thi Nang Vimanmek,** otherwise known as the Celestial Residence. This 81-room all-teak palace is thought to be the largest teak pavilion in the world. Tours are run from 9:30 a.m. to 4 p.m.

6. SHOPPING

It may not have the reputation of Hong Kong or Singapore, but Bangkok will dazzle you with both elegant and exotic shopping opportunities. The city's many markets, ranging from the most primitive to ultra-chic modern malls, offer even the most world-weary shopper unusual, high-quality goods at extremely reasonable prices. Thailand is internationally renowned for its excellent silk and precious stones (including sapphires and rubies) as well as fine gold jewelry, but less known in the Western world are its enormously appealing handcrafts and antiques (including Khmer and Burmese work), finely carved teak sculpture, bronze, niello, and silverware, as well as leather goods made from the country's many unusual reptiles. (U.S. travelers should be aware of their country's strict Customs laws against bringing back items made from skins of animals and reptiles on endangered species lists.)

HELPFUL HINTS: There are a few rules concerning shopping in Thailand. First, be prepared to bargain; it's the accepted mode of commerce in all but the very best stores. Second, if you plan on purchasing an expensive item, do your research by shopping in several stores to determine a range of prices for similar goods. When you're ready to buy, you'll have a much better idea how much you should ultimately pay for a given object. Third, try to check out the store you intend to buy from with local people. This is tricky, because so many places pay commissions that you never know whether you're getting straight information; however, if you have friends in the city who know about individual shops or you have a trusty concierge, you'll be one giant step ahead.

One place to begin your research is a handy guide published by TAT entitled *Official Shopping Guide,* which is revised frequently and confers on listed establishments the status of a reliable, quality business. Actually, a commission reviews a vast number of shops in Bangkok and only recognizes those that operate on a high standard with fair trading practices. We suppose this is the Thai equivalent of the Better Business Bureau.

WHERE TO SHOP: There are many shopping areas in Bangkok, so it's advisable to plan your shopping itinerary with a map. Once again we recommend Nancy Chandler's excellent *Map of Bangkok* also known as *The Market Map and Much More.* This is an indispensable guide to some of Bangkok's best stores and shopping regions. The map is on sale at most bookstores and in many hotel newsstands. If you're serious about shopping, buy this map!

Most major hotels have shopping arcades. In many cases, these contain quality shops with respectable reputations, though their prices are often much higher than those in less upscale neighborhoods. The best arcades, in our opinion, are those at the **Oriental and Regent Hotels.** Similar price and quality goods are found in the high-end malls, particularly at **River City,** located next to the Royal Orchid Sheraton. **Siam Square** and the nearby **Mah Boon Krong Center** are centrally located and thoroughly modern shopping malls with a tremendous range of goods.

Specific streets or areas are known for excellent shopping. Among these are the **Chinatown streets off Sampeng Lane,** where one finds the so-called Thieves Market, the Pahurat cloth market, and a million and one notions stands; the compact **Bangrak Market,** behind the Shangri-la Hotel; **Sukhumvit Road** with its upscale antiques and handcrafts shops as well as bookstores; **Silom and Surawong Roads,** between the Oriental and Lumpini Park; **Thewarat Market,** the wholesale flower outlet; and the new **weekend market** at Chatuchak Park.

Bangkok also supports several **department store** chains with the **Central** as the largest; the most accessible branches are on lower Silom Road, Ploenchit Road near the Meridian President, and off the highway near the airport, next to the Hyatt. We also like browsing in the glitzy **Thai Tokyu** department store in the Mah Boon Krong Center.

Of course, we couldn't conclude a section on shopping choices in Bangkok without mentioning **street vendors.** Though they are hardly the most reliable purveyors of goods, you can nearly always purchase delightful souvenirs from these dealers, and if you're a good bargainer, at the lowest prices in Bangkok. The best stalls are along Silom Road, near the Silom Village, near the Nana Hotel off Sukhumvit, Soi 4, and in Chinatown.

HANDCRAFTS: An excellent outlet for Thai, Burmese, and Lao handcrafts is the **House of Handicrafts,** located at 20A on the second floor of the Sukon

Court, at 46 North Sathorn Rd. across from the YMCA (tel. 234-3021). They carry exceptional hand-carved and painted puppets and dolls as well as other traditional Thai crafts, including fine textiles. They also have a smaller outlet in the Regent of Bangkok arcade. The **Lotus** shop in the same arcade carries fine Thai and Tibetan textiles.

One of our favorite all-purpose shops is the **Thai Home Industries,** a short walk from the Oriental Hotel on Oriental Avenue (tel. 234-1736). The energetic elderly women who run this expansive emporium carry a wide range of Thai crafts including bronze work, spirit houses, carved wooden ornaments, and other decorative objects. Nearby on the second floor of the Oriental Plaza is the **Anong Gallery** (tel. 235-7991), where you can purchase modern clothing fabricated with hill-tribe embroidered material.

The royal family, in their ongoing effort to encourage production of Thai handcrafts, sponsors several stores in Bangkok. The **Chitrlada Shop** in the Oriental Plaza Arcade as well as the **Hill Tribe Foundation** at the Srapatum Palace sell good-quality Thai and hill-tribe crafts at reasonable prices.

ANTIQUES: If you intend to purchase antiques, you should know that certain items, such as Buddha images, cannot legally be taken out of Thailand and Thai Customs is extremely vigilant on this point. Also, there are a great many well-crafted fakes that sell at prices fetched by originals; if you plan on buying an expensive item, be sure to purchase it from a reputable dealer. Unfortunately, that will not guarantee its authenticity but at least you'll have a better chance of finding the genuine article. Below are some of the shops that we feel carry aesthetically pleasing objects.

The oldest antique shops in Bangkok are **Monogram I and II** (tel. 235-1875), located in the Oriental Hotel and the nearby Oriental Arcade. We found some gorgeous carved wooden sculpture and finely embroidered Burmese tapestries here, but be warned that the prices are as high here as anywhere in Bangkok. **Peng Seng,** a venerable antique shop located at 942/1-3 Rama IV Rd. (tel. 233-1891), near Jim Thompson's, is also popular with collectors.

It used to be that Charoen Krung (New Road) and the smaller outlet roads near the Oriental were lined with antique shops. Though there are still many dealers in this congested area, some of the finest shops moved to the notable **River City shopping mall,** creating Bangkok's greatest concentration of high-end antique galleries. If you want to get a taste of what Thai antiques are like, head here for you're certain to find something to your taste among the many, many shops. Be warned that the River City shops are, like the Monogram stores, the most expensive in the city. We like several shops on the fourth and third floors. On the fourth floor, in Suite 438-440 is **Charoon Antiques** (tel. 235-2972), which sells lovely stone friezes, a large quantity of Khmer sculpture, and other Thai statuary. On the same floor, in Suite 452, is a shop run by **Piak Padungsiriseth** (tel. 235-2972), which has superb wood sculpture. Again on the fourth floor, in Suite 446 is **The Old Time** (tel. 235-2973), with many Khmer stone sculptures and impressive antique furniture. On the third floor, in Suite 306, is **Chinawat Antiques** (tel. 235-2970), which presents its elegant wares in a more tasteful manner than the other glitzy shops. We judged many of their goods to be true art objects, worthy of a superior collection. Nearby, in Suite 304, is the **Golden Triangle,** a shop quite unlike anything else in River City. This simple boutique carries antique textiles and hill-tribe clothing, reminding us more of the fine shops in Chiang Mai than the outlets in Bangkok.

Asian Heritage, located at 57 Soi 23, off Sukhumvit Road (tel. 392-0672), displays expensive furniture, sculpture, and art in a private Thai home. The proprietress speaks excellent English and will ship purchases to the United States. We also found some fine objects at reasonable prices at **Noi Umpawa,** on Sukhumvit Road between Soi 14 and Soi 16.

JEWELRY: Bangkok, which serves as a major trading point for both sapphires and rubies, just may have some of the best jewelry values in Southeast Asia, if only because these highly marked-up gems pass through fewer hands. In addition, the overall quality of gold and silver work throughout the country is excellent. Both metals' price is set by international commodity exchanges, so don't expect any bargains there, but labor is inexpensive and exceptionally talented, making jewelry a good buy in Thailand.

In days past, the most popular item was the princess ring, a tiered decorative band with a myriad of stones; the typical configuration includes a ruby, emerald, topaz, garnet, sapphire, moonstone, and brown zircon. One can still find this traditional souvenir, but today there is an enormous range of work, from a simple gold chain or string of pearls to contemporary designs festooned with fabulously expensive gems destined for showrooms along Fifth Avenue in Manhattan. Again, the best advice is to shop around at several stores before buying, so that you can compare both quality and price.

Before mentioning any specific places by name, we were told repeatedly by knowledgeable locals that nearly all jewelers who display their work in the very best hotel shopping arcades produce fine-quality work at fair prices. Those singled out were the many shops in the **Dusit Thani** arcade as well as those at the **Regent of Bangkok.**

One of the more reliable jewelers in Bangkok is Uthai Daengrasmisopon, who runs **Uthai's Gems,** located at 28/7 Soi Ruam Rudee, off Ploenchit Road (tel. 253-8582); Uthai has been a jeweler for 32 years, 7 at his own outlet. Uthai's shop was referred to us by staffers at the American and British embassies as well as by local friends. Upon visiting we found lovely one-carat sapphire rings in a 14-karat-gold setting for about $200; a comparable ruby ring runs about $800. Uthai sells princess rings for $85. His gold chains are handcrafted in 22-karat-gold and are priced by weight with an added fixed charge for workmanship. We were impressed with the amount of custom work that Uthai performs; he generally allows two days to a week for most pieces. Uthai also runs a mail-order business, so you can send photographs of pieces you'd like copied and he can accommodate your request. We highly recommend this shop.

Johnny's Gems, in Chinatown (tel. 222-1706), is one of Bangkok's oldest and largest jewelry emporia, and it enjoys a fine reputation for reliability and price. The added virtue of Johnny's is that they will shuttle you between their store and your hotel.

Among the other reliable dealers in Bangkok are **A.A. Jewelry,** at 104 Siam Square (tel. 251-4920); **New Universal,** at 1144-46 New Rd. (tel. 234-3514); and for pearls, **Tok Kwang,** at 224-6 Silom Rd. (tel. 233-0658).

SILK: It's nearly impossible to mention silk in Thailand without referring in some way to Jim Thompson (see Jim Thompson's House in "What to See and Do in the City"), the legendary American who founded the modern Thai industry of silk weaving. Even if you don't visit his company's elegant shop, the **Jim Thompson Thai Silk Company,** at 9 Surawong Rd. (tel. 234-4900), most competitors will compare their workmanship and price with his goods, giving you yet another reason to visit this near tourist attraction. If you're looking for top-drawer goods, including finely woven cotton, Thompson's is the place—but expect to pay for the pleasure. Kyle had a long-sleeve shirt made (four yards of single-weight printed silk) for about 1,750 baht ($70). She also bought some scarves for 175 baht ($7) each, as well as wonderful silk pajamas for 2,400 baht ($96). John bought a tie for 400 baht ($16) and some pillow covers for 475 baht ($19). Jim Thompson Thai Silk Company is open every day from 9 a.m. to 8 p.m.

The other big silk outlet, **Shinawatra,** is at 94 Soi 23, off Sukhumvit Road (tel. 258-0295), with branches in Chiang Mai and Pattaya. Here you'll find good-quality material at prices slightly lower than Thompson's.

We also like **Home Made Thai Silk,** at 45 Soi 35, off Sukhumvit Road (tel. 258-8766). The quality of their silk is excellent and it's the only shop we found where you can see silk being woven.

There are also very good silk outlets in the international hotel shopping arcades.

SHOES AND LEATHER GOODS: Many people leave Bangkok wearing shoes and cowboy boots made from ostrich, elephant, snake, alligator, or other exotic leathers. We found a huge range of shoes and boots made from these materials at **S.P. Bootery,** in the River City shopping complex (tel. 235-2966). There are many such shops along New Road near the Oriental that also carry wallets (for about $10) and purses. Prices for boots range from $75 to $300.

Many shoe stores will also custom-make footwear and carry other leather accessories. Try **Patou,** in the Indra Shopping Center on Ratchadamri Road (tel. 251-3971), for finely crafted shoes; they sell locally produced Charles Jourdan and other high-fashion shoes. Another excellent outlet for shoes, boots, and a full range of leather accessories is **Chao Phrya Bootery,** at 116/3 Silom Rd. (tel. 234-1226); they also have a branch at 266-268 Sukhumvit Rd., near Soi 19. In addition to their large inventory, they also do efficient custom work.

BRONZE/NICKEL WORK: Most of the major handcrafts, silk, or jewelry shops also carry bronze (or bronze and nickel alloy) flatware. We loved the hand-made quality and weight of these Thai-designed sets. We purchased a complete set for 12 at **Uthai's Gems,** including every possible implement, for $150. There are many different sets available at the **Thai Home Industries Shop** for similar prices. Be aware that such sets weigh up to 50 pounds and will have to be shipped home; expect to pay an additional $50 for postage.

7. NIGHTLIFE

Bangkok has one of the livelier nightlife scenes in all Asia, with a range of activities that should satisfy anyone. Probably the most popular evening events are the displays of Thai classical dance and music held at various restaurants (see "Dining"). For those who want to venture into other aspects of local culture, what follows is but a sample of evening alternatives.

TRADITIONAL CULTURE: The **National Theater,** near Sanam Louang, close to the National Museum (tel. 221-5861), presents demonstrations of Thai classical dancing and music with performers from the School of Music and Dance in Bangkok. These performances are generally much superior to those at the tourist restaurants and hotels. Performances are held on the last Friday of the month and on special occasions; call for the current schedule. One can also see demonstrations at the Oriental Hotel twice a week; in addition to dancing, the show includes examples of Thai boxing and sword fighting.

THAI BOXING: We are big fans of Thai boxing and heartily recommend it to anyone with an interest in genuine Thai culture.

There are two major stadia for boxing: **Lumpini Stadium,** on Rama IV, in the park of the same name, and **Rajadamnoen Stadium,** on Rajadamnoen Road. Bouts begin at 6 p.m. and go well into the evening. There are fights every night of the week, alternating between the two venues. Admission ranges from 125 baht ($5) to 550 baht ($22).

MOVIE THEATERS: There are movie theaters at nearly all of the shopping centers and malls in the city, such as Siam Square. Most of the main cinemas show recently released English-language films, some dubbed, others with subtitles. Ask your concierge to call the theater to determine whether the film is being shown in English. The American University Alumni (tel. 252-4021) and the British Council both show older films in English. Additionally, scan the local English-language tabloids for movie advertisements; they usually list all films shown in English.

DISCOS AND NIGHTCLUBS: Bangkok has a complete offering of discos from the elegant to the funky. The sophisticated crowd usually heads for **Diana,** at the Oriental (tel. 236-0400), or **Bubbles,** at the Dusit Thani (tel. 233-1130). Expect to pay between 350 baht ($14) and 400 baht ($16) for a two-drink cover price.

The most popular danceteria in Bangkok is the **Palace** on Viphavadi Rangsit Hwy. (tel. 278-5161), an enormous club frequented by the city's wildest youth. On the Thonburi side, try **Paradise Disco.** If you're out that way, **Hollywood,** in the Hyatt Central Plaza Hotel (tel. 541-1234), is also quite popular.

A more locally frequented nightclub and dance spot is the **Mandarina** (tel. 233-4980), at the Mandarin Hotel, which has a live singer and band belting out Thai and international tunes. There's a 140-baht ($5.50) cover charge weekdays, 275 baht ($11) on the weekend.

BARS: All the international hotels have very elegant bars. We particularly like the **Palm Court** at the Shangri-la for the view over the Chao Phrya River. The **Bamboo Bar** at the Oriental is a great rendezvous point for world travelers.

At Soi Patpong 2, **Bobby's Arms** (tel. 233-6828) is much frequented by the English crowd and features boisterous drinking and sing-alongs; they have Dixieland jazz every Sunday night at 8:30 p.m. **Napoleon's Lounge,** at 76 Patpong Rd. (tel. 236-4999), has jazz every night beginning at 7 p.m. **Firecat,** in Patpong, is quite popular with the local community; drinks are 60 baht ($2.50) and there's no cover charge.

One of the more popular bars with travelers on the cheap is **Woodstock** (also known as the **Rock 'n' Roll Bar**), at 210-213 Nana Plaza off Sukhumvit on Soi 4 (tel. 252-9174). They also have a food menu and rock videos.

GAY BARS: Bangkok, of course, has a large gay bar circuit. Among the top places are the **Super A Cocktail Lounge,** on Soi Anumanrachaton off Surawong Road; **My Way Gay Bar,** at 944/4 Rama IV Rd., with three floors of entertainment; **Bangkok Garden,** at 108/3 Sukhumvit Rd., Soi 49; and the **Silver Fox,** at 1/11 Sukhumvit Rd., Soi 24.

SEX CLUBS AND MASSAGE PARLORS: The song "One Night in Bangkok" was a huge international hit in 1985 and, though it was actually about chess (from the musical, *Chess*), the song was spiritually celebrating the naughtiest aspect of life in Bangkok. Since the 1960s—and particularly since the Vietnam War—Bangkok has served as the sin capital of Asia, with sex clubs, bars, massage parlors, and prostitutes concentrated in two districts, Patpong and so-called Soi Cowboy. Patpong Road is perpendicular to Silom and Suriwong Roads and functions as an international sex street fair. Soi Cowboy is located between Soi 21 and Soi 23 off Sukhumvit Road and is a less concentrated version of Patpong. There are V.D. clinics in both areas, as well as many dispensing pharmacies.

Two new sex club zones are the Nana Entertainment Plaza on Soi Nana, off Soi 3 Sukhumvit Road, and Washington Square, near Soi Cowboy.

Sex Clubs

It's just about impossible to wander around Patpong without a hawker approaching you with a laminated menu card, displaying the evening program at one of 75 or so sex clubs. The shows vary a bit, but you'll get the gist of it with the following: "Woman smoke cigarette. Woman and razor blades. Woman opens Coke bottle. Woman and Ping-Pong balls. Woman uses chopsticks. Woman and live fish." Yes, it's all here in Patpong. The shows tend to be pretty routine, though if you've never seen it, this is the place. Most clubs, such as Pink Pussycat, Cleopatra, Super Star, King's Castle, and James Bond, have two shows a night; the first begins at 10 p.m., the second goes on at midnight.

A Word of Warning: Most places try to get you in the door (always upstairs; downstairs is for seminude go-go dancing only), promising that there is no cover charge. Forget it! When you order your first drink they'll try to hit you with an outlandish bill, including a cover charge. Politely inform your waiter that you were told there wasn't such a charge and that you'll be happy to leave if there is a problem. They will haggle with you and, ultimately, you'll settle on an equitable price, but it's always best to ask in advance about charges for drinks, admission, show, and cover. Expect to pay about 300 baht ($12) for admission and a drink.

Massage Parlors

If you want to try a traditional medical massage, head for the school at Wat Po (see "What to See and Do in the City"); otherwise you can visit the health club at your hotel.

Another kind of massage heavily advertised in Bangkok is a body massage at any one of the city's hundreds of "modern" massage parlors. A body massage is not meant to relax your limbs—it involves the masseuse using her whole body, thoroughly soaped, to massage the customer. If one wishes, a "sandwich," with two masseuses, can also be ordered.

Nearly all massage parlors are organized along the same lines. Guests enter a lobby where there is a coffeeshop/bar and several waiting rooms where young Thai women, with numbers pinned on their blouses, sit on bleachers behind windows. Guests can examine the women from a distance and select their masseuse. Both guest and masseuse take a room in the building and typically spend between one and two hours on a massage. Rates for a hand rub run about 250 baht ($10); a body massage runs about 500 baht ($20), with a sandwich costing about 1,000 baht ($40). These rates are all negotiable and should include a long session. Most massage parlors are open from 5 p.m. and close at midnight. Among the most popular places are Darling, on Soi 12 off Sukhumvit Road, well known with local executives; Cleopatra, near the Imperial Hotel; Atami, at 1573 New Petchaburi Rd.; and La Cherie, at 25-35 Suriwong Rd.

Warning

Although Bangkok hosts many semi-licit and illicit activities, two that deserve special mention are drugs and AIDS. The waft of marijuana and the easy availability of other controlled substances shouldn't signify to any interested tourist that drugs are tolerated by the local authorities. The police frequently clamp down on both sellers and buyers, and ignorance of the law is not an accepted defense. As for AIDS, though the government claims there is scant incidence of the disease in Thailand, logic suggests that there is far more than is claimed.

8. DAY TRIPS FROM THE CITY

If you have time, there are plenty of easy day trips that can be taken from Bangkok. Favorite excursions include various cruises along the Chao Phrya to the more distant klongs as well as to the ancient capital of Ayutthaya, north of Bangkok, and the Bang Pa-In Summer Palace, which is on the way. History buffs will be drawn to the famous bridge over the River Kwai, at nearby Kanchanaburi in the east, in the heart of some of Thailand's lushest countryside, dotted with waterfalls. For those interested in animals, there are two crocodile farms of note, one near an exquisite rose garden. And if you're looking for a beach, you might want to head south to Hua Hin or, southeast, to Pattaya (see Chapter XX).

DAY TRIPS ON THE RIVER: Several river tours venture outside Bangkok. The *Oriental Queen,* a luxurious cruise boat operated by the Oriental Hotel (tel. 236-0400), leaves the Oriental Pier every day at 8 a.m. for the old capital city of Ayutthaya. Buses meet the boat in Ayutthaya for tours of the city ruins and the lovely Bang Pa-In Summer Palace. At 5 p.m. the buses leave for the two-hour return trip to Bangkok. You can also reverse the trip, traveling up by bus and returning by boat. Cost is 950 baht ($30) per person, including lunch, tour, and full transportation.

A cheaper excursion to Ayutthaya is offered by the **Chao Phrya Express Company** (tel. 222-5330). Boats leave the Maharaj Pier (off Maharaj Street, north of the Grand Palace) at 8:30 a.m. on Saturday, Sunday, and holidays. The Chao Phrya boat stops at the Thai Folk Arts and Handicraft Center, the Bang Pa-In Summer Palace in Ayutthaya, and the Pai Lom Temple, a sanctuary for open-bill storks (the best time to visit is from December to June). The all-day excursion is very popular with locals and costs a reasonable 160 baht ($6.50) per person, meals not included. There is no guide on this tour.

Another fascinating river trip is to the still authentic **Damnoen Saduak floating market** in Ratchaburi, about 109 km (68 miles) south of Bangkok. Most travel agents can arrange a tour there, in conjunction with a trip to the tallest Buddhist monument, the 380-foot-tall **Phra Pathom Chedi** (Great Golden Chedi) in Nakhon Pathom, the most ancient Dvaravati center and oldest town in Thailand. To do it on your own, take a bus for Damnoen Saduak from the Southern Bus Terminal on Charan Sanitwong Road. They leave every 20 minutes from 6 a.m., cost about 50 baht ($2) each way, and take about two hours. Leave early, since market activity peaks between 8 a.m. and 10 a.m. From the Damnoen Saduak station, walk along the canal or take a water taxi for 15 baht (60¢) to the floating market. You can also rent a boat for about 375 baht ($16) to 630 baht ($25.25) and explore it more fully. As always, negotiate with the driver and settle the price before you leave.

THE ANCIENT CITY: Imagine a giant map of Thailand spread over 200 acres, with the country's major landmarks built in miniature. This is what you'll find at the Ancient City. This instant tourist site was built on an empty rice field several years ago and is visited mainly by organized bus tours, though you can certainly go on your own. The Ancient City is open daily from 8:30 a.m. to 6 p.m.; admission is 60 baht ($2.50). The Ancient City is located at Kilometer 33 on the Sukhumvit Hwy., Samut Prakan province. For more information, contact the Ancient City Co., on Ratchadamnoen Avenue in Bangkok (tel. 222-8143).

CROCODILE FARM: There are two crocodile farms within metropolitan Bangkok. The first is three kilometers (two miles) from the Ancient City, at Kilometer 30 on the Sukhumvit Hwy. At this croc farm (tel. 395-0477) there are over 30,000 snappers, both fresh- and saltwater varieties. In addition to the crocodile display, there is a show in which handlers wrestle them in murky ponds. The crocodile farm is open daily from 8 a.m. to 6 p.m.; feeding takes place around 5 p.m. Admission is 100 baht ($4).

The other farm, a relatively new establishment called the Samphran Crocodile Farm and Zoo (tel. 294-5211), is half a mile north of the Rose Garden (see below). This 22-acre complex offers a garden-like environment and the usual croc-handling show. Hours are 9 a.m. to 6 p.m., with show times at 11 a.m. and 2 p.m.; admission is 100 baht ($4).

THE ROSE GARDEN COUNTRY RESORT: Besides its rose garden, this attractive if somewhat touristy resort is known for its all-in-one show of Thai culture that includes Thai classical and folk dancing, Thai boxing and sword fighting, and cock fighting. A convenient way for visitors making a brief visit to Thailand to digest some canned culture, it's a popular spot on the typical tourist circuit. Hours are 8 a.m. to 6 p.m. daily. Admission to the garden is 15 baht (60¢), and to the show, 175 baht ($7).

Surprisingly enough, the restaurant is very good and very appealing as it overlooks the Nakorn Chaisri River filled with islands of water hyacinth, affording an opportunity to watch the ever-flowing Thai river life. The tom yam kung and the green curry will set the taste buds afire; the pad thai noodles are good and so, too, is the somewhat strange-looking but very tasty spicy pla krob salad (dried fish with tamarind sauce). Main courses run 35 baht ($1.50) to 60 baht ($2.50). For more information, call 253-0295.

AYUTTHAYA: Only 72 kms (44½ miles) north of Bangkok, Ayutthaya has to be one of the great highlights of any trip to Thailand. Although most people take the standard day tour from Bangkok that allows only a few hours in Ayutthaya, this ancient city deserves more time, particularly to experience it at dawn and dusk. For 417 years from when it was founded in 1350 by King U-Thong, it was Thailand's capital and the seat of 33 kings of various dynasties. In its heyday, until the mid-18th century when it was destroyed by the Burmese, it was the Pearl of the East, a vast majestic city with three palaces, 400 splendid temples on an island threaded with 35 miles of canals—a city that mightily impressed European visitors. Traces of the two major foreign settlements can still be seen today. The Portuguese first arrived during Rama II's reign in 1511, and a collection of religious objects, coins, porcelain, clay pipes, and skeletons can be seen at the Settlement's memorial building. The Japanese are remembered by a recently erected stone with an inscription and a hall and gate.

There is something hauntingly sad about Ayutthaya. In 1756 after a 15-month siege, it was totally destroyed by the Burmese. Today every temple site testifies to the hatred that can drive human beings to rampant and wanton destruction. Here stands a whole row of headless Buddhas, there a head lies caught in the roots of a tree. It's as if each figure were torn limb from limb. Some of the temples are still being rescued from the jungle.

Getting There

There is both bus and train service from Bangkok. Trains leave Bangkok's Hua Lamphong Station, Rama IV Road, 20 times daily from 4:30 a.m. The trip takes 1¼ hours and costs 20 baht (80¢) in third class. Buses leave from the Northern Bus Terminal on Phaholyothin Road, every 30 minutes from 6 a.m. The one-hour trip costs 35 baht ($1.50).

The tours to Ayutthaya leave from the Oriental Hotel pier daily at 8 a.m. and visit Bang Pa-In also. You can choose to go by the *Oriental Queen* cruiser and return by air-conditioned coach or vice versa. Tickets, including buffet lunch, cost 950 baht ($38).

Getting Around

A minibus from the train station into town will cost about 8 baht (30¢). You can also hire a minibus for about 300 baht ($12) per day. Better yet, hire a long-tail or another boat and see the city the leisurely way. Cost? About 30 baht ($1.25) per hour.

What to See

You might start at the two branches of the National Museum. The main one is the **Chao Sam Phraya Museum,** on Rojana Road near the junction of Sri Sanphet Road. It houses some impressive antique bronze Buddha images, carved panels, religious objects, and other local artifacts. The other, the **Chandra Kasem Palace,** is itself a splendid building constructed in 1577 during the reign of King Maha Thamaraja, the 17th Ayutthaya monarch, as his son's residence (King Naresuan). It was totally destroyed but later restored by King Mongkut, who stayed here whenever he visited Ayutthaya. Objects on display include some very beautiful gold artifacts, jewelry, carvings, Buddhas, and domestic and religious objects from the 13th to the 17th century. Both museums are open Wednesday through Sunday from 9 a.m. to 3 p.m.; closed Monday and Tuesday.

Near the Chandra Kasem Museum, **Wiharn Phra Mongkol Bopit** houses Thailand's largest seated bronze Buddha in a somewhat cramped viharn built in 1956 in the style of the original, which was destroyed in 1767. It was either brought from or copied from Sukhothai and supposedly erected here in 1615 by King Ekatosaroth, in honor of his brother, Naresuan, who later drove the Burmese from Sukhothai in the 16th century and pursued them into Burma, after which they remained for 160 years at relative peace.

The old royal palace, **Wang Luang,** was totally destroyed by the Burmese, although the foundations of the three main buildings can still be made out and the visitor can only be impressed by the sheer size of the compound. Close by stands **Wat Phra Sri Sanphet,** originally built in 1448 to serve as the king's private chapel (the equivalent to the Emerald Buddha temple in Bangkok) and renovated in both the 16th and 17th centuries. The huge 55-foot-high bronze standing Buddha was originally cast in 1500 during the reign of the ninth king, Ramathipodi, and covered with gold. In 1767 the Burmese tried to melt the gold and the resultant fire destroyed the image and the temple. Still, the replica is awesome. Nearby is a line of three Sri Lankan–style chedis built during the 15th century to enshrine the ashes of three Ayutthaya kings.

To the east of the royal palace, the prang of **Wat Phra Ram** soars into the sky. Originally built in 1369 by King Ramesuen, second King of Ayutthaya, the remainder of the complex is in ruins.

Also to the east of the royal palace, the **Wat Mahathat,** at the corner of Chee Kun Road and Naresuan Road, built in 1374 during the third king's reign, overwhelms with the tragic proportions of its destruction. The site is strewn with Buddhas broken off at the neck or at the base of the torso; somber Buddha images litter the ground, some propped up, others clutched by tree roots. The giant prang is also truncated and only half its original size.

Opposite Wat Mahathat stands **Wat Rajaburana,** which was built in 1424 and has been splendidly restored. The prangs and chedis are magnificent and have retained some of the original stucco. When the prang was excavated, bronze Buddha images and votive tablets as well as golden objects and jewelry were found in its two crypts. There are also mural paintings, rows of seated Buddhas, standing disciples, and *Jataka* (tales from the Buddha's former lives) scenes in the four niches, as well as a frieze of heavenly beings and some Chinese scenes. Both are severely damaged despite restoration.

A very large impressive Buddha can be seen at **Wat Phanan Choeng,** a temple that was built in 1324, 26 years before King U Thong founded Ayutthaya. The image is 62 feet high and more than 45 feet from knee to knee. See also the small adjacent Chinese temple, a memorial to a Chinese princess who was betrothed to the King of Thailand and who committed suicide when he failed to attend her arrival.

Across the river from Wat Phanan Choeng, **Wat Suwan Dararam** is visited by the present royal couple when they visit Ayutthaya. It was built by Rama I. The murals and door panels depicting stories from the *Ramakien* are quite beautiful; note also the carvings on the roof beams.

On the Lopburi side of the river, **Wat Na Phra Mane** survived the destruction of Ayutthaya and is worth visiting to see the black stone Buddha dating from the Dvaravati Period, as well as the principal Buddha fully decorated in regal attire.

Back on the main site on the other side of the river, one chedi serves as a moving reminder of the role that women have often played in Thai history, in a country where they were expected to serve alongside men in war. Only a chedi and a statue remain of a temple built to commemorate **Queen Suriyothai,** who was killed when she intervened in a duel that her husband was fighting on elephantback with a Burmese general.

Don't miss **Wat Yai Chai Mongkol,** located a few minutes outside Ayutthaya. It's a beautifully tended temple that was built by King U Thong in 1357 for meditation. The massive pagoda was built in 1592 by King Naresuan after he defeated the Burmese by killing their crown prince in single-handed combat on elephants.

Set a little distance from the other main temple sites, **Wat Chai Wattanaram** is still being restored, and traces of the jungle—roots and branches—straggle around the many chedis and prangs. The whole complex has an overgrown, haunted air about it and that deep sense of tragedy that is the essence of Ayutthaya.

Accommodations and Dining

The selection is small. Among the best of these small, modest hotels is the **Uthong Inn,** 210 Moo 5, Tambon Rojana Road (tel. 035/242618), with its neat, clean carpeted rooms with air conditioning. The front-desk personnel are accommodating and the hotel provides laundry service. There's also a restaurant attached. Double rooms rent for 400 baht ($16) to 700 baht ($28).

Near the boat landing and Chan Kasem Palace, the **U Thong Hotel,** 86 Uthong Rd. (tel. 035/251136), has basic, clean rooms for 300 baht ($12) to 500 baht ($20).

The **Thai Thai,** 13/1 Naresuan Rd. (tel. 035/251505), has 27 adequate rooms and charges a low 250 baht ($10) to 350 baht ($14) double per night.

A convenient **restaurant** is located right across from the entrance to Wat Maha That. It's pleasant enough and offers a combination Chinese/Thai menu. A meal for two with beer will cost about 220 baht ($8.75).

For a more scenic setting, try **Ruenpae,** a floating riverfront restaurant to the north of the Pridi Damrong Bridge (tel. 251807). It offers a typical Thai/Chinese menu with such dishes as steamed fish in plum sauce, roasted chicken with salt, Nanking soy cake, grilled prawn, and beef with chili, priced from 30 baht ($1.25) to 50 baht ($2). Dinner for two will run about $6 to $9.

There's a similar floating restaurant, **Pae Krung Koa,** 4 Uthong Rd. (tel. 241555), to the south of the bridge. It's similarly priced.

For real budget dining, try the small food shops near the Hua-Raw and the Chao Prom markets.

BANG PA-IN: Only 61 km (38 miles) north of Bangkok, this royal palace is usually combined with Ayutthaya into a one-day tour. In our view, the palace is not that interesting and if you have to choose, your time would be better spent exploring Ayutthaya fully. Originally the temple and palace at Bang Pa-In were built by Ayutthaya's King Prasat Thong in the mid-17th century. When Bangkok became the capital it was abandoned until King Mongkut began returning occasionally in the mid-19th century. His son, King Chulalongkorn, stayed there every year and constructed the royal palace as it is seen today.

The architectural style mixes Thai with very strong European influences. The building that stands in the middle of the lake is the **Phra Thinang Aisawan Thippa-At.** Behind it, in Versailles style are what were the king's apartments, which today serve as a hall for state ceremonies. The other building of note is the

Phra Thinang Wehat Chamrun, a Chinese-style building where the members of the court generally resided during the rainy and cool seasons. Inside are a series of richly decorated rooms in the Chinese style. Also worth visiting is the **Phra Thinang Withun Thatsuna,** an observatory on a small island that affords a fine view of the countryside from the top.

While you're here across the Chao Phraya River, the remarkable Gothic-style **Wat Nivet Thamaprawat,** built during King Chulalongkorn's reign, is worth seeing.

Bang Pa-In is open daily except Monday and Friday from 8 a.m. to 3 p.m. Admission is 12 baht (50¢). Minibuses leave Ayutthaya regularly beginning at 6 a.m. from Chao Prom Market, Chao Prom Road. Fare is about 12 baht (50¢) and the trip takes about 50 minutes. The tour from Bangkok's Oriental also stops here.

NAKHON PATHOM: En route to Kanchanaburi, about 60 km (37 miles) west of Bangkok, the chedi of Nakhon Pathom's Phra Pathom soars like a golden bell into the sky. It's actually made of orange tiles, is the world's tallest Buddhist monument, and marks the spot where Buddhism was introduced to Thailand 2,300 years ago. Walk all the way around the central chedi and observe the many smaller shrines, some with very appealing reclining or seated Buddhas.

Note: The Floating Market at Damnoen Saduak is about 40 minutes south of Nakhon Pathom, so that you can either combine the two sites into a one-day trip; or stop at Nakhon Pathom en route to Kanchanaburi.

KANCHANABURI: This city, near the famous bridge over the River Kwai, is located in what has to be some of Thailand's most beautiful scenery. Along the river the mountains rise in misty haze; the jungle stretches away too, waterfalls abound, and as you drive along the road you'll pass fields of tapioca, tobacco, sugarcane, tamarind, mango, papaya, banana, and palm trees. In the old town you'll find the river lined with floating restaurants where you can while away the hours gazing at the river and its mountain backdrop. Kanchanaburi stands at the junction where two tributaries—the Kwai Noi and the Kwai Yai—meet and form the Mae Klong River.

Information

The **TAT Office** is on Saeng Chuto Road (tel. 034/511200). The **telephone area code** is 034.

Getting There

Non-air-conditioned buses leave Bangkok's Southern Bus Station every 15 minutes from 5 a.m. to 7:30 p.m., for a fare of 30 baht ($1.25), and air-conditioned buses leave every hour from 6 a.m. to 9:30 p.m., for a fare of 65 baht ($2.50). Trains leave from Thonburi Station, Bangkok Noi, at 8 a.m. and 1:55 p.m. The trip takes about 2½ hours and costs 55 baht ($2.25). Or you can take the special tourist trains that leave on Saturday, Sunday, and holidays, stopping 40 minutes in Nakhon Pathom to view the earliest and tallest Buddhist stupa in Thailand, and 30 minutes at the River Kwai bridge. At Nam Tok Station minibuses take visitors to Khao Phang Waterfall round trip and then the train proceeds to Kanchanaburi for a 45-minute stop before returning to Bangkok. The trains leave at 6:15 a.m. and arrive back at Hualumpong Station at 7:30 p.m. Fares are 95 baht ($3.75). Reservations recommended.

What to See

Before going out to see the bridge itself, stop at the **Jeath museum** in town in the precincts of Wat Chaichumphon. Constructed to resemble the prisoners' barracks, it's a sobering and moving witness to the horrors of war and the terrible suffering of the prisoners of war who built the railway and bridge. The railway was built to maintain the Japanese army in Burma. It was a crucial supply and communication link built to replace the alternative sea route via the Strait of Malacca that had been closed by the Allies. The name Jeath is an acronym of the initials of those nationalities that built the railway—Japanese, English, American, Australian, Thai, and Hollanders. The museum is filled with photographs, personal mementoes, and newspaper accounts of their lives—recording the tortures that they were subjected to by the Japanese, the malnutrition, the disease, and the despair. They were fed a handful of rice a day, worked half-naked and barefoot digging earth to dump onto the rising railbed only to have it washed away; they were tormented by the 100° heat and insects. They died of dysentery, malaria, beriberi, cholera. The Japanese had originally calculated that it would take five to six years to complete the 425-km (264-mile) track, but they reduced that calculation to 18 months for the POWs. In fact it was finished in a year. Some 16,000 men, mostly British, Australian, and American, died—27 for every kilometer of track. Another 100,000 Burmese, Chinese, Indians, Indonesians, Malays, and Thais—forced labor—were also killed by disease and starvation and were buried in unmarked graves at the places where they dropped dead. It's said that the prisoners and laborers built the bridge so badly in the hope that it would collapse. The museum is open daily from 8:30 a.m. to 4:30 p.m.

Also in town, near the railroad station, you can stop by the **Kanchanaburi War Cemetery,** where every stone tells a story of loss. Many of the 6,982 graves are those of young men in their 20s and 30s who died so far from home. The epitaphs are intensely moving. Another cemetery, a few miles out of town contains close to 2,000 graves.

About 2½ miles from Kanchanaburi, the **Bridge over the River Kwai** is well touristed. You can walk across it looking toward the mountains of Burma as you go. For some it's a nerve-racking experience, because you'll be walking along rickety railroad ties laid on an open grid structure that allows you to see the water below. So many people cross the bridge in both directions that you have to plant your feet very carefully while you let each other pass. The bridge was brought from Java and assembled by Japanese prisoners. It was bombed several times and rebuilt after the war, but the curved spans of the bridge are the originals. If you visit during the River Kwai Bridge Week, you can also see a son et lumière spectacle. This is usually held at the end of November or the beginning of December.

OTHER NEARBY SIGHTS. Among Thais, the surrounding area is widely known for its natural beauties such as Erawan Waterfall and National Park, Sai-Yok National Park, and La Wa Cave. Undoubtedly, the best time to visit these areas is during the rainy season or shortly after its end when the cascading waterfalls are in full flood. The **La Wa Cave** is about 75 km (45 miles) from town along Rte. 323; **Sai-Yok National Park** is about 104 km (62 miles) along the same route; its focal point is its waterfall, Sai Yok Yai, often celebrated in Thai song and verse. You can take a boat to these two places from Pak Saeng Pier at Tam-Bon Tha-Saow. The round trip will take about four hours and cost about 125 baht ($5). Buses to Sai Yok take about two hours and cost 28 baht ($1.10).

Farther along Rte. 123 there's also **Dawadung Cave** (110 km, 68 miles), the **Hin Dat Hot Springs** (130 km, 80 miles), and the remote three-tiered waterfall **Pha Tat.**

The most popular attraction about 65 km (40 miles) along Rte. 3199 is **Erawan Waterfall and National Park.** The waterfall is 1¼ miles long and drops down seven tiers, creating a series of ponds and streams; it's a great bird and butterfly sanctuary. Buses leave from the bus terminal in Kanchanaburi on Saeng Chuto Road (tel. 511-387) for Erawan Waterfall. The trip takes about 1½ hours. The fare is 22 baht (90¢). Buses to Sai Yok take about 2 hours and cost 28 baht ($1.10).

Along Rte. 3086, 31 miles north, in the Bo Phloi area you can observe the **mining of sapphires.** From the roadside you may spy the wooden framework of a winch and see people filling wheelbarrows with rock-hard lumps of earth. It's amazing to see a person emerge from one of these wells using a tree limb minus its branches as a ladder. If they're lucky after washing through the mud, they may find blue or black sapphires and earn a day's living. Travel another 30 miles or so north along the same route and you'll come to Than Lot Cave and Traitrung Waterfall in **Than Lot National Park.**

Where to Stay

The best and most fun place to stay is at one of the several traditional-style floating resorts down on the river. You'll stay either in a bamboo hut on a floating raft or back on shore in a bamboo hut on stilts with a large rectangular porch at the front. You sleep on the floor and use communal Asian-style toilets.

About 25 miles west along the river from Kanchanaburi, **River Kwai Jungle House,** 3788 Tharur, Thamaka, Amphoe Sai Yok (tel. 034/561052 or 561429; in Bangkok, 02/279-2040 or 279-3083), is one such resort. Here, you're in the forest; there are mango trees, clumps of bamboo and bougainvillea, turkeys and chickens pecking at the dust, and a couple of pet monkeys for company. There is also an open dining area serving Thai specialties. If you take the train from Bangkok, the management will have you picked up at the Kanchanaburi train station. Prices, including three meals a day, are 550 baht ($22) single, and 925 baht ($37) double. You'll need a flashlight as the grounds are poorly lit.

Another similar-style place is **River Kwai Farm,** about 20 miles from town. Rates are 550 baht ($22) with meals. For information, contact River Kwai Farm Co., 16/6 Soi Pipat, Silom Road, Bangkok (tel. 02/235-6433 or 234-7435).

Paekarn Resort is also on the riverbank, but not really in a jungle area. The accommodations are also less rustic, having modern Western bathrooms with tiled showers. Each cabin is made of bamboo and sleeps four on platforms equipped with mattress and pillow. The cost is 1,000 baht ($40) per cabin per night. To make arrangements to stay here, go to Paekarn Floating Restaurant in Old Kanchanaburi. A long-tail boat will transport you to the resort for 250 baht ($10).

If you're not up for such simple accommodations, there's the **River Kwai Village,** Amphoe Sai Yok, Kanchanaburi, about 43 miles from the bridge; the Bangkok address is 1054/4 New Petchburi Rd. (tel. 02/251-7552 or 251-7828). It's a rather depressing so-called Western-style resort. Accommodations are in single-story buildings. Our room was barely adequate, with a water-stained toilet bowl, torn curtains, stained trash cans, cold water, and signs of black mold on the walls. The air conditioning worked though, the beds were firm, and the furnishings typical Formica. The choice accommodations here, in our opinion, are found down a steep incline on floating rafts on the river. The restaurant is cheap and cheerful and serves adequate Thai and Western food. Doubles are 650 baht ($26).

Dining

Our favorite dining spots lie all along the river in Old Kanchanaburi. Pick any one of the very attractive floating restaurants on Riverside Road. At **Restaurant Paekarn,** Riverside Road (tel. 514-0612), try the delicious green curry with prawn, or the sweet-and-sour beef, or chicken with basil, or pork with cashew nut. Dishes cost 35 baht ($1.50) to 70 baht ($2.75).

Ban Naur, also on Riverside Road (tel. 512326 or 511722), has similarly priced dishes—shrimp with lemongrass, steamed whole fish on lemongrass and salted prune, beef with shredded eggplant and hot pepper, and rice noodles fried with pork, dried shrimp, and tomato sauce are just a few of the highlights.

At the bridge itself, expect to pay a little more at the **River Kwai Floating Restaurant.**

HUA HIN: About 200 km (124 miles) or a 3½-hour drive from Bangkok, Hua Hin is a delightful small fishing village and favorite royal resort, originally "discovered" by King Rama VI and then by Rama VII, who built a summer palace here in the '20s. Wander along the fine, white sandy beaches, strolling south to Stone Head (Hua Hin) with its Khao Takiab hill topped with a temple. Go into town in the early evening to view the fishermen at the docks unloading their catch in large baskets, mending their nets, and fixing their boats before going out on another fishing expedition. Stroll along the narrow streets and peer through the open doors of the wooden houses—into rooms ajumble with beds, tables, scooters, and TVs—homes that often double as stores. Also, stop by the Hua Hin Royal Golf Course near the station, a sight in itself. There are two buildings —one a super-elegant stop for the royal train only and the other for us simple folks. If you're not staying at the famous Railway Hotel, you may want to stop by for a drink at this lovely resort. In the film *The Killing Fields,* it was used as the double for Phnom Penh's leading hotel that had served as the headquarters for foreign journalists. Hua Hin also has a night market that's fun to visit.

A Side Trip

South of Hua Hin on the coast, **Sam Roi Yot** (300 peaks) **National Park** with its marshland and lakes offers particularly exotic waterfowl, the Kaeo and Phraya Nakhon caves, and Sai Cave with impressive stalactites and stalagmites. The caves can be reached by a 10- to 15-minute boat ride from Bang Phu, a nearby fishing village.

Information

Tourist Information Center is at 6k/2 Damnoenkasem Rd. (tel. 032/ 512120), open daily from 8 a.m. to 6 p.m.

Getting There and Getting Around

Some 15 air-conditioned buses a day from Bangkok's Southern Terminal on Charansanitwong Road leave every hour from 6 a.m. on. Fare is about 90 baht ($3.50) and the trip takes about four hours. Eight trains a day leave from Bangkok's Hua Lampong Station. Fare is 220 baht ($8.75) in first class, 80 baht ($3.25) in second class.

Walk or rent a bicycle from the place across from the Hua Hin Bazaar on Damneonkasem Road for about 50 baht ($2) an hour. A samlor to anywhere in town will not cost more than 25 baht ($1).

Where to Stay

The most elegant and the most convenient place to stay is the **Hotel Sofitel,** Damneonkasem Road, Hua Hin (tel. 032/511012), the masterfully restored old 1923 Railway Hotel, a two-story Thai-Victorian structure, decorated with fretwork and built in an L-shape with a pavilion open on both sides that serves as the reception area. Paths lead through lush gardens dotted with topiary, past the pool and cabaña down to the beach. Old-world accents include the original switchboard (for display only). The 60 rooms, each off the veranda, have been restored carefully, retaining the teak floors and wainscoting, high teak ceilings, and brass switches, but adding all the modern conveniences—air conditioning, telephone, TV, mini-bar, and large tiled terraces. In the tiled bathrooms there are showers and the original porcelain taps are still in place. Another 100 rooms have been added in the same style, minus the high ceilings; there are also villas available with two bedrooms, two bathrooms, and a living room. For dining there's the '30s-style railway café as well as three restaurants—Thai, seafood, and a brasserie. Facilities also include two tennis courts, two swimming pools, and mini-golf (free transit is given to the golf course). Singles or doubles cost 1,875 baht ($75) to 2,750 baht ($110).

About a mile from town, the **Royal Garden Resort,** 107/1 Phetkasem Beach Rd. (tel. 032/511881 to 511884), is a full-facility resort attracting many British and German tourists. The 210 modern rooms furnished with rattan and equipped with mini-bar, telephone, and TV, also have terraces overlooking the large central pool and the beach beyond. The Market is the top restaurant; there's also a pizza parlor and coffeeshop. Tennis courts, water-sports center (windsurfing, sailing, and skiing), table tennis, and a small disco complete the facilities. Singles go for 1,875 baht ($75) to 2,600 baht ($104); doubles, for 2,000 baht ($80) to 2,750 baht ($110). Add 375 baht ($15) during peak season from November 1 through April.

The **Royal Garden Village,** another resort about 3 miles from Hua Hin, is also being constructed and will open in late 1988. The designs call for several traditional Thai-style buildings each housing six or so rooms. It, too, will have full facilities.

Back in town **The Jed Pee Nong,** 17 Damneonkasem (tel. 032/512381), is so clean it sparkles. The open lobby is inviting with its rattan furnishings, tile floors, and adjacent café area. The rooms are carpeted, clean, and furnished with bed, dresser, and a bathroom with shower. Singles or doubles are 300 baht ($12) with fan and 425 baht ($17) with air conditioning.

A RESORT IN NEARBY CHA AM. About nine miles from Hua Hin, the **Regent Cha Am Beach Hotel,** Cha Am Beach, Petchburi (tel. 032/471483), is a large 550-room full-facility resort. Accommodations are in four-story modern buildings built in a triangular layout with one side overlooking the central pool and ocean and the other offering a view of the distant mountains. Rooms are typical modern style with rattan and bamboo furnishings, TV, telephone, air conditioning, mini-bar, full tiled bath, and balcony. Similar appointments are found in the 35 round thatch-roofed cottages located down on the beach. The facilities are extensive—including babysitter, health club, bicycles, eight tennis courts, two squash courts, two pools (one Olympic size), games room, and more. Restaurants include the Tapien Tong seafood restaurant, the open-air Lom Fang Lake for local Thai cuisine and seafood, a 24-hour café serving good Thai food, a coffeeshop, and a poolside snackbar; at night a disco opens up. Single or double rooms range from 1,500 baht ($60) to 1,750 baht ($70), depending on the view; cottages begin at 2,000 baht ($80). Prices for table d'hôte meals are 175 baht ($7) for American breakfast, 275 baht ($11) for lunch, and 350 baht ($14) for dinner.

CHAPTER XVIII

CENTRAL THAILAND'S HISTORICAL LEGACY

□ □ □

1. PHITSANULOK
2. SUKHOTHAI AND SI SATCHANALAI

Central Thailand incorporates the vast Central Plain, known as the great rice bowl of the country. It's the source of Thailand's major crop and the source of the country's wealth. Washed by rivers, including the Chao Phrya, the land sweeps on with rice field after rice field in which the farmers work from season to season. It's where you will discover much traditional Thai culture and it's where the Thai kingdom was first founded.

1. PHITSANULOK

The city of Phitsanulok is set on the banks of the Nan River and bisects Thailand's north and central provinces, in the country's fertile rice belt. If you're planning an all-encompassing tour of northern Thailand, Phitsanulok is roughly equidistant between Chiang Mai and Bangkok, and is an ideal base for visiting Sukhothai, 58 km (35 miles) northwest of the city, and Si Satchanalai. Because of this strategic location, the city enjoys prosperity and some historic importance.

The area is surrounded by a seemingly endless array of rice paddies, particularly delightful in the late spring. Houseboats and long boats ply the Nan and the Song Kwai Rivers, connecting with the Chao Phrya and feeding into the Gulf of Siam. Some of the flat-bottom vessels transport rice south to the capital for export. Agricultural markets bring swarms of peasants into the city's thriving market and keep the traders' coffers full.

Phitsanulok is the birthplace of King Naresuan (the Great) and his less famous brother, Prince Ekatosarot. The Ayutthaya king is legendary in Thai history for his gallant defense against the forces of the invading Burmese army during the 16th century. There are many paintings of his hand-to-hand fighting, on elephants, with a Burmese crown prince. Other Ayutthaya kings used Phitsanulok as a staging and training ground for battles with the Burmese, and for 25 years it served as the capital of the Ayutthaya kingdom.

It certainly isn't the most attractive city in Thailand, but Phitsanulok has some of the friendliest people we met anywhere in the country. The Thai sense of hospitality transforms this otherwise bland, modern city into a relatively homey place. Nearly all of the city was destroyed by fire in 1959, and concrete and steel have replaced carved teak and painted stucco. Miraculously, about the only thing that survived is the town's most important site, Wat Mahatat, and with it the most venerated Buddha image in the region, Phra Buddha Chinarat. Don't miss it.

ORIENTATION: The town is fairly compact, with the majority of services and sights for tourists concentrated along or near the east bank of the **Nan River.** The river itself is the town's most picturesque asset, with houseboats moored to its banks and klongs shooting off its tributaries. There is also a market along the lower banks. A **cable car** bridges the two shores; the ride costs a modest 3 baht (12¢) each way. The PTT and the post office are near the cable-car terminal. **Phyalithai Road,** which runs perpendicular to Phuttabucha Road along the river, leads directly to the **Clock Tower,** the town's most central landmark. The other central artery is **Boromtrilokanart Road** (named after the 15th-century Ayutthaya king who lived and was crowned in Phitsanulok; the name is spelled differently on every map we've ever seen, but this is a good approximation!). This major commercial street begins along the lower banks of the river, angles to the middle of town, around the Clock Tower, and ends along the upper bank, near Wat Mahatat and the museum. The **train and bus stations** are 2 ½ blocks east of the Clock Tower, near the Amarintr Nakorn Hotel, at Naresuan and E-Katodros Roads.

USEFUL INFORMATION: The **TAT office** (tel. 055/252742) is located on the street level at 209/7-8 Surasi Trade Center on Boromtrilokanart Road, near the Clock Tower. The office is open daily from 8:30 a.m. to 4:30 p.m. The main **police station** is located nearby at the intersection of Naresuan Road and Boromtrilokanart Road; for emergencies, call 199 or 191. The main medical facility is the **Buddhachinnarat Hospital** (tel. 252570 or 252630), which serves the entire province. The **telephone area code** for the Phitsanulok region is 055.

Unlike many of the larger, more tourist-oriented towns, Phitsanulok has few banks to exchange foreign currency. The most conveniently located branch is the **Bangkok Bank,** one block from the Clock Tower; hours are 9 a.m. to 3:30 p.m. Monday through Friday. We found no banks with extended hours, so you'll have to change money at your hotel (watch out for the lower rate). The **General Post Office** is on Phuttabucha Road, along the river near the cable car. The **PTT** is set just down from the post office, along the river; they are open 24 hours. The **Sidra Book Shop** on Naresuan Road has a good collection of English-language books including guidebooks. You can get your camera repaired at **Tamachart,** located between the police station and the Clock Tower. The main department store is **Topland,** across from the police station, where you can buy nearly anything.

GETTING THERE: You'll find frequent plane, train, and bus service between Bangkok and Phitsanulok.

By Air

Thai Airways flies between Phitsanulok and Bangkok twice daily; the one-way fare is 720 baht ($28.75) for the 35-minute flight. There are also connecting flights between Chiang Mai and Phitsanulok three times daily for 505 baht ($20.25), but be aware that the flight makes many stops and takes over three hours. There is an evening connecting flight from Phuket and Surat Thani to Phitsanulok via Bangkok. There is also connecting service between Phitsanulok and Chiang Rai, for 660 baht ($26.50), and to Mae Hong Son for 715 baht ($28.50). Thai Airways maintains an office in Phitsanulok at 209/27-28 Boromtrilokanart Rd. (tel. 258020), near the TAT office.

By Train

There is daily train service from Bangkok to Phitsanulok on both the **express** and the **rapid** trains. The express takes six hours and departs Bangkok at 6 p.m., while the rapid takes eight hours and departs at 3:45 p.m. A **sleeper** is available, but should be reserved as early as possible. The price of a second-class, one-way, air-conditioned sleeper (on the express only) is 373 baht ($15); a first-class seat costs 292 baht ($11.75), plus a 30-baht ($1.25) supplement if you ride the express. Tickets can be reserved at the Bangkok Railway Station (tel. 223-7020) up to 30 days in advance. The Northern Line also runs express and rapid trains to Chiang Mai on a daily basis. In Phitsanulok you can call 258005 for local train information.

In addition to the normal trains, there is a special Diesel Railcar operated by **Khaem Inn Travel** (tel. 251997, or 223-7010 in Bangkok) that runs three times daily between Bangkok and Phitsanulok. The fare is 205 baht ($8.25) each way for an air-conditioned car; the trip takes about six hours.

By Bus

There is frequent bus service between Phitsanulok and Bangkok on an air-conditioned **public bus.** Buses depart from the Northern Bus Terminal in Bangkok (tel. 279-4484) and arrive in Phitsanulok at the local terminal (tel. 258-0555). There are also private companies offering transportation services. **Phitsanulok Yan Yon Tours** (tel. 258647, or 245-7481 in Bangkok) and **Thavorn Farm** (tel. 258526, or 511-3673 in Bangkok) run daily trips between Phitsanulok and the capital. If you take an air-conditioned bus, arrange to have the bus company shuttle you from your hotel in Bangkok to the Northern Terminal. The trip takes five hours. There are also connecting buses between Phitsanulok and Chiang Mai, Mae Hong Son, and Chiang Rai.

GETTING AROUND: It's unlikely that you'll spend much time in Phitsanulok, but if you do, there are several easy and inexpensive transportation options. **Samlors (tuk-tuks)** are common and cheap. The fare within the town should run about 45 baht ($1.75) for an hour-long ride. **Taxis** are available, and a cab from the airport runs about 25 baht ($1). Note that the higher-priced hotels run their own pickup service at the airport.

You'll most likely want to take a trip from Phitsanulok to Sukhothai and Si Satchanalai. **Phitsanulok Tour Center** (tel. 242206) rents cars by the day or week; expect to pay 1,300 baht ($52) per day, including insurance. **Rung Thong Tour** (tel. 259973) offers a private car with driver to Sukhothai (where they will wait while you see the sights) and back for 1,300 baht ($52). There is frequent (nearly on the hour) and inexpensive air-conditioned bus service to Sukhothai for 19 baht (75¢); but note that the bus only runs to the modern town of Sukhothai and not to the Sukhothai Historical Park, which can only be reached by another 12-km (7½-mile) bus trip. You can hire a tuk-tuk for the short trip for about 45 baht ($1.75).

There are public buses to Si Satchanalai and Sawankhalok that depart from the station across from the Sukhothai Hotel; the fare is 19 baht (75¢). Contact the TAT office for the latest schedule and prices.

ACCOMMODATIONS: There are no luxury or first-class hotels in the city but there are several acceptable moderate and budget-class hotels that are far superior to anything in the surrounding towns. Nearly all hotels cater to the many large European tour groups that visit Sukhothai, so make sure to reserve ahead.

The best of Phitsanulok's lodgings is the **Pailyn Hotel,** located on Boromtrilokanart Road (tel. 055/252411), one block from the river. The Pailyn is the newest hotel in town, and its bright and airy marble lobby gives it a certain panache. The rooms are utterly plain, but clean and fairly quiet. In keeping with the personality of the town, the staff is especially gracious and helpful. A double room runs 800 baht ($32), 60 baht ($3) less for a single.

The only hotel in Phitsanulok possessing a swimming pool is the **Rajapruk,** three blocks from the train station at 99/9 Pha-Ong Dum Rd. (tel. 055/258477). The hotel is a bit older and more worn than the Pailyn, and like its competitor, the guest rooms are spartan but clean. Doubles run 800 baht ($32).

Similar accommodations can be found at the **Thep Nakorn Hotel,** 43/1 Sri Thamtraipidok Rd. (tel. 055/251817), set between the Clock Tower and the train station. Nothing fancy here, but at 550 baht ($22), it's a decent value.

The **Amarintr Nakorn Hotel,** within sight of the train and bus stations (tel. 055/258588), was built at the beginning of Phitsanulok's mini hotel boom back in 1972, but it still is an acceptable choice for convenient lodging. For 550 baht ($22) it offers clean rooms and air conditioning.

The **Nanchao Hotel,** 242 Baromtrilokanart Rd. (tel. 259511 to 259513), has adequate rooms that rent for 350 baht ($14) double. The hotel has a restaurant.

DINING: Before we discuss the eating options in Phitsanulok, you should know about a local specialty, the so-called Nam Wa banana. This is actually a sun-dried banana baked with honey, and it's absolutely delicious. A small box of these morsels runs a modest 17 baht (70¢) and can be found at Sala 10, at Rattana near Wat Mahatat.

As for more hardy dining, **Saw Lert Rot,** at 4/5 Arthitayawongse Rd. (tel. 258442), serves excellent Thai and Chinese cuisine. They suggested ordering their fried chicken and we loved it. For a most intriguing setting, try **Song Kwai,** a dining room in a houseboat moored on the Nan River. The food, like that at Saw Lert Rot, is both Thai and Chinese and of fine quality. We also like **Thiparos,** at 9 Sai Lue Thai Rd. (tel. 258200), for their finely prepared Cantonese dishes. All of these suggested restaurants are modestly priced.

If you want to dine al fresco, head for the daytime goods and produce market along the river. At night this busy spot becomes a food-stall market with a myriad of delectable and inexpensive eating options.

WHAT TO SEE AND DO IN THE CITY: The highlight of any visit to Phitsanulok is touring **Wat Phra Sri Ratana Mahatat (Wat Yai)** and paying homage to its brilliant bronze, late-Sukhothai-era Phra Buddha Chinarat. The bot that houses this most revered of Buddhas is a prize example of traditional Thai architecture, with the three eaves overlapping one another to emphasize the nave. The elongated, low extensions to the side articulate the central structure, adding a layer of elegance to this well-preserved monument. The powerful-looking image inside the bot was cast in 1357 under the aegis of the Sukhothai King Mahatammaracha and is enhanced by the exquisite black-and-gold columns and backdrop of the wat. (Phitsanulok supports a Buddha statue-making business, and it's hardly surprising that this image has served as a model for ideal representations of the Buddha.) The most distinctive element of the Buddha is the regal-looking halo surrounding the central figure as well as the perfect expression of controlled tranquility. We enjoyed following the painted murals on the walls illustrating the life of the Buddha as well as the two *thammas* (pulpits) to the side of the central Buddha. The wat is nearly always packed with worshippers paying their respects to the Buddha, and praying for a healthy mind and body. Before leaving, be sure to examine the excellent late-Ayutthaya Period mother-of-pearl inlaid doors leading into the chapel; they are similar to those in the Royal Chapel in Bangkok and were added to the building in 1756 as a gift from King Borommakot of Ayutthaya.

Other than the main bot, the most distinctive architectural aspect of the temple grounds is the Khmer-style prang, rebuilt by King Boromtrilokanart, behind the central bot. The gilding on the top half of the prang is probably recent, but it complements the Khmer form of temple décor. Notice also the Buddhist statuary in and around the prang. There is a small museum in the compound that houses a good collection of Sukhothai- and Ayutthaya-era Buddhas.

When we visited the wat last year we happened to be there during the Buddha Chinarat Festival, held annually on the sixth day of the waxing moon in the third lunar month (usually sometime between late January and early February). This event transforms the wat into a cultural circus, with well-wishers, dancers, monks and abbots, children, and tourists all converging on the temple grounds for a six-day celebration.

The wat is open daily from 8 a.m. to 5 p.m.; during the Buddha Chinarat Festival, from 8 a.m. to midnight.

From Wat Mahatat, you might want to stroll along the banks of the **Nan River,** lined with semipermanently moored houseboats (Song Kwai or "Two River" City). From here you can take the **cable car** to the other side of the river to view the monument to Naresuan and the city and provincial buildings. Farther along the river is the **day market** with a panoply of everyday items, produce, and a scattering of hill-tribe crafts for sale at relatively low prices. There is also a daily market 1½ blocks from the train station. Just a short distance, on the southern outskirts of the town, is the **Buddha Casting Factory and Folk Museum,** a kitschy treat for those who want to see how local craftspeople fabricate a 40-foot-tall statue. The Folk Museum aspect of the excursion is on the modest side; however, it will give you a more accurate picture of Thai peasant life.

If you're interested in Khmer-style architecture, you may want to journey three miles south to **Wat Chulamanee,** the oldest temple in the Phitsanulok area. Like the prang at Wat Mahatat, this Khmer-built spire was rebuilt by King Boromtrilokanart after his instruction in the architecture of nearby Sukhothai. The wat was restored in the 1950s and is studied particularly for its fine laterite cactus-shaped prang and the elaborate stucco designs decorating the structure.

NIGHTLIFE: Phitsanulok has the usual set of Thai town evening diversions including discos, bars, nightclubs, and markets. Of the discos, **Studio 54** at the Pailyn, **Talk of the Town** at the Rajapruk, and **Sarina** at the Nanchao hotels are the most popular. The Amarin Nakorn hosts the **Amarin Nightclub** where patrons can "rent" partners by the hour to hit the dance floor for 90 baht ($3.50) per hour. Music is supplied via live band and alternates between contemporary and ballroom dancing.

If you want to take a samlor (bicycle trishaw) tour of the town, you can rent a vehicle and hire a driver for about 70 baht ($2.75); stops include the fruit market, the Clock Tower, the train station (an old British engine is on display), and the banks of the Nan River.

2. SUKHOTHAI AND SI SATCHANALAI

The emergence of Sukhothai ("Dawn of Happiness") in 1238 as an independent political state signified not only the birth of a unified kingdom, but also symbolized the genesis of Thailand itself. It was here that the Thai people established the first monarch, Phor Khun Bangk Klang Hao, as King Sri Indrathit, and it was Sukhothai that would become the country's most influential religious and cultural center. Today Sukhothai is Thailand's preeminent site, especially after the massive ten-year effort by UNESCO to preserve its magnificent monuments.

If you are keen on discovering the country's most impressive archeological site, go no farther, for what Borobudur is to Indonesia and Ankgor Wat is to Cambodia, Sukhothai is to Thailand.

Si Satchanalai is another richly endowed Sukhothai city, thought to have been built at the same time as its more famous neighbor. The ancient city is on a similar scale as Sukhothai but its 22 monuments aren't nearly in as fine a state of repair; nevertheless, it is absolutely worth a detour and some visitors are more taken with it because of its very sense of decay. Near Si Satchanalai an exciting Thai-Australian excavation of early ceramic kilns is being undertaken by the University of Adelaide.

If you're traveling from Phitsanulok, the drive takes you across wide plains where there are rice paddies, cotton fields, and mango and lemon groves. Most of the peasants still use ancient methods of farming, including water buffalo and manual plow, though some have purchased tractors (which locals call the "iron buffalo").

ORIENTATION: Sukhothai Historical Park is located 7½ miles from the modern town of Sukhothai. The new town isn't particularly distinguished, but it does offer useful services. The town is built along the banks of the Yom River and is best traversed by tuk-tuk.

Si Satchanalai is built along the Yom River, 56 km (35 miles) from Sukhothai and 17 km (10½ miles) from Sawankhalok.

USEFUL INFORMATION: Sukhothai has no TAT office; however, there is tourist information and currency exchange in the Bangkok Bank during normal business hours. The closest TAT office is located in Phitsanulok (tel. 055/252742). The same is true for a major hospital: in the event of an emergency, call the Buddhachinnarat Hospital (tel. 252570 or 252630) which serves the entire province. The telephone area code for the Sukhothai region is 055.

GETTING THERE: There is bus service between Bangkok and Sukhothai approximately ten times daily, departing from the Northern Bus Terminal (tel. 279-4484). Buses operate nearly every hour for the shuttle between Phitsanulok and Sukhothai; the fare is 19 baht (75¢) for the air-conditioned coach. If you wish to fly or take a train, you must stop in Phitsanulok and take local transportation to Sukhothai.

ACCOMMODATIONS: Only a couple of miles from the Historical Park are the **Thai Village Houses,** at 214 Jarod Vithitong Rd. in the Muang Khao (old city) (tel. 055/612752), set in the privately owned Sukhothai Cultural Center (a kind of mini mall). The quarters are actually teak bungalows, quite attractive from the outside, but spartanly furnished inside. We had really hoped that the management would take the idea of living in a traditionally built Thai home all the way, but alas. . . . Still, we enjoyed our stay here and would recommend it to anyone who wants to make an extended visit to the site. Room rates run 350 baht ($14) to 450 baht ($18), depending on the size of the bungalow. The Nam Khang is an unexceptional restaurant on the premises. However, the Boonchu Antique Shop is a first-rate emporium with some marvelous examples of locally produced (old) sangkaloke pottery for sale.

The **Raj Thani,** at 229 Carot Vithi Thong Rd. (tel. 055/611031), offers the only acceptable lodgings in the new town. The public spaces and guest rooms are relatively clean and the décor is exceptionally plain. An air-conditioned double room runs 450 baht ($18).

DINING: For Thai food in the new town, try the **Rat Thani Café** in the Rat Thani Hotel. We particularly like the **Dream Café,** on Ratuthit Road, for its décor, including a fine collection of antique ceramic pieces from archeological sites in the area (selected pottery is for sale). The food is a pastiche of Thai, Chinese, and American, including burgers, beer, and ice cream sundaes. A typical meal of pad Thai (noodles and vegetables) with beer will cost 80 baht ($3.20).

The **Rik Kaeng Wang House,** across the Yom River from the archeological headquarters in Si Satchanalai, serves pretty good Thai food in an attractive setting.

WHAT TO SEE AND DO: The two main sites are the Sukhothai Historical Park and the ancient town of Si Satchanalai. There are numerous chedis and wats in the area, particularly in the hills around ancient Sukhothai; however, most guides will not take you for fear of bandits. One side trip that is quite engaging is a tour of the archeological site where an Australian and Thai team is unearthing a series of kilns dating from the 13th century.

Sukhothai Historic Park

In 1978 UNESCO named Sukhothai a target for preservation of world culture and heritage, along with Venice, Borobudur, Mohenjodaro, Carthage, and Nubia. With strong support from the Thai government, a team of international and regional archeologists and art historians have been trying to preserve the most significant repository of Thai culture.

HISTORICAL BACKGROUND. Until the mid-13th century Sukhothai was a Khmer outpost, largely uninhabited by ethnic Thais. With a growing threat that Kublai Khan might expand his empire from Burma, the Thais were on the verge of being squeezed out of their own land. Two powerful Thai princes banded together to defend the central plains against Khmer forces. They defeated the Khmer army and discouraged Kublai Khan from entering the territory. Thus was born the kingdom of Sukhothai in 1238.

During the next two centuries the Thai kingdom was to expand to roughly its present borders from the northwest in Burma to Cambodia in the east and south to present-day Malaysia. Since then Thailand has never relinquished that land to a foreign power.

The Sukhothai kingdom also codified what became the main ingredients of Thai culture, largely accumulated from disparate foreign sources. Buddhism came from Sri Lanka, and to a lesser extent, Burma and India; Hinduism came from India; ancestor worship originated in China. The administrative system is thought to have been derived from the Mongols. Social customs and cultural forms were strongly influenced by the Khmer (the written language, for example, was adapted from Khmer). Combined, they became distinctly Thai.

Sukhothai, under King Ram Khamhaeng, also known as Rama the Strong, was a diplomatic and trading center as well as a principal center of Buddhism. Sukhothai was also a free-trade area, a fact that boosted its economy: a Sukhothai manuscript proclaims, "Whoever wants to trade in elephants, so trades. Whoever wants to trade in horses, so trades. Whoever wants to trade in silver and gold, so trades. . . . Whoever cultivates the fields, possesses them." As strong as free trade was, nothing was as dominant a force in ancient Sukhothai as was Buddhism.

All the influences that created Thai culture were combined at Sukhothai in the form of religious temples and monuments, statues and decoration. Here, in a 25-square-mile rectangle, 300,000 inhabitants, a thriving economy, and a strong spiritual drive forged Thailand's greatest national treasure.

The so-called Sukhothai-style Buddha is perhaps the most notable of artistic achievements. The walking figure, graceful in movement yet impassive in expression, is most characteristic of the driving force of Buddhist Sukhothai faith. Seated Buddhas reflect the victory over illusion and are utterly transcendent, powerful images that no doubt created strong impressions on medieval Thais.

The buildings were influenced both by Khmer-style structures as well as northern Thai chedis and viharns. The production of celadon-colored pottery, called Sawankalok, was once thought to have been developed as a result of Sukhothai's contact with Chinese traders and craftsmen. Now, with research at Si Satchanalai, there is some evidence that this renowned process originated in the Sukhothai area, and was a product of Thai craft.

Eight monarchs of the Phra Ruang Dynasty ruled Sukhothai, yet the kingdom began to wane as early as 1365 when it was overshadowed by the growing power of Ayutthaya. Within another 50 years Sukhothai was just another vassal state and its golden era was exhausted.

By the 18th century the Ayutthaya rulers who had once honored Sukhothai by rebuilding some of its most important monuments moved south to establish their new capital in Bangkok. Sukhothai was abandoned to the farmers to cultivate and to use for grazing. A new city of Sukhothai was established, and with it, the fate of the ancient capital was sealed for almost 200 years.

VISITING THE SITE. You can reach the site by taxi, private car, or bus (see "Getting There"), but once there you might consider renting a **bicycle;** they run 30 baht ($1.25) and are available near the entrance. We enjoyed visiting the site in the early morning and in the early evening. At those times there are fewer buses and groups, and the site seems that much more serene, not to mention cooler. At night, Sukhothai is known as a local lovers' lane; early in the morning, it's the area's best jogging park. The site is open every day from 8 a.m. to 5 p.m.; admission is 25 baht ($1).

Before exploring the site, stop at the **Ramkhamhaeng National Museum,** where there are maps and guidebooks for sale, a detailed model of the area, and an admirable display of Sukhothai and Si Satchanalai archeological finds largely culled from the private collection of the abbot of Wat Ratchathani. The museum is open from 9 a.m. to noon and 1 to 4 p.m. Wednesday through Sunday.

A network of walls and moats defines the perfect rectangle that is the central city. (It is thought that the original moat connected Sukhothai with Si Satachanalai.) At one of the gates along the wall, King Ramkamhaeng installed a bell, which if rung would indicate that a subject required judicial intervention to settle a dispute.

Begin your exploration of the ancient city at the central area where you'll find Wat Mahatat and the Royal Palace. **Wat Mahatat** is part of the royal compound and, accordingly, is the most extraordinary and largest monument in the park, a multi-chedi edifice that is dominated by a 14th-century lotus-bud tower and encircled by a moat. Surrounding this unique Sukhothai-style chedi are several smaller towers of Sri Lankan and Khmer influence and a grouping of Buddhist disciples in the adoration pose. Before its removal to Bangkok in the 18th century, an imposing cast-bronze seated Buddha was placed in front of the reliquary (today this image, Phra Si Sakaya Muni, is on display in the capital at Wat Suthat). The viharn that housed this figure was built in 1362 by King Lithai. The small viharn to the south contains a fine Ayutthaya-era Buddha. Be sure to examine the lowest platform of the large chedi on the south side of Wat Mahatat for its excellent stucco sculpture. There are also murals worth noting in the crypt of this chedi. During our investigation of about 200 chedis we were taken with two elegant Sri Lankan–style stupas (equivalent to Thai "chedi") at the southeast corner of the site; scout out the site and you're sure to find some gems. Some of the best architectural ornamentation in Sukhothai is found on the upper, eastern-facing levels of the niche pediments in the main reliquary tower. Dancing figures, Queen Maya giving birth to Prince Siddhartha, and scenes from the life of the Buddha are among the best-preserved details.

Head east and you'll arrive at the **Royal Palace.** Although this once-grand complex contained the throne and stone inscription of King Ram Kamhaeng (there is a copy in the Ramkamhaeng Museum; the original is in the National Museum in Bangkok), today it is a shambles.

If you continue south you'll come to the 12th-century **Wat Si Sawai,** a Hindu shrine that was later converted to a Buddhist temple. The architecture here is distinctly Khmer, with the three Lopburi-style prangs commanding center stage. The viharns around the central cactus-shaped towers are of more traditional Sukhothai design.

Wat Traphang Ngoen is west of Wat Mahatat, set in its own pond. Though the remains are few, other than an attractive chedi, the vistas of the surrounding monuments are among the most superb in the park.

Take the road north, past Wat Mahatat, to **Wat Chana Songkram** where there is a Sri Lankan–style stupa of note. Nearby is **Wat Sa Si** with its similarly influenced Sri Lankan chedi and viharn set on a small island in Traphang Takuan pond. Take a moment to examine the stucco Buddha in the fore viharn.

The remainder of monuments worth seeing are outside the central park. Most of the interesting monuments are to the north. If you leave the park at the northern (San Luang) gate and continue about 150 yards, you'll arrive at **Wat Phra Phai Luang,** most notable for its Khmer prangs and superb carving. The layout is similar to Wat Si Sawai with three prangs; however, the state of preservation is considerably rougher, with only the northern tower still showing off its exquisite stucco decoration. This monument was originally a Hindu shrine and was once graced with a lingam, a phallic sculpture placed in Shiva temples. Later it was converted into a Buddhist sanctuary as evidenced by the mondop, a square building containing a Buddha image with illustrations of the four postures of the Buddha: sitting, standing, reclining, and walking. Other Buddhist structures are now in ruins, with the exception of a pedestal with images of seated Buddhas.

One of the more astonishing monuments in Sukhothai is found at **Wat Si Chum,** where there is a 45-foot-tall Buddha in the pose of Subduing Mara. If you don't suffer from claustrophobia or acrophobia, climb up the narrow airless passageway to the top.

Si Satchanalai

The stone inscription found at Sukhothai referred to Si Satchanalai as a protectorate of King Ram Khamhaeng, leading some to speculate that this ancient city was built by the legendary Sukhothai monarch. Most historians believe, however, that Rama I expanded a city that was well established by the 13th century, possibly built by Khmer settlers, or even earlier. During the Ayutthaya Period the town was known as Sawankhalok (now the nearest modern town) for the area's legendary industry. During the height of the Sukhothai kingdom, Si Satchanalai was famous for its ceramic Sawankhalok ware, which was exported throughout Asia.

Like Sukhothai, Si Satchanalai is built along the banks of the Yom River, which was crucial to the development of the ceramics industry. So important was this trade to the city that there were literally over a thousand kilns operating along the river. Today these kilns are being excavated by a Thai-Australian team led by a trio of archeologists from the University of Adelaide. Their findings contradict the prevailing view that Chinese traders brought the method of producing celadon to Sukhothai in the 13th century. Instead they hypothesize that ceramic manufacture began over 1,000 years ago at Ban Ko Noi, just four miles north of Si Satchanalai, making it an indigenous Thai form. (If you are eager to see this team at work, contact the Si Satchanalai Historic Park office or the TAT about making a visit; the site is a short tuk-tuk ride from the old city.)

There are 22 monuments in the old city of Si Satchanalai, ranking it well below Sukhothai in importance, yet the quality of the buildings and the relative isolation of the site add to the allure.

VISITING THE SITE. One must cross the Yom River to enter the old city where, like Sukhothai, there are laterite and earthen ramparts and a moat.

The first two monuments that you'll encounter, Wat Chang Lom and Wat Chedi Chet Thaew, are the most impressive in the city. **Wat Chang Lom** is distinctly Sri Lankan, with its characteristic stupa and 39 laterite elephant buttresses (it's unusual in Thailand to find so many elephant sculptures still intact). If you ascend the stairs, you can walk around the base of the stupas and admire the 19 Buddhas that are installed in niches above the terrace. The history of this wat relates to the discovery of the Buddha's relics at the site during the reign of King Ram Khamhaeng. The king built the temple to commemorate the event, and it is described in the stone inscription found at Sukhothai.

Just to the south is **Wat Chedi Chet Thaew,** a complementary complex to the more regal Wat Mahatat at Sukhothai. Like its more famous cousin, Wat Chedi Chet Thaew is distinguished by a series of lotus-bud towers and rows of chedis thought to contain the remains of the royal family. Many of the chedis are adorned with stucco decorative images, and some have traces of color.

The balance of monuments within the ancient city walls are worth inspecting, though nothing compares to **Wat Phra Si Rattana Mahatat,** located about half a mile southeast of the bridge. The most prominent feature of this 13th-century temple is the Khmer-style prang, thought to date from the renovation made under the rule of the Ayutthaya King Borommakot in the 18th century; the original structure probably was of classical Sukhothai design. The highlight of this monument is the exterior carving and sculpture, in particular a superb walking Buddha done in relief. Some of the more delicate fragments of the wat, including very rare wooden doors, have been removed to the museum in Sukhothai.

The site at Si Satchanalai is open daily from 8 a.m. to 5 p.m.; admission is 25 baht ($1).

CHAPTER XIX

CHIANG MAI AND THE NORTHERN HILLS

□ □ □

1. ORIENTATION
2. USEFUL INFORMATION
3. ACCOMMODATIONS
4. DINING
5. WHAT TO SEE AND DO IN THE CITY
6. DAY TRIPS FROM THE CITY
7. SHOPPING
8. NIGHTLIFE
9. TREKKING IN THE NORTHERN HILLS

It would be difficult to find a city in Thailand that reflects more of the country's rich cultural heritage and modern aspirations than Chiang Mai. Dating back to the 13th century, Chiang Mai was the capital of Lan Na Thao (Kingdom of One Million Rice Fields), the first independent Thai state. The area has also been home for centuries to hill-tribe people including the Akha, Karen, Lahu, Lisu, Hmong, Yao, and the descendants of the Mon-Khmer people. These tribes farm the 3,300-foot-high fertile terrain, living lives that seem to belong to another century.

Aspects of the past are reflected in wats ablaze with the color of saffron and abuzz with the chanting of monks, traditional markets selling handcrafts and artifacts, streets lined with skillfully built teak houses, and vestiges of a system of walls and moats originally constructed for defense. Yet Chiang Mai is a thoroughly modern city, Thailand's second city after Bangkok, and one with the usual blessings and shortcomings of contemporary life. One of the most significant recent changes has been the displacement of tribal people in the nearby hills and valleys to make way for the development of retirement- and vacation-home communities.

Each year in early February the city hosts one of the nation's most extravagant pageants, the Chiang Mai Flower Festival, replete with floats, traditional and modern music, food stalls selling delicious foods, and masses of orchids, jasmine, and roses. In April the city celebrates again, this time marking the traditional Thai New Year (Songkran Festival), with lively processions and religious ceremonies. Chiang Mai is also renowned for the beauty and grace of its women; it's a joy to listen to these enchantresses speak with their lilting, melodic dialect.

Because of its temperate climate (similar to the hill stations in nearby Burma) and central location, Chiang Mai is an excellent base for exploring the north of Thailand. One of the most popular side trips is a trek through the hilltribes region, where small groups either head north toward Chiang Rai and the Golden Triangle or northwest to more remote Mae Hong Son.

The hot season lasts for only two months, during March and April. During the rest of the year the weather is pleasant, far cooler than Bangkok; at night, from November to February, a sweater is often required.

HISTORICAL BACKGROUND: In the late 13th century King Mengrai, the son of King Lao Meng of nearby Chiang Sean, consolidated his rule by uniting several Thai tribes that had migrated from southern China. He built his original capital in Chiang Rai in 1262. Mengrai, whose brilliant rule was aided by useful alliances, saw a threat in Kublai Khan's Mongol incursions into Burma and quickly formed an alliance with Sukhothai in the south. The Lanna Thai king moved to consolidate his position when he vanquished the vestiges of the Mon empire in Hariphunchai and, in 1296, moved his new capital south to what is now Chiang Mai. There is a monument to King Mengrai, across from Wat Phan Tao, where he was supposedly struck by lightning and killed in 1317.

For the next century Chiang Mai prospered. The kingdom grew, taking in most of the present-day northern provinces, and with Sukhothai as its ally, was able to repulse any significant attack from its Khmer and Mon neighbors. With the rise of Ayutthaya came the eventual destruction of the Sukhothai Empire and Chiang Mai and the Lanna Thai's guarantor of power. Ayutthaya forces repeatedly tried to take Chiang Mai, but the kingdom did not yield. Instead, Chiang Mai strengthened itself, and from the late 14th century until the eventual fall to the Burmese in 1556, it enjoyed tremendous affluence and influence. Many of the most renowned wats were built during this period.

After 200 years of relentless warfare with the Burmese, Chiang Mai and the Lanna Thai Kingdom were destined for ruin. Even after King Taksin recaptured Chiang Mai from the Burmese army in 1775, the city and its inhabitants were so weakened that Taksin had those few who had survived moved to nearby Lampang. For two decades Chiang Mai was literally a ghost town, bringing an end to its kingdom.

A new line was begun in 1796 when King Rama I appointed a local prince the governor of the reestablished Chiang Mai. The city was formally incorporated into the modern Thai state in 1938.

1. ORIENTATION

The site of medieval Chiang Mai was chosen by a triumvirate of 13th-century kings, representing the Lanna Thai, powerful Sukhothai, and Phayao kingdoms. Always keen to spot metaphysical spirits and signs, the royals selected an area that was inhabited by a triumvirate of forces symbolized by two white barking deer, two white sambar deer, and a family of white mice. The chosen tract was on a fertile plain bordered by the Mae Nam Ping River to the east and the verdant, cool Doi Suthep Mountains to the west, and was to be called Nopphaburi Si Nakhonphing Chiang Mai (the formal title of the new city).

The **Old City** was completely surrounded by a massive wall and a moat.

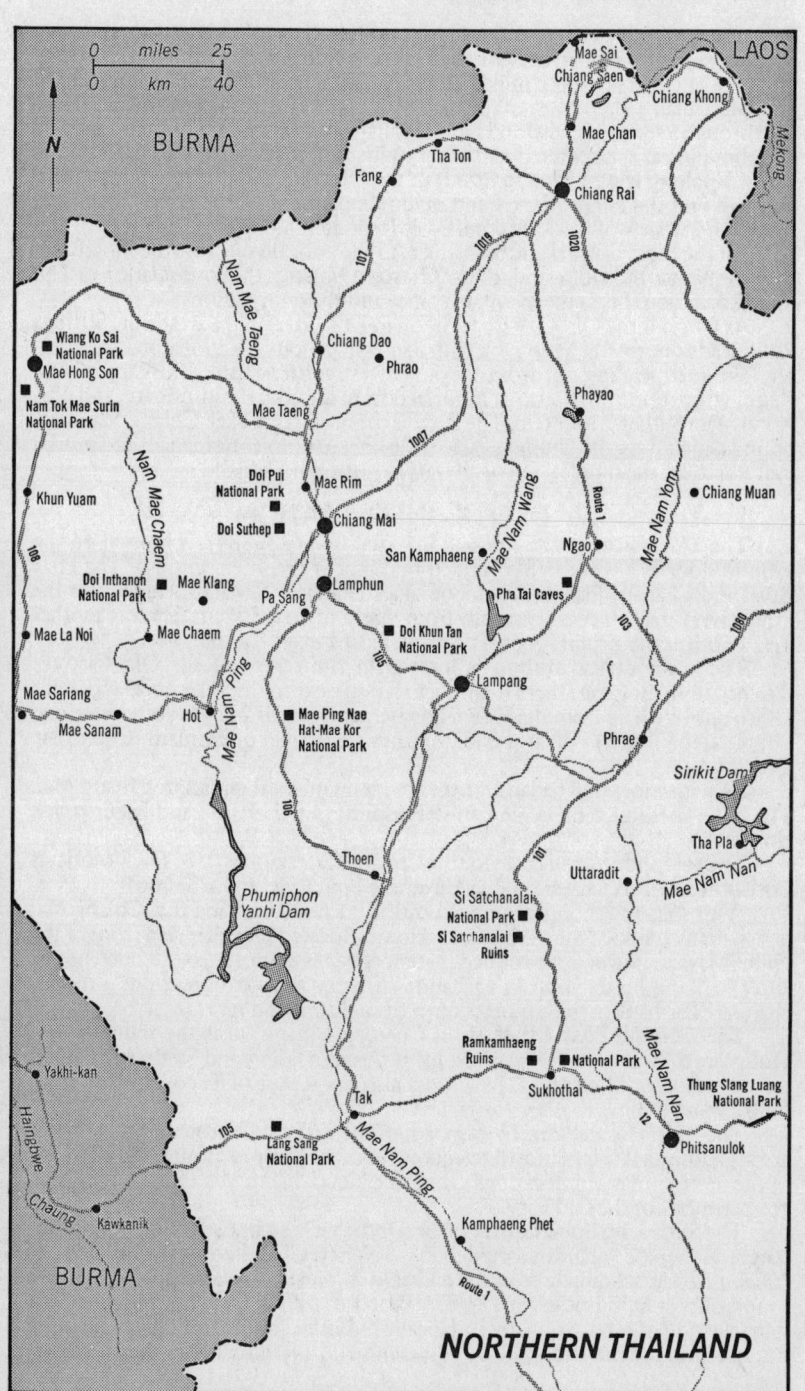

NORTHERN THAILAND

Only the moat survives today (and it was rebuilt in the 18th century), and only the restored gates remain as reminders of the original wall. Within the Old City are three of the area's more important wats, Wat Chedi Luang, Wat Phra Singh, and Wat Chiang Man. Most of the major streets radiate from the Old City (passing through a series of gates) and fanning out in all directions. The main business and shopping area is centered in the half-mile stretch between the six gates on the east side (along **Moon Muang Road)** of the Old City and the Ping River. Here you will find the Night Market and many shops, some of the better hotels and restaurants, a slew of trekking companies (especially along Tha Phae Road), and some of the most picturesque backstreets in the area. If you cross the Ping River over the **Nawarat Bridge** and follow **Charoen Muang** (the continuation of Tha Phae Road) you'll pass the main post office and the train station.

As you exit the Old City from the Suan Dok Gate on the west side, **Suthep Road** leads out to Wat Suan Dok with its justly famous traditional massage center. The road leading out from the northwest corner of the Old City is **Huai Kaeo,** where one finds a strip of modern hotels, the zoo, the university, and ultimately Doi Suthep Mountain. The latter is the most regal of all Chiang Mai compounds, including the Phuping Palace (the king's summer residence) and nearby Wat Phrathat, the most sacred of all wats in northern Thailand.

2. USEFUL INFORMATION

The **TAT office,** at 135 Praisani Rd. (tel. 053/235334), is housed on the ground floor in a wonderful rounded building at the intersection of Tha Phae Road and Charoen Prathet Road, one block from the Nawarat Bridge (over the Ping River). The office is open daily from 8:30 a.m. to 4:30 p.m. There is another TAT booth at the airport, open daily from 8:30 a.m. to 8 p.m.

The main **police station** is located in the center of the Old City on Ratchadamnoen Road; there is another station next to the Telephone and Telex Office one block up from the TAT. For emergencies, call 221444; otherwise you can reach the **Tourist Police** at 235490 (they are located on Samlarn Road in the Old City).

As with most of Thailand, there are many medical clinics in Chiang Mai. The main medical centers are **Lanna Hospital** (tel. 211037) and **McCormick Hospital.**

The **telephone area code** for the Chiang Mai region is 053. The **American Consulate** is on Wichayanon Road, near the Ping River (tel. 235566).

With so many shopping opportunities, it's not surprising that Chiang Mai has so many **banks.** One of the most centrally located branches is in front of the Night Market; however, be warned that most banks do not keep extended hours. After banking hours you can exchange currency at your hotel or at a money changer. The bank at the airport is open from 8 a.m. to 8 p.m.

The **General Post Office** is on Charoen Muang, near the train station. Hours are 8:30 a.m. to 4:30 p.m. Monday through Friday and 8:30 a.m. to noon on weekends and holidays. The airport also has a post office, open daily from 8:30 a.m. to 8 p.m.

The **PTT** is located one block north of the TAT on Charoen Prathet. There are six additional international telephone booths scattered around the city (one of the more convenient locations is near the New Chiang Mai Hotel on the eastern perimeter of the Old City).

The **Suriwong Book Center** on Sri Dornchai has a fine selection of English-language books, including guidebooks. Nancy Chandler's colorful *Map of Chiang Mai* is absolutely essential and sold in most bookstores in the area. We found ours at **D.K. Books,** at 234 Tha Phae Rd. (tel. 235151), where there is a fine selection of internationally and locally published books in English. If you're interested in the hill tribes, we can't recommend anything better than *Peoples of* *the Golden Triangle* by Paul and Elaine Lewis (London: Thames and Hudson, 1984). This is an extraordinary source book, containing detailed descriptions and color photographs of the main tribes residing in and around the north. Don't miss it! John Hoskin's *Chiang Mai and Northern Thailand* (Hong Kong: Hong Kong Publishing Co., 1984), is a good companion for those who want to explore the small towns in and around the Chiang Mai province.

GETTING THERE: Until the 1920s, when the railway's Northern Line was completed, one traveled to Chiang Mai either by long boat or by elephant. Either way, the trip took over two weeks and was considered fairly arduous. Today getting to Chiang Mai is a snap, with frequent flights, direct train service, and daily caravans of buses.

By Air

Chiang Mai is connected to Bangkok five times daily via **Thai Airways,** for a one-way fare of 1,275 baht ($51). There are also connecting flights between Chiang Mai and Phitsanulok three times daily for 505 baht ($20.25). There are three flights a day between Chiang Mai and Mae Hong Son and two a day to Chiang Rai, for 310 baht ($12.50) and 300 baht ($12) respectively. The Thai Airways office is located at 240 Prapokklao Rd. in Chiang Mai (tel. 211541).

Dragonair flies directly from Hong Kong to Chiang Mai every Wednesday and Saturday; their representative in Chiang Mai is **Golden Tour,** at 17/3 Charoen Pratwet Rd. (tel. 252031).

Thai International Airways maintains an office in Chiang Mai at the Saeng Tawan Theater Building on Chang Klan Road (tel. 234150).

By Train

There is daily train service from Bangkok to Chiang Mai on both the express and the rapid trains. The express takes 12 hours and departs Bangkok at 6 p.m., while the rapid takes 15 hours and departs at 3:45 p.m. Sleepers are available but should be reserved as early as possible. The price of a second-class round-trip air-conditioned sleeper (on the express only) is 940 baht ($37.50). A third-class round-trip seat on the rapid train runs 265 baht ($10.50). Tickets can be purchased at the Bangkok Railway Station (tel. 223-7020) up to 30 days in advance. In Chiang Mai you can telephone 242094 for local train information.

By Bus

Approximately 18 different companies offer air-conditioned bus service between Bangkok and Chiang Mai, with frequent departures. There are also public buses running eight times a day. If you're in Chiang Mai, it's best to check with a travel agent or to go to the Bangkok bus terminal at the Anusarn Shopping Center, off Chang Klan Road, for specific times. All buses to Chiang Mai depart from the Northern Terminal in Bangkok. If you take an air-conditioned bus, arrange to have the bus company shuttle you from your hotel in Bangkok to the Northern Terminal. The fare runs approximately 260 baht ($10.50) and the trip takes nine hours. There is also frequent bus service between Chiang Mai and Mae Hong Son, Phitsanulok, and Chiang Rai.

GETTING AROUND: When Carl Bock traveled to Chiang Mai in 1882 he wrote about the introduction of carriages: "I doubt, however, if, when the novelty of the thing died away, the people would care to adopt this mode of locomotion in preference to elephant-riding. . . . Even then, roads would have to be constructed for this purpose and the Laosian is not yet educated up to that high pitch of civilization." Much has changed. Not only are there carriages, but there are taxis, tuk-tuks, private cars, bus, minibuses, and best of all, bicycles.

If you have the stamina, the most efficient mode of transportation in and around Chiang Mai is via **bicycle**. The town is basically flat, there is a good network of roads (the "Laosians" have obviously progressed), the distances aren't too great, and it's terrific exercise. Many guesthouses rent bikes. We found very serviceable machines at the **Chiang Mai Guesthouse,** 91 Charoen Prathet (tel. 053/236501), where a day's rental runs 25 baht ($1). Other guesthouses around Tha Phae Road, in the Old City, also rent bikes, or if you're feeling bold, motorcycles for about 175 baht ($7). (Check to make sure you have the necessary insurance.) Expect to leave your passport or credit card as security.

After biking, the ubiquitous **tuk-tuk** is the next best option. The fare within Chiang Mai is always negotiable, but expect to pay about 50 baht ($2) for an hour-long ride. The local red **minibuses** cost 5 baht (20¢) for in-town destinations. The minibus to Wat Prathat on Doi Suthep Mountain charges 35 baht ($1.50) on the way up and 25 baht ($1) for the ride down. **Taxis** are not the most efficient vehicles for navigating Chiang Mai's twisting streets (and there aren't very many around), but a cab from the airport is a good idea. Expect to pay 75 baht ($3) to your hotel. Alternatively you can take the **Thai Airways limo** (really a minibus) for 25 baht ($1).

If you plan to tour outside of Chiang Mai there are several options. **Hertz,** at 442 Charoen Muang Rd. (tel. 235496), rents cars, with or without driver, by the day or week. **Avis** has an office at 14/14 Huai Kaeo Rd. (tel. 222013), opposite the Chiang Mai Orchid Hotel, with similar service. Self-drive rental rates range from $30 to $75 a day or $180 to $450 a week for unlimited kilometers. Expect to pay a driver from $6 to $10 an hour, with a three-hour minimum.

There is frequent and inexpensive **bus** service to the nearby villages of Saraphi, Lamphun, and Pa Sang, as well as Hang Dong; contact the TAT for the latest schedule.

FESTIVALS IN CHIANG MAI AND THE NORTHERN TOWNS: As

elsewhere in Thailand, there seem to be so many festivals that even without planning you're likely to run into one during your travels. Here are brief descriptions of a few of the major events.

February

The **Flower Festival** in Chiang Mai, one of the highlights of the year, celebrates Chiang Mai's undisputed position as the "Flower of the North" with a mammoth parade, concerts, flower displays and competitions, a food fair, and a beauty contest. The actual parade, the focal point of the festival, consists of flower-laden, often wat-shaped floats (orchids, roses, carnations, and daisies), marching bands, smiling beauties, dancing and drumming hill tribes people, impatient children, and a flower-garlanded elephant or two. The pace is decidedly Asian, not nearly as rushed as the Macy's Thanksgiving Day Parade, for example. The streets are jammed as spectators cling to or climb onto anything to get a clear view of the procession. The route begins at the Nawarat Bridge and snakes through town, culminating at Buak Hat Park in the southwest corner of the Old City.

The park itself is the location for most of the other events. Among them is an exquisite orchid competition/display, as well as demonstrations of flower arranging. The park is also the venue for the annual beauty pageant, with the late-evening crowning of Miss Chiang Mai Flower Festival.

As with any other festival there is an incredible assortment of food stalls selling such favorites as dried plums, grilled corn, sticky rice, popcorn, and (yes, even in Chiang Mai) Belgian waffles!

The **Chiang Rai Festival** takes place around the second week of February and it, too, has a long list of festivities. The festival is known for its special display of hill-tribe culture and a fine market. Those in the know claim it's the single most important gathering of tribal people in all of Thailand.

April
The **Songkran (Water) Festival** takes place on April 13, marking the Lanna Thai New Year. Most of the ceremonies take place at the wats, where water is sprinkled over Buddhas, monks, elders, and tourists, all to ensure good fortune. The Songkran Festival is celebrated in all of the northern provinces and is a most joyous event.

May
The end of May is **lychee season** in nearby Chiang Rai and a festival is held in honor of the harvest. There is a parade, lychee competition and display, lots of food (including you know what), and a beauty contest to find Miss Chiang Rai Lychee Nut. The festivities take place in Kho Loi Park. Consult the local TAT for details.

August
The **Longan Fair** in Lamphun celebrates that town's most favorite fruit, and yes, there is a Miss Longan competition. (For additional information, see the section below covering Lamphun).

September
Nan province sponsors a **boat race** with wildly decorated crafts zipping down the Nan River. The race is run seven days after the Rains' Retreat, marking the beginning of the dry season.

3. ACCOMMODATIONS
Unlike Bangkok, there are no luxury-class hotels similar to the Oriental or the Hilton, nor any first-class hotels either; however, Chiang Mai has many good moderately priced hotels and guesthouses, and many more budget choices, making a visit to the city far more affordable than Bangkok.

An Important Note: During the Flower Festival prices rise steeply, anywhere from 85% to 150% above the prices that are quoted below.

MODERATELY PRICED ACCOMMODATIONS: Most of the highest-priced hotels are concentrated in one of two areas: in the business district near the Ping River or to the west of the Old City on Huai Kaeo Road. The area around the business district, though closer to the heart of Chiang Mai (in both location and spirit) and the Night Market, is bound to be a bit noisier than the west-side neighborhood. The strip on Huai Kaeo Road is fairly undistinguished, but it's a convenient tuk-tuk ride away from the action in the Old City.

Around the Old City and the Business District
The ten-story **Chiang Mai Plaza Hotel**, at 92 Sri Donchai Rd. (tel. 053/252050), completed in 1986, is a typical bland modern Western-style hotel. Although it's moderately priced, many of its features are found in higher-category lodgings. The cavernous (and cold) lobby is so enormous that the few islands of furniture seem a bit lost in the acres of brilliantly polished granite. Accommodations are tastefully furnished and utterly clean; all rooms have the usual hi-tech amenities. There is a good-sized pool on the second floor and a small shopping arcade. The hotel is in town, but just far enough away, toward the Ping River, to be out of the congestion. Single rooms are 1,750 baht ($70); doubles are 2,000 baht ($80).

When the **Mae Ping Hotel,** Sri Donchai Road (tel. 053/251060), opened in late 1988, it added to the Chiang Mai skyline another tower-style hotel with 350 rooms and 50 suites, all with super-modern conveniences. Among the planned facilities, are an Italian restaurant, coffeeshop, nightclub, shopping arcade, swimming pool, and business center.

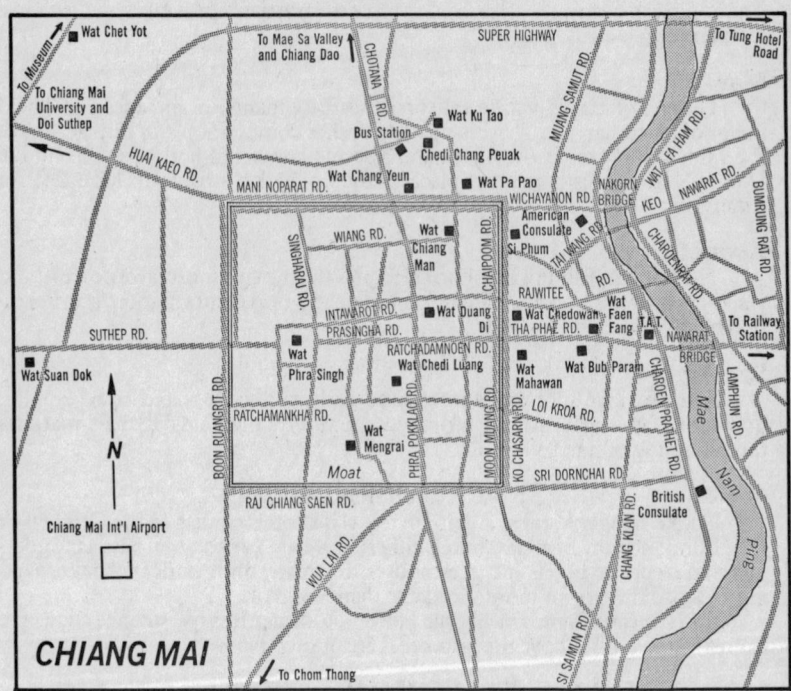

The **Dusit Inn,** at 112 Chang Klan Rd. (tel. 053/251033), the northern cousin of Bangkok's Dusit Thani, is a first-rate moderately priced hotel located less than 200 yards from Chiang Mai's famed Night Market. This is an ideal spot for those who enjoy being in the thick of things but want all the creature comforts: air conditioning, television, mini-bar, tasteful furnishings—all with an element of luxury. We found the hotel staff particularly helpful and courteous. The lobby is warmly elegant with many Thai objets d'art adorning the walls. The rooms are of good size, clean, and though not absolutely new, well maintained. The Dusit has a pool, a bar, and a splendid Chinese restaurant, Jasmine (most delicious for its lunchtime dim sum). Standard double rooms rent for 1,800 baht ($72), singles are 1,510 baht ($60); deluxe rooms go for 2,400 baht ($96).

Next door to the Dusit, at 110 Chang Klan Rd., the **Hotel Suriwongse** (tel. 053/236733) is one of Chiang Mai's better values. Its clubby lobby, paneled with carved dark hardwood and carpeted in a muted purple tone, gives it a richness that belies its moderate price. Rooms are of adequate size, but are equipped with first-class amenities. Unlike the woody decorative scheme downstairs, the colors in the upstairs guest areas are cheerier off-white and green pastel. The hotel's northern-style restaurant, Fueng Fah, is well regarded and very popular. Doubles run 1,660 baht ($66); singles are 1,430 baht ($57).

The moderately priced **Chiang Inn Hotel**, at 100 Chang Klan Rd. (tel. 053/235655), is located very close to the Night Market, at the opposite end from the Dusit and the Suriwongse. The hotel is set back from the street and minimizes your chances of being disturbed by street noises at night. The accommodations are quite acceptable, though not up to the highest standard in this price category. All 175 rooms are clean and have air conditioning, television, and mini-bars. The compact lobby is certainly a busy place, with a cocktail bar, piano bar, check-in area, and restaurant. Twin-bedded rooms rent for 1,900 baht ($76); singles are 1,480 baht ($59).

Around Huai Kaeo Road

The **Rincome Hotel,** 301 Huai Kaeo Rd. (tel. 053/221044), is one of our favorites in Chiang Mai because it retains a traditional Thai atmosphere. A member of Thailand's largest chain, Siam Lodge Hotels, it just might be their best. The lobby and rooms are all finely decorated with examples of local handcrafts, as are the staff: the helpful women behind the desk wear elaborately embroidered vests; the public spaces are adorned with Burmese tapestries and carved wooden sculpture (particularly white elephants); guest rooms have carved accents and moldings and sport locally made painted umbrellas and framed embroidery on the walls. Rooms are both spotlessly clean and comfortable. The grounds are expansive, containing two swimming pools and a tranquil garden. In addition, the handsome teak restaurant serves good food, and the Rincome has a few interesting shops in its arcade. All in all, at 1,663 baht ($66) for a single and 2,000 baht ($80) for a double, the Rincome Hotel is a fine value.

Since it opened, the **Chiang Mai Orchid,** at 100-102 Huai Kaeo Rd. (tel. 053/222099), has garnered a fine reputation for its facilities and friendly service. It deserves it. The rooms are pleasantly appointed with local woodcarvings, the lobby and other public spaces are festooned with flowers of various sorts (of course, there's a liberal scattering of orchids), and furnished with clusters of chic, low-slung rattan couches and chairs. Dark-wood lanterns add to the visually striking lobby. Within the Orchid's complex are a pool, a decent shopping arcade (there's a better mall across the street), several restaurants, a disco, and a cocktail lounge dubiously called the Opium Den. Low-floor single rooms are 1,510 baht ($60) and high-floor singles are 2,100 baht ($84), with doubles running 1,660 baht ($66) and 2,400 baht ($96) respectively. If you intend to stay at the Orchid during the high season, it's advisable to make a reservation as early as possible.

BUDGET HOTELS: As with the moderately priced lodgings, most of the hotels are either centered in the Old City or the business district, or along Huai Kaeo Road.

Around the Old City and the Business District

The **River View Lodge,** 25 Charoen Prathet Rd., Soi 2 (tel. 053/251109 or 251110), is tucked away down on the riverbank and is run by a delightful couple. The lawns stretch down to the river and the property has a deck where you can sit outside and have breakfast. The attractive building of white stucco has a row of dormers, each gable decorated with local Thai carving. The 36 rooms show a personal touch—the teak furniture was locally crafted, the lamp bases are locally modeled Buddha images, and there are traditional woodcarvings above the beds. They have tile floors and contain table, chairs, dresser, telephone, air conditioning, and bathroom with shower. Our favorite room is the small one with its own garden terrace. In the airy, tiled restaurant you'll be served traditionally prepared home-style cuisine as well as European-style food. This really is a home-away-from-home kind of place. Singles or doubles range from 600 baht ($24) to 660 baht ($26.50), depending on whether you have a river view. Only a five-minute walk from the Night Market.

Even if you don't stay at the **Chiang Mai President,** 226 Wichayanon Rd. (tel. 053/251025), you might want to take a look inside. It's wild. Carved wooden elephant-head tables, plenty of mirrors, flashing lights, marble, tiles made in imitation of wood relief, painted murals on elevator doors, live Thai singers—you name it and it's likely to be found somewhere in this hotel's front-end circus. It's too bad that the "let's throw it on the wall and see if it sticks" décor isn't carried out upstairs or we'd undoubtedly recommend this for those on the kitsch circuit. Instead the rooms are only of acceptable quality compared to its similarly priced competitors. The President (we kind of wondered which president inspired this) is very popular with European tour groups and those looking for an entertaining evening right at their own front door. Singles and doubles rent for 525 baht ($21).

Even though it's not fancy, another favorite budget choice is the **Chiang Mai Guesthouse,** 91 Charoen Prathet (tel. 053/236501), a 28-room inn overlooking the Ping River. The setting is fairly idyllic: a small garden-and-courtyard compound near the river that's just a five-minute walk to the Night Market and some of the city's best restaurants. There are many variations on the room configurations, though all are clean, some are large, many have bathrooms, a few have views, and most have air conditioning. The room prices reflect these various options, with rates ranging from 125 baht ($5) sharing a bath to 275 baht ($11). The Guesthouse also has very serviceable bicycles for rent at 30 baht ($1.25) a day. Their small restaurant is an ideal spot for a peaceful breakfast or snack. Highly recommended. Call ahead for reservations.

The ever-popular **Diamond Hotel,** built near the banks of the Ping River at 33/10 Charoen Prathet (tel. 053/234153), is a good budget choice both for its location and price. The seven-story building normally hosts group visitors from Europe and the lobby is often filled with French and German travelers. Rooms are simple but clean, and some have river views. Though the hotel has a comfortable, homey feel, it's getting a bit worn. Nevertheless, for the budget traveler the Diamond is a good choice. Doubles run 830 baht ($33); singles cost 650 baht ($26). One of the most favored aspects of the Diamond is its two restaurants (see "Dining"), the White Orchid and Lanna Khan Toke.

If the Chiang Mai Guesthouse is fully booked or you want to match the convenience and price, try the **Galare Guest House** at 7-7/1 Charoen Prathet, Soi 2 (tel. 053/233885), near the Night Market. Rooms are in a Thai-style building with broad, covered verandas glistening with polished teak and rattan furniture, overlooking a pleasant garden and courtyard. Though the rooms are small, they are comfortable and tastefully furnished. The real value rooms have attached toilets and showers and air conditioning (but no phone) for 300 baht ($12) double. Galare also offers a no-frills restaurant under a covered deck overlooking the river, as well as a number of choices for organized treks to hill-tribe villages near Chiang Rai and Mae Hong Son. They can also arrange local tours of Chiang Mai.

The **Prince Hotel,** at 3 Tai Wang Rd. (tel. 053/236744), is another budget choice located a short tuk-tuk ride from the Night Market. The rooms and public spaces have touches of local style, and the facilities are clean but aging. Rooms have televisions and come with fan or air conditioning. Singles with fan run 480 baht ($19), and with air conditioning, 815 baht ($33); doubles run 485 baht ($19) and 970 baht ($39) respectively.

Located one block from the Mae Nam Ping River, the 180-room **Pornping Hotel,** 46 Charoen Prathet (tel. 053/235099), bustles with activity, primarily focused at its coffeeshop with live music. The hotel is popular with Chinese guests, and we have observed some very spirited card games in the corner of its homey lobby. The public spaces are of the polished marble, glass, and mirror variety (that is, Hong Kong style). The rooms aren't quite so glitzy, though they are air-conditioned. The service tends to be a bit brusque. Singles and doubles rent for 980 baht ($39) in the standard category, with deluxe accommodations renting for 1,485 baht ($59).

Around the Train Station

Going away from town in an easterly direction, about half a mile from the Ping River near the train station, is the 150-room **Royal Park,** at 471 Charoen Muang (tel. 053/242755). This bright white, six-story hotel is popular with many Asian groups, which gives it a bit more of an exotic atmosphere than is warranted by its rather nondescript interior. Rooms are clean, air-conditioned, and of decent size; they also have televisions and balconies. There is a pool downstairs and a pretty little garden in the rear. For 750 baht ($30) single or 875 baht ($35) double, the Royal Park is an acceptable alternative.

Right around the corner from the Royal Park is the attractive **Nantawan Guesthouse,** 50/1 Thunghotel Rd., where a double room runs 300 baht ($12). Like the Royal Park, this is a budget alternative if you need to stay near the train station.

Around Huai Kaeo Road

The **Holiday Lodge, Chiang Mai,** 16/16 Huai Kaeo Rd. (tel. 053/210-9014), opened in 1987 and offers 70 rooms in well-kept buildings set in a U-shape around a pool and garden where you can view the outline of Doi Suthep in the distance. The possibilities are particularly attractive here because they include an eight-person dormitory room with teak bunks, a four-person room furnished with dresser, table, and chairs as well as bunks, and of course, the typical double, including a very large queen-size with its own TV. All rooms have air conditioning, bath/shower, and telephone. Dormitory accommodations are 180 baht ($7.25) per person; regular doubles are 725 baht ($29) and the extra-large queen is 875 baht ($35). The hotel has a decent casual restaurant as well as a comfortable TV lounge off the pastel-colored lobby. The management is very friendly.

Sri Tokyo, on the road that runs along the western perimeter of the Old City at 6 Boon Ruangrit (tel. 053/213899), is a recently built high-rise near the far ritzier Orchid. The rooms are fairly compact, as are the lobby and pool. It's as if everything here is done at 80% of "normal" size. Though somewhat diminutive, lodgings are amply furnished with bamboo and rattan beds, tables, and chairs. All rooms are equipped with air conditioning and television. One unique design feature of the Sri Tokyo, other than its odd proportions, is that all the floors are open-air along the sides, allowing for good cross ventilation but a wee too much noise. Choose your room carefully; you'll sleep better. Singles or doubles run 850 baht ($34) a night.

It may be a bit tough to find, but the 31-room **YMCA,** at 2/4 Mengrairatsamee Rd., off Hutsadhisawee Road near the Thai Public Library and just a few blocks from the Orchid (tel. 053/221819), offers clean, quiet, and hospitable rooms to many a long-distance traveler. As with most Ys, there's a fairly wide selection of rooms ranging from private rooms with air conditioning and shower to dorm-style beds sharing a common bath. Rates are 280 baht ($11) for the top-of-the-line down to 75 baht ($3) for a bed in a three-person room. The YMCA also has a family room that runs 475 baht ($19) with fan, 555 baht ($22) with air conditioning. Use of the Y is included in the price.

Midway along the Huai Kaeo strip is the four-story **Chiang Mai Hills Hotel** (tel. 053/221255), which offers a lot for its budget prices: spacious rooms, sauna, swimming pool, two restaurants, and massage. Accommodations are clean, though lacking in style. Doubles go for 900 baht ($32), while singles run 750 baht ($30).

The **Chiang Come Hotel,** set off Suthep Road at 7/35 (tel. 053/211020), is near the Suan Dok Gate on the west side of the moat. Located in more of a residential neighborhood than the Huai Kaeo Road hotels, this budget inn is very quiet, though a tad isolated. The hotel caters largely to a middle-class Asian clientele with only a few Europeans to be seen. Perhaps these regional visitors know something about value, because the Chiang Come, with rooms going for 625 baht ($25) single and 690 baht ($28) double, is a very reasonable deal. Though not fancy, the rooms are clean and cool.

When you enter the grounds of the 98-room **Chiang Mai Resort Hotel,** at 99/9 Huai Kaeo Rd. (tel. 053/222122), a short distance from Chiang Mai University, you might imagine that Motel 6 has a branch in Chiang Mai. It really does have that "Let's just pull off the road, dear" feel. The rooms are spartanly furnished, though equipped with the essentials: air conditioning, hot water, and shower. Single and double rates are the same, 500 baht ($20).

The 156-room **Phucome Hotel,** at no. 21 on the Huai Kaeo strip (tel. 053/211026), was built in 1985 but already has signs of wear. Everything is spic and span and the staff is certainly eager to please, but you'd do well to inspect your room before committing. This five-story inn charges 825 baht ($33) for a standard single or double.

4. DINING

Northern-style cooking differs from that of the south primarily because of the influences of the various ethnic minorities (including the Burmese) who live in the area. Even the Chinese food is different, reflecting the number of Muslims who have migrated south from Yunnan Province (there are many restaurateurs from Kunming). Among the most distinctive dishes are sticky rice (often served in a knotted banana leaf), khao soi (a spicy, curried broth with vegetables and egg noodles), and many other meat and fish curries. The formal northern meal is called Khan Toke, the name referring to the custom of sharing a variety of entrees with guests around low tables. Most of the restaurants that serve in the Khan Toke style combine a dance performance with the meal, making it a full evening's entertainment. Chiang Mai is also blessed with wonderful street food and food markets (there's a fine one next to the Night Market). As usual, check to see that the ingredients (especially the oil) and cooking utensils are clean, and then go to it.

Like Bangkok, Chiang Mai has many restaurants serving both local and international cuisine. If you're in the mood for French, for example, don't despair —it's here and it's moderately priced.

NORTHERN THAI EVENINGS: A popular dining room where guests can sample the food and dance of northern culture is **Lanna Khan Toke** on Charoen Prathet Road (tel. 234153). The restaurant, popular with groups, is housed in a Victorian-style building upstairs from the White Orchid, a Chinese eatery. Guests remove their shoes before entering the wooden room, and sit on comfortable pillows at a low table. The menu is fixed and usually includes sticky rice, cap moo (fried pork skins), kang kai (a meat-and-vegetable curry), stir-fried chicken, larb (minced beef with chili peppers), and namprik ong (a spicy pork-and-vegetable dish). After dinner, everyone adjourns to the lower-floor amphitheater for a program of traditional northern dances. The price for dinner and dancing is 210 baht ($8.50) per person. Because many groups attend the Lanna Khan Toke, it's a good idea to phone ahead for reservations. Dinner begins at 7 p.m.

A similar type of meal is served at the **Old Chiang Mai Cultural Center,** on Wua Lai Road (tel. 235097); if you call, they'll often arrange to pick you up at your hotel. The Cultural Center has craftmaking displays from the hill-tribe villages as well as shops. Prices are about the same as at Lanna Khan Toke. Nearby is a Thai herbal massage center, which sounds like just the thing before a khan toke meal and dance performance. Dinner begins at 7 p.m.

THAI CUISINE: One of northern Thailand's food specialties is chicken gai yang (for years, we've been eating it in New York as "Chickens Die Young"), a honey-grilled fowl that puts Colonel Sanders to shame. Chiang Mai's best is, appropriately, the **Honey Chicken Restaurant,** located next to the Pornping Hotel on Charoen Prathet. An order of this delicacy is 40 baht ($1.50) for a large plate, enough for two. The key to gai yang is certainly the sauce, a sweet and slightly hot condiment that should be used liberally. Continuing on the chicken theme, try the spicy chicken soup with plump and abundant mushrooms. The atmosphere at this open-air restaurant is totally casual, and you'll find mostly Thai locals with only a few farangs. A real value: Dinner for two should run 115 baht ($4.50).

Suthasinee Khao Soi, at 134/10 Chang Klan Rd. (no telephone), isn't easy to find and they close early (before 9 p.m.), but if you want to try some very authentic khao soi, this is a sure bet. A bowl of this spicy and aromatic noodle-and-vegetable concoction will set you back a modest 12 baht (50¢), but this is a big-time taste sensation. This isn't a touristy place, so if you have a hard time finding it, just ask any resident for Khao Soi and they'll likely point you in the right direction.

Our two favorite **food markets** where there are ample opportunities to sample local favorites are located on the corner of Loi Kroa Road and Chang Klan near the Night Market and the Somphet Market on northwest interior perimeter road in the Old City. At night, try the food stalls on Moon Muang Road at the southwest corner of the Old City. There is a row of outdoor restaurants and stalls on the other side of the moat at the gate near Loi Kroa Road.

If you're out touring and find yourself near Wat Suan Dok, you might want to visit a branch of the local **Rote Yiam Noodles** chain, where you can eat an inexpensive bowl of beef noodles or try their Lampang khao soy (a curried noodle soup).

Up the hill toward Doi Suthep, at 65 Suthep Rd. you come to the **Galae Restaurant,** set in an enviable location overlooking a lake with shade trees and outdoor dining. In the evening you can sit out under the moon and the stars, dining by candlelight. The place is famous for the beef that's cooked on a spit with dried chili, lemon juice, and garlic sauce.

If you're looking for fresh fish, try the **Nang Nual Seafood Restaurant,** 27/2 Koa Klang Rd. (tel. 235771). Though they serve a varied international menu including Western and Chinese cuisine, we enjoy their Thai-style fish dishes. The setting is exotic—guests dine in a garden with a waterfall. Two should expect to spend about 345 baht ($13.75) for a complete meal.

Saving one of the best for last, **Baan Suan Restaurant,** at 51/3 San Kamphaeng (tel. 234116), is an ideal lunch or dinner option for those who are scouring this busy road for exotic shopping bargains. The physical layout is spacious with both outdoor and indoor seating (air-conditioned) in a traditional teak house. The menu is varied with typical northern Thai dishes mixed with Burmese and other regional entrees. We particularly loved their Burmese curries, steamed pomfret with plum sauce, and Chiang Mai sausage. Dishes cost 45 baht ($1.75) to 70 baht ($2.75). Two can eat here for about 230 baht ($9.25). Baan Suan is open daily from 11 a.m. to 2:30 p.m. and 6 p.m. to midnight.

VEGETARIAN CUISINE: It's hard to categorize the **Whole Earth Restaurant,** located down the street from the Chiang Mai Plaza Hotel at 88 Sri Dornchai Rd. (tel. 232463). The food, not strictly vegetarian but leaning in that direction, is Thai, Chinese, and Indian. The restaurant is housed in a modern hardwood, glass, and concrete building with an interior that's in line with the nearly exclusively Western crowd that it attracts (much like its Bangkok cousin of the same name). In the evening there is often an acoustic guitarist strumming mellow tunes. If this sounds like a heavy farang scene, it is; at our last meal here, we sat next to a couple who talked about the high cost of coops in Manhattan. But don't be put off, the food is fine. If you're looking for an evening of Asian food in the Western style, then the Whole Earth Restaurant will satisfy.

West of the Old City, at 11 Suthep Rd. (across from the Medical School), is the cheap and wonderful **Mansavirat Vegetarian Restaurant** (no telephone), where two can sup on Thai noodles and vegetables for less than 65 baht ($2.50)! Open daily for breakfast and lunch only.

CHINESE CUISINE: On the first floor of the Dusit Inn, a short way from the Night Market on Chang Klan Road, **Jasmine** (tel. 251033) is an intimate, quiet, and tastefully decorated Cantonese restaurant that specializes in dim sum. These delicately made and only mildly spiced dumplings are steamed in baskets and served immediately. Most baskets contain two to four pieces and cost about 14 baht (55¢). The variety of dim sum changes often, but there are normally 12 different kinds from which to choose. Two people will be amply fed for 115 baht ($4.50). At dinner or lunch, the usual Chinese entrees can be ordered from the menu. House specialties include bird's-nest soup, barbecued pig, crystal prawns, crab claw casserole, minced squab with lettuce, and bean curd with black mushrooms. If you select from the menu, a great and exotic Chinese feast should cost about 345 baht ($13.75). Jasmine is open daily and accepts all credit cards.

The **White Orchid** is the downstairs neighbor of Lanna Khan Toke on Charoen Prathet (tel. 234153), but it offers Chinese food only. Diners are served around large tables, where ten can sup comfortably. For the farang, be assured that the restaurant can easily accommodate couples or small groups. You can either sit under the covered pavilion or outside in the garden café overlooking the river. We enjoyed a sensational meal including Peking duck, roast duck, sliced noodles with shrimp, chicken with cashews, and stir-fried mixed vegetables. Dinner (or lunch) for two should cost 115 baht ($4.50) to 230 baht ($9.25), depending on the entree. The White Orchid is open from 11 a.m. to 2 p.m. and 5 to 10:30 p.m. daily.

WESTERN CUISINE: At **Le Coq d'Or,** 18-20 Chaipoom Rd. (tel. 252605), we enjoyed the best French food that we found anywhere outside Bangkok. Although the owner-chef is Swiss, the restaurant could have been plopped down here from Alpine France with its cozy wood beams, tile floors, upholstered red French chairs, and French country artifacts. The beef was the most tender that we tasted anywhere in Thailand, and according to the chef, the locally raised cattle have been developed by the Thai army in cooperation with the French. The food is classic French, from the appetizers—goose pâté, shrimp cocktail, escargots in butter and herbs, consommé with sherry—to the desserts, which include pear Belle Hélène, soufflé Grand Marnier. The main courses, too, run from filets of sole with lemon and capers or whole red snapper to duck à l'orange and rack of lamb. Prices range from 175 baht ($7) to 325 baht ($13). A really fine dinner for two with a decent bottle of wine will cost about 1,500 baht ($60). A place to go when you can't take any more chili and beer or Mekhong (rice whisky). Open daily for lunch from noon to 2 p.m., and for dinner from 7 to 10 p.m.

Near Wat Chiang Man, Lung Thaworn ("Uncle Eternity") is a cultivated, older gentleman who for 12 years was a cook at the French Embassy. He still prepares a mean coq au vin and other French specialties at his **Lung Thaworn Restaurant,** located on Wiang Kaeo Road (no telephone). We loved his tomato soup and nicely grilled meat. The restaurant is not much more than a food stand with tables and covered with what looks like a temporary canopy. Two can eat for less than 175 baht ($7). Lung Thaworn is open daily from 8 a.m. to 10 p.m.

Down the street you'll find cheap steaks and baked potatoes in a very informal environment at **Ban Rai Steaks,** just a stone's throw from Wat Chiang Man.

Dining is al fresco behind the rustic wooden gates of the restaurant. A meal for two will cost under 260 baht ($10.50); open daily for lunch and dinner.

Back on Charoen Prathet at no. 71, along the Ping River, is one of Chiang Mai's prettiest restaurants, **Le Chalet** (tel. 236810). The restaurant is set in a wonderfully constructed two-story teak house surrounded by a rustic garden. The menu is French/continental and the food is okay for the price 130 baht ($5.25) to 165 baht ($6.50). Two should expect to pay about 600 baht ($24).

One of the more picturesque settings for dining and drinks is on the east bank of the Ping River, across from the Chinda Hospital. The **Riverside** (tel. 243239) is just fine for Western food (they serve Thai dishes as well), but most people come here for the view and music. We've heard everything from Cole Porter piano tunes to Hank Williams ballads strummed on a 12-string.

If you're craving Italian food (don't laugh, we've had good Italian food all over Thailand!), you'll have to head out Huai Kaeo Road to no. 100/63 and the **Babylon Restaurant** (no telephone). The Babylon is rather far, opposite the entrance to Chiang Mai University, but it's a good bet for those who are staying on upper Huai Kaeo. We loved their pasta and pizza, both delicious and extremely inexpensive. For pizza in town, try **Daddy's Pizza,** down Chang Klan Road near the Saengtawan Cinema on Sri Dornchai.

Looking for a game of darts, draft beer, and an English ambience? Search no farther than 88 Huai Kaeo Rd., just up from the Rincome Hotel, for **The Pub** (tel. 211550). The menu is fairly authentic pub food and the atmosphere is Thai-English homey.

We found two German restaurants, both with refreshing draft beer. The **Alt Heidelberg** (tel. 222034) is just up the street from the Chiang Mai Orchid, while the **Haus Munchen,** at 115/3 Loi Kroa Rd. (tel. 234027), is around the corner from the Night Market. You can eat wurst and other German favorites (including homemade brown bread), drink draft beer, as well as check in with the German expatriate community in these two popular hangouts.

5. WHAT TO SEE AND DO IN THE CITY

Chiang Mai offers superb sightseeing, shopping, trekking, elephant riding, rafting, and bicycle riding all within a compact geographical area. No matter what you choose, be sure to explore the city: stroll along the Ping River and into the Old City, visit the food and flower markets, search for elegant teak homes, and stop along the way to sample some of the world's best street food.

THE HISTORICAL SIGHTS: Except for Bangkok, Chiang Mai has the greatest concentration of exquisitely crafted wats in the country. If you start in the early morning you can see all of the principal sights in one day, particularly if you travel by bicycle or tuk-tuk. The following is a one-day itinerary beginning in the Old City. This tour is by no means exhaustive; there are hundreds of wats, shrines, and other sites of interest. These are simply the few highlights that are a "must" for anyone interested in Buddhist culture.

If you have rented a bicycle near the Tha Phae Gate or at one of the guesthouses, it normally makes the most sense to begin at **Wat Chedi Luang** on the corner of Ratchamankha Road and Phra Pokklao. Actually there are two wats of interest at this site. Wat Chedi Luang is a complex dating from 1411 when the original chedi was constructed by King Saen Mamuang. The already-massive edifice was expanded in the middle of the 15th century, only to have the structure ruined by a severe earthquake in 1545, just 11 years before the fall of Chiang Mai to the Burmese (it was never rebuilt). A Buddha still graces its exterior; it's not unusual to spot a saffron-robed monk contemplating the Buddha as he circles the chedi. The remarkable nagas, guarding the stairway entrance to the typical northern viharn, are exceptionally ornate and ferocious. Next to the tall gum tree on the left as you enter the compound is the shrine honoring Sao Inthakhin, also referred to as the city's pillar. It is believed that the upkeep of this wat is directly related to the well-being of Chiang Mai. During festivals, young girls often sell small birds trapped in rattan cages. It's a Buddhist custom to set them free—known as making merit—bringing good fortune to the liberator. You can buy into this good-luck ritual for about 6 baht (25¢). The other wat on the grounds is the attractive **Wat Phan Tao**, with its wooden viharn and bot, reclining Buddha, and fine carving on the eaves and door. After leaving the temple, walk around to the monks' quarters on the side, taking in the row of traditional, dark-wood northern architecture as well as the delightful landscaping.

Depart via the northernmost exit, opening onto Ratchadamnoen Road, and continue until it brings you into the grounds of **Wat Phra Singh**. The wat was built during the zenith of Chiang Mai's hegemony over the north; consequently it became one of the more important shrines in the city. Today it's still the site of many important religious ceremonies, and there are many monks in attendance (we found the monks here to be especially friendly and curious; if the opportunity is available, strike up a conversation with one of the students). King Phayu, of Mengrai lineage, built the chedi in 1345, principally to house the cremated remains of King Kamfu, his father. As you enter the grounds, head to the right toward the 14th-century library. Notice the graceful carving on the base and the characteristic roof line with four separate elevations. The sculptural *devata* (Buddhist spirits) figures, in both dancing and meditative poses, are thought to have been made during King Muang Kaeo's reign in the early 16th century. On the other side of the temple complex is the 200-year-old Lai Kham ("Gilded Hall") viharn, housing the venerated image of the Phra Singh or Sihing Buddha, brought to the site by King Muang Ma in 1400. Pay particular attention to the frescoes, illustrating the stories of Sang Thong (the Golden Prince of the Conchshell) and Suwannahong. These images convey a great deal about the religious, civil, and military life of 19th-century Chiang Mai (you might want to ask the guard to close the windows to reduce the glare for a better look) during King Mahotraprathet's reign.

The next stop, at **Wat Suan Dok** (originally called Wat Puppharama), is on Suthep Road. Take either road out of Wat Phra Singh leading to the Suan Dok Gate and continue straight for about a mile; Wat Suan Dok will be on your left. We like this complex less for its architecture (the buildings, though monumental, are undistinguished) but for the contemplative spirit of this former garden of the 14th-century Lanna Thai monarch, King Ku Na. Unlike most of the other wats (which are often considered more tourist attractions than working temples and schools), Wat Suan Dok houses quite a few monks, many of whom seem to have completely isolated themselves from the frenzy of the outside world. Among the main attractions in the complex are the bot, with a very impressive Chiang Saen bronze Buddha dating from 1504 and some garish murals; the chedi, built to hold the miraculous relics of the Buddha prophesied by Sumana Thera (the same monk who inspired Wat Phra That on Doi Suthep), a renowned monk of the late 14th century; and a royal cemetery with some splendid shrines. If you're so inclined, traditional Thai herbal massage (like that at Wat Po in Bangkok) is offered on the grounds of the wat. Also, there are several khao soi and noodle stands outside the temple; you might want to backtrack a few blocks on Suthep Road for good, cheap vegetarian fare at Mangsavirat Restaurant. Otherwise head to Huai Kaeo Road for more restaurants (see "Dining").

To reach the next location, continue up Suthep Road (go west) for a short distance to Nimmanahaeminda Road. Turn right and continue for about half a mile, going past the Rincome Hotel on Huai Kaeo. Cross Huai Kaeo, making a quick left and then a quick right, joining the so-called Super Highway (you can very comfortably ride a bike on the wide shoulder). On your left, about half a mile up the Super Highway, is one of the most elegant sites in all of central

Chiang Mai, **Wat Chet Yot** (also called Wat Maha Photharam). The chedi was built during the reign of King Tilokkarat in the late 15th century; his remains are in one of the smaller chedis. The unusual design of the main rectangular chedi with seven peaks is not of Thai inspiration, but was copied from a temple in nearby Burma (the temple also has architectural elements of Chinese Yuan and Ming origin, as well as Indian influence). However, the extraordinary proportions, sculptured relief on the base, and the juxtaposition of the other buildings make Wat Chet Yot ("Seven Spires") a masterpiece. We were particularly drawn to the angelic and seemingly levitating devata figures carved into the base of the chedi. The Lanna-style Buddha, hidden in the center, was sculpted in the mid-15th century, the same date as the wat in general. A door inside the niche containing the Buddha leads to the roof on which rests the Phra Kaen Chan ("Sandlewood Buddha"). There is also a nice vista of the temple and grounds from up top. (Note: Only men are allowed to ascend the stairs.) With such a strong spiritual ambience, it's most appropriate that a meeting of the World Sangkayana took place here in 1477 to revise the doctrines of the Buddha. The modern-looking viharn, next to the chedi, was constructed in 1981.

To return to the Old City, continue on the Super Highway, make a right turn on Chotana Road, entering through the Chang Puak Gate. Make a left on Wiang Kaeo and **Wat Chiang Man** will be on your left. (This is another good eating opportunity, with Lung Thaworn and Ban Rai Steaks very near to the site; see "Dining.") This wat, thought to be Chiang Mai's oldest, was built during the 14th century and was the home of King Mengrai. Like many of the wats in Chiang Mai, this complex reflects an architectural style incorporating native Lanna with other influences from other important centers of Buddhism. In this case, some of the structures look to be influenced by Ceylonese (Sri Lanka) designs: notice the typical row of elephant supports. Wat Chiang Man is most famous for its two Buddhas: Phra Sritang Khamani (a miniature crystal image known as the White Emerald Buddha) and the marble Phra Sri-la Buddha. We also enjoyed the pure sound of the small bells atop the spires of the chedi. Unfortunately, the viharn that safeguards these religious sculptures is almost always closed; however, it's open on Sunday and holidays.

OTHER SIGHTS: If you plan to go trekking or have an interest in the hill-tribe people in the surrounding area, you might want to visit the **Tribal Research Institute,** located two miles from the Old City off Huai Kaeo Road, on the grounds of Chiang Mai University. The institute conducts research, publishes excellent books and brochures, coordinates trekking groups, and runs an informative small museum devoted to the ethnographic legacy of the northern tribal groups. The museum is open Monday through Friday from 8:30 a.m. to 4:30 p.m.

Half a mile farther up Huai Kaeo is the **Zoo,** Thailand's largest, though hardly the most impressive. There is also a children's playground and a park-like arboretum in the hilly and cool setting. You might consider stopping here for a picnic before going up the 12-km (7½-mile) switchback road to Doi Suthep and the Phuping Palace.

6. DAY TRIPS FROM THE CITY

If you have time for only one day trip, we recommend taking a minibus up to Wat Phra That and touring Suthep Mountain. If you have more time, you might want to journey to Lamphun, Chiang Rai, Mae Hong Son, or to an elephant work camp.

WAT PHRA THAT AND THE ROYAL PALACE: The jewel of Chiang Mai is Wat Phra That, set atop Doi Suthep, some nine miles from the Old City and (2½ miles) from Phuping Palace, the summer residence of Thailand's royal family. This is one of four royal wats in the North, occupying one of the most breath-taking sites in all of Chiang Mai province. Doi Suthep is over 3,300 feet high and can be quite cool, even when it's warm down in the city. The mountain is covered with forests, waterfalls, and flowers and is an ideal picnic stop.

Wat Phra That was built to house a relic of the Buddha that was prophesied and found by Sumana Thera in the 14th century. During the installation of the relic in Wat Suan Dok (in the Old City), Sumana Thera discovered that the holy object had split in two, with one part equaling the original in size. A decision was made, in order to honor the miracle, to build another wat to house the "new" relic. King Ku Na placed the relic on a howdah of a sacred white elephant and let him wander freely through the hills. After several false starts, the prophetic pach-yderm blew his horn three times, made three counterclockwise circles, and knelt down. A site had been found atop Doi Suthep. The original chedi was built to a height of 26½ feet. Subsequent kings added to it, first by doubling the size, and then by adding layers of gold and other ornamentation to the exterior. Other structures were raised to bring greater honor to the Buddha and patron. Of these the most remarkable is the naga staircase, added in 1557, 290 steps leading up to the wat. The road winding up the mountain was the last major addition (making it far easier than the five-hour climb), finished in 1935 by Kruba Srivichai (a Lanna Thai monk) and thousands of volunteers after only 175 days of excavation and grating.

The best way to reach the wat is to take the minibus from Chang Puak (White Elephant) Gate on the northern side of the moat. The fare is 35 baht ($1.50) going up and 25 baht ($1) for the descent. The ride is curvy and cool, so plan on bringing a sweater. The bus stops at the base of the naga staircase. The climb is 290 steps and it really is part of the site and experience. For those who'd rather not, there's a motorized gondola that will lift you to the top for a modest 6 baht (25¢). Whether you take the stairs or not, the nagas (with their incredibly long scaly bodies) deserve careful examination as they comprise one of the most dramatic approaches to a temple in all of Thailand (try to ignore the many shops selling trinkets at the base). Within the temple grounds the sanctity of the pil-grimage becomes more apparent. Most Thai visitors come here to make an offer-ing and be blessed. The usual offerings are flowers, candles, and small squares of gold leaf that are applied to one's favored Buddha or to the exterior of a chedi. Believers kneel down in worship, often shaking prayer sticks or burning incense, as they attend to their ritual. It's not unusual to see a Westerner take part in these public ceremonies.

The architecture and site plan are extraordinary; from every vantage point the view is gorgeous. We delighted in the gilded-copper gold-leaf-covered deco-rative umbrellas around the central chedi and the murals showing scenes from the life of the Buddha. It's advisable to come in the early morning or evening to avoid the crowds.

If you're lucky (we never are), you can enter the grounds of the **Phuping Palace,** the summer home of the king and his family, to tour the reputably fabu-lous gardens. All we can say is that if members of the royal family are visiting admission is verboten; otherwise you can tour the garden on the weekends from 8:30 a.m. to 4:30 p.m.

LAMPHUN: Just 26 km (16 miles) south of Chiang Mai, this ancient city was founded in 663 by the Mon Queen Chammadevi as the capital of Hariphunchai. Throughout its long history Lamphun was fought over and often conquered. Be-fore Chiang Mai was settled, Lamphun was one of the leading powers of the north. In the 13th century, the overlord of the city, Ai Fa, built a canal linking Lamphun's Kuang River with the Mae Nam Ping, creating a link with growing Chiang Mai. After taking complete control over the city he treasonably delivered it to a rival king, Muang Rai, marking the advent of Lamphun's decline.

Like the Old City in Chiang Mai, the main attractions here (aside from the legendary women) are the historical buildings, including some excellent Dvaravati-style chedis, 9th-century wats, and a fine museum. Lamphun, as well as Pa Sang to the south, is also known for its excellent cotton and silk weaving and for a unique and tasty fruit called a longan. On the second weekend in August, Lamphun goes wild with its **Longan Festival,** celebrating with a parade of floats decorated only in longans, a fruit exhibition and market, and a beauty contest to select that year's Miss Longan.

If you're looking for silk and cotton, visit the row of **silk merchants and workshops** on Lamphun-Lee Road, including Suchada and Nandakwang, and Nandakwang Laicum; we'd also recommend Suvaree at 206 Rob Muang Rd. and Thielmnil at 439 Pa Sang-Lee Rd. In addition to the silk outlets in San Kamphaeng, the textiles produced in Lamphun are much sought-after by the discerning.

If you have a car, are driving to Lamphun, and have an interest in medicine, you might want to take a detour off Rte. 1008, to the **McKean Rehabilitation Institute.** This is a fascinating leprosy clinic and park dating from the beginning of this century. The clinic is set on an island and you can drive the circumference in a few minutes. There are tours conducted daily from 8 a.m. to 4 p.m. Monday through Friday and 8 a.m. to noon on Saturday.

Getting There

The most direct way to get to Lamphun is by car, taking the old highway, Rte. 106, straight to the town; there is a faster superhighway to the east, but you'll miss the lovely tree-lined road. Buses run to Lamphun and Pa Sang, leaving from the east side of the Nawarat Bridge in Chiang Mai, along the Ping River.

The Historical Sights

The first stop should be **Wat Phra That Hariphunchai,** the highlight of Lamphun and one of the most striking temples in all of Thailand. The central chedi, in Chiang Saen style, is over 200 feet high and dates from the 9th century, when it was built over a royal structure. The multitiered umbrella at the top is gilded with gold (indicating something of great value hidden inside the stone structure) while the exterior of the chedi is faced with bronze. Also of interest in the temple complex are an immense bronze gong (reputedly the largest in the world), several viharns (rebuilt in the 19th and 20th centuries) containing Buddha images, and a smaller structure that enshrines the supposed four footprints of the Buddha (in legend, he visited a hill about ten miles from the town where he left his footprints; the site is marked by Wat Phra Bat Tak Pha). During the full-moon day in May, there is a ritual bathing for the Phra That.

Across the street from the wat is the **Hariphunchai National Museum,** housing a wonderful collection of Dvaravati- and Lanna-style votive and architectural objects. The museum is open Wednesday through Sunday from 9 a.m. to 4 p.m.

Wat Chammadevi (Wat Kukut) is located less than half a mile northwest from the center of Lamphun. The highlights here are the late-Dvaravati-style chedis (thought to be similar to those at Buddha Gaya in India), Suwan Chang Kot and Ratana, built in the 8th and 10th centuries respectively. The chedis are remarkable both for their design as well as for the standing Buddhas that adorn the four corners of the structures. The wat itself was built by King Mahantayot, the son of Queen Chammadevi, in honor of his mother, the founder of the Hariphunchai kingdom.

PA SANG: If you continue down Rte. 106 another five miles you'll reach Pa Sang. Like Lamphun, Pa Sang is noted for its fine weaving, particularly of cotton thread. Small workshops are open for viewing, as are stands that sell locally woven textiles. The Lamphun bus continues to Pa Sang, making it an easy day trip from Chiang Mai.

LAMPANG AND THE ELEPHANT-TRAINING SCHOOL: Lampang,
notable for its magnificent Burmese temples, is located off the H11 superhighway, about 40 miles southeast of Lamphun. There is frequent bus service from Chiang Mai for 30 baht ($1.25); the stop is at the eastern terminal, just over the Nawarat Bridge on Charoen Rat Road and the trip takes about 2½ hours. In past descriptions the town was famous for its exclusive reliance on the horse and carriage for transportation, a throwback to its 19th-century European legacy. Now, however, the few horses look out of place among the darting tuk-tuks and motorcycles and the modern town offers little in the way of enchantment.

Don't let that put you off, for Lampang is graced with some of the finest Burmese temples in Thailand: **Wat Phra Keo Don Tao,** the supreme 18th-century Burmese temple in the country with its impressive carved wooden chapel and Buddha, once the repository for the Emerald Buddha (before it was moved to Bangkok) and, reputably, a strand of the Buddha's hair; **Wat Chedi Sao,** so named for its 20 Burmese-style chedis, picturesquely set in a rice field near the banks of the Wang River; on the other side of the river, **Wat Sri Chum** and **Wat Sri Rong Muang,** two exquisite Burmese temples; and 20 km (12 miles) to the south, **Wat Lampang Luang,** considered one of the finest examples of northern religious architecture.

Our favorite activity in the region is the demonstration at the **Young Elephant Training Center,** located 54 km (33 miles) east of Lampang, run by the Veterinary Section of the Northern Timber Work Department of the Forest Industry Organization. Unlike many other elephant camps, mostly set up for tourists, this is actually a working concern. The three- to five-year-old elephants train at this facility to harvest hardwoods, specifically teak, in the government-controlled forests. There are about 100 elephants at any one time at the center, all supervised by a veterinary staff and an experienced group of *mahouts* (handlers and trainers). Among the tasks that the elephants learn are bathing (the Huai Mae La provides enough water for frolicking), pushing logs with both trunk and tusks, log-hauling, walking in procession, piling logs, and crouching down to allow mahouts to mount and dismount, as well as learning their various commands. Elephants train throughout the year, except during the hot season from March to May. (Sometimes the school has no elephants in training, so check with the TAT office in Chiang Mai before heading out just to see the elephant camp.) The actual training and demonstration period runs from 7 to 11 a.m., every day except holidays.

DOI INTHANON NATIONAL PARK: Thailand's tallest mountain—
8,575 feet—is Doi Inthanon. The mountain and a series of waterfalls are protected in over a 360-square-mile national park that is only 47 km (29 miles) from Chiang Mai. The area also offers both Karen and Hmong tribal villages and elephants working in the field, making this a most popular day-trip destination for residents of Chiang Mai.

Doi Inthanon Road climbs 48 km (30 miles) to the summit of the mountain. Along the way you may stop at the 100-foot-high Mae Klang Falls (a popular picnic spot with food stands) and nearby Pakan Na Falls (less crowded). The latter requires a bit of climbing along a path. The main road continues up to the top where there is a fine view and two more falls, Wachirathan and Siriphum, both suitable for exploration.

If you travel by private car, take Rte. 108 south through San Pa Tong (if you want, you can take an eight-mile side trip to Lamphun on Rte. 1015). Continue south where there are signs in English that will direct you to the national park.

Larger buses and minibuses run to the village of Chom Thong from the Chiang Mai Gate, on the southern perimeter of the Old City. From Chom Thong you will have to take another minibus to the national park; expect to pay about 100 baht ($5) per person, plus the park entrance fee, from Chom Thong. Camping, with proper permits, is allowed in the park. Before going, check with the TAT office for the schedule and regulations.

MAE SA VALLEY: Another lovely area, though certainly more developed than the Doi Inthanon National Park, is the Mae Sa Valley, about 20 km (12 miles) northwest of Chiang Mai. The valley is being developed as a tourist resort, but it still has an unhurried feel with its elephant show (including rides), a cascade, and a nature park, as well as orchid nurseries. The public bus runs from Chang Puak (White Elephant Gate), on Chotana Road, about 300 yards north of the northern perimeter of the Old City. If you have a car, take Rte. 107 north to Mae Rim. Then proceed west on Rte. 1096, making sure to stop at the orchid farms, just after the Adisara Fish Restaurant.

CHIANG DAO: This town 56 km (35 miles) north via Rte. 107, offers, after the training school in Lampang, the most pleasant and authentic **Elephant Training Camp.** The adventure begins as you cross the rope bridge and walk the trails through the forest to the camp. After the elephants bathe in the river, demonstrations are given of log-hauling and log-rolling. Read the pamphlet that's available —elephant lore is fascinating. After the show, you can climb into a howdah and take a safari across the Ping River, and through the forest to a Lisu village. It's a two-hour trip, costs 475 baht ($19) each, and requires advance reservations. The show begins daily at 9 a.m. and 10 a.m. Prices are 50 baht ($2) for adults and 25 baht ($1) for children; rides are 12 baht (50¢) additional. A minibus runs every 20 minutes from the bus station, Chang Puek.

Lest you think we've forgotten about all matters historical, think again, because Chiang Dao has one of Greater Chiang Mai's more fascinating sites. Ten miles beyond the elephant camp and beyond the town is the **Chiang Dao Cave** (also known as Wat Tham Chiang Dao). The road from town leads through a wonderful stretch of hardwood forests and open land, finally ending at a delightful parking lot (you'll understand when you arrive) below the opening of the cave. Inside the cave are a series of Buddhist statues, including a 12-foot-long reclining Buddha. Among the most impressive are a row of five seated Buddhas in the first cavern. The cave itself extends well into the mountain, making it a spelunker's delight, but a forbidden zone for all but the brave and the experienced. Admission is 7 baht (30¢).

A Resort in the Hills

About two hours north of Chiang Mai, **Chiang Dao Resort,** 28 Village 6, Tombol Ping Kong, Amphoe Chiang Dao, Km. 100, Chiang Mai-Fang Hwy., is an attractive resort set on 80 acres of woodlands. The Chiang Mai office is at 104-8 Rajawong Rd. (tel. 053/236995 or 232434). Accommodations consist of chalets housing from one to eight people, that are sited around a lake. Each has modern furnishings, bathroom, balcony, and stone fireplace for log fires on cold nights. Wooden walkways link the various parts of the resort, which includes two restaurants. Rates go all of the way from 700 baht ($28) for two to a whopping 8,000 baht ($320) for a villa fit for a king.

7. SHOPPING

It's virtually impossible to visit Chiang Mai, if not all of northern Thailand, without leaving laden with purchases. From contemporary handcrafts made by Yao, Karen, Hmong, Akha, Lahu, and Lisu hill people to 14th-century celadon pottery, Chiang Mai is a shopper's paradise. In fact, the Night Bazaar (Market) is considered by some to be the city's premier attraction. Even if you aren't an inveterate shopper you'll have a ball watching those who are do their best at haggling with locals over precious souvenirs.

As in the rest of Thailand, except in the most modern shops bargaining is the rule. Shop around, compare prices, decide what you want to pay, and in most cases, subtract a substantial percentage for your opening bid. There is no rule. Sometimes prices are hiked up 200%, while at other times prices are listed at close to the ultimate price. If you're prepared to negotiate a bit, you're bound to find an acceptable price. Don't be intimidated by the process: after a while it becomes a regular part of shopping, and something like a sport.

THE NIGHT MARKET: There is actually a modern, antiseptic three-story building called the Night Bazaar, but the concept of Chiang Mai's night market extends well beyond the confines of that singular complex. Many of the city's shops remain open throughout the evening, especially those that line Chang Klan Road, on which the Night Bazaar is located. These stalls have grandiose names, like Harrods (with the familiar logo, of course) and most carry Bangkok-produced counterfeits of international name-brand clothing, watches, luggage, and music or video cassettes. One can pick up a skillfully manufactured "Lacoste" shirt, faithfully reproduced, for about 55 baht ($2.25). If so desired, the little alligator logo alone goes for 12 baht (50¢), giving label-conscious consumers the opportunity to express their fashion statements. It's all here.

Inside the Night Bazaar building (with the currency-exchange booth prominently placed at the entrance, as a gatekeeper of sorts) there are primarily modern, mass-manufactured goods, with an occasional stand selling wonderful tribal chachkas. The range is from low-cost Thai fashions that are pretty good to typical souvenirs that are pretty schlocky. If you're more interested in handmade items, head for the top floor where a few of the booths and shops carry locally produced handcrafts. Some of the shops in the Night Bazaar are open throughout the day, but most open at around 6 p.m. or so and stay open until 10:30 p.m. or whenever the last paying shopper departs.

If you have any complaints that you wish to register with the authorities regarding "unsportsmanlike conduct" in the shopping game, rest assured that the Tourist Police booth, on the sidewalk at the foot of the stairs leading up to the Bazaar, is staffed throughout buying hours.

HILL TRIBE AND BURMESE HANDCRAFTS AND ANTIQUES:
Chiang Mai is a center for the sale of tribal crafts because of its proximity to the Golden Triangle. Goods from Burma (often smuggled), Laos, northern Thailand, and even Cambodia find their way into the stores and markets of the city, mostly via Chinese traders. Generally, the newly made items are still of fairly high quality, particularly those made in the more remote provinces; however, it is the older objects and textiles that are real treasures. Workmanship tends to be significantly better, dyes are natural, and there is greater attention to traditional designs. As one can imagine, the scarcity of these older handcrafted items has significantly driven prices up over the past few years, so if you want an expertly made woven belt with silver trinkets, for example, be prepared to pay over $100.

The best advice before buying anything is to shop around. The variety of stores in Chiang Mai is astonishing, so that you'll find similar items in other shops. We liked a few of the shops on Tha Phae Road, between the gate of the same name and the river. One of the best shops for high-quality tribal crafts, and in particular, textiles, is **Anongporn**, at 208-10 Tha Phae Rd. (tel. 236654). The selection here seems almost endless with display cases bulging with goods. Intricately embroidered Hmong collars, colorful Akha jackets and bags, and

Mien coats are but a fraction of their textile supply. We also admired their small selection of silver jewelry, including belts, bracelets, necklaces, and silver beads. Not only is the selection of older items so special, but the quality of their newly made goods seems to be higher than what sells in the typical market stalls. Prices are comparable to what you'll find in other area stores. Plan on spending some time here.

The quality and prices are about as high as you'll find in Chiang Mai, but if it's traditional Thai and Burmese antiques that you crave, look no farther than **Maneesinn Antiques** at 289 Tha Phae Rd. We were especially impressed with their collection of exquisite lacquerware and baskets. The shop is rather small, but the selection of small furniture, woodcarving, and sculpture is impressive.

You'll have to go a bit out of the way to find the elegant home of **Duangjitt Thaveesri,** but inside the gate is a stunning display of antique textiles and silver housed in a traditional teak house. Duangjitt is a distinguished woman who has spent her life collecting fine works of Thai and tribal clothing and woven material (she also participates in organizing the Chiang Rai Festival, where there is an especially good market). It's a misnomer to call her house a shop, though many items are for sale, because it feels more like a private museum with Duangjitt as your highly learned guide. Duangjitt's house is at 29/4 Tung Hotel Rd. (it's actually set back from the road near the Irrigation Department), several long blocks east of the Ping River; if you wish to visit, it is essential to telephone ahead (tel. 242291) to make sure that someone is there. Duangjitt also operates two small shops in the arcades at the Orchid and Rincome Hotels.

They only sell newly made goods at **Thai Tribal Crafts,** at 208 Bumrung Rat Rd., but we found a few first-class bargains. The store was established to give local craftspeople an opportunity to sell their goods directly to the consumer without using a middleman. After visiting several such stores around Chiang Mai, we felt that this shop had the best selection and quality, even though many of their items are a little on the cute side. Thai Tribal Crafts is the northern distributor of the excellent book, *Peoples of the Golden Triangle* by Paul and Elaine Lewis (London: Thames and Hudson, 1984). Prices are similar to those in the Night Bazaar. Thai Tribal Crafts is open Monday through Saturday from 9 a.m. to 5 p.m.

Down the road at 200/1-3 Bumrung Rat Rd. is another of Chiang Mai's better antique shops, **Borisoothi Art Gallery** (they also have a branch in the River City mall in Bangkok). The store is vast and the collection encompasses an enormous range of goods of varying quality, including some great Khmer, Laotian, and antique Thai sculpture. We recommend looking at their woodcarving and fine celadon up front and the displays in the back rooms. Like Maneesinn, prices are high, so use your best bargaining skills and you might end up with a real treasure.

In the Night Market, seek out **Siam Gallery,** at no. 60 on the second floor. Although the prices may be higher here, the quality is excellent and the authenticity assured.

SILVER AND CERAMICS: Thai craftspeople are excellent silversmiths, often sought out by international jewelry companies to manufacture high-quality designs. Though the price of silver is set by international standards, the cost of labor to fashion it into jewelry is a major cost component, making Thai silver a bargain. In addition to jewelry, many studios produce flatware and silver bowls, often elaborately decorated. The best area for shopping for silver is Wua Lai Road (Rte. 108), about two miles south of the Chiang Mai Gate, on the south side of the Old City. **Siam Silverware,** at 5 Wua Lai Rd., is one of the larger dealers. Thai ceramics, often done in imitation of traditional celadon shapes produced in Sukhothai and Si Satchanalai, are also much prized by visitors to the north. There are several showrooms on Wua Lai Road, including **Chiang Mai Sankaloke** and

Pleatpun Sankaloke. For a better selection, try the **Mengrai Kilns** at 31/1 Ratuthit Rd., on the east side of the Ping River near the Chiang Mai Gymkhana Club. Mengrai Kilns produces fine, handcrafted reproductions of celadon ware.

SAN KAMPHAENG ROAD AND BO SANG: Take San Kamphaeng Road (Rte. 1006) out of Chiang Mai, traveling due east for about four miles, and you'll discover a road lined with shops and showrooms that extends for another 4½ miles. Before setting out on your shopping extravaganza, you might want to plan on getting a bite to eat. We heartily recommend Baan Suan Restaurant (see "Dining") near the Chiang Mai end at 51/3 San Kamphaeng Rd.

One of the first shops is **Chiang Mai Tasanaporn,** located at 123 Mu 3, San Kamphaeng Road, specializing in woodcarving, one of the region's real specialties. You can watch the craftsmen fashioning the most intricate carving with simple hand chisels. Popular items to purchase are cocktail cabinets and elephants, but for our money the teak coffee tables with masterfully carved scenes from the *Ramakien* are most exquisite. These last will cost about 23,000 baht ($920), but it's well worth it, for you won't find craftsmanship like this anywhere and it will quickly become a treasured heirloom.

You can watch the silversmiths hammering and polishing at **Chiang Mai Silverware,** 62/10-11 Sankampaeng Rd. (tel. 246037). Much of the work is ornate and the prices are steep, although you can purchase tiny herb pots for as little as $5. A single demitasse spoon costs around $15, and picture frames run as high as $200.

At **Thai Shop,** 106 Moo 3 Sankampaeng Road (tel. 245733), you can observe the making of bronzeware, a handsome substitute for silverware, but one that you must be careful about when purchasing, because some vendors do not use enough nickel or, indeed, use any bronze. Here, at Thai Shop, the product is 3% nickel, 79% copper, and 18% tin, making for a positively handsome, gleaming product. A service for 12 with 144 pieces costs about $175, considerably less than real silverware. The shop also sells lacquerware, some of which is coated with an eggshell application, while other pieces are hand-painted. The whole process takes many months as each of the 19 coats of lacquer is applied and allowed to dry.

On the other side of the street, about half a mile east is **Shinawatra Thai Silk,** an extremely good outlet that is only rivaled by Jim Thompson in Bangkok. Shinawatra (they also have a branch across from the Chiang Mai Orchid Hotel at 14/4-8 Huai Kaeo Rd.) sells one- and two-ply silk in addition to upholstery-grade material. Expect to pay 300 baht ($12) for a square meter of two-ply silk and 400 baht ($16) for upholstery-grade silk.

Beyond Shinawatra, on the same side of the road, is a cluster of northern-style teak houses serving as an antiques mall, with little shops selling Thai and Burmese objects, woodcarvings, and textiles. Several shops sell newly made tribal crafts.

The road continues for about half a mile before intersecting with Rte. 1014, leading into the hamlet of **Bo Sang** (also known as the Umbrella Village). Here you can observe women making the paper and the bamboo frames for the umbrellas, and then hand-painting them with traditional Thai scenes or floral patterns. If you like, you can bring rough sketches of a design and they will duplicate it for you. Several workshops are open to the public and umbrellas are, of course, for sale. This is a standard stop on the bus-tour route, so you might want to leave this for the end of the day to miss the majority of group tourists.

If you return to the San Kamphaeng Road intersection there are a number of roadside basket merchants that carry finely made wares. Just beyond that is **Boon Lacquerware,** one of the best in Chiang Mai. After passing several other silvermaking and tribal crafts shops, you'll arrive in **San Kamphaeng,** a tiny village known for its fine cotton and silk. As with Bo Sang, there are several work-shops where you can observe the weaving process and buy locally made fabric. Many local women told us that they buy much of their silk for dressmaking here in San Kamphaeng. Shop around to compare prices and quality.

JADE/JEWELRY: There's one shop that is worth visiting at the base of Doi Suthep and that is **Orchid and Jade Factory** (tel. 211-7674), which has a solid reputation and supplies Gumps in San Francisco among others. Although the Chinese and traditional Thai prefer green jade, the superior Burmese jade or jade-ite (as opposed to nephrite, Chinese jade) does in fact come in gold, white, red, and orchid. The owner displays some beautiful jewelry and carved standing pieces. A well-cut pendant will cost anywhere from $80 for an unusual blue jade to $120 and up. The shop also sells rubies, sapphires, and other semiprecious stones.

BASKETRY: About 8½ miles south of Chiang Mai on Rte. 108 is the village of **Hang Dong.** Shops displaying an extraordinary array of Thai basket weaving line either side of the road. Some of the shops are actually part of the residences of the basket weavers. Very little English is spoken here but you can do quite well with hand gestures and a rudimentary knowledge of Thai numbers. There are steam-ers, strainers, sticky-rice holders, traps, furniture, etc. There are no middlemen here to take a commission, so bargaining is easier.

8. NIGHTLIFE

Although shopping is a prime evening activity, Chiang Mai does not lack other diversions. Many people sample Thai food and dancing at a khan toke din-ner. If that doesn't suit your tastes, try one of the following activities.

BARS: Most bars have some form of live entertainment, usually a folk or coun-try singer (yes, Western country music has hit Chiang Mai). One such place is the **Riverside Bar and Restaurant,** 9-11 Charoen Rat Rd., along the banks of the Ping River, **Harmony Pub and Music Chamber,** near the Night Bazaar, has Thai singers doing Western favorites. The **Karen Hut,** at 13 Chiang Moi Rd. (near the New Chiang Mai Hotel), also has live music and is among the more popular places in town.

GAY BARS: Again, Chiang Mai isn't nearly in the same league as Bangkok, but there are several gay bars. One of the most popular is the **Siamese Cat Cocktail Lounge,** at 19/39 Singharaj Rd. There is a show on weekend nights from 11 p.m. to midnight.

DISCOS AND NIGHTCLUBS: The Pornping Hotel has the **Bubbles Disco** with a live band. It's nothing great, but if you want to dance, it's adequate. The top four hotels—the Chiang Mai Plaza, Dusit Inn, Orchid, and Rincome—all have discos where they play top international hits. When we were there last, the **Plaza** at the Chiang Mai Plaza was the most popular. Expect to pay 110 baht ($4.50) for a cover charge. Drinks are extra.

Chiang Mai has a few larger nightclubs, where you can dance with an escort (female), drink, and watch a Thai floor show. Among the most popular are **Hon-ey Chiang Mai** (for both club and massage), out on the Super Highway across from Wat Chet Yot; the **Blue Moon** (also club and massage), and **Hennessy.** Be-fore going in, make sure you understand all the charges, as they often mount up faster than you anticipate.

MASSAGE PARLORS: There is no one street as in Bangkok or Pattaya, but if you want to try a Thai massage there are several options. **Rinkaew Povech,** at 183/4 Wua Lai Rd. (tel. 234565), near the Old Cultural Center, offers traditional herbal massage for men and women. An hour massage runs 250 baht ($10). **Hat Thep,** above the Blue Moon Night Club on Moon Muang Road (tel. 214818), also offers traditional-style massage.

Sayuri, on Soi 2, Bumrung Rat Road (tel. 242361), has both body and hand massage for 750 baht ($30) and 450 baht ($18) respectively. If you are in the market for more than the usual fare, inquire of any concierge, a taxi or tuk-tuk driver, or ask at a massage parlor.

THAI BOXING: It isn't for everyone, but you can soak up more of the authentic Thai experience by attending an exhibition of Thai boxing than in nearly any other venue. The ring is set in a rope-and-canvas cordoned area. Inside, the promoter grabs a microphone and chants the names of the boxers over blaring loudspeakers, hawking potential spectators. As fight time approaches, the crowd swarms in, divided between ringside for 120 baht ($4.75) and standing room for 45 baht ($1.75). Serious fans hover over the tables where the fighters are being oiled, massaged, taped, and counseled, hoping to gain some slight edge on the unofficial betting line. Betting begins just before a bout opens and continues through the fight, with bets shifting so many times it's a wonder that anyone can keep track. The stakes for winning a match range from about 2,000 baht ($80) to 20,000 baht ($800), depending on the ranking of the boxers. The boxing itself usually begins around 9 p.m. and lasts into the early-morning hours. The first slug fests are between flyweights—kids really, who look about 12 to 14 years old. Heavyweight fights begin in the late evening. Unlike Western-style boxers, the fighters who are more likely to win are flexible and have long, lean bodies. The bouts last three rounds, the last being the most feverish. No sooner is a match over than the next begins. Spectators move in and out of the arena to get food, or more likely, to down a quick drink. The whole scene has the feel of a Thai country fair. There are few if any farangs at such events—most tourists see only "boxing demonstrations" as part of a total program of Thai culture—but if you want to take in something indigenous, try a night of Thai boxing. Check with the TAT for the latest schedule (they usually have them two or three nights per week) and location.

9. TREKKING IN THE NORTHERN HILLS

Trekking around Chiang Mai is a relatively new phenomenon. Until the middle 1970s few people took to the trails, preferring the dramatic peaks in Nepal, Pakistan, and India to the low foothills of the Himalayas. Those few who did headed for the Golden Triangle, at the borders of Thailand, Burma, and Laos, attracted by the concentration of indigenous and nomadic hill tribes and their traditional culture. Many of these trekkers were also lured by the Golden Triangle's illicit opium fields, tended by tribal people and sold by the factions of the Kuomintang armed forces and the publicity-shy, so-called Shan warlord, Khun Sa.

Today hundreds of people head north every week, with organized tours along well-beaten paths, to Akha, Karen, Lahu, Lisu, Hmong, and Yao villages, all within a two- to three-day Jeep ride and walk away from Chiang Mai. Nearly all tours combine treks with river rafting and elephant walks, adding a kind of visceral thrill to the often-gruelling hikes.

Trekking has become so organized that a coordinating meeting is held each month to examine the number of tourists visiting each village and to restrict the flow of trekkers on well-trafficked trails (prices are fixed, as well, at these "trade" meetings). If this sounds like trekking has lost some of its pioneer spirit, it has and it hasn't. It is true that many of the villages and their tribal residents now depend on revenue generated by treks and, accordingly, don traditional costumes, perform music and dancing and other ceremonies, produce crafts, and offer the obligatory opium pipe to well-paying Western guests. And it is true that most treks visit the same places, increasing the likelihood of running into other groups. But if you are willing to journey to the more esoteric destinations you can still explore territories little known to any but the most knowledgeable adventurer.

TREKKING COMPANIES: The TAT publishes a list of trekking companies that operate out of Chiang Mai. As of 1988 there were 37 different travel agencies that arranged treks and even more agencies that booked other companies' trips. In other words, the problem isn't finding a trek (there are several leaving every day), it's finding one that perfectly combines experienced and knowledgeable guides, an intelligent itinerary, a compatible group, appropriate timing, and an acceptable price. Trekking companies go in and out of business with regularity (though there are a few "established" outfits), so it will take some effort for you to find one that suits your needs; plan on spending a whole day in Chiang Mai just for doing your research. We think it's more important to understand what you should look for in a particular trek rather than recommending one company over another. Fortunately, most of the agencies are concentrated along Tha Phae Road and Moonmuang Road, so you won't have to run all over the city to find trekking outfitters.

The Guide

If there is one single element of a trek that will make or break the experience, it is the guide. An increasing number of hill tribe people are serving as guides, and that's all to the good. They often speak a myriad of tribal dialects, know the best trails, are well informed about the area and people, and are usually pretty interesting characters themselves. Several friends raved about Mr. Chiang Comlai, who works with **Pinan Tours,** at 235 Tha Phae Rd. (tel. 053/236081), as one of the best in the business. Other locally recommended companies include **Galare Travel Service,** 54-56 Tha Phae Rd. (tel. 053/236237); **Singha Travel,** 277 Tha Phae Rd. (tel. 053/233198); and **S. T. Tour,** 143/18 Super Highway, c/o Lanna Villa (tel. 053/222174). Before signing on to a trek, it's a good idea to meet your prospective guide; ask questions and don't be pressured into taking a trek with a guide about whom you harbor some doubt.

READER'S TOURING SELECTION: "We had a really good guide and went for eight days, hiking over the Burmese border. **Folkways Trekking,** at 257 Tha Phae Rd. in town (tel. 053/232169), waited for a group to gather and organized this trek" (Stan Mendoza, New York, N.Y.).

The Itinerary

The next issue is the itinerary. Several well-known agencies, like **Summit Tours,** 164-166 Tha Phae Rd. (tel. 053/233351), offer prepackaged routes that leave on a regularly scheduled basis. If you intend to stay on the better-traveled trails, you should have no problem finding a company to accommodate you; however, if you intend to climb to the more remote spots, you might either have to arrange a custom tour (more expensive) or call around to see if anyone happens to offer such a trip. If you do intend to visit the Golden Triangle, most trekking companies offer a two- or three-day trek. For those who want to travel east to Phayao or Nan, or northwest to Mae Hong Son, you will have to dig a little to find an appropriate outfit. Many trekking companies (such as Pinan Tours) will arrange custom trips for you, even on short notice, with a corresponding increase in price. If you can't stand the idea of trekking, but want to visit some of the hill-tribe villages, inquire about Jeep trips.

Nearly all trekking outfitters list the various hill-tribe villages that are included in their itineraries. They advertise the names like car salesmen drolly reading out standard features of a new model. Try to read as much as you can (if you like, start with out section on the ethnicity and geography of the tribes) and decide for yourself which groups you'd most like to visit.

Most treks start with a Jeep or minibus drive to the head of the trail. Such trips can take a full day, depending on how far your destination is from Chiang Mai. Plan on spending a minimum of two or three days for a nearby trek and between five days and two weeks for the more remote spots.

The Group

We've heard about more trips being transformed into wonderful experiences (and occasionally, disasters) by the composition of the group. Certainly if you plan on taking a short trip, the personality of the group is less important than if you're on a two-week jaunt with five other people, but don't underestimate group dynamics. If you're planning a long, arduous trip, try to meet your fellow travelers before committing; you might find that they aren't up to the rigors of the adventure or, conversely, you may not meet their expectations. Of all the criteria that we use, this is the most difficult to assess. Group size is another critical factor. Try to find an agency that limits the number of people to about ten per trek.

The Season

Seasonality plays some part in trekking, especially if you don't want to trudge through rain and mud. The dry and cool season runs from November to February; it will likely rain throughout the rest of the year. If you travel by improvisation, as we do, be assured that you can find some trek leaving Chiang Mai nearly anytime. Plan on spending a full day in Chiang Mai to locate a suitable trekking agency. If you need to make reservations, contact the TAT and explain your specific needs to them. They often know the schedules of the larger trekking outfits and can make suggestions.

The Price

The last criterion is price. Here, as with everything in Thailand, some negotiating is in order. Visit a few of the Tha Phae Road or Moon Muang Road agencies to determine the current price, find one that you might want to join, and offer about 30% less than the average asking price. On our last visit, Pinan Tours had a four-day/three-night trek to the area around Mae Hong Son for 1,225 baht ($49); a three-day/two-night trek ran 1,050 baht ($42).

When inquiring about price it's important to determine what the price includes, and more important, what it doesn't. Typically, trekkers' fees will pay for food for the group. On some trips there will be opportunities to stop in restaurants, where you'll be expected to pay. We found a couple of budget operators who insisted that trekkers pay separately for transportation to and from the trail head. Some companies provide sleeping bags, when needed, free of charge, while others rent them for a fee. And of course, expect to pay for your opium cocktail hour with the village headman; it's the proper thing to do.

Most companies charge for trekking frills, such as elephant walks and river rafting. Again, Pinan charges 250 baht ($6) additional for an extended elephant walk and 250 baht ($6) for a rafting adventure. The best policy is to ask about all of these things before signing up, as there is nothing worse than discovering expensive "hidden" charges.

ETHNICITY AND GEOGRAPHY OF THE HILL TRIBE REGION:

Thailand's 420,000 tribal people live in nearly every province in the country (except for a large swath around Bangkok), yet two areas account for the largest numbers. A few of these ethnic minorities inhabit the southern edge of Thailand in the jungles around the Malaysian border, but the greatest number reside in the lower hills and high valleys of the north. Most tribes migrated from China or Tibet to Burma, Laos, and Vietnam, and ultimately settled in Thailand's northern provinces such as Chiang Rai, Chiang Mai, Mae Hong Son, Phayao, and Nan. Some of the tribes seem to be indigenous to the region (that is, they have occupied areas within Thailand for hundreds of years), while others are nomadic, responding to agricultural and trade fluctuations as well as political strife.

The six main tribes are the Akha, Hmong, Karen, Lahu, Lisu, and Mien, and each tribe has subgroups that are linked by historical lineage, language, costume, social organization, and religion.

Hill tribes are divided into two linguistic categories: Sino-Tibetan and Austro-Asiatic. Only the Mon-Khmer speak a dialect of the latter category. In addition, tribes are divided geographically into lowland or valley dwellers who grow cyclical crops, such as rice or corn, and high-altitude dwellers who grow opium poppies. The so-called indigenous tribes are those that tend to inhabit the lower terrain, while the nomadic groups generally occupy higher ground, above 3,300 feet. Many of these highland minorities, such as the Akha (Kaw), Lahu (Mussur), Lisu (Lisaw), Hmong (Meo), and Mien (Yao), have experienced problems with opium addiction. The Thai government has tried, with only limited success, to wean these ethnic minorities away from cultivating opium poppies, both for health reasons as well as international pressure to stem the heroin trade.

Nearly all tribal villages have a headman who performs most of the political and social functions, including welcoming guests. The high-altitude villages exist as a convenience for growing poppies and are led by village elders or a shaman who consult spirits. If there is a change in condition—agriculturally, from disease or death, or as a result of security (there are bandits in the area)—the whole village may disband and move to a more advantageous location. Villages also break up over internal disputes, leading the inhabitants to wander in families and take up residence in a new region. Most often the social unit is characterized as the extended family; this is especially true among the Hmong and Yao, who practice polygamy. The larger villages also host a local trader, usually of Chinese or Thai extraction, who funnels the opium into the lucrative pipeline. During cultivation months, tribal and Thai contract laborers (many of whom are addicts) will temporarily reside in the village, taking opium in lieu of cash for their work.

Highland minorities believe in spirits, and it is the role of the shaman, or head religious figure, to read into every situation the workings of the spiritual pantheon. The ghosts of ancestors (often associated with the Chinese), the spirits of the cosmos, the soul of an animal—all contribute to the fortune of individuals, families, villages, crop harvests, and weather. Most villages practice rites that are meant to appease these spirits, with the shaman or headman chosen to determine the problem, prescribe the solution, and perform the ritual. Remarkably enough, neither the shamans nor the headmen are considered to be of higher stature than the other villagers. They merely render a service and are on equal footing with all other inhabitants. If a shaman or headman becomes too grandiose in his political aspirations, the villagers will often collectively decide to disband.

Karen

The 250,000 Karen are the largest tribal group in Thailand, accounting for over half of all tribal people living in the country. In nearby Burma it's estimated that there are over four million people of Karenic descent (and of Buddhist belief), many of whom have settled along the Thai-Burmese border (the Burmese government often battles the Karen people for control over the region). In Thailand the Karen are geographically dispersed, living as far north as Chiang Rai and as far south as Kanchanaburi. Among the Karen are several subgroups: the Sgaw (White Karen), the Pwo (also White Karen), Kayah (Red Karen), and Pa O (Black Karen). The Sgaw and Pwo represent 95% of Karen tribespeople, with the other two groups living in remote areas of Mae Hong Son.

The Karen have lived in Thailand since the 18th century, though they date their culture back to the 8th century B.C. Based on their language and mythology scholars place their geographic origin west of Tibet. There is a wonderfully self-deprecating theme in Karen life: the great spirits gave bounties to all people, but the Karen were watching the crops; wisdom was dispensed by the deities in written form, but the Karen lost the paper; and so forth.

Today the Karen engage in swidden agriculture, an excellent form of land rotation that is being threatened by overpopulation. The crops themselves are watched over by a ritual landlord who makes sacrifices to the spirits. The most commonly mentioned spirit to placate is the so-called Crop Grandmother, who sits perched on the stumps of felled trees. The major deity is the Lord of Land and Water, and it is to him that most sacrifices are made. Karen tribes mostly occupy lower-lying areas, and are not significant growers of opium poppies.

The Karen are among the most assimilated among the hill tribes of Thailand, making it difficult to identify them by any outward appearance; however, the more traditional tribespeople wear silver armbands and don a beaded sash and headband.

Hmong(Meo)

The Hmong are a nomadic tribe scattered throughout Southeast Asia and China. About 65,000 Hmong live in Thailand, with the greatest number residing in Chiang Mai, Chiang Rai, Nan, Petchabun, and Phrae provinces; there are approximately four million Hmong living in China. Like the Karen there are several subgroups residing within Thailand: the Hmong Daew (White Hmong) and the Hmong Njua (Blue Hmong) are the two main divisions, with the Hmong Gua Mba (Armband Hmong) a subdivision of the Hmong Daew. The latter group, which only recently entered Thailand from Laos, is currently concentrated in refugee camps near the border. The Hmong speak a Sino-Tibetan dialect that uses many words from Chinese. As with other ethnic minorities (especially the Mien, with whom the Hmong have a deep affinity), the Chinese attempted to restrict the freedom of the fiercely independent Hmong to speak their language and pursue their non-Han social customs.

In Thailand, the Hmong generally dwell in the highlands where they cultivate opium poppies at a rate greater than any other tribal group; corn and rice are also grown as subsistence crops. It's not unusual to find Yunnanese living in a Hmong community, as the Chinese have traditionally served as a conduit for opium in Thailand. The Hmong are also excellent animal breeders; their ponies are especially prized. As with other nomadic tribes, the Hmong maintain much of their wealth in silver jewelry. Thick silver neck rings, earrings, bracelets, and rings are worn and displayed. Neck rings are given to Hmong babies as a sign of their acceptance into the material world. During the December New Year festival, families wear their silver jewelry and ornaments in a fabulous display of craftsmanship. The women are particularly distinctive with knotted, long dark hair woven with horse or human hair switches to create an enormous bun on top of the head. Though most men take one wife, it is a sign of wealth to take two.

As with most of the other tribes, the Hmong are pantheistic and rely on shamans to perform spiritual rites. Shamans practice animal sacrifice and perform many rituals in the event of a spiritual emergency (they make house calls) by contacting the spirit world in a trance-like state. They place particular emphasis on the spirit of doors: doors for entering and exiting the human world, doors to houses, doors to let in good fortune and to block bad spirits, and doors to the afterlife. At the same time the Hmong are ancestor worshippers, again an echo from their Chinese past.

Like the Chinese, with whom they resided for so many centuries, the Hmong are an entrepreneurial lot, and they are beginning to move down from the hills to pursue a less rigorous and more profitable life in other occupations. But as long as the lucrative opium trade continues, the Hmong will remain in the highlands, cultivating poppies.

Lahu (Mussur)

The Lahu people, of which 40,000 abide in Thailand, are a fractured group with a great many subdivisions. The differences are absolutely apparent from the clothing worn by the various Lahu tribespeople. Some costumes are elegantly embroidered, others plainly colored and unadorned; some have sewn-on silver ornaments, other outfits are brightly colored—all are different, but all are Lahu. The two main bands are the Laho Na (Black Lahu) and the Lahu Shi (Yellow Lahu), with the Lahu Hpu (White Lahu), La Ba, and Abele comprising a minuscule number. To make matters more confusing, the Lahu do not use surnames, though a few villages are now adopting Thai names. Like the Hmong, most Lahu villages are set above 3,300 feet in the mountains around Chiang Mai, Chiang Rai, Mae Hong Son, Tak, and Kaphaeng Phet, where poppies, dry rice, corn, and other cash crops are grown.

The Lahu first entered Thailand during the late 19th century, having migrated from southwestern China and, later, into Burma. Their language, Lahu Na, is so well accepted in the highlands that other tribal people, as well as Yunnanese Chinese, have adopted it as their common tongue. The Lahu are skilled musicians, and their bamboo and gourd flutes are the most common instrument (we bought such a flute in the Night Market in Chiang Mai; it makes a lovely sound and is easy to play). These flutes are often used by young men to woo the woman of their choice. The Lahu also fashion bamboo into water pipes for irrigating crops.

If any tribe reflects the difficulties of maintaining a singular cultural identity in the tumult of migration, consider Lahu religion as an example: originally animist (indigenous), they adopted the worship of a deity called G'ui sha (possibly Tibetan in origin), they borrowed the practice of merit (boon) from Buddhism (Indian or Chinese), and ultimately incorporated Christian (British/Burmese) theology into their belief system. Today the various branches of Lahu practice many forms of their religion; however, there are some constants. G'ui sha is the supreme being who created the universe and rules over all spirits. Spirits inhabit animate and inanimate objects, making them capable of benevolence or evil, with the soul functioning as the spiritual force within people. In addition, they practice a kind of Lahu voodoo as well as following a messianic tradition. The best time to witness Lahu rituals is at their festive New Year (contact the guide services to determine the exact date).

Mien (Yao)

Even more than the Hmong, the Mien (thought to be a corrupted form of "barbarian" in Chinese) are closely connected to their Chinese past. The tribe is thought to have originated in southern China where they incorporated the Han language and writing style into their own. Many Mien legends, history books, and religious tracts are recorded in Chinese. The Mien people also assimilated ancestor worship and a form of Taoism into their theology in addition to celebrating their New Year on the same date (relying on the same calendar system) as the Chinese.

There are now estimated to be 33,000 Mien living in Thailand, concentrated in Chiang Rai, Phayao, Lampang, and Nan provinces. The Mien are still numerous in China as well as in Vietnam, Burma, and Laos. Like the Hmong, tens of thousands of Mien fled to northern Thailand from Vietnam and Laos after the end of the Vietnam War.

Mien farmers do not rely on opium poppies (though some do grow them); instead they cultivate dry rice and corn. The women produce rather intricate and elegant embroidery, which often adorns their clothing. Much of Mien religious art appears strongly influenced by Chinese designs, particularly by Taoist motifs, clearly distinguishing it from other tribes' work.

Courting rituals appear absolutely libertine in comparison with Western traditions. Young men and women are free to have premarital sexual relations, and it is common for several children to be born before a couple is actually wed. The compatibility of birth dates between the proposed husband and wife are extremely important and a form of astrology is used to determine this. As long as an agreeable price can be found for the bride, nearly anything goes. Adoption of other Mien children or children from other suitable tribes is common practice among Mien clans.

Lisu (Lisaw)

The Lisu are one of the smaller ethnic minorities in northern Thailand, representing less than 5% of all hill-tribe people. They arrived in Chiang Rai province in the 1920s, migrating from nearby Burma. The Lisu occupy high ground, usually above 3,300 feet, allowing them to grow poppies for the opium harvest as well as other subsistence crops. Lisu people, like their Chinese cousins (many have intermarried), are reputed to be extremely competitive and hardworking. Paul and Elaine Lewis, in their *Peoples of the Golden Triangle*, claim that they "travel in large boisterous groups. When selling they employ the hard-sell technique. When buying they are vociferous bargainers." Even their clothing is brash, incorporating a multitude of brightly colored tunics, embellished with hundreds of silver beads and trinkets. All of which is to say that the Lisu are achievers.

The Lisu also live well-structured lives. Their rituals rely on complicated procedures and expect much from the participants. Everything from birth to courtship to marriage to death is ruled by an orthodox tradition, liberally borrowed from Chinese ideas. In such a structured, achievement-oriented society, it is not surprising that the Lisu have the highest suicide rate among Thailand's tribal people.

Akha (Kaw)

Perhaps of all the tradition-bound tribes, the Akha, accounting for only 3% of all minorities living in Thailand, have maintained the most profound connection with their past. At great events in one's life, the full name (often over 50 generations of titles) of an Akha is proclaimed, with each name symbolic of a lineage dating back over a thousand years. All aspects of life are governed by the Akha Way, an all-encompassing system of myth, ritual, plant cultivation, courtship and marriage, birth, death, dress, and healing. Equally significant is the continuity of the Akha Way: each Akha can depend on an absolutely certain past and uphold the present to ensure the future.

It may be that the strength of the Akha Way is the key to maintaining the identity of such a nomadic people, for the Akha are widely spread throughout southern China, Laos, Vietnam, and Burma. The first Akha migrated from Burma to Thailand in the beginning of the 20th century, originally settling in the highlands above the Mae Kok River in Chiang Rai province. Now they are moving down to lower heights in search of more arable land. They are so-called shifting cultivators, depending on subsistence crops and raising domestic animals for their livelihood.

We found the clothing of the Akha among the most attractive of all the hill tribes. Skillful embroidery on simple black jackets is the everyday attire for both men and women. During festivals, especially over the four-day New Year in December, women don decorative headdresses embellished with silver baubles, feathers, colorful beads, and coins. The Akha shoulder bags are similarly adorned and are of exceptional quality.

The Akha are ancestor worshippers, but they also attach great importance to separating the human world from the spirit world. In each village, large open gates are built and consecrated to symbolize the segregation of these two worlds, in effect trying to create harmony through isolation. Sadly, it will take more than metaphysical isolation to secure their culture from the intrusions of modern life.

CHAPTER XX

SOUTHERN THAILAND: THE BEACHES

□ □ □

1. PATTAYA
2. KOH SAMUI AND SURAT THANI
3. PHUKET

Thailand's beaches, along the Andaman Sea and the Gulf of Thailand (also known as the Gulf of Siam), are world-renowned for their clean white sand, palm groves, and warm salt water. Less known are the glorious opportunities for exploring the underwater sea life and coral treasures, fine windsurfing and sailing, and the region's exquisitely simple seafood cuisine. For decades few but the brave and the hardy ventured to the often-primitive Thai beaches, but today most areas are served by a sophisticated tourism infrastructure and indulgent accommodations. No area with a sandy crescent is protected from the hotel developer's hand, but there are still areas that are relatively undeveloped and absolutely splendid.

Pattaya is the oldest and most decadent of Thailand's southern resorts. Phuket, the country's fastest-developing tourist destination, has the finest coastline of any accessible part of the country. It's also the jumping-off point for Koh Pi Pi, a secluded and comely hourglass-shaped island that is in vogue for those looking to escape the throng. The most remote of the three beach areas is Koh Samui, Thailand's second-largest island, off the eastern coast from Surat Thani. Since the mid-1970s Koh Samui has been the exclusive enclave of trekkers and energetic travelers who relish the opportunity of an extended visit on an island where thatched huts, walks along the beach, and an easy, uncomplicated life define the local style.

1. PATTAYA

Imagine lifting Bangkok's notorious Patpong district whole and transplanting it to a gentle seaside resort some two hours south of the capital. Discos, massage parlors, transvestite clubs, bars with scantily clad Thai teens—all conveniently jammed together along a beachfront strip, a legacy of an era when the town was the R & R capital of Thailand for Vietnam-weary American troops. That's Pattaya.

Now imagine another impression of Pattaya: a sophisticated retreat from

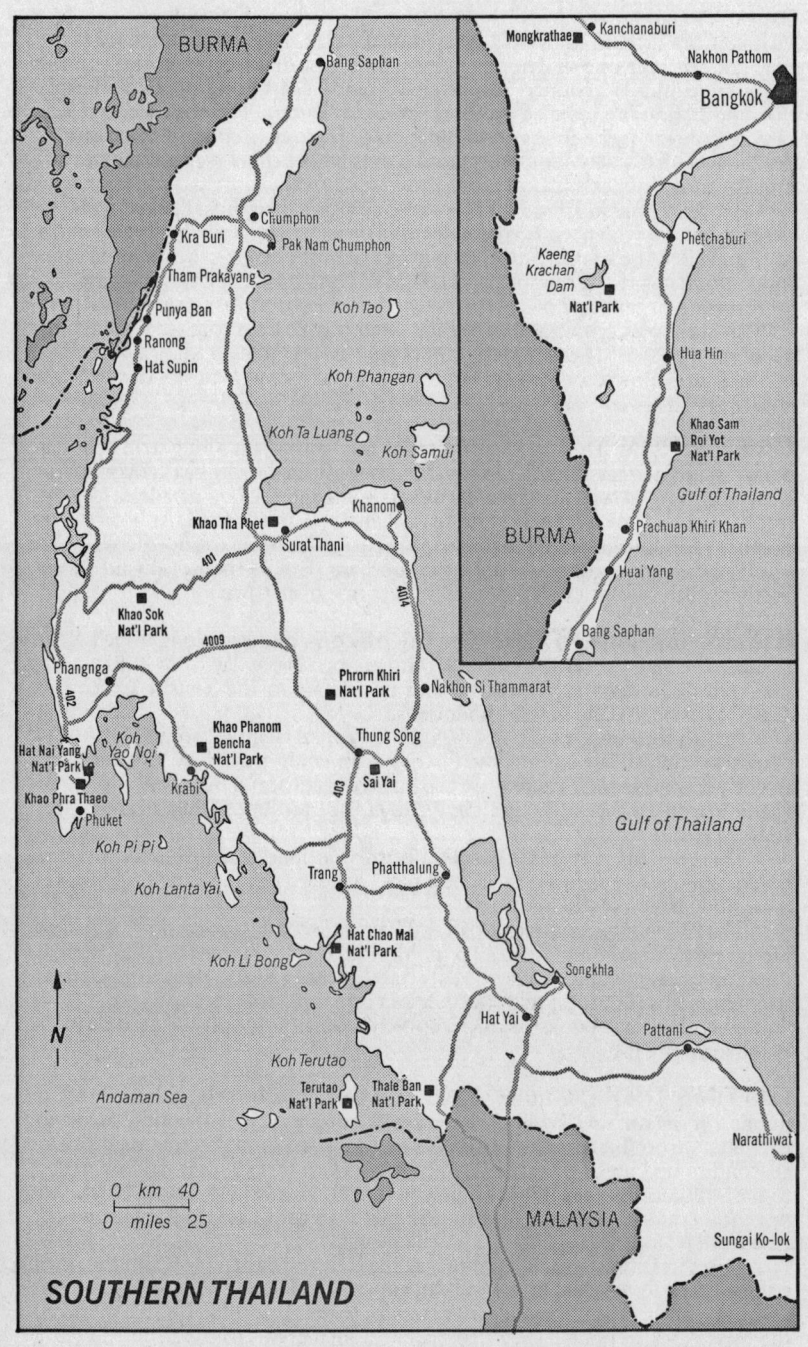

SOUTHERN THAILAND

Bangkok's frantic pace where sprawling, well-manicured, seaside gardens host visitors from around the world who want to relax, take in breathtaking vistas, play golf, or visit one of Thailand's best, and least developed, beaches. In this vision, one finds the country's finest new luxury resort hotel and enough isolation and tranquility to suit a monk. That is also Pattaya. Perhaps the most accurate description is the strange combination of these two, contradictory images. And maybe that's why sometimes honky-tonk, other times elegant, Pattaya still attracts hordes of guests.

For years Bangkok residents have made Pattaya their most favored weekend destination, as evidenced by the vast number of Florida-style high-rise condominiums. Because of the enormous number of buses making the 2½-hour commute, not a surprising number of them go to Pattaya for the day, most often for windsurfing or sailing; however, it's the international tourist groups (that typically spend a week or two as part of their infamous Thai sex tour) that seem most visible in the town. The common sight of an oversize farang leading a petite Thai country girl-cum-escort through the town is testament to Pattaya's freewheeling spirit.

ORIENTATION: The best way of envisioning Pattaya is as a long strip of hotels, bars, restaurants, agencies, and shops built opposite a narrow beach overlooking a bay. **Central Pattaya Road** bisects **Beach Road** and the two parallel streets behind the strip, **Pattaya Second Road** and **Pattaya Third Road.** At both the far northern and southern ends of the strip are two bluffs. Over the northern side are several quiet resort hotels, and on the southern flank is the Royal Cliff Hotel. Farther south is Jomtien Beach, a 15-minute ride from town.

USEFUL INFORMATION: The **TAT office** is midway along Beach Road (Tanon Chaihat) (tel. 038/428750), and is open every day from 8:30 a.m. to 4:30 p.m. The **Tourist Police,** located next door to the Tourist Office (tel. 429371), is open daily on a 24-hour basis.

Pattaya is equipped with a multitude of medical facilities ranging from V.D. clinics to sophisticated centers with CAT scan equipment. The two most frequently recommended centers are the **Pattaya Memorial Hospital,** on Pattaya Klang Road (tel. 429422), and the **Pattaya International Clinic** on Soi 4 (tel. 428374).

There are many **moneychanging booths** around town. In addition, area **banks** often stay open past their 3:30 p.m. standard closing time (as late as 10 p.m.) for currency exchange.

The **PTT** is between Beach Road and Pattaya Second Road on Soi Post Office. Hours are from 8:30 a.m. to 4:30 p.m. Monday through Friday and 8:30 a.m. to noon on weekends and holidays. Many travel agents will also book long-distance telephone calls. The local **telephone area code** for Pattaya is 038.

There is a small bookstore, **D.K. Book House,** near the post office next to the Royal Garden Hotel.

GETTING THERE: Getting to Pattaya is best done by **bus,** either private or public, for the roughly 2½-hour drive. Buses operate every half hour from 6 a.m. to 10 p.m. from Bangkok and from 6 a.m. to 9 p.m. from Pattaya. Most private air-conditioned buses will arrange to transport you from your hotel in Bangkok to the Southern Bus Terminal, where you transfer to a Pattaya-bound coach. The price for a one-way ticket is 65 baht ($2.50), 115 baht ($4.50) for a round-trip ticket. All major travel agencies can issue tickets.

Buses in Pattaya use the terminal at the Regent Marina Hotel on the north end of Beach Road. **Thai International Limousine Service** (tel. 423140), open 24 hours, offers private car-and-driver service to the airport for 1,875 baht ($75); the trip takes two hours. They also operate a smaller bus to the airport in Bangkok three times a day for 225 baht ($9). Both services will arrange to pick you up from your hotel in Pattaya. Other private companies also serve the airport for 125 baht ($5) and make use of the Regent Marina Bus Terminal.

GETTING AROUND: Transportation in and around Pattaya is best left to the roving **minibuses.** These converted open-bed trucks with facing wooden bench seats cruise along the streets stopping for any would-be passengers (a gentle honking of the horn alerts you to their presence). The fare within Pattaya is a very reasonable 5 baht (20¢); fares to far-flung beaches, such as Jomtien, run anywhere from 10 baht (40¢) to 30 baht ($1.25), depending on your skill as a negotiator. (Note: Drivers will insist on 30 baht, as that is the posted fare, but be assured that they have taken less.) Some hotels have their own minibuses, but they charge as much as 20 baht (80¢) for the same bumpy ride.

For those who dare, **motorcycles** rent for 150 baht ($6) a day, inclusive of insurance, and are available all along the beach strip and Central Pattaya Road.

Rental cars are available through a travel agent or hotel concierge, rates are approximately $60 per day including insurance.

ACCOMMODATIONS: Pattaya went through a hotel boom during the Vietnam War years to lodge soldiers on R & R. Since then many of these establishments have become just a bit worn and some are in serious decline. One particularly bright note is the newest hotel on the Pattaya scene.

As we go to press, the following hotels announced plans to open in Pattaya in 1989. **Ambassador,** Jomtien Beach; **Dusit Resort,** Pattaya Nua; **Pattaya Park Beach,** Pattaya Park; **Sheraton,** Jomtien Beach.

A Luxury Choice

For many years the Royal Cliff Hotel (tel. 038/421421), built on the bluff south of the town, was the standard of style in the honky-tonk of Pattaya. Now the Royal Cliff Hotel is the Royal Cliff Beach Resort and within its confines is the spiffy **Royal Wing,** treated both by guests and its capable Swiss management as a separate entity from the original. The level of service is more personal, the rooms are more regally appointed, and the facilities are state of the art. The Royal Wing is as opulent as the Shangri-la in Bangkok—in other words it represents the pinnacle of Hong Kong–style glitz. The white marble lobby is tastefully adorned with contemporary Asian decorative motifs, combining Thai and Chinese influences. Each guest, upon arriving, is met by an assistant manager, registered and personally escorted by that very courteous attendant to the residential rooms. All rooms have two balconies and command fine vistas of Pattaya Bay. The room décor, like the lobby, is ultra-clean and bright, with pastels softening the mood.

Down at beach level is an irregularly shaped pool that looks like something designed by Jean Miró. The bridges and waterfalls add an exotic touch to this already-plush palace. The beach itself is rather small, but uncrowded and well maintained. Particularly alluring is the poolside Benjarong Restaurant, with peach-colored upholstery and polished bleached marble floors. The menu is continental with just a hint of Thai.

Each of the 84 suites, other than those that a pasha, his entourage, and their friends might require, runs 5,600 baht ($224) for single or double occupancy.

The Moderately Priced Range

Given the regal lineage of the Royal Wing, it's not surprising that its parent, the **Royal Cliff Beach Resort** (tel. 038/428612), is Pattaya's top first-class selection. The 700-room hotel, located on the same grounds as the Royal Wing on the southern end of town, was built and upgraded in phases: the main building, constructed in 1976, houses four terraced stories of suites and was recently refurbished; the nine-story structure was built a year later and it, too, is undergoing renovation. Nearly all rooms have views of the bay and offer spacious accommodations and terraces. An elevator effortlessly transports guests from the upper reaches of the precipice down to the clean (for Pattaya) sandy beach. The hotel has two main restaurants: a 24-hour coffeeshop up in the lobby area and an extremely handsome grill decorated in neo-Colonial Thai teak style. Though the Royal Cliff has a nine-hole golf course, management usually shuffles its guests over to the Siam Country Club, the country's premier course. Given the size of this expansive resort, it's not surprising that their staff numbers over 1,300.

Room rates are rather complicated, given the varying types of lodgings that the hotel has to offer, but you can count on spending 2,100 baht ($84) to 3,150 baht ($126) for a double and 3,500 baht ($140) to 5,320 baht ($213) for a suite. Be sure to request a room with a view.

Unlike many of the "international"-style resort hotels, the **Grand Palace,** 1 Sunset Strip on the northern end of Beach Road (tel. 038/429901), retains a touch of local ambience. As you enter its serene courtyard lobby, an imposing seated Buddha, replete with flower offerings and joss sticks, bids you welcome. Rooms are well appointed with bleached wood paneling, marble baths, and the normal technological features. Rates for single and double occupancy are the same, the difference in room prices relates to views, bay at 1,945 baht ($77.75) or garden for 1,540 baht ($61.50). Both views are well worth the price. The Grand Palace's location, on the north side at the edge of the strip, is roughly equivalent to the southside Siam Bayshore in that both are close to the action, but far enough away to sample the quiet life of a more secluded Thai resort.

Perhaps the finest hotel along the middle of the Pattaya beach strip is the **Siam Bayview** (tel. 038/418728), sister of the Siam Bayshore Hotel. As you enter from the beach side you'll walk past their well-kept garden, swimming pool, and terraced fountain. Unlike its many wilting neighbors, the Bayview is of recent vintage and is kept up to snuff by an attentive staff. All of its 270 rooms are equipped with air conditioning, TV, and phone. The hotel has two fine tennis courts. Singles and doubles range from 1,680 baht ($67.25) to 2,100 baht ($84), depending on size and location of rooms.

Located at the far southern end (quieter than the north) of Pattaya Beach Road and set in its own 22-acre park-like grounds is the **Siam Bayshore Hotel** (tel. 038/428730), completely renovated in 1985. The lobby is an impressive four-story atrium planted with giant fan palms. Overall, it makes a distinct impression much like the Bayview, as a well-groomed establishment. Blue-and-white low-rise buildings punctuate the sprawling grounds that are circuitously connected by garden paths and bridges. There are two pools, two tennis courts, and a great many organized activities. Double rooms run 2,100 baht ($84); singles, 1,680 baht ($67.25).

Looming above the Beach Road, just north of Central Pattaya Road, is the high-rise **Montien Hotel** (tel. 038/428155), offering perhaps the best sea and mountain vista of the "strip" hotels. (The Montien is owned and operated by the same group that operates the fine hotel of the same name in Bangkok.) The multilevel lobby, grand and open-air, is decorated in overstuffed wicker and rattan, a style echoed in all guest rooms. The grounds are well manicured and the place, much like Pattaya itself, always seems to buzz with activity. As with other hotels of its category, the Montien offers the usual amenities: air conditioning, TV, pool, and tennis courts. The best rooms are those that face the water, costing 2,100 baht ($84) a night for two, 1,800 baht ($72) for one. Subtract 300 baht ($12) for a mountain-facing room.

The **Asia Pattaya,** about a ten-minute drive from the hurly burly of the beach strip, several miles past the Royal Cliff, on the way to Jomtien Beach (tel. 038/428602), offers immaculate grounds, rooms that are aging but well kept, and numerous amenities. Among them is a nine-hole golf course and a clean private beach. The Asia also runs its own disco with a DJ and, often, a live band. If this sounds like the Asia is a mite self-contained, it may be due to its isolation from town. If you don't mind the relative seclusion, the Asia Pattaya is a fine choice. Rooms with a view of the water run 2,240 baht ($89.50); those that overlook the mountain are 1,820 baht ($72.75).

The **Wong Amat Hotel** (tel. 038/418118), like most of the recommended Pattaya lodgings listed in this guide, is on the periphery of the noisy downtown scene. Specifically, this park-like resort hotel is on the far northern side of town off Pattaya Nakma Road. The 207 rooms are of varying age and quality, so those in the newer section are preferable. European travel groups often claim the largest number of rooms, due in some part to its affiliation with the Golden Tulip chain, so it's advisable to make a reservation before venturing. All rooms are equipped with air conditioning and other refinements. The Wong Amat, like others of its ilk, offers tennis courts, a putting green, a pool, its own private beach, and a full complement of dining rooms. Room rates for single travelers are 1,540 baht ($61.50), 1,680 baht ($67.25) for two.

The **Novotel Tropicana,** 45 Beach Rd. (tel. 038/428645), is a low-rise, motel-style, pale-yellow inn smack in the middle of the Beach Road strip. Though this friendly lodging is on the worn side it still retains a comfortable, beachside ambience, particularly because of its two pools and garden leading out to the strip. Double rooms run 1,820 baht ($72.75).

Budget Accommodations

The **Palm Garden,** on the corner of Naklua and Beach Road on the north side of Pattaya (tel. 038/429386), is an excellent budget selection. Its 120 rooms are simply furnished, but the hotel is quite clean and offers the same amenities of the flashier, higher-priced inns. Though not set on the beach, the Palm Garden is a short walk away. The pool is large and the garden well kept. At 630 baht ($25.25) for a single or double, the Palm Garden represents good value. Similar accommodations, though on an even more modest scale, are available at the related lodgings near the 2nd Road, the **Palm Village** (tel. 038/428153) and the **Siam Pattaya Hotel** (tel. 038/428580). Prices are similar to the Palm Garden.

If plain décor and spotlessly clean accommodations at a budget price are what you seek, the unassuming **Thai Palace Hotel,** set on the back road near legendary Alcazar's (tel. 038/423062), just might fit the bill. This recently built 40-room inn has air conditioning and a decent-size pool, all for 560 baht ($22.50) for single or double occupancy. Request a room facing away from the roadway; you'll sleep better if the incessant motorcycles aren't within easy earshot.

The **Pattaya Inn,** on Soi 2 between Beach Road and Pattaya 2nd Road (tel. 038/428400), is typical of the town's many budget hotels, though a bit cleaner than average. Its 100 rooms aren't equipped with TVs, but air conditioning is standard. At 700 baht ($28) for one or two guests, the Pattaya Inn is an acceptable alternative.

At Jomtien Beach

Jomtien is where the windsurfing and sailing cognoscenti of Bangkok escape. Huge condos, built to house these wealthy merrymakers, threaten to overwhelm this mushrooming beach community. But for the moment it's still a fun place to spend a short holiday in the sun. If you want to escape the bustle of the

Pattaya strip, consider taking a 40-baht ($1.50) excursion south to lovely Jomtien Beach.

Set in a lush garden, across a dirt road from some of the area's best windsurfing, are the **Sugar Hut Bungalows,** at 45/4 Moo 12 (tel. 038/423160), similar in style to what one finds at Koh Samui and in the more primitive parts of Phuket. These Thai bungalows, with rattan walls, thatch roofs, and wooden floors, are built high on stilts to avoid floods and tides. Each bungalow is equipped with a bathroom and fan and rents for 785 baht ($31.50) for one or two people. One of the treats of staying at the Sugar Hut Bungalows is that it's attached to the serenely perfect Sugar Hut Restaurant (see below), the finest eatery in the area.

Far less interesting architecturally, but still a very good value, is the **Surf House International,** 44/45 Jomtien Beach Rd. (tel. 038/422398). Each of the 36 simple, clean, and air-conditioned rooms runs 630 baht ($25.25) for two, 560 baht ($22.50) for the solo traveler. Like most of the Jomtien accommodations, the Surf House seems to attract a younger, beach-loving crowd than those who frequent the Pattaya for indoor activities. Most rooms have balconies and water views; request a seaside room on the top floor and you'll be rewarded with a fine, yet low-cost, panorama.

DINING: Though Pattaya isn't a culinary center of Thailand, with European-based outlets outnumbering those featuring local fare, there a few excellent Thai establishments that should be on any gourmand's itinerary.

Thai Cuisine

Set off the tacky Beach Road strip on Soi 5 is **P.I.C. Kitchen** (tel. 422773). P.I.C. stands for Pattaya International Clinic, which is situated directly across from the restaurant on Soi 4. Be assured that the restaurant bears no relation, either in style or substance, to the hospital. Actually P.I.C. is as tasteful a place as we found in all of Pattaya. The ambience and menu is quite similar to its sister restaurant, Sugar Hut at Jomtien Beach. The food is so delicious and the atmosphere so perfect—a comfortable Thai palace set in a quiet garden—that one could eat every meal here during a stay in Pattaya and be perfectly content. Our favorite dishes include deep-fried crab claws, spring rolls, spicy eggplant salad, mixed fried vegetables with oyster sauce, fried chicken with cashews, and steamed white snapper on a bed of vegetables, ginger, and salted prunes. Dinner (or lunch) runs about 250 baht ($10) to 375 baht ($12.50). P.I.C. Kitchen is open daily for breakfast, lunch, and dinner; all credit cards are accepted.

Most of Pattaya's restaurants cater to European tastes, but **Samsak Restaurant,** at 22 Soi 4 off Beach Road (tel. 428987), cooks mainly Thai dishes from an extensive list of entrees. The restaurant is an unadorned covered pavilion with an abundance of chirping birds providing the background music. Of their more exotic fare we enjoyed hormak pla shawn, a variety of steamed fish mixed with curry paste and served in a coconut; kai hor bai toey, chicken wrapped in pine leaves; and beef with garlic. Dinner for two ranges from 250 baht ($10) to 435 baht ($17.50). Samsak is open daily from 11 a.m. to 1 a.m.

Locals rave about a place called **Pa,** located somewhere in the northern end of town, off Naklua Road. We couldn't find it and the only minibus driver who recognized the name just smiled but refused to take us there. If anyone finds it and could file a report, we'd love to hear from you!

Continental

Dolf Riks, who presides over a café of the same name halfway between the Regent Marina and Pattaya Bowl (tel. 428269), is an Indonesian-born Dutch restaurateur who's also a bit of a character. He owns Pattaya's oldest restaurant, specializing in both Indonesian and European dishes. Although Dolf's menu changes with his whims, he normally serves an Indonesian rijsttafel, seafood in a clear broth with wine, a Spanish garlic soup, and ramekin Madras, an oven-baked curry ragoût. The restaurant caters primarily to a European clientele and is open daily from 11 a.m. to midnight. Reservations are recommended only during the high season. Dinner for two will run about 625 baht ($25).

For those who thirst for a German-style beer hall, **Deutsche Haus** is also recommended.

At Jomtien Beach

The **Sugar Hut Restaurant,** located in Jomtien Beach on the same grounds as the bungalows of the same name (tel. 422600), will most likely fulfill all of your fantasies of exotic tropical dining on a Southeast Asian beach. Actually, this Thai-style teak, open-air pavilion is set back from the sand, separated by a well-kept garden. Oleanders and palms and the sound of birds add to the already magical ambience. The food itself is traditional Thai in spirit, with fish and seafood the suggested entrees. We savored a meal of sumptuous steamed crab claws, mixed seafood in a spicy broth, and a blend of fresh papaya and pineapple juice, all for about 310 baht ($12.50) for two. Supping at the Sugar Hut Restaurant is a special treat.

Less elegant and slightly cheaper dining is available next door at **Suan Tarn,** also known as Copacabana.

NIGHTLIFE: Unlike most places, "nightlife" lasts all day long in party Pattaya, even though things really crank up in the evening hours.

Girls, Girls, Girls

As far as relations between the sexes go, Pattaya is hardly a subtle place. A casual stroll down the Beach Road after sundown reveals a market for flesh that would satiate a bear. Open-air bars, topless bars, sex shows, and streetwalkers all brazenly advertise their trade and are alluringly available. Most of the action takes place in the bars, where topless dancers hoof on an island bar. Each dancer wears a number and is available "after the show" for a fee. Sometimes, exuberant drinkers less than delicately place money on the bodies of their favorite dancers; it's not surprising to see a kinetic piggy bank undulating to the beat.

No survey could possibly canvas all establishments that cater to the predominantly male sexual appetite (and if one could even care to accomplish such a task, the information would inevitably be out of date); however, we list two places to give an idea of the flesh trade. At the **Baby A-Go-Go** drinks are on the high side with a Thai Singha beer running 75 baht ($3), but each drink seems to be accompanied by three or four teenage girls who massage your shoulders and hang onto your arms, legs, and other appendages. As of 1988, **Blackout** was the up-and-comer in the competitive Pattaya scene. The décor is more sophisticated than most and the music just a bit more current. Drinks cost about the same as at Baby A-Go-Go.

The fee system works something like this: pay about 550 baht ($22) to the club owner to take the "escort" outside; pay between 400 baht ($16) and 500 baht ($20) as a "guest charge" at the hotel, where the escort's ID will be kept for security; and 500 baht ($20) to 700 baht ($28) for in-room entertainment.

Gay Bars

Pattaya, like Soi Cowboy and Patpong in Bangkok, has many clubs catering to a gay crowd. Those that were in favor as of 1988 were **Boss, Cockpit,** and **Homex.** In addition, there are several gay escort services.

Discos

For those who just like to dance, rest assured that Pattaya has plenty of places to "groove to the pirated sounds of this and yesteryear." **Disco Duck,** much admired by visiting Thai teenagers, in the Pattaya Resort Hotel, and **Marina Disco,** in the Regent Marina Hotel, are the current favorites.

Transvestite Clubs

Pattaya has not one, but two grand-scale transvestite clubs: **Tiffany,** on Second Pattaya Road (tel. 422700), and the **Alcazar Cabaret,** also on Second Pattaya Road (tel. 428746). The show lasts about an hour, with three shows offered nightly. Both places deliver a similar performance with a score of coy, fan-waving boys adorned in flowing silk gowns and traditional Thai costumes performing untraditional dances.

Massage Parlors

Most of Pattaya's massage parlors are located on Second Road. **Rainbow** and **Physical Massage** are two of the most prominent.

Warning

As in Bangkok, Pattaya hosts many semi-licit and illicit activities; two that deserve special mention are drugs and AIDS. We repeat our warning: the waft of marijuana and the easy availability of other controlled substances shouldn't signify to any interested tourist that drugs are tolerated by the local authorities. The police frequently clamp down on both sellers and buyers, and ignorance of the law is not an accepted defense. In regard to AIDS, though the government claims there is scant incidence of the disease in Thailand, logic suggests that there is far more than is claimed.

BEACHES: The town beach, along Pattaya Beach Road, is unfortunately quite polluted and not recommended for swimming; however, those beaches at the extreme ends of town are cleaner. A better choice for bathing is **Jomtien Beach,** about 15 minutes south of the town and well connected by minibus. Windsurfers rent for 125 baht ($5) per hour, and the beach is long and sandy with a few scrubby trees for shade.

Local travel agencies advertise boat excursions to nearby islands with promises of better beaches. We are sorry to say that few, if any, are better than Jomtien. If you are serious about finding a great beach, consider taking a day trip to nearby Koh Samet.

KOH SAMET: The island of Samet is blessed with long, fine sandy beaches that rival those on Phuket and Koh Samui, and outshine anything to be found in metropolitan Pattaya.

The island's northern half is triangular with a long tail leading to the south, looking somewhat like a kite. Most of the beaches are on the east coast of the tail and are progressively cleaner as you head south, away from the ferry dock. Although the tail is only about half a mile wide, there are few paths that connect the two coasts. Passengers alight from the ferry on the east coast where there are ten beaches, each linked by a dirt path. The most popular, closest, and dirtiest beach is south of the jetty, Ao Thian or Candlelight Beach. Up north, on the west coast, is Ao Phrao (a.k.a. Paradise Beach), which is the most isolated on the island. Nearly the entire western coastline is uninhabited as there are few ways to get there other than by sea.

The island is dry, so all drinking water is transported by those oft-running ferries. Because there is so little water, hotel developers have been shy about commercializing this little sandy utopia; however, plans are afoot to build a major desalinization plant that would ultimately lead to a building boom. For now most visitors who intend to spend the night stay in clean bungalows without any frills ranging in price from 315 baht ($12.50) to 625 baht ($25). Others head back to the mainland to stay in Ban Phe.

Getting There

Getting to Koh Samet from Pattaya is quite easy. Buses depart Pattaya from the Regent Marina Station three times daily, making the one-hour journey to Ban Phe and connecting with a ferry that reaches Koh Samet some 40 minutes later. The cost of the bus is 150 baht ($6) one way, 250 baht ($10) for a round-trip ticket; the ferry costs 25 baht ($1) each way, and operates every 30 minutes during the high season.

2. KOH SAMUI

The island of Samui lies 84 km (52 miles) off Thailand's east coast in the Gulf of Thailand, near the mainland commercial town of Surat Thani, about 420 miles south of Bangkok. For well over 100 years Samui was visited by Chinese merchants sailing down from Hainan Island in the South China Sea. They traded for the island's two most profitable products, coconuts and cotton. Though co-conuts grow throughout Southeast Asia, those from Koh Samui are among the most coveted, principally for their flavor. To this day Samui sends over two mil-lion coconuts a month to Bangkok. (One fascinating sidelight of the harvest is that islanders have trained monkeys to climb the lanky fruit trees and shake off the coconuts. Much of the fruit is used for making oil, a process that involves scraping the meat out of the shell and drying and pressing it to produce a sweet oil.) This rich agricultural tradition continues to the present day, and visitors to the island still see trucks laden with yellow and green coconuts, fresh from har-vesting.

That Koh Samui is both isolated (until 1988 there was no air service to the island) and agriculturally rich has made it a relatively late entry in Thailand's ro-bust tourist derby. It was only 10 or 15 years ago that the first backpackers set foot on the island's magnificent beaches; the majority of tourists at that time opted for the still-nascent resorts of Phuket and, to a lesser extent, Pattaya. Fortunately, Koh Samui has yet to be fully invaded by the mega-resort developers, though it takes little imagination to chart Samui's destiny.

For now, at least, what Koh Samui offers is a idyllic tropical retreat with clean, warm water and beaches catering to all tastes, each with a simple, homey network of bungalows, primitive to luxurious.

The season on Samui is from mid-February through mid-November when the heat isn't excessive and the stormy winds have calmed. During that period, locals consider March through July as the prime months. During the balance of the year either the monsoon is on and it's extremely rainy or the winds turn fierce and make the water rough for swimming.

ORIENTATION: Though it's the country's third-largest island, with a total area of 90 square miles, the entire coastline of Samui can be toured by car or motorcycle in about two hours. The island is hilly and densely forested, with co-conut palms dominating the flora. Both the car-ferry and express boats arrive on the west coast, in or near (depending on the boat) **Nathon,** the largest town. Nearly all of Samui's fine beaches are on the north or east coasts, necessitating a short ride to your ultimate destination. With one exception, the island's only paved road follows the coastline.

The best of the northern beaches is at **Mae Nam Bay,** directly opposite near-by **Koh Phangan.** The northeast corner of Samui, between Thong Sai and Choeng Mon Bays, offers a delightfully punctuated coastline with rocky out-crops alternating with perfect sandy crescents. The long east-coast stretch between **Chaweng and Lamai beaches** is the most popular destination for visitors and, consequently, where you'll find the greatest concentration of bungalows. The southern coast is home to the island's small fishing fleet, dating back to the era of the China trade. Only one road bisects the island, leading to Na Muang Falls, a modest, but lovely waterfall in the interior. The west coast has a few sandy strips, but the busy boat traffic and resulting exhaust emissions lessen the appeal.

USEFUL INFORMATION: There is no TAT office on Koh Samui (the nearest agency is in Surat Thani), but the **Tourist Police** office in Nathon (tel. 077/421245 or 424281) is open daily on a 24-hour basis.

Nathon is also home to the island's major **hospital** (tel. 421230).

There are several **change booths** in Nathon. In addition, the **Thai Farmers Bank** and the **Siam City Bank** often stay open past their 3 p.m. closing time (as late as 6 p.m.) for currency exchange.

The **post office** is on the northern end of the waterfront street. There is no central telephone exchange on Koh Samui; all calls are made on radio telephones. Most travel agents in Nathon can book telephone calls. The local **telephone area code** for Koh Samui is 077.

Songserm Travel Center (tel. 077/421228), the operator and ticket agent for the express boats, will book phone calls, confirm airline tickets, and make reservations for destinations throughout Thailand; Songserm is located on the second street, one block north of the express boat pier.

There is a small bookstore/coffeeshop, **Buayaem's,** on the second street in Nathon.

Many people in villages throughout the island will collect, wash, and deliver laundry for about 5 baht (20¢) per shirt. Some enterprising Samuians actually walk the beaches in search of farangs with dirty clothes to clean.

Many **shops,** particularly on the second street in Nathon, sell inexpensive beachwear and suntan lotion.

There is a **Catholic church** on Samui, to the north of Nathon, that conducts Sunday mass at 8:30 a.m.

GETTING THERE: For years the only way to get to Samui was to travel to Surat Thani and take the ferry or express boat. Now there is a new alternative.

By Air

Those who flock to Koh Samui year after year shiver when they hear about a proposed airport, connecting the island with Bangkok and beyond. After years of maneuvering, Koh Samui finally has a genuine airport, still not in service, suitable for turbo-prop planes. How this quantum leap in the development of Samui's infrastructure will affect the state of things is anyone's guess, but the new times are soon to come. Sahaon Air is planning to make the commute from Bangkok, but they'll first have to overcome well-organized local resistance. At presstime, the airlines was still negotiating landing rights.

Another route to the area is to fly from Bangkok or Phuket to Surat Thani. From there you can take either an express boat or a ferry. There are daily flights on **Thai Airways** from Bangkok for 1,380 baht ($55.25) and from Phuket for 300 baht ($12).

By Train

Again, the idea is to take the train from Bangkok to Surat Thani and to transfer to Samui by boat. There are normally seven trains a day making the 13-hour journey to Surat Thani. The State Railway of Thailand (tel. 223-7020 in Bangkok) offers a special train that departs Bangkok at 6:30 p.m. and arrives in Surat Thani at 6 a.m. That leaves enough time to catch the express boat at 7:30 a.m. A second-class sleeper costs 354 baht ($14.25); second-class seats run 254 baht ($10.25).

By Bus
There are many buses running between both Bangkok and Phuket to Surat Thani. Air-conditioned buses from Bangkok run 225 baht ($9), while minibuses from Phuket make the four-hour trip for 200 baht ($8) inclusive of the ferry ticket.

By Express Boat
The most efficient way to get to Koh Samui from Surat Thani is to take the express boat. Boats leave the Songserm (tel. 077/272928) express boat pier three times daily, at 7:30 a.m., noon, and 2:30 p.m., for the two-hour shuttle to the island. The express boats land at Nathon where mini-trucks eagerly await the new load of holiday makers. Tickets cost 60 baht ($2.50) for a one-way trip, 100 baht ($4) for a round trip. Returning boats from Koh Samui depart daily at 7:30 a.m., noon, and 3 p.m.

By Car-Ferry
The oldest mode of transportation to Samui is the car-ferry that departs from Donsak, about 70 km (43 miles) south of Surat Thani. If you intend to bring a car over to the island, get to the ferry at least an hour before departure time to get your vehicle on line. Otherwise you might be forced to take the next boat. Those who travel without a car can pick up a minibus from either the airport, the Samui Tour office at the Taifah Hotel opposite the train station (tel. 077/311042), or at the Samui Tour office at Baandon (tel. 077/272452), which will transport you to the Donsak port. Boats depart twice a day from the train station at 6:20 a.m. and 7:15 a.m., and four times a day from Baandon at 8 a.m., 9:30 a.m., 3 p.m., and 5 p.m. The total trip takes two hours and 20 minutes from Surat Thani to Koh Samui.

The boat arrives at the ferry jetty, four miles south of Nathon. There is a large open-air restaurant attached to the ticket office and a plethora of noodle stands nearby. As you alight from the ferry and walk down the pier, you'll come to a parking lot where signs for various parts of the island correspond to waiting buses and mini-trucks.

The ferry departs from Koh Samui at 7:30 a.m., 12:30 p.m., 2:00 p.m., and 4 p.m. A one-way ticket is 50 baht ($2) per passenger and 175 baht ($7) for a car and driver.

SURAT THANI: The town of Surat Thani offers little of interest to tourists other than as a transportation hub to Koh Samui and Koh Phangan; however for those with an extra day or two in their itinerary there is an interesting day trip to be made. Approximately 7½ miles away from the town is **Suan Mokkha Phalaram,** a renowned Buddhist retreat that conducts programs in English. This center of meditation is led by its abbot, Bhikkhu Buddhadhas, who often travels around Thailand teaching the ways of the Buddha. The retreat has limited accommodations for visitors who wish to spend more time (call the TAT for additional information; see below).

Useful Information
For information about Surat Thani, Koh Samui, and Koh Phangan, contact the **TAT office,** at 5 Talad Mai Rd. in Surat Thani (tel. 077/281828), down the street from the Wang Tai Hotel. The TAT office is open daily from 8:30 a.m. to 4:30 p.m. The **Tourist Police** (tel. 077/281300) is open 24 hours to handle emergency calls.

The largest concentration of **banks** is near the pier for the boats to Koh Samui, near the night market.

Accommodations

The best lodgings in town are found at the **Wang Tai Hotel,** at 1 Talad Mai Rd. (tel. 077/273410). Though the accommodations are on the modest side, this high-rise hotel on the edge of Surat Thani's busy center area is a comfortable inn for a short stay. The hotel has a pool, mini-golf course, and various restaurant options. Twin-occupancy rooms run 770 baht ($30.75); singles are 630 baht ($25.25). All rooms have air conditioning and TVs.

For about the same rates, but not quite on the same level as the Wang Tai, are the **Siam Thani** (tel. 077/273081) and the **Siam Thara** (tel. 077/273740), both near the center of the town.

Dining

Usually there would be nothing special to recommend to interested eaters in a typical southern Thai town such as Surat Thani. Fortunately, Surat Thani boasts a wonderful regional dish that is not to be missed by even the most casual diner. The oysters harvested off the coast are as succulent and gigantic as one could ever imagine. Most restaurants in town serve these gastronomic gems, for what seems to a jaded Westerner, at a pittance. Oysters are served raw, with a spicy Thai sauce as an accompaniment, or cooked hot-pot style in a broth with vegetables. Either way, they are one of the gustatory highlights of the country.

Among the recommended restaurants in Surat Thani are **Chayhwai, Sunhieng,** and **Yim Yim,** all specializing in both Thai and Chinese cuisine.

GETTING AROUND: The most efficient way to get around the island is to take the roving **mini-trucks** that cruise the major arrival and departure points. The trucks advertise their destinations with colorfully painted signs to such beaches as Lamai, Chaweng, and Mae Nam. If you wish to visit a site off the beaten track (or simply one not mentioned on a vehicle), ask the driver of the appropriate truck if he will make a detour to your requested stop. Most buses operate on an as-needed basis. It's a good idea, if you're going to a far-flung destination, to inquire as to the departure time of the last operating bus. The one-way fee is 20 baht (80¢).

Alternatively, you can rent **motorcycles and Jeeps,** both in Nathon and in the various beach communities, for 190 baht ($7.50) and 625 baht ($25) respectively. Most of the rental agencies in Nathon are on the waterfront strip. The Thong Sai Bay Hotel is soon to be an Avis affiliate.

There are a few **radio taxis** for hire; your hotel, if equipped, can call them for you. Some of the upper-bracket hotels will arrange to meet you at the ferry depots upon arrival.

Koh Samui Divers, located on the second street in Nathon (tel. 077/ 421273), supplies equipment and instruction for those who wish to explore the waters off Samui and the many nearby islets.

BUNGALOWS: If you've read the description of bungalows in the introduction to the Thailand portion of this book, you might want to know about the local style on Koh Samui; they're a bit different. Most of the bungalows on Samui are made from palm, rattan, and bamboo, built in a simple A-frame or lean-to shape. Most have no interior bathroom or air conditioning. What you get for your 45 baht ($1.75) to 210 baht ($8.50) is a one-room affair with a bed, a fan, and a small terrace. At the moment, several of the earliest bungalow complexes (most have between 10 and 20 units) are plowing their profits back into their real estate and building more modern cottages. These rent for between 140 baht

($5.50) and 420 baht ($16.75), and often include a cold-water shower, toilet, and in some cases, air conditioning. Don't be surprised if you go to rent a bungalow and you're offered a range of accommodations; many of these establishments are a veritable patchwork of huts in many styles.

Nearly all the bungalows on Samui are built on the edge of the water, mainly on Chaweng, Chaweng Noi, Lamai, and Mae Nam beaches. Nearly all have a simple restaurant where meals tend to be extremely inexpensive. Few, if any, of the bungalows have telephones, so reservations are nearly impossible. One suggestion is to write in advance and upon response, enclose a deposit for the first few night's tariff.

We love names, and our current favorites among the over 100 island listings are: "Big Buddha Bungalows," "Calm," and for the nostalgia crowd, "Ziggy Stardust." Please write if you unearth one with an interesting moniker.

AROUND THE ISLAND: Although both the car-ferry and express boats dock near Nathon, the island's largest town, it is by no means where you should stay if you've come to sample Samui's fine beaches. Instead, head to one of the destinations on the opposite coast or up to the north.

Nathon

As for Nathon, notwithstanding the ferry trade, it's a very typical Thai town, especially so on the third street. There you'll find a morning market, the usual motorcycle repair shops, a Chinese temple, and in the alley leading to the temple, a brothel with a sign written in Thai that warns, "If the door is closed, don't knock." The third street also has two good, very inexpensive noodle shops where two can dine for 35 baht ($1.50); there is a vegetarian restaurant on the second street with entrees running about 12 baht (50¢).

One of the more fascinating aspects of life on Samui is **buffalo fighting.** These contests take place on festive occasions only, typically New Year's Day, Chinese New Year, and during the Songkran Festival. The fights consist of buffalos chasing each other, locking their horns, and wrestling the other to the ground. Rarely do they injure their opponents, though fans have been known to get trampled upon by a rampaging buffalo on the loose. The event is quite festive, with gold leaf applied on the horns of the beasts and festive ribbons and banners placed around the area. Like other aspects of Thai sports, buffalo fighting is very much tied to gambling.

Mae Nam Bay

Set midway between the east and west coasts on the northern perimeter (facing nearby Phangan Island), Mae Nam Bay hosts a relatively isolated beach and few bungalow villages. It was only a few years ago that the first bungalows appeared at Mae Nam, so the scene is far more tranquil than that at Chaweng. The names of the bungalows at Mae Nam say it all: "Peace," "Silent," and "Friendly." The beach itself is on par with Lamai, long and sandy. Normally this beach enjoys milder weather during the stormy months than the more densely developed east coast.

Of the accommodations, the most interesting is **Phanarm Inn II,** run by a local headman called "Black Moon." Mr. Moon collects animals and houses them in a mini-zoo that adjoins his bungalow hamlet. The highlight of the zoo is his rare Thai Kang monkey that peers out at night like an owl from its home in a tree. Deer, exotic birds, and a bear or two round out the menagerie. Rooms for humans aren't nearly so wondrous, with the typical accommodation amounting to a simple bungalow with a sink, toilet, fan, and bed. Rooms rent for 112 baht ($4.50) to 420 baht ($16.75), depending on facilities. As with most such set-ups, there is a restaurant attached to the bungalow complex.

Wat Phrayai (Big Buddha)

The gold-tiled Big Buddha sits atop a small islet connected by a 300-yard dirt causeway near Bang Ruk. The Buddha is of recent vintage, built in 1970, as are the polychrome smaller Buddhas in various positions situated around the periphery. Though the Big Buddha has little historic value, it's an imposing presence above the northeast side of the island and is one of Samui's primary landmarks. If you climb the steps to the base you'll have fine views of Samui's irregular coastline.

There are a number of souvenir shops in the parking lot leading to the Big Buddha that carry shells, beads, and locally made handcrafts at modest (and bargainable) prices. As you leave the parking lot, don't forget to notice the psychedelically painted Sea Demon storybook figures set in the water.

Built midway between Mae Nam and the Big Buddha is one of the island's older inns, the **Nara Lodge.** All of its 30 motel-style rooms have bathrooms and balconies, and some are equipped with air conditioning. The Nara Lodge is quite clean and the grounds, with a well-watered lawn, concrete pathways, and an acceptable beach, give it a slightly suburban ambience. Rooms with fans run 420 baht ($16.75), while those with air conditioning rent for 840 baht ($33.50). A new resort is planned near the Nara Lodge and should be ready for occupancy when you arrive.

Thong Sai and Choeng Mon Bays

The island juts out at the northeastern shore with rock formations creating private coves and protected swimming areas. The geology is reminiscent of the rough and irregular coastline along the Maine shore (if you can imagine some sort of tropical New England), though on a much reduced scale. Waves pound the rocks, sending up explosions of white foamy water, and the resulting tidal pools reveal a myriad of marine life.

THONG SAI. One such cove is at Thong Sai, where virtually the entire area is dominated by a single resort. As of this writing, the **Thong Sai Bay Hotel** (tel. 077/272222, extension 204) is the most luxurious accommodation on Koh Samui. The hotel is divided into two parts: the first is a cluster of first-class whitewashed cottages built up on a rocky bluff overlooking the bay; the second is a low-rise building that houses guest rooms, lobby, and a restaurant. Many of the cottages are duplexes, with a bathroom (hot and cold water) and bedroom on the upper floor, and a sitting area leading out to a bamboo-covered terrace on the lower level. These really are like suites. The rooms are tastefully decorated with furniture made of bamboo, rattan, and local grown gnarly wood.

Perhaps what's so remarkable about the Thong Sai Bay Hotel, aside from the contrast with everything else on the island, is that it's both low-key and very private, resting comfortably above its own beach bordered by rocks on each side. In addition to a satisfactory restaurant, the hotel offers guests a boat to tour the island, water-sports equipment, and a car-rental service through Avis. At 2,240 baht ($89.50) a night for a single and 2,520 baht ($100.75) for a double, the Thong Sai Bay Hotel is a real discovery.

CHOENG MON. If you proceed down the beach to the southern end of Thong Sai beach, you'll come to a fairly formidable set of rocks (they can be climbed safely if you wear decent footwear). Just over these craggy cliffs is arguably the finest beach on the whole island, Choeng Mon. This gracefully shaped crescent is about a half mile long. Palm trees reach right to the water's edge and are densely packed as you move inland. The sand is powdery in contrast to the slightly pebbly beach at Thong Sai. Swimming is excellent, with few rocks near the central shore. Across from the far southern tip of Choeng Mon is a deserted island with an excellent beach. You can swim or, if the tides are right, walk to the island, but be careful of the rocks that are much in evidence at the periphery of Choeng Mon. Connected to the island is an even smaller islet, where on the far side you'll discover an abandoned house.

Although there were, as of late 1988, only a few bungalows, we expect to see more along this prime coastline. Among the best lodgings available on Choeng Mon is **Su's Place,** run by a Thai-German management team. Su is a thoroughly engaging Thai woman who doubles as gracious host and accomplished chef. Each of Su's 15 bungalows is larger than the normal Koh Samui variety and is attractively decorated with rattan floor and wall coverings. The bed is set on a platform (very advanced by island standards) and the bathroom is completely tiled. With a cold-water shower, toilet, and fan in the room, it's quite a bargain for 420 baht ($16.75) per bungalow. The restaurant, specializing in Thai and Chinese cuisine, is tops on the beach, and if that's not enough, Su's Place also has its own mini-zoo. An excellent value!

Another slightly less costly alternative is **Chat Kaeo Resort,** a modest set of 280-baht- ($11.25)-a-night bungalows. The rooms are equipped with a shower but no fan. Several guests we spoke with praised its restaurant.

Farther up the beach are the only other bungalows at Choeng Mon, **P.S. Villas,** which rent for similar rates at Chat Kaeo.

Yai Noi Bay

The coastal road cuts inland along this section of the eastern coast, along Phung Bay, where the shoreline is rugged and impassable. The next beach of any consequence is at Yai Noi, where there is another attractive lodging alternative, the **Coral Bay Resort** (tel. 279-7573 in Bangkok). The 60-acre grounds of this moderately priced 45-bungalow unit lead to a fine, fairly quiet beach. Each bungalow, done on an upscale version of the island's more primitive model, is built of local wood and rattan and features "cathedral ceilings." Terraces look out directly to the beach or to a garden; the remainder of the land is dominated by coconut trees. As with most accommodations on Koh Samui, the hotel features a bar and restaurant with acceptable fare. The price for an air-conditioned bungalow is 1,260 baht ($50.50), 1,120 baht ($44.75) with a fan.

Chaweng Yai and Chaweng Noi Bays

Along with Lamai, the two Chawengs are the most popular destinations on Koh Samui. When you visit Chaweng you'll understand the attraction: the beach extends for about three miles and is an ideal place to swim, windsurf, jog, or just sunbathe. Nowadays the average tourists along Chaweng are no longer just the intrepid on their way to Koh Samui, Chaweng, and Lamai. There are a few families here and there, as well as an increasing number of European retirees. Still, the greatest number of inhabitants along this stretch are the young, many of whom are on the Southeast Asian circuit. The fare served at the bungalow restaurants caters to this group, with natural foods and magic mushroom omelets in predominance.

ACCOMMODATIONS AT CHAWENG YAI. The 30-unit **Pansea** (tel. 077/2356075) is set amid the multitude of bungalows along busy Chaweng Yai Beach. Each room, built in the island cabaña style, is air-conditioned, has a hot-water shower, and is furnished rather plainly. Among the amenities are a restaurant and a huge selection of aquatic sports equipment, suitable for windsurfing, snorkeling, and sailing. The Pansea operates on a half-board (breakfast and one other meal) basis; singles cost 2,380 baht ($95.25) per night; doubles are 2,940 baht ($117.50).

Of excellent value and on a par with the Pansea but nearly 1,400 baht ($56) cheaper is the **Village** (tel. 077/272222). The Village is owned and operated by Thomas Andereggen, a Swiss hotel manager, and Patchree Vialette, a Thai architect who designed the hotel and its companion establishment, the White House. Each of the 20 bungalows has a bathroom with cold water only and a fan. The interiors are scrubbed whitewash. Rooms are spacious and prettily appointed. We enjoyed three aspects of life at the Village: first, it has a delightful garden, with a gazebo, that leads out to the beach; second, an active restaurant/bar that overlooks the beach; and third, a genuinely friendly staff. At 910 baht ($36.50) a night, the Village is a fine value.

Just a bit down the beach at Chaweng is the Village's companion, the **White House** (tel. 077/272222). The name derives from the days when the land had only a white house built on it, prior to construction of ten attached bungalow-style rooms. The accommodations are similar to the Village, with the same tasteful décor and warm service. Rooms rates are according to size and location, with standard rooms renting for 770 baht ($30.75) to 925 baht ($37) and larger facilities going for 1,050 baht ($42) to 1,190 baht ($47.50), the latter mini-suites. Again, a very good value.

A much less expensive alternative is the **Joy** bungalow, next door to the Lightning Disco, where rooms rent for about 140 baht ($5.50).

ACCOMMODATIONS AT CHAWENG NOI. The newest and most luxurious resort on this vast coastline is the **Imperial Chaweng Hotel,** set on a terraced hill overlooking Chaweng Noi Beach (tel. 077/272222, extension 204). Like most of the island, the hotel is built in a grove of coconut palms that extend to the sandy shore. All 80 attached hotel-style rooms have a sea view and easy access to the beach. Amenities in these spacious quarters include air conditioning, television, refrigerators, and large balconies. We particularly enjoyed the eccentrically shaped saltwater swimming pool that seems just about to spill over into the bay. Single rooms run 1,960 baht ($78.50) and doubles are 2,240 baht ($89.50). The hotel is owned and operated by the same group as the Thong Sai Bay Hotel, so it's possible to make reservations there or at the Imperial Hotel (tel. 252-0450) in Bangkok.

Lamai Bay

The beach on Lamai Bay is comparable to that on Chaweng, and people often don't discriminate between the two other than for selected accommodations. Though there are a great many bungalows at Lamai, there are few that exceed the least expensive, most primitive standard, and therefore Lamai is more popular with travelers who stay for long periods of time. Among the best bungalows we found are the **Weekender, Aloha,** and **Golden Sand,** in order of quality. Bungalows at these establishments run between 250 baht ($10) and 420 baht ($16.75).

One of the nighttime attractions of Lamai is the **Flamingo Disco,** an oversize duplex cabaña that often has live music and dancing on a concrete floor. The Flamingo is open daily for dinner from 4 to 9 p.m. and for dancing from 9 p.m. to 3 a.m. There is a massage parlor behind the disco; massages run 100 baht ($4) per hour.

Big Rock

Koh Samui's famed Big Rock, also known as Grandmother and Grandfather, is at the far southern end of Lamai Beach. Many people are struck by the phallic shape of Grandfather rock. These huge boulders spill into the sea and are great for climbing and watching the tides. There is a small café near the Big Rock.

Na Muang Falls and the Southern Coast

The island road forks at Bang Nam Chuet, with the western road heading across the interior of the island and connecting with the coast road near the ferry jetty. Along the way the road climbs past **Na Muang Falls,** a rather diminutive but pleasant waterfall that makes for a nice picnic stop. The other fork continues south, leading to the Chinese trading ports on Bang Kao Bay. There is a finely built, century-old, Chinese-style teak house several miles east of the port. The family that owns the house harvests coconut trees with two trained monkeys, both of which can be seen in their yard. Ask a local to direct you to the old house.

There is a modest port on the southwest corner of Samui where boats ply the waters to nearby Dog Island and the pearl farm. **Dog Island** earned its name because, apparently, no dog could survive on this plot of land (not, as popular legend has it, that on windy days passengers become sick as a dog). The pearl island represents a nascent effort at pearl cultivation, much like its counterpart off Phuket.

West Coast

One of Samui's better beaches, though on the puny side, is the private cove at **Laem Phang Ka** on the southern tip of the west coast. There are only a few bungalow villages cropping up here, with more promised in the future. From this point on the island, the road cuts inland until a crossroad cuts back to the ferry jetty. Only a few miles up is Nathon; however, many Thai families stop for picnics at **Hin Lat Falls,** a rather uninteresting and littered site that supplies the town with its drinking water. If you climb up the rocks away from the throng the area is far less crowded and considerably cleaner.

EXCURSIONS FROM KOH SAMUI: Many travelers to Samui are repeat visitors, most of whom remember when there were only a few bungalows and generally primitive conditions. For those in search of Samui of yesteryear, a trip to **Koh Phangan** may be in order. Phangan Island is about two-thirds the size of Samui and similar in terrain and flora. Most tourists head for the sandy beach at Hat Rin on the southern tip, avoiding the coral reefs and the ferry dock (at Thong Sala pier) on the west coast. Though Phangan is less developed than Samui there are still over 50 bungalow villages scattered over the island. The price range for lodging is lower than on Samui, with average accommodations running between 30 baht ($1.25) and 210 baht ($8.50).

Another popular excursion is to the **Ang Thong Islands National Marine Park.** All-day tours sail to these 40 craggy, verdant islands, known chiefly for their dramatic grottos, remote sandy beaches, and wildlife, particularly birds. The National Park Authority authorizes camping on the islands.

Getting to Koh Phangan and Ang Thong

Getting to Koh Phangan is easy enough. Two boats a day, at 10:30 a.m. and 3 p.m., make the 45-minute journey for 35 baht ($1.50). Returning to Samui is more complicated, because the ferry departs at 6 a.m. and 11:30 a.m., making it impossible to visit on a day trip.

The trip to Ang Thong can be arranged through nearly any travel agent on the island and runs 190 baht ($7.50). The Ang Thong cruise operates every Wednesday, Saturday, and Sunday.

3. PHUKET

It's hard to keep up with Phuket. No other Thai destination is changing so rapidly: what one experiences today may soon become a distant memory. In its pristine state, this island in the Andaman Sea, 572 miles from Bangkok, is almost an idyllic place: long sandy beaches (some with dunes), warm, clean water, excellent snorkeling and scuba-diving (with exotic fish and coral reefs), ideal windsurfing conditions, mountains for climbing, and the best seafood in all of Thailand. For years Phuket has been Thailand's finest resort destination.

Yet during the past five years the Thai government has granted economic incentives to encourage developers to shape the island into an international-class resort. Hotels, some enormous, are taking over every beach where once only low-ly bungalows stood. As groups pour in from Singapore, Hong Kong, Germany, and Italy, out go the vanguard of backpackers to nearby Koh Pi Pi or Koh Samui on the gulf. As of this writing, six major resort complexes are under construction, with untold others on the way.

What complicates the issue is that many of the resorts, though certainly not all, are disarmingly attractive, often elegant places. If anything, Phuket learned much from the excesses of Pattaya. The Miami Beach strip of concrete and steel is rarely seen on Phuket. In its place are serene bays framed by tastefully designed retreats that are modeled after hillside villas or luxury bungalows. True, it's nearly impossible to find a totally secluded beach, but in its stead are extremely comfortable facilities with a high level of service—not a bad trade-off.

To further complicate the evolution of Phuket, offshore tin mining, once a thriving industry on the island, is making a comeback due to rising mineral prices in the international market. The future portends a three-way battle among mining interests, the tourism lobby, and ecologists.

The season on Phuket extends from September to March with the four-month stretch between November and March representing the prime months. From April to August the monsoon strikes the island, making it less than hospitable for farangs in need of a soothing beach-bound furlough.

THE VEGETARIAN FESTIVAL: Each province in Thailand has its special festival, usually harkening back to far more primitive times and rituals. The Vegetarian Festival on Phuket dates only from the beginning of the 20th century and is of Chinese origin. The genesis of this festival relates to a visiting troupe of Chinese performers, imported from the mainland to entertain tin miners. Many of the actors were stricken with a disease that forced the company to cease performing. Several members of the troupe were convinced that those who had contracted the ailment were being punished for not practicing their traditional Taoist rites. A remedy was proposed: for nine days and nights all the performers would eat only vegetables and observe the religious rites they had neglected. Of course, all the actors recovered and locals considered the entire episode a minor miracle.

Today the Vegetarian Festival is marked by a series of special events, some of spectacular and magical interest. Strict observers eat only vegetarian food, often distributed by the island's five Chinese temples (most tourists visit the two that are centered in Phuket town). During the nine-day period, all participants wear only white clothing. But the most fascinating aspect of the festival are the series of religious rites including fire-walking, climbing razor-sharp ladders, and piercing the body with sharp implements. All of these acts are performed under hypnosis and are startling to witness.

The festival begins on the first day of the ninth Chinese lunar month, so that in 1989 it will begin on September 30 and in 1990 on October 18.

ORIENTATION: Phuket is Thailand's largest island, and its terrain is vast and varied. Wide veldt-like plains give way to lush forests dense with mangroves, rubber, and palm trees. One can imagine the island with lions, tigers, and rhinoceros roaming the interior, before the Thais settled here in the 13th century. Hills dominate much of the island, in places punctuating gentle beach coves with craggy rocks spilling down from the slopes. From nearly any high point on Phuket you can see the enormous number of nearby islands and islets, among them, hourglass-shaped Koh Pi Pi off the southern shore. That Phuket is so hilly explains the origin of its modern name, derived from the Malay *Bukit* or mountain. In parts of the interior, open-pit mining for tin and other metals has scarred the land.

The town of Phuket, located in the southeastern quarter, is the commercial and transportation nexus of the island, a bustling spot with an active produce market. Although most, if not all, local buses go to Phuket town (usually called Phuket), this is not where most visitors are drawn to stay. Phuket is inland, noisy with the din of buzzing motorcycles and often fiery hot. Instead, head for the shore where the blazing sun, fine white sand, and refreshing sea will lure you to stay longer than you had planned.

The most attractive beaches are on the west coast, extending from Nai Harn, on the southern tip of the island, to Bang Tao, approximately 30 km (19 miles) north. The greatest number of bungalows and newly built resorts are in between these two along the Kata, Kata Noi, Karon, Karon Noi, Patong, and Surin corridor. A coastal road that links these beaches is slated to be completed in the near future. At present, travel between some of the beaches necessitates a detour to Phuket.

In the northern and inland sections of the island there is a remarkable contrast between Phuket of the past and of the future. Peasants still work the fields with water buffalos and basic tools, while along the perimeter of these centuries-old farms, road crews tear up the agricultural lanes to create wide, modern thoroughfares for the tourist trade to come.

USEFUL INFORMATION: The **TAT** is headquartered in the center of Phuket town, at 73-75 Phuket Rd. (tel. 076/212213), and is open every day from 8:30 a.m. to 4:30 p.m. They also maintain a desk at the airport with the same hours. The **Tourist Police,** located next door to the tourist office (tel. 212468), is open daily on a 24-hour basis. There is also a Tourist Police office in Patong Beach (tel. 321182). The police **emergency** telephone number is 199.

Warichira Hospital (tel. 211786 or 211114) serves Phuket and the surrounding area; there is also a ten-bed clinic at Patong (tel. 321444).

Pharmacies are located in Phuket and Patong and, with limited supplies, in major hotels around the island.

Banks are located only in Phuket, Patong, and at the airport. The airport bank is open daily from 9:30 a.m. until the arrival of the last flight of the day. (There is also an airport information booth, open until the last flight, that dispenses current data on available hotels.) Most hotels in other areas will change money but at lower rates.

The **PTT** is on Montri Road in Phuket and, with the Overseas Telephone Office around the corner on Phang Nga Road, is open 24 hours. The local **telephone area code** for Phuket is 076.

English-language books and magazines are available at **Patong International Books** in the New Shopping Arcade in Patong.

Phuket Center Tour, on Rasada Road (tel. 212892), and **Sun and Sand Tour,** in the Pearl Hotel on Montri Road (tel. 211044), both organize excursions around the island as well as serving as rental agents for boat companies. For information about diving equipment and excursions, see the sections concentrating on Patong and Kata Noi.

GETTING THERE: Phuket is well connected, not only to other points in Thailand, but also to major cities around Southeast Asia. A reliable travel agency in Bangkok with an office in Phuket is Seatran, 1091/157 Metro Shopping Center, New Petchburi Road, Bangkok 10400 (tel. 02/253-5307); in Phuket: 6 Phangna Road, Amphoe Mnang, Phuket 83000 (tel. 076/211-809).

By Air

Thai Airways (tel. 211195) flies twice daily from Bangkok for 1,470 baht ($58.75) each way. Flights return from Phuket for the one-hour flight back to Bangkok.

There are direct flights from Surat Thai to Phuket for 300 baht ($12). The half-hour flight is scenic, as it crosses verdant southern Thailand. Thai Airways also has flights to Penang for 1,030 baht ($41.25), Hong Kong 7,560 baht ($302) daily, and to Kuala Lumpur for 1,700 baht ($68).

Many hotels and bungalows provide a van for those arriving from the airport for transfer to various points on the island; expect to pay 60 baht ($2.50) to 180 baht ($7.25). There is limousine service from the airport to the Thai Airways office on Ranong Road in Phuket for 50 baht ($2). The public bus operates on an infrequent basis for 18 baht (70¢).

By Bus or Car

There is frequent bus service between Bangkok and Phuket. The air-conditioned bus from Bangkok costs 299 baht ($12) for the 14-hour ride. The public bus has seven departures daily from the capital and costs 165 baht ($6.50). Buses between Surat Thani and Phuket run six times daily for 61 baht ($2.50); the overland trip takes about six hours. There is also minibus service between the two cities. Taxis to Surat Thani are available for about 180 baht ($7.25). The taxi stand is in front of the Pearl Cinema on Phang Nga Road.

GETTING AROUND: Transportation throughout Phuket is by **minibus** or van. Nearly all routes pass through Phuket town. Most buses stop at the public market off Rasada Road, down from the Fountain traffic circle. Fares to the most popular destinations range from 15 baht (60¢) to 25 baht ($1). Buses usually run whenever there is a full load of passengers or produce.

Within Phuket, **tuk-tuks,** at 8 baht (30¢) for any in-town destination, and **taxis** are an inexpensive mode of transportation. Tuk-tuks can also be hired for longer distances; a five-passenger tuk-tuk from Phuket to Patong, for example, costs 125 baht ($5).

Motorcycles are extremely popular on Phuket; they rent for 180 baht ($7.25) a day and are available in Phuket on Rasada Road and at all the main beach resorts. Rental **Jeeps,** for 650 baht ($26) a day, are also available on Rasada Road in Phuket and at the beaches and hotels.

Car rentals are available in Phuket at **Pure Car Rental,** opposite the Thavorn Hotel (tel. 211002), for 1,300 baht ($52) a day excluding gasoline. There are two additional car-rental outlets operating in hotels in Patong: the **Avis** affiliate at the Phuket Cabaña Hotel (tel. 321138) and the Patong Merlin Hotel (tel. 321070).

PHUKET: Even if you don't stay in Phuket, a walk through the markets or along side streets (notice the early-20th-century Sino-Portuguese architecture), a visit to the crocodile farm or Thai boxing stadium, or a stop at one of the two Chinese temples makes a diverting tour.

Some people prefer to be based in Phuket, taking daily bus trips to different beaches, instead of being centered in one resort. Others arrive on the island only to find that the beach resort hotels are filled to capacity. In either case, if you stay in Phuket there are some worthy options.

Accommodations

The best of the in-town alternatives is the **Phuket Merlin Hotel,** set away from the center at 158/1 Jawaraj Rd. (tel. 076/212866). Though only a short 8-baht (30¢) tuk-tuk ride from downtown, a stay at the "suburban" Merlin is, in comparison to its rivals, serenity itself. The brick high-rise hotel was built in 1981 and sports a snazzy wood and polished-stone lobby. The best values are the superior singles and twins for 1,050 baht ($42) and 1,260 baht ($50.50) respectively. The hotel offers a free shuttle bus to Patong Beach, where there is a companion hotel. If you are looking for luxury but don't want to pay Patong prices—the equivalent twin room at the Patong Merlin is 1,550 baht ($62)—a stay at the Phuket Merlin is an attractive option.

In the same category, the **Pearl Hotel,** on Montri Road (tel. 076/211044), is a decent value. Rooms are clean, modestly furnished, and well maintained. The small garden at the back is the most exotic part of the hotel with its artificial waterfalls cascading into the pool. Superior doubles run 1,240 baht ($49.50); singles are 1,090 baht ($43.50).

The **Thavorn Hotel,** at 73 Rasada Rd. (tel. 076/211333), is the choice budget option in town. The spotless, clubby, dark-wood lobby underscores the attention that staff and management pay to the upkeep of the hotel. The rooms, particularly the twins, are spacious and appointed with carpeting and air conditioning. At 650 baht ($26) for a double room, the Thavorn is an excellent value. The only drawback, and it's a common complaint in town, is noise; ask for a room facing the back and you're bound to sleep better. We recommend it highly.

A rather nondescript inn, the **Imperial Hotel** at 51 Phuket Rd. (tel. 076/212311), offers modestly priced accommodations. Rooms with fans, at 350 baht ($14), are a better value than those with air conditioning for 550 baht ($22). Again, request a room away from the street.

The **Montri Hotel** at 12/6 Montri Rd. (tel. 076/219936), is another acceptable budget option. Double rooms with air conditioning and hot water are clean and a reasonably good value at 500 baht ($20). For those who need less luxurious digs, rooms outfitted with fans and cold water cost 275 baht ($11). Noise is a problem in the area around the Montri as well.

Dining

Phuket is known for its excellent seafood, but the restaurants in town, mostly catering to local clientele, serve more inexpensive cuisine. Thai and Chinese restaurants abound. We enjoyed a fine midday meal at **Kaw Yam,** at 1/1 Thungka Rd., around the corner from the Phuket Merlin Hotel (a ten-minute tuk-tuk ride from the center). The friendly staff serve attractive and well-prepared Chinese and Phuket specialties from a tidy kitchen. A plate of crispy fried Singapore noodles wrapped around fresh Phuket giant shrimp (presented with a sweet dipping sauce) was a marvel of taste and texture. Two people can eat a full meal here for 400 baht ($16). Kaw Yam is open daily for lunch and dinner.

Other recommended eateries in town are **Lame Thong,** on Montri Road (tel. 211269), for Chinese food; **Nai Yao,** on Phuket Road (tel. 212175), also with Chinese fare; **Mae Porn,** on Phang Nga Road (tel. 212106), for Thai food; **Lai An Lao,** on Rasada Road (tel. 211245); **Rooftop,** at the Pearl Hotel (tel. 211044); and **Tien Kong,** at the Phuket Merlin Hotel (tel. 212866).

ACTIVITIES AROUND THE ISLAND: Phuket offers a wide assortment of experiences. Backpackers and campers will want to head north to Nai Yang National Park and Beach, just a few miles from the airport. Those in search of an active party scene will undoubtedly find Patong the ideal destination. The beaches south of Patong, namely Karon and Kata, attract a more sedate crowd, those who enjoy fine swimming and diving, and who seek a more reclusive base.

The South Coast

One of Phuket's more fascinating sites is the **Marine Biological Research Center** on Phanwa Cape, on the very southeast tip of the island, about four miles from Phuket town. Here you will find the Phuket Aquarium with a vast array of indigenous sealife on display in glass tanks. One of the keen interests of those at the center is the cultivation and reintroduction of sea turtles into the Andaman Sea (see the later section on Nai Yang Beach). The display is open daily from 10 a.m. to 4 p.m. for a modest fee.

Some of the earliest development on the island began on the southern tip of the island extending from Chalong Bay to Rawai Beach and Nai Harn Beach. **Chalong Bay** is seven miles from Phuket and, like Rawai, suffers from the past dredging of offshore mining. The beaches that once were wide and sandy now tend to be muddy and unattractive. Many visitors now pass through the port on Chalong Bay to take the short trip to Koh Pi Pi. If you find yourself in Chalong Bay and need a bite to eat, try Kan-Eng II (tel. 216288). **Wat Chalong,** located on Chao Fa Road, is one of the island's most revered Buddhist sanctuaries because of the role of its abbot in 1876 in defending the island against a rebellion by miners.

The beach at Rawai is not on a par with other island beaches and doesn't warrant a special visit. If for some reason you do decide to stay in the area, there are suitable accommodations. Among the best is the **Phuket Island Resort** (tel. 076/215950), a 231-room hotel complex that commands admirable views from its perch at Lame Ka of the palms, beach, and nearby islands. The resort is equipped with all kinds of outdoor diversions and is isolated from other megacomplexes. Single rooms with air conditioning run 1,220 baht ($48.75); doubles are 1,440 baht ($57.50).

Nai Harn Beach

Those who have visited Phuket in the past speak nostalgically of the days on Nai Harn Beach when it was the quintessential tropical Shangri-la with just a few simple bungalows dotting an otherwise perfect beach. Today the bungalows are so jammed together that it's more like a beach slum. Ironically, what may salvage Nai Harn from its own tawdriness is its latest development, the **Phuket Yacht Club** (tel. 076/214020). Perched above the northern edge of Nai Harn, looking down at its more modest neighbors, is a luxurious beach resort that rivals anything on the island. From its pagoda-style entryway to the terraced gardens overflowing with pink and white bougainvillaea, the Yacht Club reeks of confident preeminence. All 108 rooms, ranging in price from 3,500 baht ($140) for a single to 4,200 baht ($168) a double, enjoy fine views of the beach and the Andaman Sea beyond from their well-landscaped balconies. Rooms are spacious and decorated with cheerful fabrics and wicker furniture. TV, air conditioning, a marvelous pool, and the hotel's own Chinese junk that cruises the island round out this resort's features, and by our estimates make it the best accommodations of Phuket.

It's impossible to see from nearby Nai Harn beach, but half a mile beyond the Phuket Yacht Club along a dirt road is the 38-bungalow compound called the **Jungle Beach Resort** (tel. 076/215929), opened in 1987. Actually the bungalows are set in a natural cove above Ao Sane Beach, but there is no other access other than from Nai Harn. The setting is absolutely equatorial: at night monkeys swoop down from the hills and climb the resort's trees; during the long rainy season, water cascades over the rocks to form natural waterfalls. The bungalows, ranging in price from 1,400 baht ($56) to 1,650 baht ($66), are equipped with fans and air conditioning, hot and cold water, and a large deck. The Jungle Beach Resort isn't for everyone, but it is exotic, very private, and a reasonable value. If you choose to stay here, it's advisable to phone ahead so that they can arrange a transfer from the airport or town, for 180 baht ($7.25) and 25 baht ($1) respectively.

Kata and Karon Beaches

These are among the island's most attractive beaches stretching from Kata to Karon, about 20 km (12½ miles) southwest of Phuket town and several miles north of Nai Harn. Suntanned bodies stretch out against a sand dune backdrop, while fishing fleets put out to sea and farmers tend their crops. You know you're in Thailand here unlike at some other hermetically sealed sites.

The two beaches are separated by a rocky promontory, but they are quite similar, in both ambience and development. A few bungalows, primitive to luxury, interrupt the long coastline and an occasional behemoth (Club Med and the

Arcadia Hotel, for instance) weighs in along the shore, but in between the mammoth development and the horizon is a perfectly hospitable zone. The coral and rocks near the shore are home to numerous fish and underwater creatures, and the beach itself is inviting. We particularly enjoy the late-afternoon transition to night on Karon Beach. Here the languishing sun casts a soft hue over the palms, while fishing boats set sail for their evening's work. You can't beat a long walk along these shores during this magical hour.

Yet even with its impressive physical appeal, Kata and Karon highlight just how the island is changing, most notably in the attitude of the local people. Here they seem just a bit less friendly, perhaps standoffish, and far more eager to cash in on the visitor than in other parts of Thailand. Since many of the tourists coming to these beaches are Europeans, particularly Germans and Italians, the restaurants have retreated from serving Thai food and cater to a more distinctly Western palate. In the clubs, bars, and restaurants it's more likely that you'll hear the Talking Heads than Thai music (or eat fish and chips instead of tod man pla).

During the day the beaches resemble a kind of embryonic Saint-Tropez. Rows of rented beach chairs and umbrellas line the fine white sand, not yet packed together but the trend is unmistakable.

KATA BEACH ACCOMMODATIONS. Right now, the **Kata Thani Hotel** (tel. 076/216632) is the only structure on lovely Kata Noi Beach, a stark contrast to the nearby beach at Kata and farther north at Karon, with their low-rent bungalows sandwiched between deluxe high-rise palaces. Because of its unique position, the low-rise Kata Thani can afford to be a bit more restrained in its level of luxury. The rooms in the hotel building (the recommended lodgings) and bungalows are clean, modern, and tastefully decorated with dark varnished pine logs. The hotel also has a sizable pool, around which is an outdoor bar and restaurant. A wide, well-mowed lawn divides the main hotel facilities from the beach, lending a gracious air to this fine resort. Doubles with a sea view cost 2,400 baht ($96); singles are 2,120 baht ($84.75).

It seems that whenever a resort boasts a Club Med it signifies that the place has arrived on the international jet-set map. Apparently, little Kata Beach can count itself among the chosen. Sitting regally, in its own sealed compound, the 300-room **Kata Beach Club Méditerranée** (tel. 076/212901) commands an enormous and enviable piece of beachfront real estate. In typical Club Med fashion, the Kata Beach facility is so completely equipped that contact with the outside world is hardly required. A full range of water sports is available, and if you do feel compelled to wander off, various excursions around the island are offered. The luxury-style resort is now managed by a Thai group and enjoys a fine reputation for service and facilities. Special kudos are in order for the food, including bountiful locally caught Phuket seafood. The soup-to-nuts price for all of this adult frolicking is 2,500 baht ($100) per person. Children under 12 pay half price.

Located directly on Kata Beach, the **Kata Inn** (tel. 076/212892) is the middle child of the Kata Thani, Kata Inn, Kata Inn 85 family. The hotel offers reasonably comfortable bungalows, most with air conditioning and hot water. The inn has a pleasant outdoor restaurant overlooking the beach. Bungalows rent from 1,050 baht ($42) to 1,925 baht ($77), depending on location and if equipped with air conditioning. Though it isn't nearly as private as the Kata Thani, the inn is still an acceptable alternative on the Kata shore.

The **Marina Cottage** (tel. 076/212901) is situated on the cusp of Kata and Karon beaches on a north-facing promontory. The cottages are a bit more comfortable than the next-door Kata Inn 85, and the price reflects the difference, with a bungalow renting from 700 baht ($28) to 1,900 baht ($76), depending on location and facilities (air conditioning). The hotel is also home to the area's only P.A.D.I. International Diving School, which conducts classes, rents equipment, and leads expeditions around the island reefs. Our only gripe with the Marina Cottage is that the staff tends to be less amiable than you might expect at a typical Thai inn; nevertheless, most guests claim to have enjoyed their stay at this well-situated hotel.

The **Kata Inn 85** (tel. 076/215728) is set just below the Marina Cottages and is an ideal resting spot for those on a budget who long to escape the throng at other nearby beaches. The bungalows are modest in size and décor, but for 750 baht ($30) to 950 baht ($38), depending on the view, the Kata Inn 85 is a good value.

KARON BEACH ACCOMMODATIONS. Literally on the beach, the **Phuket Arcadia Hotel** (tel. 076/21481 to 21486) is a modern full-facility resort that opened in late 1987. The low-rise and high-rise buildings are constructed so that every one of the 255 rooms has a view of the beach and ocean. Each room is attractively, if somewhat blandly, furnished and offers all the standard comforts: TV with video, mini-bar, air conditioning, telephone, radio, balcony, and bathroom with amenities like shampoo and soap. For casual dining there is a café serving Thai, Chinese, and Western cuisine and a poolside snackbar. The Tai Kong restaurant specializes in the locally caught seafood. For after dinner, there's also a lounge and disco. Sports facilities include an outdoor pool, tennis courts, putting green, water sports like windsurfing, and a games room. The landscaping is a little stark, but give it time. Additional features include 24-hour room service and also on-call medical service. Singles run 2,150 baht ($86) to 2,875 baht ($115); doubles, 2,400 baht ($96) to 3,100 baht ($124). Meals are extra.

We visited the **Thavorn Palm Beach Hotel** (tel. 076/215557) very shortly after it opened, and if the energy and optimism of the staff has been sustained, then you should enjoy a high level of service. Most of the 60 deluxe rooms are poised above the dunes of Karon, with fine views from the balconies. Though the interior décor of the hotel is minimal, individual rooms are fully equipped with the hi-tech amenities largely reserved for big-city lodgings. The pool is particularly inviting. Accommodations run 2,125 baht ($85) for a twin and 1,875 baht ($75) for a single.

Set directly on Karon beach, dunes and all, the **Karon Villa** (tel. 076/212709) is an ever-expanding hotel and bungalow compound. A new series of sea-view bungalows were opened in 1987. Guest rooms are good values at 1,150 baht ($46) for a single and 1,375 baht ($55) for a double; for a deluxe room add 500 baht ($20). At that price you can look forward to air conditioning, a spotless bathroom, TV, and a reasonably spacious room. The hotel has a fine outdoor bar/restaurant where you can sip exotic drinks while the sun sets or dine to classical Thai music. All in all, the Karon Villa is a winner.

DINING AT KATA AND KARON BEACHES. Most travelers eat at their hotel or bungalow, but there are numerous dining choices, especially at Karon. The **Suchavadee Restaurant,** at the Karon Villa (tel. 212709), serves a wide range of international dishes as well as Phuket seafood. A lobster costs about 175 baht ($7), depending on the season. If you'd rather stop by for a drink, we heartily recommend the mai tais as well as fresh fruit concoctions.

Along the unmarked street (Patak Road) heading away from the beach near the Karon Inn, there is a concentration of home-style restaurants that cater to a largely European crowd. Most of these establishments display their seafood in stalls along the road so that you can comparison-shop for price (they often vary wildly, especially according to season). The most venerable of these establishments (and equal to the rest for its quality of food) is the **Sunset.** The Thai chef has cooked in Europe and understands the taste buds of his clientele. A delicious mixed-seafood platter, beer, and banana split (we told you!) runs 155 baht ($6.25) per person for an ample amount of food. The Sunset also runs its own laundry service, and it's not surprising to see diners walk up to the counter to deposit dirty clothes before chowing down. We were struck by the summer-camp atmosphere and wondered if they served punch and cookies.

Two other notable eateries are the **Sawasdee**, where barbecued seafood is the house specialty (don't miss the tiger prawns), and the restaurant at the Marina Cottage, both located along the Karon beach strip.

Back in Kata, the preeminent dining establishment is **Jack and Joy**, around the corner from the Kata Inn on Phang Nga Road (tel. 211838). This modern-looking dining room serves fine Thai and international dishes, including local seafood.

A French-Flavored Thai Resort at Relax Bay

Tucked away alone on this secluded bay with a 600-yard-long beach and backed by 40 acres of lush tropical greenery, the **Meridien, Phuket**, P.O. Box 277, Phuket 83000 (tel. 076/321480 to 321485), is an alluring resort that combines Western and traditional Thai architectural elements. The basic U-shaped design ensures that 80% of the 470 rooms face the ocean. The modern furnishings in each room are of rattan and teak. Amenities include color TV with video, radio, mini-bar, air conditioning, telephone, personal safe, balcony with wooden sundeck chairs, and a bathroom equipped with hairdryer and clothesline. The dining possibilities are varied. There are in fact six restaurants: the formal Le Phuket's, featuring gourmet cuisine that blends French inspiration with Thai ingredients; the Pakarang, overlooking the hotel's seawater lagoon, which specializes in charcoal-grilled seafood; the Nopparat, offering themed buffets; a French-style café serving Thai specialties; a poolside snackbar; and a twice-daily barbecue. Afternoon tea is served in the Similian Lounge while the Tonson Bar is a romantic spot overlooking the sea for before-dinner cocktails or after-dinner drinks. Other entertainments include the discothèque and the many demonstrations and performances of traditional Thai arts that are given in the delightful open lobby. For sports enthusiasts there's plenty going on: two swimming pools, one a huge 12,000-square-foot saltwater lagoon; seven-hole mini-golf, putting green, and driving range; two squash courts; four tennis courts; a fitness center; a variety of indoor games; yoga, aerobics, and jogging; plus many water sports—scuba-diving, snorkeling, windsurfing, canoeing, and fishing. Singles range from 2,400 baht ($96) to 2,600 baht ($104); doubles, from 2,600 baht ($104) to 2,850 baht ($114). A surcharge of 300 baht ($12) applies from mid-December to mid-January. A shuttle service runs to Patong Beach, Phuket town, and the airport.

Patong Beach

Your attitude toward Patong will depend on your expectations and how you compare it to other destinations you have visited. When we first visited this thriving beach resort we had just made a pilgrimage to that capital of sun and sin, Pattaya. The word on the circuit was that Patong was finished, succumbing to the lure of hotel development and the titillation business. Yes, Patong does have a proliferation of hotels and guesthouses, and yes, the nightlife scene includes a number of go-go girl bars and massage parlors, but Patong is still a very far cry from the excesses of Pattaya. The beach is outstanding and generally not too crowded. The water is normally clean, except when storms wash debris onto the shore. There are enough, but not too many, hotels on the beachfront, and the many seafood restaurants will satisfy any palate (even if you don't care for seafood). Patong is not a virgin island paradise, but it's loads of fun for those who seek a modicum of action.

UPPER-BRACKET ACCOMMODATIONS. The **Coral Beach Hotel**, 104 Moo 4 (tel. 076/321106), stands high on the rocks above the throng of Patong. It's the only true deluxe lodging in the area, and as such, offers a few exotic amenities such as squash, badminton, and tennis courts as well as a fitness club. The rooms are finely appointed and service seems to be at a high level. Our only hesitation about this very handsome complex is its proximity to the beach. The swimming area immediately adjacent to the hotel is fine for snorkeling, due to the rocky reef, but you'd do well to walk down the hill to Patong or farther south to Relax Bay for a sandy beach. During the high season the Coral Beach Hotel requires half board (breakfast and one other meal) with double rooms running 2,800 baht ($112); singles cost 2,200 baht ($88).

Many of Patong's hotels are fairly simple, beachside bungalows. The best of them are comfortable, but often of anonymous character. In contrast to these, the **Patong Merlin,** on the beachfront strip at 99/2 Moo 4 (tel. 076/321070), has an abundance of style. The spacious open-air lobby is done in Thai fishing décor replete with nets, swordfish on the wall, and a brass wheel. Rough-hewn beams support the structure and rattan chairs and sailors' trunks fill out the space. The rooms are similarly adorned, but include air conditioning, TVs, and balconies, the best of which overlook the pool and a gorgeous center court garden. With doubles running 1,540 baht ($61.50) and singles at 1,300 baht ($52), the Merlin represents an excellent seaside value.

Built on the northern end of the Thaweewong Road strip, the **Phuket Cabaña Hotel** (tel. 076/321138) is a tasteful complex of Thai island cabins with loads of character: exposed wood beams, dark lacquered bamboo, rattan wall coverings, and stone floors. Though the cabins are packed together, the closeness of the beach combined with the hotel's enticing pool and rates of 1,250 baht ($50) to 1,750 baht ($70) a night makes this one of Patong's most attractive lodgings.

There's also a typical **Holiday Inn** right here on Patong Beach, at 86/11 Thaweewong Rd. (tel. 076/321020). The modern concrete-block buildings contain 280 rattan-furnished rooms, all appointed with air conditioning, color TV, and telephone. The resort fronts the beach, offers a range of water sports including diving, as well as tennis and swimming in a large irregularly shaped pool. There are two restaurants, one specializing in seafood and German-style cuisine, the other a coffeeshop with a pool terrace. Singles are 1,875 baht ($75); doubles, 2,125 baht ($85). Suites begin at 3,500 baht ($140).

The **Banthai Beach Resort** (tel. 076/211421), built in 1986 along Thaweewong Road, is a curious and wonderful melding of an American "cozy court" motel and Thai bungalows. The rooms are of a Howard Johnson-"no surprises" variety but with lots of Thai knickknacks. The exterior design motif includes a spirit house, traditional Thai roof lines, and imitation thatch walls. We really enjoyed the ersatz quality of the place; someone had a sense of humor to build this. The rooms are immaculately clean and staffed by a friendly team. They also have Thai classical dancing at their Sala Thai Restaurant. At 1,975 baht ($79) for a superior double and 1,300 baht ($52) for a single, the Banthai Beach Resort is a fun seaside inn.

The **Safari Beach Hotel,** on Thaweewong Road near the Banglai intersection (tel. 076/321230), is a low-rise, 30-room inn where the buildings are arranged in the shape of a horseshoe set around a pool. The décor is, in typical Patong fashion, nondescript, but as compensation the beach is directly across the street. All rooms are equipped with all the usual amenities, including air conditioning. During the high season rooms rent for 1,875 baht ($75), single or double.

The **Patong Beach Hotel** also on Thaweewong Road but on the southern end of the strip (tel. 076/211426), is an average hotel that's popular with European tour groups. Within its grounds are a pool, tennis courts, and a restaurant and disco, all clean but lacking in any distinct style. Of course, the beach is a stone's throw from the rooms, but if you're looking for something more luxurious or Thai you might be better off elsewhere. High-season doubles cost 1,200 baht ($48); singles are 1100 baht ($44).

Only the superior rooms are worthwhile at the **Seagull Cottage,** located next to the Patong Merlin at the far southern end of Thaweewong Rd. (tel. 076/321123). These are attached accommodations with rattan wainscotting, air conditioning, and television. They aren't wildly interesting or elegant guest quarters, but at 1,600 baht ($64) are a better value than the 1,050-baht ($42) bungalows. All rooms at the Seagull have names, such as Jimmy or Kathy, rather than numbers—strange but true.

BUDGET ACCOMMODATIONS. The **Club Andaman,** set across the street from the beach on Thaweewong Rd. (tel. 076/321102) is a budget-priced northside hotel, whose grounds are landscaped with squat, full coconut trees and rows of tall, skinny palms. This park-like hotel is set apart from the other strip hotels, lending it a private aura. Although the grounds are generous, the accommodations are comfortable if not luxurious. Clean, well-kept Thai bungalows with fans or air conditioning range from 1,135 baht ($45) to 1,740 baht ($70). For the price and the quiet location Club Andaman is a fine value, and it's still only a three-minute walk to the beach.

Nearby, also on Thaweewong Road, is the **Thara Patong** (tel. 076/321135), set across the street from the Cabaña Hotel. The Thara is really two hotels. The first is a conglomeration of clean, rattan-covered bungalows that are a good budget choice. These rooms come with fans and hot water, a happy compromise given their 600-baht ($24) tariff. For another 450 baht ($18) you can stay in the second tier, modern (and less enchanting) air-conditioned rooms that are as tidy as the bungalows. The staff at the Thara Patong is friendly and the small garden is a delight, ranking it among the best budget options.

Located directly on the beach, midway along the Thaweewong strip, the **Patong Bay Garden Resort** (tel. 076/321297) is a modest inn for such a grand name. Its simple but cozy lodgings rent for 800 baht ($32) to 950 baht ($38) a night, single or twin. Comparable accommodations are found at the **Holiday Resort,** on the south end of the beach strip (tel. 076/321101). These bungalows are set back about 50 yards from the beach. The rooms are functional, spartan, and clean. Doubles or singles are 575 baht ($23) for fan-cooled rooms and 975 baht ($39) for air-conditioned quarters. The 15 modern, prefab bungalows run 1,200 baht ($48) each.

DINING. As with the hotels, most of Patong Beach's restaurants line the seaside road. The restaurants have amazingly similar menus, though there is some difference in price and quality. We recommend sampling the island's incomparable seafood, especially the more exotic varieties, including our favorite, tiger prawns.

Patong Seafood, near the Safari Beach Hotel (tel. 321247), is typical of the many open-air seaside eateries. Absolutely casual in ambience, this very basic restaurant serves a full range of locally caught Andaman specialties. Among them are the much-heralded Phuket lobster at 40 baht ($1.50) per 100 grams (about a quarter pound) and the scarcer tiger prawn at 46 baht ($1.75) per 100 grams. Unlike some of Patong's other seafood restaurants, the manager here buys directly from fishermen and tends to price his entrees a bit lower than most. It is open daily for lunch and dinner.

UNDERWATER SPORTS. Many visitors come to Phuket for the fantastic diving off its many coral reefs. If you want to dive, Patong has many diving shops that offer everything from instruction to equipment rentals to individual chartering. **Fantasea, Santana,** and **Ocean Diver** are all on the beachfront strip and can arrange a full range of undersea adventures. The **Phuket International Diving Center** is based in the Coral Beach Hotel (tel. 321106) and offers the same service.

Bang Thao Bay

On a perfect, secluded bay, 22 km (13½ miles) from Phuket town, the **Dusit Laguna,** 390 Srisoontorn Rd. (tel. 076/311320 to 311329), is a stylish modern resort that also manages to be traditional and intimate at the same time. The resort faces the beach and is flanked by two lagoons. The landscaped gardens include tropical foliage and a waterfall, and contribute to the peaceful harmony of the place. The 240 rooms are tastefully furnished and have mini-bars, TVs, private balconies, and large bathrooms with amenities. The cuisine is high quality too. The centrally located JunkCeylon grill room specializes in Phuket fresh seafood and meats; the RuenThai Thai restaurant, overlooking the South Lagoon, offers regional dishes from all over the country. The Laguna Café affords a full view of the pool, waterfall, and gardens, and is pleasant for breakfast lunch or dinner. There's also an al fresco barbecue terrace, a disco, and a couple of lounges for sundown cocktails overlooking the water. Sporting facilities are extensive: water sports (windsurfing, waterskiing, sailing, diving); two pools, one specially designed for kids; putting greens; two tennis courts; and outdoor games including giant chess. Singles are 2,200 baht ($88); doubles, 2,450 baht ($98). Suites begin at 4,600 ($184). Note the peak-season surcharge of 500 baht ($20) per night.

Nai Yang Beach

If you've flown to Phuket and happened to look south as you came in to land, you might have noticed an extraordinary expanse of pristine shoreline, framed by a dense forest of palms, casuarina, and other indigenous flora. This is the **Nai Yang National Park** and it's an ideal destination for those who truly want to leave the crowds behind. There are a few bungalows; many people choose to camp.

Nai Yang is also known for its participation on **National Fish Species Multiplication Day** (no, fish do not do arithmetic; and no again, we didn't name this holiday) when the Marine Biological Research Center on Phuket releases its crop of sea turtles back into the Andaman Sea. Sea turtles ranging in size from huge (about 100 pounds) to humongous (1,500 pounds) swim the waters around Phuket, but without protection against fishermen. If not for the efforts of the Marine Biological Center these creatures would probably be extinct from local waters. April 13, during the Songkran holiday, marks the day when all animals are to be released, thus it is fitting that the holiday should coincide with National Fish Species Multiplication Day. There are organized activities on this day, and if you happen to be on the island you should make a special trip to see these miraculous animals.

Mai Khao Beach

Like Nai Yang, Mai Khao is a marvelous beach on the northeastern shore that is even closer to the airport. The beach itself is Phuket's longest and is most known as the site where sea turtles lay their eggs from October to February.

Inland Sites

As the road heads inland from the airport, it passes **Wat Phra Thong (Golden Buddha),** the most sacred shrine on the island. It is here that a boy who tethered his water buffalo to a post mysteriously contracted a disease. The post, it was later discovered, was the top of a huge, golden Buddha that was buried deep in the ground. For some reason, only the top part of the image was excavated and a temple was built to house the statue. Legend has it that those who tried to unearth the submerged portion of the Buddha were attacked by hornets and other insects. The buried Buddha is glazed with gold-leaf stucco as a protective coat over the solid-gold image beneath.

Just a few miles east is the **Khao Phra Thaeo Wildlife Park,** which is most noteworthy for Ton Sai falls, a lovely spot to stop for a cool break on a blisteringly hot day. The park is home to a menagerie of birds and other fauna, as well as a variety of palm that is unique to the island.

KOH PI PI: If you find the whole scene on Phuket too much for your overtouristed soul, an extended excursion to the Pi Pi Islands just might be the primitive escape you need. There are actually two Pi Pi's set in the Andaman Sea, **Pi Pi Don** and Pi Pi Le, both very close to one another. The first is where most travelers head, both for its sensational beaches and simple accommodations. Rocky **Pi Pi Le** is known for its crystalline water, colorful coral formations, and wide assortment of undersea life. The contour of the island is so pronounced that it has the appearance of a Chinese rock sculpture. The water between Phuket and Koh Pi Pi can be rough; sometimes boats don't make the voyage, waiting for a more placid sea. The best time to visit is from November to January when the Andaman is tranquil and the weather ideal.

Pi Pi Don, which most people refer to simply as Pi Pi, is an hourglass-shaped islet so thin-waisted that it appears that you could jump from one side of the island to the other. There are long beaches on both sides. The best way to see this unique formation is to take the Mountain View Trail, which starts at the fishing village and continues along a marked path. The hike takes about 45 minutes to the top, but the vista is unforgettable.

The boats that ply the waters from Chalong Bay on Phuket to Koh Pi Pi dock at the fishing village. Nearby, about a 15-minute walk away, is **Long Beach,** where there is fine snorkeling and swimming.

Accommodations are fairly primitive on the island. Typical of these lodgings is **Pi Pi Andaman,** a recently built bungalow complex where many travelers hunker down for an extended stay. The rooms are in Thai style with fans; toilets and showers—outside the huts—are shared.

Pee Pee Island Village, 158/20 Yaowaraj Rd. (tel. 076/215014), has 60 or so traditional Thai-style bungalows on the beach, each of bamboo and thatch, but with modern bathrooms. Facilities also include a restaurant and bar. Rates are 600 to 900 baht ($24 to $36). Long boats at the landing make daily excursions to remote points on the island as well as sailing the waters around Pi Pi Le.

Getting to Koh Pi Pi

The trip to Koh Pi Pi takes 1½ hours from Chalong Bay. Boats leave Phuket at 8:30 a.m. and arrive at Koh Pi Pi at 10 a.m., daily. Also Aloha Tours (tel. 076/216726) operates a daily ferry leaving at 9 a.m. Roundtrip fare is 750 baht ($30). Excursion boats also depart from Krabi for the 1½-hour journey, leaving at 1 p.m. and arriving at Koh Pi Pi at 2:30 p.m.; cost is 750 baht ($30) roundtrip.

WHO'S WHO AMONG THE RAMAS. The Thai people truly revere their royal family as anyone who is there on the celebration of King Chulalongkorn Memorial Day can testify. One senses that the relationship of Thais to their monarchs is not based simply on respect but resonates on a deeply personal level. Each monarch is remembered for his particular personality and character as well as his actions. You will often hear particular monarchs referred to in conversation, so here to help you identify them are some brief facts about each.

RAMA I: The founder of the Chakri dynasty, he reigned from 1782 to 1809. He established Bangkok as the capital modeling it after the previous capital of Ayutthaya, which had been destroyed by the Burmese. He recovered much of the territory that had been lost including Chiang Mai and Sukhothai. He ordered the building of Wat Suthat to house the gilded Buddha that he had brought back from Sukhothai.

RAMA II: A great patron of the arts, Rama II ruled from 1809 to 1824. He began the building of Wat Arun and reopened Thailand to European contact.

RAMA III: The major issue that he faced during his reign from 1824 to 1851 was colonization by the European powers.

RAMA IV: Prince Mongkut ascended to the throne at the age of 47 after having spent many years as a wandering monk and as abbot at Wat Bovornives. Having studied Western languages and ways, he was able, through clever diplomacy, to prevent Thailand from falling under European control. He understood the need for modernization and is known in the West as the King who employed the English governess Anna Leonowens to teach his children.

RAMA V: This is the same Chulalongkorn the Great whose memory is celebrated on October 23. Beloved by his people, he was a great reformer, who released the people from their obligation to prostrate themselves before him and abolished slavery. He ceded a large portion of territory that previous monarchs had conquered, notably Laos, Cambodia, and four Malay provinces to France and England. By doing this he secured peace and independence from the colonial powers and was able to begin the industrial development of the country. He reigned from 1868 to 1918.

RAMA VI: He ruled from 1918 to 1925 and was best known for his academic achievements—translations of Shakespeare and Molière and the continued Europeanization of the country.

RAMA VII: His reign, from 1925 to 1935, was brief and turbulent. The Depression severely affected the Thai economy and helped set the scene for a "bloodless revolution" that ended the absolutism of the monarchy and left the king in effect a puppet. He abdicated in 1935.

RAMA VIII: Crowned as a young boy in 1935, educated in the West, he returned to assume his duties at the age of 20 in 1945 but died mysteriously in his Bangkok palace the following year.

RAMA IX: The current king Bhumiphol was born in Cambridge, Massachusetts. Crowned in 1950, he assumed his duties in 1951 and has captured the hearts and minds of his people, particularly because he seems to appreciate and love the countryside and the life of rural Thailand. He has commiserated with them and ministered to them in times of natural disaster and has fostered many ecologically sound rural development projects, such as fish farming.

PRENTICE HALL TRAVEL TITLES ON ASIA: This first edition of *Frommer's Dollarwise Southeast Asia* covers Burma, Hong Kong, Indonesia, Malaysia, Singapore, and Thailand in detail, but there are several other Prentice Hall titles that you may also want to consult.

In the Frommer series you'll find *India on $25 A Day, Dollarwise Japan and Hong Kong,* the *Touring Guide to Thailand,* and the *Touring Guide to Hong Kong, Macau and Singapore.*

Asian titles in the Insight Guide series include the recently published *Rajasthan,* plus backlist favorites, *Bali, Burma, Hong Kong, India, Indonesia, Java, Korea, Malaysia, Nepal, The Philippines, Singapore, Southeast Asia, Sri Lanka, Taiwan,* and *Thailand.*

In the American Express series, there are guides to *Tokyo* and *Hong Kong, Singapore and Bangkok.*

The Baedeker series includes volumes devoted to *Bangkok, Hong Kong, Singapore,* and *Tokyo,* and a country guide to *Japan.*

And for the business traveler, there are *Economist Business Traveller's Guides* to *China, Japan,* and *South-east Asia.*

Recently updated and now available, the first English-language editions of the famous nineteenth-century French guidebook series, the Guides Bleus, on *China* and *Japan.*

Prentice Hall Travel books can be purchased at bookstores or ordered directly from the publisher at One Gulf + Western Plaza, New York, NY 10023.

Index

Amarapura (Burma), 68
Ang Thong (Thailand), 601
Ava (Burma), 69
Ayutthaya (Thailand), 533–5

Bali (Indonesia), 233–73
  beach resorts: *see* Kuta Beach; Nusa Dua; Sanur *below*
  culture of, 237–41; performing arts, 239–40; religion and ritual, 238–9; visual arts, 240–1
  Eastern, 267
  etiquette, 262
  golf resort, 266–7
  Kuta Beach, 249–54; accommodations, 249–52; orientation, 249; restaurants and nightlife, 252–3; shopping, 254; sights and attractions, 253–4; tourist information, 249
  map, 242
  Northern, 265–7
  Nusa Dua, 254–6
  orientation, 233–4
  Sanur, 241, 243–9; accommodations, 243–6; restaurants, 246–8; shopping, 248; sights and attractions, 248
  South-Central, 262–5; Batubulan, 263–4; Celuk, 264; Denpasar, 262–3; Goa Gajah (the Elephant Cave), 264–5; Mas, 264; Tampaksiring, 265; Ubud, 265
  tourist information, 234–5
  transportation to, 235–6; from Yogyakarta, Surabaya, and Ngadisari, 231–2
  transportation within, 236–7, 262
  Ubud, 256–61; accommodations, 257–60; history of, 256–7; orientation, 257; restaurants, 261; shopping, 261; sights and attractions, 260–1; tourist information, 257; transportation to and within, 257
  Western, 269–70
Bali Aga villages (Indonesia), 268
Baliem Valley (Indonesia), 307–11
  sights and attractions, 316–17
Bandung (Indonesia), 208–11
Bangkok (Thailand), 482–540
  ABCs of, 489–95
  accommodations, 495–505; budget, 503–4; first-class, 498–500; guesthouses, 504–5; luxury, 495–8; moderately priced, 500–3; near the Oriental Hotel, 501, 503–4; near the railroad station, 502; near the Royal Palace, 501–2; near Sukhumvit Road, 502
  day trips from, 531–40; Ancient City, 532; Ayutthaya, 533–5; Bang Pa-In, 535–6; crocodile farm, 532; Hua Hin, 539–40; Kanchanaburi, 536–9; Nakhon Pathom, 536; on the river, 532; Rose Garden Country Resort, 532–3
  history of, 483–4
  map, 484–485
  nightlife, 529–31
  orientation, 483, 485
  restaurants, 505–15; American, 514; budget, 507–8; Chinese, 510–11; fast-food, 509–10, 515; French, 513–14; health food, 512; highlights, 505–6; at the hotels, 507; Indian, 511; Italian, 514–15; Japanese, 511; moderately priced, 506–7; seafood, 512–13; Thai, 506–10; with traditional dancing, 508–9; Vietnamese, 511–12; Western, 513–15
  shopping, 525–9; antiques, 527; bronze/nickel work, 529; handcrafts, 526–7; helpful hints, 526; jewelry, 528; shoe and leather goods, 529; silk, 528–9; where to shop, 526
  sights and attractions, 515–25; cock, beetle, and fish fighting, 525; Dusit Zoo and the Celestial Residence, 525; Grand Palace, 518–19; Jim Thompson's house, 522; Kamthieng House, 523–4; kite fighting, 525; Lak Muang (City Pillar), 520; landmarks and neighborhoods, 483, 485; markets, 524; National Museum, 519–20; Red Cross Snake Farm, 525; royal barges, 516; Tai Chi, 525; Vivanmek Mansion, 523; Wang Suan Pakkard, 521–2; Wat Arun (Temple of Dawn), 521; Wat Benjamabophit (the Marble Wat), 522–3; Wat Bovornives, 523; waterways, 515–16; Wat Mahatat, 519; Wat Phra Keo (the Emerald Buddha), 517–18; Wat Po (Temple of the Reclining Buddha), 520–1; Wat Suthat, 523; Wat Traimit (Temple of the Golden Buddha), 524
  tourist information, 494
  transportation to and within, 485, 487–9

Bang Pa-In (Thailand), 535–6
Bang Thao Bay (Thailand), 612
Batak Highlands (Indonesia), 282
Batubulan (Indonesia), 263–4
Batu Ferringhi (Malaysia), 373, 375
Batur (Indonesia), 266
Biak (Indonesia), 311
Bogor (Indonesia), 207–8
Boma (Indonesia), 317
Borneo (Malaysia), 393–411
  map, 394
  Sabah, 404–11; accommodations, 406–7; nightlife, 411; orientation, 404–5; restaurants, 407; shopping, 411; sights and attractions, 407–11; tourist information, 405; transportation to and within, 405–6
  Sarawak, 393–404; accommodations, 397–8; history, 393, 395; orientation, 395; restaurants, 398–9; shopping, 403–4; sights and attractions, 399–403; tourist information, 395–6; transportation to and within, 396–7
Borobudur (Indonesia), 223–5
Brastagi (Indonesia), 281
Bratan, Lake (Indonesia), 267
Bromo, Mount (Indonesia), 230–31
Bukittinggi (Indonesia), 293–4
Burma, 23–75
  ABCs of, 34–44
  currency, 36–7; exchange chart, 30
  economy of, 27
  festivals and holidays, 38–9
  geography of, 24
  history of, 27–30
  Inle Lake: see Taunggyi below
  itineraries, 30–31
  language of, 26, 40–1
  Mandalay, 62–70; accommodations, 65; day trips and excursions from, 68–70; history of, 63; map, 56; orientation, 63; restaurants, 65–6; shopping, 67–8; sights and attractions, 66–7; tourist information, 63–4; transportation to and within, 64–5
  map, 25
  Pagan, 54–62; accommodations, 57–8; history, 55; map, 56; orientation, 55; restaurants, 59; sights and attractions, 59–61; tourist information, 55; transportation to and within, 55, 57
  people of, 24, 26–7
  religion of, 26–7
  Taunggyi and Inle Lake, 70–5; accommodations, 73–4; map, 56; restaurants, 74; sights and attractions, 74–5; tourist information, 71;

transportation to and within, 71–3
  tourist information, 43–4
  transportation to and within, 31–4
  see also Rangoon

Cameron Highlands (Malaysia), 364–5, 367–8
Candi Dasa (Indonesia), 268
Candi Mendut (Indonesia), 225
Candi Sukuh (The Erotic Temple) (Indonesia), 227
Carita Beach (Indonesia), 207
Celuk (Indonesia), 264
Cha Am (Thailand), 540
Chaweng Noi Bay (Thailand), 600
Chaweng Yai Bay (Thailand), 599–600
Cheung Chau (Hong Kong), 137
Chiang Dao (Thailand), 571
Chiang Mai (Thailand), 551–76
  accommodations, 557–62; budget, 559–62; near Huai Keo Road, 559; moderately priced, 557–9; near Old City and business districts, 557–8; near train station, 561
  day trips from, 567–71; Chiang Dao, 571; Doi Inthanon National Park, 570–1; Lampang and the elephant-training school, 570; Lamphun, 568–9; Mae Sa Valley, 571; Pa Sang, 569–70; Wat Phra That and royal palace, 567–8
  history of, 552
  map, 558
  nightlife, 575–6
  orientation, 552, 554
  restaurants, 562–5; Chinese, 564; Northern Thai, 562; Thai, 563; vegetarian, 563–4; Western, 564–5
  shopping, 571–5; basketry, 575; hill tribe and Burmese handcrafts and antiques, 572–3; jade/jewelry, 575; night market, 572; San Kamphaeng Road and Bo Sang, 574–5; silver and ceramics, 573–4
  sights and attractions, 565–7; festivals, 556; Thai boxing, 576
  tourist information, 554–5
  transportation to and within, 555–6
Choeng Mon Bay (Thailand), 598–9
Cing Chung Koon Temple (Hong Kong), 136

Densapar (Indonesia), 262–3
Desa Besakih (Indonesia), 268–9
Dieng Plateau (Indonesia), 227
Doi Inthanon (Thailand), 570–1

Gilimanuk (Indonesia), 270
Goa Gajah (the Elephant Cave) (Indonesia), 264–5

Hong Kong, 76–144
  ABCs of, 86–92
  accommodations, 92–101; budget, 98–9; first-class, 95–7; on Hong Kong Island, 95–6; hostels and dormitories, 99–101; Kowloon, 96–7; luxury, 92–3, 95; moderate, 97–8
  currency, 88; conversion table, 80
  excursions from, 135–44; China, 138–9; Macau, 139–44; new territories, 135–7; outlying islands, 137–8
  history of, 77–9
  map, 82–3; Central District, 94
  nightlife, 133–5
  orientation, 80–1
  restaurants, 101–15; Cantonese, 104–7; Chinese, 103–11; Chiu Chau, 110–11; continental, 113–14; Dim Sum, 105–6; fast food, 114–15; highlights, 102–3; Indian, 112; Japanese, 111; Mongolian, 108; Peking, 107–8; seafood, 109–10; Shanghai cuisine, 109; Southeast Asia cuisines, 112–13; Szechuan, 108–9; vegetarian, 111; Vietnamese, 111–12; Western, 113–15
  shopping, 122–33; art and antiques, 124–5; cameras, computers, and electronics, 125–6; carpets and rugs, 126; ceramics, crystal, porcelain, 126; clothing, 126–8; exotica, 128; eyewear and optical, 128; factory outlets, 128–30; markets, 131–2; smoking supplies, pen, lighters, 132; souvenirs, 132–3; tips, 123–4
  sights and attractions, 115–21; Aberdeen, 117, 118; cultural, 119–21; festivals and holidays, 88–90; harbor tours, 115–16; museums, 119–20; Repulse Bay, 117, 118; Stanley, 117–19; Star Ferry, 115; Victoria Peak, 117
  sports and recreation, 121–2
  tourist information, 91–2
  transportation to and within, 81, 84–6
Hong Kong Island accommodations, 95–6
Hua Hin (Thailand), 539–40

Indonesia, 5, 145–318
  ABCs of, 157–63
  books about, 163
  culture of, 150–5; Adat, 150; arts and crafts, 152–4; Batik arts, 152–3; cuisine, 154; etiquette, 150; Gamelan music, 150; performing arts, 151–2; Wayang theater, 151–2

  currency, 158; conversion table, 155
  economy of, 148
  history of, 149–50
  itineraries, 155
  language, 161, phrases, 163–4
  map, 146–47
  people of, 148
  Samosir Island, 282; accommodations, 284; restaurants, 285; sights and attractions, 285–6; transportation to, 282; festivals and holidays, 159–60
  sights and attractions: *see specific places*
  tourist information, 163
  transportation to and within, 155–7
  see also Bali; Irian Jaya; Jakarta; Java; Sulawesi; Sumatra
Inle Lake (Burma), 76–5
  accommodations, 73–4
  orientation, 70–1
  restaurants, 74
  sights and attractions, 74–5
  tourist information, 71
  transportation to and within, 71–3
Irian Jaya (Indonesia), 305–18
  Baliem Valley, 307–11
  Biak, 311
  history of, 306–7
  Jayapura, 311–14
  orientation of, 306
  Sentani, 314–15
  Wamena and environs, 315–17

Jakarta (Indonesia), 165–99
  ABCs of, 172–5
  accommodations, 175–80; budget, 179–80; first-class, 177–8; hostels and guesthouses, 180; luxury, 175–7; moderately priced, 178–9
  excursions from: Krakatoa, 205–7; Pulau Seribu, 203, 205
  history of, 165–7
  map, 168
  nightlife, 198–9
  orientation, 167
  restaurants, 180–7; Chinese, 184; continental, 185–6; fast food, 186–7; highlights, 181–2; Indian, 184; Indonesian, 182–4; Japanese, 185; Korean, 184–5; Thai, 184; Vietnamese, 184; Western, 185–7
  shopping, 195–8; antiques and curios, 197–8; bargains, 197; Batiks and woven fabrics, 195–6; department stores and malls, 196–7; jewelry, 197; woodcarving, 196
  sights and attractions, 187–95; Ancol Dreamland, 194; Fatahillah Square, 192–3; Istiqlal Mosque, 189–90; Merdeka Square, 189; National

Jakarta: (cont'd)
Monument, 188–9; National Museum, 190; Old Batavia, 193–4; Pasar Burung, 195; Pasar Ikan, 192; Ragunan Zoo, 194; Soekarno monuments, 188; Sunda Kelapa, 191; Taman Fatahillah, 192; Taman Mini Indonesia Indah, 190–1
tourist information, 174–5
transportation to and within, 167, 169–71
see also Yogyakarta
Java (Indonesia), 200–32
Central, 223–7; Borobudur, 223–5; Candi Mendut, 225; Candi Sukuh (The Erotic Temple), 227; Dieng Plateau, 227; Pawon, 225; Prambanan and environs, 225–7
Eastern, 227–31; Mount Bromo, 230–1; Solo (Surakarta), 227–30
history of, 201–2
map, 204
orientation, 202–3
transportation to and within, 202–3
West, 207–11; Bandung, 208–11; Bogor, 207–8
Jayapura (Indonesia), 311–14
Jiwike (Indonesia), 317
Jomtien Beach (Thailand), 589–90, 591

Kanchanaburi (Thailand), 536–9
Karon Beach (Thailand), 606, 608–9
Kata Beach (Thailand), 606–9
Kintamani (Indonesia), 266
Klungkung (Indonesia), 267
Koh Phangan (Thailand), 601
Koh Pi Pi (Thailand), 613
Koh Samet (Thailand), 592–3
Koh Samui (Thailand), 593–601
bungalows, 596–7
excursions from, 601
orientation, 593–4
sights and attractions, 597–601; Big Rock, 600; Chaweng Noi Bay, 600; Chaweng Yai Bay, 599–600; Choeng Mon Bay, 598; Lamai Bay, 600; Mae Nam Bay, 597; Na Muang Falls and the southern coast, 600–1; Nathon, 597; Thong Sai Bay, 598; Wat Phrayai (Big Buddha), 598; west coast, 601; Yai Noi Bay, 599
Surat Thani, 595–6
tourist information, 594
transportation to and within, 594–6
Komodo Island (Indonesia), 272–3
Kota Bharu (Malaysia), 379–81, 383
Kota Kinabalu (Malaysia), 407–9
Kowloon (Hong Kong), 96–7, 116
Krakatoa (Indonesia), 205–7
Kuala Lumpur (Malaysia), 339–63

ABCs of, 344–9
accommodations, 349–52
history of, 339–40
map, 341
nightlife, 362–3
orientation, 340
restaurants, 352–6
shopping, 359–62
sights and attractions, 356–9
tourist information, 346–8
transportation to and within, 340, 342–4
Kuala Terengganu (Malaysia), 380–4
Kuantan (Malaysia), 382–4
Kuta Beach (Indonesia):
accommodations, 249–52
nightlife, 253
orientation, 249
restaurants, 252–3
shopping, 254
sights and attractions, 253–4
tourist information, 249

Lamai Bay (Thailand), 600
Lamma (Hong Kong), 137–8
Lampang (Thailand), 570
Lamphun (Thailand), 568–9
Lantau (Hong Kong), 137
Lok Ma Chau (Hong Kong), 136
Lombok (Indonesia), 270–2
Lovina (Indonesia), 266

Macau, 5, 139–44
accommodations, 141–2
history of, 139–40
orientation, 140
restaurants, 142–3
sights and attractions, 143–4
transportation, 140–1
Macau (China), 5
Mae Nam Bay (Thailand), 597
Mae Sa Valley (Thailand), 571
Mai Khao Beach (Thailand), 612
Malacca (Melaka) (Malaysia), 384–91
accommodations, 387
history of, 384–5
orientation, 385
restaurants, 387
shopping, 391
sights and attractions, 388–91
tourist information, 385–6
transportation to and within, 386–7
Malaysia, 5, 318–91
ABCs of, 328–37
books about, 337–8
currency, 331; conversion chart, 324
customs, 331
economics of, 321
festivals and holidays, 333–4
geography of, 319–20
history of, 321–3

Malaysia (cont'd)
  itineraries, 324–5
  language of, 320–1; phrases, 330
  peninsular, 364–91; Cameron High-
    lands, 364–5, 367–8; east coast,
    379–84; Malacca (Melaka),
    384–91, 384–91; map, 366; Pe-
    nang, 368–79
  people of, 320
  politics of, 323–4
  religions of, 321
  sights and attractions: *see specific places*
  tourist information, 336–7
  transportation to and within, 325–7
  see also Borneo; Malacca; Kuala Lumpur;
    Penang; Sabah; Sarawak
Mandalay (Burma), 62–70
  accommodations, 65
  day trips and excursions from, 68–70
  history of, 63
  map, 56
  orientation, 63
  restaurants, 65–6
  shopping, 67–8
  sights and attractions, 66–7
  tourist information, 63–4
  transportation to and within, 64–5
Mapi 5 (Indonesia), 317
Mas (Indonesia), 264
Maymyo (Burma), 69–70
Medan (Indonesia), 278–81
Mingun (Burma), 69
Minnan Thu (Burma), 61
Mount Bromo (Indonesia), 230–31
Mount Popa (Burma), 61

Nai Harn Beach (Thailand), 606
Nai Yang Beach (Thailand), 612
Nakhon Pathom (Thailand), 536
Nathon (Thailand), 597
Nias Island (Indonesia), 287
Nusa Dua (Indonesia), 254–6
Nusa Penida (Indonesia), 267–8

Padang (Indonesia), 291–3
Padangbai (Indonesia), 268
Padang Sidempuan (Indonesia), 287–8
Pagan (Burma), 54–62
  accommodations, 57–8
  history, 55
  map, 56
  nightlife, 62
  orientation, 55
  restaurants, 59
  shopping, 62
  sights and attractions, 59–61
  tourist information, 55
  transportation to and within, 55, 57
Popa, Mount (Burma), 61
Papar (Malaysia), 408–9

Parapat (Indonesia), 283–4
Pa Sang (Thailand), 569–70
Paton Beach (Thailand), 609–12
Pattaya (Thailand), 584, 586–92
  accommodations, 587–90
  beaches, 592
  nightlife, 591–2
  orientation, 586
  restaurants, 590–1
  tourist information, 586
  transportation to and within, 586–7
Pawon (Indonesia), 225
Penang (Malaysia), 368–79
  accommodations, 372–4
  history of, 368–9
  nightlife, 378–9
  orientation, 369
  restaurants, 374–5
  shopping, 378
  sights and attractions, 375–8
  tourist information, 369–70
  transportation to and within, 370–2
Penelokan (Indonesia), 265
Phitsanulok (Thailand), 541–5
  accommodations, 543–4
  nightlife, 545
  orientation, 542
  restaurants, 544
  sights and attractions, 544–5
  tourist information, 542
  transportation to and within, 542–3
Phuket (Thailand), 601–13
  accommodations, 604–5
  orientation, 602–3
  restaurants, 605, 605
  sights and attractions, 605–13; Bang
    Thao Bay, 612; inland sites,
    612–13; Kata and Karon Beaches,
    606–9; Koh Pi Pi, 613; Mai Khao
    Beach, 612; Nai Harn Beach, 606;
    Nai Yang Beach, 612; Patong Beach,
    609–12; south coast, 605–6; vege-
    tarian festival, 602
  tourist information, 603
  transportation to and within, 603–4
Pikhe (Indonesia), 316–17
Prambanan (Indonesia), 225–7
Pugima (Indonesia), 317
Pulau Seribu (Indonesia), 203, 205
Puncak (Indonesia), 208

Rangoon (Burma), 45–53
  ABCs of, 34–44
  accommodations, 48–9
  day trips from, 53
  festivals and holidays, 38–9
  history of, 45–6
  map, 47
  orientation, 46, 48
  restaurants, 49–51

Rangoon (*cont'd*)
  shopping, 53
  sights and attractions, 51–3
  tourist information, 44, 46, 48
  transportation to and within, 48
Rantepao (Indonesia), 302–4

Sabah (Malaysia), 404–11
  accommodations, 406–7
  map, 394
  nightlife, 411
  orientation, 404–5
  restaurants, 407
  shopping, 411
  sights and attractions, 407–11
  tourist information, 405
  transportation to and within, 405–6
Sagaing (Burma), 68
Samosir Island (Indonesia), 282–6
  accommodations, 284–5
  restaurants, 285
  sights and attractions, 285–6
  transportation to, 283
Sangeh (the Monkey Forest) (Indonesia),
  270
Sanur (Indonesia), 241, 243–9
  accommodations, 243–6
  restaurants, 246–8
  shopping, 248
  sights and attractions, 248
  tourist information, 241
Sarawak (Malaysia)
  accommodations, 397–8
  history, 393, 395
  map, 394
  nightlife, 404
  orientation, 395
  restaurants, 398–9
  shopping, 403–4
  sights and attractions, 399–403
  tourist information, 395–6
  transportation to and within, 396–7
Sentani (Indonesia), 314–15
Shatin (Hong Kong), 135–6
Sibolga (Indonesia), 287
Sinatma (Indonesia), 317
Singapore, 5, 412–56
  ABCs of, 420–5
  accommodations, 425–32; budget,
    430–1; first-class, 428–30; hostels,
    431–2; luxury, 426–8
  currency, 422; conversion chart, 415
  customs, 422
  history of, 413–15
  map, 416–17
  nightlife, 455–6
  orientation, 415, 418
  restaurants, 434–40; Chinese, 434–6;
    continental, 438–9; fast food, 440;
    Hawkers Centres, 434; highlights,
  433; high tea, 439–40; Indian,
    436–7; Japanese, 437–8; Malay and
    Nonya, 436; Singapore-style, 434;
    Western, 438–40;
  shopping, 449–55; Asian handcrafts,
    454–5; department stores, 451–3;
    downtown, 453; electronics, 453;
    ethnic neighborhoods, 454–5;
    malls, 453; Marina Square and Raf-
    fles City, 453; Orchard Road,
    451–3; tips, 450–1
  sights and attractions, 440–9; Arab
    Street, 441; for children, 448; Chi-
    natown, 442–3; colonial heritage,
    444–5; cultural, 441–4; festivals
    and holidays, 423; harbor and the
    Islands, 448–9; Little India
    (Serangoon Road), 443; National
    Museum and Art Gallery, 443–4;
    Peranakan Palace, 444; tours, 448;
    zoos, parks, and gardens, 446–8
  tourist information, 425
  transportation to and within, 418–20
Singaraja (Indonesia), 266
Si Satchanalai (Thailand), 549–50
Snake Island (Malaysia), 408
Solo (Surakarta) (Indonesia), 227–30
Southeast Asia:
  history of, 6–7
  itineraries, 16–17
  map, 2–3
  planning your trip, 9–15; adventure
    travel, 11–12; with children, 15;
    educational travel, 13; getting there,
    9–13; health care, 14–15; study
    tours, 11; visas and travel docu-
    ments, 13–14
  religions of, 7–9
  transportation to, 9–13
Sukhothai (Thailand), 545–9
  accommodations, 546
  orientation, 546
  restaurants, 546–7
  sights and attractions, 547–9
  tourist information, 546
  transportation to and within, 546
Sulawesi (Indonesia), 296–305
  map, 290
  Rantepao, 302–4
  Tana Toraja, 296–9, 302–5; culture
    of, 296–8; Rantepao, 302–4; sights
    and attractions, 304–5; transporta-
    tion to, 298–9
  Ujung Pandang, 299–302
Sumatra (Indonesia), 274–89, 291–6
  map, 275
  North, 274–82; Batak culture, 276–7;
    Batak Highlands, 282; Brastagi,
    281; Medan, 278–81; transporta-
    tion to and within, 277–8

Sumatra (*cont'd*)
  trans-Sumatra overland, 286–8
  West, 288–9, 291–6; Bukittingi, 293–4; Minangkabau culture, 288–9, 294–6; Padang, 291–3; transportation to and within, 289, 291
Surat Thani (Thailand), 595–6

Taman Ayun (Indonesia), 269–70
Tampaksiring (Indonesia), 265
Tanah Lot (Indonesia), 269
Tana Toraja (Indonesia), 296–9, 302–5
  culture of, 296–8
  Rantepao, 302–4
  sights and attractions, 304–5
  transportation to, 298–9
Tao Fong Shan (Hong Kong), 136
Taunggyi (Burma), 70–5
  accommodations, 73–4
  orientation, 70–1, 70–1
  restaurants, 74
  sights and attractions, 74–5
  tourist information, 71
Thailand, 5, 458–613
  ABCs of, 469–80
  Bangkok: *see* Bangkok
  books about, 480–1
  central, 541–9; Phitsanulok, 541–5; Sukhothai, 545–9
  Chiang Mai: *see* Chiang Mai
  currency, 469–70, 473; conversion chart, 465
  economy of, 461–2
  festivals and holidays, 475–6
  geography of, 458
  history of, 462–5
  itineraries, 466
  language, 477; words and expressions, 471–2
  language of, 460
  map, 459; northern, 553
  northern, 576–83; Akha (Kaw), 582–3; ethnicity and geography of hill tribe; region, 578–83; festivals, 556–7; Hmong (Meo), 580–1; Karen, 579–80; Lahu (Mussur), 581; Lisu (Lisaw), 582; map, 553; Mien (Yao), 581–2; trekking companies, 577–8
  people of, 458–9
  politics of, 465
  religions of, 460–1

  southern, 584–613; Big Rock, 600; Chaweng Noi Bay, 600; Chaweng Yai Bay, 599–600; Choeng Mon Bay, 598; Koh Samui, 593–601; Lamai Bay, 600; Mae Nam Bay, 597; map, 585; Na Muang Falls and the southern coast, 600–1; Nathon, 597; Pattaya, 584, 586–92; Phuket, 601–13; Thong Sai Bay, 598; Wat Phrayai (Big Buddha), 598; west coast, 601; Yai Noi Bay, 599
  tourist information, 479–80
  transportation to and within, 466–9
Thiyipyitsaya (Burma), 61
Thong Sai Bay (Thailand), 598
Tirta Gangga (Indonesia), 268

Ubud (Indonesia), 256–61, 265
  accommodations, 257–60
  history of, 256–7
  orientation, 257
  restaurants, 260
  shopping, 261
  sights and attractions, 260–1
  tourist information, 257
  transportation to and within, 257
Ujung Pandang (Indonesia), 299–302
Ulu Watu (Indonesia), 269

Vietnam, 12–13

Walesi (Indonesia), 317
Wamena (Indonesia), 315–16
Wesaput (Indonesia), 317
Wong Tai Sin Temple (Hong Kong), 136–7

Yai Noi Bay (Thailand), 599
Yogyakarta (Indonesia), 211–23
  accommodations, 214–17; budget, 216–17; first-class, 214–15; moderately priced, 215–16
  history of, 211–12
  orientation, 212–13
  restaurants, 217–19
  sights and attractions, 219–23; cultural, 219–20; Museum Sonobudoyo, 222; Sultan's Palace, 220–1; Water Castle, 221–2; Wayang Kulit puppets, 219
  tourist information, 213–14
  transportation to and within, 212, 213